AN INCOMPLETE EDUCATION

AN INCOMPLETE EDUCATION

Judy Jones & William Wilson

BALLANTINE BOOKS

NEW YORK

Portions of this book originally appeared in *Esquire*.

Grateful acknowledgment is made to the following for permission to reprint previously published
material:

City Lights Books, Inc.: excerpt from the poem "The Day Lady Died" by Frank O'Hara.
Copyright © 1964 by Frank O'Hara. Reprinted by permission of City Lights Books, Inc.

Farrar, Straus & Giroux, Inc.: excerpt from the poem "For the Union Dead" from *For the Union
Dead* by Robert Lowell. Copyright © 1960, 1964 by Robert Lowell. UK rights administered by
Faber & Faber, Ltd. Reprinted by permission of the publishers.

Henry Holt and Company, Inc. and Jonathan Cape, Ltd.: excerpts from the poems "Nothing
Gold Can Stay" and "Directive" by Robert Frost from *The Poetry of Robert Frost*, edited by
Edward Connery Lathem. Copyright 1923, 1947, © 1969 by Holt, Rinehart and Winston, Inc.
Copyright 1951 by Robert Frost. Copyright © 1975 by Lesley Frost Ballantine. Reprinted by
permission of the publishers and the Estate of Robert Frost.

Harper & Row Publishers, Inc.: excerpt from the poem "Daddy" from *The Collected Poems of
Sylvia Plath*, edited by Ted Hughes. Copyright © 1963 by Ted Hughes. Reprinted by permission
of Harper & Row Publishers, Inc.

Page 659 constitutes a continuation of the copyright page.

LIBRARY OF CONGRESS CATALOGING-IN-PUBLICATION DATA

Jones, Judy, 1946–
An incomplete education.

Includes index.
1. Handbooks, vade-mecums, etc.   I. Wilson, William, 1948–   . II. Title.
AG105.J64   1987   031'.02   86-91572
ISBN 0-345-29570-6

Text design by Beth Tondreau
Photo editor: Cheryl Moch
Manufactured in the United States of America

20   19   18   17   16   15

ACKNOWLEDGMENTS

The authors would like to thank the following, all of whom contributed their energies, insights, and expertise (even if only three of them know the meaning of the word "deadline") to the sections that bear their names:

Owen Edwards, Helen Epstein, David Martin, Jon Pareles, Karen Pennar, Henry Popkin, Michael Sorkin, Judith Stone, James Trefil, Ronald Varney, Barbara Waxenberg, Alan Webber, Mark Zussman.

And we'd love it if you'd send a dollar apiece to:

Esquire veterans Byron Dobell and Christopher Buckley; Ballantine editors Joëlle Delbourgo and Ann La Farge; and Douglas Jones, Alfred Lowman, Alix Nelson, Michael O'Brien, and Michael Stout.

CONTENTS

INTRODUCTION

It's like this: You're reading the Sunday book section and there, in a review of a book that isn't even about physics but about how to write a screenplay, you're confronted by that word again: *quark*. You have been confronted by it at least twenty-five times, beginning in at least 1978, but you have not managed to retain the definition (something about building blocks), and the resonances (something about threesomes, something about birdshit) are even more of a problem. You're feeling stymied. You worry that you may not use spare time to maximum advantage, that the world is passing you by, that maybe it *would* make sense to subscribe to a third newsweekly. Your coffee's getting cold. The phone rings. You can't bring yourself to answer it.

Or it's like this: You *do* know what a quark is. You can answer the phone. It is an attractive person you have recently met. How are you? How are you? The person is calling to wonder if you feel like seeing a movie both of you missed the first time around. It's *The Year of Living Dangerously*, with Mel Gibson and that very tall actress. Also, that very short actress. "Plus," the person says, "it's set in Indonesia, which, next to India, is probably the most fascinating of all Third World nations. It's like the political scientists say, 'The labyrinth that is India, the mosaic that is Indonesia.' Right?" Silence at your end of the phone. Clearly this person is into overkill, but that doesn't mean you don't have to say something back. India you could field. But Indonesia? Fortunately, you have cable—and a Stouffer's lasagna in the freezer.

Or it's like *this:* You know what a quark is. Also something about Indonesia. The two of you enjoy the movie. The new person agrees to go with you to a dinner party one of your best friends is giving at her country place. You arrive, pulling into a driveway full of BMWs. You go inside. Introductions are made. Along about the second margarita, the talk turns to World War II. Specifically, the causes of World War II. More specifically, Hitler. Already this is not easy.

But it is interesting. "Well," says another guest, flicking an imaginary piece of lint from the sleeve of a double-breasted navy blazer, "you really can't disregard the impact Nietzsche had, not only on Hitler, but on a prostrate Germany. You know: The will to power. The Übermensch. The transvaluation of values. Don't you agree, old bean?" Fortunately, you have cable—and a Stouffer's lasagna in the freezer.

So what's your problem? Weren't you supposed to have learned all this stuff back in college? Sure you were, but then, as now, you had your good days and your bad days. Ditto your teachers. Maybe you were in the infirmary with the flu the week your Philosophy 101 class was slogging through *Zarathustra*. Maybe your poli-sci prof was served with divorce papers right about the time the class hit the nonaligned nations. Maybe you failed to see the relevance of subatomic particles given your desperate need to get a date for Homecoming. Maybe you actually *had* all the answers—for a few glorious hours before the No-Doz (or whatever it was) wore off. No matter. The upshot is that you've got some serious educational gaps. And that, old bean, is what this book is all about.

Now we'll grant you that educational gaps today don't signify in quite the way they did even ten years ago. In fact, when we first got the idea for this book, sitting around *Esquire* Magazine's research department, we envisioned a kind of intellectual *Dress for Success,* a guidebook to help reasonably literate, reasonably ambitious types like ourselves preserve an upwardly mobile image and make an impression at cocktail parties by getting off a few good quotes from Dr. Johnson—or, for that matter, by not referring to Evelyn Waugh as "she."

Yup, times have changed since then. (You didn't think we were still sitting around the *Esquire* research department, did you?) And the more we heard people's party conversation turning from literary matters to money-market accounts and condo closings, the more we worried that the book we were working on wasn't noble (or uplifting, or profound; also long) enough. Is it just another of those bluffers' handbooks? we wondered. Is its guiding spirit not insight at all, but rather the brashest kind of one-upmanship? Is trying to reduce the complexities of culture, politics, and science to a couple hundred words each so very different from trying to fill in all the wedges of one's pie in a game of Trivial Pursuit? (And why hadn't *we* thought up Trivial Pursuit? But that's another story.)

Then we realized something. We realized that what we were really going for here had less to do with competition and power positions than with context and perspective. In a world of bits and bytes, of reruns and fast forwards, of information overloads and significance shortfalls (and of Donald Trump and bagpersons no older than one is, but that's another story) it feels good to be grounded. It feels good to be able to bring to the wire-service story about

Reagan's dream of packing the Supreme Court a sense of what the Supreme Court is (and the knowledge that people have been trying to pack it from the day it opened), to be able to buttress one's comparison of Steven Spielberg and D. W. Griffith with a knowledge of the going critical line on the latter. In short, we found that we were casting our vote for grounding, as opposed to grooming. Also that grounding, not endless, mindless mobility, turns out to be the real power position.

And then something really strange happened. Setting out to discover what conceivable appeal a Verdi, say, could have on a planet that was clearly—and, it seemed at the time, rightly—dominated by the Rolling Stones, we stumbled into a nineteenth-century landscape where the name of the game was grandeur, not grandiosity; where romanticism had no trashy connotations; where music and spectacle could elicit overwhelming emotions without, at the same time, threatening to fry one's brains. No kidding, we actually *liked* this stuff! What's more, coming of age in a world of T-shirts and jeans and groovy R & B riffs apparently didn't make one ineligible for a passport to the other place. One just needed a few key pieces of information and a willingness to travel.

And speaking of travel, let's face it: Bumping along over the potholes of your mind day after day can't be doing much for your self-esteem. Which is the third thing, along with power and enrichment, this book is all about. Don't you think you'll feel better about yourself once all those gaps have been filled? Everything from the mortifying (how to tell Keats from Shelley) to the merely pesky (how to tell a nave from a narthex)? Imagine. Nothing but you and the open road.

Before you take off, though, we ought to say something about the book's structure. Basically, it's divided into chapters corresponding to the disciplines and departments you remember from college (you were paying *that* much attention, weren't you?). Not that everything in the book is stuff you'd necessarily study in college, but it's all well within the limits of what an "educated" person is expected to know. In those areas where our own roads weren't in such great repair, we've called on specialist friends and colleagues to help us out. Even so, we don't claim to have covered everything; we simply went after what struck as the biggest trouble spots.

Now, our advice for using this book: Don't feel you have to read all of any given chapter on a single tank of gas. And don't feel you have to get from point A to point B by lunchtime; better to slow down and enjoy the scenery. Do, however, try to stay alert. Even with the potholes fixed, you'll want to be braced for hairpin turns (and the occasional five-car collision) up ahead.

AN
INCOMPLETE
EDUCATION

AMERICAN STUDIES

Contents

Flag drill, farmworkers' camp, Caldwell, Idaho, 1941.

American Literature 101

A FIRST-SEMESTER SYLLABUS

You signed up for it thinking it would be a breeze. After all, you'd read most of the stuff back in high school, hadn't you?

Or had you? As it turned out, the thing you remembered best about *Moby Dick* was the expression on Gregory Peck's face as he and the whale went down for the last time. And was it really *The Scarlet Letter* you liked so much? Or was it the Classic Comics version of *The Scarlet Letter*? Of course, you weren't the only one who overestimated your familiarity with your literary heritage; your professor was busy making the same mistake.

Then there was the material itself, much of it so bad it made you wish you'd signed up for "The Nineteenth Century French Novel: Stendhal to Zola" instead. Now that you're older, though, you may be willing to make allowances. After all, the literary figures you were most likely to encounter the first semester were by and large only moonlighting as writers. They had to spend the bulk of their time building a nation, framing a constitution, carving a civilization out of the wilderness, or simply busting their chops trying to make a living. In those days, no one was about to fork over six figures so some Puritan could lie around the Hamptons polishing a screenplay.

Try, then, to think only kind and patriotic thoughts as, with the help of this chart, you refresh your memory on all those things you were asked to face—or to face again—in your freshman introduction to American Lit.

JONATHAN EDWARDS (1703–1758)

Product of: Northampton, Massachusetts, where he ruled from the pulpit for thirty years; Stockbridge, Massachusetts, where he became an Indian missionary after the townspeople of Northampton got fed up with him.

Earned a Living as a: Clergyman, theologian.

High-School Reading List: The sermon, "Sinners in the Hands of an Angry God" (1741), the most famous example of "the preaching of terror."

Jonathan Edwards' church, Northampton, Massachusetts.

College Reading List:

Any number of sermons, notably "God Glorified in the Work of Redemption by the Greatness of Man's Dependence on Him in the Whole of It" (1731), Edwards' first sermon, in which he pinpoints the moral failings of New Englanders; and "A Faithful Narrative of the Surprising Work of God" (1737), describing various types and stages of religious conversion. Also, if your college professor was a Fundamentalist, a New Englander, or simply sadistic, one or two of the treatises, e.g., "A Careful and Strict Enquiry into the Freedom of the Will" (1754), or the "Great Christian Doctrine of Original Sin Defended" (1758). Not to be missed: a dip into Edwards' *Personal Narrative*, which suggests the psychological connection between being America's number-one Puritan clergyman and the only son in a family with 11 children.

What You Were Supposed to Have Learned in High School:

Edwards' historical importance as quintessential Puritan thinker and hero of the Great Awakening, the religious revival that swept New England from the late 1730s to 1750.

What You Didn't Find Out Until College:	What Edwards thought *about*, namely, the need to get back to the old-fashioned Calvinist belief in man's basic depravity and his total dependence on God's goodwill for salvation. (Forget about the "covenant" theory of Protestantism; according to Edwards, God doesn't bother cutting deals with humans.) Also, his insistence that faith and conversion be emotional, not just intellectual.

BENJAMIN FRANKLIN (1706–1790)

Product of:	Philadelphia, Pennsylvania.
Earned a Living as a:	Printer, promoter, inventor, diplomat, statesman.
High-School Reading List:	The *Declaration of Independence* (1776), which he helped draft.
College Reading List:	*The Autobiography of Benjamin Franklin* (1771–1788), considered one of the greatest autobiographies ever written; sample maxims from *Poor Richard's Almanack* (1732–1757), mostly on how to make money or keep from spending it; any number of articles and essays on topics of historical interest, ranging from "Rules by Which a Great Empire May Be Reduced to a Small One," and "An Edict by the King of Prussia" (both 1773), about the colonies' Great Britain problem, to "Experiments and Observations on Electricity" (1751), all of which are quite painless.
What You Were Supposed to Have Learned in High School:	Not a thing. But back in grade school you presumably learned that Franklin invented a stove, bifocal glasses, and the lightning rod; that he established the first, or almost the first, library, fire department, hospital, and insurance company; that he helped negotiate the treaty with France that allowed America to win

independence; that he was a member of the Constitutional Convention; that he was the most famous American of the eighteenth century (after George Washington) and the closest thing we've ever had to a renaissance man.

What You Didn't Find Out Until College:

That Franklin had as many detractors as admirers, for whom his shrewdness, pettiness, hypocrisy, and nonstop philandering embodied all the worst traits of the American character, of American capitalism, and of the Protestant ethic.

WASHINGTON IRVING (1783–1859)

Washington Irving's house, Tarrytown, New York.

Product of:

New York City and Tarrytown, New York.

Earned a Living as a:

Writer; also, briefly, a diplomat.

High School Reading List:

"Rip Van Winkle" and "The Legend of Sleepy Hollow," both contained in *The Sketch Book* (1820).

College Reading List:

Other more or less interchangeable selections from *The Sketch Book*, *Bracebridge Hall* (1822), *Tales of a Traveller* (1824), or *The Legends of the*

Alhambra (1832), none of which stuck in any-one's memory for more than ten minutes.

What You Were Supposed to Have Learned in High School:

That Irving was the first to prove that Americans could write as well as Europeans; that Ichabod Crane and Rip Van Winkle's wife both got what they deserved.

What You Didn't Find Out Until College:

That Irving's grace as a stylist didn't quite make up for his utter lack of originality, insight, or depth.

JAMES FENIMORE COOPER (1789–1851)

Product of:

Cooperstown, New York.

Earned a Living as a:

Gentleman farmer.

High-School Reading List:

Probably none; *The Leatherstocking Tales*, i.e., *The Pioneers* (1823), *The Last of the Mohicans* (1826), *The Prairie* (1827), *The Pathfinder* (1840), and *The Deerslayer* (1841), are considered grade-school material.

College Reading List:

Social criticism, such as *Notions of the Americans* (1828), a defense of America against the sniping of foreign visitors; or "Letter to his Countrymen" (1834), a diatribe written in response to bad reviews of his latest novel.

What You Were Supposed to Have Learned in High School:

That Cooper was America's first successful novelist and that Natty Bumppo was one of the all-time most popular characters in world literature. Also that *The Leatherstocking Tales* portrayed the conflicting values of the vanishing wilderness and encroaching civilization.

What You Didn't Find Out Until College:

That the closest Cooper ever got to the vanishing wilderness was Scarsdale, and that, in his day, he was considered an insufferable snob, a reactionary, a grouch, and a troublemaker known for defending slavery and opposing suffrage for everyone but male landowners. That eventually, everyone decided the writing in *The Leatherstocking Tales* was abominable but that during the 1920s Cooper's social criticism began to seem important and his thinking pretty much representative of American conservatism.

RALPH WALDO EMERSON (1803–1882)

Product of: Concord, Massachusetts.

Earned a Living as a: Unitarian minister, lecturer.

High-School Reading List: A few passages from *Nature* (1836), Emerson's paean to individualism, and a couple of the *Essays* (1841), one of which was undoubtedly the early, optimistic "Self-Reliance." If you were spending a few days on Transcendentalism, you probably also had to read "The Over-Soul." If, on the other hand, your English teacher swung towards an essay like "The Poet," it was, no doubt, accompanied by a snatch of Emersonian verse—most likely "Brahma" or "Days." (You already knew Emerson's "Concord Hymn" from grade-school history lessons, although you probably didn't know who wrote it.)

College Reading List: Essays and more essays, including "Experience," a tough one. Also the lecture "The American Scholar," in which Emerson called for a proper American literature, freed from European domination.

What You Were Supposed to Have Learned in High School: That Emerson was the most important figure of the Transcendentalist movement, whatever that was, the friend and benefactor of Thoreau, and a legend in his own time; also, that he was a great thinker, a staunch individualist, an unshakable optimist, and a first-class human being, even if you wouldn't have wanted to know him yourself.

What You Didn't Find Out Until College:

That you'd probably be a better person if you *had* known him yourself and that almost any one of his essays could see you through an identity crisis, if not a nervous breakdown.

NATHANIEL HAWTHORNE (1804–1864)

Nathaniel Hawthorne.

Hawthorne's house, Concord, Massachusetts.

Product of:

Salem and Concord, Massachusetts.

Earned a Living as a:

Writer, surveyor, American consul in Liverpool.

High-School Reading List:

The Scarlet Letter (1850) or *The House of the Seven Gables* (1851); plus one or two tales, among which was probably "Young Goodman Brown" (1846) because your teacher hoped a story about witchcraft would hold your attention long enough to get you through it.

College Reading List:

None, since you were expected to have done the reading back in high school. One possible exception: *The Blithedale Romance* (1852) if your prof was into Brook Farm and the Transcendentalists; another: *The Marble Faun* (1860) for its explicit fall-of-man philosophizing.

What You Were Supposed to Have Learned in High School:

What the letter *A* embroidered on someone's dress means.

What You Didn't Find Out Until College:

That Hawthorne marked a turning point in American morality and a break from our Puritan past, despite the fact that he, like his ancestors, never stopped obsessing about sin and guilt. Also, that he's considered something of an underachiever.

EDGAR ALLAN POE (1809–1849)

Edgar Allan Poe's cottage, New York City.

Product of:

Richmond, Virginia; New York City; Baltimore, Maryland.

Earned a Living as a:

Hack journalist and reviewer.

High-School Reading List:

"The Raven" (1845), "Ulalume" (1847), "Annabel Lee" (1848), and a few other poems, probably read aloud in class; a detective story: "The Murders in the Rue Morgue" (1841) or "The Purloined Letter" (1845), either of which you could skip if you'd seen the movie; one or two of the supernatural-death stories, say, "The Fall of the House of Usher" (1839) or "The Masque of the Red Death" (1842), either of which you could skip if you'd seen the movie; a couple of the psychotic-murderer stories, e.g., "The Tell-Tale Heart" or "The Black Cat" (both 1843), either of which you could skip if you'd seen the movie; and a pure Poe horror number like "The Pit and the Pendulum" (1842), which you could skip if you'd seen the movie. Sorry, but as far as we know, they still haven't made a movie of "The Cask of Amontillado" (1846).

College Reading List:

None; remedial reading only, unless you chose to write your dissertation on "The Gothic Element in American Fiction."

What You Were Supposed to Have Learned in High School:

That Poe invented the detective story and formulated the short story more or less as we know it. That maybe poetry wasn't so bad, after all. Also, that Poe was a poverty-stricken alcoholic who did drugs and who married his thirteen-year-old cousin, just like Jerry Lee Lewis did.

What You Didn't Find Out Until College:

That once you're over seventeen, you don't ever admit to liking Poe's poetry, except maybe to your closest friend who's a math major; that while Poe seemed puerile to American critics, he was a cult hero to European writers from Baudelaire to Shaw; and that, in spite of his subject matter, Poe still gets credit—even in America—for being a great technician.

HARRIET BEECHER STOWE (1811–1896)

Product of:

Litchfield and Hartford, Connecticut; Cincinnati, Ohio; Brunswick, Maine.

Earned a Living as a:

Housewife.

High-School Reading List:

Uncle Tom's Cabin (1851–2).

Harriet Beecher Stowe.

College Reading List:

The Pearl of Orr's Island (1862) and *Old Town Folks* (1869), if your professor was determined to make a case for Stowe as a novelist. Both are considered superior to *Uncle Tom's Cabin.*

What You Were Supposed to Have Learned in High School:

What happened to Uncle Tom, Topsy, and Little Eva. That the novel was one of the great catalysts of the Civil War.

What You Didn't Find Out Until College:

That you'd have done better to spend your time reading the real story of slavery in *My Life and Times* by Frederick Douglass. That the fact that you didn't was just one more proof, dammit, of the racism rampant in our educational system.

HENRY DAVID THOREAU (1817–1862)

Product of:

Concord, Massachusetts, and nearby Walden Pond.

Earned a Living as a:

Schoolteacher, pencil maker, surveyor, handyman, naturalist.

High-School Reading List:

Walden (1854), inspired by the two years he spent communing with himself and Nature in a log cabin on Walden Pond.

College Reading List:

"Civil Disobedience" (1849), the essay inspired by the night he spent in jail for refusing to pay a poll tax; *A Week on the Concord and Merrimack Rivers* (1849), inspired by a few weeks spent on same with his brother John, and considered a literary warm-up for *Walden;* parts of the *Journal,* inspired by virtually everything, which Thoreau not only kept but polished and rewrote for almost twenty-five years—you had fourteen volumes to choose from, including the famous "lost journal" which was rediscovered in 1958.

What You Were Supposed to Have Learned in High School:

That Thoreau was one of the great American eccentrics and the farthest out of the Transcendentalists, and that he believed you should spend your life breaking bread with the birds and the woodchucks instead of going for a killing in the futures market like your old man.

What You Didn't Find Out Until College:

That *Walden* was not just a spiritualized *Boy Scout Handbook,* but according to twentieth-century authorities, a carefully composed literary masterpiece. That, according to these same authorities, Thoreau *did* have a sense of humor. That Tolstoy was mightily impressed with "Civil Disobedience" and Gandhi used it as the inspiration for his *satyagraha.* That despite his reputation as a loner and pacifist, Thoreau became the friend and defender of the radical abolitionist John Brown. And that, heavy as you were into Thoreau's principles of purity, simplicity, and spirituality, you still had to figure out how to hit your parents up for plane fare to India.

Henry David Thoreau's house, Concord, Massachusetts.

HERMAN MELVILLE (1819–1891)

Product of:

New York City; Albany and Troy, New York; various South Sea islands.

Earned a Living as a:

Schoolteacher, bank clerk, sailor, harpooner, customs inspector.

High-School Reading List:

Moby Dick (1851; abridged version, or you just skipped the parts about the whaling industry); *Typee* (1846), the early bestseller, which was, your teacher hoped, sufficiently exotic and action-packed to get you hooked on Melville. For extra credit, the novella *Billy Budd* (1824).

College Reading List:

Moby Dick (unabridged version), *The Piazza Tales* (1856), especially "Bartleby the Scrivener" and "Benito Cereno"; and the much-discussed, extremely tedious *The Confidence Man* (1857).

What You Were Supposed to Have Learned in High School:

That *Moby Dick* is allegorical (the whale = Nature/God/the Implacable Universe; Ahab = Man's Conflicted Identity/Civilization/Human Will; Ishmael = the Poet/Philosopher) and should be read as a debate between Ahab and Ishmael.

Herman Melville's house, Albany, New York.

What You Didn't Find Out Until College:

That Melville didn't know *Moby Dick* was allegorical until somebody pointed it out to him. That his work prefigured some of Freud's theories of the unconscious. That, like Lord Byron, Norman Mailer, and Bob Dylan, Melville spent most of his life struggling to keep up with the name he'd made for himself (with the bestselling *Typee*) before he turned thirty. And that if, historically, he was caught between nineteenth-century Romanticism and modern alienation, personally he was pretty unbalanced as well.

MARK TWAIN (1835–1910)

The Twain family.

Product of:

Hannibal, Missouri; various Nevada mining towns; Hartford, Connecticut.

Earned a Living as a:

Printer, river pilot, newspaper reporter, lecturer, storyteller.

High-School Reading List:

The Adventures of Huckleberry Finn (1884). Also, if you took remedial English, *The Adventures of Tom Sawyer* (1876).

College Reading List:

The short story "The Celebrated Jumping Frog of Calaveras County" (1865), as an example of Twain's frontier humor; the essays

"Fenimore Cooper's Literary Offenses" (1895, 1897) and "The United States of Lyncherdom" (1901), as examples of his scathing wit and increasing disillusionment with America; and the short novel, *The Mysterious Stranger* (1916), for the late, bleak, embittered Twain.

What You Were Supposed to Have Learned in High School:

That *Huckleberry Finn* is the great mock-epic of American democracy, marking the beginning of a caste-free literature that owed nothing to European tradition. That this was the first time the American vernacular had made it into a serious literary work. That the book profoundly influenced the development of the modern American prose style. And that you should have been paying more attention to Twain's brilliant manipulation of language and less to whether or not Huck, Tom, and Jim made it out of the lean-to alive. Also, that Mark Twain, which was river parlance for "two fathoms deep," was the pseudonym of Samuel Langhorne Clemens.

What You Didn't Find Out Until College:

That Twain grew more and more pessimistic about America—and about humanity in general—as he, and the country, grew older, eventually turning into a bona fide misanthrope. And that he was stylistically tone-deaf, producing equal amounts of brilliant prose and overwritten trash without ever seeming to notice the difference.

The Beat Goes On

A HUNDRED YEARS' WORTH OF MODERN AMERICAN POETRY

So much of what we've all been committing to memory over the past lifetime or so—the words to "Help Me, Rhonda" typify the genre—eventually stops paying the same dividends. Sure, the beat's as catchy as ever. But once the old gang's less worried about what to do on Saturday night than about meeting child-support payments and stemming periodontal disease, it's nice to have something more in the way of consolation, perspective, and uplift to fall back on. Good news: All the time you were glued to the car radio, a few people with a little more foresight were writing—and what's more, printing—poetry, some of which is as about as Zeitgeisty as things get.

It is, however, a little trickier than the Beach Boys. For one thing, it's modern, which means you're up against alienation and artificiality. For another, it's poetry, which means nobody's just going to come out and say what's on his mind. Put them together and you've got modern poetry. Read on and you've got modern poetry's brightest lights and biggest guns, arranged in convenient categories for those pressed for time and/or an ordering principle of their own.

THE FIVE BIG DEALS

EZRA POUND (1885–1972)

Profile: Old Granddad . . . most influential figure (and most headline-making career) in modern poetry . . . made poets write modern, editors publish modern, and readers read modern . . . part archaeologist, part refugee, he scavenged past eras (medieval Provence, Confucian China) with a mind to overhauling his own . . . in so doing, masterminded a cultural revolution, complete with doctrines, ideology, and propaganda . . . though expatriated to London and Italy, remained at heart an American, rough-and-ready, even vulgar, as he put it, "a plymouth-rock conscience landed on a predilection for the arts" . . . responsive and rigorous: helped Eliot (whose *The Waste Land* he pared down to half its original length), Yeats, Joyce, Frost, and plenty of lesser poets and writers . . . reputation colored by his anti-Semitism, his hookup with Mussolini, the ensuing charges of treason brought by the U.S. government, and the years in a mental institution.

Motto: "Make it new."

A colleague begs to differ: "Mr. Pound is a village explainer—excellent if you were a village, but, if you were not, not." —Gertrude Stein

Favorite colors: Purple, ivory, jade.

Latest books read: Confucius, Stendhal, the songs of the troubadours, the memoirs of Thomas Jefferson.

The easy (and eminently quotable) Pound:

> There died a myriad,
> And of the best, among them,
> For an old bitch gone in the teeth,
> For a botched civilization,
>
> Charm, smiling at the good mouth,
> Quick eyes gone under earth's lid,
>
> For two gross of broken statues,
> For a few thousand battered books.
>
> from *Hugh Selwyn Mauberley*

The prestige Pound (for extra credit):

> Zeus lies in Ceres' bosom
> Taishan is attended of loves
>   under Cythera, before sunrise
> and he said: "Hay aquí mucho catolicismo—(sounded catoli*th*ismo)
>   y muy poco reliHión"
> and he said: "Yo creo que los reyes desaparecen"
> (Kings will, I think, disappear)
> That was Padre José Elizondo
>   in 1906 and in 1917
> or about 1917
>   and Dolores said "Come pan, niño," (eat bread, me lad)
> Sargent had painted her
>   before he descended
> (i.e., if he descended)
>   but in those days he did thumb sketches,
> impressions of the Velásquez in the Museo del Prado
> and books cost a peseta,
>   brass candlesticks in proportion,
> hot wind came from the marshes
>   and death-chill from the mountains. . . .

from *Cantos,* LXXXI (one of the Pisan Cantos, written after World War II while Pound was on display in a cage in Pisa)

T. S. (THOMAS STEARNS) ELIOT (1888–1965)

Profile: Tied with Yeats for most famous poet of the century . . . his masterpiece *The Waste Land* (1922), which gets at the fragmentation, horror, and ennui of modern times through a collage of literary, religious, and pop allusions . . . erudition for days: a page of Eliot's poetry can consist of more footnotes and scholarly references than text . . . born in Missouri, educated at Harvard, but from the late 1910s (during which he worked as a bank clerk) on, lived in London and adopted the ways of an Englishman . . . tried in his early poetry to reunite wit and passion, which, in English poetry, had been going their separate ways since Donne and the Metaphysicals (see page 186) . . . his later poetry usually put down for its religiosity (Eliot had, in the meantime, found God); likewise, with the exception of *Murder in the Cathedral,* his plays . . . had a history of nervous breakdowns; some critics see his poetry in terms not of tradition and classicism, but of compulsion and craziness.

Motto: "Genuine poetry can communicate before it is understood."

A colleague begs to differ: "A subtle conformist," according to William Carlos Williams, who called *The Waste Land* "the great catastrophe."

Favorite colors: Eggplant, sable, mustard.

Latest books read: Dante, Hesiod, the *Bhagavad Gita,* Hesse's *A Glimpse into Chaos,* St. Augustine, Jessie L. Weston's *From Ritual to Romance,* Frazer's *The Golden Bough,* Baudelaire, the Old Testament Books of Ezekiel, Isaiah, and Ecclesiastes, Joyce's *Ulysses, Antony and Cleopatra,* "The Rape of the Lock," and that's just *this* week.

The easy (and eminently quotable) Eliot:

The opening lines of "The Love Song of J. Alfred Prufrock," the let-us-go-then-you-and-I, patient-etherised-upon-a-table, women-talking-of-Michelangelo lead-in to a poem that these days seems as faux-melodramatic and faggy—and as unforgettable—as a John Waters movie. (We'd have printed these lines for you here, but the Eliot estate has a thing about excerpting.)

The prestige Eliot (for extra credit):

Something from the middle of *The Waste Land,* just to show you've made it through the whole 434 lines. Try, for example, the second stanza of the third book ("The Fire Sermon"), in the course of which a rat scurries along a river bank, the narrator muses on the death of "the king my father," Mrs. Sweeney and her daughter "wash their feet in soda water," and Eliot's own footnotes refer you to *The Tempest,* an Elizabethan poem called *Parliament of Bees,* the World War I ballad in which Mrs. Sweeney makes her first appearance (ditto her daughter), and a sonnet by Verlaine.

WILLIAM CARLOS WILLIAMS
(1883–1963)

Profile: Uncle Bill . . . at the center of postwar poetry, the man whom younger poets used to look to for direction and inspiration . . . smack-dab in the American grain . . . determined to write poetry based on the language as spoken *here,* the language he heard "in the mouths of Polish mothers" . . . avoided traditional stanza, rhyme, and line patterns, preferring a jumble of images and rhythms . . . spent his entire life in New Jersey, a small-town doctor, specializing in pediatrics . . . played homebody to Pound's and Eliot's gadabouts, regular guy to their *artistes*—the former a lifelong friend, with whom he disagreed loudly and often . . . wanted to make "contact," which he took to mean "man with nothing but the thing and the feeling of that thing" . . . not taken seriously by critics and intellectuals, who tended, until the Fifties, to treat him like a literary Grandma Moses . . . *Paterson* his *The Waste Land.*

Motto: "No ideas but in things."

A colleague begs to differ: "A poet of some local interest, perhaps." —Eliot. "Anti-poetic." —Wallace Stevens.

Favorite colors: Blue, yellow, tan.

Latest books read: Keats, Pound's *Cantos*, Allen Ginsberg's *Howl*.

The easy (and eminently quotable) Williams:

> so much depends
> upon
>
> a red wheel
> barrow
>
> glazed with rain
> water
>
> beside the white
> chickens.

"The Red Wheelbarrow"

The prestige Williams (for extra credit):

> The descent beckons
>   as the ascent beckoned
>   Memory is a kind
> of accomplishment
>   a sort of renewal
>   even
> an initiation, since the spaces it opens are new
> places
>   inhabited by hordes
>   heretofore unrealized,
> of new kinds—
>   since their movements
>   are towards new objectives
> (even though formerly they were abandoned)
> No defeat is made up entirely of defeat—since
> the world it opens is always a place
>   formerly
>   unsuspected. A
> world lost,
>   a world unsuspected
>   beckons to new places
> and no whiteness (lost) is so white as the memory
> of whiteness

from *Paterson,* Book 2 ("Sunday in the Park"), Section 2

ROBERT FROST (1874–1963)

Profile: The one who got stuck being popular with readers outside college English departments . . . but not just the "miles-to-go-before-I-sleep" poet; as one critic said, "sees the skull beneath the flesh" . . . born in California, where he spent his boyhood: the New England accent just a bit of a fraud . . . recreated, in his poems, the rhythms of actual speech, the actions of ordinary men . . . "got" nature, tradition, and anxiety . . . his tone sad, wry, and a little narcissistic . . . eventually carved out an elder-statesman role for himself in official American culture . . . isolation, limitation, and extinction were favorite themes . . . said to have been a creep to his wife and son (who committed suicide) . . . for better or worse, hard not to memorize.

Motto: "We play the words as we find them."

A colleague begs to differ: "His work is full (or said to be full) of humanity." — Wallace Stevens.

Favorite colors: Teal blue, slate gray, blood red.

Latest books read: The King James Bible, Thoreau's *Walden*, Hardy's *Tess of the D'Urbervilles*.

The easy (and eminently quotable) Frost:

> Nature's first green is gold,
> Her hardest hue to hold.
> Her early leaf's a flower;
> But only so an hour.
> Then leaf subsides to leaf.
> So Eden sank to grief,
> So dawn goes down to day.
> Nothing gold can stay.
>
> "Nothing Gold Can Stay"

The prestige Frost (for extra credit):

> . . . Make yourself up a cheering song of how
> Someone's road home from work this once was,
> Who may be just ahead of you on foot
> Or creaking with a buggy load of grain.
> The height of the adventure is the height
> Of country where two village cultures faded
> Into each other. Both of them are lost.

And if you're lost enough to find yourself
By now, pull in your ladder road behind you
And put a sign up CLOSED to all but me.
Then make yourself at home. The only field
Now left's no bigger than a harness gall.
First there's the children's house of make-believe,
Some shattered dishes underneath a pine,
The playthings in the playhouse of the children.
Weep for what little things could make them glad. . . .

from "Directive"

WALLACE STEVENS (1879–1955)

Profile: With Yeats and Eliot, billed as a great "imaginative force" in modern poetry . . . self-effacing insurance executive who spent a lifetime at the Hartford Accident and Indemnity Company, writing poetry nights and weekends . . . didn't travel in literary circles (and was on a first-name basis with almost no other writers); did, however, manage to get into a famous fistfight with Ernest Hemingway while vacationing in Key West . . . believed in "the essential gaudiness of poetry" . . . his own verse marked by flair, self-mockery, virtuoso touches, aggressive art-for-art's sakeishness . . . in it, he portrayed himself as the aesthete, the dandy, the hedonist . . . held that, since religion could no longer satisfy people, poetry would have to . . . had the sensuousness and brilliance of a Keats (cf., as the critics do, Frost's "Wordsworthian plainness").

Motto: "Poetry is the supreme fiction, madame."

A colleague begs to differ: "A bric-a-brac poet." —Robert Frost.

Favorite colors: Vermilion, chartreuse, wine.

Latest books read: A Midsummer Night's Dream, the poetry of Verlaine, Mallarmé, and Yeats, Henri Bergson's *On Laughter.*

The easy (and eminently quotable) Stevens:

I placed a jar in Tennessee,
And round it was, upon a hill.
It made the slovenly wilderness
Surround that hill.

The wilderness rose up to it,
And sprawled around, no longer wild.
The jar was round upon the ground.
And tall and of a port in air.

It took dominion everywhere.
The jar was gray and bare.
It did not give of bird or bush,
Like nothing else in Tennessee.

"Anecdote of the Jar"

The prestige Stevens (for extra credit):

Ramon Fernandez, tell me, if you know,
Why, when the singing ended and we turned
Toward the town, tell why the glassy lights,
The lights in the fishing boats at anchor there,
As the night descended, tilting in the air,
Mastered the night and portioned out the sea,
Fixing emblazoned zones and fiery poles,
Arranging, deepening, enchanting night.

Oh! Blessed rage for order, pale Ramon,
The maker's rage to order words of the sea,
Words of the fragrant portals, dimly-starred,
And of ourselves and of our origins,
In ghostlier demarcations, keener sounds.

from "The Idea of Order at Key West"

THE FIVE RUNNERS-UP
MARIANNE MOORE (1887–1972)

If "compression is the first grace of style,"
    you have it.

from "To a Snail"

Has been called "the poet's poet" and compared to "a solo harpsichord in a concerto" in which all other American poets are the orchestra . . . has also been called, by Hart Crane, "a hysterical virgin" . . . in either case, was notorious for staring at animals (pangolins, frigate pelicans, arctic oxen), steamrollers, and the Brooklyn Dodgers, then holding forth on what she saw . . . believed in "predilection" rather than "passion" and wanted to achieve an "unbearable accuracy," a "precision" that had both "impact and exactitude, as with surgery" . . . watch for her quotes from history books, encyclopedias, and travel brochures . . . original, alert, and neat . . . appealed to fellow poets, including young ones, with her matter-of-fact tone, her ability to make poetry read as easily as prose.

JOHN CROWE RANSOM (1888–1974)

—I am a gentleman in a dustcoat trying
To make you hear. Your ears are soft and small
And listen to an old man not at all. . . .

from "Piazza Piece"

Finest of the Southern poets (he beats out Allen Tate and Robert Penn Warren), and the center of the literary group called the Fugitives (mention tradition, agrarianism, and the New Criticism and they'll read you some of their own verse) . . . liked the mythic, the courtly, the antique, and flirted with the pedantic . . . small poetic output: only three books, all written between 1919 and 1927 . . . founder and editor, for over twenty years, of the *Kenyon Review*, arguably the top American literary magazine of its day . . . at his worst, can be a little stilted, a little sentimental; at his best, devastatingly stilted and wonderfully ironical . . . worth reading on mortality and the mind/body dichotomy.

E.E. (EDWARD ESTLIN) CUMMINGS
(1894–1962)

. . . the Cambridge ladies do not care, above
Cambridge if sometimes in its box of
sky lavender and cornerless, the
moon rattles like a fragment of angry candy

from "[the Cambridge ladies who live in furnished souls]"

Innovative in a small and subversive way . . . the one who used capital letters, punctuation, and conventional typography only when he felt like it, which helped him convince a considerable readership that what they were getting was wisdom . . . the son of a minister (about whom he'd write "my father / moved through dooms of love"), he sided with the little guy, the fellow down on his luck, the protester . . . has been likened to Robin Hood (the anarchist), Mickey Spillane (the tough guy), and Peter Pan (the boy who wouldn't grow up) . . . wrote love poems marked by childlike wonder and great good humor.

HART CRANE (1899–1932)

The photographs of hades in the brain
Are tunnels that re-wind themselves, and love
A burnt match skating in a urinal.

from *The Bridge* ("The Tunnel")

Wanted, like Whitman, to embrace the whole country, and was only egged on by the fact that he couldn't get his arms around it . . . his major poem *The Bridge* (that's the Brooklyn Bridge, a symbol of the heights to which modern man aspires), an epic about, as Crane put it, "a mystical synthesis of 'America' "; in it you can hear not just Whitman, but Woody Guthrie . . . as somebody said, found apocalypse under rocks and in bureau drawers . . . "through all sounds of gaiety and quest," Crane claims he hears "a kitten crying in the wilderness" . . . a homosexual who, at thirty-three, committed suicide by jumping overboard into the Gulf of Mexico.

ROBERT LOWELL (1917–1977)

The Aquarium is gone. Everywhere
giant-finned cars move forward like fish;
a savage servility
slides by on grease.

from "For the Union Dead"

One of the New England Lowells (like James Russell and Amy) . . . discussed the intricacies of the Puritan conscience, then converted to Catholicism . . . his principle subject the flux, struggle, and agony of experience . . . was interested in "the dark and against the grain" . . . lived a high-profile personal life (political stress, marital strain, organized protest, mental illness) . . . even so, managed to outlive and outwork such equally troubled colleagues and intimates as Delmore Schwartz, Randall Jarrell, Theodore Roethke, and John Berryman . . . gave poetry a new autobiographical aspect and a renewed sense of social responsibility . . . aroused greater admiration and jealousy, for the space of twenty years, than any other contemporary American poet.

ROOTS: FOUR PRIMARY INFLUENCES

THE ROMANTICS: Wordsworth, Shelley, et al. (see pages 188–89 and 191–92). The line of descent starts here, with all that talk about the importance of the imagination and the self. Don't tell your modern-poet friends this, though; they probably follow Yeats and Eliot in repudiating the early nineteenth century and would rather date things from Whitman and/or the Symbolists.

THE SYMBOLISTS: Rimbaud, Verlaine, Mallarmé, and the rest of the Frogs, plus the young Yeats. (Poe and Baudelaire were forerunners.) Believed there was another world beyond the visual one, a world of secret connections and private references, all of which just might, if you gave them a shove, form a pattern of some kind. Thus drunken boats and "fragrances fresh as the flesh of children." Gets a little lugubrious, but don't we all? Anyway, they made poetry even more an affair of the senses than the Romantics had done.

WALT WHITMAN: Founding father of American poetry. Charged with the poetic mission ("I speak the password primeval"), he raised all the issues that modern poetry is about: experimentation with language and form; revelation of self; the assumption that the poet, the reader, and the idea are all in the same room together and that a poem could make something happen. Hyperventilated a lot, but people on the side of freedom and variety are like that.

EMILY DICKINSON: Founding mother of American poetry; as William Carlos Williams put it, "patron saint" and "a real good guy." Reticent and soft-spoken where Whitman is aggressive and amped. Short lines to Whitman's long ones, microcosm to his macrocosm: "The brain is wider than the sea." Gets you to see how infinity can mean infinitely small as well as infinitely big.

HOOTS: FOUR TWENTIETH-CENTURY POETS NOT TO TOUCH WITH A TEN-FOOT STROPHE

First, Edna St. Vincent Millay, Our Lady of the Sonnets, who, in 1923, beat out—with three slender volumes, including one titled *A Few Figs from Thistles*—T. S. Eliot's *The Waste Land* for the Pulitzer Prize; but who, subsequently, despite former boyfriend Edmund Wilson's efforts to save her, began to seem, "ah, my foes, and oh, my friends," very silly. Also, Amy Lowell, dragon to Millay's sylph, whom Eliot called "the demon saleswoman of poetry" and whom Pound accused of reducing the tenets of Imagism to "Amygism"; you may remember, from tenth-grade English, her musings on squills and ribbons and garden walks. Now she doesn't even make the anthologies.

Then, Carl Sandburg, who catalogued so memorably the pleasures of Chicago, his home town ("City of the Big Shoulders," and so forth), who almost certainly liked ketchup on his eggs, but who was, even back then, accused— by Robert Frost, hardly an innocent himself—of fraud; better to go with Will Rogers here, or Whitman (whom Sandburg consciously imitated). Finally, Edwin Arlington Robinson, whose "Richard Cory" and "Miniver Cheevy" we can recite whole stanzas of, too, which is precisely the problem. Picture yourself in a room full of well-groomed young adults, all of whom, if they chose, could swing into "Miniver loved the Medici, / Albeit he had never seen one; / He would have sinned incessantly / Could he have been one."

OFFSHOOTS: FIVE CULT FIGURES

Five poets, no longer young (or even, in a couple of cases, alive), who are nevertheless as edgy, angry, and/or stoned as you are.

ALLEN GINSBERG: Dropout, prophet, and "Buddhist Jew," not necessarily in that order. "America I'm putting my queer shoulder to the wheel." His most famous works, *Howl* (about the beat culture of the Fifties, the second part of which was written during a peyote vision) and "Kaddish" (about his dead mother, this one written on amphetamines). Some critics see him in the tradition of William Blake: a spiritual adventurer with a taste for apocalypse, who saw no difference between religion and poetry. As William Carlos Williams said in his intro to *Howl*, "Hold back the edges of your gowns, Ladies, we are going through hell."

FRANK O'HARA: Cool—but approachable. At the center of the New York School of poets (others were John Ashbery, James Schuyler, and Kenneth Koch), and a bridge between artists and writers of the Sixties. Objected to abstraction and philosophy in poetry, preferring a spur-of-the-moment specificity he called "personism." Had a thing about the movies, James Dean, pop culture in general; and his poems prefigure pop art. Thus, in "The Day Lady Died," lines like, "I go on to the bank / and Miss Stillwagon (first name Linda I once heard) / doesn't even look up my balance for once in her life. . . ." Run down by a dune buggy on Fire Island.

ROBERT CREELEY: One of the Black Mountain poets, out of the experimental backwoods college in North Carolina where, back in the Fifties, the idea of a "counterculture" got started. Kept his poems short and intimate, with titles such as "For No Clear Reason" and "Somewhere." His most famous utterance: "Form is never more than an extension of content." (Stay away from the prose, though, which reads like Justice Department doublespeak.) The consummate dropout: from Harvard—twice, once to India, once to Cape Cod—with additional stints in Majorca, Guatemala, and, of course, Black Mountain. "If you were going to get a pet / what kind of animal would you get."

SYLVIA PLATH: Her past is your past: report cards, scholarships (in her case, to Smith), summers at the beach. In short, banality American-style, on which she goes to town. May tell you more about herself than you wanted to know (along with Robert Lowell, she's the model of the confessional poet); watch especially for references to her father ("marble-heavy, a bag full of God, / Ghastly statue with one grey toe / Big as a Frisco seal. . . ."). Wrote *The Bell Jar*, autobiographical—and satirical—novel of an adolescent's breakdown and attempted suicide. Married to English poet Ted Hughes, she later committed suicide herself. The new style of woman poet (along with Anne Sexton and Adrienne Rich), a cross between victim and rebel.

LEROI JONES, a.k.a. Imamu Amiri Baraka: Started off easy, doing graduate work at Columbia and hanging out with his first wife (who, as it happened, was white) in Greenwich Village. Subsequently turned militant: "We must make our own / World, man, our own world, and we can not do this unless the white man / is dead. Let's get together and kill him, my man, let's get to gather the fruit / of the sun." Moved first to Harlem, then to Newark (where he'd grown up). Looked to jazz, to Africa, to the black experience for strength; took up wearing dashikis and speaking in Swahili. Likewise to be noted: his plays, especially *Dutchman* (1964).

American Intellectual History, and Stop That Snickering

EIGHT AMERICAN INTELLECTUALS

The French have them, the Germans have them, even the Russians have them, so by God why shouldn't we? Admittedly, in a country that defines "scholarship" as free tuition for quarterbacks, intellectuals tend to be a marginal lot. Jewish, for the most part, and New York Jewish at that, they are accustomed to being viewed as vaguely *un*-American and to talking mainly to each other—or to themselves. (The notable exception is Norman Mailer, an oddball as intellectuals go, but a solid American who managed to capture the popular imagination by thinking, as often as not, with his fists.) The problem is precisely this business of incessant thinking. Intellectuals don't think up a nifty idea, then sell it to the movies; they just keep thinking up more ideas, as if that were the point.

GERTRUDE STEIN (1874–1946)

Our man in Paris, so to speak, Stein was one of those rare expatriates who wasn't ashamed to be an American. In fact, for forty-odd years after she'd bid adieu to Radcliffe, medical school, and her rich relatives in Baltimore, she was positively thrilled to be an American, probably because her exposure to her compatriots was pretty much limited to the innumerable doughboys and GIs she befriended (and wrote about) during two world wars—all of whom, to hear her tell it, adored her; and to the struggling-but-stylish young writers for whom she coined the phrase "The Lost Generation" (Hemingway, Sherwood Anderson, et al.), who were happy to pay homage to her genuine wit and fearless intellect while scarfing up hors d'oeuvres at the Saturday soirées at 27 rue de Fleurus (an address, by the way, that's as much to be remembered as anything Stein wrote). True, Hemingway later insisted that, although he'd learned a lot from Gert, he hadn't learned as much as she kept telling everyone he had. True, too, that if she hadn't been so tight with Hemingway and Picasso (whom she claimed to have "discovered"), the name Gertrude Stein might today be no more memorable than "Rooms," "Objects," or "Food," three pieces of experimental writing that more or less sum up the Gertrude Stein problem. The mysterious aura that still surrounds her name has less to do with her eccentricity or her lesbianism (this was Paris, after all) than with the fact that most of what she wrote is simply unreadable. Straining to come up with the exact literary equivalent of Cubist painting, the "Mama of Dada" was often so pointlessly cerebral that once the bohemian chic wore off, she seemed merely numbing.

RECOMMENDED READING: *Three Lives* (1909), three short novels centered on three serving women; an early work in which Stein's experiments with repetition, scrambled syntax, and lack of punctuation still managed to evoke her subjects instead of burying them. *The Autobiography of Alice B. Toklas* (1933), the *succès de scandale* in which Stein, adopting the persona of her long-time secretary and companion, disseminated her opinions on the famous artists of her day with great good humor and, the critics said, an outrageous lack of sense. Also, give a listen to *Four Saints in Three Acts* (1934), an opera collaboration with Virgil Thomson that still gets good notices.

EDMUND WILSON (1895–1972)

A squire trapped in the body of a bulldog. Or do we mean a bulldog trapped in the body of a squire? Anyhoo, America's foremost man of letters, decade after decade, from the Twenties until the day of his death. Erudite and cantankerous, Wilson always steered clear of the teaching positions and institutional involvements that all other literary critics and social historians seemed to take refuge in, preferring to wing it as a reviewer and journalist. The life makes good reading: quasi-aristocratic New Jersey boyhood, Princeton education (and start of lifelong friendship with F. Scott Fitzgerald), several marriages, including one to Mary McCarthy (whom he persuaded to write fiction), robust sex life, running battles with the IRS (over unpaid income taxes) and Vladimir Nabokov (over Russian verse forms), the nickname "Bunny." Plus, who else went out and studied Hebrew in order to decipher the Dead Sea Scrolls (Wilson's single biggest scoop) or ploughed through a thousand musty volumes because he wanted to figure out the Civil War for himself?

Bunny, you see, was determined to get to the bottom of things, make connections, monitor the progress of the Republic, and explain the world to Americans and Americans to themselves, all with the understanding that it could be as much fun to dissect—and hold forth on—Emily Post as T. S. Eliot.

RECOMMENDED READING: *Axel's Castle* (1931), a booklength study of the symbolist tradition in Europe and a good general introduction to Yeats, Eliot, Proust, Joyce, et al. *To the Finland Station* (1940), a booklength study of the radical tradition in Europe and a good general introduction to Vico, Michelet, Lenin, Trotsky, et al. *Upstate* (1972), an old man's meditation on himself, his life, and his imminent death.

LIONEL TRILLING (1905–1975)

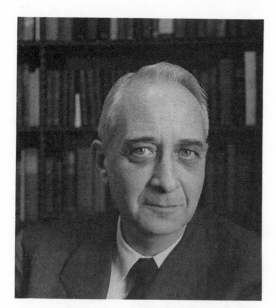

Self, society, mind, will, history, and, needless to say, culture. It can be a bit of a yawn, frankly, especially when you really only wanted him to explain what Jane Austen was up to in *Mansfield Park,* but at least you'll find out what liberalism—of the intellectual as opposed to the merely political variety—is all about. A big Freudian, also a big Marxist, and affiliated with Columbia University for his entire professional life, Trilling worries about things like "the contemporary ideology of irrationalism" (this in the Sixties, when the view from Morningside Heights wouldn't hold still, and when Trilling himself was beginning to seem a little, uh, over the hill); "our disaffection from history"; and, more than anything else, the tensions between self and society, literature and politics, aesthetics and morality. A touch rueful, a little low-key, Trilling wasn't constantly breaking out the port and the bon mots like Wilson, but his heart was in the right place: He cared about the nature and quality of life on the planet, and probably would have lent you the guest room if, as one of his undergraduates, you'd gotten locked out of the dorm.

RECOMMENDED READING: *The Liberal Imagination* (1950), the single most widely read "New York" critical work, which, under the guise of discussing literature, actually aimed, as Trilling said, to put liberal assumptions "under some degree of pressure." *The Middle of the Journey* (1947), his one novel, about political issues (read Stalinism) confronting American intellectuals of the day; loosely based on the life of Whittaker Chambers. *Sincerity and Authenticity* (1972), late Trilling, especially the concluding examination of "the doctrine that madness is health."

HANNAH ARENDT (1906–1975)

Back in the Fifties she seemed like an absolute god-send—a bona fide German intellectual come to roost in the American university system at a time when intellectuals had the kind of clout that real estate developers have today. Not only did Arendt actually condescend to *talk* to her students at Princeton (where she was the first woman professor ever), and Columbia, and Berkeley, and so on, but she saw nothing demeaning in writing about current events, bringing to bear the kind of Old World erudition and untranslated Latin and Greek phrases that made Mr. and Mrs. America feel they could stand tall. She wasn't afraid to take on the looming postwar bogey-men—war crimes, revolution, genocide—and, as it seemed at the time, wrestle them to the ground with the sheer force of her Teutonic aloofness, her faith in the power of the rational, her ability to place un-speakable events in the context of a World View and a History that, inevitably, brought us home to Plato and the moderation-minded Greeks. Granted, she was a little too undiscriminating about her audience, a little too arbitrary in her assertions, and a little too sweeping in her generalizations for many of her fellow political philosophers. And she was a little too intent on forging order out of chaos for our taste: When it came to distinguishing between "labor," "work," and "action," or reading 258 pages on the nature of "think-ing," we decided we'd rather merengue. Still, who else dispensed so much intellectual chicken soup to so many febrile minds? Who else thought to point out, amid the hysteria of the Nuremberg trials, that perhaps Adolf Eichmann had not acted alone? And when Arendt had an insight, it was usually a lulu—like the notion that even nice middle-class folks were capable of monstrous acts of destruction. The latter idea gave rise not only to her now-famous phrase, "the banality of evil," but, it is generally agreed, to the New Left which, of course, later disowned Arendt as a flabby bourgeois.

RECOMMENDED READING: *The Origins of Totalitarianism* (1951), a dense, some-times meandering study of the evolution of nineteenth-century anti-Semitism and imperialism into twentieth-century Nazism and Communism; still the classic treatise on the subject, it was, surprisingly enough, a bestseller in its day. *Eichmann in Jerusalem: The Banality of Evil* (1963), with which she made a lot of enemies by insisting not only that Eichmann didn't vomit green slime and speak in tongues, but that he didn't even get a fair trial. *The Life of the*

Mind (1977), her unfinished magnum opus, two volumes of which were published posthumously; as one critic pointed out, it may fall short of chronicling the life of the mind, but it does a bang-up job of chronicling the life of Arendt's mind.

PAUL GOODMAN (1911–1972)

True, he was an anarchist, communist, draft dodger, sexual liberationist (and confirmed bisexual), as well as den father to the New Left, but Paul Goodman still comes off sounding an awful lot like Mr. Novak. Talk about soft-spokenness, talk about lending a hand, talk about talking it out: Goodman is *there* for the "kids," as he calls them, including the "resigned" beats and the "fatalistic" hoods, plus everybody else who's going to wind up either dropping out or making Chevy tail fins on an assembly line. Humankind is innocent, loving, and creative, you dig? It's the bureaucracies that create the evil, that make Honor and Community impossible, and it's the kids who really take it in the groin. Thus goes the indictment of the American social and educational systems in Goodman's *Growing Up Absurd* (1960), the book that made him more than just another underground hero. But to get the whole picture, you'll also have to plow through his poems, plays, novels, magazine pieces, and confessions; his treatises on linguistics, constitutional law, Gestalt therapy, Noh theater, and, with his brother, city planning; plus listen to him tell you about his analysis and all those sit-ins. A renaissance man in an era that favored specialization, Goodman never lost his sense of wonder—or of outrage. And one more thing: If your parents used to try to get you to watch them "making love," it may well have been on Goodman's say-so.

RECOMMENDED READING: *Growing Up Absurd*, of course. And, if you liked that, *The Empire City* (1959), a novel with a hero perversely named Horatio Alger and a lambasting of the Thirties, Forties, and Fifties. *Five Years: Thoughts in a Useless Time* (1967), his journal of late-Fifties despair. And "May Pamphlet" (1945), a modern counterpart to Thoreau's "Civil Disobedience."

NORMAN MAILER (1923–)

Although he probably wouldn't have wowed them at the Deux Magots, Mailer, in the American intellectual arena, is at least a middleweight. Beginning in the mid-Fifties, when he took time off from his pursuit of the Great American Novelist prize to write a weekly column for *The Village Voice* (which he co-founded), he has probably been our most visible social critic, purveyor of trends, attacker of ideologies, and promoter of the concept of the artist as public figure. Operating as a sort of superjournalist—even Mailer has never claimed to be a man of letters—he proceeded to define new waves of consciousness, from "hip" to the peace movement to feminism, just as (though never, as his detractors point out, before) they hit the cultural mainstream. Like a true New Journalist, he was forever jumping into the action, taking risks, playing with the language, and making sociological connections. Unlike other New Journalists, however, he came equipped with a liberal Jewish background, a Harvard education, considerable talent as a novelist, and enough ambition to make him emperor, if only he'd been a little less cerebral and a lot less self-destructive. By the late Sixties, he'd hit on the strategy (soon to become an M.O.) of using narcissism as a tool for observation and commentary, a device which seemed both to validate a decade or so of personal excess (drugs, drink, fistfights, and the much-publicized stabbing of his second wife) and to set him up as the intellectual successor to Henry Adams. Later, he got himself into debt, wrote second-rate coffee-table books, launched an unsuccessful campaign for the mayoralty of New York City, married too many women, sired too many children, made too many belligerent remarks on TV talk shows, got behind one of the worst causes célèbres ever (Jack Abbott), spent a decade writing a "masterpiece" no one could read (*Ancient Evenings*), and generally exhausted everyone's patience. Still, it's worth remembering that, as *Time* magazine put it, "For a heady period, no major event in U.S. life seemed quite complete until Mailer had observed himself observing it." Moreover, it's hard to think of anyone who managed to explore the nature of celebrity in the media age from so many different angles—and lived to tell the tale.

RECOMMENDED READING: *Advertisements for Myself* (1959), a collection of combative essays and mean-spirited criticism of fellow writers, which marked the beginning of Mailer's notoriety; read it for the two acknowledged masterpieces: "The White Negro" and "The Time of Her Time." *Armies of the Night* (1968), Mailer's account of the anti-Vietnam War march on Washington; his most widely read nonfiction book and the debut of the narrator-as-center-of-the-universe format. *Miami and the Siege of Chicago* (1969), more of the same, only different; an attempt to penetrate to the heart—or lack thereof—of the Republican and Democratic conventions. *The Executioner's Song* (1979), the Pulitzer Prize–winning saga of convicted murderer Gary Gilmore; Mailer's comeback after all those coffee-table books and, as one critic suggested, his single foray into punk literature.

NOAM CHOMSKY (1928–)

Sometimes it's a mistake to try to make connections. For instance, there's not much point in trying to derive Jane Fonda, the leftwing political activist and Mrs. Tom Hayden, from Jane Fonda, the Hollywood actress who starred in *Klute* and *Barbarella*. Or vice versa. Likewise, although it's only natural to want to connect Noam Chomsky, the linguist and philosopher, with Noam Chomsky, the political observer and outspoken critic of American society, it's not going to get you very far. The latter Chomsky went on the most memorable of the Vietnam peace marches and spoke out repeatedly against "the military–industrial complex" and American foreign policy in Southeast Asia; chided the "liberal intelligentsia" for rationalizing the worst excesses of the politicians and technocrats; and suggested, back when Henry Kissinger was up for a Columbia professorship, that the former Secretary of State and professional *éminence grise* was fit to head only a "Department of Death." The former Chomsky held forth on the subject of generative—a.k.a. transformational—grammar, with its deep and surface structures, and on the nature of the mind itself. Simply put, Chomsky believes that man's capacity for mastering language, specifically its grammatical structure, is innate, as genetically determined as his digestive system or his sex drive. The result: All of us constantly (and painlessly) use sequences and combinations of words that we have never heard before, much less learned. Chomsky singlehandedly managed to bring linguistics front and center, transforming it (you should pardon the expression) from an academic specialty practiced among moribund American Indian tribes and sleepy college sophomores into the subject of heated debate among epistemologists, behavioral psychologists, child-development theorists, and the French, but that doesn't mean he didn't accumulate his share of detractors. Some complained that he makes the human consciousness sound suspiciously like an Apple computer; others note that he never really defined what he meant by "deep structure," the psychic system from which our spoken language is generated and of which any sentence or group of sentences is in some way a map. Critics also tend to find his political thinking strident, flat, brittle, opinionated, and, in the final analysis, not all that bright.

RECOMMENDED READING: Try *Language and Mind,* a series of three lectures Chomsky gave at Berkeley in 1967, for his clearest statement on the relations between his theory of language and his theory of human nature; follow with *Topics in the Theory of Generative Grammar* (1966), an easy-to-understand statement of his basic linguistic notions. *Aspects of the Theory of Syntax* (1965) is the classic statement of Chomsky's mature theory, but if you stood even the eentsiest chance of being able to read it you wouldn't in a million years be reading *this.* Many of the early political essays are collected in *American Power and the New Mandarins* (1969); a more recent collection is *Towards a New Cold War* (1982).

SUSAN SONTAG (1933–)

She delineated a new aesthetic, heavy on style, sensation, and immediacy. For Sontag (the Sontag of the Sixties, that is) art and morality had no common ground and it didn't matter what an artist was trying to say as long as the result turned you on. For everyone from the *Partisan Review* crowd to the kids down at the Fillmore, she seemed like a godsend; she not only know where it was at, she *was* where it was at. A serious thinker with a frame of reference to beat the band, a hard-nosed analytical style, and subscriptions to all the latest European journals, she would emerge from her book-lined study (where she had, presumably, been immersed in a scholarly comparison of Hegel's philosophical vocabulary, Schoenberg's twelve-tone theory, and the use of the quick cut in the films of Godard), clad in jeans, sneakers, and an old cardigan, to tell the world it was OK to listen to the Supremes. Maybe you never *did* understand what Godard was getting at—at least you knew that, if Sontag took him on, he, too, was where it was at. Ditto Bergman, Genet, Warhol, Artaud, John Cage, Roland Barthes, Claude Lévi-Strauss, Norman O. Brown, and the government of North Vietnam. Eclecticism was the hallmark of Sontag's modernist (today, read postmodernist) sensibility. A writer with all the grace and subtlety of a guerrilla commando issuing proclamations to a hostile government, she has come under heavy attack from her critics—who are a lot more outspoken now than they were back when they were still hoping to get invited to the latest Happening—for her political naïveté (and revisionism); for the uncompromising vehemence of her assertions; and for suffering, as one writer put it, "from the recurring delusion that life is art." To which her fans reply that Sontag's ability to get all these reactionary types so hot under the collar is exactly what makes her a national treasure.

RECOMMENDED READING: *Against Interpretation* (1966), a collection of essays that includes some of her best-known works, e.g. the title piece, "On Style," and "Notes on Camp." *Styles of Radical Will* (1966), another nonfiction grab bag whose high points are a defense of pornography ("The Pornographic Imagination"), a lengthy discussion of Godard ("Godard"), and one of her most famous—and certainly most readable—essays, "Trip to Hanoi." *On Photography* (1977), the book that won her a large lay audience and innumerable enemies among photographers (and that helped a lot of people feel they finally knew what to make of Diane Arbus). Sontag has also written fiction, in the trippy, content-eschewing style of the French *nouveau roman*, and a couple of screenplays, notable for their lack of plot and characterization.

AND EIGHT PEOPLE WHO, AMERICAN OR NOT, HAD IDEAS WHOSE TIME, IT SEEMED AT THE TIME, HAD COME

MARSHALL McLUHAN (1911–1980)

"The medium is the message," of course. That is, the way we acquire information affects us more than the information itself. The medium is also, as a later version of the aphorism had it, "the massage": Far from being neutral, a medium "does something to people; it takes hold of them, bumps them around." Case in point—television, with its mosaic of tiny dots of light, its lack of clarification, its motion and sound, and its relentless projection of all of the above straight at the viewer, thereby guaranteeing that viewer an experience as aural and tactile as it is visual. And high time, too. Ever since Gutenberg and his printing press, spewing out those endless lines of bits of print, the eye had gotten despotic, thinking linear, and life fragmented; with the advent of the age of electronics man was at last returning to certain of his tribal ways—and the world was becoming a "global village." There were those who dismissed McLuhan (for the record, a Canadian) as less a communications theorist cum college professor than a phrase-mongering charlatan, but even they couldn't ignore entirely his distinction between "hot" and "cool" media (it's the latter that, as with TV or comic books or talking on the phone, tend to involve you so much that you're late for supper). Besides, McLuhan had sort of beaten his critics to the punch: Of his own work, he liked to remark, "I don't pretend to understand it. After all, my stuff is very difficult."

R. BUCKMINSTER FULLER (1895–1983)

"An engineer, inventor, mathematician, architect, cartographer, philosopher, poet, cosmogonist, comprehensive designer, and choreographer" was how

Fuller described himself; for a few other people "crackpot," "megalomaniac," "enfant terrible," or "Gyro Gearloose" did as good a job more economically. Convinced that man, through technology and planning, could become super- man and "save the world from itself"; that "Spaceship Earth" was a large mechanical device that needed periodic tuning; that "the entire population" of that earth "could live compactly on a properly designed Haiti and comforta- bly on the British Isles"; that the geodesic dome, a sphere composed of much smaller tetrahedrons, was the most rigorously logical structure around; and that he himself had "a blind date with principle," "Bucky" flew tens of thousands of miles annually, visiting Khrushchev's Moscow and everybody else's college campus with equal élan, waving excitedly from behind Coke- bottle glasses for up to six hours at a time. (Annually, that is, except for the year during which he refused to speak at all, to anybody, including his wife.) His ultimate conclusion: The universe is governed by relatively few principles and its essence is not matter but design.

KATE MILLETT (1934–)

Whatever their personal feelings about women in combat boots, you'd have thought men would be open-minded enough to admit that, for a chick, Millett had guts. An academic turned activist, and one of those unstoppable Catho- lics-in-revolt, she was always willing to walk it like she talked it. While Betty Friedan, the supply-sider of sisterhood, was still dressing for success and biting her nails over whether or not it was OK to have lesbians as friends, Millett was out in full drag, holding the Statue of Liberty hostage, chronicling her affairs in vivid—not to say tedious—detail, and telling women it was time to get out from underneath, not just figuratively, but literally. But it all paid off eventually; *Sexual Politics* became a bestseller, its once-revolutionary thesis was accepted as basic feminist canon, men started having trouble getting it up, and Betty Friedan began to wonder if having your own corner office and your own coronary was really all it was cracked up to be.

MALCOLM X (1925–1965)

The Last Angry Negro, before everybody stopped saying Negro, Brother Malcolm (né Malcolm Little and a.k.a. Red, Satan, Homeboy, and El-Hajj Malick El-Shabazz) was one of the first to come right out and tell the world what he *really* thought of honkies. Although, in his days as a radical, which, in what was to become a trend, followed closely on his days as a dealer/pimp/burglar/convict/Muslim convert, Malcolm never actually *did* much, he managed, through sheer spleen, to scare the socks off Whitey, make Martin Luther King reach for the Excedrin, and provide a role model for a generation of black activists who were ready to put their muscle where Malcolm's mouth had been. Whatever folks thought of his politics, everyone had to admit that Malcolm had charisma: At one point, the *New York Times* rated him the country's second most popular campus speaker, after Barry Goldwater. Malcolm mellowed considerably after Elijah Muhammad booted him out of the Black Muslims (and Muhammad Ali dropped him as his Personal Spiritual Advisor). Unfortunately, it wasn't long after that that he was gunned down by an informal firing squad hired, various rumors had it, by the Muslims, the U.S. government, or the Red Chinese. Whatever—he was immortalized by the bestselling autobiography ghostwritten by Alex "Roots" Haley.

ERNESTO "CHE" GUEVARA (1928–1967)

The peripatetic Argentine revolutionary who became a model of radical style and, along with Huey Newton, one of the seminal dorm posters of the Sixties. Although he did have a catchy nickname (it translates, roughly, as "Hey, you") and a way with a beret, the main points to remember are that he was the Number Two man, chief ideologue, and resident purist of the Cuban revolution; and that he wrote *the* book on guerrilla warfare. He also showed all the kids back in Great Neck that a nice middle-class boy from Buenos Aires, with a medical degree, no less, could make good defending the downtrodden in the jungles of the Third World. His split with Fidel over the latter's cop-out to Soviet-style materialism (Che was holding out for the purity of Chinese Marxism) didn't hurt his reputation, either; nor did going underground for a couple of years, during which, it later turned out, he was in all the right places—North Vietnam, the Congo, various Latin American hot spots. Unfortunately, his revolutionary theories were a little half-baked, and when he tried to implement them down in Bolivia, he ran smack into the Bolivian army—a colonel of which summarily executed him, thereby creating an instant martyr.

HUNTER THOMPSON (1939–)

The one journalist you could trust back when you were a sophomore at the University of Colorado. A sportswriter by training and temperament (he was

Raoul Duke in *Rolling Stone* magazine), Hunter, as we all called him, became a media star by inventing "Gonzo Journalism," a reportorial style that was one step beyond New Journalism and two steps over the edge of the pool. Gonzo Journalism revolved around drugs, sex, and the patent impossibility of Hunter's ever meeting his deadlines, given the condition he was in. It assumed that all global events were engineered to (a) make you laugh, (b) make you famous, or (c) kill you. For the record, Hunter really did fear and loathe Richard Nixon, with whom he shared the rampant paranoia of the day; by the time he'd finished cataloguing the various controlled substances he'd supposedly ingested to ease the pain of the 1972 presidential campaign, he was a shoo-in as the Walter Cronkite of the Haight-Ashbury set. By the end of the decade, though, the joyride was over. Dr. Gonzo, sent to Saigon to cover the evacuation, took one look at the genuine carnage around him, filed his expense report, and caught the next plane for home. Moreover, college kids started thinking that maybe there *was* life outside Hunter's hotel room; worse, history rounded a bend and they discovered John Belushi.

WILHELM REICH (1897–1957)

Brilliant but dumb, if you know what we mean, and certainly, by the end, not playing with a full deck. His early Marxist-Freudian notions made some sense, such as the idea that you can't revolutionize politics without revolutionizing the people who make them, or that thinking about yourself constantly can make you neurotic. Frankly, his emphasis on the regenerative powers of the orgasm seemed a little simpleminded even at the time, but it wasn't until his discovery of Orgone Energy—the life force which he found to be bluish-green in color—that some of us got up and moved to the other end of the bus. Before you could say "Deadly Orgone Energy," Reich was babbling about cosmic orgone engineers—"CORE men"—from other planets and comparing himself to such historic martyrs as Jesus, Socrates, Nietzsche, and Woodrow Wilson (that "great, warm person"). He died in a federal penitentiary in 1957, convicted of transporting empty Orgone Boxes across state lines.

GEORGE IVANOVITCH GURDJIEFF (1874–1949)

The Paul Bunyan of mystics, Gurdjieff spent twenty years pursuing "truth" through the wilds of Asia and North Africa, crossing the Gobi on stilts, navigating the River Kabul on a raft, clambering blindfolded through vertiginous mountain passes, chatting up dervishes and seers, unearthing a map of "pre-sand" Egypt, digging through ruins, hanging out in a secret monastery, and soaking up ancient wisdom and esoteric knowledge. If you're wondering what he learned, we suggest you do the same; Gurdjieff certainly isn't going to tell you: His summa, *All and Everything*, is 1,266 pages in search of an editor. You could try wading through the explications of P. D. Ouspensky, the Russian mathematician who was Gurdjieff's top disciple for a while, remembering, however, that Gurdjieff thought Ouspensky was an ass for trying to explicate him. Never mind. Just ask yourself, "Would I really buy spiritual guidance from a man who once raised cash by dyeing sparrows yellow and selling them as canaries?" If your answer is no, you probably would have missed the point anyway.

Family Feud

A BRIEF HISTORY OF AMERICAN POLITICAL PARTIES

The symbology (donkey and elephant, Tip O'Neill and George Bush) seems carved in stone and the structure (wards and precincts, national committees and electoral colleges) as intrinsically American as a B.L.T. Imagine your surprise, then, when we remind you of something you learned for the first time back in fifth grade; namely, that this nation of ours, purple mountain majesties and all, began its life without any political parties whatsoever. George Washington—whose election in 1788 had been unanimous and unopposed, and who at one point found himself being addressed as "Your Highness the President"—was above even thinking in terms of party loyalty. The rest of the Founding Fathers considered "factions," as they put it, straightening their periwigs, to be unscrupulous gangs hell-bent on picking the public pocket. James Madison, for instance, while an old hand at lining up votes and establishing majorities on specific issues, assumed that those majorities would (and should) fall away once the issue in question had been resolved.

But then there was Alexander Hamilton, who, having managed to dictate foreign policy to Washington and domestic policy to Congress for the better part of two administrations, finally gave Madison and Jefferson no choice but to take action against him. Hamilton was a Northerner, a federalist (as opposed to a state's rightser), an industrialist, a venture capitalist, and a power broker. Jefferson you know about: Southerner, agrarian, progressive, and all-around renaissance man. Thus began the power struggle that would result, by 1796, in the formation of two rival parties—Hamilton's Federalists and Jefferson's Democratic Republicans, ancestors of our Republicans and Democrats, respectively.

The blow-by-blow (including how Jefferson bested Hamilton and what the difference between Jeffersonian and Jacksonian democracy is) we'll save for another time. In the meantime, take a look at this chart for the big picture:

Round 1	**DEMOCRATIC REPUBLICANS*** (1796, Jefferson, Madison, et al.— the South and landowning interests)	**FEDERALISTS** (1792, Hamilton, John Adams, et al.— the North and commercial interests; gone by 1816)

TIME OUT: Monroe's factionless "Era of Good Feelings," 1817–1824

Round 2	**DEMOCRATS*** (1832, Andrew Jackson—as above, plus small farmers, backwoods types, "little guys" in general)	**NATIONAL REPUBLICANS** (1828, J. Q. Adams, Henry Clay—as above, plus border-states residents; gone by 1832)
		WHIGS (as above, plus anti-Jacksonian Democrats)
Round 3		**REPUBLICANS*** (1856, Abraham Lincoln—Northerners, urbanites, business types, factory workers, blacks)
Round 4	**DEMOCRATS*** (FDR—dominant 1932 through 1960s, Northeasterners and Southerners, city dwellers, blue-collar workers, Catholics, liberals, ethnics)	**REPUBLICANS** (Midwesterners, businessmen, farmers, white-collar workers, Protestants, the "Establishment")

*Dominant party.

Note that for almost 200 years the same two parties, variously named, have been lined up against each other; third parties—Teddy Roosevelt's Bull Moose, Robert LaFollette's Progressive Action, Strom Thurmond's Dixiecrats, and more recently, George Wallace's American Independence—while a godsend for political commentators trying to fill column inches, have had surprisingly little success with the electorate. Nor is this a country where we think much of (or where most of us could define) coalition as a political form.

As to how you can distinguish Republicans from Democrats today, we'll content ourselves with quoting from a letter from a friend: "Republicans hire exterminators to kill their bugs; Democrats step on them. . . . Democrats buy most of the books that have been banned somewhere; Republicans form censorship committees and read the books as a group. . . . Democrats eat the fish they catch; Republicans hang theirs on the wall. . . . Republicans tend to keep their shades drawn, although there is seldom any reason why they should; Democrats ought to and don't."

Back to you, George.

American Mischief

FIVE TALES OF AMBITION, GREED, PARANOIA, AND MIND-BOGGLING INCOMPETENCE TO RIVAL WATERGATE

THE TWEED RING: The gang of crooked politicians that ran New York City like a private kingdom throughout the mid-1800s. Led by William Marcy "Boss" Tweed and operating through Tammany, New York's powerful Democratic political machine, these boys were the stuff old gangster movies are made of. Although the "boss" system was widespread in those days and political machines were always, by their very nature, corrupt (essentially, they provided politicians with votes in return for favors), none could match the Tweed Ring for sheer political clout and uninhibited criminality. During its reign, the group bilked the city out of at least $30 million (a conservative estimate); Tweed himself got $40,000 in stock as a bribe for getting the Brooklyn Bridge project approved and a lot more for manipulating the sale of the land that is now Central Park. He also got himself elected to the state senate. The Ring was finally broken in the 1870s through the dogged efforts of the *New York Times*, *Harper's Weekly* cartoonist Thomas Nast (whose caricatures helped demolish Tweed's gangster-with-a-heart-of-gold public image), and Samuel Tilden, a Democratic reformer with his eye on the Presidency. Tweed died in prison; though his name is now synonymous with political corruption, some commentators point out that without crooks like him, there never would have been enough incentive to get this country built.

CRÉDIT MOBILIER: One of the worst financial scandals on record, this tacky affair took place during the notoriously incompetent presidency of Ulysses S. Grant and revolved around the building of the Union Pacific Railroad. Its most visible villain was Oakes Ames, a director of the railroad and a member of the House of Representatives. When Congress agreed to pick up the tab for building the Union Pacific, Ames, who knew the job could be done for much less than the amount granted, got together with some other stockholders to form the Crédit Mobilier, a dummy construction corporation. They used the company to divert excess funds into their pockets. By the time the project was completed in 1869, it was heavily in debt and Ames and his friends had skimmed about $23 million in profits. To be on the safe side, Ames passed out Crédit Mobilier stock to some of his favorite Congressmen. Then, in one of those priceless moves that make history, he wrote a letter to a friend telling him he'd distributed the stock "where it would do the most good" and listing the names of the lucky recipients. Naturally, the newspapers got hold of the letter, and you can guess the rest. Note, however, that although the list implicated officials as high up as the Vice President, none was ever prosecuted. In fact, some historians now wonder what the big fuss was about. After all, they say, what's a few million dollars in the nation's history? They got the job done, didn't they? Yes, but on the other hand, who rides the Union Pacific anymore?

TEAPOT DOME: An oil scandal that took place during the administration of Warren G. Harding, generally acknowledged to have been one of the most worthless presidents ever. Secretary of the Interior Albert B. Fall persuaded Harding to give him control of the U.S. naval oil reserves at Elk Hill, California, and Teapot Dome, Wyoming. A year later, Fall secretly leased the reserves to the owners of two private oil companies, one in exchange for a personal "loan" of $100,000, the other for $85,000 cash, some shares of stock, and a herd of cattle. It wasn't long before the secret leaked and everybody

JUGGERNAUT.

was up before a Senate investigating committee. In yet another remarkable verdict, all three men were acquitted, although Fall was later tried on lesser charges and became the first cabinet member ever to go to prison. Meanwhile, the public was outraged that the Senate had prosecuted at all; this was, as you'll recall, the Roaring Twenties, when everyone was busy doing the Charleston or making shady deals themselves. Even the New York newspapers accused the Senate of character assassination, mudslinging, and generally acting in poor taste.

THE SACCO–VANZETTI CASE: People still seem to take this one personally. Nicola Sacco and Bartolomeo Vanzetti were Italian immigrants accused of murdering two people during an armed robbery in Massachusetts in 1920. The trial, which took place in the wake of the wave of national hysteria known as the "Red Scare," was a joke; the public was paranoid about immigrants and the presiding judge made it clear that *he* knew what to expect from people who talked funny. To make matters worse, Sacco and Vanzetti were avowed anarchists who both owned guns. Although there was no hard evidence against them, they were convicted and sentenced to death. The case became an international cause célèbre, and people like Felix Frankfurter, John Dos Passos, and Edna St. Vincent Millay spent years pressing for a retrial. When Sacco and Vanzetti were finally electrocuted in 1927, everyone was convinced that the whole liberal cause had collapsed. In the end, liberalism didn't die, of course, and Sacco and Vanzetti became martyrs, with poems and plays written about them. Unfortunately, modern ballistics tests conducted in 1961 seemed to prove conclusively that the fatal bullet used in the robbery did indeed come from Sacco's gun. Never mind, it still looks like Vanzetti might have been innocent.

THE PUMPKIN PAPERS: A misnomer, refering to the Alger Hiss case. It is essentially another story of red-baiting and questionable goings-on in the courtroom, but nobody, except the principal characters, feels all that bad about this one; they just love to argue about it. In 1948 Alger Hiss, a former high official in the State Department, was accused by Whittaker Chambers, a senior editor at *Time* magazine and a former spy, of helping him deliver secret information to the Russians. Nobody believed Chambers until Richard Nixon, then an ambitious young lawyer out to make a name for himself, took on his case. Soon afterward, Chambers suddenly produced five rolls of incriminating microfilm (not "papers" at all) that he claimed to have hidden inside a pumpkin on his Maryland farm. These, along with an old typewriter supposedly belonging to Hiss, were the famous props on which the case against him rested. Nixon pushed hard, and the government bent the law in order to try Hiss after the statute of limitations on the alleged crime had run out. He was convicted and served almost four years in jail; Nixon's fortunes were—or seemed to be—made. The case just won't die, however; new evidence and new theories keep popping up like ghosts in an Edgar Allan Poe story. On the one hand, nobody quite believes that Hiss was entirely innocent; on the other hand, they're *sure* Nixon wasn't.

Famous Last Words

TWELVE SUPREME COURT DECISIONS WORTH KNOWING BY NAME

Why worth knowing? Because in a country with a 200-year-old constitution that was never very nuts-and-bolts in the first place, executive and legislative powers that cancel each other out, and a couple hundred million people all talking at once, it can be mighty tricky to tell our rights from our wrongs, much less make either stand up in court. In the end, none of us really knows what's a freedom and what's a felony until nine elderly Justices have adjusted their robes, scratched their heads, and made up their minds.

The Supreme Court in 1921. That's Justice Brandeis in the back row, far left; Oliver Wendell Holmes seated, second from right.

MARBURY v. *MADISON* (1803)

You may know this one only by name, given the catchy alliteration and the fact that we've all had a lot on our minds since 1803. Nevertheless, this was the single most important decision ever handed down by the Court because it established the right of judicial review, without which there wouldn't *be* any Supreme Court decisions worth knowing by name.

The plot gets complicated, but it's worth the effort. John Marbury had been appointed a district-court judge by outgoing President John Adams. In the hubbub of changing administrations, however, the commission—the actual piece of paper—never got delivered. When the new secretary of state, James Madison, refused to honor the appointment, Marbury appealed to the Supreme Court to issue a writ of mandamus, which would force the new administration to give him his commission. Now forget Marbury, Madison, and the meaning of the word mandamus for the moment; what was *really* going on was a power struggle between John Marshall, newly appointed chief justice of the Court and an unshakable Federalist, and Thomas Jefferson, newly elected president of the United States and our most determined anti-Federalist. Marbury's had been only one of innumerable last-minute judgeships handed out by the lame-duck Federalists in an effort to "pack the courts" before the anti-Federalists, who had just won the elections by a landslide, swept them into permanent oblivion. Understandably, the anti-Federalists were furious at what they considered a dirty trick. To make matters even worse, Marshall himself was one of these so-called "midnight judges," appointed just before Jefferson's inauguration; and, as it happened, it was Marshall's brother who had neglected to deliver Marbury's commission in the first place.

By all standards of propriety, Marshall should have been vacationing in Acapulco while this case was being argued. Instead, he wrote the opinion himself, managing to turn it into the classic mix of law and politics that approaches art. First, he declared that Marbury was theoretically entitled to his commission. Second—and here's the twister—he *denied* Marbury's petition on the grounds that the part of the law that allowed the Supreme Court to issue writs of mandamus in this sort of case was unconstitutional, and therefore null and void.

The results: (1) Marbury got to keep his dignity, if nothing else; (2) Jefferson was appeased because Marbury didn't get the job; (3) the Court avoided a confrontation with the president it would certainly have lost, since it didn't have the power to enforce a writ of mandamus even if it had had the power to issue one; and (4) most importantly, the Court officially established itself as the final arbiter of the constitutionality of any law passed by Congress, and it did so by righteously *denying* itself a power. This last point made the Court the effective equal—in a checks-and-balances sort of way—of both Congress and the president. And let's not forget that (5) Marshall came away from the case looking like the soul of judicial integrity, not only because he'd rejected a Federalist place-seeker, but because the law he'd overturned was a Federalist law. This left him free to spend the next thirty-five years interpreting the Constitution and shaping American history according to his own brilliant, but decidedly Federalist, views.

McCULLOCH v. MARYLAND (1819)

Why should you care about a case that prevented the state of Maryland from taxing notes issued by the Second Bank of the United States? Because what was really in question was the constitutionality of the Bank itself; and the Bank brouhaha was symbolic of the major preoccupation of the day: Who was going to run this show, the federal government or the individual states? Had John Marshall not had his way, we might have ended up as a loose confederation of states that couldn't see eye-to-eye on anything, and that certainly wouldn't have had a prayer of beating the Russkies in a missile race.

The controversy over the establishment of the First Bank of the United States was still smoldering in the hearts of states' rights advocates when this new outrage came along. They argued that by incorporating the Second Bank, Congress had exceeded its constitutional powers and that, in any event, the states could tax whatever they wanted to as long as it was on their turf.

Marshall, who, as you'll recall, was an ardent Federalist with a vision of a strong Union, scored the biggest win of his career with this one. In upholding the constitutionality of the Bank's incorporation, he managed to fire off several statements that subsequently became classics of American law. For instance, he deftly worked the opposition's argument—that nowhere in the Constitution was Congress specifically empowered to charter a bank—into the premise that the Constitution speaks in a broad language so that it can be "adapted to the various crises of human affairs." He also claimed that the sovereign people had made the central government supreme over all rivals within the sphere of its powers, and concluded that the Maryland tax was invalid because "the power to tax is the power to destroy," and it just wouldn't make sense to let a supreme power be destroyed by an inferior one. He neatly summed up the whole thing:

> Let the end be legitimate, let it be within the scope of the Constitution, and all means which are appropriate, which are plainly adapted to that end, which are not prohibited but consist with the letter and spirit of the Constitution are constitutional.

Thus, with a few well-chosen words, Marshall not only proclaimed, once and for all, the supremacy of national over state government (well, there was still the Civil War to come, but the theory, at least, was now down on paper), he also established both the federal government's—and, by extension, the Court's—right to make what was henceforth to be known as a "loose construction" of the Constitution. Which, of course, is another way of saying it's anybody's ball game.

DRED SCOTT v. SANFORD (1857)

Yes, Dred Scott was a slave; no, he had nothing to do with John Brown or Harpers Ferry. Nearly everyone seems to have a mental block here, so let's get the story straight, even if it is a bit of a downer. Dred Scott was a Missouri black who sued his master, claiming that he had been automatically freed by having been taken first to Illinois, a free state, then to the Minnesota Territory, where slavery had been forbidden by the Missouri Compromise.

The case was a real cliff-hanger; not only did the Court take forever to decide, but, given the year, there was, naturally, a lot more at stake than one man and a few legal loopholes. The whole country was waiting to see who would ultimately get control of the new western territories. If the slave states succeeded in institutionalizing slavery there, it would mean more votes and political power for the agrarian South. If the antislavery states got their way, it would mean an even greater concentration of power for the industrial North; in which case, the South threatened, it would secede.

Finally, Chief Justice Roger Taney delivered the opinion for a predominantly Southern Court. First, he ruled, Negroes were not citizens of the United States (they had, as he put it, "no rights any white man was bound to respect") and were not, therefore, entitled to go around suing people. Petition denied. The Court could have stopped there but it chose to go for the extra point: Scott, it declared, couldn't possibly have been freed by his stay in the Minnesota Territory because Minnesota wasn't free territory. In fact, Congress had no right to create free territory since, in so doing, it had violated the Fifth Amendment by depriving Southerners of their right to property. Ergo, the Missouri Compromise was unconstitutional, null, and void. The South, naturally, saw this as the Supreme Court's shining hour, while Northerners began to mutter that maybe there was a higher law than the Constitution, after all.

HAMMER v. DAGENHART (1918)

Once the Civil War had dispatched the federal/state power struggle, the Court turned its attention to the country's latest concern: getting rich. Making

America wealthy involved yet another wrestling match, this time between government and business. Now the justices leapt into the ring, headed straight for the big-money corner, and spent the remainder of the "Gilded Age" utilizing their now-considerable repertoire of judicial maneuvers to defend vested wealth against government interference. From Reconstruction through Depression, they handed down a series of decisions that succeeded in blocking federal and state regulations, promoting the principle of laissez-faire, and generally helping the rich get richer. By the early twentieth century, the Court found itself pitted not only against government, but against what it saw as the menace of socialism (the growing labor movement) and the clamor of the masses (social reform).

Hammer v. *Dagenhart* was one of the more memorable illustrations of the spirit of the age. In it, the Court overturned a Congressional act designed to limit child labor. The act prohibited interstate or foreign commerce of commodities produced in factories employing children under fourteen and in mines employing children under sixteen. (If the legislation seems a bit roundabout, it's because the Court had already ruled it unconstitutional for Congress to interfere in the manufacture of goods in any way.) The suit, by the way, was brought by Dagenhart, who had two sons working in a North Carolina cotton mill and who was determined to keep them there. Describing himself as "a man of small means" with a large family to feed, Dagenhart claimed that he needed the boys' pay "for their comfortable support and maintenance." The Court's unshakable conservatism and consistent success in such cases blocked social legislation for years and finally led to Franklin Roosevelt's notorious efforts to "pack the court" with justices friendly to the New Deal. The Court did eventually bow to public pressure for reform, of course, so feel free to hold it responsible (along with the Democrats) for the development of the "welfare state."

SCHENCK v. *UNITED STATES* (1919)

The case that set the bottom line on freedom of speech and, in so doing, gave Justice Oliver Wendell Holmes the opportunity to make one of the Supreme Court's most historic statements:

> The most stringent protection of free speech would not protect a man falsely shouting fire in a theatre and causing panic. . . . The question in every case is whether the words are used in such circumstances and are of such a nature as to create a clear and present danger that will bring about the substantive evils that Congress has a right to prevent. It is a question of proximity and degree. . . . When a nation is at war many

things that might be said in time of peace are such a hindrance to its effort that their utterance will not be endured so long as men fight and that no Court could regard them as being protected by any constitutional right.

The principle of "clear and present danger" became one of the rare justifications for restraining freedom of speech. In the case at hand, it was used to deny the petition of John Schenck, a young man arrested for distributing pamphlets arguing against the legality of the draft. In the Thirties and Forties, it became the basis for prosecuting many people whom the government considered politically subversive.

BROWN v. *BOARD OF EDUCATION OF TOPEKA* (1954)

The decision that, theoretically at least, ended school segregation, although Little Rock was still three years down the road. *Brown*, which was the umbrella for five separate segregation cases from five different states, was the petition brought on behalf of eight-year-old Linda Brown, whose father was tired of watching her take the schoolbus to a blacks-only Topeka school every day when there was a whites-only school within spitting distance—so to speak—of their home. The Court's decision overturned the principle of "separate but equal" facilities it had established with *Plessy* v. *Ferguson* back in 1896. Separate but equal was the doctrine that had, for sixty years, allowed segregationists to insist that they weren't implying that Negroes were inferior just because they didn't want to eat, wash up, or share a bus seat with one. Only slightly less controversial than the Scopes trial, *Brown* attracted friend-of-the-court briefs from everyone from the American Jewish Congress to the AFL-CIO, but the main characters to remember are:

1. Thurgood Marshall, the NAACP lawyer who argued for the petitioners and who later became the Supreme Court's first and, to date, only black Justice.
2. Dr. Kenneth B. Clark, the black New York psychologist who made the courts safe for psychosociology by introducing as evidence his now-famous "dolls experiment." Clark had shown a group of black children two dolls, one black and one white, asking them to choose the doll they found prettiest and would most like to play with, and the doll they thought looked "bad." The children's overwhelming preference for the white doll was seen as proof that segregation was psychologically damaging to black children.
3. Chief Justice Earl Warren, who proved his talents as an orchestrator of men by herding eight feisty justices and nine more or less dis-

similar viewpoints together to form one unanimous opinion; to wit, that "separate educational facilities are inherently unequal." Unanimity, which Warren believed essential in such an explosive situation, subsequently became the hallmark of all Supreme Court decisions on racial equality.

4. President Dwight D. Eisenhower, who was so unsympathetic to the cause of desegregation that the Court, knowing it couldn't count on him to enforce its decision, put off elucidating the how-to's of the opinion for a whole year. At that point, in *Brown II*, it made the cautious, and ultimately disastrous, declaration that the Southern school districts must undertake desegregation measures "with all deliberate speed," a phrase which many Southern school districts chose to interpret as sometime in the afterlife.

BAKER v. *CARR* (1962)

All about reapportionment, but don't go away, we won't bore you with the details (unless of course, you'd *like* to know that Baker was the disgruntled voter, Carr the election official, and the setting was Tennessee). Besides, Earl Warren claimed that this was the most important decision of his not unremarkable tenure as chief justice. What you need to grasp: that the country's demographics had changed over the years but its election districts hadn't, so that small towns and rural areas were consistently overrepresented while cities were underrepresented. This put power firmly in the hands of minority and special-interest groups, who were determined to keep it that way. The Court had long refused to get involved in the "political thicket" of voting rights, but with *Baker* v. *Carr*, it plunged in and decided that unequal election districts were discriminatory and violated the Fourteenth Amendment. This, and the armload of reapportionment cases that followed, not only gave us the phrase "one man, one vote" (or, as more progressive historians would have it, "one person, one vote"), it also shifted the country's center of gravity from the hinterlands to the cities.

MIRANDA v. *ARIZONA* (1966)

The rights of the accused, especially the right to counsel, the right to remain silent when taken into custody, and the right to be informed of one's rights, were at stake here. But you already know this if you've ever watched network television. You may also know that the Miranda rule makes cops snarl and gives the D.A. ulcers. Miranda was the culmination of a series of decisions designed to protect the accused before trial, all of which got their muscle from the exclusionary rule (i.e., throwing out evidence that doesn't conform to tight judicial standards) and none of which won the Warren Court much popularity with law-and-order fans.

The issue is, in fact, a sticky one. Consider it, for instance, from the point of view of Barbara Ann Johnson. One day in 1963, Johnson, an eighteen-year-old candy-counter clerk at a movie theater in Phoenix, was forcibly shoved into the back seat of a car, tied up, and driven to the desert, where she was raped. The rapist then drove her back to town, asked her to say a prayer for him, and let her go. Soon afterwards, the police arrested twenty-three-year-old Ernesto Miranda, a high school dropout with a criminal record dating back to the time he was fourteen. Miranda had already been convicted of rape in the past. Johnson identified him in a lineup. Miranda then wrote out a confession, stating that it was made with full knowledge of his rights. He was convicted and sentenced to forty to fifty-five years in prison, despite his court-appointed lawyer's contention that his client had been ignorant of his right to counsel. An appeal to the state supreme court failed, but the Supreme Court's decision set Miranda free. Miranda and the ACLU were naturally appreciative of the Court's libertarian stance; Barbara Ann Johnson, less so. But not to worry. Miranda was later reconvicted on new evidence. He served time in prison, was released on parole, and was stabbed to death in a Phoenix bar ten years after the Court's landmark decision. And stay tuned: If the Burger Court didn't really make chopped meat of this and most of the other Warren Court rights-of-the-accused provisions, conservatives can still pin their hopes on the Rehnquist Court.

A BOOK NAMED JOHN CLELAND'S "MEMOIRS OF A WOMAN OF PLEASURE" v. MASSACHUSETTS (1966)

Fanny Hill goes to Washington, there to help the Court formulate its three-pronged definition of obscenity. Henceforth, the burden was on the censors to prove that a work in question (a) appealed to prurient interest, (b) was patently offensive, and (c) was utterly without redeeming social value. The result: Pornographers took to making "medical films" prefaced by passages from Shakespeare.

FURMAN v. *GEORGIA* (1972)

Capital punishment outlawed, in one of the longest (243 pages) and most tortured (a 5–4 split and nine separate opinions) decisions of the Court's history. Never mind the gory details of Furman, which was only the lead case among five involving rapes, murders, and rape-murders. More to the point are the four separate arguments the Court was asked to consider as bases for declaring the death penalty unconstitutional:

1. The death penalty was imposed in a discriminatory manner; statistics showed that it was usually black and poor people who died, whereas middle-class whites simply hired the kind of lawyers who could get them off.
2. The death penalty was imposed in an arbitrary manner, with no clear criteria for deciding who would live and who would die.
3. Because it was so seldom used, the death penalty never really functioned as an effective deterrent.
4. Society's standards had evolved to the point where the death penalty, like branding and the cutting off of hands, constituted "cruel and unusual punishment."

To make matters more painful, there had already been an informal moratorium on executions in 1967, so that 600 people now sat on death row, awaiting the final decision. Even those justices who favored capital punishment squirmed at the idea of having *that* much blood on their hands.

In the end, the Court took the wishy-washy stance that capital punishment was unconstitutional *at that time* because it was arbitrarily and capriciously imposed. Only two justices out of the five-man majority thought the death penalty was cruel and unusual punishment. The Court's decision left everyone confused as to what to do next—but not for long. Within three years the people of some thirty-five states had redesigned their death-penalty laws to get around the Court's restrictions, thereby disproving at least one of the petitioner's arguments: that society had evolved beyond the death penalty. In 1975, the Court ruled on the existing laws in five states and found only one (North Carolina's) to be unconstitutional. Still, no one wanted to cut off the first head. It wasn't until 1977, when Gary Gilmore broke the ice by insisting that the state of Utah stand him in front of a firing squad, that anyone was executed. The first involuntary execution took place in 1979, with the electrocution of John Spenkelenk, who had been reprieved by the *Furman* decision seven years earlier.

ROE v. *WADE* (1973)

The decision that legalized abortion as part of a woman's right to privacy (although Justice Blackmun, who wrote the majority opinion, spent many months trying to prove that abortion was part of the doctor's right to privacy). According to the opinion, the state only has the right to intervene when it can prove it has a "compelling interest," such as the health of the mother. As for the fetus, its rights can only begin to be considered after the twenty-sixth week of pregnancy. Not the most airtight of Supreme Court opinions, this one is still under constant and ferocious attack. The state of Texas, for instance, filed a petition for rehearing, comparing the assertion that a fetus was not a person to the Court's decision that Dred Scott was not a person.

UNIVERSITY OF CALIFORNIA REGENTS v. *ALLAN BAKKE* (1978)

The clearest thing to come out of this, the Court's first affirmative-action case, was that it probably was not a good idea to try to stage a media event around a Burger Court decision.

The storyline, in case you lost it in all the confusion, was as follows: Allan Bakke, a thirty-eight-year-old white engineer, had twice been refused admission to the University of California's medical school at Davis, despite a 3.5 college grade-point average, which was well above the 2.5 required for white applicants and the 2.1 required for minorities. Concluding that he'd been passed over because of Davis's strict minority admissions quota, Bakke took his case to the Supreme Court, charging reverse discrimination. The media jumped all over *Bakke*, in part because it was the first time affirmative action had been tested in the courts, and everyone was anxious to see how much the mood of the country had changed—for better or worse—since the Sixties; in part because the Burger Court's somewhat shoddy civil-rights record promised to lend an edge to the whole affair.

The outcome, however, was a two-part decision that merely left most people scratching their heads. The Court declared itself firmly behind the principle of affirmative action, but just as firmly behind Bakke's right to get into medical school. In effect, it said: Principles, yes; quota systems, no. Some civil-rights groups decided to take this as a resounding success, others as a crushing blow; ditto the opposition. Some said it left the door open for future affirmative-action measures (there are other ways to promote racial balance besides quota systems, the Court pointed out, and no one was ruling out an institution's right to take race into account as one factor among many when deciding on an applicant's qualifications). Others insisted it left an even wider margin for businesses and universities to discriminating against minorities. Some legal scholars pointed out inconsistencies and downright lapses of reason in the justices' opposing opinions (the Court was split 5–4); others declared the everyone-gets-to-take-home-half-a-baby decision a fine example of judicial wisdom.

Although the haziness of *Bakke* pretty much insured that the courts would be gnawing on affirmative-action cases for years to come, it was the press that was really left holding the bag. Screaming headlines that contradicted each other ("Court Votes 'Yes' to Bakke"; "Court Votes 'Yes' to Affirmative Action") just made a lot of newspapers look silly and, after a couple of frustrating go-nowhere specials, TV reporters had to conclude that legal ambiguities did not make for optimum prime-time fare.

ART HISTORY

Contents

Marcel Duchamp's "L.H.O.O.Q." (a cheap French pun translating roughly to "she's got a hot ass"), a.k.a. "Mona Lisa With a Moustache."

Ten Old Masters

In a way, we're sorry. What we had really wanted to do was talk about our ten *favorite* painters. Then we got to thinking that it should be the ten painters whose stock is currently highest, who are most in vogue in a crudités-and-hired-bartenders way. (Whichever, you'd have heard about Piero della Francesca, Caravaggio, Velásquez, and Manet, all notably absent here.) Then we realized that, if you were anything like us, what you really needed was remedial work, not a pajama party or a year in finishing school. So, here they are, the ten greatest—we suppose that means something like "most seminal"—painters of all time.

GIOTTO (GIOTTO DI BONDONE)
(c. 1266–c. 1337)

Giotto's "Deposition."

As the little girl says in *Poltergeist:* "They're heeere!" By which we mean artists who sign their work, travel in packs, and live lives about which something, and sometimes too much, is known. Before Giotto (that's pronounced "JOT-to"), the artist hadn't counted for any more than the stonemason or the glassblower; from here on in, he'd be accorded a degree of respect, authority, and press unknown since ancient Greece. Also in abeyance since the Greeks: the human body, about which the courtly and rigid Byzantines—Giotto's only available role models—had felt some combination of ashamed and uninterested. Giotto, out of the blue (and we're waist-deep in the Middle Ages, remember), turned mannequins into people, dry Christian doctrine into vivid you-are-there narrative, mere colored shapes into objects that seemed to have weight and volume, and his native Florence into the art world's red-hot center for the next 250 years. No painter would prove either as revolutionary or as influential as Giotto for six centuries, at which point Cézanne opined that eyewitness-style reporting on life might not be the ultimate artistic high.

KEY WORKS: The Arena Chapel frescoes in Padua, thirty-three scenes from the lives of Christ and the Virgin Mary and her folks.

COLLEAGUES AND RIVALS: Duccio, from neighboring Siena, where life was conservative, aristocratic, and refined, and where ballots were cast for beauty rather than truth.

MASACCIO
(TOMMASO DI SER GIOVANNI DI MONE)
(1401–1428?)

Played Elvis Presley to Giotto's Frank Sinatra. That is, Masaccio took his predecessor's 3-D realism and put some meat on it, encouraged it to flex its muscles and swivel its hips, enlarged the stage it was playing on, and generally shook the last vestiges of middle age(s) out of the whole performance. Thus begins the Renaissance, the era that rediscovered Greece and Rome; that posed the questions "Why?," "How?," and "So what?"; that promoted such novelties as humanism, freedom, and the idea of leading a full life; and that—casting its gaze on the lot of the artist— came up with a support system of studios, patrons, and apprentices. With Masaccio (a nickname that translates roughly to "Pigpen"), we're at that Renaissance's heroic beginnings, smack-dab in the middle of boom-town, no-holds-barred Florence, and we're watching as the new sciences of perspective and anatomy encourage painters to paint things as they appear to the eye. That doesn't, however, mean you're going to get off on Masaccio the way you got off on Elvis. For one thing, Masaccio died at twenty-seven, before he'd really done all that much. For another, until recently most of his extant work was in rough shape or badly lit (those damned Italian churches) or both. Most importantly, few of us these days are wowed by perspective and anatomy. As a result, Masaccio is what art historians call a "scholar's painter." But it was his stuff and nobody else's that Leonardo, Michelangelo, et al., back in the mid-fifteenth century, were ankling over to the Brancacci Chapel to take a long hard look at.

Masaccio's "The Expulsion from Paradise."

KEY WORKS: *The Holy Trinity with the Virgin, St. John, and Donors* (Sta. Maria Novella, Florence), *The Tribute Money* and *The Expulsion from Paradise* (both Brancacci Chapel, Sta. Maria del Carmine, Florence).

COLLEAGUES AND RIVALS: In this case, not fellow painters, but an architect, Brunelleschi, and a sculptor, Donatello. Together, the three ushered in the Renaissance in the visual arts.

RAPHAEL (RAFFAELLO SANZIO)
(1483–1520)

Button up your overcoat. That chill you're feeling, coupled with the fact that, if you took History of Art 10A, he was the one you got hit with the week before Christmas vacation, means that it's impossible to smile brightly when the name Raphael comes up, the way you do with Leonardo da Vinci and Michelangelo—the two contemporaries with whom he forms a trinity that is to the High Renaissance what turkey, ham, and Swiss are to a chef's salad. That said, the thing about Raphael is—and has always been—that he never

Raphael's "The School of Athens."

makes mistakes, fails to achieve desired effects, or forgets what it is, exactly, he's supposed to be doing next Thursday morning. He *perfected* picture painting, the way engineers perfected bridgebuilding or canal digging or satellite launching; each of his canvases is an exercise in balance, in organization, in clarity and harmony, in coherence and gracefulness. For 400 years, right through the nineteenth century, Raphael was every painter's idol; lately, though, he's begun to seem a little bland, as well as a lot sticky-fingered, absorbing and assimilating and extracting from other artists (especially Michelangelo) rather than trying to figure things out for himself. Note: With the High Renaissance, painting packs its bags and moves from Florence to Rome, where the papacy will take over the Medicis' old Daddy Warbucks role, and where Raphael—handsome, tactful, and possessed of a good sense of timing—will earn his reputation as the courtier among painters, a fixture at the dinner parties of popes and princes.

KEY WORKS: The early Madonnas (e.g., *Madonna of the Goldfinch*, Uffizi, Florence), the portrait of Pope Leo X (Pitti Palace, Florence), and especially the murals in the Stanza della Segnatura (Rome), then the Pope's private library, and especially the one entitled *The School of Athens*.

COLLEAGUES AND RIVALS: Michelangelo and, to a lesser extent (at least they weren't constantly cat-fighting), Leonardo.

TITIAN (TIZIANO VECELLIO)
(1477–1576)

Welcome to Venice—opulent, voluptuous, pagan, on the profitable trade route to the Orient, given to both civic propaganda and conspicuous consumption—where light and color (as opposed to Florence's structure and balance) are the name of the game. With Titian, the most important of the Venetians, painting becomes a business, a dog-eat-dog profession with agents and p.r. people and client mailings, a business in which religious and political demands are nothing next to those of the carriage—make that gondola—trade. Titian was versatile (he did everything an oil painter could do, from altarpieces to erotica, from straight portraits to complex mythologies) and obscenely long-lived (it took the plague to bring him down, at something like ninety-nine), and he dominated the art scene for seventy-five years, with his flesh-and-blood, high-wide-and-handsome approach. He presided at the divorce of painting from architecture and its remarriage to the easel, and assured that the primary medium of the new union would be oil on canvas. Don't

Titian's "Venus of Urbino."

expect rigor or even real imagination from the man, though; what's on display here are energy and expansiveness. Prestige point: In his old age, Titian, whose eyes weren't what they used to be, began painting in overbold strokes and fudged contours, encouraging modern critics to praise his newfound profundity and cite him as a proto-Impressionist, a man who painted how he *saw* things, not how he knew them to be.

KEY WORKS: It's the corpus, not the individual canvas, that counts. Right up there, though: *Madonna with Members of the Pesaro Family* (Frari, Venice), *Rape of Europa* (Gardner Museum, Boston), *Venus of Urbino* (Pitti Palace, Florence), and *Christ Crowned with Thorns* (Alte Pinakothek, Munich).

COLLEAGUES AND RIVALS: Giorgione, who played sensualist, die-young Keats to Titian's long-lived, Spirit-of-the-Age Wordsworth.

EL GRECO
(DOMENICOS THEOTOCOPOULOS)
(1541–1614)

He was, in the words of Manet, "the great alternative." Though of late El Greco's been positioned as the seasoned thinker, rather than the God-happy wild man, either way he was too much of an anomaly to have real impact on his contemporaries—or to found a school of Spanish painting. (Both of those would have to wait for Velásquez to come along, a few years later.) In fact, it's the twentieth century that's made El Greco's reputation, applauding his distortions—especially those gaunt, tense, strung-out figures—and his creation of an inward, fire-and-ice world, complete with angst and hallucination. From Van Gogh through the young Picasso and the German Expressionists, up to the American Abstract Expressionists of the Forties and Fifties, all of whom had a big I-gotta-be-me streak, El Greco has served as a patron saint. A little history: "El Greco" was the nickname given to this footloose Greek ("Greco," get it?) by the citizens of rarefied, decaying Toledo, Spain, when he arrived there after a boyhood spent among Byzantine icons, followed by stints in Venice (where he

El Greco's "Toledo in a Storm."

glanced at the Titians) and Rome (where he offered to redo Michelangelo's Sistine Ceiling). Which is funny, inasmuch as we tend to think of his vision as more Spanish than anybody's but Cervantes'. For art historians, he holds two records: "Last of the Mannerists" (those anticlassical eccentrics who knew you couldn't top Raphael at the perfection game, and decided to put all their chips on weirdness instead) and "most disturbingly personal painter ever." Critics go into raptures over his "incandescent"—some prefer "phosphorescent"—spirituality. But, hey, no problem: Here's a painter you'll always be able to recognize on any wall in any museum in the world.

KEY WORKS: First and foremost, *Burial of Count Orgaz* (Santo Tomé, Toledo), the largest and most resplendent El Greco. Also: *Toledo in a Storm* and *Cardinal Niño de Guevara* (both at the Metropolitan, New York), the latter a portrait of Spain's menacing, utterly unholy-looking Grand Inquisitor. ⸙

COLLEAGUES AND RIVALS: Like we say, none among his contemporaries. But forms, with Velázquez and Goya, the trinity of Great Spanish Painters.

PETER PAUL RUBENS (1577–1640)

Not an anal retentive. From factory headquarters in Antwerp (now Belgium, then still the Spanish Netherlands), Rubens, the "prince of painters," purveyed his billowy, opulent, robust, and sensual portraits, altarpieces, landscapes, historical tableaux, and mythological treatments to the Church, the town fathers, private patrons, and virtually every royal household in Europe. (It helped that he was as much a diplomat as an artist, entrusted with secrets of state by, among others, the Infanta of Spain, and hence provided with entrée to all the best palaces.) To be associated with the name Rubens: First, success beyond anybody's wildest dreams: financial, professional, and personal. Second, Flemish painting, which began with the restrained van Eyck, proceeded through Bosch and Brueghel, and reached its culmination now, an art that was drumming up a full-tilt Catholic sumptuousness even as its north-of-the-border Dutch cousin was becoming more and more Protestant and bourgeois. The third is the concept of the baroque, the organizing principle behind all seventeenth-century art—dynamic, emotional, exuberant, and asymmetrical in all those places where the classicism of the High Renaissance had been static, poised, and balanced; a principle that, among other things, decreed that the work of art was greater than the sum of its parts. Anyway,

Rubens' "The Judgment of Paris."

Rubens created and created and created, and if his altarpieces didn't seem particularly mystical or his bacchanals all that wild and crazy, still, there was enough sheer activity in each of them that you couldn't really squawk. For the conscientious: There's always the chance that you'll forget which painting is Rubens' and which is Titian's (and anyone who tells you that's impossible because the two men are separated by a hundred years and half of Europe is lying). Just remember that Titian subordinated the whole of his painting to its parts, Rubens the parts to the whole; that Titian valued serenity, even in an orgy scene, Rubens tumult; and that Titian painted the equivalent of Vassar coeds, Rubens Ziegfeld showgirls.

KEY WORKS: As with Titian, it's the shooting match, not the individual shot. However, *The Judgment of Paris* (National Gallery, London; that's his second wife in the middle); the Marie de' Medici series (Louvre, Paris; thirty-six panels' worth of commemoration); and the late landscapes (various museums), with the Rubens family chateau in the background, will give you a sense of his range.

COLLEAGUES AND RIVALS: A rung down the ladder, Anthony van Dyck, the portraitist of aristocrats, especially English ones, and Rubens' one-time assistant.

REMBRANDT VAN RIJN (1606–1669)

Rembrandt's "Self Portrait."

The son of a miller and a baker's daughter, with a face—famous from over a hundred self-portraits—much likened to a loaf of bread. But, as Miss Piggy, herself every inch a Rubens gal, might say, *quel* loaf of bread. The man who manipulated tonality (lights and darks, to you) and eschewed contour better than anybody ever, Rembrandt was also the painter who realized, first and most fully, that the eye could take in a human figure, the floor it was standing on, the wall behind it, plus the flock of pigeons visible through the window in that wall without having to make any conscious adjustments. (If we were talking automotive, rather than art, history, Rembrandt would be the advent of the automatic transmission.) More than *that*, even, Rembrandt was the very model of the sensitive and perceptive person, as some of us used to say sophomore year, taking the sober, commonplace Dutch panorama—guild hall and slum, merchant and beggar—and portraying it in all its poignancy and detail; even Christianity, the inspiration for the other half of the Rembrandtian output, becomes, in his hands and for the first time since Giotto, an affair for ordinary men and women. And if all that's not enough, Rembrandt's still the answer most game show contestants would come up with when asked to name a famous painter. Historical generalization: Rembrandt (and the rest of the seventeenth-century Dutch, who had no popes or patrons farming out commissions) turned out the first art to be consumed exclusively by us mere-mortal types, paintings that were to be tucked under your arm, carried home, and hung over the living-room sofa.

KEY WORKS: Many. The ones that come up over and over are *The Night Watch* and *The Syndics of the Cloth Guild* (the latter adopted by the Dutch Masters cigars folks; both, Rijksmuseum, Amsterdam) and a pair of late self-portraits (1659, National Gallery, London; 1660, Kenwood, London). And you'll need one of the religious paintings, perhaps *Return of the Prodigal Son* (Hermitage, Leningrad).

COLLEAGUES AND RIVALS: Lots of them; painting and painters were as much in evidence in seventeenth-century Holland as they'd been in fifteenth-century Florence. You should know Frans Hals (impulsive, with a predilection for people hanging out and getting drunk) and Jan Vermeer (intimate, with a predilection for people opening mail and pouring milk). Everybody else is categorized as a "Little Dutchman," a genre painter specializing in landscapes, still lifes, portraits, or interiors.

CLAUDE MONET (1840–1926)

The problem is, you're dealing with two legendary reputations (and that's not counting M*a*net, Monet's cool-ass contemporary). The first Monet is the Father of Impressionism. You remember Impressionism: the mid-nineteenth-century movement that grabbed an easel and a handful of paintbrushes and announced it was going outdoors; that attempted to capture the spontaneous and transitory effects of light and color by painting with the eye (and what it saw), rather than with the mind (and what it knew to be true); that couldn't have cared less about form, in the sense of either composition or solidity; that was initially reviled by the conservative French critics and artgoing public; and that wound up becoming, in our century, the most popular, most cooed-over style of painting ever. The second Monet is the great-uncle of Modernism, the man who—getting progressively blinder and more obsessed with reducing the visible world to terms of pure light—eventually gave up form altogether and

Monet's "Terrace at Sainte-Adresse."

took out the first patent on abstraction; it's this Monet the avant-garde has tended to prefer. Note to those wondering what happened to the eighteenth century: You shouldn't exactly forget about it, but any hundred-year period whose biggest box-office draw is Watteau is strictly optional.

KEY WORKS: For the Impressionist Monet: at your discretion. Try *Terrace at St. Adresse* (1866, Metropolitan, New York) or *Impression—Sunrise* (1872, Musée Marmottan, Paris). For the proto-Modernist Monet: the touchstones are the Rouen Cathedral series (1894, Metropolitan, New York, and Museum of Fine Arts, Boston, among others) and the water lilies series (1899, 1904–1925, Museum of Modern Art, New York, and Carnegie Institute Art Museum, Pittsburgh, among others).

COLLEAGUES AND RIVALS: The only "true" Impressionists besides Monet are Pissarro and Sisley. Manet is a proto-Impressionist, among other things. Degas and Renoir are quasi-Impressionists. Cézanne, Seurat, Van Gogh, and Gauguin are post-Impressionists. And Toulouse-Lautrec is played by José Ferrer, on his knees, with his feet strapped to his buttocks.

PAUL CÉZANNE (1839–1906)

This is a test. Pass it—that is, "get" what Cézanne was up to, maybe even like it—and chances are you'll have no trouble with "modern" art, abstraction, alienation, and all. Flunk it—that is, wonder what the fuss is about and move immediately on to Van Gogh and/or Gauguin—and you've got big problems ahead of you. As to what Cézanne *was* up to, exactly: First, he was rejecting Impressionism (note that he's an exact contemporary of Monet), not only its commitment to transience and to truth-as-what-the-eye-sees, but its affiliation with the bourgeoisie and the boulevards; Cézanne wanted to infuse some gravity, even grandeur, back into painting. Second, he was refuting classical "one-point" perspective, which makes the viewer the person on whom everything converges and for whom everything is done. For Cézanne "seeing" was a process, a weighing of choices, not a product. (He also decreed color, not line, to be the definer of form; geometry, not the needs of composition, to be its basis; and the laws of representation to be revokable at will.) Third, he was singlehandedly reversing the pendulum swing towards representational "accuracy" that Giotto had set in motion 600 years before; from here on in, *how* you perceive is going to count for more than *what* you perceive, the artist's modus operandi for more than the illusions he can bring off. Granted, this is pretty heavy stuff, but at least the paintings are sensuous, inviting, and still of the world as we know it.

The sledding gets rougher with Picasso and the Cubists, up next.

KEY WORKS: Any still life. Ditto, any view of Mont Sainte-Victoire, in Cézanne's native Provence, *the* mountain in art history. Ditto, any and all scenes of card players. And the portraits of his wife and himself. In general, the later a Cézanne, the bigger a deal it's likely to be—also the more abstract. A lot of people consider *Bathers* (1898–1905, Philadelphia Museum of Art) the painter's summa, but follow his example and come to it last.

Cézanne's "Still Life with Apples."

COLLEAGUES AND RIVALS: The other three Post-Impressionists: Seurat (the one with the thousands of little dots), Van Gogh (him you know), and Gauguin (of Brittany and Tahiti).

PABLO PICASSO (1881–1973)

Try to rise to the occasion. God knows, the critics and commentators try, labeling Picasso, among other things, "the charging bull of modern art," "that Nietzschean monster from Málaga," and "the walking scrotum, the inexhaustible old stud of the Côte d'Azur." Be all that as it may, you've got to understand something about Cubism (which has nothing to do with actual cubes, and everything to do with seeing things in relationship to one another, simultaneously, and from more than one vantage point at a time, with the result that you may find yourself looking at a teacup, say, or a bird cage, both head on and from the air). And something about celebrity (Picasso, towards the end, enjoyed a fame no painter, not even worldlings like Raphael and Rubens, had ever known, complete with bastard heirs, sycophantic dealers, and *Life* magazine covers). Beyond those two basics there's the energy, the fecundity, the frankness, the no-flies-on-me penchant for metamorphosis and the consequent welter of styles (one critic counted eighty of them, and that was back in the early Fifties), the mythologizing (watch for Minotaurs, nymphs, and river-gods), and, in a personal vein, the womanizing (he was notorious for classifying his lady friends as either "goddesses or doormats"). You should know that Cézanne and the primitive sculpture of Africa and pre-Christian

Picasso's
"Les Demoiselles d'Avignon."

Spain were big influences and El Greco a lesser one; that the "pathetic" Blue and "wistful" Rose periods predate Cubism per se; that the appeal of collage—literally, "gluing"—was that it got scraps of modern life right inside the picture frame; that Picasso claimed to "paint forms as I think them, not as I see them" (let alone as they looked); and that the painting after 1950 (not the sculpture, however) was once judged to be lacking in intensity.

KEY WORKS: *Les Demoiselles d'Avignon* (1907, Museum of Modern Art, New York), arguably the most "radical" of all paintings, and *Guernica* (1937, Prado), last of the great "political" paintings. Also, a sculpture; try *The Guitar* (1912, Museum of Modern Art), all metal sheets and empty spaces.

COLLEAGUES AND RIVALS: Georges Braque, who once commented that he and Picasso were "roped together like mountaineers," but who wound up playing Ashley Wilkes to his friend's Rhett Butler. For the record: Juan Gris and Fernand Léger are the two other ranking Cubists; Henri Matisse (see under "Fauvism"), the other great painter of the century; Marcel Duchamp, the alternative role model (see under "Dada") for young—and subversive—artists; Salvador Dali (see under "Surrealism"), the fellow Catalan who valued publicity and the high life even more than Picasso did.

The Leonardo/ Michelangelo Cribsheet

	Leonardo da Vinci	Michelangelo Buonarroti
full name	Leonardo da Vinci	Michelangelo Buonarroti
dates	1452–1519	1475–1564
address	Florence, then Milan, finally Paris	Florence, then Rome
nickname	"The First Modern Man"	"Il Divino"
quote	"Intellectual passion drives out sensuality."	"The more the marble wastes, the more the statue grows."
mindset	universal and diffuse, enigmatic and elusive	narrow and single-minded, passionate and thorny
the Italian word for the above, approximately	*misteriosità*	*terribilità*
at heart not a painter so much as a . . .	scientist and philosopher	sculptor and architect
he most wanted to . . .	understand	create
the work celebrated the world over	*Mona Lisa, Last Supper*	The Sistine Ceiling (especially *The Creation of Man*), the statue of David

The Leonardo/Michelangelo Cribsheet

the works you can get points for knowing about	one of the scientific drawings from the *Notebooks*, as below	one of the lesser sculptures, like an unfinished *Slave,* or something architectural, like Rome's Campidoglio

Italian art term most likely to crop up in a discussion of his work	*sfumato* (see page 82)	*contrapposto* (see page 79)
when he wrote, he . . .	jotted down descriptions of his experiments	composed sonnets to his lovers
gay?	yup; major boyfriend a hustler who stole his drawings and then sold them, ditto the outfits Leonardo bought him	yup; major boyfriend handsome, learned, thoughtful, and from a good family; affair said to have been "platonic," however
beard?	right, like the one on the bagperson in the Penn Station men's room	sure, like the one on the crack dealer in Washington Square

Practical Italian for the Gallery-Goer

Artwise, New York may be having a field day, but it's Italy that had a High Renaissance. Which means that if it's snob appeal you're after, you're going to have to learn to roll your *r*s a bit. Here's your basic lesson:

chiaroscuro (kee-ahr-e-SKEWR-o): Literally means "bright-dark" in Italian and describes the technique, in painting or drawing, of modeling three-dimensional figures by contrasting or gradating areas of light and dark. Leonardo da Vinci was among the first to use chiaroscuro to break out of the tradition of flat, one-dimensional outlining of figures. One of the great achievements of the Renaissance, chiaroscuro soon became part and parcel of painting. Rembrandt is the acknowledged master of the technique; if you want a more recherché example, try Caravaggio.

Chiaroscuro: Caravaggio's "The Musicians."

contrapposto (kohn-tra-POH-stoe): In sculptures of the human form, the pose in which the upper body faces in a slightly different direction from the lower, with the weight resting on one leg. Contrapposto was originally the Greeks' solution to the problem of balancing the weight of the body in sculpture in a way that was both architecturally reasonable and a little interesting. (The earlier formula had been the frontal, static pose, in which the legs were treated like two columns with the torso set squarely on top of them and the head balancing on top of that. The Greeks, rightly, found this boring and stupid.) Renaissance

Contrapposto: Cristofano da Bracciano's "Orpheus."

sculptors revived the Greek formula, renamed it, and added dynamic tension by making the placement of body parts more extreme and contrasting. This may seem like picky technical stuff to you, but it was a watershed in the history of art. Contrapposto is all over the place in Renaissance sculpture, but the example you can't get away with ignoring is Michelangelo's *David*.

fresco: This was *the* method for painting indoor murals, from the days of the Minoan civilization in Crete right up to the seventeenth century. It involves brushing water-based pigments onto fresh, moist lime plaster (*fresco* means "fresh" in Italian), so that the pigment is absorbed by the plaster as it dries and becomes part of the wall. Fresco painting reached its peak during the Renaissance, when artists had the backing—and the backup crews—to allow them to undertake the kind of monumental works the technique is best suited to. Today, it's also referred to as "buon fresco" or "true fresco," to distinguish it from "secco" or "mezzo" fresco, a later method of painting on dry plaster that allowed artists to get similar results with less trouble. Frescoes abound in European art history, but some of the most famous are Michelangelo's, in the Sistine Chapel; Raphael's, in the Stanza della Segnatura and the Loggia of the Vatican; and Giotto's, at the Arena Chapel in Padua. During the 1930s and 40s, the WPA Federal Arts Project commissioned a couple thousand frescoes, mostly for municipal buildings and mostly forgettable.

Impasto: Van-Gogh's "Self Portrait."

impasto: The technique of applying thick layers or strokes of oil paint, so that they stand out from the surface of a canvas or panel: also called "loaded brush." Such seventeenth-century painters as Rubens, Rembrandt, Velázquez, and Frans Hals used impasto to emphasize pictorial highlights; in the nineteenth century, Manet, Cézanne, Van Gogh, and others used it more extensively for texture and variety. Some modern painters, including de Kooning and Dubuffet, took to laying the paint on with a palette knife or simply squeezing it directly from the tube. (One does not, it should be clear, create impasto with water colors.)

morbidezza (MOR-buh-DETZ-uh): Literally, "softness," "tenderness." Used to describe the soft blending of tones in painting—by Correggio, for instance—or rounding of edges in sculpture, especially in the rendering of human flesh. On a bad day, could seem to degenerate into effeminacy and sickliness.

pentimento: A painter's term (and Lillian Hellman's) derived from the Italian word for "repentance," and referring to the evidence that an artist changed his mind, or made a mistake, and tried to conceal it by painting over it. As time goes by, the top layer of paint may become transparent, and the artist's original statement begin to show through. Pentimento can often be found in seventeenth-century Dutch paintings, in which the artists commonly used thin layers of paint to obliterate an element of a composition—one of the children, say, in an interior—only to have its ghost reappear behind a lady's dress or a piece of furniture a couple hundred years later. One of the most famous examples of pentimento is the double hat brim in Rembrandt's portrait *Flora.*

Pentimento: Rembrandt's "Flora."

putto [plural: *putti*] (POO-toe; POO-tee): Those naked, chubby babies that cavort through Italian paintings, especially from the fifteenth century on. Putto means "little boy" in Italian, and originally the figure was derived from personifications of Eros in early Greek and Roman art; by extension, the term came to apply to any naked child in a painting. Putti were very popular in Renaissance and Baroque paintings, where they stood for anything from Cupid, to the pagan attendants of a god or goddess, to cherubim celebrating the Madonna and child.

Putti in Veronese's "Mars and Venus United by Love."

quattrocento; cinquecento (KWA-tro-CHEN-toe; CHINGK-weh-CHEN-toe): Literally, "the four hundred" and "the five hundred"; to art buffs, the fifteenth and sixteenth centuries, respectively. In other words, the Early and the High Renaissances.

sfumato (sfoo-MAH-toe): Comes from the Italian word for "smoke" and describes a method of fusing areas of color or tone to create a soft, hazy, atmospheric effect, not unlike the soft focus in old Hollywood movies. Sfumato is most often mentioned in connection with Leonardo and his followers.

sotto in su (soh-toe-in-SOO): This one is good for a few brownie points; it means, approximately, "under on up," and describes the trick of painting figures in perspective on a ceiling so that they appear extremely foreshortened, giving the impression, when viewed from directly underneath, that they are floating high overhead instead of lying flat in a picture plane. Sotto in su was especially popular in Italy during the Baroque and Rococo periods (seventeenth and eighteenth centuries), when lots of people were painting ceilings and trying to create elaborate visual illusions. The names to drop: Tiepolo, Correggio, Mantegna.

veduta (veh-DOO-tah): Means "view"; in this case, a detailed, graphic, and more or less factual view of a town, city, or landscape. Vedute (note the plural) were in vogue during the seventeenth and eighteenth centuries, when the artists who painted, drew, or etched them were known as "vedutisti." A variation of the veduta was the *veduta ideata* ("idealized"), in which the realistic elements were juxtaposed in such a way as to produce a scene that was positively bizarre (e.g., Canaletto's drawing of St. Peter's in Rome rising above the Doge's Palace in Venice). The vedutisti to remember: Canaletto, the Guardi family, Piranesi.

Six -ism's, One -ijl, and Dada

YOUR PERSONAL GUIDE TO EUROPEAN ART MOVEMENTS BETWEEN 1900 AND HITLER

B e grateful we edited out Orphism, Vorticism, Suprematism, and the Scuola Metafisica at the last minute.

FAUVISM

Henri Matisse, "Blue Nude." (1907)

Headquarters: Paris and the South of France.

Life Span: 1905–1908.

Quote: "*Donatello chez les fauves*!" ("Donatello among the wild beasts!"), uttered at the Salon d'Automne by an anonymous art critic upon catching sight of an old-fashioned Italianate bust in a roomful of Matisses.

Central Figures: Henri Matisse, André Derain, Maurice de Vlaminck, all painters.

Spiritual Fathers: Paul Gauguin, Henri "Le Douanier" Rousseau.

Salient Features: Raw, vibrant-to-strident color within bold black outlines; moderately distorted perspective; an assault on the Frenchman's traditional love of order and harmony that today reads as both joyous and elegant; healthiest metabolism this side of Dr. Pepper commercials.

Keepers of the Flame: None (though Matisse is a big, and ongoing, influence on everybody).

EXPRESSIONISM

Ernst Ludwig Kirchner,
"Street, Dresden." (1908)

Vassily Kandinsky,
"Black Lines." (1913)

Headquarters:	Germany.
Life Span:	1905–1920s.
Quotes:	"He who renders his inner convictions as he knows he must, and does so with spontaneity and sincerity, is one of us."—Ernst Kirchner.
	"Something like a necktie or a carpet"—Wassily Kandinsky, of what he feared abstract art might degenerate into.
Central Figures:	In Dresden (in "The Bridge"): Kirchner, Emil Nolde, Karl Schmidt Rottluff, painters. In Munich (in "The Blue Rider"): Kandinsky, Paul Klee, Franz Marc, painters. Under the banner "New Objectivity": George Grosz, Otto Dix, Max Beckmann, painters. Confrères and honorary members: Arnold Schoenberg, composer; Bertolt Brecht, dramatist; Franz Kafka, writer.
Spiritual Fathers:	Vincent van Gogh, Edvard Munch, Friedrich Nietzsche.
Salient Features:	A tendency to let it all—pathos, violence, morbidity, rage—hang out; distortion, fragmentation, Gothic angularity, and lots of deliberately crude woodcuts; the determination to shake the viewer up and to declare Germany's artistic independence from France. Down in Munich, under Kandinsky—a Russian with a tendency to sound like a scout for a California religious cult—abstraction, and a bit less morbidity.
Keepers of the Flame:	The abstract expressionists of the Forties and Fifties, today's "neo-expressionists," and a barriorful of graffiti artists.

CUBISM

Georges Braque, "Soda."
(1911)

Headquarters:	Paris.
Life Span:	1907–1920s.
Quote:	Anonymous tasteful lady to Pablo Picasso: "Since you can draw so beautifully, why do you spend your time making those queer things?" Picasso: "That's why."
Central Figures:	Picasso, of course, and Georges Braque. Also, Juan Gris and Fernand Léger, all painters. Guillaume Apollinaire, poet.
Spiritual Father:	Cézanne.
Salient Features:	The demise of perspective, shading, and the rest of the standard amenities; dislocation and dismemberment; the importance of memory as an adjunct to vision, so that one painted what one knew a thing to be; collage; analytic (dull in color, intricate in form, intellectual in appeal), then synthetic (brighter colors, simpler forms, "natural" appeal); the successful break with visual realism.
Keepers of the Flame:	Few; this half-century has gone not with Picasso but with Duchamp.

FUTURISM

*Umberto Boccioni,
"Unique Forms of
Continuity in Space."
(1913)*

Headquarters: Milan.

Life Span: 1909–1918.

Quotes: "A screaming automobile is more beautiful than the 'Victory of
                        Samothrace.' " "Burn the museums! Drain the canals of
                        Venice!"—Filippo Tommaso Marinetti.

Central Figures: Marinetti, poet and propagandist; Giacomo Balla and Gino Sever-
                        ini, painters; Umberto Boccioni, sculptor and painter; Antonio
                        Sant'Elia, architect.

Spiritual Father: Georges Seurat.

Salient Features: Dynamism, simultaneity, lines of force; vibration and rhythm
                        more important than form; exuberant, optimistic, anarchic; human
                        behavior as art. Had an immediate impact bigger than Cubism's—
                        on Constructivism, Dada, and Fascism.

Keepers of the Flame: Performance artists (who likewise stress the theatrical and the eva-
                        nescent), conceptualists.

CONSTRUCTIVISM

Naum Gabo, "Column."
(1923)

Headquarters:	Moscow.
Life Span:	1913–1932.
Quotes:	"Engineers create new forms."—Vladimir Tatlin.
	"Constructivism is the Socialism of vision."—László Moholy-Nagy.
Central Figures:	Tatlin, sculptor and architect; Aleksandr Rodchenko, painter and typographer; El Lissitzky, painter and designer; Naum Gabo and Antoine Pevsner, sculptors.
Spiritual Fathers:	Kasimir Malevich, Lenin, Marinetti.
Salient Features:	Art as production, rather than elitist imaginings, and squarely in the service of the Left; abstract forms wedded to utilitarian simplicity; rivets, celluloid, and airplane wings; the State as a total work of Art.
Keepers of the Flame:	None: the State ultimately squashed it.

DE STIJL ("THE STYLE")

Piet Mondrian, "Composition 7."
(1937–1942)

Gerrit Rietveld, armchair.

Headquarters: Amsterdam.

Life Span: 1917–1931.

Quote: "The square is to us as the cross was to the early Christians."—
                    Theo van Doesburg.

Central Figures: Van Doesburg and Piet Mondrian, painters; Gerrit Rietveld and
                    J. J. P. Oud, architects.

Spiritual Father: Kandinsky.

Salient Features: Vertical and horizontal lines and primary colors, applied with a
                    sense of spiritual mission; Calvinist purity, harmony, and sobriety;
                    purest of the abstract movements (and Mondrian the single most
                    important new artist of the between-the-wars period); say "style,"
                    by the way, not "steel."

Keepers of the Flame: Minimalists.

DADA

Marcel Duchamp, "Fountain." (1917)

Headquarters:	Zurich (later Berlin, New York, and Paris).
Life Span:	1916–1922.
Quotes:	"Like everything in life, Dada is useless." "Anti-art for anti-art's sake."—Tristan Tzara.
Central Figures:	Zurich: Tzara, poet, and Jean Arp, painter and sculptor. New York and Paris: Marcel Duchamp, artist; Francis Picabia, painter; Man Ray, photographer. Berlin: Max Ernst, George Grosz, Kurt Schwitters.
Spiritual Father:	Marinetti.
Salient Features:	Anarchic, nihilistic, and disruptive; childhood and chance its two most important sources of inspiration; the name itself a nonsense, baby-talk word; born of disillusionment, a cult of nonart that became, in Berlin, overtly political.
Keepers of the Flame:	Performance artists, "happenings" and "assemblages" people, conceptualists.

SURREALISM

Salvador Dali, "The Persistence of Memory." (1931)

Headquarters: Paris (later, New York).

Life Span: 1924–World War II.

Quote: "As beautiful as the chance meeting on a dissecting table of a sewing machine and an umbrella."—Comte du Lautréamont.

Central Figures: André Breton, intellectual; Louis Aragon, Paul Eluard, writers; Jean Cocteau, writer and filmmaker; Luis Buñuel, filmmaker. Abstract wing: Joan Miró, painter. Explicit wing: Salvador Dali, Yves Tanguy, Max Ernst, René Magritte, painters.

Spiritual Fathers: Sigmund Freud, Giorgio de Chirico, Leon Trotsky.

Salient Features: Anti-bourgeois, but without Dada's spontaneity; committed to the omnipotence of the dream and the unconscious; favored associations, juxtapositions, concrete imagery, the more bizarre the better.

Keepers of the Flame: Abstract expressionists, "happenings" people.

Twelve Young Turks

W ell, not really Turks. In fact, the Old World has nothing to do with it. For the last forty years, it's America—specifically, New York—that's been serving as the clubhouse of the art world. Now shake hands with a dozen of its most illustrious members. That's Jackson Pollock in the Stetson and Laurie Anderson in the P. F. Flyers.

JACKSON POLLOCK (1912–1956)

Jackson Pollock's "One." (1950)

Don't settle for the "cowboy" legend, in which Pollock—the most talked-about artist of the last forty years—blows into New York City from Cody, Wyoming, riding his canvases like broncos and packing his frontier image like a six-gun. Granted, the man had a rowdy streak, spattering, flinging, and dripping paint by day and picking fights in artist's bars by night, but his friends always insisted that he was a sensitive soul; inspired by the lyricism of Kandinsky and steeped in the myths of Jung, all he wanted was to be "a part of the painting," in this case "all-over" painting, with no beginning, no end, and no center of interest. Some nomenclature: "Action painting" is what Pollock (alias "Jack the Dripper") did, a particularly splashy, "gestural" variant of abstract expressionism, the better-not-hang-this-upside-down art turned out by the so-called "New York School."

MARK ROTHKO (1903–1970)

Declaring that he painted "tragedy, ecstasy, doom, and so on," Rothko was pleased when people broke down and cried in front of The Work—and withdrew from an important mural commission for New York's Four Seasons restaurant because he couldn't stand the idea of them eating in front of it. Here we're in the presence of abstract expressionism's so-called "theological" wing (which also sheltered Barnett Newman and Clyfford Still), typified by—in addition to a fondness for monasticism and bombast—large, fuzzy-edged rectangles of color, floating horizontally in a vertical field. Renunciation is the keyword. In a sense, minimalism begins here, with Rothko.

WILLEM DE KOONING (1904–)

The *other* "action" painter, and the most famous New York School artist (even if he was born in Holland) after his Wyoming colleague. De Kooning never totally lost faith in recognizable imagery—most notably, a gang of big-breasted middle-aged women (of whom he later said, "I didn't mean to make them such monsters")—and never tossed out his brushes. But he did paint in the same hotter-than-a-pepper-sprout fever, allowing paint to dribble down the canvas, as soup down a chin, and he did reach beyond where he could be sure of feeling comfortable.

DAVID SMITH (1906–1965)

Was to postwar sculpture what Jackson Pollock was to postwar painting (and, like Pollock, was killed at his peak in an automobile accident). Influenced by the work of Picasso and by a summer vacation he'd spent as a welder in a Studebaker factory, and intent on glorifying, rather than apologizing for, the workaday world, Smith constructed his work instead of casting or molding it. The result: shapes that are "ready-made" rather than solid, arrangements that look provisional instead of stately, and a mood that is anything but monumental. Whereas the Englishman Henry Moore (the other "sculptor of our time") always seemed to be making things for museum foyers and urban plazas, Smith's work is more likely to rise, oil-well-style, from a spot nobody could have guessed would be home to a work of art.

ANDREW WYETH (1917–)

Of course, not everybody really wanted *Woman II* over the breakfront or *Cubi XVIII* in the front hall. For those thus resistant to Art, but still desirous of something pretty and expensive, there was Andrew Wyeth, working in the American realist tradition of Grant "American Gothic" Wood and Edward "All-Night Diner" Hopper, and given to painting in a manner middlebrow critics liked to call "hauntingly evocative," as with the much-reproduced *Christina's World*. As to whether Christina is trying to get away from the house (à la *Texas Chainsaw Massacre*) or back to it (à la *Lassie, Come Home*), don't look at us. Don't look at Wyeth for too long, either: You'll lose all credibility as intellectual, aesthete, and cosmopolite.

ROBERT RAUSCHENBERG (1925–)
JASPER JOHNS (1930–)

Counts as one selection: Not only were Rauschenberg and Johns contemporaries, not only did they together depose, without really meaning to, the reigning abstract expressionists, they also, for a time, cohabited. However, they couldn't have been less alike, temperamentally and philosophically. Think of them as a vinaigrette dressing. Rauschenberg is the oil: applied lavishly, sticking to everything, rich, slippery, viscous. Probably best known for his so-called "combines" (like this free-standing angora goat, with a tire around

Robert Rauschenberg and "Monogram." (1955–59)

its belly), he scoured the streets and store windows of downtown Manhattan for junk; believed that art could exist for any length of time, in any material, and to any end; and, as one critic said, "didn't seem house-trained."

Johns, by contrast, is the vinegar: poured stintingly, cutting through everything, sharp, stinging, thin. In his paintings of flags, targets, stenciled words and numbers, and rulers—all as familiar, abstract, simple, and flat as objects get—he endowed the pop icons of the twentieth century with an "old master" surface, reduced painting to the one-dimensionality it had been

Jasper Johns and "Three Flags." (1958)

hankering after for a generation, and got to seem sensuous, ironic, difficult, and unavailable—all those hipper-than-hip things—in a single breath. Together, Rauschenberg and Johns did for art (whose public, such as it was, had been getting tired of not being able to groove on the stuff Rothko, de Kooning, et al. were turning out) what the Beatles did for music. Note: Rauschenberg and Johns are usually billed as proto-"pop" artists; the former is not to be confused with "pop" artists Roy Lichtenstein (the one who does the paintings based on comic-book panels) and Claes Oldenburg (the one who does the sculptures of cheeseburgers and clothespins).

ANDY WARHOL (1928–1987)

Needs no introduction here. But forget for a minute Andy, the albino in the silver fright wig, the guy who painted the Campbell's soup cans and the Brillo boxes, Liz and Marilyn; who made underground movies like *The Chelsea Girls* and *Flesh;* who founded *Interview* and took Studio 54 as his anteroom; and who got shot in the gut by Valerie what's-her-name. Concentrate instead on Warhol, the tyrant and entrepreneur, the man who taught the art world about the advantages of bulk (a few hundred was a *small* edition of his prints, and the 200th of them was presented, promoted, and, inevitably, purchased, as if it were the original) and who persuaded the middle class that hanging a wall-sized picture of a race riot, or an electric chair, or an automobile accident, or Chairman Mao, over the couch in the family room not only was chic, but made some kind of sense. More recently, there were the commissioned portraits: Not since Goya's renditions of the Spanish royal family, it's been observed, has a group of people who should have known better so reveled in being made to look silly.

FRANK STELLA (1936–)

"All I want anyone to get out of my paintings . . . is the fact that you can see the whole *idea* without any confusion. What you see is what you see." Thus spake Frank Stella, who'd learned something from Jasper Johns, and who would go on, while still in his twenties, to help launch the movement known as minimalism, according to some the most self-consciously American of all the -isms (and according to others the last, wheezy gasp of modernism itself). The idea was to get away from the how-often-have-you-seen-this-one-before literalness of pop and back to abstraction—a new abstraction that was fast, hard, flat, and hauntingly unevocative. Key words here are "self-referentiality" and "reduction"; the former meant that a painting (preferably unframed and on a canvas the shape of a lozenge or a kite) had no business acknowledging the existence of anything but itself, the latter that the more air you could suck out of art's bell jar the better. By the Seventies, Stella would be making wall sculptures of corrugated aluminum and other junk, cut by machine then crudely and freely painted, that relate to his early work approximately as the movie *The Cotton Club* relates to *The Godfather*.

CHRISTO (1935–)

Obsessed with *empaquetage*—in plain English, wrapping—the Bulgarian-born Christo spent years practicing on bicycles, trees, storefronts, and women friends before moving on to a section of the Roman Wall, another of the Australian coastline, and, eventually, a 1,250-foot-wide valley somewhere in Colorado (this in 250,000 square feet of bright orange nylon, for upwards of $400,000). Why, you're wondering, "wrap" a valley? It's part of what some critics dubbed the "New Scale" (Christo himself calls it "public art"), a move to take art out of the studio and away from the "Uptown Museum-Gallery Complex" simply by making it too big for studios, museums, and galleries to hold. It's also a good way to get media attention, make money (Christo issues stock in himself, redeemable in working drawings), and, as with so much before it, *épater les bourgeois,* in this case whole families of them driving cross-country to Disneyland.

LAURIE ANDERSON (1947–)

"Our plan is to drop a lot of odd objects onto your country from the air. And some of these objects will be useful. And some will just be . . . odd. Proving that these oddities were produced by a people free enough to think of making them in the first place. . . ." That's Laurie Anderson speaking. She of the red socks and the white high-top sneakers, the seven-hour performance pieces, the lights-up-in-the-dark electric violin, the movie clip of an American flag going through the fluff-dry cycle, the Kodachrome slide of the dog and the little girl in a playsuit, curbside. Anderson is a performance artist and as such, yokes music with visuals, cliché with poetry, electronics with sentiment, slide shows with outrage. Like Christo, performance artists do what they can to take art out of the institution; unlike Christo, they tend to quote that indefatigable old avant-gardist John Cage, who years ago declared art to be a way "simply" to make us "wake up to the very life we're living." And if you're thinking seven hours of anyone is an awfully long time, even with the movies and the backup band, you may be right.

JULIAN SCHNABEL (1951–)

Julian Schnabel and "St. Francis in Ecstasy." (1980)

Guess what: Painting—after ten years of conceptualism and minimalism, of typewriter art and pebbles glued to gallery walls—is back. So's expressionism (see page 84). So's the human figure. And the art world once again takes in Europe. Still, New York is where any ambitious young artist feels he can really breathe free, and it's this young American who for a time loomed the largest and used up the most oxygen. Julian Schnabel, for better or for worse the biggest-deal painter since Jackson Pollock, specializes in Ping-Pong-table-sized canvases covered with cupboards' worth of broken crockery, yards of cheap velvet, lots of thick, gucky paint, and the occasional pair of antlers. Also, as Mark Rothko might say, in "tragedy, ecstasy, doom, and so on"—or what passes for same.

Raiders of the Lost Architecture

A RACE-WALKER'S GUIDE TO THE GREEK TEMPLE AND THE GOTHIC CATHEDRAL

You don't have to be standing in front of the Parthenon to be suffused with all those old doubts about what's Doric and what's Ionic—and where to look, approximately, when somebody calls your attention to the frieze; almost any big-city post office can make you feel just as stupid. Ditto, Chartres, naves and narthexes, and even a moderately grandiose Catholic—or Episcopal—church. In fact, a little practice here at home isn't such a bad idea *before* you hit Athens, Paris, and points in between.

GOTHIC ELEVATION

Cross

Finial

Crocket

Louver Window

Tower

Belfrey

Belfrey Floor

Gallery

Running Mold/Running Ornament

Double Lancet Window

Clerestory

Rose Window

Triforium

Tracery

Mullion

Dripstone/Head Mold

Portal

CROSS SECTION OF NAVE

GOTHIC FLOOR PLAN

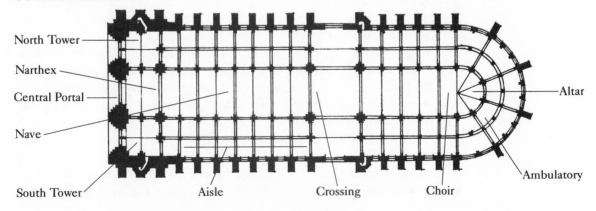

North Tower

Narthex

Central Portal

Nave

Altar

South Tower

Aisle

Crossing

Choir

Ambulatory

Real-Estate Investment for the Aesthete

2,482 RMS, RIV VU

Contributor Michael Sorkin assesses the choicest styles, hottest architects, primest buildings, and pithiest sayings of modern architecture.

FIVE MODERN STYLES

Architectural fashion is like any other: it changes. The difference is that architects are forever looking for a Universal Style, something suitable for every occasion. This is hardly a new impulse. The folks who brought you the Doric order and the Gothic cathedral had something similar in mind. However, while it may have taken hundreds of years to put up Chartres, a smart-looking Hamptons beach house can get done practically overnight. As a result, stylistic turnover is nowadays a tad accelerated.

The International Style

A coinage of the early Thirties, this label recognized that modern architecture actually did have a "style" and was not, as many had argued, simply a force of nature. The movement's major perpetrators tended to argue that their work was essentially "rational," that what they did was as scientific as designing a dynamo or a can opener. Le Corbusier, the most vigorous polemicist of the time, promoted the gruesome slogan, "A house is a machine for living." Thanks to which analogy, machine imagery is one of the hallmarks of the style, especially anything with vaguely nautical overtones such as steel railings and shiny metal fittings. Also popular were glass-block-and-strip windows mounted flush with a facade. International Style buildings are almost invariably white and conceived in terms of planes—like houses of cards—rather than in terms of the solidity of neo-classical and Victorian architecture, against which many of these architects were reacting. (A sense of mass, it is often said, was replaced by one of volume.) Key monuments include Gropius's buildings for the Dessau Bauhaus (1926), Le Corbusier's

Villa Savoye (1929), and Aalto's Paimio Sanitorium (1928). In the Seventies, the style was much appropriated by restaurants: For a while there, it was next to impossible to dine out without staring at a wall of glass blocks from your Breuer chair.

The Bauhaus, Dessau, Germany; Walter Gropius, architect.

The Yale Art and Architecture Building; Paul Rudolph, architect.

Brutalism

The name, like so much in the modernist lexicon, comes from the French, in this case *béton brut*. Which is not, as you might suppose, an after-shave, but rather unfinished concrete, the kind that shows both the grain of the underlying wooden formwork and lots of rough edges. The French have a special genius for referring to the presumed ardors of the natural—"Eau *Sauvage*"—and nature has always emitted strong vibes, one way or the other, for modern architects. This is no doubt because the ideological basis for modern architecture (as for everything else worthwhile) comes from the Enlightenment and its problem child, Rationalism. On the one hand, it's resulted in a lot of buildings that look like grids; on the other, in a preoccupation with a kind of architectural state of nature, like that which preoccupied Rousseau. (Perhaps this is why renderings of modern buildings so often feature lots of trees.) Brutalism represents a reaction to the flimsy precision of the International Style, a reversion to roughness and mass. Characteristics include larger expanses of concrete, dungeonlike interiors, bad finishes, and a quality of military nostalgia, a sort of spirit-of-the-bunker that might have gone down happily on the Siegfried Line. The style—popular in the Sixties and early Seventies—has pretty much taken a powder, but it's left behind the likes of Paul Rudolph's Art and Architecture Building at Yale University and Kallman and McKinnell's Boston City Hall.

Expressionism

A style whose day was, alas, brief. Concurrent with Expressionism's flowering in the other arts, architects (mainly German, mainly in the Twenties), managed to get a number of projects built in a style that will be familiar to you from *The Cabinet of Dr. Caligari* (see page 148). As you will recall, with Expressionism, things tend to get a little skewed, not to mention a little sinister, with materials often seeming to be on the point of melting. More than any other, this is the style that best embodies the kind of Looney Tunes sensibility, with its working out of the aberrations of the unconscious, that we all identify with the fun side of Twenties Berlin. The two greatest works in the genre are Erich Mendelsohn's Einstein Tower, an observatory in Potsdam that looks like a shoe; and Hans Poelzig's interior for the Grosses Schauspielhaus in Berlin, an auditorium that looks like a cave. The latter was commissioned by theatrical impresario Max Reinhardt, no slouch when it came to the visual. Expressionism is easily the funkiest of the modern styles.

The AT&T Building; Philip Johnson and John Burgee, architects.

Postmodernism

A kind of portmanteau term (no relation to John Portman, the architect of all those ghastly hotels with the giant atriums), meant to describe a condition as much as a style, the condition of not being "modernist." As you have undoubtedly noticed, "modern architecture" has lately come in for more than its share of lumps, and architects are shamelessly scrambling to disavow what most of them only a few years ago thought was the cat's pajamas. Postmodernism's most exemplary figure is Philip Johnson, the architect of the cocktail circuit and the leading arbiter of architectural fashion. His premier contribution is a New York skyscraper headquarters for American Telephone and Telegraph that looks a lot like a grandfather clock, allegedly the result of the postmodernist preoccupation with "history." Two camps here. First is the group who respond to the vogue by sticking a Corinthian column or similar bric-a-brac in the foyer. Their preferred color is salmon. Second is the group who used to be modernists and continue to build in exactly the same way, claiming that they are now postmodern because they are choosing to build in a historical style which simply happens to be modern. Their favorite color is white.

The Chicago School

Not to be confused with the Chicago School of Criticism, which is known for its neo-Aristotelianism, or the Chicago School of Economics, which is known for its monetarism. The Chicago School of Architecture, which flourished around the turn of the century and comprised such immortals as William Le Baron Jenney, Dankmar Adler, Louis Sullivan, Daniel Burnham, and John W. Root, is widely touted as having been the source for modern architecture, American branch, and as having invented the skyscraper. Lecturers often show slides of the Monadnock Building (Burnham and Root, 1892) and the Seagram Building (Mies van der Rohe, 1958) side by side to demonstrate this lineage, citing such shared attributes as simplicity, regularity, and structural candor. This isn't really wrong, but it's not quite that simple, either. Most standard architectural historians take the technological determinist line with regard to the birth of the skyscraper. For them, the seminal event in the history of American architecture is the invention of cheap nails which made possible the "balloon frame" (houses made of lightweight timber frameworks, nailed together and easy to erect) which in turn led—via the Bessemer steel-making process and the Otis elevator—to the rigid steel frame, and thence to the profusion of tall buildings that sprang up in Chicago like mushrooms after a shower. This formulation may be too simple, but there's no doubt that the Chicago architects made the first concerted and systematic effort to find new forms for the new type of building, often with lovely results.

FIVE MODERN ARCHITECTS

What would architecture be without architects? The five listed here constitute the generally agreed-upon list of the modern immortals.

Ludwig Mies van der Rohe (1886–1969)

Mies van der Rohe (always referred to simply as "Mies") is the one behind all those glass buildings, most famously the Seagram Building in New York. Although Mies is hardly to blame for it, one of the big problems with this kind of architecture is that it is fairly easy to copy, and that while one such building on a street may be stunning, fifty of them are Alphaville. The reason for the ease of imitation is that Mies was essentially a classical architect. That is, like the Greeks, he invented a vocabulary (cognoscenti use linguistics jargon as often as possible when talking about architecture) of forms and certain rules about how those forms could be combined, all of which he then proceeded to drive into the ground. Although his early work was influenced by Expressionism (as with the famous glass skyscraper project of 1921) and de Stijl (the brick houses of the Twenties), projects after the early Thirties were more and more marked by precision, simplicity, and rectilinearity. Prime among these is the campus for the Illinois Institute of Technology in Chicago, first laid out in 1939, on which Mies continued to work through the Fifties. To sound knowledgeable about Mies, you might admire the way in which he solved that perennial architectural problem, the corner.

The Seagram Building;
Ludwig Mies van der Rohe, architect.

Le Corbusier (1887–1965)

Le Corbusier (a.k.a. "Corb" or "Corbu," depending on where you went to school) is a self-appropriated pseudonym of obscure meaning, like "Liberace." His real name was Charles Édouard Jeanneret. Like so many architects, Le Corbusier was something of a megalomaniac, who, perhaps because he was Swiss, thought that unhygienic old cities like Paris would be better off if they were bulldozed and replaced by dozens of sparkling highrises. Fortunately, Parisians ignored this idea, although it did achieve enormous popularity in the United States, where it was called "urban renewal." On the other hand, Corb's buildings were superb. His early houses, including one for Gertrude Stein and her brother Leo at Garches, outside Paris, are legendary, supreme examples of the International Style, the most definitive of which is the Villa Savoie of 1929 (a big year indeed for modern architecture). Later in life, Corb discovered Cubism and concrete, and things began to change noticeably. Instead of thin planes and relatively simple geometries, Corb got into thick walls and sensuous, plastic shapes. Of this later work the best known is Notre

Dame en Haut, a church whose form was inspired by the kind of headgear Sally Field wore as the Flying Nun. Towards the end of his life Corb did get to do an entire city: Chandigarh in India.

Walter Gropius (1883–1969)

To be perfectly frank, Gropius was not really such a hot designer. He was, however, the presiding genius of the Bauhaus, which, you scarcely need to be told, was the Shangri-la of modern architecture. Which makes Gropius, we guess, its Sam Jaffe. The Bauhaus—*bauen* (to build) plus *haus* (just what you'd imagine)—was designed by Gropius and is his most memorable work, the epitome of the International Style. During its brief life, before it was closed by Hitler (whose views on modern art and architecture we won't go into here), the Bauhaus was a virtual Who's Who of the modern movement, a home to everyone from Marcel Breuer to László Moholy-Nagy. Its curriculum, which was ordered along medieval master–apprentice lines, embraced the whole range of the practical arts and its output was staggering in both quality and quantity. After it was shut down, Gropius (and most everyone else associated with it) came to the United States, bringing European modern architecture with them. This was either an intensely important or utterly dreadful development, depending on where you went to architecture school and when. Gropius was married to a woman named Alma, who was also married to Gustav Mahler and Franz Werfel, although not concurrently, and who is sometimes described as the first official groupie.

Frank Lloyd Wright (1869–1959)

By his own admission, Wright was the greatest architect of all time. More than any other modernist, he went through several distinct stylistic phases. The conventional view is that the initial, so-called "prairie" style was his best. A college dropout, he worked for a time in the office of the Chicago architect Louis Sullivan before setting up on his own in Oak Park, a town he proceeded to virtually carpet with his work. This early output—mainly houses but including such gems as the Unity Temple (1906) and the Larkin Building (1904)—was, despite European as well as Japanese influences, at once very modern and very American, deriving its essence from Wright's near-mystical sense of the plains. Unique in proportion, detail, and decoration, these projects also "articulated" space in a new way. Rather than thinking of architecture as segmented, Wright perceived it as continuous and flowing, not as so many rooms added together but as a sculptable whole. Wright's later houses preserve this spatial sensibility but come in a welter of styles, ranging from zonked-out International to Mayan. The best known house from Wright's middle period is Falling Water (1936), built over a waterfall in Pennsylvania and designed, according to legend, in less than an hour. Many people confused by the disparity between the prairie houses and something like the Guggenheim Museum or the Marin County Civic Center find late Wright perplexing. Although Wright was, like Le Corbusier, a power freak, his version of Utopia—which he called Broadacre City—was somewhat less threatening, resembling, as it does, the suburbs. Wright ran his office, which still exists, along feudal lines. The man currently in charge was married to Stalin's daughter, Svetlana.

Alvar Aalto (1896–1976)

Aalto, the hardest drinker among the twentieth-century masters, came from Finland, where dipsomania is the national pastime, and which has, unaccountably, produced more modern architects per capita than any other country. After the customary neoclassicist dalliance, Aalto took up the International Style and produced a number of masterpieces in a personalized version of same. The most important of these are the legendary Viipuri Library and the Paimio Sanitorium, both dating from the late Twenties. The Viipuri Library, now in territory occupied by the Soviets, had an auditorium with a beautiful undulating (and acoustically sound) wooden ceiling—the first instance of an Aalto trademark. No discussion of Aalto can omit mention of the tremendous responsiveness of his buildings to their particular (generally cold) environments, especially the way they introduce and modulate natural light. Of the five immortals, Aalto is the most unabashedly sensuous and tactile, full of swell textures and gorgeous forms. Aalto's best formal move was probably a fan shape, which allowed him to orient various rooms for best exposure to the sun over the course of the day; to illustrate this form in conversation, hold your hand parallel to the ground and stretch the fingers. As who wouldn't be, coming from Finland, Aalto was big on the use of wood both in his buildings and in his famous bentwood furniture. Unfortunately, most of Aalto's work—like the great Saynatsalo Town Hall (1952)—is located in places whose names are completely unpronounceable. This forces people to refer constantly to the several projects (e.g., the Imatra Church) that they *can* pronounce.

FIVE MODERN BUILDINGS

The Barcelona Pavilion

Built for an exposition in 1929, this is modern architecture's holy of holies, a status further enhanced by the fact that the pavilion was torn down shortly after it was built; such are the rules of expositions. What this means is that everything everyone knows about it must be received from photographs, the preferred medium of architectural communication. The Barcelona Pavilion—did we mention that it's by Mies?—is one of the most distinguished examples of a "free plan," that is, a plan not primarily based on the symmetrical imperative but rather on a sensibility derived from Suprematism and de Stijl (see page 88), yielding something rather like a collage. The result: spaces that flow and eddy, moving through large openings and expanses of glass into the out-of-doors and right on down the street. The Barcelona Pavilion is also remembered for its modern attitude toward materials. While retaining the International Style's predilection for crisp lines and planes, Mies enriches their formal potential by the use of a variety of posh materials, including chrome, green glass, polished green marble and onyx, and travertine. Many conclusions to be drawn here. First, the building affirms the displacement of craft (the hand) by precision (the machine); instead of carving the stone, Mies polished it. Second, Mies treats the surfaces of planes not as deep and solid (like a Gothic church) or as smooth and white (as in so much International Style shtik) but as highly reflective, like glass; in the Barcelona Pavilion, everything either reflects or gets reflected, then gets reflected again in two shallow pools, one inside and one out. Finally, this was the occasion for the design of the famous Barcelona chair, the most definitively upscale piece of furniture ever.

Clockwise, from upper left: The Barcelona Pavilion (1929); Carson, Pirie, Scott (1904); The Chrysler Building (1930); The Robie House (1909); L'Unité de' Habitation (1952).

L'Unité d'Habitation

Finished in 1952, this is the best of Corb and the worst of Corb, always referred to simply as "the Unité" despite the fact that there are actually three of them. (The original is at Marseilles, the other two at Nantes and Berlin.) So what is it? Well, you might say that it was an apartment house with social cachet, the result of an idea whose time had come. Also gone, some thirty years before. Back in the good old days of modernism, when architecture was seen as an instrument for progressive political transformation, architects talked about building "social condensers" and theorized vaguely about how people would learn to live in happy collective harmony if only they had the right kind of structures in which to do it. Corb, having glommed on to this idea, thought that if the whole countryside were dotted with "Unités" of his own design, everyone would get on fine. Fortunately, he was only able to build the three. By itself, the Marseilles Block (as some call it) is notable for a number of reasons, some social and others—the important ones—formal. The social program includes a shopping arcade on an upper floor, recreation and day care on the roof, and interior "streets" (big corridors, really) on every other floor: a variety of conveniences designed essentially to imprison. Formally, things are more positive and provide a golden opportunity for learning some key vocabulary words. Let's start with *pilotis*, the big legs on which the entire building is raised. Corb thought that these would free the landscape from the building (it's supposed to flow uninterrupted underneath), but they had the reverse effect. The Unité is constructed in *béton brut* (we've had this one already), and its heavily sculpted facades incorporate *brise-soleils* (sun screens) and are heavily *polychromed* in primary colors. The roof vents, chimneys, elevator housings, and such are done in free-form shapes; together they make for a lovely silhouette.

The Robie House

The Robie House (1909) is the finest example of Wright's "prairie" style work. "Prairie" style was both a style and—as with so much great art—an anxiety. At the turn of the century the prairies still abutted Chicago and Wright had them on the brain: their endless flatness, their windsweptness, and, dare we say, their romance. As a result, the longness and lowness of prairie buildings (Wright was not the only architect so moved) is fairly easy to understand. Other elements, including decorative treatments and Wright's characteristic "flowing space," bespeak such influences as an early dose of Japanese architecture and a stint in Louis Sullivan's office. The Robie House itself is long, low, and brick. A tightly controlled but asymmetrical bi-level plan, a mature application of Wright's geometrical decoration, vertical windows arrayed in strips, and a low hipped roof each does its bit. Next time you stroll past the Guggenheim with a friend, mention the Robie House and how incredible you find it that one architect could have done both.

Carson, Pirie, Scott

Designed by Louis Sullivan and built between 1899 and 1904, the Carson, Pirie, Scott department store (originally built as the Schlesinger and Meyer department store) is the hottest product of the Chicago School. Why? For starters, it has great structural clarity, which is to say, it is easy to "read" the underlying steel structure in the lines of the facades, which look like an arrangement of posts and beams filled in with glass. The proportions of the structural "bays" (the distance between columns, framed by floors above and below) are on the long side, a proportion that is considered particularly "Chicago." That old bugbear, the corner, is dealt with especially neatly by Sullivan who, in effect, inscribes a cylinder there, accelerating the window proportions to help zing the viewer around the block. Less frequently noted is the incredible decoration that covers all surfaces (not counting the windows, dummy). Indeed, Sullivan was a great apostle of ornamentation, and the intricate system he finally arrived at was not so very different from Art Nouveau.

The Chrysler Building

The good news is that it's once again OK to like the Chrysler Building. For years seen as a detour on the way to boring modernism, we now acknowledge that the flowering of Art Deco (after the 1925 Exposition des Arts Décoratifs in Paris), which took place in the Twenties and Thirties, was one of the high points in modern design. In every sense, Deco's highest point is the Chrysler Building, designed by William Van Alen and, briefly, the tallest building in the world. It is still the most beautiful, most "classic" skyscraper ever built. The convention in talking about skyscrapers is to analogize them to classical columns, with their three-part division of base, shaft, and capital, or, if you prefer, beginning, middle, and end. The Chrysler is great because it succeeds at all levels. The lower portion contains a handsomely decorated lobby and dramatic entries, well related to the scale of the street. The shaft makes use of an iconography based, appropriately enough, on automotive themes (flying tires, a frieze of Plymouths) and the crown is that wonderful stainless steel top, the skyscraper's universal symbol.

FIVE MODERN MAXIMS

After all, what's a style without a slogan? Here are our favorites.

LESS IS MORE: Mies van der Rohe's coinage. Mies is undergoing something of a revival today, so it's sort of okay to use this, provided you keep your delivery ironic. On the other hand, postmodernist wags have had so much fun turning it on its head—More is more, Less is a bore, etc.—that some circumspection is advised.

ORNAMENT IS CRIME: Adolf Loos penned this goody (Anita wasn't the only aphorist in the family), an obvious reaction to fin de siècle excess. Given the recent upsurge of interest in ornament, be *sure* to keep your delivery ironic.

FORM FOLLOWS FUNCTION: The functionalist credo, generally attributed to Mies, but actually used by several eminences, including Louis Sullivan. The earliest use appears to be by Horatio Greenough, a mid-nineteenth-century Yankee sculptor remembered for his statue of George Washington in a peek-a-boo toga.

THE PLAN IS THE GENERATOR: Corb's version of the above. It means you should start (if you happen to be designing a building) from the floor plan, with all its implications of rational relationships, rather than impose some sort of "artistic" vision on a building a priori. Fortunately, Corb did not always practice what he preached.

ROAM HOME TO A DOME: From Bucky. Buckminster Fuller (see page 41), that is, the apostle of geodesic domes, Dymaxion houses, positive effectiveness, and other benign nonsense. And meant to be sung to the tune of "Home on the Range." No doubt you'll be keeping your delivery ironic.

Snap Judgments

An intelligent, if highly jaundiced, view of photography, by contributor Owen Edwards.

No one really knows that much about photography, and no one is even particularly sure what he likes. The history of the medium is so short—Nicéphore Niépce made the first photograph, a grainy little garden scene, in

1827 (though if you point out that Thomas Wedgwood might have been first, in 1802, many will be impressed)—that its salient points can be picked up in an afternoon. And the exact nature of photography is so much in dispute that you can call it an art (or a virus) without much danger of being wrong. Indisputably, however, there are categories, giving such comfort as categories do, and here's what you ought to know about each.

LANDSCAPE

Everything you need to say about landscape photography is Ansel Adams. The straight, somewhat unimaginative wisdom holds that Adams is the greatest landscape photographer ever. The revisionist stance is that Adams is passé by about a century, and that after Timothy O'Sullivan photographed the West following the Civil War, landscape was played out as a theme anyway. The latest neorevisionism, however, says it's OK to like Adams even if he *is* the Kate Smith of photography. Or you can end the discussion by saying that the only great landscape pictures nowadays are being made by NASA robots in the outer limits of the solar system.

FASHION

Though it was discovered only recently that fashion photographers might be artists, no one has ever mistaken them for plain working stiffs. The first fashion photographer of note was Baron de Meyer. His title was suspect, but useful nevertheless; he created the archetype of the social photographer, the inside man who not only knew about haute couture, but knew the women who could afford it. Then Edward Steichen came along and did a better de Meyer. (Steichen always did everything better; when in doubt, say Steichen.) Then a Hungarian photojournalist named Munkacsi appeared in the mid-Thirties and revolutionized fashion photography by making his models run along beaches and jump over puddles. Then Richard Avedon got out of the Coast Guard and did a better Munkacsi. And from then on, it's been a gentle slide downhill, since nobody's ever done a better Avedon. Not even Avedon.

FINE ART

The answer to the tedious and irrepressible question, "Is photography art?" is yes, but almost never when it thinks it is. Most of the avowed art photographers of the nineteenth century are considered quaint at best, grotesque at worst, while the pictures that have pried money out of the arts endowments look like what Fotomat promises not to charge you for. The great photographic art has been made by people doing something else. By Eugène Atget, trying to document Paris, or August Sander trying to codify all the faces in Germany. It's perfectly safe, then, to dismiss any art photographer as hopelessly misguided. Except Man Ray, who was really a painter, and so can't be blamed for his failures. And László Moholy-Nagy, who discovered that the more things you did wrong, the better the photograph looked.

The great muddler of art photographers is also the medium's most revered saint, Alfred Stieglitz, who, early in this century, encouraged his fellow Photo Secessionists to blur, draw on, scratch, or otherwise manipulate their pictures to ensure that the hoi polloi would know they were artists. Stieglitz, by the way, was not Steichen, though even people with vast collections of lenses continue to think so. Steichen was a disciple of Stieglitz who fell out of favor

Left: Edward Steichen, "The Flatiron Building." Below: Man Ray, "Nusch Éluard."

when he began to make a bundle in advertising. (Stieglitz, being a saint, was not much fun.) In 1961, Stieglitz discovered Paul Strand's unmanipulated masterpieces, decided that his followers were hopeless and misguided, and consigned them to oblivion. The resulting confusion has never quite cleared up.

FINE ART, ABSTRACT DIV.

Abstract photography is a disaster, invariably boring. Though photography is by nature an *abstract* of reality, it's always of something, so that attempts to make it of nothing seem silly. The viewer wants to know what he's looking at, leans closer and closer, and ends up frustrated and peeved. The closest thing to true abstraction a photographer can manage is to take something and make it *look* like nothing. Most grants are awarded to photographers who are good at doing that.

FINE ART, STILL LIFE DIV.

The most overrated still-life photograph in the universe is Edward Weston's jumbo-sized pepper, made in the classic More-Than-Just-a-Vegetable style that has since accounted for half a century of abysmal amateur efforts. (Weston is probably the most overrated photographer, too, in large part due to the efforts of sons, lovers, and half the population of Carmel, California, to keep the legend alive.) The real contest for World's Greatest Still-Life Photographer is between Irving Penn, who studied drawing and illustration with Alexei Brodovitch in Philadelphia, and Hiro, who worked as a photographer for Brodovitch at *Harper's Bazaar*. (Remember Brodovitch—he was tough, selfish, often drunk, said "If you look through the viewfinder and see something you've seen before, don't click the shutter," and was guru to two generations of great photographers.) Everybody knows about Penn; his prints are second in price only to Adams's (but his are worth it). Few people know about Hiro except the knowing.

PHOTOJOURNALISM

This is the most problematic kind of photography for everybody, especially Susan Sontag. It's what most people think of when they think of photography

at all, and what most photographers start out wanting to be, and then spend a lifetime trying to retire from. The word—an awful-sounding hybrid (why not journography?)—was invented by Henri Cartier-Bresson so that he wouldn't be accused of making art while he made art, and it wrongly implies that one or more photographs can tell a story. Without words—usually a thousand or more—pictures are powerful but dumb.

Life magazine started the whole myth of photojournalism's storytelling power, but in truth *Life* was just a very good illustrated press, in which photographs were never allowed to wander unattended. The patron saint of photojournalists is Lewis Hine, who made pictures of child laborers and sweatshops at the turn of the century. Its greatest hero was W. Eugene Smith, who combined an honest concern for human suffering with a canny eye for dramatic composition and lighting, and a very cranky disposition. Both Hine's work and Smith's are currently fetching very good prices at art auctions. So much for yesterday's news.

PORTRAITURE

Cartier-Bresson (and various others) observed that after the age of forty, we have the faces we deserve. Portrait photographers tend to divide up between those who hide the evidence, and those who uncover it. Bachrach and Karsh represent the first group, Avedon and Penn the second. Portraits of known people are more interesting than all the rest because we have a chance to decide whether what we see jibes with what we think we know about them. Thus, the outrage and/or delirium caused by Avedon's warts-and-all celebrities. The best of the nineteenth century portraitists, and one of the best ever, was Nadar, a Parisian hobnobber whose pictures of that great self-imagist Sarah Bernhardt are unparalleled. Then again, since faces are the landscapes of lives, the best portrait ever made is probably mouldering in your family attic. Should an argument develop over who is the Greatest Portraitist of Photography, come down staunchly on the side of the aforementioned August Sander, a German who wandered the Walds before World War II, chronicling his countrymen in a series of haunting stereotypes. Add Manhattan neurosis and the Age of Anxiety and you have Diane Arbus.

DOCUMENTARY

In one way or another, all photographs are documentary, so all photographers are documentarists. Some, of course, are more so than others. A documentary

photographer is a photojournalist whose deadline is a hundred years hence; posterity is the point. The first great large-scale documentary work was done by Matthew Brady and a group of photographers he hired to cover the Civil War (including Timothy O'Sullivan, who, as has been noted, later played the first, best notes in what has become the Ansel Adams songbook). The most famous and exhaustive documentary project was the misery-loves-company team put together by Roy Stryker to photograph sharecroppers, sharecroppers, more sharecroppers, and occasional other types during the Great Depression. This led to the discovery of the placebo effect in photography: If we take everybody's picture, maybe they'll go away and leave us alone.

Ironically, one of the great working-class heroes of documentary photojournalism was Walker Evans, a patrician sort who did much of his paying work for *Fortune* magazine. It seems highly likely that Evans viewed the whole idea of photography with some embarrassment, since many of his pictures are of empty rooms, or of people from behind.

SURREALISM

In one way or another, all photographs are surreal, too, since that isn't actually Uncle Frank smirking on the beach, but just a little slip of paper coated with chemicals. But some photographers insist on being official surrealists. The harder they try to put things together in odd and unsettling ways, the more miserably they fail. The problem is that life as we know it is already odd and unsettling. So for true surrealism, we are right back with documentary photography—especially when done by people who know where to look for the kind of juxtapositions the rest of us pretend we don't see. Robert Frank was a great unofficial surrealist, as was Diane Arbus. Bill Brandt isn't bad, though the credit is due mostly to the fact that he's a genius at the terrible print. The reigning king of the official surrealists is Frederick Sommer, who lives in Arizona and produces about one print a year, more or less, spending the rest of the time giving lectures, receiving grants, and collecting disciples. In terms of overall rankings, Sommer is the 10,094th best photographer in the world, although he is the 37th best in Arizona.

WOMEN

The best of all women photographers is my aunt Isabel, who for several years was the only person on earth who could take my picture without causing me to vanish instantly. Other notable women are:

Lisette Model, one of the world's smallest photographers, who had such a gravitational attraction to large people that her first pictures made in the

resorts of southern France look like monuments come to life. As is the case with certain gifted photographers, Modell was as good as she would ever get on the first day of her career. She has been called the mentor of Diane Arbus, which she used to admit and deny at the same time, for reasons known only to her.

Imogen Cunningham, who lived so long that rumors circulated that she had been archivally processed. Like photographs, photographers almost inevitably benefit from great age (although they fade, their value inevitably rises). Cunningham was never anything but all right, but she had covered so much time and territory that eventually she became the art-photography world's unofficial mascot, a position she labored at by becoming adorably "feisty." As a result, feisty old Johnny Carson displayed her to the world on "The Tonight Show," shocking the millions who thought women photographers look like Faye Dunaway.

Berenice Abbott, who made the best portrait ever of James Joyce, and single-handedly saved the work of Atget from the trash bin, and who, whether she liked it or not, became an institution without ever being a great photographer.

Helen Levitt, almost unknown, shy, brilliant, virtually invisible in shabby coat and furtive mien, who crept around New York for forty years or more taking in street life. She's a genius in black-and-white or color, and when you state emphatically that Levitt is America's greatest woman photographer, you will have the rare pleasure of being both esoteric and right.

CELEBRITY

Last and least among photographers are the paparazzi. But while it is perfectly all right to hold them in contempt, it's not OK to ignore them; they know where life is going. And, for that matter, *Life*. Andy Warhol predicted that someday everybody would be famous for fifteen minutes—the paparazzi work hard at reducing that to 1/125th of a second. Valedictorian of all celebrity photographers is Ron Galella, who has been sued by Jackie Onassis, punched by Marlon Brando, and deplored by even the most deplorable of his subjects. None of this has affected him adversely. He's not allowed to get as near Jackie as he used to, when he goes after Brando he wears a football helmet, and he can't get into the new Palladium any more easily than he got into the old Studio 54, but life isn't bad for Ron; he's enough of a celebrity now to have his own faithful paparazzi. Let's face it, the celebritymongers are slime. But the way things are going, someday they will be artists. So when you sneer, smile.

Economics

T H R E E

Contents

A good day on the stock market—a month before the Crash of '29.

Now, What, Exactly, Is Economics, And What Do Economists Do, Again?

E conomists are fond of saying, with Thomas Carlyle, that economics is "the dismal science." As with much that economists say, this statement is half true: It *is* dismal.

An equally helpful definition of economics was offered by American economist Jacob Viner, who said, "Economics is what economists do."

More to the point, perhaps, is the fact that economics concerns itself with the use of resources. It is about changes in production and distribution over time. It is about the efficiency of the systems that control production and distribution. It is, in a word, about wealth. This alone should be enough to engage our attention.

Over the past decade or so, economics has experienced a substantial surge of interest and notoriety. Suddenly economists are finding themselves not only studying wealth but also enjoying it. This is largely a result of their current relationship with politicians. Where once rulers relied on oracles to predict the future, today they use economists. Virtually every elected official, every political candidate, has a favorite economist to forecast economic benefits pinned to that official's or candidate's views.

Besides, even if being in a position to feel on top of current events doesn't constitute a sufficient lure, people still want to be able to understand why it takes their bank three weeks to clear an out-of-state check. Not that, as contributor Alan Webber is about to show, the economists are necessarily ready to tell them.

EcoSpeak

O ne reason economics is so hard to get a grip on is that economists speak in tongues whenever possible. They are, after all, being paid to come up with a lot of fancy guesswork, and they know how important it is to keep everyone else guessing about what they're guessing about since, in the end, your guess is as good as theirs. Anyway, here's what a few of their favorite terms really mean.

PROFIT: To get a firm grasp of profit and its counterpart, loss, you might consider the Biblical quotation, "What does it profit a man if he gain the world but lose his soul?" For an economist, the correct way to answer this question would be to calculate the revenues received from gaining the world and subtract the costs incurred by losing one's soul. If the difference (known as "the bottom line") is a positive number, you have a profit.

CETERIS PARIBUS: One of the things economists like to do is analyze a complicated situation involving a huge number of variables by changing one and holding the rest steady. This allows them to do two things: first, focus on the significance of that one particular element, and second, prove that a pet theory is correct. "Ceteris paribus" is the magic phrase they mutter while doing this. It means, literally, "Other things being equal."

FACTORS OF PRODUCTION: Ordinary people talk about resources, the things—like land, labor, or capital—used to make or provide other things. Economists talk about factors of production.

COMMODITIES: This is the stuff that gets produced using, you guessed it, factors of production. Commodities generally fall into two categories: goods, which are tangible, and services, which are not. An easy way to remember this distinction: These days, goods are Japanese and services are American; they make cars, we make lawyers.

CONSUMPTION AND PRODUCTION: Consumption is what happens when you actually use commodities; production is what happens when you make them.

DEMAND AND SUPPLY: Demand is the amount of anything that someone wants to buy at any particular price; supply is the amount that someone wants to sell at any particular price. Economists have a lot of fun making you guess what happens to the relationship between supply and demand when the amounts or the prices change. More on this game later.

EXTERNALITIES: Effects or consequences felt outside the closed world of production and consumption. In other words, things like pollution. Economists keep their own world tidy by labeling these messes "externalities," then banishing them.

FREE-MARKET ECONOMY VS. PLANNED ECONOMY: In the former, decisions made by households and businesses, rather than by the government, determine how resources are used. Vice versa and you've got the latter. As long as you are living in the United States, it's probably a good idea to associate a free-market economy with the good guys, a planned economy with the bad guys. If you find yourself in Bulgaria or parts of Cambridge, Massachusetts, simply reverse the definition to get with the prevailing theology.

GROSS NATIONAL PRODUCT (GNP) VS. GROSS DOMESTIC PRODUCT (GDP): GNP is a dollar amount (in the U.S., an enormous one) which represents the total value of everything produced in a national economy in a year. If the number goes up from year to year, the economy is growing; divide that number by the number of people living in the country and you get per capita income. An alternative measure, GDP, leaves out foreign investment and foreign trade and limits the measure of production to the flow of goods and services within the country itself. As a result, some economists believe it affords a more accurate basis for nation-to-nation comparisons. Either way, GNP or GDP, the basic idea is that more is better.

HUMAN CAPITAL: At first blush, "human" and "capital" may seem like strange bedfellows. But in the land of economics, human capital refers to the investments that businesses make in their workers, such as training and education, or, more broadly, to the asset to the firm represented by the workers and their skills.

INDIFFERENCE CURVE: This shows all the varying combined amounts of two commodities that a houshold would find equally satisfactory. For example, if you're used to having ten units of peanut butter and fifteen of jelly on your sandwich, and you lose five units of the peanut butter while gaining five of the jelly, and the new sandwich tastes just as good to you as the old one, you've located one point on an indifference curve.

INFLATION: One of the chief villains of current events, inflation is most simply understood as a rise in the average level of all prices. Getting the definition down is one thing; getting the rate of inflation down is another.

LAISSEZ-FAIRE: It seems that whenever economists want to describe an imaginary world, they turn to a foreign language (see "ceteris paribus," above, or try to read the Annual Report of the Council of Economic Advisors to the President). Literally translated "let do," this phrase invokes the notion of an economy totally free of government intervention, one in which the forces of the marketplace are allowed to operate freely and where the choices driving supply and demand, consumption and production are arrived at naturally, or "purely." A kind of economic Fantasyland.

LONG RUN VS. SHORT RUN: It's appalling, but economists take even perfectly obvious terms like the "long run" and the "short run" and try to invest them with scientific meaning. The short run refers to a period of time too short for economic inputs to change, and the long run refers to a period of time, as you may have guessed, long enough for all of the economic inputs to change. The terms are important when you get to thinking about how individuals or companies try to adapt to circumstances—and whether or not they can do it. For some economists, the long run, in particular, comes in handy when defending a pet theory. For example, during times of economic downturn and high unemployment, economists might argue against any form of government intervention, saying that "in the long run" the marketplace will adjust to correct the situation. The problem, of course, is that most people live "in the short run," and that, as economist John Maynard Keynes once cautioned, "In the long run, we're all dead."

MACROECONOMICS VS. MICROECONOMICS: Further evidence of the tendency of economists to see things in pairs. Here, "macro" is the side of economics that looks at the big picture, at such things as total output, total employment, and so on. "Micro" looks at the small picture, the way specific resources are used by firms or households or the way income is distributed in response to particular price changes or government policies. One problem economists don't like to talk about is the difficulty they have in getting the two views to fit together well enough to have any practical application.

MARKET FAILURE: This is one of a number of terms that economists use to put down the real world. Here's the way it works: When things don't go the way economists want them to, based on the laissez-faire system (see above), the outcome is explained as the result of a "market failure." That way, it's not the economists' fault—they had it right, it's the market that failed.

MIXED ECONOMY: Another term for economic reality, the "mixed economy" is the middle ground between the free market (the good guys) and the planned economy (the bad guys). When you look around a country like the U.S. and see the government manipulating the price and availability of money and energy, legislating a minimum wage, and so on, you have to conclude that ours is not really a free market. But neither is it a centrally planned economy. Grudgingly, economists have decided that what it is is a mixed economy, a kind of economic purgatory they will have to endure while they pray for ascension to the free market.

OPPORTUNITY COSTS: The idea behind the line, "I could've had a V8." In economics, there is a cost to using your resources (time, money) in one way rather than another (which represented another opportunity). Think of it this way: There is an opportunity cost associated with your studying economics instead of a really useful subject like podiatry.

PRODUCTIVITY: Another of the big words in the field, productivity, simply defined, is a measure of the relationship between the amount of the output and that of the input. For example, when you were in college, if it took you two days (input) to write your term paper (output) and it took your roommate one day to hire someone to write his term paper, your roomie's productivity was twice yours—and he probably got a better grade.

VALUE ADDED: A real comer in the world of economics, the value added is a measure of the difference of the value of the inputs into an operation and the value of the product the operation yields. For example, when Superman takes a lump of coal and compresses it in his hands, applying superforce to turn the coal into a perfect diamond, the value added, represented by Superman's applied strength, is significant. The term explains how wealth is created; it's also what you use to justify all those hours you've been putting in on the Super-Pullover machine.

VALUE-ADDED TAX: Like the name says, a tax on the value added. At each stage of the value-added chain, the buyer pays and the seller collects, a tax based on the value of the services added at that stage. The tax is rebated on exports and paid on imports. It is also known by its noneconomics name: a sales tax.

EcoThink

Now that you can talk like an economist, the next step is to learn to think like one. The good news here: Economics is a closed system; internally it is perfectly logical, operating according to a consistent set of principles. Unfortunately, the same could be said of psychosis. What's more, once having entered the closed system of the economist, you, like the psychotic, may have a hard time getting out.

THE FOUR LAWS OF SUPPLY AND DEMAND: Economics as physics—something like the laws of thermodynamics brought to bear on the study of wealth. Basically, these four laws say that when one thing goes up, the other thing goes down, or also goes up, or vice versa, depending. When demand goes up, the price goes up; when demand goes down, the price goes down; when supply goes up, the price goes down; when supply goes down, the price goes up.

THE THEORY OF PERFECT COMPETITION: If the four laws of supply and demand are economics as physics, this is economics as theology. The theory holds that firms always seek the maximum profit; that there is total freedom for them both to enter into and to leave competition; that there is perfect information; and that no business is so large as to influence its competitors unduly. It is, according to economic dogma, a situation in which neither firms nor public officials determine how resources are allocated. Rather, the market itself operates like an "invisible hand" (see "Adam Smith," below). And if you buy that one, there's this bridge we'd like to talk to you about.

THE PRINCIPLE OF VOLUNTARY EXCHANGE: Comes under the heading how-to-make-even-the-simplest-idea-sound-important; also known as people buying and selling to get what they want.

THE THEORY OF COMPARATIVE ADVANTAGE: The basis for much of our thinking about international trade. Most simply, it says that everyone's economic interests are served if each country specializes in those commodities which its endowments (natural resources, skilled labor, technology, and so on) allow it to produce most efficiently, then trades with other countries for *their* commodities. The classic example: Both England and Portugal benefit if England produces woolens and Portugal produces port and the two countries trade their products—rather than both countries trying to produce both products. Once you've arrived at an understanding of the theory of comparative advantage, the next thing to think about is how it is that Japan—without natural resources, native technology, or capital—became dominant in steel, cars, motorcycles, TVs, and Gobots. The answer may tell us more about the theory of comparative advantage than it does about the Japanese.

THE THEORY OF RATIONAL EXPECTATIONS: Maintains that people learn from their mistakes. It is illustrated by the story of the economics professor who was walking across the campus with a first-year economics student. "Look," said the student, pointing at the ground, "a five-dollar bill." "It can't be," responds the professor. "If it were there, somebody would have picked it up by now."

THE THEORY OF REVEALED PREFERENCE: Another of those laws that stipulate how people are *supposed* to behave. According to this one, people's choices are always consistent. In other words, once you have revealed your preference for a pepperoni pizza over a Big Mac, you'll always choose the pizza, provided it's available. Reduce it to this level, and it's easy to see the limits of the theory.

ECONOMIES OF SCALE: At the heart of manufacturing strategy since the days of Henry Ford. The principle is a simple one: With big factories using long production runs to make a single commodity, you can reduce manufacturing costs. In addition, the more you repeat the same operation, the cheaper it becomes. Following this principle, American factories have turned out some very cheap goods, indeed.

THE PHILLIPS CURVE: Had everything going for it. Based on data compiled in England between 1861 and 1957, this theory held that when inflation goes down, unemployment goes up and vice versa. For politicians, it was an invaluable guide: If you had too much unemployment, you let inflation go up and—presto!—down went unemployment. If inflation was raging out of control, you put a few people out of work and down went inflation. All in all, a handy little tool. Then along came stagflation, which combined high unemployment with high inflation, and the Phillips curve turned into the Phillips screw.

EcoPeople

ADAM SMITH (1723–1790)

The first economist, this Adam Smith was an actual person, not some contemporary telejournalist's pseudonym. His historic book, *An Inquiry into the Nature and Causes of the Wealth of Nations* (1776), propounded the idea that competition acted as the "invisible hand," serving to regulate the marketplace. His theories, some of them derived from observations he made while visiting a pin factory, would prompt skeptics to ask, "How many economists can dance on the head of a pin?"

DAVID RICARDO (1772–1823)

With Malthus (see below), a leader of the second generation of classical economists. Early on, Ricardo made a fortune in the stock market when he ought to have been going to school. He next gravitated to economics, where his lack of education, naturally, went undetected. In his most famous work, *The Principles of Political Economy and Taxation* (1817), he advanced two major theories: the modestly named "Ricardo Effect," which holds that rising wages favor capital-intensive production over labor-intensive production; and the theory of comparative advantage (see "EcoThink," above).

THOMAS MALTHUS (1766–1834)

A clergyman who punctured the Utopianism of his day by cheerfully predicting that population growth would always exceed food production, leading, inevitably, to famine, pestilence, and war. This "natural inequality of the two powers" formed, as he put it, "the great difficulty that to me appears insurmountable in the way to perfectability of society." Malthus's good news: periodic catastrophes, human perversity, and general wretchedness, coupled with the possibility of self-imposed restraint in the sexual arena, would prevent us from breeding ourselves into extinction.

JOHN STUART MILL (1806–1873)

A child prodigy, Mill learned Greek when he was three, mastered Plato at seven, Latin and calculus by twelve; at thirteen he digested all that there was of political economy, of Smith, Malthus, and Ricardo. For the next twenty years he'd write; in 1848 (noteworthy also for the publication of the *Communist Manifesto* and a passel of revolutions, see page 556) he published his *Principles of Political Economy, with Some of Their Applications to Social Philosophy*. A couple of critics complained that the book was unoriginal—"run-of-the-Mill"—and that Mill's mildly Socialist leanings (he argued for, among other things, trade unions and inheritance taxes) were antithetical to the Spirit of England. Many more, though, appreciated his making the distinction between the bind of production and the flux of distribution—how, while we can produce wealth only insofar as the soil is fertile and the coal doesn't run out, we can distribute it as we like, funneling it all towards the king or all towards the almshouse, taxing or hoarding or, for that matter, burning it. Sociopolitical options took a seat next to economics' abstract—and absolute—laws, and ethics eclipsed inevitability. Mill would be revered as a kind of saint (and *Principles* serve as the standard economics textbook) for another half century.

JOSEPH SCHUMPETER (1883–1950)

An Austrian who came to America in the early Thirties and whose best-known work was published a decade later, Schumpeter is remembered today as the man who argued that government should not try to break up monopolies, that, in fact, a monopoly was likely to call into existence the very forces of competition that would replace it. This dynamic, labeled the "process of creative destruction," is now much brandished by more conservative political and economic observers, who use it to explain to old industries why it's OK for them to go out of business. "Don't think of it as bankruptcy and massive unemployment," the rationale goes. "Think of it as 'creative destruction.' "

JOHN MAYNARD KEYNES (1883–1946)

The most influential economic thinker of modern times, known to his close friends and intimates as Lord Keynes (remember to pronounce that "kanes"). Pre-Keynesian economists believed that a truly competitive market would run itself and that, in a capitalist system, conditions such as unemployment would be temporary inconveniences at worst. Then along came the Great Depression. In 1936 Keynes published his major work, *The General Theory of Employment, Interest, and Money* (now known simply as *The General Theory*) in which he argued that economics had to deal not only with the marketplace but with *total* spending within an economy (macroeconomics starts here). He argued that government intervention was necessary to stimulate the economy during periods of recession, bringing it into proper, if artificial equilibrium (the New Deal and deficit spending both start here). Keynes's system, brilliant for its time, has proved less valuable in dealing with modern inflation, and has been considered officially obsolete ever since Richard Nixon declared himself a Keynesian back in 1971. More recently, however, Ronald Reagan's supply-side economists set Keynes up in order to knock him down again in an uprising known in economics circles as "The Keynes Mutiny."

JOHN KENNETH GALBRAITH (1908–)

One of the first (and certainly one of the tallest) New World economists to give a liberal twist to the field's dogma. In his *The New Industrial State* (1967), Galbraith, a Canadian, argued that the rise of the major corporation had short-circuited the old laws of the market. In his view, such corporations now dominated the economy, creating and controlling market demand rather than responding to it, determining even the processes of government, while using their economic clout in their own, rather than society's, interests. More traditional economic thinkers have agreed that Galbraith is a better writer than he is an economist.

Five Easy Theses

Even though economies are always in flux, economic theories aren't built to turn on a dime. As a result, it doesn't take long for even the most hallowed hypothesis to stand exposed as just another version of the Emperor's New Clothes. Here, for the record, a few items we've recently found balled up on the floor of the Emperor's closet.

THE LAFFER CURVE: Economist Arthur B. Laffer's much-applauded hypothesis, rumored to have been first sketched on the back of a cocktail napkin, which states that at some point tax rates can get so high—and the incentive to work so discouraging—that raising them further will reduce, rather than increase, revenues. The converse of this theory, popularly known as supply-side economics, maintains that a government, by cutting taxes, actually gets to collect more money: this version has been widely credited with creating the largest deficit in American history.

KONDRATIEFF LONG WAVE CYCLE: Obscure theory dating from the Twenties and periodically enjoying a certain gloomy vogue. Nikolai Kondratieff, head of the Soviet Economic Research Center, postulated that throughout history capitalism has moved in long waves, or trend cycles, which last for between fifty and sixty years and consist of two to three decades of prosperity followed by a more or less equivalent period of stagnation. Kondratieff described three such historical cycles, and when economists dusted off his graphs and brought them up to date in the 1960s and 1970s, they found his theories to be depressingly accurate. According to their predictions, we were all in for another twenty years with no pocket money. The Russians, by the way, weren't thrilled with

Kondratieff's hypothesis either, since it implied that the capitalist system, far from facing impending collapse, would forever keep bouncing back like a bad case of herpes. Sometime around 1930, Kondratieff was shipped off to Siberia and never heard from again.

ECONOMETRICS: Yesterday's high-level hustle. Econometrics used to mean studies that created models of the economy based on a combination of observation, statistics, and mathematical principles. In the Sixties, however, the term referred to a lucrative mini-industry whose models were formulated by computer and hired out to government and big business to help them predict future trends. Government, in fact, soon became the biggest investor in econometrics models, spending millions to equip various agencies to come up with their own, usually conflicting, forecasts—this, despite the fact that the resulting predictions tended, throughout the Seventies, to have about the same record for accuracy as astrology. Today, econometrics models are still expensive and still often wrong, but they're accepted procedure and nobody bothers making a fuss about them anymore.

MONETARISM: One of the two major schools of thought currently feeding advice to political leaders on how to control inflation. Monetarists favor a laissez-faire approach to everything but the money supply itself (see below); they have misgivings about social security, minimum wages, and foreign aid, along with virtually every other form of government intervention. They stress slow and stable growth in the money supply as the best way for a government to ensure lasting economic growth without inflation, and they insist that, as long as the amount of money in circulation is carefully controlled, wages and prices will gradually adjust and everything will work out in the "long run" (see "long run," above). Monetarism owes much of its appeal to one of its chief proponents, Nobel Prize–winning economist Milton Friedman, whose theories are generally acknowledged to form the backbone of Prime Minister Margaret Thatcher's economic policy in Britain. Liberal critics say Friedman owes his own appeal to the fact that he looks like everyone's favorite Jewish uncle.

NEO-KEYNESIANISM: Monetarism's opposite number, a loose grouping of economists who are less inclined to wait for the "long run." The Neo-Keynesians argue that there are too many institutional arrangements—things like unions and collective-bargaining agreements—for wages and prices to adjust automatically. They maintain that the best way for a government to promote growth without inflation is by using its spending power to influence demand. Who wins in the Monetarist/Neo-Keynesian debate seems less important than the fact that each side has found someone to argue with.

Action Economics

OR, PUTTING YOUR MONEY WHERE THEIR MOUTHS ARE

So much for theory. Although no self-respecting economist ever dispenses with it entirely, there *are* areas of economics in which interpreting—or inventing—economic gospel takes a back seat to delivering on economic promises. That is, to keeping things—money, interest and exchange rates, deficits—moving in what's currently being perceived to be the right direction. Here, contributor Karen Pennar explains what some of those promises (and some of those directions) are. Come to terms with them and you'll be ready to queue up for her tour of the markets, stock and otherwise, where action turns into hair-raising adventure.

THE FEDERAL RESERVE BOARD

Known in financial circles as the Fed (and not to be confused with the Feds), this government body, our central bank, wields enormous control over the nation's purse strings. In fact, it's said that the Fed's chairman is the second most powerful man in Washington. He and his six colleagues, or governors of the Federal Reserve Board, direct the country's monetary policy. Simply put, they can alter the amount of money (see "Money Supply") and the cost of money (see "Interest Rates"), and thereby make or break the economy. When the Fed tightens, interest rates rise and the economy slows down. When the Fed eases, interest rates fall and the economy picks up. Or so it used to be. The balancing act is so difficult, and the Fed so mistrusted, that these days its actions often have a perverse effect. So much for simplicity.

Many swear that the Fed is the root of all economic evil. In his landmark work, *A Monetary History of the United States, 1867–1960* (co-authored by Anna J. Schwartz), Milton Friedman placed blame for the Great Depression squarely on the Fed (for tightening too much). He hasn't stopped berating it since, and he has plenty of company. Beating up on the Fed is a popular sport—unfair perhaps, but understandable. A little history: The Fed, created in 1913 by an act of Congress, grew steadily in strength during the Depression years. By the 1950s, it had evolved into an independent force, free of the pressures of Congress and the president. Checks and balances for the economy, you might say.

This explains why the Reagan administration has had a love–hate relationship with the Fed, praising it when interest rates are falling, then cursing it when interest rates climb. Members of Congress, similarly, are often frustrated by the Fed's independence, and periodically threaten to limit its autonomy.

But the Fed has proven blissfully immune to criticism. It can always point an accusing finger at Congress and the President, blaming them for fiscal irresponsibility, that is, for tax and budget policies that foul up the economy. Fed chairman Paul Volcker did this when Reagan was winning legislators' hearts and minds, and he was on pretty firm ground. The name-calling and mud-slinging will continue, and the Fed will go about its business, watching over the nation's banks and monetary affairs. If bankers squirm and politicians scream, so be it. When nobody likes what you're doing, reasons the Fed, you must be doing something right.

MONEY SUPPLY

This is what the Fed is supposed to control but has a hard time doing. The money supply comes in many shapes and sizes, and it has undergone many transformations. If you figure what you've got in your wallet and your bank account (assuming you're not a Rockefeller), multiply that by the number of American adults, add to that an estimate of corporate America's cash and bank deposits, you've got a pretty good idea of the basic money supply—over $600 billion at the Fed's last count. The Fed, by daily manipulation, can alter that number. And, though it might be a matter of months, everyone ultimately feels the effect of the Fed's actions. If the Fed releases less money into the economy, in-

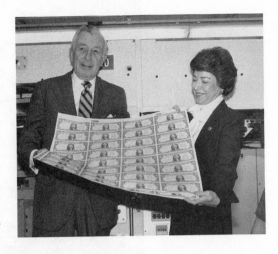

terest rates rise, corporate America borrows and produces less, workers are laid off, and everyone's spending is cut back. When the Fed pumps more money into the economy, the reverse happens. And if it moves too far in one direction or another, the Fed can create a depression (the result of too much tightening) or hyperinflation (the result of too much easing.)

So the next time you hear someone talk about the money supply, pay attention. But don't panic if you hear that it fell by, say, $10 billion in one week. (The Fed, with masterful understatement, is the first to admit that the money supply behaves erratically.) Instead, find out what its growth rate has been over the last six months or so. Then worry.

INTEREST RATES

A pair of Gucci shoes costs $150. A BMW 320i retails for $17,000. A one-bedroom Manhattan apartment rents for $1,200. What do all of these items have in common? They're expensive commodities. So is money. Some years, if you want to borrow $10,000 from your friendly banker, you have to pay about 14% interest, or $1,400 a year, on top of the $10,000 principal you owe. If you've got a mortgage, the rate may be lower, say 10% or 12%, but—well—variable. That means you could get a nasty shock in five years and be paying 16% on your mortgage. Of course, you could be pleasantly surprised and be paying a mere 8%.

It's hard to believe that interest rates hovered around 2% until 1950, and only hit double digits in 1974. What happened? The Vietnam War, wage and price controls, a quadrupling of oil prices, a flabby Fed, and a ballooning budget deficit. You're safe blaming any or all of these for eventually pushing prices up. Including the price of money. Now, when inflation has finally slowed down, interest rates are still pretty high. Why haven't interest rates fallen further? Because many people still doubt that inflation is licked, so they build a risk premium into interest rates. Basically, for interest rates to fall, you've got to believe. And most of us are agnostic at best when it comes to the economy.

THE TWIN DEFICITS

Do you live beyond your means? That is, do you spend more than you earn, borrow money to pay off credit card bills, then borrow money to pay off what you've borrowed? If you do, you're in the best of company. The U.S. government runs a deficit. In fact, it runs two deficits—one with its own citizenry, and one with the rest of the world. The deficits are different, because they are measured by separate accounting systems, but most economists will tell you that they are related, because if one of them wasn't so large, the other one wouldn't be either.

First, that deficit Uncle Sam runs within its borders, known as the budget deficit. In fiscal year 1985 (which ended September 30, 1985), the U.S. government spent a record $212 billion more than it raised in revenues, meaning that it was *in the red* by that amount. And there seems scant hope that the government will be able to reverse its profligate ways, despite unending debates in Congress over formulas for budget cutting.

Now every good New Deal Democrat knows that deficit spending is good—within reason. It pumps up the economy, just like how when you buy a car on credit, you're helping Detroit. But the problem is that the government has to borrow money to spend beyond its means, and it borrows from you and me. And corporate America. The near-daily borrowing fix that the government has to get overwhelms the credit markets, keeping interest rates high because lenders to the U.S. government want to be well rewarded for shouldering all that debt. And high interest rates make for an appealing investment—which is where the other deficit comes in.

Foreigners lend the U.S. lots of money, because they buy a lot of that Treasury debt. Where do they get the money? From us. In 1985, the U.S. bought nearly $150 billion *more* of goods and services than the rest of the world bought from us. The strong dollar had a lot to do with this—it made our exports expensive for foreigners and imports cheap for us. So what's wrong with these deficits? Well, a lot of problems (economists like to call them distortions) crop up. Like interest rates staying stubbornly high. Or U.S. workers losing their manufacturing jobs because of imports. It's a bit like debt is for individuals—a little is OK, a lot gets you in trouble.

FLOATING CURRENCIES

You may not remember, but figuring out a restaurant bill in France used to be easy (paying it was another matter). Just over a decade ago, foreign exchange rates, or the price of foreign currencies in U.S. dollars, were fixed. For long stretches of time—years in some cases—the ratio of dollars to French francs, or German marks, or whatever—simply didn't change. Occasionally there would be an official devaluation of a foreign currency, making it cheaper for foreigners, which meant they could get more francs for a dollar. Or there would be a revaluation, making the currency more expensive, which meant they could get fewer marks for a dollar. These rare changes were the result of large shifts in the amount of goods and services traveling in and out of a country, or in the flow of money and investments.

But in the late 1960s and early 1970s, these flows became enormous, and the delicate international financial system devised after World War II (named the Bretton Woods system after the New Hampshire town where the finance ministers gathered) became strained beyond repair. So currencies cut loose and traded wildly on markets. We don't have pure floating rates, as free-market thinkers such as Milton Friedman would like, because governments buy and sell their own currencies to stabilize exchange rates. But it's still a far cry from the old days. Just a look at the swings the dollar has taken—surging up 50% in four years then retreating most of the way—tells the story.

THE GOLD STANDARD

Economists always seem to be searching for an elixir, and not a few seem to think they have found it in the gold standard. The funny thing is that the gold standard is one of the oldest concepts around, and one that many thought was dead and buried. Only now, with economies beset by volatile markets, high interest rates, and rising deficits, the idea has been revived.

Under the gold standard, all countries once valued their currencies in gold, making paper convertible into gold and setting currency exchange rates on the basis of that convertibility. This country had a "pure" gold standard—done away with by Franklin Delano Roosevelt in 1933—under which any citizen could turn in his paper currency for gold. Then there was a modified gold standard, under which the dollar was tied to gold at $35 an ounce, and other currencies were tied to the value of the dollar. Nixon killed that off in 1971.

Adoption of a gold standard would force automatic adjustments on the U.S. and on its trading partners. It would also enrich or devastate, depending on whom you believe, the world's top gold producers, South Africa and the U.S.S.R. (who incidentally are also the world's top diamond producers, but do you hear anyone touting a diamond standard?). Gold, so the argument goes, has intrinsic value, while paper does not. When Cambodians fled Pol Pot's regime, they carried few possessions but all their gold. People understand gold, its proponents say, and a gold standard would make our economic policymakers in Washington honest. Somehow, this all works in the realm of theory. But today's

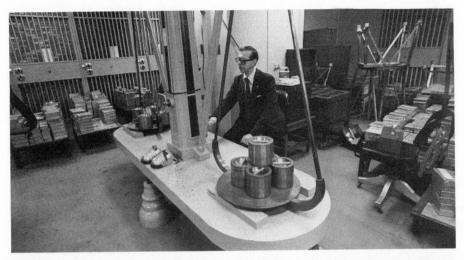

gold-pushers are like octogenarians who remember the good old days but forget about gas lamps and outhouses. The mechanistic inflexibility of the gold standard is what forced us to go off it: Stabilization could be damaging, what with people turning in their cheap paper currency for gold and sending economies into severe contractions.

There was concern in 1981 that Reagan's Gold Commission would send us back to the financial dark ages. But even that venerable group of economists and citizens opted not to turn back the clock. If the economy gets worse, inflation rebounds, and interest rates climb still higher, we may hear more about a gold standard. Don't hold your breath waiting for it to happen.

Adventure Economics

OR, PUTTING YOUR MONEY WHERE YOUR MOUTH IS

Because so many people share in the national pastime known as playing the market (which means, of course, the stock market, and refers specifically to the granddaddy of them all, the New York Stock Exchange), it's worth your while to know the rudiments. The way to do that is to follow the stock tables in your newspaper and read the daily market summaries. The tables may look like hieroglyphics and the summaries may read like Chinese, but you can decode them with a little help. And if you're really ambitious, you can learn about a few other markets—like the bond and futures markets—and think of yourself as a financial polyglot.

THE STOCK MARKET

A *stock* represents a share, or fractional ownership, in a company, and a very fractional one indeed. Large companies have tens of millions of shares outstanding. Companies sell stocks (the first time they do it's called going public) because they need other people's money. With a strong base of stockholders' equity, as the pool of ownership is known, a company can buy machinery, fill orders, pay its executives handsomely (and its workers not so handsomely), and even borrow money.

Stock comes in two forms—common and preferred. The difference lies chiefly in dividend policy (see below), but is also important when a company liquidates. Then the preferred shareholder is, as the designation implies, in a better position than the common shareholder.

A *dividend* is the reward, or payoff, a company gives the stockholder for investing in it. It's actually a piece of the profits, but don't imagine for a minute that all the profits are distributed proportionally. No way: Profits must be plowed back into the company's operations (and, some might say, into executives' pockets). But something has to be given to the investor who helped make things happen, so dividends of anywhere from a few cents to a few dollars per share are handed over quarterly. The company sets the dividend rate, and every so often may decide to toss a few more coins shareholders' way. But a company, if it is in poor financial shape, may also suspend paying dividends on common stock, or cut a dividend. The company, however, must distribute dividends in full to preferred stockholders before it pays common stockholders, so it is the latter who get their dividends axed first in a pinch.

A *capital gain* is the profit you make on the sale of your ownership in a company, provided the company has done well, its stock is in demand, and its stock price has risen: You hit big in the market.

A *loss* is a loss. Today—or the day you bought stock—was not your day.

The *stock market* is where winners and losers get together. Sometimes it seems like a party, other times like a wake. Big winners and losers determine the mood, because the real market makers are pension funds, banks, corporations, and other money managers, all known as institutional investors. The little guy is just that, and he tends to get swept up or under the tidal waves institutional investors create. The cardinal rule of any market, the stock market included, is buy low, sell high, but if everyone did that successfully, there'd be no markets to speak of. For any person who buys low, there's somebody selling low, and for anyone selling high, there's someone willing to buy high. Why? Because of expectations and greed. A person selling low is trying to cut his losses and figures the worst is yet to come, so it's time to bail out. And a buyer shelling out big bucks is convinced that stock prices will go still higher, and he wants to cash in, even if belatedly.

The *herd instinct* accounts for the tidal waves and derives from the fact that people are always looking over their shoulders to see what the next guy is doing. And more often than not, for no good reason, they figure he must be right and they must be wrong. Institutional investors suffer this market paranoia in the worst way, so you see how a herd can form and really trample the market. Since institutions invest in many names, stock prices across the board tend to move in line with each other during big market swings. That's what people mean when they say the market moved up or down. All sorts of things can affect the herd, from a change in tax legislation to a political assassination. But the herd can take on a life of its own, as it did in August 1982 and, in a very different mood, in September, 1986. Even with little evidence of improvement in a foundering economy, and with scant relief from lower interest rates, people can decide to buy, and hope to win big.

If you'd watched the stock tables during those September 1986 days, the numbers would have told the story. "Market indicators" is a good place to start—it'll give you an overview of the market. Here's how you'd read the results for September 11, 1986.

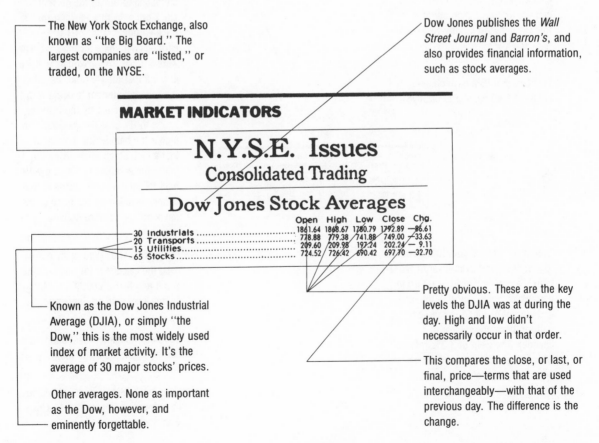

The New York Stock Exchange, also known as "the Big Board." The largest companies are "listed," or traded, on the NYSE.

Dow Jones publishes the *Wall Street Journal* and *Barron's*, and also provides financial information, such as stock averages.

MARKET INDICATORS

N.Y.S.E. Issues
Consolidated Trading

Dow Jones Stock Averages

	Open	High	Low	Close	Chg.
30 Industrials	1861.64	1868.67	1780.79	1792.89	—86.61
20 Transports	778.88	779.38	741.88	749.00	—33.63
15 Utilities	209.60	209.98	197.24	202.24	— 9.11
65 Stocks	724.52	726.42	690.42	697.70	—32.70

Known as the Dow Jones Industrial Average (DJIA), or simply "the Dow," this is the most widely used index of market activity. It's the average of 30 major stocks' prices.

Other averages. None as important as the Dow, however, and eminently forgettable.

Pretty obvious. These are the key levels the DJIA was at during the day. High and low didn't necessarily occur in that order.

This compares the close, or last, or final, price—terms that are used interchangeably—with that of the previous day. The difference is the change.

There are other averages, calculated by other firms, but none really compares with the Dow, which holds a mystical fascination for anyone remotely interested in the stock market. By and large, however, any representative average should tell the same story with different numbers—that is, on a day when the Dow was up, they should be up too.

So much for the big picture. How about those ten IBM shares you inherited from Uncle Eddy? Look up IBM—it's a big company, the stock is "blue chip" because of size, reputation, and clout, so it'll be listed on the Big Board. (That fledgling company your neighbor invested in is probably a "penny stock," so called because it usually costs a few cents to buy; you'll find it listed OTC, or over the counter, only if it's been bought or sold on a given day.) Back to the big time. Here's what IBM looked like at the close of business on September 11, 1986:

Just a barometer. It shows IBM's trading range for the past year. Look at these two numbers and check against "last" column. You can see IBM is trading about midway between its fifty-two-week high and low.

This tells you IBM pays shareholders $4.40 per share, each year.

This measures the number of times by which IBM's latest twelve-month earnings (per share) must be multiplied to obtain the current stock price. With a PE ratio (or price-earnings ratio) of 13, earnings per share for the past year were $10.70. (Approximately. Keep in mind that the PE ratio, as listed, is a rounded number to begin with.) PE ratios are cited by those in the know. VERY broadly speaking, the higher the better. But remember that a high stock price divided by miniscule earnings can also give a high PE, and all that means is that people have bid up the price of the stock on the basis of nothing.

Even if you've held your IBM shares for ten years and plan never to sell, there's an implicit yield or return to you, which fluctuates with the price and current dividend (remember both of those are subject to change). The yield of 3.2% reflects what percent the annual dividend, $4.40, is of the closing price, $139¼.

Multiply by 100. (You really don't need the calculator for this one.) You'll find that 2,860,600 IBM shares were sold on September 11.

Obvious. Remember last and closing mean the same thing.

How much IBM gained, calculated by comparing September 11 close with September 10 close.

52-Week				Yld	PE	Sales				
High	Low	Stock	Div	%	Ratio	100s	High	Low	Last	Chg.
24¾	16½	IntAlu	.72	3.7	15	64	19⅜	19⅛	19⅜	— ⅜
161⅞	122¼	IBM	4.40	3.2	13	28606	142⅞	138¼	139¼	— 4⅞
36¾	23⅜	IntCtrl	.50	2.0	17	124	25½	25	25¼	— ⅜
48⅞	29	IntFlav	1.16	3.1	18	1406	39⅜	36½	37¾	— 1⅞

The stock market isn't the only market around. There's the *options market*, where people buy and sell the rights to buy and sell stocks, believe it or not. This way, for less money than it would take to actually buy stocks outright, people can play the market. Without ever owning a stock, they can win big or lose big on its movement. Playing the options market can be (if that's possible) even more of a crapshoot than playing the stock market.

Also a dicey game, for some, though a very useful tool for others, is the *futures market*. This market was originally devised to help out farmers and manufacturers who used farm products. Contracts for future delivery (within a few months) of grains, pork bellies, and assorted other items could be bought and sold, providing a hedge against anticipated rising costs or falling revenues. But the market has burgeoned in recent years with the inclusion of a host of new contracts (from foreign exchange to stock indices) and scores of new players. Today hardly anyone active in the futures market takes actual delivery on a contract. The fastest growing component of the market is in financial futures—Treasury bills and the like—because roller-coaster interest rates are still another cost businessmen want to hedge against and speculators bet against.

Once the staidest of them all, the *bond market* has been hopping recently because of that same familiar culprit—ricocheting interest rates. Used to be, a company that wanted to fix its borrowing costs for ten or twenty years would borrow money from investors by issuing bonds. The U.S. Treasury did the same, as did thousands of municipalities and the nation's fifty states. The investor would buy the bond, receive a fixed amount of interest each year from the issuer, and get back his principal when the bond "matured." Bonds were boring because nothing changed. Prices were steady because interest rates were steady. If interest rates moved slightly higher, the resale price of the bond, or its price on the secondary market, moved a notch down. No big deal.

Today everything has changed. Borrowing fixed-rate money for twenty years, not to mention lending it, takes phenomenal courage. And even ten years looks like a long stretch. Who knows where interest rates will be ten or twenty years from now? And what about the interim, when you may want to sell the bond? The nightmarish guessing game has turned the market into a churning mass, with buyers and sellers tripping over each other to secure mere fractions of a percentage point in interest. Lower rates have made the market "rally," that is, bonds have recouped some of their lost value and prices are higher—but no one is settling in for the long (read 20-year) haul just yet.

So much for the markets. If you feel like dipping your big toe in, be forewarned: The old adage that you should never invest more than you can afford to lose still holds true. In fact, truer than ever. Leave the fancy stuff and the big bets to the old hands. After all, they know more than you.

Or do they?

Economic Punchlines

OR, PUTTING YOUR MOUTH WHERE YOUR MOUTH IS

In the past, all the good jokes were about doctors, lawyers, and politicians, but now that economists control the politicians and make more money than the doctors and lawyers, it's they who've become the butt. As it happens, the jokes themselves are far too long to recount here. Which means you'll have to be content with the punch lines:

Joke 1: "Do you have any idea how many economists you have to kill just to get a pound of brains?"

Joke 2: "Who do you think was responsible for creating all this chaos in the first place?"

Joke 3: "The economist says, 'First, assume the existence of a can opener.'"

Joke 4: "The good news is that the bus just went over the edge of the cliff. The bad news is that there were three empty seats on it."

CHAPTER

FILM

Contents

Careers in filmmaking: Worth the bus fare to Hollywood?

Remedial Watching for the Baby-Boom Generation

It's one thing when they try to get you on opera: You really *can* simply wave your passport in their faces and announce that that isn't what we do here. It's quite another when they hit you with movies, which are as American in genesis and allure as you are. *Birth of a Nation* got you down? Or *Potemkin*? Or *Citizen Kane*? This'll help.

THE BIRTH OF A NATION
(AMERICAN, 1915)

Director

D. W. (David Wark) Griffith. The original and still, to some, the greatest. Newcomers to Griffith (and, obviously, to film history, in which he is always a long Chapter 3, right after "The Movies Are Born" and "The Movies Find a Public") may, however, appreciate a couple of touchstones. The first: Thomas Edison. Like him, Griffith was a practical genius, a boy-scientist type who wanted to solve the problem, not promulgate the theory. The second: Charles Dickens. Like *him*, Griffith was sentimental, melodramatic, and hopelessly Victorian. Though a reactionary in terms of his subject matter (big moments in history, American rural and domestic life, moral-religious allegories) and a philistine when it came to "art," he single-handedly propelled movies out of the realm of stage-bound theatricality and into that of the cinematic. He also realized, a full decade before anybody else even got around to thinking about it, the possibilities of the new medium, and contributed its two most basic techniques: the cross-cut (in which we watch a little of one scene, then a little of another, then back to the first, etc., in a way that suggests simultaneous action) and the close-up (in which we get to feel we know, and are maybe not so very different from, the characters up there on the screen). *Birth of a Nation* and *Intolerance* (1916, an interweaving of stories of cruelty from four different civilizations, from Babylonian times to D. W.'s own) are the "core" Griffith; cultists, by contrast, dote on *Broken Blossoms* (1919). Ironical note: Griffith lived too long, with Hollywood first stripping him of his creative freedom, then forcing him to edit the botched efforts of other directors, and finally refusing even to take his phone calls. He died, forgotten, in a Hollywood hotel room.

Story

Nation—in the form of two families, the abolitionist Stonemans of Pennsylvania and the plantationist Camerons of North Carolina, who are, despite their differences, great friends—is torn apart by Civil War. Reconstruction proves even worse: Negroes are uppity; Flora Cameron (Mae Marsh)—a.k.a. the Little Sister—jumps off cliff to avoid being raped by Gus, an emancipated house slave; and it takes the Ku Klux Klan, led by Ben Cameron—a.k.a. the Little Colonel—who, by the way, is in love with Elsie Stoneman (Lillian Gish), to set things right. Stay put for the climax: cross-cuts between two simultaneous Klan rescues, one of Elsie, whom a mulatto with a heavy black-supremacy rap wants to make "queen" of an all-black empire; the other of the entire Cameron family, with a Stoneman thrown in for good measure, from a cabin being besieged by Negroes and carpetbaggers.

What All the Fuss Was About at the Time

Nobody had ever seen anything remotely like this: a three-and-a-half-hour epic, with a coherent plot, persuasive performances, chase scenes, camera movement for days, brimming over with emotion and what appeared to be ideas; plus, it had been budgeted at an unheard of $100,000 and cost an equally unheard of $2 a head to see. Without warning, movies emerged from the penny arcades into respectability. The era of the "feature film" was born and with it the pattern for the "blockbuster," in which huge sums of money are invested in the hopes of even huger returns at the box office. Needless to say, not all the East Coast reviewers thought much of the movie's bathetic story, simple-minded thesis, and overwritten title cards (e.g., "Bitter memories will not allow the poor bruised heart of the South to forget"). And the racism riled black and liberal viewers: There were riots in New York, Boston, and Chicago; city fathers demanded cuts; and Jane Addams and the president of Harvard, among others, wrote chiding letters. All the brouhaha did, though, was (a) incite Griffith, himself the son of a Kentucky colonel, to counterattack, first with pamphlets and then with *Intolerance*—in his opinion proof positive that *he*, at least, was free from prejudice; (b) suggest to anybody who'd managed to keep his cool just how inflammatory this new medium could be; and (c) fuel the movie's publicity and box-office operations. Not that *Birth* needed a shot in the arm; it was an immediate hit. As President Wilson said, "It is like writing history with lightning."

What All the Fuss Is About Today

Some people are still stuck on the racism, but most of us have moved on to Griffith as fashioner of the "grammar and rhetoric" of film, from his stockpiling of technical devices to his discovery that the emotional content of a scene, rather than its physical setup, determined where to place the camera and when to cut. Then there was his overall success with actors—how he got them to function as an ensemble as well as to underact (for the times, it was underacting)—and his particular success with those contrasting types of womanhood, Lillian Gish (idealized femininity, purity, frailty) and Mae Marsh (the girl next door). *Birth* is also a valid historical document, not of Civil War days, but of the country fifty years later, still in reaction to that war. None of which makes for easy viewing: Birth (ditto *Intolerance*) has most modern audiences watching the minute-hands of their wristwatches.

THE CABINET OF DR. CALIGARI (GERMAN, 1919)

Director

Robert Wiene, but don't give him another thought: He was a one-shot and he got the job only because Fritz Lang was tied up making something called *The Spiders*. Instead, be mindful of the screenwriters, a Czech named Hans Janowitz, who'd happened to witness a sex murder in Hamburg's Reeperbahn, and an Austrian named Carl Mayer, who'd been examined once too often by army psychiatrists during World War I; the set designers, a four-man contingent headed by Hermann Warm, who used expressionist principles and techniques to create the movie's warped, angular look, going so far as to paint in, rather than throw, those eerie lights and shadows; and even the producer, Erich Pommer, who financed the whole crazy package and hoped the public would bite.

Story

Check out the frame-tale setup: Patient in mental hospital tells elaborate and horrifying story of weird, heavily bespectacled carnival-circuit hypnotist (Werner Krauss), who controls lurching somnambulist, Cesare (Conrad Veidt), inducing him to commit series of murders. His story told, patient freaks out and is taken to office of mental hospital's benign director, who, in the course of examination, puts on pair of horn-rimmed spectacles and . . .

What All the Fuss Was About at the Time

German intellectuals liked the sick settings, the way a madman's fantasy life had been translated into visual terms; French intellectuals went one step further and coined the term *caligarisme,* which they used to describe cinema that was abstract, like a "painting in motion," rather than realistic narrative of natural events in natural settings—a useful enough idea in a postwar world that was striking almost everyone as sinister and unworkable. This sort of distortion was not unknown in the theater, of course. The amazing thing was that now a movie camera was eschewing reality, apparently no longer interested in recording the "look" of things, the very purpose it had been devised for. But apart from getting the intellectuals going and setting a certain standard for future "art" films, *Caligari* would not seriously influence the course of movies.

What All the Fuss Is About Today

For horror-movie aficionados, this is the granddaddy, happily fleshed out with mental illness (persecution, hallucination, breakdown) and the chilling ambiguities generated by the tale-within-a-tale format. More than mere horror, however, *Caligari* purveys the kind of weirdness that fuels cultism: Here's a way to get the jump on friends who are still gaga over Kafka or, what's worse, *The Rocky Horror Picture Show*. Then, there's the movie's inherent appeal for painters and set designers: Unlike other classics of the cinema, this is one in which stagecraft and painted flats, rather than camera movement and dynamic editing, do the job—and get the credit. Finally, it's a traditional favorite of sociologists and portent readers; German film theorist Siegfried Kracauer, for instance, sees in it the beginnings of a "cortège of monsters and tyrants" that would eventually culminate in Hitler.

NANOOK OF THE NORTH
(AMERICAN, 1922)
Director

Robert J. Flaherty. Boy with a camera (and a Jean-Jacques Rousseau streak), intent on revealing the essence and the quality of life as it was then being lived in such exotic outposts as the frozen Arctic (*Nanook*), the South Seas (*Moana*), the barren, storm-tossed islands off Ireland's west coast (*Men of Aran*), and the bayous of Louisiana (*The Louisiana Story*). The first—and most legendary—of the documentary filmmakers, he sidestepped studios and story lines for what he could observe out there on his own. Intense and gentle; paragon of integrity; like Renoir (whom he helped smuggle out of France and into America during the War), a "poet" among directors.

Story

Eskimo family—stalwart Nanook, jolly wife Nyla, two small children, plus infant in pouch of Nyla's sealskin parka—survives elements and sculpts nature as best it can on shores of Hudson Bay. Very cold, shores of Hudson Bay. And crawling with seals. Sequences to note: Family emerges from kayak, one by one, like circus midgets from a tiny car; Nanook, at trading post, goes wild over phonograph and tries to eat phonograph record; Nanook, on big ice floe, stands alone at edge, spearing fish; Nanook builds igloo, from (just as you'd always suspected) blocks of compacted snow. But we bet you didn't know he was going to install a chunk of frozen river as a window.

What All the Fuss Was About at the Time

Unpredictably, a big commercial, as well as critical, hit. Of course, it helped that the picture opened in New York in the middle of one of the hottest Junes on record; but beyond that, viewers couldn't get over the way they were invited not only to travel to a distant clime, but to look into somebody else's mind and heart. Plus, everybody wanted to know how Flaherty had done it, had lived for months in subzero temperatures, a thousand miles from the nearest restaurant, photographic supply store, oral surgeon, whatever—and had gotten all these Eskimos not only to trust him, but to take direction (a matter that bothered some critics so much that they charged Flaherty with misusing "facts"). Then there was Nanook himself: the bright eyes, the continual smile, the weather-beaten face. Within a matter of months, Eskimo pies were being sold on both sides of the Atlantic, and words like "igloo," "kayak," and "anorak," formerly known only to anthropologists, were popping up in grade-school civics texts and sporting-goods store windows. Too bad Nanook couldn't have basked in his new fame: He died of starvation, out there on the ice, shortly after the film was released.

What All the Fuss Is About Today

Three things. First, the documentary tradition, of which Flaherty is held to be the father; how it was discovered that dramatic content could be derived from the depiction of fact, how documentary is both more "real" and more "respectable" than the fiction film. Second, Flaherty as counterpoint to Hollywood, as the great director who, unlike Griffith and Stroheim, wasn't crushed by it; and who, unlike Sternberg, didn't collaborate with it; but who simply abandoned it for places where he couldn't be reached by phone. Third, the final product, a triumph of structure, editing, and sympathy, even if he did force all those Eskimos to wear skins and furs that were more Eskimoish than anything they'd ever pick out for themselves.

THE LAST LAUGH (GERMAN, 1924)

Director

F. W. (Friedrich Wilhelm) Murnau. Most revered director of Germany's Golden Age, which was conceived in the rubble of World War I, thrived through the heady days of the Weimar Republic, and withered away in the early Thirties, the result either of Hitler's crackdown on creative types or of Hollywood's buying them all up, or both. A pupil of Max Reinhardt, the German genius of the stage, Murnau jettisoned the expressionism and eerieness of *Caligari* days and began serving up bratwurst-and-boiled-potatoes realism. (Even his 1922 *Nosferatu*, based on Bram Stoker's *Dracula*, used everyday, business-as-usual, port-city-of-Bremen settings.) Hollywood got its hands on Murnau, too: He made *Sunrise,* about a young wife threatened by her unbalanced husband, for Fox in 1927, then collaborated with Flaherty on a quasi-documentary South Seas drama called *Tabu* (1931). Only forty-three, he died in a car crash a week before *Tabu*'s premiere, thereby affording film historians a favorite example of directorial careers nipped in the bud.

Story

Dignified old man (Emil Jannings) at top-drawer hotel is exalted by braided and epauletted uniform that is part and parcel of job. One morning he arrives at work to find that new, young doorman is hailing cabs, lugging suitcases, etc., and that he has been demoted to washroom attendant and must wear simple white smock. More humiliation follows, especially at home, where old man had formerly been treated like grand duke and is now treated like dirt. Not to worry: Tacked-on happy ending has him inheriting fortune of rich American hotel guest and dining sumptuously in hotel dining room.

What All the Fuss Was About at the Time

Hailed by American critics as "the best film in the world," *Laugh* was also a big popular success. Jannings's performance, if broad, was a great crowd-pleaser; besides, the world on screen looked real again, instead of like some crazy—and probably subversive—artist's nightmare. But the biggest impact was technical, and Hollywood felt it more deeply than that from any other foreign film: Suddenly, the movie camera was actually *moving,* up and down, forward and back, through the lobby of the hotel and out onto the street—even in simulation of the shakiness of a hangover, tracking and tilting and swinging and twirling. Freed from its fixed tripod (though not yet provided with cranes and dollies), it had become flexible and aggressive, had become—as the film historians like to observe—an actor.

What All the Fuss Is About Today

The situation's been in hand for a while now—unless you're stranded in a roomful of N.Y.U. film students, all of whom will be noting, in addition to the moving camera and the realism, the fact that said realism is subjective (i.e., filtered through the consciousness of the central character) and that there is a great deal of attention being paid to his emotional and psychological state. Even nonstudents, though, tend to marvel at how easy this movie is to watch, how modern in its narrative flow. Moreover, the story is told without so much as a title card, so efficient and eloquent are the visuals—until, that is, a series of cards announce (and apologize for) the tacked-on, trumped-up ending. Poignant oddity: The signs in the washroom, which are printed in Esperanto, a token of Murnau's conviction that cinema (at the time still silent) was destined to level the linguistic barriers between nations.

GREED (AMERICAN, 1924)

Director

Erich von Stroheim. More precisely, either Erich Oswald Hans Carl Marie Stroheim von Nordenwald, son of a colonel on the Austrian general staff and himself a former officer in the Austro-Hungarian cavalry; or Erich Oswald Stroheim, son of a Prussian-Jewish hatter who'd emigrated to Vienna, and himself a former frustrated foreman in his father's straw-hat factory—depending on whether you believe Stroheim's own publicity or its subsequent debunkers. Either way, the man who, as director and genius, suffered more than anybody else at the hands of Hollywood. A meticulous craftsman who exceeded budgets and audience's attention spans as a matter of course, he met his nemesis in profits-minded Irving Thalberg. Of the eight-and-a-half films he managed to turn out in over fifteen years of directing, all but the first two were mutilated by studio cutters, one was taken away from him in mid-production, and a couple weren't even released. Even so, he remains, after Griffith, the most influential director Hollywood turned out in the years before talkies. (The other bottom-line Stroheims: *Foolish Wives*, 1922, and *The Wedding March*, 1928.) Also an actor, both in the Teens (when he invariably portrayed nasty, stiff-backed Huns and was billed as "the man you love to hate") and, following the asphyxiation of his directing career, in such classics as Renoir's *Grand Illusion* (as the aristocratic Colonel von Rauffenstein) and Billy Wilder's *Sunset Boulevard* (as Norma Desmond's butler and playmate).

Story

From Frank Norris's turn-of-the-century naturalistic novel *McTeague*. San Francisco dentist (that's McTeague), practicing without a license, fixes tooth, then courts and marries sweet young thing (Zasu Pitts), who, at their engagement party, learns she's won $5,000 in lottery: the beginning of the end. A long and elaborate wedding banquet (a scene in which, among other things, a funeral cortege can be glimpsed through an open window) follows, along with boredom, estrangement, blackmail, penury, murder, and a Death Valley climax, in which ex-dentist and blackmailer fight and die like dogs. Interspersed with above: shot of long bony arms, belonging to no one in particular, clutching at pile of gold coins.

What All the Fuss Was About at the Time

The Stroheim method: How he'd shot the Death Valley scene *in* Death Valley (in 132° heat); how he'd made the cast and crew live in the San Francisco house they were using as a set; how he kept his actors working till four in the morning; how no detail, no bit of atmosphere, no bow in the direction of verisimilitude was, for this man, too much. (For other movies, he'd demand that a life-size replica of Monte Carlo be built, that his movie archdukes wear only authentic medals and have crests on their—perforce—silk underwear.) The fact that he'd submitted a forty-two-reel (i.e., ten-hour) movie, edited it to twenty-four reels under duress, then sat back and watched as the studio hacked it—and all its subplots, bit parts, symbolism, and narrative continuity—to ten reels and two-and-a-half hours. Also, the subject matter (avarice and human degradation, dirty dishes and unmade beds, à la Zola) which had one popular critic branding the film "a vile epic of the sewer," another "the sour crème de la sour crème." The few colleagues who'd seen the original forty-two reel version were dumbstruck, enthralled; anybody who saw the ten-reel one had a hard time knowing what was going on. A monumental commercial failure.

What All the Fuss Is About Today

The Stroheim legend—the man more than the movie. How he, a hatter's son, created himself: the aristocratic past, the monocle, the super-erect posture, the extra-long cigarettes. The fact that while the only version of the film we have is the two-and-a-half hour one, the complete screenplay *does* exist, along with a few extra stills—a constant provocation to cinephiles, who keep hoping one of Stroheim's own original forty-two-reel prints, with coins, fillings, picture frames, and a canary allegedly hand-tinted in gold, will turn up. How we still don't know whether a ten-hour movie version is, aesthetically, let alone commercially, possible. Then there's the object lesson for young directors: If Michael Cimino had paid attention to the Stroheim case, would he have made *Heaven's Gate?* Finally, for the trivia buffs, the realization that Zasu Pitts hadn't always played ditzy manicurists.

THE GOLD RUSH (AMERICAN, 1925)

Director

Charlie Chaplin. Tripped over his own mystique. The product of a Dickensian English boyhood (complete with drunken father, insane mother, orphanages, and floggings), Chaplin never stopped acting out his anxieties regarding food, security, social injustice, ostracism, bullies, and the human condition. Touring America in a music-hall act, he had been discovered by Mack Sennett, who employed him in a series of shorts, as a puppet and pratfaller. Within a year, Chaplin had evolved the "Tramp" persona, with a cane, a hat, floppy shoes, and a pair of Fatty Arbuckle's trousers as props, and negotiated a contract to make his own pictures. Ahead lay, in addition to enormous popular success, the acclaim of the culturati; his conviction that he *was* the Little Man, the Tragic Clown; a loss of touch with his fans, who were being provided with fewer and fewer laughs and more and more sentiment; increasingly "heavy" films (*City Lights*, 1931; *Modern Times*, 1936; *Monsieur Verdoux*, 1947; *Limelight*, 1952) that garnered mixed reactions; several marriages, most notably his last one, to Eugene O'Neill's daughter Oona; deportation from the U.S. as a Communist sympathizer; a couple of less-than-successful English-made movies, à la *A Countess from Hong Kong* (1966); and official rehabilitation in the form of a special Oscar in 1972. He died in 1977.

Story

The Lone Prospector (Chaplin) joins mass trek to frozen Alaska gold fields; that's him looking out at you from the lower lefthand corner of the group picture. Arrives pursued by bear, and with frying pan spanking buttocks at every step. Is isolated in tiny cabin in blizzard with two larger and hungrier prospectors; eats own shoe. Meets dance-hall Girl and falls in love, but is stood up on New Year's Eve, in course of which he dreams he spikes two hard rolls with forks and causes them to do variety of dances (famous sequence, this). Cabin almost falls over cliff. Strikes gold. Boards ship for San Francisco. Runs into Girl, who, it turns out, loves him back.

What All the Fuss Was About at the Time

To a degree, comedy in general. Chaplin was simply the favorite in a rag-tag, anyone-can-play segment of the industry that boasted Langdon, Lloyd, Laurel and Hardy, and—the only one now regarded as being in Chaplin's league—Buster Keaton. Primed, the public applauded. To a degree, Chaplin in general, too. The first movie-spawned personality to be widely regarded as a genius, as well as the first international movie star, Chaplin fueled an icons-and-memorabilia industry that compares favorably with those of Mickey Mouse, the Beatles, and E.T. The Little Man confronting power and wealth, less hostilely than ambivalently, appealed to the little man in everybody; the only difference was *they* couldn't use every last bit of their bodies to convey the pathos, whimsy, and acuity of it all. As for *The Gold Rush* itself: Great moments (the bear, the shoe, those rolls, the precipitously placed cabin), with a nice thematic unity that critics had not yet started complaining was undermined by too episodic a structure.

What All the Fuss Is About Today

Most of it's in the backlash. Chaplin hasn't been artistically discredited, exactly, but he's been made to seem self-serving, even circumscribed. The big beneficiary is Keaton, whose *The General* has replaced Chaplin's *The Gold Rush* and *Modern Times* on all-time ten-best lists, as critics rushed to prefer the former's athletic naturalness and sense of film's "possibilities" to the latter's balletic self-consciousness and solipsism. Not that anybody's denying Chaplin's genius—only his modesty, sincerity, and devotion to the genre. Flashiest critical line for the undecided to take: that Chaplin, unlike Keaton, put the exterior world behind him—at the expense of his popularity—and lived out of "the interior, almost schizophrenic relationship between director and actor." (That's Andrew Sarris, by the way.) A saner tack: Be moved by the grace, the eloquence, the expressiveness of Chaplin's fingertips, and appreciate how he, like Griffith and Orson Welles, bridges the gap between movies as art and movies as entertainment.

POTEMKIN (RUSSIAN, 1925)
Director

Sergei Eisenstein, to movies what Freud is to psychology: the theoretician who's never been surpassed, the practitioner who's never been entirely superseded. Also, like Freud, the right man in the right place (in this case, Russia) at the right time (the fifteen turbulent years following the Revolution, during which Soviet films were the most exciting in the world). You may feel he's manipulating you and he is: Eisenstein subscribed to Lenin's belief that art could influence politics and that "the most important of all the arts, for us, is cinema"; saw that it could not only capture reality, but transmute it, less through the stories it told than through bold imagery, stylized compositions, and, most of all, rhythmic editing. Only twenty-six when he made *Potemkin* (Russians and purists pronounce that Po-*TYOM*-kin, by the way), Eisenstein would live both to employ his genius and to suffer for it. Under Stalin he was alternately purged and reinstated a couple of times a decade until his death in 1948; as personally devastating was his sojourn in Hollywood in the early Thirties, during which he made conversation with Charlie Chaplin and Mary Pickford, posed for press photos with Rin Tin Tin, collaborated unsuccessfully with Theodore Dreiser and Upton Sinclair, and watched his dream of filming an epic about Mexico from Toltec days to the present be sandbagged by the capitalists. Other seminal Eisenstein: *Strike* (1924), *Ten Days That Shook the World* (a.k.a. *October;* 1927), the two-part *Ivan the Terrible* (1942–1946).

Story

It's 1905. Sailors on the tsarist battleship *Potemkin*, anchored off the Black Sea port of Odessa, grow tired of, among other things, maggots in their meat. Group of them rebels and is ordered shot by firing squad made up of their mates. "Brothers! Who are you shooting at?" shouts rebels' ringleader, and rebellion becomes shipwide mutiny. As it happens, the citizens of Odessa— workers, mothers with baby carriages, bearded university professors, plus an amputee and an unforgettable old lady with pince-nez—see rightness in all this, and gaily assemble on the broad white steps in the middle of the town, where, within five minutes, they are gunned down and trampled on by a couple of hundred Cossack soldiers. But the spirit of revolution lives on. In the final segment, the *Potemkin* races toward an imperial squadron, prepared to do battle. Guns are drawn on it, but, in the nick of time, it runs up flags spelling out "Join us." The fleet does not fire. Everybody cheers.

What All the Fuss Was About at the Time

First off, that *Potemkin* didn't look like a movie, didn't look staged (as the high-artifice films that were coming out of Germany did) or even acted; in fact, it read as a newsreel. Second, that it was such powerful stuff: Nobody who's seen the Odessa Steps sequence will ever forget it (or admit that he has, anyway). Of course, that's not to say that he'll be aware of what went into it: on the one hand, of Eisenstein's commitment to "actuality," to using real people rather than actors (a furnace man as the ship's doctor, a gardener as the ship's priest, and sailors as the sailors) and shooting on location rather than in the studio; on the other, of his clever and intense use of montage, a kind of hyperrhythmic editing in which Image A (shot of boots of soldiers marching relentlessly toward top of steps) is juxtaposed with Image B (shot of woman protesting soldiers' butchery) in such a way that the audience anticipates and becomes psychologically involved with a third, as yet unseen Image C, resulting from the "collision" of the first two. Thinkers pointed out that this was really just the application of the principles of dialectical materialism to art, but that wasn't what had Mary Pickford, Douglas Fairbanks, and Cecil B. De Mille making pilgrimages to Moscow, or young American intellectuals sitting night after night in Eighth Street movie houses. This movie seemed to be ushering in the twentieth century, taking up where Griffith had left off. With *Potemkin*, cinema had at last given up the theatrical, and the literary, and spoken in its own language. And, in just five reels and eighty-six minutes, it blew you away besides.

What All the Fuss Is About Today

The montage is still right in there: How, without it, is any true *cinéaste* going to go on to deal with, say, Godard? An even bigger come-on: the fact that this exciting, dynamic, idealistic, ideological, brave era of Soviet movie-making didn't last; that Eisenstein and his colleagues would, within five years, be branded formalists and decadents by Stalin and company and that Soviet film would take a nosedive into banality. (Of course, the same thing was taking place in Germany under Hitler, but at least the Germans—producers, directors, actors, screenwriters, cameramen, and, for all we know, hair-and-makeup people—relocated to Hollywood.) Finally, there's the sheer power of it all. Even if the story seems a little cartoonish, the idea of Eisenstein defining an art form, seizing the moment, defying hubris and Hollywood is *very* Promethean. For those who prefer the statistical angle: With Renoir's *La Règle du Jeu* and Welles's *Citizen Kane*, *Potemkin* is one of the three movies guaranteed to show up, decade after decade, on every international critic's all-time ten-best list.

THE PASSION OF JOAN OF ARC
(FRENCH, 1928)

Director

Carl-Theodor Dreyer, a Dane then working in Paris. And that's not all: The set designer was a German (Hermann Warm, from *Caligari* days), the cameraman a Pole, and the star, Maria Falconetti, an Italian, but the picture, from subject matter to aesthetics, is strictly French. Spoken of in the same hushed tones as Griffith, Eisenstein, and Renoir, but for most of us, even harder to get down with. Three possible ins: the supernatural angle (Dreyer's obsessed with witches and vampires, even if he does see them as all-too-human martyrs), the Bergman connection (having learned to tolerate one Scandinavian's bottomless guilt and pain, you shouldn't have too much trouble plugging into another's), and the old sympathy ploy (Dreyer, unappreciated in his own lifetime, could pursue his art only by dint of the money he made as manager of a Copenhagen movie theater, never got to make a movie about the life of Christ, never got to work in Hollywood like his mentor Griffith, etc., etc.). Other vintage Dreyer: *Vampyr* (1932), *Day of Wrath* (1943), and *Ordet* (1955).

Story

Based on actual trial records that, in 1928, had just come to light: A series of five grueling cross-examinations, culminating in the execution, at the stake, of Joan (Falconetti), but not before giant close-ups have told us everything we ever wanted to know about Joan and her accusers (among them Antonin

Artaud, pre-"Theater of Cruelty," as the only compassionate one). But plot isn't the point here. Go instead for the passion, in this case, almost equal parts eroticism and religious persecution.

What All the Fuss Was About at the Time

The camerawork, especially as it fixed on faces (not to mention Joan's dirty fingernails) rather than action and events, faces that fill the screen and come complete with sweat, tears, wrinkles, warts, and spittle, and are thrown into even higher relief by the starkness of the sets and the dead whiteness of the sky. And, equally, Falconetti's performance as Joan: the way she managed to emanate sainthood, sorrow, and suffering, all without benefit of makeup—or, for that matter, much in the way of hair. (As one of Dreyer's assistants said, "It was a film made on the knees.") An enormous success with the critics, who hailed it as the ultimate silent film, the distillation of a de-

cade of creative filmmaking in Europe; the man from the *New York Times*, for instance, announced that it made "worthy pictures of the past look like tinsel shams." Banned in Britain, by the way, for its depiction of English soldiers stealing Joan's ring and sticking their arrows into her arm.

What All the Fuss Is About Today

Ignore the comparisons of *Passion* to various musical forms (most often an organ fugue); what you really have to grasp is the fact that this, of all the standard masterpieces of world film, is the one that separates the sheep from the goats, the aesthetes from the philistines, the devotees from the hangers-on. The former have largely shut up about Falconetti, who was so drained by this film she never made another. But they still can't get over those faces. Ditto the wild blend of fleshiness and spirituality. If you must find fault, cite the title cards—so disruptive, so unnecessary, and so emblematic of the silent film's increasing frustration at not being able to speak. By all means, point out that sound had already arrived in France as Dreyer began *Passion*, and that, had he succeeded in obtaining financing, the last great work of silent film might have been the first great masterpiece of the sound era. Then finish your espresso and go home.

L'AGE D'OR (FRENCH, 1930; ENG. TITLE, *THE GOLDEN AGE*)

Director

Luis Buñuel. The Spanish maverick who, yoking the outrageous with the matter-of-fact, the blasphemous with the banal, managed to parlay one of the least flashy—and, frankly, least cinematic—of directing styles into a career that, a half-century later, was still going strong. In 1930, though, Buñuel was just getting started, having arrived in Paris five years earlier with his friend and fellow surrealist Salvador Dali. The year before, the two had collaborated on *Chien Andalou*, the seventeen-minute manifesto-on-film, having nothing to do with either dogs or Andalusians, in which a girl's eye gets slashed with a razor, a man's hand is shown crawling with ants, and dead burros lie sprawled across two grand pianos. Now they undertook something more ambitious: an hour's worth of denunciation, obsession, and mania, financed by the famous French "angel," the Vicomte de Noailles. Dali, who wasn't the easiest man in the world to work with (he'd try to convince you, for instance, that his waxed moustache served as an antenna for his muse, then turn around and expect you to buy a painting from him), had gotten that much worse since all the *Chien* notoriety, and lasted only a day on the *L'Age* set. Despite the credits (and with the exception of one gag, in which a man walks with a large stone on his head), the film is pure Buñuel.

Story

May as well begin with the documentary footage of the scorpions. Not that it prepares you for the bandits, or the Majorcans, or the fellow kicking a violin down the street. In a way, it *does* prepare you for the man and his mistress, though not necessarily for the mud they're rolling in. Things are a little more upbeat at the marquis's party (ignore the kitchen fire and the gamekeeper who shoots his little boy) especially once the man and mistress get out to the garden, where they try to have sex while seated in two wicker garden chairs. Try, that is, until he is summoned inside to take the minister's phone call and she busies herself with the toe of the statue. At some point somebody throws a Christmas tree, an archbishop, a plough, a bishop's crook, a stuffed giraffe, and several pillowfuls of feathers out a window. Then, before you know it, we're leaving a chateau in the company of four worn-out orgiasts; look for a cross, covered with snow and festooned with a woman's hair. The End—accompanied by a happy little Spanish march, the kind you might hear at a bullfight.

What All the Fuss Was About at the Time

Le bourgeois wasn't just épaté—he was livid. A fun-house mirror full of the pressures and postures of the day, *L'Age* pilloried Church, State, and Establishment, and monkeyed with morals, manners, and bodily functions. To get it past the censors, Buñuel had had to position the film as "the dream of a madman"; now he billed it as "a desperate, passionate appeal to murder." Although it took a few weeks for the news to get around, eventually gangs of Fascists, Catholics, and anti-Semites broke into the theater, threw stink bombs and purple ink at the screen, and slashed the paintings by Dali, Max Ernst, and Man Ray hanging in the lobby. Then the right-wing press got in on the action, along with the police chief. The film was banned, and Buñuel was branded a subversive. He went back to Spain and made a scathing documentary called *Land Without Bread*, likewise banned; he wouldn't direct another movie for fifteen years.

What All the Fuss Is About Today

Unlike *Chien*, which seems a little on the adolescent, "look-ma-no-hands" side, *L'Age* comes across as fresh, stringent, biting, if anything enhanced by all that's gone on between then and now. It's your single best introduction to (a) avant-garde cinema (marked by its fondness for abstraction, its eschewal of narrative, and its overall flakiness), (b) surrealism (with all its jarring, illogical literalness, plus more Freudian bric-a-brac than you can shake a phallus at), and (c) Buñuel himself (whose later themes, targets, and preoccupations it sets in motion). The other avant-garde—and quasi-surrealist—film of the period: Jean Cocteau's *Blood of a Poet* (also 1930, also financed by the Vicomte de Noailles), a "poem on celluloid," according to Cocteau, featuring a mouth in a drawing that comes alive, a hermaphrodite with a "Danger de Mort" sign in its crotch, and a fatal snowball fight. After its rhapsodizing and self-congratulation, you'll appreciate Buñuel's outrage all the more.

STAGECOACH (AMERICAN, 1939)

Director

John Ford. The grand old man of American movies. Gruff, big-hearted, meditative Irishman with a taste for folklore and nostalgia. In many ways a throwback to Griffith (sentimental, moralistic, committed to the probing of character and motive), Ford remained, through the Forties and Fifties, the single most important director whom Hollywood didn't totally undo. Instead it gave him four Oscars (for *The Informer*, 1935; *The Grapes of Wrath*, 1940; *How Green Was My Valley*, 1941; and *The Quiet Man*, 1952), plus a couple more for his wartime documentaries. He also received, in 1973, the first of the American Film Institute's Life Achievement Awards, a fitting tribute to a man who, over the course of fifty years, made some 130 movies (including silents), the majority of which dealt with the American experience—the history, the dream, the legend—in one form or another, most notably the western. You can complain that Ford's maudlin and simplistic; you can regret that he ever took on such highfalutin, arty projects as *Informer* and *Grapes;* and you can explain how, unlike his confrère Howard Hawks (more on him in a minute), he needed a strong screenwriter at his side, but you can't not stand up when he enters the room.

Story

Grand Hotel with sagebrush and on wheels. Stagecoach in question is bound for Cheyenne; on board are a former Confederate officer turned cardsharp (John Carradine), an alcoholic doctor (Thomas Mitchell, who'd played Scarlet O'Hara's father that same year), a prostitute (Claire Trevor) who's just been run out of town, a timid whiskey salesman, an escaped convict, a bank embezzler, and, of course, the pregnant wife of a cavalry lieutenant, who refuses to speak to the prostitute. Andy "Jingles" Devine is the driver. Along the way they're joined by the Ringo Kid (John Wayne), who's lost his horse; both the prostitute and the doctor undergo radical transformations (he becomes Marcus Welby); the army wife gives birth; the Apaches attack; the cavalry comes to the rescue; and, finally, in Cheyenne, the Ringo Kid settles an old score with the Plummer boys, then rides off with the prostitute to start a new life.

What All the Fuss Was About at the Time

The western, already an established Hollywood genre, gained new respectability. It also gained a form, a flexibility, and an overall relevance: Now "prestige" directors could make westerns without being accused of slumming. John Wayne, previously no great shakes, became a star—as did Monument Valley, the tract on the Utah–Arizona border with all those buttes, mesas, and sandstone spires; both would figure in many John Ford westerns to come, notably the so-called "cavalry trilogy" (*Fort Apache, She Wore a Yellow Ribbon,* and *Rio Grande*). Literary types got to note the resemblance to Guy de Maupassant's short story *Boule de suif,* about a prostitute traveling in a carriage with a bunch of bourgeois during the Franco–Prussian War, while everybody else in the theater watched for the Indians to mass on the horizon.

What All the Fuss Is About Today

To be honest, there isn't much. *Stagecoach* was remade in the Sixties, with Ann-Margret in the Claire Trevor role, but the fact that we're even telling you that shows you how little news there is here. And even the western—a big deal as recently as the Fifties—has been replaced, both as entertainment and as myth, by high-tech and sci-fi. But *Stagecoach* is still the best choice for those who want in on the Ford mystique, an important first stop on anybody's road toward the bitter, dark (and cultish) *The Searchers*. Do be careful with the important Ford/Hawks polarity. Born in 1895 and 1896, respectively, they both made westerns (Hawks was even smart enough to hire Ford's boy, John Wayne) and they both hung around forever, with Peter Bogdanovich hounding them for interviews and dinner invitations every step of the way. But Hawks was never the Establishment favorite Ford was (no Academy Awards, for instance, unless you want to count a "special" one) perhaps because he eschewed art for action, sentimentality for cynicism, the safe idea of woman-as-Maureen-O'Hara for the sexy idea of woman-as-Lauren-Bacall. With no folklore and great humor (Ford had none), Hawks made at least one film in every important Hollywood genre: the gangster picture (*Scarface*), the screwball comedy (*Bringing Up Baby*), the *film noir* (*The Big Sleep*), the musical (*Gentlemen Prefer Blondes*), and, yes, the western (*Rio Bravo*). He wasn't an innovator, as Ford could be when he chose, but he was the most artless of the great Hollywood directors—so craftsmanlike, so in control as to be "invisible." And it was Hawks, not Ford, who stopped those *Cahiers du Cinéma* French boys dead when they first discovered Hollywood.

LA RÈGLE DU JEU (FRENCH, 1939; ENG. TITLE, *THE RULES OF THE GAME*)

Director

Jean Renoir. The grand old man of world cinema, impossible to dislike and even harder to disparage. Had his ups (sunny, unfettered childhood overseen by his father, Pierre Auguste, the Impressionist painter; unbroken lifetime string of supportive women and creative collaborators, what he called his *équipe;* at least one film that was both a popular and critical smash, namely the 1937 *La Grande Illusion,* about national loyalties and class affinities in a World War I German prisoner-of-war camp). And his downs (majority of his films misunderstood and cold-shouldered at the time they were released; *Règle,* his masterpiece, first butchered, then withdrawn, finally bombed to smithereens; personal inability to cope with Hollywood during his exile there in the Forties). Words to brace yourself for in any discussion of Renoir: humanism, realism (and/or naturalism), lyricism; luminosity, spontaneity, generosity; nature, artifice, civilization. What they're really trying to say: that Renoir's heart was in the right place, that he took the long view, that he cared about people (especially his actors, for the sake of whom he was willing to sacrifice plot, dialogue, or technique), that he had an artist's soul as well as eye and winked at his audience with both, that he understood how—as one of the characters in *Règle* puts it— "The terrible thing is that everyone has his own reasons." Basic Renoir, in addition to *Règle* and *Illusion*, the two big guns: *Boudu Saved from Drowning* (1932; the inspiration for *Down and Out in Beverly Hills*), *A Day in the Country* (1936), *The Southerner* (1945; about a family of sharecroppers, the best from his Hollywood period), *The River* (1951; shot in India), *The Golden Coach* (1952; in which Anna Magnani plays an actress on tour in eighteenth-century Peru).

Story

Rich marquis throws elaborate country house party for high-toned friends; sex, games, and the chase on everybody's mind, notably those of marquis, marquis's wife, her aviator lover, marquis's mistress, estate gamekeeper, his wife the lady's maid, and poacher new to the neighborhood. (Also of the party: Octave, the friend of the family, played by Renoir himself.) In the course of the week or two that everyone's together, there's a hunt (watch for the beaters flushing the rabbits and pheasants), elaborate theatrics and a fancy-dress ball, the shooting of the aviator by the gamekeeper, and a tour of the marquis's collection of wind-up toys.

What All the Fuss Was About at the Time

To begin with, that Renoir had gotten carried away. Because of bad weather and casting problems, *Règle* wound up costing twice what it was supposed to; plus it ran 113 minutes and the front office insisted it be shaved down. Also, what with Europe in a tizzy and war about to break out, a lot of people weren't much in the mood for what Renoir called "an exact depiction of the bourgeois of our time"; for the ultranationalists and anti-Semites among them, the presence of a Jew (the marquis) and an Austrian (the marquis's wife) in the cast was the last straw. Then there were those who merely found the movie immoral, decadent, or incomprehensible. More footage was cut. Even so, *Règle* was banned as demoralizing; when the Nazis arrived on the scene, it was banned all over again. To add insult to injury, in 1942 the Allies inadvertently destroyed the film's original negative. (English-speaking audiences wouldn't get to see the painstakingly reconstructed complete version until the late Fifties.) In the meantime Renoir had fled to America; by the time he returned to France in the early Fifties his spirit was broken.

What All the Fuss Is About Today

Half the crowd raves about how dazzling, complex, brilliantly structured and ironic it is; the other half about its richness, sensuality, egalitarianism, and drollness. Then they get down to specifics: the multiple viewpoint, how *Règle* doesn't root for one side or the other in the class war, how it was the first psychologically sophisticated film in which the notion of good people and bad people was completely eliminated. Alternatively, Renoir's use of the deep focus, in which the camera pulls back to show us a landscape as clear and sharp as the characters busily ensnaring each other in the foreground—a perfect way to probe human relationships, establish man's interaction with the world, and engage the viewer by bringing him into the field of action. Or maybe you prefer to think of Renoir as the spiritual leader of the French cinema, whose artistry and humanity served, in the Thirties, as the only alternative to Hollywood brashness and glamour. If you aren't swept away by any of the above, at least be mindful of Renoir's enormous influence on the next generation of filmmakers, from Truffaut and the New Wave in France, to the neo-realists (De Sica, Rossellini, et al.) in Italy, to Satyajit Ray, who's never stopped talking about how he met Renoir when the latter was filming *The River* on the banks of the Ganges. Finally, there's critic Pauline Kael, who points out how *Règle* foreshadows all those jaundiced house-party movies of the Sixties—*L'Avventura, La Dolce Vita, Last Year at Marienbad*—in which the big house symbolizes the remains of European civilization.

CITIZEN KANE (AMERICAN, 1940)
Director

Orson Welles. The wunderkind: *Kane*, which he produced, directed, wrote (sort of), and starred in, all at the age of twenty-five, remains the most impressive directorial—and entrepreneurial—debut in movie history. Keep in mind that Welles already had an outsize reputation when he got to Hollywood, as an actor and director for the stage (he had founded the Mercury Theater in 1937) and radio (he was the force behind the weekly Mercury Theater of the Air); it was this reputation that accounted for (a) the degree of artistic and financial control he was given on *Kane*, and (b) the degree of suspicion and dislike Hollywood instinctively felt for him. After *Kane*, which turned out to be a commercial failure and a public-relations fiasco, it was all downhill. His next (and next best) film, *The Magnificent Ambersons* (1942) was re-edited in his absence, and everything from then on suffered from either funding or quality-control problems. Still, nobody's had more influence on young filmmakers over the last forty years. Many of them see Welles as a titan, committed to art and personal vision, eager to experiment with storytelling and cinematography, a man brought down by nothing less than hubris.

Others see him as a big chubby boy, given to overstatement, unnecessary camera movement, and half-baked profundity; a man done in by simple egomania. Our favorite summation of Welles: that of Herman J. Mankiewicz, co-author of the *Kane* screenplay, who, observing the big man on the set one day, was heard to mutter, "There, but for the grace of God, goes God." Other Welles you might consider turning out for: *The Lady from Shanghai* (1948), *Macbeth* (1948), *Touch of Evil* (1958), *Mr. Arkadin* (1962), *The Trial* (1963), *Chimes at Midnight* (1966, with Welles as Falstaff).

Story

Never a dull moment. Media baron and thwarted politician Charles Foster Kane (played by Welles and based largely on William Randolph Hearst) dies, in bedroom of fabulous castle home, Xanadu (cf. San Simeon), with "Rosebud" his last spoken word. Cut to "March of Time"-style newsreel acquainting us with the outline of his overscale, somewhat unsavory, and absolutely enigmatic life. Cut to newspaper office, whence young reporter is dispatched to discover essence of same, especially as it might be summed up by word "Rosebud." He visits library established by Thatcher, Kane's childhood guardian (George Couloris), where he reads of Kane's youth and, of course, this being the twentieth century, of Kane's mother (Agnes Moorehead); then interviews, in succession, Kane's business manager (Everett Sloane), Kane's best friend (Joseph Cotten), Kane's mistress (Dorothy Comingore), and Kane's majordomo at Xanadu. Loads of flashbacks, in which we observe Kane run newspaper, stir up war with Cuba, marry niece of President (Ruth Warrick), meet toothachy mistress and attempt to turn her into diva, run for office. But reporter never finds out what "Rosebud" means. We do, though: After everybody's gone home, camera registers it as name of sled, now being consigned by workmen to Xanadu's furnace, that Kane hit Thatcher in stomach with when, so many years ago, latter tried to separate him from mother.

What All the Fuss Was About at the Time

Prime example of a film undone by advance publicity, most notably attempts by Hearst to suppress, buy up, calumniate, etc., *Kane*. He succeeded in making distribution a nightmare for parent studio RKO and in infuriating, boring, and perplexing enough people so that, when the film finally came out, it died on the vine. (Hollywood, ever vulnerable in the manners-and-morals department, and fearing another Fatty Arbuckle-type scandal, got so roiled it booed *Kane* at the Academy Awards every time one of its nine nominations came up; that year John Ford's *How Green Was My Valley* was the big winner.) Then there was Welles the man, the sacred monster, the virtuoso, who in *Kane* did with the moving picture almost everything that could be done with it, yanking his audiences forward and backward in time, montaging sound as well as image, plunging his camera through, say, the skylight of a New Jersey cabaret rather than using the front door—and then, on top of the pyrotechnics, starred in the thing himself. Scandal and bravura—but *Kane* remained out of circulation from its initial release till its late Fifties art-house revival.

What All the Fuss Is About Today

Welles and *Kane* zoom to very top of 1972 *Sight & Sound* international critics poll! The most written about, most controversial movie ever! America on map as producer of sound films to rival Europe's! The one American talking picture that "seems as fresh today as the day it opened"! (That last is Pauline Kael, whose *The Citizen Kane Book* is required reading for zealots.) On the other hand, you can, as far as fashioning a personal reaction to *Kane,* do better. Revel in the film's unabashed theatricality, its sleight of hand, its highly visible "insides." Note the polished camera work of Gregg Toland, the Bernard Herrmann score. Suggest that *Kane* hints at the insanity implicit in American pop culture—and American life—as broadly as a Busby Berkeley musical number. Or Richard Speck. Get behind Kael's assertion that screen-

writer Mankiewicz is the real genius behind *Kane;* then cite Peter Bogdanovich's refutation of same. And rather than alluding to Rosebud (a gimmick in
the film, a cliché in film talk), take as your favorite scene the one in which old
Bernstein, Kane's business manager, reminisces about seeing the girl in the
white dress on the Jersey ferry: "She didn't see me at all," he says, "but I'll
bet a month hasn't gone by since, that I haven't thought of that girl."

For Extra Credit

THE THIRTEEN NEXT-BIGGEST-DEAL MOVIES THEY MADE BEFORE YOU—OR STEVEN SPIELBERG—WERE BORN

1. *The General* (Buster Keaton, 1926). Now widely held to be the best of all
    Twenties comedies, bar none. (In case you hadn't noticed, Keaton's no
    longer playing Jonson to Chaplin's Shakespeare.) The reasons: action
    that's all of a piece, rather than episodic and "taped together" (Southern
    engineer gets back the supply train Yankee soldiers have hijacked, as
    well as his girlfriend, who was accidentally aboard), plus technique that
    integrates character and environment, incident and existence, instead of
    just capturing a few brilliant pantomimes on celluloid. Unlike Chaplin,
    Keaton doesn't mime, emote, or ingratiate—he merely stares, a man up
    against a whole army (not just the town bully), with a face as quintessen-
    tially American as Abe Lincoln's (cf. Chaplin's Old World one) and a girl
    who's more pain in the ass than Holy Grail.

2. *Mother* (Vsevolod Pudovkin, 1926). Soviet movies aren't just Eisenstein.
    In fact at the time, many critics preferred the work of his contemporary
    Pudovkin, who was lyric and emotional where Eisenstein was epic and
    intellectual, and who, as Dwight Macdonald remarked, used his shots as
    a novelist uses words rather than, à la Eisenstein, as a musician uses
    notes. Case in point: *Mother,* Pudovkin's masterpiece, the tale of a
    woman who, tricked by the police into betraying her own son (who's in
    league with a bunch of striking workers), learns that radicalism is the only
    way to fly; it's all from a Maxim Gorky story you may know in its

subsequent *Mother Courage* incarnation. To be noted: The professional actors (cf. Eisenstein's insistence upon using nonprofessionals); the fact that the movie's hero, while symbolic, is nevertheless an individual (cf. Eisenstein's masses); the way in which montage here is a function of "linkage," of shots being used like so many building blocks (as opposed to Eisenstein's dialectical "collision" of images).

3. *Metropolis* (Fritz Lang, 1926). As *Caligari* begot the horror film, *Metropolis*—futuristic and allegorical—generated the sci-fi one. Here we're in a city (said to have been inspired by Lang's first shipboard view of New York), built on two levels, one for the rich, with skyscrapers and hanging gardens and air taxis, the other—subterranean and prisonlike—for the workers who keep the aboveground society going. The story, which is perfectly preposterous, concerns a banker's son who decides to go live with the workers, whereupon he falls in love with a girl named Maria. Do note, however, the sets (not that it's easy to miss them) and the way in which the cast of hundreds is made to function more as scenery than as crowd. As for Lang: he's a tough nut, and a bitter one (half-Jewish, he'd fled Germany even though Hitler wanted him to stay and make pro-Nazi movies), with a penchant for criminality and angst, the guilty innocent and the femme fatale.

Life underground in "Metropolis."

4. *Napoléon* (Abel Gance, 1927; full title, *Napoléon vu par Abel Gance*). The highlight of the 1927 Paris movie season, when the original seven-hour version premiered at the Paris Opéra. Also, the highlight of the 1981 New York movie season, when a painstakingly reconstituted four-hour version (by movie scholar Kevin Brownlow, egged on by Francis Ford Coppola), was shown at Radio City Music Hall. You're up against two things here. The first is scale: from the 6,000 extras and 150 sets, to the nicely matched ambitions of subject Napoleon and director Gance, to the sheer enveloping scope of the tripartite, fifty-feet-by-twelve-and-a-half feet screen. The second is technology. Gance's Polyvision, as wraparound as Cinerama, in fact predates it by thirty years. What's more, scholars see *Napoléon* as a clearinghouse for silent screen techniques (Gance wasn't known as the French Griffith for nothing) and tend to be especially overwhelmed by his moving cameras, sometimes handheld, sometimes suspended by wires, sometimes strapped to horses, pendulums, or, we're told, dancers' bellies.

5. *Pandora's Box* (G. W. Pabst, 1929). By the other "Golden Age" German director who, along with Murnau and Lang, you maybe should have heard of. Not Pabst's most famous movie (that would be *Joyless Street* or his bastardization of Brecht's *The Threepenny Opera* or maybe *Kameradschaft*, about German miners who rescue French ones), but probably your best investment. For one thing, it'll prepare you for the big-deal Alban Berg opera *Lulu*, all about sex and parasitism. For another, it'll afford you the chance to watch American actress Louise Brooks, recently rediscovered, do her thing as Lulu. The movie goes on forever before Lulu, having devoured her fifth or sixth mate, praying-mantis style, and now down and out in London, meets her match in Jack the Ripper; but there are enough high-perversity moments along the way to keep most of us latter-day sexual sophisticates satisfied.

6. *The Blue Angel* (Josef von Sternberg, 1930). Perverse, psychoerotic saga of how cabaret queen Lola Lola (Marlene Dietrich), who sings "Falling in Love Again" several times a night and spits into her mascara, transforms poor, respectable Professor Rath (Emil Jannings) into a whimpering clown given to doing his chicken imitation in front of an audience of vindictive former pupils. May give you another interesting insight or two into the frenzy and murkiness of Twenties Germany; will certainly acquaint you with the von Sternberg mystique—the visual bravura; the aspirations toward high art and European culture; the all-in-the-same-breath preoccupation with glitter and gutter; and, of course, with Dietrich, whom von Sternberg subsequently brought to Hollywood and di-

Showgirl (Marlene Dietrich) ensnares educator (Emil Jannings) in "The Blue Angel."

rected in a string of cult classics full of veils, nets, fog, and smoke. After their collaboration petered out in the mid-Thirties, von Sternberg ceased to count for much, but the personal legend, the mastery of cinematic illusion and sexual delusion, the commitment to languor and decadence at a time when other directors were trying to say something meaningful about society, vouchsafe him classic status.

7. *Earth* (Aleksandr Dovzhenko, 1930). For those desiring a glimpse of the Russian countryside beyond what they got in *Dr. Zhivago.* Dovzhenko, the third genius of Soviet silent film, stands apart from his illustrious colleagues: The son of an illiterate Ukrainian peasant, he taught himself filmmaking, didn't choose to theorize, and had a predilection for the folkways, nicely blended with poetry and satire. His movie world has less to do with montage than with horses that talk (in title cards, of course), paintings of military heros that roll their eyes, and animals who, as one critic notes, sniff the air and smell the revolutionary spirit. In *Earth,* his masterpiece, one's confronted by nature, life, death, childbirth, and a farm in the process of being collectivized. Unfortunately, the shot in which a group of peasants urinate into a tractor's radiator to keep it from boiling over has been removed from the foreign-release prints.

8. *Le Million* (René Clair, 1931). Breezy, flirtatious tale of Parisian artist Lothario who leaves winning lottery ticket in pocket of sports jacket, subsequently lent by soft-hearted girlfriend to passing thief, who happens to run second-hand clothing store on the side, where jacket is purchased by touring Metropolitan Opera tenor. Somehow, everybody (and all his friends) winds up onstage at the opera that night, then goes back to the hero's garret for an *8½*-style snake dance. Stylized (somewhere between ballet and puppet theater), and a musical (perhaps the first in which the music really carries the story forward), *Million* is immensely likable; it's also the prototype for the Marx Brothers' *A Night at the Opera*. Watch what you say about Clair, though. A founding father of the talking picture and considered a paragon of levity and wit as recently as twenty years ago, he's now written off by many as a fluffhead who relied too much on special effects.

9. *Trouble in Paradise* (Ernst Lubitsch, 1932). The plot doesn't recount well (in a sentence, male-female pair of jewel thieves, impersonating aristocrats, set up French perfume heiress) and the stars are disappointingly second-order (Herbert Marshall, Miriam Hopkins, Kay Francis). But you'll find out, in no time flat, what those "Lubitsch touches" are: the "dry sparkle" of language and sexuality; the "artless" wit, visual and

Jewel thieves (Herbert Marshall and Miriam Hopkins, right) ensnare perfume heiress (Kay Francis) in "Trouble in Paradise."

otherwise; the "moderne" period sense; the ellipsis, the polish, the perfectionism; the total grasp of Americans' preoccupation with sex and money; the caress. Lubitsch (according to Andrew Sarris, "the least Germanic of German directors as Lang was the most Germanic") was also the only silent-era director Hollywood imported from Europe whom it didn't wind up disappointing, defeating, or, as in the case of Murnau, sending home for burial. Gliding easily from silents to talkies, he pioneered the cinematic, as opposed to the theatrical, musical, adapted himself to Hollywood business ways, coaxed intelligent performances out of empty Hollywood heads, and kept the champagne flowing.

10. *Zéro de Conduite* and *L'Atalante* (Jean Vigo, 1933 and 1934). Counts as one selection: The revival houses always show them together (*Zéro* is only forty-five minutes long); besides, having seen the two of them, you'll have seen Vigo, who died when he was only twenty-nine. One of those poetic rebel types, constantly being compared with Rimbaud and James Dean, he defies categorization and gives the avant-gardiste goose pimples; after Renoir, he's the single biggest deal in the first golden age of French filmmaking. *Zéro*, a study of revolt and freedom in a boys' boarding school, is alternately real and surreal, and so virulently antiestablishment that it was banned, from the critics' screenings in 1933 (during which fistfights broke out) until after the Liberation. Today's critics like to note the debts owed to it by such subsequent boys' school pictures as Truffaut's *The Four Hundred Blows* and Lindsay Anderson's *If . . . .* *L'Atalante*, about a couple of newlyweds attempting to adjust to life together on his river barge, is a less experimental, more commercial affair, adapted from somebody else's screenplay and tarted up with a *Man and a Woman*–type theme song; but it's still pure Vigo: imaginative, iconoclastic, clear-headed.

11. *Triumph of the Will* (Leni Riefenstahl, 1936). The official film record, ordered by Hitler himself, of the sixth Nazi Party Congress, held in Nuremberg in 1934. The prologue has der Führer en route, flying in his airplane over the waiting city, then descending Messiah-like, out of the clouds, and subsequently marching blithely by tens of thousands of Nazi soldiers, who might as well be soldier ants. Torchlight parades; Brown Shirts and Black Shirts, listening transfixed one minute, *Sieg Heil!*-ing the next; naked-from-the-waist-up Hitler Jugend; speeches; some drilling of the troops; even dinner time. Of course we'll never know for sure whether Hitler really had a crush on the red-haired dancer-skier-actress to whom he encharged the making of movies on his political conventions

and on the 1936 Olympics, but she stands enshrined as one of the few truly creative types (and the *only* truly creative woman type, everyone but Susan Sontag seems agreed) to work in the medium.

12. *Henry V* (Laurence Olivier, 1944). The first of the trio of Shakespeare films he directed and starred in (the others are *Hamlet*, 1948, and *Richard III*, 1956); the first time Shakespeare was ever made into a good movie; and the first sign from England—apart from Hitchcock and the documentarists—that that country could bring anything at all to the art of the sound film. What's in it for you? Well, there's the sheer gloss on the enterprise, from its unprecedented $2 million budget through the Olivier screen presence (in this case, under a haircut that Grace Jones would be proud to have come up with). There's the enchantment of the movie's structure, which features a camera traveling over a model of early seventeenth-century London, on into the hexagonal Globe Theatre, where, get this, the premiere performance of *The Chronicle Historie of Henry the Fifth* is just getting underway. Finally, there's the play itself: You get a free crack at *Henry V* (see page 200) and its "Once more unto the breach, dear friends" and "We few, we happy few, we band of brothers" speeches. On the other hand, you're not going to recognize anybody in the cast besides Olivier (no Gielgud, no Richardson, etc.). And you aren't fighting the Battle of Britain as audiences felt *they* were when the movie first came out; if a lump in the throat or a surge of feeling is what you're after, you stand a better chance of acquiring it at *Close Encounters*.

13. *Les Enfants du Paradis* (Marcel Carné, 1945; English title, *Children of Paradise*). A lot of movie: sumptuous sets recreating the Paris of Balzac; six central characters (most notably the mime Baptiste, played by Jean-Louis Barrault; the ham actor Lemaître, played by Pierre Brasseur; and the courtesan Garance whom they both love, played by the legendary Arletty); two distinct acts; a whole set of art-is-life, life-is-art, play-within-a-play-within-a-movie undercurrents; and a running time of three hours and fifteen minutes. Either you love the "literary," deliberately old-fashioned style of this superromantic, superfatalistic spectacle or you side with Truffaut and the New Wave (see below) and wonder how a director, still in his early thirties, for crying out loud, could make such a reactionary, pretentious piece of crap. Whichever, *Enfants* is an eyeful, concocted by Carné and the poet/screenwriter Jacques Prévert, one of the most celebrated pairs of screen collaborators ever.

French, Likewise Hollywoodese, for the Movie-Goer

Don't know the grip from the gaffer—or from the dolly? How about the gaffer from the auteur? And what's a McGuffin for, anyway? Read on.

First, the French. The two most important terms are *montage* and *mise en scène*, and, for cinema buffs, they're opposed. *Mise en scène* (literally, "put into the scene") refers to everything that takes place on the set: direction of actors, placement of cameras, deployment of props, choice of lenses, and so on. *Montage* can mean, simply, "editing," or it can mean the kind of creative editing that, à la Eisenstein, juxtaposes specific shots so as to create whole new meanings. For what it's worth, film-theory fans point out that realists prefer *mise en scène*, expressionists *montage*.

Next, three terms rooted in the Fifties and Sixties. The (1) *Cahiers du Cinéma* reference you occasionally trip over is to a film magazine (literally, "Notebooks of the Cinema") founded by, among others, the French theorist André Bazin, and contributed to by, among others, such (2) *Nouvelle Vague* (or "New Wave") directors as François Truffaut, Jean-Luc Godard, Eric Rohmer, and Claude Chabrol, all of whom were determined to do in, once and for all, the talky, theatrical, studio-crafted movies of France's postwar years. For inspiration, they went back a generation to the more spontaneous, more heart-felt Thirties of Renoir, Clair, and Vigo, who, in their opinion, constituted the "authentic" French tradition. They also cast their gaze on Hollywood, on Hitchcock and Hawks and a clutch of other, less prominent directors. Soon they, like their mentors, would be seen as the prime forces, the (3) *auteurs* (literally, "authors") behind their movies, mediating style, theme, and technique through a single consistent vision. Truffaut first used the term in 1958; Andrew Sarris, film critic for *The Village Voice*, is most responsible for promoting the *auteur* theory in this country.

Two more French terms, by the end of which we'll find ourselves at the corner of Hollywood and Vine. The first is *cinéma vérité* (the second word means "truth"), which can be used loosely to describe almost any kind of documentary technique (including the application of such techniques to fictional subjects), or strictly to describe movies that—starting in the Sixties—were made with lightweight (and hence very mobile) equipment, two-person camera-and-sound crews, and extensive on-camera interviewing.

The other French term: *film noir* (the second word means "black"), a term

François Truffaut, hanging ten on the nouvelle vague.

coined by French critics to describe the kind of Hollywood gangster picture in which the crooks aren't so much bad as sick, and the passions run dark and brooding. John Garfield was the *film noir* protagonist par excellence, Gloria Grahame or Shelley Winters its abused, and no-better-than-she-should-be, female lead.

John Garfield, film noir protagonist par excellence.

Shelley Winters, as the women men loved to abuse.

Another genre term—strictly American—worth noting: *screwball comedy,* which reached its height in the Thirties, in such films as *Bringing Up Baby* (1938, directed by Howard Hawks, with Katharine Hepburn and Cary Grant), and which focused on sexual relationships, madcap action, and verbal oneup-manship, usually among the upper class, and which is to be opposed to the *slapstick comedy* of the silent era. The one other genre-related term not imme-diately obvious: Alfred Hitchcock's *McGuffin,* the plot element or device that, according to him, drives the plot and fuels the audience's interest, but that can be ignored once it's served its purpose (for instance, the whole Janet Leigh, love-and-money business at the beginning of *Psycho*).

Then there's the technical, get-to-know-your-cameraman vocabulary. Here, it's a seminal—and tricky—distinction between the *zoom* and the *track* that's most worth paying attention to. Both describe ways of following a moving subject with a camera, the zoom with a lens that automatically refocuses to allow for a variable distance between camera and subject (and subject and background), the track with a moving camera, usually mounted on rails, that maintains a single focus on—and consequently a constant distance from—its subject. Tracking is as a result a steady process; zooming a fast, somewhat arhythmic one in which distant objects can be magnified, or close ones moved rapidly away from.

A *pan* is what a stationary camera does when it wants to survey its vicinity, simply moving on its axis from left to right, or right to left. Other stationary shots include the *tilt* (the camera moves up or down) and the *roll* (the camera lies on its side and maybe turns over). Pans are common, tilts less so (just as one looks up less often than one looks to the side), rolls least common of all, in general relegated to "trick" shots, up to and including the one in which Fred Astaire, in *Royal Wedding,* seems to be dancing on the ceiling.

Also an issue: Getting from one scene to another. Here the choices include the *fade out* (the image gradually goes to black) followed by the *fade in; a dissolve* superimposes one image on another, so that the screen is never en-tirely image-free. With a *wipe,* more common in Thirties movies than in contemporary ones, an image appears to wipe off a preceding one. Of course, transition can also be effected by out-and-out cutting. A *jump cut* within a scene gets us from point A (hero enters room) to point B (hero flops down on bed at far side of room) without forcing us to watch him walk by his desk, his bureau, and his bulletin board with the pennants pinned to it. *Cross-cutting* establishes a feeling of parallel action by cutting repeatedly from one scene (and mood, and set of characters) to another.

About the equipment: The *boom* is a traveling arm used to hold the micro-phone above the actors (and, with any luck, out of the frame), the *dolly* a set of wheels on which the camera is mounted so as to be able to "track."

And the personnel. The *gaffer* is the chief electrician. The *grip* builds the sets and rigs the lights. (The gofer makes Danish and Xerox runs.) As for that most mysterious of all cinema terms, *best boy,* we're sorry to report that he plays neither page to the director's knight nor paramour to the leading lady. All he does is assist the gaffer, a reminder of just how workaday studio, as opposed to *Cahiers,* life can be.

LITERATURE

Contents

"Enemies of the Book," drawing by Gustave Doré.

A Whirlwind Tour of British Poetry

IF IT'S TUESDAY, THIS MUST BE BROWNING

Don't even think of unpacking. Just wash out yesterday's socks, then prepare to get a grip on six hundred years of poetry in motion.

GEOFFREY CHAUCER

Bifel that in that seson on a day,
In Southwerk at the Tabard as I lay,
Redy to wenden on my pilgrimage
To Canterbury with ful devout corage,
At night was come into that hostelrye
Wel nine and twenty in a compaignye
Of sondry folk, by aventure yfalle
In felaweshipe, and pilgrimes were they alle
That toward Canterbury wolden ride.
The chambres and the stables weren wide,
And wel we weren esed at the beste.
And shortly, whan the sonne was to reste,
So hadde I spoken with hem everichoon
That I was of hir felaweship anoon,
And made forward erly for to rise,
To take oure way ther as I you devise.

from "The General Prologue,"
The Canterbury Tales (1386–1400)

The first wave of English poetry (give or take *Beowulf*), the tales-within-a-tale being shared by twenty-nine pilgrims en route to the shrine of Saint Thomas à Becket in Canterbury provide a bard's-eye view of social classes, economic levels, and personality disorders in medieval England. Note that the Tabard, where the pilgrims spend their first night out, is one of the famous inns of literature. And that the pilgrims, from the Knight to the Wife of Bath to the Miller, will manage to seem as recognizable a bunch of human types as the ensemble in a movie like *Nashville*. Note, too, that three hundred years after the Norman Conquest, French words are almost as integral to Middle English (that's what Chaucer's writing in) as Anglo-Saxon ones. Speaking of which, if you're going to tackle the *Tales* at all, you might as well go for the authentic Middle English version rather than a lame modernization (although you'll certainly need all the footnotes you can find). And try reading the "Prologue" aloud; once you get the hang of it, Chaucer's English is surprisingly melodious, even if it does sound a little like Norwegian.

EDMUND SPENSER

He there does now enjoy eternall rest
And happie ease, which thou doest want and crave,
And further from it daily wanderest.
What if some little paine the passage have
That makes fraile flesh to feare the bitter wave?
Is not short paine well borne, that brings long ease,
And layes the soule to sleepe in quiet grave?
Sleepe after toyle, port after stormie seas,
Ease after warre, death after life does greatly please.

from *The Faerie Queene* (1590–1596)
Book I, Canto 9

With characters like King Arthur, Queen Elizabeth, Venus, the Angel Gabriel, Adam and Eve, and Despair (that's him above, trying to convince somebody to commit suicide), *The Faerie Queene* isn't just England's first epic, it's also its first theme park. Though Spenser meant to write twelve books, each celebrating a different knightly virtue, he managed to finish only the first six—to almost nobody's chagrin. Wildly uneven, *The Faerie Queene* can go on for pages without producing a single line, image, or insight you care about, then dazzle you by summing up (and sometimes even solving) the sort of personal problem you've spent the last five sessions trying to thrash out with your shrink. The two main themes (both fleshed out allegorically, with characters and scenery embodying historical events and ideas): medieval chivalry (already, in Spenser's day, pretty much a memory) and Protestant Christianity (still, in Spenser's day, requiring some getting used to). But don't worry too much about who's supposed to be Mary Tudor and who's supposed to be Francis Drake. Better to keep moving, just the way you would at Six Flags Over Texas.

JOHN DONNE

Our two souls therefore, which are one,
  Though I must go, endure not yet
A breach, but an expansion,
  Like gold to airy thinness beat.

If they be two, they are two so
  As stiff twin compasses are two;
Thy soul, the fixed foot, makes no show
  To move, but doth, if th' other do.

And though it in the center sit,
  Yet when the other far doth roam,
It leans and harkens after it,
  And grows erect, as that comes home.

from "A Valediction: Forbidding Mourning" (1633)

The first and best of the Metaphysical poets, Donne broke away from the conventions of the Elizabethan sonnet and the courtly love poem to invent a poetry characterized by a dense, almost incomprehensibly learned style, extremely complicated imagery, a zillion offbeat references to the arts, sciences, crafts, and daily life of the times, and a fractured meter and syntax that were meant at times to sound conversational, at other times simply to knock your socks off. His poetry tends to be ironic and erotic or heartfelt and impassioned, depending on which of his two favorite obsessions—love or death—he is focusing on at the time (love, naturally enough, in the early poems; death later on). In both he is wise and intellectually astute, and in the love poems—more precisely, the dissection-of-the-psychology-of-love poems—he's not only sharp and smart, he's also more modern than you are. Metaphysical poetry enjoyed a brief vogue in the early seventeenth century, but Donne didn't really come into his own until the twentieth.

JOHN MILTON

High on a throne of royal state, which far
Outshone the wealth of Ormus and of Ind,
Or where the gorgeous East with richest hand
Showers on her kings barbaric pearl and gold,
Satan exalted sat, by merit raised
To that bad eminence; and, from despair
Thus high uplifted beyond hope, aspires
Beyond thus high, insatiate to pursue
Vain war with Heaven; and, by success untaught,

His proud imaginations thus displayed:—
  "Powers and Dominions, Deities of Heaven!
For, since no deep within her gulf can hold
Immortal vigour, though oppressed and fallen,
I give not Heaven for lost: from this descent
Celestial Virtues rising will appear
More glorious and more dread than from no fall,
And trust themselves to fear no second fate!—"

from *Paradise Lost* (1658–1665) Book II

Milton claimed to have written it to "justify the ways of God to man," but you'd be smart to interpret it as his attempt to one-up Homer, Virgil, and Dante; an outcry by a no-nonsense Puritan against the high-flown Church of England; and an exercise in style-as-substance, with loftiness the upshot in both departments. The most celebrated English poet after Shakespeare, Milton erected a major edifice, gilded and soaring, where Spenser had gone for sheer acreage. Keep three things in mind as you read: (1) it's still the Renaissance, at least up north, that time during which man was trying to get a bead on who he (or she) was even as he (or she) sought to outperform the Greeks and Romans at their own games; (2) it's not the theology that matters most here, it's the scheme, sweep, effect; and (3) you aren't the only one who thinks Milton's Satan is infinitely more interesting than Milton's God. Time a problem lately? Forget *Paradise Lost* and read "Lycidas," Milton's bite-size elegy on the death of a sailor friend—sweet and intimate, yet abristle with the kind of poetic conviction you came to him for in the first place.

ALEXANDER POPE

  Know then thyself, presume not God to scan;
The proper study of mankind is man.
Placed on this isthmus of a middle state,
A being darkly wise, and rudely great;
With too much knowledge for the sceptic side,
With too much weakness for the stoic's pride,
He hangs between; in doubt to act, or rest;
In doubt to deem himself a god, or beast;
In doubt his mind or body to prefer;
Born but to die, and reasoning but to err;
Alike in ignorance, his reason such,
Whether he thinks too little, or too much;
Chaos of thought and passion, all confused;
Still by himself abused, or disabused;
Created half to rise, and half to fall;
Great lord of all things, yet a prey to all;

Sole judge of truth, in endless error hurled:
The glory, jest, and riddle of the world!

from *An Essay on Man* (1733–1734)
Epistle II

Poor Pope: He was a hunchback, he was barely five feet tall, and he was a Catholic, on account of the last of which he stands outside the Grand (read Protestant) Tradition of English poetry. His revenge: being more epigrammatic than anybody ever (with the possible exception of Oscar Wilde) and so quotable you don't even know you're quoting him—e.g., "A little knowledge is a dangerous thing," "Damn with faint praise," "Fools rush in where angels fear to tread," and so on through column after column of Bartlett's. Historical note: This is the Augustan Age (also starring Swift, Addison, and Steele; so-called because London now thought it was the equal of Augustus's Rome), a conservative, well-ordered era when rhyming couplets, fine manners, powdered wigs, and elaborate gardens were all you needed to get a reputation as a tastemaker. Not that Pope was himself one of the smugs. For sheer venom, spleen, and bile, his satires still haven't been beat.

WILLIAM WORDSWORTH

Our birth is but a sleep and a forgetting:
The Soul that rises with us, our life's Star,
    Hath had elsewhere its setting,
      And cometh from afar:
    Not in entire forgetfulness,
    And not in utter nakedness,
But trailing clouds of glory do we come
    From God, who is our home:
Heaven lies about us in our infancy!
Shades of the prison-house begin to close
    Upon the growing Boy
      But he
Beholds the light, and whence it flows,
    He sees it in his joy;
The Youth, who daily farther from the east
    Must travel, still is Nature's Priest,
    And by the vision splendid
    Is on his way attended;
At length the Man perceives it die away,
And fade into the light of common day.

from "Ode: Intimations of Immortality" (1807)

A revolutionary in a revolutionary age and the first of the Romantics (Coleridge, Byron, Keats, and Shelley were the others, Blake a precursor), Wordsworth hated Pope, arguing that memory counted for more than wit, imagination for more than reason, and nature for more than gazebos and topiary hedges. Visual, subjective, and basically all het up, he introduced a style he thought of as conversational (though you won't), favored an everyday, even a tabloid sort of subject matter (look for lyrics written to "The Idiot Boy," "The Mad Mother," and "The Female Vagrant"), and redefined poetry famously as "emotion recollected in tranquillity." Two big don'ts: Don't think you have to read *The Prelude,* his longest, most ambitious, and most lethal poem. And don't adopt him wholesale as your mentor: Wordsworth-the-revolutionary is notorious for having turned into Wordsworth-the-reactionary, a nasty old man given to campaigning against the abolition of slavery, the reform of Parliament, and the prevention of cruelty to animals.

ROBERT BROWNING

I, painting from myself and to myself,
Know what I do, am unmoved by men's blame
Or their praise, either. Somebody remarks
Morello's outline there is wrongly traced,
His hue mistaken; what of that? or else,
Rightly traced and well ordered; what of that?
Speak as they please, what does the mountain care?
Ah, but a man's reach should exceed his grasp,
Or what's a heaven for? All is silver-gray
Placid and perfect with my art: the worse!
I know both what I want and what might gain,
And yet how profitless to know, to sigh
"Had I been two, another and myself,
Our head would have o'erlooked the world!"
　　No doubt.

from "Andrea del Sarto" (1855)

His contemporary, Tennyson, got most of the attention at the time, but lately it's Browning who's become the hero, for blazing the trail of Modernism in poetry with his jagged-edged dramatic monologues (in which the speaker reveals things about himself he has no idea he's revealing) and his jazzy beat. Jettisoning the confessional style of the Romantics in favor of first-person narrative, Browning, though pre-Freud, manages to come across with a fair amount of sexual heat and even more psychoanalyzable content. On the negative side:

He tries too hard ever to seem cool or commanding; he can drift off into stupid, just-what-you'd-expect-from-a-Victorian moralizing; and sometimes he sounds as if he thinks he's writing for children. Personal note: Before he got famous, he was Mr. Elizabeth Barrett.

WILLIAM BUTLER YEATS

That is no country for old men. The young
In one another's arms, birds in the trees
—Those dying generations—at their song,
The salmon-falls, the mackerel-crowded seas,
Fish, flesh, or fowl, commend all summer long
Whatever is begotten, born, and dies.
Caught in that sensual music all neglect
Monuments of unageing intellect.

An aged man is but a paltry thing,
A tattered coat upon a stick, unless
Soul clap its hands and sing, and louder sing
For every tatter in its moral dress,
Nor is there singing school but studying
Monuments of its own magnificence;
And therefore I have sailed the seas and come
To the holy city of Byzantium.

from "Sailing to Byzantium" (1927)

Yeats is generally ranked as one of the greatest—oh, let's just go ahead and say *the* greatest—of twentieth-century poets. Partly mystical, partly earthy, and partly just plain Irish, he saw himself and his generation as the Last of the Romantics, and resisted all further categorization. His poetry varies from period to period, as does what can be deduced of his philosophy, but it tends to be made up of anecdotal material—some of it autobiography, some of it folklore, some of it occult theory, some of it current events—overlaid by symbolism and sensuality, all honed for maximum precision. Although he got bad press for becoming a Fascist later in life, he did not, like Wordsworth, turn into a bore, and his "mature" period is considered his best. In fact, he's the poet laureate of old age, a subject with which he became obsessed, and several of his better-known poems, like the one above, provide models for growing old.

HOW TO TELL KEATS FROM SHELLEY

John Keats

Percy Bysshe Shelley

Keats is the one you'd play racquetball with. He wasn't happy exactly, but he was better adjusted and less the outcast than Shelley, and it shows. (As a kid, Keats had been noisy and high-spirited, a bit of a hellion; Shelley was always coming home from the playground in tears.) Keats wrote letters that his friends couldn't wait to get, and that literary critics and biographers delightedly pore over alongside his poetry; Shelley wrote letters in which he talked about himself a little too much, and it's his essays—philosophical, high-flown, full of abstractions—that the scholars note. Of all the Romantic poets, Keats has worn the best, his stock never varying by more than a point or two; Shelley's has wavered significantly, ever since T. S. Eliot branded his poetry "an affair of adolescence" and Lionel Trilling said he "should not be read, but inhaled through a gas pipe." Be that as it may, it's Shelley, high-principled and far-sighted, you'd want by your side at the barricades.

As for the poetry, Keats's is sensuous, concrete, and concentrated, with art-for-art's-sake overtones. (It was he, after all, who wrote, " 'Beauty is truth, truth beauty,'—that is all / Ye know on earth, and all ye need to know," though there's some question as to whether he was being sarcastic.) Keats was a craftsman, with no theory to speak of; it's a commonplace to compare him, in the richness and confidence of his language, to Shakespeare, as in these lines, from "Ode to a Nightingale":

> Thou wast not born for death, immortal Bird!
>   No hungry generations tread thee down;
> The voice I hear this passing night was heard
>   In ancient days by emperor and clown:
> Perhaps the selfsame song that found a path
>   Through the sad heart of Ruth, when, sick for home,
>   She stood in tears among the alien corn; . . .

Shelley's poetry is less solid, more shifting and translucent, more volatile. Unlike Keats, who was at home in the world of things and who was capable of both greed and earthiness, Shelley was able to say of himself, "You know, I always seek in what I see the manifestation of some thing beyond the present and tangible object." (He was also able to address an unsuspecting skylark, "Hail to thee, blithe Spirit!") A radical, full of black despair, Shelley, like Wordsworth, was deemed "a voice of the age." This is how that voice sounds, in the early "Hymn to Intellectual Beauty":

> I vowed that I would dedicate my powers
>   To thee and thine—have I not kept the vow?
>   With beating heart and streaming eyes, even now
> I call the phantoms of a thousand hours
> Each from his voiceless grave: they have in visioned bowers
>   Of studious zeal or love's delight
>   Outwatched with me the envious night—
> They know that never joy illumed my brow
>   Unlinked with hope that thou wouldst free
>   This world from its dark slavery, . . .

Shelley had the more interesting—and a marginally longer—life. Born an aristocrat (whereas Keats's father owned a livery stable), he came to be regarded as an atheist, a revolutionary, and an immoralist; he was, in addition, married to Mary Wollstonecraft Godwin, daughter of the radical social philosopher William Godwin and author of *Frankenstein,* with whose half-sister Byron would later have a much-remarked-on affair. Keats didn't hang out with Shelley and Byron, was preoccupied with the financial and medical problems of his brothers, and had a traumatic relationship with a girl named Fanny Brawne. Both Keats and Shelley died miserably, Keats in Rome in 1821 from tuberculosis, Shelley off the Italian coast in 1822 when his boat was swamped in a squall. Keats was twenty-six, Shelley thirty.

Triple Play

You say the dishes are done, the kids are in bed, and the VCR is broken? Good: This is your opportunity to take a few minutes and bone up on literary devices. And we don't mean foreshadowing and onomatopoeia. *They're* for high-school sophomores. If you want to sound like an adult, it's wit, irony, and ambiguity you've got to be able to field—and every so often manifest. But what, exactly, are they? We don't blame you for not being sure; each is booby-trapped in some way. The first has a complicated history, the second comes in too many shapes and sizes, and the third leaves you wondering whether it's good or bad. To, er, wit:

WIT

At its best, it's—as you've doubtless heard—like a rapier: fast, clean, intensely civilized. And it's immediately recognizable: Oscar Wilde, Dorothy Parker, and Tom Stoppard are witty; Groucho Marx is funny, even trenchant, but too interested in being *un*civilized to be witty; nor is Joan Rivers (too scattershot, too sloppy); nor is *Vanity Fair* Magazine, which seems to have confused being brilliant with sounding British (and civilization with celebrity).

But that's lately. In past centuries, the word was both more incendiary and more central, and how you used it revealed which side of the politico-literary fence you were on. From its original Anglo-Saxon sense of "mind, reason, intelligence," it

Oscar Wilde

had come by Elizabethan times to be used of anything clever or ingenious, especially if it was also a little bizarre, paradoxical, or farfetched. The Metaphysical poetry of John Donne (see page 186), in which, as Dr. Johnson noted, "the most heterogeneous ideas are yoked by violence together," was the height of wit in this sense—which was soon being equated with the spirit of poetry itself. So far, so good.

Enter the Augustans of the eighteenth century, who, enamored of the classical proportions and strictures of ancient Rome, had other plans for the word, insisting that, properly used, *wit* tended not toward bizarrerie but, rather, eloquence and precision. Alexander Pope (see page 187) used the word at least forty-six times in his *Essay on Criticism,* most memorably in the lines "True wit is nature to advantage dressed, / What oft was thought, but ne'er so well expressed"; John Dryden said, among other things, that wit, "like a nimble spaniel, beats o'er and ranges thro' the field of memory, till it springs the quarry it hunted after." Their point: that everybody should stop associating wit with the Metaphysicals (whom the Augustans loathed, and who wouldn't be reconstructed until T. S. Eliot spoke up for them a couple of centuries later) and start associating it with *them.*

The nineteenth century didn't care much for the word *wit* (preferring, among others, *imagination*) and allowed it to languish, to the point that it was soon synonymous with mere levity; Matthew Arnold, for instance, struck Chaucer— not to mention Pope—from the list of great poets because he was "witty": He lacked high seriousness. Now the word, like the Metaphysicals—not to mention Pope—has achieved respectability once more: It's not that high seriousness is out (like heavy meals), just that getting it said fast, and maybe even piquantly, is, like the perfect sorbet or the perfect chèvre salad, very much in.

IRONY

Socrates

Unlike *wit,* its meaning, or rather bundle of meanings, has held fairly steady over time: Always it's implied that there are two sets of listeners keyed in to the same statement, story, or piece of information, and that one of them gets it—sees it for what it is, in all its poignancy or complexity or awfulness—and the other one doesn't. If you're in the former set, congratulations: The ability to recognize irony, especially in writing (where there are no facial expressions or vocal inflections to help it, and you, along), has for centuries been regarded as one of the surest tests of intelligence and sophistication.

The word derives from *eiron,* one of the basic character types in Greek drama, the trickster who pretends he's ignorant, thereby provoking somebody else to reveal his most ludicrous side. Not that this technique was confined to the stage: Socrates, for instance, acted the part of the *eiron* when he asked those apparently pointless, naïve questions of his students, only to demolish the kids in the end. Thus was born *Socratic irony*, where those who are in on the game smile knowingly as their master's feigned ignorance routs dogma, superstition, and/or popular wisdom.

More common is *dramatic irony*, also called *tragic irony*, where the audience knows something—or many things—the characters onstage don't, and consequently can read doom into all the innocent, trivial remarks they make. You know: Oedipus vows revenge on the murderer of his father, and all of us (whether because we're already familiar with the tale, as even children were in ancient Greece, or whether because the omniscient chorus spilled the beans while Oedipus was out of earshot) gasp.

Verbal irony, by contrast, is no more complicated than calling a three-hundred-pound linebacker Tiny, or saying "Brutus is an honorable man" when what you really mean is that he's a junkyard dog. It is, though, more complicated than sarcasm, which is almost always heavy-handed and caustic (and spoken), and it can sometimes leave you wondering what, exactly, the intended meaning is. It can also be extremely moving, as when Mercutio says, of his death-wound in *Romeo and Juliet*, "No, 'tis not so deep as a well, nor so wide as a church door; but 'tis enough, 'twill serve."

For the graduate student: You'll also want to take note of *cosmic irony*, where God mocks, thwarts, or sports with us mere-mortal types; the classic example here is the last sentence of Thomas Hardy's *Tess of the D'Urbervilles:* "The President of the Immortals, in Aeschylean phrase, had ended his sport with Tess." And of *romantic irony*, especially prominent—as the name suggests—in the early nineteenth century, in which the author reveals that his characters are just fictions, after all, being created and manipulated by him, as in Byron's long satiric poem "Don Juan" (pronounced, just this once, JOO-en).

And everybody: Given that you've bothered to read (and we to write) all of the above, promise you'll stop saying, "It's ironic" when all you mean, really, is that it's a little odd.

AMBIGUITY

You're right to be suspicious of it in a contract, even in a conversation. But ambiguity—from the Latin *ambi-*, "both," plus *agere*, "drive"—is, it turns out, not such a bad thing in literature, especially poetry, where nobody has to choose between meanings the way he might have to in a courtroom or on a street corner. Classic example: in Shakespeare, Hotspur's drumming up antagonism to Henry IV by saying, "We must have bloody noses and crack'd crowns / And pass them current too"—where the crowns in ques-

William Empson

tion are first of all coins, second heads, and third what kings wear, and where a single word thus manages to hint at the action, and the most important theme, of the play.

The final authority on ambiguity, by the way, is William Empson, the British literary critic who wrote, in 1930, *Seven Types of Ambiguity*, still beloved of English professors and comp-lit grad students, where he defined ambiguity as "any verbal nuance, however slight, which gives room for alternative reactions to the same piece of language." The seven types, for the record, range from seemingly unconnected meanings contained in a single word, to alternative meanings that together clarify an author's state of mind, to a statement that's so obviously loopy that the reader has no choice but to invent his own meaning.

Empson goes on and on about all this, but all you have to worry about remembering is that, even in poetry, ambiguity can be a good thing (involving, in Empson's words, "intricacy, delicacy, or compression of thought") or a bad one (reflective of "weakness or thinness of thought"). That, and not using *ambiguous* when what you really mean is *ambivalent*—when you mean somebody is *feeling* conflicted about something, is of two minds about it: Language exhibits ambiguity; people feel ambivalence.

Bellying Up to the Bard

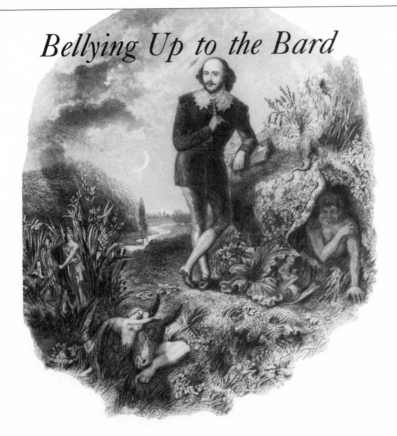

It's not just that we don't know much about Shakespeare-the-man; it's not just that what he wrote presents so many obstacles (the overwhelming textual complexities, the outmoded theatrical conventions, the fact that the heroes have all been played by Richard Burton); it's that there's so much riding on having a meaningful relationship with him. Sorry, we can't do much more than make the introductions; what the two of you do in the clinches is your problem.

In the meantime, whether things ultimately work out for you or not, you still ought to know what the plays are all about. Like everyone else, we've divided them up into four categories. Also, we've asked Henry Popkin, a Shakespeare-scholar neighbor of ours, for some deep background on one play from each category, plus a once-over of the rest. Still don't know what to make of the whole business? Take a look at what some other literary titans have had to say about Shakespeare over the years.

As to who it is, precisely, that you're spending time with here, well, that's been the source of endless gossip. Skeptics have ascribed authorship of Shakespeare's plays to everyone from Francis Bacon and the seventeenth earl of Oxford to an Arab sheik named Zubair.

THE HISTORIES

Shakespeare's history plays—there are ten of them—tell the story of England from the end of the fourteenth century to the reign of Henry VIII, father of Elizabeth, the woman who gave us the adjective "Elizabethan." (One, about Bad King John, is set roughly two centuries earlier than the rest.) It's hard to find a contemporary analogue to what Shakespeare was doing in his histories, obsessed as they are with civil strife and rebellion, with "order and degree." The historical novel comes to mind, of course. But in terms of the popularity these plays enjoyed, the way they came out in installments, and the extent to which they focused on certain rich, ingrown, and acrimonious families, it's probably *Dallas, Dynasty,* and *Falcon Crest* we really should be talking about.

Close-up: *Henry IV*, Part I

Can honour set to a leg? No: Or an arm? No: Or take away the grief of a wound? No. Honour hath no skill in surgery then? No. What is honour? A word. What is in that word honour? Air. A trim reckoning! Who hath it? He that died o' Wednesday. Doth he feel it? No. Doth he hear it? No. 'Tis insensible then? Yea, to the dead. But will [it] not live with the living? No. Why? Detraction will not suffer it. Therefore, I'll none of it. Honour is a mere scutcheon—and so ends my catechism.

act 5, scene 1

Laurence Olivier as Hotspur

A play that got away from its author. While surely intended to focus on Hal, the future Henry V, as the embodiment of the perfect prince, a model of courage, common sense, and fidelity to his father, King Henry IV, it winds up lingering most fondly over—and etching most sharply—the volatile young rebel Hotspur and the Rabelaisian old reprobate Falstaff. Granted, the former, full of foolhardiness and childish resentments, and the latter, with his steadfast refusal to take anything to heart beyond simple self-preservation, could not have governed England (at least not an England we could bear living in), but we'd rather share a pot of ale with either than with Shakespeare's cold-blooded paragon.

The first half of the play enforces the contrasts by cutting back and forth between the conspiracy that Hotspur, his father, and his uncle—the redoubtable Percy family, who had helped Henry IV depose Richard II and now think themselves unfairly ignored—lead against the King, and the highway robbery being planned by Falstaff. Hal eventually scotches both schemes, thwarting Falstaff's plan to rob the King's treasury at Gadshill and Hotspur's plan to rob him of his realm at Shrewsbury. The dual successes may make a man of Hal, but they don't make him any more endearing.

The genius of the play lies in its integration of something like realistic comedy into a chronicle-play format and in its depiction of Falstaff—equal parts wit and fool, philosopher and con man, hypocrite and debunker. In fact, Falstaff was such a favorite of Elizabethan audiences that he was brought back in both *Henry IV*, Part II and *The Merry Wives of Windsor* (and his death reported at the beginning of *Henry V*). Critics disagree on whether Falstaff is a coward or not, and on whether he really expects his lies to be believed, but the majority of them maintain not only that he is the most superbly rendered comic figure in all of Shakespeare, but that, in six centuries of English literature, only Chaucer's Wife of Bath gets off anywhere near the same number of good lines.

The Other Histories

Henry VI, Parts I, II, and III—Early Shakespeare, set against a background of England's sixty-three-year-long Wars of the Roses, between the House of Lancaster and that of York, and guaranteed to induce such objections on the part of the uninitiated as: What's the plot? Who's the hero? Isn't there too much going on? And how can you do that to Joan of Arc? The three-part sequence examines the problems created by a king who is weak and who has only a dubious title to his throne. Shakespeare would deal more neatly with the same issues a few years later, with *Richard II*, his study in weak character, and *Henry IV*, his study in dubious title.

Richard III—You may want to think of it as *Henry VI*, Part IV. No shades of gray here: Richard is totally evil. He's also totally entertaining, and ascends to the throne by slaughtering a clutch of its legitimate heirs. Eventually he's

---

I remember, the Players have often mentioned it as an honour to *Shakespeare*, that in his writing, (whatsoever he penned) he never blotted out a line. My answer hath been, would he had blotted a thousand.

Ben Jonson

overthrown—by a prince not in the least evil and much less entertaining, but whose dynastic claims are impeccable, whose marriage ends the Wars of the Roses, and whose granddaughter will turn out to be Elizabeth I. The best scenes: Richard's wooing of the Lady Anne and the downfall of the Duke of Buckingham, his early supporter. The most famous lines: "A horse! a horse! My kingdom for a horse!" and "Now is the winter of our discontent / Made glorious summer by the sun of York."

King John—He of the Magna Carta, which means another history with, instead of a royal hero, a royal villain. But not without a hero altogether: That's the Bastard Faulconbridge, son of Richard the Lion-Hearted. More rhetoric here than poetry, it's often said, specifically much noodling about such contemporary political issues as the rights and duties of kings, the wisdom of inheritance by primogeniture, and the relation of secular rulers to spiritual ones.

Richard II—Richard loves to play at being king and gets off some rather good poetry on the subject, but he is the victim of indecision, effeminacy, and bad advisors, and he is eventually overthrown by the hard, efficient Bolingbroke, who'll take the throne as Henry IV. The first really developed "tragedy of character" in the English drama—and the first of the four parts of Shakespeare's second, or mature, history cycle, to be followed by the two halves of *Henry IV* and *Henry V*. Most famous speech, hands down: "This happy breed of men, this little world, / This precious stone set in the silver sea." Runner-up: "For God's sake, let us sit upon the ground, / And tell sad stories of the death of kings."

Henry IV, Part II—In which Prince Hal is required to reject the irrepressible Falstaff for the sake of higher duty: "Reply not to me with a fool-born jest: / Presume not that I am the thing I was." Comedy looms larger here than history, though, and Falstaff (especially with Hotspur gone) larger than any other three characters put together. Perhaps to make Hal look better, the play also gives us a really shameless opportunist in the person of his brother John.

Henry V—Prince Hal, now a hero-king, conquers France. His old drinking buddies get the worst of it again, being unfavorably contrasted with a cross

> *S*hakespear, (whom you and ev'ry Play-house bill
> Style the divine, the matchless, what you will)
> For gain, not glory, wing'd his roving flight,
> And grew immortal in his own despight.
>   Alexander Pope

section of doughty British soldiers (reminiscent of the bomber-crew movies of World War II, with Wales and Scotland corresponding roughly to Brooklyn and Chicago). The two most famous lines: "Once more unto the breach, dear friends, once more," and "We few, we happy few, we band of brothers."

Henry VIII—This play, Shakespeare's last, has had its problems: Shakespeare didn't write it alone; the portrait of the King is blurry; and the Globe Theater burned down when wadding from onstage cannon charges ignited during its production. Still, the characters of Katharine of Aragon and Cardinal Wolsey have managed to catch the occasional fancy of actors and/or audience.

THE COMEDIES

It helps to keep in mind that, during the Renaissance, a play did not have to be a barrel of laughs to be called a comedy; any drama with a happy ending and a generally optimistic point of view fulfilled the requirements. If the plot also revolved around a temporarily troubled love affair, you had romantic comedy, the genre that, from about 1595 to 1600, was Shakespeare's forte and that hit its peak with his three so-called "joyous" comedies, *Much Ado about Nothing*, *As You Like It*, and *Twelfth Night*, all of which satisfied their audiences' desire for escapist entertainment. After 1600, with a more somber mood reigning in England and theater audiences becoming both more sophisticated and more cynical, the tone of the plays changed; the three "problem" comedies, *Troilus and Cressida*, *All's Well That Ends Well*, and, especially, *Measure for Measure*, hardly seem like comedies at all, except for those inevitable—and barely believable—happy endings.

Close-up: *Twelfth Night*

> What is love? 'tis not hereafter;
> Present mirth hath present laughter;
>   What's to come is still unsure:
> In delay there lies no plenty;
> Then come and kiss me, sweet and twenty,
>   Youth's a stuff will not endure.
>
>   act 2, scene 3

Illyria is a center of self-indulgence, a morass of misplaced love and the rejection of life—or the overeager embracing of it, sometimes by the same person. Its duke, Orsino, wastes most of his energy being lovesick over Olivia, who has spurned him. She, having renounced life to mourn her dead

Twelfth Night

brother, switches over to another losing proposition, a fixation on Cesario, who is really Viola in drag. Malvolio, obsessed by self-love, is soon convinced that Olivia is as crazy about him as he is about himself.

That most of the major characters spend most of the play mooning about or making fools of themselves is not surprising, given that *Twelfth Night* is the closest thing Shakespeare ever wrote to a *musical* comedy—someone is forever breaking into a pavane or one of those apparently tuneless Elizabethan ditties (like the one above), and nearly everyone in the play seems to be taking a holiday, like they did in old Fred Astaire–Ginger Rogers movies—in fact, *Twelfth Night* was named for a holiday, the twelfth night of Christmas.

Viola, of course, is taking a holiday from her true identity by dressing up as a man. But although Malvolio and Sebastion also disguise themselves, very little of this play's comic effect depends on mistaken identity. Instead, its humor comes from the human failings of its characters. It is the characters—even the minor ones—that really make *Twelfth Night:* The sensible Viola is probably Shakespeare's most lovable heroine, and the conceited, priggish Malvolio is the character everyone remembers best, partly because narcissists were rare in Elizabethan drama and partly because the rather cruel way he's treated by the other characters was immensely satisfying to Elizabethan audiences and wrings sympathy from modern ones.

*S*hakespeare approximates the remote, and familiarises the wonderful; the event which he represents will not happen, but if it were possible, its effects would probably be such as he has assigned; and it may be said, that he has not only shown human nature as it acts in real exigencies, but as it would be found in trials, to which it cannot be exposed.

Samuel Johnson

The Other Comedies

The Comedy of Errors—This very early, uncharacteristically farcical comedy, drawn from two Roman plays by Plautus, gets most of its laughs from mistaken identity, with a sprinkling of marriage jokes thrown in. What's surprising is that, as pure sitcom, it still works on the modern stage.

The Two Gentlemen of Verona—An interesting forerunner of the kind of romantic comedy that Shakespeare was to make one of his distinctive genres, exhibiting all the imaginable extremes of fidelity, gallantry, and melancholy, as if the dramatist was staking out the boundaries within which his subsequent comedies would be enacted. In Valentine and Proteus, the "two gentlemen" whose friendship turns to rivalry, and Silvia and Julia, their lady friends, he also begins to formulate his method of using contrast to establish character.

Love's Labours Lost—Lots of learned wit, not all of it easily decipherable by contemporary audiences, in this story of a king and three courtiers who undertake a rest-and-study cure but quickly change their plans when a princess and her three ladies-in-waiting turn up. Shakespeare's attention keeps shifting—probably a sign that the play kept being rewritten.

The Taming of the Shrew—Let's not kid ourselves; this *is* a male-chauvinist play: Petruchio does eventually subjugate the self-willed Katharina. The best that can be said for her, finally, is that she learns to exchange clever remarks with him, but she must submit totally on every issue that counts. Shakespeare's treatment of his heroine, however, merely reflects the standard Elizabethan view of a woman's place according to which, Petruchio really does Kate a favor by forcing her to accept her proper role. By the way, in those days, *shrew* was pronounced "shrow," which explains why many of the play's rhymes seem a bit off.

A Midsummer Night's Dream—Shakespeare's first comic masterpiece is a compliment to love, but a back-handed one, given the quarrelsome marriage of Oberon and Titania, the marriage by conquest of Theseus and Hippolyta, the lampooning of tales of true love in the play within a play, and the mismatched infatuations in the forest. All of which makes it hard to tell the difference between love and lunacy. In Puck, the beneficent goblin, and Bottom, the weaver, who winds up with an ass's head, Shakespeare created two of his most memorable minor characters.

---

*L*ike a miraculous celestial Light-ship, woven all of sheet-lightning and sunbeams.
Thomas Carlyle

The Merchant of Venice—In this double plot, the courtship of Portia pits the true values of Belmont, her home, against the false values of Venice, which thinks life is all about gold, silver, and justice (as opposed to mercy). Although the play is classed as a romantic comedy, the emphasis is more on friendship than on love, and the question of the anti-Semitism inherent in Shakespeare's portrayal of Shylock always gets more attention than either.

Much Ado About Nothing—The witty exchanges of the unwilling lovers Benedict and Beatrice make for much of this comedy's charm. On the other hand, Claudio's bitter denunciations of Hero, the woman he so recently adored, tend to distress modern audiences with their cruelty. As the title suggests, confusions and misunderstandings abound, compounded by the two monumentally incompetent constables, Dogberry and Verges.

As You Like It—We're in the idyllic Forest of Arden, to which all the good characters have fled from the corrupt court. Our backpackers include: the young nobleman Orlando, who falls in love with Rosalind, daughter of the banished duke (and the first of Shakespeare's self-reliant, no-nonsense heroines), Rosalind's cousin Celia, Jaques (always referred to as "the melancholy Jaques"), and the fool Touchstone. The exiles praise the free life of the forest, but, except for Jaques, they all jump at the chance of going back to civilization.

The Merry Wives of Windsor—Said to have been written in response to Queen Elizabeth's request to see Falstaff in love. If so, the monarch got short weight. This is Falstaff bereft of his wit, and he's not in love, or even in lust, just prodded by vanity and greed. Amiable enough on the whole, however, and the only play in which Shakespeare presents (and defends) the life of his own middle class.

Troilus and Cressida—A romance with an unfaithful woman (Cressida) conducted in the middle of a war (Trojan) over another unfaithful woman

---

*S*hakespeare's name, you may depend on it, stands absurdly too high and will go down. He had no invention as to stories, none whatever. He took all his plots from old novels, and threw their stories into a dramatic shape, at as little expense of thought as you or I could turn his plays back again into prose tales. That he threw over whatever he did write some flashes of genius, nobody can deny: but this was all. Suppose anyone to have had the dramatic handling for the first time of such ready-made stories as Lear, Macbeth, &c. and he would be a sad fellow indeed, if he did not make something very grand of them.
George Gordon, Lord Byron

(Helen). War and love are shown to be equally vicious and destructive. Or, as Thersites says, "Lechery, lechery; still wars and lechery; nothing else holds fashion." This play squeaks through as comedy on a technicality: The two principals are still alive at the end.

All's Well That Ends Well—Classed, along with *T & C* and *Measure*, as one of the "dark" or "problem" comedies, said to mirror the increasingly pessimistic side of Shakespeare and/or Elizabethan England. This one is the lightest of the three and Helena one of the most endearing of Shakespeare's heroines. Having cured her king of an ailment that baffled the court physicians, she sets out resolutely to track down (and bag) her man, a self-centered nullity under the influence of his friend, the boastful and opportunistic Parolles. That she wants him at all is problematic, but then, Shakespeare never said love had to be reasonable.

Measure for Measure—Scholars like to roll out religious allegory to explain this play, but even with the special pleading it can seem bitter and cynical. The Duke appoints his deputy, Angelo, to clean up the mess he has made in Vienna. Why can't he do it himself? Doesn't he see through Angelo's hypocrisy? If so, he is at fault for putting Vienna at the deputy's mercy. If not, he is incompetent. Isabella's refusal to lay down her virginity to save her brother is understandable, but must she then tell him about it? Isn't the Duke's revenge for Lucio's verbal insults a bit excessive? And what real satisfaction can anybody take in a finale in which sordidness is converted to happiness by fiat? Are you starting to see the problem? Do you care?

I keep saying Shakespeare, Shakespeare, you are as obscure as life is.
Matthew Arnold

---

*W*hat is he? You might almost answer, He is the earth . . . the globe . . . existence. . . . In Shakespeare the birds sing, the rushes are clothed with green, hearts love, souls suffer, the cloud wanders, it is hot, it is cold, night falls, time passes, forests and multitudes speak, the vast eternal dream hovers over all. Sap and blood, all forms of the multiple reality, actions and ideas, man and humanity, the living and the life, solitudes, cities, religions, diamonds and pearls, dunghills and charnel houses, the ebb and flow of beings, the steps of comers and goers, all, all are on Shakespeare and in Shakespeare; and, this genius being the earth, the dead emerge from it.
Victor Hugo

THE TRAGEDIES

Amazingly, nineteenth-century audiences preferred the comedies; it's only the twentieth century that has been so impressed by Shakespeare's tragedies—at least, with those four tragedies generally acknowledged as his greatest: *Hamlet, Othello, Macbeth,* and *King Lear.* All of these were written between 1601 and 1606, after Shakespeare began leaning toward heavily symbolic, multilayered plots that clearly juxtaposed good and evil. Combine these elements with the kind of psychological complexity that only a terribly unhappy character can put across, and you can see why the tragedies jibe so nicely with the modern sensibility.

Close-up: *King Lear*

Blow, winds, and crack your cheeks! Rage! Blow!
You cataracts and hurricanoes, spout
Till you have drench'd our steeples, drown'd the cocks!
You sulphurous and thought-executing fires,
Vaunt-couriers to oak-cleaving thunderbolts,
Singe my white head! And thou, all-shaking thunder,
Smite flat the thick rotundity o' the world!
Crack nature's molds, all germens spill at once,
That make ingrateful man!

act 3, scene 2

If you have tears, prepare to shed them now. Though this line comes from *Julius Caesar,* it applies best to *King Lear,* which, increasingly, scholars and critics have come to regard as the most bitter, bleak, and pessimistic—as well as the greatest—of Shakespeare's tragedies.

"King Lear, *act I, scene 1*," *painted by Edwin Austin Abbey.*

The play's opening events hardly prepare us for the bombshells that follow. Retiring from power and dividing his kingdom, Lear relies, outrageously, on a single test—his daughters' public declarations of love. Offended by this silliness, Cordelia, his favorite and the only one of his three daughters who is genuinely devoted to him, brusquely rejects his demand. That's all it takes to propel Lear—and us—inexorably through five acts of unspeakable anguish, culminating in the deaths of both Lear and Cordelia. And why? Not just because Lear has a dumb view of human relations. The fact is that this is a terrible world, filled with evil and unimaginable cruelty. What comfort there is doesn't derive from anything as trivial (and as unattainable) as a happy ending, but from the warmth and joy Lear and Cordelia feel when they are temporarily reunited. Lear has learned a lot, but the tuition was a killer.

There is nothing halfhearted about the play's tragic effects; no one gets hurt just a little. Lear, having abdicated, doesn't shuffle off to a tower room to do jigsaw puzzles; he is driven out, crazed, to seek shelter on the heath in a raging storm. Cordelia is hanged in prison. Gloucester's punishment for being misled about his legitimate son, Edgar, and for being faithful to his king is to be blinded—onstage.

King Lear is full of the kind of significant parallels Shakespeare liked to use to reinforce his effects. Gloucester is a second tragic father, also brought to grief for failing to distinguish between his good and bad children. Lear, judging his daughters' devotion to him by the number of knights they will allow him, is repeating his original mistake of trying to measure love. Meanwhile, a virtual symphony of madness is being played out in the delirium of Lear, the feigned lunacy of Edgar, and the addled wisdom of the Fool, who pretty much sums up the moral of the play when he tells Lear, "Thou shouldst not have been old till thou hadst been wise."

The Other Tragedies

Titus Andronicus—Lots of blood and gore, with about as much substance as a Charles Bronson movie and a similar cumulative effect—that is, if you can imagine Bronson as a victorious Roman general who sets out to avenge the rape and mutilation of his daughter, Lavinia. Not a play to win raves from the critics, who like to think of it either as the work of a young Shakespeare out to have a hit at any cost, or as not the work of Shakespeare at all.

Romeo and Juliet—The world's most famous star-crossed lovers play out the world's worst run of luck. Although it contains some beautiful poetry and a couple of brilliantly developed minor characters (Mercutio and the Nurse), and despite the moralizing of twentieth-century remakes like *West Side Story*, this one is really just what it appears to be—a classic tearjerker.

Julius Caesar—Ruined for most of us by being taught in high school, when we were too young to care about anyone as noble and good as Brutus, whose tragedy this really is. (We were just confused and irritated when the title character got killed off in the middle of the action.) True, the plot is more straightforward than most of Shakespeare's, but the play's austerity isn't for sixteen-year-olds.

Hamlet—The Master's shot at one of the big box-office genres of his day—the revenge tragedy, in which, nine times out of ten, a treacherous murder is avenged by a tireless pursuer, with plenty of carnage along the way. Shakespeare's addition of a psychological and philosophical dimension, and his creation of a hero who thinks so much that he can't get the job done, have, however, sufficed to keep this version off the drive-in circuit.

Othello—All about the deceptiveness of appearances. Othello's black exterior is no guide to his noble character. "Honest Iago" is untrustworthy. Desdemona, who is innocence itself, gets smeared. And Cassio, who has been fooling around with a courtesan, is really a fine fellow after all.

Macbeth—Don't fall for the victim-of-circumstances line. Not only does Macbeth murder his king and slaughter a whole family of innocents, but the business about his wrestling with his conscience has been greatly exaggerated. He worries only about the practical consequences, not the ethical implications, of his evil deeds. When his wife judges him to be "too full o' th' milk of human kindness," she doesn't mean what we mean by kindness, and besides, she's hardly an authority on the subject.

Antony and Cleopatra—Overly complex, perhaps, but then, Shakespeare had a lot to deal with here: the decline and fall of Antony, who, although he's the victim of his own unbridled passion, can't be made to seem a total fool; the development of Cleopatra from a selfish little twit into someone whose death-by-asp moves us; and the depiction of Rome and Egypt as two different and opposing worlds, without the benefit of split-screen technology.

Timon of Athens—A kind of morality play about worldly vanity. Timon, a nobleman, goes broke entertaining his friends, who then refuse to have anything to do with him. He becomes a hermit and a cynic, whom, for all practical purposes, we can forget about. An acknowledged mess, *Timon* was probably tinkered with beyond recognition.

Coriolanus—At last, a tragedy in which *both* sides repel us—the aristocratic Coriolanus with his *noblesse oblige* and his contempt for the masses, and the scheming tribunes who play on those masses' foolishness, fickleness, and gullibility. Because of its ambiguity, the play has been easy to use propagandistically; it was staged as a pro-Fascist parable in France between the wars, and later rewritten from a Marxist perspective by Bertolt Brecht.

THE ROMANCES

"Romances" is what scholars call the four comedies that Shakespeare wrote after his prosperous company took over the Blackfriars Theatre in 1608 and began requiring texts different from those he had been supplying earlier. More wistful, more melancholy, and more atmospheric than anything that had preceded them, the Blackfriars plays were staged at night in a closed, artificially lit environment, and cost considerably more money. Their wealthier, better-educated audience expected emotional, heart-wrenching poetry, extravagant incident, extended suffering, and perilous escapes—then a happy ending.

Close-up: *The Tempest*

Scene from The Tempest, *rendered by Henry Fuseli.*

> . . . These our actors,
> As I foretold you, were all spirits and
> Are melted into air, into thin air;
> And, like the baseless fabric of this vision,
> The cloud-capped towers, the gorgeous palaces,
> The solemn temples, the great globe itself,
> Yea, all which it inherit, shall dissolve,
> And, like this insubstantial pageant faded,
> Leave not a rack behind. We are such stuff
> As dreams are made on, and our little life
> Is rounded with a sleep. Sir, I am vexed.
> Bear with my weakness; my old brain is troubled.
> Be not disturbed with my infirmity.
> If you be pleased, retire into my cell
> And there repose. . . .   act 4, scene 1

The Tempest is the last play wholly written by Shakespeare. As a result, generations of readers have viewed it as the culmination of his vision, identifying Prospero, the magician and duke-in-exile, who now presides over a desert island, with the playwright, and the play itself with Shakespeare's farewell to his art and subsequent retirement to Stratford. This may or may not have been conscious on Shakespeare's part, but certainly *The Tempest* represents a heartfelt return to naïveté after the complexity and weight of the great tragedies.

Here's the plot: Prospero seizes an opportunity to get back at his usurping brother and restore himself as Duke of Milan. He creates a storm and shipwreck, netting not only the brother, but also a fit suitor for his daughter, Miranda; the suitor's father, the King of Naples; the suitor's father's brother, likewise treacherous; and all their retainers. Conspiracies ensue, some "upstairs," some "downstairs," but Prospero's magic is sufficient to vanquish all comers. Ultimately *The Tempest*, like all the romances, is a play of reconciliation, and Prospero turns benign and forgiving. He arranges a marriage that unites two previously hostile families—and presents a masque that elegantly celebrates that marriage. (Appropriately, the play helped to celebrate the betrothal of King James's daughter, Elizabeth.)

When Shakespeare wrote *The Tempest*, he had been reading travelers' tales and was mindful of a recent shipwreck that had taken place off Bermuda. He must also have been thinking about the practical effects of such travelers' activities; accordingly, *The Tempest* is in some respects a parable of colonialism. In the two creatures who had greeted Prospero after his own shipwreck years earlier (and who then became his servants), we have the perfect image of the good and the bad native: Ariel cooperates and serves his master by helping to oppress the rest of the population, while the bestial Caliban (a near anagram for *cannibal*) instigates the archetypal colonialist nightmare by trying to rape Miranda. All of which raises larger issues, i.e.: Is nature superior to civilization and, by extension, to art? And in which state—nature or civilization—is man nobler?

---

*T*he fact is, we are growing out of Shakespeare. Byron declined to put up with his reputation at the beginning of the nineteenth century; and now, at the beginning of the twentieth, he is nothing but a household pet. His characters still live; his word pictures of woodland and wayside still give us a Bank-holiday breath of country air; his verse still charms us; his sublimities still stir us; the commonplaces and trumperies of the wisdom which age and experience bring to all the rest of us are still expressed by him better than by anybody else; but we have nothing to hope from him, and nothing to learn from him— not even how to write plays, though he does that so much better than most modern dramatists.

George Bernard Shaw

The Other Romances

Pericles—Apparently an old play only partially rewritten by Shakespeare, and the first of the romances, complete with wonderful adventures in strange places, long separations, deaths not real but feared, etc., etc. Consider Marina, unpredictably saved from a murderer by pirates, sold by her rescuers to a brothel, and so resolute in her purity that she's able to convert the brothel's patrons. Realism it's not, but it has a certain archaic charm.

Cymbeline—An odd concoction, mingling Celtic Britain and ancient Rome, with a plot that is no more than a machine for producing sensations, overflowing with abductions, disguises, magic potions, and mistaken identities. The central story pits Princess Imogen, daughter of King Cymbeline of Britain, against the new queen, her stepmother, who's determined that Imogen marry her cloddish son Cloten. Still to come: Imogen's "seduction" by Iachimo, a kind of cut-rate Iago; her encounter with her two long-lost brothers; her mistaking Cloten's headless body for that of her true husband, Posthumus; and the dream sequence, featuring a personal appearance by Jupiter.

A Winter's Tale— The fact that a character exits "pursued by a bear" is no more outrageous than King Leontes's sudden, entirely unmotivated jealousy of his wife, Hermione, or her decision to teach him a lesson by turning into a statue for sixteen years. Then there's the matter of Bohemia, notoriously landlocked, having been issued a seacoast. In other words, the events of the play are patently fantastical, contributing to an atmosphere that is part fairy tale and part allegory, in which we travel from court to countryside, from winter to summer, and from death to life.

I do not believe that any writer has ever exposed this *bovaryisme*, the human will to see things as they are not, more clearly than Shakespeare.
T. S. Eliot

*W*hen I read Shakespeare I am struck with wonder
That such trivial people should muse and thunder
In such lovely language.
D. H. Lawrence

FIVE DEFINITIONS (OUT OF FIVE THOUSAND OR SO) THAT MIGHT MAKE THE GOING A LITTLE EASIER

DIE—Can mean "to come in lovemaking: to have an orgasm." This is what Benedick means in *Much Ado about Nothing* when he says, "I will live in thy heart, die in thy lap, and be buried in thy eyes." Heady knowledge, but use it sparingly: *Die* usually means "to die."

FOOL—Often a term of endearment, as it is at the end of *King Lear* when Lear says, "My poor fool is dead." He means Cordelia, not the Fool, whose absence from the latter part of the play nobody ever bothers to explain.

HORNS—The adornment and symbol of the cheated-on husband, the cuckold. Alluded to when Othello says, "I have a pain upon my forehead here." More often, the basis of the favorite family of jokes among the Elizabethans, who seemed to think any reference to horns was in and of itself uproarious.

HUMOUR—Mood, idiosyncrasy, temperament. Bottom in *A Midsummer Night's Dream* means the first when he says, "Yet my chief humour is for a tyrant." (He likes to play tyrants.) Never as in our "sense of humor." But in making *humour* such a prominent word in *The Merry Wives of Windsor,* Shakespeare was probably giving a nod to Ben Jonson, who in such plays as *Every Man in His Humour,* popularized a more formal concept of the "four humours": When phlegm, or blood, or yellow bile, or black bile is dominant in somebody, he is rendered phlegmatic, or sanguine, or choleric, or melancholic, rather than "good-humoured," i.e., emotionally balanced.

QUICK—In addition to the meaning we're most familiar with ("acting with rapidity"), can mean "vital, vigorous, full of energy"; "sharp, piercing"; or—here's the important one—"living, endowed with life," and, by extension, "pregnant." Hence a phrase like "the quick and the dead" and a line like, in *Love's Labour's Lost,* "The poor wench is cast away; she's quick; the child brags in her belly already."

THE SECOND MOST FAMOUS ENGLISH PLAYWRIGHT

That would be George Bernard Shaw, who lived about three hundred years after Shakespeare and who beats out Christopher Marlowe, Ben Jonson, William Congreve, Richard Brinsley Sheridan, and Oscar Wilde for the slot. True, he's not really English, but Anglo-Irish. And, unlike Shakespeare, he's not just a dramatist (or, more precisely, a dramatist with a taste for sonnet sequences). He's an insatiable critic, a prolific letter writer, and an indefatigable social reformer. A know-it-all with a sense of humor, Shaw took it upon himself to lecture (and upbraid) his era on his era, and went on doing so from the late nineteenth century to his death in 1950.

The plays are of varying degrees of heaviness, acerbity, and outrage, with varying ratios of polemic to farce. Even a relatively benign one like *Pygmalion* (the basis for *My Fair Lady*) manages to send up the class structure, relations between the sexes, and the idea of education. In the early *Widowers' Houses* and *Mrs. Warren's Profession*, Shaw skewers slum landlordism and prostitution, respectively; in *Major Barbara*, soup-kitchen evangelism; in *Heartbreak House*, the human species and civilization in general. Shaw's masterpiece (or, as his critics would have it, his attempt at a great play): *Saint Joan*, in which the famous martyr is revealed as a model of clear-eyed common sense.

In all the plays, Shaw's intention is to shake his audience's complacency, challenge its hypocrisy, and demonstrate how anybody who isn't part of the solution is de facto part of the problem. And neither the problem nor the solution is, in Shaw's hands, what you may have begun by thinking it was. Thus, he writes in a preface, *Mrs. Warren's Profession* was written "to draw attention to the truth that prostitution is caused, not by female depravity or male licentiousness, but simply by underpaying, undervaluing, and overworking women so shamefully that the poorest of them are forced to resort to prostitution to keep body and soul together."

Three cautions when approaching Shaw: Wit is one of his hallmarks, but it's in the service of intellect rather than simple entertainment; don't expect a cascade of Oscar Wilde–style epigrams and absurdities from him. Then: It's easier to read Shaw than to see it performed; in fact, with their explicit and endless stage descriptions, his plays can verge on novels, and a lot of the arguments repay (and require) study. Finally: Remember the adjective form of Shaw's name— *Shavian*, with a long *a*.

Let's Pause for a Moment and Consider Boswell's Life of Johnson

He received me very courteously; but it must be confessed that his apartment, and furniture, and morning dress, were sufficiently uncouth. His brown suit of clothes looked very rusty; he had on a little old shrivelled unpowdered wig, which was too small for his head; his shirt-neck and knees of his breeches were loose; his black worsted stockings ill drawn up; and he had a pair of unbuckled shoes by way of slippers. But all these slovenly particulars were forgotten the moment that he began to talk.

Published in 1791, James Boswell's *The Life of Samuel Johnson, LL.D.* is still the greatest biography in the English language and a gold mine of conspicuous erudition. In fact, in the days, not so very long ago, when people aspired to intellectual superiority the way they currently yearn for vast real estate holdings, the ability to quote Boswell quoting Johnson constituted the basic literacy test in some (admittedly preposterous) social circles.

Don't look for a story line; just think of the book as a talk show with a particularly entertaining guest and an interviewer who knows enough to shut up and listen. And don't let the scholarly reputation scare you off; Johnson the eighteenth-century savant seemed awesome even to his contemporaries, but making him accessible was Boswell's mission in life.

Essentially a quick succession of close-ups of Johnson holding forth, the biography is three-dimensional and so fast-paced that you may feel like you're being whisked from one dinner party to another without ever having time for a cigar. Before the evening's over, however, Johnson will have come alive, and, although none of his aphorisms will help you get rid of cellulite or make a killing in corn futures, you'll probably find both his unshakable moral certitude and his way with words fortifying.

Keep in mind that Johnson was not only a great conversationalist but the author of the *Dictionary of the English Language*—which he wrote, by himself, over the course of eight years, after reading every notable piece of English literature from Shakespeare's time to his own day and jotting down all the words he thought needed explaining—and a famous "Preface to Shakespeare," among a great many other works. Also that Boswell was no ordinary biographer but a man obsessed with his subject, a writer whose prodigious memory, application, and style revolutionized the genre.

Finally, you might want to memorize a few bits of Johnsonese yourself, just in case intellectual snobbism comes into vogue again during your lifetime. Here are some good ones to toss off in the drawing room, bearing in mind, of course, that your timing, as well as your delivery, must be impeccable:

If he does really think that there is no distinction between vice and virtue, why, sir, when he leaves our houses let us count our spoons.

Sir, a woman preaching is like a dog's walking on his hind legs. It is not done well; but you are surprised to find it done at all.

A man of genius has seldom been ruined but by himself.

That fellow seems to me to possess but one idea, and that is a wrong one.

No man but a blockhead ever wrote except for money.

A cow is a very good animal in the field; but we turn her out of a garden.

Patriotism is the last refuge of a scoundrel.

Were it not for imagination, sir, a man would be as happy in the arms of a chambermaid as a duchess.

Worth seeing? Yes, but not worth going to see.

He is not only dull himself, but the cause of dullness in others.

I have found you an argument; I am not obliged to find you an understanding.

It is better to live rich, than to die rich.

A Bedside Companion to the Nineteenth-Century English Novel

In general, English novels of the nineteenth century are a lot easier to read than, say, Faulkner; they don't ask much more of you than sheer stick-to-it-iveness. But there *is* the problem of understanding what all those characters are traipsing across, riding in, and being offered a glass of. Not to mention the varieties of clergy and degrees of aristocracy they always seem to be bumping into. And then there's the money. Herewith, a partial exegesis of seven difficult areas in Austen, Dickens, Thackeray, Eliot, Meredith, Trollope, Hardy, and, yes, the Brontës.

THE TOPOGRAPHY: PICKING YOUR WAY THROUGH THE COUNTRYSIDE

In general, it's gentle. And it's Anglo-Saxon: No buttes, mesas, or steppes need apply.

"The Cornfield" by John Constable.

At the Seashore

STRAND—Land bordering a river, lake, or sea; a beach. But especially the area between tidemarks (which means the body of water is more often than not the ocean). In London, the street called the Strand occupies the former shore of the Thames.

SHINGLE—A stretch of beach covered with loose, smooth pebbles and little or no sand. Also, the pebbles themselves.

BIGHT—A bend or indentation in a shoreline (sometimes used of a bend in a river, as well). Therefore, a wide bay formed by such a bend. From an Old English word that meant bend or angle, including those of the body, like the inside of the elbow and the armpit.

In the Woods

GLADE—A clearing in a forest where the sunlight shines down between tall trees. Has a strong positive charge: A glade is a pleasant place to be. (*Glade* is related to *glad,* and originally meant "bright.")

COPSE—A thicket of small trees or shrubs. It derives from the French *couper,* "to cut." Emotionally neutral: One might use it as a trysting-place or as a source of kindling wood. Also called *coppice.*

GROVE—This one's second nature, but don't lose sight of its salient feature: no undergrowth.

On the Moor

MOOR—A broad track of open land, usually high but poorly drained, with patches of heath (see below). An expansive, potentially threatening place: Lots happens, emotions run high, limits are hard to set, and Heathcliff goes at it with Cathy.

HEATH—In common parlance, synonymous with *moor,* but refers more specifically to that part of a moor that is not quite so soggy, and, not totally surprisingly, covered with heather.

FEN—Flat, swampy land; a bog. But especially the kind of swampy land where peat forms, hence a frequent component of moors. The Fens are certain low-lying districts in central England, not far from Cambridge.

In the Meadow

SWARD—Basically, any land covered with grassy turf, whether man-made (a lawn) or natural (a meadow); a wide expanse of green. Usually in heavily forested, densely populated, or somewhat arid areas, swards stand out by contrast. Also spelled *swarth*.

LEA—A grassland or meadow, especially one that's gone untilled for a while, as in Gray's "The lowing herd winds slowly o'er the lea." Also spelled *ley* (both forms are pronounced either "lee" or "lay"), it's more aggressively poetical than most of these terms.

SWALE—The thing is, it's cool. Either it's cool because it's shady, or it's cool because it's moist, if not out-and-out marshy. Or both. (They don't always say which.) Also spelled *swail*.

In the Valley

VALE—A broad, low-sided valley, generally with a good-sized stream running through it. (By extension, it's the world as a scene of sorrows, with that stream turned into tears.)

DALE—Same as vale, though both more intimate (it's not always broad) and more upbeat (as in the expression "up hill and down dale"). A related word is *dell*, guaranteed to be both secluded and woodsy.

GLEN—From a Gaelic word meaning "mountain valley." Now any steep, narrow valley, generally remote and unfrequented—unless by elves.

In the Hills

DOWNS—A plural form (or, less frequently, *down*, the singular). An expanse of hilly, grassy upland, good for grazing. Also, the short-wooled sheep developed there. After the Downs, two parellel hill ranges in southern England.

WELD—The same open, rolling country, but with lots of woods. After the Weald, a once-forested area of Kent, Surrey, and Sussex, in southern England. Say "weeld." (From the same root: *wold*, an elevated tract of open country or moorland, not necessarily wooded, as in the Cots*wold*s.)

TOR—England's short on mountains, and this is about as rugged as the landscape gets: a rocky peak, craggy hill, or—at its least dramatic—a pile of rocks on top of a hill.

TARN—A small mountain lake without significant tributaries. Wordsworth and D. H. Lawrence liked to pause by same.

By the Lake

MERE—Not just the lakes of the Lake Country (e.g., Windermere, Grasmere, Buttermere). Can be as small as a pond, and is sometimes used of a marsh. Water's what's important: The word is related to the Latin word for "sea."

RILL—A small brook or stream, a rivulet. No big deal, but your mere's probably fed by a few.

WEIR—A fence, enclosure of stakes, wattle, or what-have-you placed in a stream to trap fish. On a larger scale, a dam placed across a river or canal to raise or divert the water or to regulate its flow.

On the Farm

CROFT—A small enclosed field or pasture near a house. Sometimes the whole farm, if it's small and down on its luck (a tenant farm, for instance).

STILE—A set of steps or rungs up one side of a fence or hedge and down the other, of a sort that a person can negotiate easily but a cow can't.

THORP—Where they'll try to take you on Saturday night: the nearest small town or village. They may instead call it a *ham* or a *wick*. Look for all three words, now archaic, as elements in English place names.

At the Manor

CHASE—A privately owned, unenclosed game preserve. It's here that one rides to hounds. And that Lady Chatterley dallies with the gamekeeper.

HEDGEROW—A closely planted row of bushes, shrubs, or trees meant to function as a fence or boundary, or as a deliberate interruption of the view. One might make use of a stile to get over a low-slung hedgerow—though ideally not while a guest at a great estate. Save that kind of behavior for your weekend at the croft.

SHIRE—Another word for each of the counties into which England is divided. But the Shires is specifically the fox-hunting district of central England, consisting mainly of Leicestershire and Northamptonshire. Bear in mind, too, that "county life" counted (and counts) for a great deal in England: If one couldn't dazzle London, one might still dazzle one's shire.

In the Garden

BOWER—A shaded, leafy recess, an arbor, into which one withdraws to read or think, and which may be either natural or man-made. (Also, in poetry, a rustic cottage or similar country retreat, or simply a private chamber, even a boudoir.) Spenser's Bower of Bliss is the legendary one, but it's the rare country house that doesn't provide something that passes for a bower.

GAZEBO—A pavilion in the middle of a garden, usually trellised, latticed, cupolaed, and gingerbreaded within an inch of its life. The idea is to stand in it and look all around you: The word is a fanciful takeoff on the Latin future-tense construction, and means roughly, "I shall gaze."

HAHA—A staple in Jane Austen novels. It can be a moat, or just a fence, stone wall, or hedge sunk into the ground; either way, it encloses a garden or park without impairing the view. So called after the presumed exclamation of somebody encountering a particular haha for the first time.

THE CLASS STRUCTURE: THE DUKE AT THE TOP OF THE STAIRS

Frankly, it's a relentless business. Also, complicated and patently unfair. And that's today. In the nineteenth century, things were considerably worse; just ask Becky Sharp, Elizabeth Bennet, or Pip. But before you do, glance over this table, which, begging your pardon, sir or ma'am, begins just where you'd expect it to: at the very top.

The Royals

A class—and a law—unto themselves. Even now, there are those who consider everyone not born into it—and that includes dukes, duchesses, and the Queen Mother—little better than commoners.

KINGS AND QUEENS—Inaccessible, perhaps, but easy to pick out in a crowd, especially in the nineteenth century, during which there were only four of them. Victoria (reigned 1837–1901) needs no introduction here. Before her came a couple of Georges (between them, they reigned 1760–1830) and one William (IV, 1830–1837). N.B.: The younger George (who would become George IV) ruled from 1811–1820 for his father (III), who was declared hope-

"The Coronation of Queen Victoria" by Sir George Hayter.

lessly insane. This period—the Regency—was one of social complacency, moral laxity, and ostentatious display; provided abundant opportunities for clotheshorses and adventurers; and, in a way, provoked Victorianism.

Upon meeting the king or queen: Bow or curtsy—depending on your gender, not theirs—and say, "Your Majesty." Thereafter, say, "Sir," or "Ma'am."

PRINCES AND PRINCESSES—Although in fairly wide use on the Continent (French princes, for instance, are usually *not* royal and rank below dukes), in England the titles are reserved for the children of the sovereign and—feminists take note—those of his grandchildren who are descended through his sons; a ruling queen typically makes her husband a prince, too. (The grandchild provision explains today's Princess Alexandra, a granddaughter of George V through her father, the Duke of Kent; the husband one explains Prince Philip.) In the nineteenth century two princes figured prominently: George, the prince regent, and Albert, Victoria's husband, the prince consort. Prince of Wales is, as you've heard, the title traditionally conferred on the sovereign's oldest son.

Upon meeting a prince or princess: Bow or curtsy and say, "Your Royal Highness," subsequently, "Sir" or "Ma'am."

The Nobles

Or, as the English like to say, the peers of the realm, each of whom passes on his title—or, as often, package of titles—to his oldest son. Originally the whole business had to do with ownership of land, discharge of feudal obligations, and the wielding of actual power rather than with mere wealth and privilege. For the last few centuries, though, it's meant only that such hereditary peers (who come in five strengths), together with a few "life" peers (who come in only one and whose titles are not bequeathable) and Church of England bigwigs, sit together in the House of Lords and continue, with their wives and children, to provide England with her lords and ladies—and her much-debated class system. (The mnemonic you'll need to remember the five-tiered structure is "Do men ever visit Boston?") N.B.: A duchess, marchioness, etc., is most often the wife of a duke, marquess, etc.; however, if a woman is the oldest daughter of a duke (etc.) in a family with no male heirs, she becomes a duchess (etc.) "in her own right".

DUKES AND DUCHESSES: A very big deal, head and shoulders above the other degrees of the peerage. Historically, throughout Europe dukes controlled vast areas—like Bavaria and Normandy—and pretty much called their own shots. This was never the case in England, where the first duke wasn't created until 1338, but even so, they're a rare and much-deferred-to breed, a couple of dozen in number. There are a few "royal dukes," too, relatives of the sovereign like the late Duke of Windsor or the present Dukes of Gloucester, Kent, and York, who seem to like having a title beyond the "prince" that's theirs by birth. The title has also served as a reward for military heroes, like the Dukes of Marlborough and Wellington.

Upon meeting a duke, say, "Your Grace." His wife, the duchess, is "Your Grace," too.

MARQUESSES AND MARCHIONESSES: First of all, it's "MAR-kwiss" (even when spelled *marquis,* in the French manner) and "MAR-shuness," and it comes from "march," an old word for a border territory. The title wasn't well received at first (the first and second honorees complained that "Marquess is a strange name in this kingdom"), but eventually, with Tudor persistence, it gained acceptance. Formerly a reward for viceroys of India upon their return home, and, in 1917, a compensation to relatives of George V when he made them give up their obviously inappropriate German titles, there are almost as few marquesses around as there are dukes.

Upon meeting a marquess—or anybody from the four lower grades of the peerage— say, "My Lord." Call his wife "Madam."

EARLS AND COUNTESSES—William the Conqueror tried, back in the eleventh century, to substitute the Continental title *count,* but nobody bit: They were all too fond of the distinction between *eorl,* an Old English word meaning "man of position," and *ceorl,* an Old English word meaning "churl"; besides, *earl* was the only hereditary title around at the time, and it damn well *should* have a native flavor. (Women, on the other hand, seem to have had less resistance to the chic French import—hence *countess*.) Today there are a couple of hundred earldoms; particularly effective prime ministers, like Disraeli, the earl of Beaconsfield, and Anthony Eden, the earl of Avon, are rewarded with them when they retire.

VISCOUNTS AND VISCOUNTESSES: That's "VYE-count" and "VYE-countess," and the title originally designated the fellow who stood in for the count or, more precisely, given that this is England, the earl. (The *vis-* is like the *vice* in *vice-president*.) The most recently instituted of the five grades (1440), it's the accepted way to say thank you to a good speaker of the House of Commons.

BARONS AND BARONESSES: Low men on the peerage totem pole, taking in, originally, those Englishmen whose ancestors had fought, during the Middle Ages, in Wales, Scotland, and France, and, more recently, a number of industrialists and trade-union leaders (who are generally given the title only for life). As demonstration of their lack of precedence, barons are never referred to by their title, merely as Lord So-and-so. (For the record, the sequence goes, the duke of U, the marquess of V, the earl of W, the viscount X, and Lord Y.) Lord Y's wife is, similarly, Lady Y, never the baroness.

AS FOR THE KIDS—In general, only the oldest son comes out on top—though not until the old man kicks off. In the meantime, if that old man is a duke, marquess, or earl, the son is awarded a "courtesy" title, one of his father's lesser ones, to use: e.g., the son of a still-living duke of Wellington would be titled the Marquess Duoro until the major title comes free; eldest sons of viscounts and barons just have to wait. They, and everyone else in the second generation, make do—most of them for life—with what's called a courtesy style. If you're lucky (Daddy's a duke or marquess), you're "Lord" or "Lady": Lord John Brown, Lady Mary Brown (daughters of earls are "Ladies" too). If you're not so lucky, you get a simple "The Hon." (read: "The Honourable") to put before your name: The Hon. John Doe, The Hon. Jane Doe. As for the grandchildren: They're on their own unless they belong to the oldest son.

The Lesser Nobles

Or, depending on your point of view, the titled commoners. They come in two sizes: the baronet and the knight; don't look for either in the House of Lords.

BARONETS— Literally, "little barons." In 1611, King James I, needing capital, instigated "a new dignitie between Barons and Knights," open to anyone whose paternal grandfather had borne arms, who possessed an annual income of at least a thousand pounds, and who was willing to make a £1,095 down payment. While these Johnny-come-latelies were not, under any circumstances, to think of themselves as noble, they were encouraged to adopt the style Sir John Lately, Bt., and they could pass their title on to their—that's right—oldest son. *Vanity Fair*'s Sir Pitt Crawley—dirty, cynical, coarse—is one side of the baronet story.

Say: "Sir John." His wife is "Lady Lately."

KNIGHTS—The knight was the most significant figure in the feudal system, a mounted horseman who fought for his liege lord and defended the honor of his lady. For a while now, it's been the most frequently conferred "dignity" in England by far; allows the male recipient a "Sir" (his wife is "Lady") and the female recipient a "Dame" (her husband gets nothing); but wouldn't you know, it's guaranteed for one lifetime and one lifetime only.

Say: As with a baronet. Plus, "Dame Agatha."

The Gentry

They can be of birth as high and breeding as fine as the nobility; in fact, many of them are the descendants of that nobility's younger sons and daughters. But there's no getting around the fact that, as intimidating as their manners and as awesome as their fortunes may be, they are sadly lacking in one thing: titles. As the people at *Burke's* point out, they're the only untitled aristocracy in the world.

ESQUIRES—In the Middle Ages, the esquire (or squire) attended the knight and carried his gear. Once the Middle Ages were over, though, somebody decided that the category might be usefully applied to—and we quote—"the sons of peers, the sons of baronets, the sons of knights, the eldest sons of the younger sons of peers, and their eldest sons in perpetuity, the eldest son of the eldest son of a knight, and his eldest son in perpetuity, the king of arms, the herald of arms, officers of the Army or Navy of the rank of captain and upwards, sheriffs of counties for life, J.P.'s of counties whilst in commission, serjeants-at-arms, Queen's counsel . . ." and, well, you get the picture: It's a catchall, really, albeit one with connotations of both rank and real estate, and a way of appeasing any number of people who would otherwise risk seeming, in the eyes of the world, no better than their neighbors. It didn't really work out, though. While the Victorians jealously reserved *esquire* for the landed gentry, and withheld it from commercial and industrial types with too much and too new money, by the start of this century, the word had lost—through careless usage—almost all its distinction. Today the entire male population of Britain and Ireland is regularly so addressed (an "Esq." after their name taking the place of a "Mr." before it) by mail-order houses and book clubs.

A note on *squires:* Not so much an honor or even a slot in the hierarchy as a way of life. They were the big country landowners who exercised authority and financial leverage over their districts or villages, like Squire Western in *Tom Jones.* A paternal lot, who spoke in broad provincial dialect, rode to hounds, and weren't necessarily esquires (although they were certainly gentlemen; see below), the squirearchy was extinguished in England by the increasing taxes and creeping urbanism of the nineteenth century.

GENTLEMEN—Historically, of "gentle" birth, entitled to bear arms, owning at least three hundred acres of land, but lacking the larger distinction of being an esquire, let alone a knight or better. For more than a century now the word has had almost no agreed-upon meaning at all (as that old curmudgeon, H. W. Fowler, lamented, "We are all of us esquires now, and we are none of us gentlemen"), but in Jane Austen's day it was still something to keep in mind: Mr. Collins was considered an appropriate suitor for Elizabeth Bennet precisely because he was a gentleman, even though he was also a fool, a clergyman, and her cousin. (And Charlotte Lucas, a knight's daughter, no less, was happy to land him.)

And So On

Ugh: Mostly peasants, servants, grooms, tradesmen, and the like. Obviously, you won't be paying *them* your respects: It's enough that you're civil (but firm) with them and occasionally throw a little business their way. Nevertheless, there are a handful of folks whom, while they aren't gentry, mind you, one just might consider having a dance or two with on a slow Saturday night. They are the . . .

YEOMEN—And here we pass from what is basically the upper middle class to what is, at most, the middle middle one—small, independent farmers who, like the squirearchy, would be forced out of existence by the pressurized ways of nineteenth-century life, but who up until their demise as a class had a reputation for being sturdy and hardworking, sometimes even educated, and possessed the kind of integrity that England is always tapping you on the shoulder to tell you it has. Respectable, landowning, and they could vote, but Emma Woodhouse (see page 241) wouldn't let poor Harriet Smith marry one.

THE CLERGY: SAY AMEN, SOMEBODY

One of the quainter, and more confusing, fixtures in your nineteenth-century novel is the local clergyman. On the one hand, it was apparently hard to arrange an evening of whist without deferring to the rector; on the other hand, his wife always seemed to show up wearing someone's cast-off frock. Or was that the vicar's wife? And why, pray tell, wasn't the curate invited?

RECTOR—The head clergyman of a country parish, who had rights to the parish lands and owned its tithes. He held his post for life and could pass it on to his sons. In the eighteenth century, most rectors were the children of farmers and tradesmen, with no social status to speak of, but by the beginning of the nineteenth century, enough of them had made a killing in local agriculture to turn the clergy into a fit calling for the younger sons of gentry. As a result, the nineteenth-century rector was usually an educated gentleman who, in theory at least, was the social equal of the local squire, with whom he was expected to play cards and go grouse hunting. He functioned as if he were a landowner and often devoted most of his time to raising crops more profitably while his underpaid assistants ran the church. In reality, however, most rectors had neither the independent income, nor the knack for turning a profit from parish lands, necessary to keep up a gentleman's lifestyle. They were often dependent on upper-class patrons who treated them like poor relations. The classic example of this type of rector is, once again, the insufferable Mr. Collins, who spends his life fawning upon his patroness, the Lady Catherine de Bourgh.

VICAR—A sort of free-lance parson who stands in for a dead or absent rector or who heads a parish in which the tithes belong to someone else (e.g., the local squire). The vicar lived in a vicarage instead of a rectory, collected an allowance or salary in lieu of tithes, had no control over the land, and was only a transient (which is to say, he hadn't been established in the neighborhood for generations). In terms of education and breeding, however, he was the equal of a rector and, if he had a big enough independent income, could one-up him. After tithes were abolished in England in 1936, the terms *rector* and *vicar* became synonymous.

PARSON—A very general term (thought to derive from the French *personne*, which, reassuringly, means "person") for the head of a parish—i.e., a rector or a vicar—or for any Protestant minister below the rank of bishop who has enough authority to conduct religious services.

CURATE—Assistant to the rector or vicar, who usually did most of the tedious church work of the parish. Members of the "inferior clergy," curates were known for being poor, insecure, and a little uncouth; in your novel, the curate will probably have a large brood of ragged children for whom the gentle heroine is constantly making up baskets of provisions. Don't confuse the English curate with the French *curé*, or "parish priest." (And *le vicaire* is conversely, *le curé*'s assistant.)

BEADLE—A minor parish officer who ushers people in and out of Sunday services, delivers messages for the parson, and generally keeps the parishioners, especially the small boy parishioners, in line. In short, a sort of church constable.

SEXTON—A kind of dignified janitor, who takes care of church property, rings the church bells, and digs the graves.

THE DRINKS: WHAT TO SERVE WITH THE OYSTERS, THE SOUP, THE FISH, THE SAVOURY, THE GAME, THE TRIFLE, AND THE CIGAR

First, you need to know that upstairs, the lords and ladies drank wine, bottles and bottles of it. Oh, a gentleman in need of fortification might have the occasional brandy or, if the day was hot and he was in a democratic mood, a beer, but wine was, for centuries, the traditional beverage of the upper classes. In the nineteenth century, when French wines became available again for the first time in a hundred years and vintage wines were all the rage, any gentleman worthy of the name was expected to keep a well-stocked cellar, to provide six or seven varieties with dinner, and to deal with them as a connoisseur. As Routledge's *Etiquette for Gentlemen* put it back in 1865, "How to eat soup, and what to do with a cherry-stone are weighty considerations when taken as an index of social status; and it is not too much to say, that a man who elected to take claret with fish, or ate peas with his knife, would justly risk the punishment of being banished from good society." We agree, in principle . . . but what's claret?

CLARET—The British term for any red Bordeaux wine (luckily, they call their Burgundy Burgundy). Claret has a special niche in the English heart because back in the Middle Ages, when Eleanor of Aquitaine married Henry Plantagenet (see page 549), Bordeaux and its vineyards became British possessions. Ever since, claret has been the preferred table wine in upper-class British households. Even during the Francophobic eighteenth century, when the English monarchy tried to replace the French wine trade with that of the Portuguese, the French managed to smuggle claret into England by shipping it via Portugal. Still, claret didn't really come into its own in England until the nineteenth century, and the onset of the vintage-wine obsession. Claret was served with several different courses at Victorian dinners, and it was standard practice to have a few bottles on hand for high tea. Toward the end of the century, when society began to regard the seven-wine dinner as a bit excessive, claret, along with champagne, became the all-around dinner wine, and some young lords even began to substitute it for port as an after-dinner drink.

PORT—The drink of choice of the upper class; a sweet, red, fortified wine originally from Oporto, in Portugal. Although early port was simply mediocre Portuguese table wine, Portugal (as Britain's oldest continuous ally) always got such favorable trade agreements, and shipped so much wine to England, that eventually the English got used to the stuff. The *cult* of port, however, didn't start until the nineteenth century, by which time the Portuguese had learned two important things: One, if they put the wine in a flat-sided bottle and left it lying around for a long time, it tasted better; and two, adding a little brandy not only helped it "travel," but also provoked an altogether more enthusiastic response from the consumer. Before long, the British nobility was passing the port, tenderly decanted, with the venison, the game, the cheese, and again with dessert; and gentlemen looked forward to tossing off another glass or two (which in the parlance of the day meant at least a bottle apiece) after the ladies had retired to the drawing room. This, by the way, was vintage port that had been aged at least twenty years, the absolute minimum before the wine was considered fit to drink. It was traditional for the well-heeled Victorian father to lay down a pipe of port (about 140 U.S. gallons' worth) at the birth of his son or godson, to be opened after the boy's twenty-first birthday. The equivalent gesture today, in terms of generosity, might be to present the boy with a kilo of cocaine.

HOCK—Although hock originally referred to wine from the area around Hochheim, Germany, it became a general British term for any white Rhine wine. In Victorian times, hock's place was on the dinner table, in its traditional green glass, next to the claret with the roast meat course and the dessert.

SACK—At various points in British history, sack referred to a dry white wine from Spain or the Canary Islands, or to a heavy, sweetened, amber-colored wine from any of several Mediterranean wine-producing regions. Very popular in Shakespeare's day, it eventually gave way to sherry-sack, or sherry.

SHERRY—The world's most popular fortified wine. Sherry comes from Spain, although the British are, in a way, its adoptive parents. Real sherry, according to them, comes from Andalusia, Spain (the name "sherry" is an anglicization of Jerez, the capital of the sherry region), the way real champagne comes from the Champagne region of France. The British have always preferred the *finos*, the light, dry sherries, which makes the best aperitifs. Americans, by contrast, are mainly familiar with the *olorosos*, the second, and inferior, type of sherry, which is sweet, heavy, earthy, and the basis for brands like Harvey's Bristol Cream. There's no such thing as a vintage sherry, but *finos* can be very elegant; the Victorians used to like them with the fish and soup at the beginning of a meal, and again at the end, with dessert. They believed sherry should be properly decanted and served in ordinary wine glasses, never in those thimble-sized "sherry glasses" common today. Amontillado, which you probably remember from Edgar Allan Poe's horror story, is a medium dry sherry, halfway between a *fino* and an *oloroso*.

MADEIRA—A heavily fortified white wine from the Portuguese island of Madeira. This was one of the first fortified wines to make it big in England, having arrived in the seventeenth century along with the Portuguese bride of Charles II, Catherine of Braganza. (Actually, Catherine brought the whole island as part of her dowry, but Charles, who was having a cash-flow problem at the time, settled for money instead.) Catherine loved to sip Madeira in the morning as she munched a slice of Madeira cake; before long all the fashionable ladies of the kingdom got into the habit of tossing off a little glass to get the day started, a practice that lasted well into the Victorian era. As a result, Madeira, besides being a standard dessert wine, had a reputation as a ladies' drink. For the record, Madeira comes both dry and sweet; malmsey, in a butt of which Richard II allegedly drowned his two innocent little nephews, was one of the sweet varieties.

SAUTERNE—The greatest of the white Bordeaux wines, grown in the Sauternes region of the province of Bordeaux. It is a sweet, intense, fruity wine served, then and now, with dessert.

TOKAY—Another sweet dessert wine; as you can see, the end of a Victorian dinner was a little like the climax of a fireworks display, with five or six wines being presented simultaneously, along with the cakes. This one is golden brown and comes from the town of Tokay, or Tokaj, in Hungary.

NEGUS—Back in Samuel Pepys's time, this was a simple mixture of wine, water, and sugar named for one Colonel Negus, whose accomplishments are somewhat vague. Johnson and Boswell (see page 214) drank about a bottle of negus apiece every night. Later, because port was the wine most commonly used to make the concoction, negus came to mean mulled port.

MEAD—A sweet, fermented honey or honey-flavored wine the Babylonians were drinking back in 2000 B.C. (For your trivia collection: They declared mead the official wedding drink, stipulating that the bride's parents be required to keep the groom well supplied with "the wine of the bee" for the month following the marriage; that month became known as *honeymonth*, hence our *honeymoon*.) It was a great favorite of the ancient Britons, who believed in its powers as an intoxicant, a medicine, and an aphrodisiac. For centuries, making mead was a sort of cottage industry in English monasteries. It began to die out, partly because Henry VIII suppressed the monasteries and partly because the English honeybee went into a slump. Samuel Pepys caught Charles II drinking metheglin, a kind of spiced mead, as late as the seventeenth century, but the wine became virtually extinct after that. Two reasons to know what it is: You're sure to run across the term somewhere in English Lit., and recently, in a fever of nostalgia, mead-making became a British cottage industry all over again.

So much for the goings on upstairs. Downstairs and out on the farms, respectable working folk were consuming vast quantities of beer (in 1876 alone, they downed thirty-four gallons for every man, woman, and child in the country). Beer drinking was not only respectable, it smacked of patriotism; nearly everyone brewed his own at home (or rather, *her* own—brewing was considered woman's work) from local English barley. What's more, it was a lot safer than drinking from the typhoid-ridden public water systems, which is why ten-year-old boys at Eton and Harrow drank beer for breakfast as a matter of course. Naturally, with a lifetime of beer drinking—and custom-beer drinking at that—behind one, some very specific tastes arose, such as:

BITTER—A traditionally English and still very popular type of draught, or keg, beer (although now you can find it in little bottles) that is light, dry, strong, and relatively high in both hops and alcohol content (compared, that is, with the lager-type beers favored in the U.S.; bitter is neither the strongest nor the bitterest beer in England). Always ordered as "a pint of bitter," which will get you a tankard, and never to be confused with bitters, the root extract used to spike a cocktail.

PORTER—A dark brown, heavily hopped brew with a 6 to 7 percent alcohol content (most U.S. beers average 3 to 6 percent) and a taste of roasted malt. Porter, which was originally called "porter's beer" or "porter's ale," probably because it started out as a drink for porters and other common laborers, was an exception to the nineteenth-century trend toward lighter, less alcoholic beers, and it became one of the great pop hits of its time. Rumored to be more healthful than beer, it was a big favorite with actresses and singers, who swore by its salutary effects on their voices, and one election campaign revolved around the slogan "Peace, Plenty, and Porter." It turned out to be just a flash in the pan, though; today porter is virtually extinct.

STOUT—An even stronger, more heavily hopped version of porter. This one managed to hang on, thanks to the Guinness family, with whom the word *stout* is now more or less synonymous.

As for the class distinctions of beer (which, by the way, is the same thing as ale in Britain), they're a little tricker than those of wine. Although, on the whole, beer was a working-class drink, it did have its fans among the upper echelons, including the residents of certain colleges at Oxford and Cambridge—most of which had their own breweries—who became famous for producing a very dark, semi-lethal collector's item called "Audit Ale." Moreover, the rise of the big English breweries around the beginning of the nineteenth century changed the whole picture. Great fortunes were made and, with them, great families, whose members suddenly bore titles and sat in the House of Lords. Under the circumstances, beer drinking pretty much had to become socially acceptable. Today, among beers, anything goes, with the possible exception of a sweetish variety called "mild," which still has a faintly low-class image.

Meanwhile, sailors and other rough trade, when they weren't drinking beer, were downing:

GROG—Any liquor, but especially rum, that's been diluted with water. Grog was named after Admiral Edward Vernon (whom the sailors called "Old Grog" because he always wore a grogram coat), who gave the order that the daily rations of rum aboard Her Majesty's ships be diluted. Pretty soon, taverns catering to sailors had taken up the practice, and grog became what one settled for when one couldn't afford a stiffer dose.

And at the bottom of the barrel, so to speak, the wretched rabble were killing themselves with bad English GIN. Gin had been promoted back at the start of the eighteenth century by William of Orange, who considered it the perfect drink for the workingman, forgetting, for the moment, that the only decent gin was still being produced in Holland and was much too expensive for poor people. So the lower orders bought what they could afford, lured by the promise of getting "drunk for a penny, dead-drunk for two-pence, and straw for nothing" (meaning that the pub owner would drag them to the cellar to let them sleep it off), and for the rest of the century, gin drinking leveled the poor like a plague. By the mid-nineteenth century, the gin epidemic had begun to taper off, except for the curious defection of many respectable working-class women from beer to gin, after which gin was nicknamed "Mother's Ruin."

THE CARRIAGES: WHEELS OF FORTUNE

In the nineteenth century, one's carriage, or carriages, had as many social connotations as one's car, or cars, do in Los Angeles today. (Of course, back then, one had to be at least moderately upper crust to own a carriage at all.) Yet most of us, faced with the mention of a cabriolet, are at as much of a loss as Jane Eyre would have been at the mention of a Volvo station wagon. The following guide may be of some help; keep in mind, however, that *all* carriages were custom-made, and hybrids abounded.

PHAETON—Any of a bewilderingly large family of four-wheeled open carriages that marked the carriage's turning point from means-of-transportation to status symbol. The earliest models, the eccentric and risky Highflyers, inspired the prince regent—and eveyone

Phaeton

else—to take up driving as a sport. Later, when the regent, now George IV, became too fat to climb into the original version, a low phaeton (pronounced "FAY-ut-en") was devised. Drawn by docile ponies, the low phaeton became the only acceptable vehicle for a lady to drive.

CURRICLE—A racy little Italian import, also fashionable during the Regency, when young gentlemen prided themselves on being accomplished "whips." Two-wheeled, and drawn by a pair of horses instead of just one, curricles were built for speed. They were used for both town and country driving and became very popular in the trendy aristocrat's version of drag racing.

CABRIOLET—The sports car of its time; superseded the curricle as the carriage for the fashionable man-about-town. Considered the perfect bachelor's carriage, it held two passengers comfortably, sheltered by a hood with a curtain that could be drawn for privacy. Relatively economical since it was pulled by only one horse, the cabriolet nevertheless allowed for a certain amount of ostentation: One could—and did—equip one's carriage with the largest,

Cabriolet

finest horse one could find, accessorized, in case anyone missed the point, by the tiniest available groom.

BROUGHAM—The discreet, black, coachman-driven affair used by nervous peers in old Jack-the-Ripper movies. Simple, practical, and dignified, the brougham (pronounced "broom" or "BROO-em") was named after its originator,

Brougham

Landau

Lord Brougham, the lord chancellor of England. It was the one major innovation in coach-making under Queen Victoria, reflecting the shift to a more sober, moralistic mood, and it remained England's most popular closed carriage throughout the Victorian era.

VICTORIA—A French import, known on the other side of the Channel as a "Milord." This was another very popular, coachman-driven town carriage but, being open, or at most equipped with a folding hood, it was used mainly in summer. A great favorite with Victorian ladies, it was light, low, elegant, roomy, and easy to

Victoria

climb into, and it came with sweeping mudguards to protect voluminous skirts.

LANDAU—The nineteenth-century equivalent of a limo, the landau (pronounced "LAN-dow") was second in formality to the closed town coach (the nineteenth-century equivalent of a stretch limo). A large four-horse carriage used for long-distance travel and formal-dress occassions,

it held four passengers seated opposite each other (which led to its sometimes being called a "sociable-landau") and had a jointed hood that could be raised or lowered, as with a hard-topped convertible. At its most elaborate, the landau was led by two postillions and accompanied by two liveried outriders; all six horses were perfectly matched, of course.

BAROUCHE—Like a landau in structure and status but, because its folding hood covered only one of its seats, used almost exclusively as a summer carriage. The fact that owners usually liked to drive their barouches themselves also made them a little less formal than landaus. But the barouche is the one you'll find most often referred to in novels, marking ceremonial occasions, family outings, and sporting events. The snobbish Mrs. Elton, in Jane Austen's *Emma*, never misses a chance to tell everybody that her brother owns one, and Mr. Pickwick first meets amiable old Mr. Wardle while the latter is climbing out of his for a family picnic.

Barouche

GIG—The Volkswagen of the Victorian era; a light, open, one-horse carriage that carried one or two passengers perched directly above the two wheels. Not particularly elegant but com-

Gig

pact, economical, and maneuverable, gigs became increasingly popular as the century wore on. The country doctor, for one, nearly always drove up in his gig. Not acceptable for town use.

DOGCART—As popular as a suburban station wagon, and used in much the same way. Originally built to hold a sportsman's dogs in a ventilated storage boot beneath the seat, the dogcart had a fold-up footboard that could double as a seat, thereby accommodating four passengers back to back. Since practicality, not fashion, was what counted in country vehicles, most landowners kept at least one dogcart on the estate.

WAGONETTE—A big, plain, open wagon of a thing, with bench seats inside, made specifically for family excursions in the country. Although not elegant, wagonettes were very much in vogue for a while; Queen Victoria and the earl of

Chesterfield didn't mind owning them, and King Louis Philippe once sent Victoria the French version, called a *char-à-banc*, as a gift.

POST CHAISE—The gentlemanly alternative to sharing legroom in a large mail or passenger coach. One hired the post chaise in stages, from inn to inn. They were always painted yellow and were traditionally driven postillion by an elderly postboy dressed in a yellow jacket and a beaver hat. Although this was considered the first-class way to travel long distances, anyone looking for the equivalent of flying the Concorde had to own the private version of the post chaise, called a traveling chariot, emblazoned with the family crest.

HANSOM CAB—The "Gondola of London"; the vehicle hired taxi-style by Sherlock Homes and any other gentleman who couldn't afford, or didn't want, to keep a private carriage. For a

Hansom Cab

long time, hansoms were considered quite dashing; no respectable lady would be caught dead riding alone in one, or with any man other than her husband.

THE MONEY: A GUIDE FOR PICKPOCKETS, WASTRELS, AND FORTUNE HUNTERS

As some of you no doubt remember, David Copperfield was born with a caul, that is, with a portion of fetal membrane encasing his infant head, believed in those days to be a sign of good luck and a safeguard against drowning. David's mother having just been widowed (and financially reduced), the caul "was advertised for sale, in the newspapers, at the low price of fifteen guineas." A solitary bidder "offered two pounds in cash, and the balance in sherry," and subsequently the caul "was put up in a raffle . . . to fifty members at half-a-crown a head, the winner to spend five shillings." It was won by "an old lady with a handbasket, who, very reluctantly, produced from it the stipulated five shillings, all in halfpence, and twopence halfpenny short."

Now, how much money did the raffle realize—more than the desired fifteen guineas or less? And how much did the old lady pay? And what's a guinea anyway? We're glad you asked. Herewith, a guide to the intricacies of the English monetary system, back when England was calling the shots.

POUND—Or, more formally, the pound sterling, for over nine hundred years a symbol and index of Britain's power, wealth, and determination to get her way in the world. Originally, equivalent to a pound-weight of silver pennies, called sterlings (or "little stars," after the mark each was stamped with), later simply the basic unit of English currency—currency that was not foreign, not colonial, not debased, but "sterling," or lawful. It came in the form of a pound note (paper) or a sovereign (gold coin). The slang term is *quid*, always in the singular, and the sign, equivalent to our $, is a crossed *L*, £, from the first letter of *librum*, the Latin word for pound. Divided, prior to 1971's shift to decimals, into shillings and pence.

SHILLING—Twenty of them used to make up a pound, before they were discontinued in 1971. In its mood, not unlike our quarter: Lots of routine daily business was done in them; books, lunches, shoeshines, magazines, and gloves bought. Abbreviated *s.*, as in 12*s.*, or symbolized by a slash, as in 12/-, "twelve shillings even." The slang term is *bob.*

PENNY—In the plural, *pence,* twelve of which used to make up a shilling (and 240 a pound). Now the pound comprises one hundred *new* pence (or one hundred "p," pronounced "pee"). Used to be available in several denominations, among them the ha'penny (or halfpenny), tuppence (or twopence), thrippence (or threepence), fourpence (also called a groat), and sixpence (also called a tanner, also a teston). Abbreviated *d.*, from the Latin *denarius*, an old Roman coin. Thus £8 3s. 8*d.*—or, alternatively, £8/3/8—is eight pounds, three shillings, and eight pence.

There you have the basic units, simple enough provided you can remember there are twenty shillings in a pound and twelve pence in a shilling and not the other way around. But, as you know, the English don't like things to be *too* simple. So we have:

GUINEA—A little bigger than a pound—one shilling bigger, to be precise. At first a coin, made from gold from Guinea, with a little elephant stamped on it and meant to be employed specifically in the Africa trade. Since 1813, simply a unit—£1 1s.—traditionally used to state such quantities as professional fees, subscription amounts, and the value of pictures, horses, and estates. A "prestige" way of stating the cost of something, as well as a way of understating, pyschologically—à la $9.98—that cost.

FLORIN—A silver coin, with a flower on it, worth two shillings.

CROWN—Likewise silver, with a you-know-what stamped on it. Worth five shillings. (A half crown is, obviously, 2 1/2 shillings.)

FARTHING—A quarter of a penny. And still less worth having: the MITE—an eighth of a penny.

So Mrs. Copperfield advertised the caul for £15 15*s.* She received a £2-plus-sherry offer (not alluring, given that her own sherry was already on the market). At the raffle, fifty people paid 2 1/2 shillings (or a half crown) each, £6 5*s.* altogether. The old lady came up with an additional 5*s.*, less 2 1/2*d.* Total: £6 9*s.* 9 1/2*d.*, or considerably less than half the amount that had at first been asked. On the other hand, those were the days when a pound sterling was really a pound sterling.

Talking about what money will buy is tricky enough in one's own country on the day one is actually considering spending some of it. Arriving at exact equivalences over the decades and across national boundaries is almost impossible. Still, certain generalizations can be made. Among them:

(1) that inflation is not the inexorable force recent history—and especially recent British history— would lead us to believe it is. Since 1661, prices in Britain have alternately risen and fallen, fallen and risen, and only in the last generation gone haywire. While there was considerable inflation during the early part of the nineteenth century (what with the Napoleonic Wars), by the 1820s, things had pretty much leveled off. In fact, in 1911, on the eve of World War I, a pound would buy more than it did on the eve of the Great Plague of 1665.

(2) that international events gravely affect how many francs or dollars or quetzals the pound—or any other unit of currency—is worth. Around the time of the American Revolution, a pound brought between $4.50 and $5.00; that figure shot up to $12.00 during the American Civil War, returning to "normal" during 1880, not falling to a new "normal" level of about $2.50 until after World War II. Today it's worth well under $2.00.

(3) that not only does the perceived "formal" value of the pound fluctuate, so does the living standard of the society it serves, not to mention the degree to which transfer of cash, as opposed to, say, barter, or the providing of room and board by an employer, accounts for how that society spends its money. Thus, as the nineteenth century drew to a close, though few people were making more than a couple of pounds a week, just one pound would buy: six bottles of whiskey or thirty gallons of fresh milk or the rent of a shop or house for nearly a month or fifteen pairs of serviceable ladies' shoes.

(4) that not only do the perceived formal value of the pound and the living standard of the society fluctuate, so do buying habits, human needs, and customs of the country. For instance, money seems to go further in an agricultural society than in an industrial one; in a part of the country—or of the century—that boasts a lot of gardens and pastures, where the price of tomatoes, milk, and brussels sprouts seldom packs much of a wallop, than it does in town. Then, too, if there are no music halls or gin mills within a twenty-mile radius of your house, you don't allow for many evenings out in your entertainment budget.

All that said, let's look a little more closely at Dorothea Brooke, the heroine of George Eliot's *Middlemarch* (see page 241), who, in 1832, the year the First Reform Bill was passed by Parliament, can be overheard describing herself to a distraught Lydgate (who's just lost four or five pounds at the billiard table) as having "seven hundred a-year of my own fortune, and nineteen hundred a-year that Mr Casaubon left me, and between three and four thousand of ready money in the bank." Keeping in mind that a few years before, it has been estimated by a journal of the day, a family could live on a minimum income of one guinea a week, provided they didn't drink or "seek entertainment," you can see that this makes Dorothea—while no Barbara Hutton—a very wealthy woman. Moreover, not only was an 1832 pound worth at least fifteen of today's pounds, it *went* further, and living standards were lower, especially in Dorothea and Lydgate's small, not-yet-industrialized, north-of-England town. Given all of this, our Miss Brooke had an annual income that was the equivalent of at least $75,000 a year, with another $115,000 in her savings account, which, since she owned her own home and didn't care about jewels or parties, was more than enough to endow hospitals, found a village, and bail Lydgate out. As to where her income came from—that is, what it meant to have "seven hundred a-year" in the first place—you should know that rents on the land he owned were the major source of every aristocrat's income (as they still are for, say, Prince Charles). Of course, there were such things as a commercial class (relegated to London and other big cities), as profit, interest, and investment, but most country folk didn't get embroiled to any great extent: Better to "live on" one's own estate, in both senses of the phrase.

THE NAMES: ENGLISH AS A SECOND LANGUAGE

So we say Lord Tomato and they say Lord Tomahto; what's the big deal? We all speak the same language, right? Wrong. It turns out that *they* speak English and we just translate, more or less successfully, as you'll see from the following list of well-known names.

1. Bolingbroke (as in Henry IV's surname): BOLL-in-brook
2. Pepys (as in Samuel, the diarist): PEEPS
3. Cowper (as in William, the poet): COOP-er
4. Crichton (as in James, the Scottish Renaissance man known as "the Admirable Crichton," as well as all British families named Chrichton or Chreighton, and even the American novelist, Michael): CRY-ten
5. Cockburn (as in Alicia, the eighteenth-century wit; Sir Alexander, the nineteenth-century lord chief justice of England; plain old Alexander, the twentieth-century expatriate journalist; plus Cockburn Harbour and Cockburn Sound): CO-burn

Two Scottish cities:
6. Edinburgh: ED-in-burra
7. Glasgow: GLAZ-ko or GLAZ-go

Two place names that are easier to pronounce correctly if you don't smoke:
8. Marlborough: MARL-burra or MAR-burra
9. Pall Mall: PELL-MELL

One whose correct pronunciation may sound like an affectation, but isn't:
10: Queensberry (as in the marquis of): QUEENS-bry (and that's MAR-kwis)

One case of the language doing a double take:
11. Magdalen and Magdalene (the college at Oxford and the college at Cambridge): pronounced like "maudlin," which derives from the name Magdalen

And a few that follow rules:
12. The county names ending in *cester*—drop the *c* and the letter preceding it: Gloucester, Worcester, Leicester: GLOSS-ter, WOOS-ter, LESS-ter, also, their alternative names:
    Gloucestershire, Worcestershire, Leicestershire: GLOSS-te-sher, WOOS-te-sher, LESS-te-sher
13. The *wich*es—drop the *w*: Norwich, Woolwich, and the tip-off, Greenwich: NOR-ich, WOOL-ich, GREN-ich
14. The *wick*s—ditto: Northwick, Southwick, Warwick, Smithwick: NORTH-ick, SOUTH-ick, WAR-ick, SMITH-ick
15. A London *wark* that can get you coming and going: Southwark: SUTH-erk

16. The *ers*—say "ar" (but stay on your toes; the rule doesn't always apply): Berkeley (as in George, the Irish philosopher; Sir William, the colonial governor of Virginia; also, the former earldom and the square), Berkshire (the county), Derby (the borough, the earldom, and the English horse race): BARK-lee, BARK-sher, DAR-by. And a tricky one: Hertford: HAR-ferd

Finally, a couple of instances in which they insist on speaking English when they should be speaking French:

17. Beauchamp (as in Guy de, Richard de, Thomas de; London's Beauchamp Place, and Beauchamp Tower in the Tower of London): BEECH-em

18. Beaulieu (the town and the abbey): BYOO-lee

And, the ultimate in inscrutable British English:

19. Cholmondeley (a common last name): CHUM-lee

Guess Who's Coming to Dinner?

TWELVE FICTIONAL CHARACTERS WITH WHOM YOU SHOULD HAVE AT LEAST A NODDING ACQUAINTANCE

Literature does have its practical applications. For instance, suppose you're at a dinner party and you overhear your hostess describing you to the person on your left as "a real Baron de Charlus." What do you say to your new acquaintance? And how should you feel about your hostess? Or yourself? See below.

Baron de Charlus (from Proust's *Remembrance of Things Past*): A closet case. An aristocrat who travels in the best society, the Baron cultivates his image as a woman chaser while dating an eclectic assortment of boys on the sly. French aristocrats do this all the time, of course, but the Baron suffers from such a virulent strain of depravity that it not only leads him into scandal, it makes him prematurely senile.

Cousin Bette (from Balzac's *Cousin Bette*): An aging spinster consumed by hatred. An ugly duckling who, for various reasons, never metamorphosed into a swan, Bette is dependent on her relatives and is, therefore, forced to hide her envy and bitterness behind a facade of goodwill. She's nobody's fool, however; secretly, she's dedicated her life to ruining other people's.

Father Zossima (from Dostoevsky's *The Brothers Karamazov*): A famous church elder, holy and ascetic, who teaches a doctrine of love and forbearance. When he dies, a miracle is expected, but instead, his body begins to decompose almost immediately. Cynics point to this as a sign that his teachings were false. Ask yourself (*a*) if your hostess is a cynic, and (*b*) if you've had a checkup recently.

Isabel Archer (from James's *The Portrait of a Lady*): An intelligent, vivacious, high-minded American girl who's off to Europe in search of her Destiny. Which is to say she's headed for trouble. Isabel has her faults: She's naïve and a little presumptuous, she gets huffy when criticized, and she could do with a lesson or two in picking her friends. Still, you can't blame her for wanting to get out of Albany.

Julien Sorel (from Stendhal's *The Red and the Black*): A brilliant, hypocritical young parvenu. A misfit determined to make it in a society he despises, Sorel uses his love affairs to get ahead and almost manages to become a successful cad. He is both too smart and too sentimental for his own good, however; ultimately, he self-destructs.

Dorothea Brooke (from Eliot's *Middlemarch*): A young woman of great intelligence and integrity who longs to devote herself to a worthy cause. Her idealism gets her into a disastrous marriage with Mr. Casaubon, a menopausal scholar who can't see the forest for the trees. Dorothea's a sweet kid, but she really ought to lighten up a bit.

Alexey Vronsky (from Tolstoy's *Anna Karenina*): The dashing young officer for whom Anna Karenina abandons her husband, child, and respectable society life. Vronsky isn't really a bad sort, he just isn't neurotic enough to cope with a tragic love affair. He really does seem to take it hard when Anna throws herself under the train that's taking him away to war. Heck, all the poor guy wanted was a little space.

Emma Woodhouse (from Jane Austen's *Emma*): "Handsome, clever, and rich, with a comfortable home and a happy disposition," Emma has "lived nearly twenty-one years in the world with very little to distress or vex her." Too bad she's a terrible snob, an incurable gossip, a cold fish, and utterly blind both to her own faults and to the mess she makes trying to run everyone else's life.

Stephen Dedalus (from Joyce's *A Portrait of the Artist as a Young Man* and *Ulysses*): Well, you can take this one of two ways, as the critics have. On the one hand, Stephen may be a pretentious aesthete, an egomaniacal little prig who only *thinks* he's an artist. On the other hand, he may have talent. At any rate, he's not a bore; he has depth, intelligence, an abundance of Catholic guilt, a driving need to find a father figure, and a striking resemblance to James Joyce.

Eustacia Vye (from Hardy's *The Return of the Native*): Caution: Contents Under Pressure. Eustacia is stuck out on the heath with nothing to do and no one to talk to until Clym Yeobright comes home from Paris. Seeing him as her ticket to glamour and adventure, she marries him. Unfortunately, all he wants to do is teach school and spend quiet evenings in front of the fire. After a period of making herself and everyone else miserable, Eustacia drowns herself in a bog.

Marlow (from Conrad's *Lord Jim, Heart of Darkness,* and other tales): The narrator of long stories, usually told late at night over booze and cigars, in which one or another of Conrad's outcasts works his way through some agonizing and frequently fatal moral dilemma. Although Marlow claims to be baffled by whatever it is that "causes me to run up against men with soft spots, with hard spots, with hidden plague spots, by Jove! and loosens their tongues at the sight of me for their infernal confidences," he is really a sleuth of the soul, as perpetually on the lookout for a knotty problem as Ted Koppel.

Mrs. Ramsay (from Woolf's *To the Lighthouse*): Somebody's ideal of womanhood. Loving, tender, sensitive, instinctual, compassionate, and efficient, she copes gracefully with eight children, a demanding husband, a steady stream of houseguests, and the village poor—all on a tight budget—and still manages to age so beautifully that everyone who meets her wants to paint her portrait or carry her bundles. If you're anything like her, give us a call.

Three Important-Sounding Fallacies (and Two Important-Sounding Other Things) You May or May Not Want to Watch Out For

PATHETIC FALLACY

A phrase coined by the British critic and essayist John Ruskin to call attention to the tendency on the part of second-rate poets to attribute to nature the emotions and motivations of human beings. Ruskin cites a passage from a poem of the day, "They rowed her in across the rolling foam— / The cruel, crawling foam," then comments dryly, "The foam is not cruel, neither does it crawl. The state of mind which attributes to it these characters of a living creature is one in which the reason is unhinged by grief." However, while this practice might have struck Ruskin as, in his word, "morbid," *pathetic fallacy* is now a fairly neutral term used to designate any nature-as-human image, whether convincing (as in the hands of Shakespeare or Keats) or absurd (as above). Look for a lot of pathetic fallacy in the Romantic poets (where mountains mourn and fields smile) and in the novels of Thomas Hardy.

INTENTIONAL FALLACY

Or don't believe everything the author tells you—especially if he's trying to explain why he's written the book or play or poem at hand. For instance, Milton, up front in *Paradise Lost,* tells us he wants to "justify the ways of God to men." Don't (according to critics William K. Wimsatt, Jr., and Monroe Beardsley, who came up with the term *intentional fallacy*) count on it. And even if it's true, if that's precisely why Milton thinks he wrote his epic, so what? Who *cares* why he thought he wrote it? The Big Critical Issue here: Which counts more, the Author or the Work? Intentional fallacy was a favorite thing of the New Critics of the forties and fifties, who, having been force-fed historical and biographical background material when they were kids, now insisted on "close readings of the text." In other words, forget the Author, forget his Period; it's you and the night and the music. And the Critic, of course.

AFFECTIVE FALLACY

The flip side of the intentional fallacy, and likewise introduced by Wimsatt and Beardsley, who now warned against the "confusion between the poem and its *result* [what it *is* and what it *does*]"—i.e., it doesn't matter whether the night and the music (and the Critic) make you feel amorous, or melancholy, or afraid of the dark. Your emotional response to the poem or story or whatever doesn't matter any more than how the poet or novelist or whoever felt as he wrote it. How you react isn't the point; the poem (etc.) is the poem. Is the poem. Note that (*a*) the affective fallacy is what some critics think happens when somebody puts a lot of emphasis, as Aristotle did, on a goal like catharsis (see page 260), and (*b*) both the intentional and affective fallacies are battle cries, not neutral terms like *pathetic fallacy,* and not open-and-shut cases.

OBJECTIVE CORRELATIVE

T. S. Eliot's idea. It means that a good poet, playwright, or novelist doesn't write, "H-m-m, how sad, even pathetic, that girl looks, the one over there by that rock, who lives, I think, by the River Dove"; he says instead, at least if he's Wordsworth, "A violet by a mossy stone." Eliot maintained that the objective correlative—the concrete and specific image—is "the only way of expressing emotion in the form of art," and he defines it as "a set of objects, a situation, a chain of events which shall be the formula of that *particular* emotion, such that when the external facts, which must terminate in sensory experience, are given, the emotion is immediately evoked." Whatever; she still looks sad to us.

NEGATIVE CAPABILITY

Hard to get a clear definition here, even though everybody from F. Scott Fitzgerald to service-magazine journalists behaves as if he knows exactly how and when to deploy it. The phrase is Keats's, and he kept using it in letters to friends in slightly different, and slightly vague, senses. Somebody must have called him on it (not that it did much good), because, in 1817, Keats glosses "negative capability" in yet another letter: ". . .that is, when a man is capable of being in uncertainties, Mysteries, doubts, without any irritable reaching after fact & reason." Lionel Trilling (see page 34) interpreted this to mean "a way of dealing with life," "to make up one's mind about nothing—to let the mind be a thoroughfare for all thoughts," to trust the subconscious and not "try too hard in coming at a truth." F. Scott's reading of it (in *The Crack-Up*) was a little different: "The test of a first-rate intelligence is the ability to hold two opposed ideas in the mind at the same time, and still retain the ability to function. One should, for example, be able to see that things are hopeless and yet be determined to make them otherwise." Other people seem to think negative capability is related to empathy. Or integrity. Or objectivity. Anyway, according to Keats, Shakespeare had a lot of it. Who knows? So might you.

Three Twentieth-Century Novels to Reckon With

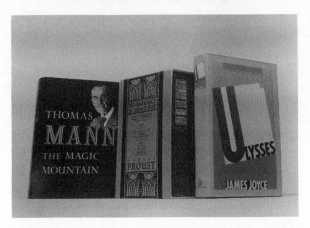

Sure they're long, and none of them's exactly a cliff-hanger. But that doesn't mean you have to spend the rest of your life tiptoeing around these monuments of High Modernism, one English, one French, one German.

ULYSSES (1922)
JAMES JOYCE

What did his limbs, when gradually extended, encounter?

New clean bedlinen, additional odours, the presence of a human form, female, hers, the imprint of a human form, male, not his, some crumbs, some flakes of potted meat, recooked, which he removed.

If he had smiled why would he have smiled?

To reflect that each one who enters imagines himself to be the first to enter whereas he is always the last term of a preceding series even if the first term of a succeeding one, each imagining himself to be first, last, only and alone, whereas he is neither first nor last nor only nor alone in a series originating in and repeated to infinity.

The novel as cab ride: potholes, gridlock, minority-group parades, plus the springs are shot and the driver's smoking a cigar. The trick is to sit back, ignore the meter, and try not to anticipate the destination. Go easy on yourself: Linearity—getting from A to B—was never much on Joyce's mind and it doesn't have to be much on yours either. More than any other, this is a book not to stand on ceremony with.

But it is a book to be careful around. An eyes-in-the-gutter, *Life*-goes-to-a-bad-dream mutant of a novel, it's still every bit as off-putting as you found it the first time around. (The passage above, from the "Ithaca" chapter, in which Leopold Bloom—an advertising-space salesman in 1904 Dublin, exhausted husband to Molly, would-be father to Stephen Dedalus, and twentieth-century analogue to Ulysses, a.k.a. Odysseus (see page 251), the most down-to-earth yet cunning of the Greek heroes—comes home and goes to bed, is as easy as the going gets.) The basic problem with *Ulysses* is, of course, that there's too much in it: the *Odyssey*-mimicking structure, the linking of each of the eighteen episodes with a different academic discipline *and* a different bodily organ, the symbols and allusions, the puns and parodies, the cast of dozens (all Irish and all voluble), the determination to do it all, both expressionistically and documentarily, and in eighteen hours and forty-five minutes, no less. Then there's Joyce himself, who, while he may be, as Eliot pronounced, "the greatest master of language in English since Milton," is also a show-off of the worst, third-grader-with-a-father-who-writes-for-television sort.

Two tips: Don't be afraid to browse. Find an episode you like. *Then* graze; let Joyce's precise, unflagging, comic, and consolational portrayal of life take hold. And don't be proud: A guide, like Stuart Gilbert's *James Joyce's "Ulysses"* or Harry Blamires's *The Bloomsday Book*, both of which provide page-by-page assistance, will help you over the rough patches.

REMEMBRANCE OF THINGS PAST
(1913–1927)
MARCEL PROUST

. . . since the accident to her jaw, [Mme. Verdurin] had abandoned the effort involved in real hilarity, and had substituted a kind of symbolical dumb-show which signified, without endangering or even fatiguing her in any way, that she was "laughing until she cried." At the least witticism aimed by any of the circle against a "bore," or against a former member of the circle who was now relegated to the limbo of "bores"—and to the utter despair of M. Verdurin, who had always made out that he was just as easily amused as his wife, but who, since his laughter was the "real thing," was out of breath in a moment, and so was overtaken and vanquished by her device of a feigned but continuous hilarity—she would utter a shrill cry, shut tight her little bird-like eyes, which were beginning to be clouded over by a cataract, and quickly, as though she only just had time to avoid some indecent sight or to parry a mortal blow, burying her face in her hands, which completely engulfed it, and prevented her from seeing anything at all, she would appear to be struggling to suppress, to eradicate a laugh which, were she to give way to it, must inevitably leave her inanimate. So, stupefied with the gaiety of the "faithful," drunken with comradeship, scandal and asseveration, Mme. Verdurin, perched on her high seat like a cage-bird whose biscuit has been steeped in mulled wine, would sit aloft and sob with fellow-feeling.

The novel as flotation tank. Except that it feels more like you're suspended in mayonnaise than floating on water, and, far from sensory deprivation, it's sensory inundation that the experience winds up being all about. Your host(s): Marcel, a fictitious first-person narrator as well as the author whose name appears on the cover. The length of your session: three thousand pages, distributed over seven dense volumes, five resonant locales, half a dozen impressive drawing rooms, and between seven and ten major love affairs (depending on whether you count Marcel's infatuation with his mother and his grandmother as one or two, and his passionate discovery of his literary calling, on page two thousand nine hundred and something, at all).

Begin (and, if you must, end) with *Swann's Way,* the first volume in the heptology; for conversational purposes, at least, you'll have read Proust. You won't meet many people who've made it through the whole thing; besides, the narrative eventually comes full circle, and virtually all its important themes and characters are presented here. Shifting back and forth in time and space, the narrator first recalls his childhood in the relatively innocent town of Combray, then goes on to tell of the doomed obsession of Robert Swann, an elegant dilettante, with an unworthy tart named Odette de Crécy. (Later, all the characters will exchange roles and masks until they're unidentifiable, and everyone you've met along the way will either die or turn out to be gay.) This segment will also give you a perfectly adequate take on Proust's prose style; in fact, by the time you come stumbling back into the sunlight, you'll feel positively intimate with the interminable, serpentine sentences; the constant, unstoppable metaphors, analyses, and digressions; and the schizophrenic shifts from gloomy reverie to bitchy social comedy—all in a way that you'll find hard to explain to your roommate.

Chic and snobbish, Proust is nevertheless out to alter consciousness, to make the impossible connections, to demonstrate the relationships, real or illusory, between transcendence and trendiness, art and love, the self and the other, people and birds: His theories of relativity give Einstein's a run for the money.

THE MAGIC MOUNTAIN (1924)
THOMAS MANN

They even took Karen, one afternoon, to the Bioscope Theatre in the Platz—she loved it all so very much. The bad air they sat in was offensive to the three, used as they were to breathing the purest; it oppressed their breathing and made their heads feel heavy and dull. Life flitted across the screen before their smarting eyes: life chopped into small sections, fleeting, accelerated; a restless, jerky fluctuation of appearing and disappearing, performed to a thin accompaniment of music, which set its actual *tempo* to the phantasmagoria of the past, and with the narrowest of means at its command, yet managed to evoke a whole gamut of pomp and solemnity, passion, abandon, and gurgling sensuality. It was a thrilling drama of love and death they saw silently reeled off; the scenes, laid at the court of an oriental despot, galloped past, full of gorgeousness and naked bodies, thirst of power and raving religious self-abnegation; full of cruelty, appetite, and deathly lust, and slowing down to give a full view of the muscular development of the executioner's arms. Constructed, in short, to cater to the innermost desires of an onlooking international civilization. . . .

The novel as triathlon, with politics, philosophy, and science where the bike, the water and the foam-rubber inner sole should be. Not hard to read, exactly: Unlike Joyce and Proust, Mann—ever the burgher, never the bohemian—gives you a crystal-clear picture of the action; while things get strange, they're never unrecognizable. But you do need mucho endurance to get through the lectures on duty and rationalism and Marxism and Eros and vitalism, each delivered by a different Old World spokesperson with an ax to grind.

Itself exhausted, yet moving relentlessly from minute to minute, week to week, and finally year to year, *The Magic Mountain* keeps its hero, the "unremarkable" Hans Castorp, virtually immobile in a sanitarium for the tubercular, located high in the Alps in the days "before the Great War." The sanitarium, of course, is Europe and Castorp's fellow inmates are Europe's dispossessed: progressive radicals, reactionary Jesuits, cat-eyed Russians. Everyone's a patient. And a captive. Ditto the reader. And the amazing thing about the book is that, as a Munich woman wrote to Mann, "I was not bored by your novel, and with every page I read I was astonished that I was not bored."

If you don't get bored, it'll be despite Mann's craftsmanship (labored, ham-fisted) and storytelling technique (old-fashioned, digressive), and because of his subject, which couldn't be more to the point: art, alienation, and apocalypse. Mann, an architect (to Proust's painter, Joyce's sculptor), has taken a condemned site—all that rotting yet reassuring pre–World War I culture—and built a skyscraper on it. And everybody from J. Alfred Prufrock to Woody Allen has had lunch in its ground-floor restaurant.

Gifts from the Greeks

A FEW ENRICHING IDEAS FROM THE CLASSIC CLASSICAL CIVILIZATION

HOMERWORK

True, the scholars can't be sure that he was really blind, that he was really a wandering minstrel, that he really wrote both (or either) the *Iliad* and the *Odyssey,* or that he even really existed. For the record, most of the scholars now seem to believe that there were two poets at work here, the *Odyssey* poet having been preceded (and influenced) by the *Iliad* poet, and some of them seem to think that *homer* was an archaic Greek verb meaning "to set to verse." Whatever; given how old you—not to mention the poems—are, it's probably easier just to go on filing them under the name Homer and hoping for the best.

What we do know: that both poems are epics, telling memorable, larger-than-life stories in memorable, larger-than-life language; that both concern the Trojan War (but, even taken together, tell only a small part of the story of that war); that they were almost certainly composed sometime in the eighth century B.C., nearly four hundred years after the events they describe; and that they were meant to be recited, not read.

We also know that Western literature begins here. Not only have the *Iliad* and the *Odyssey,* like the Old Testament, never been dropped from the syllabus, they're the cornerstone for the whole epic tradition: Virgil's *Aeneid,* Dante's *Divine Comedy,* Milton's *Paradise Lost,* down through—with the emphasis on the "down"—Joyce's *Ulysses* (see page 246). None of which makes for the world's easiest read; those embarking on same are advised to bear in mind that (a) people in the eighth century B.C. thought of people in the twelfth century B.C. as being bigger, stronger, and better acquainted with the gods than they themselves were (result: a degree of overstatement, and of man/god interaction, that's less just for effect than it is from the heart), and (b) all those "wine-dark sea"s, "rosy-fingered dawn"s, and "Poseidon, shaker of earth"s, while they might have you nodding off, helped both the poet remember his lines and the audience get into the mood (after all, you didn't object when Billy Joel sang "don't go changing" twenty-five times in the same song).

Attention, please: While you don't really have to read both (or either) the *Iliad* and the *Odyssey,* you'd be advised to at least have an opinion as to which you like better; some people will even treat your preference as a short-form personality inventory. Which is precisely why we've prepared the chart below, *Iliad* on the left, *Odyssey* on the right:

Iliad

Odyssey

	Iliad	*Odyssey*
Setup	Prepare to stay put: a bleak, embattled beach outside the gates of Troy (a.k.a. Ilium—hence the title—in present-day Turkey), in the last months of the ten-year siege the Greeks have undertaken to avenge the wifenapping of luscious Helen from Spartan king Menelaus by Trojan prince Paris	Don your life jacket: thousands of nautical miles and dozens of ports of call, over the course of ten years and much of the eastern Mediterranean, as Odysseus—one of the heroes of the siege of Troy—tries to get home to Ithaca
Main Characters	The Greek Achilles (your basic tragic hero, noble in all things and dashing to the max, but too proud and vengeful for his own good) and the Trojan Hector (a hero himself, stuck fighting a war neither of his own making nor worthy of him)	Odysseus (alias Ulysses, prudent, resourceful, and a born survivor), his son Telemachus (left at home for twenty years, trying to keep things together while wondering where his father—and his sense of self—is), his wife Penelope (long-suffering, likewise resourceful, fending off a clutch of suitors by weaving and unweaving her prenuptial tapestry)
Supporting Cast	On the Greek side: Agamemnon (the king and general, brave but flusterable), Ajax (the consummate soldier, strong, daring, not too swift), Odysseus (see opposite), Patroclus (sweet and gentle, Achilles's "special" friend); on the Trojan side: Priam (king of Troy, father of both Hector and Paris); hovering over all: most of the gods and goddesses, rooting for one team or the other	The fantastical creatures (the women are especially memorable) Odysseus encounters along the way, like Calypso, Circe, the Sirens, the Cyclopes, Scylla and Charybdis, etc., etc.; the kings Telemachus preps under, Nestor (wise and seasoned) and Menelaus (courtly and considerate); Penelope's suitors, as a group; the goddess Athena, presiding over the whole and protecting Odysseus and company

	Iliad	*Odyssey*
Plot Summary	Agamemnon and Achilles quarrel over distribution of booty; Achilles goes off to sulk in tent; war goes on without him; Patroclus, wearing Achilles' armor, is slain by Hector; Achilles, in rage and despair, slays Hector; Achilles and Priam weep together at Hector's funeral	Double (but simple) plot: Odysseus tries—and tries and tries—to get home as Telemachus defies suitors and finally sets out in quest of him; two (characters and plots) are finally united on Ithaca; father and son slay suitors
Genre	Tragedy (said to be ancestor of the drama)	Comedy (said to be ancestor of the novel)
Themes	Manliness, force, duty, *arete* (see page 260); war (obviously), including fighting, killing, plundering; the male impulse	Sensitivity, longing, home and family; the quest for identity and intimacy; the roles of wit and luck, treachery and loyalty; the female principle
Structure	An examination, lasting 16,000 lines, of a single, well-defined incident in the Trojan War (and including neither the war's beginning nor its end); focused, unified, selective	The double plot, natch, plus 12,000 lines of stories from everybody you meet along the way; more episodes than a year's worth of *Love Boat*s; complex, inclusive, digressive
Tone	Sublime, intense	Sophisticated, wry
Rating	Preferred throughout antiquity; the aristocratic choice (everybody in it is an aristocrat or a god, and everybody who listened to it was probably one, too)	Favorite of contemporary readers (as borne out by trade-paperback sales figures); the popular choice (a vote for people in all shapes and sizes, including women, and with all manner of tales to tell)

But don't cast your ballot now; better to read a passage or two in each, decide which speaks to what's going down at the moment for you. (Try Priam's speech to Hector, *Iliad*, Book XXII, lines 25–76; with the *Odyssey* you're better off skimming till you find something you like.) Then take sides. And one more thing: Hit a dull or a bumpy spot—in the *Iliad*, the *Odyssey*, or anyplace else where for the most part you've been getting a smooth ride—and you can invoke the favorite formula of academics and book reviewers everywhere, coined by the Roman poet Horace in the first century B.C.: "Even Homer nods."

HERO WORSHIP

Of the four great Greek heroes in the days before the Trojan War—before, that is, Agamemnon and Achilles and the *Iliad*—one poses no problem. That's Hercules. The other three are at least as worthy but, scanted by Hollywood, they're short on fan clubs. Here, then, is the rundown on Perseus, Theseus, and Prometheus.

Perseus first, whose father was Zeus—making him a demigod as well as a mere hero—and who is the one who slew Medusa, she of the snakes-for-hair and the petrifying (literally) countenance; and who rescued Andromeda from the sea monster. With Perseus, we're in what reads like a fairy tale (complete with wingèd sandals, magic sack, a cap that makes its wearer invisible, and so on). We're also in what could pass for a matriarchy: From his boyhood on, women loom large in Perseus's story, beginning with his mother, Danaë, (whom Zeus had gotten pregnant by covering her in a, you should pardon the expression, golden shower), continuing through the three Gray Women (whom Perseus tricked into revealing vital information by stealing the single eye they shared), the three Gorgons (of whom Medusa was one), and Andromeda (who wouldn't have been sea-monster bait if *her* mother, Cassiopeia, hadn't bragged in front of a god about her own beauty). Scholars compare Perseus to Saint George, who likewise slew a dragon and rescued a princess. If Hollywood were to decide to do the Perseus story, they could do worse than cast Sting in the role.

Theseus is in every way more difficult; the great Athenian hero, celebrated not only in myth but in three plays by Euripides and one by Sophocles, he has a legend that doesn't self-contain. Or, as the Athenians themselves used to say, awestruck by the sheer number of his exploits and enterprises, "Nothing without Theseus." Unlike Perseus, Theseus was pure mortal; his father was King Aegeus of Athens, after whom the Aegean Sea would be named. His best-known early adventure was slaying the Minotaur (the half-bull, half-man monster who lived in the labyrinth on Crete) with the help of the princess Ariadne and her ball of thread; his best-known late one had him dealing with his wife Phaedra's infatuation with his son by a previous marriage, Hippolytus. In between there range an ongoing friendship with Hercules, an encounter with Medea, a war with the Amazons, the slaying of Procrustes (with the one-size-fits-all guest-room bed), the forgiving of Oedipus, and much, much more. Quasi-legendary, quasi-historical, Theseus is also an intellect, a man of conscience and compassion, and a father to his people—more King Arthur than just another knight. It's a part that calls for Jeremy Irons.

The most difficult (and the most senior) of all is Prometheus. Son of one of the Titans, the first wave of rulers in prehistoric Greece, predating Zeus, Hera, Poseidon, and the rest of the Olympians, not to mention the mortals, by at least a generation, Prometheus (literally, "foresight") helped Zeus over-throw their shared ancestors. In gratitude, the new gods delegated Prome-theus to create man out of clay. Not knowing when to stop, Prometheus then stole fire from the sun, with the help of which he was able to breathe wisdom (plus a little of what we now call style) into his new creation. Not surprisingly, Zeus saw the fire business as a combination of disloyalty and audacity. Prome-theus was chained to a rock, where an eagle pecked daily at his liver, until Hercules finally set him free.

Several things here: First, note that Prometheus pursues and receives fire (a.k.a. inspiration), and is hence a poet; that he has flown in the face of the tyranny of established power, and is hence a rebel; and that his predicament prefigures the Crucifixion, and he is hence a martyr and proto-Christ-figure. Various ages have made various big deals of all this, most notably Aeschylus in the trilogy *Prometheus Bound, Prometheus Unbound,* and *Prometheus the Fire Bringer;* and, in the Romantic Age, Goethe, who saw Prometheus as a symbol of man's creativeness and independence of spirit, and Shelley, who wrote *Prometheus Unbound,* part psychodrama, part political allegory, and all anti-establishment hullabaloo. (In it, Prometheus, like Lucifer in *Paradise Lost,* is a rebel with a cause, and Jupiter/Zeus, like Milton's God, literal-minded and overbearing.) So what are you to make of your cousin's new fiancé when she describes him as "Promethean"? Well, he's either artistic or he's martyred or he's mad as hell; on the other hand, knowing your cousin, he may just wear an earring. And whom should we cast in *The Prometheus Story*? David Bowie, maybe. Or Bruce Springsteen. The point is, the actor's not only got to be bankable, he's got to be able to sing.

A word about Hercules: Sure, he's strong. Also simple, blundering, brash, and big. But he's not *just* about strangling snakes, killing lions, diverting rivers through stables, and spelling Atlas for a while. He also has a great midcareer mad scene, was known to dress up in drag, and eventually commits suicide. Which is why we think we'll be talking not to Sly Stallone's agent about the Hercules remake, but to William Hurt's.

TWO GUYS FROM DELPHI

Of the myriad gods and goddesses who habitually messed with the Greeks' heads, only two are still worth getting steamed up about. Apollo, tagged "the most Greek of all the gods," was the god of light, inventor of medicine, master musician, number-one archer, ideal of manly beauty, and symbol of all that was cool, civilized, and rational in Greek life. Like the young JFK, he had a flashy pedigree (son of Zeus and Leto; twin brother of Artemis), wielded enormous political power, had numerous love affairs, and was widely admired for his ability to dispense impartial justice and play a mean game of touch football (or its ancient Greek equivalent) with equal panache. He was definitely a representative of the Establishment, but then, being the law-and-order candidate was no social handicap during the Golden Age, and Delphi, the seat of his oracle, was both a religious shrine and the political power center of Greece.

Dionysus, by contrast, was an arriviste among Greek gods. Although he was fathered by Zeus, his mother, Semele, was a mortal, and no one was ever really sure where he'd spent his presumably wild youth, before he arrived on the Greek mainland and started raising hell. While Apollo passed his time inculcating high moral principle and urging moderation in all things, Dionysus and his followers roamed the hills celebrating sex, drugs, and rock 'n' roll. (Actually, as far as we know, the Greeks weren't into hash, coke, or acid at the time, but Dionysus was the god of wine, a substance that, being new to the populace, amounted to the same thing.) Before long, Dionysus had amassed enormous popular appeal and a huge following of bored Greek housewives who were delighted at the chance to slip away from their looms for a night of dancing, shrieking, and ripping small animals to shreds with their teeth. The point, for these Dionysian groupies, was *enthousiasmos,* a state of transcendent ecstasy in which possession was nine-tenths of the fun. Interestingly, the conservative male power structure (we know, we know) was prepared to tolerate these periodic lapses from wifely virtue; instead of banning the Dionysian revels, it simply co-opted them. Dionysus was given his own place of honor at Delphi, time-sharing with Apollo on an alternating six-month basis, and the celebrations became official state occasions. Since Dionysus doubled as the god of drama, these rites turned into theatrical events at which plays were presented as offerings to the god—and there you have the beginnings of theater as we know it.

It may have seemed an unlikely partnership even at the time, but the Apollo/Dionysus alliance worked tolerably well for the Greeks. Having made Dionysus an official element of state religion, they were in a position to regulate his behavior, making him less threatening and more socially acceptable as Greek life became more conservative and rationalistic.

In a way, the rivalry between the two gods didn't really start until the nineteenth century, when Nietzsche, in his *Birth of Tragedy,* contrasted what he saw as the primitive, creative, emotional "Dionysian" state of being, where life is dominated by music, dance, and lyricism, with the formal, analytical, coldly rational, and ultimately static "Apollonian" state, in which art and originality are squelched. Later, Spengler picked up on this notion in *The Decline of the West,* where he theorized that the uninhibited Dionysian element was the mark of a culture on the rise, the overcivilized Apollonian one the beginning of the end. In the 1960s and early 70s, these characterizations fueled a lot of radical theater and caused a great many people to take off their clothes in public; eventually, however, the Dionysian element began to lose its rough edges once again, and everybody put his or her clothes back on and went to work on Wall Street.

YOU SAY YOUR FATHER SACRIFICED YOUR SISTER, YOUR MOTHER AMBUSHED YOUR FATHER, YOU SLAUGHTERED YOUR MOTHER, AND NOW YOU'VE GONE BLIND AND ARE BEING CHASED AROUND THE COUNTRYSIDE BY THREE BLOOD-SOAKED WOMEN WITH SNAKES FOR HAIR? IS THAT WHAT'S BOTHERING YOU, BUNKY?

Not every civilization has the taste for tragedy that the ancient Greeks had. Not only did they invent the genre, but many critics insist that, in all of Western literature, there have been only four truly great tragic poets, three of whom wrote within fifty years of one another in Periclean Athens, a city whose population, not counting slaves (who didn't have much time to write poetry), was roughly equal to that of present-day Dogpatch. Although this traffic jam of talent has never been adequately explained, it probably stemmed from the Greeks' need to blow off steam (see *catharsis*, below) after trying to behave rationally all day instead of sacrificing virgins and praying to rocks the way their ancestors had. In fact, it was part of the function of tragedy to help the man on the street make sense of a lot of decidedly *irrational* gods and goddesses—who were holdovers, for the most part, from more primitive times—while purporting to pay homage to them.

In the absence of public television, it was also up to the tragic poets to combine enlightenment with entertainment. Aeschylus and Sophocles pulled this off with great success; Euripides, on the other hand, was a box-office flop. Nevertheless, given the right translation, all three still have the power, not necessarily to make you cry (if that's all you're after, you can make do with *Imitation of Life*), but to inspire the "pity and awe" that Aristotle considered hallmarks of any tragedy worth the price of admission. Reading the three in sequence will also give you a bird's-eye view of mankind jockeying for its current position at the center of the universe.

Aeschylus (525–456 B.C.): The granddaddy of Greek tragedy, Aeschylus (ES-ku-lus) was the first playwright to get some real action going by putting two actors onstage at the same time, instead of making audiences listen to one man rapping interminably with a chorus (and, of course, the Greek chorus didn't do high kicks; it just talked). In fact, action was Aeschylus's strong suit. He was a master of the bold stroke—the stirring speech, the grand gesture, the relentless buildup of tension followed by the inevitable thwack of the ax. If he is a little heavy on febrile metaphor ("Behold the orphaned children of the eagle father, now that he has died in the binding coils of the deadly viper, and the young he left behind are worn with hunger of starvation, not full grown to bring their shelter slain food, as their father did") and a little light on verisimilitude (Electra recognizes her long-lost brother, Orestes, by the fact that their footprints match), he is still the tragic poet best equipped to make the hairs stand up on the back of your neck. Armed with the charge-forth morality of the war hero (which, in fact, he was, having participated in the Athenian victory over Persia; see page 566), he never wastes time questioning the motivation of the gods, who seem to get their kicks from making mankind cry Uncle, or of his characters, none of whom is notable for thinking things through when there's a suicidal act of courage to commit before breakfast. Nietzsche, one of history's three or four most prominent definers of tragedy, saw Aeschylus's plays as the pinnacle of the form, an expression of the "reaffirmation of the will to live in the face of death." Certainly, his plays are page-turners, and the vision of Clytemnestra boasting that not only has she just slaughtered her husband, the king, but that if she were the teensiest bit less circumspect she'd drink a toast with his blood, does provide a refreshing alternative to the latest Woody Allen movie.

Sophocles (c. 496–c. 406 B.C.): The biggest box-office success of the three tragedians, Sophocles was also the most innovative (he put yet a third actor onstage, thereby thickening the plot considerably; wrote the first self-contained tragedies—as opposed to the trilogies, the Greek version of the mini-series, that audiences were accustomed to; and even came up with the idea of using painted sets), as well as the most craftsmanlike. Although he, too, based his plays on traditional myths, he wasn't opposed to tinkering with the conventions a bit in order to make the stories more believable: There are no matching footprints in *his* version of the Electra-Orestes reunion; Orestes simply tells Electra who he is. Sophocles is also considered by far the best poet of the lot, an artist who was more interested in perfecting the form than in proving a point. Not that he didn't have a point to prove; as the undisputed champion of the status quo, he virtually defined the poetic tradition of Apollonian classicism (see "Two Guys from Delphi," above). When his heroes come to grief, it's because they've failed—albeit through no fault of their own—to follow one of Apollo's two favorite maxims: "Know thyself," and "Nothing to excess." Still, by ascribing his protagonists' inevitable downfall to some fatal flaw of character (see *hamartia*, below) rather than to a fit of pique on the part of some Idi Amin–like deity, Sophocles scored a subtle point for man as more than a spear-carrier in the shaping of his own destiny. Whether Greek audiences grooved on this new power position or just appreciated solid workmanship, they awarded Sophocles some twenty first prizes—and never anything less than a second—at the annual Dionysian festival at which all Greek tragedies made their debut. Aristotle proclaimed Sophocles's *Oedipus Rex* the most perfect of all tragedies; modern critics call his work Greek drama at its most rational, most balanced, and, as some like to point out, most middle-aged.

Euripides (480 or 485–406 B.C.): Last born of the trio, Euripides had the misfortune to come of age as the sun began to set on Athenian democracy. While the older generation was still holding pep rallies for the glory that was supposed to be Greece, he started taking potshots at the gods, the established order, and the growing Athenian penchant for power-tripping. Partly because of his vehement anti-authoritarianism, and partly because of his willingness to get so upset over individual human suffering, Euripides is considered the most modern of the tragedians. Psychologically, he was certainly ahead of his time. His characters seem more neurotic than heroic; they're continuously aware of the fact that they're in pain and they never let us forget it, either. Unfortunately, this didn't play as well in the fifth century B.C. as it does nowadays. Euripides ended up a bitter recluse, having won only five first prizes at the Dionysian festivals. In fairness to his audiences, it must be said that he really wasn't the playwright his predecessors were; his plots tend to drift, his pace to drag, and his protagonists to exit the stage more often than not via a *deus ex machina*, literally carried off to meet their destinies by gods and goddesses who suddenly flew in on invisible wires. A couple of millennia later, however, Euripides was to become the ancient-Greek-poet-of-choice for a whole roster of 1960s protest groups, who used his *Trojan Women* to underscore the horror of napalming babies in Vietnam, and his *Medea* to explain why they were burning their bras.

SPEAK ANCIENT GREEK LIKE A NATIVE: TAKE THIS SIMPLE QUIZ

How Is Greek Tragedy Different from the Six O'Clock News?

In Greek tragedy, whenever a construction crane crushes a hapless shopper or a successful politician butchers his next of kin, you'll generally find, in lieu of a camera crew, the following elements:

HAMARTIA—Usually translated as "fatal flaw" (or "error" or "shortcoming"), it's what, according to Aristotle, it takes to be a tragic hero. Sometimes hamartia can verge on vice, sometimes it can seem a misstep no more shameful than choosing the wrong door on a game show. In either case, it functions like a renegade gene, biding its time until the moment is right to bring some otherwise healthy individual to his or her knees. Hamartia is a necessary component of tragedy because, Aristotle reasoned, there is no point in witnessing the destruction of a man who is thoroughly virtuous, on the one hand, or thoroughly corrupt, on the other.

HUBRIS—Everybody's favorite example of hamartia. It adds up to arrogance or pride, although it can start out as an essentially harmless character trait taken to extremes, or, according to some critics, as merely a hero's attempt to express too much in the way of human vitality and choice, thereby violating the social—or the cosmic—order.

NEMESIS—What's going to get a hero whose hubris starts showing. Originally, Nemesis was a quasi-goddess who epitomized righteous anger at a breach of the rules and who liked to mete out punishments. Subsequently, a hero's highly specific, individual, and thoroughly inevitable undoing.

CATHARSIS—The experience of purgation, or purification, of the emotions that Aristotle claimed tragedy could be counted on to produce, thereby rendering it socially useful. Ideally, catharsis is something that both hero and audience will undergo simultaneously, although it's going to hurt the hero a lot more. Of course, we've lost the volume in which Aristotle explained what catharsis was, exactly, but don't let that stand in the way of your having a good cry.

How Is an Ancient Greek Like a Native Californian?

Both base their way of living on the concept of *arete*, or inborn capacities, the development of which is, for each, the highest purpose of the individual. (The classic example of arete is the acorn that always has it in it to be a mighty oak.) The Greek assumed, however, that arete had as many social as personal reverberations and that, given all the freedom in the world to develop one's potential, one would naturally develop it in a way that was best for everyone. Self-actualizing as it may be, leaving one's spouse and children to marry one's eighteen-year-old freshman composition student probably wouldn't have counted as full-fledged arete for the Greeks.

What's Love Got to Do, Got to Do with It?

The Greeks wrote the book on forms of affection, and Western civilization hasn't done much but muddy the waters ever since. Our umbrella-term *love* didn't exist back in fifth-century Athens; instead there were seen to be three very distinct and powerful love-related forces at work in the world: *eros* (what we would call "sexual love," only more complex), *philia* (what we would call "friendship," but ditto) and *agape* (what we would call "love of God" or "love of God's creatures" if we ever gave it a second thought). Having organized the whole business from the ground up, the Greeks were able to appreciate its subtleties: Eros, for instance, while it is the basis for our word *erotic*, didn't just refer to the feelings evoked by pornographic vases (or videos) or even to the heat generated between men and women (for that matter, the Greeks gave more credence to the heat generated between men and men), but to all sorts of passions, including spiritual ones, that were based on a yearning for union or self-fulfillment; it also recognized the fact that fulfillment inevitably neutralized desire. The social implications of philia can't even be translated into English, and under the joint heading eros/philia the Greeks had room for a whole roster of good feelings, ranging from kindness toward creatures of the same race (*physike*) to benevolence toward guests (*xenike*). On the other side of the cosmic coin was agape (say it like "canapé," sort of), which implied the giving of affection without expecting anything back, and which was soon twisted beyond recognition by overenthusiastic Christian theologians. None of this is to say that the Greeks' clearheaded perspective was responsible for their minuscule divorce rate, only that the Greeks spent a lot of time thinking about the meaning of love, whereas the rest of us have opted just to dance to it.

MUSIC

W.S.PRESTON.

Contents

Imperial Ladies' Orchestra, Hoag Lake Theater, Woonsocket, Rhode Island; Miss Lizzie A. Otto, directress.

Classical Music for the Disconcerted

PLAY IT AGAIN, SAM—AND THIS TIME WE'LL TRY TO LISTEN

Ten paradigmatic works, offered as a map for the ear by contributor Jon Pareles.*

JOSQUIN DESPREZ: *LA DÉPLORATION SUR LA MORT D'OCKEGHEM*

IOSQVINVS PRATENSIS.

For most regular concertgoers, music before Bach is a mystery. Even a lot of early-music fans think of it simply as intensely dulcet, fa-la-la-filled madrigals and jaunty dances played on nasal instruments. But that's not all there is to it. This is, after all, music that has survived almost five centuries; one way to enjoy it is to savor its alienness. Its structures can seem whimsical or perverse, as with "cantus firmus" pieces whose important melody is the slowest-moving part, in the bass. And early harmonies sound a little off today, both because the tuning of instruments has changed and because the fifteenth-century ear had its own notions of dissonance and consonance. So, early music moves in mysterious ways—often, it just seems to mosey along, coming to a rest here and there, then moseying on again via the occasional utterly peculiar turn. *La déploration sur la mort d'Ockeghem*, by the Fleming Josquin Desprez, is the sound of the Middle Ages becoming the Renaissance. Johannes Ockeghem, who died in 1495, was the last great medieval composer, writing seamless, otherworldly pieces, all of whose parts moved independently. Josquin's requiem piece for him, with "Requiem aeternam" as its cantus firmus, begins as an homage to Ockeghem, then changes to the more modern style: clearer phrases, voices sometimes echoing each other, something akin to modern chords. In half a century, there would indeed be madrigals; a century after that, Bach would be born.

Pro Cantione Antiqua, London; Archiv 2533 145

* Jonathan Pareles is a music critic of *The New York Times*.

JOHANN SEBASTIAN BACH: MASS IN B MINOR, BWV 232

Bach was the greatest Baroque composer because he was also the last Renaissance composer; that is, he wrote brilliantly in both the newfangled *concertante* style—with a clear separation of melody and accompaniment, in forms built from contrasting sections— and the older, free-flowing counterpoint. Written between 1733 and 1748 (Bach died in 1750), the Mass is a virtual Bach encyclopedia, with each chunk of text set as the composer saw fit. It has solo arias; sections in which voices and instruments intertwine; massive concertante choruses in which solo and instrumental groups trade off with full chorus and the Baroque orchestra of strings, organ, recorders, oboes, bassoons, trumpets, and drums; and sublime, complex fugues, pieces in strict counterpoint derived from the staggered entrances of the theme, or "subject." Some arias, such as the "Agnus dei" for alto and the "Domine Deus" for soprano, tenor, and recorder, are so devout it's hard to remember that Bach was only a Lutheran.

Nikolaus Harnoncourt, cond. Concentus Musicus Wien, Telefunken 6.35019/SKH 20

WOLFGANG AMADEUS MOZART: SYMPHONY NO. 41 IN C MAJOR ("JUPITER"), K. 551

In *Lucky Jim*, Kingsley Amis called Mozart's music a "skein of untiring facetiousness." Maybe. But not the "Jupiter." True, its themes are typically Mozartian question–answer pairs, ever so neatly balanced. And, as with most classical symphonies, each movement proceeds duly away from, then back to, its starting point. (In sonata form, used in first movements of symphonies and sonatas, themes are introduced, taken for a ride, then returned home safe and sound.) But in Mozart's music, the process is displayed with diagrammatic clarity and absolute poise. Even when the writing seems effortless, it moves forward; its symmetries pull it ahead gracefully yet inevitably, disturbing their own balance, only to set it straight again. The three final symphonies Mozart wrote in summer, 1788 (the "Jupiter" is the last one) are the peak of classical form, congenial and precise. At his best, Mozart wasn't facetious—he was Olympian.

Karl Böhm, cond. Berlin Philharmonic, Deutsche Grammophon 138 815 SLPM

LUDWIG VAN BEETHOVEN: PIANO SONATA NO. 29 IN B FLAT MAJOR, OPUS 106 ("HAMMERKLAVIER" SONATA)

When the movies show Beethoven in creative agony, the soundtrack ought to be the "Hammerklavier," which took him two years to write (1817–1818) and blew the roof off the sonata while honoring its form (see Mozart). The "Hammerklavier" is an obsessive work, longer and probably more difficult than any previous piano sonata, yet so concentrated that almost every detail, large and small, derives from a single idea: in musical terms, a chain of descending thirds. Like the iodine crystal that seeds a cloud, that idea generates not only all of the sonata's themes, but its harmonic plan and even the relation between movements. Beethoven's relentless logic leads him far afield (the Adagio has moments that sound like Chopin) but he never, ever, rambles. Despite its length, the "Hammerklavier" is no-frills writing with a vengeance.

Wilhelm Kempff, piano; Quintessence PMC-7130

FRÉDÉRIC CHOPIN: TWENTY-FOUR PRELUDES, OPUS 28

In some of the greatest salons of all time, Chopin was *the* salon pianist. He was much loved for his pianistic technique, and for the sense of melancholia in even his most triumphant pieces. He was also a harmonics pioneer, charting extraordinary new chords. Like most of his contemporaries, Chopin was better at writing tunes than at sustaining large-scale structures; unlike them, he had the sense to concentrate on miniatures (the preludes, waltzes, mazurkas) and on extended miniatures (ballades, nocturnes, polonaises). In 1839 he completed the twenty-four preludes—one in each major and minor key, just like Bach's *The Well-Tempered Clavier;* none is longer than five minutes, most under two. Each is a gem: the C Minor, whose chord sequence was stolen for the *Fame* theme song; the E Minor, with its sustained melody floating above an astounding sequence of chords; the lithely filigreed E Flat Major; the vociferous, breakneck, where-the-hell-are-we-going G Minor. Chopin doesn't make more of his ideas than he ought to; if thirty-three seconds is enough, that's where the prelude ends. A few composers could take the hint.

Maurizio Pollini, piano; Deutsche Grammophon 2530 550

PETER ILYICH TCHAIKOVSKY: CONCERTO IN D FOR VIOLIN AND ORCHESTRA, OPUS 35

Think of Romantic man, alone and heroic, bending a universe to his will—what better analogue than the concerto? The soloist faces the orchestra and battles it with his virtuosity until, finally, they join in triumphant partnership. From Mozart's time, the concerto had been a star vehicle, but the classical-era composers at least remembered that the orchestra existed. By the time Tchaikovsky wrote his Violin Concerto in 1878, the orchestra is lucky to get a few rumbles and forebodings in edgewise before the soloist enters with his first sweet, soulful melody. That tune comes back as a rabble-rousing march, complete with trumpets, but not before a tear-jerking second theme and considerable violinistic showing-off. The showing-off is the point, of course. After a short, tearful Andante, the concerto's finale is a violin decathlon. Upon hearing the premiere, Vienna's top critic wrote: "The violin is no longer played but rent asunder, beaten black and blue." What fun.

Leonid Kogan, violin; Constantin Silvestri, cond. Paris Conservatoire Orchestra, Seraphim S-60075

ARNOLD SCHOENBERG: *PIERROT LUNAIRE*, OPUS 21

Schoenberg blueprinted quite a bit of twentieth-century chamber music with his 1912 song cycle, *Pierrot Lunaire*. Loony (or, if you prefer, moon-drunk) Pierrot the harlequin drifts through Albert Giraud's twenty-one poems to the sinuous dissonances of a "broken consort," instruments from different families: piano, flute, clarinet, violin, and cello. The poems are declaimed in *Sprechstimme*, literally "speak-sing," which Schoenberg devised as a combination of song's melodic contours and speech's indeterminacy. After *Pierrot,* Schoenberg (along with Anton von Webern) went on to further compress and systematize atonal pointillism in the serial or twelve-tone style (see page 277), all the rage in the latter twentieth century. Meanwhile, the instrumentation, *Sprechstimme,* text-centered form, tiny musical gestures, and atonality all gave other composers ideas. So did Pierrot's lightheadedness.

Jan DeGaetani, voice; Arthur Weisberg, cond.
Contemporary Chamber Ensemble,
Nonesuch H-71251

IGOR STRAVINSKY: *LE SACRE DU PRINTEMPS* (*THE RITE OF SPRING*)

The Rite of Spring is Tarzan among the classics: pagan, ill-mannered, passionate, suffused with jungle rhythms. No wonder there was a riot at the 1913 premiere, where it backed a Diaghilev ballet that Stravinsky never much liked. What the vociferous audience missed, however, was the music's astonishing intricacy and delicacy. Between its percussive, brassy climaxes—the rite ends with a young girl dancing herself to death—*Le Sacre* is deeply melodic without an atom of sentiment (the bassoon call that opens the piece may haunt you forever). Stravinsky studied orchestration with Rimsky-Korsakov (of *Scheherezade* fame), but turned all the old tricks inside out, using woodwinds in particular to achieve an eerie, pungent sound. Half a century later, *Le Sacre* is still galvanizing for audiences and hellishly difficult for orchestras and conductors. It has, moreover, left its mark. Leonard Bernstein brought its choppy rhythms to Broadway in *West Side Story,* and its obsessively repeated motifs, energizing harmonies that barely move, predicted today's minimalists.

Pierre Boulez, cond. Cleveland Symphony, Columbia MS 7293

BÉLA BARTÓK: THE SIX STRING QUARTETS

String quartets, historically, are a composer's most rigorous private utterances; with just two violins, viola, and cello there's no room for anything but purest form expressed in intimate counterpoint. The six string quartets Bartók wrote between 1908 and 1939 are, with Beethoven's final six, the form at its most intense. Bartók's sum up his growth from an impressionable pan-European eclectic to a visionary native (in this case Hungarian) voice. In the first three, Bartók puts the squeeze on received lyricism: He reduces themes to angular motifs; develops those motifs with merciless concision; replaces comfortable Europeanisms with dissonances and rhythms out of Hungarian folk tradition. The third quartet, his shortest, is so distilled and dramatic it feels like a single indrawn breath. For the final three, Bartók loosens up a bit, singing in the atonal phrases of his own new language. Along the way, he uses every bit of the string quartet's sonic vocabulary, including sliding notes and glassy harmonics and grainy *col legno* (playing with the wood of the bow), yet never sounds as if he's showboating because every effect is at the service of the whole.

The Juilliard String Quartet, Columbia D3S 717

TERRY RILEY: IN C

It's only a page or two of music, a collection of fifty-three motifs in the key of C. Any number of musicians, the more the better, can play it without a conductor. While somebody plunks out steady Cs on a keyboard, the other musicians play a motif, repeat it for some time, then move on to the next one. They all listen to each other so that no one gets too far ahead or behind. And the nigh-miraculous result is a monumental work: a rich, pulsing C chord encompassing ceaseless activity, change within stasis. It's minimalism, or trance music, or process music, or going-nowhere music, or cooperative music, or whatever you want to call it. Because it's so warmly consonant, minimalism has attracted a new audience to contemporary music; because it ignores most classical ideas of form and drama, it has the old guard outraged. CBS MS 7178

The Parts of an Orchestra, Dummy, Once and for All

Actually, you have a right to be confused; orchestra structures come and go—as they've been doing for about three centuries—and a conductor will add or subtract instruments at the drop of a baton, depending on the demands of the piece to be performed. In general, however, when people today say "symphony orchestra," they mean pretty much what they meant in the nineteenth century, and what you see below. Of the four sections of instruments, the string section is the largest, most important, and usually the most continuously played. Woodwinds are second in the pecking order; they add color and sometimes carry the melody. The brass, which acts as the muscle, or amplifier, in those swelling, passionate passages, is generally used sparingly. And, of course, the percussion section provides the beat. If you still don't know a cornet from a clarinet study this page, then clip and pin to your sleeve.

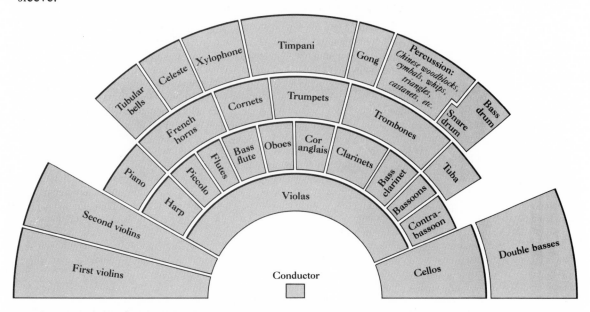

STRINGS: First and second violins (they're all the same instruments, they just play different parts), violas, violoncellos (or simply cellos), double basses, and, sometimes, a harp.

WOODWINDS: Piccolo, flutes, clarinets, oboes, cor anglais, bassoons, contrabassoon.

BRASS: French horns, cornets, trumpets, trombones, tuba.

PERCUSSION: Timpani, bass drum, snare drum, cymbals, triangles, assorted instruments such as wood blocks, castanets, gongs, glockenspiel, etc.

Practical Italian for the Concertgoer

First, there are the words indicating the speed and volume at which a composition is to be played; we've ranged them from the least to the most:

SPEED

grave (=solemn) largo (=wide, broad)	very slow
adagio (=at ease)	quite slow
lento	slow
andante (=walking)	steady, flowing
andantino	either somewhat faster or somewhat slower than andante, depending on your conductor's reading of that diminutizing suffix
moderato	moderate
allegretto	moderately fast
allegro (=cheerful)	fast
vivace	lively
presto	fast
prestissimo	very, very fast

VOLUME (with abbreviations)

pianissimo (pp)	very soft
piano (p)	soft
mezzo piano (mp)	sort of soft
mezzo forte (mf)	sort of loud
forte (f)	loud
fortissimo (ff)	very loud

Note: More "p"'s or "f"'s can be added as desired by the composer; there are even "pppppp" passages in Tchaikovsky's "Pathétique."

CHANGE IN SPEED

accelerando	getting faster
ritardando rallentando	getting slower

CHANGE IN VOLUME

crescendo	getting louder
decrescendo diminuendo	getting softer

You've noted that the Italians like to qualify things. Sometimes they do this with suffixes (that *-issimo*, for instance, means "very," *-ino* and *-etto* both mean "a little"). Sometimes they use whole words, as with:

molto	much
meno	less
mezzo	half
poco	a little
non troppo	not too much

But that's just the basic, strike-up-the-band stuff. Other, less blatantly quantitative terms, in simple alphabetical order, include:

a cappella (literally, "as in church"): Used of vocal music without instrumental accompaniment, even though instrumental accompaniment has been common in churches since the Middle Ages.

arpeggio (from the Italian for "harp"): A broken chord in which the notes are played in succession so as to recall—on a piano, violin, whatever—a harpist "sweeping" the strings.

cadenza (literally, "cadence"): A passage in a concerto (and a display of virtuosity, florid, brilliant, or both) in which the solo instrument plays without the orchestra. It was up to the performer to decide to execute a cadenza until the time of Mozart; now always indicated by the composer.

cantabile (from the Italian for "singing"): In a flowing style.

coda (from *cauda,* "tail"): A concluding, rounding-off section to a piece of music, or a portion of it.

da capo (literally, "from the head"): An indication that a previously played section of music is to be repeated.

glissando (from an Italian version of the French *glisser,* to slide): Sliding from note to note, as by running one's fingers over the keys of the piano, strings of the harp, etc.

legato (literally, "bound together"): Describes a smooth performance without accentuated notes (cf. *staccato,* below).

obbligato (literally, "obligatory"): Denotes some indispensable part: an elaborate embellishment of a main melodic line, an instrument that's critical (but subordinate) to a vocal performance. Careful: Some people use the term to signal precisely that element which *can* be dispensed with; the point is, according to them, if it's a key support, it can't also be the heart of the matter.

pizzicato (literally, "pinched"): Directs that, with stringed instruments, the strings are to be plucked with the fingers, not bowed.

rubato (literally, "robbed"): Indicates that a player should "play around" with a given tempo, marginally accelerating or relaxing it, for effect; sometimes one hand—on a piano keyboard—might play "normally," the other go with the *rubato*. Also known as swaying the rhythm.

scherzo (literally, "joke"): A sped-up form of the minuet, much beloved of Haydn and Beethoven. Common today as a component of sonatas, symphonies, etc.

sforzando (literally, "forced"): Designates a note to be played with special emphasis.

staccato (literally, "detached"): Opposite of *legato* (above), with notes to be played in a sharp, highly differentiated manner.

tessitura (literally, "texture"): Refers to the basic range of a part, vocal or musical, excluding any very high or low notes.

toccata (literally, "touched"): A piece that shows off the "touch," originally often used of a trumpet fanfare, now more often of a free-form keyboard piece.

tremolo (from the Italian for "tremulous"): A "trembling" effect, either from the rapid repetition of a single note (by, say, fast backwards-and-forwards "bowing") or from the rapid alternation of two notes more than a whole tone apart.

vibrato (literally, "shake"): A rapid, slight wavering of pitch.

Five Composers Whose Names Begin With the Letter P

WE'D HAVE THROWN IN PAGANINI, BUT WE KNOW HOW BUSY YOU ARE

GIOVANNI PIERLUIGI DA PALESTRINA (1525–1594): No pioneer. A native Roman who composed almost entirely for the Church, Palestrina wrote masses, motets, and hymns in the same polyphonic texture—where separate strands of melody, each provided by an independent voice, count for more than the harmony they go to make up—that characterizes all music composed before 1600. But if he only marks the end of the medieval era, with all its ritual and mysticism, rather than the dawn of a new one, Palestrina's still one of the most important figures before Bach and Handel. Think of him as the Homer of music.

Suggested listening: *Missa Papae Marcelli* (King's College Choir, Seraphim S-60187), *Song of Songs* (Cantores in Ecclesia, Michael Howard, cond.; L'Oiseau-Lyre SOL338/9).

FRANCIS POULENC (1899–1963): Wrote avant-garde music with the working man in mind. Poulenc belonged to that group of irreverent young composers called the Six, a fixture of between-the-wars Paris (Erik Satie, who'd made a career of irreverence was the group's sponsor; it also included Darius Milhaud and Arthur Honegger). Against authority (in this case, traditional French good taste), fond of jazz and the music hall, susceptible to the Dadaist and Surrealist movements in art, these guys would all be hanging out on the Lower East Side today. Of the Six, Poulenc was the most gaminlike, mischievous and flippant, squarely on the side of everyday music for everyday people. Who'd have predicted that, by the late Fifties, he'd be writing opera and religious music?

Suggested listening: Songs (including "Les fiançailles pour rire" and "Cinq poèmes de Max Jacob"; Decca Argo ZRG804), Mass in G (Bernstein, New York Philharmonic, Columbia M-34551).

SERGEI PROKOFIEV (1891–1953): One of three Russian composers of this century you can't not know something about. Despite some youthful iconoclasm (and an ongoing astringency), Prokofiev is about as accessible as good twentieth-century music gets: melodious but not bland, rhythmic but not blatant.

He may also be the first classical composer you ever heard, if your first-grade teacher played you *Peter and the Wolf* the way ours did. The other two de rigueur Russians: Igor Stravinsky (see also page 269, with as many moods, phases, and ego needs as Picasso), and Dmitri Shostakovich (the heir to Tchaikovsky, but also the number one product—and victim—of Soviet musical training and strictures).

Suggested listening: *Classical Symphony*, Opus 25 (London Symphony Orchestra, Angel S-37523), *Alexander Nevsky* (the movie score; LSO, Angel S-36843), *Romeo and Juliet* (the ballet; LSO, Angel S-37020).

GIACOMO PUCCINI (1858–1924): If Italy were on fire and only a single Italian opera could be saved, it wouldn't be one of Puccini's. Though there's no arguing with *La Bohème, Tosca,* and *Madame Butterfly* at the box office, they can, next to the best of Verdi, strike bona fide opera lovers as a little, well, vulgar. A showman and crowd-pleaser (not to mention a pirate who wasn't above stealing an idea or two from a colleague), Puccini has had his greatest influence on the development of the popular musical theater.

Suggested listening: For extra credit, *Turandot* (the last Puccini opera, with the Chinese-princess heroine; Birgit Nilsson, Renata Tebaldi, et al., RCA LSC-6149).

HENRY PURCELL (1659–1695): First, the good news. Purcell is virtually the only pre-twentieth-century English composer you have to know anything about at all. Now, the bad news. You *do* have to remember that it's pronounced PURS-el, with the accent up front. For his short life (he died at 36), Purcell was the great Baroque master, not only of English music, but of European music in general; technically brilliant, exceptionally versatile, he was the first winner of the coveted Wünderkind Award that would later go to Mozart. Purcell's gifts included an ability to adapt musical composition to the peculiar inflections of spoken English; it's rumored that, had he lived a little longer, he'd have made something of English opera.

Suggested listening: *Dido and Aeneas* (the opera; Archiv 198424), *Theatre Music* (including "Abdelazer," "Distressed Innocence"; Academy of Ancient Music, L'Oiseau-Lyre DSL0504).

The Day the Music Died

ATONALITY, TWELVE-TONE THEORY, AND SUCH

Depending on whether you're one of the cognoscenti or just an average listener, atonality is either the biggest breakthrough of the twentieth century or what's wrong with modern music. Before you can understand what atonality *is,* however, you have to know a little about what it isn't—namely, tonality. Think, for a moment, of how nicely "do re mi fa sol la ti do" fit together—that's tonality for you. It has to do with the idea that, of the twelve tones in a chromatic scale (all the notes from, say, one C to another on the piano keyboard), only seven have a natural affinity for, hence are capable of sustaining meaningful relationships with, each other. These tones interact as family members, experiencing their little tensions (dissonances) from time to time, but managing to work things out between themselves (consonances), and always, ultimately, gravitating toward one restful "home" note (the tonic), which determines their key. Such groupings—orderly, reassuring, full of familiar emotional associations—are the basis of tonality and of virtually all Western music from Bach to Brahms.

In the early 1900s, however, the Viennese composer Arnold Schoenberg, heavily influenced by Wagner (who had played around with dissonance in *Tristan und Isolde),* by twentieth-century malaise, by German Expressionism, by the radical thinking then rampant in Vienna, and by his own Teutonic angst, began to chafe under the old tonal tradition—and under the idea that music was supposed to make people feel better. In 1921 he did the first really new thing in 300 years of musical history: He threw out tonality altogether and composed an opus in which he gave equal importance to all twelve tones of the chromatic scale. In order to keep his early compositions from slipping naturally into tonality, Schoenberg filled them with dissonance, in much the same way German Expressionist painters filled their paintings with the grotesque: Dissonance broke up the notes, kept them from forming cliques, as it were, and evoked a kind of unrelieved tension—near hysteria, in fact—which seemed right for the times.

There was still the problem of how to hold a piece together without tonality, however. Schoenberg eventually solved it by inventing the twelve-tone row, which became the basis for twelve-tone, or dodecaphonic, music, as well as for later serial music. Composing with twelve tones is a little like playing a very complicated board game, minus the entertainment value. First, the composer decides on a row—a particular order for the twelve pitches. The row then becomes the basic material of the piece, with variations unfolding according to a very specific set of rules. It can, for instance, be played forward, backward, upside-down, or upside-down and backward, so long as the whole row is played through before any of the tones is sounded again. (Are you beginning to see why twelve-tone music has failed to capture the popular imagination?) In short, the twelve-tone form was a necessarily arbitrary, highly intellectual way of exerting control over the chaotic elements of atonal compositions, of imposing the strictly rational over the basically irrational.

Later, the idea of the tone row as the organizing principle of a piece led composers to attempt to exercise the same kind of control over all the elements of a piece: pitch, rhythm, timbre, dynamics, you name it. This all comes under the heading "serial music," which can include, but isn't limited to, twelve-tone and atonal forms. Absolute control! To the public, this was simply not an idea whose time had come; to many critics, it was an idea whose time had come and gone. In fact, the whole business of atonal and serial music shouldn't worry you too much; only composers really understand it and they rarely talk to anyone but each other anyway. Just keep in mind that atonality aims at a whole new concept of what music, and listening to music, is all about, and be aware that, silly as serial music can get at times, virtually every modern composer has flirted with its various forms at some point in his or her career—as contributor Ronald Varney documents here.

TUNEBUSTERS

In 1899, after trying in his early compositions to out-Wagner Wagner, the twenty-one-year-old Arnold Schoenberg composed a string sextet entitled *Transfigured Night*. It was a milestone in the history of music, perhaps the first really atonal work.

In 1904 Alban Berg and Anton von Webern, also Austrians, apprenticed themselves to Schoenberg in Vienna and became the two chief disciples of his radical musical teachings. While Berg, handsome and aristocratic, always displayed somewhat romantic tendencies in his composing, Webern, squinty-eyed and professorial, would become more daring and radical than the master himself. In 1910, with these two firmly under his wing, Schoenberg crowed, "In ten years, every talented composer will be writing this way, regardless of whether he has learned it directly from me or only from my work."

In 1912 Schoenberg composed *Pierrot Lunaire* (see also page 268), a fully atonal, slightly bizarre song cycle which is considered his masterpiece. About it, Leonard Bernstein wrote: "This is a piece which never fails to move and impress me, but always leaves me feeling a little bit sick. This is only just, since sickness is what it's about—moon-sickness. Somewhere in the middle of this piece you have a great desire to run and open a window, breathe in a lungful of healthy, clean air."

Berg, though not prolific, wrote three works that have become recognized as major additions to the classical repertoire: his *Violin Concerto* and two operas, *Wozzeck* and *Lulu*.

The enigmatic Webern concentrated on chamber music, emphasizing silence as much as sound in almost painfully short works that reduce music to its barest elements. His *Six Bagatelles* for string quartet is only three and a half minutes long. Other works, like his *Variations* for orchestra or *Symphony for Chamber Orchestra*, seem to last a lifetime. "The pulverization of sound into a kind of luminous dust" is the way Virgil Thomson described one of Webern's pieces.

It is ironic that, of atonality's Big Three, Schoenberg probably enjoyed the least success. During the 1930s he fled Germany and wound up in Los Angeles, where he taught at UCLA and continued to compose. He died in 1951, embittered by his lack of recognition. And when atonal music and the twelve-tone theory swept Europe and the United States during the Fifties and Sixties, it was Webern, not Schoenberg, who was hailed as the high priest of atonality. Webern's works were so influential, in fact, that they prompted a binge of international experimentation. Some examples:

Iannis Xenakis: One of the most often booed of modern composers. Has written music based on far-out theories from math and engineering.

Pierre Boulez: Noted for his contempt for every composer in history (except himself, the Big Three, and maybe a few of his own followers). Has generally sought in his music a sound expressing, as he puts it, a "collective hysteria and spells, violently of the present time."

John Cage: Achieved renown for cramming all kinds of junk, from bits of wood to weather-stripping, into his "prepared pianos" and then having the pianist strike the keys at random. Tireless in his efforts to do away with the role of the composer. Known for two particularly eccentric works: *Imaginary Landscape No. 4*, in which twelve radios are "played" by twenty-four performers; and the most famous silent piece in history, *4'33"*, in which a pianist sits silently at the keyboard for four minutes and thirty-three seconds, creating a sort of musical vacuum in the concert hall. Also fun: his *0'0"*, to be played "in any way to anyone."

Karlheinz Stockhausen: A specialist in electronic music. Like Cage, explores the outer frontiers of musical pointlessness. In the epic cycle *Gold Dust,* asked the performers first to starve themselves for four days while living in complete isolation. Then, in his own words, to "late at night, without conversation beforehand, play single sounds, without thinking which you are playing, close your eyes, just listen."

The atonality craze that began after Webern's death in 1945 was, by the mid-70s, already winding down. The music had become incredibly complicated; audiences felt increasingly bored and alienated by it; and the composers found themselves with nothing more to say on the subject. Today's generation of avant-garde composers, such as Philip Glass (see page 287) and Steve Reich, while still in the atonal tradition, are writing music that is less grating and more hypnotic.

Still, two things must be said for atonality: It broke classical music wide open, and it left audiences reeling. Neither has recovered.

—Ronald Varney

Beyond BAY-toe-v'n and MOAT-sart

It's not that music is strewn with unpronounceable names; in fact, if you can fake your way in French, remember a handful of basic German pronunciations (like the two in the title), and treat all Italian proper names as if they were varieties of pasta, you'll do fine. There are, however, a few classic pitfalls.

1. The sole Brazilian composer to achieve international status: Heitor Villa-Lobos (AY-tor VEE-la LOW-bush).

2. The German expatriate composer, now best known for his theater work: Kurt Weill (VILE).

3. The two Czechs, one best known for his symphonies, the other (see page 286) for his operas, Antonin Dvořák and Leoš Janáček (AN-toe-neen DVOR-zhock and LEH-osh YAN-a-check).

4. The highly polished turn-of-the-century French composer: Camille Saint-Saëns (ka-ME-YA sanh-sawnhs; lots of nasality, please, and only one vowel sound in "Saëns").

5. The only really important pre–twentieth-century English composer: Henry Purcell (PURS-el).

6. The Hungarian-born conductor: Sir Georg Solti (GAY-ork SHOAL-tee). While we're on the subject, "Georg," the German form of the name, is always so pronounced, while "Richard," as in Wagner, is RICK-art. To say RITCH-erd when you've gone to all the trouble of saying VOG-ner is, you'll agree, a little silly.

7. The New Zealand–born soprano: Kiri Te Kanawa (KIR-ee Tuh-KON-a-wa). And then there's the one about how Barbara Walters calls her "Kiwi."

8. Finally, those two composing, conducting, no-longer-enfants-terribles of contemporary music, one French, the other American: Pierre Boulez (see page 279) and Leonard Bernstein (it's boo-LEZ and BERN-stine (stein, as in Steinway).

Opera for Philistines

350 YEARS OF OPERA AT A GLANCE

THE ITALIANS

Invented opera, the Mediterranean equivalent of baseball, c. 1570. Encouraged enthusiastic audience participation. Had knack for creating catchy tunes. Ruled the roost until the twentieth century.

THE COMPOSER	THE OPERAS

Claudio Monteverdi (1567–1643)
Opera's first musical genius; turned early academic theory into stage success by hitting his audiences where they lived. Speak his name with respect.

Heavy on recitative and short on show stoppers, but the passion and musicianship still come across; highly respected museum pieces. The masterpieces, *Orfeo* and *L'Incoronazione di Poppaea*, continue to draw an audience.

Alessandro Scarlatti (1660–1725)
One of the fathers of classical opera; a scholar's composer. Historical landmark only.

Of the 115 he wrote, about 70 are extant and you've never heard of any of them. Big deal in their day, however. Established opera as a going concern. Laid structural foundation for *opera seria*—serious opera, Italian style, of the seventeenth and eighteenth centuries, with heroic characters, tragic predicaments, usually mythical settings, strictly delineated arias and recitatives.

Gioacchino Antonio Rossini (1792–1868), Vincenzo Bellini (1801–1835), Gaetano Donizetti (1797–1848)
Hottest composers of their time; big box-office draws.

Rossini's *The Barber of Seville* was the pinnacle of *opera buffa* (comic opera about common people and everyday life, usually revolving around boisterous romantic intrigues; a reaction against the stuffy formality of *opera seria*). Bellini and Donizetti, on the other hand, were rivals in the *bel canto* category (see page 291). Major entries: the former's *Norma*, the latter's *Lucia di Lammermoor*. Donizetti's operas were sloppier, but contained more memorable tunes and the most sentimental atmospheres. Bellini's works were more meticulous but thin on storyline and orchestrally clumsy; he might have won in the end, but he died young.

Giuseppe Verdi (1813–1901)

Mr. Opera; the greatest Italian composer in a predominantly Italian art form. Like Shakespeare, had innate sense of theater: instinct for constructing plot, creating character, moving action along, suffusing the whole with universal themes; wrote unforgettable melodies. Of humble origins; a patriot. Changed the nature of traditional Italian opera simply by outgrowing it.

For the most part, melodramas that transcend their genre. Any Verdi opera is considered a class act, but the three of his "middle period," *Rigoletto*, *Il Trovatore*, *La Traviata*, are the most popular; *Aïda* is the grandest; *Otello* and *Falstaff*, his one comedy, are the prestige choices, both "mature Verdi."

Giacomo Puccini (1858–1924)

Most bankable composer ever. The Steven Spielberg of opera. (See also page 276.)

Superficial, sentimental, borders on the vulgar and, in some cases (notably *Turandot*), the perverse. But *Tosca*, *La Bohème*, and *Madame Butterfly* are supremely accessible, undeniably heartrending, and laden with catchy tunes. Watch for the earmarks of *verismo*, the trendy gutter realism of the period.

THE GERMANS

Heavily into symbolism, weighty themes, philosophical and sometimes erotic undertones, and, after Wagner, orchestration. Top of the charts in the twentieth century.

THE COMPOSER

THE OPERAS

Christoph Willibald von Gluck (1714–1787)

Opera's first great reformer; attempted to streamline the form, do away with the florid excesses of *opera seria*, create a balance of power between drama and music. Of great historical, but little practical, importance, since no one followed his lead.

Formal, well balanced, critically respected, and largely forgotten because they lack immediate musical appeal. You're not likely to see *Orfeo ed Euridice* or *Iphigénie en Tauride*, at least where opera houses depend on audiences to pay their expenses.

Wolfgang Amadeus Mozart (1756–1791)

No great innovator, but had that magic touch; personalized and humanized opera and succeeded in balancing all of its pain-in-the-neck elements. A master musician, a sophisticate, a "natural." With Verdi and Wagner, forms the triumvirate of opera "greats."

Remember Mozart's three great "Italian" operas: *Le Nozze di Figaro*, a comedy with political overtones; *Così fan tutte*, a sexual farce, sort of, that scandalized all but late-twentieth-century audiences; and *Don Giovanni*, the greatest example of Mozart's unconventional mix of tragedy and comedy. The two "German" operas to know about are *Die Entführung aus dem Serail* (*The Abduction from the Seraglio*) and *Die Zauberflöte* (*The Magic Flute*, which some critics consider the most perfect opera ever written). Both are advances on the traditional German "singspiel," a loose construction of popular and folk tunes, and together laid the foundations for indigenous German opera.

Ludwig van Beethoven (1770–1827)

The Romantic genius; wrote only one opera, but it's a doozy.

Fidelio took nine years to write, blazed no new trails, and has some serious problems in the structure department; still, it's Beethoven, it's big-time, and to its admirers, it's the greatest opera ever written. It is also, in its moralistic themes, the polar opposite of the frivolous immorality Herr B. deplored in Mozart.

Richard Wagner (1813–1883)

Opera's towering intellect, its second Great Reformer (this one had influence in spades), and the pinnacle of German Romanticism. A megalomaniac and a visionary.

Wagnerian "music drama" (his term) aimed at a union of all theatrical arts: poetry, drama, music, and stagecraft. Major innovations: symphony-scale operatic orchestration (and singers powerful enough to be heard over it); the dripping-with-significance leitmotif (an orchestral theme recurring throughout a work and representing a particular character or idea). All Wagner operas are narcotic, hypnotic, and very, very long. *Tannhäuser* is considered the most accessible, *Parsifal* the least. In between, remember *Tristan und Isolde*; the four-opera *Ring* cycle; and the lone comedy, *Die Meistersinger von Nürnberg*. All are full of psychosexual undertones and all are holy, holy, holy.

Richard Strauss (1864–1949)

Most popular composer of the turn of the century. Not to be confused with Johann Strauss, "The Waltz King," although Richard capitalized on the association by sprinkling his operas with waltz tunes.

Lovely, easy-to-swallow operas that made lots of money. *Salomé* is best remembered as a succès de scandale, *Der Rosenkavalier* for its pretty waltzes.

Alban Berg (1885–1935)

Probably the most important modern opera composer; an experimentalist working with atonality and post-Freudian themes (see also page 278.)

His two operas, *Wozzeck* (pronounced VOY-chek) and the unfinished (but recently reconstructed) *Lulu* are both highly cerebral, avant-garde works with complex musical structures unlike anything you ever thought of as opera. Don't bother looking for melodies (there aren't any), but the plots are full of sinister sexuality and twentieth-century angst.

THE FRENCH

In it for the spectacle: the storyline, the costumes, the courtly dances, the divine special effects, and *le pauvre* who gets boiled in oil in the second act.

THE COMPOSER

THE OPERAS

Giacomo Meyerbeer (1791–1864)

A German who went to Paris and wrote the most successful French operas of his time. The master of grand opera. His works are now rarely performed.

Les Huguenots, the best known and longest lived, is grand opera par excellence. The dominant style in nineteenth-century France, grand opera was long, epic, historical, and loaded with spectacle, always including a ballet or two and usually at least one massacre. Never the most subtle or best-knit of plots, but large, expensive, and exciting.

Louis-Hector Berlioz (1803–1869)

Either France's greatest opera composer or a genius *manqué*, depending on taste. Much maligned in his own day ("The French wanted talent, not genius," says a critic). Brilliant anti-Wagnerian opera theorist; unconventional, unclassifiable. Remains a controversial figure.

No two alike, though all aimed at drama *through* music (as opposed to the Wagnerian ideal of drama *and* music); *Benvenuto Cellini*, an early, resounding failure, cut short his operatic career; *Les Troyens* (*The Trojans*), his "gigantic masterpiece," brought vindication in the twentieth century.

Charles François Gounod (1818–1893); Georges Bizet (1838–1875)
Each wrote one masterpiece.

Gounod's *Faust,* once ubiquitous, has dropped down the charts recently, but is still one of the few French operas performed all over the world. Bizet's *Carmen* is the most famous example of *opéra comique* (the French alternative to grand opera; not necessarily humorous, although usually equipped with a happy ending; the term applied to any opera that included spoken dialogue) and, although often badly produced, one of the most popular operas ever.

THE ENGLISH

Always a bridesmaid, never a bride.

THE COMPOSER

Henry Purcell (1659–1695)
England's Great White Hope. Alas, he died young. (See page 276.)

George Frideric Handel (1685–1759)
German-born, naturalized Englishman who lived in London and wrote mainstream Italian operas. Because he and they were so successful, gave English colleagues a permanent inferiority complex.

Benjamin Britten (1913–1976)
England's postwar contender; not in the Hall of Fame just yet, but the best they've got and the only modern English composer whose name you're likely to hear. Known for eclecticism, passionate music, a feeling for the human predicament.

THE OPERAS

Dido and Aeneas, the only English opera to rank as a world masterpiece.

Quintessential *opera seria;* of Handel's many operas, a few are still performed, e.g. *Orlando, Giulio Cesare, Rinaldo.* Beautiful music, lame dramas, highly formalized structures; once considered white elephants, now have a limited but enthusiastic following.

Peter Grimes and *Billy Budd* are his two well-known, full-scale operas; lack of English opera tradition and consequent lack of funding resulted in chamber (small) operas such as *The Turn of the Screw, Let's Make an Opera, The Beggar's Opera* (a remake), etc.

THE RUSSIANS

Had a penchant for collective singing, heroic themes, folk idioms; can get as gloomy as a rainy day in Vladivostok.

THE COMPOSER	THE OPERAS
Modest Petrovich Moussorgsky (1839–1881) Mother Russia's number one operatic son.	His one complete opera, *Boris Godunov*, based on a play by Pushkin, is considered uniquely Russian in the way Dostoevsky is considered uniquely Russian; original, both musically and dramatically, impassioned, nationalistic, imbued with intense feeling for the "Russian people." Also, a little grim.
Peter Ilyich Tchaikovsky (1840–1893) Educated in the West; the first to pour Russian themes and melancholia into Western classical molds.	His masterpiece, *Eugene Onegin*, has moments of greatness but is criticized for being "too pretty."

THE CZECHS

Passionate, colorful, high on folklore.

Bedřich Smetana (1824–1884)
Czech patriot; one of the leaders of the movement toward nationalistic opera; a major force behind development of a Czech style.

The Bartered Bride, a colorful peasant comedy, is the only one of his works well known outside the homeland. His other operas tend more toward the heroic than the folksy, their patriotism troweled on.

Leoš Janáček (1854–1928)
Former cult figure, increasingly recognized as a master composer.

Lyrical, theatrical, and thoroughly accessible, his operas have run into trouble because translating opera from the Czech is no mean feat. The composer's humanism, love of nature, and obsession with folk idioms and speech rhythms are evident in his three best-known works, the tragic *Jenufa*, the fantastical *Makropoulos Affair*, and the pantheistic *Cunning Little Vixen*, with its cast composed entirely of animals.

THE AMERICANS

Have suffered from Old World/New World schizophrenia; worked it out in a diversity of styles and genres. Keep trying.

THE COMPOSER

Douglas Moore (1893–1969)
Minor explorer of American regionalism and roots.

Virgil Thomson (1896–)
Sophisticated music critic and composer who made brief forays into opera.

Gian-Carlo Menotti (1911–)
Well-known Italian-American lightweight; forthright defender of opera as mass entertainment and promoter of television as operatic medium.

Philip Glass (1937–)
Postmodernist with a predilection for hypnotic repetition, electronic technology, and mixed-media effects.

THE OPERAS

The Devil and Daniel Webster, from Benét's literary tall tale, and the folkloric *Ballad of Baby Doe*, popular with touring companies and university music clubs.

Four Saints in Three Acts and *The Mother of Us All*, two charming, cerebral, short operas, notable for the cachet of Gertrude Stein's collaboration.

A long string of hits, of which the most famous are *The Medium*, a melodramatic supernatural thriller; *The Consul* and *The Saint of Bleecker Street*, serious operas about, respectively, political refugees and religious skepticism; and *Amahl and the Night Visitors*, the first opera to be written for television, perfect Christmas family fare.

Einstein on the Beach and *Satyagraha*, the former a marathon collaboration with then-wunderkind Robert Wilson, having something to do with relativity theory; the latter all about (sort of) Gandhi and passive resistance.

Eleven Arias to Sing in the Shower

BRING YOUR OWN SOAP

TOSCA (Puccini) act 2, "Vissi d'arte": Famous singer (that's Tosca) and her painter boyfriend fall into the clutches of evil police chief. He threatens to liquidate boyfriend unless she submits to his advances. She protests: "Vissi d'arte, vissi d'amore, non feci mai / Male ad anima viva!" ("Love and music, / these I have lived for, / Nor ever harmed a living being!")

RIGOLETTO (Verdi), act 3, "La donna è mobile": Dad, a court jester (Rigoletto), tries to shield daughter from worldly corruption. Things start to slide when an old count puts a curse on him. After Dad's boss, the lascivious Duke, seduces his daughter, Rigoletto forces her to eavesdrop with him while the Duke reveals his true misogynist colors: "La donna è mobile / Qual piuma al vento / Muta d'accento / E di pensiero." ("Woman's fidelity / Turns like the weather, / Sways like a feather / Tossed in the breeze.") Aria recurs later, revealing to Rigoletto that it is murdered daughter, not murdered Duke, he carries in the sack on his back.

LUCIA DI LAMMERMOOR (Donizetti), act 3, "Spargi d'amaro pianto" (just refer to Lucia's "Mad Scene"): Girl's brother tries to pressure her into marriage to bolster fading family fortunes. Forges letter announcing her true love's engagement to another woman. Plan backfires; on her wedding day, she goes bananas, stabs her tutor, and wanders babbling among the wedding guests. "Spargi d'amaro pianto / Il mio terrestre velo. Mentre lassù nel Cielo lo pregherò per te." ("Ah, shed your bitter tears / over my earthly remains. But meanwhile in Heaven above I will be praying for you.")

LA TRAVIATA (Verdi) act 1, "Sempre libera": Young man loves dying courtesan; Dumas' "La Dame aux Camélias" retold. Violetta contemplates possibility of returning Alfredo's love and leading a pure and simple life. Then she has second thoughts: "Sempre libera degg'io / Follegiare di gioia in gioia. . ." ("Ever lightsome, ever free, / Flitting on from joy to joy. . .")

DIE WALKÜRE (Wagner) act 1, "Winterstürme" ("The Spring Song"): Hapless brother and sister, fall guys for the gods, are reunited after years of misery and loneliness. They fall in love. Things seem to be picking up. Little do they know . . . "Winterstürme wichen / Dem Winnemond, / In milden Lichte / Leuchtet der Lenz." ("Winter storms have waned in / the joyful May. / The spring is shining, / mild is his light.")

DON GIOVANNI (Mozart), act 1, "Madamina" (also known as "Leporello's Catalogue Aria"): Life in the fast lane with the notorious ladies' man (we're talking about Don Juan here, in case you don't speak Italian). After one particularly close shave, the Don leaves his servant, Leporello, to entertain a vengeful victim. Leporello tries to make conversation: "Madamina, il catalogo è questo, / Delle belle che amo il padron mio." ("Little lady, this is the catalogue / Of the Ladies my master has loved.") Best known for its refrain: "Ma, in Ispagna, son già mille e tre!" ("But in Spain, one thousand and three!")

NORMA (Bellini), act 1, "Casta Diva": Love among the Druids. High Priestess (Norma) has swapped sacred chastity for the affections of a Roman proconsul. Now she's left to contend with a guilty conscience, two illegitimate kids, and a crowd of restless locals itching for a rumble with the Romans. Craving peace (for the moment—she'll feel less pacific when she hears that the proconsul plans to leave her for a younger priestess), Norma invokes the Moon: "Casta Diva, casta Diva, che in argenti / Queste sacre, queste sacre antiche piante / A noi volgi il bel sembiante." ("Chaste Goddess, chaste Goddess, who makes silver / These ancient, sacred trees / Turn toward us thy lovely face.")

FIDELIO (Beethoven) act 1, "Abscheulicher": Wicked governor imprisons political opponent. Opponent's wife, in drag, gets job as jailkeeper's assistant. Overhears governor's plot to assassinate husband. Is understandably upset: "Abscheulicher! Wo eilst du hin? Was hast du vor? / Was hast du vor im wilden Grimme?" ("Monster! Whither is thy haste? / What designs breed thy rage?")

LA BOHÈME (Puccini), act 1, "Che gelida manina": Four carefree young artistes share substandard garret. The sensitive poetic one meets consumptive little embroideress from garret next door. Notices, as they proceed to fall in love, that she seems a bit under the weather: "Che gelida manina / Se la lasci riscaldar." ("Your tiny hand is frozen. Let me warm it into life.")

LE NOZZE DI FIGARO (Mozart), act 1, "Non so più cosa son": Sexual intrigue, sexual revenge, marital infidelity, the breakdown of the class system—an Italian "Upstairs, Downstairs." Here, the young page Cherubino describes what it feels like to discover his hormones: "Non so più cosa son, cosa faccio, / Or di fuoco, ora son di ghiaccio. . ." ("I can't give you a good explanation / For this new and confusing sensation.")

CARMEN (Bizet), act 2, "La fleur que tu m'as jetée" (known as Don José's "Flower Song"): Gypsy femme fatale (Carmen) seduces honorable young officer of the guard, leading him to betray his sweetheart and his post to join a band of smugglers. After doing time for helping Carmen escape from police, the hapless Don José, destined to be ditched for a toreador, pledges his love: "La fleur que tu m'as jetée / Dans ma prison m'était restée. / Flétrie et sechée, cette fleur / gardait toujours sa douce odeur. . ." ("The flower you threw me / Stayed with me in prison. / And though its bloom was swiftly gone, / Its haunting fragrance lingered on.")

Practical Italian for the Operagoer

diva: Literally, "goddess": a great lady of the opera, a legend. The highest accolade given to a female singer, usually by adoring fans or an ecstatic press. Ranks above the more restrained "prima donna," which, properly speaking, simply refers to the leading lady of an opera company.

recitativo: (Actually, you're better off using the English "recitative," unless you happen to be in Milan.) Refers to the speechlike vocal sections used to advance the action in an opera, as opposed to the more lyrical, anchoring arias, duets, etc. In most pre-Wagnerian opera, the *recitativo* was kept rigidly separated from the moments of pure "song," and, if allowed to go on too long, had a tendency to make audiences drowsy. Later composers began to blur the boundaries between the two.

libretto: The text, or lyrics, of an opera; also a "little book" (the literal meaning of the word) containing the lyrics, a synopsis of the plot, and often, an accompanying translation. In the early days of opera, librettos (in Italian, *libretti*) were reduced to pocket size so that they could be carried to the theater to help spectators follow the words of an opera during a performance. This custom was made possible by the fact that, at the time, house lights were habitually kept on throughout the performance; if further illumination was needed, audiences were sold little candles that attached to the tops of the librettos.

bel canto: Means, literally, "beautiful singing" and refers, historically, to the type of singer-dominated opera prevalent in Italy throughout the seventeenth and eighteenth centuries. In *bel canto* opera, pure vocal technique was emphasized, usually at the expense of drama and orchestration. With the advent of nineteenth century Romantic opera (and, in particular, Verdi's sweeping melodramas) the genre fell out of favor and was rarely heard until Maria Callas helped to revive it in the 1950s. Bellini's *Norma* and Donizetti's *Lucia di Lammermoor* are considered pinnacles of the *bel canto* style.

coloratura: A fake Italian word (possibly derived from the German "*koloratur*") indicating elaborate ornamentation of the melodic line; a kind of vocal acrobatics consisting of runs, trills, and added flourishes, and demanding exceptional speed and agility on the part of the singer. A coloratura soprano is one who specializes in this type of singing. Joan Sutherland is the best-known contemporary example and is, some say, one of the greatest coloratura singers of all time.

Opera Houses

THE HEAVY HALF DOZEN

TEATRO ALLA SCALA (MILAN)

Built in 1776 and named for a duchess, not a ladder, La Scala is still Italy's premiere opera house, despite Mussolini's efforts to transfer the operatic action to Rome. Like most major European houses, La Scala was bombed during World War II; the theater was rebuilt along the old Baroque lines—horseshoe-shaped auditorium, elaborate decor, seats stacked vertically to the ceiling—and reopened in 1946. The house gained points through its close association with Verdi in the nineteenth century, but nearly everyone agrees that its "Golden Age" came during the on-and-off directorship of Toscanini, between 1898 and 1929; it had another flowering during the 1950s, when Maria Callas reigned as "La Regina della Scala" and both Visconti and Zeffirelli worked on productions.

According to Western critics, La Scala has been in decline since the early 1970s when it became a hangout for Communists. Now the management is accused of substituting ideological standards for aesthetic ones, of discriminating against singers who aren't party members and against works it considers "fascist" (Puccini, for instance). We wouldn't want to comment on the validity of these accusations, but we will say that out of eighteen or so operas produced at the house each season, at least five or six are usually Russian. Still, La Scala is La Scala, legendary for its high production standards, huge repertory, and endless internal squabbles. Note: Audiences here are quite restrained, by Italian standards; in other parts of Italy it is said, scornfully, that the Milanese "sit on their hands" during performances. La Piccola Scala, housed in the same building, opened in 1956; it seats only 600 (the main house accommodates over 2,000) and specializes in chamber and experimental operas better suited to its size.

ROYAL OPERA HOUSE, COVENT GARDEN (LONDON)

Now the dowager queen of British opera, Covent Garden didn't really come into its own until after World War II. Although it was traditionally known for its star-studded seasons and blue-blooded audiences, its performances were generally dismissed as more social than serious, its productions as more opulent than tasteful. During the war, the theater was converted to a dance hall, thanks to a lack of public support that still makes English opera buffs wince in humiliation. After opera was reinstated in 1946, the resident company had to contend with a virulent inferiority complex due, in part, to the stream of foreign guest artists by which it was continually being upstaged, and in part to the way everyone kept pointing to the humble Sadler's Wells company as the place where British opera history was *really* being made. During the 1950s, however, singing standards at Covent Garden were upgraded and production standards became, at the very least, dependable.

Never quite as secure as the Royal Ballet, with which it shares headquarters, the Royal Opera has, for years, been hampered by a series of financial crises—but then, what British institution hasn't? The present theater, which opened in 1858, is the third to have existed on the site, which was originally a convent garden (hence the name), and, until 1974, the central fruit and vegetable market of London.

STAATSOPER (VIENNA)

One of the most venerable opera houses and, according to some, the most important, the Staatsoper (or State Opera) has three distinct advantages over its rivals: (1) its location in what has been, since the seventeenth century, the music capital of the world; (2) its resident orchestra, the Vienna Philharmonic, which has been called "the world's supreme musical instrument"; and (3) a combination of generous government subsidies and high ticket prices which allow it to hold a super-long annual season and to present more operas during that time than any other house (in some years more than twice as many as the Met, three times as many as Covent Garden). On the other hand, the Staatsoper, and the Viennese in general, are notoriously conservative; although they insist on high standards, they won't brook innovation. Consequently, history is preserved here, not made, and the Staatsoper's reputation, for better or worse, is based on rigidly traditional productions of the classics, especially works by the perennial Viennese favorites, Wagner, Mozart, and Richard Strauss.

The original theater, built in 1869 to house the already successful Vienna Court Opera, was partially destroyed during World War II; although the rebuilt version, which opened in 1955, still boasts an ornate facade and a lobby and grand staircase not unlike those of the Paris Opéra, the new auditorium is pencil-plain modern and not particularly attractive.

FESTSPIELHAUS (BAYREUTH, W. GERMANY)

Technically, Bayreuth, as it is universally known, is a festival, not a house, but it *is* one of the great operatic centers of the world, so let's not split hairs. Remember that it's pronounced BY-royt, unlike the capital of Lebanon, and that the name is virtually synonymous with that of Richard Wagner, who envisioned it as the ideal theater, supervised its design and construction, and ran it until his death. (His body, along with that of his father-in-law, Franz Liszt, is buried on its grounds.) After he died, Bayreuth was run by successive generations of Wagners and since its opening in 1876, has been devoted exclusively to the production of Wagnerian opera. Design-wise, the theater was revolutionary for its time. It was, in a sense, the first democratic opera house, eschewing the old Baroque box-and-tier system in favor of a fan-shaped auditorium with continuous rows of seating that provided uniformly good sightlines and spectacular acoustics. Under the direction of Wagner's grandson Wieland, Bayreuth exchanged opera's traditional naturalistic, painted backdrops for minimal sets and sophisticated lighting, calculated to evoke atmosphere and universal themes rather than specific locales. The technical innovations here have, for some time, provided standards for modernist theater design throughout the world.

L'OPÉRA (PARIS)

Probably the most sumptuous opera house in the world, l'Opéra (formally, l'Académie Nationale de Musique) was, at its 1875 opening, certainly the biggest. Designed as a monument to Second Empire architecture by Charles Garnier (and sometimes called "le palais Garnier"), the house peaked between 1885–1906, then promptly went into a seventy-year decline. Its enormous stage and machine-laden backstage area, tailor-made for the spectacular processions, elaborate special effects, and ornate ballets the French had loved so much during the heyday of grand opera (when Verdi, working in Paris, contemptuously referred to the theater as "la grande boutique"), now played host to an endless string of shoddy productions complemented by second-rate singing. By mid–twentieth century, l'Opéra had become just another elaborate piece of bric-a-brac on the Parisian landscape, as essential to the production of opera as the Eiffel Tower to the production of oil.

Since the early 1970s, however, l'Opéra's honor has been restored; not only has the house staged a comeback, it has made a name for itself as a showcase for experimental operas and for innovative, often controversial restagings of the classics. Today, its "failures" (a production of the *Ring* cycle, for instance, that drew boos and hisses from conservative audiences) tend to be as newsworthy as its "successes" (like its glamorous, history-making productions of Berg's *Wozzeck* and *Lulu*). As for the theater itself, it remains one of the great Parisian tourist attractions, noted particularly for its Grand Staircase—so grand, in fact, that it usurps valuable seating space.

METROPOLITAN OPERA HOUSE
(NEW YORK)

The original opened on Broadway in 1883 when a group of wealthy business-men, irritated because they couldn't get boxes at the Academy of Music, decided to start their own theater. Despite its early policy of producing all operas in German, the Met had, by the turn of the century, shown a knack for attracting the biggest operatic guns of Europe (Caruso, Mahler, and Tosca-nini, among others) and the richest patrons of its home town (the Vanderbilt clan alone took up five private boxes). In 1966, the company moved to con-temporary glass-and-marble headquarters at Lincoln Center for the Perform-ing Arts. The new theater drew raves for its acoustics, its huge warren of backstage rehearsal and administrative rooms, and its state-of-the-art technical facilities (the *New Yorker* music critic called it "the most efficient factory for the production of opera ever devised"); some pans for its less-than-perfect sightlines; and a mixed bag of gasps and snickers for the two huge Chagall murals adorning the Great Hall. Today the Met is one of the two or three most prestigious and important opera houses in the world, although hardly the most adventurous. Next door, at the decidedly less glamourous New York State Theater, the plucky New York City Opera plays Betty to the Met's Veronica.

A Night at the Opera

MANNERS AND MORALS FOR THE MTV GENERATION

Granted, you'd feel more comfortable if you'd absorbed opera etiquette as a tot, sitting between Mummy and Daddy at La Scala or Covent Garden. Just remember that the prospect of going to the opera is a lot more intimidating than the actual experience, and that, in America at any rate, at least half the audience will be made up of late-bloomers like yourself. It does help, however, to know the rules of the game:

1. *Memorize the plot before you go.* This will only take a minute, given the complexity of most opera plots (but watch out for *Rigoletto*), and nearly everyone's written a book summarizing them. Opera, as you'll recall, is supposed to be the perfect combination of music *and* drama, and you'll find it enormously helpful, as the curtain goes down on *Aïda,* for instance, to know why that nice young man and his girlfriend are still hanging out in the basement.

2. *Bring a libretto.* If you can't borrow it from the local library, you can usually buy one at the box office on the night of the performance. Cram during intermission. No one will expect you to understand even a third of what's being sung onstage, but after all, the librettist didn't deliberately write the lyrics in a language you wouldn't understand; he meant them to enhance the appeal of the songs, and, as in the best of Broadway musicals, they often do.

3. *Don't clap until the people around you do.* The moments of silence in an opera don't always signal breaktime; very often, the singer pauses for effect, or to indicate that something dramatic is about to happen, or to heighten the intensity of an orchestral interlude, which, by the way, is to be paid attention to. Opera orchestras, unlike Doc Severinsen and his boys, don't expect to have to play through applause.

4. *Go ahead and voice your enthusiasm,* if the spirit moves you, at the end of a well-executed aria. Strictly speaking, you're supposed to shout "Bravo!" if the singer is a man, "Brava!" if it's a woman, but American audiences tend to take a unisex approach, shouting "Bravo!" to everyone indiscriminately, and the singers don't seem to mind. (Just, please, refrain from yelling "Bravissimo!" which is simply pretentious. Some of the people around you may be doing it, but you don't want to know them.)

5. *Don't spend a lot of time worrying about what to wear*, unless you're going to La Scala, or have an invitation to share a box at the gala with the Duke and Duchess of Bedford. Jeans, of course, are inadvisable (although not unheard of). And while we agree that arriving in diamonds and satin with a liveried footman to help one out of one's carriage can make the whole opera-going experience more meaningful, outside Milan, and especially in America, most people opt for comfort and just try to have clean hair.

6. *Don't choose Wagner your first time out.* Later, maybe, you'll come to relish sitting in the dark for four hours contemplating the erotic implications of death and listening to music that (to the untrained ear) all sounds alike. Right now, it's OK to go for one of the crowd-pleasers, maybe something by Puccini or Verdi (although, if we had to choose between them, we'd recommend the Verdi; they'll both make you cry, but even a novice will sense the presence of Quality). Some obvious possibilities:

Aïda, which, for sheer grandeur and pageantry, can't be beat; if the music doesn't get you, you can still groove on the elephants.

Carmen, the world's most popular opera, and one of the most accessible; this is a real *musical*, complete with Spanish dances and lots of gypsy flavor. It does, however, bring with it the risk of shoddy production values and over-weight leading ladies.

The Magic Flute, a spectacular fairytale, written to please ordinary people, not just opera buffs. The plot's so hare-brained that you won't lose anything by not understanding German, and as pure entertainment it is, like any Mozart, a shoo-in.

Norma, one of the greatest "singer's operas." It's harder to recommend this one; the plot's clumsy and you may not go for the *bel canto* style. Given the right cast, however, the music can take your breath away; besides we've always had a thing about Druids.

PHILOSOPHY

Contents

Socrates, about to swig the hemlock, in Jacques-Louis David's 1787 you-are-there evocation of his death.

Philosophy Made Simplistic

Philosophy is the study of everything that counts, just as those ancient Greeks, who were as interested in the structure of matter and the existence of God as they were in the nature of good, always said it was. Today, though, what with the pressures of specialization (not to mention the glut of Ph.D.'s), the physicists have walked off with matter and the theologians with God, leaving the philosophers either to go on pondering "What is good?" or to become computer programmers. Don't tell *them* that, though; they still think they have the last word on anything that falls within one or more of the following five areas of classical philosophical investigation:

1. *Logic:* What's valid, what's invalid; what can profitably be argued and proven, what can't; how to test a categorical syllogism; how not to keep making silly mistakes all the time. Or, as Tweedledee says in *Through the Looking Glass,* "Contrariwise, if it was so it might be; and if it were so, it would be; but as it isn't, it ain't. That's logic."

2. *Ethics:* Which actions are right and which ends are good. Moreover, is the rightness of actions inferable from the goodness of their consequences? And while you're on the subject, is the virtuousness of a motive to be inferred from the rightness of the actions that it tends to prompt? Also, is it less bad to shoplift from K-Mart than from the corner hardware store even though the salesperson at K-Mart explained the fine points of home rewiring to you and the guy who runs the hardware store doesn't know a switch from a socket? And other more or less practical aspects of human conduct.

3. *Aesthetics:* Beauty and art and taste, standards and judgments and criticism, Aristotle and Oscar Wilde and Christie Brinkley. Why do we like what we like? Does art per se exist, or is it just patches of color and hummable tunes and words in a row? Is the point of a work of art that it be representative of something, or that it express its creator's identity, or that it engage its audience? And is there a relationship between what's beautiful and what's good?

4. *Epistemology:* Do we *really* know anything and, if so, what? And how do we know it? And how do we know that we know it? And how do we know that we know that we know it? etc. Note: Ever since Wittgenstein (see page 325), formal philosophical inquiry has been centered less on classical epistemology and more on language, less on the question, "How do you know?" and more on the question, "What do you mean?"

5. *Metaphysics:* The big one; the search for (and ransacking of) ultimate categories, with, as its goal, an understanding of the all-inclusive scheme of things otherwise known as the world and of the part man

plays within it. Past discoveries have included existence, essence, time, space, God, self, and cause. Stay tuned. But don't hold your breath: A lot of philosophers now characterize metaphysics as "over-poetic" and "prescientific."

Got Another Minute or Two?

Philosophy is, as befits the so-called "queen of sciences," rife with -ologies and -isms. Of these, let's take a closer look at three of the former (and you've already had epistemology, don't forget) and two of the latter.

Ontology is literally the study of being (the cancer specialty is on*c*ology), and is sometimes used interchangeably with metaphysics. Depending on whom you listen to, it's either the most generic and abstract of all intellectual inquiries or it's a compilation of pseudo-problems only a fool would tackle. If you must field (or wield) the word, keep in mind that it implies getting to the heart of the matter, to the very essence of something. So, an ontology of the cinema would proceed by taking the thing called "moving pictures" and contrasting it with still photographs and with paintings, with television, with the landscape viewed through the windshield of a moving car. It would talk about other activities revolving around lenses and editing; other art forms undertaken collectively and enjoyed communally. (What it wouldn't deal with: Eisenstein, Hollywood in the Thirties, Jean-Luc Godard's career, censorship, the "zoom," what makes a movie fun to watch, or the insipidity of Oscars night.) Careful: *Ontology* is a word strictly for intellectual big-spenders.

Two -ologies have to do with final affairs. One, *eschatology* (not to be confused with *sca*tology, a preoccupation with excrement or talking dirty), describes any doctrine or system focused on such end-of-the-line matters as death, the afterlife, immortality, and redemption. William Buckley has even described Communism as an eschatological system because it deals in a "millennial vision" of peace and equality, en route to which the present is just a way station, life less a process than a partial product.

The other, *teleology*, is applied to a belief in, or study of, an overall purpose, design, or end (*telos*, in the Greek), usually in nature. Teleologists like to invoke results as reasons: Of course the giraffe has a long neck, argued the pre-Darwinian biologist and teleologist, Lamarck (see page 526); he needs it to reach the tender leaves he feeds on. Teleology tends to thrive in systems structured around the existence of an active God, intent on revelation (see page 335). And to be treated as anathema by scientists.

Still With Us?

Great! Of the -isms, by far the most important are the diametrically opposed idealism and materialism, neither of which has its everyday meaning here.

Idealism stipulates that the nature of reality is completely bound up with mind and consciousness and thought, that your leg and your bandanna and your patriotism and Bruce Springsteen and his leg and his bandanna and his patriotism cannot be dealt with—perceived or proven to exist—except through the activity of your (or somebody's) knowing mind.

Materialism maintains that all entities—including everybody and everybody's leg and everybody's bandanna and everybody's patriotism *and* everybody's mind—can only be explained in terms of matter and energy, atoms and electrons. Thus had Madonna sung about being a material*ist* girl, she'd have been casting her vote not for net gloves and dangly earrings but for molecules over perceptions. Which, come to think of it, was more or less what she was doing anyway.

Rating the Thinkers

A CONSUMER'S GUIDE TO TWENTY PHILOSOPHERS

PLATO (c. 427–c. 347 B.C.)

Best-Known Works: The *Dialogues,* especially the *Apology, Crito,* and *Phaedo* (a trilogy about the imprisonment and death of Socrates); the *Symposium* (on the nature of love); and the *Republic* (on the principles of government).

Readability: Too bad you were asked to read the *Republic* at an age when you couldn't wait to get back to *Lord of the Rings.* As philosophers go, Plato is a live wire; the *Dialogues* read like screenplays, complete with sets, props, characters, and, of course, dialogue. True, that ancient Greek frame of reference takes some getting used to but, as with any vintage movie, switching into another mindset is half the fun.

Qualities of Mind: Abstract, absolutist, imaginative, moralistic, ironic; intellectually better equipped to walk on water than build bridges.

Catchphrases: The allegory of the cave (see page 327), philosopher-kings.

Influence: Metaphysics on a grand scale, from the world's greatest rationalist. Postulated the existence of a supreme order of archetypal, universal ideas, or pure Forms, of which all our existing forms and ideas are only cheap, transitory reflections; these paradigmatic Forms are independent of, and inaccessible to, sensory experience, and are only perceivable through the power of the mind. Plato's confidence in the possibility of reasoning or conceptualizing one's way to Truth, together with his mistrust of knowledge obtained through the senses, pretty much defines philosophical rationalism, then and now. He is also our only source—albeit an unreliable one—for the teachings of Socrates.

Personal Gossip: A rich young aristocrat who could afford to spend his time contemplating pure Ideas. His real name was Aristocles; Plato was a nickname meaning "broad," which may have referred to his forehead, his waistline, or the scope of his ideas. And yes, he was probably gay.

Current Standing: Some contemporary philosophers would agree with Alfred North Whitehead's remark that "Philosophy is only a series of footnotes to Plato." (But, then, no one can appreciate a philosopher-mathematician like another philosopher-mathematician.) Neither empiricists nor fitness buffs much go for his denigration of sensory experience, however, and, on the whole, Aristotle, a nuts-and-bolts type, seems more acceptable to the modern mind.

ARISTOTLE (384–322 B.C.)

Best-Known Works: Organon, Physics, Politics, Rhetoric, Poetics, Nichomachean Ethics.

Readability: If you enjoy reading leases, you'll love Aristotle; every thought is examined in detail and every detail meticulously numbered. To be fair, you should remember that his only extant works are treatises which were probably intended as lecture notes; his early popular works have been lost.

Qualities of Mind: Lucid, learned, practical, didactic, analytical, versatile. Dante called him "The master of those who know."

Catchphrases: The Golden Mean, the Unmoved Mover (see page 334), the Dramatic Unities, entelechy, catharsis (see page 260).

Influence: The roots of modern science and, probably, Western civilization. Discarded Plato's abstractions in favor of observation and analysis of the physical world. Systematically studied and categorized virtually everything: astronomy, physics, anatomy, physiology, psychology, natural history, political science, rhetoric, art, theology, whatever. Planted the ideas of the pursuit of happiness (a thoroughly modern, success-oriented morality, which tacitly relegates virtue to the level of a means to an end) and the Golden Mean (or "moderation in all things," a doctrine that, as Bertrand Russell pointed out, appeals mainly to the respectable middle-aged). Established the West's first, and until recently, only, systematic study of logic. Still associated with modern concepts of scientific analysis, although many of his conclusions put scientists on the wrong track for a couple thousand years.

Personal Gossip: Student of Plato (remember the order: Socrates taught Plato, Plato taught Aristotle); teacher of Alexander the Great, who apparently didn't pay much attention to him.

Current Standing: Plato's opposite number and of the two, the leader in a science-minded age.

SAINT AUGUSTINE (354–430)

Best-Known Works: Confessions, The City of God.

Readability: Not difficult, exactly, but after reading seven pages on the wickedness of stealing a pear, or two chapters on the putative differences between good demons and bad demons, you may decide you'd rather spend your time discussing, say, fluoridation of the water supply with someone closer to your own age.

Qualities of Mind: Scholarly, fevered, guilt-ridden, dogmatic, idealistic.

Catchphrases: City of God, city of man.

Influence: Cornerstone of the Christian Church; attempted a rational defense of Christianity in light of the fall of the Roman Empire and tried to fit all of history into a Christian framework. Sometimes called the founder of theology. Gave us ideas of separation of Church and State and of history as progression toward a goal (see page 537). Biggest influence on Christian thinking, and especially on Roman Catholicism, after St. Paul. Wrote the first self-analytical autobiography, precursor of the genre as well as of the modern introspective novel.

Personal Gossip: Had a long-term mistress and an illegitimate child before his mother, St. Monica, finally talked him into becoming a Christian.

Current Standing: Out of date, but he had soul. Admired by Platonists (since he was an outspoken Plato fan himself) and by contemporary Protestant theologians in search of "the essence" of Christianity.

SAINT THOMAS AQUINAS (1225–1274)

Best-Known Works: Summa Theologica, Summa Contra Gentiles.

Readability: Elaborate and extremely formal; do not drive or operate heavy machinery while reading.

Qualities of Mind: Learned, dogged, systematic, analytical; they didn't call him "The Prince of Scholastics" for nothing.

Catchphrases: His epithet: "The Angelic Doctor."

Influence: Constructed the second great synthesis of Christian thinking, which superseded Augustine's as of the thirteenth century. Championed Aristotle, as opposed to Plato, and based his theology more on concrete analysis of this world than on irrational faith in the next. Reinterpreted Aristotle's ideas in Christian terms. Effected the classic integration of reason and revelation, proved conclusively the existence of God, and split hairs more brilliantly and systematically than nearly all his Scholastic colleagues. Provided the Catholic Church with much of its official dogma, then and now.

Personal Gossip: When he was a teenager, his mother had him locked up for two years to prevent him from becoming a Dominican monk. He escaped and joined the order anyway. He later became very famous and very fat.

Current Standing: A lesson in the rewards of thoroughness; beyond that, unless you're a Catholic priest, take him with a grain of salt.

NICCOLÒ MACHIAVELLI (1469–1527)

Best-Known Works: The Prince, Discourses.

Readability: A piece of cake; Machiavelli was forced to earn his living as a writer, so he understood the importance of keeping his audience awake.

Qualities of Mind: Shrewd, pragmatic, insightful, cynical.

Catchphrases: The chief foundations of all states . . . are good laws and good arms.

Influence: Revolutionized political philosophy and shocked idealists by adopting a purely secular, scientific perspective toward statecraft; left out questions of morality altogether in order to focus, reporterlike, on what was, not what should have been. Wrote the classic how-to book for aspirants to power (*The Prince*). Based principles of government on the assumptions that man is fundamentally bad and that the end justifies the means. Was the rare philosopher whose name became a household word, in his case, synonymous with deception, unscrupulousness, and cunning.

Personal Gossip: A politician himself (as well as author and historian), Machiavelli wrote *The Prince* in an unsuccessful attempt to curry favor with the reigning Medici, who didn't like him and who probably never read it. (Among those who *did* read it: Mussolini, Hitler, Lenin, and Stalin.) For a more balanced, and more honest picture of his ideas, read the *Discourses*.

Current Standing: His political views are more acceptable in our era than in any since his own; nowadays anyone who disagrees with him is assumed to be hypocritical or naïve. Considered a first-rate social scientist, but as a pure thinker, superficial, inconsistent, and generally shaky.

RENÉ DESCARTES (1596–1650)

Best-Known Works: Discourse on Method, Meditations on First Philosophy.

Readability: Rolls right along; philosophy with a sense of style for a change. Descartes writes like an intelligent adult addressing other intelligent adults. His prose, some say, is to the French language what the King James Bible is to the English.

Qualities of Mind: Sophisticated, independent, lucid, methodical, individualistic.

Catchphrases: Cogito ergo sum.

Influence: Marks the point at which the world decided to go modern. Was determined to make a clean sweep of all the comfortable old assumptions, to take nobody's word for anything, to doubt everything in order to find something he could be sure of. Came up with the famous bottom line, "I think, therefore I am." Most important for his emphasis on the *way* we know things, which made him "father of the scientific method." Insisted on the complete separation of mind and matter (which would later split philosophy into warring camps) and on the purely mechanistic nature of the physical world.

Personal Gossip: Who can gossip about a mathematician? This was the kind of guy who would move rather than allow his friends to drop by and interrupt his train of thought.

Current Standing: Seminal figure of modern philosophy; usually off-base (who says "I am" just because "I think," and how do I *know* I think, anyway?) but always inspiring.

JOHN LOCKE (1632–1704)

Best-Known Works: An Essay Concerning Human Understanding, Second Treatise on Government.

Readability: Boring but bearable; like reading the Declaration of Independence, which, in fact, borrowed from his phraseology as well as from his ideas.

Qualities of Mind: Modest, sensible, utilitarian, tolerant.

Catchphrases: The mind as *tabula rasa* (blank page), the system of checks and balances, the labor theory of value, laissez-faire, the rights of man, "Knowledge is the perception of the agreement or disagreement of two ideas."

Influence: As a political philosopher, was the theoretical architect of what we call democracy; gave us basic liberal ideals (the primacy of the pursuit of happiness, the belief in the natural rights of man) and specific principles of government (majority rule, checks and balances). As a pure philosopher, was the first to stress epistemology, the study of *how* we know things. Pioneered modern empiricism, declaring that the mind at birth is *tabula rasa*, that there are no such things as innate ideas, that all ideas come to us through our senses from the material world—a science-oriented way of thinking that opted for limited, but immediately usable, knowledge of everyday reality.

Personal Gossip: A physician who came to prominence, politically and philosophically, when he chose the winning side (William of Orange, see page 550) in the Glorious Revolution of 1688.

Current Standing: No towering intellect, just an eminently reasonable man with a head full of ideas whose time had come. A propounder of popular, rather than profound, political theories, the validity of which depend largely on how one feels about liberal democracy.

BARUCH SPINOZA (1632–1677)

Best-Known Works: Ethics.

Readability: Just conquered the Matterhorn? Looking for a challenge? Welcome to the *Ethics*, a deadly morass of euclidean definitions, axioms, theorems, and demonstrations of the impossible. Too bad; Spinoza could be a rather eloquent writer. We're told that if you can get through the whole thing—twice—it starts to grow on you.

Qualities of Mind: Analytical, realistic, idealistic, mystical, rational, patient, rigorous, determined.

Catchphrases: Sub specie aeternitis (in the light of eternity); all determination is negation.

Influence: The world's most sensible mystic. Constructed the first thoroughly logical, consistent metaphysical system and made the first attempt at an objective, scientific study of human behavior. Carried all arguments to their logical conclusions, even when those conclusions meant trouble. A pantheist and a pure determinist, who believed, as all good mystics do, in the oneness of the universe, in the supremacy of immutable natural law, in the necessity of learning to go with the flow. Had no followers, but his freethinking religious views helped pave the way for the Enlightenment.

Personal Gossip: Excommunicated (and formally cursed with all the curses of Deuteronomy) by the Jewish community in Holland for refusing to keep his heretical thoughts to himself. Socially ostracized, he earned his living as a lens grinder, wrote philosophy on the side, and is best remembered for behaving, all the way to his deathbed, like a saint.

Current Standing: Nobody doesn't like Spinoza; he was smart, hardworking, and holy, one of the few intellectuals on record to have actually lived by his beliefs. Bertrand Russell called him "the most lovable of philosophers." On the other hand, the idea of bowing quietly to Natural Law has never been big box office in the West.

GOTTFRIED WILHELM VON LEIBNIZ
(1646–1716)

Best-Known Works: Monadology, Principles of Nature and of Grace, Theodicy.

Readability: Uninviting: dry, precise, businesslike; moves fast and seems likely to snap at you if you can't keep up.

Qualities of Mind: Rigorous, dynamic, logical, systematic, concise, humorless.

Catchphrases: Windowless monads, pre-established harmony; also Voltaire's parodistic phrase "This is the best of all possible worlds."

Influence: One of the great "Continental rationalists," mainstream thinkers of the seventeenth century. Invented the infinitesimal calculus, founded the first system of symbolic logic, furthered the development of exact logical analysis. A metaphysician in the tradition of Descartes, he created the famous analogy of the Cartesian Clocks, which postulates that mind and body do not interact, but only seem to, because they are synchronized by God. Publicly espoused a philosophy that was pious, logical, and somewhat simpleminded, for which he was caricatured as Dr. Pangloss in Voltaire's *Candide*. Secretly spent his life trying to perfect a brilliant, complex mathematical system that aimed at replacing thought with calculation.

Personal Gossip: An ambitious hypocrite who kept his best work secret and published whatever would make him popular with his employers. Admired and was influenced by Spinoza, whom he denounced as soon as it seemed expedient.

Current Standing: Considered by many to be one of the greatest logicians of all time. Although nearly all of his conclusions are either totally implausible or hopelessly obsolete, his methods for arriving at them are models of clearheadedness.

DAVID HUME (1711–1776)

Best-Known Works: Enquiry Concerning Human Understanding; A Treatise of Human Nature and the simplified version of the first book thereof, *An Enquiry Concerning Human Understanding.*

Readability: Lucid, compact, direct; refreshing, though not, as Hume had hoped, riveting.

Qualities of Mind: Rigorous, no-nonsense, consistent, honest.

Catchphrases: The science of man. Also, Kant's famous remark that reading Hume "awakened me from my dogmatic slumbers."

Influence: The Scottish skeptic who took Locke's empirical arguments to their logical conclusion (which Locke had neglected to do) and wound up doubting our ability to know anything at all. That the sun will rise tomorrow morning, according to Hume, is not something we *know,* but something we *believe,* simply because it has risen every other morning. Effectively deflated metaphysical pretensions, made philosophers very nervous about their assumptions, and made it clear that the Age of Reason had arrived at a dead end.

Personal Gossip: A cheerful, easy-going sort, despite his skepticism; one of the few men capable of maintaining a friendship with Rousseau (although Rousseau did turn on him in the end). Always wanted to be a famous writer.

Current Standing: A watershed and a warning signal; has forced all subsequent philosophers to look before they leap. No self-respecting philosopher can wholly accept his conclusions (i.e., that we can't know anything), but none has entirely succeeded in refuting his arguments, either.

IMMANUEL KANT (1724–1804)

Best-Known Works: Critique of Pure Reason, Critique of Practical Reason, Critique of Judgment.

Readability: Confirms your worst fears. Kant wrote exclusively for his learned colleagues and succeeded in making even *their* eyes glaze over. Will Durant compared him to Jehovah, saying "He speaks through clouds, but without the illumination of the lightning flash."

Qualities of Mind: Scholarly, complex, profound, moralistic, systematic, earnest.

Catchphrases: The categorical imperative, transcendental logic, "thing-in-itself" (*Ding-an-sich*).

Influence: Put Germany on the map as an intellectual power (and lent it the pedantic tone for which it soon became notorious); made sweeping revisions in nearly all branches of philosophy, thereby inspiring other philosophers to stop bickering among themselves and get serious about thinking again. Effected what he called a "second Copernican revolution": The origin of the world as we know it, he insisted, is the human mind itself, which, far from being tabula rasa, has an inherent structure through which we filter all experience and which imposes its own order on the world of phenomena (though not on the real/ideal world of "things-in-themselves," which is unknowable). Likewise, humans have an innate awareness of moral law, in the form of the categorical (i.e., unconditional) imperative (i.e., command), a sort of bottom line ethical "ought." In attempting to make the world safe for both God and science, Kant managed to restore some dignity to the idea of the human mind; also to destroy the credibility of traditional metaphysics (since we can't "know" any external reality that isn't colored by our own "knowing"), to make modern philosophy more subjective than objective (and to prefigure such radically man-centered movements as existentialism), and to widen the rift between philosophy and the physical sciences.

Personal Gossip: The archetypal academic philosopher; a retiring, studious little man who didn't travel, never married, and lived a life of such extreme regularity that, according to legend, the citizens of his home town used to set their clocks by his daily walks.

Current Standing: One of philosophy's All Stars, with Plato, Aristotle, and, if the judges are in a generous mood, Hegel. Often called "the founder of modern philosophy," which is not to say that anyone totally accepts—or ever accepted—his theories, but that every subsequent philosopher has teethed on them. Also, that his complex theories foreshadowed such hip twentieth-century systems as structuralism (see page 330).

GEORG FRIEDRICH WILHELM HEGEL
(1770–1831)

Best-Known Works: Phenomenology of Spirit, The Philosophy of Right, Lectures on the Philosophy of History (compiled and published posthumously).

Readability: The nadir of German prose; pompous, pedantic, obscurantist; every statement is qualified, as is every qualifying statement, and Hegel doesn't stop short of inventing his own words. Not only don't you have to read him, you should feel free to snigger when anyone suggests it.

Qualities of Mind: Abstruse, academic, methodical, with mystical leanings.

Catchphrases: The dialectic (thesis vs. antithesis leads to synthesis), Absolute Spirit.

Influence: Took Kant's mind-ordered world from the human level to the cosmic one, creating a totally awesome system into which all past, present, and future experience *and* thought fit together rationally in an encompassing dialectic that is constantly evolving toward supreme self-consciousness, or Absolute Spirit. At which point we'll know everything and see God. Plenty of energy and ambition here, not to mention enormous clout: By the end of the nineteenth century, most academic philosphers of any stature were Hegelians, which is to say they embraced, theoretically, the notion of Change, accepted Strife as essential to Progress, saw things as Parts of a Whole and themselves as characters in the Unfolding of History, argued dialectically, and tended to think in capital letters. They probably would have continued to run amok with the notion of Absolute Spirit if Marx and Engels hadn't come along and sold the world on Absolute Economics instead.

Personal Gossip: None, really, except that for a man whose philosophy could so easily be read as revolutionary at the outset, Hegel had become notoriously conservative by middle age. A classic example of what money, fame, and a few favors from the King of Prussia can do.

Current Standing: There *had* to be a backlash; by the early twentieth century Hegel's complexity and that crazily incomprehensible prose had made him a laughingstock among many philosophers. Nowadays, he's been more or less restored to a top-shelf position in the Philosophers' Hall of Fame, although his thinking is still mistrusted as leading to a glorification of the state over the individual and an end-justifies-the-means immorality.

ARTHUR SCHOPENHAUER (1788–1860)

Best-Known Works: The World as Will and Idea, Essays.

Readability: No problem: sure-footed, vigorous prose, with plenty of examples, analogies, and, at moments, wit; often quotable.

Qualities of Mind: Cultured, pessimistic, arrogant, embittered, individualistic.

Catchphrases: The world is my idea.

Influence: The first to come right out and insist that there was something more important than knowledge or intellect: namely, will, and specifically, the will to live (Nietzsche and Freud were both to be influenced by this concept). Believing that will was inherently evil, he argued that the best one could strive for was renunciation of desire, a temporary absence of pain through the contemplation of high art (which made him very popular among artists), and, with any luck, the eventual extinction of the species. His rejection of the action-minded, essentially bourgeois confidence of the nineteenth century presaged the individualistic despair of the twentieth.

Personal Gossip: Spent twenty-five years without speaking to his mother, a literary lady who'd disliked him (although she continued to foot the bills) ever since she heard that two geniuses could not exist in the same family. Had a reputation for meanness and spent most of his life alone, save for the company of his dog (the authorities disagree here; it may have been a cat), whom he named Atma, or "World-Soul."

Current Standing: His system is generally regarded as a mishmash of oversimplifications and inconsistencies, peppered with a few brilliant insights; still, thanks to those insights and his skill in presenting them, he's been designated a historical landmark and, as one of the few pessimists in the history of philosophy, is considered something of a curiosity.

SØREN KIERKEGAARD (1813–1855)

Best-Known Works: Either/Or (more dramatic than theoretical), *Fear and Trembling, Sickness Unto Death.*

Readability: A bit gristly (*you* try chewing on reflections like "Dread is a sympathetic antipathy and antipathetic sympathy"), but it has its moments.

Qualities of Mind: Melancholy, unorthodox, God-oriented, imaginative.

Catchphrases: The leap into absurdity.

Influence: No one paid much attention at the time; the idea that there were *no* reliable guidelines for human action, that one could only hope for enlightenment by committing oneself to a God who might very well never give one the time of day, just seemed like one man's personal problem. But once twentieth-century alienation had set in and people had begun wondering why they should get out of bed in the morning, Kierkegaard started to make sense. In the hands of Sartre and Camus, his belief in God was replaced by a belief in the Void, the whole philosophy was given a leftist twist, and before you knew it, everyone in Paris was carrying on like characters out of *Last Year At Marienbad*.

Personal Gossip: Poor Søren; but what could you expect with that Fall-of-the-House-of-Usher childhood and those spindly legs? Even so, people shouldn't have made fun of him the way they did, especially about that painful broken engagement. (On the other hand, he did ditch *her*.)

Current Standing: Acknowledged as the "founder" of existentialism (although existentialism is less a philosophical system than a bad mood), and a brilliant thinker whose neurosis was prophetic.

WILLIAM JAMES (1842–1910)

Best-Known Works: Principles of Psychology, The Will to Believe and Other Essays, The Varieties of Religious Experience, Pragmatism.

Readability: Chatty, colloquial, and direct; like an entertaining dinner guest.

Qualities of Mind: Cultured, commonsensical, optimistic, moralistic (New England Puritan variety).

Catchphrases: The will to believe, the cash-value of ideas (also, in a more literary vein, stream of consciousness, the bitch-goddess success).

Influence: Almost put America on the map as an intellectual presence. Pioneer of pragmatism, our first indigenous school of thought. Attempted to make philosophy relevant by abandoning the search for absolutes in favor of a will-it-cut-down-trees approach to ideas. Theorized that reality is whatever we make it, that truth is tantamount to effectiveness, ditto goodness (thus, if believing in God makes you a better person, then God exists), and that philosophy should stick to answering questions that have a "cash-value," i.e., that will make a significant difference in people's lives. Set the tone for much subsequent twentieth-century philosophy.

Personal Gossip: Older brother of Henry James. Was a famous psychologist before switching to philosophy. Center of a clique of brilliant Harvard intellectuals. Attempted suicide in adolescence (more proof that bad things happen to good people).

Current Standing: One for our side; an American philsopher who won't embarrass you at black-tie dinners. Whatever his limitations as a systematic thinker, he made up for them by being well rounded.

FRIEDRICH NIETZSCHE (1844–1900)

Best-Known Works: Thus Spake Zarathustra, The Will to Power (beware posthumous additions by his sister), *Twilight of the Idols, Ecce Homo* (his autobiography).

Readability: Looks easy enough; used ordinary language, specialized in short spurts and aphorisms, pulled no punches (sums up Socrates, for instance, as "the patron saint of moral twaddle"), but style is overheated and dense; reads a little like Norman Mailer in his apocalyptic mode.

Qualities of Mind: Impetuous, irreverent, individualistic, elitist, unstable.

Catchphrases: The will to power, transvaluation of values, *Übermensch*, God is dead.

Influence: One of the most flamboyant and controversial philosophers ever, vehemently opposed to virtually all established culture and morality. A prophet who announced the demise of God (and, more importantly, of all absolutes), prophesied the World Wars (or something very like them), warned of democracy's tendency to promote conformity and suppress excellence; also, favored selective breeding. A cultural historian whose perceptions about unconscious human drives paved the way for Freud's. Insisted that the dominant force of history is the "will to power," and advocated a "transvaluation of values" in which the traditional "feminine" virtues espoused by Christianity (submission, compassion, being nice to other people) would be joined with "masculine" virtues (courage, strength, toughness) in a morality that aimed at greatness rather than goodness. Hoped for the ascendancy of the *Übermensch,* or superman, in whom Dionysian instinct and dynamism would be perfectly integrated with Apollonian reason and ethics (see pages 254–56). Has been variously interpreted—and misinterpreted—as a spokesman for Fascist, Nazi, anti-Nazi, Romantic, anti-Romantic, and existentialist doctrines.

Personal Gossip: A frail, sickly boy raised in a household of pious women. Became a classics scholar. First an ardent admirer, then bitter enemy of Wagner. Went hopelessly insane at age forty-four. His sister, who had problems of her own, later distorted some of his writings, making him sound more racist than he really was.

Current Standing: It's no longer fashionable to call him the Antichrist, to blame him for World War II, or even to dismiss him as a brilliant but sophomoric "literary philosopher." These days, he's admired as a visionary theorist of language and knowledge. On the whole, however, philosophers are still busy trying to figure out exactly what he was driving at.

HENRI BERGSON (1859–1941)

Best-Known Works: Time and Free Will, Creative Evolution, Matter and Memory (see also *On Laughter,* a minor but famous work).

Readability: Smooth and seductive; Bergson was a master of visual imagery who didn't believe in arguing a point when he could paint a watercolor of it instead. You'll probably be wafted along in happy agreement with him, but good luck afterwards trying to explain what you've read.

Qualities of Mind: Suave, sophisticated, mystical, optimistic, artistic.

Catchphrases: Élan vital.

Influence: The chic philosopher of Europe between the wars. Combated the depressingly mechanistic, deterministic, shut-up-and-reproduce outlook of Darwinism with his mystical "vitalism." Viewed human history as a contest between the inertia of matter (associated with reason, conservatism, laws, and social pressure) and the creative energy—or *élan vital*—of living things (associated with intuition, art, charisma, and the mysteries of life). Everyone was delighted to have some version of free will restored and to be given such a clear-cut distinction between people and rocks. His theories had a great impact on artists, political activists, and socialites: Shaw appropriated his concept of *élan vital* and Proust used his mystical concept of time and memory as the basis for *Remembrance of Things Past.* The party ended with the outbreak of World War II, however, when everybody began to prize sanity over spontaneity again.

Personal Gossip: Proust was best man at his wedding.

Current Standing: Developed appealing theories that, though not without merit, are taken with a grain of salt. Reason is still at a premium, after all.

Moreover, it's understandably difficult for any philosophy department to embrace a mystic, particularly one who, instead of producing a coherent system of thought, chooses to describe life as a "shell bursting into fragments which are again shells."

ALFRED NORTH WHITEHEAD (1861–1947)

Best-Known Works: Principia Mathematica (with Bertrand Russell), *Science and the Modern World, Adventures of Ideas.*

Readability: Perfectly accessible, provided you stick to the latter two, which were written for the layman.

Qualities of Mind: Idealistic, mystical, religious, balanced, thorough, disciplined.

Catchphrases: The philosophy of organism, occasions and becomings.

Influence: A mathematician turned metaphysician; his work with Russell produced the first new system of logic since Aristotle, the *Principia* which, whether or not one cares about that sort of thing, is considered one of the great intellectual monuments of all time. On his own, worked out the most comprehensive metaphysical system of this century ("the philosophy of organism"), a synthesis of idealism, empiricism, mysticism, mathematics, God, Darwin, and Bergson, to name just a few. Aimed at a general theory that would, in the best metaphysical tradition, explain absolutely everything, and one that would make it OK for God to exist in the modern world. His philosophy, which revolved around theories of change and actualization of potentiality, is now called "process theology."

Personal Gossip: Reputed to have been a kind man whose wife was a great help to him, although they were always worrying about money.

Current Standing: Universally admired for the pure scope of his understanding, his balanced intelligence, his ability to incorporate dualities into vast schemas without getting silly, and his unwavering faith in the possibility of total understanding. But since no subsequent philosopher has shared that faith, and so few of them believe in God, his metaphysics is already obsolete.

LUDWIG WITTGENSTEIN (1889–1951)

Best-Known Works: Tractatus Logico-philosophicus, Philosophical Investigations.

Readability: Bedside reading for Bauhaus fans; oddly and intriguingly structured, especially the *Tractatus*, which was intended as a model of clarity and has the added advantage of being only seventy-five pages long. Not the kind of book you can't put down, but if you're in the right mood, it reads a little like poetry.

Qualities of Mind: Intense, penetrating, exacting, original, analytical.

Catchphrases: Language games; Whereof one cannot speak, thereof one must be silent; Don't ask for the meaning, ask for the use.

Influence: Seminal—and central—figure in linguistic analysis, one of the dominant trends of modern philosophy (and Cambridge's answer to sloppy French existentialism). Was convinced that language creates a picture of the real world and that most philosophical problems are merely the result of philosophers' misuse of language; experience only *seems* complicated because of our confused descriptions of it, which represent knots in our understanding. Untangle the knots and, according to the theory, philosophical questions will simply dissolve. Was notable for having formulated two separate philosophical systems, the second of which (called ordinary language philosophy) refuted the first (logical atomism, or picture theory). Was a major influence on yet another group of moderns, the logical positivists.

Personal Gossip: A rich kid who gave away his inheritance because, he said, he didn't want his friends to like him for his money. Quit philosophy after finishing his first book, spent a few years teaching grade school in the Alps and contemplating suicide. Built a mansion for his sister which is considered outstanding architecture. Could whistle difficult passages of music from memory. Took up philosophy again and became a cult hero at Cambridge.

Current Standing: Early Wittgenstein gets raves for sheer brilliance, even though no one is into logical atomism anymore; his later work gets mixed reviews, but the subject is still hot stuff in England and America. On the whole, a prestige philosopher.

JOHN DEWEY (1859–1952)

Best-Known Works: Democracy and Education, Reconstruction in Philosophy, The School and Society.

Readability: No laughs, no tears, just earnest American textbook prose.

Qualities of Mind: Robust, practical, down-to-earth, zealous, democratic.

Catchphrases: Progressive education, learning by doing.

Influence: An intellectual activist, a thinker for the heartland, and one of the dominant American philosophers of the century. Conceived of philosophy as an instrument for guiding human action, and turned James's theoretical pragmatism into an applied science, using pragmatic principles to help resolve contemporary social issues. Developed a biology-based theory of knowledge, emphasizing the problem-solving nature of human thought processes and the importance of experimentation in learning. Famous for using these theories to reform the American educational system, rejecting learning by rote in favor of learning by doing. A champion of collective social power.

Personal Gossip: None.

Current Standing: The thoroughly relevant philosopher. Hard to criticize him on the basis of his ideas because these were never supposed to be eternal verities; even harder to argue with his success in implementing them. Pragmatism itself is still open to debate; Bertrand Russell accused Pragmatists of "cosmic impiety" in making truth out to be nothing more than a tool for human use, and warned that Dewey's "intoxication" with social power was the greatest danger confronting modern man. All we know is, Johnny *still* can't read.

Toys in the Attic

FIVE FAMOUS PHILOSOPHICAL MIND GAMES

ZENO'S ARROW: One of the best known of the paradoxes with which a whole contingent of early Greek logicians liked to amuse themselves; this one illustrated the impossibility of motion or change. The flight of an arrow, said Zeno, is an apparent example of motion. But at any given moment of its flight, the arrow is either where it is or where it is not. If it moves where it is, it must be standing still, and if it moves where it is not, then it can't be there; thus it can't move. This sort of thing drove Zeno's friends crazy, of course, but it also provoked a crisis among metaphysicians, who were, for a long time, concerned with reconciling the basic features of permanence and change. It also gave rise to a vast literature that set about trying to prove, disprove, or avoid Zeno's conclusions. In fact, you could probably still get a lively dinner-table conversation going on the subject today, given the right crowd and plenty to drink.

PLATO'S CAVE: The famous allegory with which Plato, using Socrates as his mouthpiece, tries to explain the nature of human knowledge. Picture, says Socrates, a bunch of people who've spent their whole lives chained up in an underground den, unable to turn around. Behind them a fire is blazing, but all they can see are their own shadows on the wall of the cave in front of them. Never having seen anything else, they naturally mistake these shadows for reality. In the same way, the rest of us mistake the world as we know it for the real world, whereas the objects, and even the qualities, of this world are only shadows of the pure forms that exist in the realm of ideas. Now, what does this mean for you? It means, for example, that somewhere above us in that realm of forms and ideas, there is one, and only one, perfect automobile, of which the lemon you've been driving is merely a crude imitation (you probably suspected something of the sort already). By training your mind to contemplate the idea of the perfect driving machine rather than the expensive heap of scrap metal in your driveway, you can eventually struggle up out of the cave into the sunlight where you'll see the car with perfect clarity. True, you will then be confined to driving the idea of the car on the idea of a highway, but Plato never claimed that being a philosopher was easy, and at least you can be pretty certain you'll never encounter much traffic in the realm of ideas.

BURIDAN'S ASS: A famous stumbling block to the concept of free will. An ass, placed equidistant from two identical bundles of hay, has no basis for choosing one over the other and ends up starving to death. Although it was first suggested by Aristotle in connection with astronomy, the image is traditionally attributed to the medieval French philosopher Jacques Buridan, who claimed that a man must choose that which his reason tells him is the greater good, but that he may delay making a decision until his reason has had sufficient time to gather all the information it needs. Actually, it's a starving dog that Buridan refers to; the ass was his critics' idea.

OCCAM'S RAZOR: "Entities ought not to be multiplied, except from necessity." The maxim for which William of Occam, the Franciscan scholar, is best remembered. Actually, Occam never really said this, but he did say, "It is vain to do with more what can be done with fewer," which adds up to the same thing; moreover, he did uphold the principle of eliminating all unnecessary facts or hypothetical entities in analyzing a subject, and he *did* dissect every question as if with a razor.

PASCAL'S WAGER: The pragmatic approach to God, and Pascal's attempt to save the skeptical soul through common-sense reasoning. Basically, his argument goes: OK, so you'll never know for sure whether or not God exists, it's all a cosmic game of heads or tails. But you have everything to gain and nothing to lose by betting on His existence. Remember, you're only staking one finite, so-so little life—no, not even that, only the way you *live* that life—against a chance to win an infinity of an infinitely happy life. If you win (if God exists), you've won everything; if you lose (if God doesn't exist), you haven't really lost a thing. And don't say you'd rather not play, because you have no choice; you're already in the game.

Dueling Dualities

TWO PAIRS OF CONCEPTS DEAR TO THE HEARTS OF PHILOSOPHERS, LOGICIANS, LITERARY POSEURS, AND INTELLECTUAL BULLIES EVERYWHERE

DEDUCTION VS. INDUCTION: Begin by forgetting what Sherlock Holmes used to do; to a philosopher, deduction is much more serious and far-reaching than being able to guess Watson was at his club all day because it's been raining and his clothes aren't wet. So what is it? It's a formal argument that assumes one or more principles as self-evident, then, following rigid rules and forms and proceeding from the general to the specific, infers one or more conclusions from those principles. The example you've heard before: "All men are mortal. Socrates is a man. Therefore, Socrates is mortal." Pay attention to that form. It's called a syllogism, and it's deduction at its most classic—though you can substitute Michael J. Fox for Socrates if you want.

Induction, by contrast, is empirical, factual, ordinary-feeling; it makes use of experiment and/or experience—the scientific method, if you will—to arrive at an inference and proceeds from the specific to the general. When you make an induction, you begin by recording instances, monitoring behavior, counting noses. If you go out to dinner at a Mexican restaurant a dozen times and each time you wake up at 3 A.M. with horrible indigestion, you may well induce that your digestive tract can't take Mexican food, at least not late at night. Of course, you could be wrong; maybe you'd have gotten sick those nights anyway, or maybe it's the particular Mexican restaurant, not Mexican food in general. Or maybe your roommate is poisoning you and trying to make it look like Mexican food. Don't worry, though: Unlike deduction, which, assuming its premises are sound, is certain, absolute, and airtight, induction is about mere probabilities; its success depends on how accurately you observe and over how many cases.

Historical note: For at least 200 years philosophers have been looking for a logical proof for why induction works as well as it does or, failing that, even just an orderly way to think about it. No soap. About the closest anybody's come to actually legitimatizing it as a philosophical entity, as opposed to a useful day-to-day skill, is John Stuart Mill, who cited "the uniformity of nature" as one reason why induction has such a good track record. Of course, that nature is uniform is itself an induction, but Mill was willing to give himself that much of a break.

Sometimes the line between deduction and induction is clear-cut: For instance, noting (with many a famous philosopher) that the sun always rises, you may have deduced it from the laws of planetary motion, or you may have induced it from the last 3,000-odd dawns. Sometimes you think you spot incest: After all, whoever first said that all men are mortal must surely have felt the need to do a little field work first, thereby inducing deduction's single most famous premise. But the flavors of the two will always be distinctive: Deduction is, in the end, all about the axiom ("A triangle has 180°"), while induction has the ring of the maxim ("Faint heart ne'er won fair lady").

A PRIORI VS. A POSTERIORI: In a way, we're back with deduction and induction. That is, a priori knowledge is based on assumption-as-bottom-line, on belief that doesn't depend on experience for validation, on "general principles" of the two-plus-two-equals-four, no-plant-can-get-up-and-walk variety. And, like deduction, it's absolute. A posteriori knowledge derives from observation, of the this-box-is-red, everybody's-sentimental-on-Valentine's-Day variety. You get to it after (*post-*) looking around for yourself. (Your professor probably added that a priori reasoning proceeds from cause to effect, a posteriori reasoning from effect to cause, but that seems like a harder way to think about the whole business.) A good example here, and we owe it to English grammarian, lexicographer, and all-round curmudgeon H. W. Fowler: Browning's famous line "God's in his heaven—all's right with the world" would be interpreted by an a priorist to mean "Given we know there's a god, the state of the world must be OK," by an a posteriorist to mean "The world's so obviously OK, there's got to be a god." Caution: A priori thinking can have negative connotations in some circles, implying arbitrary judgments based on preconceived notions.

What Was Structuralism?

AND WHY ARE WE TELLING YOU ABOUT IT NOW THAT IT'S OVER?

Structuralism was a French intellectual movement that peaked in the Sixties. Because it was French, as opposed to, say, German, it had automatic chic and cachet. And because it was French, as opposed to, say, English, it was a problem for the Anglo-Saxon mind right from the start.

Even less focused, less definable, and less happy-go-lucky than existentialism (its immediate predecessor on university daises and at Left Bank café tables), structuralism wasn't a philosophy exactly, but a *method,* a way of analyzing and, with any luck, understanding things. Many, many things. Everything, in fact. As such, it cut across academic disciplines and art forms, from linguistics and anthropology (its two major incubators), to literary criticism, film, history, and sociology, to psychology and politics.

Structuralists believed, fervently and at great length, that (a) the component parts of any system have meaning only in terms of their relations to one another; that (b) those relations tend to be binarily organized, i.e., to involve a pair (or many pairs) of terms, each half of which is parallel, or opposed, or inverted, or equivalent, or duplicative, or whatever, with regard to the other; and that (c) all cultural phenomena, from linguistic structures to kinship practices, table manners to skirt lengths, wrestling to insanity, and so on, long into the Paris night, are governed by the same principles, and hence related to each other. They, as well as all patterns of human behavior, are codes in which are reflected the inherent structuring tendencies of the human mind. And they directly reflect the ways in which the mind sorts, clusters, and mediates every image, every stimulus, every bit of information it stumbles across. Pay close enough attention to these phenomena, ask the right questions, construct the appropriate "model," the structuralists urged, and eventually you couldn't help getting to the bottom of things.

Structuralism had its beginnings in linguistics, in the work of the Swiss (but French Swiss, if you get our drift) linguist Ferdinand de Saussure, who observed, among other things, that the "signifier" c-a-t was an arbitrary way of calling attention to the "signified" concept of cat and an even more arbitrary way of designating Muffin over there, the "referent." And that all that kept c-a-t from being c-o-t or b-a-t was a single sound, more specifically, a single sound difference, enough of which differences together went to allow us to encode meaning in language—arbitrarily, granted, but with a high degree of success. Also, how to decode meaning. And, what's more, Saussure hinted knowingly, it's not just language. We "understand" Coke in terms of its not being Pepsi, a mimosa in terms of its not being a Bloody Mary, Top-Siders in terms of their not being motorcycle boots.

Saussure, who died in 1913, had been very provocative. But outside the linguistics community, which he'd provided with a whole new lease on life, it took decades for the news to trickle down to intellectuals-at-large. Enter Claude Lévi-Strauss, the anthropologist (and the high priest of structuralism), the publication of whose *Elementary Structures of Kinship* in 1949 launched the structural phase of anthropology. For the next thirty years, Lévi-Strauss chis-

Claude Lévi-Strauss

eled away at primitive cultures and mythologies (as he called them) as if no white man had ever seen a clay pot or a loincloth or an incest taboo before.

Picture him, for instance, in residence among the Bororo Indians of central Brazil, dealing with their every routine, from cooking to marital fidelity, as if each were a language, a system of communication, structured by unconscious but absolutely binding and consistent laws, laws that were binary in nature (as suggested by two of Lévi-Strauss's better known working titles, "The Raw and the Cooked" and "From Honey to Ashes").

Of course, the Bororo Indians could themselves have applied the structuralist method to an analysis of Parisian department-store layouts or social-kissing practices, had they cared to make the trip. The method is, you understand, up for grabs, employable by anybody who's familiar with it precisely because it is rooted in the structures of the mind. Or, as Lévi-Strauss himself put it, "We do not claim to show how men think in myths, but how myths think themselves in men, and without their knowledge. . . . Myths think themselves among themselves." In fact, Lévi-Strauss had already sorted through a lot of those myths, eventually decreeing the existence of units called mythemes, the equivalent in culture of phonemes, the lowest-common-denominator elements of speech.

Structuralism was an attempt to apply science to areas where it had never been applied before, to banish the old belles-lettres approach to literary criticism, the old pencil-and-notebook approach to anthropology, the old roots-and-prefixes approach to linguistics. But it also had certain Marxist overtones (as what French intellectual movement does not?): By questioning the codes—of behavior, of meaning, of authority—it implicitly questioned who had power and why we went along with his having it. Its real beauty, though, lay in its ordering principles. Lévi-Strauss would hear everybody's folk tales and kinship-system stories, thousands and thousands of variations of a theme, and, working structurally, reduce them to a few potent—and lucid—"systems of difference."

Roland Barthes, the bottle imp of Paris intellectual life from the Fifties until his death in 1980, could watch a wrestling match or a Molière play, read a fashion magazine or a novella by Balzac, spend an hour at a striptease parlor or several months in Japan, and break the experience down into its component, binarily opposed parts—many of which would then be interchangeable from spectacle to spectacle, experience to experience. Other structuralists worth knowing about: Michel Foucault, the French historian (see page 547), decoder of insanity, imprisonment, sexuality, and other "marginal" social institutions; Jacques Lacan, the French psychoanalyst (see page 418), who maintained that the unconscious is structured the same way a language is; and Umberto Eco, the Italian scholar and cultural commentator, a specialist in semiotics, or communication through signs, a variant of structuralism that emphasized subject matter over methodology. (Sometimes called structuralists, but not exactly in this way: Noam Chomsky, the American linguist, and Jean Piaget, the French child psychologist.)

So, why have we chosen to lecture on structuralism, given that it's pretty much yesterday's papers? Two reasons. First, it's the immediate ancestor of—and the force behind—*post*structuralism, a.k.a. deconstruction, likewise an invention of the French

Roland Barthes

(and very hot just now, as these things go) and likewise a way of getting inside something, usually called a "text," then shaking it up a bit. The poststructuralists are led by philosopher Jacques Derrida; included (before their deaths) "late" Barthes, "late" Foucault, and "late" Lacan; and now maintain a transatlantic clubhouse at Yale. *Their* method, in the words of one convert, is "to disturb" a work "along its own fault lines"; to question all such supposedly self-evident structures as superior/inferior, in/out, original/belated, man/woman; to accuse all systems—power structures no less than paragraph structures—of being propped up from the inside and, get this, of unwittingly betraying, under cross-examination, exactly how, and how much, they are propped up.

The poststructuralists, unfortunately, are even harder on most Anglo-Saxon minds than the structuralists were. Even Barthes, the most genial of them, could turn out a sentence like: "A text is not a line of words releasing a single 'theological' meaning (the 'message' of the Author-God), but a multidimensional space in which a variety of writings, none of them original, blend and clash." And check out, when you have a few days, Derrida on *différance*, "a differing that's also a deferral."

So, why else have we chosen to lecture on structuralism, not to mention poststructuralism? Reason two (and let's not lose sight of the binary nature of our own minds, please) is simple: Questioning authority, and wondering not only who's in charge here but why we're behaving as if he (or she) *really* were in charge, is, in the Eighties, just a simple survival tactic.

Three Well-Worn Arguments for the Existence of God

These old chestnuts mark the point at which philosophy—which supposedly bases its arguments on reason—and theology—which gets to call in revelation and faith—overlap. The result, as you'll see, sounds an awful lot like wishful thinking.

THE COSMOLOGICAL ARGUMENT: This one dates all the way back to Aristotle's theory of motion and encompasses Thomas Aquinas's version, known as the argument from contingency and necessity. We know from experience that everything in the world moves and changes, said Aristotle (or simply *exists*, said Aquinas), and everything that moves, or exists, has a mover, i.e., a cause, something that precedes it and makes it happen. Now, we can trace lots of things in the world back to their immediate causes, but there is always another cause behind them and another behind *them*. Obviously, said Aristotle & Co., we can't keep tracing effects back to causes indefinitely; the buck has to stop somewhere, there has to be one cause that isn't, itself, caused by something else, or one entity that existed before all the others could come into existence. This first cause, the Unmoved Mover, is God. The cosmological argument, widely accepted for centuries, started running into snags when Hume decided that the whole principle of cause-and-effect was a mirage. Later, Kant made matters worse by pointing out that, while there may be cause-and-effect in *this* world, we don't get to assume that the same holds true out there in the Great Unknown. Today, critics counter the cosmological argument by pointing out that there's no reason to assume we *can't* have an infinite series of causes, since we can construct all sorts of infinite series in mathematics. Also that the argument never satisfactorily dealt with the question any four-year-old knows enough to ask, namely, Who made God?

THE ONTOLOGICAL ARGUMENT: This is an example of the old philosopher's dream of explaining the nature of the universe through sheer deduction (see page 329); also, of how slippery a priori reasoning can get. The argument, which probably originated with St. Anselm back in the Middle Ages and which hit its peak with Descartes, Spinoza, and Leibniz, the Continental Rationalists of the seventeenth century, runs as follows: We can conceive of perfection (if we couldn't, we wouldn't be so quick to recognize imperfection) and we can conceive of a Perfect Being. God is what we call that Being which embodies all imaginable attributes of perfection, the Being than which no greater Being can be conceived. Well, if you're going to imagine a Perfect Being, it stands to reason that He exists, since a Perfect Being that didn't exist wouldn't be as perfect as a Perfect Being that did, and isn't, therefore, the most Perfect Being you can imagine. (Is He?) Hence, by definition, God exists. (Doesn't He?) If you're still awake at this point, you may already have noticed that the ontological argument can be criticized for begging the question; that is, it assumes, at the outset, the very thing it purports to prove. Still, when you think about it, the argument is not nearly as simpleminded as it appears. Just where *did* you get your idea of a Perfect Being if you're so sure no such thing exists?

THE TELEOLOGICAL ARGUMENT, OR THE ARGUMENT FROM DESIGN: You've probably heard this one before. The gist of it is that simply by looking around you can see that the world is a strange and wondrous place, something like an enormous machine with millions of perfectly made and perfectly interlocking parts. Now, nobody but an underground filmmaker would claim that such a structure could be the result of mere chance. For metaphysicians from Plato and Aristotle to eighteenth-century Enlightenment thinkers, enamored of the mechanical symmetry of the universe, and nineteenth-century ones, enamored of the biological complexity of same, the idea that there had to be a Mind behind all this magnificent order seemed pretty obvious. The teleological argument survived for so long partly because the world *is* a pretty amazing place, and partly because the argument's validity never depended on the idea that God is omniscient or omnipotent, only that He's a better planner than the rest of us. However, as Hume, the great debunker, was to point out, even if we could assume the existence of a Cosmic Architect who was marginally better at putting it all together than we are, such a mediocre intelligence, which allowed for so many glitches in the plan, would hardly constitute God. And then along came the mathematicians again, pointing out that, according to theories of chance and probability, the cosmos just might be an accident after all.

POLITICAL
SCIENCE

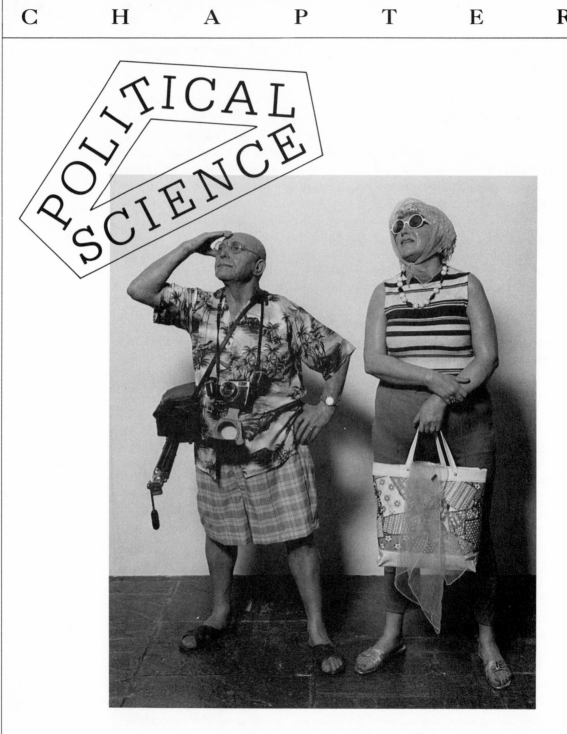

E I G H T

Contents

"Tourists" by Duane Hanson.

What You Need to Know Before Answering a Personals Ad in the International Herald-Tribune

A NERVOUS AMERICAN'S GUIDE TO LIVING AND LOVING ON FIVE CONTINENTS

ARGENTINA

THE LAYOUT: South America's second biggest country (after Brazil), with topography ranging from lush tropical forests (the Gran Chaco, near the Brazilian border) to arid, windy steppes (Patagonia, home of some sheep, a lot of oil rigs, and a few luxury hotels). Argentina has plenty of rich farmland, copious mineral deposits, and, at its top and bottom, a lot of wide-open spaces. That's because most Argentines have gone off to live in the Pampa, the central grasslands where the gauchos used to roam, the cattle still graze, the wheat grows, and most of the manufacturing is done. In fact, a large percentage of them have set up housekeeping over by the coast, in Buenos Aires, Argentina's version of Paris, ditto Miami Beach, where one can gaze out of the window of one's high-rise apartment (unless one happens to live in a shanty on the outskirts of town) and dream of Swiss bank accounts waiting beyond the horizon.

THE SYSTEM: A federal republic and a constitutional democracy, with a president elected by indirect vote, a bicameral legislature, and a constitution modeled more or less on our own. At least, that's what it's supposed to be. Ever since 1930, however, when the military first acquired the habit of overthrowing the elected government whenever things seemed to be getting out of hand, the system has, more often than not, been whatever the junta-of-the-month has deemed necessary. It hasn't seemed to matter much to the man in the street; no one has put any stock in constitutional guarantees since Juan Peron, the popular demagogue and Mussolini fan, proved, back in 1949, that a constitution was just a piece of paper, easily rewritten once you were the boss.

WHAT YOU NEED TO KNOW TO READ THE NEWSPAPERS: Stick to the arts and real-estate sections; everything else is bound to be bad news. Take the economy, for instance. (You might as well take it; you're paying for it. Saddled with the third largest foreign debt in the world, Argentina only manages to stay afloat by borrowing more whenever the notes come due.) The economy is so calamitously out of control as to seem, to the casual observer, like an act of God. To the Argentines themselves, however, for whom bitter factionalism is mother's milk, the state of the economy is obviously somebody's—that is, somebody *else's*—fault: the voracious trade unions, always demanding higher wages and paralyzing industry with strikes and violence; the businessmen, trying to eke out more profits by raising prices, then investing the extra pesos overseas; the money-guzzling public industries, many of them run by the military and therefore untouchable; or the military itself, 80,000 strong with no foreign enemies in sight and a certain standard of living to maintain. Naturally, no one wants to read about the economy for long, and it's almost exhilarating when the terrorist groups, right-wing, left-wing, or both, start livening things up. That's nearly always followed by another military coup, and once the generals are in power again, no one has to read any more bad news because all the grumpy journalists and editors just seem to *pfffft!* disappear.

WHAT YOU NEED TO KNOW IF YOU'RE DATING AN ARGENTINE: Wondering why your date never introduces you to any of his or her friends? Don't take it personally. Your date's old school chums may have been among the 9,000 or so *desaparecidos* who were kidnapped, murdered, and thrown into mass graves by the ruling junta in the 1970s and early 1980s. But there's no need to be nervous. The generals—a few of them anyway—have been locked up and the streets are safe again (although if a Ford Falcon with no license plates tries to pick you up, you might want to hop on the nearest bus). You and your date can have a fine time by yourselves since, despite its Alice-in-Wonderland economy, Argentina still manages to maintain the highest standard of living in Latin America. Why not go for a stroll down one of Buenos Aires's fashionable boulevards, stop off at a charming sidewalk café for a "Chéburger" and a $5 cup of coffee, then do a little shopping (plenty of designer jeans here) or go see a show (also plenty of nightlife)? Just remind your date to bring along twice as much money as you think you'll need; inflation can run to over 1,000 percent annually, and by the time you get downtown, your date's peso could be worth half what it was when you left home.

WHAT YOU NEED TO KNOW TO MEET YOUR DATE'S PARENTS: Don't expect flounced skirts and castanets; most Argentines are proud of their European roots, and your date's parents are probably just back from a shopping spree in Milan (a big percentage of the population is of Italian descent). Do expect them to be slightly aloof and possibly a little defensive. Argentines are aware that their country is a notorious underachiever, and they resent the way the U.S. moved in to corner the very world markets they feel *they* should have had. Nor were they pleased when we tried to get them to join our grain embargo against the Russians. The way they see it, *we* don't buy their wheat, so who were we to ask them to give up their biggest customer? Don't get all huffy and patriotic about it, though; your date's parents are anything but Communist sympathizers. In fact, you'll want to figure out just how far to the right they lean before you start gushing about how much you enjoyed seeing *Evita* on Broadway. If they're working class, you're probably on safe ground. They'll undoubtedly be Peronistas who'll love to reminisce about the good old days when Peron and his movie-star wife came down to the factories and threw coins to the adoring crowds. But if they're middle class, you may end up having to sit through a tirade about how the Perons' corruption and fascist tactics are what ruined the country in the first place. Obviously, you won't want to mention the Falklands (oops! they're called the Malvinas here), those little islands off the southeastern coast that have been under British sovereignty for 150 years, since it was there that the military decided to make the ill-conceived grandstand play that brought down the government and humiliated the whole country in the eyes of the world. Your best bet: Stick to discussing Jorge Luis Borges, a native son, and enjoy your steak.

CAMBODIA

THE LAYOUT: A big, saucer-shaped rice paddy flanked by mountains and watered by monsoons, just right for nurturing a peaceful little farming nation. But the neighborhood is what really counts, and it's a lousy one. The Thais, on one side, and the Vietnamese, on the other, have been wandering into the backyard for centuries. Now, with the former a U.S. ally, the latter solidly Communist, and the Chinese hiding out in the shrubbery, Cambodia might as well go jump in the Gulf of Siam.

THE SYSTEM: Cambodia—officially, the Khmer Republic—hasn't had anything that could legitimately be called a system since Prince Norodom Sihanouk was deposed in 1970. Sihanouk, a slippery character who nevertheless got Cambodia out from under the thumb of the French and campaigned to keep his country out of the Vietnam debacle, had abdicated the throne in favor of his parents in order to take practical control of the country (first as premier, then as chief of state) while preserving the monarchy. He was replaced, after a military coup, by his erstwhile second-in-command, Lon Nol, a corrupt right-winger tacitly backed by the United States. Lon Nol, in turn, was knocked out of the ring by Pol Pot, a fanatical Communist revolutionary openly backed by Peking. Pol Pot was overthrown in 1979 by invading Vietnamese, who installed a puppet regime under Heng Samrin. If you're clever about picking sides, *you* might be the next ruler of Cambodia.

WHAT YOU NEED TO KNOW TO READ THE NEWSPAPERS: That with friends like it's got, Cambodia could use a real ally, and it isn't likely to find one on this planet. Sure, Thailand let a couple hundred thousand refugees and guerrilla fighters camp on its borders, but the Thais, who have their own problems, have made it clear that they're not about to sign any adoption papers. China and the United States lend a hand by funding insurgents trying to drive the Vietnamese out of Cambodia. That, you'll recall, is the same United States that secretly bombed Cambodia from 1965 to 1973, and whose unauthorized incursions into Cambodian territory brought the Vietnamese war into the country in the first place. And that's the same China that backed the psychopath Pol Pot and his Khmer Rouge, the army of fanatical Cambodian Communists that slaughtered at least 2 million of their compatriots and utterly demolished the country's economy. Then there's the Soviet Union, one of the few countries that sends nonmilitary aid to the folks inside Cambodia. It's not that the Band-Aids and aspirins aren't welcome, just that true gratitude toward a conqueror—even one that conquers by proxy—is a rare quality. Even if you can't quite see who's going to win what out of all this (and be prepared for the players to change their strategies at any moment), you shouldn't have any trouble figuring out who's going to lose.

WHAT YOU NEED TO KNOW IF YOU'RE DATING A CAMBODIAN: Your date may be a little edgy, since he or she lives in a country occupied by 160,000 or so of its traditional enemies, the Vietnamese. Your date may also be gone a lot; unless you're invited along, don't ask too many questions. He or she is probably out blowing up bridges for one of the three guerrilla groups still operating in the countryside or hiding out across the Thai border. If you *are* invited along, definitely ask questions; specifically, which guerrilla group is your date working for? If it's Prince Sihanouk's band, no sweat; Sihanouk, who is admittedly out of his league when he tries to play the big powers off against each other, may well have Cambodia's interests at heart and has, at any rate, managed to hang on longer than anyone else. If it's either of the other groups, however, kiss your date goodbye and promise to write. One, the apparently well-meaning Khmer People's National Liberation Front, serves mainly as cannon-fodder, and the other is the same Khmer Rouge that tortured babies for faulty ideology during the last regime. And speaking of babies, don't be surprised if your date seems to be rushing you a bit on that score; the government is encouraging Cambodians to propagate as fast as they can, to fill the population void left by the irrepressible Khmer Rouge.

WHAT YOU NEED TO KNOW TO MEET YOUR DATE'S PARENTS: Brush up on your high school French. True, the Cambodians were only too happy to break away from the French Union back in the mid-Fifties, but they'd barely waved goodbye to the last boatload of bureaucrats before all these strangers started marching into the country. And at least the French, who were around for five centuries, showed some appreciation for Cambodia's Indian heritage—it was French scholars, after all, who rebuilt Angkor Wat. The Vietnamese, on the other hand, got their ideas of civilization from China; they act like Cambodia's culture were some kind of embarrassment—which is pretty much how Cambodians view Vietnamese culture, too. Speaking French will also remind your date's parents of their son, the doctor, who was supposedly killed, along with the rest of the professionals and intellectuals, when the Khmer Rouge were in power but who, it's now rumored, may really be alive and well and living in Paris. It's all rather disorienting. To cheer up your date's parents, get them to show you around Phnom Penh, still a beautiful old city, if a bit decayed, and one of the few places in Asia where you don't have to worry about drinking the tap water, since there isn't any. Stroll through some of the lovely French villas, being careful not to trip over the squatters sleeping on the sidewalk, then have an early dinner at one of the city's terrific French restaurants. On second thought, make that lunch; you want to be sure to get back to your hotel (one of the three in town at which you, as a foreigner, will be allowed to stay) in time for the 5 P.M. curfew.

CANADA

THE LAYOUT: The second largest country in the world (after the Soviet Union, Canada's other superpower neighbor), but with only a few more residents than the state of California. Indeed, space, sheer space, is the salient feature here, with cold a close second: The latter (*not* enhanced television reception, since Canada recycles American programming anyway) explains why 75 percent of the population huddles within 100 miles of the United States border. Ontario is the most populous, most prosperous, most powerful, most urban, and most industrialized (also, most resented) of the ten provinces and two territories that go to make up the country; it also has the capital, Ottawa, and the biggest, most cosmopolitan city, Toronto. Quebec is the largest and second most populous province, with what used to be the biggest, most cosmopolitan city, Montreal, plus the bulk of the whopping 28 percent French-Canadian minority. Lately, the four western provinces, formerly no more glamorous than North Dakota, have been making themselves over with the proceeds from all the oil and minerals they sit on. The Maritimes, north of New England, on the other hand, simply make do, with fishing, coal mining, ship building, and federal subsidies.

THE SYSTEM: A federal union—a very loose federal union, in which the prime minister (for most of the last twenty years, that was Pierre Trudeau, the Johnny Carson of world political leaders; now it's somebody named Brian Mulroney) tries to convince his countrymen that Canada's future is as a strong, united nation rather than a confederation of shopping centers, while the ten provincial premiers plump for priorities—and an identity—that are, in a word, provincial, and tell the prime minister to keep his goldarned hands off their oil, uranium, nickel, asbestos, natural gas, and/or newsprint. Also in the picture: a governor-general who represents Queen Elizabeth II, the official head of state, but he—and, for that matter, she—is purely a figurehead. There are two major political parties, the Liberals (Trudeau's one of those) and the Progressive Conservatives (like Mulroney, with the emphasis on the second half of the phrase), and a two-house legislature, modeled on Britain's Parliament, of which the important half is the elected House of Commons; the Senate is merely appointed, and by the governor-general at that.

WHAT YOU NEED TO KNOW TO READ THE NEWSPAPERS: That a lot of the action is in that provinces-versus-Ottawa tension. It's the goad (also the high) in Canadian politics, and it helps explain why Quebec gets to hold referendums on whether or not to secede from the rest of the country and why Alberta (the most dynamic of the western provinces) gets to claim that not only her oil, but her oil revenues, oil-development program, and oil-marketing strategy, are her own business, and not Ottawa's. Part of the problem is that Canada was created, in the mid-1860s, not from within, by patriots, but from without, by a jittery Britain, worried about containing a reunited United States, and that there's never been a revolution or a civil war—or even a serious *project*—to help forge a Canadian identity. The other part of the problem is that Canada's federal government possesses only those powers not already accorded the provinces (the reverse of the states'-rights setup here), which means that the provinces are firmly in control of health, education (a big issue in a bicultural country), natural resources, interprovince commerce, and quite a few other matters. As for that French-English tension: Things have pretty much quieted down since De Gaulle, on a 1967 visit, stepped out on the balcony and declared, "Vive le Québec libre!" True, René Lévesque and his Parti Québecois tried (and failed) in 1980 to whip up majority support for "sovereignty" for Quebec, but separatism—and the spectre of a new, independent, volatile, and Gauloises-puffing neighbor just north of Vermont—is simply not the topic it used to be.

WHAT YOU NEED TO KNOW IF YOU'RE DATING A CANADIAN: You need to know a joke or two, that's what you need to know. (Those Canadian nights are long, and your date's likely to be glum, shy, repressed, and painfully decent.) We suggest, for an icebreaker, "Funny, Canada could have had British government, French culture, and American proficiency. So how come you wound up with French government, American culture, and British proficiency?" When the laughter's died down, remind your date of the time *Maclean's,* the Canadian biweekly, ran a contest in which readers were asked to complete the phrase, "As Canadian as . . . ," and the winning entry was "As Canadian as possible under the circumstances." Finally, quote the English poet Rupert Brooke, who, on a North American visit a few decades ago, observed, "Canada is a live country—live, but not, like the States, kicking." At this point, your date should be ready to regale you with his description of those very States as "the land of bilk and money"; alternatively, he may want to review with you the fine points of his company's pension program: It's never too early to start planning for a secure future, after all. Now, assuming you're still awake, let your date know that you know that all the cultural currents don't flow from south to north. Say thanks to your date for John Kenneth Galbraith, Saul Bellow, Joni Mitchell, Lorne Green, and Anne Murray, among others, as well as for the invention of insulin, pablum, and basketball. Of course, the above advice holds true only if your date is an English-speaking Canadian. If he's a French-speaking one (in which case, he'll probably be just as glum, but less shy, repressed, and decent), you'll have your hands full trying to sing the national anthem in French at the same time you dodge his advances: French-Canadians, you see, are worried about declining birth rates—this after years of a fertility so relentless and intimidating that non-French Canadians began speaking of the "revenge of the cradle." And those *nuits canadiennes* are no less *longues* in Quebec.

WHAT YOU NEED TO KNOW TO MEET YOUR DATE'S PARENTS: First, that you're as likely to be served tea and biscuits as coffee and apple pie: Canada is still playing up, rather than muting, its ancestry. And it's not just that Elizabeth-as-head-of-state business, either; turns out, for example, that their version of Memorial Day weekend centers on Queen Victoria's birthday (which even the English have stopped bothering with). Moreover, it was just a few years ago that London mailed them back the original of the British North America Act, the 1867 document that serves as Canada's constitution and that had been the last vestige of Canada's official—and totally surreal—"colonial" status vis-à-vis Mother England. Second, that while you probably won't be found unworthy as a suitor, you do have a few teensy p.r. problems to work out, including acid rain, a Canadian dollar that in seven years has gone from being worth more than its south-of-the-border counterpart to being worth thirty cents less, and the fact that the U.S. controls, through corporate investment and subsidiaries, more than half of all Canadian mining and manufacturing. Then, what *can* you say about all those north-of-the-border Burger Kings and Kentucky Fried Chickens, not to mention the *National Enquirer*s in the supermarket checkout rack? But don't panic. If you, unlike your government, play it cool (remembering neither to tip your date's father when he opens the front door nor to expect to borrow the family car for the weekend), the parental blessing's virtually assured.

ETHIOPIA

THE LAYOUT: Located in the Horn of Africa, just across the Red Sea from Saudi Arabia and the Yemens, Ethiopia is a Christian nation flanked by Moslem states and a Marxist stronghold with both feet in Black Africa and its face turned toward the Middle East. Mostly high country studded with mountains, cut by valleys, and fringed at its outer edges by semi-desert, with the kind of topography that encourages guerrilla fighting and makes it virtually impossible to get from one place to another without ruining a set of tires. Its two perpetual hotspots: Eritrea, in the north, a former Italian colony, now an Ethiopian province and the country's only access to the sea; and the Ogaden in the southeast, a desert area that cuts deep into the midsection of Somalia and is both ethnically and culturally Somalian. More recent headaches: Tigre, another northern province now clamoring to secede, and the Sudan, the neighbor that gives sanctuary to Ethiopian rebels.

THE SYSTEM: Just your average biblical empire until 1974. That was when Emperor Haile Selassie (whose name, reggae fans, was Ras Tafari until his 1930 coronation), who claimed royal descent from King Solomon and the Queen of Sheba, was deposed by the Provisional Military Administrative Council, better known as the Dirgue. For the next few years, the Dirgue busied itself replacing Selassie's feudal state with "scientific socialism," a one-party Marxist system complete with collective farms, nationalized property, and tight government control of the economy. Bitter infighting among the Dirgue's 120 members led, in 1977, to a shootout from which Colonel Mengistu Mariam emerged as the country's leader. He's ruled with an iron hand ever since, backed by the Soviet-styled Ruling Workers' Party and the largest standing army in Black Africa.

WHAT YOU NEED TO KNOW TO READ THE NEWSPAPERS: That the U.S. frets about having a Marxist outpost so close to the Persian Gulf, especially one that spouts so much pro-Soviet propaganda and has so much influence over the rest of Black Africa, and that the stories in your local newspapers are likely to reflect this discomfort. You heard less about famine in the north during Haile Selassie's reign, although millions starved during 1973–1974, when he botched the distribution of U.S. aid at least as badly as the current government did the last time around. But Selassie maintained close ties with the U.S. and only "cordial relations" with the U.S.S.R., a situation that was reversed as soon as the Dirgue took over. Ever since Ethiopia's 1977–1978 war with Somalia, the Soviets have been footing the bill for the government's neverending battles with secessionists in Eritrea and Tigre, and in the Ogaden. Whether Mengistu really thinks the Russians offer a model government for a nation of African subsistence farmers, or whether he merely wants to keep Soviet guns and ammo coming while he replaces the country's traditional chaotic wretchedness with a home-grown Marxist system, gives the newsweeklies something to debate in the absence of any real information out of Addis Ababa.

WHAT YOU NEED TO KNOW IF YOU'RE DATING AN ETHIOPIAN: Don't bother to write; your date can't read. Government claims that illiteracy's been reduced to just under 40 percent are probably wishful projections; 85 percent of the people were illiterate just a couple of years ago, and most of them would have been too busy trekking to refugee camps in the interim to spend much time in school, even if there were any schools. Don't try to make small talk, either, unless you're fluent in Amharic (the official language) or in Gallgina, Tigrina, or one of 100-odd local dialects. And don't bother to pack any fancy clothes; your date lives in a country with one of the lowest standards of living in the world. Do bring sensible shoes; if you're lucky, your date will own a few oxen and a government-issued plow and there will have been enough rain recently to warrant your spending many hours together out in the fields. Also bring hiking boots; if you're not so lucky, your date will be among the 30 million Ethiopians being forced to relocate, either as part of the government's vast resettlement program, designed to move large segments of the population from the parched north to the wide open south, or in the move known as "villagization," aimed at getting the peasants off their remote farms and into more easily controlled communities. In either case, you'll be traveling by foot with little food, and there's a good chance that if you do survive long enough to get where you're going, there'll be absolutely nothing—no house, no job, and certainly no hot meal—waiting for you when you arrive.

WHAT YOU NEED TO KNOW TO MEET YOUR DATE'S PARENTS: First, get your prejudices straight: The Ethiopians have contempt for the Eritreans (who consider themselves Arabs) and the Eritreans loathe their Ethiopian oppressors. The Ethiopians look down on the local Somalians (whom their great Emperor Menelik, back in the nineteenth century, labeled "the cattlekeepers for the Ethiopians") and the Somalians revile the Ethiopians. Second, be careful what you say. If your date's parents are Christians and members of the Coptic Church, they're likely to be wary of anything but the most innocuous how-was-choir-practice small talk, since the Church is now under the watchful eye of the government. And they may have pretty ambivalent feelings toward the Church itself, which, in pre-Marxist days, held 85 percent of the land and viewed them, quite literally, as serfs. If they're Moslems, they'll probably be all steamed up about the fact that the Christian infidels have always treated them as rabble, even though they make up an equal percentage of the population. Your best bet: If your date's parents seem mainstream and reasonably comfortable, admire the new propaganda billboards dotting the landscape and speak of Colonel Mengistu as the country's savior. If your date's parents live up in the mountains, in the desert, or in a heavily fortified underground city, wear your "Born in the U.S.A." T-shirt and watch out for low-flying Soviet aircraft.

FRANCE

THE LAYOUT: It's the second largest country in Europe (counting the Soviet Union), and the location's nice—friendly neighbors, water views on three sides—but, of course, the facilities are hardly modern. The five famous rivers (the Seine, Loire, Rhine, Rhône, and Garonne) aren't the great commercial waterways they were back when boats were smaller, and despite repeated efforts at decentralization, all roads still lead, literally and figuratively, to Paris. Still, the place has character. Although recent governments have tried to carve the country into tidy, homogeneous administrative *départements*, everyone continues to divide it, mentally, into the same *anciens provinces* (Normandy, Brittany, Burgundy, Gascony, etc.) they were pledging fealty to back in the Middle Ages. (When chatting up the waiter in your local bistro, remember that Provence is the name of a particular province—the one with the Riviera in it—and that, to a Frenchman, everything that isn't Paris is "les provinces.")

THE SYSTEM: France is now on its Fifth Republic. The four earlier republics, dating from the French Revolution, were ended by Napoleons I and III, the collaborationist Vichy government during World War II, and Charles de Gaulle, respectively. Each had its own constitution and a somewhat different internal organization. (Given that only de Gaulle, with his imperious personality, his incessant talk of "la gloire de la France," and his intimidating height, was able to make any of these republics take root, you may be justified in suspecting that the French are ambivalent toward the whole idea of a republic and keep wondering if they might not, after all, prefer a king.) France is headed by a president elected for seven years—although even de Gaulle knew enough to step down midway through his second term—who has the strongest powers of any elected head of state; among these are the power to dissolve the National Assembly annually, to challenge existing laws, and to handpick his own prime minister, thus presumably assuring the latter's loyalty. However, the four major political parties (one conservative, one centrist, one socialist-but-not-all-*that*-socialist, and the feistiest Communist party in Western Europe) can regroup into complicated and potent patterns; when such a coalition is both strong and hostile to the presidency, it can pit president and prime minister against each other, and cause the whole system to strain at its seams.

WHAT YOU NEED TO KNOW TO READ THE NEWSPAPERS: That on the international front, France is no team player. Determined to take what it sees as its rightful place among the superpowers (third on the dais, next to the U.S. and the Soviet Union), it has, especially since de Gaulle, adopted a foreign policy aimed at asserting its independence from American and Russian influence and at creating a strong Europe with—who else?—itself at the helm. It fought for the creation of the European Common Market; exploded its own atomic bomb back in 1960; withdrew militarily from NATO in 1966, kicking both U.S. and NATO forces out of the country; was one of the first to recognize the government of mainland China (long before we did); and makes a point of maintaining a "special relationship" with whichever radical Middle Eastern faction no one else is speaking to at the moment. If the French do seem to have a special feeling for the underdog (they've appointed themselves spiritual advisors to any number of struggling Third World countries), it may be a matter of residual paternalism (up until a little over twenty years ago, when France still had its empire and its *mission civilatrice*, many of these countries were dutifully singing the "Marseillaise" while the locals slapped *plastique* bombs on the walls of French colonial headquarters) or simply of their enduring pride in the fact that the French Revolution was, after all, the revolution that started it all.

WHAT YOU NEED TO KNOW IF YOU'RE DATING A FRENCHPERSON: Be prepared to discuss, for hours on end, politics, philosophy, foreign policy, the politics of philosophy, the philosophy of politics, the politics and philosophy of foreign policy, the early films of Jean-Luc Godard, and what's wrong with the New York art scene. Be conversant with trendy intellectual theories (see page 333, for some tips on Post-Structuralism), keeping in mind that intellectuals are to your date what rock stars were to you and your friends back in high school. With any luck, your date will be a student or graduate of one of *les grandes écoles;* if so, you'll not only get taken to the best restaurants, you'll also be privy to what the leaders of France are really thinking, en masse, behind their partisan rhetoric. Otherwise, your date may well be unemployed, given the government's policy of letting failing industries sink without a trace in order to try to modernize the economy. Don't worry; thanks to France's ferocious unions, you'll eat very well on your date's unemployment compensation— which may be as much as 90 percent of his or her former salary. Anyway, being out of work will allow you and your date plenty of time to demonstrate for causes. If you like seeing your name in the newspapers, try joining the adventuresome Greenpeace environmentalist group; if you prefer something a little more off the beaten track, however, the Breton Liberation Movement might be just the ticket.

WHAT YOU NEED TO KNOW TO MEET YOUR DATE'S PARENTS: That almost anything you say is going to precipitate a history lesson. The French can recall the pecking order of the Merovingian dynasty or the events that led up to the Third Empire as clearly as you can remember your last love affair, and they're likely to be a good deal more entertaining on the subject; nothing will give them more pleasure than to share the memories of their illustrious past with an ignorant American who hasn't got one of his own. Relax, enjoy your *boeuf bourguignon,* and hope that the talk doesn't turn to current events. This will inevitably lead to an anti-American harangue revolving around what your hosts regard as America's disastrous foreign policy and "the serious threat of Anglo-American hegemonism" in general; to a family feud over French politics or the latest excesses of the Pope (and don't be surprised when either of these takes a xenophobic or anti-Semitic turn at the drop of a hat); or, perhaps worst of all, to a passionate discussion of French literature during which, the one time you do manage to get your two centimes in, everyone at the table will leap to correct your grammar.

INDONESIA

THE LAYOUT: Wins the most-fragmented-nation award: six large and 13,662 lesser islands, strung necklace-style along the equator, just south of Indochina. (Java's the most important of them, but you've heard of Sumatra, Bali, Borneo, and New Guinea, too.) Lushly tropical, with torrential rains, machete-proof jungles, snakes, tigers, crocodiles, etc. Also, volcanic, fertile, and full of Asia's most enticing assortment of natural resources, including oil. The fifth most populous country in the world, and the most populous Moslem one, with more people than Egypt, Iran, Turkey, and the Arabian Peninsula combined. Ethnically complex, however, with over 250 mutually unintelligible languages; fortunately, almost everybody's agreed to speak something called Bahasa Indonesia, much touted locally as the "purest" form of Malay.

THE SYSTEM: Another soldier state. This one bills itself as a limited democracy, with a powerful president, elected by the People's Consultative Congress (almost 200 members of which are presidentially appointed, making Indonesia a great country in which to be the incumbent). Current president, now serving his fourth five-year term: Suharto, a former general whose power base remains solidly the army, in his opinion a "sociopolitical agent of development" as much as a military force.

WHAT YOU NEED TO KNOW TO READ THE NEWSPAPERS: That, since World War II ended and first the Japanese, then the Dutch got out, Indonesia's history has revolved around two men and two men only: Sukarno and Suharto. The former, flamboyant and high-profile, fought for its independence, guided it to nationhood, became (in 1949) its first president, and went on to take his place, with Nehru, Nasser, Tito, and Nkrumah, in the pantheon of "nonaligned" leaders. At home, he adopted the authoritarian system he called "guided democracy," dissolved existing political parties and decided to rule by decree, and left the economy pretty much to fend for itself. Abroad, he flirted heavily with the Chinese Communists, "confronted" neighbor Malaysia, grabbed the western part of New Guinea from the Dutch, and withdrew in a snit from the UN, the only nation ever to do so. An abortive pro-Communist coup against the anti-Communist military in 1965 gave strongman Suharto his chance: He removed Sukarno (implicated as an engineer of the coup), slaughtered 300,000 Indonesian Communists, turned his back on Peking, made nice with such pro-West neighbors as Thailand, Singapore, Malaysia, and the Philippines, dug for oil, rejoined the UN, fixed his attention, more or less successfully, on such matters as political stability, national consolidation, and economic planning, and called the whole program the "New Order." His two p.r. blunders: gobbling up the tiny adjacent Portuguese colony of Timor and treating its population—already ragged and run-down—worse than Portugal had; and, more recently, rewarding loyal relatives and friends with lucrative business deals in a way that makes some people think of Ferdinand Marcos.

WHAT YOU NEED TO KNOW IF YOU'RE DATING AN INDONESIAN: That your date's country is, despite its surprisingly low profile and predilection for sarongs, a potential Third World model and a force to be contended with. It's tricky, though: You might point out how experts on economic development say that "the mosaic that is Indonesia" is one of the two most baffling of developing nations (the other being "the labyrinth that is India"). The single biggest problem: how to achieve equality and unity among all those islands. Java, for instance, has way too many people for its size (more than 80 million, or about 60 percent of the total population), yet efforts to relocate a few of them in the underpopulated "Out Islands" haven't been very successful. Worse, big and rich Sumatra, with most of the oil but not that many people, feels it's doing all the work while Java—site of Djakarta, the capital, with its political life and supper clubs—has all the fun. Indonesia's big advantage: that array of natural resources, coupled with a talent for merchandising them that Macy's might envy. Thus it's segued from its "exotic" period (spices and indigo), to its "setting up house" period (tea and coffee, tobacco, palm oil, rubber, tin, sisal, and tropical hardwoods), to its current trendy oil-and-petroleum-by-products period, and, even as we speak, is probably readying copper, bauxite, and natural gas for when the oil runs out. Of course, if you're dating a university student, chances are he'll resent the exploitation, repression, and corruption of the present (as well as the former) regime, so steer clear of "economic miracle" talk. And be braced for the occasional show of independence; your date may, for instance, want to point out how his country, unlike, say, Thailand and the Philippines, is not a "client state" of your country.

WHAT YOU NEED TO KNOW TO MEET YOUR DATE'S PARENTS: You should probably first determine whether they are, like 90 percent of the population, Moslem, and if so, how Moslem. No Indonesian is going to quote the Ayatollah Khomeini at you, but a few of them are keyed up about the way Suharto has finagled Moslems out of political power, not to mention his decision to put the Javanese mysticism he favors on a par with Islam. Also, just because you once spent an idyllic three days exploring the museums and canals of Amsterdam, don't make the mistake of talking sentimentally about Indonesia's former long-term landlord. From the seventeenth century on, neither particularly broad-minded nor particularly lenient, the Dutch showed their absolute worst side when they refused to get out even after the war for independence had largely been won. Watch your tongue on the subject of the Japanese, as well: Indonesia (then still the Dutch East Indies) spent most of World War II as the centerpiece of Tokyo's "Greater Co-Prosperity Sphere."

ITALY

THE LAYOUT: Unlike Orion or the Great Bear, Italy actually resembles the thing it's supposed to look like, an old boot, high-heeled and in need of resoling, trying to kick Sicily across the Mediterranean. You can, for convenience' sake, pinpoint Rome about midway up the shin and Florence just behind the kneecap. You'll run into trouble when you hit northern Italy, though, where a cloud of smoke seems to be issuing from the top of the boot. Don't let it throw you; northern Italians would just as soon not share an image with the backward Mezzogiorno (i.e. everything south of Rome; pronounced METSO-jyorno), and smoke is a perfectly appropriate symbol for the industrial heart of the country. The way the smoke seems to be disappearing into the rest of Europe makes sense, too, given northern Italy's historical ties with France and Austria. Across the top of the country stretch the Alps, nice for skiing but never very effective at discouraging foreign invaders. The Apennines, running the length of the country, served for centuries to keep Italy region- rather than nation-minded and to make it virtually ungovernable (remember that Italy, like Germany, only came together as a country 100 years ago). To the west, in mid-Mediterranean, lies the big, barren, mineral-rich vacationland of Sardinia, which is not only an integral part of Italy but a reminder of how times have changed in this part of the world; Sardinia has belonged, in various periods, to Genoa, Pisa, Spain, and Savoy, and was a kingdom on its own for a while, encompassing Turin. Just above Sardinia is the island of Corsica which, though Italian by culture and temperament, belongs, uneasily, to France.

THE SYSTEM: The world's most fluid parliamentary democracy, with a president elected every seven years and a new premier appointed, it seems, every Wednesday. There have, at any rate, been forty-odd governments since the end of World War II, when Italy ceased to be a chaotic monarchy. Pluralism is the name of the game here; everyone has something to say and no one listens to anyone else for very long. The dominant Christian Democrat and numerous lesser parties form complicated coalitions the way some people play combinations at the track. How long any of these lasts, however, usually depends on whether or not the PCI, the strongest Communist party in the West, has been invited to participate, and on how adept the party leaders are at not getting caught with their hands in the cookie jar. (The fact that Parliament has the right to use a secret ballot on everything except votes of confidence has not, traditionally, fostered moral rectitude among the country's leaders; nor has the elaborate patronage system that props up some of the more fragile coalitions.) Each of Italy's twenty regions has its own bicameral government which, on one hand, keeps business humming on the homefront whenever the national leadership falls apart and, on the other, adds to the bureaucratic red tape and the general impossibility of getting things done. Meanwhile, inside Rome's city limits, the Pope holds court as absolute monarch of the Vatican City, which issues its own currency, postage stamps, and passports.

WHAT YOU NEED TO KNOW TO READ THE NEWSPAPERS: That you might be better off *not* reading the newspapers. What with terrorist attacks, economic upheavals, government scandals, underworld vendettas, strikes, floods, earthquakes, and volcanoes, Italian headlines can make you want to book the next flight to Zurich. But it pays to keep your cool. Before you know it, the terrorists are captured, the economy rallies, a new government forms overnight, the courts crack down on the Mafia, the buses start running again, and thousands of Neapolitan earthquake victims become so attached to their prefab metal shelters that they refuse to move into new government housing. As for the economy, you won't get the real story by reading the stock market pages. Most Italians—including many who are officially unemployed or "disabled"—make their rent through the country's hugely profitable "submerged economy," made up of businesses small enough to be exempt from taxes and union restraints and businesses that don't, legally, exist at all. None of this is to say that life runs smoothly in Italy, only that a history of near-continuous warfare and of domination by every variety of despot seems to have strengthened the country's resistance to disaster and heightened its appreciation of crisis. And its track record doesn't look so bad when you realize that it's only been an industrialized nation since the 1940s. Another appearance not to be fooled by: Italian Communism, which functions more like the workers' rich uncle than like anybody's Big Brother, and which, in the wake of Poland and Afghanistan, allowed itself to be virtually excommunicated by Moscow rather than alienate its hometown constituency.

WHAT YOU NEED TO KNOW IF YOU'RE DATING AN ITALIAN: Not much, if your date's a man. A recent survey showed that Italian men still want their women to be "sweet and affectionate" homebodies, and almost 30 percent of them insist they'd never marry anyone who wasn't a virgin. If you're dating an Italian woman, however, you might want to review all the arguments for the E.R.A. Italian feminism may be mild by American standards, but it's become enough of an issue to be adopted by the Communist Party, which has been touting women's rights in an effort to attract the new Italian yuppie vote. (And unless you want to look like a real cluck, don't forget that both divorce and abortion have been legal in Italy since the 1970s, no matter what the Pope says.) Once you've got gender taken care of, there's locale to consider. If you're dating a Milanese, for instance, it will pay to study up on the latest Italian fashion magazines and dress accordingly, in deference to the fact that the fashion and textiles industries are among the biggest profit-makers in the country. If your date lives in Turin, congratulate him or her on the way Fiat's pulled into the black and prepare to discuss the pros and cons of the *scala mobile*, the law that ties wage hikes to price increases, allows your date to buy those new snakeskin shoes, and has, for years, crippled the Italian economy. In the Mezzogiorno, you can skip all these formalities, provided you drive a big car.

WHAT YOU NEED TO KNOW TO MEET YOUR DATE'S PARENTS: Well, again, that will depend. In the north, you should know something about Italian history; for instance, how to pronounce "Risorgimento" (the *s* sounds like a *z*), the nineteenth-century struggle to get out from under foreign rule and unify the country. You should know that Venice wasn't always a mecca for honeymooners; that back when it was the trade link to the Orient, it was one of the world's richest states and one of the few in these parts to resist enemy invasion. You should know a little something about Renaissance art, of course, especially if your date's folks are Florentines (see page 76), and you ought to be able to tell your Guelphs (supporters of the popes) from your Ghibellines (supporters of the Holy Roman Emperors). In other words, you may have to crack a few textbooks. In the south, relax. Italians on the whole read fewer newspapers than other Europeans, and the illiteracy rate in the Mezzogiorno still hovers between 20 and 30 percent. Here, however, you'd better learn to love your date's family, because you'll be seeing a lot of them. For one thing, your date will almost certainly live at home, thanks to the chronic housing shortage. For another, *familismo* is stronger than ever these days; a lot of people insist it's what really holds the country together. How do you get the family to like you? Simple. If you're not a Catholic, lie and say you are. (But don't rave about the Pope; Italians never entirely trust the papacy and they feel particularly put off by the current pontiff, who's never at home when they come to visit.) Then cultivate a priest or a Communist politician who can provide someone in your date's family with a *raccomendazione*. With one of these, your date's kid brother can get a job—or an old-age pension; without it, he could spend the rest of his life selling bootleg American cigarettes behind the train station.

JAPAN

THE LAYOUT: Doesn't call itself Nippon (literally, "land of the rising sun") for nothing; this is as Far East as it gets. And as isolated. A 1,000-mile archipelago sweeping away from the Asian mainland, Japan is separated from its nearest neighbors (and former territories), the Koreas, by the Sea of Japan. Nearly everyone lives on one of the four main islands: Honshu, Hokkaido, Shikoku, and Kyushu—that's 120 million people, or half the population of the U.S., packed into an area about the size of Montana. And now that so many of them have moved down to Honshu's Pacific coast, to Osaka, the former capital, or more likely, to Tokyo, the present one, to get a job in a big corporation, most Japanese watch the rising sun from over a neighbor's shoulder.

THE SYSTEM: A constitutional monarchy, symbolically headed by the Emperor Hirohito who, though persuaded, after World War II, to disclaim direct descent from the sun goddess, still represents what may be the world's longest unbroken chain of royal rulers—1,500 years' worth (although few of them, ever had any real power in Japan). Under the current constitution, drafted by the occupying Allied forces in 1946 and tactfully accepted by the Japanese in 1947, the Diet, or parliament, consists of a 252-member House of Councilors and a House of Representatives about twice that size. The Diet elects the prime minister who, with his eighteen-member cabinet, makes up the executive branch. Because the conservative, pro-business Liberal Democratic Party has had control of the Diet since 1955, whoever is elected (more precisely, agreed upon by a few LDP elders) to head the party is a shoo-in for prime minister. Although the LDP leadership is both fragmented and fractious, the Japanese talent for reaching consensus, combined with the fact that party members in Japan's stratified society are not only professional politicians but old college drinking buddies, allows transitions in government to take place with a minimum of fuss.

WHAT YOU NEED TO KNOW TO READ THE NEWSPAPERS: That, like Britain, Japan developed as an island nation, adjacent to but isolated from a continent loaded with big-power countries. That, consequently, it, like Britain, didn't have to worry about being invaded; instead, it had the luxury of devoting itself to its own development while its neighbors wasted time, money, and psychic energy building up their defenses and patrolling their borders. And that you'd probably be better off viewing Japan as the catalyst of a new, global, technological revolution—just as Britain was the major force behind the industrial revolution—than getting hot under the collar every time you read about another Japanese marketing success. Reassure yourself, too, that while Japan's protectionist trade policies and deadbeat attitude toward defense may well amount to shirking global responsibilities, the country does have legitimate economic problems. Not the least of these is a near-total dependence on outside sources for raw materials, including oil, which makes the whole economy vulnerable to political tremors in the rest of the world, especially in the Middle East.

WHAT YOU NEED TO KNOW IF YOU'RE DATING A JAPANESE: Plenty. Japanese newspapers have five to six times the circulation of their American counterparts, so your date's probably going to know a good deal more about what's going on in the world than you do. You might score a few points by reeling off everything you learned in your college survey course on Medieval European Literature, but don't count on it. Your date's never had more than a two-month summer vacation since kindergarten; while you and your friends were out shoplifting at the five-and-dime, he was boning up on English and Western Civ. in a special cram school, hoping to make the grades that would put him on the fast track to Tokyo University or some other prestigious college and thence, to lifetime employment with a status corporation. Of course, if your date's still in school, he's likely to be snappish or suicidal or both. The pressure to make grades is so intense that teen suicide and graduation-night head-bashing are common. (Don't worry about any of this if your date's a girl, though. Japanese women were only force-fed the vote by the constitutional revision of 1947, and feminism is hardly on the march here. Your date may want a job, but only to kill time until she gets married.) If your date is one of the lucky ones who landed a post with Mitsubishi or some other corporate giant, expect to have a ball at company picnics and hootenannies (sing-alongs are a national obsession), although these will be about the limit of your social life. Your date will be working late six days a week, commuting at least three hours a day, and getting fall-down drunk with his cronies whenever he gets a little free time. If your date *does* have more than a few hours to spend with you—and if he seems a little dazed—he may have gotten stuck working in one of Japan's distressed industries, like steel or coal mining, that have been forced to take the unheard of step of laying off workers. If so, remember this isn't Detroit; that cup of coffee you'll be lingering over together is going to run you about $7, American.

WHAT YOU NEED TO KNOW TO MEET YOUR DATE'S PARENTS: How to keep from bumping into things. Your date's parents are not only going to be a lot smaller than you, they'll also be considerably more accustomed to moving around in tight spaces, since the average Japanese apartment is about half the size of the average American one. If you want to please your date's parents, rush (careful of that tea table!) to assure them that you are, unfortunately, only able to visit their magnificent country for a very short time; that, in fact, you will almost certainly never see them again after next Thursday. This will prevent them from having to arrange a hasty marriage between your date and the suitable young Japanese man or woman next door (about half the marriages in Japan are still arranged by parents) in order to prevent any possibility of your joining the family. It's not your table manners, abominable as these may be by their standards; it's just that you're, well, different. Japan is such a closed—some critics come right out and say racist—society that when the Japanese government finally offered permanent asylum to 3,000 Vietnamese boat people, the boat people politely declined, explaining that they felt they'd fit in better in the United States. Don't be too hard on your date's parents. Remember that the Japanese had had absolutely no exposure to Western thinking before the Meiji Restoration—which came in the wake of Admiral Perry's forcing Japan to open it's doors to foreign trade (see page 557) and which launched the country on its beat-them-at-their-own-game strategy of appropriating Western technology—began flooding them with it in 1868. And keep in mind that it was the very cohesiveness of Japanese society that allowed a tiny island with no resources to launch its "New Order," the dream of empire that, at its peak during World War II, expanded the limits of Japan to include what is now Taiwan, Indonesia, Indochina, Thailand, Burma, Korea, Manchuria, the Philippines, part of the Soviet Union, and virtually every Pacific island group within torpedo distance.

MEXICO

THE LAYOUT: South of the border—and no border ever separated two more contrasting standards of living than the U.S.-Mexico one. Not that there isn't a lot of contrast *within* Mexico, too: between tropical coastal lowlands and chilly inland mountain ranges; between a few huge, unmanageable cities (most notably Mexico City, on the verge of wresting the "world's largest" title from Shanghai) and tens of thousands of remote rural communities; between the rich, who may or may not fly to Houston for the day to shop, and the poor, who may or may not make their living by picking through smoldering trash heaps. In area, the third largest country in Latin America (after Brazil and Argentina), and with 82 million people—113 million expected by the year 2000—the second most populous (after Brazil).

THE SYSTEM: A blend of democracy and authoritarianism, with the emphasis on the latter. Technically a federal republic, with contending political parties, but dominated since 1929 by the Institutional Revolutionary Party (P.R.I.) to the virtual exclusion of all others. The President enjoys almost mystical power, a little in the manner of the Aztec emperors and Spanish viceroys who preceded him; of course, *they* didn't have to step down after six years in office. Because members of the Senate and Chamber of Deputies must do likewise, and because in Mexico the legislature is pretty much a rubber stamp for the president, the country's politicians are more attracted to the bureaucracy than to electioneering—or to getting things done.

WHAT YOU NEED TO KNOW TO READ THE NEWSPAPERS: That after four or five years of oil boom (and hog-heaven prosperity), Mexico, the world's fourth-largest producer of the stuff, has been plunged into full-throttle economic crisis, complete with skyrocketing inflation, dwindling foreign-exchange reserves, and a peso worth roughly one-twentieth what it was worth a decade ago. That it owes $24 billion to commercial banks in the U.S. and that every year it seems less and less able to pay it. That something like 94 percent of all U.S. illegal-alien arrests—a couple of million a year (and that's just the *arrests*)—involve Mexicans hoping to land a job harvesting tomatoes in the Sacramento Valley or watering some gringo's garden in Beverly Hills for the $3.35 an hour it would take them a whole day to earn back home. That Mexico is the largest supplier of marijuana and heroin to the U.S. market, and a conduit for a third of its cocaine. That the P.R.I. has won every single Mexican election, no matter what the level, for the last fifty-seven years. That Mexico no longer seems like such a great model of maturity and civilian rule. That the U.S. shares a 1,952-mile border with Mexico. That, in short, as foreign-policy headaches go, "Mexican stability" ranks, in the minds of many diplomats, second only to "the Soviet menace."

WHAT YOU NEED TO KNOW IF YOU'RE DATING A MEXICAN: That he may not be in the best of moods. If he's rich, there's no problem: You'll have the choice of the duplex in town, the hacienda in the hills, or the villa on the coast, and there's the Learjet to get from one to the other by. If he's middle class, he'll be annoyed by government corruption, conspicuous consumption, and the 70 percent rent increase on his two-bedroom apartment; he'll also be so disenchanted by not only the P.R.I. but the largely toothless opposition parties, including the Communists, that, far from shouting Ché-style slogans, he'll probably be bingeing on burritos again. (If he's from Chihuahua, up north, on the other hand, he may have helped organize election-fraud sit-ins and boycotts a couple of years ago.) If he's an urban squatter, still reeling from last year's inflation rate of 90 percent (and the stench from the open sewers), he may or may not have had temporary work lately, and may or may not be able to buy you a Coke (ounce for ounce, at least six times as expensive as gasoline). If he's a rural peasant, he's probably contemplating joining his cousins as an urban squatter, and you may find yourself being asked to help him move—or to smuggle him across the border in the trunk of your car. In any event, plan to be introduced to lots of little brothers and sisters, whether in the coastal villa or the two-room cardboard shack: The birth rate in Mexico is a hefty 2.9 percent, and almost half of Mexico is less than sixteen years old.

WHAT YOU NEED TO KNOW TO MEET YOUR DATE'S PARENTS: That, well-mannered as you are, there's almost sure to be a problem. The scars from the Texas and the Mexican-American Wars of the last century still aren't completely healed, and it doesn't help that the real estate north of the Rio Grande that we grabbed from Mexico back then has become primer and primer. You might remind your date's parents that we're *all* imperialists, really, and that Mexico herself is built on the bones of old Aztecs, Toltecs, and Mayans; this approach will backfire, however, if your date is of predominantly Indian, rather than Spanish, ancestry. You can't go too far wrong if you praise Mexico's political stability (don't slip and say "stasis" instead), making it clear that you don't for a minute put it in the same category with the banana republics of Central America on the one hand or the totalitarian regimes that used to dominate South America on the other. Beam at any mention of the 1910–1917 revolution, which broke the power of the old aristocracy, brought about a strong constitution and broad-based political system, and got the Church pretty much off everybody's back. Marvel at the country's cultural record (in art, architecture, and literature, especially) and at its position of leadership throughout the Spanish-speaking world. If none of the above works, offer to smuggle everybody, Mom, Dad, date, and all unmarried siblings, across the border in the trunk of your car.

NICARAGUA

THE LAYOUT: The biggest country in Central America and the one with the fewest mouths to feed (about 3 million). There's plenty of variety to the landscape—mountains, lowlands, virgin forests, two huge lakes, and a torrid, swampy Caribbean coast—but most of it's been abandoned for a little volcano-studded strip of land between the mountains and the Pacific. Nicaragua is one of four Central American countries (the others are Honduras, El Salvador, and Guatemala; Panama and Costa Rica have their own problems) that are so bound together by history, social conditions, climate, and the fact that they all share a little isthmus the size of Montana, that what happens to one can't help but rattle the others. As a result, ideology tends to count for more than nationalism in this part of the world, and observers, both inside and out, have reason to view the area as prime domino-theory territory.

THE SYSTEM: In 1933, when the U.S. Marines finally pulled out, after hanging around for eleven years protecting U.S. commercial interests, they left Anastasio Somoza García in charge of the National Guard. Before you could say "Latin American dictatorship," Somoza had turned the Guard into his personal militia, arranged for the assassination of his rival, General Sandino (the guerrilla leader for whom the present-day Sandinistas are named), and made himself president. For the next forty-five years, the Somoza clan ran Nicaragua more like a shady family business than a country. Finally, in 1979, after years of guerrilla fighting, Sandinista revolutionaries overthrew the Somoza dynasty and replaced it with a three-man junta. After elections held—and, according to some, admittedly cranky, Western observers, rigged—in 1984, Daniel Ortega, former coordinator of the junta, became president. He shares leadership with a nine-member Sandinista directorate; a National Assembly exists, but is virtually powerless.

WHAT YOU NEED TO KNOW TO READ THE NEWSPAPERS: That you'll pretty much have to go on one of those fact-finding visits if you expect to get any feel for what's really happening down there, and even if you do, you won't learn much. The Sandinistas may be, as they keep insisting they are, repressive only because they're so beleaguered by Contra raids and U.S.-instigated economic problems. But, things would have been tough enough even without interference from the north, given the fact that a bunch of under-age guerrilla-fighters were suddenly faced with turning the Somoza's family-owned sweatshop into a functioning national economy. Given, too, the uneasy marriage that made the revolution in the first place: middle-class professionals and businessmen hoping for reform, on the one hand; Marxist ideologues vowing a radical transformation of society, on the other. You're not wrong to notice something familiar about the Sandinistas' end-justifies-the-means rhetoric. But you also get to have a feeling of *déjà vu* when daily evidence shows the U.S. to be engaged in yet another "secret war." Reading the newspapers, at this point, may just be a matter of picking sides and rooting for your team, even when you know it's playing dirty.

WHAT YOU NEED TO KNOW IF YOU'RE DATING A NICARAGUAN: What kind of Nicaraguan? A Sandinista? Get ready to memorize the usual Marxist propaganda, to meet a lot of nice Cubans and even more nice gringos (you'll recognize the former because they'll be trying to make themselves invisible; the latter will be snapping photos and asking loads of questions), and to spend a good deal of time hanging around the barracks drinking soda with your date's army buddies. If you feel like making yourself useful, you can always volunteer to help vaccinate the kids in the local barrio, or you could head out to the countryside to train teachers. (No need to feel inadequate; a little reading and writing is all you'll need to know, along with a few of the Party slogans you've picked up at the barracks.) What if your date's a Contra? Well, you'll already be out in the countryside—mostly next door, in Honduras or Costa Rica—commandeering chickens from the locals. You may have to ambush a busload of civilians or two, just to earn your keep. And your date may seem like a bit of a hick; many of the Contras are peasants who, until they were recruited, lived so removed from all the revolutionary ruckus that they've never known who they're fighting, or why; they just do what they're told. Or your date might turn out to be a Miskito Indian who joined the Contras because he's pro-U.S. or because he'd been driven from his home by the Sandinistas. Whoever you're with, you'll probably find some time during the day to play games. Remember that 65 percent of Nicaragua's population is under age 35; most of the soldiers are younger than that; and when they're not out trashing villages or shooting down civilians, kids still want to have fun.

WHAT YOU NEED TO KNOW TO MEET YOUR DATE'S PARENTS: That they're probably mestizos, of mixed European and Indian ancestry, like nearly 70 percent of the population, and that they've spent their whole lives picking cotton, bananas, or coffee beans and being treated like dumb animals by the folks up at the hacienda. They may have had high hopes for the revolution at some point (or they may not have known it was going on), but by now, they're resigned to things being pretty much the way they've always been, only with less to eat. They may be feeling a little more unsettled than usual, especially if they live in an area of heavy fighting or if they're among the families with one kid fighting for the Sandinistas and one for the Contras. And they really will be upset if the priest doesn't come out to the village anymore. The Catholic Church in Nicaragua, one of the most radical in Latin America, played a major role in revolutionizing the rural peasants, but even Nicaraguan priests have to talk to the Vatican sometimes, and the Vatican has recently turned thumbs down on preaching Marx to the locals. Don't, however, feel free to make cynical, antireligious remarks. Some Cuban teachers tried to in the early days of the revolution, and that was the end of Cubans in Nicaraguan classrooms.

NIGERIA

THE LAYOUT: It's the biggest, fanciest house on the block, granted, but the block's in shantytown, consisting of nine ramshackle converted colonies crowded together in a row and looking for all the world as if their stilts are about to give way. In fact, they were all carved out of the mangrove swamp a century ago by imperialists who were thinking more about the administrative convenience of their respective motherlands than about sensible zoning, and nearly all of them are having to struggle to remain standing as nations. Nigeria's the one at the far end, just before you turn the corner into Equatorial Africa. A former British colony surrounded by former French colonies, it extends farther north than its neighbors and is geographically more diverse: swamps and tropical forests in the south, grasslands and savannas in the center, semidesert in the far north. With somewhere between 80 and 95 million inhabitants, it's also the most populous country on the continent.

THE SYSTEM: After gaining independence in 1960, Nigeria became, in 1963, a federal republic comprising four more or less self-governing territories—North, West, and East Nigeria (later known as Biafra), and the Federal Territory of Lagos—loosely bound together under a weak central government. When north-south hostilities broke out in 1966, the Supreme Military Council moved in to take over. Martial law held things together, through two attempted coups and a political assassination, until 1979, when the old parliamentary government was replaced by a U.S.-style presidential system and the country was reorganized into nineteen states in an effort to defuse regional antagonisms. At the end of 1983, another military coup put Nigeria's presidential democracy out of its misery. The general in charge of the new government was himself toppled in 1985. The latest general seems to have things well in hand, but you might want to wait until he's stuck it out a little longer before you memorize his name. Don't worry, you'll probably have at least until Oct. 1, 1990, the date on which the military has promised to turn the country back over to the people.

WHAT YOU NEED TO KNOW TO READ THE NEWSPAPERS: That Nigeria's got lots of oil—a particularly pure, particularly desirable variety of oil—and was, in the Seventies, a Cinderella nation for which sudden wealth created as many problems as it solved (e.g., an unstable, overspecialized economy; a boom-town atmosphere of high inflation, widespread corruption, and unrealistic expectations; and a government that, when subsequently faced with a depressed world oil market, was left holding a bag of ambitious promises it could no longer afford to keep). Nigeria's also got unification headaches: 250 ethnic groups that can't understand each other's lingo (including three big ones that don't much like each other), and a north-south split that led to civil war back in the Sixties, when the people of the southeast tried to secede and form the Republic of Biafra, only to be barricaded inside their own barren (but oil-rich) land, where thousands of them starved to death. And speaking of failures to communicate, Nigeria doesn't get along all that well with its neighbors either, particularly Cameroon, with whom it is perpetually bickering over offshore oil rights.

WHAT YOU NEED TO KNOW IF YOU'RE DATING A NIGERIAN: Don't wait for your date to call; there are plenty of telephones in Nigeria but they hardly ever work. Going to the movies will almost surely be a hassle, too. Your date may have a car, but you'll have a hard time finding gas for it, unless you're in Lagos, in which case you'll spend most of the day stuck in a traffic jam, known locally as a "go-slow." And we do mean "day;" although the military has taken to shooting armed robbers, you'd be crazy to venture out after dark in a cash economy with skyrocketing urban unemployment and shortages on virtually everything. If you like your date, you probably won't mind staying home and watching the electricity flicker on and off. Speaking of your date, do make allowances if he or she seems a bit excitable, not to say psychotic. How do you think you'd feel if you had one foot in tribalism and the other in twentieth-century slum-living, plus a brand new television that doesn't work because no one in the country can afford to import parts anymore?

WHAT YOU NEED TO KNOW TO MEET YOUR DATE'S PARENTS: If they live in the city, they'll probably speak English, the official language, but out in the country, anything goes. It's just as well; the minute you opened your mouth, you'd just put your foot in it. If they live in the north, they're undoubtedly Hausas or Fulanis, conservative and aggressively Moslem. The Hausas are resentful because they were once a ruling class (if you go to visit, you might still see a sultan or two in full regalia), and now, just because they never moved to the cities and sent their kids to public schools, no one asks their opinion on anything anymore. If they're from the southwest, they'll be relatively sophisticated Christian Yorubas, who've been feeling paranoid ever since the Hausas and other Moslem groups (who make up about half of Nigeria's total population) started clamoring for Islamization of the whole country. And if they call one of the southeast territories home, they may well be activist Ibos, who feel chronically put-upon because so much of Nigeria's oil is dug out of their land and yet even in the good old days they never, they insist, got more than a tiny sliver of the profits in return. Don't mention Biafra, whoever you're talking to; the very name still conjures up hard feelings and, despite all the minor irritations, everybody really is trying harder to get along with one another now.

PAKISTAN

THE LAYOUT: Say hello to the Subcontinent (make sure there are no Pakistanis in the room before you go calling it the *Indian* Subcontinent), where anything can happen and something involving the death of millions usually does. Pakistan, the slab at the western border angling down from the Hindu Kush mountains to the Arabian Sea, marks the spot at which the Moslem and Hindu worlds collide. West of Pakistan are the rich relations: Iran and the Middle Eastern gang, all reassuringly Moslem, if a bit . . . unbalanced. Directly east is the gaping maw of India, Pakistan's Mommy Dearest. (And way over to the east, across about a thousand miles of India, you'll find the long-suffering pariah that used to be known as East Pakistan, now called Bangladesh.) Looming overhead are the two big feet of Asia: the Soviet Union, currently crunching down on what used to be the buffer state of Afghanistan, and China, whose toes nudge Pakistan's perenially inflamed Kashmir region ever so gently. Terrain-wise, Pakistan itself is nothing to write home about; apart from the mountains, it's mostly irrigated desert and waterlogged alluvial plain, divided into four provinces—Punjab, Sinh, Baluchistan, and the Northwest Frontier—that are chronically at odds with each other.

THE SYSTEM: Apparently, that's for Allah to know and the rest of us, including the Provisional Military Government, to find out. Back in 1947, when Pakistan was carved out of the old British India as a homeland for its Moslems, India inherited the colonial version of British parliamentary democracy more or less intact, while Pakistan inherited fond memories and a lot of soldiers trained in the Indian army. As a result, government here is very much in the Argentine mold—a few years of civilian floundering habitually culminating in a military takeover. Last time around, in 1977, it was Prime Minister Zulfikar Ali Bhutto, a Peron-like populist demagogue, who got bumped (and, in 1979, bumped off). His successor, Gen. Muhammad Zia ul-Haq (who swore he'd only be around for ninety days), has since made himself president, put elections off indefinitely, and outlined a new constitution that pretty much does away with the old parliamentary system without explaining what's to replace it. Looks like it will be some sort of presidential system with one, or maybe a few, vice presidents; a 350-member advisory council made up of, you know, businessmen, unions, whoever; and all the old political parties except for Bhutto's. Growing opposition, led by Bhutto's Radcliffe-educated daughter, Benazir, may mean further upheaval ahead.

WHAT YOU NEED TO KNOW TO READ THE NEWSPAPERS: That with Iran down the tubes and the Soviets in Afghanistan, Pakistan suddenly moved to the "A" list for White House parties. While it seems to be enjoying its new-found prestige as a front-line state—mediator for its Moslem brothers in Afghanistan, despite the fact that for years the two countries have been squabbling over their common border—and its military-aid package from the U.S., Pakistan's not about to do anything that might really offend the Russians. Actually, although global strategy in this part of the world may seem fairly obvious to the outside observer (the Russians descending glacier-like toward the Arabian Sea and the Persian Gulf; the U.S. hurriedly trying to patch up old snubs and strengthen Pakistan against the assault), the Subcontinent itself still operates on the level of a schoolyard feud; the superpowers may like to behave as if they're over-seeing a grown-up game of chess, but the players all have slingshots hidden under their shirts. Pakistan continues to think the real threat comes from India, who already acts as if she owns the Subcontinent and is secretly biding her time until she can devour all Moslem children. India, for her part, insists that the Soviet invasion of Afghanistan was a *defensive* move. Fact is, she is a little paranoid about Moslems and what's more, she's still furious with the U.S. for acting as if we preferred Pakistan right from the start. While you're trying to sort out who hates whom the most, keep in mind that India's already got the Bomb and Pakistan's working on it.

WHAT YOU NEED TO KNOW IF YOU'RE DATING A PAKISTANI: That you may be headed for heartbreak because your date's just using you to get his green card. Pakistan is a remittance economy, and manpower is its most profitable export. In fact, whole segments of the government bureacracy are devoted to fina-gling the best possible deals on visas—student visas easily extendable in this country, dependents welcome in that one, that sort of thing. Don't be too hard on your date; if he stayed home, he'd have nothing to do but hang around the bazaar all day, getting into trouble and exacerbating the housing shortage. On the other hand, if you're dating a Moslem woman, you ought to have your head examined. Moslem women don't date; you're either going to ruin some innocent girl's life (virginity still counts here) or get caught messing around with somebody's wife, which, under Zia's reinstated Islamic law, will get you 100 lashes.

WHAT YOU NEED TO KNOW TO MEET YOUR DATE'S PARENTS: That they may take your money and use your medical facilities, but they'll never let you marry their daughter. If you insist on trying to ingratiate yourself, you might ask where they hail from; most of the older generation emigrated from somewhere else after World War II. Don't be surprised, though, if they seem a little bummed out. Pakistan, as Moslem paradise and ideal state, is beginning to strike even Pakistanis as one of those things that seemed like a good idea at the time (the fact that the Moslem paradise they had in mind only existed back in the Prophet's time, and that even *that* one only lasted thirty-two years, might have tipped them off that it wasn't all going to be smooth sailing). Don't think you're going to score any points by waxing enthusiastic over Zia and his Islamization movement; Bhutto may have been a corrupt son of a bitch, but he was a real friend to the working man—he gave a lot of power to the trade unions and knew just where and when to donate the odd pair of temple doors. It was probably a mistake to hang him, given that his family is still alive and kicking, and revenge is a time-honored Islamic tradition.

SAUDI ARABIA

THE LAYOUT: 830,000 square miles of desert like you wouldn't believe, with temperatures routinely in excess of 118°F and nary a river, stream, or hotel bar in sight. The oil fields are in the east, over near the Persian Gulf; the Moslem holy cities of Mecca and Medina are in the west, over near the Red Sea; Riyadh, the capital, is in the big middle chunk, the traditional preserve of the Sauds, the country's ruling family; and to the south is the bone-dry Empty Quarter, the Rub al Khali, which even the Bedouins avoid. In fact, only one percent of the country is suitable for growing so much as a date palm. A single statistic says it all: Gasoline cost, the last time we checked, 31 cents a gallon; mineral water, $5.

THE SYSTEM: A feudalistic monarchy, even if the country is only half-a-century old. The royal family, consisting of something like 4,000 princes and an equal number of princesses, is descended from Abdul Aziz ibn Saud, the man who, back in 1932, established a kingdom out of a patchwork of rival desert tribes and a couple of shards of the former Ottoman Empire. Ever since, he and a succession of his sons and grandsons (kingship always passing through the first king, rather than the current one) have ruled with absolute authority. The current King is named Fahd, and the defense minister, the interior minister, and the governor of the capital are all his brothers, the crown prince his half-brother, and the foreign minister his nephew. (Not for nothing do the Israelis grumble, "It's not a country, it's a family".) Also in the picture: a twenty-five-man Council of Ministers that the king gets to appoint himself and—this sounds good on paper, but think twice before you ask for one—the monthly *majlis,* or audience with the king, at which the king (or, more likely, his locally based son-in-law) hears any and all gripes anybody in the kingdom cares to make. The other authority in this patriarchal, rabidly Islamic nation: the *ulama,* the religious scholars and priests, who function not only as clergy but also as the national judicial system, meting out punishments Koran-style and sometimes even overriding the monarch. Plans for a more popular "consultative assembly" are reportedly being studied, but don't hold your breath.

WHAT YOU NEED TO KNOW TO READ THE NEWSPAPERS: That the Saudi Arabians are the world's third-largest oil producers (after the Russians and the Americans), even if they are today pumping fewer than half the number of barrels per day they were pumping back in 1980, and that they've been the key member of the dreaded OPEC (see page 389) ever since its founding in 1960. That, in the Seventies, it looked as if Saudi Arabia would be filling Egypt's shoes as leader of the Arab world, but that—the result of traditionalism, isolationism, and an unwillingness to commit—that never happened. That, in the Eighties, it looked as if Saudi Arabia would be buying up most of Europe and the U.S., but that—the result of the fall in the demand for oil abroad and a financial crash at home—that never happened. That Saudi Arabia nevertheless believes in Arab solidarity, subsidizing, among others, Syria and the Palestine Liberation Organization, and backs Iraq in the war with Iran (whom, in the person of the proselytizing Ayatollah Khomeini, it loathes and fears), but that it also thinks its American connection is the only thing keeping the Russians (already entrenched in Yemen to the south, Ethiopia across the Red Sea, and Afghanistan over yonder) from camping out along its Persian Gulf pipelines. That, as allies go, Saudi Arabia can't be counted on for a whole helluva lot, but that, more than ever these days, you take what friends you can get, especially if they're relatively stable and very rich.

WHAT YOU NEED TO KNOW IF YOU'RE DATING A SAUDI ARABIAN: If your date's a girl, she'll be a nurse, a teacher, a princess, or unemployed—there aren't many professional options for Saudi women, though a lot of them do go to college. She may also, depending on her family and home town, still be wearing the veil; even so, don't rule out the occasional present, easily selected at, say, the Yves Saint Laurent boutique in Jiddah or the Christian Dior one in Riyadh. If you're dating a boy, things will be that much easier—especially if he's a member of, friend of, or supplier to the royal family, in which case he's making money hand over fist in contract commissions. In any event, you won't be hard up for creature comforts: Most families own an air conditioner, a washing machine, a radio, a TV, and, if they live in town, four or five video recorders. Important social note: If invited to the annual King's Camel Race, in which 2,704 camels cover a 22 km. course, don't bring a flask to the track. Lately the Saudis have been cracking down on alcohol and drugs, and Americans can no longer count on a suspended sentence in place of the prescribed flogging. True, the flogging isn't as bad as it is in, say, Pakistan, given that the flogger has to hold the hefty Koran under his whip arm and the floggee gets to wear a T-shirt, but forty lashes is still forty lashes.

WHAT YOU NEED TO KNOW TO MEET YOUR DATE'S PARENTS: A couple of Arab words will prove that your heart's in the right place. To *majlis* and *ulama*, which you already know, add *hajj*, the pilgrimage to Mecca, Muhammad's birthplace, which every Moslem is enjoined to make at least once in his life, and *salat al-fajr*, which has nothing to do with light lunches and everything to do with dawn prayers. Abdul Aziz will still be talked of, and how he united Saudi Arabia "by the will of Allah and the strength of his right hand." Don't, however, allude to his oldest son, Saud (who was deposed in 1964 for wantonness and incompetence), and be respectful if the name Faisal comes up (he returned the country to moral rectitude and fiscal responsibility, and was assassinated in 1975 by a nephew in the middle of an otherwise routine *majlis*). You might lament the passing of the Bedouins, those nomads of yore, falcons perched on their wrists and salukis prancing at their sides, who are now down to a population roughly that of Hartford. Or you might simply gape at the modernization—Toyota dealerships, traffic jams, and airports that make the Dallas/Fort Worth one look like LaGuardia—that's so in evidence all over the peninsula.

SWITZERLAND

THE LAYOUT: Small, landlocked nation of central Europe, sealed off top and bottom by mountain ranges (the Jura and the Alps) and on either side by lakes (Geneva and Constance), and full of edelweiss, brass cowbells, rushing streams, snow-capped peaks, ski resorts, and, it turns out, fallout shelters. Derives its languages and tastes in literature from its neighbors: The western sector (focused on Geneva) speaks French; the central and eastern sectors (focused on Zurich), constituting the bulk of the country, speaks German; and the south gesticulates in Italian.

THE SYSTEM: Federal republic, officially known as the Swiss Confederation. Probably the most direct and most genuine democracy going, with lots of referendums (Should we be forced to have seatbelts in our cars? Should we have federal riot police? Should we send the "guest workers" back to Spain and Turkey?), citizens' initiatives, and gung-ho government at the state and local levels. (The states in this case are called cantons, and there are twenty-six of them, each with its own constitution, budget, and laws.) A two-house parliament selects the president and vice president, who spend most of their time greeting foreign dignitaries and toasting visiting dance troupes. Real power, both political and economic (not that it's easy to tell the difference in Switzerland), is concentrated in the hands of a few hundred industrialists, farmers, bankers, trade union leaders, and the like, who hammer out consensuses in "preparliamentary commissions." Political parties exist, but have agreed to agree on most issues.

WHAT YOU NEED TO KNOW TO READ THE NEWSPAPERS: That while Switzerland is devoutly neutral, that doesn't mean it's the least bit pacifist. Not only does it have a long history of supplying mercenaries to the rest of Europe (of which the Swiss Guards in the Vatican are the last vestige), it maintains an army reserve of 650,000, with every able-bodied man in the country on twenty-four-hour call until he's fifty. And, unlike the rest of us, it's determined to survive the nuclear holocaust that's so obviously around the corner: Mandatory home fallout shelters do interim duty as laundry rooms and wine cellars; networks of underground hangars edge all major cities, ready to disgorge jet fighters; and storage vaults concealed behind fake rocks will safeguard, thank you very much, at least some of the gold that gives Switzerland, with a paltry 6 million people, the third largest holdings in the world, after the U.S. and West Germany. As for its day-to-day prosperity, everything you've heard about it—the proficiency at making clocks, watches, and chocolates, the deftness at handling money (Switzerland has a higher per-capita income than anybody except three Arab mini-states), the forty-four-hour work week—is true. All this with no natural resources to speak of beyond water.

WHAT YOU NEED TO KNOW IF YOU'RE DATING A SWISS: That all that materialism, conservatism, isolationism, and early-to-bed-early-to-rise stuff can begin to get a person down. Who, after all, wants to feel that he's living in a clinic? (And who could *really* be proud of the fact that he's a citizen of the one European country that might never be mentioned in a college-level European-history textbook and not even be missed?) Even if your date seems content to follow Papa in the watchmaking, banking, or pharmaceuticals business, you'll still want to sound him out on such potentially divisive issues as why it took women until 1971 to get the vote in Switzerland (at least in most of Switzerland; women in a couple of cantons still don't quite have it); and whether he really feels that laundering money for Arab sheiks and American mafiosi is a proper occupation for a nation that can't stop patting itself on the back for its probity and charm. You'll also want to check with him on what ever became of the Movement of the Discontented, the Zurich-based youth gang who occupied the steps of the opera house and pelted everybody with eggs after they heard that 60 million francs were to be spent restoring the opera when *they* didn't even have a club house. Not, obviously, that it's all that easy growing up and old in a country where only 7 percent of the population attends college and everybody else is expected to go off to trade school, then spend the rest of his life making cuckoo clocks and sweeping the front walk. In short, don't buy your date's seeming complacency without first thumbing through his canceled checks to see how much he spends every month on his shrink.

WHAT YOU NEED TO KNOW TO MEET YOUR DATE'S PARENTS: Well, Switzerland is Europe's oldest republic, and that's nice. Also, it's been officially neutral in every conflict since 1815, and that's nice, too, provided you don't get hung up on how, as a neutral, it sold corn, wheat, and armaments to the Nazis and made a bundle shipping munitions on its strategically located Germany-to-Italy railways. On second thought, best not to rock the boat at Sunday dinner. So before you get going on WW II (or the ethics of unnumbered bank accounts), compliment your hosts on keeping such a neat country and on their reputation as a haven for émigrés, of both the rich and fashionable and the dissident and brooding varieties. (Visitors this century have included Thomas Mann, James Joyce, Solzhenitsyn, Lenin, and Tristan Tzara.) Don't yourself expect necessarily to be taken to your date's parents' bosom, however: Many a Swiss mother to this day advises her daughter not to marry "foreign"—a category that includes not only the world beyond the Alps but those areas within them that don't speak the same language she does.

TAIWAN

THE LAYOUT: Small, teardrop-shaped island—a.k.a. Formosa (and, officially, the Republic of China)—located less than a hundred miles off the southern coast of the *other* China. One of the most crowded countries in the world, and, because of the rugged and heavily forested Chungyang mountain range running spinelike down the island, things are even more congested than they at first sound: 18 million people eat, sleep, love, plow, and make transistor radios in an area considerably smaller than Connecticut.

THE SYSTEM: Under martial law since 1949, when, pursued by a zillion Communist Chinese, Generalissimo Chiang Kai-shek withdrew his Kuomintang (i.e., Nationalist Chinese) forces from the mainland and set them down here to catch their breath before reclaiming the 4 million square miles of ground they'd lost. Four decades later, they're still waiting. As a result, the island's governed not only despotically, but provisionally. An elected National Assembly and a clutch of *Yuan* (or councils), also elected, do most of the work, but since these bodies were created to represent all of China, and since 95 percent of China now sits on the other side of the Formosa Strait, real elections can't logically be held until the KMT recovers the mainland. Consequently, terms of office go on forever, and a lot of delegates pull up to the Assembly senile and/or in wheelchairs. Chiang remained head of the KMT (which turned into *the* local political machine, with opposition candidates allowed to campaign only in a loose coalition called the *dangwai*, "outside the party") and his country's only president until he died in 1975; today his son, Chiang Ching-kuo, himself no spring chicken, is in charge.

WHAT YOU NEED TO KNOW TO READ THE NEWSPAPERS: That Taiwan painted itself into a corner when it didn't simply secede from the mainland, but instead went on touting itself as the only legally constituted government of all China and made everybody choose between it and its big, volatile neighbor. (Of course, if it *had* announced it was seceding, it couldn't have told the native Taiwanese that the occupation of their island would just be temporary, but you can't have everything.) For years, things went Taiwan's way: The West endorsed its "we-are-China" stance, not only keeping it in the UN but preserving its veto power in the Security Council. Trouble started in 1964 when France (*naturellement*) recognized Mainland China and "derecognized"—as the Taiwanese say—Taiwan. In 1971, after years of ever-narrower General Assembly votes, Taiwan was ousted from the UN altogether; in 1972, Nixon visited Peking; and in 1978, Carter severed relations with Taipei and normalized them with Peking, withdrawing U.S. forces from the area and demoting its embassy to an "unofficial" mission, staffed by retired diplomats, though pointing out that the U.S. still wouldn't look favorably on a third party's invading the place. As to the really big question of whether or not the two Chinas will ever get together again: Keep in mind that while both the Nationalists and the Communists believe with all their hearts that island and mainland are destined to be reunited one day, Taiwan thinks it'll happen only after Peking comes to appreciate the virtues of making transistor radios and watching prime-time soaps, too. Forget the so-called "Hong Kong model," by which, in 1997, Britain will cede its crown colony (and profit center) to the Commies; the last time Comrade Deng suggested that, if Taiwan would agree to become an autonomous region within *his* China, it could keep its own government, capitalist system, and even army, the Nationalists muttered things like "Once a jackal, always a jackal," then canceled delivery on several crates of telephone equipment the old man had ordered.

WHAT YOU NEED TO KNOW IF YOU'RE DATING SOMEBODY FROM TAIWAN: Avoid the harsher realities, namely, that Taiwan is, as nations go, an orphan, an outcast, and a sitting duck. Instead, concentrate on the Confucius-meets-Horatio-Alger, electricity-comes-to-straw-hut side of the picture: how Taiwan (along with fellow "Gang of Four" countries South Korea, Hong Kong, and Singapore) has in the past decade overtaken even the developed nations in whole areas of trade and manufacturing. Provide assurances of ongoing American interest in and commitment to Taiwan, and while you're obviously in no position to promise anything like the jet fighters they keep angling for, you can point to the fact that military tensions in the area are at their lowest ebb since the late Forties and to the unlikelihood of America's deserting Taiwan when American banking and industry have so many billions of dollars invested there. If all that doesn't do the trick, get the date laughing at Red China's amphibious inadequacies and how obvious plans for an invasion of Taiwan by sea would be to everybody. If you must, remind him that his country, thanks in part to a program undertaken with fellow pariahs Israel and South Africa, is on the verge of nuclear capability. Oh, and don't worry too much about the language barrier: The chances are pretty good that, even if your date didn't go to college in America, he'll be able to talk as if he did.

WHAT YOU NEED TO KNOW TO MEET YOUR DATE'S PARENTS: That long before the economic miracle, long before Chiang Kai-shek and the KMT, there was an island, a beautiful island, called Taiwan, full of people, beautiful people, called Taiwanese—and that, despite the post-1949 influx of 2 million Chinese Nationalists, they still constitute over 80 percent of the island's population. Long-suffering (as well as slightly lacking in imagination), they've had to deal not only with the Nationalists, in the course of whose arrival many thousands of Taiwanese were killed, but for fifty years before that with the Japanese, and before *that* with the Spanish, Dutch, and Portuguese. Taiwanese parents may, as a result, chafe secretly at their enforced subservience to virtually everyone (and see you as but the latest colonialist oppressor), even as they flaunt their present high standard of living and increased political visibility and mix you a Tom Collins. Nationalist parents serve martinis, and may still insist on talking about how great things will be when they finally get that mainland back.

TURKEY

THE LAYOUT: East meets West—or tries to. Most of Turkey's in Asia, of course (where it goes under the name of Anatolia, a big bulbous peninsula that borders Russia and Iran to the east, Syria and Iraq to the south), but note, too, that European mouthful, which mostly serves as a poignant reminder of how the Turks used to police the Balkans all the way up to Hungary. Istanbul (originally Byzantium, then Constantinople) sits on the crack, the strategic Bosporus Strait, which, along with the Dardanelles Strait farther west, controls traffic from the Russian-owned Black Sea clear to the Mediterranean—a passage long coveted by Russia, itself bereft of a warm-weather port (and, it goes without saying, as volatilely Eurasian as Turkey). The other difficult neighbor is Greece, a thorn in Turkey's side since at least the Trojan War, back when Anatolia was still Asia Minor. Inland you'll find Ankara, the capital, at which point fertile plains turn into heavy-duty mountains, many of which are populated by such determinedly non-Turkish groups as the Armenians and the Kurds.

THE SYSTEM: In theory, a republic ever since 1923, when a defeated Ottoman Empire contracted itself into modern Turkey, with a president, prime minister, and parliament elected by universal suffrage. Until 1947, though, Turkey had only a single political party, and for at least a decade after that the incumbent government tended to announce who'd won at the polls before actually bothering to count the votes. Then there's the army, which, in the past three decades, has engineered three military coups and dispensed a whole lot of martial law. Today, there's once again a general in charge—though he did go to the trouble of getting himself elected president—who, over his seven-year term, can dissolve parliament, call new elections, veto legislation, convoke the cabinet, and clamp down on the universities. Other power players: the National Security Council (a military body with statutory authority to tell the civilian cabinet exactly how little it thinks of their latest idea) and the prime minister (currently Turget Özal, a short, pudgy, bespectacled fellow, about whom more below).

WHAT YOU NEED TO KNOW TO READ THE NEWSPAPERS: That exoticism (minarets, opium, a non-European language, and *falaka*, the custom of beating political prisoners on the soles of their feet) notwithstanding, Turkey has done everything it can think of to become a full-fledged member of the European community, and that it feels pretty ripped up about the ongoing rejections. Not out-and-out rejections, exactly: Turkey does belong to NATO, after all (and provides its second largest land army, after the U.S.), and can expect to have its application for full membership in the Common Market reviewed with a straight face. It's the little things: The way Turkish "guest workers" in Germany and Sweden and Switzerland are always made to feel that their seams are crooked, for instance; or the fact that the West seems intent on sympathizing with Greece in the still-going-strong Greco-Turk rivalry (most recently being played out on the nearby island of Cyprus); or the tone of voice in which the U.S., a few years back, demanded that Turkish farmers plow under their poppies, a traditional cash crop. Of course, the West wasn't exactly wrong all those years to be looking askance at a neighbor where terrorism, political assassination, warring Moslem sects, and permanently unfinished apartment complexes were simply pieces of the landscape, or to be worrying about an ally chronically on the verge of bankruptcy. Since the Shah of Iran bit the dust, though, Turkey—about all that now stands between Russia and the Middle East—hasn't seemed quite such an embarrassment, especially given all its military installations, supply depots, and listening posts along Russia's sensitive southwestern border. And don't agonize too much over Turkey going the way of Iran: The experts will tell you that Turkey (a) has no Shah figure to serve as a target for unified opposition; (b) over the past half-century has played religion down to the extent that it's a force only among extremist groups; and (c) began to modernize much earlier (and much less frantically) than Iran, resulting in a wider distribution of wealth and a stabler middle class.

WHAT YOU NEED TO KNOW IF YOU'RE DATING A TURK: First of all, that he's probably in the army. The military plays a unique role in Turkey: It's a political force (and virtually a political party), it's the single most cohesive element in Turkish life (many of whose other elements have been known to carry bombs and machine guns in their briefcases), and it's a time-honored way for a young man to get ahead. So if your date gets a little overheated when he talks about who his favorite generals are, don't roll your eyes: The Turkish military is to be seen as a progressive force, the obvious heir to Kemalism—the modernist, secular, pro-Western spin given the new nation by its soldier-founder. (Even the most recent coup was no South American, take-what-you-can-get-while-the-other-side-is-having-its-siesta affair. The Turkish generals, fed up with a parliament unable to do so much as elect a president, revive the stagnant economy, or combat the thirty-deaths-a-day street violence, simply acted—as they'd done so many times before.) If, however, your date *isn't* a soldier, brace yourself for a discussion of economics, of how Turkey has stopped trying to sell things (including itself) to Europe and started selling them to the Middle East, including Saudi Arabia, Syria, and both Iraq and Iran, where, at least, it stands a chance of making some money and maybe even becoming a regional power. This, clearly, is the opposite of Kemalism, Eastern- (as opposed to Western-) looking, and with an inherently Islamic bias. *This* date will be a fan of prime minister Özal, the highest-profile Turk in fifty years, and angling for a cabinet post rather than a military commission. This date may also be female: Although arranged marriages, complete with dowries, are still fairly routine in Turkey, women routinely compete for most job listings, including those for government ministers and university professors.

WHAT YOU NEED TO KNOW TO MEET YOUR DATE'S PARENTS: Don't force yourself to rhapsodize about the old Ottoman Empire, which in its glory days (before it became "the sick man of Europe") stretched from Budapest to Baghdad, from Algeria to the Arabian peninsula; the Turks are themselves ambivalent about it at best. Besides, almost every vestige of it was obliterated by Mustafa Kemal, later known as Kemal Atatürk (literally, "Father Turk"), who, after the Empire's final dismemberment following Turkey's ill-fated alliance with Germany in World War I, got Westernization rolling. By his death in 1938, he'd rallied the army and prevented Turkey's asphyxiation at the hands of Greece (who'd had the good sense to side with the Allies); established state industries; changed the written form of Turkish from Arabic to Latin script; broken the stranglehold of the Moslem religion; abolished the wearing of fez, turban, and veil; given women the right to vote; and insisted that everyone come up with a last name (example: "Atatürk"), just like the ones they had on the other side of the Bosporus. As a result, Turkey has been that rarity, a

Westward-minded Moslem—although, and this is important, *not* Arabic—nation. Oh, and steer clear of any discussion of Turkey's house minorities, the Armenians in the northeast (whom it came down hard on in the Twenties, and who are now paying it back by lobbing grenades at Turkish diplomats and tourist offices) and the Kurds in the southeast (who, like the Kurds in neighboring Iraq, Iran, and Russia, keep thinking that having their very own nation is a perfectly reasonable idea).

WEST GERMANY

THE LAYOUT: Even without East Germany, manages to have more people (62 million), more neighbors (nine), and a bigger gross national product ($659 billion) than any other European country except the Soviet Union. Flat and Protestant up north, hilly and Catholic down south (the latter tendencies culminate in the Alps of Bavaria), West Germany—like Italy—is crawling with cities, including dirndled Munich, bell-bottomed Hamburg, pinstriped Frankfurt, and mascaraed Düsseldorf, all of whom compete for cultural, financial, and/or industrial primacy. West Berlin (she's the one in the leather miniskirt) is an airplane ride away and is *not* the capital; that's Bonn (in something from a mail-order catalog). This fact, coupled with a 600-mile border with East Germany and Czechoslovakia, makes West Germany talk a lot about military and/or diplomatic blackmail and practice its own intense brand of détente, known locally as *Ostpolitik* (see below). For the record, the Ruhr Valley, over near Holland, is the manufacturing heart of the country; the Rhine flows right through it, en route to the North Sea.

THE SYSTEM: Federal republic, made up of ten *Länder* (or states), with powers similar to those of American states (no accident, this; the U.S. was *the* postwar influence here) and a two-house legislature, the important—and elected—half of which is the Bundestag. There's a president, but the big deal is to be chancellor (like Konrad Adenauer, Willy Brandt, and the two Helmuts, Schmidt and Kohl). As in so many European countries, the vicissitudes of coalition—rather than the reversals of election—are the basis for the shifts in political power. Here the major players are the conservative, pro-Western Christian Democrats (currently in power) and the moderate, leftward-drifting Social Democrats, plus the liberal Free Democrats (many fewer in number, but with a history of manipulating both of the above) and the far-right Christian Socialists of Bavaria. Newer to the scene: the disenchanted, pro-life, -trees, and -the-individual, anti-NATO, -nukes, and -economic-growth "Greens," some of whom are just now turning forty.

WHAT YOU NEED TO KNOW TO READ THE NEWSPAPERS: That West Germany (formally, the Federal Republic of Germany) turns out to be a lot less Western than we've all been thinking of it as. In fact, it's only since 1945 and the three-power Allied occupation of half of a nation less than a hundred years old that anybody's been lumping it together with its Atlantic-looking neighbors and assuming that the Germans want roughly what the English, French, Dutch, etc., do. Before that, the country had been regarded as something "other," neither Western (all craft guilds and plashing fountains) nor Eastern (all onion domes and howling wolves). Granted, West Germany has done itself proud with its imitation of the American model in matters of government and industry; its close collaboration with traditional enemy France in matters of culture and commerce; and its integration into the European Community, in the course of which it became somebody you could once more invite to weddings. But it still abuts its severed eastern half, and, through her, registers the pulse of Poland, Russia, and even Asia, and if it wants to practice *Ostpolitik* ("*Ost*" = "east," by the way), economically and psychologically, nobody should really be gaping: Preserving the dialogue with Russia is always—Poland and Afghanistan or no Poland and Afghanistan—going to be a high priority among the Germans. (In fact, those are the only foreign affairs the Germans, who lack France's nuclear capability, "blue-water" navy, African and Mideast interests, and silver tongue, conduct.) Then there's the matter of NATO in general and the U.S. in particular: Germany worries that, what with all those medium-range "Euromissiles" deployed on its soil, America means to fight its battles in Bremerhaven—or what's left of Bremerhaven. Anyway, given that younger Germans no longer perceive Russia as The Enemy; that the German economic miracle is yesterday's news; that polls show Germans to be the most anxious and self-involved of all Common Marketers; that half of all German newspaper headlines read "The Beginning of the End"; and that you can't roll home from the rathskeller without tripping over a family of Turkish guest workers—is it any wonder that West Germany, once America's European yes-man, now sometimes turns querulous and shifty?

WHAT YOU NEED TO KNOW IF YOU'RE DATING A WEST GERMAN: Pack the Reeboks and the Benetton sweatsuit. Turns out that dating a West German is an awful lot like dating an American, and that these days the kind of American it's most like dating is a yuppie. (Five years ago, the kind of American it would have been most like dating was a campus radical, but that was back when the Greens were still young and vibrant and before it had become painfully obvious that no matter how vigorously you protested the deployment of medium-range nuclear weapons on your soil, it wasn't ultimately going to do any good.) So, brace yourself for bars and discothèques with jacket-and-tie dress codes (including one in West Berlin actually called Yuppies Inn), for fraternity parties, for church on Sundays (expect your date to nudge you happily when the choir sings Bach), for conversations about the joys of high-profile individual performance (local hero: Boris Becker, the tennis star), and for the whole middle-class getting-and-spending thing you've been saddled with yourself. On the other hand: Lower-middle-class types are still capable of getting mad and blowing off steam, especially when they don't get that job in the ball-bearing factory they'd been counting on. But neither are they going to have much money to take you places and buy you things, and you know how that works *your* nerves.

WHAT YOU NEED TO KNOW TO MEET YOUR DATE'S PARENTS: Oy. Make that "ach"—no sense getting off on the wrong foot. Basically, you have your work cut out for you. It's not that your date's parents don't like Americans, it's just that there are so many potential conversational land mines, of which the Holocaust is only the most obvious. Also avoid the subject of "unification," which they'll know you know they know every government in the world is determined at all costs to prevent; an *un*divided Germany still, forty years later, evokes images, if not of goose-stepping brown-shirts, at least of 80 million efficient, obedient, indefatigable Germans kissing the frau goodbye at five A.M., grabbing the old lunch bucket, and heading for the job in the munitions plant. You *could* talk culture: German was, after all, the language of that intellectual holy trinity, Marx, Freud, and Einstein, nor is there any ignoring Kant and Hegel and Goethe and Nietzsche, not to mention all the composers, but even that will backfire if someone in the group wonders aloud where all that culture ever *got* Germany. (It's all such dark, heavy, unrelenting stuff, not a bit like the French and English legacies, with their upbeat Matisses and six-and-a-fraction precious volumes of Jane Austen.) Which reminds us, try not to compare Germany to other countries in any respect, and especially don't compare her to France. While it's true they're the best of friends these days, too much talk of her more glamorous neighbor may remind Germany how (a) she doesn't have twelve centuries of consolidated national identity and purpose to fall back on, and (b) nobody ever watched her with envy and appreciation when she took to the dance floor. By all means, don't mention the Weimar Republic, Germany's between-the-wars go at democracy; that was the period when a loaf of bread cost a wheelbarrowful of marks, as well as when Hitler managed to get himself named chancellor, and, half-a-century later, the allusion can still induce panic.

YUGOSLAVIA

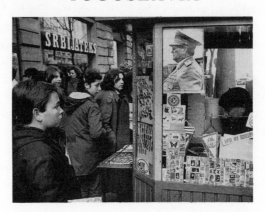

THE LAYOUT: Thick forests, fertile plains, lush valleys (including that of the Danube, as much a presence here as in the rest of the Balkan Peninsula), a stunning coastline, and fairly respectable mountains. Alternatively, a crazy quilt of eight nationalities, five languages, three religions (not counting atheism), and two alphabets, hastily stitched together by the Allies at the end of World War I in an effort to account for long-seething Slavic nationalism on the one hand, and the amputated appendages of the defeated Austro-Hungarian and Ottoman Empires on the other. With a name that translates literally as "Land of the South Slavs," Yugoslavia serves as home to Slavic souls south of Poland and Czechoslovakia and west of Russia and Bulgaria.

THE SYSTEM: A Communist state, and an Eastern European one, yes, but *not* a Soviet satellite. Under Josip Broz Tito, its first and only president-for-life (his ended in 1980, after thirty-five years in office), Yugoslavia successfully defied Russia, whirling itself out of the Soviet orbit and creating its own brand of Communism, heavy on private ownership of land and industrial "self-management." With Tito gone, a nation used to one-man rule (the jury's still out on whether that man was benevolent or brutal) is now run by committee. There's a nine-member "collective" presidency (which includes somebody from each of the country's six constituent republics and two dependent provinces, as well as the head of the League of Communists), with a one-year presidential term in constant rotation among the nine, plus a twenty-three-member Party Presidium and a two-house legislature—making it almost impossible for even a Yugoslav to know who the boss is. Pay attention to those six republics, though: Each has its own flag, foreign-affairs apparatus, banks, courts, language, and way of doing things, and each is theoretically free to secede from the union at any time.

WHAT YOU NEED TO KNOW TO READ THE NEWSPAPERS: First off, that the six republics have a tendency to distrust one another—and that's putting it mildly. For the fact that Yugoslavia has held together at all there's, once again, Tito to thank: By raising the standard of living and putting Yugoslavia's name in lights both as a defier of Stalin and as a linchpin in the neutral-nations movement of the Sixties, he got a lot of Yugoslavs' minds off how most effectively to hate their neighbor. Unfortunately, given foreign debt, inflation, unemployment, and the fact that a rich, industrious north still looks down its nose at a poor, benighted south (cf. Italy), intramural resentments are once more in full bloom. So's separatism: The Croatians are reasonably quiet now, but in the southern province of Kosovo, with a concentration of ethnic Albanians and a standard of living about one eighth that of the north's, things have been tense ever since 1981, when a student at the University of Pristina dumped the contents of his tray on the cafeteria floor, setting off a chain of riots and rumors, the latter culminating in fears that Albania would annex Kosovo, Bulgaria grab Macedonia, and the Russians eventually wind up with access to that all-weather port on the Mediterranean they've been hankering after for centuries. On the other hand, the death of Tito hasn't led to disintegration, just inertia; the Russians are busy in Africa and Afghanistan; and whose economy, besides Japan's and Switzerland's, isn't a perennial problem anyway?

WHAT YOU NEED TO KNOW IF YOU'RE DATING A YUGOSLAV: That, while they live in a country no bigger than Wyoming, Yugoslavs come in a variety of flavors. The Slovenes, in the far north, are the hard-working and liberal-minded ones, with the highest per capita income; chalk this up in part to their long history of Austrian domination, and don't be surprised if your date turns up in lederhosen and talking about the dangers inherent in the political manipulation of photography. The Croatians are almost as productive, and considerably less Germanicized; also, they have all the prettiest seacoast (including the resort towns of Dubrovnik and Split) and what passes for a sense of humor. Careful, though: Lately a lot of young Croatians, frustrated with being Yugoslavs, have become super-Catholics. The Bosnians are landlocked, stubborn, and may bristle noticeably when you ask them to point out the intersection in Sarajevo, their capital, where World War I began; also, they're the ones who are becoming the Islamic fundamentalists. The Serbs, in by far the most plentiful supply, boast the national capital, Belgrade; also, in the old, nineteenth-century days, when Slav nationalism was just getting off the ground, it was the small, independent kingdom of Serbia that provided a rallying point for everybody else. As a result of all this, Serbs think of themselves as the heart and soul of the Yugoslav enterprise and can get a little big for their britches. The Montenegrins are mountain folk, make better soldiers than workers, and tend to be tall. The Macedonians get stuck with the "poets-at-heart" label; don't flinch at the peasant drag.

WHAT YOU NEED TO KNOW TO MEET YOUR DATE'S PARENTS: Don't let all the cafés and the slivovitz fool you: These folks know from suffering. First there were the Austrian and Turkish landlords, in evidence through the end of World War I, at which point the short-lived Kingdom of the Serbs, Croats, and Slovenes (note the billing) was decreed. Then there was Hitler. Concomitant with him was the virtual civil war between Tito's Nazi-hating Partisans and the Communist-fearing Četniks, chauvinistic Serbian royalists loyal to the exiled King Peter II. (Silver-lining department: At least it was the Partisans, and not the Soviets, who liberated the country at the end of World War II, which was all that kept it from going the way of Poland, Hungary, Czechoslo-vakia, etc.) Then there was Tito himself, who, while promoting shopping sprees and summer cottages, also had a history of jailing dissidents and purg-ing liberals. Still, at least he provided a center. Now, what with centrifugal force on the one hand and sluggishness on the other, Yugoslavs worry that the entire country could disappear, without the Russians so much as lifting a finger. Or as a joke recently making the rounds of Belgrade has it: "Question: What do we do if the Russians attack? Answer: We fight back. Question: But what do we do if they don't?"

Dead-Letter Department

ACRONYMS—AND ACRIMONY— FROM HERE TO HONSHU

Countries have always banded together in times of war, forming alliances that are usually less ideological than they are expedient. But it wasn't until the League of Nations took shape, right after World War I, that every-body began to think membership in some larger order might be a good idea in and of itself. Now the world is one big Club Méditerranée, a paradise for joiners, swingers, lodge brothers, and nymphomaniacs (and a place where, as often as not, you can pay for your drinks with beads). The UN, successor to the League, is the most comprehensive world organization: Only Switzerland, the two Koreas, Taiwan, a handful of European mini-states, and another of South Pacific island nations don't belong. Beyond that teem military alliances, economic unions, ethnic orders, industrial organizations, and social and charitable societies. Here's a look at those among them that—always modern, occasionally trendy—tend to do business under their initials alone.

NATO (NORTH ATLANTIC TREATY ORGANIZATION)

Gidget takes the Grand Tour. Formed 1949, with Berlin under Soviet blockade and the Communist world looking pretty monolithic, by the U.S., Canada, and ten European nations: Britain, France, Italy, Belgium, the Netherlands, Luxembourg, Norway, Denmark, Iceland, and Portugal. This grouping was the West's bottom line in the old days, before the age of economic miracles and the Common Market, and while war and rubble-strewn residential neighborhoods were still on everybody's mind. A military-defense treaty providing for mutual assistance in the event any member of the alliance was attacked, NATO was also a way of letting the world know what side of the fence you were on, even if your local Communist party was threatening to take over and even if you didn't strike your neighbors as particularly tidy or reliable at the time. Greece and Turkey joined in 1952, vouchsafing the "free world" 's southern flank; West Germany signed on in 1955. France, ever testy and suspicious, withdrew its military forces from joint military command in 1966, though sticking by the alliance in spirit; still, headquarters had to be moved from lovely Fontainebleau to prosaic Brussels. Lately there's been a lot of talk about "paralysis of will" and "failure of common outlook" within NATO, as well as about whether (a) the U.S. would really risk all its big cities "to save Rotterdam" in the face of some Soviet diplomatic-military blackmail move; and (b) Europe, and especially West Germany, should allow U.S. medium-range missiles, the first capable of reaching Soviet targets from Europe itself, to be stationed on its soil. In the plus column: Spain just decided to join up, the first new member since Cold War days.

Note: As for CENTO (Central Treaty Organization) and SEATO (Southeast Asia Treaty Organization), forget about them. Created by analogy with NATO, and consisting of the U.S., Britain, France, and those Asian states willing to get behind the regional containment of the Soviet Union, they've long been inactive and are now officially defunct (CENTO as of 1979, SEATO as of 1977).

EC (EUROPEAN COMMUNITY)

Gidget looks on as Monique, Gina, Ilsa, and Katrinka decide to bury the hatchet and lend each other their second-favorite sweaters. An umbrella organization established by degrees in 1952, 1958, and 1967, the EC integrated three earlier European "communities," including the so-called "Common Market."

Return with us now to '52, when six industrialized nations of Western Europe—France, Italy, West Germany, and the Benelux countries (Belgium, the Netherlands, and Luxembourg)—pooled their coal and steel resources in the European Coal and Steel Community (ECSC), which permitted the ready flow of those two commodities across international boundaries, under the direction of a "High Authority" to which each nation surrendered just a little bit of its sovereignty. Now it's 1958, and the coal-and-steel plan has worked so well that the same six nations decide to drop a few more formalities and restrictions. They form the European Economic Community (abbreviated EEC, nicknamed the Common Market, or the "Inner Six"), which aims to eliminate *all* internal tariff barriers, to hit upon a unified policy with regard to the rest of the world, and to allow money and workers to move freely within the six nations' frontiers. Also created then: the European Atomic Energy Community (Euratom), which provided for the pooling of peacetime atomic resources and research. Both the EEC and Euratom were structured along the same supranational "High Authority" as the ECSC; the merger of the three in 1967 resulted in the full-blown European Community (EC).

Sounds pretty tame, we know. Still, with this series of voluntary suturings on the part of a clutch of shell-shocked, no-longer-great nations of Europe, a new economic power was born to the west of the Soviet Union, a strong ally was created to the east of the U.S., and—in one bold stroke—any number of old European rivalries, suspicions, and potential conflicts were smoothed over. Moreover, Germany, once accepted into the set-up, began to feel respectable again, France got to feel like the boss of something again, and everybody got to feel like they *belonged*.

The rest of Europe couldn't help wondering if it wasn't missing out on something big. It was. In 1973, Britain, Ireland, and Denmark became full members of the Common Market (and, by extension, the European Community); Norway would have, but pulled out a few minutes before the induction ceremony, when a referendum showed that a majority of Norwegians opposed membership. In 1981, Greece joined, then, five years later, Spain and Portugal; Turkey is currently lined up, pen in hand, hoping to do likewise. This isn't Utopia we're talking about: Political integration seems less and less likely with every passing year (and every new member), and it's not easy welcoming those poor, agriculture-heavy, and not-always-stable nations of southern Europe into your club when that club's main activity is prosperity. But the European Community is still a bona-fide modern miracle, a coup—however indirect—of postwar diplomacy and economic planning.

EFTA (EUROPEAN FREE TRADE ASSOCIATION)

The sorority for those coeds who didn't want to lend each other sweaters, and were happier singing madrigals, throwing pots, and gazing into the fire than dating football players. Formed 1960, by Britain, Denmark, Norway, Sweden, Switzerland, Austria, and Portugal. Spurred on by the success of the Common Market, the so-called "Outer Seven" wanted to promote economic expansion and trade, but screwed up their noses, each for her own reasons, at even the whiff of political integration. The seven eliminated tariff restrictions among themselves, but went on maintaining separate tariff structures with the outside world, an arrangement that allowed Britain to continue within the Commonwealth system of trade preferences. Iceland joined in 1971, and Finland's been an associate member since 1961; Britain and Denmark, you'll recall, pledged the rival sorority in 1973, Portugal a decade later.

COMECON (COUNCIL FOR MUTUAL ECONOMIC ASSISTANCE)

Natasha cleans up the yard and ties the children to a tree. Established 1949, by Russia and her Eastern European satellites: Poland, East Germany, Hungary, Czechoslovakia, Bulgaria, Romania, and Albania. Originally Stalin's method for making renegade Yugoslavia (Communist, but outside Soviet control) feel left out and threatened; gradually, however, in the Khrushchev era, COMECON began to see Western Europe—and not poor Yugoslavia—as its main goad and target. (Albania, a fan of Red China's, was expelled in 1961; Mongolia joined in 1962 and Cuba in 1972.) As for the meanings of "mutual" and "assistance," don't press your luck: Keep in mind how Khrushchev, back in the Fifties simply announced that Hungary and Czechoslovakia were to make things in factories, Bulgaria and Romania were to farm, and that was that. The military counterpart to COMECON (and equivalent to NATO) is the Warsaw Pact, in which the Soviet Union plays the part of the U.S., East Germany plays the part of West Germany, and Romania is France.

OECD (ORGANIZATION FOR ECONOMIC COOPERATION AND DEVELOPMENT)

A few of the girls get together to plan a charity ball, but spend most of the meeting-time having lunch. The successor to an earlier grouping of eighteen Western European nations, established in 1948 to oversee postwar reconstruction. Assumed its present shape in 1961, when the U.S. and Canada signed in, and all twenty nations, already solidly committed to helping themselves, vowed to turn their attention to the "developing" nations and proceeded to lend them money, pat them on the back, and serve as role models. Japan, Australia, New Zealand, and even Finland eventually joined; Yugoslavia is an associate member. Housed in an elegant chateau just off Paris's Bois de Boulogne that once belonged to the Rothschilds, the OECD has little trouble attracting delegates.

ANZUS (AUSTRALIA/ NEW ZEALAND/ UNITED STATES COUNCIL)

Gidget goes Down Under. Signed in 1951, this tripartite security treaty provided for mutual assistance should any of the three signatories be the victim "of an armed attack in the Pacific area." For Australia and New Zealand, the moment marked a slight turning away from Mother England, who no longer seemed like such a dynamite champion of anybody, including herself, and a turning towards the U.S. For the U.S., it was all part of the Asian-Pacific game plan: Two days later a similar pact was signed with the Philippines, and, the next week, yet another with Japan. Lately there's been talk of how much sense it would make to integrate Japan into ANZUS—and of how New Zealand wants no part of America's nuclear umbrella.

OAS (ORGANIZATION OF AMERICAN STATES)

Gidget flies to Rio. Also to Buenos Aires, Mexico City, Bogotá, Santo Domingo, and Tegucigalpa. The most recent Pan-American "arrangement," built on the foundations of the 1910 Pan-American Union, and meant to promote the joint welfare, protect everyone's sovereignty, settle disputes, and generally get the job done—most often railroading anti-Communist resolutions through the annual conferences, a trend that continued right through the expulsion of Castro's Cuba from the organization. Hemisphere relations now seem a little less one-sided than they used to, though, and the OAS is no all-for-one, one-for-all love-in; if there's been a major theme lately, it's not mutual solidarity, but human-rights abuses. An anomaly for the discerning: Canada has never belonged to the OAS or to any of its predecessor so-this-is-the-New-World bodies. And stay awake: Don't confuse this OAS with the other OAS—Organisation de l'Armée Secrète—the terrorist group out to get De Gaulle during the Algerian war for independence, defunct since the early Sixties.

OPEC (ORGANIZATION OF PETROLEUM EXPORTING COUNTRIES)

Abdul goes to Caracas—or at least he did in 1960, when delegates from Iran, Iraq, Kuwait, Qatar, and Saudi Arabia converged on the capital of Venezuela, where they agreed to check overdevelopment by the Western oil companies and to maintain steady—and coordinated—prices. Soon they were joined by Ecuador, Indonesia, Gabon, Nigeria, Algeria, Libya, and the United Arab Emirates; the oil companies were on their way out (though not down); oil cost $40 a barrel instead of $3; and, on account of the preponderance of Arab states among the oil producers, what started out as a trade cartel began to take on intense international political significance. Not that the Arabs agree on that much. Or that it's easy to give a dinner party for thirteen and serve something that Indonesia, Algeria, Gabon, and Ecuador all like. By the mid-Eighties, though, thanks to new oil discoveries and reduced oil consumption in the West, and to dissension within OPEC, the cartel's power seemed pretty much broken.

OAU (ORGANIZATION OF AFRICAN UNITY)

Gidget's forced to have second thoughts about all the terrible things she said to the daughter of the black family who tried to get into Gidget's parents' country club. Founded in 1963 at a Pan-African conference; consists of some

Clockwise from top: The European Community (EC), a.k.a. the Common Market; the Association of Southeast Asian Nations (ASEAN); the Organization of African Unity (OAU); and the Organization of Petroleum Exporting Countries (OPEC).

fifty members—every country on (or just off) the African continent, except South Africa and its Namibia (or, as Gidget used to say, Southwest Africa). A little like the OAS except that there's no United States to intimidate everybody else, and no one's first language is Spanish. Given the way Africa was carved up by its colonial landlords of the last century—with total disregard for history or tribal loyalties—a lot of OAU energies are spent on redressing boundary grievances and determining who legitimately owns or, more likely, doesn't own whom. (Morocco's annexation of the once Spanish Western Sahara and South Africa's intractability with regard to Namibia are recent agenda items.) If you're invited, wear your tribal robe over your three-piece suit and bring along a burnous; OAU conferences get a little schizophrenic.

ASEAN (ASSOCIATION OF SOUTHEAST ASIAN NATIONS)

Gidget sits reading *Vogue;* somewhere in the South China Sea, a shrimp fisherman sneezes. For the connoisseur of international groupings. Included not only as proof that you never know who's going to invite whom into his house for a brainstorming session, but also as perhaps the premier example of the impact the Common Market phenomenon has had around the world. Formed in Bangkok in 1967, by Thailand, Malaysia, Singapore, the Philippines, and Indonesia, but didn't meet, not even once, until 1976, by which time the U.S. had pulled out of Vietnam, leaving a vacuum in the area, and the five of them decided to create a "zone of peace, freedom, and neutrality." (The sultanate of Brunei joined in 1984.) Basically an economic union—although regional economic integration hasn't really gotten anywhere, and their trade is only 16 percent among themselves anyway—ASEAN is decidedly nonmilitary and barely political. On the other hand, it's still, *faute de mieux,* the major anti-Communist force in the area, maintaining a reasonably solid front against Communist encroachments, even if it can't decide whether Russia, encamped in Vietnam and Cambodia, or China, looming over all, is the bigger threat.

A Trio of Geographical Clarifications for a Nation that, Frankly, Would Rather Skateboard

WHY EVERY MIDDLE AMERICAN DOESN'T BELONG TO THE MORAL MAJORITY

One way to divide up the Western Hemisphere is to snap it in two just a little below its narrowest point, the Isthmus of Panama. (Not for nothing did they decide to dig the canal there, rather than across, say, Honduras.) This gives you two big pieces: North America, which includes Canada, the United States, Mexico, Central America, the West Indies, and, up top, Greenland, still owned by Denmark; and South America, which includes the continent's twelve independent nations (ranging in size from Brazil, the fifth-largest country in the world, to Suriname, the former Dutch Guiana), plus French Guiana and the notorious Falkland Islands.

On the other hand, there are the times when a person wants to speak collectively of his southern neighbors (more and more of whom are, we grant you, trading in the metaphor of neighborhood for a substandard three-room apartment right down the block). Now the term of choice is Latin America, and it takes in everything from Mexico and Cuba all the way to Chile and Argentina. Everything, that is, that speaks a Romance language, which leaves out most current and former British colonies, likewise Dutch ones, as well as the U.S. Virgin Islands; Puerto Rico, though, is Latin American.

South-of-the-border breaks down in other ways, too. Central America is the seven nations stretching from Guatemala and Belize, which you may remember as British Honduras, to Panama. Middle America—however ridiculous the term sounds in light of all those old double-knit-polyester jokes—includes, in addition to Central America, both Mexico and the countries of the Caribbean (a.k.a., more or less, the West Indies; see box), regardless of language and colonial past. South America we've already talked about.

Now, what if you want to point only to those people in Latin America who speak Spanish—i.e., the Mexicans, the Central Americans, the residents of Cuba, Puerto Rico, and the Dominican Republic (*not* Haiti, next door, which speaks a free-form version of French), plus almost everybody in South America except the various Guianans and the Brazilians (the last of whom speak Portuguese)? Then you'll say Spanish America, or better, given that the U.S. kicked Spain out of Cuba and Puerto Rico, its last New World holdings, in 1898, Hispanic America.

ISLANDS IN THE STREAM

A few nice distinctions for revolutionaries and winter vacation-goers. First, don't think that Caribbean and West Indian are exact synonyms. The West Indies (which disappointed Columbus by not turning out to be the East Indies, that is, present-day Indonesia) includes all the Caribbean islands (from the Caribee Indians whom Columbus found living there, the source, also, of our word "cannibal") *plus* the Bahamas, which aren't any more in the Caribbean than Fort Lauderdale is. The Caribbean Islands themselves break down into two big groups: the Greater Antilles (Cuba, Jamaica, Hispaniola, which is shared by Haiti and the Dominican Republic, and Puerto Rico; called "Greater" because they're adult-sized), and the Lesser Antilles (everything else, none of it with much heft). The Lesser Antilles break down in turn into the Leeward Islands (e.g., the Virgins, Antigua, Guadeloupe) and the Windward Islands (e.g., Grenada, Martinique), plus Barbados, Trinidad and Tobago, and Curaçao and the rest of the Dutch Antilles. Bermuda, by the way, is not a West Indian island at all, but a flyspeck of a British colony a few hundred miles off the coast of North Carolina, all pink stucco houses and shetland sweaters. If you're heading there for a February vacation (or a revolution), you've made a terrible mistake.

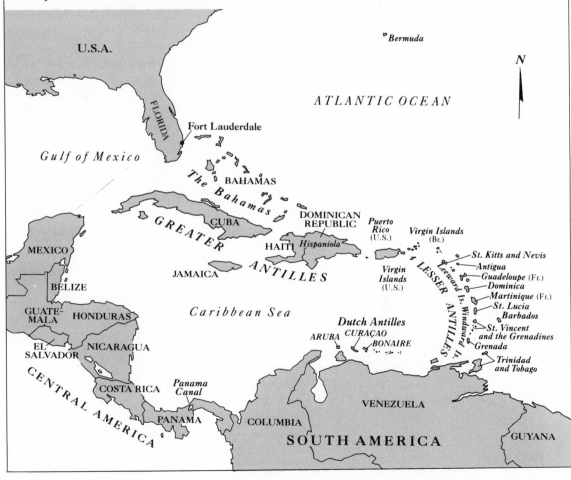

WHY ENGLAND, WHILE ADMITTEDLY A ROYAL THRONE OF KINGS AND A LITTLE WORLD, IS NOT EXACTLY A SCEPTRED ISLE OR A PRECIOUS STONE SET IN THE SILVER SEA

It isn't a sceptred isle or a precious stone set in the silver sea because it's only a *part* of that isle and that stone. The other parts are called Wales (to the west) and Scotland (to the north), and together the three have made up a single country since the 1707 Act of Union between England (which had already swallowed up Wales) and Scotland. It was called "Great" less out of copy-writer's overkill than to distinguish it from "Little Britain," better known as Brittany, across the channel in France, which had been named and settled by Celts driven out of "historic" Britain by the Germanic Angles and Saxons in the fifth and sixth century. Not to be outdone, evidently, the Angles came up with "England."

No, we're not finished. The British Isles is the name for the islands of Britain and Ireland taken together, along with such outlying island groups as the Shet-lands and the Orkneys and the British possessions of the Isle of Man and the Channel Islands. The United Kingdom is the formal name for the nation you now won't be referring to as England; its full name is the United Kingdom of Great Britain and Northern Ireland. (It was known as the United Kingdom of Great Britain and Ireland from 1801 until southern Ireland—a.k.a. the Irish Free State, a.k.a. Eire—pulled out in 1922.) Today, both "Britain" and "the U.K." are accepted shorthand forms for "United Kingdom."

No, we're not finished. The British Empire, which at its height, just after World War I, took in 450 million people spread over 14 million square miles (a quarter of the earth's population and land surface), from Canada to Ceylon, Ireland to Iraq, Australia to Antigua, and which the sun was supposed never to set on, hasn't existed since 1947, when India and Pakistan became indepen-dent, and when "British Commonwealth" seemed like a more diplomatic heading under which to be bearing what remained of "the white man's burden." Now, unless you're a reactionary yourself, you'd do well to call it "the Commonwealth," more formally "the Commonwealth of Nations," no "British" about it.

No, we're not quite finished. British—the adjective—can be used of the island of Britain and the people who live on it, assuming you don't want to be more specific and say English, Welsh, or Scottish (which, for what it's worth, is preferred by most Scots to "Scotch," unless it's broth or whisky you're talking about); the Northern Irish are Irish, not British, but begorrah, and we'd best not be opening that one up. A person who lives in Britain is a Brit*o*n, as opposed to a Br*e*ton, which is a person who lives in Brittany (or Bretagne, as the French like to say). Britishers is what Americans sometimes call Britons, who find the word mildly funny. Be all that as it may, you'll still probably choose, with most Britons, to refer to Prince Philip's wife not as "Her Britannic Majesty" but as "the Queen of England."

WHY THE ORIENT EXPRESS NEVER GOT TO TOKYO

Nobody uses "Near East" much anymore as a way of indicating that part of Asia and Africa that comprises Turkey, Cyprus, Syria, Lebanon, Israel, Jordan, Egypt, Iraq, and the countries of the Arabian Peninsula. "Middle East" (or, more folksily, "Mideast") is still going strong, however, and takes in all of the above, as well as Libya and the Sudan, Ethiopia and Somalia (the so-called Horn of Africa), Iran and Afghanistan—plus, if you're British and have a fondness for days of Empire, India, Pakistan, Sri Lanka (formerly Ceylon), Nepal, Bangladesh, and even Burma, now usually lumped together as the "Indian Subcontinent."

"Arab World," an expression that varies in popularity according to whether the Arabs are speaking to one another at the time, leaves out Israel, obviously; it also leaves out Iran (which is Moslem but not Arab), Ethiopia (which is full of Christians and blacks), Turkey (which is full of Turks, who, incidentally, in the days of the Ottoman Empire, played landlord to the entire neighborhood), and all points beyond. On the other hand, "Arab World" very definitely includes Tunisia, Algeria, and Morocco, which together with Libya form a strictly regional grouping called the Maghreb, from the Arabic word for "west," which is where they lie with regard to Egypt and Arabia, secular and spiritual Arab headquarters, respectively. "Arab League" is the loose political association of Arab states throughout the region, Morocco to Iraq, Lebanon to Somalia, with Arab nationalism its raison d'être; "United Arab Republic," you may remember, was the short-lived union of Egypt and Syria.

So much for now. There's also a sizable back list of geographical names, any of which can pop up without much warning. "Palestine" got a new lease on life with the PLO; historically, it describes the territory defined roughly by present-day Israel, from Biblical times to its British mandate following World War I, with bits of Jordan (formerly, Transjordan, "across the Jordan [River]")

and Egypt thrown in. Asia Minor ("Little Asia") is essentially Turkey, at least the 95 percent of it that's not in Europe and that's also today known as Anatolia. The Fertile Crescent arches from the Mediterranean coast of Syria in the west to Iraq and the Persian Gulf in the east; like the Nile Valley, it's a famous Cradle of Civilization, especially the Mesopotamian portion of it, centered on the plain bounded by the Tigris and the Euphrates rivers. The Levant (from the French word for "rise," which the French obviously assumed the sun did there) is the eastern tier of the Mediterranean, Greece to Egypt, but especially the Syria/Lebanon portion of it, which the French got as *their* mandate following World War I.

Which brings us to the term "Orient" itself, from the Latin word for "rise," a term that, until this century, was used invariably to designate Turkey, Arabia, Egypt, Persia (our Iran), Palestine, etc., *not* China, Japan, Korea, and the Philippines, which were known then, as they still are today, as the Far East. This shouldn't come as a surprise: The fellows in whose honor "We Three Kings of Orient Are" was written weren't, after all, shoguns.

PSYCHOLOGY

N I N E

Contents

Undergoing an analysis, Hollywood-style, in the early talkie Secrets of a Soul.

Herr Doktor, What's Wrong With Me?

A GUIDE TO NEUROSIS, PSYCHOSIS, AND PMS

Somebody—was it Freud or one's freshman-year roommate?—defined a neurotic as a person who could neither love nor work, but who was still, nine days out of ten, able to get around. In other words, whatever trouble he may be having with unresolved anxiety, guilt, or revulsion, a neurotic remains capable of coherent speech, good manners, tasteful outfits, and what psychologists—or was it one's freshman-year roommate?—call reality-testing.

The neurotic (unlike the psychotic, about whom more in a minute) is not out of his mind. If anything he's too much in it, condemned to try to use his neurotic symptom (the obsessive-compulsive's ritual handwashing, for instance) as an outlet for the least objectionable part of an objectionable impulse and, usually, as a barrier against the enactment of the rest of that impulse as well. Where do these objectionable impulses come from? Childhood sexual wishes, mostly, some as early as in-crib masturbation and feces-smearing, some later and directed against the parents, nearly all of which proved painful or unwieldy and were repressed, that is, chased out of consciousness and "forgotten." As if all that weren't enough, the fledgling neurotic's libido—his sex drive and primary energy source, lying inside him, as Freud pointed out, like so much crude oil—regresses, finding safer, more manageable satisfactions in an earlier, less intimidating stage of sexual development.

Don't take it personally. This one-two punch is the fate of almost everybody, and it generally connects with us in mid-Oedipus complex, just when we're trying to catch the bus for kindergarten. But not everybody has to deal with it all over again later. That chore falls to the adult for whom adult-style goings-on—or the lack of them—have become so painful, so unwieldy that he reinstitutes the long-dormant repression-and-regression process. Tied to a period and a pattern in the past, with things going badly now, he repeats, or acts out, over and over and over again, the trauma he can't "remember." As Freud once sighed, "Today, neurosis takes the place of the monasteries, which used to be the refuge of all whom life had disappointed or who felt too weak to face it."

Like cancer, the other mythic disease of the century, neurosis is a grab bag of ailments, syndromes, and prognoses, with a complex causation closely linked to individual susceptibility. Reach in and you're likely to pull out one of the following, divided here, as they were in Freud's day, between the "transference" and the "narcissistic" varieties.

The transference neuroses, also known as the classical neuroses, were the ones Freud thought psychoanalysis could actually cure. They include:

HYSTERIA: from the Greek word for womb, used, pre-Freud, to designate only certain female disorders; subsequently applied to any disorder in which anxiety is converted into bodily paralysis or a sensory disturbance like blindness.

PHOBIA: in which anxiety is projected onto a single class of things (wide open spaces, say, or little white mice) that are then scrupulously avoided.

OBSESSION: where talismanic doing, fussing, straightening, and sometimes just plain thinking are used to express frustrated sexual energy; ritual hand-washing is the well-worn example here.

The reason these are called "transference" neuroses is that the analyst, by roughly recreating the original childhood conflict and acting as a stand-in for hard-pressed, erratic Mommy and/or Daddy, allows the patient to "transfer" submerged emotions onto him and work through the conflict one more time—this time within the safety and consistency of the analysis.

The good news: The phobic, the hysteric, or the obsessive can usually regain (after several years of analysis and tens of thousands of dollars) all the energy that was formerly at the service of his neurosis.

The bad news: These days, there aren't all that many classic hysterics, phobics, and obsessives around to be cured; seems that sexual liberation has pretty much thinned the ranks.

The narcissistic neuroses, with considerable shading (and a little fudging) on the part of the psychoanalytic community, correspond to what we think of as psychoses. These tend to manifest themselves not in terms of a single easy-to-identify symptom but rather a diffuse, fugitive "feeling" and include, traditionally (i.e., according to Freud):

MELANCHOLIA: severe depression, with or without its manic counterpart in tow.

DEMENTIA PRAECOX: our schizophrenia, called "praecox," or premature, because of its typical onset in postadolescence.

PARANOIA: projection (a defense mechanism we'll be getting to in the next session) magnified and embellished to the point of delusion, usually of either the somebody's-out-to-get-me-and-he's-poisoned-the-tap-water or the I-am-the-King-of-Prussia-off-with-their-heads sort.

In all of them, the ego is not merely under siege; it's long gone. And the chances of recovery are not so hot. The person with the narcissistic neurosis—whose sexual wishes had never developed to the point of being attached to Mommy and/or Daddy; who had instead remained, literally, "stuck on himself"—couldn't, according to Freud, be reached by the analyst either. It's true that some analysts led by a couple of latterday Viennese named Heinz Kohut (see page 415) and Otto Kernberg, have shifted the emphasis of their work from Oedipus to Narcissus, from castration anxiety to self-love, and from Victorian-era sexual repression to Me-decade grandiosity, enough so that there's some hope for the narcissist. But he remains a tough cure.

Confidential to all you schizophrenics out there (and you know who you are): Hang tough! Granted, it's not easy having regressed to the ultimate narcissism, an infantile state in which everything you see, touch, or hear reads as an extension of you. And, yes, your mind is split, between a tiny little normal person with a wee small voice who recalls how nice things used to be, and the population of ten randomly selected Bosch canvases plus your entire junior high school. In fact, if our century still admits of madness as something certifiable, you've got it. But look on the bright side: Nobody can accuse you of having repressed anything. You're living it, baby.

Footnote for fetishists, devotees of S & M, homosexuals, and perverts of all stripes: No, you are not, according to Freud, neurotics. Perversion, while marked by regression to some soft, unchallenging, essentially self-involved state (or occasionally by one's never having moved beyond that state at all), does not involve repression, conflict, or the batting around of the ego by the super-ego and/or the id. You may be perfectly happy. Probably not, though: Most perverts wind up with their share of independently generated neuroses, too. And that's a little like working double shifts. Or do we mean both sides of the street? We'll think about it while we're washing our hands.

Oh, and we were just kidding about the PMS.

Eleven Ways to Leave a Mother

I f Hollywood were to make a movie out of the structure of your mind, they wouldn't be wrong to cast Jack Nicholson as the id, Robert Duvall as the ego, and, oh, Christopher Reeve as the superego. The id's always going to leer, mug, and try to get its way. The ego's always going to come across with the subtlest (simultaneously most restrained and most inventive) acting, only occasionally exuding false nobility and/or martyrdom. And the superego's always going to register as a bit of a stiff, a sometimes well-intentioned, sometimes despotic outsider.

Whereas you're born with your id, seat of the instincts and repository of libido, in full swing, your ego comes together only gradually. Once in place, it has to integrate sensory perceptions, modulate voluntary movement, keep tabs on the instincts that are penned up in the id next door, and provide for their, as well as its own, pleasure, all without ever losing sight of reality. Sometime in the course of childhood, as early as age five or six, the superego takes shape, incorporating the early influences of parents and teachers; thenceforth, on top of everything else, you're saddled with conscience, morality, and a tendency to come down on yourself at the worst possible moments.

So the ego is up against the id (which wants to disobey it), the superego (which tries to make it feel bad), and the outside world (which, on some days, is enough to make you scream). To the extent that it is a strong and healthy ego, it attempts to honor the demands of all three. To do so, even the well-endowed ego makes compromises, adopting special techniques called defense mechanisms, so that, when confronted with certain demands, it doesn't have to panic, self-destruct, or assume the fetal position. By actively intervening, the ego thereby transforms what it or the world or the superego views as bad into something neutral or better.

This "armor-plating of character," as Wilhelm Reich (see page 429) described it, is innocent enough in moderation; it is also virtually inescapable. But when defense mechanisms become too powerful, so encumbering character that it can't make it down the hall to the bathroom, problems ensue. You'll get a sense of those problems when you take a look at this rundown of the most celebrated defense mechanisms. The comment on the right reflects how each might be employed by a nine-year-old boy who's angry at his father and who, natch, feels guilty about feeling angry—not that he's necessarily in touch with either the anger or the guilt, let alone the defense mechanism.

1. *repression*   "H-m-m? I don't know what you're talking about."

Whoever represses simply forgets—blissfully (unless, that is, the repressed material resurfaces). Repression may be the most potent defense mechanism of all; certainly it is the best at combatting sexual wishes. Other defense mechanisms, some psychiatrists say, simply do the work it leaves undone.

2. *regression*   "Goo. Flubba dada?"

To regress is to revert to an earlier, less threatening stage of psychosexual development; its a basic prerequisite for most neuroses and all perversions. It needn't result in talking baby talk, but it gets you—and your ego—off the hook by taking you back to a time when things were easier, still merely anal, say, and you didn't have to worry about being castrated by Daddy just because you happened to love Mommy.

3. *projection*   "Oh, no, I'm not mad at Daddy. *Mommy* is mad at Daddy."

The anger is attributed to someone else; guilt and anxiety thus become unnecessary. Projection doesn't alter the nature of the feeling: It gets rid of it by pushing it out into the world, to the same degree that repression would bury it. Projection can be dangerous, though; it's this defense that causes you to hear censuring voices. Those voices are only your super-ego, of course, but *you* don't know that.

4. *denial*   "You must be crazy. I'm not mad at Daddy."

This is the wholesale falsification of reality, and the flip side of repression. Whereas repression severs the ego from internal pressures, denial severs it from those of the outside world. It's perfectly normal—desirable, even— in children; in adults (for whom full-scale fantasy lives are no longer practical), denial can indicate advanced mental illness.

5. *reaction formation*   "Mad at Daddy? I *love* Daddy! Where is he anyway? I want to sit in his lap."

Here you convince yourself that the exact opposite of something awful and unacceptable is, in fact, true, then replay your revised version of it a zillion times a day. A veteran reaction formationer (most often an obsessive-compulsive) becomes excessively solicitous of the person he hates, often instituting elaborate ceremonial acts to keep his true feelings at bay.

6. *reversal*   "Mad at Daddy? Daddy's mad at *me!*"

This one's as old as the first conflict between ego and instincts; in fact, it, along with repression, was one of the first defense mechanisms your young ego used. (You used it yourself in first grade: It's the "you're dumb-no-*you're*-dumb" of the playground.) Like displacement (below), it is usually invoked as a preliminary to more complicated defensive maneuvers.

7. *displacement*   "Mad at Daddy? I'm mad at Rags. Bad dog!"

The emotion is transferred from a dangerous object, who can retaliate, to a safe one, who can't. As with reversal, it's usually a first step: The ego, having gone this far, will probably give things at least one more twist—

regression, say, or reaction formation. Otherwise, you might figure out how you really felt.

8. *isolation*   "Yes, I guess I'm mad at Daddy. It would be fun to shoot him and watch him die. May I have some more milk and cookies, please?"

Recognition minus affect: You don't bother to deny, repress, or reshape the traumatic emotion, you just disconnect from it. You can talk about it without feeling a thing.

9. *intellectualization*   "Well, yes I am mad at Daddy. I'm probably wishing him dead so that I can have Mommy all to myself, which, of course, is quite normal at my age."

Isolation for smart people. In this one, also known as "rationalization," you overthink the problem in order to avoid making contact with the emotion or anxiety behind it.

10. *undoing*   "Uh-oh, I'm very mad at Daddy. I'd better go line up all my teddy bears so they're *exactly* even with the squares on my rug."

Here, an action is meant to expiate an emotion, or an earlier action, that the ego can't bear to deal with. Undoing can involve actually canceling something out (for instance, shopping yourself bankrupt, then returning everything you've bought) or magically doing so, through a compulsive (and apparently unrelated) ritual.

11. *sublimation*   "Mad at Daddy? Excuse me, I really must get this finger painting finished."

Of all the mechanisms of defense, the only truly desirable one. By the time it's acquired, the super-ego's well in place, channeling the libido into some useful endeavor, transforming the instinctually gratifying into the socially useful. Artists are alleged to be the biggest sublimaters around, expressing in paint, clay, or guitar riffs what the rest of us take out on our stomach linings. Freud said it best, of course:

> [The artist] opens out to others the way back to the comfort and consolation of their own unconscious sources of pleasure, and so reaps their gratitude and admiration; then he has won—through his phantasy—what before he could only win in phantasy: honour, power, and the love of women.

Return With Us Now to a Quiet Side Street

in a Working-Class Neighborhood in Turn-of-the-Century Vienna, Where,
in a Darkened Second-Floor Room, a Man With a White Beard
(and a Nosebleed) Beckons You to Lie Down on a Horsehair Sofa.
And Please, Feel Free to Say Whatever Comes Into Your Mind . . .

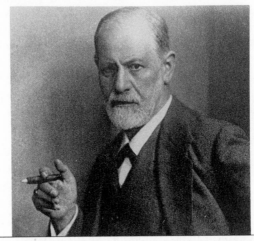

FREUD AND HIS FOLLOWERS

Freud, like the philosophers who preceded him and the psychoanalysts—and, for that matter, the physicists—who followed, struggled to formulate a system for solving the mysteries of the soul. What he came up with: a therapeutic procedure that would, he hoped, help recover those dark, submerged parts of man's being that force him into a lifetime of repetitive action and ritual discontent. For Freud, this procedure called for the patient (henceforth known as the analysand) to lie on the couch for fifty-five minutes and relate anything that came to mind, no matter how silly, shameful, or self-incriminating. If the treatment was often, literally, nightmarish for the analysand, it was no day at the beach for the analyst, either. As Freud warned, "No one who, like me, conjures up the most evil of those half-tamed demons that inhabit the human breast and seeks to wrestle with them, can expect to come through the struggle unscathed."

He didn't. Nor, presumably, did five of his most prominent disciples. All of whom undergo, on the following pages, short-term treatment with contributor Barbara Waxenberg, Ph.D.

SIGMUND FREUD (HIMSELF)

In the beginning there was Freud—or as he is universally labeled, Freud himself, with the pronoun wired inextricably to the noun. Not to refer to him this way immediately reveals you to be a parvenu on the psychoanalytic scene. To establish your credentials among the cognoscenti, you must, whenever some arcane metapsychological point is discussed, ask whether the speaker is referring to the early writings (1895–1900) or to the middle phase (roughly 1900–1910); that is, to theories which Freud himself (see how it's done?) revised in his later papers. It also adds a bit of heft to throw in such remarks as "Yes, but in 'On Narcissism' or in 'Analysis Terminable and Interminable,' Freud himself said . . ."

It was in the early period that Freud made some of his most revolutionary contributions: the nature of the unconscious, the mechanisms of repression and resistance, the phenomenon of transference, the significance of dreams ("the royal road to the unconscious," as he put it), and the method of free association. He also developed his seduction theory, the belief that neuroses stemmed from actual sexual assaults on young children, a theory he later abandoned in favor of the belief that such traumas were not real events, but fantasies that stemmed from unconscious wishes. This recasting of seduction, exploitation, and betrayal from an external event to an internal conflict-laden desire was to color Freud's sense of what psychoanalysis was all about; henceforth, he would emphasize the idea of intrapsychic forces over the individual and his environment. This was to remain the dominant bias of psychoanalysis until it was challenged by Otto Rank and Sándor Ferenczi in 1925 and, much more vehemently, by Harry Stack Sullivan a decade later. It tied psychoanalysis to an instinctual-drive theory, rooted in biology and based on sequential phases of infant sexuality. It also laid the groundwork for viewing the Oedipal conflict as a universal experience, pivotal in human development.

The word *metapsychology* has been defined as a psychological theory that cannot be verified or disproved by observation or reasoning. Which is to say, its verifiableness can be eternally argued. The further removed from consensus the theory is, the more easily it remains enshrined in the hearts of its followers. So it is with Freud's instinctual-drive theory. For Freud, the instinctual drive acts as a constant and inescapable force that creates a state of tension that one works at reducing. Although man (and woman, but Freud was notoriously puzzled about what, exactly, women want) is regulated by the pleasure principle, pleasure is more or less defined as the absence of excitation. So much for fun and games in turn-of-the-century Vienna. Instincts have a source of excitation within the body, an aim (the removal of excitation) and an object (the means by which the satisfaction of the aim is achieved). In the Freudian model, this object need not be a person, although everyone would probably agree that if the desired "object" turns out to be a statue or a French poodle, one is wasting one's time and libidinal energies or losing one's marbles.

In tracing the stages of human development, Freud postulated that erotic feeling is first experienced in the mouth, the newborn's primary source of pleasure; later shifts to the anus, where enjoyment is derived from the retention and expulsion of feces; and ultimately, at about age three or four, to the genitals, in the so-called phallic stage. Under normal conditions, interest in these organs progresses in orderly sequence. Fixation occurs when, as a result of trauma or constitution, libido is bound at a particular developmental stage so that some portion of it never advances beyond this point. When the person gets into trouble later on in life, he is likely to regress to the point of fixation. Adult patterns of behavior take shape according to the way each erotic phase is negotiated. For example, possessiveness, meticulousness, orderliness, and retentiveness are viewed as anal traits, while passivity and helplessness or sadism and exploitation are seen as oral ones.

The phallic period coincides with that of the Oedipus complex, which is central in the Freudian theory of neurotic development and which begins to develop at about age three, when little girls and boys decide that marrying the parent of the opposite sex and killing off the parent of the same one is a neat idea. This is often quite flattering to Mommy or Daddy, who is probably having a hard time with bulges, hair loss, and his spouse and who could do with a bit of stroking. But it can be a bit wearing on the parent rival. "When is Daddy going to die?" goes down poorly with morning coffee. The family romance begins to wear thin at about age five or six when the boy, fearing castration by his father (a bit of talion revenge), turns away from Mom, identifies with Dad, and goes back to watching television instead of primal scenes for the years of the so-called latency period, during which sexual interest is in abeyance. The fate of the girl is more complex since she's got nothing to lose, ostensibly because Mommy's already done away with her fancy equipment. And now Mommy has Daddy and Daddy's penis and everything and it's not fair! But eventually she identifies with mother, accepts the feminine role (i.e., her castration and penis envy), adopts a Cabbage Patch doll, and represses her incestuous wishes. Ho hum.

According to Freud, the bases for psychological disorder are laid down between ages one and six and all later learning is an elaboration of early conflict. In structural terms, conflicts exist among id impulses (those unconscious reservoirs of sexual and aggressive impulses constantly seeking discharge), ego defenses (which ward off the direct discharge of the impulse and its access to consciousness), and superego restrictions (the stern conscience which embodies parental and cultural standards). The embattled ego must mediate between the primitive forces of the id and the censoring, guilt-inducing power of the superego. In psychoneuroses, the ego becomes progressively less able to effect satisfactory compromises and is eventually overwhelmed. The ultimate aim of psychoanalysis is to increase the relative strength of the ego so that it can effectively deal with pressures from above and below and with external reality.

Originally, Freud postulated a life-preserving instinct and a sexual instinct. After World War I, he turned his attention more fully to the problem of repressed aggression. This gave rise to his second instinct theory, the conflict between Eros, the life-preserving instinct, and Thanatos, the death force. Both aggression and the compulsion to repeat events are, in complicated ways, related to the death instinct. Since man strives for a homeostasis in which tension is minimal, death would be the ultimate relief of this tension.

Today, while Freud's biomechanical view of human functioning has been seriously (and continually) questioned, his method of psychoanalytic inquiry, his concepts of transference, repetition, and resistance, and his theory of unconscious experience remain the cornerstones of the analytic process.

FIVE FOLLOWERS

Psychoanalysis was—and is—a rigorous undertaking, but its rigors are not exactly what they used to be. Freud saw the same twelve patients every day, six days a week (and then wrote late into the night); present-day psychoanalysts, more pleasure-seeking and self-preservative, will see a patient only three to five times a week (and then sit down to dinner). On the other hand, analyses were more compact in those days, extending from six to twelve months, rather than six to twelve years, perhaps because the array of symptoms, from hysteria to obsessional neurosis to phobia, were more amenable to treatment than today's vague anxieties, characterological issues, and "disorders of the self."

Then there are the differences that now exist between analytical schools; between, say, the Interpersonalists, who maintain that they contact the "unique individual" rather than the Freudians' "Oedipal cliché," and the Freudians, who accuse the Interpersonalists of not dealing with unconscious experience. To add to the tension, there are even theorists who point out that only a masochist, a social isolate, or a nut would accept a stranger's invitation to lie down on his couch, turn your back to him, and spill your guts while the stranger says nothing in response.

There's nothing new about such dissension; it's known in science as pluralism, and it's been characteristic of the psychoanalytic movement ever since Alfred Adler challenged Freud in 1910 over the relative importance of the sexual drives. Adler viewed the core problem as man's struggle to overcome feelings of inferiority (he coined the phrase "inferiority complex") and saw the "wish to be a complete man"—in the face of physical handicaps and environmental conflicts—as the guiding fiction behind every neurosis. Moreover, unlike Freud, who regarded society as a limitation on the individual, Adler came to see social interaction as essential to mental health. Freud, never one to take kindly to dissent, showed Adler the door (and would later refer to him cuttingly as "Dr. Alfred Adler, who was formerly an analyst").

Next to exit was Carl Jung, who also objected to Freud's heavy emphasis on sex. He saw man as influenced by higher forces (in his emphasis on a collective unconscious and his heavy use of symbolism, Jung could get pretty mystical), which conflict with his animal nature. Libido was regarded as a general life force, sexual in origin, but no longer reducible, in adulthood, to its sexual components. Jung developed a theory of character based on two fundamental personality types: the introvert who is absorbed in his inner world, and the extrovert who turns outward at the expense of private experience. For Jung, the overriding goal was always the achieving of a harmony between the conscious and the unconscious; that alone could make a person one and whole. Moreover, he argued that neurotic symptoms were not always the residue of an unhappy childhood, as Freud maintained, but were often attempts on the part of the mind to correct its own disequilibrium, and therefore could serve as pointers to a more satisfactory synthesis.

And that was just the first generation. The following pages concentrate on subsequent generations of rebellious, argumentative, and lapsed Freudians who, together, have effectively challenged the Master's view of what psychoanalysis is and what it ought to (and can) accomplish.

Melanie Klein (1882–1960): Hypothesis on Hypothesis

If prospective parents were to read Melanie Klein instead of Benjamin Spock, there would be a lot fewer babies. Klein's writings, if understood, would probably rival the pill as the most effective form of birth control yet devised. For to bear a "Kleinian baby" is to bring a potential cauldron of destructiveness and hate into the nursery, a child whose fantasies rival, in greed, malevolence and envy, those of Stephen King, Edgar Allan Poe, and the Marquis de Sade.

Briefly, Klein subdivided the first year of life into two phases; the paranoid-schizoid, in which the infant relates to anatomical parts of persons, chiefly the breast and penis; and the depressive, in which the mother is recognized as a whole person who can therefore be destroyed by the child's own hatefulness. In essence, the infant is capable of constructing elaborate phantasies (Kleinians use the *ph* spelling to express their extension of the term to the imaginings of the infant) about the good breast, which nourishes and is loved, and the bad breast, which deprives and is consequently destroyed. Don't even ask about bottle-fed babies; things are complicated enough already. Under the impact of anxiety and frustration, the child's desires and phantasies extend to the mother's entire body, which is seen as containing all kinds of goodies, including the father's penis, incorporated during intercourse. Klein writes, "The dominant aim [of the baby] is to possess himself of the contents of the mother's body and to destroy her by means of every weapon which sadism can command."

Meanwhile, the infant tries to incorporate enough good objects and substances to neutralize the bad objects and substances in his own body. There is a Jungian, as well as a Dracula-like, feeling to all this, an acceptance of some primordial, racial unconscious. The newborn enters the world with an innate sense of the existence of the mother and the contents of her body. Klein's babies live in a doggie-eat-doggie world in which punishments for destroying the bad breast or emptying the good one are anxiously anticipated. To survive in this jungle, the child wards off the dangers of the bad objects and feelings by "splitting" or separating their images from the good objects and feelings. As if this weren't bad enough, even the "good" is contaminated by primitive forces of envy, stirred up by the fact that the appearance and disappearance of the milk-laden good breast is controlled by the mother and not by the child. To pile Pelion on Ossa, bad objects seem even more malevolent because of the hatred projected onto them by the rageful, greedy child whose needs are insatiable.

This takes us up to the second half of the first year (although it might seem that a lifetime has already been lived) when, if all has gone well, the paranoid-schizoid position is superseded by the depressive position. The outstanding feature of this position is the unification of the mother; no longer safely split into good and bad entities, she becomes a single person with both good and bad features. Integration, naturally enough, brings with it despair, since the good features of the mother are now no longer protected from the child's destructiveness.

Klein took Freud's death instinct and his theories of aggression and ran with them, adding her own view of envy as a biological given. The environment contributes little, but, like a mirror, reflects the baby's own conflicts back on him. Klein did not concern herself with parental defects and sufferings; she concentrated solely on the child's destructive urges and regrets. In this, she differed from Sullivan, Karen Horney, Erich Fromm, and Erik Erikson in America, as well as from W. R. D. Fairbairn and Donald Winnicott in England. What she accomplished was to focus attention on the earliest stage of human development, before the Oedipal conflict comes into play. Although she retained Freud's drive model and his id-ego-superego terminology and regarded herself as fundamentally orthodox in approach, there is little of Freud's psychophysiology in her schema. Instead of regarding drives as discrete quantities of energy, she redefined them as passionate feelings of love and hate. She saw human life as an intense dramatic tragedy that has its roots in the infant's constitutional makeup. In this framework, the Oedipal conflict becomes more a wrestling for power and destruction than a struggle with libidinous impulses. Anxiety and guilt stem from aggressive phantasies and fear of retaliation.

Klein's work split the British Psychoanalytic Society into two factions, one loyal to her, the other to Anna Freud. Others, like Winnicott, formed a third, nonaligned group. Although Klein's views are unverifiable, the recent emphasis on the importance of pre-Oedipal life in the understanding of borderline and narcissistic disorders has lent more credence to her theories.

Harry Stack Sullivan (1892–1949): Things Are Often What They Seem

After all this meta-messing, Harry Stack Sullivan, a native American of the what-you-see-is-what-you-get school, comes as a relief. For Sullivan, what you see (and get) is all bound up with how you participate: We can only know another person in terms of how we interact with him. Where Freud concentrated on what went on within the psyche of the individual, Sullivan focused on his relationships with others.

For Sullivan, the data of psychoanalysis—the behavior of the analysand and the analyst's public and private reactions to what the patient says and does—are there to be directly observed; excluded are all hypothetical events occurring in some Never-Never Land "inside" the patient, not to mention the unconscious as an explanatory concept. Thus Sullivan, along with Clara Thompson, Karen Horney, Erich Fromm, and Frieda Fromm-Reichmann, spawned a new psychiatric movement in America, based on how a person makes sense of and responds to what is going on around him, rather than on the biological-drive theory that is the pillar of Freudian theory. In other words, to understand the individual, one must understand the network of relationships in which he is enmeshed; one must pay attention to the "interactional" rather than the "intrapsychic."

What really interested Sullivan was why people failed so badly at living productive and creative lives and, instead, stereotypically repeated the same unsatisfying actions. Perhaps influenced by the insecurities and privations of the Depression, Sullivan pared down his motivational system to two basic needs: satisfaction (both biological and emotional) and security (which he viewed as the avoidance of anxiety). The search for satisfaction inevitably propels a person toward involvement with others; Sullivan thought loneliness was the most painful of human experiences.

Like Klein's child, Sullivan's develops notions of "good" and "bad," but Sullivan saw these impressions as linked to the actual responses of the mother, not as derivatives of the fantasy life of the child. Sullivan's good mother is the nonanxious mother; his bad is a nervous or timid soul who empathically communicates her distress to the child, who then gradually learns to modify his behavior in order to modulate mommy's anxiety. Of the child's introduction to the world of malevolence and mystification, Sullivan wrote, "Once upon a time everything was lovely, but that was before I had to deal with people."

Sullivan dealt with the Self System, that configuration of traits that have been reinforced by the affirmation of the significant persons in the child's life, and the security operations the child develops in order to avoid anxiety and threats to self-esteem. Three areas are delineated: the good-me (Mommy's-smiling-and-not-all-wigged-out-and-I-feel-pretty-good-too); the bad-me (Mommy's-feeling-anxious-and-cross-and-I'm-not-feeling-too-cool-either); and the not-me (she's-flipping-her-lid and-I'm-shaking-from-head-to-toe). If Sullivan had raised children instead of cocker spaniels, he might have added the category who-me, as in did-you-glue-all-your-underwear-together? Who-me? But he didn't. And he didn't.

The Self System acts as a steering mechanism directing the child toward experiences that are associated with parental approval and freedom from anxiety, and away from ones that have met with disapproval and are subsequently blocked out of awareness. From all of this arises a pattern of I-You interlocking behaviors: If I act weak and helpless, then You, like my parents, must be solicitous and caretaking. If I am adorable, You must be admiring, and so on. Sullivan labeled these pairings "parataxic integrations": They become rigidified and dominate adult life, sometimes almost completely overlaying one's perceptions of the real people in one's life, who, stripped of their individuality, are seen as echoes and shadows of parental figures.

Donald W. Winnicott (1896–1971): The "Good-Enough Mother" of the Year

Winnicott is every reader's fantasy (with an *f*) of all that a good mother should be. Few practitioners could engage the heart and mind of a child so directly, poignantly, and empathically as this psychoanalyst, who had spent forty years as a pediatrician. (This nourshing holds true for grown-up children as well.) As for the mystique of psychoanalysis, Winnicott once wrote, "In doing psycho-analysis, I aim at:

>   Keeping alive
>   Keeping well
>   Keeping awake

I aim at being myself and behaving myself." Good advice in any ball park. Like Spencer Tracy, he knew his lines and didn't bump into the furniture.

From Winnicott's perspective, man's core problem lies in his struggle to arrive at an existence which is his and his alone but which, at the same time, allows for intimate contact with others. Intimacy, however, is an inherently limited affair. "At the center of each person is an incommunicado element, and this is sacred and most worthy of preservation. This core never communicates with or is influenced by the external world."

Life begins not with the infant but with the infant-mother pair, with the crucial developmental factor being the currents of empathic understanding that flow between caretaker and fledgling. It is the responsibility of the former to mediate between the inner world of the child and the environment about him. In plain language, she's got to help him to feel safe, for whether or not the child develops a real self will profoundly affect the nature and state of every problem the adult experiences. The mother must initially be exquisitely attuned to the physical and emotional needs of the infant as if an invisible band stretched between the two of them. She must respond when called and refrain from impinging when not needed. In such an environment, offered continuous nurturance, the infant enjoys a seemingly omnipotent position, in which whatever he imagines for himself is followed by the mother's presentation of the desired object. He is the source of all creation and can, through the magic of hallucinating what he wants, will his own satisfactions. Given this sunlit enchantment, he gradually becomes able to tolerate longer and longer separations from the mother without experiencing the terror of annihilation. Ultimately, he develops the capacity to be alone. Later comes the capacity for concern. Concomitantly, the mother awakens from a period of "maternal preoccupation" and begins to note with some astonishment that the world continues to function beyond the walls of the nursery. Bliss has ended.

Motherhood in this framework of empathic bonding is a hard row to hoe. Myriad pitfalls exist, predominantly linked to failure to respond to the infant's hallucinatory experiences (need to nurse, be caressed, be comforted, etc.) or to too much interference or overstimulation when the child would prefer to be alone, staring at the ceiling. The mother must be able to contain both the child's dependency and the aggressiveness that is an inevitable accompaniment to the process of separation, without becoming overwhelmed or counteraggressive. She must also be able to respond to his need to play.

In the worst-case scenario, the infant becomes compulsively attuned to the needs of others, primarily the mother, and in order to survive, develops what Winnicott terms a "false self." The "false self" contacts and complies with the directives of others, while his "true self" becomes dissociated, goes underground, and protects itself by remaining hidden. The psychoanalyst must provide what the parents failed to offer, a holding environment that is durable, attentive, and responsive, a *symbolic* re-creation of early mother-child interaction but not an actual regression to the patient's early years. And, like the "good" mother, he must be able to survive the inevitable assaults of the analysand without being annihilated. In this safety, the patient's true self can emerge.

Heinz Kohut (1913–1981): Mirror, Mirror on the Wall

Over and over the wheel must be invented. Although it is obvious that psychoanalytic theories overlap, they are promulgated as if they have sprung full-blown from the heads of their creators, products of parthenogenesis and not of union.

So it is with the concept of empathy, pretty much derided when touted by Carl Rogers (nondirective counseling) or Franz Alexander ("corrective emotional experience"). It was viewed then as a surface phenomenon, secondary in the therapeutic bag of tricks, soothing and supportive but hardly such stuff as psychoanalyses are made of. But in the last decade, empathy has had quite a revival; given clout and respectability by a former president of the American Psychoanalytic Association, it now gets star billing.

What has created all this furor is the spread of borderline and narcissistic personality disturbances. Modern patients suffer from wounded self-esteem, shift rapidly from adoration to abhorrence and from grandiosity to despair, and are far more fragmented and eruptive than the hysterics and obsessives for whom the psychoanalytic method was devised. Until recently, they were considered to be beyond the pale of insight-oriented psychoanalytic treatment. But lately there has been a rush to modify technique to embrace this more disturbed population (You can hardly find a conference that does not focus on the problems of treating the "difficult" patient.). Cynics might remark that the psychoanalyst had either to widen his scope or take down his shingle since the popularity of other forms of treatment (psychotherapy, behavior modification, encounter groups, and medication) has made the intensity, duration, and cost of psychoanalysis far less appealing. Where psychiatry was once a highly regarded medical specialty, it is now far down on the preference lists of medical students.

And so along came Kohut (the aforementioned president of the distinguished A.P.A.) and his "disorders of the self," by which he meant defects in the sense of inner cohesion and continuity. In his 1971 volume, *The Analysis of the Self*, Kohut straddled two positions: On the one hand, he maintained his allegiance to Freud by holding to the instinctual drive theory and to the conviction that Oedipal issues were central in tracing the origins of the structural neuroses; on the other, he established a parallel path of narcissistic development that allowed him to concentrate on the relationships established in earlier stages of human evolution. In the system that Kohut eventually constructed, man's search became a struggle to develop a cohesive and integrated self.

With Kohut, we are confronted once again with a baby in need of empathic response, but in this theory, parental figures are referred to as self-objects, signifying that the child is not yet able to differentiate himself from other objects in his world. Like Sullivan, but using different terminology, Kohut saw the child as experiencing the feeling states of these self-objects. The way that self and self-objects interrelate determines whether a cohesive or a fragmented self will emerge.

What the child requires of these self-objects is the mirroring of his capacities; he needs to sense that the self-objects can enjoy his exhibitionistic displays and are present as continuous, nurturing, empathic, and respectful figures. In addition, the growing child needs to be able to idealize at least one of his parents, to feel that the self-object that he's tightly tied up with is a swell human being. Although it seems simplistic in light of the complexity of interfamily relationships, Kohut sees the self as based on these two polarities of experience—admiring and being admired. Failure to develop at least one aspect, either mirroring or idealization, ultimately leads to a defective sense of self and the inability to maintain a consistent sense of self-esteem, that is, to narcissistic pathology.

Thus Self Psychology began with an effort to bring the narcissistic disorders within the purview of psychoanalysis. This widening of the net yielded a different set of data, largely concerned with relational issues and, since the self-systems of these patients were more primitively organized, a different series of transference and countertransference reactions to deal with. Kohut never completely dispensed with drive theory, although he waffled quite a bit on the subject. But his system, unlike Freud's and Klein's, does not rest on a conflict model. Even the Oedipal conflict, the heart of the Freudian matter, is avoidable if the parent-child interaction is a salutary one. Furthermore, Kohut viewed the Oedipal period not in terms of a triad of sexuality, hateful jealousy, and guilt, but as a growth stage in which the child derives joy from exercising new capacities and mastering new challenges. Where Freud saw Guilty Man who fears castration as a consequence of sexual rivalries, Kohut saw Tragic Man whose anxiety lies in the threat of annihilation.

In working with patients who present narcissistic pathology, the analyst initially acts as a self-object, providing the empathic responses that were missing in the patient's early life, and presents him or herself as a person who can be, and who will allow himself to be, idealized. Like small children preening before their mothers, these patients look to their analysts as one looks in a mirror in order to see one's reflection and to bask in a sense of specialness. Or they may adore and experience themselves as merged with these exalted beings, feeling strong and secure as long as this bonding is maintained. Growth occurs largely through experiencing a relationship that supplies what the parents failed to supply, rather than through the power of verbal interpretation. Ultimately, because an analyst is as flawed and as short-tempered as anyone else, the patient begins to view the deity in a more realistic light and correspondingly sees himself and his own capacities more clearly.

The encouragement of mirroring and idealizing transferences sets Kohutians apart from classical theorists, particularly right-wing Freudians who regard the model as far too supportive and nurturant. Although some of Kohut's theoretical positions resemble Sullivan's (e.g., the emphasis on the self and on early one-on-one patterns of relationships), his definition of the analytic stance differs markedly from that of the Interpersonalists. The latter are far more likely to address themselves to, (and sometimes to trample on) the weeds and flowers that are clearly visible in the garden, rather than the fragile shoots that are only beginning to emerge from the ground.

Jacques Lacan (1901–1981): Enfant Terrible

What do you do with the *Écrits* of Jacques Lacan when you've got three years of college French at best and a vocabulary maintained largely from reruns of *Breathless*? While Lacan's confrères nudge one another in the ribs and roll their eyes over such Gallic ticklers as his extended verbal play on Le Nom du Père (alternatively, God the Father, the father as definer of law, or modestly, Lacan himself as definer of psychoanalysis), its homophone, le non du père (the father's "No!" or the absent father) and its extension, les nonnes du père (Lacan's singularly devoted female disciples), you, mon pauvre petit, stand outside the charmed circles feeling alienated and perplexed.

Reading Lacan requires, along with your degree in the language, familiarity with Freud, Heidegger, Hegel, Sartre, the structural linguists, and the structural anthropologists. And that's just to *read* him. Understanding requires a good deal more. It is disheartening, however, after wading through his *Stade de Miroir*, ferreting out the true meaning of the Other (not at all what you'd suppose), and distinguishing full from empty speech, to learn from Stuart Schneiderman that since Lacan has emphasized the centrality of the spoken word in the analytic cure, his theories cannot be transmitted through the written one. *"The only way to learn the correct application of Lacan's theories to psychoanalysis is through supervision by a member of the Freudian School of Paris"* (italics his). So it looks like you'll also need an airplane ticket.

Basic to Lacan's theories is his insistence that the unconscious is structured like a language. What exactly Lacan means by this is rather obscure, and his intention is clearly (and this is the only clear thing about Lacan) to keep things that way. It takes a certain amount of chutzpah to take a hypothetical construct and authoritatively define its structure, but Lacan was never famous for diffidence. Any man who can begin the following sentence with the phrase "to put it in a nutshell" is not going to let you off easy:

> To put it in a nutshell, nowhere does it appear more clearly that man's desire finds its meaning in the desire of the other, not so much because the other holds the key to the object desired, as because the first object of desire is to be recognized by the other.

Through his style, Lacan explicates his thesis; that is, through enigmas within conundrums inside rebuses, he demonstrates the quirkiness of the unconscious. Or maybe not.

Lacan highlights the fact, that regardless of the metapsychology of the practitioner, "psychoanalysis has only a single intermediary: the patient's Word." He believes Freud's greatest contribution was an understanding of the way language is structured and a recognition that the unconscious can be reached through the process of free association. But for Lacan, the unconscious is the structure hidden behind the patient's discourse, since in the process of speaking he moves further away from himself. In the act of describing how you think or feel, you no longer experience what you are describing. The unconscious cannot, therefore, be revealed through conscious speech, but can only be tapped into through "gaps" in discourse: forgetting, misuse of words, slips of the tongue, puns, dreams, etc. Lacan returns to the Freud of *The Psychopathology of Everyday Life* and *The Interpretation of Dreams* for the bedrock of his theories.

More poetically, in the words of a follower:

> The unconscious is not the ground which has been prepared to give more sparkle and depth to the painted composition: it is the earlier sketch which has been covered over before the canvas is used for another picture. If we use a comparison of a musical order, the unconscious is not the counterpoint of a fugue or the harmonics of a melodic line: it is the jazz one hears despite oneself behind the Haydn quartet when the radio is badly tuned or not sufficiently selective. The unconscious is not the message, not even the strange or coded message one strives to read on an old parchment: *it is another text written underneath and which must be read by illuminating it from behind or with the help of a developer.*

But what has intrigued Americans about Lacan is not his theoretical formulations, which approach incomprehensibility, but his waiting room, which had something of the flavor of a dentist's. Also of Grand Central Station. Not for Lacan the ordered fifty-minute schedule of the modern psychoanalyst; his practice was of a whimsical character. He was known to throw a patient out after a few minutes of idle associations, to extend a session according to his fancy, or to keep a patient hanging around all day if this seemed appropriate. A depressed patient might be treated with the consulting room door open (so that the man might remain in contact with the other sufferers in the corridor) for ten-minute sessions at intervals spread out over the day until his despair lifted. Lacanians defend their erratic ways in terms of "logical punctuations," that is, sessions defined by the needs of any given analysand on any given day. It makes sense, but it's a hell of a way to run a railroad.

CRUMBS FROM THE MASTER'S TABLE: QUOTATIONS FROM THE WRITINGS OF SIGMUND FREUD

Analysis almost seems to be the third of those "impossible professions" in which one can be quite sure of unsatisfying results. The other two, much older-established, are the bringing-up of children and the government of nations.

Analysis Terminable and Interminable (1937)

I do not think our successes can compete with those of Lourdes. There are so many more people who believe in the miracles of the Blessed Virgin than in the existence of the unconscious.

New Introductory Lectures on Psychoanalysis (1932)

A culture which leaves unsatisfied and drives to rebelliousness so large a number of its members neither has a prospect of continued existence nor deserves it.

Future of an Illusion (1928)

We believe that civilization has been built up, *under the pressure of the struggle for existence*, by sacrifices in gratification of the primitive impulses.

Introductory Lectures on Psychoanalysis (1916–1917)

I then made some short observations upon the *the psychological differences between the conscious and the unconscious*, and upon the fact that everything conscious was subject to a process of wearing-away, while what was unconscious was relatively unchangeable; and I illustrated my remarks by pointing to the antiques standing about in my room. They were, in fact, I said, only objects found in a tomb, and their burial had been their preservation: the destruction of Pompeii was only beginning now that it had been dug up.

Notes Upon a Case of Obsessional Neurosis (1909)

In girls the motive for the demolition of the Oedipus complex is lacking. Castration has already had its effect, which was to force the child into the situation of the Oedipus complex. Thus the Oedipus complex escapes the fate which it meets with in boys: it may be slowly abandoned or dealt with by repression or its effects may persist far into women's normal mental life. I cannot evade the notion (though I hesitate to give it expression) that for women the level of what is ethically normal is different from what it is in men. Their super-ego is never so inexorable, so impersonal, so independent of its emotional origins as we require it to be in men. Character-traits which critics of every epoch have brought up against women—that they show less sense of justice than men, that they are more often influenced in their judgments by feelings of affection or hostility—all these would be amply accounted for by the modification in the formation of their super-ego which we have inferred above.

Some Psychical Consequences of the Anatomical Distinction
Between the Sexes (1925)

A man who has been the indisputable favorite of his mother keeps for life the feeling of a conqueror, that confidence of success that often induces real success.

Life and Works of Sigmund Freud, vol. 1, by Ernest Jones (1953)

One might compare the relation of the ego to the id with that between a rider and his horse. The horse provides the locomotor energy, and the rider has the prerogative of determining the goal and of guiding the movements of his powerful mount towards it. But all too often in the relations between the ego and the id we find a picture of the less ideal situation in which the rider is obliged to guide his horse in the direction in which it itself wants to go.

New Introductory Lectures on Psychoanalysis (1932)

Where id was, there shall ego be.

New Introductory Lectures on Psychoanalysis (1932)

A woman who is very anxious to get children always reads *storks* instead of *stocks*.

The Psychopathology of Everyday Life (1901)

Occasionally I have had to admit that the annoying, awkward stepping aside on the street, whereby for some seconds one steps here and there, yet always in the same direction as the other person, until finally both stop facing each other . . . conceals erotic purposes under the mask of awkwardness.

The Psychopathology of Everyday Life (1901)

When a member of my family complains that he or she has bitten his tongue, bruised her finger, and so on, instead of the expected sympathy I put the question, "Why did you do that?"

The Psychopathology of Everyday Life (1901)

FRUITS OF THE MASTER'S LABORS: FIVE FAMOUS FLIPPED-OUT CASES

ANNA O.: A compendium of hysterical symptoms from paralysis to hydro-phobia, and famous within the profession as a study in the pitfalls of counter-transference, the thing that happens when your shrink starts reacting neuroti-cally to *you*. Actually, Anna began as the patient not of Freud, but of his colleague Josef Breuer, who abruptly terminated treatment when his wife became jealous, suspecting that the twenty-one-year-old girl was experiencing more than just catharsis on the couch. Breuer was called to Anna's bedside that same night to find her thrashing about in the throes of false labor, convinced she was pregnant with his child. The next day, Frau Breuer whisked away her guilty, overinvested husband for some extended R & R in New York. Freud later picked up on the "cathartic method" Breuer had been using—more or less successfully—with Anna, and Anna herself went on to become Germany's first social worker (although no one is quite sure what that fact has to do with her treatment).

LITTLE HANS: A five-year-old who wouldn't go out of doors for fear a horse would bite him. The case is remarkable because Freud saw Little Hans only once, and treated the boy by proxy through his father. The trouble had started when Hans was three-and-a-half and his mother tried to discourage him from masturbating by warning him—as mothers did in those days—that if he didn't keep his hands where they belonged she'd send for the doctor to "cut off your widdler and then what will you widdle with?" Little Hans, who was developing quite a fascination with widdlers in general, had not failed to notice that horses had great big widdlers and that his mother had none. Before you knew it, horses, Mommy, and the possibility of castration were all mixed up with his fears of competing with his father. Guided by Freud, Little Hans's father reassured the boy and was eventually able to help him overcome his phobia, thereby becoming, himself, simultaneously part of the problem and part of the solution. What's more, Little Hans grew up to be a musician, just like his dad.

DORA: One of Freud's most famous cases—and reads like a soap opera. Dora, a teenager in the "first blossom of youth," was sent by her father to Dr. Freud for treatment of various hysterical symptoms linked to a dastardly proposition made to her by a neighbor, Herr K., whose wife, it just so hap-pened, was having an affair with Dora's father. To complicate matters further, Dora looked to Frau K. as a surrogate mother, since her own mother was too preoccupied with scrubbing and cleaning to pay any attention to her family.

Dora's father asked Freud to "bring Dora to reason," by which he meant keep her quiet. Dora, a spirited eighteen-year-old, listened to a lot of talk about her shameful sexual feelings and none whatsoever about the web of deceit she was caught in. After eleven weeks of analysis and two famous dreams, she quit treatment, seriously hurting Freud's feelings. Still, much later, he realized he'd learned two important lessons from the case, namely, that hysterics tended to reveal an awful lot through dreams and free association and that it paid to mistrust what he labeled the patient's "flight into health," a speedy but only temporary improvement in the early stages of analysis. Dora, on the other hand, got considerably less out of her treatment, and grew up to be a frigid, unhappy man-hater.

THE RAT MAN: Not a sci-fi character, head of rat, body of man, but an army officer who became violently agitated when he heard a fellow officer describing an exotic form of punishment in which a pot of rats was overturned on a man's naked buttocks and left to gnaw their way through the anus. The officer immediately began to imagine this happening to either his father or the woman he loved, and soon he developed a complicated obsessional system to prevent it, despite the fact that his father had been dead for several years and his lady friend was safe at home darning socks. The dénouement of the case involved a lot of wrong turns by both patient and analyst and a good deal of linguistic play on the word "rat," but eventually Freud helped restore the man to health, in time for him to be killed a year later in World War I. Freud used the case to illustrate the mechanism of displacement (see page 404) and the sadistic anal eroticism that he believed underlay most cases of obsessional neurosis.

THE WOLF MAN: A rich young Russian in a state of complete helplessness who could make contact with reality only after he'd emptied the contents of his intestines with an enema. The case is famous because Freud concentrated on little but the child within the man and treated the "infantile neurosis," at the expense, some say, of the adult patient. The nickname derives from a childhood dream in which the patient opened his eyes to see six or seven white wolves with tails like foxes' sitting quite still on the branches of a large walnut tree outside his window. The deciphering of the dream involved catching Mommy and Daddy busily engaged in a primal scene (Freud's term for the sex act as witnessed by a child), with intercourse occurring doggie-style. Freud made considerable progress with the Wolf Man, but when the patient became too enamored of the analytic process, Freud fixed a date for termination: one year, no matter what. Resistance crumbled, analysis proceeded apace, and the Wolf Man went home to Russia. He returned to Freud after the Revolution, destitute, homeless, and once again a fruitcake, thereby proving that reality counts, too.

Hello, Jung Lovers

No, we haven't forgotten you. And yes, you—and Carl Gustav—deserve more than an offhand paragraph or two in a Freudian's tribute to Freud (see page 406). Of course, we can't expect to make up here for decades of benign neglect, second bananadom, and jokes about flying saucers. But we can arrange to quote your man a little bit, remind you of some of his favorite terms, and say a word or two about what he stood for.

He is, happily, almost as quotable as Freud, although you can't always be sure, when you summon him up, whether it's a lecture hall or a hot tub you'll find yourself ensconced in. The lecture-hall Jung sounds something like this:

> The more the critical reason dominates, the more impoverished life becomes; but the more of the unconscious and the more of myth we are capable of making conscious, the more of life we integrate. Overvalued reason has this in common with political absolutism: under its dominion the individual is pauperized.

The hot-tub Jung sounds more like this:

> Somewhere there was once a Flower, a Stone, a Crystal, a Queen, a King, a Palace, a Lover and his Beloved, and this was long ago, on an Island somewhere in the Ocean 5,000 years ago. . . . Such is Love, the Mystic Flower of the Soul. This is the Center, the Self.

Among the terms Jung came up with: "collective unconscious" (the deep, species-wide layer of the psyche underlying the personal unconscious) and "archetypes" (the mythic images and motifs that go to make up the collective unconscious); the "complex" (a group of interrelated, and emotionally charged, ideas or images); "individuation" (not so very different from our self-actualization, and a process that involves coming to terms with the thinking/feeling and intuition/sensation axes that together determine the four psychological "types"); the pairs "extrovert/introvert" and "anima/animus" (the latter alluding to the woman-inside-every-man and the man-inside-every-woman); the "active imagination" (by dint of which one writes or paints one's unconscious fantasies, and a staple of Jungian analysis); "synchronicity" (a meaningful coincidence of two causally unrelated events); and the "Self" (the very center of one's being).

If Jung sometimes gets a little trippy, well, that's one of his endearing qualities. To Freud's tight-ass reductionist, always looking for a scientific reason for everything, always talking about repression, always rooting about in the muck of the past, Jung is loose-limbed and open-minded, an expansionist. He's committed to the spirit, to exploring art, religion, philosophy, and borderline phenomena from alchemy to ESP. He believes in the future (even at those moments that he isn't feeling so optimistic about it). And when it does strike him as right to stop and think about what's gone before, he's more interested in construing it as rich mythology than as stifling autobiography.

Getting Straight

*A CORNUCOPIA OF CURES, CRAZES, AND QUICK FIXES**

Chances are that you, your boss, your cousin, and most of your friends have contributed their share to the annual $3 billion that Americans sink into psychotherapy. As a result, you may already know that our 29,000 psychiatrists are licensed physicians who charge as much as $150 for as few as forty-five minutes of their time; that our 26,000 clinical psychologists hold

---

* Held aloft by contributor Helen Epstein.

doctorates in psychology but are not M.D.'s; that our 31,000 mental-health social workers hold neither degree and often may not be covered by your health insurance; and that there are thousands of lay therapists in business with no certification whatsoever.

Of course, none of this really helps explain *why* Americans are so obsessed with psychotherapy. What's the matter with families and friends? Why must we pay strangers to pay attention to us? Are we certifiably crazier than citizens of other nations?

Perhaps it's because the United States is a free country, and a little freedom can be dangerous to mental health. Are the French, after all, routinely called upon to choose between thirty-eight varieties of ice cream? Are the Japanese constitutionally bound to the pursuit of happiness? Must either consider a panoply of alternatives—graduate school, hang-gliding, etc.—to the allegedly inevitable process of growing up?

Ironically, psychotherapy is a European invention. The word derives from the Greek, means "treatment of the soul," and first achieved prominence in turn-of-the-century Vienna (see page 406). Before World War II, therapy had been deemed appropriate mostly for the bona-fide crazies. But the Sixties underlined the inadequacy of such an absolutist point of view: It was increasingly difficult to determine who was sane for one thing, and, for another, there was a new market for "awareness," "authenticity," and "self-realization." Psychotherapists obligingly opened their doors and created new styles, indeed new schools. Today, as a result, over 300 types of therapy are available in the U.S.

The oldest is *psychoanalysis,* the "talking cure" discovered by Josef Breuer and developed by Sigmund Freud for middle-class Viennese ladies suffering from hysteria (page 401). Whether or not you will be able to transform "hysterical misery into common unhappiness" (as Freud put it) can't be predicted. There are few, and inconclusive, studies of success rates in analysis, although first-person accounts, often disguised as novels, abound. At four times per week and $75 a (bargain) session for eleven (current average) years, the cost comes to $154,000, but with inflation, health insurance, and tax deductions that's not so bad—considering how well you get to know yourself.

Psychoanalytically oriented psychotherapy is psychoanalysis adapted for people who won't lie down and/or can't take the time. In POP, your therapist may shed the Dr. an analyst insists on in favor of Don or Sue, and may even call you by your given name. Your sessions may occasionally run over fifty minutes; you may not have to pay for sessions you miss; and because sessions are scheduled only once or twice a week, you may ask to have them changed around if you win the lottery and decide to go to Bali.

Instead of allowing you to ramble on uninterrupted (or fall into stony si-

lence) about your emotionally distant mother, the therapist will interrupt you
and talk about what you have/haven't said. POPers have all studied Freud but
many draw on the work of such defectors from the Master as Alfred Adler (see
page 409), Harry Stack Sullivan (page 412), Karen Horney, Wilhelm Reich
(page 429), or Carl Jung (page 424), who either disagreed with Freud or
abandoned him altogether. Like analysts, POPers decorate their offices with
Persian carpets, off-white furniture, and innocuous art. Like analysts, they
will be interested in hearing you explore that limitless well of material—your
childhood—as well as occasional items from your daily life and the newspapers (an assassination maybe, or a particularly evocative war) *if* it has personal associations and you don't begin to intellectualize as a "defense" against
getting to your true feelings (see page 405). POPers are in general more liable
than analysts to tell you exactly what tricks you are using to avoid "taking
responsibility," such tricks as "denying" your feelings, "resisting" your therapist, "acting out" old patterns, and "projecting" your state of mind onto the
bus driver. In therapy, you "work it through."

Nor does it have to take eleven years to work it through. Lately there has
been a strong push toward "short-term dynamic therapy" (spearheaded by a
farily prominent analyst named Judd Marmor) which sets firm deadlines and
specific goals in an effort to spur the patient's will to be well. With the patient
anxious about, say, his upcoming wedding, the STDT therapist will typically
not only interrupt and guide, he'll also raise questions calculated to provoke
anxiety, e.g., "Is it possible that your mother is jealous of your fiancée? Are
you afraid that your father is secretly furious about your wedding?" Thus
encouraged to confront his true feelings, simultaneously relating them to past
events and working to solve the problem at hand, a patient can, while still
following Freud, "get it all out" in something like eight or nine sessions ($30
to $60 a session), usually in the out-patient clinic of a large hospital or univer-
sity health service.

If at this point it's sounding as if we all think too much, consider *Gestalt*,
which is German for "configuration" and which aims to get around what you
say to how you feel. Developed by Fritz Perls, of Esalen Institute fame (yet
another apostle gone astray) during the 1940s, Gestalt dismisses Freud's concern with the There and Then in favor of the Here and Now. It throws what
we lay people call thinking, dreaming, assuming, guessing, and wishing into
one category called Fantasy and disparages it. Instead, the patient (usually
called "client" in these precincts) is urged to discover his five senses, the key
to Perceptual Reality.

According to Gestalt, simple awareness of one's moment-to-moment sensations is therapeutic. A session involves tuning out the "background" of life and focusing on the distinct "figure" or problem that's bothering you Right Now. One step beyond the POPer, the Gestalt therapist will find out your nickname, will touch as well as talk to you, and may invite you out for coffee later. You will not be allowed to sit back and retell your favorite stories of trial or abandonment. Rather, you will be interrupted after every few words with a question like: "Why are you smiling as you describe your father's funeral?"

When you try to answer, you'll likely be interrupted again by a warning to stay in the Here and Now. Gestalters don't want you to mess things up by using your brain. Instead they provide props on which to act out your feelings. These may include stuffed animals, pillows, and empty chairs to serve as substitutes for other people, other situations, or your other selves. These objects can be stroked, scratched, or pummeled without fear of retaliation. And while you are punching out the ex-lover you have imaginatively placed in the empty chair, your therapist is giving you lots of feedback on what all three of you, him included, are feeling.

Gestalt may be experienced one-on-one or in a group, one or more times a week. Like psychoanalysis and POP, its goal is to make the patient stop repeating "sick" patterns of behavior, get rid of emotional "garbage," and "take responsibility" for his life. Additionally, Gestalt aims to facilitate "fuller living," with regard to which the therapist serves not only as guide but as model. Consequently, a Gestalt shrink can be expected to be warm, open, caring, sensually on the ball, and persuaded of everyone's inherent ability to "grow and change." You may forget such basic skills as where to cross the street and how to eat lobster, but with luck you'll learn to be completely Here Now.

Feeling tense with confusion (or disapproval), sweating, or suffering stomach aches? Then maybe *bioenergetics* and/or *biofeedback* is for you. These therapies focus neither on the Where and When or the Here and Now, but on manipulating physiology to change emotional patterns.

Bioenergetics owes its beginnings to Wilhelm Reich, another Freud dropout, who had begun to work on "character armor" and the "energy economy of the body" in the 1940s. The goal of bioenergetics (as well as of such Reich-influenced therapies as Rolfing and the Alexander technique) is to relax this armor, deepen the patient's breathing, and release his "life force"; the latter entails getting in as many orgasms as possible. Sessions take place once or twice a week, often involving special dress and/or undress as well as intensive patient-therapist interaction. The patient performs special exercises; the therapist questions, comments, and makes physical adjustments designed to "break through" and "unblock" energy. The exercise might be pounding a mattress with a tennis racket (to unleash feelings of rage) or draping oneself (stomach up) over a padded stool and panting (to get in touch with suppressed pelvic cravings). Patients are required to sing, sigh, hum, laugh, cry, shout, or hiccup in order to specify the kind of energy they are releasing at the moment. They may also talk.

In biofeedback, they often do not talk at all. Once the therapist and patient have discussed the offending physiological problem (breaking out in hives when faced with a date, heading for the washroom when asked a direct question), the patient is hooked up to monitoring machines which translate agitation into quantifiable—and visual—terms. If the patient is suddenly forced to think of unpleasant things, the dials swing to the right; as the patient employs biofeedback relaxation techniques, the dial returns to the safe, low readings. The patient is told to ignore the details of the anxiety-provoking situation and simply work on getting the salient physiological process (blood-vessel, sweat-gland, or stomach-acid activity) back to normal. Whereas bioenergetics teaches the "release" of tension, biofeedback teaches its "control." Usually practiced once a week, it has the distinction of being among the shortest-term therapies (six months on the average). With no audience, there is little incentive for the patient to procrastinate, and while it is not recommended for anybody trying to decide among ice cream flavors or career choices, it is said to do wonders for migraines.

B.F. Skinner

Behavior therapy is the only major form of psychotherapy in the United States to have developed independently of the Viennese analysts. It draws partly on the work of Ivan Pavlov, whose experiments with dogs and drooling might ring a bell, partly on the work of B. F. Skinner, who examined the cause-and-effect relationship between environment and behavior. Starting from the proposition that all behavior is learned, behaviorists believe that they can fix anything that's wrong with you, provided you follow a special regimen. Such a therapist doesn't care what you call each other. He also has little or no use for "transference" or "energy" or, as far as that goes, any explanation you might offer for your difficulties. According to a behaviorist, neurotic symptoms—especially phobias, obsessions, compulsions, and a wide range of sexual problems—are simply learned bad habits. His job, he believes, is to help you unlearn them and to replace them with new, more productive patterns. And he wants immediate results.

You have trouble riding elevators or airplanes? Crossing bridges? Cracks in the sidewalk? No problem: First they'll "desensitize" you, then reeducate you. Want to stop choosing psychopaths for friends? Lose weight? Start jogging? The behaviorists have a system, a set of homework assignments, clearly defined "goals," and all the assurance in the world that you can do it.

Behavior therapy has an infinite variety of applications. In sex therapy, partners learn how to express, and reinforce, what each finds pleasurable; in assertiveness training, you may be taught to walk into a coffee shop and ask for a glass of water without ordering so much as a corn muffin. You will be expected to do reading, keep a journal of your homework assignments and their consequences, and, most of all, behave the way the therapist and you have decided you should. How you feel at the moment doesn't matter; whether you've succeeded in changing the way you act does. But, because of the way feelings and behavior tend to dovetail, you're expected to start feeling better, too.

A new variant of behavior therapy is *cognitive therapy*, although what it sets out to modify isn't so much behavior as thought and attitude. A relatively short-term (six weeks to three months) treatment developed by Aaron Beck of the University of Pennsylvania, it's based on the premise that a person's thought processes (and the linguistic structures that underlie them) go a long way in determining psychological disturbances. In Beck's view, a depressed person, for instance, through a process of distortion and exaggeration, has misinterpreted reality. The resulting thoughts (e.g., that he has nothing to offer anybody, that he's the lowest of the low) have become automatic and entrenched. Solution: Make the person aware of the automatic—and ultimately the invalid—nature of his "cognitions." Sessions are forty-five minutes long and cost from $15 to $50.

Doubtless you're longing to retreat to a discussion of some less messy subject, like Art or maybe the Politics of Philosophy. Fine, but don't think that means there's no such thing as *family therapy*, in which whole families allow their actions to be scrutinized, sometimes videotaped and then rearranged. Or *art, music, dance, video* and *biblio therapies*, in which painting, singing, dancing, watching TV, and reading books, respectively, serve as the catalysts for the releasing of emotion.

Probably, too, you'll want to skip such fashions as *transactional analysis*, which involves figuring out what kinds of "scripts" you might be "buying into," and *primal scream therapy*, in which large numbers of screamers congregate on mattresses and throw themselves against padded walls. Instead, focus on the American tradition of self-betterment, the problem of moving into a postindustrial world, and the pragmatic idealism that has in the past produced better can openers, taller basketball players, and more amendments to the Constitution. And, during working hours, anyway, do your best to keep the lid on.

RELIGION

Contents

Frontispiece to Book I of Milton's Paradise Lost *(see page 186), 4th edition, 1688.*

Those Old-Time Religions

DIVINE TO SOME, MERELY FABULOUS TO OTHERS

Have you ever noticed how prophetic revelation seems to give some people a new lease on life at about the same time others their age are gearing up for midlife crisis? Buddha, Jesus, and Zoroaster all got the Message when they were hovering around thirty, a birthday that, we assume, must have signaled middle age back when people started begetting as teenagers. True, Muhammad was forty when he first chatted with the Angel Gabriel, but then Islam as a whole was a late bloomer. So if you still feel, after scanning the great faiths outlined here, that the monotheisms of the West and the polytheisms of the East all leave you cold; that you can't really get behind karma, nirvana, yin and yang, the Holy Trinity, or separate dishware for meat and dairy; that you're as nervous and irritable and determined to file for divorce as ever; that you wish you could believe in something but you don't know what it is— our advice is: Stay loose and keep your eyes fixed on the heavens.

JUDAISM

17 million believers, mostly in Israel and the United States.

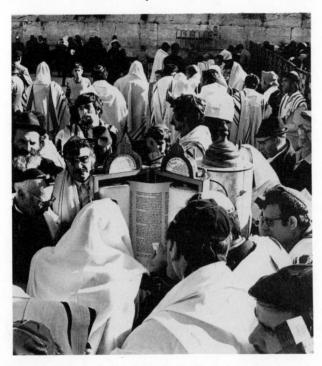

It's c. 1700 B.C. Heaven is crowded with divinities of the Moon, Sun, Stars, Trees, and Irrigation, as well as with various celestial dog-and-pony acts. Enter a Sumerian named Abraham, who insists that there is only one Almighty God, and that all the others will have to go. As it happens, it's Abraham who has to go, thereby setting up an extraordinarily fatiguing pattern of Jewish exile that will repeat itself for the next 4,000 years. But not to worry: Abraham's God, Yahweh (don't say it out loud), has made him a Covenant he can't refuse—the right, for himself and his progeny, to dwell in the Land of Canaan (later renamed Palestine) in perpetuity, in return for living clean and sticking to this newfangled idea of monotheism. Packing up his kin and his kitchen utensils, Abraham resettles in the Promised Land, on the other side of the Euphrates, thereby earning the name Hebrew (from an ancient word meaning "the other side") and sowing the seeds of unrest in the Middle East.

But all that's family history; Judaism as a more or less organized religion didn't really get rolling until Moses led a group of transplanted Hebrews out of slavery in Egypt and trekked with them back to the Promised Land. Moses took his orders directly from Yahweh, who was quite clear about what he expected from the Jews, issuing directives on everything from ethics ("Thou shalt have no other god before me," "Thou shalt not kill," etc.) to health standards ("Forget pork"). The shalts and shalt nots were recorded, along with a lot of divinely revealed history, in the Torah, later translated into the first five books of the Old Testament.

If this is beginning to seem like an awfully long story (and we're only up to about 1300 B.C.), try to be patient; in the absence of a national identity or reasonably tolerant neighbors, history had to suffice to keep Jewish tradition alive throughout the next several millennia of persecution, exile, and general *tsurus*. History, that is, and the law, as embodied in the Torah and buttressed by the scholarly commentaries on same later collected in the Talmud (the number two book of Judaism).

Because Jewish law and tradition evolved as a kind of Survivor's Guide to Life on a Hostile Planet, Judaism is (with the exception of certain mystical reinterpretations of the Scripture known as the Cabala) somewhat more practical and here-and-now-oriented than many other religions. The key event behind this survivalist mentality: the Diaspora, originally referring to the destruction of the Temple of Jerusalem in 856 B.C. and the subsequent exile of the Jews to Babylonia (the first "Babylonian Captivity"), later to the chronic dispersion of the Jews across the face of the earth. Other key terms: Zionism, the political movement that aimed at making good Yahweh's original Covenant through the establishment of a Jewish homeland in Israel; and Orthodox, Conservative, and Reform, the three branches of American Judaism.

Orthodox Jews try to uphold all of the ethical and practical imperatives of traditional Judaism as they've been handed down in the Torah and Talmud—light the Sabbath candles every Friday night; be in temple early the next morning; don't travel, telephone, touch money, or pose for pictures on the Sabbath; use separate cooking utensils for meat and dairy dishes, etc. Conservative Jews observe the moral rules of traditional Judaism but have adapted many of the everyday ones to suit modern life. They'll light the candles on important holidays and go to temple as often as they can manage it; they won't work on the Sabbath but see nothing wrong with getting up early to drive to Grandma's house, where they will probably upset Grandma by suggesting she fry salami and eggs in the same pan for breakfast. Reform Jews uphold only the ethical values of Judaism, believing that the practical taboos no longer serve the purposes for which they were intended a few thousand years ago. They probably don't own any Sabbath candles, may spend Friday night partying with their Gentile friends at the country club (which didn't allow them in until a few years ago), and will stop on the way to Grandma's house the next day for a chilidog with cheese.

CHRISTIANITY

1 billion followers: 600 million Roman Catholic; 63 million Eastern Orthodox; 370 million Protestant. Dominant in Western Europe and the Americas.

The first Christians weren't Christians at all, of course, but Palestinian Jews who, smitten with Jesus of Nazareth's notions about universal love, the brotherhood of man, and redemption through faith, saw nothing particularly disloyal or disruptive in regarding themselves as Jews for Jesus. It wasn't until Jesus's followers began recruiting non-Jewish converts, who insisted that circumcision was weird and Christ divine, that Christians and Jews started giving each other dirty looks across the bazaar.

Although it's never easy to launch a new world religion, the early Christians had a particularly tough time of it, beset, as they were, by a lot of internal bickering over who, exactly, Jesus was, and by any number of competitive pagan religions bent on co-opting the Savior for their own nefarious purposes—notably the Gnostics, with their salvation-through-revelation occultism and their predisposition to see Good and Evil in very black-and-white terms. In fact, most early Christian doctrine was formulated as a defense against total incoherence; hence its tendency towards dogmatism and the Christian establishment's later habit of excommunicating anyone who didn't toe the party line. There was also the problem of the ruling Romans, who, not in the least obsessed with distinguishing true Christians from false ones, simply declared open season on all of them.

It wasn't until the fourth century, when the Emperor Constantine himself converted to Christianity, that Christians were transformed from persecuted underdogs into imperial pets. After the construction of Constantinople as Christian capital and arts center, a new yuppie constituency began replacing the original slave, peasant, and humble-laborer devotees. In A.D. 325, the church was rich enough to host its first ecumenical council, out of which came the Nicene Creed, which affirmed, mainly, belief in the Holy Trinity and which is still the basic statement of faith for most Christians. By the end of the century, Christians had put together a testament of their own, comprising the four Gospels, the Acts of the Apostles, twenty-one epistles, and the Revelation of St. John the Divine. (They'd already appropriated the entire Old Testament, plus the Apocrypha, a collection of writings retrieved from the cutting-room floor and never accepted as official canon.)

Success didn't eliminate dissent within the ranks, however. In 1054, after a few centuries of squabbling over such issues as whether or not art was cool (remember the biblical injunction against graven images), the Pope of Rome excommunicated the Patriarch of Constantinople, and the Church was henceforth split into Roman Catholic and Eastern Orthodox divisions. Today, the two Churches differ mainly in decor (the Eastern Orthodox Church got the Byzantine domes and the elaborate mosaics; the Roman Catholics got the Gothic cathedrals and the Renaissance art collection), style (the Eastern Church still goes in for interminable masses, showstopper rituals, and the burning of extravagant amounts of incense), language (Greek and local vernacular in the East; Latin, and lately, local vernacular in the West), their attitudes toward the Immaculate Conception (not bloody likely, according to the E.O.C.), and, of course, the infallibility of the pope.

More fussing and fighting in the West led, in the fourteenth century, to the Great Schism, during which two rival popes ruled simultaneously, one from Rome, one from Avignon; and in the fifteenth century to the Reformation, when Luther, Calvin, Zwingli, et al., fed up with Church corruption, split Western Europe into Catholic and Protestant factions.

Today, Protestant sects (there are about 250 of them) dominate much of northern Europe and the old British Empire, and maintain a slight edge over Catholicism in the United States, while the Catholic Church has pretty much cornered the market in France, Italy, Spain, and Latin America. The twentieth century ecumenical movement hopes, someday, to put all the pieces of the Church back together again. In the meantime, the combined Catholic-Protestant head count still matters, since Christianity, as anyone who has ever opened the door to a Seventh-Day Adventist knows, is one of the great missionary religions of the modern world.

ISLAM

550 million believers, according to the World Almanac; 1 billion, according to the Islamic Center, Washington, D.C. Dominant in Arab world, Turkey, Iran, Afghanistan, Pakistan, and Indonesia.

Oops. Did we say it's never easy to launch a new world religion? We overlooked Islam (you can bet it won't happen again), the youngest of the monotheistic megafaiths. In A.D. 622, its official birthdate, Islam was little more than a gleam in the prophet Muhammad's eye; less than 200 years later, it was the power behind an empire that stretched from Spain to India. Of course, Muhammad didn't really start from scratch; as a Bedouin trader living on the outskirts of Mecca, he'd already picked up a lot of gossip about Judaism and Christianity by the time he was ready to start having divine revelations of his own. As a result, Islam bears an uncanny likeness to its two predecessors, though with variations that, from the beginning, made it highly appealing to the common man (and we do mean *man*) as well as to certain fierce desert tribes prepared to appreciate Muhammad's policy of winning through decapitation.

The main attraction of Islam (Arabic for "submission to the will of God") is its utter simplicity. Your average Moslem (Arabic for "one who submits") can get to Heaven, not by striving for some quasi-mystical and pretty much unattainable state of grace, but simply by following the Five Pillars of Islam. First and most important of these is the affirmation of faith, in the words "There is no God but Allah and Muhammad is His prophet." Say this with real feeling just once in your life and no one can accuse you of not being a true Moslem (although only you and Allah will know for sure). Two: Pray five times a day, turning toward Mecca (no need to check your watch; just listen for the call of the muezzin and hit the ground when everyone else does). Three: Fast from sunup to sundown throughout the entire month of Ramadan (and, if you're a well-to-do twentieth-century Moslem, binge-eat into the wee hours). Four: Make the hajj, the pilgrimage to Mecca, at least once if you can afford it (luckily, you no longer have to travel on foot or by camel; flights leave daily from most major cities). Five: Give alms, unless you're so poor you have to beg them. And if you want to earn bonus points to ensure a smooth entry into Heaven, simply contrive to die while fighting a Holy War.

In case you get confused, you can look up the essentials in the Koran, the one and only sacred text of Islam, which contains the words of Allah as revealed to Muhammad. You may find the going a bit tricky, however, since Muhammad wrote in a rhythmic Arabic that's completely untranslatable. Join the club; three quarters of the Moslem world is now composed of non-Arabs, and none of them can read their own Scriptures, either. Anyway, most of the Koran is devoted to retelling the stories of the Old and New Testaments from the Moslem—that is, the correct and uncorrupted—point of view. (For instance, the five great early prophets were really Adam, Noah, Abraham—the first Moslem—Moses, and Jesus. Alexander the Great was a prophet, too, and Muhammad was the last to carry Allah's divine word to man; and that's Allah, by the way, not Yahweh, which must have been some sort of typo.) The Koran won't give you much detail about ethical behavior or daily ritual; for that, you'll have to turn to the Hadith, the collected sayings of Muhammad, which, almost everyone acknowledges, are probably not authentic.

The Moslem world is meant to be a theocracy, and it's in the who's-running-the-show department that Islam splits into its only two major sects, Sunni and Shi'ite. The Sunnis, who comprised about 90 percent of all Moslems today, are the ones you don't hear much about; conservative and relatively tolerant, they believe in rule by tradition and consensus. The Shi'ites are the radical reformers who, like fundamentalist Christians, are convinced the world is going to hell in a handbasket; they are given to dire proclamations, strict proscriptions, and the cutting off of hands in the public square. The Shi'ites believe in rule by imams, or leaders, of whom the ayatollahs compose a sort of middle-management cadre.

From its inception, Islam has had great success in winning converts in hot, arid, impoverished countries where the natives are susceptible to a lot of shouting and sword-brandishing, and to the promise of a Heaven that, unlike home, consists of green meadows and babbling brooks. Another lure: Traditional Islam is basically egalitarian and flexible; follow the simple rules and nobody is going to torture you for heresy or shun you because of the color of your skin. Feminists, pacifists, and drunk drivers, however, need not apply.

ZOROASTRIANISM

250,000 believers, mostly Parsis living in India.

You pretty much had to be there—Persia, in the sixth century B.C. that is—to get the full flavor of Zoroastrianism as Zoroaster conceived it. (Actually, as he conceived it, it was called Zarathustrianism; Zoroastrianism is the Greek translation.) By the time it became the state religion of Persia, in A.D. 226, Zoroaster's own mother wouldn't have recognized it. But use your imagination. Picture yourself trying to settle down and run a peaceful little ancient farm while surrounded by a zillion nature gods perpetually vying for your attention. You could spend half the day sacrificing to gods of twigs and pebbles and the like just to get in a decent harvest, and you still wouldn't have a clue as to how to behave nicely or raise your kids. Zoroaster eliminated a lot of the time-wasting twig worship while adding a relatively coherent moral dimension to daily life. It's true that Zoroastrianism, in its earliest form, was mainly concerned with increasing the harvest and ensuring the happiness and well-being of various farm animals; nevertheless, it was as subtle and sophisticated an ethical system as anything you'll find in . . . well, wherever you look for ethical systems nowadays.

Zoroaster trimmed the pantheon of Persian gods to two warring ones: Ahura Mazdah, a.k.a. Ormuzd, the Creator and God of Goodness and Light; and Ahriman, God of Evil and Darkness. Ahura Mazdah is attended by six lesser deities, or archangels, or *ahuras*, or abstract qualities, take your pick, who translate roughly into Good Thought, Highest Righteousness, Divine Kingdom, Pious Devotion, Salvation, and Immortality. Ahriman, naturally, has his own entourage of evil spirits, called *divs* or *daevas*. Human beings, by their thoughts and actions, can side with Goodness, Light, and Life or with Evil, Darkness, and Death, and, by doing so, participate in the ultimate destiny of the Universe. Up to a point. The catch—and what makes Zoroastrianism different from the purely dualistic religions that were all the rage in ancient times—is that eventually, Ahura Mazdah is going to win. This makes for a nice, if somewhat complicated, marriage of free will and determinism—and, eventually, for a kind of happy ending.

Daily life for a Zoroastrian was nevertheless a very risky business, with evil spirits lurking everywhere. Near-constant ritual purification was necessary to ward off the forces of corruption, darkness, and death. At the same time, Ahura Mazdah's elements, fire, water, and earth—all of which are reverenced but not, as any modern Zoroastrian would be quick to tell you, worshipped—had to be particularly well protected from contamination; hence the spooky "Towers of Silence" on which Zoroastrians placed their dead so as not to defile the earth. But physical corruption and defilement were also linked to evil mental states, thought being a very powerful force in the Zoroastrian cosmos. At some point, as you can see, it all becomes a bit much for the modern Western mind to grasp. (Although you can bone up on the purification rituals, along with a lot of songs, hymns, and liturgies, in the Zoroastrian scriptures, the *Zend Avesta*, it's so fragmentary, so corrupted, and so old that you still won't know your forces of Light from your forces of Darkness, much less be able to tell who's winning.) The Eastern mind, on the other hand, seems to do very nicely with it. When Persian Zoroastrianism was wiped out by Moslem hordes in the eighth century, a small group of Zoroastrians escaped to India, where incessant ritual purification is never a bad idea. Now known as Parsis and concentrated in and around Bombay, they've become one of the wealthiest, best-educated, and most-respected minority groups in a society that doesn't normally reward strangeness *or* strangers.

HINDUISM

465 million believers, mostly in India.

Very old: Predates all other world religions, except Judaism, by centuries at least. Also, very disorganized: Has 330 million gods, more than enough for every family to have its own; a couple of dozen sects; a clutch of holy books; plenty of rituals, ceremonies, and spiritual disciplines; and neither a historical founder nor any consensus as to what, exactly, religious practice consists in. In a sense, Hinduism seems easy—tolerant, inclusive, undemanding, with an embarrassment of color, pageantry, and paths to Brahman, the Infinite Being (and ultimate reality) you eventually want to be at one with. Easy, that is, assuming you're not infelicitously placed within the caste sytem and stuck being a servant or a peasant; or infelicitously placed without it and stuck being an untouchable—or a pig or a mosquito.

The paradox here: You have plenty of time (in fact, as many lifetimes as you need) and plenty of ways to work out the release of your soul from the world and the ultimate rendezvous with Brahman. But there's a real chutes-and-ladders feeling to the game plan and, rather than getting to simply shake the dice, you're always being judged on how nicely you behaved on your last turn. In other words, your karma—literally, "action"; figuratively, a kind of cosmic system of cause-and-effect—determines your rise (and fall) in caste, through life after life, incarnation after incarnation until you finally get to the top of the board and the end of the game.

Along the way, be prepared to deal with the most prominent of the gods (each of whom, incidentally, is a manifestation of Brahman, and many of whom have subsidiary manifestations of their own): Shiva the Destroyer, a.k.a. the Cosmic Dancer; Vishnu the Preserver, a.k.a. Krishna, a.k.a. Buddha; and Shakti the Divine Mother. And with a couple of important sets of books: the Vedas, those ancient scriptures, written in Sanskrit, that lay the groundwork for Hinduism and culminate in the *Upanishads* or "secret doctrine"; and the *Mahabharata,* the longest poem in the world, containing India's favorite religious text, the *Bhagavad Gita,* a dialogue between the god Krishna and a soldier named Arjuna. And with any and all animals, especially cows, bulls, monkeys, and snakes (each of which you'll be nice to, since it, like you, is probably on its way up or down). Of course you'll visit Benares and bathe in the Ganges. And you may go Tantric, embracing that branch of yoga (from a Sanskrit word meaning "to join" and related to our "yoke") that seeks enlightenment through, among other procedures, a style of sensual love-making in which "each is both." Needless to say, you'll also be on the lookout for gurus, mantras, mandalas (the former chanted, the latter painted), and sutras (treatises on various aspects of the *Vedas,* the Kama Sutra section of which may remind you of Tantric yoga classes).

Not that Hinduism is all easy-listening. You'll also be expected, en route to Brahman, to give some thought to *maya* (originally, "might"), the illusion that the shapes and structures, the things and events we perceive with our senses in some way stand for reality—otherwise known as confusing the map with the territory. Problem is, as long as we're under the spell of *maya* and think we're separate from our environment, we're going to be bound—and pushed around—by karma, and once again find ourselves being issued an end-of-lifetime report card. At which point, according to Hinduism (and for that matter, Buddhism, warming up in the bullpen), the whole business begins again.

BUDDHISM

250 million believers, mostly in Southeast Asia, China, Korea, and Japan.

Take Hinduism. Subtract the caste system, downplay the gods, the ritual, and the Play-Doh colors, and substitute Nirvana for Brahman. Now add the Four Noble Truths, the Noble Eightfold Path, the Three Baskets, and the Great Wheel, and transport the whole business from India to points south (Sri Lanka), east (Burma, Thailand, and Indochina), and north (Nepal, Tibet, China, Mongolia, Korea, and Japan). Refuse to take any questions on the origin of the world or the nature of the divine and insist that everybody in the group work, quietly on his own, towards feeling better about himself through a program of pity, joy, kindliness, and meditation.

It's not that Buddhism is abstemious, exactly (the robes *are* saffron, after all, and representations of the Buddha several stories high and made of gold), just that there's a pared-down quality to it and that it comes down hard in all the places where Hinduism is free-form and assimilative. In part this is because Buddhism had a single founder (and hence an indisputable source and role model), Siddhartha Gautama, the so-called "historic" Buddha, son of a sixth-century B.C. Indian prince, who proceeded to renounce worldliness in favor of enlightenment, of the middle way (between extremes of self-indulgence and self-denial), and, eventually, of Nirvana itself—a word that means, literally, a "going out," as of a candle when there's no more wick to burn, and, figuratively, liberation from all desires, cravings, and "becomings," from suffering and from the endless round of lifetimes and selves. And in part it's because Buddhism, as a missionary religion (like Christianity and Islam), had to travel light, both to maximize its chances of getting over the mountains and through the rainforests and to leave its converts some room to use their imaginations.

Basically, these converts fall into two camps, roughly established (cf. Catholicism and Protestantism) along north/south lines. The southern camp (Sri Lanka, Southeast Asia) practice a form of Buddhism known as Hinayana (or "Little Vehicle"), characterized by orthodoxy (what the historical Buddha said goes), austerity, and a concept of salvation based on one's own right living. The northern camp (Nepal all the way to Japan) practice Mahayana (or "Great Vehicle"), which postulates that the Buddha is not just historical but divine and that nobody—not even a bodhisattva, two thirds of the way to being a Buddha himself—is going to enter into Nirvana until every last one of us is ready to enter into Nirvana. Two important subcamps of Buddhism: the Lamaism of Tibet, in which the Dalai Lama called the shots until Communist China threw him out, and the Zen Buddhism of Japan, transplanted from China, in which *satori*—the attainment of enlightenment, plain and simple, through intuition rather than intellect—is the name of the game, prepared for in activities like judo, calligraphy, flower arranging, and so on, and embodied by the *koan*, a paradoxical observation of the sound-of-one-hand-clapping variety.

Careful: It's often hard to remember what's basically Hinduist, what's Buddhist. Not only did Hinduism spawn Buddhism, it then glommed on to a lot of what the Buddhists had gone on to say and think. So you get nirvana, karma, mantra, tantra, and yoga, not to mention Buddha himself, in both packages (though usually not in the same strengths). Do try to remember that there are now almost no Buddhists in India itself. And that whereas the spirit of Hinduism is theatrical and clubby, that of Buddhism is no-nonsense and do-it-yourself.

TAOISM and CONFUCIANISM

35 million believers, mostly in China.   *160 million believers, likewise.*

Let's begin with yin and yang. You remember yin and yang: the two poles of experience, joined in a symmetric union, a continuous cycle; yang the bright, creative, male, heavenly force, yin the dark, receptive, female, earthly one, each of the two containing the seed of its opposite. Note that we're not talking Western-style opposites here, of the true-false, good-bad variety, but something more like harmony, balance, completeness, fulfillment.

Turns out, that's pretty much how Confucianism and Taoism work. Each founded in the sixth century B.C. (and thus predating the arrival of Buddhism in China by roughly 700 hundred years), and each equipped with its own legendary sage, the two together sum up, play to, and care for the Chinese character as we know—or think we know—it. Confucianism is practical, social, ethical, full of advice on how to behave in the world, father to son, husband to wife, ruler to subject, older friend to younger friend; more code than creed, with no churches or clergy in sight. Taoism is mystical, devoted— even more than Buddhism (though probably less than Zen)—to transcending everyday life and finding the *tao*, the path, the way of the natural order. Nor did the Chinese fall into the trap of doing some schematic Type A–Type B thing with the two. Rather, they chose to emphasize Confucianism when they were educating their kids, then convert to Taoism when they got older in the hopes of regaining the spontaneity that had been squelched by a lifetime of honoring social conventions and playing by the rules.

Confucius—K'ung Fu-tse, or "Grand Master K'ung," back home in China—was, you don't have to be told, particularly good with the one-liners: "It is only the wisest and the stupidest who cannot change," "The proper man understands equity, the small man profits," "Silence is a friend who will never betray," and so on, enough of them to fill the *Lun Yü*, or *Analects*, Confucianism's basic reference work. Lao-tzu—the "Grand Old Man" (literally) of Taoism, said to have once baffled Confucius in philosophical debate—had a more enigmatic style, as befits a religion determined to transcend: "Without going out of the door, one can know the whole world. Without peeping out of the window, one can see the *tao* of heaven. The further one travels, the less one knows." His collection is called the *Tao Te Ching (The Way of Virtue)*. The *I Ching* (or Book of Changes), by the way, which you once may have been in the habit of consulting on days when the Tarot wasn't working out, and which is as much about yin and yang as everything else in the country is, predates both men; Confucius even based some of his teachings on it.

So, Confucianism is yang: practical, masculine, dominant, active. Taoism is yin: intuitive, feminine, yielding, passive. The Confucians wanted to get the job done, keep the wheels greased, make sure the system held up for another few hundred generations; the Taoists to lead a perfectly balanced life in harmony with the tao and to leave artifice and conformity in the dust.

Not that it stayed so simple. First, threatened by Buddhism, Taoism sacrificed all the understatement to eye appeal and sheer numbers. Buddhism had thirty-three different kinds of heaven, so Taoists came up with eighty-one. Taoism took over some of the Buddhist gods and restored others from the old folk religions it had supplanted (including the City God, the Wealth God, and the Kitchen God), and developed a lively interest in selling charms, reading fortunes, and sponsoring secret societies. Today, it's still sect-and-society mad, a religion of the semiliterate and the eternally hopeful. Confucianism, too, once it had eliminated the examination system it ran to keep those civil-service candidates on their toes, seems to have had an identity crisis. Both are outlawed in the People's Republic today (it especially didn't help Confucianism that Confucius was a feudal aristocrat), but *we* know that's just a phase of the cycle, don't we?

SHINTOISM

65 million believers, mostly in Japan.

The Hammacher-Schlemmer of Eastern religions: Full of odd and largely useless items, as well as old and demographically undesirable shoppers, and, perhaps most important, overshadowed by Bloomingdale's up the street (that would be Buddhism, a sixth-century import from China via Korea; that there are as many Shintoists as there are today is due in part to sheer force of habit and in part to the fact that most of them are practicing Buddhists, too).

The religion of ancient Japan, Shintoism—from *shin-tao*, the later Chinese equivalent of the Japanese *kami-no-michi*, or "way of the gods" (Japan had no written language until it appropriated China's in the fifth century A.D.)—developed out of a combination of nature and ancestor worships, sometime around 700 B.C. The religion had a complex pantheon of *kami*, or gods, led by a Supreme Sun Goddess and including guardian household spirits; presiding tree-, river-, rock-, and village-divinities (including *kamikaze*, the "divine wind"); deified emperors; and miscellaneous national heroes.

A set of customs and rituals rather than a moral or philosophical system, Shintoism puts a lot of stress on purity, especially bodily cleanliness, and obedience; makes little of life after death and a lot of self-versus-nonself thinking; and fosters the belief that, since the Japanese have occupied their island pretty much by themselves for as long as anybody can remember, they are all related to each other, to their royal rulers, and to the Supreme Sun Goddess herself. It's these last planks in the Shintoist platform that had so many Japanese committing harakiri for their emperor in World War II and Douglas MacArthur banning Shintoism as an instrument of the state, while allowing it as a religious sect, shortly thereafter.

The Good Book as Good Read

Sorry; as far as we know, Video Scripture hasn't hit the market yet. But the written Word itself offers some pleasant surprises, especially if you've been avoiding it since Sunday School days. It is, for instance, tailor-made for short attention spans: You can easily absorb a verse or two while waiting for the cash machine and half a dozen psalms on a short bus-ride home. It's chock-full of the kind of homespun wisdom and thoughtful advice you'd be lucky to get in a year's subscription to your favorite lifestyle magazine. It puts any number of book and movie titles into perspective. And given a choice between contemplating "Mother Eats Baby in Bizarre Devil-Worship Ritual!" at the supermarket checkout counter or any one of the passages below, we know which *we* think makes for a nicer day. Being sentimentalists at heart, we also opt for the King James Version whenever possible, as we've done here.

1. There were giants in the earth in those days; and also after that, when the sons of God came in unto the daughters of men, and they bare children to them, the same became mighty men which were of old, men of renown.*

Genesis 6:4

2. By the rivers of Babylon, there we sat down, yea, we wept when we remembered Zion.**　　　　　　　　　　　　　　　　　　　Psalms 137:1

3. A little sleep, a little slumber, a little folding of the hands to rest, and poverty will come upon you like a vagabond and want like an armed man.

Proverbs 6:10

4. I am a brother to dragons, and a companion to owls. My skin is black upon me, and my bones are burned with heat. My harp also is turned to mourning, and my organ into the voice of them that weep.　　　　　　Job 30:29–31

---

* For the record, they're talking about the time before the Flood.

** Properly associated not with reggae music, but with the first Babylonian Captivity (see pages 436 and 464).

5. I returned, and saw under the sun, that the race is not to the swift, nor the battle to the strong, neither yet bread to the wise, nor yet riches to men of understanding, nor yet favour to men of skill; but time and chance happeneth to them all.*   Ecclesiastes 9:11

6. Or ever the silver cord be loosed, or the golden bowl be broken, or the pitcher be broken at the fountain, or the wheel broken at the cistern.**
                                                                    Ecclesiastes 12:6

7. For they have sown the wind, and they shall reap the whirlwind: it hath no stalk: the bud shall yield no meal: if so be it yield, the strangers shall swallow it up.†   Hosea 8:7

8. And why beholdest thou the mote that is in thy brother's eye, but considerest not the beam that is in thine own eye?   Matthew 7:3

9. For we brought nothing into this world and it is certain that we can carry nothing out.   I Timothy 6:7

10. Faith is the substance of things hoped for, the evidence of things not seen.   Hebrews 11:1

11. Be not forgetful to entertain strangers, for thereby some have entertained angels unawares.   Hebrews 13:2

12. And when he had opened the seventh seal, there was silence in heaven about the space of half an hour.††   Revelation 8:1

---

* Ecclesiastes (Greek for "preacher") is now believed to have been the nom de plume of a wealthy, kindly old cynic who lived around 200 B.C. For a long time he was considered too materialistic, pessimistic, and agnostic to be included in the Bible at all; naturally, he is a big favorite with modern readers.

** The subject here is old age and death, about which Ecclesiastes worried a lot. The rest of the passage is also worth remembering: "Then shall the dust return to the earth as it was: and the spirit shall return unto God who gave it."

† Spoken of the errant people of Israel who were, as usual, off worshipping false idols and wallowing in luxury while the kingdom collapsed into political confusion and Assyrian armies gathered ominously to the north.

†† The seventh seal is the last of those which secure the great book held in God's right hand. It is being opened, at the moment in question, by a lamb with seven eyes and seven horns.

The Good Book as Good Business

We know, if we think about it, that God didn't speak to His Biblical scribes in seventeenth-century English prose; that the King James version of the Bible is not carved, Cecil B. De Mille–style, in stone. This allows for considerable diversity of opinion about how He said whatever it was that He said. It also makes for a Bible-publishing industry that has churned out 2,500 English-language versions alone over the past couple of centuries and that continues to ring up an estimated $180 million in sales each year.

Some of this superabundance of Scripture is justified. For one thing, new discoveries of ancient texts and more sophisticated methods of interpreting them have allowed scholars to correct errors in earlier translations. For another, some people sincerely want to get the Word across to a new generation of readers with considerably different literary needs. Then there's simple chauvinism: Every sect and denomination now seems determined to have its own version of things, translated by its own scholars, to present to its own faithful. So, as scrambled eggs and fried-egg sandwiches have been joined by the Egg McMuffin and Croissan'wich, next to the King James and the Revised Standard versions, we now have such bestsellers as *The Good News Bible* and *The Book*. Here, contributor David Martin provides a brief critical guide to ten Bibles, complete with samples of how each handles two familiar Biblical passages.

THE KING JAMES BIBLE (a.k.a. the Authorized Version): Retains its popularity more for sentimental than for utilitarian reasons. Despite ongoing revisions, it still presents translation problems and some of the language, already slightly outdated when it was published in 1611, is now so archaic that it's impossible to decipher without divine guidance. But it's beautiful stuff, whatever it means, and it did help shape the English language for the next couple of centuries. If you have no purist hang-ups, the abridged and heavily annotated collegiate version known as *The Dartmouth Bible* can make the going a whole lot easier.

THE REVISED STANDARD VERSION: An American reworking of the King James Bible, issued between 1946 and 1952. Proponents praised it for cleaning up the King James's language and many of its textual errors. Detractors said it still retained too many archaisms, while fundamentalists blamed the Commies for its supposedly weakened stance on the divinity of Jesus, the integrity of the Trinity, and the historicity of the Virgin Birth. Has become, as the name implies, the familiar version of the Bible in the United States and probably throughout the English-speaking world.

THE NEW ENGLISH BIBLE: Published in 1970 by the Oxford and Cambridge University Presses, and a totally new translation from the original texts. Instead of a word-for-word translation, though, which produces what has come to be known as "Bible English," this goes meaning-for-meaning and favors contemporary idiom; as a result, it's clearer than the King James but also wordier. Its Anglicisms—"truckle to no one," "meal-tub," "throw on the stove,"—can drive an American crazy.

THE JERUSALEM BIBLE: Brought out in 1966 and heralded as the first Roman Catholic translation in English, from the original text rather than from the Latin Vulgate. An excellent piece of scholarship, it includes book-by-book introductions and notes on archeology, geography, theology, and language that are considered by many to be the most complete of those in any one-volume Bible. The doctrine is relatively liberal, although Catholic dogma does creep into the notes (e.g., on 1 Corinthians 7: "Virginity is a higher calling than marriage, and spirituality more profitable").

THE NEW AMERICAN BIBLE: The first translation from the original texts for *American* Catholics, and a surprisingly undogmatic one. A word-for-word translation, it can get a bit ponderous, but does clean up a lot of archaism.

THE LIVING BIBLE: Completed in 1971, and comes in various versions. (The one for Catholics is called *The Way: Catholic Edition*, and for blacks there's—honest—*Soul Food*.) Literally a paraphrase, *The Book*, as it's now called, has been criticized extensively for its careless treatment of the geography, history, and language of the times, as well as for some of the theological conclusions of its author, Kenneth N. Taylor. Some people also take exception to having *The Book* touted on bumper stickers. No beauty here: The Psalms are done in prose, the Song of Solomon as some kind of a dramatic reading among several speakers, and its colloquial style is sitcom-flat: "Hey, who's that girl over there?," "Martha was the jittery type."

THE GOOD NEWS BIBLE (Today's English Version): The American Bible Society's popular illustrated model, designed to be easily understood by absolutely everyone, including newcomers to the English language. The translation is accurate enough, but the style is strictly newspaperese.

THE NEW INTERNATIONAL VERSION: Published in 1978 with a strikingly familiar format. When someone speaks, there are quotation marks; when the speaking voice changes, so does the paragraph—just like in a James Michener novel. The translation itself, neither literal nor paraphrase, is innocuous, and the theology, conservative evangelical.

VERSION	FROM PSALMS 23	FROM ECCLESIASTES
The King James Bible	The Lord is my shepherd; I shall not want. He maketh me to lie down in green pastures: he leadeth me beside still waters. He restoreth my soul . . .	Vanity of vanities, saith the Preacher, vanity of vanities: all is vanity.
The Revised Standard Version	The Lord is my shepherd, I shall not want; he makes me to lie down in green pastures. He leads me beside still waters; he restores my soul.	Vanity of vanities, says the Preacher, vanity of vanities! All is vanity.
The New English Bible	The Lord is my shepherd; I shall want nothing. He makes me lie down in green pastures, and leads me beside the waters of peace; he renews life within me.	Emptiness, emptiness, says the Speaker, emptiness, all is empty.
The Jerusalem Bible	Yahweh is my shepherd, I lack nothing. In meadows of green grass he lets me lie. To the waters of repose he leads me; there he revives my soul.	Vanity of vanities, Qoheleth says. Vanity of vanities. All is vanity!
The New American Bible	The Lord is my shepherd, I shall not want. In verdant pastures he gives me repose: Beside restful waters he leads me; he refreshes my soul.	Vanity of vanities, says Qoheleth, vanity of vanities! All things are vanity!

VERSION	FROM PSALMS 23	FROM ECCLESIASTES
The Holy Scriptures	The Lord is my shepherd; I lack nothing. He makes me lie down in green pastures; He leads me to water in places of repose; He renews my life.	Utter futility!—said Koheleth—Utter futility! All is futile!
The The New King James Version	The Lord is my shepherd; I shall not want. He makes me lie down in green pastures; He leads me beside the still waters. He restores my soul . . .	"Vanity of vanities," says the Preacher. "Vanity of vanities, all is vanity."
The Living Bible	Because the Lord is my shepherd, I have everything I need! He lets me rest in the meadow grass and leads me beside the quiet streams. He restores my failing health.	In my opinion, nothing is worthwhile; everything is futile.
The Good News Bible	The Lord is my shepherd; I have everything I need. He lets me rest in fields of green grass and leads me to quiet pools of fresh water. He gives me new strength.	It is useless, useless, said the Philosopher. Life is useless, all useless.
The New International Version	The Lord is my shepherd, I shall lack nothing. He makes me lie down in green pastures, he leads me beside quiet waters, he restores my soul.	"Meaningless! Meaningless!" says the Teacher. "Utterly meaningless! Everything is meaningless."

THE HOLY SCRIPTURES: Completed in 1982, and the first translation from Hebrew by Jewish scholars since the Septuagint, the Hebrew-to-Greek translation of the Old Testament done more than 2,200 years ago (and so called because it was the work of 72 scholars). While more formal than many Christian translations, it is very literal and reads well aloud (the novelist and rabbi Chaim Potok served as literary coordinator).

THE NEW KING JAMES VERSION: An attempt to update the King James. It restored certain parts of the original seventeenth-century text, which had been inadvertently changed, and modernized some of the language—"sheweth" to "show," "thy" to "your," for example. On the whole, though, the translation tends to vulgarize the prose without making it all that much more accessible. Also available in paperback, in a version marketed as *The Bible*, with commentaries on everything from stress to drugs to homosexuality.

Bible Baedeker

A MERCIFULLY BRIEF WHO-WHAT-AND-WHERE GUIDE TO THE HOLY LAND

SIX IMPORTANT PLACES THAT BEGIN WITH THE LETTER *G*

GILEAD: A fertile, mountainous region east of the Jordan River, between the Sea of Galilee and the Dead Sea. Badlands of a sort, Gilead (with its colonizers, the Gileadites) was both cut off from the rest of the country and open to attack by hostile neighbors. This was the home of the outlaw king Jephthah and of the prophet Elijah. King David fled to Gilead to escape the rebellion led by his son Absalom, and it was here that the Syrian Laban caught up with his fugitive son-in-law Jacob. The region was known for its spices, myrrh, and balm, which prompted the prophet Jeremiah, seeking a cure for the decline of the Hebrew nation, to ask his famous rhetorical question: "Is there no balm in Gilead? Are there no physicians there?" Poe's narrator in "The Raven" was even more skeptical, wondering: "Is there balm in Gilead?"

GAZA: A town that spelled trouble for Israel right from the start. Located on the plain between the Mediterranean Sea and western Israel that is now known as the Gaza Strip, this began as an Egyptian garrison town and was later one of the five great cities of the Philistines. In fact, it's where the Philistines brought Samson to blind him, after his betrayal by Delilah (hence the title of Aldous Huxley's novel *Eyeless in Gaza*); Samson retaliated by bringing down the Philistine temple on top of them all. Later, the unlucky town was besieged, first by Alexander the Great, then during the wars of the Maccabees, and again during the Crusades. Although the exact location of ancient Gaza is unknown, modern Gaza is the principle city of the Gaza Strip, the impoverished area which, since the 1940s, has been the site of massive Palestinian refugee camps and the scene of endless clashes between Egyptians, Israelis, and Arab guerrillas.

GEHENNA: A corruption of the Hebrew Ge-Hinnom, the valley outside Jerusalem where, during various periods, the Jews slipped into the pagan rite of human sacrifice. The practice was to burn one's child, usually the firstborn, as an offering to the fire god, Moloch. God was, naturally, appalled by the custom; according to Jeremiah, he laid a curse on the place, changing its name to "the valley of slaughter" and promising: "I will make this city desolate, and a hissing; every one that passeth thereby shall be astonished and hiss, because of all the plagues thereof. And I will cause them to eat the flesh of their sons and the flesh of their daughters, and they shall eat every one the flesh of his friend in the siege and straitness . . ." (Jeremiah 19:8). Later, Gehenna became synonymous with Hell, as in Rudyard Kipling's verse: "Down to Gehenna or up to the throne / He travels fastest who travels alone."

GOSHEN: There have always been too many Goshens to keep track of. One was a region of Egypt, probably located in the northeast part of the Nile delta, where Joseph settled his father, Jacob, and all of Jacob's offspring, after returning from his exile in Egypt. During this period they were under the protection of the Pharaoh, but over the next four centuries the Jews living in Goshen became the slaves of the Egyptians. (When Moses finally came along and delivered them from slavery, they headed directly east, it's thought, to a place called the Sea of Reeds, not, as it says in the Bible, to the Red Sea.) Another Goshen probably refers to the hill country near the Negev, once occupied by Joshua's army; this is the one from which we got the expression land o' goshen. And then, of course, there's Goshen, Indiana and Goshen, Connecticut.

GETHSEMANE: The olive grove, or garden, on the western slope of the Mount of Olives, east of Jerusalem, where Jesus underwent his "agony" (during which, as he prayed, "his sweat was as it were great drops of blood falling down to the ground," Luke 22:44), where he was visited by an angel, and where, soon afterward, he was betrayed by Judas and arrested. In the Bible, the garden seems to be under a kind of spell, which causes the disciples to fall asleep repeatedly while Jesus struggles with temptation. You've seen the spot as a backdrop in religious paintings.

GOLGOTHA: The same as Calvary; the place where Jesus was crucified. (Golgotha derives from the Hebrew, and Calvary the Latin, word for "skull.") It was somewhere just outside the walls of Jerusalem, although no one knows the exact location. Ever since St. Helena discovered what she believed to be a piece of the cross in the area in A.D. 327, the site has traditionally been placed within what is now the Church of the Holy Sepulchre. There is a hole in the ground inside the church where the cross was supposed to have been set.

FIVE FAMILIAR CHARACTERS WHO WON'T STAY PUT

ABSALOM: King David's handsome third son, who killed his half-brother Amnon to avenge the rape of his sister. He was eventually pardoned by David, who was partial to him and probably overpermissive. Later, Absalom "stole the hearts of the men of Israel" and conspired to overthrow the king. During the decisive battle, Absalom's hair got caught in the branches of an oak tree, and his mule rode out from under him. As he hung there helplessly, one of David's men finished him off, despite the king's orders that his son's life be spared. David's cry upon hearing the news—" O my son Absalom, my son, my son Absalom! Would God I had died for thee, O Absalom, my son, my son!" —is the classic father's lament. Absalom, as a symbol of the son who brings his father grief, was used by Dryden in his satirical "Absalom and Achitophel" and by Faulkner in his novel *Absalom, Absalom!*

ISHMAEL: Son of Abraham conceived when Abraham's wife Sarah, for years unable to have a child, finally sent her Egyptian maid Hagar in to sleep with her husband. Later, Sarah became pregnant with Isaac and, in a fit of jealousy, had Hagar and Ishmael cast out into the wilderness to die. God came to their rescue, however, by providing a well at Beer-sheba. Ishmael grew up in the wilderness under God's protection and became the first Arab. (The story is sometimes used to explain the bad feeling between Jews and Arabs.) Ishmael is a symbol of the outcast, because of the line in the Bible that reads: "And he will be a wild man; his hand will be against every man, and every man's hand against him." Melville gave the name Ishmael to the narrator of *Moby Dick*, the philosophical schoolmaster who took to the sea every time he soured on the world. Captain Ahab, by the way, also comes directly from the Old Testament: He was Jezebel's husband, a king who succumbed to idol worship.

JOB: The most put-upon person in the world; a healthy, happy, prosperous, and godly fellow who, for no apparent reason, suddenly has his family and his possessions wiped out and is himself covered with boils. His wife advises him to "curse God and die," and his friends sit around with him all day urging him to repent for his sins, assuming that he must have done something wrong to bring all this misery down on himself. (The expression "Job's comforters" refers to the kind of friends who, when times are bad, manage to make them worse.) Job never gives in, however; his point is that God doesn't always have to make sense to us, that He doesn't always punish evil and reward righteousness but can do whatever He wants. God, in the end, decides that Job has passed the test and rewards him handsomely. Writers from Dostoevsky to O'Neill have wrestled with the theme of Job's suffering, and Archibald MacLeish retold the story in modern terms in his play *J.B.*

SUSANNA: The heroine of a famous courtroom drama reported in the Old Testament Apocrypha. A beautiful and virtuous young married woman, she is accused of adultery by two lecherous elders whose advances she's spurned. They claim to have seen her with a young man while she was bathing. She is just about to be found guilty and stoned to death, when young Daniel comes to her rescue. Asking to be allowed to cross-examine the elders, he proceeds to demolish their testimony, Perry Mason–style. Justice wins out; Susanna is saved and the elders are stoned. The story was a favorite subject of Renaissance painters, who usually chose to depict the part of the story that takes place in the bath, since that allowed them to produce a religious work and paint a gorgeous nude model at the same time. Susanna reappears as a figure in Wallace Stevens's poem "Peter Quince at the Clavier."

MARY MAGDALEN: An elusive figure, one of several Marys who were devoted to Jesus. She is known to have been possessed by "seven demons," which Jesus exorcised, and to have been present when He was crucified, when He was buried, and again when His tomb was found empty. Beyond that, her story is a series of mixups. She may or may not have been the sister of Martha, and she probably wasn't really a harlot; the latter slander came from the fact that she took her name from Magdala, her home town, which was a seaport with a bad reputation. She may have washed Jesus's feet, but then again, it may have been another Mary who did that. At any rate, she became a saint and a symbol of repentance, and she gave us the word "maudlin," which means "tearful," and the French "Madeleine," the name and the cookie. In paintings, she's usually the one with the red hair.

FOUR PAIRS OF GROUPS WHO KEEP STEPPING ON EACH OTHER'S TOES

Not everybody was alone with his problems, his family, or his God in the Holy Land. The following preferred to travel in packs—packs that, like Democrats and Republicans or Oreo and Hydrox, were not always immediately distinguishable from each other.

APOSTLES AND DISCIPLES: There were twelve of each, but not quite the same twelve. While Judas is always counted as a disciple, he didn't, according to the best sources, make the apostles roster, where he was replaced by some-

"The Sacrament of the Last Supper" by Salvador Dali.

body called Matthias. Strictly speaking, the disciples were *students* of Christ (from the Latin word for "pupil"), the apostles His *envoys* (from the Greek for "send away"). Paul is often added to the list of primary apostles, and Judas sometimes retained, swelling the group to fourteen. Also, the principal missionary to a country is sometimes designated its apostle: St. Patrick is the apostle of Ireland.

SERAPHIM AND CHERUBIM: First of all, they're not those plump babies you see in Renaissance paintings. In the Old Testament, a cherub had anywhere from one to four faces and either one or two pairs of wings, and was closer to a beautiful young man than to a toddler; God sat among or just above the

A pair of seraphim, one with head, one without—and each with a full complement of wings.

cherubim. A seraph, by contrast, had three pairs of wings, hovered over the throne of God, had a reputation for zeal and ardor, and was the very highest-ranking of the nine "choirs" of angels. (Or, as Isaiah once remarked, "I saw the Lord seated on a throne. . . . About him were attendant seraphim, and each had six wings; one pair covered his face and one pair his feet, and one pair was spread in flight.") In art, seraphim are most often red-toned and may carry a candle; cherubim, the second highest-ranking, tend to be blue and sometimes have books. Both are depicted as mere heads, surrounded by the appropriate number of wings. For the record, the nine grades of angel, divided into three hierarchies, are, from highest to lowest: seraphim, cherubim, and thrones, all of which surround God in perpetual adoration; dominions, virtues, and powers, which together govern the stars and elements; principalities, which protect the kingdoms of the earth, and archangels and angels, which carry messages. Angelology, surprisingly, was a fairly exact science.

PHARISEES AND SADDUCEES: The two great Jewish religious sects and political parties. As far as Jesus was concerned, both were bad news: literal-minded, cold, and hypocritical. But the Pharisees, even if they did think they were holier than everybody else, were at least recognizable fellow human beings. The intensely nationalistic majority sect, they were interested in getting their message to the people and determined to pay as much attention to the Oral Law as to the Written one, which meant they campaigned for the ideas of an afterlife, resurrection, Day of Judgment, and Messiah. The Sadducees believed in none of the above, or for that matter in angels: They accepted only the Hebrew Scriptures, rejecting all oral tradition, elaborate though it had gotten to be. They were mostly upper-class types, supplemented by priests, they were much stricter than the Pharisees (who were themselves ten times as bad as your least favorite grade-school teacher), and they weren't very popular, even when marked on a curve. (It didn't help that, not believing in any future punishments in heaven, they doled out harsh legal ones on earth.) The strife between the Pharisees and Sadducees ended in Roman intervention and domination, but at least the Pharisees made it into the second century A.D.; their ideas underlie many aspects of Orthodox Judaism today. Figuratively, of course, a pharisee is a self-righteous hypocrite. There is no such thing as a lowercase Sadducee, a reflection of the fact that they were the minority party, that they'd died out by A.D. 70 (the year the Romans destroyed Jerusalem), and that they left nothing of particular interest, philosophically or stylistically, to either Jew or Christian.

ASSYRIANS AND BABYLONIANS: The bad guys (Mesopotamian division), each of whom was responsible for one especially traumatic dislocation of the Jews. The Assyrians (who predominated during the eighth and seventh centuries B.C., who lived in the mountainous north of the Tigris-Euphrates river valley, whose capital was Nineveh, and who did all those bas-reliefs of winged beasts and heavily bearded humans) were militaristic and wanted nothing more than to fight all day, every day. Their most telling blow against the Jews was the taking captive, in 722 B.C., of the ten northern tribes of Israel, whom they then proceeded to scatter over the Assyrian desert. These so-called Lost Tribes have subsequently been identified with the peoples of Ethiopia, Latin

America, and Afghanistan, not to mention high-caste Hindus and Japanese, the Indians of the Eastern Seaboard, and, most endearingly, the English. Major Assyrian kings: Sargon, Sennacherib, and Assurbanipal. The Assyrians were eventually defeated by an alliance of Persians and Babylonians (see below). You can read about them in 2 Kings 16–19.

The Babylonians (who predominated during the sixth century B.C., who lived on the fertile plain in the south of the Tigris-Euphrates valley, whose capital was Babylon, who are sometimes referred to as the New Babylonians— or even the Chaldeans—to distinguish them from a much earlier Babylonian civilization under Hammurabi and who built the Hanging Gardens), were fighters, too, but they were also fatalists and sensualists, which in the end did them in. Their most devastating move against the Jews is called the Babylonian Captivity (or the first Diaspora), and involved the two tribes of Judah, just south of Israel, tens of thousands of whom were forced into exile in and around Babylon in 586 B.C. The Babylonian king par excellence: Nebuchadnezzar. His son was defeated by the Persians. You can read about the Babylonians in 2 Kings 20–25, and in Daniel (where Shadrach, Meshach, and Abednego are thrown into the fiery furnace, where Daniel is thrown into the lions' den, where the handwriting shows up on the wall, and where Nebuchadnezzar goes temporarily insane and eats grass, "like oxen").

Seven People Not to Bother Sharing Your Old God-Spelled-Backwards Insight With

FIVE ARE GERMANIC PROTESTANTS WHO WON'T THINK IT'S FUNNY, ONE'S AN AUSTRIAN JEW WHO'S ALREADY BEEN STRUCK BY IT HIMSELF, AND ONE'S A FRENCH CATHOLIC WHO MIGHT JUST TRY TO GET YOU TO PUBLISH YOUR FINDINGS

And they're all theologians, engaged in an ages-old attempt to talk rationally about the Word, the Way, and the Messiah, while, like the rest of us, keeping an eye on things down at city hall and out in the 'burbs.

KARL BARTH
(Swiss, Calvinist, 1886–1968)

Not a whole lot of fun. For starters, he'd had it with the liberal Protestant theology of the preceding century, an I'm-OK-Thou-Art-OK affair that put man and God on roughly the same footing and that burbled a lot about human progress. God, said Barth, is not only totally divine, totally supreme, and totally transcendent (i.e., nothing like the rest of us), He's also totally unknowable except through His revelations, the times and places for which, by the way, He chooses all by Himself. So forget worrying about how you should "talk with God": It's not even an option. Concentrate instead on your own sinfulness, because that—not the goodness and dignity the liberals so liked to emphasize—is man's true nature. You can call all of the above "neo-orthodoxy." Or you can call it "crisis theology," Barth's catchphrase for how faith derives not from front-pew smugness but from front-line peril, in this century specifically from the dislocations and devastations of two world wars. But you'd be smart to let it go at that. The alternative—attempting to dip into Barth's *Church Dogmatics*, twelve volumes' worth of the bottom line on revelation, creation, reconciliation, redemption, and the like—is, as reading experiences go, the equivalent of chewing a mouthful of bubble gum studded with broken glass.

PAUL TILLICH
(German Emigrant to U.S., Lutheran, 1886–1965)

Thoroughly modern and more or less human. Tillich viewed theology as a perfectly natural, perfectly personal endeavor, with a built-in man-asks-God-answers format. In many ways the opposite number of Barth, who saw God as wholly-other and transcendent, way out there (and not at home anyway), Tillich sees Him as, if maybe still way out there, at least willing and able to make the trip in from time to time. God has presence, not just existence; in fact, He's both the source and the goal of everything, the "Ground of Being" in Tillich's famous phrase, and religion is the "sacred depth," the unifying center of every aspect of life. Drawing on then-trendy existentialism and psychoanalysis as well as on philosophy and theology proper, Tillich attempted to redress Barth's obsession with the "revelatory" pole of Scripture and tradition by dancing round and round the "situational" one of what this century has dealt us. As a result, his work—most notably the three-volumed *Systematic Theology* and the chattier, slightly autobiographical *The Boundaries of Our Being*—is full of discussions of culture, society, ethics, and current events. Keep awake especially for raps on Christian socialism and something called theonomy, through which Tillich hoped we could all unite our own beings with the Ground of Being, and in so doing resolve the conflict between the individual and the state. Not that human truth is ultimate—just that the human condition is worth addressing oneself to.

RUDOLF BULTMANN
(German, Lutheran, 1884–1976)

The debunker. Specifically, the man who set out to "demythologize" the New Testament, stripping it of the myths that second- and third-generation Christians had encrusted it with back when Jesus's death was still news and nobody wasn't privy to at least one first-hand account of the Resurrection. Insisting that there was no point in continuing the nineteenth century's search for a "historical" Jesus, yet understandably reluctant to throw the baby (that would be Christ's, and Christianity's, essential "message") out with the bath water, Bultmann turned to a succession of techniques to get the worshiper-friendly effects he wanted. Among them: form criticism, a Biblical-research style that asks why a specific Gospel narrator would choose to relate a miracle when he could equally well have thrown in a parable or a bit of scenic description; hermeneutics, a way of interpretatively updating a text—like the New Testament—so that it bears on and reads for a whole new tribe or generation; and, like Tillich, Christian existentialism, the midcentury movement committed to reassessing religious doctrines and traditions in terms of sheer human interest. A reasonable enough program, you say? Not to Bultmann's critics, who argued that it cut into not only the box-office appeal of Jesus but the big-daddy authority of God.

REINHOLD NIEBUHR
(American, Evangelical, 1892–1971)

Not easy to pigeonhole: A theologian who was able to make the connection between sin and politics and an activist who thought history had more to do with irony than with progress. A pragmatist, certainly, and a Midwesterner, the bulk of whose career was, nevertheless, spent teaching Applied Christianity at Union Theological Seminary in New York City. Also, an aphorist of sorts: The so-called "Serenity Prayer"—"God, give us grace to accept with serenity the things that cannot be changed, courage to change the things . . ."—is vintage Niebuhr. Nor is it any easier trying to slot the man according to what he opposed: the Babbittry underlying American business life and the American dream; the naïveté of liberal Protestants who thought improving society really brought the Kingdom of God any closer; the emphasis that Barth put on the supernatural; the emphasis that Tillich put on the here-and-now; anybody who thought grace was for Christians only; totalitarianism; unthinking pacifism;

pride; and complacency, to name just a few. It's not *wrong* to think of him as a "Christian socialist," manning the sociopolitical barricades, meeting power with power, seeing that justice is done, but you should keep in mind that the neoconservatives also claim him as a role model. Anyway, he was a second-generation American (and not all that heavy-duty a theoretician), and he believed that sin is basically a misuse of human freedom; that "values" and "judgments" have to be understood in terms of a person's circumstances (Niebuhr is the father of "contextual ethics"); and that while you have a responsibility to fight for what's right you don't always count on winning.

DIETRICH BONHOEFFER
(German, Lutheran, 1906–1945)

The martyr. Hanged by the Nazis (but not before he'd smuggled enough letters out of his prison cell to flesh out what would become a transatlantic bestseller), Bonhoeffer knew all about horror, repression, outrage, and the deft turn-of-phrase. It was "cheap grace," an early effort, that first aroused attention; it characterized "comfortable" Christianity, the kind that costs its followers little or nothing in the way of abnegation, hardship, or lack of popularity, and was opposed to the genuine (and expensive) grace that active, exclusive discipleship under Christ entails. Bonhoeffer would later plead for a secular, "religionless" Christianity, directed towards "man come of age," with an emphasis on this world rather than the next, freedom instead of obedience, and "behavior not belief." Such an approach to religion (a word he didn't much go for, by the way) would appeal to men not where they were weak but where they were strong and in "the marketplace of life" rather than "outside its city limits." (The last turn-of-phrase is ours, but we think he'd—and maybe He'd—approve.) Not such good ideas, per Bonhoeffer: metaphysics, in which men speculate after God in the interstices of scientific knowledge; psychotherapeutic and existentialist approaches to Christianity; and too much "inwardness," whether on the mystical or the merely pietistic model. All things considered, and despite his premature death, Bonhoeffer's probably had a bigger (and a more international) response than any other modern theologian: Not only are there file cabinets full of "Bonhoeffer Literature" consisting mainly of readers' correspondence, with a few scholarly tracts and cult items thrown in, there's also a Bonhoeffer Society that holds regular congresses and keeps those cards and letters coming.

MARTIN BUBER
(Austrian, Jewish, 1878–1965)

This century's most important Jewish religious thinker—for the record, "theologian" is pretty much a Christian label—at least among Protestants and Catholics. (Jews had problems with his iron-out-the-differences, Arab-Israeli-cohabitation approach to Zionism; his Hasidic taleteller persona and all that quaint straight-from-the-Cabala lore; not to mention the fact that the Christians seemed to like him so much.) The best-known Buber bequest: The "I-Thou" relationship, which can only be undertaken with "the whole being" and "in total openness to the other"; which is opposed to the obviously less desirable "I-It" relationship; and which is how we're meant to get along not only with each other but with God—for Buber not an object of belief, but the subject, the "Eternal Thou." In fact, because, as he saw it, each little daily I-Thou moment, even the shopping mall ones, had Eternal Thou reverberations (how we behave to each other is how we're behaving towards God) don't be surprised when Buber filibusters about interpersonal relations, public life, politics, community versus society, and life on the kibbutz, all at least as intricately bound up with religion as going to temple ever was. Be prepared, too, for a lot of existentialist imagery: the walk on "the narrow ridge," modern man "at the edge," and a bundle of "abysses," including those between Israel and the Arabs, Jews and Christians, friendship and alienation. Not the scholar's scholar, exactly, but Buber is hands-down the person's person.

PIERRE TEILHARD DE CHARDIN
(French, Catholic, 1881–1955)

Out there—a doer as much as a thinker, and a mystic into the bargain. Trained not only in theology but in paleontology, Teilhard had been in on the discovery of Peking man, then got himself into trouble when he tried to make sense of the find. From most people's point of view, it's hard to see what anyone could dislike about the idea that science and religion aren't irreconcilable; and the notion that human evolution never stopped, just moved indoors, seems like simple common sense. The Catholic Church, though, had other ideas: Teilhard was enjoined from publicizing, in his lifetime, his theory of cosmic evolution—in which, according to him, man has come to have a guiding hand—and his conviction that belief in same does not entail a rejection of Christianity. (He was also packed off to Africa.) Still, nobody can deny that, at least posthumously, Teilhard got off a few good ones, most notably in *The Phenomenon of Man;* among them were the terms "noösphere" (the realm or domain in which the mind does it all, modeled on—and destined to supplant—mere biosphere) and "Omega point" (variously interpreted as the integration of all personal consciousness and as the second coming of Christ). Anyway, turns out you weren't the only one who wondered how come, if all the birds and animals already existed in the Garden of Eden, there could also be dinosaur tracks up the road.

science

Contents

Miss Helen Richman of Chicago Illinois, shows models of the crystal formations of four substances as they would appear under a high-powered microscope.

Out of the Cyclotron,
Into the Streets

Some scientific terms yearn for a notoriety greater than the university community or the industrial complex can provide. Bored with having a precise, agreed-upon meaning known only to a few white-coated old lab technicians, they set their caps at becoming indispensable to Woody Allen and Barbara Walters. They may lose a little of their cogency in the process, but they sure do get around.

Catalyst

"You know," Jerry Rubin once told a reporter from *New York* magazine who was doing a piece on his "networking salons," "Abbie used to call me the catalyst when we were at the Chicago 7 trial. I guess that's what I am." Well, up to a point. In chemistry, a catalyst has to satisfy two separate requirements. The first is that it promote, enhance, or speed up a chemical reaction. This it does by combining, on the molecular level, with each of the active ingredients involved, bringing them into certain contact with each other, rather than waiting for their chance collision. The second requirement is that, though it furthers a reaction, it remain itself unchanged, unspent, and unaccounted for afterwards. (Enzymes, those protein molecules that figure in the chemical reactions of living organisms, meet both these requirements and are hence the body's catalysts.) Now, while Jerry Rubin may be adept at bringing people together and while he may make things move faster than they otherwise would, he's hardly the retiring, self-effacing, or even particularly consistent type. In short, he's more reactant than catalyst. And that goes double for Henry Kissinger.

Centrifugal force

The "center-fleeing" tendency that comes over a ball when it's being spun at the end of a string, a liquid like blood or milk when it's undergoing separation in a centrifuge, or you when you're taking a curve in a car that's going too fast. Essentially, the effect is one of being pulled away from the center of a specific orbit, to a degree based on the mass of the object in question, the speed at which it's traveling, and the radius of its path. It is the complement of centripetal, or "center-seeking," force, which can be gravitational, mechanical, or electrical in nature, and which is what keeps the ball, the blood, the milk, and you from being somewhere over the Atlantic Ocean by now. Both terms pop up all over the place: A historian, for instance, might tell you that Thomas Jefferson's sympathies lay with the centrifugal, not the centripetal, forces of the new nation—with rural life, farming, and the decentralization of powers rather than with urban life, manufacturing, and the centralization of them.

Clone

No need to panic. Coined by a horticulturist in 1903, "clone" simply describes a genetic copy of an individual organism, arrived at by a style of asexual reproduction in which the nucleus of a cell from the body of the single parent is stimulated to start dividing all by itself. Strawberries naturally send out clones to take root at a distance from the parent plant; gardeners routinely help other specimens along by cutting, grafting, and budding them. Cloning became a big deal when biologists made a whole new frog from the DNA in the nucleus of an intestinal epithelial cell of an old one. Given the extreme difficulty of manipulating mammalian eggs without damaging them (along with the obviously knotty ethical issues involved), it's unlikely that any human clones will soon join the ranks of the strawberries and the frogs—and the bacteria, cauliflower, roses, mice, and zebra fish. Not that you won't go on hearing the word used to evoke fear (of, say, the mad dictator who clones an army of himselves) or, more frequently, simple contempt (as for brigades of yuppies in Reeboks and pearls).

Fission *and* Fusion

They're both nuclear reactions (i.e., they change the structure of an atomic nucleus) and they both represent what happens when Einstein's famous $E = mc^2$ is acted out. In fission, which is behind atomic bombs, nuclear reactors, and radioactivity, the nucleus of a big uranium atom is split into smaller parts when struck by a free neutron. Uranium is the fuel of choice because it "splinters" readily, releasing two or three more neutrons, which in turn strike and splinter neighboring uranium nuclei in a chain reaction. The result: energy; also, Chernobyl.

In fusion, which is behind starlight, sunshine, and the hydrogen (a.k.a. thermonuclear) bomb, and which scientists hope someday to adapt to nuclear energy production, the nuclei of two little hydrogen atoms are joined together, or fused, at temperatures approaching 50,000,000°C, to form a single, heavy helium nucleus, ejecting high-speed neutrons in the process. In both fission and fusion, the atoms resulting from the splitting and the joining, respectively, weigh slightly less than the ones that went into the process. It's this difference in mass that has been converted into the energy.

So why not forget dangerous, dirty fission and get behind controllable, clean fusion? Because fusion, while it works nicely on the sun, requires temperatures higher than we've been able to achieve here on earth except, so far, in the hydrogen bomb, which is triggered by fission (in the form of an atomic bomb) at its core anyway. Still, given that fusion, once perfected, could churn out energy equivalent to 300 gallons of gasoline from a gallon of sea water, you can expect the scientists to stay on the case. In the meantime, bear in mind that fusion is both more natural and more powerful than fission, packing the kind of wallop and carrying with it the degree of conviction that, in ward politics as in the lab, results from putting things together, not tearing them apart.

Half-life

The fixed, invariable amount of time it takes half of an original sample of a radioactive substance like uranium, radium, or carbon-14, to break down, decay, fall to pieces—which all such substances do, nucleus by nucleus. Although scientists can never tell which specific nucleus is going to end it all next, they are surprisingly exact when it comes to predicting the overall rate of change. (It's a little like demographers noting that Buffalo or Detroit is losing population at such-and-such a rate without being able to say which family is going to leave town next.) For instance, the half-life of Uranium 238 is 4.5 billion years, which means that at the end of that time a pound of the stuff will have dwindled to half a pound; after another 4.5 billion years, to a quarter of a pound; after yet another 4.5 billion years, to an eighth of a pound, and so on. Useful to geologists in determining the age of rock specimens (and, by extension, of the planet), half-life also has popular applications: Girls with streaked blonde hair may speak of the half-life of meaningful relationships in their crowd.

Mass

Forget about weight. Forget about volume. Mass—which physicists define as the quantity of matter in a body—is the adult way of coming to grips with the question "How big?" (Weight is simply the measure of the force of gravity acting on that body and, unlike mass, tends to vary, sometimes inconveniently, from place to place. As for volume, some make do without: Electrons, for instance, have mass and no volume at all.) Of course, mass and energy have been shown—by Einstein, in his formula $E = mc^2$ (see page 483)—to be roughly the same thing. Which brings us to the dog-eared phrase "critical mass": In a nuclear chain reaction it's the minimum quantity of fissionable material (see above) necessary to keep those neutrons popping and those nuclei alert. In *Business Week*, by analogy, it's the minimum level of potency or density you have to be at if you're really going to perform. Thus marketing types might pinpoint a magazine's critical mass at the moment its circulation becomes large enough to attract national advertisers.

Matrix

It was at one of Jerry Rubin's salons that a woman from Metromedia said, "I delight in networking and matrixing. I'm not here to meet men." Although only a fool would claim to know exactly what she meant, we *can* fill you in on "matrices" (note plural). From a Latin word that meant first "pregnant animal" and later "womb," a matrix is the place where something is generated, contained, and/or developed. The word is used of, among other things, the rock that a fossil or gemstone is found embedded in; the band of formative cells in your nails and teeth; an industrial mold; and, in mathematics, a rectangular array of elements, for example,

$$\begin{matrix} 2 & 4 & 11 \\ 5 & 5 & -3, \end{matrix}$$

where those elements are shorthand for some larger picture (they may, for instance, be the coefficients in a pair of linear equations that are meant to be considered together), and where they are less significant taken one by one than as a composite. In time, computer types picked up on the word, too, applying it to the point at which input and output leads intersect. That Metromedia woman: Apparently she preferred the potentially fruitful exchange of information or ideas to the potentially fruitless one-night stand.

Osmosis

When fluid passes through a membrane from one side, where there's a lower concentration of a particular particle, to the other, where there's a higher concentration of the same particle, that's osmosis. Essentially, it's an attempt to reach equilibrium, which biological systems, not unlike yourself, find to be a highly desirable state; in this case, equilibrium will ensure the identical number of particles per cubic whatever of fluid on both sides of that semi-permeable (but selective) membrane without any of the particles having to move a muscle. "Learning by osmosis" is likewise automatic, imperceptible, effortless.

Parameter

In mathematics—economics, too—a quantity that varies with the conditions under which it recurs, but that is, for the time being and within the context of the current problem, both constant and knowable. In life, a parameter is the measuring stick we have at hand, whose own length isn't exactly set (it may be a yardstick today and a foot-rule tomorrow) but which nevertheless helps us define, estimate, or describe the totally unknown quantity in the next room. Take the queuing consultant called in by the Museum of Modern Art to help with "flow" during a Picasso retrospective. "Using parametric analysis of the number of people per painting and square feet per person," he explained, "I advised the museum on queuing line layouts and admissions-per-hour." A good use of the word: The parameters here were the existing estimates of how many people could, at a major museum exhibit, look at a painting at the same time and how much space they needed to do it; those guidelines, however, were understood to be subject to change (the mark of a good parameter), depending on canvas size, hanging technique, desirability of standing close to or away from the work, intrinsic interest of a particular painting or roomful of them, etc. Not everybody does so well with the word, however: Press secretaries, for instance, tend to speak of the "parameters" of a problem when all they mean is that problem's distinguishing features. And even careful speakers use it as a substitute for "outer limit," when the word they really want may be "perimeter."

Quantum

Originally, anything that could be counted or measured (from a Latin word meaning "how much"). In physics, quanta—the plural form—came to refer to the discontinuous series of little packets in which light sometimes travels. Quantum theory, which dates from 1900, when Max Planck (see page 527) proposed it as a way of accounting for the emission of light by a body so hot that it's luminous (a poker thrust into a fire, for instance) and which underlies quantum mechanics (see page 490), was in complete contradiction to the then-prevailing wave theory of light. Later, both theories, like the Certs twins, would prove to be right, neither alone sufficing to explain light, which sometimes travels in waves (like a river) and sometimes travels in quanta (like raindrops), but never does both at the same time. As for the phrase "quantum leap," it's an abrupt, usually unpredictable change or step—as with an electron's sudden transition from one fixed orbit to another as it circles an atom's nucleus—but it's not necessarily an enormous one. Properly, a quantum leap (or jump) in, say, the number of terrorist incidents is not about size but suddenness.

Quark

Of the several hundred subatomic particles out of which physicists tell us all matter is made, the quark is the most evasive, the most piquing, and the most basic—so small as to have no size, so simple as to have no internal structure. Of course, nobody's managed to shake a quark loose for closer inspection (the most they've been able to do is hit a few over the head with beams of electrons), but that hasn't stopped scientists from insisting that quarks, like black girl groups of the Sixties, usually travel in threes and carry electrical charges that are multiples of $\frac{1}{3}$; from attributing to them properties they call "color" and "flavor"; from giving them such first names as "up," "down," "strange," "charm," "bottom," and "top"; or from positing the existence of mirror-image, or anti- , quarks. Quarks bond with other quarks in such standard combinations as protons (two up quarks and a down quark), neutrons (two down quarks and an up quark), pi mesons, mesons, baryons, kaons, and so on(s)—all the other subatomic particles, in fact, except leptons (a category that includes electrons, muons, and neutrinos), which are themselves so "elementary" as not to be able to be further broken down. Despite the whimsicality (the word itself is borrowed from a song in Joyce's *Finnegans Wake*, "Three quarks for Muster Mark," where it may refer to the squawking of birds, their excrement, or both), quarks pack a mean intellectual wallop. They imply that nature is three-sided, and that such dualist constructions as time/space, mind/body, and either/or miss the point. Specks of infinity on the one hand, building blocks of the universe on the other, quarks represent science at its most ambitious—also its coyest.

Symbiosis

The perfect relationship—assuming you're not all that interested in relating to whomever it is you've chosen to settle down with. Take, for instance, the case of the rhinoceros and the yellow tickbird. The tickbird dines on parasites infesting the rhinoceros's horny skin; the rhinoceros itches less and is warned of danger when the tickbird, sharp-eyed and skittish, abandons him for the nearest tree. Or there's the lichen, that exemplary union of alga, which brings home the bacon (it knows how to photosynthesize), and fungus, which keeps the house (it stores moisture the alga needs and scoops out the rock they're living on to make a bungalow).

In such classic instances of symbiosis ("life together"), both parties benefit but in very different ways, each compensating for the other's shortcomings, rather than duplicating his talents. Although it's tempting to appy the word to, say, the S & M relationship being worked out nightly in the apartment down the hall, you weaken its meaning when you do so. The sadist and the masochist complement each other, all right, but they're deriving too much the same benefit—sexual gratification—from their joint undertaking to qualify as a bona fide symbiosis, a label that should be saved for arrangements between partners with widely divergent priorities.

Synapse

It's the junction—a microscopic gap, actually—of two neighboring neurons, or nerve cells. And there are loads of them: An average neuron in the human brain has somewhere between 1,000 and 10,000 synapses with nearby neurons, some of which are responsible for thinking, some of which are responsible for moving, and some of which are, for better or for worse, simply blank. When a nerve impulse reaches the synapse, there to jump across to the adjacent nerve cell, it's given a nudge along by an electrically triggered squirt of a chemical. Some chemicals enhance, others inhibit; ditto painkillers, tranquilizers, and recreational drugs. The adjacent nerve cell reacts accordingly, either getting all excited itself and relaying the message to a muscle, a gland, or yet a third nerve cell, or giving it the cold shoulder. Caution when using the word: A synapse is properly a place, at most a transaction. It is not in itself a full-scale neural event, and it is even less a good synonym for what is portrayed in comic books as a little light bulb going off over somebody's head.

Synergy

Like Gestalt (see page 427), another the-whole-is-greater-than-the-sum-of-its-parts manifesto. But at least this one is backed up by lab reports and an etymology you can understand: the Greek *syn-* + *ergos,* "together working." At its most scientific, synergy refers, in biology, to the relationship between "agents" whose combined physiological clout outweighs the sum of their individual jabs; thus booze and barbiturates, ingested together, will knock you out faster and more totally than can be predicted by adding up what each of them does to you on its own. From biology, it's a short step to the boardroom, where executives decide that, by merging with the like-minded types across town, they can pull in a market share in excess of their two individual ones put together.

Valence

In chemistry, a measure of the combining power of a specific element, equal to the number of different chemical bonds one atom of that element can form at any given time. All atoms feel most secure when they have a complete outermost electron shell, and they'll go to great lengths to achieve one, borrowing elements from or sharing them with other atoms. For this reason neon, with an outer shell that's full-up at birth, is highly unreactive—so chemically aloof, in fact, that, along with helium and argon (among others), it's been dubbed one of the "noble gases." Carbon, by contrast, with an outer shell of eight electrons only half filled, is a born joiner and an unabashed swinger, almost always requiring more than a single relationship to feel safe and provided for. It's largely as a result of this capacity for interaction that you hear so much about carbon in chemistry circles. As for your valence, broadly speaking it's your capacity—and tendency—to interact with the others out there. Just remember, you don't *have* to go to bed with them.

Keeping Up With Cosmology

In the second century A.D., Ptolemy, a Greek working out of Alexandria, Egypt, codified all ancient astronomical beliefs and made a momentous pronouncement: The earth was the center of the universe, around which the sun, the planets, and the stars all revolved, and beyond the orbit of the most distant star lay the empyrean, the place where angels and immortal spirits dwelled. Rigorously mathematical and highly persuasive, the Ptolemaic system was accepted by virtually all educated Europeans until Copernicus's treatise *On the Revolution of the Heavenly Spheres* (published posthumously in 1543) broke the news that, far from nestling cozily at the center of things, it was the earth that was doing the revolving, a theory that was soon to be embroidered and enlarged upon by Tycho Brahe (see page 528), Kepler, Galileo, and Newton. Exit angels and immortal spirits. Enter uncertainty, relativity, quarks, leptons, gluons, the strong and weak forces, the Big Bang, and the search for our cosmic roots. Here, with an update: contributor James Trefil.

Since the late 1920s, we've known that other galaxies are moving away from our own. The obvious explanation for this is that the universe as a whole is expanding. Because every expansion has to start somewhere, it's also obvious that if we reverse the expansion and follow the galaxies backwards in time, to the tune of some 15 billion years, there will come a point at which all the matter in the universe is crammed into a very tiny space. The appearance of the universe from a single infinitely dense point of matter is what we call the Big Bang.

Astrophysicists tend to dislike obvious explanations like this, which is why, throughout the Fifties and Sixties, there were all sorts of theories that attempted to explain expansion without the Big Bang scenario. But new evidence came in, these alternate theories bit the dust, one by one, and today hardly anyone disputes the Big Bang.

The thing about the Big Bang as far as modern physics is concerned is that when the universe was younger, it must have been hotter. Compressing matter always makes it heat up (try touching the barrel of a tire pump after it's been used). Higher temperatures also mean that the building blocks of matter, such as atoms, move faster and collide more violently. Thus, when the universe was younger, its constituent parts were bumping into each other with much higher energy than they do in our own relatively frigid era.

When matter is subjected to high temperatures, two important things happen. First, it changes form. Heat an ice cube and you get water, heat the water and you get steam. If you heat a collection of atoms enough, the collision will become so violent that their electrons will be torn loose and you'll have a new form of matter—a collection of negatively charged electrons and positively charged nuclei. The sun is made up of this sort of matter.

The Ptolemaic concept of the universe.

A twentieth-century view of the solar system.

The second important temperature-induced change has to do with the creation of new particles via Einstein's famous formula, $E = mc^2$. The theory of relativity tells us that matter and energy are interchangeable—given enough of one, you can convert it into the other. Thus, when a bit of a uranium nucleus is converted into energy in a nuclear reactor, the end result is sufficient electrical current to run your house. Conversely, every day, in giant particle accelerators throughout the world protons and electrons are brought up to almost the speed of light and allowed to collide with a target. The result: The energy of the particle is converted into mass and new particles are created in the collision.

In this early, high-temperature universe, then, we expect two things to happen: Existing forms of matter will change form and exotic new forms of matter will be created from the available energy. But there's one other result we might also expect: that the fundamental forces—the way bits of matter interact with one another—will also change.

The Early Universe

One way of measuring the extent of our knowledge about the universe is to ask how close to the beginning we can get in our description of the events that formed it. In the 1920s, for example, we knew enough about atoms to get to within 500,000 years of creation. By the Fifties, the development of nuclear physics had allowed us to come within three minutes. Today, thanks to our understanding of elementary particles, we can get to within a fraction of a second—a fraction so small we need a different way of writing numbers to describe it. We can talk about time between 10^{-35} (that's a decimal point followed by thirty-four zeros and a one) and 10^{-43} (forty-two zeroes and a one) seconds after the Big Bang. In fact, only one hurdle remains before we get to the moment of creation itself.

The best way to picture the evolution of the universe is to think of a cloud of highly compressed steam. If you let it go, it will expand, cooling off as it does so. When it cools to 212°F it will condense into droplets of water. If it continues to expand and cool it will reach another critical temperature—32°F—at which point the water will freeze into ice. The same thing happened with the universe as would happen with the steam, except that the transitions that correspond to condensation and freezing are both more numerous and more complicated.

Although a few intrepid theorists have speculated on how the initial collection of matter that eventually became the universe came into existence, there is no firm scientific opinion on this subject; right now the question is simply beyond our knowledge. With regard to the first 10^{-43} seconds of the universe—the time elapsed before the first major "freezing"—we're in a little better shape. Although there is no generally accepted theory that describes matter at the temperatures that existed then, we can still make out some of its salient features. Most striking was a tremendous simplicity. Instead of the large number of basic particles we see in matter today, there was just one kind—the so-called superparticle. Instead of the four basic interactions (more on this later), there was only one way for matter to interact. Everything was as economical and as elegant as it could be. It's been downhill ever since.

At 10^{-43} seconds, the first "freezing" occurred. Two broad classes of particles appeared—one group similar to the electron, the other similar to the photon (the "particle" which makes up visible light); quarks (see page 479) first appeared at this time as well. The force of gravity became distinguishable from the other forces. During the period from this freezing down to 10^{-35} seconds, the universe may or may not have conformed to something called the grand unification theory (GUT). This theory, first developed in the mid-1970s, is being subjected to intensive experimentation right now. (More on it later, too.)

During freezings at 10^{-35} and 10^{-10} seconds, respectively, the universe became steadily more differentiated and more complex. At around 10^{-4} seconds (a tenth of a millisecond), the free quarks that had been roaming the universe condensed into the elementary particles that are the building blocks of matter as we know it. At three minutes, these elementary particles started to collect to form the nuclei of atoms. Finally, at 500,000 years, the final major transition occurred. The first electrons attached themselves to those nuclei to form simple atoms. In each of these cases, the transition to a new form of matter occurred as soon as the temperature had dropped to the point at which the interparticle collisions no longer had sufficient energy to disrupt the fragile new structure.

The 15 billion years that have elapsed since then have seen the formation of galaxies and stars and the development of life. During this period, all of the chemical elements heavier than helium, including the iron in your blood and the carbon in your DNA, were made, in stars that later died, returning their contents to the interstellar medium, where they were taken into the nascent solar system. Still, from the point of view of fundamental physics, all of the interesting events in the history of the universe were over by the time it was a few minutes old. In fact, it takes longer to describe what happened than it took the universe to undergo the actions described.

What Matter Is Made of

The best analogy for how we are coming to understand matter is the peeling of an onion. We peel off one layer and penetrate to a deeper one, only to discover that there is yet another to work on. The first layer was peeled off our onion in 1805, when British chemist John Dalton published the modern atomic theory of matter. He showed that the enormous variety of substances that surround us is made up of only a few different chemical elements, each of which has its own type of atom. In the early twentieth century the second layer was peeled off when the structure of the atom was revealed. All of the different kinds of atoms, it was argued, were made up of only three kinds of elementary particles—protons and neutrons in the nucleus and electrons orbiting the nucleus; this picture of the atom would become more or less standard. For a while, its inherent simplicity seemed to be clouded when it was found that there were not just two types of particles inside the nucleus, but hundreds. Most of these appeared and disappeared too quickly to be seen, but they could be produced independently in accelerators.

In the mid-1960s, yet another layer was peeled off. It was pointed out that the myriad elementary particles are actually made up of a small number of still more basic entities called quarks. Unlike the protons and neutrons that make up the nucleus, the quarks that make up the protons and neutrons cannot be seen as free particles. The grand unification theories postulate that once the quarks condensed into particles, 10^{-4} seconds after the Big Bang, they were forever confined in their new homes. It's a good thing the theories make this prediction, because no one has yet produced an experimental result which is universally accepted as evidence for the discovery of a "free" quark.

The Fundamental Forces

Physics is the study of matter and motion. Thus the quest for the fundamental building blocks of matter that led to the quarks is only half the picture. The other half has to do with the way that matter in all stages behaves, i.e., interacts with itself. Up until the beginning of this century, physicists had been able to find only two fundamental forces in nature—the force of gravity and the force associated with electricity and magnetism. In this century, studies of the nuclear and subnuclear world have produced two more fundamental forces, neither of which is part of our everyday experience. One of these, the strong force, is what holds all the elementary particles together in a nucleus. The other, the weak force, operates in many situations in nature, the most familiar being the slow radioactive decay of some unstable nuclei and particles. These four forces are a varied lot. Some, like electromagnetism and gravity, act over long distances. Others, like the two nuclear forces, act only over distances about the width of a nucleus or less. They also differ markedly in strength, with the strong being the strongest, followed by the electromagnetic, weak, and gravitational forces.

Despite these apparent differences among the forces, the great advances in physics over the last decade and a half have been made by theorists who believe that the differences are only apparent, and that the forces are actually *identical*. There are important historical precedents for this view. Isaac Newton gave us the first in the seventeenth century, when he showed that the same force which, in your backyard, causes an apple to fall to the ground also holds the moon and planets in their orbits. In so doing, he reversed two millennia of Western thought, during which scientists had seen no resemblance between earthly and celestial gravity. Yet Newton's Theory of Universal Gravitation, which attributes the motions of both planets and apples to a mutual attraction that exists between all objects possessing mass, says that despite apparent differences, the two forces are, at bottom, the same. We say that Newton unified the two forces of gravity and, because of the term "gravitational field," we say that Newtonian gravity is an example of a "unified field theory."

In 1968, Steven Weinberg (then at MIT) took an important step toward the unification of the forces when he theorized that the weak and electrical forces were unified (i.e., essentially identical), and that apparent differences between them were due more to the present low temperature of the universe than to anything fundamental to their natures. The result was a reduction in the number of basic interactions in nature from four to three. Since 1968, enough predictions of this particular unified theory have been confirmed that it is now accepted by everyone.

The new idea which made this particular advance possible is called the gauge principle. In essence, this principle states that the correct theory of nature must be one in which it is not significant if different observers come up with different definitions of things that can be defined arbitrarily. For example, the principle suggests that the correct theory of gravity is one in which the amount of energy you expend getting to the top of a cliff is the same whether you go straight up its side or take a more gradual, winding path. Theories like that of the electro-weak interaction, which incorporates the gauge principle, are said to be gauge theories.

Gauge theories and unification go hand in hand, and, once Weinberg had shown the way, a further unification was not long in coming. The grand unification theory mentioned above is the latest. In the GUT, the strong, electromagnetic, and weak forces are all considered to be fundamentally the same. In addition to allowing us to retrace the history of the early universe, the GUT makes a number of important predictions that are being tested right now. The most startling is the statement that the proton, hitherto thought to be the absolutely stable building block of nuclei, actually decays (although over a very long time period). Major experimental efforts now underway to detect such an elusive decay are an important test of the grand unification theory.

Gravity: Odd Man Out

Given this history, it would seem that the next step is obvious. All we have to do is use the same techniques to bring gravity into the fold and we'll have the ultimate theory, in which all forces of nature are brought together under the same roof. Such a theory would probably be called superunified, since the adjective "grand" is already spoken for.

Unfortunately, this is one of those easier-said-than-done things. Our current concept of gravity centers on Einstein's General Theory of Relativity, and the concept of force used in this theory is radically different from the concepts used to describe the other three forces. To understand the frontier problem in theoretical physics these days, then, we have to know something about relativity.

The first thing to realize is that there are actually two theories of relativity. The simplest, called the special theory, was published in 1905. It is not a theory of gravitation, but most of the other effects associated with relativity are incorporated into it. The equivalence of mass and energy, the twin paradox (which stated that a twin who went on a long space journey at high velocity would be much younger when he returned than his brother who stayed home), and the increase of mass with speed were all predicted by this theory. It is well verified experimentally; in fact, every time an accelerator delivers a burst of particles, every time a reactor produces a kilowatt of energy, the theory is verified anew.

The general theory was published in 1916. It is anomalous in science because it was accepted with only a few experimental tests, the most familiar being the bending of starlight as it passes the edge of the sun.

Both theories are based on a single principle, called, appropriately enough, the principle of relativity. It states that any two observers will discover the same laws of physics in action, regardless of their relative motion, no matter how different the picture may *look* to the two of them. The special theory is restricted in that the two observers can't be accelerating, whereas the general theory holds for any observers, accelerating or not. Since gravity produces acceleration, it can be treated only in the context of the general theory.

To grasp the picture of the gravitational interaction that arises we need another analogy. Imagine a rubber sheet held taut at the edges. (This is the image most often used to discuss Einstein's curved,

CHECKING IN WITH QUANTUM MECHANICS

Quantum mechanics is the name given to the theory, developed in the 1920s, which describes the behavior of matter on the atomic and subatomic level. It has been the subject of a spate of books and articles, each purporting to show that accepting quantum mechanics requires some basic change in our thinking about the world. Some authors tell us that we have to turn to Eastern mysticism because of it, others that it teaches that the presence of consciousness is required for the world to function. One writer has claimed that quantum mechanics demands the downfall of patriarchal societies.

There's no question that the world of the electron is different from our own. For starters, in our everyday experience, we're accustomed to being able to observe something without changing it. We can watch a bowling ball roll along, confident in the knowledge that the light beams bouncing off it and hitting our eyes won't deflect it from its path. In our everyday world, the possibility of continuous observation allows us to assume that the ball moves smoothly from one point to the next.

In the subatomic world, things are different. The only way to observe a particle is to bounce another particle off it, and this must necessarily disturb the original particle. It's as if the only way we could determine the position of a bowling ball was by bouncing another bowling ball off it. In which case, its smooth, continuous, predictable motion toward the pins could not take place.

In the subatomic world, the act of measurement changes the system being measured, giving rise to what is known as the Heisenberg Uncertainty Principle. The principle tells us that if we choose to measure one quantity (e.g., the position of an electron), we inevitably alter the system itself and therefore can't be certain about other quantities (e.g., how fast the electron is moving). Since an interaction is involved in every measurement, and since measurements are involved in observations, physicists sometimes say that the act of observation changes the system. This is a reasonable statement, provided you realize that it's the interaction of particles, not the conscious observer, that is important. Consciousness has nothing to do with quantum mechanics, although there are plenty of people who misinterpret the principle to suggest that it does.

That probing matter affects its form and behavior is only part of the weirdness inherent in quantum mechanics. Equally bizarre: that some particles exist so briefly that they are not real but "virtual," and that the universe as we know it is based on chance and randomness at the subatomic level.

four-dimensional space-time continuum.) If we drop a heavy weight on the sheet, the sheet will deform, developing a depression in the area of the weight. If we shoot a marble across the sheet, it could well become trapped in this depression, circling round and round the heavier weight. In general relativity, a large object (such as the earth) distorts the fabric of space and time in just the same way that the heavy weight distorts the sheet. Other objects (such as the moon) react to this distortion by going into orbit. The important point about this view of gravity is that it is purely geometrical—it does not involve any dynamic concept of force. It's this difference between gravity and the other fundamental forces that makes the development of a truly unified field theory so difficult.

There's one more thing to say about relativity. Not only does it *not* imply that "Everything is relative," in fact, the whole point is that, even though different observers may see events differently, there is still a firm and unchanging bedrock in nature—a bedrock made up of the laws of physics.

Riding Herd on the Life Sciences

They're a skittish lot, and ornery to boot, always fighting among themselves, wandering off into the chaparral, grazing near precipices, or popping up unexpectedly with a brood of wacky hybrid offspring in tow. Nobody warned you back in Biology 101 that once you took them on, you'd never be able to turn your back on them again for a minute. (Or that everything you'd learn about them would turn out to be wrong, or at least outdated, just when you needed it most.) Here contributor Judith Stone wrestles a few of bio-sci's meanest subjects to the ground, in an effort to restore some sense—possibly illusory and definitely fleeting—of mastery and control.

ALL IN THE FAMILY

"Descended from monkeys?" the Bishop of Worcester's wife is said to have cried after hearing about Darwin's startling new theory of evolution. "My dear, let us hope it isn't true! But if it is, let us pray it doesn't become widely known!"

Well, the skeleton's been out of the closet for 126 years now, and today anthropologists have a fairly clear, though unfinished, picture of the human family tree, based on fossil remains. Like all mammals, we ultimately trace our roots back to a tiny, shrewlike creature that inherited the earth after the dinosaurs disappeared abruptly and mysteriously 65 million years ago. As the shrew's progeny diversified, tree dwellers developed such dandy gimmicks as binocular vision, hands that could grasp, and brains efficient enough to handle all that swinging. This ape line seems to have forked between 10 and 4.5 million years ago; one group stayed apes, the other eventually became us.

About 15 million years ago, the planet's climate cooled; steamy forests gave way to grassy savannas. Those tree dwellers who came down for a look eventually became the family *hominidae,* of which our subspecies, *Homo sapiens sapiens,* is the only remaining member. A hominid family album would feature the venerable ancestors below, including the two most talked about celebrity fossils, a petite creature named Lucy, from 3.6 to 3.2 million years young, and a 1985 find, a skull about the same age, which obviously should have been nicknamed Ethel. The study of this pair may yield information that further alters our picture of human evolution. And keep in mind that scientists could any day discover bones that rewrite history; in fact, *Fredus flintstoniensis* may have turned up by the time you read this.

NAME: ***Ramapithecus*** (from Rama, the Indian god-hero, and *pithecus,* Greek for ape)
TIMEFRAME: Lived from 15 million to 8 million years ago.
VITAL STATS: Stood three feet high and weighed forty pounds; tiny brain. Remains found in Asia, Europe, and Africa.
COMMENTS: Probably the first hominid, but no one can be positive since we

have only teeth and jawbones to go by. These suggest that *Ramapithecus* could handle not only the soft fruits of the wet forests, but also the chewier snacks of the grasslands—evidence that it may have come down from the trees, semi-erect, to stroll and nosh. Note: Anthropologist David Pilbeam believes that *Ramapithecus* was an ancestor of neither humans nor apes, but a dead-end line. Watch this developing story. In any event, there's a several-million-year gap in the fossil record between *Ramapithecus* and its next relative.

NAME: ***Australopithecus afarensis*** (*Australo,* southern; Afar, a region in Ethiopia)
TIMEFRAME: Disputed—from 3.6 million to 2.9 million years ago.
VITAL STATS: Walked upright, had apelike jaw, fairly human body and brain of about 400 cubic centimeters; about four feet tall. Probably lived much like a chimp.
COMMENTS: In 1979, in Ethiopia, anthropologist Donald Johanson found a female skeleton he dubbed Lucy, after the Beatles' song "Lucy in the Sky With Diamonds." Her age, originally gauged at 3.6 million years, indicated that she was a new species whose bones seemed built for walking erect. Johanson believes her to be the ancestor, not only of later australopithecenes, who eventually died out, but of another branch of hominids which became humans. Anthropologist Richard Leakey thinks that common ancestor will prove to be an even older, as yet undiscovered species, a view that was given a boost when chemical analysis showed that Lucy was about 400,000 years or more younger than had at first been thought. If so, some scientists argue, then Lucy isn't a member of a previously unknown species, but a slightly pea-brained *Australopithecus africanus*.

NAME: ***Australopithecus africanus***
TIMEFRAME: Between 3 million and 1.3 million years ago.
VITAL STATS: Three to four feet tall, brain size about 600 cubic centimeters, indicating development of language and analytical skills.
COMMENTS: See below.

NAME: ***Australopithecus robustus***
TIMEFRAME: Slightly younger than *A. africanus*—or overlapping.
VITAL STATS: Larger and heavier-boned, at five feet, 130 pounds. Big grinding teeth and ridged skulls.
COMMENTS: Scientists have thought that *A. robustus*, descended from *A. africanus*, in turn gave rise to another rugged species, *A. bosei*. But the recent discovery in Kenya of the 2.5 million-year-old skull of an *A. bosei* (or someone very much like him), several hundred thousand years older than any other fossil of that species, suggests that *robustus* and *bosei* lived at the same time

and may even have been members of the same species, and that instead of descending from *africanus*, all three were contemporaries. Furthermore, the new *bosei* skull resembles those of larger examples of *A. afarensis*, chums of Lucy that Johanson found in a group of thirteen. They may actually have been members of different species. It's possible that *afarensis, bosei,* and all the other australopithecenes lived at the same time, overlapping instead of descending from each other in an orderly fashion. That would mean that Leakey is right, and we have to look beyond Lucy for an older relative who spawned both australopithecenes and us.

NAME: ***Homo habilis*** ("handy man")
TIMEFRAME: About 2 million years ago.
VITAL STATS: Four and a half feet tall, 64 to 100 pounds, brain weight about 750 cubic centimeters. Higher forehead indicates developed frontal and temporal lobes, and thus greater reasoning powers.
COMMENTS: Handy man was the first hominid routinely to use tools. So far, the first of the human line diverging from the australopithecenes for which we have fossil evidence.

NAME: ***Homo erectus*** ("erect man")
TIMEFRAME: From 1,500,000 to about 400,000 years ago.
VITAL STATS: Nearly our size, with smaller jaw and higher forehead than his forebears. Despite name, not the first to stand upright.
COMMENTS: Produced the first hand axes, and was the first to make use of fire and shelter—the rude beginnings of culture. Able to concentrate and to plan ahead.

NAME: ***Homo sapiens*** ("wise man")
TIMEFRAME: From about 400,000 to about 100,000 years ago.
VITAL STATS: Flatter faces, bigger brains (about 83 percent the size of ours); but still had bulging brow ridges.
COMMENTS: No miracle makeovers here; *H. erectus* segued slowly into *H. sapiens.* He cooked his food, made wooden tools, and may have launched language. (The word "sauté" did not appear for millions of years, however.)

NAME: ***Homo sapiens neanderthalensis*** (after the Neander Thal—or "valley"—of Germany, where they were first discovered)
TIMEFRAME: From about 150,000 to 40,000 years ago.
VITAL STATS: Not hunched brutes, as popularly believed; the first skeleton, found in 1856, just happened to be that of a big, arthritic specimen. Came in many varieties, from incredible-hulk types to those who might pass for modern people.

COMMENTS: Generally accepted as a subspecies of *H. sapiens*. Probably the first humans to conduct funerals, as evidenced by remains of flower pollen at a Neanderthal gravesite. The Neanderthals disappeared mysteriously about 35,000 years ago, to be replaced by the Cro-Magnons, a hipper subspecies of *H. sapiens* responsible for the celebrated cave paintings in Lascaux, France. Nobody knows whether the Neanderthals died out, were killed, or simply intermarried themselves into oblivion.

NAME: ***Homo sapiens sapiens*** ("wise, wise man")

TIMEFRAME: From about 40,000 years ago to today and perhaps even tomorrow.

VITAL STATS: Look in the mirror. Your brain probably logs in at about 1,350 cubic centimeters and you wouldn't kick yourself out of bed.

COMMENTS: Our subspecies, right or wrong. Its members were hunter-gatherers until relatively recently; they domesticated animals 18,000 years ago, invented agriculture 12,000 years ago, founded cities only about 5,000 years ago, and didn't invent the pet rock until the mid-twentieth century.

THE SPLICE OF LIFE

Genetic engineering is a process that inserts genes from one living organism into the cells of another, thereby custom-tailoring them to do work they weren't designed for. (But they still won't do windows.) For example, thanks to genetic engineering, or recombinant DNA technique, millions of bacteria are kept busy churning out precious human insulin. Scientists build the microfactories by slipping the human gene responsible for the creation of insulin into *E. coli*, a mild-mannered bacterium found in our digestive tract. So far, genetic engineering has been most successful with microorganisms and plants; science is still working on the problem of getting genetically altered DNA back into a human cell. Someday, however, we may be able to replace, remove, or repair bad genes, like the ones responsible for such diseases as cystic fibrosis, sickle cell anemia, and perhaps even cancer.

To understand how genetic engineering works, you've got to know about deoxyribonucleic acid, or DNA, three letters even more important than MSG or HBO. First, go back to the days when you were a swinging single cell—a fertilized egg whose nucleus contained forty-six particles called chromosomes, twenty-three from each parent, carrying the coded information for all your inherited characteristics, from hair color to disease susceptibility. As your cell divided, each new cell was issued forty-six identical chromosomes (except your reproductive cells, which, in anticipation of future mating, have only twenty-three apiece). The strandlike chromosomes are made up of several thousand genes, each responsible for a particular trait. And the genes are composed of DNA, the chemical that runs the show, controlling all life processes. All living things have DNA in every cell. (The exception: Some viruses contain only a chemical cousin of DNA called RNA.) Indeed, it has been said that if the instructions coded in one person's DNA were written out, they would fill 1,000 encyclopedia-sized volumes. You might want to wait for the movie.

In 1953, Francis Crick and James Watson earned a Nobel Prize for discovering that DNA is shaped like a spiral staircase, the famous double helix. Phosphates and sugars form the railing of the staircase, and pairs of four nitrogen bases in various combinations form the steps—up to about 3 billion of them in human DNA. The order of the base pairs determines the particular characteristics of any shrub, egret, or standup comic.

Dr. James Watson, left, and Dr. Francis Crick, with their Nobel-prize-winning model of the DNA molecule.

Twenty years after this discovery, two California researchers, Stanley Cohen and Herbert Boyer, found a way to perform DNA transplants. For example, to turn bacteria into human insulin factories, DNA is first removed from a human cell and cut with special enzymes at the spot where the needed gene is found. Then, using more enzymes, the human gene is snapped into a plasmid, a strand of extra DNA found in bacterium. When the bacterium reproduces, it creates millions of copies of itself, each with the new gene. In this way, scientists are producing human insulin, growth hormone, and interferon. They may someday be able to insert the cattle gene responsible for producing muscle protein into bacteria, a glob of which would taste like steak.

There's already controversy and intrigue in the world of genetically altered organisms. In 1985, such an organism was tested for the first time outside the lab—semiofficially. A vaccine made by genetically altering a herpes virus was injected into 250 piglets. The test may have launched a golden age of agriculture—or a regulatory nightmare. What if the gene-altered vaccine goes wild, mutates, affects humans?

Gene splicing is not to be confused with cloning, replacing the nucleus of a fertilized egg with the nucleus from any cell in the body of a donor (see page 475) which upon division results in a perfect genetic copy of that donor. And don't get genetic engineering mixed up with in-vitro fertilization, the creation of test-tube babies. In that case, the ovum (or several ova) are removed from the mother, fertilized in a petri dish by a sperm from the father, and returned to the mother's womb. The world's first test-tube baby, born in England in 1978, now has a test-tube sister. (The term is unfair; the kid spends only a couple of days in a dish, as an egg ⅟₂₅ of an inch in diameter.) There are now thousands of in vitro children in the world.

In a newer procedure, so-called prenatal adoption, a woman needn't produce her own eggs. The fertilized ova of another woman, who has been artifically inseminated with sperm from the first woman's mate, can be implanted in the womb of the infertile woman and carried to term.

Yet another technique allows the freezing of fertilized and unfertilized eggs for future use. A woman may someday have her ova easy—she could deposit a fertilized egg, to be reimplanted later, once she's launched her career or sown her wild oats. Or she could rent a womb, paying someone else to carry her child. But mightn't that lead to the creation of a class of drone-moms employed by women who want to buy their way out of morning sickness?

Ah, that's just one of the ethical problems of biotechnology, the blanket term for all this fiddling around with Life Itself. Other sticklers: What if the wrong people start tampering with characteristics, like physique, building a brave new world of superjocks and ultrawimps? What if a genetically engineered microbe escapes from the lab or the test area? There are still some bugs to be worked out.

GENE-POOL ETIQUETTE

When a man makes a pass at a woman, he's trying to get into her genes, according to the briefly trendy young science of sociobiology, wildly controversial in the early Eighties and a continuing annoyance to women and others like them. Its proponents suggest that social behavior, as much as any physical characteristic, is genetic.

Darwin sparked a revolution by insisting that humans descended from apes through the process of natural selection. That is, individuals with traits that suited them to the task of reproduction lived to pass on these traits; a species improved as genetic duds were weeded out (see page 519). Sociobiologists go one step further and declare that any human behavior—from altruism to infanticide, from aggression to philandering—evolved because it somehow allowed an individual to pass on more genes to the next generation. A human being, sociobiologists say, slapping their knees and winking broadly, is just a gene's way of making more genes.

The science was spawned about twenty years ago by entomologists studying female bees who sacrificed their lives to save the swarm. How, the researchers wondered, could such altruism be adaptive? Surely the behavior couldn't help species survival in the usual way, since kamikaze bees didn't live to pass on the trait to their children. But it turned out that female bees shared more genes with their sisters than with their own offspring. The ostensible altruism of the suicidal bees selfishly assured the survival of a higher percentage of their genes. The British biologist J. B. S. Haldane was once asked if he'd die to save his brother. No, he replied thoughtfully, but he'd give up his life for three brothers or nine cousins. In other words, an animal—insect or human— is genetically programmed to choose whatever behavior stands to propel the greatest number of its genes into the next generation.

The man who has done most to apply sociobiological theory to humans, E. O. Wilson of Harvard University, stresses that genes don't ordain, they predispose, and in the context of culture. While all cultures develop distinctive adornments, for example, there's no specific gene that triggers a desire for Cartier cufflinks.

Dubbed "so-so biology" by its critics, the science is easily abused. According to sociobiologists, if a behavior exists, it must be adaptive—a rationale that could be used to excuse racism, sexism, cruelty to animals, aerobic dancing, and other unsavory behaviors. For example, University of New Mexico sociobiologists have suggested that rape evolved as an adaptive strategy for male animals who couldn't compete for mates, and is thus an option programmed into male behavior.

That's not the only reason sociobiology makes feminists blanch. The bottom line, sociobiologically speaking, is to get your genes reproduced, for which men and women have evolved different strategies. Sperm is "cheap"; men produce billions in a lifetime. Eggs are "expensive"; women produce only about 400 in a lifetime and of those, no more than about 30 are likely to be fertilized. Women always know their children are theirs; men can't be sure. So it was to a prehistoric woman's advantage to be choosy, since a lot was at stake with each egg; she needed a mate who'd stick around and protect the kids. It was to a prehistoric male's advantage to impregnate as many females as possible to ensure his genetic immortality. And why should a guy waste time dragging home meat for another guy's genes, especially when he has sperm to burn? Which, boys and girls, is why men evolved to be "naturally" promiscuous and women evolved to be "naturally" monogamous.

Sociobiologists have no way of proving their ideas experimentally. They point to the universality of certain behaviors—incest taboos, religious laws—as proof that they're genetic. Opponents point to the endless unpredictability and flexibility of humankind as proof that genes aren't the seat of power.

MANY ARE COLD, BUT FEW ARE FROZEN

Yes, the Big Chill is coming, but you won't need your industrial-strength thermal underwear for another 3,000 to 20,000 years.

Over the past billion years, the earth has experienced three long periods during which ice built up at its poles, each period made up of several 100,000-year "ice ages" when glaciers advanced to cover much of the world. These ice ages were punctuated by 10,000-year "interglacials," warm spells marked by the retreat of the vast ice sheets. We live at the end of such a temperate timeout; the last great ice age wound down about 7,000 years ago. At its peak, 20,000 years ago, glaciers encased most of North America, Europe, and Asia. Days were about eleven degrees colder than they are now, forcing humans and animals southward.

It's not hard to see that an ice age is caused by a temperature drop creating summers cool enough so that the previous winter's snow never melts. Several seasons' snows accumulate and compact to form glaciers. But what turns down the thermostat? The cold facts have been hotly debated, but the theory most widely accepted—the "astronomical" theory—states that three periodic changes in the earth's position relative to the sun seem to have launched ice ages by influencing the amount of solar radiation the earth receives.

Because of the gravitational pull of the sun and moon on the equator, the earth wobbles on its axis like a toy top slowing down. Every 22,000 years or so, it describes a circle in space. The axis also tilts, causing the seasons. When the North Pole tips away from the sun, it's winter in the Northern Hemisphere. Today, the angle of tilt is 23½°, but every 41,000 years it moves from 22° to 24° and back again. Perhaps the most important cycle is a change in the shape of the earth's orbit—from nearly circular to highly elliptical and back to circular—every 100,000 years due to the gravitational tug of fellow planets. The combined effect of these three cycles is to place the earth farther away from the sun at certain times, cooling the planet into an ice age.

If the astronomical theory makes sense to most scientists, why do some of them get all worked up about an imminent ice age? They insist that a veil of dust thrown up by manmade pollution and increased volcanic activity, together with thicker cloud cover generated by jet vapor, will lessen the amount of heat we get from the sun. (As so often happens in the wacky world of science, other people worry that some of these very same problems will make the earth too hot, not too cold.) Even if pollution and volcanoes do kick up enough dust to cause a slight drop in temperature, most scientists agree that this will not alter the primordial rhythms of the cosmos. It'll be thousands of years before the ice age gathers steam, to mix a metaphor. In the meantime, ours may ultimately be the warmest interglacial in history—dangerously warm, thanks to the greenhouse effect, below.

SOME LIKE IT HOT

Leave your car parked all day in the sun with the windows rolled up and you'll return to an interior much hotter than the air outside. That's because window glass admits sunlight but traps heat. Carbon dioxide (CO_2), the gas we exhale, has a similar physical property; it is transparent to solar radiation (sunlight) but opaque to infrared radiation (heat). We need *some* CO_2 to act as insulation, along with water vapor and ozone, an unstable form of oxygen. No sweat, as long as CO_2 stays in its current proportions, i.e., only about .03 percent of the total atmosphere.

In the last 100 years, however, the amount of atmospheric CO_2 has increased about 15 percent, thanks to the burning of coal, oil, and gas and to widespread deforestation, which has eliminated plants that would have photosynthesized thousands of tons of CO_2 into oxygen and carbohydrates. The more CO_2 in the atmosphere, the hotter we get. A rise in the global temperature of a mere 2°C to 4°C (3.6°F to 7.2°F), which some climatologists think could happen by early next century, would melt polar ice caps, causing seas to rise and submerge coastal cities; upset weather patterns, triggering droughts and floods; and decrease wind circulation, playing havoc with ocean currents and depleting the fish supply.

As is usual in the apocalypse biz, a few people see the greenhouse effect as a boon, not a bane. First of all, they insist, it won't get all *that* hot, and since CO_2 stimulates photosynthesis and increases plant yields, agricultural productivity could soar. Others think the warming trend could extend our interglacial period and even stave off the next ice age. More people, however, side with the British scientific journal *Nature,* which observed some time ago that the release of CO_2 from all those fossil fuels we've been burning may be the most important environmental issue in the world today.

Don't confuse the greenhouse effect with deodorant doom, the notion that such manmade chemical compounds as jet exhaust and fluorocarbons used as spray-can propellants (now banned in the U.S. and a few European countries, but not in the rest of the world) will destroy the ozone layer (ten miles up and twenty miles thick) that protects the planet from deadly ultraviolet and other high-energy radiation. But feel free to fret. In 1985, scientists reported a large, mysterious hole in the ozone layer over the South Pole. The hole, which has appeared for two months every winter since at least 1979, is the size of the United States and growing. It could be a transient, fluky weather phenomenon, a previously unnoticed cyclical event—or the awful thing everyone said would happen if we overdid the Aquanet.

ONE SINGS, THE OTHER DOESN'T

As the host said, rolling his eyes at the departing couple, "I don't know how they stay together. She's so left hemisphere, and he's so right hemisphere." He didn't mean that one of them's from Peshawar and the other's from Pittsburgh, but that their personalities epitomize the different ways the two halves of our brain seem to deal with the world. The left hemisphere, which controls the right half of the body, is responsible for language and logic; the right hemisphere, which controls the left half of the body, handles such intuitive, nonverbal processes as emotions and spatial relationships.

Uncovering this dichotomy earned a 1981 Nobel Prize for Roger Sperry, the Caltech psychobiologist who has experimented with people whose hemispheres had stopped speaking to each other. Ordinarily, the two halves of the brain are connected by a bundle of millions of nerve fibers, the corpus callosum, that allows signals to pass between the hemispheres and enables us to function as an integrated unit. By observing epileptics whose corpora callosa had been severed to prevent the spread of seizures, Sperry learned how the hemispheres divvy up the chores. In one classic experiment, he showed a different picture to each hemisphere simultaneously. (What the right eye sees is processed in the left hemisphere, and vice versa.) The left, verbal hemisphere was shown a picture of a knife and the right, nonverbal hemisphere was shown a picture of a spoon. Asked to *name* what he saw (to use language, a left hemisphere skill), the subject said knife. Asked to feel about with his left hand (a spatial skill, controlled by the right hemisphere) and pick up what was in the picture, the subject chose a spoon from a group of objects. The right brain didn't know what the left brain was doing.

Until recently, the division of labor between left and right seemed fairly clearcut and accounted for a variety of functions: intellect versus intuition, concrete versus abstract thinking, objective versus subjective understanding, linear versus holistic perception. But now the head honchos themselves are split on a number of issues. Most agree that in 95 percent of right-handers and 67 percent of left-handers, the left hemisphere is specialized for language. But new evidence suggests that the right brain handles some important language functions: recognizing narrative and humor—storyline and punchline, interpreting tone of voice, making metaphors. Scientists also thought that the rational left brain was definitely boss, relinquishing control to the right only during sleep and dreams. Now it appears that there may be complementary dominance: Each hemisphere has a specialty and kicks in when duty calls.

The specialization may have less to do with what the task is than with how it's done. The right hemisphere seems to be a creative generalist, trying lots of solutions until one works. The left brain seems to be a plodding specialist, good at problems that are already familiar. Physical differences between the hemispheres support this hypothesis: The right hemisphere has long fibers plugging into many different areas of the brain, so it can schmooz and tune into the grapevine to solve a problem. The left brain contains shorter fibers tapping a smaller space, allowing it to do more detailed work. Still more studies (don't these neurologists ever go to the movies?) show that the right brain handles novelty, the left brain what's old hat. Unfamiliar faces are recognized with the right hemisphere, familiar faces with the left. Seasoned telegraphers interpret Morse code with the left brain, young whippersnappers, the right. Nonmusicians recognize melodies with the right hemisphere, but musicians use the left.

One interesting bit of conjecture to come from split brain theory: the idea that *déjà vu*—the feeling that what's happening now has happened to you in the past—may be nothing more than a neurological glitch that causes information to reach one hemisphere a split second before it reaches the other, so that a single event is processed twice.

STATE OF SIEGE

In the last twenty years, researchers have pieced together a picture of what happens when a foreign invader (e.g., a virus, bacterium, or a parasite) enters the body. First, the army—our trillion white blood cells, born in the bone marrow—is alerted. These cells are of two major kinds: phagocytes ("cell eaters") that constantly patrol the body looking for intruders to devour, and lymphocytes (lymph cells), little commandos called T and B cells (B is for bone marrow, T for the thymus, a small gland in the neck where T cells mature).

The soldiers in this army communicate via special proteins called lymphokines. (Yes, of course, the military metaphor is tired, but "the body's bowling team" just won't work.) At the first sign of attack, special phagocytes called macrophages begin to swallow up the enemy, taking from each the equivalent of its dog tag—a tiny piece called the antigen, which a macrophage then displays on its own surface to attract helper T cells trained to recognize that particular antigen. (The thymus apparently has on hand a T cell able to recognize each of nature's hundreds of millions of antigens.) The macrophage secretes a lymphokine called interleukin-1, which stimulates the helper T cells to reproduce. The helper Ts in turn secrete interleukin-2, which causes the creation of still more helper T cells and of *killer* T cells, whose job it is to clobber body cells already taken over by the invader. The new helper T cells release a lymphokine that orders the production of B cells in the spleen and lymph nodes. (Gives a whole new meaning to the term "sick day," doesn't it?)

Helper T cells then produce yet another lymphokine that tells B cells it's time to stop reproducing and start making antibodies, proteins tailored to fight specific antigens. The B cells are capable of creating millions of different antibodies, which either fight the invaders or flag them so phagocytes can recognize and devour them. The helper Ts, bless 'em, also secrete gamma interferon, a lymphokine that boosts T cell activation, assists B cells in producing antibodies, and helps macrophages digest the enemy.

When the invaders are vanquished, suppressor T cells tell the rest of the immune system to call it quits. Turning off the immune response is as important as launching it; some forms of blood cancer seem to be the result of T and B cells gone wild. And the immune system can mistakenly attack the body's own cells, as in such autoimmune diseases as rheumatoid arthritis and systemic lupus erythematosus. (Allergies are basically an immune system overreaction to harmless invaders like dust and pollen.)

After the battle's over, phagocytes clean up the debris—dead cells, spilled biochemicals. Certain B and T cells, called memory cells, remain in the blood and the lymphatic system, on guard against renewed attack by the same antigen. Vaccination is a sort of basic training for memory cells; it introduces dead or weakened disease-causing substances into the body, priming memory cells so that they'll recognize the invader should it ever appear again in full force.

The good guys don't always win, of course. Cold viruses, for example, are constantly mutating to escape detection, and chemicals like asbestos overwhelm macrophages, which can't digest them. But for every bout with flu or herpes you suffer, thousands of sneak attacks have been thwarted.

There's one attacker against which the body is powerless. HIV, the virus that causes AIDS, enters the body hidden inside helper T cells, in blood or semen from an infected person. The virus apparently hijacks the victim's helper T cells when they come to investigate the intrusion. It lies dormant for months or years in these hostage T cells until they begin to divide, perhaps in response to some subsequent infection. Not only do the helper T cells fail to sound the alarm that would activate killer T and B cells, they are themselves spreading the disease. Second-wave invaders, in the form of opportunistic infections, meet no opposition when they march in for the kill.

There is, however, good news on other fronts. Researchers are harnessing the arsenal of the immune system to fight cancer. Crossing spleen and cancer cells, they've cloned the resulting hybrid to produce antibodies that scout the body for incipient tumors. These so-called monoclonal antibodies may some-day be used to deliver drugs or radiation to a diseased site in the body, bypassing healthy tissue.

Perhaps the most dramatic advances come from the new field of psychoneu-roimmunology, the study of interactions between the mind and the nervous, endocrine, and immune systems. Scientists have found, for example, that a body under stress produces an excess of the steroid cortisol. Because macro-phages coping with all that cortisol can't seem to handle other infections, we catch more colds when we're stressed out. We know that exercise seems to stimulate the brain to produce natural painkillers, called endorphins and en-kephalins, and that it might even affect T cell production. Why? And how do the brain and immune system communicate? It looks as though the brain may speak to the white blood cells through the lymphokines, the protein mes-sengers—and the white blood cells may talk back. The immune system may ultimately be found to work not just as an army, but as part of an elaborate feedback loop. Is it the body's discussion group? Its town meeting? Stand by for new metaphors.

Making a Name for Yourself in Science

EIGHT BRIGHT IDEAS THAT LIT UP THEIR OWNERS' LIVES

ARCHIMEDES' PRINCIPLE

Holds that buoyancy is the loss of weight an object seems to incur when it is placed in a liquid, and that that loss is equal to the weight of the liquid it displaces. Takes off from (but is not restricted to) the "Eureka!" business.

To recap, it's the third century B.C.; we're in Syracuse, in Sicily (for centu-ries an important Greek outpost); and the local king, Hiero II, has reason to suspect that the royal jeweler has sneaked some silver into the new, and supposedly 100 percent gold, royal crown. Hiero calls in Archimedes, who for a while is stumped. He knows that gold weighs more than silver and consequently has less volume and that the volume of a piece of pure gold and of a crown of pure gold weighing the same amount would be the same. But how to measure the volume of a strange-shaped thing like a crown? Then, pondering the problem one day in the tub, Archimedes realizes that a body immersed in liquid displaces exactly its own volume of that liquid. Measure the volume of the water that's spilled over the side of the tub and you've got the volume of the thing *in* the tub. At which point, Archimedes shouts "Eureka!" and runs home naked, where he puts first the piece of pure gold, then the crown said to be of pure gold, in a basin of water. The crown causes the water to rise higher, revealing itself to have a greater volume (and hence to be less dense, i.e., *not* pure gold). And revealing the jeweler to be guilty.

The story told, bear in mind that Archimedes' principle, as opposed to Archimedes' bath, applies not only to bodies immersed in water but to bodies floating on it, and not only to solids but to liquids and gases. It explains, in addition to why ships float, why balloons rise, and it warns that in determining what will and what won't sink, float, or fly away, both weight and volume must be considered, not to mention shape and position. If you can manage to remember anything here beyond "Eureka!" you might go for "specific gravity," the ratio of a given density of a solid or a liquid to the density of water (and of a gas to air), and a term that, while unknown to Archimedes, pretty much sums up what his principle winds up being all about.

FIBONACCI SERIES

He started with 1, as who among us wouldn't? Then he repeated it: 1,1. Then he added the two: 1, 1, 2. And he kept on adding, always the concluding pair of what was now, unmistakably, a series: 1, 1, 2, 3; 1, 1, 2, 3, 5; 1, 1, 2, 3, 5, 8. And so on, all the way to 1, 1, 2, 3, 5, 8, 13, 21, 34, 55, 89, 144. And why stop there? So, . . . 233, 377, 610, 987, 1,597, but you get the picture. Now, if you're wondering what, apart from the lack of late-night television in thirteenth-century Pisa, accounts for Fibonacci's perseverance, we can report that he was working out the solution to the problem of how many pairs of rabbits can be produced from a single pair of rabbits, if every month every pair begets a new pair, which from the second month on is itself productive, assuming that none of the rabbits die (or become bored) and each pair consists of a male and a female.

Wait, it gets interesting. Turns out that the Fibonacci series not only connects with controlled population growth, it also keeps popping up on nature walks. For instance, the ratio of scales distributed in opposing spirals around a pine cone is 5:8; of bumps around a pineapple, 8:13; of seeds in the center of a sunflower, 21:34. All of which are *adjacent Fibonacci pairs*. If nature doesn't do it for you, try culture. Seems the ratio between any two adjacent Fibonacci numbers (after 3) is roughly 1:1.618—none other than the ratio behind the celebrated Golden Section, in mathematics the division of a line segment into two parts such that the whole segment is to the larger part as the larger part is to the smaller. The Golden Rectangle, whose length and width are the two parts of a line segment divided Golden Section-style, is a big deal in art and architecture because its proportions are so satisfying to the eye, incorporating, to hear the aestheticians tell it, both static unity and dynamic variety. The classic example here is the facade of the Parthenon, but Golden Rectangles have also been found in paintings by everybody from Leonardo to Mondrian.

THE LINNAEAN SYSTEM OF
TAXONOMIC CLASSIFICATION

What's it to you whether or not we have an orderly, scientifically sound method for cataloguing plants and animals? Not much. But it comes in awfully handy for scientists who, up until the middle of the eighteenth century, had to say something like "that little yellow flower with the spots on its petals" every time they wanted to compare notes. It was the Swedish botanist Carolus Linnaeus who came up with the idea, shocking in its day, of dividing plants into twenty-four "classes" distinguished by their sex (for which he has been called "the Freud of the botanical world"), that is, according to the length and number of stamens and pistils in their flowers, then subdividing those classes into "orders" based on the number of pistils. The sexual approach made sense in light of the then-novel idea of dividing God's creatures into broad categories, called "species," according to their individual characteristics; Linnaeus grouped his species by their ability to reproduce the same characteristics, generation after generation.

Besides coming up with a game plan, Linnaeus hit on the idea of using binomial nomenclature—that is, two names, one for the genus (as in

"Homo"), one for the species (as in "sapiens")—as a shorthand labeling system to replace the cumbersome and confusing descriptive names botanists were using at the time. Then he got everyone he knew to run around frantically naming plants and animals as fast as they could, hoping to get absolutely everything in creation named before some unsuspecting botanist or zoologist somewhere used the same name for a different species, thereby messing up the system. As a result, many of these names were arbitrary, spur-of-the-moment affairs, one reason that, today, many of them strike us as unsystematic and not all that helpful.

Modern naturalists also disagree with certain of Linnaeus's categories, and, to the old "kingdoms" of "Plantae" (plants) and "Animalia" (animals) they've added a third, "Protista," to cover single-celled amoebas, bacteria, slime molds, and the like. Nevertheless, the Linnaean system, arbitrary and artificial as it may be, is still the best we've got.

BROWNIAN MOVEMENT

The zigzag, irregular dance done by minute particles of matter when suspended in a liquid; named for Robert Brown, the botanist who established its existence in 1827, while watching microscopic pollen grains float around in water. Brown noticed that although the direction any particular pollen grain would take was unpredictable, all the grains moved faster when the water got hotter and slowed down as it cooled. Einstein later did a paper on Brownian movement, theorizing that the grains were always in motion because they were being batted around by water molecules; the hotter the water, the faster the water molecules moved, and the more direct hits to the pollen grains. Eventually, Brownian movement became an important substantiating factor of the kinetic molecular theory of matter, which states that matter is composed of tiny particles (or molecules) that are constantly in motion.

THE DOPPLER EFFECT

The change in the frequency of a wave (whether of sound or of light) that occurs whenever there is a change in the distance between the source and the receiver; named for the early nineteenth-century Austrian physicist Christian

Doppler. If the source of the waves and the receiver are approaching each other (or one is approaching the other), Doppler observed, the frequency of the wavelengths increases and the waves get shorter, producing high-pitched sounds and bluish light. If the source and receiver are moving farther apart, sound waves are pitched lower and light appears reddish. (The most commonly cited example of the Doppler effect: the train whistle that screeches in the distance, dropping in pitch as it approaches the platform where you're standing.) Used in radar to track the velocity of a moving object; in astronomy to measure distances between and rotations of stars, planets, and entire galaxies; also to track satellites. When, in 1929, the astronomer Edwin Hubble noticed that the light from distant stars was becoming redder, he took this "Doppler shift" or "red shift" to mean that the stars were rushing away from earth. His conclusion, known as Hubble's Law and now generally accepted, was that the universe is expanding.

BOOLEAN ALGEBRA

Ever since Aristotle—as George Boole, the nineteenth-century English mathematician, would have been the first to tell you—language has been getting in the way of truth. That is, the way we talk, with all its inaccuracy, ambiguity, and potential for hysteria, tends to mess up the way we think.

Boole's solution: Get rid of the words altogether, instead letting symbols (*a* and *b, x* and *y, P* and *Q,* whatever; it doesn't matter that they're arbitrary as long as they're precise) stand for the components of thought, which, not entirely coincidentally, often turn out also to be the elements of formal logic. Then, manipulate the symbols mathematically, in a kind of "mental" algebra that's based on such simple operations as negation (corresponding roughly to what you and I mean by "not"), conjunction (our "and"), and alternation ("or"); and that—here's where you're supposed to stand up and applaud—always reduces things, no matter how complicated or abstruse, to either a "1" (standing for "all" or "true") or a "0" (standing for "nothing" or "false"). Thus was not only Boolean algebra born, but also the device known as the truth table (which lists all possible combinations of true and false values that can accrue in the interplay of two or more statements) and the intellectual specialty known as symbolic logic (which succeeded in wresting logic from the philosophers and delivering it over to the mathematicians).

For fifty years nobody but Lewis Carroll seems to have gotten all that turned on by Boole's "laws of thought," but those laws did, shortly before World War I, knock the socks off Alfred North Whitehead (see page 324) and Bertrand Russell, who relied on them to establish more or less persuasively that not only was logic the proper domain of mathematics, it was indeed where the latter's roots lay. Since then there's been no stemming the Boolean tide. First lawyers took to constructing truth tables in the courtroom. Then telephone-company engineers began thinking of parallel "on/off" switches and "open/closed" circuitry in 0-versus-1 terms. To the point that today it's the rare computer that doesn't proceed along the relentlessly binary lines first laid down by Boole—as stunning an example as the atom bomb of how theory, and the wackier the better, fuels technology.

MÖBIUS STRIP

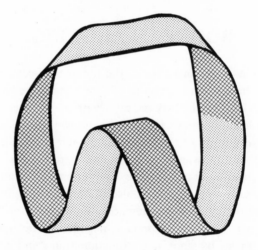

Take an ordinary flat strip of paper. Give it a half-twist. Now Scotch-tape the two ends together to form a loop. Okay, ready? Take a red Magic Marker and color in one side of the loop, and a green Magic Marker and color in the other. Whoops! That's right: The strip has only one "side"—or do we mean "one" side? Easy to construct, and hard to imagine, the so-called Möbius strip (named after the nineteenth-century German mathematician and astronomer who first described it) also reacts strangely to scissors: Cut it along a line drawn lengthwise down its middle and you'll get not two Möbius strips but a normal two-sided strip twice as long as the one you started with. (The mathematicians' explanation for this: A Möbius strip has only one edge; the cut adds a second edge and with it a second side.) Now try cutting a new strip along a line one third of the way in from its edge; we won't tell you what you'll wind up with, but it's pretty weird, too.

As to what's *really* going on here: The subject is geometric transformations undertaken in space, collectively known as topology. Superficially a series of exercises in paradox reminiscent of all those old M. C. Escher drawings, topology nevertheless crystallizes a bunch of the century's top issues. For instance, in the case of the Möbius strip, what does it purport that something that appears at a given point to be two-sided, when traced round its continuum, is in fact one-sided? One theory: that life is holistic, not reductionistic; that persisting in trying to consider everything in terms of its component parts (the brain as a collection of neurons, say) risks missing the whole (the brain as mind).

GÖDEL'S INCOMPLETENESS THEOREM

The problem here—if you, unlike most twentieth-century theoreticians, still want to look at it as a problem—is self-reference, a historic stumbling block for logicians. In 1931, the Czech-born mathematician Kurt Gödel demonstrated that within any given branch of mathematics, there would always be some propositions that couldn't be proven either true or false using the rules and axioms (statements like 1 = 1 that are accepted without proof) of that mathematical branch itself. You might be able to prove every conceivable statement about numbers within a system by going *outside* the system in order to come up with new rules and axioms, but by doing so, you'll only create a larger system with its own unprovable statements. The implication is that *all* logical systems of any complexity are, by definition, incomplete; each of them contains, at any given time, more true statements than it can possibly prove according to its own defining set of rules.

Gödel's theorem has been used to argue that a computer can never be as smart as a human being because the extent of its knowledge is limited by a fixed set of axioms, whereas people can discover unexpected truths. (Maybe; but we've met pocket *calculators* who are smarter than some of the people we went to high school with.) It plays a part in modern linguistic theories, which emphasize the power of language to come up with new ways to express new ideas. And it has been taken to imply that you'll never entirely understand yourself, since your mind, like any other closed system, can only be sure of what it knows about itself by relying on what it knows.

Fun—Or At Least a Few Minutes—With Numbers

Either mathematics is poetry, all density and precision, or it's the most flagrant type of entrepreneurship, in which nobody's satisfied until his headquarters is taller than anybody else's headquarters. Exhibit A: Numbers—the symbols we use to count up all the things around us that aren't unique or continuous—an area where mathematicians have gotten either more lyrical or more rapacious over the years, depending on how you look at it. Below, some of the number "types" they've managed to corner and/or construct for themselves.

The Number System

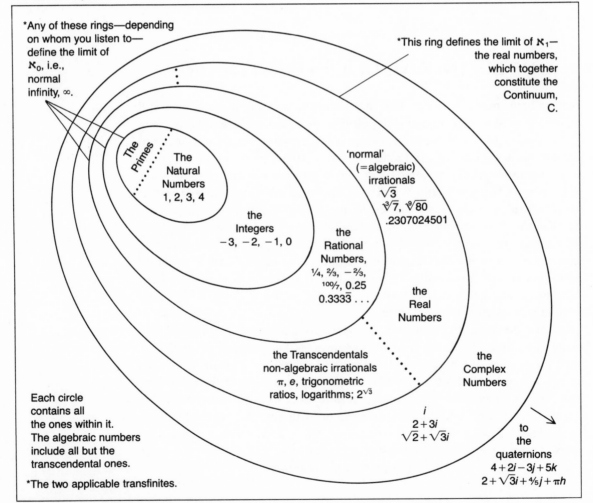

*Any of these rings—depending on whom you listen to—define the limit of $\aleph_0$, i.e., normal infinity, ∞.

*This ring defines the limit of $\aleph_1$—the real numbers, which together constitute the Continuum, C.

The Primes

The Natural Numbers 1, 2, 3, 4

the Integers $-3, -2, -1, 0$

the Rational Numbers, $\frac{1}{4}, \frac{2}{3}, -\frac{2}{3}, \frac{100}{7}, 0.25$ $0.333\overline{3}\ldots$

'normal' (=algebraic) irrationals $\sqrt{3}$ $\sqrt[3]{7}, \sqrt[8]{80}$ .2307024501

the Real Numbers

the Transcendentals non-algebraic irrationals π, e, trigonometric ratios, logarithms; $2^{\sqrt{3}}$

the Complex Numbers

i $2 + 3i$ $\sqrt{2} + \sqrt{3}i$

to the quaternions $4 + 2i - 3j + 5k$ $2 + \sqrt{3}i + \frac{1}{5}j + \pi h$

Each circle contains all the ones within it. The algebraic numbers include all but the transcendental ones.

*The two applicable transfinites.

NATURAL

NATURE: The counting numbers.

EXAMPLES: 1, 2, 3, 4, . . .

HISTORY: In use since man first felt a need to know how many of something—goats, pots, issues of *Penthouse*—he owned. Some primitive societies still make do with "one," "two," and "many."

PRACTICAL USES: Conducting censuses, scoring basketball games, seating people at dinner parties.

MATHEMATICAL RESONANCES: One of the first creative highs. The sense among early "numbers" types that they were on to something big, something real *and* abstract. Also, the inevitability of distinctions between "odd" and "even," and "cardinal" (1,2,3; the counting numbers) and "ordinal" (1st, 2nd, 3rd; the ranking numbers). Ditto, of considerations of "infinity," the quality of endlessness, symbolized as ∞, toward which the natural numbers were seen to progress.

PRIME

NATURE: Those natural numbers higher than 1 that can't be evenly divided by any number other than themselves and 1. (Opposed to the *composite* numbers.)

EXAMPLES: 2, 3, 5, 7, 11, 13, 17, . . .

HISTORY: Arduous. Also, odd. Euclid proved there was no end to the primes. Somebody else constructed a "sieve" to isolate them. Any number of Renaissance-and-later men tried to devise a formula that would generate all possible ones: no dice. Then there's the Goldbach conjecture of 1742. The largest known prime (as of a few years ago) has 3,375 digits; needless to say, they now have the computers on the case.

PRACTICAL USES: None whatsoever, unless you find yourself at a mathematicians' convention.

MATHEMATICAL RESONANCES: A thorn in the side. Mathematicians can't bear that they still don't know why primes fall where they do, or, for that matter, how many there are. Then, too, primes are just one example of sets of numbers having special properties that the Greeks and others managed to isolate. Another time we'll tell you about the perfects and the amicables.

THE INTEGERS

NATURE:
The natural numbers, plus 0 and all the negative numbers. Also called the whole numbers.

EXAMPLES:
. . . , −4, −3, −2, −1, 0, 1, 2, 3, 4, . . .

HISTORY:
Zero, an ancient Hindu innovation, arrived in Europe in Roman times, along with the Arabic numerals; it was an instant hit. Negative numbers (from the Latin *negare*, "to deny") had a harder time: If the root of an equation was less than zero, the Greeks, so flexible in other respects, called it "fictitious" and threw it out. Only in the sixteenth century did an Italian, Cardano, systematically use negative numbers, pointing out that there *can* be less than nothing—a debt, for instance.

PRACTICAL USES:
Negative numbers make debit-heavy bookkeeping elegant. Zero makes 37 different from 307 or 3,700.

MATHEMATICAL RESONANCES:
Now there was a genuine number line, stretching infinitely to both left and right. Also, all equations of the $A + x = 0$ variety could be solved. And, there was zero, with all its inherent weirdness, to think about.

RATIONAL

NATURE:
The integers, plus all fractions (or their decimal representations), positive and negative, a fraction being defined as the ratio of two integers, a/b, where $b \neq 0$.

EXAMPLES:
½, ⅕, −⅔, .25, .33$\overline{33}$, . . .

HISTORY:
The Egyptians and the Babylonians could handle fractions, though (a) they didn't know what they were doing, and (b) conservatives of the day sneered at the idea of a number like 7½, which was neither 7 nor 8. As usual, it took the Greeks to dignify, codify, and promote the idea. Since then, second nature to everybody.

PRACTICAL USES:
Measuring (as opposed to counting), dealing with continuous quantities like age, Brie, and drapery material which don't always break into convenient pieces. Also, sharing.

MATHEMATICAL RESONANCES:
A flush of pleasure: Rationals *felt* good. Besides, all linear (or first-degree) equations, of the $Ax + B = 0$ variety, now had one—and only one—solution. Geometrically speaking, all you needed was a straightedge.

REAL

NATURE:
The rational numbers, plus the zillions of irrational ones, which can't be expressed in fraction form: imperfect square, cube, and higher roots; decimals that

neither terminate nor repeat; the transcendentals.

EXAMPLES: $\sqrt{2}$, $\sqrt[3]{7}$, $\sqrt[19]{311}$; .2302030020000732 . . .; π, e

HISTORY: $\sqrt{2}$, the first irrational, was discovered by Pythagoras, c. 500 B.C., when he constructed a right angle, each of whose sides was one unit long, and measured its hypotenuse. His proof that it couldn't be put into fractional form was very upsetting, and resulted in the immediate sacrifice of a hundred oxen. π, the ratio of a circle's circumference to its diameter, wasn't proved to be irrational until 1761. In between, it was discovered that there are a whole lot more irrational numbers than rational ones.

PRACTICAL USES: With the exception of π and e, few if any, despite all the brouhaha. On the other hand, square roots are as much a part of the collective consciousness as asparagus or the march from *Carmen*.

MATHEMATICAL RESONANCES: Like arriving at your surprise party with a 102° fever: elation tempered by shakiness. But, the real numbers could be shown to correspond in a perfect, one-to-one way with all the points on a line (regardless of its length); this endless series of points was termed the Continuum (abbreviated C), and proved to be much more endless than the mere ∞ formed by the natural numbers. Also, you could now solve any quadratic (or second-degree) equation of the $Ax^2 + Bx + C = 0$ variety.

TRANSCENDENTAL

NATURE: A special category of irrational numbers: They're real, all right, but they're not algebraic.

EXAMPLES: π, e, plus all the trigonometric ratios and logarithms they give rise to; also any quantity (except 0 and 1) raised "radically," e.g., $2^{\sqrt{3}}$.

HISTORY: In 1844 the Frenchman Joseph Liouville proved the existence of transcendentals—irrationals that would not serve as solutions to any of the infinite number of polynomial equations in any of the infinite number of degrees possible—but couldn't come up with an example. In 1873 somebody else showed that e, the base of the so-called "natural" logarithms, was transcendental. In 1882 still another somebody showed the same of π. Since then, so many transcendentals have turned up that a lot of us have simply stopped answering the doorbell.

PRACTICAL USES: π (or pi, from the first letter of *perimetron*, Greek for "measurement around") is indispensable in carpentry and construction. e figures in statistics and nuclear physics, and, in the days before slide rules and pocket calculators put logarithms out of business, enjoyed a certain vogue. They tell us that trigonometric functions allow you to gauge the height of a telephone pole from the length of its shadow, but where we live all the phone lines are underground.

MATHEMATICAL
RESONANCES: The transcendental numbers constitute an infinity even greater than the algebraic ones. Also, since π is transcendental, nobody has to try to "square the circle" using only a straightedge and compass anymore. Flash: $e^{\pi i} = -1$.

COMPLEX

NATURE: The real numbers, plus all the *imaginary* ones, based on i, defined as $\sqrt{-1}$. But especially, these numbers when seen to consist of both real and imaginary components.

EXAMPLES: $3 + 2i$, $3 - \sqrt{2}i$, $0 + \sqrt{2}i$, $3 + 0i$.

HISTORY: What *do* you do with an equation like $x^2 + 1 = 0$? In 1777, Leonhard Euler, the most prolific mathematician of all time, introduced the symbol i (for "imaginary") to stand for the $\sqrt{-1}$. Like the X in "X-ray," it was both a shriek of victory and an admisson of perplexity. But imaginary numbers, like negative numbers, caught on.

PRACTICAL USES: The description and handling of vector quantities, which have not only magnitude but direction.

MATHEMATICAL
RESONANCES: The complex numbers constitute a plane and correspond in a perfect one-to-one way with the points in it (cf. the *line* of real numbers). Also, with them on board, you'll always have the solutions to polynomial equations of the $Ax^n + Bx^{n-1} + Cx^{n-2} + \ldots + Z = 0$ variety, no matter how high n gets, and you'll always have exactly the same number of solutions as the degre of n. With the complexes, man can solve any such polynomial, providing it has rational coefficients. In general, mathematicians were so excited by all of this that they couldn't not push their luck: The result was quaternions (see below).

ALGEBRAIC

NATURE: So-called because they turn up as the solutions of algebra-style equations. Which means all of the above numbers except the transcendental ones.

EXAMPLES: To reprise: 2, 0, -2, ½, $-¾$, .3333 . . . , .2302030020000732 . . . , $\sqrt[3]{7}$, $3 + 2i$, $0.5 - 3i$

HISTORY: The nineteenth century was the big one here: Gauss, Kummer, and Dedekind. Ideals, unique factorization, and Abelian number fields.

PRACTICAL USES: There were repercussions in mathematical physics, but we admit that's not rewiring the living-room lamp. Frankly, lingering over this category is probably a mistake.

| MATHEMATICAL RESONANCES: | First and foremost, a way of gathering all of the above together so that it both made sense and allowed a little breathing room. However, what was originally a scheme for investigating the solution of problems had now become a whole *thing,* an end in itself. The beat goes on. |

TRANSFINITE

NATURE:	"Styles" of infinity. And the sky's the limit.
EXAMPLES:	$\aleph_0$, $\aleph_1$, $\aleph_2$, $\aleph_3$, . . . , $\aleph_n$ (The letter is aleph, first of the Hebrew alphabet. Say "aleph-null," "aleph-one," "aleph-two," and so on. Or maintain a discreet silence.)
HISTORY:	In 1895, the German mathematician Georg Cantor worked out "the arithmetics of infinity," a whole series of endlessnesses. Aleph-null is simple infinity: the familiar ∞, roughly equivalent to the endlessness of the natural numbers (or, in some systems, the integers or even the rationals). Aleph-one is the infinity of the continuum, c, roughly all the real numbers or, depending on how you look at it, all the points in a line (or a square or a cube). Aleph-two may or may not be the endlessness of all curves. And nobody has been able to figure out what aleph-three, let alone aleph-thirty, might stand for.
PRACTICAL USES:	Hmmm?
MATHEMATICAL RESONANCES:	The mathematical imagination rents the video of *Yellow Submarine,* then goes out for Indian food. While everybody continues to talk about this one, it was really Cantor's baby, and he's with his alephs now; a kind of dead end.

THE QUATERNIONS

NATURE:	The complex number concept extended from two dimensions to four.
EXAMPLES:	$4 + 2i - 3j + 5k$, $2 + \sqrt{3}i + \frac{1}{3}j - \pi k$
HISTORY:	First suggested by William Hamilton in 1843 in response to his personal successes with complex numbers. Subsequently taken into even more dimensions—just as you suspected it would be.
PRACTICAL USES:	Engineers get into them. But you're up past your bedtime.
MATHEMATICAL RESONANCES:	The feeling that, once having learned to walk, one can run. Also fly. The lesson here is that when you extend numbers beyond the complex stage, you do so at the expense of something called permanence; one by one, properties you took for granted fall away. For instance, with quaternions, you have to give up either the role 0 plays *or* multiplicative commutativity (i.e., x times y no longer equals y times x). Say good night, Gracie.

Double Whammy

It just so happens that two of the biggest deals in modern science start with the letter *e:* entropy and evolution. Each spans two centuries (including this one), and each has the kind of reverberations that can't really be done justice to on restroom walls. These are their stories.

ENTROPY, THE LAWS OF THERMODYNAMICS, AND WHY YOU MAY HAVE BEEN FEELING TIRED AND LISTLESS LATELY

Entropy is what the Second Law of Thermodynamics is all about. Unfortunately, most of us seem to have gotten bogged down shortly after the First Law. Nothing surprising about that—understanding the First Law doesn't demand much in the way of concentration or stamina. The basic principle of thermodynamics, the branch of physics dealing with the transformation of heat into work and other forms of energy, it simply states that "energy is conserved"; that is, it's indestructible—there is always the same total amount of it in the universe. The First Law of Thermodynamics was a big deal back when people were trying to build better steam engines; today, it serves chiefly as the solid platform from which scientists and philosophers like to hurl themselves into the abyss of the Second Law.

The latter states, with deceptive simplicity, that "the entropy of the universe tends to a maximum." Already, whether you know it or not, you're in trouble. Entropy is a measure of the total disorder, randomness, or chaos in a system. In thermodynamics, it crops up every time any work gets done, since the only way any work *ever* gets done is through heat transfers—hot water coming into contact with cool air, for instance, to produce the steam that drives a steam engine. At the outset, the system is said to be at a low level of entropy: The fast-moving water molecules are distinct from the slow-moving air molecules, and the whole thing has a kind of order to it. But as the heat flows into the cooler medium—as heat naturally does—the fast-moving molecules begin to spend themselves, mixing with the slow ones until eventually all the molecules are moving at approximately the same speed. At this point, we're at maximum entropy; everything is at the same temperature, all the molecules are milling about without any particular order, and nothing more can be accomplished—the system has, literally and figuratively, run out of steam. The energy within the system is still there, but unless you separate the molecules again, returning them to a state of tension by heating some and chilling others, it can't be used to make things happen anymore.

Not your problem, you think, since your car runs on gas? Guess again, mush-for-brains. Outside thermodynamics, increased entropy—things going from a state of relative order to one of disorder—is the upshot of all natural actions. It's what happens when you let your vodka on the rocks sit around for a while and before you know it the ice cubes have melted into the vodka and the only thing worth dealing with is the lemon twist. It's what happens when you move into a nice neighborhood and within a few years it turns into the South Bronx. It's what happens to your body from about age thirty on. And, as scientists predicted back in the nineteenth century, it's what's going to happen to the universe—or at least, to our galaxy—in the scenario known as the "heat death" of the universe: Solar energy, the product of a hot sun turning in cold space, will inevitably run out, molecular chaos will prevail, and we'll all be left sitting in a lukewarm cosmic bath watching our toes decay.

You can see why the concept of entropy made the Victorians, already obsessed with keeping their corset stays in place, rather sad. Today, however, we prefer to brood about our weight and take a more objective approach to the Second Law, which has all sorts of interesting ramifications. It has, for instance, given us the "arrow of time," a metaphor that expresses the purely physical distinction between past and present; the fact that time is an observable, one-way progression from order to disorder, and not just a figment of our imaginations. If you look at two still photos of eggs, one showing them in their unbroken shells, the other, scrambled in a frying pan, you immediately know which came first; reverse the order and you know something's screwy. Time flows in one direction only. Another thing about progressive disorder: It's synonymous with increasing complexity. The picture of the eggs in their shells is neater, simpler, and easier to make sense of than the one showing a gloppy mess in the pan. These two concepts—the arrow of time and the increased complexity of high-entropy states—helped convince scientists earlier in this century that the universe did, in fact, have a beginning, and encouraged them to come up with the idea of the Big Bang (see page 483).

Entropy is also a hot topic among information theorists, who point out that increased complexity seems to add up to more, not less, order; and anyway, if it leads to richness of thought and communication, more power to it. Besides, according to the Second Law, the world should be falling apart by now, and it's not. But maybe that's because the universe is expanding; who's to say that the apparent order we see in our corner of it isn't balanced by total chaos at some other extremity? Then there's the whole business of probability, with which entropy is embroiled in a way that's enough, in itself, to make your brains hurt: There is no law that states absolutely that entropy *can't* be re-versed, that the scrambled eggs can't re-form into their shells or your body revert to a state of adolescent glory—only that the probability of any of that happening is so small as to be virtually nil. At least in the universe as we know it. But what do we know? Maybe what looks like disorder to us is really order. And then there's the fact (don't slow down now or you're lost) that the Second Law doesn't seem to operate the same way on the subatomic level, where time flows in at least two directions, if it flows at all. Oh, there's a lot more to think about, including, yes, the Third Law of Thermodynamics, but by now, you're probably mulling over the First Law again. As for us, we're smart enough to know maximum entropy once we're up to our eyeballs in it.

EVOLUTION, THE LAW OF NATURAL SELECTION, AND WHY YOU MAY HAVE BEEN FEELING STRESSED OUT AND PARANOID LATELY

Evolution—literally, "unrolling"—wasn't Charles Darwin's invention, much less his personal property (see page 525). In fact, the Enlightenment, a whole century before, had celebrated the notion of progress, a basically upbeat take on the inevitability of gradual human change. Hegel had introduced evolution into philosophy, and Marx, into politics. Even scientists—geologists and bi-ologists—had been speculating, since 1800 or so, on the evolutionary devel-opment of the earth and of the things that lived on it. What Darwin did was to make evolution come off as science—first, in his *Origin of Species,* published in 1859; later, in his *Descent of Man,* published in 1871.

By evolution Darwin meant that all plant and animal species are by their very nature mutable, able (and, more than that, under some pressure) to undergo small changes in their makeup; and that all existing plants and ani-mals have developed in such a fashion from others that went before them. Also, that all life is interrelated and subject to the same laws; and that the history of living things is a unified one, unfolding continuously over millions and millions of years.

Here is how Darwin said evolution worked: Given that nature is competi-tive, that more daisies and starfish and foxes are "produced than can possibly survive, there must in every case be a struggle for existence, either one individual with another of the same species, or with the individuals of distinct species, or with the physical conditions of life." Constantly embroiled in fights to the finish, nature is thus, in Tennyson's famous formulation, "red in tooth and claw." Nor is it about to provide any "artificial increase in food" or "prudential restraint from marriage." Darwin's conclusion: "Any being, if it vary however slightly in any manner profitable to itself, under the complex and sometimes varying conditions of life, will have a better chance of surviving, and thus be *naturally selected*." There's more: "From the . . . principle of inheritance, any selected variety will tend to propagate its new and modified form." Let such a process go on long enough, even randomly, and not just new species, but new genera, new families, and even whole new orders will be evolved.

About this thing called "natural selection." First off, it has nothing to do with conscious, intelligent, or purposeful behavior on the part of an organism; in that sense, nobody's "selecting" anything. A species changes, not through choice or will, but through chance, through the "play" of heredity. Inherit a useful characteristic—speed if you're a cheetah, strength if you're an oak tree, turn-on-a-dime savvy if you're a virus or a human being—and you'll be better set up to eat, compete, and mate; in short, to pass that characteristic along. Thus useful traits tend, more than useless ones, to be successfully passed on to the next generation, which profits from them in turn, until, in time, a whole species takes a slight turn to the right or left, *adapting* itself better to its environment, not through careful planning but through the cumulative luck of the draw. This is survival-of-the-fittest stuff; the "natural" simply points up that it's without self-consciousness on the part of the species, or intervention on the part of God.

About Darwinism. It's true that Darwin couldn't prove his theory since, as he put it, the great span of evolutionary time was simply unrecoverable. But that was OK, the circumstantial evidence—in the form of fossils, species distributions, plant and animal structure, embryology—was pretty good. And, except to the religious fundamentalists of the day, the basic setup *felt* right, just as the theory that the earth was round had felt right. What was upsetting were evolution's vibes: that nature had gone from being a sun-kissed harmony to being a tag-team wrestling match; that everything was always in flux, always on its way to becoming something else; that there was no such thing as virtue, just more and more adaptation; and that there were greater rewards for being "fit" than for being good or even for being right.

Darwinian evolution steamed intact into the twentieth century, alongside psychoanalysis and socialism, an intellectual tall-ship that had made it through the straits of Victorian England and would make it over the shoals of Scopes-trial America. In fact, in the Twenties and Thirties, it was to be both bolstered and refurbished (but not structurally altered) by the new science of genetics. You remember genetics. Derived initially from the nineteenth-century work of Gregor Mendel, the pea-planting monk who first came up with the laws of genetic inheritance, it crystallized around the discovery of the first gene (or unit of heredity), which, within fifty years, would be shown to make up the chromosome and itself to be made of DNA.

Fitted out with genetics, Darwinism passed into Neo-Darwinism. It still couldn't "prove" the theory of evolution, but now it could at least demonstrate exactly how evolution worked. Neo-Darwinism is considered a scientific "up" for two reasons: First, it gracefully ushered evolution into the twentieth century; second, it showed that the Master's basic hypothesis had stood the test not only of time but of technology. After genetics, as before it, natural selection was *still* the name of the evolution game.

*Ten Burning Questions in the History of Science** *

WERE THE ANCIENTS REALLY SCIENTISTS OR DID THEY JUST MAKE SOME LUCKY GUESSES?

Unlike the Scholastic Aptitude Test and the Graduate Record Exam, science gives credit not just for the right answers but for the method, as in "scientific method," by which the right answers are arrived at. Science, in other words, wants to see your worksheet. And by worksheet standards, the lowest grades go to the same ancient scientists who appear to have the most on the ball: Democritus, who articulated an atomic theory, and Empedocles, who believed that something more or less like evolution occurred by a process more or less comparable to the survival of the fittest. Face to face with poetic insight, real science throws up its hands.

Now, Aristotle rarely made a good guess. Aristotle believed in spontaneous generation (e.g., that a fly might arise out of a dung heap, no help from Mom and Dad). He believed that heavenly bodies were attached to rotating mechani-

---

* Posed and fielded by contributor Mark Zussman

cal spheres. (Think clear plastic.) He believed that terrestrial motion was regulated by a principle of inertia such that all bodies desired to be at rest at the center of the earth. He believed that the chemistry of things could be explained in terms of the four elements, earth, air, fire, and water. By worksheet standards, however, Aristotle gets reasonably high grades for empirical observation in zoology (he classified some 540 animal species, at least 50 of which he'd dissected) and particularly for his chicken embryology.

If you want to speak well of an ancient scientist, though, the one always to go with is Archimedes, whose virtues include not just the formulation of the principles of buoyancy (see page 503) and the lever and the finest mathematical mind before Newton but a whole lot of method in the absence of any system or metaphysics.

IS IT TRUE THAT THE ARABS KEPT SCIENCE ALIVE DURING THE MIDDLE AGES, WHILE EUROPE SLUMBERED?

Strictly speaking, this is not true. It wasn't the Arabs who kept science alive: it was the Arabic language, which played the same role in the vast spaces from Spain to India that Latin played farther to the north. Arabic was in effect the great switching station—or to put it another way, Islam made science international. Here's what the medieval Moslems did: They translated Galen, Ptolemy, Aristotle, Euclid, Hippocrates, and Dioscorides. Al-Razi, a Persian physician, wrote *The Comprehensive Book*, whose title suggests the overall range of the effort: *The Comprehensive Book* summed up everything that had been known of medicine in Greece, India, and the Middle East and some of what had been known of medicine in China.

At the battle of Samarkand in A.D. 704, the Moslems got their hands on some Chinese papermakers. They then built paper mills of their own at Samarkand and at Baghdad, and they passed the process along to Europe by way of Spain, another medieval switching station. Al-Khwarazmi, a Baghdad mathematician, borrowed our numeral system from the Hindus and then went on to develop algebra, without which the complex weight distribution of Gothic cathedrals probably couldn't have been pulled off. Someone called Leonardo of Pisa introduced Arabic numerals into Europe in 1202.

Europe, meanwhile, sat on its thumbs only in the universities. Away from the gownies, things were cracking; and even before the Renaissance happened along, Northerners had substituted trousers for the Roman toga. They had invented skis and the stirrup and the spinning wheel and the heavy-duty plough and mechanical clocks, and they had figured out how to cast iron and harness horses and make a barrel. This was the practical, nonacademic tradition that would sooner or later give the world the Connecticut Yankee, the Wizard of Menlo Park, and better things through chemistry.

DID GALILEO REALLY DROP A COUPLE OF LEAD WEIGHTS FROM THE LEANING TOWER OF PISA, THEREBY PROVING SOMETHING OR OTHER?

Galileo

By common consent, this most famous of all experiments (or, more properly, demonstrations) was a nice one, if it occurred. Aristotle had claimed that objects of different weights fall at different speeds—so, anyway, the sixteenth-century Aristotelians believed he'd claimed; and anyone with a little equipment at the top of the Leaning Tower could have shown that the Aristotelians were wrong as usual. Whether or not Galileo did drop the weights, however, has been in dispute for most of this century.

The story was first told by Galileo's last pupil, Vincenzo Viviani, who said that Galileo dropped the weights in front of an audience of the entire faculty and student body of Pisa University. But if Galileo had done so and if Aristotelian mechanics had been shown up for the fantasy it was, why isn't there a single independent account of the event in university records or in letters or memoirs? This is the question as modern scholarship puts it.

And it leads to a corollary question. If Galileo didn't drop weights from the Leaning Tower, what did he do? What he did was propagandize for the Copernican view that the earth voyages around the sun, not vice versa, and, what was worse, he did so in modern Italian, not in Latin, thereby stirring up trouble. In *The Dialogue Concerning the Two Chief Systems of the World, the Ptolemaic and the Copernican*, moreover, he made the Ptolemaic lunkhead, Simplicius, sound suspiciously like Pope Urban VIII.

As it happens, Galileo also constructed a telescope through which he discovered spots on the sun, mountains on the moon, satellites in the orbit of Jupiter, and phases of Venus; and he laid the groundwork for a modern mechanics. But if you want to remember just one thing about Galileo, remember that he was the first scientist-philosopher who routinely approached problems mathematically, by quantifying them—and also the first to get a bad case of the creeps at the thought of colors, tastes, odors, and anything else that he believed to be nonquantifiable.

DID NEWTON REALLY WATCH AN APPLE FALL,
AND IF SO, SO WHAT?
(AND IF NOT, SO WHAT?)

Here, obviously, we are onto another one of those Galileo-and-the-lead-weight questions. Sir David Brewster, one of Newton's nineteenth-century biographers, claims actually to have visited the tree the apple fell from and to have walked away with a piece of the root. Brewster also claims that in 1820, six years after his pilgrimage, the tree had decayed to such an extent that it was chopped down, the wood, however, like any other holy relic, being "carefully preserved"—in this case, by a Mr. Turnor of Stoke Rocheford. The story of course is that it was the falling apple that suggested to Newton the theory of universal gravitation, and the story, as Brewster acknowledges, was spread by Voltaire, who got it from Newton's niece, Catherine Barton. Voltaire, who wrote about Newton in detail, in fact never got to see the elderly mathematician-physicist, though, like any good journalist assigned to a palace press room, he did spend a lot of time hanging out in his sub-

Isaac Newton

ject's antechambers gathering scabrous anecdotes. The net of it is that the apple story is probably false and that the apple itself belongs in a barrel along with the one that Eve gave to Adam and the one that William Tell shot off his son's head and the golden one, inscribed "For the fairest," that Cupid tossed in the direction of Juno, Venus, and Minerva. On the other hand, how important is it whether he did or didn't watch an apple fall? Plenty of people other than Newton watched apples fall, and the theory of universal gravitation didn't occur to *them*.

The theory of gravitation, by the way, however obvious it may seem to every seven-year-old today, is in fact, on the face of it, no less implausible than the much earlier theory that the planets and the stars are attached to clear rotating spheres that make music (if only we could hear it); and, when you think about it, it's not really a lot less occult. You know, what is this spooky stuff called gravity that holds everything in place without glue, paste, screws, nails, or even spit? Newton himself said:

> That gravity should be innate, inherent, essential to matter, so that one body may act upon another at a distance through a *vacuum*, without the mediation of anything else, by and through which the action and force may be conveyed from one to another, is to me so great an absurdity that I believe no man who has in philosophical matters a competent faculty of thinking can ever fall into it.

Newton's $F = G\frac{mM}{d^2}$ was nevertheless the $E = mc^2$ of its day. What it says is that the force of attraction between any two bodies will be directly proportional to the product of their masses and inversely proportional to the square of the distance between them.

HOW COME CHEMISTRY TOOK SO LONG TO COME UP FROM THE DARK AGES?

An eighteenth-century chemistry lab

Chemistry took so long to come up from the Dark Ages because even after physics and astronomy and anatomy had assumed something vaguely like their modern contours, instruments didn't exist to isolate gases and no one troubled much to weigh or measure anything. Then a German named Stahl came along and carried the science down the dark, lonely dead-end road of the phlogiston theory. This theory held that all combustible substances had a physical component—namely, phlogiston—that was released on burning; new findings were wrenched about to fit the theory (for example, the discovery that the ash of a piece of firewood weighed more than the unburnt firewood led to the conclusion not that oxygen had been absorbed, but that phlogiston had negative weight). Which is to say that at the time of the American Revolution, chemists still believed that of the four elements of the ancients—earth, air, fire, and water—all but earth were irreducible. H_2O? Not yet. Water.

It was Antoine Lavoisier who got chemistry out of the fix. Lavoisier saw the implications of the findings of other men and worked them into a unified system. Both Joseph Priestley, an Englishman, and Karl Scheele, a Swede, had already isolated oxygen, but they failed to get straight the relationship between oxygen and either fire or water (Priestley, in fact, never gave up on phlogiston). Lavoisier saw that air was made up of two elements of which one contributed to combustion and one, nitrogen, did not. Henry Cavendish, an Englishman, combined hydrogen and oxygen to get water but concluded that water was hydrogen minus phlogiston. Lavoisier came up with the conclusion that satisfied your high-school chemistry teacher.

WHO GOT TO THE EVOLUTION THEORY FIRST, DARWIN OR THIS ALFRED RUSSEL WALLACE? AND ONCE YOU'VE ANSWERED THAT ONE, WHAT'S AN ENLIGHTENED MODERN PERSON SUPPOSED TO THINK OF POOR VILIFIED LAMARCK?

Darwin

Wallace

The first of these questions was somewhat baffling to Darwin himself. Darwin kind of thought that the evolution theory was his own intellectual property, but at home one day in June 1858, tinkering away at the future *Origin of Species,* he received from Wallace (who was in Malaya, recovering from malaria) a paper setting forth not just a theory of evolution but a theory of evolution by natural selection. And talk about spooky: The evolutionary process had been suggested to both men in exactly the same way. They had both read Malthus's *Essay on Population*, according to which an expanding human population is always pressing on food supply with the result that poverty and death are inevitable (see page 127). N.B.: It was neither Darwin nor Wallace but the philosopher Herbert Spencer who coined the Victorian catchphrase "survival of the fittest," and Alfred Tennyson, the poet laureate, who added the cheerful chorus, "For nature is one with rapine, a harm no preacher can heal."

Actually, what was at issue between the two naturalists was not who got to the theory first, but who had title to it. Darwin had started keeping his *Notebook on Transmutation of Species* in 1837. He had a first intimation of the role of adaptation in early 1838, and he added Malthus to his stewpot later that year. Wallace didn't begin to think of the transmutation of species until 1845, after he'd read Chambers's *Vestiges of the Natural History of Creation*. Wallace, however, *announced* his theory to Darwin before Darwin had published anything on evolution anywhere. This, then, would probably have been one for the lawyers, had both men not done honor to science by behaving like gentlemen. They actually praised each other.

As for poor Jean Baptiste Pierre Antoine de Monet, chevalier de Lamarck, the pity is he's remembered for his zany ideas about how an animal that stretches its neck often enough to get at leaves on high branches will sooner or later become a giraffe and—why stop there?—the acquired characteristic of long-neckedness will be passed along to its offspring. In fact, Lamarck not only got the idea of evolution out into the intellectual atmosphere, he also invented the categories "vertebrate" and "invertebrate" and he turned "biology" into an early-nineteenth-century buzzword.

HONEST, NOW, WAS LOBACHEVSKY THE GREATEST MATHEMATICIAN EVER TO GET CHALK ON HIS COAT?

This, to be sure, is what Tom Lehrer alleged of Lobachevsky in the famous song that also advises, "Plagiarize, plagiarize, why do you think the good Lord made your eyes?" Nikolai Lobachevsky not only ran the University of Kazan, he also found time to squeak through Euclid's undefended window of vulnerability, namely, the fifth axiom, which states that through a point *P*, not on a given line *l*, only one line *l'* can be drawn so that *l* and *l'* are parallel and so that they will never meet no matter how far they are extended in either direction.

Lobachevsky demonstrated that if you throw out the fifth axiom, which was never proven, even by Euclid, who didn't try, you can construct a non-Euclidian geometry in which more than one parallel line will pass through the point *P* and all the angles of a triangle will add up to less than 180°. Lobachevsky did not apparently mean his geometry as a description of the real universe, yet it is not only as internally consistent as Euclid's, it also has implications for geodesics and great circle navigation. In any case, as Einstein was later to demonstrate, the real universe *is* both weird and non-Euclidean, regardless of what Lobachevsky thought.

There is just one problem with naming Lobachevsky the greatest mathematician, etc. Carl Gauss had gotten to non-Euclidian geometry before him, concluding that geometry, "the theory of space," was no longer on a level with arithmetic, the latter being exclusively a product of mind, the former, empirical. Most people, in fact, will tell you that not only was Gauss greater, so was Newton, who invented calculus, and Archimedes, who almost invented calculus with less to go on. Archimedes, though, doesn't pass

Nikolai Ivanovitch Lobachevsky

the chalk-on-his-coat test. Archimedes didn't work in chalk. He worked in sand, ash, or, occasionally, olive oil.

WHAT DOES PLANCK'S CONSTANT HAVE TO DO WITH HEISENBERG'S UNCERTAINTY?

In a mutable world where today's $1-a-slice pizza parlor becomes tomorrow's $13-a-radicchio-salad watering hole, a constant is always a nice thing to happen on; and Planck's, though it was scoffed at when it was first offered to the scientific public in 1900, has turned out over the years to be one of those rare harborages that you can tie up at with confidence. Its numerical value, always represented by the letter *h*, is 0.00000000000000000000000006547—a mite of a thing, to be sure; but it has been confirmed by many hundreds of methods, and in a world like this one, you take what constants you can get and you put your arms around them. What Max Planck discovered is that radiant energy is given off in particles or, as he called them, quanta; it is not given off continuously. You want to find the energy quantum of light, for example—namely, the photon? You multiply *h* by the frequency of the radiation, represented by the letter *v*, and voilà—there you've got it. Historians have taken the quantum theory to be the dividing line between "classical" and "modern" physics.

Now, constancy is a lot less modern than uncertainty, so it's not surprising that, come 1927, Werner Heisenberg took Planck's constant and used it to elevate uncertainty beyond mere pose: Heisenberg made uncertainty into a basic principle of the cosmos. He observed that the closer you get to observing the velocity of a particle, the further you inevitably get from measuring its position, and vice versa. Indeterminacy of velocity times indeterminacy of position will equal roughly—you guessed it—the famous *h*. For this, Heisenberg won the 1932 Nobel Prize. But, because it seemed like a mockery of the law of cause and effect, even Einstein didn't like it much, and he went on record with the remark: "I shall never believe that God plays dice with the universe."

WAIT, YOU'RE FORGETTING THE DANES. DIDN'T THEY CONTRIBUTE ANYTHING?

It's hard to know exactly how you mean this, but let's assume you're serious. In fact, the Danes are *not* just blue cheese and prune Danish. Denmark may even have been the first country to have something like a national science policy. King Frederick II, in order to avoid-brain drain to Germany, set up the astronomer Tycho Brahe as feudal lord of the island of Hveen and provided him with the wherewithal to establish what in effect was the world's first observatory and think tank. Brahe spent twenty-odd years there making the most complete and precise survey of the heavens since the Greeks closed up shop. But when the new administration of Christian IV came along and cut off funding, he migrated anyway, to Bohemia, where he made his greatest contribution: He provided the data on the basis of which Johannes Kepler, a German and his successor as Imperial Mathematician, calculated the elliptical orbits of the planets.

Let's raise a tankard to the memory of Olaus Roemer. Roemer, in the Tycho tradition, traced the path of the planet Jupiter carefully, then used his results to calculate the speed of light, thereby beating out Aristotle, who thought that the speed of light was infinite, and Galileo, who tried to calculate a finite speed by trading lantern signals with an assistant on a nearby hilltop.

Hoist another tankard for Thomas Bartholin, who discovered the lymphatic system, and one more for his brother Erasmus, who discovered the double refraction of light through a piece of Icelandic crystal. And "skoal" to Hans Christian Oersted, who brought a compass needle close to an electrical wire, thereby stumbling on electromagnetism.

Niels Bohr won the Nobel Prize in 1922 for developing a new model for the hydrogen atom. Then—another forward march in the evolution of Danish science policy—he opened a Copenhagen Institute for atomic studies and drew theoretical physicists from all over the world, as Tycho had once drawn astronomers. Whereas Tycho's operation had been bankrolled by the Crown, however, the Bohr Institute was funded by the Carlsberg brewery.

IS SCIENCE WORTH DYING FOR?

This is a good question, and though the evidence is inconclusive, the answer is probably no. Life is sweet, and over the long haul the truth outs anyway. You can't kill a good idea whose time has come, etc. Be that as it may, the evidence strongly suggests that the average ecclesiastic does enjoy getting his hands on a scientist with a good idea (this is particularly true if the idea is expressed in such a way that laymen can understand it) and wringing the life out of it or, better yet, him.

In favor of dying for science, partisans of martyrdom used to invoke Giordano Bruno. The Inquisition gave him a chance to recant, but he wound up burning at the stake anyway. Since Socrates, no man had fought less to save his own life. Or at least that's the way Victorian press agentry told the story. Bruno had been an adherent of Copernicanism (the earth moved; the universe was infinite) but he was also of a mystical stripe (other worlds were inhabited; infinite universe was indistinguishable from infinite God). As a case for martyrdom for science, therefore, this can be thrown out on technical grounds: By modern criteria, Bruno wasn't a scientist at all. Rather, he used scientific ideas to dress up a system of hermetic magic. And, in any case, the Inquisition didn't indict him for Copernicanism; they indicted him for his lukewarm acceptance of the doctrine of the Trinity.

In 1633, thirty-three years after Bruno took the torch, Galileo was invited to have a look at the Inquisition's instruments of torture, and abjured. According to legend, he also said in an aside, *Eppur si muove:* It—that is, the earth— moves, even if you and I say it doesn't. But this doesn't make Galileo a martyr, only a brinkman. When it came to actually dying for ideas, Galileo wasn't having any.

As for Lavoisier, his head did roll in Robespierre's terror, but the case against him wasn't that he had invented modern chemistry, only that he had been a tax-collector under the *ancien régime*. Like Galileo, Lavoisier believed that ideas were worth living for, not dying for, and so informed his accusers, thereby evoking the famous response, "The Republic has no need of scientists." But this, by and large, has not been the view of scientists themselves.

WORLD HISTORY

T W E L V E

Contents

The old history-as-cosmic-juggling-act theory, illustrated here by the nineteenth-century French caricaturist Grandville.

The World According to Whom?

Gosh, so much has happened over the years. Wars and revolutions, edicts and referendums, dynasties and one-night stands, rebuffs and embraces. You'd think we'd have learned something from the whole business by now; after all, as the turn-of-the-century Harvard philosopher George Santayana admonished, "Those who cannot remember the past are condemned to repeat it." But how do you decide whose version of things you're going to buy? Well, you should begin by realizing that there's history (or, more formally, historiography), which is the writing down of everything that ever happened, and then there's the philosophy of history, which attempts to say what, exactly, that act of writing down accomplishes and/or where, eventually, the historical process itself leads; and that most "historians" do one or the other, although some wind up doing both. Beyond that, don't look at us: We've just examined everybody's celebrated account of one or more of the world's great moments and it seems perfectly obvious that everybody's lying.

SPOKESPERSONS

Ten guys, two each from five different history-minded civilizations; listen to them and you'll find out how the world—and the history biz—has been going for the past 2,500 years.

The Greeks: Herodotus and Thucydides

The Greeks got history—from their word *histor,* "learned man"—started, the same way they got philosophy and drama started, and their history, like their philosophy and drama, hits the ground running. Suddenly, it seemed obvious that events accumulated and that the past connected not only to the present but to the future. For the Greeks, the big deal was war, with a tip of the hat to revolution, and it was to wars that the two great Greek historians addressed themselves: Herodotus (c. 484–c. 425 B.C.) to the Persian ones (see page 566), which were still going on when he was growing up; Thucydides (c. 460–c. 400 B.C.) to the Peloponnesian one (likewise), which ended in 404 B.C., shortly before he did.

Both men are clear-eyed, go-with-your-instincts observers, but there the

Herodotus (left) and Thucydides.

resemblance ends. Although only a generation older, Herodotus has less in common with Thucydides than he does with Homer, who'd been dead for five centuries already. Expansive, digressive, myth-minded, insatiably curious, capable of repeating anything anybody tells him (not that he necessarily believes it himself), with, as Macaulay put it, "an insinuating eloquence in his lisp," Herodotus comes across like Truman Capote. Thucydides, on the other hand, is Gore Vidal: concentrated, critical, clinical, obsessed with his own methodology and limited in his interests, cold, aristocratic, grave. Of the two, Herodotus, who claimed in his *History* to want only "to preserve the great and wonderful actions of the Greeks and the Barbarians from losing their due meed of glory," is the good read—the one you could get into on a cross-country bus trip, where his anthropologist's impulses would seem right at home. Thucydides, who was more the political-scientist type and who hoped his *The Peloponnesian War* "would be judged useful by those inquirers who desire an exact knowledge of the past as an aid to the interpretation of the future," is the choice of assistant professors, junior senators, Op-Ed-page writers, and anybody else who requires a little status along with his relevance.

The Romans: Livy and Tacitus

It was one thing after another in that burg, and getting it all down on papyrus took priority over figuring out what the hell it meant. The top stories invariably concerned the state and the men who ran it, and they went from being exercises in glorification and myth-making in the days when Rome was still getting started (and still smelling like a rose), to displays of outrage and breast-beating a mere hundred years later. Livy (c. 59 B.C.–c. A.D. 17), who was reportedly employed by various government agencies, winds up sounding like the p.r. person with the Ancient Rome account: From Aeneas and "the founding of this great city," through Romulus and Remus, the Sabine women, Cincinnatus, Hannibal, et al., up to his own Augustan Age and "the establishment of an empire which is now, in power, next to the immortal gods," his *History of Rome* is historiography at the disposal of patriotism, even more full of drum rolls than the *Aeneid* of his contemporary, Virgil—also, it turns out, on the imperial payroll. (For what it's worth, the only other history with as many plugs for divine providence, manifest destiny, tradition, election, and generation is the Old Testament.)

Tacitus (c. A.D. 55–c. 117), the most readable as well as the most reliable of the Roman historians, gives us just as one-sided a view. His Rome is well into its decline, without a scrap of *fides, pietas,* or *clementia* to its name, a city that's part bordello, part reign of terror, and part George Romero movie. (It's Tacitus who, in the *Annals,* provides us with the lowdown on Tiberius, Claudius, Nero, and Agrippina, complete with poisoned mushrooms and ships that fall apart in the night.) Against a background of evil like you wouldn't believe, Tacitus—doing his last-moral-man routine—inveighs, exposes, and pours on the lurid details. "This I regard as history's highest function," he says, "to let no worthy action go uncommemorated, and to hold out the reprobation of posterity as a terror to evil words and deeds." With the emphasis on the latter.

The Germans: Ranke and Mommsen

Not exactly household names. Still, if anyone turned history around—made it rigorous and new—and pointed it roughly in the direction it's still moving in today, it was the Germans, who, beginning around 1800, left the Enlightenment (so glib, so self-involved, so French) doing its nails and marched purposefully off to the university library and the archeological dig. Leopold von Ranke (1795–1886) is not only the most important of these German historians, he may be the most important of all nineteenth-century historians. Determined to see every epoch in its own terms (as opposed to the terms dictated by *his* epoch), he searched for the "ideas" and "tendencies" that ruled it, comprehending rather than passing judgment, applying "scientific" principles where, before, murky humanistic ones had prevailed—a methodology he summed up in the somewhat memorable phrase *"wie es eigentlich gewesen,"* how it really was. Not that the old boy was as clinical and impartial as he'd have you think: An archconservative, who depended on the support first of Metternich, then of Bismarck, and who believed that Germany had a mission to develop a culture and a political system all its own; a Lutheran who, in his *History of the Reformation in Germany*, gave Luther the benefit of every doubt; a mystic who claimed to see "God's finger" in human affairs—he didn't travel light or bias-free.

Theodor Mommsen (1817–1903), his colleague and chief among his legatees, is, by contrast, one of those inspiration-to-us-all people. Like Ranke, a practitioner of the new objective history, he was a model of professionalism, of scholarship, and of saying what he meant. His *History of Rome* is based, not on old legends and myths, but on coins, inscriptions, and artifacts, many of which Mommsen literally dug up himself. Modest, wise, and good, he sought "to bring a more vivid knowledge of classical antiquity to wider circles." And he's the flip side to Ranke on the Days-of-Prussia l.p.: a frustrated liberal who had sided with the protesters in 1848, who deeply resented Bismarck, who deplored the beginnings of anti-Semitism in Germany, and who, when awarded the Nobel Prize for Literature in 1902, asked everyone not to clap. The times, he said, were too grave.

The Victorians: Macaulay and Carlyle

Don't make the mistake of writing Victorian England off as simply self-satisfied, all eight-course dinners and back-slapping conversations about how well things were going in the Punjab. In fact, the place was schizophrenic, divided down the middle by issues as unwieldy and unsettling as economic reform, Darwinism, industrialization (already run amok), and what to do about women. Which means, before you read any historian of the era, you'd better know which team he's playing on. Thomas Babington Macaulay (1800–1859) is self-satisfied, at peace with his age (though an outspoken critic of its culture), an influential politician, in favor of peace, liberty, property, applied science, progress, and the Industrial Revolution. He's in sympathy with the Whigs of the previous century and their descendants, the Liberals of his own day. He announces to a nation of Englishmen that they are "the greatest and most highly civilized people that ever the world saw"—and that things are only going to get better. (A lot of them listened: His *History of England from the Accession of James II* has gone through more printings than any other book in English but the Bible.) And if he's a little philistine, a little too much the bellow of the Establishment, he could still tell the kind of good story—upbeat, well-paced, easy to read—that made his constituents feel better about the nutsy times they were living through.

Not so Thomas Carlyle (1795–1881), a Scot with a sense of mystery, a

Macaulay (left) and Carlyle.

fetish for imagination, and the conviction that Macaulay's *History* was "a book to which 400 editions could not lend any permanent value." Carlyle was the era's self-appointed prophet, also its scourge, the sworn enemy of the Establishment, the Spirit of Progress, and the looking-out-for-number-one middle class. His *French Revolution*—"a wild savage Book, itself a kind of French Revolution," as he put it—which features an imaginary reporter as its narrator, has a you-are-there, docudrama quality that is as riveting, and as off-the-wall, as history, of whatever century, gets. Here, as in his biographies of Cromwell (whom he rehabilitated) and Frederick the Great (whom he adored), Carlyle's central thesis—which would be shared by Nietzsche, Shaw, D. H. Lawrence, and Wagner, and which would, rightly, be cited as a contributing factor in the rise of Fascism—was that the Hero, not the Establishment or the State, causes things to evolve, that "Universal History . . . is at bottom the History of the Great Men who have worked here."

Meanwhile, Back at the Ranch: Turner and Beard

You realize, of course, that there's an ocean between us and them, and that they're stunted and jaded and on their way out. Frederick Jackson Turner (1861–1932) realized it, and singlehandedly wrested American history not only from the Old World but from New England too, relocating it smack-dab in the middle of his own upper Mississippi Valley. For Turner, the frontier was "the cutting edge of American civilization," and American democracy and the American character the products of "the existence of an area of free land, its continuous recession, and the advance of American settlement westward." Part Walt Whitman, part Mr. Chips, Turner now stands for the turn-of-the-century national and regional values he swore by. If modern historians have long since stopped subscribing, they still remove their hats.

Charles A. Beard (1874–1948) is a tougher nut, less influential than Turner (who established a whole school of history) and more controversial. Irreverent and nonconformist, even before he studied his Marx he'd arrived at an economic interpretation of American history: The Constitution was "an economic document drawn with superb skill by men whose property interests were immediately at stake" and there was something hokey about its ratification; the Civil War had nothing to do with slavery or states' rights, but was instead the collision of the old agrarian culture with the new industrial one. All very stimulating. And, it turned out, most unsound: Beard had manipulated facts and deliberately overlooked evidence in order to prove his theory. It didn't help, either, that he preached isolationism during World War II—"American continentalism" was his term—and accused FDR of staging Pearl Harbor. Still, he got everybody thinking, he was a useful prototype for young activist intellectuals, and he obviously loved what he did. "The history of a civilization, if intelligently conceived," he says in the introduction to a bestselling textbook he wrote with his wife, Mary, "may be an instrument of civilization."

THINK TANKERS

You know the type—reclusive but bossy. These are the historians who couldn't care less about documents, artifacts, and eyewitness accounts. They're not out to reconstruct the past, but to let us in on what it, plus the present and the future, *mean*.

ST. AUGUSTINE (354–430): Forget the Persian Wars and the founding of Rome: The big events in human history have been the Fall, the Incarnation, and the Resurrection, with the Second Coming next on the agenda. History is not cyclical (Christ died only *once* for our sins), but a glorious unfolding, "the great melody of some ineffable composer." The earth is merely the footstool on which History rests her feet, the existence of man a subplot in the Divine comedy. And, through thirteen centuries and a succession of anchorpersons as persuasive as Dante and Milton, that's simply the way it was—night after night after night.

VICO (1668–1744): A poor scholar in dusty, provincial Naples, he announced to anybody who'd listen that history was not a succession of great men, a wrap-up of the millennium's top stories, or a grade-school pageant with God as director, box-office manager, or even prompter. It was, rather, the work—and the reflection—of men, men like you and me, men who can love and understand history (unlike nature, which will always remain a mystery to us) precisely because we've created it. Not content with one bombshell, Vico dropped another: Nations, like human intelligence, undergo an ordered and predictable progression, from an initial primitive stage through divine (or childish), heroic (or adolescent), and finally civil (or adult) ones. Then they die, and the process begins somewhere else. History is not a great unfolding; it is, rather, cyclical.

VOLTAIRE (1694–1778): Fed up with Augustine, with their own bishop Bossuet (whose *Histoire Universelle* parroted him), and with God, the *philosophes* made faces at, and attempted to refute, all three. Voltaire, the most unstoppable of them, in his *Essay on the Customs and the Spirit of Nations*, rejected Providence, thanks just the same; opined that events have more to do with chance than with design; and proposed a new kind of *histoire universelle* (note the lower-case letters), based on the notion that men are alike, no matter what country they live in, endowed with the same natural rights and faculties, destined to proceed along the same path of reason and enlightenment. It's a small world, after all! And mainstream history is, for the first time, worldly in spirit.

HERDER (1744–1803): The first wave in the German intellectual tide that would wash over the nineteenth century. According to this earnest Protestant pastor, the world isn't all that small, or people all that much alike. Rather, true civilization arises from native roots: It is the common people, the *Volk*, who engender a national character, the *Volksgeist*. German ways are different from French or English ones—not necessarily better, just different—and nationalism is inevitable. And one more thing: It's a mistake to treat the past as if it were the present's slightly retarded older brother, even if it does dress funny.

HEGEL (1770–1831): Not only are German ways different, they're a whole lot better. They're also the next sure thing, how history will be carried through the upcoming stage in its development from Pure Being (that was China) all the way to the Absolute Idea (the highest unity of thought, all integration and harmony, and obviously Prussia). World-Historical Individuals—heroic types who seem to embody the very nature of the transition to come—count for something, but the State is the important thing; in his *Philosophy of History*, Hegel invites it to fill the tall-and-big-men's shoes recently vacated by the

Church. As you may already have heard, the mechanism underlying the whole historical process he outlined is called the dialectic, and it, at least, isn't hard to grasp: The dominant idea, or "truth," of an epoch (its thesis), brings with it its precise negation (its antithesis); out of their sparring emerges a brand new, more or less hybrid "truth," or synthesis. (This was Marx's favorite part; see page 576.) Thus the very disunity of Germany, the fact of its being fragmented into all those little principalities and duchies, summons up the idea of unity, and *must* ultimately bring about the creation of a German state. That is, State—according to Hegel, the institutional embodiment of reason and liberty, "the march of God through the world."

SPENGLER (1880–1936): Surprise! The state isn't that big a deal, after all. In fact, the real action is all in the "culture," which passes through four historical phases (just like Vico said), eventually falling into complete, irreversible decay. And we're no exception, according to Spengler, who, in *The Decline of the West,* foresaw imminent Asiatic domination. Doom, gloom, and the dubious comfort that it's always been and always will be thus. Toynbee would agree. So, in a way, would the Nazis, to whom all this pessimism looked like a welcome mat. In fact, as early as 1918, Spengler was claiming to hear their "quiet firm step."

LEGENDS

Two major reputations—one still in vogue, one already in mothballs—you simply have to deal with.

Edward Gibbon (1737–1794)

It was at Rome, on the 15th of October, 1764, as I sat musing amidst the ruins of the Capitol, while the barefooted friars were singing vespers in the Temple of Jupiter, that the idea of writing the decline and fall of the city first started to my mind.

from *Memoirs*

The various modes of worship, which prevailed in the Roman world, were all considered by the people as equally true; by the philosopher, as equally false; and by the magistrate, as equally useful.

from The Decline and Fall of the Roman Empire

I have described the triumph of barbarism and religion.

from The Decline and Fall of the Roman Empire

Six volumes. Three thousand pages. A million and a quarter words. Accounting for 1,400 years (from "the Age of the Antonines," in the first century A.D., to the stirrings of the Renaissance) in the lives of three continents, Britain to Palestine, including both halves of the Empire and all the nations that border on it, with special attention to the rise of Christianity *and* of Islam and to the eventual "fall" of Rome into the "superstitious" Middle Ages. Considered the greatest history ever written in the English language, a glorious melding of heavy-duty scholarship and high style.

Be that—be *all* that—as it may, there are really only three things you've got to keep in mind about *The History of the Decline and Fall of the Roman Empire*. First, that Gibbon believed Christianity was the central destructive force in the collapse of Roman civilization. (Watch him excoriate it in the infamous fifteenth and sixteenth chapters.) By offering a lot of non-self-starters—"useless multitudes who could only plead the merits of abstinence and chastity" is how he puts it—the promise of a life after death, Christianity undermined the rational pursuit of both virtue and reward, thereby weakening the Empire's defenses against the barbarians, who took a more pragmatic, now-or-never approach to life. There were compounding factors, of course—imperial corruption, for instance—but it's Christianity that Gibbon nabs, tries, and sends up the river.

Second, that the book really *reads*. Granted, it proved a bit much for some people, even at the time; as the then Duke of Gloucester remarked, "Another damned, thick, square book! Always scribble, scribble, scribble! Eh, Mr. Gibbon?" For most everybody else, though, *Decline and Fall* is a great story told against a big backdrop, with a cast of characters who make prime-time soaps look subtle by comparison; a model of balance, precision, wit, and malice, veined with irony and spiced with innuendo. (Check out, especially, Gibbon's footnotes, where, somebody once remarked, it was clear he lived out most of his sex life.) And if it's sheer sonority you're after, there's at least as much of it here as in the speeches of Winston Churchill—himself a Gibbon freak.

Third, that there are implications. Gibbon believed that there existed a special connection between Rome at its height and his own England (which had, after all, just passed through *its* Augustan Age and which was about to enter its imperial heyday), and that everybody would surely like to see that connection analyzed, complete with it-can-happen-here overtones. Of course, it now seems clear—as far as ancient-modern analogies go—that the role Britain really played was Greece, leaving to America the somewhat thankless and totally grandiose role of Rome. Which is precisely why *The Portable Gibbon* deserves a place on the old bookshelf right next to *Animal Farm* and *1984*.

Arnold Toynbee (1889–1975)

Civilization is a movement and not a condition, a voyage and not a harbor.

Reader's Digest, October 1955

Successive Occurrences of the War-and-Peace Cycle in Modern & Post-Modern Western History: Premonitory Wars (the Prelude), The General War, The Breathing-space, Supplementary Wars (the Epilogue), The General Peace—Overture and four Regular Cycles, 1494–1945

Title of chart, with column headings,
A Study of History, Vol. 9

In London, in the southern section of the Buckingham Palace Road, walking southward along the pavement skirting the west wall of Victoria Station, the writer, once, one afternoon not long after the end of the First World War . . . , found himself in communion, not just with this or that episode in History, but with all that had been, and was, and was to come. In that instant he was directly aware of the passage of History flowing through him in a mighty current, and of his own life welling like a wave in the flow of this vast tide.

from *A Study of History*, Vol. 10

The historian as vicar, out to provide a little comfort (admittedly, cold comfort), in the face of a couple of world wars, the demise of the doctrine of social progress, and a universe gone all relative and weak-in-the-knees. Toynbee sets out to solace his reader with his own special combination of cosmic rhythm, faith-of-our-fathers piety, and three-ring erudition. The one-volume abridgment of his twelve-volume *A Study of History* (1934–1961) is, evidently as a result, the only theory of history ever to hit the mass-market racks. And if you come away from the enterprise less reassured than filled with a sense of impending doom, there's always the Durants.

History, per Toynbee, is not the great upward climb (as orchestrated by either God or Darwin), but a series of pulsations, pendulum swings, seasonal cycles, in which civilizations—of which our Western one is but the most recent of exactly twenty-one—rise, flourish, break down, and fall apart, the victims not only of external attacks, but also of internal failures of nerve. The basic mechanism in all this Toynbee calls "challenge and response," and he proceeds to illustrate how, from Egyptian and Sumerian times down to the present, every civilization has gradually lost its ability to cope, inevitably succumbing to such unhappiness as the "time of troubles" and, finally, the "universal state," which sounds good, but isn't (Hitler was out to create ours). Toynbee's system draws heavily on Spengler (see page 539), but for the latter's love of violence and pagan pessimism it substitutes mildness and the hope of religious salvation.

There's a lot in Toynbee to be impressed by: sweep, scope, breadth of knowledge, wealth of detail, boldness, conviction, energy, the determination to see a pattern in the tea leaves. And a lot to roll your eyes at: didacticism, long-windedness, and the determination to see the same pattern in the tea leaves in the bottom of every cup in the tearoom. Professional historians bring additional charges: twisting of the evidence, procrustean-bed methodology, untestable conclusions, "pernicious determinism." (They're especially annoyed at how, along about Volume 9, Toynbee announces that it is religion, not civilization, that is "the serious business of the human race.") And nobody, professional or passerby, knows quite how to behave when Toynbee takes time out from his system and lets fly with another of those trippy insights of his. Still, no other twentieth-century historian has known as much about as many different ages, peoples, and cultures; has made such a determined effort to see the forest even as he's counting and recounting the trees; or has been able to make history seem like quite such a big deal.

THE PARIS BUREAU

Frog historiography is a clubby affair. Not stuffy, exactly, but ingrown and with plenty of, how you say, *ton*. Even the radicals and the firebrands, once they've sat down at the old écritoire, start to behave as if they're contributing to a single grand enterprise, consolidating a single grand reputation, both of which, in case you were wondering, begin with *F*. Still, what other country can boast fifteen years of revolution, another eleven of Napoleon, plus major shakeups in both 1830 and 1848 *and* a humiliating defeat at the hands of the Prussians in 1870? With action like that, *mon cher*, you don't have to send your best minds off to sift through the debris of ancient Rome just so they'll have something to do.

The great national historian of France is Jules Michelet (1798–1874), who liked to think of himself as a child of the Revolution and of the masses who made it; who singlehandedly "resurrected" medieval France (complete with Jeanne d'Arc), intuiting and emoting what he couldn't piece together from the archives; and who bit by bit extended the story through his own day, becoming more and more bitter, and more and more biased, as he went along. His *L'Histoire de France*, in six volumes, is kind of like a magic-carpet ride (he'd

Delacroix's "Liberty Leading the People."

bought Montesquieu's old theory that geography and climate determine, among other things, form of government, and he insists on detailing every last hectare of La Belle France), kind of like a D. W. Griffith movie (he'd fortified himself with Vico's belief that it was the man in the street who made history), and—at its best—kind of like a salmon swimming upstream, trying to get back to the essence of what *was* by ignoring, as much as possible, the overwhelmingness of what *is*. He won't shut up, but the man has heart.

Not so most of his colleagues, who tend to be of an aggressively theoretical, even clinical turn of mind. There's Henri de Saint-Simon (1760–1825, the grand-nephew of the acid-tongued duke who'd skewered Louis XIV and his court), who distinguished between "critical" and "organic" phases of civilization; who plumped for the reorganization of society under a governing elite of scientists, financiers, and industrialists, with artists in place of clergymen; and who had a big influence on Marx and on John Stuart Mill. There's his disciple, Auguste Comte (1798–1857), arrogant, dogmatic, and a bit crazy, who divided history into three stages—the theological, in which God's will was how people explained things away, lasting until Martin Luther made the world safe for atheism; the metaphysical, in which natural laws accounted for everything, lasting from Luther until the French Revolution and the rise of the machine; and the scientific, in which you reject sweeping generalizations, unquestioned assumptions, and wishful thinking in general for the elegance of the observable fact and the verifiable law, meant to go on forever. Comte called this "scientific," eyes-on-the-road attitude positivism, and he promoted it nonstop; he also came up with the word for and the discipline of sociology, the study of man in society.

And there's that second-half-of-the-century duo, Hippolyte Taine (1828–

1893) and Ernest Renan (1823–1892), each devoted to cleaning out as many national bureau drawers as possible. Taine, a disciple of Comte, thought of history as "mechanics applied to psychology" and believed that if you assembled enough facts, and then were very, very on the ball, you'd be able to come up with all the laws that operated on them. He really wasn't *that* interested in counting and measuring, but that didn't stop Taine from feeding all of history, plus literature and art, into his fact processor, then setting it on "mince"; from announcing that culture is a matter of race, milieu, and moment, which together determine something called *la faculté maîtresse;* or from positing that vice and virtue are no less chemically analyzable than sulfuric acid and sugar. Renan, who was less pedantic than Taine and who wrote better besides, yoked science and religion, *raison* and *sensibilité*, attempting to explain, among other things, Christ's Resurrection without resorting to words like "divinity" and "miracle." He was a sweetheart, but he also could put you to sleep.

Are we forgetting anybody? Well, Alexis de Tocqueville (1805–1859), of course, who was more political thinker than historian, and who had the good sense to get out of France for a few years. Having set up shop in America, he drew a line between liberty and democracy, worried aloud about "the tyranny of the majority" and the distrust of excellence, and predicted, just as Comte was telling everybody about positivism for the second or third time, that, within a century, the United States would have 100 million people and would, along with Russia, be one of the world's two leading powers.

Then there are Braudel and Foucault; we'll get to them in a minute.

ROLE MODELS

A century's worth of them for the historians of tomorrow.

JACOB BURCKHARDT (1818–1897): The master craftsman. And still seminal after all these years. True, his *Civilization of the Renaissance in Italy* ignored economics, scanted the peasants, and kicked the Middle Ages while they were down, but it also came up with the understanding of the period we call "Renaissance"—of man just turning modern, learning to function as an individual, painting pictures and practicing statecraft and *knowing* that he's painting pictures and practicing statecraft—that scholars have been going on ever since. A cool, collected Swiss, with no particular ax to grind, Burckhardt took the Italy of the fourteenth through sixteenth centuries and distilled and bottled it, Borgias, *condottieri*, Michelangelo, and all.

BENEDETTO CROCE (1866–1952): The godfather. Exercised something like a benevolent intellectual dictatorship over Italy for half a century, during which he told Italians what to read and what not to read in literature, philosophy, and history. (Some of them still haven't gotten over it.) Transcendental, intuitive, and just this side of mystical, Croce wanted to defend history against the incursions of science—and to give it a nudge in the direction of fellow-feeling. Or, as he put it in his *History: Its Theory and Practice,* "The deed of which the history is told must vibrate in the soul of the historian." Himself equally the historian of aesthetic theories and of Italy, especially Naples; a fervent anti-Fascist before and throughout the War; with the shrewdest, sweetest (think Jiminy Cricket) kind of common sense: Croce is hard to resist. And even harder to read.

PIETER GEYL (1887–1966): The voice of reason. In Holland, the crossroads of Europe, where tolerance and sturdy ankles are a way of life, men make a point of taking the long and balanced view, of assessing what their larger, more ambitious neighbors are up to. Of course, Geyl can't refrain from invoking, in the same breath with Michelet, Ranke, and Macaulay, a Dutch historian named Groen van Prinsterer, but at least he quotes Agatha Christie, too. Measured, penetrating, the upholder of the standards of historical scholarship, with a style someone once likened to a "douche of cold water," Geyl rolled his eyes and delivered four lectures at the mention of Toynbee's name.

FERNAND BRAUDEL (1902–1985): Had the common touch. Heir to the so-called *Annales* school of French historiography—which said Enough, already, with the kings and the popes and the generals, let's see what the rest of us used to be up to, and which tried to bring to history some of the methods of the social sciences—Braudel cared less about, say, the Peace of Westphalia than about the fact that wolves were attacking Parisians well into the 1400s; that tea is popular only in countries where there are no vineyards; and that even rich people ate with their hands until the late eighteenth century, which, coincidentally, is also when the idea of privacy was invented. If anthropology is your idea of history, if you like minute observation against a sweeping backdrop, and if you don't care if you ever hear another *theory* of history in your life, then Braudel—either his two-volume *The Mediterranean and the Mediterranean World in the Age of Philip II* or his three volume *Civilization and Capitalism, 15th–18th Century*—is for you.

A.J.P. TAYLOR (1906–): A smart Alistair Cooke. Dubbed "the pyrotechnician of history," presumably because of his ability to hold millions of Brits spellbound while lecturing on various complex historical issues of the last few hundred years, and on the television yet. Then there are his (at last count) twenty-six books, including *English History: 1914–1945*, sometimes said to be his masterpiece; *The Trouble Makers*, about dissent and foreign policy; and *The Origins of the Second World War*, a scandal in its day inasmuch as it portrayed Hitler as a traditional German statesman rather than a ravening warmonger, and laid a lot of blame at the doorsteps of Britain and France. All of which suffices to make him the most widely known British historian since Macaulay. Industry gossip: Even with the popularity *and* the productivity, Taylor in 1957 lost out on Oxford's Regius Professorship of Modern History to Hugh Trevor-Roper, the *other* British historian of our times, nicknamed "the sleuth of Oxford," who'd been one of the front liners in the attack on Taylor's *Origins*. You can bet Taylor cackled to himself, though, when Trevor-Roper made the mistake, in 1983, of certifying as genuine the sixty Hitler diaries for which *Stern* and *Newsweek* had paid a forger several million dollars.

ISAIAH BERLIN (1909–): Mister—make that Sir—Sagacity. Born in Latvia, raised in England, and canonized at Oxford, he's all for choices (the harder the better) and "the painful conflicts and perplexities of the disordered freedom of the world beyond the [prison] walls." Once just another philosopher, now a historian "of ideas," of thinking about thinking, Berlin is a thorough-going liberal, a dyed-in-the-wool pluralist, and a fearless crusader against determinism and "historical inevitability" (he rolls his eyes at the mention of Toynbee's name but is above discussing him as an individual case). Naturally, he's also a champion of the intellectual underdog, the thinker (Vico is his favorite) who is out of synch with, because ahead of, his time. Caution: While he's been positioned as "the don who can't write a dull essay," be on your guard against sentences as long as freight trains and the creepily casual dropping of the biggest names of the last couple of millennia, Plato to Pasternak and Newton to Nijinsky.

BARBARA TUCHMAN (1912–): Twenty-twenty hindsight. Not only does Tuchman see both doom and folly everywhere—in France's wrongheaded strategy during the opening days of World War I in *The Guns of August;* in the primed-to-explode energies of fin-de-siècle Europe and America in *The Proud Tower;* in the chaos of the disaster-ridden fourteenth century in *A Distant Mirror*—she can't wait to rub everybody's nose in it. Though she's a pretty good storyteller (she's even been compared with Gibbon in terms of clarity and conviction) with a knowledge of how to excite public—as opposed to merely academic—

outrage and debate on behalf of her field, Tuchman's character-is-fate expositions of morality can get on a person's nerves. A bigger problem (but don't let
on we're the ones who told you): She usually doesn't wind up proving, after
700 or so pages, the thesis she posited with such elegance way back in chapter
one.

RICHARD HOFSTADTER (1916–1970): Good buddy. The first major American historian who didn't come from either a small
town in the Midwest or a long line of Bostonians, Hofstadter's
the product of New York City, and he never stopped thinking
in the cultural and political—and faintly radical—terms he
learned there. Interested in such contemporary phenomena as
the New Deal, McCarthyism, paranoia, the plight of the
American intellectual, and Barry Goldwater; easygoing and
personable (he wore clip-on bow ties and hitched up his
trousers a lot); willing to admit that the picture he'd painted
was subject to change without official notice ("I offer trial
models of historical interpretation"): Hofstadter wrote to figure
out what he really thought—and to share it with you, bro.

MICHEL FOUCAULT (1926–1984): Velvet fist in an iron glove.
Tended to ask, but usually didn't stick around to answer, the
bravest, vaguest, and thorniest kinds of questions: What are
the "discourses" that inform, say, our attitudes toward sexuality or our treatment of the insane? How do the "discourses"
emerge? What rules do they obey? How and why do they
change? Foucault, who has been claimed by both the structuralists and the poststructuralists (see page 330) and who described himself as a "historian of systems of thought," kept
two generations of Parisian Marxists and American graduate
students guessing as to what the correct answers were, without
himself ever being pinned down—like a particularly outrageous drag queen (as one insiders' simile has it) foiling the
arrest attempts of a whole squad of policemen. While it seems
clear that Foucault never did a whole lot of library research
into madness, sexuality, prison, hospitals, or anything else,
and while some of his insights seem like plain showing off,
you'll want to pay attention to his notion of the *episteme*—from
the Greek word for "knowledge," a sharp break between one
historical period and another, marked by the end of one intellectual framework and the beginning of a new one, as when

the Age of Reason, reviewing the differences between what was normal and what wasn't, decided to reclass the insane (who in the Middle Ages had been thought of as inspired), this time behind bars. Ditto, to his belief (heartfelt, incidentally) that the subtlest problem in the world, and the one most worth studying, is the relationship between liberty and social coercion, or, stated the way Foucault used to state it, between power and truth.

Fun Couples

JUSTINIAN AND THEODORA (married, A.D. 525): The team that made the Byzantine Empire what it isn't today. A couple of climbers (he came from peasant stock and worked his way up to the throne; she was the daughter of a bearkeeper at the Hippodrome), they're a classic example of what the right woman can do for a man. Justinian had energy (he was the one about whom it was first said "The emperor never sleeps"), personal appeal, and a knack for recognizing talent when he saw it. He was, however, an unstable egomaniac and an intellectual lightweight. Theodora was a troublemaker, but she had the requisite brains and nerve to keep Justinian in the imperial driver's seat. While she was alive, he consolidated the empire, drove out pesky barbarians, established the famous Justinian Code, and initiated most of the architectural feats associated with Byzantine glory. After she died (of cancer, in 548), he spent the rest of his reign tinkering.

HELOISE AND ABELARD (married, c. 1118): What a tear-jerker! Peter Abelard was the most celebrated logician, theologian, and teacher of his day, and the biggest ego in medieval France. Taking a shine to young Heloise, the brilliant 17-year-old niece of a canon at the university, he finagled a job as her tutor and promptly seduced her. After she gave birth to a son named Astrolabe (don't look at us, we weren't consulted), the couple were married, but secretly, to avoid damaging Abelard's career. Heloise went home to live with her uncle, who became increasingly freaked out over the whole affair. He took to slapping Heloise around on general principle, and finally hired a couple of thugs to sneak into Abelard's room at night and castrate him. This hurt Abelard's pride. He crept off to become a famous teacher somewhere else, write controversial scholarly treatises, and establish an order of literary nuns, of which Heloise eventually became the abbess. Poor Heloise, who was forced to take the veil, never got to spend more than five minutes with her husband after that fateful night in Paris, but she and Abelard did publish the love letters that substituted for sex for the rest of their lives; centuries later, these inspired the epistolary novel, if that's any consolation.

HENRY II AND ELEANOR OF AQUITAINE (married, 1152): Not only did they form the most potent concentration of forces in feudal Europe, but their relationship contained enough sex, power, and ambition to fuel a Broadway play and a Hollywood movie. Eleanor was thirty, Henry nineteen when they met. She saw in him a lusty young adventurer, the future King of England. He saw in her the chance for a brilliant political alliance (England was no prize in those days and she did happen to own—personally—more than half of France). Two towering egos, they spent the next twenty years intimidating the neighbors and trying to dominate each other. He turned England into a respectable kingdom; she ran Aquitaine. He fought the Church; she patronized the arts. He ran around with other women; she sponsored young troubadors. Finally, she talked her sons into making war on their father; he won and had her thrown in jail for fifteen years. She had the last laugh, though; she outlived him.

FERDINAND AND ISABELLA (married, 1469): It was a Catholic ceremony. The bride, Isabella of Castile, was the product of a Gothic-novel childhood—gloomy castle, demented mother, sexually depraved half-brother and all—but she didn't let that stand in her way when the throne of Castile was up for grabs. The groom, Ferdinand of Aragon, was dashing, dynamic, and due to inherit the province next door, plus Sicily, Sardinia, Naples, and the Balearic Islands. They were a perfect match, a couple of high-stakes players sitting on a lot of undeveloped real estate. To tame the local nobles and instill a sense of family loyalty, the couple decided to start the Spanish Inquisition. This, combined with the expulsion of the Jews and Moors, the conquest of Grenada, and the high returns on Isabella's investment in Christopher Columbus (with whom she was almost certainly *not* having an affair), did the trick. Spain became the most fearsomely Catholic country in the world and the most ironclad monarchy in Europe, and Ferdinand and Isabella, "the Catholic kings," became the best argument for or against marrying within your own faith, depending on your point of view.

WILLIAM AND MARY (married, 1677): Now here's a boring couple. Paragons of Protestant restraint, they nevertheless managed to undermine the whole concept of absolute monarchy. William (that's William of Orange) was a stolid, sensible Dutchman; fatherless, childless, humorless, and utterly devoid of table manners, he seemed incapable of any passion except a rabid hatred of the French. He was imported by the English Parliament to unseat Mary's father, the Catholic James II, which he did in a bloodless victory of political maneuvering over Divine Right known as the Glorious Revolution. Thanks in part to the obedient Mary, who was merely William's safe-conduct to the English throne, Parliament gained supremacy over the crown, England became securely Protestant again, and William, who didn't care a fig for the crown, for England, or for Mary, got to pursue his impossible dream: snuffing out all things French from the face of the earth.

NAPOLEON AND JOSEPHINE (married, 1796): An unlikely match, but it seemed to work. He was a short Corsican soldier six years her junior with minimal connections, few social graces, and no money in the bank. She was a seductive Creole from Martinique with two children, expensive tastes, and one of the most fashionable salons in Paris. His family loathed her. She wasn't impressed with him, either, but her politically prominent lover encouraged the match. Two days after the wedding he marched off to conquer Italy. She stayed home, shopped, and had affairs with younger men. He put up with her infidelities and her laziness and found comfort in the vast empty spaces of her mind. She put up with his rages and his round-the-clock workdays and worshipped him from across the room. For thirteen years they lived happily in the fast lane. He conquered most of Europe, rearranged the rest, and had himself crowned Emperor. She took to wearing Empire-waist dresses and bought more hats. He never did manage to get her pregnant, though, and in the end he annulled the marriage to hitch up with an eighteen-year-old Austrian princess who bore him an heir. Too bad; it broke Josephine's heart and, as it turned out, he needn't have bothered.

FRANKLIN AND ELEANOR ROOSEVELT (married, 1905): The closest we ever had to a king and a queen. Or to a pair of kings, but let's leave Eleanor's sexual preferences out of this, shall we? FDR *did* have a dictatorial streak, what with the New Deal, the way he tried to butt into the Supreme Court's business, and his getting us into the war. But don't forget that demagoguery was in flower in those days and it could've been worse: We could've had Huey Long. Besides, Franklin gave us Eleanor, who was a great lady in spite of those sensible shoes. Not content with planting memorial shrubs, she was even more of a reformer than he was; in fact, some people called her a Communist—an understandable mistake, given her holier-than-thou attitudes and

the fact that she didn't see anything intrinsically wrong with "Negroes." This was more a partnership than a marriage, really, and sometimes it seemed more like a rivalry than either. But isn't that, after all, the American Way?

MAO TSE-TUNG AND CHIANG CH'ING (married, c. 1938): They showed the West that Chinese Communists can have marital problems, too. He was already on his third wife when he met her; she was a struggling Shanghai actress who'd been through one husband and several, well, mentors. For nearly thirty years she was content to type his lecture notes and appear in public as Madame Mao. Then, in 1966, she suddenly emerged as first deputy leader and chief witch hunter of the Great Proletarian Cultural Revolution. For the next ten years she publicly purged bourgeois reactionism from the arts while privately screening Greta Garbo movies for her friends. Mao, who lived elsewhere, kept in touch by sending her cryptic notes and right-thinking poems. In 1977, a year after his death, she was arrested as one of the "Gang of Four," charged with plotting to become "the new empress," and expelled from the Party as a "bourgeois careerist, conspirator, counter-revolutionary, double-dealer, and renegade." Her death sentence was suspended and, when last heard from, she was still serving time in a Chinese prison.

Vintage Years

1453

The Hundred Years' War (actually the Hundred and Sixteen Years' War, but who's counting?), between England and France, is over. So are: chivalry (the armor couldn't stand up to the new English longbow, plus most of the knights had come to seem more greedy than valiant); Joan of Arc (burned at the stake, but she really *had* singlehandedly saved France); and the illusion that England, the loser, sort of, and France, the winner, sort of (even though the former, an underpopulated little island, had, in the course of the war, managed to win possession of most of the latter, the biggest, fattest country in Europe, only to be routed at the end) were destined to be a single nation. By war's end, too, kings are firmly back in the saddle after two centuries of cagey maneuvering on the part of the nobility and its parliaments (and of their own royal ineptitude). And the Middle Ages are teetering on the brink of Modern Times.

"Joan of Arc," by Rubens.

1598

Henry IV of France issues the Edict of Nantes, promising French Protestants, or Huguenots, the same civil and religious rights that French Catholics had. Unlike England, where the Catholic minority had no rights at all, and Germany, where religion was all about grabbing a free city or a principality and imposing your own creed on it, France was suddenly, and out of the blue, behaving like a grown-up. For this, there is Henry to thank, a former Huguenot (and a particularly savvy one), who, having been crowned king, realized that if he wanted to be let inside the gates of heavily Catholic Paris, he was going to have to make a few concessions—the occasion for his religious con-

*The Peace of
Westphalia.*

version and for his famous observation, "Paris is well worth a Mass." Make a
note of Henry IV (born Henry of Navarre): He's the most popular and most
fondly remembered of all the French kings (except maybe for St. Louis, back
in the Middle Ages), he was the first politician ever to make use of the slogan
"a chicken in every pot," and he was the founder of the Bourbon dynasty,
laying the foundations for the absolutism of the Louis (see page 558) who
followed him. Unfortunately, Henry was assassinated in 1610; the Huguenots
would get theirs, too, in 1685, when Louis XIV revoked the Edict of Nantes
and France started to pretend it had never even heard of religious tolerance.

1648

The Peace of Westphalia ends the Thirty Years' War, the most destructive
war yet. Wave good-bye to the medieval world-view, the Counter-Reforma-
tion, wars of religion, the Holy Roman Empire, Germany's prospects for the
next two hundred years, and Spain's prospects, period. Brace yourself for the
triumph of secular thinking, the ascendancy of France (in the person of Louis
XIV), and a new age of pluralism, in which nobody will even pretend Europe
has any overriding unity, spiritual, political, or other, and in which states will
behave like the discrete, self-interested entities they are.

1762

Jean-Jacques Rousseau publishes his *Social Contract*. His glorification of the
common man, the "noble savage," had already managed to make breast-feed-

Rousseau, center, ventures into society.

ing fashionable again (and would later encourage Marie Antoinette to dress up as a milkmaid). Now Rousseau, feeling alienated as ever—he was Swiss, Protestant, and paranoid, among other things, and nobody wanted to play milkmaid with *him*—describes a society in which he thinks men, himself included, could be happy: Individuals would surrender their natural liberty to one another, fusing their individual wills into a General Will, which, rather than a king or even a parliament, would be the true sovereign power. With his *Social Contract,* Rousseau becomes the prophet of both democracy and nationalism; in just a few years, the ideas he set forth in it will help to bring about the French Revolution. The book is not, however, a bestseller.

1815

The Congress of Vienna puts its stamp on Europe. The four Great Powers—England, Russia, Prussia, and Austria—having finally managed to write finis to Napoleon's plan for a France that stretched from Madrid to Moscow now sit down and work out a "balance of power" that will pretty much prevail until the First World War. Not that the diplomats who gathered in Austria's capital—the shifty Prince Metternich, the crafty Baron Talleyrand, and so on—were all that forward-looking; in fact, most of them, intent on squashing the liberalism and nationalism and democracy that had sprouted in the aftermath of the French Revolution, were downright reactionary. But neither were the diplomats dopes: The Treaty of Vienna wisely let France off fairly easy (applause here for Talleyrand, who knew an opening when he saw one),

*The Paris barri-
cades, 1848.*

deeded over to Britain the best and the brightest colonial empire, smoothed over the rivalry between Prussia and Austria for domination of the German-speaking world, and resolved the issue (for at least the next couple of generations) of who'd push Poland around. And, for a hundred years after the incredible (and exhausting) brouhaha of the French Revolution and Napoleon, there was—if you leave aside the insurrections of 1830 and 1848 (see below) and a few eensy localized conflicts like the Franco-Prussian War of 1870—peace.

1848

Barricades and cobblestones, radicalism and the June Days. All over Europe—Paris to Budapest, Copenhagen to Palermo—the existing order is challenged, and sometimes overturned, only to be back still pretty much on top a few months later. (Britain and Russia alone missed out on the chaos.) The issues: nationalism, constitutional government, broadened suffrage, the abolition of serfdom in the Balkans. The enemy: the ruling classes, the Catholic Church, the farflung Hapsburg influence. The result: a basic misfiring—serfs are freed, all right, but dreams of liberalism and good government bite the dust. The legacy: class hatred and national jealousy, a new toughness of mind (which the Germans, whose day is at hand, will call *Realpolitik*), and the setting of the stage for Marxism. In fact, *The Communist Manifesto* had appeared that January.

1854

Commodore Perry, an American, opens Japan. He finds there an elaborately civilized nation, much given to city life, novels, the theater, the contemplation of landscape, lacquer work, and fans. None of which stops him from threatening to open fire if the Japanese don't accede to his demands to trade with America, and on terms hugely advantageous to the latter. Ditto, to trade with everybody else in a gunboat and a cocked hat. Japan, sealed off tight-little-island-style from the rest of the world since 1640, when it had kicked out all of an earlier generation of Europeans except for a handful of Dutch merchants in Nagasaki, will soon find itself undergoing westernization in everything from the codification of its laws to the delivery of its mail. The Japanese wind up getting what they soon realize they'd really been needing all along—science, technology, bureaucracy. And they get it real fast. In fact, never have so many people undergone so profound a transformation in so few years. Or, a short century later, so succeeded in upstaging their teachers.

1945

Churchill, Roosevelt, and Stalin take another meeting, this one at Yalta, an old czarist summer resort on the Black Sea. Victory over Germany and Japan is in sight: But how are the Allied Powers to deal with the defeated? Likewise, each other? Roosevelt miscalculates, choosing to trust Stalin too much, listen to Churchill—a past master at the old spheres-of-influence, keep-your-distance style of diplomacy—too little. Russia not only gets most of Eastern Europe (not that it doesn't have one big furry boot on it already) plus parts of Japan (who it hasn't even been at war with), it gets the West's seal of approval, too. And all in the name of, talk about irony, international friendship.

Churchill, Roosevelt, and Stalin at Yalta.

Louie, Louie

I t's hard enough trying to keep track of the English Henrys and Richards; what is one to do with the crazy French monarchs who, for centuries, insisted on naming their offspring Louis? Our advice: Start small. Here, the four Louis(s) to remember, and a few things to remember them by:

THE MAN: *LOUIS XIII*
(1601–1643)

Timid, sickly, and depressed, he spent most of his life trying to assert himself; first toward his mother, the fat, silly, overbearing Regent Marie de' Medici; then toward his minister, Richelieu, on the one hand and toward Richelieu's innumerable enemies on the other. Despite his personal problems, Louis wanted very much to be a great king. History has only recently begun to do him justice, noting that he had the sense to recognize his own limitations and the guts to play second fiddle to a minister he hated for what seemed, at the time, to be the good of France.

HIS MATE:

Anne of Austria: The daughter of the King of Spain (Spain was then under Hapsburg rule), she was selected by Louis's mother, who hoped to cement an alliance between the two countries. Louis responded by ignoring Anne; it took four years for him to consummate the marriage, and twenty to father their first child. Anne had a strange life, but not the worst imaginable for a French queen; although she was perpetually at loggerheads with Richelieu, who was both arrogant and vehemently anti-Hapsburg, her husband, at least, lacked the energy to be actively unfaithful to her. She became regent once the king and his minister were dead.

HIS MINISTER:

Cardinal Richelieu: The proud, ruthless power behind the throne, whom you may best remember as the villain in Dumas's *The Three Musketeers*. Any French schoolchild would be able to recite Richelieu's famous three-point program for consolidating the power of the monarchy and the French state: Suppress the Protestants, curb the nobles, and humble the House of Austria. "Red Robe," as the Cardinal was known, succeeded, up to a point—he had a knack for crushing conspiracies and, importantly, he had the support of the king—but he nearly bankrupted the state through sheer financial ineptitude.

HIS MOTTO:

"Now I am king."

HIS CHAIR:

THE MAN: *LOUIS XIV* (1638–1715):

This little man, believe it or not, ruled the France that produced Corneille, Racine, Molière, and Pascal, and was, himself, the greatest repository of personal power in an age that was crawling with absolutist, divine-right monarchs. Short (which is why you'll always see him in heels and a mile-high wig), not pretty (that hooked nose and receding chin were the trademarks of the Bourbon dynasty), harsh, egotistical, and only moderately intelligent, he succeeded in getting himself nicknamed "The Sun King" largely because France was ripe for a leader. He did, however, have certain qualifications for the job: common sense, an ability to recognize talent, stand-out style, a strong feeling for the state, and an absolute delight in the day-to-day business of being king. Under his rule (which lasted seventy-two years, making him the longest-running monarch in French history) France became the most powerful and prestigious country in Europe, although it was financially ruined in the process.

HIS MATES:

Maria Thérèse of Spain: Louis's small, swarthy, somewhat insipid queen, whom he married to fulfill a treaty agreement. She played little part in his life, produced several children who died in infancy and one rather mediocre prince, the Grand Dauphin, who died before he could become king.

The Duchesse de la Vallière: She loved him, bore him children, and, retired, heartbroken, to a nunnery when he abandoned her.

Mme. de Montespan: An intriguer who, after replacing the Duchesse de la Vallière, managed to hang on for twelve years, and to bear the King eight illegitimate children. She fell into disgrace during the Affair of the Poisons, a court scandal involving the mysterious deaths of various nobles, among them the woman Louis had recently chosen to replace her.

Mme. de Maintenon. A pious widow in her forties, renowned for her successful literary salon. Louis gave her the task of raising his children by Mme. de Montespan. These two were friends before they were lovers; Louis, an aging libertine, admired Mme. de Maintenon's intelligence and austerity. After the death of the queen, they were married secretly. She played an important role in politics, caused a major change in the king's lifestyle, and transformed the later years of his reign—making them, some thought, slightly depressing.

HIS MINISTERS:

Cardinal Mazarin: An Italian, inherited from Louis's mother, Anne of Austria, to whom, it was rumored, he was secretly married. Mazarin's aims and policies were much the same as Richelieu's, although his style leaned more toward subtlety and unscrupulousness than open ruthlessness. His ongoing attempts to center power in the crown led to the open rebellion known as La Fronde, in which nobles and bourgeoisie nearly succeeded in toppling the monarchy, but ended by turning on each other instead. Mazarin ran the country while he lived, but after his death, the young Louis dispensed with the office of chief minister altogether and held the reins himself.

Colbert: Louis's finance minister for twenty years, he was one of the great practitioners of mercantilism, the system of building national wealth by exporting goods in exchange for gold and other precious metals. Hoping to make France economically self-sufficient, he encouraged industry, built roads, began construction of a navy, and patronized the arts, but in the end most of his programs—and his reputation—collapsed under the weight of Louis's personal extravagance.

HIS MOTTO:

"L'état c'est moi." ("I am the state.")

HIS CHAIR:

THE MAN: *LOUIS XV*
(1710–1774)

Handsome and frail, he was dubbed "le Bien-Aimé" (the Well-Beloved) by his adoring subjects early in his reign; before long, the epithet was purely ironical. Louis wasn't stupid, but he was spoiled rotten; an incorrigible débauché, he chose to flirt rather than rule. His method of governing consisted of fomenting gossip and intrigue at court and setting up an elaborate spy network, known as "le Secret du Roi," abroad. By the end of his reign, royal authority at home and French influence in Europe were just pleasant memories and Louis was, personally, the most hated man in France.

HIS MATES:

Maria Leszcynska: The daughter of a dethroned Polish king, and considerably older than Louis, she was the best that could be found in a hurry. They were married when he was fifteen, and for a while they got along fine; she was modest, sweet, and able to produce ten children in ten years. Eventually, however, she refused to sleep with the King for the sake of her health, after which she had to resign herself to being a good sport while Louis threw sexual discretion to the wind.

Mme. de Pompadour: Her bourgeois background scandalized the court more than loose morals ever could. Louis made her a marquise, and she did whatever was necessary to hang on to power for the next nineteen years. This was no small feat since, according to the history books, Louis was sexually insatiable and Mme. de Pompadour was "frigid"; she solved the problem by procuring beautiful mistresses for him. An inveterate schemer, she had a genius for stirring up trouble at court, and she helped Louis shape his disastrous foreign policy. On the plus side, she had taste and wit and was committed to encouraging artists. She provided Voltaire with support and protection and Paris with the Place de la Concorde.

Mme. du Barry: She played Lolita to Louis's Humbert. His last official favorite, la du Barry was a pretty, vivacious, rather vulgar courtesan who got on many people's nerves, but apparently meant no harm. She was, at least, an aristocrat. She reportedly sat on the arm of the royal chair during council meetings, making faces at the ministers like a pet monkey.

HIS MINISTER:

Cardinal Fleury: Already seventy when he took office, he ran the state honestly, economically, and cautiously. But he couldn't live forever; when he died in office, at the age of ninety, Louis decided not to appoint another minister in his place.

HIS MOTTO:

"*Après moi, le déluge.*" (Louis never really said this; it was a measure of his unpopularity that everyone believed he had.)

HIS CHAIR:

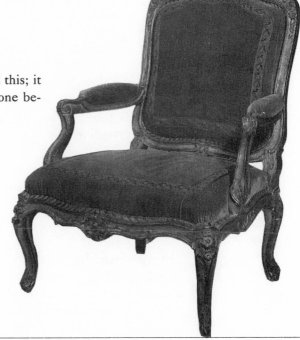

THE MAN: *LOUIS XVI*
(1754–1793)

Flabby, sluggish, humble, and shy, he was probably cut out for something, but it wasn't being king. He read slowly, danced poorly, made conversation barely at all, and always looked a mess, no matter how much trouble his valets took. Even if his piety and basic good-heartedness had been leadership qualities, Louis lacked the will to put them to work. The only things he really cared about were food, his wife, and the hunt, in ascending order. To him, a day without hunting was a day not really lived. On July 14, 1789, he wrote in his diary, "Nothing."

HIS MATE:

Marie Antoinette: She'd been the Archduchess of Austria and she was everything Louis wasn't: majestic, charming, sophisticated, proud, and frivolous. He adored her, she despised him. The fact that a genital malformation kept Louis from consummating their marriage for eight years didn't do much to keep her home at night or to make her treat him kindly. Still, rumors that she was unfaithful were probably false; she was more interested in shopping than in sex. Although her extravagance earned her the nickname "Madame Déficit," it was her Austrian background that the French found really unforgivable. In fact, letters discovered after her death revealed that the queen's mother, Maria Theresa, had had every intention of using her daughter as a tool of the Austrian government (and her meddling in politics certainly shooed the Revolution along its way), but the French had no way of knowing that at the time.

HIS MINISTERS:

Maurepas: An old courtier intent on offending no one, he missed his chance to squelch lethal court factions and refused to support the financial reforms proposed by the liberal minister Turgot because he was jealous. By the time he died, the Revolution was only eight years away.

Necker: A conservative financier who came into prominence largely because of his ambitious wife, who presided over a brilliant literary salon. He ran afoul of Marie Antoinette, and by the time he'd regained power, his orthodox financial policies were too little, too late.

HIS MOTTO:

"Let them eat cake." Not his, of course; hers.

HIS CHAIR:

Special Souvenir-Program Section

YOU CAN'T TELL THE PLAYERS—OR, IN SOME CASES, THE INNINGS—WITHOUT ONE

Persian Wars, Peloponnesian War, Punic Wars

In the *Persian Wars* (500–449 B.C.), the Greeks—most notably Athens and Sparta—defeated the greatest empire the world had up to then known, an empire that embraced not only Persia, but Asia Minor, Mesopotamia, Egypt, and much of what is today Afghanistan. The wars began in Ionia, on the Turkish coast, as a colonial revolt against the "barbarian" landlord; Athens stepped in on the colonists' side, and won a big victory at Marathon. The Spartans got involved and, with the Athenians, suffered a big (though they'd been very brave) defeat at Thermopylae; but the same year (480) the Greeks had a big naval victory at Salamis. Eventually they destroyed the Persian fleet—it was Xerxes I who suffered the defeat, his father Darius I having started the war—then pushed the Persians inland (where Alexander the Great would zap them a century later) and opened the entire Aegean to Greek shipping. Herodotus (see page 532) tells the story of the Persian Wars, which mark the coming of age of Greek nationalism and sense of superiority to the "Orient," as well as the ascendancy of Athens.

In the *Peloponnesian War* (431–404 B.C.), greedy, cocksure Athens, now the preeminent Greek city-state, and its allies, the so-called Delian League, took on spiteful, jealous Sparta and her allies, the so-called Peloponnesian League (from the Peloponnese, the southernmost Greek peninsula, which Sparta dominated). Athens, which was all about democracy and high culture and maritime trading, initially tried to wear down the resistance of Sparta, which was all about oligarchy and military discipline and living off the land. (The Persians, happy enough to see their rivals fighting, funded both sides, first one, then the other.) Ultimately, the war ruined Athens, which made a lot of miscalculations (and wasn't helped by a plague, in which Pericles, its leader, died, or by the revolt of several allies). Sparta, triumphant, took over the Athenian empire, where it did away with voting and playwriting; though it wasn't able to control Athens for long, Sparta remained the dominant power in ancient Greece for another thirty years. Thucydides, who wrote about it (see page 532), calls the Peloponnesian War the worst disturbance in Greek history, but then he hadn't met the Romans.

In the *Punic Wars* (three of them: 264–241 B.C., 218–201 B.C., and 149–146 B.C.), those Romans were able to finish off their "hated city," Carthage, in present-day Tunisia, a rival for trade and empire throughout the western Mediterranean. ("Punic" is from the Roman word for Phoenician, Carthage having been settled by the Phoenicians in the ninth century B.C.) In the first Punic War, Rome, which had just succeeded in showing the rest of the Italian peninsula who was boss, kicked Carthage out of Sicily (then grabbed Sardinia and Corsica while nobody was looking) and came to appreciate the value of naval power. In the second Punic War, Hannibal, a Carthaginian, invaded Rome from Carthaginian Spain by crossing the Alps, but wound up getting wedged into the toe of Italy's boot. Rome relieved Carthage not only of Spain but also of its fleet, then invaded the city itself. This was the end of Carthaginian commercial and imperial greatness, though the place didn't go down the tubes completely. Didn't, that is, until the third Punic War, in which Rome—incited by Cato the Elder's famous *Carthago delenda est* ("Carthage must be destroyed") speech—first blockaded, then conquered the city, taking it apart house by house and stone by stone, and finally ploughing the whole place under. The survivors became slaves and the surrounding lands, the Roman province of Africa. That same year (146 B.C.), Greece was annexed. Rome was off and running.

Middle Ages, Dark Ages, medieval times, feudalism

The *Middle Ages* are the thousand years that elapsed between the fall of the Roman Empire in the West in A.D. 476 and the onset of the Renaissance in Italy in about 1500. Scholars subdivide the Middle Ages into the Early Middle Ages (476 to 900 or 1000, the central figure of which is Charlemagne), the High Middle Ages (900 or 1000 to around 1300), and the Late Middle Ages (1300 to 1500); together the three periods account for the millennium that separates the Ancient world from the Modern one.

The Dark Ages is what Renaissance people, looking down their aquiline noses, called the whole of the Middle Ages. Scholars, however, stepping in once again, preempted the term for the Early Middle Ages only, arguing that the five centuries after the year 1000 weren't, give or take the Hundred Years' War, the Crusades, the Spanish Inquisition, and the Great Plague, really as bad as all that.

Medieval times—or the medieval era, or whatever—is simply, and literally, a Latinate way of saying "Middle Ages," from the Latin *medius*, "middle," plus *aevum*, "age." And *feudalism* describes not a period of time but a political system that prevailed during it, in which vassals (the ancestors of our nobles) pledge fealty (our loyalty) to their liege lord (our king) exchanging their service in time of war for inheritable fiefs (our real estate). As it happens, feudalism was in effect in most of Europe from about the tenth century until the end of the fourteenth. But while it coincides with much of the Middle Ages, that doesn't mean you get to substitute one term for the other.

Thomas Aquinas, Thomas à Becket, Thomas à Kempis, Thomas More

All four are saints. Think of them as the scholastic, the martyr, the mystic, and the humanist, respectively. But let's do this in chronological order.

Thomas à Becket, a twelfth-century Englishman, is the martyr. After a somewhat loose-living youth, during which he gave his friend King Henry II (see page 549) every reason to think he'd make an easygoing enough Archbishop of Canterbury, Becket fooled everybody, including himself, by either, depending on whom you talk to, getting religion or going on a power trip. Anyway, he interfered enough with Henry's attempts to consolidate national power at the expense of the Church that he wound up being assassinated in 1170 in Canterbury Cathedral. Thus began a martyrdom that would see immediate baronial rebellion (and the consequent withering of royal power), subsequent canonization, an enormous and centuries-long tourist industry (it's Thomas's shrine that Chaucer's pilgrims are headed for), plus all those plays (by Tennyson, Eliot, and Anouilh) and movies (with Richard Burton and Peter O'Toole).

Thomas Aquinas, a thirteenth-century Italian, is the scholastic, one of that breed of philosophers who liked to argue about how many angels could dance on the head of a pin and, regardless of *that* answer, whether or not they had navels. In a sense, he transcended the genre (see page 308), managing to channel some of that endless Q-and-A energy into arguing with the real dopes about how faith couldn't be endangered by reason, which meant it wasn't a sin to go on thinking. Known to some as the Angelic Doctor, to others—the result of the slowness of his delivery—as the Dumb Ox.

Thomas à Kempis, a fourteenth-century German, is the mystic. Purported author of something called *The Imitation of Christ*, which charted the progress of the individual soul up to and including its union with God, in fact he spelled big trouble for the Catholic Church. After all, emphasize enough how we can all commune directly with God in perfect solitude, without need of words, worship, or sacraments, let alone church property, and a few of us are going to stop showing up on Sunday. This wasn't Kempis's intention (he still honored the Church's *pattern* of salvation), but it got Martin Luther, among others, thinking.

With *Thomas More*, we're back in England and it's the sixteenth century. A northern humanist, like the Dutchman Erasmus and the Frenchman John Calvin (see below), he took Renaissance energy—which tended to be employed down in Italy to make beautiful things and explore the infinite riches of the human personality—and thought about God, society, science, and human nature. A statesman (and the author of *Utopia*, his version of which was a severe and snobbish agricultural community with plenty of slaves to take care of the degrading stuff), he, like Becket, was put to death for refusing to do his king's bidding. Required by Henry VIII to sign the 1534 Act of Supremacy, which declared the English monarch to be the "Protector and Only Supreme Head of the Church and Clergy of England," thereby getting England out from under the thumb of the Pope *and* allowing Henry to get his divorce from Catherine of Aragon, More demurred. He was offed the following year and canonized four centuries later.

John Wyclif, John Huss, John Calvin, John Knox

Another group who, basically, gave the Catholic Church a bad time. *John Wyclif*, an Englishman teaching at Oxford, had noticed, like Thomas à Kempis, that it was possible to do without the elaborate possessions of a church and, if you were devout by nature, even without priests. The difference is that in 1380 or so, he, unlike Kempis, said as much, furthermore recommending that everybody simply go home and read the Bible, which he just happened to have translated into English.

John Huss, a Bohemian from central Europe who lived at about the same time, took things one step further by turning his ritual-resistant Hussites from a religious group into a Czech national movement in protest of German supremacy in the area. Both Wyclif and Huss were branded as heretics.

John Calvin, a Frenchman who lived from 1509 to 1564, is a much bigger deal. A generation younger than Luther, he experienced a sudden conversion at the age of twenty-four, joined forces with the religious revolutionaries, and published his *Institutes of the Christian Religion*, addressed—unlike Luther's writings—not just to Germans but to everybody who was dissatisfied with the existing Roman setup. Because Calvin did so much with the idea of predestination (God had chosen some people to be saved, others to be damned; you knew who you were, and that was that, don't even bother to struggle), Calvinists tended to be militant, uncompromising, self-righteous—i.e. Puritans. They also refused to recognize the subordination of church to state or the laying down of rules by any king or parliament. Rather, Christians should, according to Calvin, Christianize the state, as Oliver Cromwell would do a century later in England. In the meantime, Calvinism took root in France (the Huguenots were Calvinists) and spread not only to England and Germany, but to the Netherlands, Poland, and Hungary, too.

In Scotland, *John Knox*, a particularly sober-sided type who would give Mary, Queen of Scots, a bad case of the shakes, made Calvinism—later called Presbyterianism—the established Scottish religion.

Jacobean, Jacobite, Jacobin, Jacquerie

All four come from the Latin given name Jacobus, the ancestor of our "James" (and the Frenchman's "Jacques"). *Jacobean* describes the period—rich, exuberant, and increasingly cynical—during which the Stuart king James I ruled Britain, right after Elizabeth. More a cultural term than a historical one, it evokes the late, great tragedies and romances of Shakespeare; the grisly, overwrought drama of his contemporaries John "The Duchess of Malfi" Webster and John "'Tis Pity She's a Whore" Ford; the poetry of Donne and the Metaphysicals; and, natch, the King James Version of the Bible.

Jacobite describes those Brits who, several decades and an expulsion or two later, were trying to get James I's Stuart descendants—Scottish, Catholic, and firm adherents of the divine right of kings—back on the English throne. Even with a lot of collaboration on the part of the French and a couple of out-and-out invasion attempts, via Scotland, in 1715 and 1745, the Jacobites, who'd hoped to turn the clock back by a century or so, didn't so much as get the minute hand moving. The net impact of their scheming was the stripping down of the traditional Scottish Highlands clans and the banning of kilts and bagpipes for thirty years.

Today, "Jacobite" is pretty much relegated to the history books (except when used, impishly, of Henry James fans). *Jacobin,* by contrast, still shows up in the odd George Will or Mary McGrory column. Originally, it signified the most radical of the essentially well-educated, middle-class revolutionaries during the French Revolution (who'd met in an old Jacobin, or Dominican, monastery in Paris); it embraced such subgroups as the Girondists and the "Mountain"; and it included almost every French revolutionary leader you ever heard of: Robespierre, Marat, Danton, Condorcet, St. Just, etc. Eventually, the Jacobins were found—by the rabble, the *popular* revolutionaries like the sans-culottes (so called because they went around not in knee-breeches but in trousers)—to be insufficiently militant, and most of them wound up, like the royalists before them, at the guillotine. Today, "jacobin" is used to describe radicals, or extreme leftists, who are determined to carry on the revolution at any cost; who like to talk political theory into the wee hours; and who, in general, have contempt for the will of the majority, the persons-in-the-street, believing that it's *they*, the intelligentsia, who are best equipped to call the shots. The Bolsheviks, behind Russia's 1917 revolution, are this century's most famous jacobins.

Oldest of all is *jacquerie*, from Jacques, the generic French nickname for a peasant, used to describe an insurrection of peasants, such as was first set off in France in 1358, a response to the economic hardships brought about by the Black Death and the Hundred Years' War (see page 553). Similar massive uprisings took place in England, most notably Wat Tyler's rebellion of 1381, during which, shaking their pitchforks, peasant spokesmen wondered aloud why some people were rich and fancy, others poor and drab—or as they put it, in a famous couplet, "When Adam delved and Eve span / Who was then a gentleman?"

Puritans, Pilgrims, Dissenters, Roundheads

The *Puritans* were the extreme, Calvinistic Protestants—as opposed to the moderate, Church-of-England ones—in seventeenth-century England. The *Pilgrims* were those Puritans who left England for Holland in 1608, arriving at Plymouth Rock in 1620. The *Roundheads* (so called because of their close-cropped hair) were the Puritan followers of Oliver Cromwell in the 1640s war between the forces of Parliament (spearheaded by Cromwell) and those of the king, Charles I, whose followers had long hair, wore too much lace and cologne, and were known as Cavaliers. By the 1650s, *Dissenters*, a broader term that took in a variety of anti-Church-of-England nonconformists, was how you would have designated the fellows you used to think of as Puritans.

Diggers, Levellers, Luddites, Chartists

British antiestablishmentarians, all. The *Levellers* (many of whom were, for the record, Puritans) and the *Diggers* were both fixtures in Cromwellian England. The former pushed for almost-universal male suffrage, a written constitution, subordination of Parliament to the will of the voters and other things it would take the American and French Revolutions (and another century) to get a real taste of. The latter thumbed their noses at the idea of private property and went around occupying and occasionally cultivating other people's land.

The *Luddites* were rioters who took to destroying machinery in the factories of northern England between 1811 and 1816; especially averse to textile machines, they blamed the impact of the Industrial Revolution for their unemployment and misery. Their leader was Ned Ludd.

The *Chartists* were a working-class group, named after the People's Charter they'd drafted in 1838, advocating, among other things, universal adult male suffrage, the secret ballot, equal electoral districts, the annual election of the members of the House of Commons, and the payment of salaries to those members so that you wouldn't have to be independently wealthy to be able to spend your days in session there. The Chartist movement died down as the result of opposition from the government and from businessmen, as well as from internal dissension. But, unlike the Diggers, the Levellers, and the Luddites, the Chartists had at least gotten a lot of smart, influential people to listen. Their full program would be in place shortly after World War I.

Whigs, Tories

Both arose (like so much else) in seventeenth-century England in response to the controversy surrounding the pro-French, pro-Catholic policies of Charles II. The *Whigs*—also known as the Country Party, made up of the biggest-deal aristocrats, always eager to weaken a king since it automatically strengthened *them*, and backed by the middle class and the merchants of London—wanted to see Charles II (not to mention his even more Catholic brother, James II, due to succeed him) checked. They stood for the supremacy of Parliament and for religious toleration. The *Tories*—also known as the Court Party, consisting of the lesser aristocracy, the country squires, and the Anglican clergy—supported Charles and were suspicious of the Whigs' commercial leanings, among other things.

Of course, neither the Whigs nor the Tories was anything like an organized political party back then (even taken together, there were only a few thousand of them), but by the next century they would be the two leading parties of the country, and would remain so, right through the nineteenth century, when the Tories renamed themselves Conservatives and the Whigs renamed themselves Liberals.

Both terms were less than complimentary in origin, and were in each case first used by the opponents of the faction in question. A "whig" was originally a Scottish cattle rustler, a "tory" an Irish plunderer. You don't hear much about Whigs these days, but even now, in England, a Tory is a mildly hostile name for a conservative, especially a right-wing one.

colony, protectorate, dominion, territory, mandate, trusteeship, dependency, possession

Enjoy them while you can; the era of imperialism is winding to a stop. The familiar word here is *colony*, but it has an edge: A colony, strictly speaking, consists of a company of people transplanted somewhere for the purpose of settling it; as a result, a colony should have a fair sprinkling of faces that remind you of what folks look like back in the Mother Country. (Canada was a colony of Great Britain's, whereas in China—except for Hong Kong, another colony—Britain just had a lot of treaties and trading concessions in effect.) In a *protectorate*, an imperial power doesn't claim to be settling anything; it just strides in and takes over in the name of the existing ruler, presumably to save him and his subjects from other, less noble-minded imperial powers. A *dominion* is a specifically British concept, used of a particularly well-regarded colony that, while still tied to the mother country, was largely self-governing—Canada, Australia, and New Zealand, for example; today, the dominions are independent (which is not to say the queen isn't still constantly popping by). *Territory* applies to a portion of a country—usually remote and undeveloped, like Canada's Yukon and Northwest Territories—that's not deemed ready to become a full-fledged state or province.

A *mandate* is what the victorious Allied Powers handed out to themselves from the former empires of the defeated Central Powers after World War I. Thus Britain got Palestine and Trans-Jordan; France, Syria and Lebanon; Japan, some of Germany's former holdings in the Pacific; and—abbreviating the list somewhat—South Africa got the former German colony of Southwest Africa, a.k.a. Namibia, which is the only mandate still in existence. The same thing happened after World War II, except this time the United Nations supervised the doling out of former Italian and Japanese possessions, plus assumed responsibility for the mandates. Today, the Trust Territory of the Pacific, administered by the U.S. (which, just between us, seems very reluctant to let go of it), is the only remaining *trusteeship*.

A *dependency* could be any of the above, plus the little sheikdom or sultanate whose foreign affairs you're helping to handle even though you don't claim to own it. If you did, it—like colonies, protectorates, dominions, etc.—would be a *possession*, and you would be both occupying and controlling it.

The Boer War, the Boxer Rebellion

We know you think you know—and you're probably right. But today's Boer War and Boxer Rebellion are tomorrow's Persian and Punic Wars, so let's run through them just to make sure.

The Boers (from the Dutch word for "farmer") were the descendants of the Dutchmen who'd originally settled the Cape of Good Hope, the southern tip of Africa, in the seventeenth century. After 1815, when England annexed the Cape according to the terms of the Congress of Vienna (see page 555), the Boers, simple, old-fashioned folk, made the "great trek" inland and cleared the Transvaal and the Orange Free State in an effort to get away from the British. They didn't think much of slavery or miners or adventurers or fortune-hunting Englishmen. Unfortunately, the English, in the course of their planning for a Cape-to-Cairo railway, now found themselves confronted by two little Boer republics just where a few hundred miles of track were supposed to go down. The discovery of gold and diamonds in the Transvaal pressurized matters further. Brits poured in, the Transvaal refused to pass the bills that would allow the Brits to build their mines, the Brits started to terrorize the Boers, and Europe started screaming about British bullying. (The German emperor, William II, even sent a telegram to the president of the Transvaal congratulating him on having staved off the British raiders "without having to call for the support of friendly powers.") Three years later England went to war with the two Boer republics, and over the course of the next three years, conquered them in the *Boer War* (1899–1902). Incorporated into the British Empire, but with various of their institutions (including their language, Afrikaans) pretty much intact, the Boers soon found themselves a part of the Union of South Africa, today's Republic of South Africa, about which we'll not get going here. Britain, for her part, found herself the least popular nation in Europe—which encouraged her to rethink matters enough to present herself as an acceptable potential ally for a war that, it would turn out, was only a decade away.

The *Boxer Rebellion*, which also broke out in 1899 and which also involved Britain, along with every other Western power with a stake in China—formerly a proud empire, now weakened, demoralized, and on her last legs. Seems a Chinese secret society bent on revolution and named something like the Order of Righteous Harmonious Fists (the Westerners doubled over with laughter at the nickname "Boxers") had besieged all the Western legations—French, Russian, and German, as well as British—in northern China, killing missionaries and railway workers, as well as Chinese converts to Christianity. The European powers, joined by Japan and the U.S., sent an international force against the Boxers, squashing them in very short order. The victors made things even harder on the Chinese, hitting them with, among other things, a bill for $330 million. The upshot: The Chinese government decided it was high time to join its neighbor Japan in a Westernization program. And younger Chinese, deciding it was high time to get rid of both the foreigners *and* the government, rallied to a fellow named Sun Yat-sen. It was the beginning of a Chinese revolution that, with time out for World War II, would go on for half a century.

Redshirts, Brownshirts, Blackshirts, Black and Tans

The *Redshirts* were Garibaldi's (he'd gotten the wool for them cheap from the government of Uruguay, whose independence he'd helped secure), and with them he helped achieve the unification of the modern nation of Italy in the early 1860s. The *Brownshirts* were Hitler's; they constituted the *Sturmabteilung*, or SA, the Nazi "stormtroops." The *Blackshirts* were also Hitler's, in the persons of his elite *Schutzstaffel*, or SS, the "security echelon," but he'd gotten the idea from Mussolini, who'd first come up with the idea for color-coded private militias. The *Black and Tans* were Britain's, recruited to fill vacancies in the Royal Irish Constabulary caused by the killing or intimidation of its native-Irish members during the Troubles of 1919–1923; themselves given to terrorist tactics (and named after a local breed of hound), the Black and Tans wore khaki uniforms and black belts.

epoch, era, age, eon, period

Epoch and *era* present the big stumbling block here, because almost nobody uses them anymore the way the historians meant them to be used. Which is: An epoch is the date of an occurrence that starts things going in a new direction or under new conditions (i.e., a point in time). An era is the time during which what started as an epoch continues, building steam, gaining momentum, becoming established—at which point you've got a *period,* an era that's run its course and is ready for another epoch-making event. An *age* is pretty much an era (the Age of Reason, the Era of Good Feeling: both have a sense of center to them); an *eon* any immeasurably, even infinitely long time. Anything else? Well, a *cycle* is a succession of periods followed by another, similar succession. And your *birthday* is the day you were born, celebrated with a cake in most Western countries.

Note to geology majors: You shouldn't have to be reminded—and no one else cares—that the geologic time scale's largest division is the eon (one or more eras), followed by the era (one or more periods), the period (one or more epochs), and the epoch. Thus, one—that is, you—speaks of the Pliocene epoch of the Tertiary period of the Cenozoic era. Right?

Reds

Contributor Michael Sorkin casts a cold eye on the men—and the woman—who took Karl Marx's more or less straightforward theory of history and did so much thinking, rethinking, second-guessing, and arguing among themselves as to what he really meant, didn't mean, might have meant, and ought to have meant that poor Marx had no choice but to confess, famously and fairly early on, "Je ne suis pas un Marxiste." But first, a look at the old boy, Marxist or not, himself.

KARL MARX (GERMAN, 1818–1883)

Marx, and Marxism, didn't simply happen. A German, born in 1818, Karl Marx was influenced by the social ideas that came out of the French Revolution, the economic ideas that came out of the British Industrial Revolution, and, especially, by the philosophical ideas that were now coming—and coming and coming—out of Germany as it emerged into the European high noon. In fact, Marx can himself be thought of as one in an ever-lengthening line of German philosophers, the most notable of whom was Hegel (see page 317), to whom he—along with other "Young Hegelians" like Engels—was much devoted in his youth and from whom he picked up the very useful dialectical method. Like any philosopher, Marx was interested in the big questions, and the one his system "solves" is that most basic quandary of history; namely, what makes it go, and where. Marx answers the question by taking dialectics (Hegel's thesis-antithesis-synthesis dynamic) and combining it with materialism, the half of philosophy that says matter constitutes, and has precedence over, mind. The result, as if you didn't know: dialectical materialism.

In a nutshell, Marx's argument is that economic relationships are the basic forces in history and that it is only around them that the whole complex of social relationships arises. Marx called these two interrelated aspects the economic "base" and the social "superstructure." As a materialist, he felt that the "relations of production"—the basic setup and reciprocal interaction among those people or classes who are doing the work and making (or not making) the money—defined by the "base" decreed the "general character of the social, political, and spiritual processes of life. It is not the consciousness of men that determines their existence, but, on the contrary, their existence that determines their consciousness." (Those who really know their Marxism like to observe along about now how Marx has found Hegel "standing on his head" and—by insisting that actualities come before ideas, that the mind doesn't conceive of freedom, then decide to go out and found a Greek city-state, but the other way around—is here "setting him on his feet again.")

There's one more very big issue: As with all dialectics, change is part of the very nature of things; a force necessarily calls its opposite into being. For Marx, the social system—the superstructure, as it were—contains within itself the seeds of "contradiction," leading to a disequilibrium with the economic base and, eventually, to the overthrow of the whole business—in other words, revolution; also progress. Watch how it works: Material conditions (agrarian industrial, whatever) spawn economic classes. Thus, at some point, there'd been a feudal, or landholding, class, which, according to the theory, got top-heavy and overwhelmed by a bourgeois, or commercial, class. Now, in plain sight of Marx and anybody else whose eyes were open, that bourgeoisie was calling into being *its* dialectical antithesis, the proletariat. In fact, the more bourgeois a country was, the more it was going to become proletarian: The busier the factories, the bigger the laboring class. Eventually, with all these bourgeois types devouring each other in their race to get ahead, the proletariat will see its chance and take over, "expropriating the expropriators," "seizing the levers of production," and abolishing private property. Marx thinks he sees this coming in 1848, but he's wrong; society isn't quite ready to become classless, the state to "wither away," or religion—"the opiate of the people," the only thing that keeps them from protesting the grimness of their lives by promising all of them another one later—to pack its bags and leave town.

Of course, the theory is much more complicated than that. (Simplified descriptions like the foregoing are the basis for what is commonly called "vulgar Marxism.") In fact, Marx devoted his life to elaborations on all of the above, producing a vast body of work, vastly documented and vastly ramified. But Marx knew that he couldn't change the destiny of the world just by hanging out in the library. He was also a revolutionary who held that theory must be joined with practice. "Philosophers have studied the world," as he put it, "but the problem is to change it." So Marx organized. He lectured and made speeches. He went to meetings and debates. Eventually, he went west, to London and Paris, more evolved than any German city was and hence that much closer to the inevitable revolt. He wrote newspaper articles (Marx was for a time the European correspondent for the New York *Tribune*). He, with his family, starved and got deported. And he, with his friend Engels, wrote *The Communist Manifesto*—perhaps the most stirring and incendiary document ever. "The proletarians have nothing to lose but their chains," it concludes. "They have a world to win. Workers of the world, unite."

Marx had a lot of faith in these proletarians, the class of wage earners capitalism was, in effect, fleecing. Not only were they destined to rise up and overthrow the system, they were the harbingers of everything Marx was working toward—initially a new socialist order in which the oppressed would be freed and wealth would be distributed on the principle of "to each according to his needs, from each according to his ability." Ultimately, this workers' state would "wither away," leaving no oppressive institutions to mediate among people; in the meantime, it was to be governed, in Marx's phrase, by a "dictatorship of the proletariat."

But while Marx was probably just trying to describe the class content of the regime, many subsequent self-avowed Marxists have seen it otherwise, warming especially to the possibilities of that first word, "dictatorship." Such, as with so many other great thinkers, has been the fate of Marx: He has been interpreted. As his work attained the stature of holy writ, his disciples—and his exegetes—multiplied. Marx became a dogmatist's dream. His work (enormous, changing, and incomplete: *Das Kapital*, his magnum opus, was never finished) has been battled over by countless factions, each of which claims to know the "real" Marx. As a result, the first thing most Marxists want to know about other Marxists is which side they're on. The following may provide some clues.

FRIEDRICH ENGELS (GERMAN, 1820–1895)

Friedrich Engels was the perfect collaborator: patient, intelligent, articulate, enthusiastic, and rich. The son of a wealthy textile manufacturer, he was, for many years, in charge of the Manchester branch of his family's factory. This not only enabled him to send regular checks to Marx (often the one thing standing between the Marx family and destitution), it also gave him a fine vantage point from which to survey the course of mid-nineteenth century capitalism, providing grist for such works as *The Condition of the Working Class in England.* In truth, Engels's work is inseparable from that of Marx (they wrote successive drafts of *The Communist Manifesto,* and Engels ghosted many of Marx's *Tribune* articles), and he proved Marx's staunchest defender in the years after his death. Largely self-educated, Engels was not as deep a thinker as Marx but he was a brilliant polemicist, and his ongoing fascination with science, particularly Darwinism, made him even more adamant than his colleagues about the inevitability of capitalism's downfall. Perhaps his most enduring contribution, however, is the elaboration of the idea of the "relative autonomy" of the superstructure, the notion that it could interact with the base, sometimes actually pushing it along a bit, if only for a limited period. Through such subtle divergences as these Engels started a trend toward revisionism—the customary perjorative for any and all tampering with Marx—that would soon become standard operating procedure.

VLADIMIR ILYICH LENIN (RUSSIAN, 1870–1924)

With Lenin, as with Perle Mesta, the key word is party—in this case, the Communist Party. Lenin (né Ulyanov) was the revolutionary's revolutionary. He wed Marxism—up to that point, don't forget, a Western doctrine—to a strong, and absolutely Russian, tradition of false names, forged passports, and invisible ink. Then, incredibly single-minded, he proceeded to put everything through the sieve of revolutionary practice in the belief that any issue could be resolved in response to the query: "Is it good for the revolution?" Tireless as a propagandist, prolific as a writer, incomparable as an agitator, and merciless as an adversary, Lenin emerged as the leader of the Bolshevik (or "majority") faction of the

Russian Communists, and became, after the October, 1917, Revolution, the first head of state of the new Russia. His version of the dictatorship of the proletariat tended to emphasize the dictatorship. As he saw it, authority was to be exercised not by the unwieldy mass of proletarians, but by a surrogate: the Communist Party proper, composed of dedicated and knowledgeable people who could both understand the proletarian world view and act as its instrument. In fact, according to Lenin, there couldn't be any revolution at all without such a powerful vanguard party to get things organized. There was, needless to say, disagreement on this, which Lenin, who died on the job, never saw resolved. Even so, his heirs had him embalmed and placed on display in Red Square, where he remains an object of necrophiliac admiration to this day.

ROSA LUXEMBURG (POLISH, 1871–1919)

Rosa Luxemburg ("Red Rosa" as she came to be known) was the great champion of revolutionary orthodoxy. Considerably more leftist than Lenin and the Bolsheviks, she vigorously assailed their revisionism, most notably over the issue of party organization. Luxemburg pushed for what she called "spontaneity," the kind of worker-originated impulse that resulted in things like general strikes and that upbraided Lenin for his opportunistic advocacy of "ultra-centralism," arguing that "Revolutionary tactics cannot be invented by leaders, they must develop spontaneously—history comes first, leaders' consciousness second." And "We must frankly admit to ourselves that errors made by a truly revolutionary labor movement are infinitely more fruitful and more valuable than the infallibility of the best of all possible central committees."

Luxemburg's major theoretical work is *The Accumulation of Capital*, which attempts to supplement Marx by establishing a precise economic argument for the inevitability of the collapse of capitalism. To make a long story short, she contends that the contradiction between capitalism's reliance on noncapitalist markets and its tendency to destroy its noncapitalist environment can only lead to its ruin. The Leninist camp attacked her for this theory, which they twisted into the "automatic collapse of capitalism" and branded as "fatalistic." Luxemburg would not live to see her reputation totally besmirched—by Stalin—since she and her friend Karl Liebknecht (with whom she founded the Spartacus League, predecessor of the German Communist Party) were murdered while under arrest by the German authorities.

JOSEF STALIN (RUSSIAN, 1879–1953)

What can you say about Stalin except that he was one of the worst pieces of bad news since the Flood? Born Josef Dzhugashvili, he soon changed his name to Stalin ("Man of Steel"), which you'd think would have given someone a clue to his mettle. On assuming power, Stalin's interpretation of the dictatorship of the proletariat turned out to be even simpler than Lenin's: dictatorship by Stalin. His legacy includes the Gulag, the Cult of Personality, the show trials, the purges, mass starvation, a police state, and the industrialization of the Soviet Union. It is to this last that Stalinists tend to point when citing his achievements. Except among the three of them, however, "Stalinist" is considered a term of abuse. When Stalin died, he was put on display next to Lenin until people had second thoughts some years later and removed his corpse to less high-toned surroundings.

LEON TROTSKY (RUSSIAN, 1879–1940)

Like Lenin and Stalin, Leon Trotsky (né Bronstein) changed his name. On other points they had less in common. One of the revolutionary "old boys" (though a relatively late joiner of the party, for which he was given much grief), Trotsky organized the Red Army after the revolution and led it to success in the ensuing civil war. Energetic and smart, he was one of the key men around Lenin, despite differences over the role of the Party. Under Stalin, he was not only not key, he was not even around very long, sent into exile by the jealous despot. The issue over which they nominally came to blows was Trotsky's theory of "permanent revolution," which was in conflict with Stalin's espousal of "socialism in one country." Trotsky had what might be called a "process" view of revolution. He felt that the success of the one that Russia was having depended on its continuous expansion, both within Russia and in other European nations. "Socialism in one country," as you may have guessed, held that nurturing the revolution at home was the top priority. The question was finally resolved by one of Stalin's agents, who put an ice pick through Trotsky's skull. Like so many other things, though, "Trotskyism" was mainly a fiction invented by Stalin (though fervently believed by Trotsky and a few others) out of sheer paranoia. Not that Trotsky was such a prize, either, being rigid, doctrinaire, and even brutal, although he *was* a fine writer and the author of the definitive account of the 1917 Revolution. Should someone call you a "Trot," however, it's to the former attributes that he or she is probably alluding. Remember also that a "Trotskyite" is a "Trotskyist" to a Stalinist.

MAO TSE-TUNG (CHINESE, 1893–1976)

Mao Tse-tung's was the last truly great cult of personality. Beside him, such upstarts as Tito, Khaddafi, and Barbra Streisand pale into insignificance. Indeed, among Marxists, Mao's was the last of the great isms. Mao surely helped all of this along by being as brilliant an aphorist as he was a revolutionary, stirring untold billions of Chinese with lines like "The world is progressing, the future is bright, and no one can change the general trend of history," "We know the pear only by eating it and we know society only by participating in the class struggle," and "Some play the piano well and some badly, and there is a great difference in the melodies they produce."

What makes it all so special? To start with the obvious, Mao's Marxism is uniquely Chinese, with dialectics as much indebted to Taoist yin and yang as to Hegel. But Mao's major contribution is the idea of peasant revolution. In the late 1920s Mao broke with the orthodox view that the proletariat was the only revolutionary class and proposed, to the consternation of the Soviets, that the peasantry play the leading role—a strikingly apt idea in a country which had jillions of oppressed peasants and scarcely a prole. Mao also departed from theoretical orthodoxy by emphasizing the importance of the superstructure. Later, this was to lead to the so-called "Hundred Flowers Campaign" (which encouraged people to criticize the Party and which rapidly got out of hand) and to the so-called "Cultural Revolution" (which encouraged people to criticize the Party and which rapidly got out of hand). In the West, nobody much is a Maoist anymore, probably because you can only say "The revolutionary is like a fish swimming in the sea of the people" so many times before beginning to feel a little silly.

GEORG LUKÁCS (HUNGARIAN, 1885–1971)

If you're determined to go after bourgeois culture with a Marxist cleaver, the work of Georg Lukács is indispensable. Lukács (that's pronounced LOO-kahsh) provided the first serious evaluation of Hegel's role in Marx's thought, revising then-current views of dialectics. No intellectual lightweight, he argued that the historical interaction of subject and object is the basic form of dialectics, insisting in *History and Class Consciousness*, his major work, that a developed class consciousness would impel the proletariat to become both the subject and the object of history. As he put it, proletarian dialectics implies an idea of consciousness which "is not the knowledge of an opposed object but is the self-consciousness of the object *the act of consciousness overthrows*, the objective form of the object."

Another riveting concept of Lukács's is "totality." Bourgeois society, he insisted, tends to destroy the possibility of images of the whole, forest-for-the-trees-style, preventing proletarians (among others) from acquiring true knowledge of reality. Dialectics is the answer, because "only in this context which sees the isolated facts of social life as aspects of the historical process and integrates them in a totality, can knowledge of facts hope to become knowledge of reality." Which brings us to the idea of *reification*, the one thing to remember about Lukács should you choose to remember anything at all. Reification (a concept Marx had introduced in his discussion of the fetishism of commodities in *Das Kapital*) is the process by which bourgeois society transforms social relations into commodity relations, the process by which people become mere objects, and it's the real culprit behind our inability to grasp the totality of things.

ANTONIO GRAMSCI (ITALIAN, 1891–1937)

Antonio Gramsci is everyone's favorite Marxist, as poignant and congenial a figure as the movement has spawned. A hunchbacked scholar and man of action who was in on the founding of the Italian Communist Party, he spent the last ten years of his brief life in a Fascist prison, where he managed to write the appropriately named *Prison Notebooks*, his major legacy. A lengthy sentence allowed him to focus his attention on theoretical questions and, over the years, he constructed a Marxist philosophy of culture, in the process becoming the great theoretician of the superstructure.

Perhaps one of the reasons for Gramsci's current popularity in academic footnotes is the great emphasis he places on the significance of intellectuals, whom he saw as the leading agents of ideology, an indispensable (and heretofore counter-revolutionary) force in preserving the dominance of the ruling class. This ideological ascendancy he called "hegemony," the central Gramscian cocktail-party concept. The danger of hegemony lies in the way it sneaks in everywhere, so much so that the *Weltanschauung* of the ruling class comes to seem like simple common sense. To combat this, Gramsci urged proletarians and other progressive elements to struggle to create a counterculture (sound familiar?) which would challenge the hegemonic domination of the prevailing ideology. In opposition to Lenin—obsessed with the seizure of governmental control—Gramsci envisioned a cultural, educational role for the Party. In the Sixties, in the U.S., however, Gramsci's countercultural ideas wound up resulting less in Party than in partying.

HERBERT MARCUSE
(GERMAN-BORN AMERICAN, 1898–1979)

Marcuse is one of ours, local hero to a generation whose Marxism tended to be closer to Groucho's than Karl's. Never mind his early work on Hegel, Marcuse's great contribution was the joining of politics with sex, a conjunction that would come to be virtually synonymous with the Sixties. Abandoning Freud's pessimistic view of society (with so much labor-saving technology everywhere you looked, who needed the repression and sublimation that used to get us all to the factory on time?), Marcuse held that we could finally afford to liberate Eros, to eroticize all human relations. This sounded good.

Marcuse was also popular around the campus because of his implacable opposition to positivism, empiricism, and formal logic, the ABC's of your typical college curriculum. He stood for the union of Logos, more or less "reason," with Eros, again, which, rather than the union of subject and object à la Lukács, he saw as the main job of dialectics and which he felt would make for freedom and happiness. Marcuse was a Meher Baba among Marxists, a utopian apostle of good times. He was also keen on pointing out who was keeping whom from having any fun—the reified, "one-dimensional" society which, with its pluralist "repressive tolerance," tried to make it look as if we had options but which really only offered the terrors of conformity. You needed violence to overthrow this, violence which Marcuse believed would be wielded not by the industrial proletariat (which had been bought off), but by people who were *really* outside the system, like racial minorities and students. No wonder the kids loved him.

LOUIS ALTHUSSER (FRENCH, 1918–   )

Of contemporary Marxist theorists, the hardest one to read is Althusser, which may account for his recent vogue. Althusser is the main proponent of a hybrid of structuralism (see page 330) and Marxism, a combo he opposes to old-fashioned Hegelo-Marxism as well as to more recent Marxist humanism. Basically, Althusser focuses on Marx's later work (the humanists celebrate "the young Marx," Marx the "poet" and the Utopian, the messianic and "hip" Marx), citing an "epistemological break" between the early writings, hopelessly mired in our old friend the "subject," and the mature ones, in which Marx was finally able to get down to something that might be the basis of a real *science*.

After explaining how to give Marx the properly "symptomatic" reading (paying attention, like the psychoanalyst, to both what is said and what gets left out), Althusser explains how the object of knowledge is different from the *real* object. This process—equivalent to knowledge working on *its* object—he calls "theoretical practice." Such theoretical practice, when applied to society, leads inevitably to a view of society as a totality (you remember "totality"), which can, however, be broken down—not into a vulgar base/superstructure scheme, but into a tripartite division of economy, politics, and ideology, each of the three relatively autonomous but all of them united in a larger "structure of structures." Or, as Althusser says, "The whole existence of structure consists of its effects."

As you may have gathered, these structures are very complex and have very complex relationships. Althusser calls particular relationships among them *conjunctures*, and reasons that any specific conjuncture is likely to be, in his memorable term, "overdetermined." Which is to say, complex—also, slightly redundant. This is the one Althusserian concept you may actually be able to use: If you are late to work because your mother called, you couldn't find your contact lenses, *and* the bus broke down, your lateness might be said to be overdetermined.

Otherwise, should you actually meet an Althusserian, there's not much you can do. In a pinch, try asking by what criterion he or she *knows* historical materialism is scientific. Failing that, the charge of Stalinism may prove useful. In any case, Althusser proves our basic point as well as the next Marxist: Nobody really understands Marx any better than you do.

Four Cautionary Tales

*EACH OF THEM CONSIDERABLY MORE
SOBERING THAN THE ONES KARL MALDEN
AND THE AMERICAN EXPRESS PEOPLE
TRY TO SCARE YOU WITH*

THE DREYFUS AFFAIR

A national disgrace and a landmark in the history of modern France. In 1894, Capt. Alfred Dreyfus, a wealthy Jewish officer in the French artillery, was accused of having betrayed secrets to the Germans. Although the evidence against him was slim, rabid anti-Semitism in the military prompted a court-martial to convict him of treason and sentence him to life imprisonment on Devil's Island. Great applause from the public. Two years later, Col. Georges Picquart, chief of army intelligence, discovered new evidence pointing to the innocence of Dreyfus and the guilt of one Ferdinand Esterhazy, a major in the army and a notorious adventurer. The military, however, was unwilling to admit its error and opted for a cover-up. Picquart was silenced and the authorities refused to reopen the case. Dreyfus's brother made a few discoveries on his own, however, and soon the whole affair turned into a major political issue, with all France divided into two factions: the Dreyfusards and the anti-Dreyfusards (for which, read pro-republic, anticlerical liberals and royalist, militarist conservatives, respectively). The former group included a number of intellectual—and a scattering of political—big guns, including Émile Zola, Georges Clemenceau, and Anatole France, who, although determined to redress the injustice, were actually less concerned with the plight of Dreyfus himself, who was still languishing on Devil's Island, than with discrediting the rightist government. The anti-Dreyfusards, who included no small number of reactionaries and out-and-out bigots, felt obliged to resort to perjury and intimidation to protect their idea of patriotism.

The plot continued to thicken. Major Esterhazy was finally tried and acquitted by a court-martial. An outraged Zola wrote his famous open letter beginning *"J'accuse,"* for which he was promptly sentenced to jail. He escaped to England. Major Henry, an army intelligence officer who, it now turned out, had forged much of the evidence used against Dreyfus, committed suicide. Esterhazy followed Zola's lead and escaped to England. A Dreyfusard became premier. Dreyfus was retried, convicted again by a military court—this time, found "guilty with extenuating circumstances." Great hue and cry from the public. The President of France finally stepped in and pardoned Dreyfus, but by this time, pardon wasn't good enough. The public was still up in arms, and demands for Dreyfus's complete exoneration were coming in from all over the world. Finally, in 1906, he was cleared, and, in 1930, his innocence was proven by the publication of secret German papers showing that Esterhazy had, in fact, been the culprit.

The repercussions of *"l'affaire Dreyfus"* were enormous. It discredited the royalist elements in France, brought the left-wing to political power, gave rise to a period of rabid antimilitarism and anticlericalism, hastened the separation of church and state, and exposed the extent and depth of French anti-Semitism. And for at least a decade, the country remained split between die-hard anti-Dreyfusards and righteous Dreyfusards, many of whom were neighbors or members of the same family, who would no longer sip a *vin du pays* together. As for poor old Dreyfus, he was promoted to the rank of major and decorated with the Legion of Honor, but he had a hard time readjusting to army life. He died in obscurity in Paris in 1935.

THE SARAJEVO ASSASSINATION

June 28, 1914: The visiting Archduke Francis Ferdinand, heir to the Austrian throne, and his wife, Sophie, are shot dead in the streets of Sarajevo, the capital of Bosnia, for centuries under Turkish rule but since 1878 a part of the Austro-Hungarian Empire. The assassin is a young Bosnian revolutionary named Gavrilo Princip, member of the Black Hand, a secret society headquartered in the kingdom of Serbia, just next door. The murder has the characteristic irony of many political assassinations, since the Archduke was, himself, something of a Serbian-rights activist. One month later, Austria, delivering an outrageous ultimatum to the Serbian government, demands to be allowed to participate in suppressing anti-Austrian feeling in Serbia and in punishing any conspirators in what has turned out to be an assassination plot involving officials of the Serbian government. When the Serbs tactfully rebuff the ultimatum, Austria declares war. As a result of the elaborate, if somewhat tenuous network of alliances that existed at the time, Germany declares war on Russia and France and Great Britain declare war on Germany, all within a week. By the end of the month, Japan is engaged against Germany, too, and three months later, Turkey jumps in on the side of the Germans and Austrians, an alliance known as the Central Powers. World War I is in full swing, and all because a fanatic from some weird little country nobody ever heard of blew away a man who wasn't even a monarch yet.

Obviously, blaming World War I on what happened at Sarajevo is like blaming Norman Bates's slasher impulses on Janet Leigh's turning on the hot water. Europe had been on the verge of a nervous breakdown since at least the turn of the century as a result of both family and personality problems dating back to the 1870s. That was when Germany, having just trounced the French in the Franco-Prussian War, started angling for its own place in the sun among the powers of Europe. In order to consolidate the new German position and forestall any thoughts of revenge on the part of the French, Bismarck, then Germany's chancellor, ran around forging secret alliances with anyone who'd let him in the door; specifically, the Hapsburgs, who were looking for an ally against the Russians in their attempt to grab a bigger piece of the Balkans, and the Italians, who liked the idea of siding with a winner. Virtually everyone else was offended by the Germans, who struck them not only as parvenus, but as too ambitious, truculent, and devious to make acceptable neighbors. Bismarck's Triple Alliance turned an undercurrent of resentment into out-and-out paranoia. Pretty soon France, Russia, and Great Britain had formed, not anything as formal as an alliance (Britain was too determinedly isolationist for that) but an *entente cordiale,* known thereafter as the Triple Entente, whereby each would pitch in to help out if either of the others was attacked by members of the Triple Alliance. This didn't make the Germans, who now saw themselves surrounded by potential enemies, any easier to get along with. By the early 1900s, every major power had armed itself to the teeth, and Europe was divided into two camps, each nervously waiting for the other to draw first.

In such a high-stress situation, a German unexpectedly scratching his ear might have been enough to set things off, but there was a better catalyst: the Balkans. A cluster of wild, backward countries that had only recently gotten out from under the thumb of the crumbling Ottoman Empire, the Balkans were the object of perpetual rivalry between the Russians and the Austro-Hungarians, both of whom were on their last legs without realizing it, and were, therefore, semi-hysterical much of the time. The Austrians, in particular, were crazy to keep trying to throw their weight around the Balkan Peninsula, much of which was inhabited by angry Slavs—Serbs, Croatians, Bosnians, and Slovenes—who saw themselves as a single nationality and who, being quasi-Orientals who still depended on garlic to ward off vampire attacks, felt closer to the Russians than to the Austrians, who looked down on them as ethnically inferior.

Thanks largely to the Serbs, who had a tendency to register discontent by forming secret societies and committing terrorist acts, both rival empires were, by 1914, ready to be driven around the bend. An assassination was just the ticket. It was also the chance the Germans had been waiting for. Fed up with being treated, as they saw it, as second cousins, and convinced that the Russians, who had been notoriously unreliable allies up to that point, wouldn't fight, they gave full rein to their ambitions—and to the military strategy they'd already had prepared for ten years. As for Great Britain, it felt honor-bound to declare war on Germany when German troops invaded Belgium on their way to smash the French. At this point, no one was thinking clearly and everyone was wishing the whole business would just go away. But, as the British historian A. J. P. Taylor noted, politicians and generals had a hard time keeping up with each other's point of view in those days and before they knew it, the heads of state had lost control. "Their sensations, when diplomacy collapsed," writes Taylor, "were those of a train passenger who sees the express thundering through the station at which he intended to alight."

And that's only what was happening on the surface. Behind all these global neuroses was the new-found conviction, born out of the traumatic effects of Darwinism (see page 518) on human consciousness, that Nature was a struggle for survival of the fittest; that, in the case of people, the fittest meant the best-armed; and that, under the circumstances, war was inevitable anyway. Those who still hoped this wasn't true tended to believe that enormous military strength on all sides would act as a deterrent, and that common sense would surely prevail. Wrong again. Not only was World War I out of control virtually from the beginning, it went on for four years, and it wound up signaling the end of European domination of the world.

THE SPANISH CIVIL WAR

World War II broke out officially on September 1, 1939, when the Nazis overran Poland, but it had really been going on for the better part of a decade. Germany had already, you may recall, invaded Austria and Czechoslovakia, adding a few million additional Germans—some happy about it, some not, and some not even exactly German—to her empire, as Britain and France stood huffily by. Italy was entrenched in Ethiopia and Albania, and Japan in China's Manchuria. The League of Nations protested from time to time, but, puhleez, who cared what the League of Nations thought? The saddest, wrenchingest events of the proto-War period, though, took place in Spain—for over a century Europe's backwater, self-contained, aloof, apathetic with regard to the rest of the continent, unenviable, even contemptible, in its eyes.

Civil war didn't break out until 1936, but for the preceding five years, since King Alfonso XIII was driven out in a fairly uneventful revolution, Spain had been feeling shaky. The new republican government, pledged to economic and social reform and determined to propel the country out of the eighteenth century and into the twentieth, moved against the Church (separating it from the State, which it had been pushing around since at least the Inquisition); broke up a few of the big landed estates, redistributing the acreage among the peasants; and gave a degree of local autonomy to the Catalans, in and around Barcelona, as well as to the Basques. Frankly, it was all a case of too-little-too-late, at least in the eyes of the extremists (anarchists and communists, mostly). But it was more than enough to infuriate the priests and the land-owners, not to mention the former royalists, who were upset anyway. In 1933, the government fell into the hands of the rightists, who themselves proved both ineffectual and inflammatory: A simple miners' strike was put down with more than your average brutality, and the Catalans were sent to their rooms without any supper.

Okay, now it's 1936. New general elections. All the leftist types (republicans, socialists, communists, anarchists, trade-union members) join in a Popular Front against all the rightist types (monarchists, priests, landowners, army officers, and Fascists, known locally as Falangists). The leftists beat the rightists at the polls—but it's *very* close. Even so, the leftists push ahead with their vision of the new Spain, figuring that reconciliation was a luxury, or an impossibility, or that it damn well could wait—this part isn't so clear.

Next thing you knew, the military (never a factor to be discounted in Spain) had acted; revolts at Spanish army bases in Morocco, led by General Francisco Franco, resulted in what amounted to an invasion of Spain, with almost all the soldiers siding with their officers—and the rightists. Thus the battle lines were drawn: the leftists, or Republicans, sometimes called the Loyalists, were concentrated in the south, which tended to be poor, in the industrial region around Barcelona, and in Madrid, the capital; the rightists, or Nationalists, sometimes called the Rebels (even though they were the Establishment types), were strongest in the ancient—read strongly Catholic—heartland of Spain, plus Galicia, in the northwest corner.

Even without the foreign intervention, which we'll be getting to in a minute, it would have been an especially appalling civil war. Neither side behaved itself particularly well; the Republicans, at their worst, raped nuns, cut off the ears of priests, and fought savagely and treacherously among themselves. The Nationalists came in the night and shot in the dark, with the result that whole villages weren't around in the morning; their most famous victim was the Spanish poet García Lorca. In the end, some 600,000 Spaniards would die, with many more permanently crippled, still others in exile, never to return.

But it was the Great Powers—Hitler and Mussolini on the side of the Nationalists, Stalin on the side of the Republicans—who, by taking a local amateur production and turning it into a dress rehearsal for bigger things, made sure the civil war turned into chapter-length world-history-book stuff. The Germans and Italians sent troops (the Italians over 50,000); the Soviets technicians and military advisors; both sides as much equipment—tanks, planes, guns—as they could pack up, with the emphasis on those items that still needed to be tested on the battlefield. The British and French, again, hung back, though plenty of Brits, French, Americans, and others went to Spain as volunteers, usually on the Republican side.

A lot more happened in the course of the Spanish Civil War, which lasted until 1939, by which time the Nationalists, led by Franco, had crushed the Republicans. Guernica, in the Basque country, was bombed by the Nationalists, or at least by the Germans (Picasso got it down on canvas); General Mola tossed off his famous "fifth column" line (about how he had four columns of soldiers encircling Madrid, and a fifth column infiltrating and undermining it from within); and Ernest Hemingway completed his research for *For Whom the Bell Tolls*.

But what really mattered was what the war had crystallized: The splitting of the world into Fascist and anti-Fascist camps; the proof that Germany and Italy could work nicely together in a Rome-Berlin Axis; the general belief that not just war, but War, was inevitable. Also to be noted: The arrival on the world scene of Generalissimo Franco, a brilliant military strategist and so-so politician, who, far from attempting to conduct Spain into the twentieth century, would, over the course of the next forty years, insulate her from the rest of the world and immunize her to the present.

DIEN BIEN PHU

Years later, nearly everyone would agree that France's colonial ambitions in Indochina had been doomed from the start, that her seven-and-a-half-year war in the region had been a series of disastrous misjudgments and miscalculations, and that her empire had been little more than a grand illusion since at least the end of World War II. But it wasn't until the total defeat of its forces at the North Vietnamese garrison of Dien Bien Phu in May, 1954, that the French government was forced to drop its blindfold and admit that the game was over. And no sooner had the smoke cleared than the American government crept back to the battlefield, retrieved the blindfold, and tied it securely over its own eyes.

The area now called Vietnam had always been the biggest headache in France's Indochinese empire. The territory was divided, geographically and culturally, into two native kingdoms, Tonkin and Annan, in the north, and a colony, Cochin China, in the south, a fragmentation that made communication difficult and administration awkward. What was worse, the peoples of the north, the center of Viet culture, were proud, feisty, and subversive by nature; they had never been ones to bow and smile when outsiders tried to take over their turf. By the time Japan invaded Indochina in 1940, the French had already spent a couple of decades putting down village rebellions, scattered resistance groups had begun to coalesce into a Communist-dominated nationalist underground, and Ho Chi Minh had learned some valuable lessons in organization and strategy. When the Japanese took the keys to the country away from the French, who were too busy keeping up with the war in Europe to put up much of a fight, and turned them over to the Vietnamese, the struggle for control in the north was effectively over, although none of the major powers realized it at the time.

The nationalist Communists, by then known as the Viet Minh, didn't waste any time. Keeping discreetly out of the way of the Japanese, they spread the faith in the villages and fortified their positions in the countryside. When Japan surrendered in 1945, Ho Chi Minh had consolidated enough power to declare himself head of the Democratic Republic of Vietnam.

This, however, was not what the Allies had in mind. Determined to restore European equilibrium by boosting France's fractured self-esteem, they decided to give her back her colonies, sending the British to take over Saigon and Chinese troops to recapture the north. Enter, at this poing, Gen. Vo Nguyen Giap, soon-to-be hero, from the nationalists' point of view, of two Vietnamese wars. Giap raided the local arsenals for the weapons left behind by the French and Japanese and made as much trouble as he could for the occupying French and Chinese forces. For the next few years the war in Vietnam consisted of inconclusive skirmishes and lots of military bungling on both sides, with the Viet Minh learning the hard way that conventional warfare was not their strong suit and the French continually trying to launch surprise raids on an enemy they couldn't see.

The nature of the enterprise began to change in 1949, when the Reds took over China. Ho Chi Minh suddenly found himself with an ally at his back and a steady supply of artillery pouring in from both China and the Soviet Union. The United States began to talk about keeping the Communist threat within safe perimeters. Vietnam was suddenly everyone's business. General Giap, for one, was heartened. Ho had long ago declared himself ready to lose ten men for every one of the invaders, and Giap made good the promise, launching a series of ferocious assaults that decimated his own forces but did, at least, have the effect of setting French nerves on edge and driving French troops back to fortified positions. Eventually, it also led them to make their fatal mistake.

Hoping to draw enough fire to exhaust the Viet Minh's resources and weaken their position in the rest of the country, the French decided to play on the enemy's aggressiveness by setting up 15,000 men in a defensive position at Dien Bien Phu, near the Laotian border of North Vietnam. Although the 15,000 men stationed at the fortress could only be supplied by air, the French, who, by this time, were being heavily backed by the United States, were confident that they could hold out indefinitely. What they didn't count on could, and has, filled volumes; for instance, the amount of Russian and Chinese heavy artillery that had gotten through to the Viet Minh, and the Viet Minh's ability to use it; the dense vegetation surrounding the fortress, which made it impossible to see the enemy, much less destroy its supply lines from the air; and the United States' refusal to respond to France's last-ditch appeals for help by sending its own air power to the rescue. Dien Bien Phu was besieged for 55 days, beginning in March 1954, and on May 7, the French surrendered completely. Although the Viet Minh had suffered more casualties, they had won the war. The French defeat led directly to the Geneva Conference, at which France was forced to grant independence to Laos, Cambodia, and Vietnam, thereby ending her empire in Indochina.

In hindsight, the lessons of Dien Bien Phu seemed pretty clear, at least to some people. On the military level, it demonstrated the futility of depending on superior manpower and technology to overcome a well-armed, thoroughly entrenched guerilla force fighting on difficult terrain and prepared to make outrageous sacrifices to defend a homeland. In terms of global politics, it showed just how much trouble a country could make for itself when it confused grandiosity with ideology.

The United States seemed, for a minute or two, to get the message. President Eisenhower had, after all, refused to get directly involved in the Vietnam conflict without the approval of Congress and the Chiefs of Staff had already declared the whole territory of Indochina to be "without decisive military objectives." But U.S. policy in the region had never been characterized by clear thinking or consistent action and pretty soon Eisenhower was focussing more on his "falling dominoes" speech and the Red Terror instead of on what had just happened at Dien Bien Phu, even though the Russians and Chinese had already stopped speaking to each other and it was unclear just where the Red Terror would be emanating from. When the Geneva Conference partitioned Vietnam into North and South along the 17th parallel, with the promise of free elections in two years to decide on possible reunification, Eisenhower decided to fight rather than let the Vietnamese, who were solidly behind Ho Chi Minh in the north and simply confused in the south, vote. J.F.K. compounded the error when he started looking around for a way to reaffirm U.S. prestige in the wake of Sputnik and save face personally after the Bay of Pigs, and somebody happened to mention that things were not going well in Saigon. By the time Johnson got into office we were headed for Dien Bien Phu all over again. History repeats itself, some people like to point out—and not just in Vietnam.

LEXICON

In the Beginning Was the Prefix

Go ahead: Amaze your doorman, dazzle your periodontist, shut your prospective brother-in-law up for good with your dextrous and inventive handling of such mind-clouding prefixes as demi-, crypto-, and, yes, even meta-. After all, you mastered re-, pre-, and dis-, didn't you?

WHO'S ON TOP?

```
arch-
vice-
co-
para-
sub-
```

Highest up is the man with *arch-* before his title, be it duke, bishop, or angel, each of whom towers over mere dukes, bishops, and angels, respectively; likewise, your archrival gives you more trouble than all your regular rivals put together. The *vice*-person— -president, -admiral, -consul, or, the only common such word written solid, viceroy—is next on the list; he's the stand-in, the understudy, the one who, along with former Secretary of State Haig, is ready to fill in in an emergency or to succeed in the event of death. The *co*-fellow, whether author or conspirator, is all for common cause (and/or shared culpability); sometimes his partner will be in the ascendancy (as with a copilot, who always has Dana Andrews playing him when the pilot is Burt Lancaster), but more often power and responsibility are evenly divided, just as it was between the co-captains of your high school football team. The *para*legal, the *para*medic, the *para*professional in general—from a Greek preposition meaning "alongside of"—are not full-fledged, licensed, or in charge, nor, at the rate they're going, will they ever be. But then some people thrive in the glorified-assistant role. (For the record, paratroopers have a different prefix to thank for their job title, the same one you see in parachute and parasol, a Latin verb stem meaning "protect, ward off.") And don't let's even consider dealing with the guys who are *sub*, as in subaltern and sublieutenant: Obviously, they don't know who *you* are or they'd never even suggest it.

WHO'S FOR REAL?

```
crypto-
quasi-
neo-
pseudo-
```

When Gore Vidal made media history by calling William Buckley a *"crypto*-Nazi" in front of millions of television viewers during the 1968 Democratic convention, he presumably meant that beneath Buckley's conservative facade lurked a fascist trying to keep the public—or himself—from seeing his true colors. At least, that's the way Buckley took it; Vidal later

A Few Hours' Worth of Remedial Work in Vocabulary, Spelling, Pronunciation, and Foreign Expressions

Contents

"The Confusion of Tongues," by Gustave Doré.

pointed out that what'd he'd actually called his archenemy was a "*pro* crypto-Nazi," in reference to Buckley's defense of the Chicago police, who were at that moment battering demonstrators with gleeful abandon in the streets outside. This version would make the cops the Nazis-in-law-enforcement-officers'-clothing; Buckley merely a sympathizer and, possibly, only a *quasi*-Nazi himself. (This "less-than-a-full-fledged-Nazi" interpretation is bolstered by Vidal's adding that, in fact, he hadn't meant to use the term Nazi at all; had he not blown his cool, he said, he would have called his opponent merely "Fascist-minded.") Because a crypto-Nazi has something to gain by keeping his real feelings hidden, and a quasi-Nazi probably isn't sure just what his real feelings are, you don't have to get out of the way of either of them quite as fast as you do some of those *neo*-Nazi organizations whose members like to parade up and down Midwestern streets in modified Luftwaffe surplus, paint swastikas on synagogues, and bash the heads of whichever minority groups they feel are polluting the race these days. In other words, the neo-Nazi is, or likes to think he is, the real thing, updated. Last and certainly least, don't worry at all about those fifteen-year-old *pseudo*-Nazi rockers who like to affect combat boots and Iron Crosses and who go around spouting a lot of racist rhetoric they picked up at the last heavy-metal concert; they're just out to scare you in the hopes of being taken seriously for a change.

WHICH CAME FIRST?

> proto-
> archaeo-
> *Ur-*

The thing that boasts *proto-* (from a Greek word meaning "first") before its name, that's which, whether protozoan, protoplasm, Proto-Germanic (linguists' jargon for the earliest form of a language, in this case German, that they've managed to reconstruct), or prototype. Vying with proto- for deftness at conferring precedence is another Greek word, *archaeo-*, which, while it's not particularly active in spur-of-the-moment word formation, does manage to connote not only "beginning," but "chief, ruler," as well (cf. arch-, above), as in archaeology and archetype.

(To split hairs for a moment, while a prototype is an early form or instance of something that then goes on to serve as a model for a whole string of subsequent somethings, the thing that came *first*, an archetype, is all that and more: It's not only as old as the hills, it's ageless. Thus, as Macaulay [see page 535] pointed out, England's Parliament is the archetype of representative assemblies; he could just as easily have said "prototype," but his point was that Parliament's still sitting there next to the Thames, a bit gray around the temples, perhaps, but a lady with no intention of retiring, and, what's more, immediately recognizable from pictures of herself as a girl. Gutenberg's printing press, on the other hand, is the prototype of the modern printing press—an early model that served and inspired an entire hemisphere—but it's not the archetype of it: Few people would see a resemblance between the two, and no printer in his right mind would want to use the original.)

Those annoyed with this Greek jockeying for position will wish to make the acquaintance of *Ur-*, like "echt" (see page 632) a German traveler who occasionally puts up at the Connaught or the Harvard Club. *Ur-* means "original, earliest, primitive," as in *Ur*-text (also spelled "ur-text," no cap, no italics, no hyphen, which lets you know the prefix is in the process of being naturalized), a text reconstructed from extant later texts. Thus, to present a symphony of Beethoven's in urtext and in urperformance is to do it with obvious mistakes unrectified and with an orchestra of the size and proportions Beethoven wrote it for. As for everything that's not *proto-*, *archaeo-*, or *Ur*, consign it to oblivion with a toss of the head, a raised eyebrow, and a prefixed *neo-*: From Neo-Platonists to Neo-Nazis, who needs 'em?

HOW BIG?

mega-
megalo-
macro-
micro-
mini-

The key prefix here, in the inflationary Eighties, is *mega-*, which, back in Greece, meant literally "million." Thus a megaton bomb has a force equivalent to a million tons of TNT and megabuck is somebody's idea of a funny way to say million dollars. (The related *megalo-*, indicating greatness or strength, without a specific numerical value, is what you get in megalomaniac and megalopolis.) Also worth noting: The opposing prefixes *macro-* (denoting largeness, length, or overdevelop-

ment, as in macroeconomics, see page 123; macrocosm, a.k.a. the universe; and macrobiotics) and *micro-* (denoting the reverse, as in microeconomics, microcosm, and microfilm). The former is still little enough known that the doorman may be impressed; the latter's debased by centuries of overuse—though it still beats *mini-*.

WHICH HALF?

bi-
semi-
demi-
hemi-
half-

All right, is a *bi*monthly magazine one that comes twice a month or one that comes every other month? There's no real consensus out there, but take our advice and use bimonthly for the every-other-month one, and call the twice-a-month a *semi*monthly. *Semi-*, derived from the Latin, means half, or sometimes a bit less—but then so do *demi-*, from the French, as in demitasse and demimonde; and *hemi-*, from the Greek, as in hemisphere. If you're indulging in creative prefixing, purists would have you choose, in any given situation, the prefix of the same nationality as the root you're attaching it to, but that doesn't account for demigod, among others. Of the three, *semi-* combines most freely, and when in doubt you can always fall back on good old native *half-*, as in half-wit, half-portion, and half gainer. Note to absurdists and Anglophiles everywhere: The British word for a sixty-fourth note (and you knew they'd have one) is hemidemisemiquaver.

TO WHAT DEGREE?

> hyper-
> hypo-

The stupidest mnemonic is all you need here, so voilà: *hyper-* has more letters, and it's the one that means "over, too much," as in hyperactive, hypertension, hyperbole, and just plain hyper. *Hypo-*, with only four letters, means "under, too little," as in hypoglycemia (too little blood sugar), hypodermic (literally, "under the skin"), and hype (from the old slang for the kind of hypodermic injection we now call a fix). Both began life as Greek prepositions, and both traveled well. *Hyper-*, in particular, is an industrious, even promiscuous prefix. Which means that *hypo-* —less seen, less understood—may be a better one to be able to throw around.

WHERE DO WE GO FROM HERE?

> meta-

Not all Greek prepositional prefixes are as graspable as *hyper-* and *hypo-*. For instance, we wanted to hold forth here on *ana-* and *cata-*, but forget it: While you can point out that they mean roughly "up" and "down," that really doesn't equip a person to savor "catalogue" or "Anabaptist." Besides, as prefixes go they're dead; only a scientist would use one to make a new word these days. Not so *meta-*, which currently is a hotter linguistic ticket than ever, our candidate for the prefixer's prefix. While it has two "flat" meanings as a simple preposition—"with, among" (cognate with English "mid" and German "mit") and "after, behind"—it's come to be equated with pursuit, quest, and change, with the person, object, or idea that transcends all existing forms, with the restless and the ineffable. Actually, this grandeur on the part of *meta-* is the result of a little philological misunderstanding: Aristotle called the book he wrote on transcendental philosophy *Ta meta ta phusika* ("the things after physics") because it followed his work on that subject, thereby ensuring that metaphysics would forever be equated with the transcendental, even though it was just a simple sequel. Not that that's stopped anybody from devoting his life—or his ego—to such pursuits as metahistory ("A historian writes the history of a period, a metahistorian compares different periods in order to derive an essence," as one scholar recently put it), metalinguistics, and even metaculture. With *meta-* in your pocket, you don't ever have to feel stagnant, flaccid, or middle-aged.

Distinctions Worth Making

*(OR AT LEAST BEING IN A
POSITION TO MAKE)*

affect *and* effect

Promise to get this one down and we'll spare you *lie* and *lay*. Affect is the verb most of the time; it implies influence: "Smoking can affect one's health; how has it affected yours?" Effect is the equivalent noun: "Smoking has had an effect on me and on my health." Sometimes, though (and here's where the trouble comes in) "effect" is the verb. When it is, it brings a sense not of mere influence, but of purpose, even impact: "I must effect my plan to stop smoking"; "By not smoking, I have succeeded in effecting my complete recovery." Of course, not drinking may also have *aff*ected your recovery—may have contributed to it, may have hastened it along—but here you're claiming that stopping smoking was what really turned things around.

Two little problems: (1) the way one *aff*ects a jaunty air or an English accent; and (2) the so-called affect (watch that noun) in psychology: all the emotional stuff surrounding a particular state or situation. But don't worry too much about them; concentrate on the difference in meaning above, which is where you stand to blow it if you're going to blow it at all.

anxious *and* eager

Famous last stand of the language purists: You're not anxious to spend a languorous evening with your oldest married friends, you're *eager* to spend it. Unless, that is, you've been sleeping with one of them for the past three months. Then you *are* anxious.

assume *and* presume

When you presume, you take for granted that something is true; when you assume, you postulate that it's true in order to go on to argue or to act. Presuming has tied up in it the idea of anticipation, of jumping the gun, of taking liberties; hence the adjective presumptuous. Assuming isn't necessarily a swell thing, either (hence the adjective self-assuming), but at least it's up-front about the fact that it has a chip on its shoulder. So, was Stanley being rude when he said, "Dr. Livingstone, I presume?" No, not really; after all, he'd been trailing the Scottish missionary and explorer for months, on assignment for a New York newspaper, and they must have at least furnished him with a photograph. On the other hand, had it turned out that the distinguished stranger standing on the shore of Lake Tanganyika was not Dr. Livingstone, but Dr. Dolittle, it's possible Stanley might have wished he'd said "assume" instead.

authentic *and* genuine

Something that's genuine hasn't been forged; something that's authentic tells the truth about its subject. In other words, you might, one Friday morning, regale your co-workers with the details of your Thursday night at the latest East Village night spot, when you'd really stayed home and watched television again; such an account would be genuine (you *are* the author of it) but not authentic (you weren't even in the East Village). Conversely, you might that same morning have been lucky enough to overhear, on the Madison Avenue bus, the account of somebody who had been at the club in question the night before, then repeated it verbatim to your co-workers; *that* account would be authentic (assuming the person on the bus was telling the truth himself) but not genuine, because you'd be passing off somebody else's good time as your own.

canonical, catholic, ecclesiastical, ecumenical, evangelical, *and* liturgical

The central word here is ecclesiastical, which means pertaining to the church or its clergy. Canonical means pertaining to church law, binding on all its members. Evangelical means pertaining to the teachings of Christ, especially the Four Gospels; easy to get from there to hitting the road for Jesus. Liturgical means pertaining to the liturgy, the whole ritual of public worship. (The lit*any* is a form of prayer in which the clergyman and the congregation alternate responses.) Catholic and ecumenical are the hard ones: They both mean universal. Ecumenical derives from a Greek word meaning "of the inhabited earth," and most often refers to councils or regulations that govern the entire church, or all of any one branch of it, or the spirit behind such councils and regulations. Catholic, from a Greek phrase meaning "in general," "in respect of the whole," has an additional sense of inclusiveness, of tastes, sympathies, interests that are all-embracing. (That's with a lowercase *c*, though; uppercase, and it's the old Popes and Hail Mary's business.) Both ecumenical, a term Protestants seem understandably to prefer, and catholic are the opposite of parochial, "of the parish."

compleat *and* complete

The first form is simply archaic; in a just world, no one would ever have to deal with it again. Unfortunately, the world's not just, and for a few centuries now, editors, publishers, and copywriters have found "compleat" to be a word that jazzed up titles and boosted sales. Isaak Walton did it first and best, back in 1653, with his *The Compleat Angler* (subtitled "Or the Contemplative Man's Recreation"), a discourse on fishing liberally laced with rural wisdom and unshakable Christian faith. Now look for, at your corner bookstore, the likes of *The Compleat Werewolf*, *The Compleat Belly Dancer*, and *The Compleat Nevada Traveler*. Used to describe a person, as in any of the foregoing examples, the word—however you spell it—is best defined as "perfectly skilled or equipped; consummate, accomplished."

compose *and* comprise

The wolves compose the pack; the pack comprises the wolves. (If you want to get passive about it, the pack is composed of the wolves, and the wolves are comprised by the pack.) In short, comprise is sort of an uptown synonym for "include"—except that a pack that comprises wolves is all-wolf, while one that merely includes them may have two hyenas and a German shepherd in it, too.

continual *and* continuous

Continuous is uncompromising: A continuous slope or vigil or downpour is steady, unbroken, invariable, without even a temporary reversal or a tiny interruption. Continual, on the other hand, allows for gaps, suggests, in fact, that something recurs at regular intervals, with time out in between: Continual showings are what you get at the movies, and continual setbacks may crop up at the rate of only half a dozen a year. Now, try to remember that continu*ous* is, in general, more seri*ous*—not to mention scientific, as in the mathematician's continuous function, the physicist's continuous wave, the astronomer's theory of continuous creation. Continu*al* is what you usu*al*ly mean; it's more figurative, describes how things seem, feel, strike an on-looker, as in Swift's "These people are under continual disquietudes, never enjoying a minute's peace of mind."

converse *and* inverse

Converse is a matter of simple transposition: "He hit me" is the converse of "I hit him"; "He had glamour but no money" the converse of "He had money but no glamour." "Inverse" is a more extreme—and a more ambiguous—business; it entails turning something inside out or standing it on its head. Thus, when two quantities vary inversely, one gets bigger as the other gets smaller; the inverse of a mathematical operation is the one that will nullify it (e.g., division is the inverse of multiplication). In logic, the inverse of a statement is attained by negating both its hypothesis *and* its conclusion: the inverse of "If Alice is drinking J&B, then she's drinking scotch" would be "If Alice isn't drinking J&B, then she's not drinking scotch"—as it happens, a logically defective, or "false," statement. (So is the converse: "If Alice is drinking scotch, then she's drinking J&B." Don't feel bad, though; the woods are full of defective inverses and converses.)

deprecate *and* depreciate

In terms of etymology, deprecate is the opposite of "pray for," depreciate is the opposite of "praise." If you put yourself down a little, you make a self-depre*cia*ting remark; if you really let yourself have it (and you know how bad you've been being lately), the remark might then, but only then, be self-depre*ca*ting. Don't expect anybody to applaud, though—either the flagellation or the preciseness of your language; this is a distinction almost nobody knows he's even supposed to be making.

discreet *and* discrete

Discreet—prudent, circumspect, just this side of walking on eggs—is what you should be when you're having an illicit love affair. Discrete (which, for what it's worth, comes from the same Latin word, *discretus,* "sifted through") means distinct, discontinuous, separate, as in "discrete entities," "discrete particles," "discrete elements," and should probably be reserved for dress-up occasions.

dock *and* pier

Don't try to walk on a dock: It's the space where a ship comes to rest and it's full of water. (Drydock makes the point nicely: Picture the space with all the water drained out of it so that the repairs can start.) The pier is what you *can* walk on; it's the structure on which the passengers stand and onto which the cargo is unloaded. Assuming, that is, the structure runs out into the water, away from the shore, preferably at a right angle to it. If it runs *along* the shore, it's technically not a pier but a wharf. P.S.: Don't mention any of this to Otis Redding.

egotist, egoist, solipsist, *and* narcissist

They're all stuck on themselves, but only two of them could tell you why. The egotist (from the Latin word for "I") couldn't: He just wants to fill you in on the details of his life, even if you have heard them all several times before. (Think of that *t* as standing for "talk.") The egoist, by contrast, might explain that self-interest is the foundation of all morality, and that it's therefore not just silly but downright antisocial *not* to put oneself first. The solipsist (from the Latin word for "alone"), who took even more philosophy courses as an undergraduate than the egoist did, would maintain that no person has any proof that anything exists outside his own mind, that each of us, like him, is totally alone with our own thoughts, and not just on rainy April afternoons, either. (As it happens, while no major philosopher has ever accepted solipsism, neither has any ever been able to refute it; Schopenhauer—see page 318—for his part dubbed it "theoretical egoism" and hoped we wouldn't worry about it too much.) The narcissist, a term of Freud's devising (see page 402), after the Greek youth who couldn't stop looking at his reflection in a pool of water, is basically going steady with himself and may not want to talk to you at all. If he does, his goal will not be to expound on the nature of his belief system, but to charm you into joining his fan club.

enormity *and* enormousness

Straightforward enough. Enormousness is the one that's a synonym for immensity: The enormousness of the cosmos. Enormity refers to something so far outside the moral *norm* (the root in both words) that it's monstrously wicked, unthinkable, the lowest of the low: The enormity of his crimes. Of course you can talk about the enormousness of somebody's crimes, too, if all you mean is they're big. But do try not to refer to the enormity of the cosmos—unless you know something we don't.

epidemic *and* endemic

An epidemic disease breaks out somewhere and eventually goes away again; an endemic disease breaks out and is still there centuries later. Cholera is endemic in parts of Asia; when it broke out in Europe, it was epidemic. (Think of it as the difference between *epi-*, "over," and *en-*, "in.") Which means that the AIDS epidemic is looking more and more like the AIDS endemic. Make that pandemic, given that it's shaping up to be in residence pretty much everywhere at once.

epigram *and* epigraph

Both words derive from the Greek preposition *epi*, meaning "upon" or "over," plus the familiar Greek word for "write," and both began by designating the kind of inscription you find on a monument or statue. Epigra*ph* still does mean that—sometimes. More often, it refers to a motto or quotation set at the beginning, or "over," the body of a book, chapter, or poem, intended to set the tone for or provide an entrée to the work to come (for instance, the snatch from Dante at the head of Eliot's "Prufrock," the "If I thought I were talking to anybody but a dead man" business). Epigra*m* never means inscription anymore; it occasionally is used of a super-short poem expressing a single acidulous thought, but usually it refers to a concise, cleverly worded, essentially antithetical statement, with a sting or twist at the end (e.g., Dorothy Parker's "If all the young ladies who attended the Yale promenade were laid end to end, no one would be the least surprised.").

To complete the picture, an epi*taph* is an inscription, always on a tombstone; an epi*logue* the little speech or poem that concludes a play, or the short section at the end of a book sketching the future of its characters—in short, the structural opposite of the epigraph.

ethics *and* morals

In early English scholarship, the two words were treated as synonyms, deriving from Greek *ethos* ("nature or disposition") and Latin *mos* (genitive form, *moris;* "custom"), respectively. Gradually, though, ethics came to be viewed as the science or philosophy of morals (see page 302), morals as the practice or enactment of ethics; as often happened in those days, the Latin-derived word was used for the real, tangible, everyday doing of something, the Greek-derived one reserved for the idealized, theoretical understanding of that doing. Today some people say "ethics" even when they mean "morals," simply because the word is that much less common. Don't pay any attention to them. Instead, save your strength to make the distinction between the adjective forms, ethical and moral. Here, moral has been tainted by the association of its opposite, immoral, with *sexual* misconduct, and as a result lost much of its range. Ethical has been left to describe all kinds of recognizable, day-to-day behavior that is, for whatever reason, proper, admirable, or just plain honest.

farther *and* further

The deal is this: Farther, etymologically, means more far; further, more to the fore, more forth. So, it's farther from Miami to Palm Beach than it is from Miami to Fort Lauderdale; plus, if you hate Florida's Gold Coast, you'll want to move farther away still—Daytona, maybe. Once you're settled in Daytona, no further steps (note the shift from literal to figurative) should be necessary. A couple of additional qualifications here. First, farther can apply as easily to time as to space: you may have packed up and left Miami farther back than you can remember. Second, there are so many cases where trying to decide which is right—farther to go or further? more far (in terms of sheer distance) or more forth (in terms of effort or visibility or prominence)?—that thinking *too* hard about the distinction, while it may help you get a grip on what you really mean, will also slow you down to the point that you never make it out the front door.

flaunt *and* flout

Don't try to tell us you were appalled—or, for that matter, listening—back when President Carter declaimed at the height of crisis, "The Government of Iran must realize that it cannot flaunt, with impunity, the expressed will and law of the world community." After all, using flaunt (of unknown origin; meaning to parade oneself ostentatiously, to be gaudily in evidence, to wave proudly, and to generally show off) when what you mean is flout (probably akin to the Old French word for flute, an instrument whose whistling noises can sometimes sound derisive; meaning to be scornful of, to show contempt for, to fly in the face of) is a problem for everybody. The confusion is understandable: Both words bespeak behavior that's excessive, inappropriate, and potentially disruptive. But remember that flaunting and flouting are, when push comes to shove, virtual opposites—acts typical of the chauvinist and the seditionist, respectively.

heathen *and* pagan

Neither's partaking in the great Judaeo-Christian tradition—yet. Pagan, though, with its classical background (from a Latin word meaning "country district"), often refers specifically to the ancient Greeks and Romans, whom it was hard even for nineteenth-century Christians to hold in total contempt; heathen is simply a slam term, directed at some poor benighted creature not yet one of us. Thus Christian missionaries go out to convert the heathens, all loincloths and pulsating jungle rhythms, while the pagans hold orgies and debate the relative merits of red and white wine and the connection between pain and pleasure. The infidel, unlike the pagan or the heathen, had a religion the European at least felt threatened by, most often Muhammadanism, well supplied with scimitars and minarets. Today, it denotes, among Roman Catholics, any unbaptized person, from heathen to Protestant.

infer *and* imply

It's a matter of where you stand, of whether you're transmitting or receiving. You imply something in a remark to a friend, who infers something from that remark. Anybody who goes around saying "What are you inferring?" is, unless he's addressing a philosopher, almost certain to be pretentious, and not all that smart.

insidious *and* invidious

The thing that's insidious (from the Latin word for "ambush") sneaks up on you; it's not only undesirable, it's stealthy and it's treacherous, like cancer. The thing that's invidious (from the Latin word for "envy") isn't subtle or sneaky, just repugnant and certain to cause trouble, in the form of ill will, resentment, or envy itself, generally directed against whoever said or did it. When Jesse Jackson called New York "Hymietown," he made an invidious (and a politically not very savvy) remark.

jealousy *and* envy

Envy is the simple one, and—along with wrath, gluttony, and the rest—one of the seven deadly and absolutely unmistakable sins. Implying both resentment and greed, it's when you first begrudge your neighbor the possession of something (ox, ass, VCR), then covet it for yourself. Jealousy is much subtler and less materialistic. At its classiest, it implies principled protectiveness, as when a father is "jealous for" his daughter's welfare, or principled intolerance, as in "a jealous God." More often, it has to do with ongoing personal rivalry, known or suspected, frequently of a sexual nature, coupled with a fear of loss or supplantation. Envy may make us behave badly, even turn us green, but it doesn't necessarily cloud our minds; jealousy always does.

mean, median, mode, *and* average

The umbrella term here is average; all the others are types of it, employed mainly by school children, sportswriters, and statisticians. Take the following numbers: 2, 4, 6, 7, 7, 8, 8, 8, 13. What you think of as the average (add them all up, divide by the number of terms you added) is, technically speaking, the arithmetic mean, here 63 divided by 9, or 7. The median is also 7, but for a different reason: 7 is the center term in the sequence, with four terms to either side of it. Statistically, the median can sometimes give a more reliable picture than the mean, for instance, when three people get a 60 on a test and one gets 100: Here, the mean—70—might make you think a successful learning experience had been going on, when in fact three quarters of the class hadn't learned much of anything, as revealed by the median—60. The mode is the least used of the three kinds of average: It's simply the term that crops up more frequently than any other, in the sequence up above not 7, but 8.

mutual *and* common

Just remember that *Our Mutual Friend,* the Dickens title, is a famous solecism, that is, a language-use blunder of a particularly blatant sort. More precisely, mutual implies exchange, interaction, reciprocity, none of which occurs when you simply share a friend with somebody else—when you have a friend in common. "Mutual admirers," on the other hand, makes perfect sense: I admire you and you admire me. We're reciprocating, we're interacting. We're provided for. We're happy. Note, though, that if somebody admires both of us, he is our common admirer—unless, of course, each of us is willing to admire him back, thereby making the admiration mutual. Careful here: Some people think they can tell how educated you are on the basis of how you handle the one word "mutual."

objective *and* subjective

If you're objective, you sacrifice your personality, your mood, and your need for attention to some higher (or at least bigger) goal: You become, say, a reporter for the *Washington Post* and you vow just to give the facts. If you're subjective, it's how you feel, where you're coming from, and what you make of the situation in Beirut, not to mention the fact that you're getting older, that your wallet was stolen last week, and that Cajun food is big, that counts: So you angle to take over Andy Rooney's spot on *Sixty Minutes.* Simple enough, we grant you, but you should know that objective and subjective are fighting words for (a) literary critics, who can't decide which of them good criticism, or, since you ask, good literature should be, let alone how to tell the difference; and (b) philosophers, who've been arguing about the subject (the active mind, the thinking agent) and the object (everything else, further analyzable into several dozen categories), the seer and the seen, the thought and the thing, ever since Aristotle.

oral *and* verbal

Quick: How do you describe a contract that two people strike over the phone? Well, sure, it's verbal. But so's any contract that uses words. The right answer is oral—spoken, as opposed to written. And don't confuse oral (from the Latin word for "mouth") with aural (from the Latin word for "ear") even if they are almost always pronounced alike.

pathos *and* bathos

Pathos, which in Greek means "suffering" or "passion," is the quality in literature or art that stimulates pity or compassion in the onlooker. Bathos, which in Greek means "depth," is a downward (and an unintentional) slide into the maudlin or the banal. Alexander Pope (see page 187) named it, in 1727, in a mock-critical treatise called "Peri-Bathous, or, Of the Art of Sinking in Poetry." One of his favorite examples, from a contemporary poem: "Ye Gods! annihilate but Space and Time, / And make two lovers happy." Equally bathetic: The description of the death of Little Nell in Dickens's *The Old Curiosity Shop* (of which Oscar Wilde remarked, famously, that only a man with a heart of stone could read it without laughing), and the motto "For God, for Country, and for Yale." The *a* is long in both words, by the way.

redundancy, tautology, *and* pleonasm

Deadwood. Redundancy is the blanket term here, describing any instance of the other two (as well as language that's merely verbose, that uses too many words even if they don't all mean the same thing). Tautology and pleonasm are both more specialized. The first, from the Greek *tauto-*, "same," repeats what is explicit in a way that suggests the speaker isn't entirely up to using the words he's chosen, and it's widely held to be indefensible. Examples: bibliography of books, visible to the eye, consensus of opinion. (It's also used in logic of the kind of assertion that sets out to prove itself through simple restatement: "This is the best poem that Sylvia Plath ever wrote; after all, none of the others is nearly so good.") The second, from the Greek *ple(i)on*, "more," is an established rhetorical device. It repeats what is already implicit by adding a word or phrase that is not, strictly speaking, necessary, although it may contribute to overall clarity, emphasis, or effect. Examples: fall down, to see something with one's own eyes, only just begun. Too much pleonasm can get on a person's nerves, but sometimes it's the point of the exercise: The Bible, for instance, is built on it.

sensuous *and* sensual

In both cases, it's the senses, not the mind, that're being gratified; sensations, not ideas, that you wind up having. Coined by Milton ("[Poetry is] more simple, sensuous, and passionate [than rhetoric]," he wrote), sensuous is today a more or less uncharged term and applies to the kind of pleasure you get from art, music, scented candles, and seedless grapes. Sensual has more to do with erotic pleasure, with the indulgence of the appetites, with gluttony, lust, and motives that aren't all they should be. Make the sens*ual*/sex*ual* connection, and the pair won't give you any trouble.

sententious *and* tendentious

You don't want to be either of these, if you can help it. The first is all about affectation and pompous moralizing, the second about the relentless proselytizing of the tract-writer.

specious *and* spurious

Good debunking words, these, possessed of an Oxford-debates-Cambridge rarefaction and spleen. Both mean "lacking authenticity or validity, counterfeit, false." Spurious also has overtones of bastardy, illegitimacy, and tends to pop up in gutsy phrases like "spurious brood." (Which isn't to say that a document or a bit of financial advice can't equally well prove spurious.) To the basic sense of rotten at the core, specious adds a veneer of charm, seductiveness, plausibility. From the Latin *species*, "outward appearance," it describes the thing that seems fair, sound, or true, but that, on closer inspection, is anything but. Specious evidence is not only false evidence, but evidence presented with intent to deceive—and, implicitly, evidence that almost succeeds in doing so.

sybarite, hedonist, *and* epicurean

The ancient Greeks are behind all three. Of the kinds of pleasure-lover they designate, the sybarite is the most blatant and unredeemed. Unlike the other two—both of whom had ancestors with Ph.D.'s—he doesn't have a thought in his head: *His* folks, wealthy Greek colonists in the southern Italian town of Sybaris, simply knew how to have a good time. A hedonist, by contrast, has an elaborate justification for his pursuit of pleasure (*hedone,* in Greek): He believes that it is, simply, the chief good, though he'll probably have his hand on your leg as he's telling you why. An epicurean may or may not be hedonistic. If he is, he'll at least yoke gratification with tastefulness, and probably put ease before orgasm. If he isn't—if he's a bona fide follower of the Greek philosopher Epicurus—you'd better not even offer him a drink. A true Epicurean (note cap), while he accepts the primacy of pleasure in life, tends to equate it with the avoidance of pain, the rational control of one's desires, and the practice of virtue, and to seek it in intellectual rather than bodily hiding places.

sympathy *and* empathy

For centuries, we English-speakers made do perfectly nicely with sympathy, "feeling with," the power to share another person's emotions, to be affected by his experiences, to walk a mile—or simply a few yards—in his shoes. No big deal: Just a little compassion, is all, and the chance every so often to cry at a movie. Empathy, "feeling into," originated in 1912 as a pseudo-Greek translation of the German psychoanalytic term *Einfühlung,* the ability to project one's personality into someone in order to understand him better. Several questions here: Is empathy a bigger deal than sympathy? Is it somehow "heavier," or just more self-conscious? Does one require special imagination or training to feel it? To use it? Should one be content feeling sympathy for Elizabeth Bennet and Holden Caulfield or have the stakes been raised to the point that sympathy is no longer enough? Is one in trouble if one's shrink has sympathy but no empathy? Empathy but no sympathy? What's it all about, Alfie? Write to us care of our publisher. Good-bye.

synecdoche *and* metonymy

Both are highly specialized forms of metaphor. Synecdoche (sin-EK-duh-kee) uses an appropriate part of something to signify the whole; thus "ten hired hands" means "ten hired workmen," and "wheels" were your father's car.

Metonymy (muh-TAHN-uh-mee; literally, "name-changing") includes, technically, all synecdoche, but most often denotes the use of an associated or outside attribute for the object or institution under discussion; thus journalists are spoken of as "the press," one steps on "the gas" as routinely as on the accelerator pedal, and an idea comes to you out of "the blue" rather than the sky. Literary critics and classical linguists still make a lot of this pair, but don't spend too much time on rhetorical devices; these days, you'll get more mileage out of being able to distinguish between MCI and Sprint.

turgid, turbid, *and* tumid

In botany, turgor (from a Latin verb meaning "to swell") is cellular rigidity as the result of a plant's having taken in too much water. By extension, turgid means swollen, inflated, enlarged; and, by further extension, pompous, bombastic. Turgid does not mean tur*b*id, which derives from the Latin word for "crowd," and means muddy, impenetrable, opaque; confused, disordered. (You can remember it from turbulent.) For better or for worse, turgid *does* mean tu*m*id, which is related to the word tumor (from another Latin verb meaning to swell), and which means swollen, inflated, enlarged; as well as pompous, bombastic. The one difference we can make out: Turgid can imply normal or healthy distention (a branch turgid with sap) and the kind of rant that at least doesn't put you to sleep. Tumid almost always has overtones of morbidity: a starvation victim's tumid stomach, a cow's tumid ulcer; figuratively, it bespeaks sheer bloat.

uninterested *and* disinterested

The former means indifferent, uncaring; the latter impartial. It's that simple.

venal *and* venial

The two have nothing to do with each other, etymologically or conceptually. Venal (from the Latin word for "sale") means open or susceptible to bribery, capable of betraying one's honor or duty for a price, obtainable by purchase rather than by merit. Venial (from the Latin word for "forgiveness") means pardonable, easily excused, minor in nature, thus "venial sin" (as opposed to the mortal variety). Suggested mnemonic: "Venal" rhymes with "penal," and prison is where bribe-takers wind up; "venial" rhymes with "genial," which you can afford to be, given that you're not going to be taken to task for your mistake.

Twenty-Six Words Not to Say Wrong

Ten where you have no choice:

1.	flaccid:	FLAK-sid
2.	heinous:	HAY-ness
3.	scion:	SIGH-en
4.	segue:	SEG-way
5.	ague:	AY-gyoo
6.	caste:	KAST
7.	dais:	DAY-is
8.	inchoate:	in-KOH-it
9.	quay:	KEY
10.	ribald:	RIB-uld

Eight where you have to choose between being unimpeachably correct (and risk sounding pretentious) or disarmingly casual (and risk sounding uneducated):

		Correct	*Casual*
11.	dour:	Rhymes with "poor"	Rhymes with "power"
12.	err:	Rhymes with "fur"	Rhymes with "fair"
13.	grimace:	Accent on second syllable: gri-MACE	Accent on first syllable: GRIM-us
14.	harass:	Accent on first syllable: HAR-ass	Accent on second syllable: huh-RASS
15.	impious:	Accent on prefix: IM-pee-ous	Accent on root: im-PIE-ous
16.	schism:	SIZZ-em	SKIZZ-em
17.	extant:	Accent on first syllable: EKS-tunt	Accent on second syllable: eks-TANT
18.	long-lived:	Long *i* (as in "life")	Short *i* (as in "live")

Four where you have to know what you mean before you open your mouth:

19.	forte:	It's one syllable (ignore the *e*) when it means strong point, two (FOR-tay) when it's the musical direction meaning loudly.
20.	bases:	More than one base? Say BAYS-es. More than one basis? Say BAYS-ees.
21.	slough:	In America, SLOO (rhymes with "goo") is preferred for the actual mire, swamp, bayou, or backwater; SLOU (rhymes with "cow") for the deep despair figuratively akin to it; SLUF is the only acceptable pronunciation when you're shedding dead skin.
22.	prophecy/prophesy:	The former's the noun and you say PRAH-fuh-see; the latter's the verb and you say PRAH-fuh-sigh.

Plus four more where which side you're on counts for more than simply being right:

23. junta: It's the Spaniards' word for "council," and they're going to want you to say HOON-ta. The British (and most of our anchorpersons) prefer JUN-ta. Our advice: Hope the Falklands war is over for good.

24. sheik: The Brits *and* the Arabs say SHAKE, and the anchorpersons, slowly but surely, seem to be coming round. The rest of us seem more at home with SHEEK, as of Araby.

25. Celtic: The Greeks (who made up the word Celtic) and the Bretons (who *are* Celtic) both spelled this with a *k;* and purists, including many British speakers, continue to make that *c* hard: KELT-ic. But then, *you* have the Boston Celtics to think about.

26. valet: It *was* French, but it's been pretty thoroughly Anglicized. Whether you say it to rhyme with ballet or with ballot depends on which way you want to be pretentious. (The latter probably wins.) Not pretentious? Then you won't be saying this word at all.

Twenty-Six Words Not to Write Wrong

We'll assume that you mastered "necessary" and "separate" back in the eighth grade, and that you remember "all right" on the grounds that it's the opposite of "all wrong." Beyond such basics, here are the twenty-six words you're most likely to go wrong on in your next business letter, interoffice memo, or screenplay. To make things just a bit more galvanizing, we've listed them in ascending order of difficulty (our criteria included rarefaction—see #20—as well as trickiness). And we've provided commentary.

1. trav*ele*r   The English do it with two *l*s, but America doesn't double-up except in accented syllables, e.g., controlled, propeller, referral.

2. princip*le*/princip*al*   They offered this one in eighth grade, too, but we were putting on Clearasil at the time. Briefly, a princip*le* is a ru*le*, and the princi*pal* (the most *important* person in your school) is your *pal*.

3. station*a*ry/station*e*ry   With the first, you're st*a*nding in one place; with the second, you're on your way to what the English still call the station*e*r's.

4. coo*lly*   First it looks right, then it looks wrong. The fact is, you're simply adding that familiar suffix, with its *l*, to the root. Likewise the double *n* in drunkenness, the double *s* in misspelling (it works with prefixes, too).

5. emba*rr*a*ss*   Two rs, two *s*s. But h*a*ra*ss*.

6. unpa*rall*e*l*ed   The archetypal trick word.

7. s*ei*ze — Forget "i before e except after c," which works for the English derivatives of the Latin *capio* ("I take") family: deceive, receipt, conceit, etc., plus others like ceiling. But: weird, sheik, inveigle. And, to muddy the waters, there's siege.

8. pre*ced*ing — OK: There are three verbs in *-ceed:* succeed, proceed, exceed. Of course, there's supersede. All the rest are *-cede,* including precede, whose present participle is therefore spelled thus.

9. nick*el* — Maybe it's just us.

10. fo*r*go/fo*r*ego — The first, meaning relinquish, uses *for-,* an old Anglo-Saxon word indicating abstention or prohibition, as in forbid, forsake, forbear. *Fore-* you know: It refers to what's gone before, as in forewarn, forebode, foregone conclusion.

11. superintend*e*nt — Likewise, correspond*e*nt, independ*e*nt. You have to memorize which are *e* and which *a:* Even knowing the Latin conjugations and their stems won't help (e.g., attend*a*nt).

12. mo*cc*asin — Those use-what's-at-hand Indians. Likewise, ra*cc*oon.

13. glam*ou*r — So far, so good. But it's glam*o*rous.

14. impost*o*r — The single hardest case of "*-er* or *-or?*" In general, learned, Latinate words take *-or,* simple Anglo-Saxon ones, *-er* (e.g., perpetrat*o*r and do*er*), but watch out for exceptions (e.g., actor and executioner).

15. des*icc*ate — If you use an adult word you can't afford to misspell it. Note the single first interior consonant, the doubled second one; it's a pattern, too, in titillate, vacillate, flagellate. But: dis*s*ipate, exagge*r*ate.

16. resus*c*itate — Your move.

17. i*n*oculate — Nothing to do with pain or injury (as in innocuous). From the Latin *in* plus *oculus* ("eye"), referring to the little eye the needle makes in your skin. For analogous reasons, which we won't go into here, it's a*n*oint.

18. sacr*i*legious — The relationship is with sacr*i*lege, not religious. Now try to remember how to spell sacrilege. (Hint: It's like privilege. Now try to remember how to spell *that.*)

19. con*s*ensus — Not a head-counting, but a coming together of feeling.

20. rar*e*fy — Also: liqu*e*fy, stup*e*fy, putr*e*fy, and their noun forms—rar*e*faction, etc.

21. prophe*s*y — The verb, which you pronounce "-sigh." The noun is with a *c.*

22. gene*a*logy — With miner*a*logy and an*a*logy, one of a handful of words that don't end *-o*logy.

23. pav*ili*on — Not helped by the French word from which it's derived, pavillon. Or by cotillion, its equally high-living cousin. Also: verm*ili*on.

24. d*y*sfunction — This prefix is Greek for "disease," not the familiar Latin one. While we're talking medicine (and *y*s), a swollen blood vessel is an aneur*y*sm.

25. bra*gg*ado*c*io — The double *g* (as in braggart) is easy enough; the problem's with the single *c,* which imitates neither the Italian suffix *-occio,* or the Spenserian character—Braggado*c*hio—from which the word derives.

26. autar*ky*   Here's a prestige distinction, and if you're ambitious you'll contrive to make it this week. Autar*chy* is absolute sovereignty, total self-control; autar*ky* (from a different Greek stem) is self-sufficiency, especially of an economic, damn-the-imports nature.

PLUS, AS AN EXTRA ADDED BONUS, SEVEN PHRASES YOU MAY NOT EVEN KNOW YOU WRITE WRONG

ba*te*d breath	That is, shortened—as in abate. No entrapment here.
p*ore* over	What you do to a manuscript. It's not the same as what you do to a stack of pancakes.
strai*t*jacket	Not "without any curves or twists," but "narrow, constricting," as in Strait of Gibraltar. Likewise, "the strait and narrow" (a famous redundancy), "strait is the gate."
ha*re*brained	Ditto, harelip.
test your met*tle*	Unless you're at the pig-iron auction.
chaise lo*ngue*	You still want one poolside, but it's a "long chair," not a lounge.
to the man*ner* born	It's all in the execution, not in the family real estate.

Mistaken Identities

ADJECTIVES WHOSE LOOKS ARE DECEPTIVE

CAPTIOUS: Perversely hard to please, given to fault-finding and petty criticism. Like your boss on a bad day. Or invalid wives in the kind of movie where the husband ends up burying the body in the basement and everyone in the audience hopes he'll get away with it.

FRACTIOUS: Peevish, irritable, cranky, or, in a more general sense, inclined to cause trouble. Often used to describe children or people who behave like them. Fractious derives from fraction; breaking or dividing is, after all, what a fractious individual is after. Not to be confused with "factious," from the noun "faction," which also can mean divisive—but for different reasons.

NOISOME: Has nothing to do with noise, quite a bit to do with smell. Means disgusting, unwholesome, unpleasant, as in "a noisome gas," or downright harmful, as in "noisome prison conditions."

FULSOME: Originally meant what you'd think it would mean: full, rich, plentiful. But eventually some people became uncomfortable with hedonism, and the "too much of a good thing" connotation crept in. Today, fulsome means offensively excessive or insincere. Fulsome praise, for instance, is the kind you get from someone who doesn't like you much but hopes you've got a job for his brother-in-law.

RESTIVE: Impatient or nervous as the result of restraint or delay. The way you used to feel when your mother said you couldn't go out with your friends, you had to stay home and clean your room. Often used to describe balky animals and mutinous crowds. Unlike "restless," restive implies resistance to outside control.

TORTUOUS: Full of twists and turns (but not necessarily excruciating ones), like the road to Shangri-la, or Alexis's thought processes, or foreign policy as practiced by Henry Kissinger.

PARLOUS: Simply a medieval contraction of perilous, which is, more or less, what it means: dangerous, precarious, risky. Archaic, but it still crops up regularly in political discussions, the sports section, and the phrase "parlous times."

PASSIBLE: Capable of feeling or suffering; impressionable. Comes from the Latin *passus*, past participle of the verb "to suffer," and is hence related to both passion and patience. Women were once considered passible creatures.

FECKLESS: Just remember that "feck" is a Scottish shortening of *effect;* feckless, therefore, means weak, ineffective, or, more commonly, childishly careless and irresponsible.

DILATORY: Has to do not with dilation but with delay; means tending to procrastinate. Can refer to a deliberate attempt to stall or simply to a bad habit. Don't confuse with "desultory," disconnected, haphazard, rambling.

MERETRICIOUS: Originally meant "like a harlot"; hence, the current meaning: attracting by false charms, gaudy, flashy, or tacky, like the meretricious appeal of the *National Enquirer,* or falsely persuasive, not to be trusted, like the meretricious promises of a Don Juan.

FORTUITOUS: Accidental, happening by chance. Not to be confused with fortunate: If you and Moby Dick both pick the same spot to swim in, your meeting will be fortuitous (neither of you planned it) but not, from your point of view, fortunate.

ENERVATING: The opposite of energizing, i.e., sapping, debilitating, depriving of strength or vitality. Lying on the beach in the hot sun all day is enervating; the cold shower you take afterwards is energizing.

GNOMIC: Means wise and pithy, full of aphorisms. But there's no way you'll ever not think of a wrinkled little guy with turned-up toes; OK, picture him saying, "Freedom's just another word for nothing left to lose." That's an example of a gnome making a gnomic statement.

Unknown Quantities

ADJECTIVES WHOSE LOOKS ARE TOTALLY INSCRUTABLE

LAMBENT: Flickering lightly over a surface, as a light or a flame; having a gentle glow, luminous. By extension, effortlessly brilliant, as in "a lambent wit." From a Latin verb meaning to lick.

PLANGENT: Striking with a deep, reverbating sound, as waves against the shore. By extension, plaintive, as in "the plangent notes of a saxophone." From a Latin verb meaning to lament.

INCHOATE: Just begun, undeveloped; immature, imperfect. From a Latin verb meaning to begin. Pronounced in-KOH-it.

JEJUNE: A word with too wide a range of meanings, from meagre, scanty, barren; to weak, insubstantial, unfortifying; to dull, insipid, childish, unsophisticated. Solution: remembering that jejune comes from the Latin word for fasting, i.e., having no food in your stomach, and that it's thus centered on a lack of nourishment. (It's also related to jejunum, the part of the small intestine that the ancient Roman medical man Galen kept finding empty when he performed autopsies, and to the French *déjeuner*, literally to break-fast.) Pronounced juh-JOON.

ATAVISTIC: Resembling one's ancestors, especially one's remote ancestors, rather than one's parents; reverting to ancestral type, as in "atavistic tendencies." From the Latin word for great-grandfather's grandfather.

HEURISTIC: Concerned with ways of finding things out or of solving problems; proceeding by trial and error; using hypotheses not to come to an immediate conclusion but to eliminate irrelevancies and modify one's take on things as one goes along, with any luck arriving at a theretofore unknown goal. Used of certain computer programs and educational philosophies; the "heuristic method" trains a student to find things out for himself. From the Greek verb meaning to find, and related to Archimedes' "Eureka!" ("I have found it").

DEMOTIC: Originally, relating to the simplified form of ancient Egyptian writing, the one most people at least stood a chance of understanding. (As such, opposed to "hieratic," of the priests.) By extension, popular, in common use. Today, also designates the colloquial form of Modern Greek. From the Greek word for "the people."

FUSTIAN: The base meaning is a coarse, thick cloth usually dyed a dark color to resemble velveteen. By extension, a derogatory term (noun as well as adjective) for an overblown, pompous, padded, and ultimately empty style of speaking or writing. From Fostat, the Cairo suburb where the cloth was first made.

HERMETIC: Pertaining to alchemy or the occult; hence esoteric. Also, airtight (as in "hermetic seal," a process developed by alchemists), protected from outside influences, hidden from view, cloistered. From Hermes Trismegistus, "Thrice-Great Hermes," author of ancient books about magic, equated with both the Greek god Hermes and the older Egyptian god Thoth.

NUMINOUS: Dedicated to or hallowed by a deity, especially a local one, as in "a numinous wood." By extension, holy, awe-inspiring, appealing to the spirit. From the Latin word for "presiding deity."

PROTEAN: Changing form easily; variable, versatile. From the Greek sea-god Proteus who knew everything but could not be pinned down and made to answer questions because he kept changing his shape, from fire to snake to water, etc. Not to be confused with two other myth-derived adjectives, "promethean" (from the Greek hero Prometheus; see page 254) and "procrustean" (from the Greek robber and villain Procrustes, of the one-size-fits-all bed).

PRIAPIC: Suffering from a persistent, and usually painful, hard-on. By extension, phallic; obsessed with masculinity or virility, generally one's own. From Priapos, the Greek god of procreation.

INEFFABLE: Unutterable, either because you can't (it's too overwhelming) or you shouldn't (it's too sacred); unable to be described in words. From the negative of the Latin verb meaning to speak out.

INELUCTABLE: Inescapable, inevitable, as in "the ineluctable modalities of the visible and the audible" with which Stephen Dedalus was obsessed in *Ulysses* (see page 246). From the negative of the Latin verb meaning to struggle against.

ALEATORY: Depending on chance (literally, on the throw of a die, *alea* in Latin, as in Caesar's *Alea jacta est,* "The die is cast"). By extension, involving random choice by an artist or a musician, as when John Cage (see page 279) used to throw the I Ching to determine which notes to play next.

OTIOSE: Originally, indolent, lazy. Today, ineffective, serving no purpose, futile. From the Latin word for "leisure."

EIDETIC: Very vivid, but not real; said of images that are perceived, wrongly, to be outside the head, experienced most often in childhood. The person with an eidetic memory summons up an image, as if on a mental screen, without necessarily comprehending it. From the same Greek word for "form" that gave us idea and idol. Conceptually related word: "oneiric," having to do with dreams, from the Greek word for "dream."

VISCOUS: Having high viscosity, yes. But does that mean it flows fast, like gasoline, or slow, like molasses? Answer: slow. A viscous substance is only semifluid; it's sticky, glutinous. From the Latin word for "bird-lime," a substance used to catch birds.

Six Mnemonic Devices

MEMORIES ARE MADE OF THESE

1. The order of the planets from the sun outward: My very earnest mother just served us nine pickles (Mercury, Venus, Earth, Mars, Jupiter, Saturn, Uranus, Neptune, Pluto).

2. The seven hills of Rome: Poor Queen Victoria eats crow at Christmas (Palatine, Quirinal, Viminal, Esquiline, Capitoline, Aventine, Caelian).

3. The twelve cranial nerves: On old Olympus's towering top, a fat-assed German viewed a hop (olfactory, optic, oculomotor, trochlear, trigeminal, abducens, facial, acoustic, glossopharyngeal, vagus, accessory, hypoglossal).

4. The Linnaean system of classification: King Peter came over from Germany seeking fortune (kingdom, phylum, class, order, family, genus, species, form).

5. Ranking order of the British peerage (see page 221): Do men ever visit Boston? (duke, marquis, earl, viscount, baron).

6. The names of the departments in the president's Cabinet: See the dog jump in a circle; leave her home to entertain editors (State, Treasury, Defense, Justice, Interior, Agriculture, Commerce, Labor, Health and Human Services, Housing and Urban Development, Transportation, Energy, Education).

"How Do You Say in Your Country 'Yearning for the Mud'?"

A STAY-AT-HOME'S GUIDE TO WORDS AND PHRASES IN THREE LANGUAGES

LATIN QUARTER: A COUPLE DOZEN DOUBLE-BARRELED PHRASES AND AN EQUAL NUMBER OF SAWED-OFF WORDS AND ABBREVIATIONS

Now that nobody even thinks about taking Greek anymore, it's Latin, actually a more or less businesslike language, that comes off as the height of erudition. And not just among lawyers, doctors, cardinals, and botanists, either. Here, all the shorthand forms (*re* to *qua*, *e.g.* to *i.e.*, *viz.* to *vide*) you'll ever need, plus our selection of the best of the big-deal phrases.

Sawed-Off Latin Words and Abbreviations

C.: Used to show that a date is approximate: "Died c. 1850." Short for *circa*, around. Also sometimes *ca*. Pronounced SIR-ka.

RE: Shorthand (and memorandumese) for "about," "concerning": "Re your comment yesterday." From *in re*, in this matter. Pronounced RAY.

CF.: Meant to get you to compare something to something else: "cf. page 20," that is, look at it with an eye to the issue at hand. From the Latin *confer*, meaning consult. If you pronounce it, say the letters, " 'cee eff' page 20."

FL.: From *floruit*, "he (or she) flourished." Shows up on the brass nameplates of old paintings when it's known when an artist worked but not when he was born (for the record, *n.*, from *natus*) or died (*ob.*, from *obiit*, literally "went to meet"). And while we're on the subject, note also: *aet.*, from *aetatis*, at the age of, for when they know how old the artist was when he did it but not the calendar year it was done, or want to emphasize the former.

MS.:   The abbreviation for *manuscriptum*, manuscript, in a footnote or bibliography. Not to be confused with *Ms.*, the magazine and form of address. More than one manuscript? MSS.

OP.:   The abbreviation for *opus*, work, used in cataloguing musical works, and designating either a single composition or a group of them that stand as a unit.

VS.:   Against, in the courtroom as the stadium. From versus, sometimes also abbreviated *v.*

D.V.:   God willing, from *Deo volente*. Admittedly not much seen these days, though show-offs of an antiquarian bent use it to mean "if nothing gets in our way."

E.G.:   For when you're about to give (or be given) a bunch of examples: "citrus fruits, e.g., orange, lemon, lime." Does not guarantee completeness of list (no grapefruit, for instance, above). Short for *exempli gratia*, "for the sake of example."

I.E.:   For when you're about to explain (or have explained to you) the nature of something: "citrus fruits, i.e., those from trees of the family *Citrus*, with an inedible rind, juicy flesh, usually in segments, and a high vitamin C content." Short for *id est*, "that is." More authoritative, less chatty than *e.g.*

N.B.:   For *Nota bene*, "note well." Calls your attention to something the writer thinks you might miss or not see the, in his opinion, enormous significance of.

QUA: "In the capacity of," "considered as," as in "the film qua film"—the film not as a story or an evening's entertainment, but as an act of movie-making, as cinema, as art. Pronounced KWAY or KWAH. From a Latin relative-pronoun form. Caution: User stands to reveal self as pretentious.

SIC: A nudge, usually parenthetical, often gloating, pointing out how a third party got something wrong or gave himself away: "In his review of the new Sylvester Stallione (sic) movie. . . . " From *sic,* "thus." Caution: User stands to reveal self as smug.

VIZ.: Used after a word or expression clearly requiring itemization. Equivalent to our "namely" or "to wit": "The citrus fruits, viz. orange, lemon, lime, grapefruit, tangerine, kumquat." (No mention of tangelo, unfortunately, but you get the point.) An abbreviation of *videlicet,* "it is permitted to see." Likewise, *sc.* or *scil.,* from *scilicet,* "it is permitted to know." Both *viz.* and *sc.,* unlike *e.g.,* guarantee they're giving you a complete rundown.

Q.E.D.: The capital letters printed triumphantly by a person who thinks he's convincingly proven what he set out to prove a paragraph—or a chapter, or a lifetime—ago. Short for *quod erat demonstrandum,* "which was to be shown." A favorite of geometry teachers and miscellaneous pedants.

R.I.P.: Right, on all the old tombstones. But it's short for *Requiescat in pace,* "May he (or she) rest in peace," *not* "Rest in peace," which is why you might see it on an old French or German tombstone, too.

ERGO: "Therefore," "hence." Unforgettable in Descartes's formulation *Cogito, ergo sum,* "I think, therefore I am" (see page 310), and un-avoidable in various mathematical proofs.

PACE: "With all due respect to" or "with the permission of," as in "Pace Mies, there are times when more is more." Used to express polite, or ironically polite, disagreement. Pronounced PAY-see (preferred by academicians) or PAH-chay (less correct, but more common).

STET: "Let it stand," "ignore all previous instructions to alter or correct," "this is, after all, how we want it." A printer's term, but one useful to anybody in a position to make—or not make—final changes. From a form of *stare,* "to stand." The opposite: *dele,* from the Latin word for "delete."

VIDE: In reference to a passage in a book, means see or consult. A short-ened version of *quod vide,* "which see," sometimes also abbreviated as *q.v.*

IBID.: One of the old term-paper nightmares. "In the same book, chapter, or passage" (i.e., the one referred to in the note immediately preceding). Short for *ibidem*, "in the same place." Doesn't, unlike *op. cit.*, short for *opere citato*, "in the work cited," require an author's name, just a page number, and doesn't send you scrolling up through the 150 preceding footnotes.

ET AL.: "And others," short for both *et alia*, "and other things," and *et alii*, "and other people." More specific than *etc.*, short for *et cetera*, "and the rest," "and so forth," and can, unlike *etc.*, be used of people.

AD HOC: "For this thing," said of something impromptu, improvised, for the matter at hand and that matter only. An ad hoc committee will probably last out only the season (or the problem); an ad hoc solution implies that somebody is—or ought to be—working on a permanent one. Cf. *pro tem*, short for *pro tempore*, "for the time being."

AD LIB.: "To the desire"; in music, a sign that somebody can play a passage, or an entire piece, as loud and as fast as he wants. In show business, and without the period, a sign that somebody forgot his lines.

PER SE: "Through itself"; intrinsically, by dint of its very nature.

PASSIM: Scattered, occurring throughout. Applied to a word, passage, or reference occurring here and there, over and over, in a specific book or author.

Double-Barreled Latin Phrases

BONA FIDE (BOH-na-FIDE or BOH-na-FIE-deh): Done or made "in good faith"; sincere, genuine.

CASUS BELLI (KAH-sus-BELL-ee): "Occasion of war." An event that justifies or precipitates war.

CUI BONO (KWEE-BOH-noh): "For whom (is it) good?" Question first posed by a Roman magistrate to make the point that one way to approach a crime is to determine who stood to gain from it. Often wrongly used to mean "For what purpose?"

DE FACTO (deh-FAK-toh): "From the fact." In reality; actual; actually in power. A de facto government is not formally elected or installed, but is firmly in control; cf. *de jure*, below.

DE JURE (deh-YOO-reh): "From the law." According to law; in principle. A de jure government is duly elected and installed, but exercises no real power; cf. *de facto*, above.

EX POST FACTO (EKS-post-FAK-toh): "From what is done afterwards." Formulated, enacted, or operating retroactively.

IN MEDIAS RES (in-MAY-dee-ahs-RACE): "Into the midst of things." Into the middle of a story or narrative; without background or preamble. A convention of the classical epic, first formulated by the poet Horace. The opposite approach is *ab ovo*, "from the egg."

MEMENTO MORI (meh-MEN-toh-MOR-ee): "Remember you must die." A reminder or warning of death; a death's head.

MUTATIS MUTANDIS (moo-TAH-tees-moo-TAHN-dees): "The things that ought to have been changed having been changed." With the necessary substitutions having been made, the indicated variances considered.

NE PLUS ULTRA (nay-ploos-UL-trah): "Not further beyond," said to have been inscribed on the Pillars of Hercules (today's Strait of Gibraltar), as a warning to ships. A farthest point, a highest pitch, a culmination; an impassable obstacle; and, implicitly, a suggestion to stay put or, better yet, turn back.

OBITER DICTUM (OH-buh-ter-DIK-tum): "Thing said by the way." Any incidental or parenthetical remark. In law, something the judge says in arguing a point, but that has no bearing on his decision. Plural: *obiter dicta*.

PARI PASSU (PAH-ree-PAH-soo): "With equal pace." Simultaneously, equally, proceeding alongside.

PERSONA NON GRATA (per-SOH-na-nohn-GRAH-ta): "Person not pleasing." Someone unacceptable within a given context.

QUID PRO QUO (kwid-proh-KWOH): "Something for something." A compensation, an even exchange; tit for tat.

SINE QUA NON (sin-neh-kwah-NOHN): "Without which not." The indispensable element, condition, or quality.

SUB ROSA (sub-ROH-sah): "Under the rose," though debate rages as to whether it was the rose Cupid gave someone as a bribe not to gossip about the affairs of Venus, or a rose carried by the Egyptian god Horus in a statue that also showed him with his finger to his lips, or some other rose altogether. Anyway, sub rosa means in confidence; with secrecy expressed or implied, clandestinely.

SUI GENERIS (SOO-ee-JEN-er-is): "Of its own kind." Peculiar, unique, not to be analyzed or catalogued along standard lines.

TU QUOQUE (TOO-KWOH-kweh): "You also." The ancient Roman version of "So are you." A response to an accusation directed personally.

ULTRA VIRES (UL-trah-VEER-ayz): "Beyond (one's) authority." Also, outside one's jurisdiction. It's well known that several successive administrations behaved *ultra vires* in Vietnam.

FOUR LATIN PHRASES FOR YOUR DAY IN COURT

CORPUS DELICTI (KOR-pus-de-LIK-tee): "The body of the crime." Tangible evidence of wrongdoing, including (but hardly restricted to) the body of a murder victim.

HABEAS CORPUS (HAY-bee-as-KOR-pus): "You have the body." A writ requiring that a person being detained be brought before a judge; meant to guard against unfair imprisonment, it constitutes one of the most celebrated features of both the British and the American legal systems.

NOLLE PROSEQUI (NOL-leh-proh-SEK-wee): "To not wish to proceed." Statement that the prosecution doesn't want to pursue matters further; the writ ending court proceedings. Shortened to "nol-pros" by fast-talking lawyers.

NOLO CONTENDERE (NOH-loh-kon-TEN-der-eh): "I don't want to fight." Plea made by a defendant that's equivalent to an admission of guilt (and that leaves him subject to punishment), but that allows him the legal option of denying the charges later.

AND FOUR FOR YOUR DAY OF JUDGMENT

DE PROFUNDIS (deh-pro-FUN-dees): "Out of the depths" of sorrow and despair, the first two words of Psalms 130 (and the title of a confessional essay by Oscar Wilde). An especially bitter cry of wretchedness.

ECCE HOMO (ek-keh-HOH-moh): "Behold the man," the words first spoken by Pilate (John 19:5) when he showed Jesus, crowned with thorns, to the mob. A name given to paintings showing Christ thus, also to an essay by Nietzsche in which he announces that he's the Antichrist.

NOLI ME TANGERE (NOH-lee-meh-TAN-geh-reh): "Touch me not," the words spoken by Christ to Mary Magdalen (see page 461) after his Resurrection (John 20:17). A name given to paintings showing Christ *thus;* also, a person or thing that can't be touched; a warning against getting involved or in the way.

NUNC DIMITTIS (nunk-deh-MIT-us): "Now lettest Thou (thy servant) depart," the words Simeon speaks to Jesus, satisfied that he'd finally seen the Messiah (Luke 2:29). A name for that canticle, the "Song of Simeon"; by extension, any permission to go. To "sing nunc dimittis" is to express one's readiness to depart or die.

FROM PRUSSIA WITH LOVE

We promise: There simply aren't that many German expressions for you—or any other non-German—to worry about. Of course, the ones that you do have to worry about tend to be a mouthful. Also, a skullful.

BILDUNGSROMAN (bil-DOONGS-row-MON): Literally, education novel. Tells the story of how somebody came of age, à la Pip in Dickens's *Great Expectations,* Stephen Dedalus in Joyce's *A Portrait of the Artist As a Young Man,* or Hans Castorp in Mann's *The Magic Mountain* (see page 249).

DOPPELGÄNGER (DOP-pul-GENG-er): "Double-goer," the ghostly double, the spiritual (or sometimes flesh-and-blood) counterpart of a living person; as in the Poe story "William Wilson."

GEMÜTLICHKEIT (guh-MOOT-lik-kite): From *Gemüt,* temperament, feeling. Implies geniality, coziness, a sense of shared well-being. The adjective form is *gemütlich.* Use sparingly: Can make you sound like your great-uncle Arthur.

GÖTTERDÄMMERUNG (GUH-ter-DEHM-er-oong): "Twilight of the gods." The last opera in Wagner's four-part *Ring* cycle (see page 283). Also, any terminal breakdown or tragic end, the louder the better.

LEBENSRAUM (LAY-bens-ROWM): "Living space." A big part of Germany's justification for its periodic invasions of its neighbors. Only slightly less convincing than our "manifest destiny."

SCHADENFREUDE (SHAH-den-FROY-duh): "Harm joy." You'll enjoy this one; god knows, you've already enjoyed the feeling—the slightly malicious, slightly guilty pleasure you register at the news of someone else's, and especially a friend's, misfortune.

STURM UND DRANG (SHTURM-und-DRAHNG): "Storm and stress." From a late-eighteenth-century German literary movement (centered on drama and involving, like so much else, Goethe and Schiller), a beat-your-breast, tear-your-hair-out reaction to pussy-footing French classicism. Now, any great emotional turmoil.

WELTANSCHAUUNG (VELT-ahn-SHAU-oong): "World view." A philosophy of life, a comprehensive version of the whole enchilada, and how it works.

WELTSCHMERZ (VELT-schmertz): "World pain." Ranges from a kind of sentimental pessimism or world-weariness to full-fledged distress and angst (a German noun so assimilated you don't even have to capitalize it anymore).

WUNDERKIND (VOON-der-kind): "Wonder child." The child prodigy, whether still a child (like Mozart when he first attracted serious attention), or already an adolescent (like Orson Welles when he made *Citizen Kane*). The *Wunderkind*, whatever his age, really does compose, direct, or appear on talk shows brilliantly—unlike the *enfant terrible* (see page 634), who's too busy making trouble to pay much attention to the quality of his performance.

ZEITGEIST (TSITE-guyst): "Time ghost." The spirit of the age, the taste and outlook of a period or a generation.

The Germans shot their wad with the nouns; their adjectives, by contrast, are short, to the point, and appealingly lowercase.

ECHT (EKKKT): Genuine, typical, the real thing. *Echt* Beatles would be, depending on your point of view, either "Rubber Soul" or "Sergeant Pepper."

ERSATZ (EHR-zahts): Substitute, artificial, not real. Ersatz Beatles might be the Dave Clark Five. (No need to set italic; now at home in English.)

VERBOTEN (fehr-BOHT-en): Forbidden, prohibited, don't even think it. In a roomful of Beatles freaks, it's not crazy to assume the Stones would be verboten (no italics).

Enjoy these German words and phrases? Well, no need to pine for more. Instead, just turn to the following pages and find: Bauhaus (page 100), Realpolitik (page 556), Leitmotif (page 283), Ding-an-sich (page 316), Übermensch (page 321), Ostpolitik (page 380), Gestalt (page 427) and Ur- (page 599).

A LIFETIME SUPPLY OF JE NE SAIS QUOI

The good news is, not as many French phrases have made it into Webster's and the OED as Latin phrases. The bad news is, there are a lot more French than Latin ones that you—and everybody else with an ax to grind or an impression to make—are going to want in on. Below, organized into categories (and getting harder as you read on), our favorites among the still-numerous contenders, each of which was selected because it (a) has no easy and/or economical equivalent in English, and hence isn't merely pretentious; (b) provides a glimpse of the notoriously agile, notoriously devious French mind at work, and hence isn't merely academic; and (c) is more or less tricky in its meaning, form, or use, and hence isn't merely self-evident, in which case we'd all have mastered it already, n'est-ce pas?

For the Freshman

BÊTE NOIRE (bet-NWAR): Literally, black beast; someone or something that one fears, dislikes, or characteristically avoids. Stronger than pet peeve, more graceful than bugbear. Note the e on noire.

DE RIGUEUR (de-ree-GUHR): Absolutely necessary; required by good form if nothing else. Two us in rigueur, a relative of our "rigor."

FAIT ACCOMPLI (fet-a-kom-PLEE): Literally, accomplished fact; a thing already consummated, so that fighting it is useless, and changing it impossible.

PAR EXCELLENCE (par-ek-sel-AHNSE): Above all others of the same type; literally, by (virtue of its) excellence. Paris is the European capital *par excellence.*

RAISON D'ÊTRE (ray-zohn-DETR): "Reason for being." Justification for one's existence.

For the Sophomore

BON MOT (bohn-MOH): Not just a "good word," but a witty remark, a memorable comment, an aphorism even. Come junior year, you'll want to take on *mot juste,* the "just word," the word that conveys what's meant more precisely than any word anybody else in the dorm could come up with.

CARTE BLANCHE (kart-BLAHNSH): "White paper," a sheet that's blank except for a signature, with the implication that its bearer can write his own deal. A blank check, yes, but also blanket permission.

COUP DE GRÂCE (koo-de-GRAHS): Literally, stroke of mercy; the death blow, delivered to someone mortally wounded. By extension, any finishing or decisive act. Watch that word *coup,* by the way; it's a favorite of the French, and it shows up again in *coup d'état,* the sudden, and often violent, overthrow of a government, and *coup de foudre,* literally, lightning bolt; figuratively, love at first sight.

ENFANT TERRIBLE (ahn-fahnt-teh-REE-bl): "Terrible child"; can refer to your standard-issue brat or to anybody, typically a young artist or writer, who causes trouble and calls attention to himself through unconventional and boat-rocking behavior. Note: Not to be confused with *Wunderkind* (see page 632).

PIÈCE DE RÉSISTANCE (pee-ess-de-ray-zee-STAHNS): From the sense of "resistance" as staying-power, endurance. By extension, something of substance, toughness, or strength. *Not,* as a lot of people seem to think, the crowning glory, the "capper" in a can-you-top-this sequence of items. At the dinner table, it's the saddle of lamb—not the cherries jubilee—that is, or ought to be, the *pièce de résistance.*

For the Literature Major

BELLES LETTRES (bell-LET-re): Serious literary writings—"beautiful letters"—more "artistic" than "intellectual," especially essays and criticism, but including fiction, poetry, and drama. Today, tends to have connotations of the artificial, the effete, the old-fashioned, of Henry James as opposed to Henry Miller.

FIN DE SIÈCLE (fahn-de-see-EH-kl): "End of century," specifically, the end of the nineteenth century, a period celebrated for its decadence in France (Verlaine, Mallarmé, Huysman, et al.) as in England (Wilde, Beardsley, et al.). Not surprisingly, the phrase is now being applied to the end of this century, too.

ROMAN À CLEF (roh-mahn-ah-KLAY): "Novel with key," in which people and events have been fictionalized, with any luck tantalizingly.

SUCCÈS D'ESTIME (sook-say-des-TEEM): A success based on reviews (or, sometimes, respect for the author's—or performer's—reputation) rather than on sales, on "esteem" rather than popular enthusiasm. Cf. *succès de scandale*, where the scandalousness, rather than the excellence, of the material is the come-on. Also, *succès fou*, a "mad" success, a smash hit.

TOUR DE FORCE (toor-de-FORS): "Turn of force," a display of virtuosity, an exhibition of skill, often undertaken by an author in a field not his own just to prove he can do it.

For the History Major

AGENT PROVOCATEUR (ah-ZHEN-proh-voh-ka-TUHR): The undercover agent who infiltrates the trade union or political party, pretending sympathy with its aims, and gets the members to do precisely those things that they can be punished or put away for.

CORDON SANITAIRE (kor-DOHN-san-ee-TAYR): The line, generally heavily guarded, between an infected area and a neighboring, as-yet uninfected one. Applies likewise to the isolating of politically sensitive subject matter.

ÉMINENCE GRISE (ay-mee-NEHNZ-GREEZ): The power behind the throne, the person who exercises his authority unofficially. Literally, "gray cardinal," after Cardinal Richelieu's private secretary, Père Joseph. Éminence, in case you're wondering, is a cardinal's honorific.

LÈSE-MAJESTÉ (lez-mah-zhes-TAY): An offense or crime against one's ruler or sovereign; treason. More commonly, any presumptuous conduct or overstepping of authority. And that's the same *les-* you see in "lesion," ultimately from a Latin word meaning to injure.

NOBLESSE OBLIGE (noh-BLESS-oh-BLEEZH): "Noble birth obligates," privilege entails responsibility. Point of honor (and *raison d'être*) for aristocrats and other *ancien régime*—or pre-Revolutionary, "former administration"—types.

At the Buffet Dinner

COMME IL FAUT (kohme-eel-FOH): "As is necessary"; used, sometimes slightly sarcastically, of behavior that is socially up to snuff. In introductions that are *comme il faut*, older people are introduced to younger ones and women to men, a little something or other said about each of them to the other, and all the rest of it.

DOUBLE ENTENDRE (DOO-bl-ahn-TAHN-dr): Literally, to hear or to understand double; in practice, a remark with a racy, spicy, off-color undertone as well as a flat, seemingly innocent surface meaning. Actually, the French themselves say *double entente*, but that's their problem.

D'UN CERTAIN AGE (duhn-sayr-tehn-AHJ): Not as imprecise as "of a certain age"; means, in fact, middle-aged at least. Used euphemistically, but that doesn't mean that a *femme d'un certain age* is, in the eyes of a Frenchman, necessarily over the hill.

FAUTE DE MIEUX (FOHT-de-MEEUH): "For want of something better"; for lack of a workable alternative, ideal, or guiding philosophy. Cf. *tant mieux*, "so much the better," and, for that matter, *tant pis*, "so much the worse," expressions of cynical resignation in the face of yet another new—and questionable—development.

PLUS ÇA CHANGE (ploo-sa-SHAHN-zhe): "The more it changes," the beginning of (and a recognized abbreviation for) the expression that is concluded by *plus c'est la même chose*, "the more it's the same thing." A worldly, even world-weary way of saying that there's nothing new under the sun, and even if there were, it wouldn't surprise *you*.

At the Black-Tie Dinner

ACTE GRATUIT (ahkt-grah-TWEE): The gratuitous act, sudden, enigmatic, and often disruptive, undertaken on impulse. So dubbed by the novelist André Gide at a time when the Surrealists (along with Gide's characters) were turning out a lot of them. Shooting a gun into a crowd with no particular goal in mind would be an *acte gratuit;* so were many of the Sixties "happenings."

FORCE MAJEURE (fors-mah-ZHUR): Literally, "superior strength." The irresistible force, totally out of your control, generally unexpected, and, most important, serving to release you from your obligations. Includes what English-speaking insurance companies call "acts of God," as well as various forms of strictly human negligence and bad judgment.

HOMME MOYEN SENSUEL (OHME-mwoy-EHN-sehn-soo-EL): The average sensual man, or, as the critic Matthew Arnold put it, introducing the phrase into English in the 1880s, the fellow "whose city is Paris, and whose ideal is the free, gay, pleasurable life of Paris." In other words, anyone who lives the life of the senses and doesn't let moral and intellectual considerations push him around. Today, though, a lot of people use it to mean not much more than "the typical man," "the man of average desires," "the man in the street."

TRAHISON DES CLERCS (trah-ee-ZOHN-day-KLAYRK): The critic and essayist Julien Benda's term (and his 1927 book title); literally, treason of the clerks, a reference to how intellectuals—writers, artists, and thinkers—have in this century betrayed themselves and each other by allowing their beliefs to be fired by political passions rather than guided by philosophical principles. To be directed at anybody who keeps losing sight of the big picture, the ultimate aim, in his desire to win this evening's argument.

ESPRIT DE L'ESCALIER (es-PREE-de-less-kahl-YEH): Not the spirit, but the *wit* of the staircase; the slicing, but also rather wise, retort to somebody else's fatuousness that you thought of only as you were on your way downstairs to the street (or upstairs to your room) after the party had ended.

And So to Bed

AMOUR-PROPRE (ah-MOOR-PROH-pr): An old phrase—literally, "self-love"—with an even wider range of meaning than the now-trendy narcissism, from simple self-esteem, to a need for admiration by others, to out-and-out conceit, to neurotic self-involvement. Don't be pleased if someone tells you you're a paragon (*un parangon*) of it.

ARRIÈRE-PENSÉE (ah-ree-AYR-pahn-SAY): Literally, "behind-thought." A famous old trap: Does not mean afterthought or hindsight. Does mean an idea or intention that is concealed, an ulterior motive, a hidden agenda.

CRIME PASSIONNEL (kreem-pah-see-oh-NELL): Crime of passion, sure, but especially murder, and especially when sexual jealousy is the motive. Two *s*s, two *n*s.

DROIT DU SEIGNEUR (dwah-de-sehn-YUHR): The right of the feudal lord, just as you'd expect, but specifically his right to sleep with the bride of any of his vassals on her wedding night.

NOSTALGIE DE LA BOUE (naws-tahl-ZHEE-de-la-BOO): "Yearning for the mud," for degradation, depravity, and your basic wallow, particularly by a person we'd all have thought was above such things, and particularly in a guess-who's-sleeping-with-whom context. Coined by a popular nineteenth-century French dramatist, it's a phrase at this point more familiar to us English-speakers than to the French, some of whom will look at you admiringly when you use it, as if you'd made it up yourself.

INDEX

ILLUSTRATION CREDITS

CHAPTER 1: 2 Library of Congress; 5 Forbes Library, Northamton, Mass.; 7 Sleepy Hollow Restorations, Tarrytown, N.Y.; 10, 11, 13, 14 Library of Congress; 15 Morris Gerber Collection, "Old Albany People"; 16 Mark Twain Memorial, Hartford, Conn.; 18 Idaho Historical Society; 20 Houghton Library/Harvard University; 21 Photographed by Charles Sheeler/Reproduced by permission of New Directions Publishing Corporation; 23 Alice Boughton/Library of Congress; 24 Hartford Insurance Group; 29 (top left) UPI/Bettmann Newsphotos; 29 (top right) The Sophia Smith Collection (Women's Historical Archive)/Smith College, Northampton, MA; 29 (bottom left) Wide World Photos; 29 (bottom right) New York Public Library; 32 Pablo Picasso, Metropolitan Museum of Art. Bequest of Gertrude Stein; 33 Wide World Photos; 34 David Moore/Black Star; 35. Wide World Photos; 36 Black Sparrow Press; 37 UPI/Bettmann Newsphotos; 38, 40 Wide World Photos; 48, 49, 51 Library of Congress.

CHAPTER 2: 64, 65, 66, 68 Art Resource; 69 Metropolitan Museum of Art. Bequest of Mrs. H.D. Havemeyer; 71, 72 National Gallery, London; 73 Metropolitan Museum of Art; 75, 76 Museum of Modern Art, New York; 77 (top) Culver Pictures; 77 (bottom left) The Louvre; 77 (bottom right), 78 (right) Art Resource; 79 (top) Caravaggio, "The Musicians," Metropolitan Museum of Art. Rogers Fund; 79 (bottom) Christofano da Bracciano, "Orpheus," Metropolitan Museum of Art. Gift of George and Florence Blumenthal; 80 Vincent Van Gogh, "Self Portrait with a Straw Hat," Metropolitan Museum of Art. Bequest of Miss Adelaide Milton deGroot; 81 (top) Rembrandt, "Flora," Metropolitan Museum of Art. Gift of Archer M. Huntington; 81 (bottom) Paolo Veronese, "Mars and Venus United by Love," Metropolitan Museum of Art; 83 Baltimore Museum of Art. The Cone Collection; 84 (left) Museum of Modern Art, New York; 84 (right) Guggenheim Museum; 85, 86 Museum of Modern Art, New York; 87 Guggenheim Museum; 88 (left) Carnegie Institute; 88 (right) Museum of Modern Art, New York; 89 Philadelphia Museum of Art: Louise and Walter Arensberg Collection; 90 Museum of Modern Art, New York; 91 (left) Hans Namuth; 91 (right) Museum of Modern Art, New York. Sidney and Harriet Janis Collection Fund; 92 Hans Namuth; 94 (top left) Leo Castelli Gallery; 94 (top right) Hans Namuth; 94 (bottom left) Collection of Whitney Museum of American Art. 50th Anniversary Gift of the Gilman Foundation, Inc., The Lauder Foundation, A. Alfred Taubman, an anonymous donor (and purchase) Acq. #80.32; 94 (bottom right) Hans Namuth; 96 Paula Court/Brooklyn Academy of Music; 97 (left) Mary Boone Gallery; 97 (right) Pace Gallery; 98–99 © Pamela Delonnay; 101 (left) German Information Center; 101 (right) Yale University; 102 AT&T; 104 Joseph E. Seagrams and sons, Inc.; 105 German Information Center; 106 Library of Congress; 108 (top left) Mies van der Rohe Archive/Museum of Modern Art, New York; 108 (middle left) Art Resource; 108 (bottom left), 108 (top right) Mildred Meade/Chicago Historical Society; 108 (bottom right) Library of Congress; 113 (left) Metropolitan Museum of Art. Alfred Steiglitz Collection.; 113 (right) Metropolitan Museum of Art. Elisha Whittelsey Fund.

CHAPTER 3: 118 UPI/Bettmann Newsphotos; 126, 127, 128 New York Public Library Picture Collection; 130 UPI/Bettmann Newsphotos; 132 Federal Reserve Board; 133 UPI/Bettmann Newsphotos; 134 Arthur Rothstein/Library of Congress; 137 Catherine Ursillo/Photo Researchers, Inc.; 139,140 New York Times; 142 Library of Congress.

CHAPTER 4: 144, 146 (right) New York Public Library, Lincoln Center; 146 (left) Library of Congress; 149, 150 Museum of Modern Art/Film Stills Archive; 153, 154, 155, 157, 158 New York Public Library, Lincoln Center; 159, 161, 162, 164 (right) Museum of Modern Art/Film Stills Archive; 164 (left), 166 New York Public Library, Lincoln Center; 169, 172 Museum of Modern Art/Film Stills Archive; 174, 175, 179 New York Public Library, Lincoln Center.

CHAPTER 5: 182 Bettmann Archive; 191 (left) National Portrait Gallery, London; 191 (right) Mary Evans Picture Library/Photo Researchers, Inc.; 193 National Portrait Gallery, London; 194 New York Public Library Picture Collection; 196 Courtesy of New Directions Publishers; 197 New York Public Library Picture Collection; 198, 202 New York Public Library, Lincoln Center; 206 Edwin Austin Abbey, "King Lear," Metropolitan Museum of Art. Gift of George A. Hearn; 213 National Portrait Gallery, London; 214 New York Public Library Picture Collection; 216 National Gallery, London; 221 Library of Congress; 233–35 New York Public Library Picture Collection; 236 American Numismatic Society; 251 (left) Courtesy, Museum of Fine Arts, Boston, William Francis Warden Fund; 251 (right) reproduced by courtesy of the Trustees of the British Museum; 256 New York Public Library Picture Collection.

CHAPTER 6: 262 Picture People; 264 Culver Pictures; 265 Library of Congress; 266, 267, 268 New York Public Library Picture Collection; 269 (top) Library of Congress; 269 (bottom), 270 (top) New York Public Library Picture Collection; 270 (bottom) CBS Masterworks; 271 © David Lindroth, Inc.; 282, 283 Library of Congress; 288–290 (left) Metropolitan Opera Association, Inc.; 290 (right) J. Heffernan, Metropolitan Opera Association, Inc.; 292 New York Public Library Picture Collection; 293 British Tourist Authority; 294 Archive/Photo Researchers, Inc.; 295 German Information Center; 296 Pierre Berger/Photo Researchers, Inc.; 297 Lincoln Center.

CHAPTER 7: 300 Metropolitan Museum of Art. Catherine Lorillard Wolfe Collection; 304, 306, 307 New York Public Library Picture Collection; 308 Culver Pictures; 309 New York Public Library Picture Collection; 310 Picture People; 311 Library of Congress; 312, 313 New York Public Library Picture Collection; 314, 315 Library of Congress; 317 Archive/Photo Researchers, Inc.; 318, 319 New York Public Library Picture Collection; 320 Library of Congress; 321 New York Public Library Picture Collection; 323 Library of Congress; 324 Wide World Photos; 325 Museum der Stadt, Vienna; 326 Wide World Photos; 332 Henri Cartier-Bresson/Magnum; 333 Susan Meiselas/Magnum; 334 Library of Congress

CHAPTER 8: 336 Duane Hanson, "Tourists," O.K. Harris Works of Art; 338 UPI/Bettmann Newsphotos; 341, 351, 356 Wide World Photos; 359, 364, 366, 369, 374, 382, 390 (top left), 390 (top right), 390 (bottom right) UPI/Bettmann Newsphotos; 390 (middle left) Wide World Photos; 393, 396 © David Lindroth, Inc.

CHAPTER 9: 398 Museum of Modern Art/Film

ABOUT THE AUTHORS

Judy Jones and William Wilson are free-lance writers and editors who live and work in New York. William Wilson went to Yale and Judy Jones to Smith, but both maintain that they got their real education in the process of writing this book.

Rôna

✦ Ellesméra

Du Weldenvarden

◆ Nädindel

Arduven

✦ Kirtan

◆ Sîlthrim

Gaena River

Eldor

Hadarac Desert

Ília Fëon ◆

Ceris ◆

Edda River

Hedarth ◆

Az Ragni

◆ Buragh

◆ Tarnag

FARTHEN DÛR

Orthíad ◆

Beartooth River

◆ Galfni

◆ Dalgon

Beor Mountains

BRISINGR

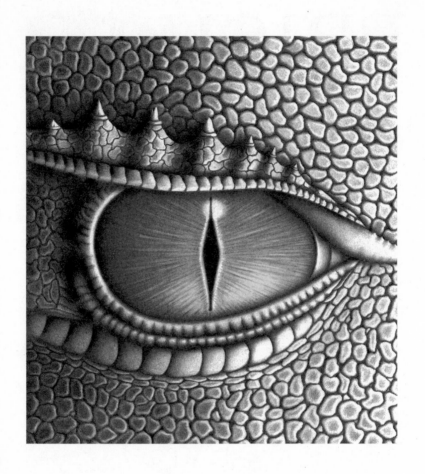

BRISINGR

or

THE SEVEN PROMISES OF ERAGON SHADESLAYER AND SAPHIRA BJARTSKULAR

INHERITANCE

BOOK THREE

Christopher Paolini

ALFRED A. KNOPF
New York

THIS IS A BORZOI BOOK PUBLISHED BY ALFRED A. KNOPF

Visit us on the Web!
www.alagaesia.com
www.randomhouse.com/teens

Educators and librarians, for a variety of teaching tools,
visit us at www.randomhouse.com/teachers

Library of Congress Cataloging-in-Publication Data
Paolini, Christopher.
Brisingr, or, The seven promises of Eragon Shadeslayer and
Saphira Bjartskular / Christopher Paolini. — 1st ed.
p. cm. — (Inheritance ; bk. 3)
Summary: The further adventures of Eragon and his dragon, Saphira, as they
continue to aid the Varden in the struggle against the evil king, Galbatorix.
ISBN 978-0-375-82672-6 (trade) — ISBN 978-0-375-92672-3 (lib. bdg.)
[1. Fantasy. 2. Dragons—Fiction. 3. Youth's writings.] I. Title.
II. Title: Seven promises of Eragon Shadeslayer and Saphira Bjartskular.
III. Title: Eragon Shadeslayer and Saphira Bjartskular. IV. Title: Saphira Bjartskular.
PZ7.P19535Bri 2008
[Fic]—dc22
2008024489

The text of this book is set in 12-point Goudy.

Printed in the United States of America
September 2008
BVG 10 9 8 7 6 5 4 3 2 1

First Edition

As always, this book is for my family.
And also for Jordan, Nina, and Sylvie,
the bright lights of a new generation.
Atra esterní ono thelduin.

CONTENTS

Synopsis of *Eragon* and *Eldest*

Eragon—a fifteen-year-old farm boy—is shocked when a polished blue stone appears before him in the range of mountains known as the Spine. Eragon takes the stone to the farm where he lives with his uncle, Garrow, and his cousin, Roran, outside the small village of Carvahall. Garrow and his late wife, Marian, have raised Eragon. Nothing is known of Eragon's father; his mother, Selena, was Garrow's sister and has not been seen since Eragon's birth.

Later, the stone cracks open and a baby dragon emerges. When Eragon touches her, a silvery mark appears on his palm, and an irrevocable bond is forged between their minds, making Eragon one of the legendary Dragon Riders. He names the dragon Saphira, after a dragon mentioned by the village storyteller, Brom.

The Dragon Riders were created thousands of years earlier in the aftermath of the devastating war between the elves and the dragons, in order to prevent their two races from ever again fighting each other. The Riders became peacekeepers, educators, healers, natural philosophers, and the greatest of all magicians—since being joined with a dragon makes one a spellcaster. Under their guidance and protection, the land enjoyed a golden age.

When humans arrived in Alagaësia, they too were added to this elite order. After many years of peace, the warlike Urgals killed the dragon of a young human Rider named Galbatorix. The loss drove him mad, and when his elders refused to provide him with another dragon, Galbatorix set out to topple the Riders.

He stole another dragon—whom he named Shruikan and forced to serve him through certain black spells—and gathered around himself a group of thirteen traitors: the Forsworn. With the help of those cruel disciples, Galbatorix threw down the Riders; killed their leader, Vrael; and declared himself king over Alagaësia. His actions forced the elves to retreat deep within their pinewood forest and the dwarves to hide in their tunnels and caves, and neither race now ventures forth from its secret places. The stalemate between Galbatorix and the other races has endured for over a hundred years, during which all of the Forsworn have died from various causes. It is into this tense political situation that Eragon finds himself thrust.

Several months after Saphira hatches, two menacing, beetle-like strangers called the Ra'zac arrive in Carvahall, searching for the stone that was Saphira's egg. Eragon and Saphira manage to evade them, but they destroy Eragon's home and murder Garrow.

Eragon vows to track down and kill the Ra'zac. As he leaves Carvahall, the storyteller Brom, who knows of Saphira's existence, accosts Eragon and asks to accompany him. Brom gives Eragon a red Dragon Rider's sword, Zar'roc, though he refuses to say how he acquired it.

Eragon learns much from Brom during their travels, including how to fight with swords and use magic. When they lose the Ra'zac's trail, they go to the port town of Teirm and visit Brom's old friend Jeod, who Brom thinks may be able to help them locate the Ra'zac's lair. In Teirm, they learn that the Ra'zac live somewhere close to the city of Dras-Leona. Eragon also has his fortune told by the herbalist Angela and receives two strange pieces of advice from her companion, the werecat Solembum.

On the way to Dras-Leona, Brom reveals that he is an agent of the Varden—a rebel group dedicated to overthrowing Galbatorix—and that he had been hiding in Carvahall, waiting for a new Dragon Rider to appear. Twenty years ago, Brom was involved in stealing Saphira's egg from Galbatorix and, in the process, killed Morzan, first and last of the Forsworn. Only two other dragon eggs still exist, both of which remain in Galbatorix's possession.

In and near Dras-Leona, they encounter the Ra'zac, who mortally wound Brom while he is protecting Eragon. A mysterious young man named Murtagh drives the Ra'zac away. With his dying breath, Brom confesses that he too was once a Rider and that his slain dragon was also named Saphira.

Eragon and Saphira then decide to join the Varden, but Eragon is captured at the city of Gil'ead and brought before Durza, an evil and powerful Shade who serves Galbatorix. With Murtagh's help, Eragon escapes from prison, bringing along with him the elf Arya, another captive of Durza's and an ambassador to the Varden. Arya has been poisoned and requires the Varden's medical help.

Pursued by a contingent of Urgals, the four of them flee across the land to the Varden's headquarters in the giant Beor Mountains, which stand over ten miles high. Circumstances force Murtagh—who does not want to go to the Varden—to reveal that he is the son of Morzan. Murtagh, however, has denounced his dead father's villainy and fled Galbatorix's court to seek his own destiny. And he tells Eragon that the sword Zar'roc once belonged to Murtagh's father.

Just before they are overwhelmed by the Urgals, Eragon and his friends are rescued by the Varden, who live in Farthen Dûr, a hollow mountain that is also home to the dwarves' capital, Tronjheim. Once inside, Eragon is taken to Ajihad, leader of the Varden, while Murtagh is imprisoned because of his relation to Morzan.

Eragon meets with the dwarf king, Hrothgar, and Ajihad's daughter, Nasuada, and is tested by the Twins, two rather nasty magicians who serve Ajihad. Eragon and Saphira also bless one of the Varden's orphan babies while the Varden heal Arya of her poisoning.

Eragon's stay is disrupted by news of an Urgal army approaching underground, through the dwarves' tunnels. In the battle that follows, Eragon is separated from Saphira and forced to fight Durza alone. Far stronger than any human, Durza easily defeats Eragon, slashing open his back from shoulder to hip. At that moment,

Saphira and Arya break the roof of a chamber—a sixty-foot-wide star sapphire—distracting Durza long enough for Eragon to stab him through the heart. Freed from Durza's spells, which were controlling them, the Urgals are driven back.

While Eragon lies unconscious after the battle, he is telepathically contacted by a being who identifies himself as Togira Ikonoka—the Cripple Who Is Whole. He urges Eragon to seek him for instruction in Ellesméra, the elves' capital.

When Eragon wakes, he has a huge scar across his back. Dismayed, he also realizes he only slew Durza through sheer luck and that he desperately needs more training. And at the end of Book One, he decides that, yes, he will find this Togira Ikonoka and learn from him.

Eldest begins three days after Eragon slays Durza. The Varden are recovering from the Battle of Farthen Dûr, and Ajihad, Murtagh, and the Twins have been hunting down the Urgals who escaped into the tunnels underneath Farthen Dûr after the battle. When a group of Urgals takes them by surprise, Ajihad is killed and Murtagh and the Twins disappear in the fray. The Varden's Council of Elders appoints Nasuada to succeed her father as new leader of the Varden, and Eragon swears fealty to her as her vassal.

Eragon and Saphira decide they must leave for Ellesméra to begin their training with the Cripple Who Is Whole. Before they go, the dwarf king, Hrothgar, offers to adopt Eragon into his clan, the Dûrgrimst Ingeitum, and Eragon accepts, which gives him full legal rights as a dwarf and entitles him to participate in dwarvish councils.

Both Arya and Orik, Hrothgar's foster son, accompany Eragon and Saphira on their journey to the land of the elves. En route, they stop in Tarnag, a dwarf city. Some of the dwarves are friendly, but Eragon learns that one clan in particular does not welcome him and Saphira—the Az Sweldn rak Anhûin, who hate Riders and dragons because the Forsworn slaughtered so many of their clan.

The party finally arrives in Du Weldenvarden, the forest of the elves. At Ellesméra, Eragon and Saphira meet Islanzadí, queen of the elves, who, they learn, is Arya's mother. They also meet with the Cripple Who Is Whole: an ancient elf named Oromis. He too is a Rider. Oromis and his dragon, Glaedr, have kept their existence hidden from Galbatorix for the past hundred years while they searched for a way to overthrow the king.

Both Oromis and Glaedr are afflicted with old wounds that prevent them from fighting—Glaedr is missing a leg and Oromis, who was captured and broken by the Forsworn, is unable to control large amounts of magic and is prone to debilitating seizures.

Eragon and Saphira begin their training, both together and separately. Eragon learns more about the history of Alagaësia's races, swordsmanship, and the ancient language, which all magicians use. In his studies of the ancient language, he discovers he made a terrible mistake when he and Saphira blessed the orphaned baby in Farthen Dûr: he intended to say "May you be shielded from misfortune," but what he actually said was "May you be *a shield* from misfortune." He has cursed the baby to shield others from any and all pain and misfortune.

Saphira makes quick progress learning from Glaedr, but the scar Eragon bears as a result of his battle with Durza slows his training. Not only is the mark on his back disfiguring, but at unexpected times it incapacitates him with painful spasms. He does not know how he will improve as a magician and swordsman if his convulsions continue.

Eragon begins to realize he has feelings for Arya. He confesses them to her, but she rebuffs him and soon leaves to return to the Varden.

Then the elves hold a ritual known as the Agaetí Blödhren, or the Blood-oath Celebration, during which Eragon goes through a magical transformation: he is turned into an elf-human hybrid—not quite one, not quite the other. As a result, his scar is healed and he now has the same superhuman strength the elves have. His features are also altered, so he appears slightly elvish.

At this point, Eragon learns that the Varden are on the brink of battle with the Empire and are in dire need of him and Saphira. While Eragon has been away, Nasuada has moved the Varden from Farthen Dûr to Surda, a country south of the Empire that still maintains its independence from Galbatorix.

Eragon and Saphira leave Ellesméra, along with Orik, after promising Oromis and Glaedr that they will return to complete their training as soon as they can.

Meanwhile, Eragon's cousin, Roran, has been having his own adventures. Galbatorix has sent the Ra'zac and a legion of imperial soldiers to Carvahall, looking to capture Roran, so as to use him against Eragon. Roran manages to escape into the nearby mountains. He and the other villagers attempt to drive the soldiers away. Numerous villagers die in the process. When Sloan, the village butcher—who hates Roran and opposes Roran's engagement to his daughter, Katrina—betrays Roran to the Ra'zac, the beetle-like creatures find and attack Roran in the middle of the night in his bedroom. Roran fights his way free, but the Ra'zac capture Katrina.

Roran convinces the people of Carvahall to leave their village and seek refuge with the Varden in Surda. They set out westward for the coast, in the hope that they can sail from there to Surda. Roran proves himself as a leader, bringing them safely through the Spine to the coast. In the port town of Teirm, they meet Jeod, who tells Roran that Eragon is a Rider and explains what the Ra'zac were looking for in Carvahall in the first place—Saphira. Jeod offers to help Roran and the villagers reach Surda, pointing out that once Roran and the villagers are safely with the Varden, Roran can enlist Eragon's help in rescuing Katrina. Jeod and the villagers pirate a ship and sail toward Surda.

Eragon and Saphira reach the Varden, who are readying for battle. Eragon learns what has become of the baby upon whom he bestowed the ill-phrased blessing: her name is Elva, and though, chronologically, she is still a baby, she has the appearance of a four-year-old child and the voice and demeanor of a world-weary adult.

Eragon's spell forces her to sense the pain of all the people she sees, and compels her to protect them; if she resists this urge, she herself suffers.

Eragon, Saphira, and the Varden ride out to meet the Empire's troops on the Burning Plains, a large swath of land that smokes and smolders from underground peat fires. They are astonished when another Rider appears astride a red dragon. The new Rider slays Hrothgar, the dwarf king, and then begins to fight with Eragon and Saphira. When Eragon manages to wrench the Rider's helm off, he is shocked to see Murtagh.

Murtagh did not die in the Urgal ambush under Farthen Dûr. The Twins arranged it all; they are traitors who planned the ambush so Ajihad would be killed and they could capture Murtagh and take him to Galbatorix. The king forced Murtagh to swear loyalty to him in the ancient language. Now Murtagh and his newly hatched dragon, Thorn, are Galbatorix's slaves, and Murtagh asserts that his oaths will never allow him to disobey the king, though Eragon pleads with him to abandon Galbatorix and join the Varden.

Murtagh is able to overwhelm Eragon and Saphira with an inexplicable display of strength. However, he decides to free them because of their previous friendship. Before Murtagh leaves, he takes Zar'roc from Eragon, claiming it is his inheritance as Morzan's elder son. Then he reveals that he is not Morzan's only son—Eragon and Murtagh are brothers, both sons of Selena, Morzan's consort. The Twins discovered the truth when they examined Eragon's memories the day he arrived at Farthen Dûr.

Still reeling from Murtagh's revelation about their parentage, Eragon retreats with Saphira, and he is finally reunited with Roran and the villagers of Carvahall, who have arrived at the Burning Plains just in time to aid the Varden in the battle. Roran fought heroically and succeeded in killing the Twins.

Eragon and Roran make peace over Eragon's role in Garrow's death, and Eragon vows to help Roran rescue Katrina from the Ra'zac.

THE GATES OF DEATH

Eragon stared at the dark tower of stone wherein hid the monsters who had murdered his uncle, Garrow.

He was lying on his belly behind the edge of a sandy hill dotted with sparse blades of grass, thornbushes, and small, rosebud-like cactuses. The brittle stems of last year's foliage pricked his palms as he inched forward to gain a better view of Helgrind, which loomed over the surrounding land like a black dagger thrust out from the bowels of the earth.

The evening sun streaked the low hills with shadows long and narrow and—far in the west—illuminated the surface of Leona Lake so that the horizon became a rippling bar of gold.

To his left, Eragon heard the steady breathing of his cousin, Roran, who was stretched out beside him. The normally inaudible flow of air seemed preternaturally loud to Eragon with his heightened sense of hearing, one of many such changes wrought by his experience during the Agaetí Blödhren, the elves' Blood-oath Celebration.

He paid little attention to that now as he watched a column of people inch toward the base of Helgrind, apparently having walked from the city of Dras-Leona, some miles away. A contingent of twenty-four men and women, garbed in thick leather robes, occupied the head of the column. This group moved with many strange and varied gaits—they limped and shuffled and humped and wriggled; they swung on crutches or used arms to propel themselves forward on curiously short legs—contortions that were necessary because, as Eragon realized, every one of the twenty-four lacked an arm or a leg or some combination thereof. Their leader sat upright upon a litter borne by six oiled slaves, a pose Eragon regarded as a rather amazing accomplishment, considering that the man or woman—he could not tell which—consisted of nothing more than a torso and head, upon whose brow balanced an ornate leather crest three feet high.

"The priests of Helgrind," he murmured to Roran.

"Can they use magic?"

"Possibly. I dare not explore Helgrind with my mind until they leave, for if any *are* magicians, they will sense my touch, however light, and our presence will be revealed."

Behind the priests trudged a double line of young men swathed in gold cloth. Each carried a rectangular metal frame subdivided by twelve horizontal crossbars from which hung iron bells the size of winter rutabagas. Half of the young men gave their frames a vigorous shake when they stepped forward with their right foot, producing a dolorous cacophony of notes, while the other half shook their frames when they advanced upon the left foot, causing iron tongues to crash against iron throats and emit a mournful clamor that echoed over the hills. The acolytes accompanied the throbbing of the bells with their own cries, groaning and shouting in an ecstasy of passion.

At the rear of the grotesque procession trudged a comet's tail of inhabitants from Dras-Leona: nobles, merchants, tradesmen, several high-ranking military commanders, and a motley collection of those less fortunate, such as laborers, beggars, and common foot soldiers.

Eragon wondered if Dras-Leona's governor, Marcus Tábor, was somewhere in their midst.

Drawing to a stop at the edge of the precipitous mound of scree that ringed Helgrind, the priests gathered on either side of a rust-colored boulder with a polished top. When the entire column stood motionless before the crude altar, the creature upon the litter stirred and began to chant in a voice as discordant as the moaning of the bells. The shaman's declamations were repeatedly truncated by gusts of wind, but Eragon caught snatches of the ancient language—strangely twisted and mispronounced—interspersed with dwarf and Urgal words, all of which were united by an archaic dialect of

Eragon's own tongue. What he understood caused him to shudder, for the sermon spoke of things best left unknown, of a malevolent hate that had festered for centuries in the dark caverns of people's hearts before being allowed to flourish in the Riders' absence, of blood and madness, and of foul rituals performed underneath a black moon.

At the end of that depraved oration, two of the lesser priests rushed forward and lifted their master—or mistress, as the case might be—off the litter and onto the face of the altar. Then the High Priest issued a brief order. Twin blades of steel winked like stars as they rose and fell. A rivulet of blood sprang from each of the High Priest's shoulders, flowed down the leather-encased torso, and then pooled across the boulder until it overflowed onto the gravel below.

Two more priests jumped forward to catch the crimson flow in goblets that, when filled to the rim, were distributed among the members of the congregation, who eagerly drank.

"Gar!" said Roran in an undertone. "You failed to mention that those errant flesh-mongers, those gore-bellied, boggle-minded idiot-worshipers were *cannibals*."

"Not quite. They do not partake of the meat."

When all the attendees had wet their throats, the servile novitiates returned the High Priest to the litter and bound the creature's shoulders with strips of white linen. Wet blotches quickly sullied the virgin cloth.

The wounds seemed to have no effect upon the High Priest, for the limbless figure rotated back toward the devotees with their lips of cranberry red and pronounced, "Now are you truly my Brothers and Sisters, having tasted the sap of my veins here in the shadow of almighty Helgrind. Blood calls to blood, and if ever your Family should need help, do then what you can for the Church and for others who acknowledge the power of our Dread Lord. . . . To affirm and reaffirm our fealty to the Triumvirate, recite with me the Nine Oaths. . . . By Gorm, Ilda, and Fell Angvara, we vow to perform homage at least thrice a month, in the hour before dusk, and then to make an offering of ourselves to appease the eternal hunger of our Great and Terrible Lord. . . . We vow to observe the strictures as they are presented in the book of Tosk. . . . We vow to always carry our Bregnir on our bodies and to forever abstain from the twelve of twelves and the touch of a many-knotted rope, lest it corrupt . . ."

A sudden rise in the wind obscured the rest of the High Priest's list. Then Eragon saw those who listened take out a small, curved knife and, one by one, cut themselves in the crook of their elbows and anoint the altar with a stream of their blood.

Some minutes later, the angry breeze subsided and Eragon again heard the priest: ". . . and such things as you long and lust for will be granted to you as a reward for your obedience. . . . Our worship is complete. However, if any now stand among you who are brave enough to demonstrate the true depth of their faith, let them show themselves!"

The audience stiffened and leaned forward, their faces rapt; this, apparently, was what they had been waiting for.

For a long, silent pause, it seemed as if they would be disappointed, but then one of the acolytes broke ranks and shouted, "I will!" With a roar of delight, his brethren began to brandish their bells in a quick and savage beat, whipping the congregation into such a frenzy, they jumped and yelled as if they had taken leave of their senses. The rough music kindled a spark of excitement in Eragon's heart—despite his revulsion at the proceedings—waking some primal and brutish part of him.

Shedding his gold robes so that he wore nothing but a leather breechcloth, the dark-haired youth sprang on top of the altar. Gouts of ruby spray erupted on either side of his feet. He faced Helgrind and began to shiver and quake as if stricken with palsy, keeping time with the tolling of the cruel iron bells. His head rolled loosely upon his neck, foam gathered at the corners of his mouth, his arms thrashed like snakes. Sweat oiled his muscles until he gleamed like a bronze statue in the dying light.

The bells soon reached a manic tempo where one note clashed

against another, at which point the young man thrust a hand out behind himself. Into it, a priest deposited the hilt of a bizarre implement: a single-edged weapon, two and a half feet long, with a full tang, scale grips, a vestigial crossguard, and a broad, flat blade that widened and was scalloped near the end, a shape reminiscent of a dragon wing. It was a tool designed for but one purpose: to hack through armor and bones and sinew as easily as through a bulging waterskin.

The young man lifted the weapon so that it slanted toward the highest peak of Helgrind. Then he dropped to one knee and, with an incoherent cry, brought the blade down across his right wrist.

Blood sprayed the rocks behind the altar.

Eragon winced and averted his eyes, although he could not escape the youth's piercing screams. It was nothing Eragon had not seen in battle, but it seemed wrong to deliberately mutilate yourself when it was so easy to become disfigured in everyday life.

Blades of grass rasped against one another as Roran shifted his weight. He muttered some curse, which was lost in his beard, and then fell silent again.

While a priest tended to the young man's wound—stanching the bleeding with a spell—an acolyte let loose two slaves from the High Priest's litter, only to chain them by the ankles to an iron loop embedded in the altar. Then the acolytes divested themselves of numerous packages from underneath their robes and piled them on the ground, out of reach of the slaves.

Their ceremonies at an end, the priests and their retinue departed Helgrind for Dras-Leona, wailing and ringing the entire way. The now one-handed zealot stumbled along just behind the High Priest.

A beatific smile graced his face.

"Well," said Eragon, and released his pent-up breath as the column vanished behind a distant hill.

"Well what?"

"I've traveled among both dwarves and elves, and nothing they did was ever as strange as what those people, those *humans*, do."

"They're as monstrous as the Ra'zac." Roran jerked his chin toward Helgrind. "Can you find out now if Katrina is in there?"

"I'll try. But be ready to run."

Closing his eyes, Eragon slowly extended his consciousness outward, moving from the mind of one living thing to another, like tendrils of water seeping through sand. He touched teeming cities of insects frantically scurrying about their business, lizards and snakes hidden among warm rocks, diverse species of songbirds, and numerous small mammals. Insects and animals alike bustled with activity as they prepared for the fast-approaching night, whether by retreating to their various dens or, in the case of those of a nocturnal bent, by yawning, stretching, and otherwise readying themselves to hunt and forage.

Just as with his other senses, Eragon's ability to touch another being's thoughts diminished with distance. By the time his psychic probe arrived at the base of Helgrind, he could perceive only the largest of animals, and even those but faintly.

He proceeded with caution, ready to withdraw at a second's notice if he happened to brush against the minds of their prey: the Ra'zac and the Ra'zac's parents and steeds, the gigantic Lethrblaka. Eragon was willing to expose himself in this manner only because none of the Ra'zac's breed could use magic, and he did not believe that they were mindbreakers—nonmagicians trained to fight with telepathy. The Ra'zac and Lethrblaka had no need for such tricks when their breath alone could induce a stupor in the largest of men.

And though Eragon risked discovery by his ghostly investigation, he, Roran, and Saphira *had* to know if the Ra'zac had imprisoned Katrina—Roran's betrothed—in Helgrind, for the answer would determine whether their mission was one of rescue or one of capture and interrogation.

Eragon searched long and hard. When he returned to himself,

Roran was watching him with the expression of a starving wolf. His gray eyes burned with a mixture of anger, hope, and despair that was so great, it seemed as if his emotions might burst forth and incinerate everything in sight in a blaze of unimaginable intensity, melting the very rocks themselves.

This Eragon understood.

Katrina's father, the butcher Sloan, had betrayed Roran to the Ra'zac. When they failed to capture him, the Ra'zac had instead seized Katrina from Roran's bedroom and spirited her away from Palancar Valley, leaving the inhabitants of Carvahall to be killed and enslaved by King Galbatorix's soldiers. Unable to pursue Katrina, Roran had—just in time—convinced the villagers to abandon their homes and to follow him across the Spine and then south along the coast of Alagaësia, where they joined forces with the rebel Varden. The hardships they endured as a result had been many and terrible. But circuitous as it was, that course had reunited Roran with Eragon, who knew the location of the Ra'zac's den and had promised to help save Katrina.

Roran had only succeeded, as he later explained, because the strength of his passion drove him to extremes that others feared and avoided, and thus allowed him to confound his enemies.

A similar fervor now gripped Eragon.

He would leap into harm's way without the slightest regard for his own safety if someone he cared for was in danger. He loved Roran as a brother, and since Roran was to marry Katrina, Eragon had extended his definition of family to include her as well. This concept seemed even more important because Eragon and Roran were the last heirs of their line. Eragon had renounced all affiliation with his birth brother, Murtagh, and the only relatives he and Roran had left were each other, and now Katrina.

Noble sentiments of kinship were not the only force that drove the pair. Another goal obsessed them as well: *revenge!* Even as they plotted to snatch Katrina from the grasp of the Ra'zac, so the two warriors—mortal man and Dragon Rider alike—sought to slay King Galbatorix's unnatural servants for torturing and murdering Garrow, who was Roran's father and had been as a father to Eragon.

The intelligence, then, that Eragon had gleaned was as important to him as to Roran.

"I think I felt her," he said. "It's hard to be certain, because we're so far from Helgrind and I've never touched her mind before, but I *think* she's in that forsaken peak, concealed somewhere near the very top."

"Is she sick? Is she injured? Blast it, Eragon, don't hide it from me: have they hurt her?"

"She's in no pain at the moment. More than that, I cannot say, for it required all my strength just to make out the glow of her consciousness; I could not communicate with her." Eragon refrained from mentioning, however, that he had detected a second person as well, one whose identity he suspected and the presence of whom, if confirmed, troubled him greatly. "What I *didn't* find were the Ra'zac or the Lethrblaka. Even if I somehow overlooked the Ra'zac, their parents are so large, their life force should blaze like a thousand lanterns, even as Saphira's does. Aside from Katrina and a few other dim specks of light, Helgrind is black, black, black."

Roran scowled, clenched his left fist, and glared at the mountain of rock, which was fading into the dusk as purple shadows enveloped it. In a low, flat voice, as if talking with himself, he said, "It doesn't matter whether you are right or wrong."

"How so?"

"We dare not attack tonight; night is when the Ra'zac are strongest, and if they *are* nearby, it would be stupid to fight them when we're at a disadvantage. Agreed?"

"Yes."

"So, we wait for the dawn." Roran gestured toward the slaves chained to the gory altar. "If those poor wretches are gone by then, we know the Ra'zac are here, and we proceed as planned. If not, we curse our bad luck that they escaped us, free the slaves, rescue

Katrina, and fly back to the Varden with her before Murtagh hunts us down. Either way, I doubt the Ra'zac will leave Katrina unattended for long, not if Galbatorix wants her to survive so he can use her as a tool against me."

Eragon nodded. He wanted to release the slaves now, but doing so could warn their foes that something was amiss. Nor, if the Ra'zac came to collect their dinner, could he and Saphira intercede before the slaves were ferried away. A battle in the open between a dragon and creatures such as the Lethrblaka would attract the attention of every man, woman, and child for leagues around. And Eragon did not think he, Saphira, or Roran could survive if Galbatorix learned they were alone in his empire.

He looked away from the shackled men. *For their sake, I hope the Ra'zac are on the other side of Alagaësia or, at least, that the Ra'zac aren't hungry tonight.*

By unspoken consent, Eragon and Roran crawled backward down from the crest of the low hill they were hiding behind. At the bottom, they rose into a half crouch, then turned and, still doubled over, ran between two rows of hills. The shallow depression gradually deepened into a narrow, flood-carved gully lined with crumbling slabs of shale.

Dodging the gnarled juniper trees that dotted the gully, Eragon glanced up and, through clumps of needles, saw the first constellations to adorn the velvet sky. They seemed cold and sharp, like bright shards of ice. Then he concentrated on maintaining his footing as he and Roran trotted south toward their camp.

AROUND THE CAMPFIRE

The low mound of coals throbbed like the heart of some giant beast. Occasionally, a patch of gold sparks flared into existence and raced across the surface of the wood before vanishing into a white-hot crevice.

The dying remnants of the fire Eragon and Roran had built cast a dim red light over the surrounding area, revealing a patch of rocky soil, a few pewter-gray bushes, the indistinct mass of a juniper tree farther off, then nothing.

Eragon sat with his bare feet extended toward the nest of ruby embers—enjoying the warmth—and with his back propped against the knobby scales of Saphira's thick right foreleg. Opposite him, Roran was perched on the iron-hard, sun-bleached, wind-worn shell of an ancient tree trunk. Every time he moved, the trunk produced a bitter shriek that made Eragon want to claw at his ears.

For the moment, quiet reigned within the hollow. Even the coals smoldered in silence; Roran had collected only long-dead branches devoid of moisture to eliminate any smoke that unfriendly eyes might spot.

Eragon had just finished recounting the day's activities to Saphira. Normally, he never had to tell her what he had been doing, as thoughts, feelings, and other sensations flowed between them as easily as water from one side of a lake to another. But in this instance it was necessary because Eragon had kept his mind carefully shielded during the scouting expedition, aside from his disembodied foray into the Ra'zac's lair.

After a considerable gap in the conversation, Saphira yawned, exposing her rows of many fearsome teeth. *Cruel and evil they may* be, but I am impressed that the Ra'zac can bewitch their prey into wanting to be eaten. They are great hunters to do that. . . . Perhaps I shall attempt it someday.

But not, Eragon felt compelled to add, with people. Try it with sheep instead.

People, sheep: what difference is there to a dragon? Then she laughed deep in her long throat—a rolling rumble that reminded him of thunder.

Leaning forward to take his weight off Saphira's sharp-edged scales, Eragon picked up the hawthorn staff that lay by his side. He rolled it between his palms, admiring the play of light over the polished tangle of roots at the top and the much-scratched metal ferrule and spike at the base.

Roran had thrust the staff into his arms before they left the Varden on the Burning Plains, saying, "Here. Fisk made this for me after the Ra'zac bit my shoulder. I know you lost your sword, and I thought you might have need of it. . . . If you want to get another blade, that's fine too, but I've found there are very few fights you can't win with a few whacks from a good, strong stick." Remembering the staff Brom had always carried, Eragon had decided to forgo a new sword in favor of the length of knotted hawthorn. After losing Zar'roc, he felt no desire to take up another, lesser sword. That night, he had fortified both the knotted hawthorn and the handle to Roran's hammer with several spells that would prevent either piece from breaking, except under the most extreme stress.

Unbidden, a series of memories overwhelmed Eragon: *A sullen orange and crimson sky swirled around him as Saphira dove in pursuit of the red dragon and his Rider. Wind howled past his ears. . . . His fingers went numb from the jolt of sword striking sword as he dueled that same Rider on the ground. . . . Tearing off his foe's helm in the midst of combat to reveal his once friend and traveling companion, Murtagh, whom he had thought dead. . . . The sneer upon Murtagh's face as he took Zar'roc from Eragon, claiming the red sword by right of inheritance as Eragon's elder brother. . . .*

Eragon blinked, disoriented as the noise and fury of battle faded and the pleasant aroma of juniper wood replaced the stench of blood. He ran his tongue over his upper teeth, trying to eradicate the taste of bile that filled his mouth.

Murtagh.

The name alone generated a welter of confused emotions in Eragon. On one hand, he *liked* Murtagh. Murtagh had saved Eragon and Saphira from the Ra'zac after their first, ill-fated visit to Dras-Leona; risked his life to help extricate Eragon from Gil'ead; acquitted himself honorably in the Battle of Farthen Dûr; and, despite the torments he no doubt endured as a result, had chosen to interpret his orders from Galbatorix in a way that allowed him to release Eragon and Saphira after the Battle of the Burning Plains instead of taking them captive. It was not Murtagh's fault that the Twins had abducted him; that the red dragon, Thorn, had hatched for him; or that Galbatorix had discovered their true names, with which he extracted oaths of fealty in the ancient language from both Murtagh and Thorn.

None of that could be blamed on Murtagh. He was a victim of fate, and had been since the day he was born.

And yet . . . Murtagh might serve Galbatorix against his will, and he might abhor the atrocities the king forced him to commit, but some part of him seemed to revel in wielding his newfound power. During the recent engagement between the Varden and the Empire on the Burning Plains, Murtagh had singled out the dwarf king, Hrothgar, and slain him, although Galbatorix had not ordered Murtagh to do so. He had let Eragon and Saphira go, yes, but only after defeating them in a brutal contest of strength and then listening to Eragon plead for their freedom.

And Murtagh had derived entirely too much pleasure from the anguish he inflicted upon Eragon by revealing they were both sons of Morzan—first and last of the thirteen Dragon Riders, the Forsworn, who had betrayed their compatriots to Galbatorix.

Now, four days after the battle, another explanation presented itself to Eragon: *Perhaps what Murtagh enjoyed was watching another person shoulder the same terrible burden he had carried his whole life.*

Whether or not that was true, Eragon suspected Murtagh had embraced his new role for the same reason that a dog who has been whipped without cause will someday turn and attack his master. Murtagh had been whipped and whipped, and now he had his chance to strike back at a world that had shown him little enough kindness.

Yet no matter what good might still flicker in Murtagh's breast, he and Eragon were doomed to be mortal enemies, for Murtagh's promises in the ancient language bound him to Galbatorix with unbreakable fetters and would forevermore.

If only he hadn't gone with Ajihad to hunt Urgals underneath Farthen Dûr. Or if I had just been a little faster, the Twins—

Eragon, said Saphira.

He caught himself and nodded, grateful for her intervention. Eragon did his best to avoid brooding upon Murtagh or their shared parents, but such thoughts often waylaid him when he least expected it.

Drawing and releasing a slow breath to clear his head, Eragon tried to force his mind back to the present but could not.

The morning after the massive battle on the Burning Plains— when the Varden were busy regrouping and preparing to march after the Empire's army, which had retreated several leagues up the Jiet River—Eragon had gone to Nasuada and Arya, explained Roran's predicament, and sought their permission to help his cousin. He did not succeed. Both women vehemently opposed what Nasuada described as "a harebrained scheme that will have catastrophic consequences for everyone in Alagaësia if it goes awry!"

The debate raged on for so long, at last Saphira had interrupted with a roar that shook the walls of the command tent. Then she said, *I am sore and tired, and Eragon is doing a poor job of explaining himself. We have better things to do than stand around yammering like jackdaws, no? . . . Good, now listen to me.*

It was, reflected Eragon, difficult to argue with a dragon.

The details of Saphira's remarks were complex, but the underlying structure of her presentation was straightforward. Saphira supported Eragon because she understood how much the proposed mission meant to him, while Eragon supported Roran because of love and family, and because he knew Roran would pursue Katrina with or without him, and his cousin would never be able to defeat the Ra'zac by himself. Also, so long as the Empire held Katrina captive, Roran—and through him, Eragon—was vulnerable to manipulation by Galbatorix. If the usurper threatened to kill Katrina, Roran would have no choice but to submit to his demands.

It would be best, then, to patch this breach in their defenses before their enemies took advantage of it.

As for the timing, it was perfect. Neither Galbatorix nor the Ra'zac would expect a raid in the center of the Empire when the Varden were busy fighting Galbatorix's troops near the border of Surda. Murtagh and Thorn had been seen flying toward Urû'baen—no doubt to be chastised in person—and Nasuada and Arya agreed with Eragon that those two would probably then continue northward to confront Queen Islanzadí and the army under her command once the elves made their first strike and revealed their presence. And if possible, it would be good to eliminate the Ra'zac before they started to terrorize and demoralize the Varden's warriors.

Saphira had then pointed out, in the most diplomatic of terms, that if Nasuada asserted her authority as Eragon's liegelord and forbade him from participating in the sortie, it would poison their relationship with the sort of rancor and dissent that could undermine the Varden's cause. *But*, said Saphira, *the choice is yours. Keep Eragon here if you want. However, his commitments are not mine, and I, for one, have decided to accompany Roran. It seems like a fine adventure.*

A faint smile touched Eragon's lips as he recalled the scene.

The combined weight of Saphira's declaration and her impregnable logic had convinced Nasuada and Arya to grant their approval, albeit grudgingly.

Afterward, Nasuada had said, "We are trusting your judgment in this, Eragon, Saphira. For your sake and ours, I hope this expedition goes well." Her tone left Eragon uncertain whether her words represented a heartfelt wish or a subtle threat.

Eragon had spent the rest of that day gathering supplies, studying maps of the Empire with Saphira, and casting what spells he felt were necessary, such as one to thwart attempts by Galbatorix or his minions to scry Roran.

The following morning, Eragon and Roran had climbed onto Saphira's back, and she had taken flight, rising above the orange clouds that stifled the Burning Plains and angling northeast. She flew nonstop until the sun had traversed the dome of the sky and extinguished itself behind the horizon and then burst forth again with a glorious conflagration of reds and yellows.

The first leg of their journey carried them toward the edge of the Empire, which few people inhabited. There they turned west toward Dras-Leona and Helgrind. From then on, they traveled at night to avoid notice by anyone in the many small villages scattered across the grasslands that lay between them and their destination.

Eragon and Roran had to swathe themselves in cloaks and furs and wool mittens and felted hats, for Saphira chose to fly higher than the icebound peaks of most mountains—where the air was thin and dry and stabbed at their lungs—so that if a farmer tending a sick calf in the field or a sharp-eyed watchman making his rounds should happen to look up as she passed overhead, Saphira would appear no larger than an eagle.

Everywhere they went, Eragon saw evidence of the war that was now afoot: camps of soldiers, wagons full of supplies gathered into a bunch for the night, and lines of men with iron collars being led from their homes to fight on Galbatorix's behalf. The amount of resources deployed against them was daunting indeed.

Near the end of the second night, Helgrind had appeared in the distance: a mass of splintered columns, vague and ominous in the ashen light that precedes dawn. Saphira had landed in the hollow where they were now, and they had slept through most of the past day before beginning their reconnaissance.

A fountain of amber motes billowed and swirled as Roran tossed a branch onto the disintegrating coals. He caught Eragon's look and shrugged. "Cold," he said.

Before Eragon could respond, he heard a slithering scraping sound akin to someone drawing a sword.

He did not think; he flung himself in the opposite direction, rolled once, and came up into a crouch, lifting the hawthorn staff to deflect an oncoming blow. Roran was nearly as fast. He grabbed his shield from the ground, scrambled back from the log he had been sitting on, and drew his hammer from his belt, all in the span of a few seconds.

They froze, waiting for the attack.

Eragon's heart pounded and his muscles trembled as he searched the darkness for the slightest hint of motion.

I smell nothing, said Saphira.

When several minutes elapsed without incident, Eragon pushed his mind out over the surrounding landscape. "No one," he said. Reaching deep within himself to the place where he could touch the flow of magic, he uttered the words "Brisingr raudhr!" A pale red werelight popped into existence several feet in front of him and remained there, floating at eye level and painting the hollow with a watery radiance. He moved slightly, and the werelight mimicked his motion, as if connected to him by an invisible pole.

Together, he and Roran advanced toward where they'd heard the sound, down the gulch that wound eastward. They held their weapons high and paused between each step, ready to defend themselves at any moment. About ten yards from their camp, Roran held up a hand, stopping Eragon, then pointed at a plate of shale that lay on top of the grass. It appeared conspicuously out of place. Kneeling, Roran rubbed a smaller fragment of shale across the plate and created the same steely scrape they had heard before.

"It must have fallen," said Eragon, examining the sides of the gulch. He allowed the werelight to fade into oblivion.

Roran nodded and stood, brushing dirt from his pants.

As he walked back to Saphira, Eragon considered the speed with which they had reacted. His heart still contracted into a hard, painful knot with each beat, his hands shook, and he felt like dashing into the wilderness and running several miles without stopping. *We wouldn't have jumped like that before*, he thought. The reason for their vigilance was no mystery: every one of their fights had chipped away at their complacency, leaving behind nothing but raw nerves that twitched at the slightest touch.

Roran must have been entertaining similar thoughts, for he said, "Do you see them?"

"Who?"

"The men you've killed. Do you see them in your dreams?"

"Sometimes."

The pulsing glow from the coals lit Roran's face from below, forming thick shadows above his mouth and across his forehead and giving his heavy, half-lidded eyes a baleful aspect. He spoke slowly, as if he found the words difficult. "I never wanted to be a warrior. I dreamed of blood and glory when I was younger, as every boy does, but the land was what was important to me. That and our family. . . . And now I have killed. . . . I have killed and killed, and you have killed even more." His gaze focused on some distant place only he could see. "There were these two men in Narda. . . . Did I tell you this before?"

He had, but Eragon shook his head and remained silent.

"They were guards at the main gate. . . . Two of them, you know, and the man on the right, he had pure white hair. I remember because he couldn't have been more than twenty-four, twenty-five. They wore Galbatorix's sigil but spoke as if they were from Narda. They weren't professional soldiers. They were probably just men who had decided to help protect their homes from Urgals, pirates, brigands. . . . We weren't going to lift a finger against them. I swear to you, Eragon, that was never part of our plan. I had no choice, though. They recognized me. I stabbed the white-haired man underneath his chin. . . . It was like when Father cut the throat of a pig. And then the other, I smashed open his skull. I can still feel his bones giving way. . . . I remember every blow I've landed, from the soldiers in Carvahall to the ones on the Burning Plains. . . . You know, when I close my eyes, sometimes I can't sleep because the light from the fire we set in the docks of Teirm is so bright in my mind. I think I'm going mad then."

Eragon found his hands gripping the staff with such force, his knuckles were white and tendons ridged the insides of his wrists. "Aye," he said. "At first it was just Urgals, then it was men and Urgals, and now this last battle. . . . I know what we do is right, but *right* doesn't mean *easy*. Because of who we are, the Varden expect Saphira and me to stand at the front of their army and to slaughter entire battalions of soldiers. We do. We have." His voice caught, and he fell silent.

Turmoil accompanies every great change, said Saphira to both of them. *And we have experienced more than our share, for we are agents of that very change. I am a dragon, and I do not regret the deaths of those who endanger us. Killing the guards in Narda may not be a deed worthy of celebration, but neither is it one to feel guilty about. You had to do it. When you must fight, Roran, does not the fierce joy of combat lend wings to your feet? Do you not know the pleasure of pitting yourself against a worthy opponent and the satisfaction of seeing the bodies of your enemies piled before you? Eragon, you have experienced this. Help me explain it to your cousin.*

Eragon stared at the coals. She had stated a truth that he was reluctant to acknowledge, lest by agreeing that one could enjoy violence, he would become a man he would despise. So he was mute. Across from him, Roran appeared similarly affected.

In a softer voice, Saphira said, *Do not be angry. I did not intend to upset you. . . . I forget sometimes that you are still unaccustomed to these emotions, while I have fought tooth and nail for survival since the day I hatched.*

Rising to his feet, Eragon walked to their saddlebags and retrieved the small earthenware jar Orik had given him before they parted, then poured two large mouthfuls of raspberry mead down his gullet. Warmth bloomed in his stomach. Grimacing, Eragon passed the jar to Roran, who also partook of the concoction.

Several drinks later, when the mead had succeeded in tempering his black mood, Eragon said, "We may have a problem tomorrow."

"What do you mean?"

Eragon directed his words toward Saphira as well. "Remember how I said that we—Saphira and I—could easily handle the Ra'zac?"

"Aye."

And so we can, said Saphira.

"Well, I was thinking about it while we spied on Helgrind, and I'm not so sure anymore. There are almost an infinite number of ways to do something with magic. For example, if I want to light a fire, I could light it with heat gathered from the air or the ground; I could create a flame out of pure energy; I could summon a bolt of lightning; I could concentrate a raft of sunbeams into a single point; I could use friction; and so forth." ·

"So?"

"The problem is, even though I can devise numerous spells to perform this one action, *blocking* those spells might require but a single counterspell. If you prevent the action itself from taking place, then you don't have to tailor your counterspell to address the unique properties of each individual spell."

"I still don't understand what this has to do with tomorrow."

I do, said Saphira to both of them. She had immediately grasped the implications. *It means that, over the past century, Galbatorix—*

"—may have placed wards around the Ra'zac—"

—that will protect them against—

"—a whole range of spells. I probably won't—"

—be able to kill them with any—

"—of the words of death I was taught, nor any—"

—attacks that we can invent now or then. We may—

"—have to rely—"

"Stop!" exclaimed Roran. He gave a pained smile. "Stop, please. My head hurts when you do that."

Eragon paused with his mouth open; until that moment, he had been unaware that he and Saphira were speaking in turn. The knowledge pleased him: it signified that they had achieved new heights of cooperation and were acting together as a single entity—which made them far more powerful than either would be on their own. It also troubled him when he contemplated how such a partnership must, by its very nature, reduce the individuality of those involved.

He closed his mouth and chuckled. "Sorry. What I'm worried about is this: if Galbatorix has had the foresight to take certain precautions, then force of arms may be the only means by which we can slay the Ra'zac. If that's true—"

"I'll just be in your way tomorrow."

"Nonsense. You may be slower than the Ra'zac, but I have no doubt you'll give them cause to fear your weapon, Roran Stronghammer." The compliment seemed to please Roran. "The greatest danger for you is that the Ra'zac or the Lethrblaka will manage to separate you from Saphira and me. The closer we stay together, the safer we'll all be. Saphira and I will try to keep the Ra'zac and Lethrblaka occupied, but some of them may slip past us. Four against two are only good odds if you're among the four."

To Saphira, Eragon said, *If I had a sword, I'm sure I could slay the Ra'zac by myself, but I don't know if I can beat two creatures who are quick as elves, using nothing but this staff.*

You were the one who insisted on carrying that dry twig instead of a proper weapon, she said. *Remember, I told you it might not suffice against enemies as dangerous as the Ra'zac.*

Eragon reluctantly conceded the point. *If my spells fail us, we will be far more vulnerable than I expected. . . . Tomorrow could end very badly indeed.*

Continuing the strand of conversation he had been privy to, Roran said, "This magic is a tricky business." The log he sat on gave a drawn-out groan as he rested his elbows on his knees.

"It is," Eragon agreed. "The hardest part is trying to anticipate every possible spell; I spend most of my time asking how can I protect myself if I'm attacked like *this* and would another magician expect me to do *that*."

"Could you make me as strong and fast as you are?"

Eragon considered the suggestion for several minutes before saying, "I don't see how. The energy needed to do that would have to come from somewhere. Saphira and I could give it to you, but then we would lose as much speed or strength as you gained." What he did not mention was that one could also extract energy from nearby plants and animals, albeit at a terrible price: namely, the deaths of the smaller beings whose life force you drew upon. The technique was a great secret, and Eragon felt that he should not reveal it lightly, if at all. Moreover, it would be of no use to Roran, as too little grew or lived on Helgrind to fuel a man's body.

"Then can you teach me to use magic?" When Eragon hesitated, Roran added, "Not now, of course. We don't have the time, and I don't expect one can become a magician overnight anyway. But in general, why not? You and I are cousins. We share much the same blood. And it would be a valuable skill to have."

"I don't know how someone who's not a Rider learns to use magic," confessed Eragon. "It's not something I studied." Glancing around, he plucked a flat, round stone from the ground and tossed it to Roran, who caught it backhand. "Here, try this: concentrate on lifting the rock a foot or so into the air and say, 'Stenr rïsa.' "

"Stenr rïsa?"

"Exactly."

Roran frowned at the stone resting on his palm in a pose so reminiscent of Eragon's own training that Eragon could not help feeling a flash of nostalgia for the days he spent being drilled by Brom. Roran's eyebrows met, his lips tightened into a snarl, and he growled, "Stenr rïsa!" with enough intensity, Eragon half expected the stone to fly out of sight.

Nothing happened.

Scowling even harder, Roran repeated his command: "Stenr rïsa!"

The stone exhibited a profound lack of movement.

"Well," said Eragon, "keep trying. That's the only advice I can give you. But"—and here he raised a finger—"if you *should* happen to succeed, make sure you immediately come to me or, if I'm not around, another magician. You could kill yourself and others if you start experimenting with magic without understanding the rules. If nothing else, remember this: if you cast a spell that requires too much energy, you *will* die. Don't take on projects that are beyond your abilities, don't try to bring back the dead, and don't try to un-make anything."

Roran nodded, still looking at the stone.

"Magic aside, I just realized there's something far more important that you need to learn."

"Oh?"

"Yes, you need to be able to hide your thoughts from the Black Hand, Du Vrangr Gata, and others like them. You know a lot of things now that could harm the Varden. It's crucial, then, that you master this skill as soon as we return. Until you can defend yourself from spies, neither Nasuada nor I nor anyone else can trust you with information that might help our enemies."

"I understand. But why did you include Du Vrangr Gata in that list? They serve you and Nasuada."

"They do, but even among our allies there are more than a few people who would give their right arm"—he grimaced at the appropriateness of the phrase—"to ferret out our plans and secrets. And yours too, no less. You have become a *somebody*, Roran. Partly because of your deeds, and partly because we are related."

"I know. It is strange to be recognized by those you have not met."

"That it is." Several other, related observations leaped to the tip of Eragon's tongue, but he resisted the urge to pursue the topic; it was a subject to explore another time. "Now that you know what it feels like when one mind touches another, you might be able to learn to reach out and touch other minds in turn."

"I'm not sure that is an ability I want to have."

"No matter; you also might *not* be able to do it. Either way, before you spend time finding out, you should first devote yourself to the art of defense."

His cousin cocked an eyebrow. "How?"

"Choose something—a sound, an image, an emotion, anything—and let it swell within your mind until it blots out any other thoughts."

"That's all?"

"It's not as easy as you think. Go on; take a stab at it. When you're ready, let me know, and I'll see how well you've done."

Several moments passed. Then, at a flick of Roran's fingers, Eragon launched his consciousness toward his cousin, eager to discover what he had accomplished.

The full strength of Eragon's mental ray rammed into a wall composed of Roran's memories of Katrina and was stopped. He could take no ground, find no entrance or purchase, nor undermine the impenetrable barrier that stood before him. At that instant, Roran's entire identity was based upon his feelings for Katrina; his defenses exceeded any Eragon had previously encountered, for Roran's mind was devoid of anything else Eragon could grasp hold of and use to gain control over his cousin.

Then Roran shifted his left leg and the wood underneath released a harsh squeal.

With that, the wall Eragon had hurled himself against fractured into dozens of pieces as a host of competing thoughts distracted Roran: *What was . . . Blast! Don't pay attention to it; he'll break through. Katrina, remember Katrina. Ignore Eragon. The night she*

agreed to marry me, the smell of the grass and her hair . . . Is that him?
No! Focus! Don't—

Taking advantage of Roran's confusion, Eragon rushed forward and, by the force of his will, immobilized Roran before he could shield himself again.

You understand the basic concept, said Eragon, then withdrew from Roran's mind and said out loud, "but you have to learn to maintain your concentration even when you're in the middle of a battle. You must learn to think without thinking . . . to empty yourself of all hopes and worries, save that one idea that is your armor. Something the elves taught me, which I have found helpful, is to recite a riddle or a piece of a poem or song. Having an action that you can repeat over and over again makes it much easier to keep your mind from straying."

"I'll work on it," promised Roran.

In a quiet voice, Eragon said, "You really love her, don't you?" It was more a statement of truth and wonder than a question—the answer being self-evident—and one he felt uncertain making. Romance was not a topic Eragon had broached with his cousin before, notwithstanding the many hours they had devoted in years past to debating the relative merits of the young women in and around Carvahall. "How did it happen?"

"I liked her. She liked me. What importance are the details?"

"Come now," said Eragon. "I was too angry to ask before you left for Therinsford, and we have not seen each other again until just four days ago. I'm curious."

The skin around Roran's eyes pulled and wrinkled as he rubbed his temples. "There's not much to tell. I've always been partial to her. It meant little before I was a man, but after my rites of passage, I began to wonder whom I would marry and whom I wanted to become the mother of my children. During one of our visits to Carvahall, I saw Katrina stop by the side of Loring's house to pick a moss rose growing in the shade of the eaves. She smiled as she looked at the flower. . . . It was such a tender smile, and so happy, I decided right then that I wanted to make her smile like that again and again and that I wanted to look at that smile until the day I died." Tears gleamed in Roran's eyes, but they did not fall, and a second later, he blinked and they vanished. "I fear I have failed in that regard."

After a respectful pause, Eragon said, "You courted her, then? Aside from using me to ferry compliments to Katrina, how else did you proceed?"

"You ask like one who seeks instruction."

"I did not. You're imagining—"

"Come now, yourself," said Roran. "I know when you're lying. You get that big foolish grin, and your ears turn red. The elves may have given you a new face, but that part of you hasn't changed. What is it that exists between you and Arya?"

The strength of Roran's perception disturbed Eragon. "Nothing! The moon has addled your brain."

"Be honest. You dote upon her words as if each one were a diamond, and your gaze lingers upon her as if you were starving and she a grand feast arrayed an inch beyond your reach."

A plume of dark gray smoke erupted from Saphira's nostrils as she made a choking-like noise.

Eragon ignored her suppressed merriment and said, "Arya is an elf."

"And very beautiful. Pointed ears and slanted eyes are small flaws when compared with her charms. You look like a cat yourself now."

"Arya is over a hundred years old."

That particular piece of information caught Roran by surprise; his eyebrows went up, and he said, "I find that hard to believe! She's in the prime of her youth."

"It's true."

"Well, be that as it may, these are reasons you give me, Eragon, and the heart rarely listens to reason. Do you fancy her or not?"

If he fancied her any more, Saphira said to both Eragon and Roran, *I'd be trying to kiss Arya myself.*

Saphira! Mortified, Eragon swatted her on the leg.

Roran was prudent enough not to rib Eragon further. "Then answer my original question and tell me how things stand between you and Arya. Have you spoken to her or her family about this? I have found it's unwise to let such matters fester."

"Aye," said Eragon, and stared at the length of polished hawthorn. "I spoke with her."

"To what end?" When Eragon did not immediately reply, Roran uttered a frustrated exclamation. "Getting answers out of you is harder than dragging Birka through the mud." Eragon chuckled at the mention of Birka, one of their draft horses. "Saphira, will you solve this puzzle for me? Otherwise, I fear I'll never get a full explanation."

"To no end. No end at all. She'll not have me." Eragon spoke dispassionately, as if commenting on a stranger's misfortune, but within him raged a torrent of hurt so deep and wild, he felt Saphira withdraw somewhat from him.

"I'm sorry," said Roran.

Eragon forced a swallow past the lump in his throat, past the bruise that was his heart, and down to the knotted skein of his stomach. "It happens."

"I know it may seem unlikely at the moment," said Roran, "but I'm sure you will meet another woman who will make you forget this Arya. There are countless maids—and more than a few married women, I'd wager—who would be delighted to catch the eye of a Rider. You'll have no trouble finding a wife among all the lovelies in Alagaësia."

"And what would you have done if Katrina rejected your suit?"

The question struck Roran dumb; it was obvious he could not imagine how he might have reacted.

Eragon continued. "Contrary to what you, Arya, and everyone else seem to believe, I *am* aware that other eligible women exist in Alagaësia and that people have been known to fall in love more than once. No doubt, if I spent my days in the company of ladies from King Orrin's court, I might indeed decide that I fancy one.

However, my path is not so easy as that. Regardless of whether I can shift my affections to another—and the heart, as you observed, is a notoriously fickle beast—the question remains: should I?"

"Your tongue has grown as twisted as the roots of a fir tree," said Roran. "Speak not in riddles."

"Very well: what human woman can begin to understand who and what I am, or the extent of my powers? Who could share in my life? Few enough, and all of them magicians. And of that select group, or even of women in general, how many are immortal?"

Roran laughed, a rough, hearty bellow that rang loud in the gulch. "You might as well ask for the sun in your pocket or—" He stopped and tensed as if he were about to spring forward and then became unnaturally still. "You cannot be."

"I am."

Roran struggled to find words. "Is it a result of your change in Ellesméra, or is it part of being a Rider?"

"Part of being a Rider."

"That explains why Galbatorix hasn't died."

"Aye."

The branch Roran had added to the fire burst asunder with a muted *pop* as the coals underneath heated the gnarled length of wood to the point where a small cache of water or sap that had somehow evaded the rays of the sun for untold decades exploded into steam.

"The idea is so . . . *vast*, it's almost inconceivable," said Roran. "Death is part of who we are. It guides us. It shapes us. It drives us to madness. Can you still be human if you have no mortal end?"

"I'm not invincible," Eragon pointed out. "I can still be killed with a sword or an arrow. And I can still catch some incurable disease."

"But if you avoid those dangers, you will live forever."

"If I do, then yes. Saphira and I will *endure*."

"It seems both a blessing and a curse."

"Aye. I cannot in good conscience marry a woman who will age and die while I remain untouched by time; such an experience would be equally cruel for both of us. On top of that, I find the thought of taking one wife after another throughout the long centuries rather depressing."

"Can you make someone immortal with magic?" asked Roran.

"You can darken white hair, you can smooth wrinkles and remove cataracts, and if you are willing to go to extraordinary lengths, you can give a sixty-year-old man the body he had at nineteen. However, the elves have never discovered a way to restore a person's mind without destroying his or her memories. And who wants to erase their identity every so many decades in exchange for immortality? It would be a stranger, then, who lived on. An old brain in a young body isn't the answer either, for even with the best of health, that which we humans are made of can only last for a century, perhaps a bit more. Nor can you just stop someone from aging. That causes a whole host of other problems. . . . Oh, elves and men have tried a thousand and one different ways to foil death, but none have proved successful."

28

"In other words," said Roran, "it's safer for you to love Arya than to leave your heart free for the taking by a human woman."

"Who else *can* I marry but an elf? Especially considering how I look now." Eragon quelled the desire to reach up and finger the curved tips of his ears, a habit he had fallen into. "When I lived in Ellesméra, it was easy for me to accept how the dragons had changed my appearance. After all, they gave me many gifts besides. Also, the elves were friendlier toward me after the Agaetí Blödhren. It was only when I rejoined the Varden that I realized how *different* I've become. . . . It bothers me too. I'm no longer just human, and I'm not quite an elf. I'm something else in between: a mix, a halfbreed."

"Cheer up!" said Roran. "You may not have to worry about living forever. Galbatorix, Murtagh, the Ra'zac, or even one of the Empire's soldiers could put steel through us at any moment. A wise man would ignore the future and drink and carouse while he still has an opportunity to enjoy this world."

"I know what Father would say to that."

"And he'd give us a good hiding to boot."

They shared a laugh, and then the silence that so often intruded on their discussion asserted itself once again, a gap born of equal parts weariness, familiarity, and—conversely—the many differences that fate had created between those who had once gone about lives that were but variations on a single melody.

You should sleep, said Saphira to Eragon and Roran. *It's late, and we must rise early tomorrow.*

Eragon looked at the black vault of the sky, judging the hour by how far the stars had rotated. The night was older than he expected. "Sound advice," he said. "I just wish we had a few more days to rest before we storm Helgrind. The battle on the Burning Plains drained all of Saphira's strength and my own, and we have not fully recovered, what with flying here and the energy I transferred into the belt of Beloth the Wise these past two evenings. My limbs still ache, and I have more bruises than I can count. Look. . . ." Loosening the ties on the cuff of his left shirtsleeve, he pushed back the soft lámarae— a fabric the elves made by cross-weaving wool and nettle threads— revealing a rancid yellow streak where his shield had mashed against his forearm.

"Ha!" said Roran. "You call that tiny little mark a bruise? I hurt myself worse when I bumped my toe this morning. Here, I'll show you a bruise a man can be proud of." He unlaced his left boot, pulled it off, and rolled up the leg of his trousers to expose a black stripe as wide as Eragon's thumb that slanted across his quadriceps. "I caught the haft of a spear as a soldier was turning about."

"Impressive, but I have even better." Ducking out of his tunic, Eragon yanked his shirt free of his trousers and twisted to the side so that Roran could see the large blotch on his ribs and the similar dis-coloration on his belly. "Arrows," he explained. Then he uncovered his right forearm, revealing a bruise that matched the one on his other arm, given when he had deflected a sword with his bracer.

Now Roran bared a collection of irregular blue-green spots, each the size of a gold coin, that marched from his left armpit down to the base of his spine, the result of having fallen upon a jumble of rocks and embossed armor.

Eragon inspected the lesions, then chuckled and said, "Pshaw, those are pinpricks! Did you get lost and run into a rosebush? I have one that puts those to shame." He removed both his boots, then stood and dropped his trousers, so that his only garb was his shirt and woolen underpants. "Top that if you can," he said, and pointed to the inside of his thighs. A riotous combination of colors mottled his skin, as if Eragon were an exotic fruit that was ripening in uneven patches from crabapple green to putrefied purple.

"Ouch," said Roran. "What happened?"

"I jumped off Saphira when we were fighting Murtagh and Thorn in the air. That's how I wounded Thorn. Saphira managed to dive under me and catch me before I hit the ground, but I landed on her back a bit harder than I wanted to."

Roran winced and shivered at the same time. "Does it go all the way . . ." He trailed off, and made a vague gesture upward.

"Unfortunately."

"I have to admit, that's a remarkable bruise. You should be proud; it's quite a feat to get injured in the manner you did and in that . . . *particular* . . . place."

"I'm glad you appreciate it."

"Well," said Roran, "you may have the biggest bruise, but the Ra'zac dealt me a wound the likes of which you cannot match, since the dragons, as I understand, removed the scar from your back." While he spoke, he divested himself of his shirt and moved farther into the pulsing light of the coals.

Eragon's eyes widened before he caught himself and concealed his shock behind a more neutral expression. He berated himself for overreacting, thinking, *It can't be that bad*, but the longer he studied Roran, the more dismayed he became.

A long, puckered scar, red and glossy, wrapped around Roran's right shoulder, starting at his collarbone and ending just past the middle of his arm. It was obvious that the Ra'zac had severed part of the muscle and that the two ends had failed to heal back together, for an unsightly bulge deformed the skin below the scar, where the underlying fibers had recoiled upon themselves. Farther up, the skin had sunk inward, forming a depression half an inch deep.

"Roran! You should have shown this to me days ago. I had no idea the Ra'zac hurt you so badly. . . . Do you have any difficulty moving your arm?"

"Not to the side or back," said Roran. He demonstrated. "But in the front, I can only lift my hand about as high as . . . midchest." Grimacing, he lowered his arm. "Even that's a struggle; I have to keep my thumb level, or else my arm goes dead. The best way I've found is to swing my arm around from behind and let it land on whatever I'm trying to grasp. I skinned my knuckles a few times before I mastered the trick."

Eragon twisted the staff between his hands. *Should I?* he asked Saphira.

I think you must.

We may regret it tomorrow.

You will have more cause for regret if Roran dies because he could not wield his hammer when the occasion demanded. If you draw upon the resources around us, you can avoid tiring yourself further.

You know I hate doing that. Even talking about it sickens me.

Our lives are more important than an ant's, Saphira countered.

Not to an ant.

And are you an ant? Don't be glib, Eragon; it ill becomes you.

With a sigh, Eragon put down the staff and beckoned to Roran. "Here, I'll heal that for you."

"You can do that?"

"Obviously."

A momentary surge of excitement brightened Roran's face, but then he hesitated and looked troubled. "Now? Is that wise?"

"As Saphira said, better I tend to you while I have the chance, lest your injury cost you your life or endanger the rest of us." Roran drew near, and Eragon placed his right hand over the red scar while, at the same time, expanding his consciousness to encompass the trees and the plants and the animals that populated the gulch, save those he feared were too weak to survive his spell.

Then Eragon began to chant in the ancient language. The incantation he recited was long and complex. Repairing such a wound went far beyond growing new skin and was a difficult matter at best. In this, Eragon relied upon the curative formulas that he had studied in Ellesméra and had devoted so many weeks to memorizing.

The silvery mark on Eragon's palm, the gedwëy ignasia, glowed white-hot as he released the magic. A second later, he uttered an involuntary groan as he died three times, once each with two small birds roosting in a nearby juniper and also with a snake hidden among the rocks. Across from him, Roran threw back his head and bared his teeth in a soundless howl as his shoulder muscle jumped and writhed beneath the surface of his shifting skin.

Then it was over.

Eragon inhaled a shuddering breath and rested his head in his hands, taking advantage of the concealment they provided to wipe away his tears before he examined the results of his labor. He saw Roran shrug several times and then stretch and windmill his arms. Roran's shoulder was large and round, the result of years spent digging holes for fence posts, hauling rocks, and pitching hay. Despite himself, a needle of envy pricked Eragon. He might be stronger, but he had never been as muscular as his cousin.

Roran grinned. "It's as good as ever! Better, maybe. Thank you."

"You're welcome."

"It was the strangest thing. I actually felt as if I was going to crawl out of my hide. And it itched something terrible; I could barely keep from ripping—"

"Get me some bread from your saddlebag, would you? I'm hungry."

"We just had dinner."

"I need a bite to eat after using magic like that." Eragon sniffed and then pulled out his kerchief and wiped his nose. He sniffed again.

What he had said was not quite true. It was the toll his spell had exacted on the wildlife that disturbed him, not the magic itself, and he feared he might throw up unless he had something to settle his stomach.

"You're not ill, are you?" asked Roran.

"No." With the memory of the deaths he had caused still heavy in his mind, Eragon reached for the jar of mead by his side, hoping to fend off a tide of morbid thoughts.

Something very large, heavy, and sharp struck his hand and pinned it against the ground. He winced and looked over to see the tip of one of Saphira's ivory claws digging into his flesh. Her thick eyelid went *snick* as it flashed across the great big glittering iris she fixed upon him. After a long moment, she lifted the claw, as a person would a finger, and Eragon withdrew his hand. He gulped and gripped the hawthorn staff once more, striving to ignore the mead and to concentrate upon what was immediate and tangible, instead of wallowing in dismal introspection.

Roran removed a ragged half of sourdough bread from his bags, then paused and, with a hint of a smile, said, "Wouldn't you rather have some venison? I didn't finish all of mine." He held out the makeshift spit of seared juniper wood, on which were impaled three clumps of golden brown meat. To Eragon's sensitive nose, the odor that wafted toward him was thick and pungent and reminded him of nights he had spent in the Spine and of long winter dinners where he, Roran, and Garrow had gathered around their stove and enjoyed each other's company while a blizzard howled outside. His mouth watered. "It's still warm," said Roran, and waved the venison in front of Eragon.

With an effort of will, Eragon shook his head. "Just give me the bread."

"Are you sure? It's perfect: not too tough, not too tender, and cooked with the perfect amount of seasoning. It's so juicy, when you take a bite, it's as if you swallowed a mouthful of Elain's best stew."

"No, I can't."

"You know you'll like it."

"Roran, stop teasing me and hand over that bread!"

"Ah, now see, you look better already. Maybe what you need isn't bread but someone to get your hackles up, eh?"

Eragon glowered at him, then, faster than the eye could see, snatched the bread away from Roran.

That seemed to amuse Roran even more. As Eragon tore at the loaf, he said, "I don't know how you can survive on nothing but fruit, bread, and vegetables. A man has to eat meat if he wants to keep his strength up. Don't you miss it?"

"More than you can imagine."

"Then why do you insist on torturing yourself like this? Every creature in this world has to eat other living beings—even if they are only plants—in order to survive. That is how we are made. Why attempt to defy the natural order of things?"

I said much the same in Ellesméra, observed Saphira, *but he did not listen to me.*

Eragon shrugged. "We already had this discussion. You do what you want. I won't tell you or anyone else how to live. However, I cannot in good conscience eat a beast whose thoughts and feelings I've shared."

The tip of Saphira's tail twitched, and her scales clinked against a worn dome of rock that protruded from the ground. *Oh, he's hopeless.* Lifting and extending her neck, Saphira nipped the venison, spit and all, from Roran's other hand. The wood cracked between her serrated teeth as she bit down, and then it and the meat vanished into the fiery depths of her belly. *Mmm. You did not exaggerate,* she said to Roran. *What a sweet and succulent morsel: so soft, so salty, so deliciously delectable, it makes me want to wiggle with delight. You should cook for me more often, Roran Stronghammer. Only next time, I think you should prepare several deer at once. Otherwise, I won't get a proper meal.*

Roran hesitated, as if unable to decide whether her request was serious and, if so, how he could politely extricate himself from such an unlooked-for and rather onerous obligation. He cast a pleading glance at Eragon, who burst out laughing, both at Roran's expression and at his predicament.

The rise and fall of Saphira's sonorous laugh joined with Eragon's and reverberated throughout the hollow. Her teeth gleamed madder red in the light from the embers.

An hour after the three of them had retired, Eragon was lying on his back alongside Saphira, muffled in layers of blankets against the night cold. All was still and quiet. It seemed as if a magician had placed an enchantment upon the earth and that everything in the world was bound in an eternal sleep and would remain frozen and unchanging forevermore underneath the watchful gaze of the twinkling stars.

Without moving, Eragon whispered in his mind: *Saphira?*

Yes, little one?

What if I'm right and he's in Helgrind? I don't know what I should do then. . . . Tell me what I should do.

I cannot, little one. This is a decision you have to make by yourself. The ways of men are not the ways of dragons. I would tear off his head and feast on his body, but that would be wrong for you, I think.

Will you stand by me, whatever I decide?

Always, little one. Now rest. All will be well.

Comforted, Eragon gazed into the void between the stars and slowed his breathing as he drifted into the trance that had replaced sleep for him. He remained conscious of his surroundings, but against the backdrop of the white constellations, the figures of his waking dreams strode forth and performed confused and shadowy plays, as was their wont.

ASSAULT ON HELGRIND

aybreak was fifteen minutes away when Eragon rolled upright. He snapped his fingers twice to wake Roran and then scooped up his blankets and knotted them into a tight bundle.

Pushing himself off the ground, Roran did likewise with his own bedding.

They looked at each other and shivered with excitement.

"If I die," said Roran, "you will see to Katrina?"

"I shall."

"Tell her then that I went into battle with joy in my heart and her name upon my lips."

"I shall."

Eragon muttered a quick line in the ancient language. The drop in his strength that followed was almost imperceptible. "There. That will filter the air in front of us and protect us from the paralyzing effects of the Ra'zac's breath."

From his bags, Eragon removed his shirt of mail and unwrapped the length of sackcloth he had stored it in. Blood from the fight on the Burning Plains still encrusted the once-shining corselet, and the combination of dried gore, sweat, and neglect had allowed blotches of rust to creep across the rings. The mail was, however, free of tears, as Eragon had repaired them before they had departed for the Empire.

Eragon donned the leather-backed shirt, wrinkling his nose at the stench of death and desperation that clung to it, then attached chased bracers to his forearms and greaves to his shins. Upon his head he placed a padded arming cap, a mail coif, and a plain steel helm. He had lost his own helm—the one he had worn in Farthen

Dûr and that the dwarves had engraved with the crest of Dûrgrimst Ingeitum—along with his shield during the aerial duel between Saphira and Thorn. On his hands went mailed gauntlets.

Roran outfitted himself in a similar manner, although he augmented his armor with a wooden shield. A band of soft iron wrapped around the lip of the shield, the better to catch and hold an enemy's sword. No shield encumbered Eragon's left arm; the hawthorn staff required two hands to wield properly.

Across his back, Eragon slung the quiver given to him by Queen Islanzadí. In addition to twenty heavy oak arrows fletched with gray goose feathers, the quiver contained the bow with silver fittings that the queen had sung out of a yew tree for him. The bow was already strung and ready for use.

Saphira kneaded the soil beneath her feet. *Let us be off!*

Leaving their bags and supplies hanging from the branch of a juniper tree, Eragon and Roran clambered onto Saphira's back. They wasted no time saddling her; she had worn her tack through the night. The molded leather was warm, almost hot, underneath Eragon. He clutched the neck spike in front of him—to steady himself during sudden changes in direction—while Roran hooked one thick arm around Eragon's waist and brandished his hammer with the other.

A piece of shale cracked under Saphira's weight as she settled into a low crouch and, in a single giddy bound, leaped up to the rim of the gulch, where she balanced for a moment before unfolding her massive wings. The thin membranes thrummed as Saphira raised them toward the sky. Vertical, they looked like two translucent blue sails.

"Not so tight," grunted Eragon.

"Sorry," said Roran. He loosened his embrace.

Further speech became impossible as Saphira jumped again. When she reached the pinnacle, she brought her wings down with a mighty *whoosh*, driving the three of them even higher. With each subsequent flap, they climbed closer to the flat, narrow clouds.

As Saphira angled toward Helgrind, Eragon glanced to his left and discovered that he could see a broad swath of Leona Lake some miles distant. A thick layer of mist, gray and ghostly in the predawn glow, emanated from the water, as if witchfire burned upon the surface of the liquid. Eragon tried, but even with his hawklike vision, he could not make out the far shore, nor the southern reaches of the Spine beyond, which he regretted. It had been too long since he had laid eyes upon the mountain range of his childhood.

To the north stood Dras-Leona, a huge, rambling mass that appeared as a blocky silhouette against the wall of mist that edged its western flank. The one building Eragon could identify was the cathedral where the Ra'zac had attacked him; its flanged spire loomed above the rest of the city, like a barbed spearhead.

And somewhere in the landscape that rushed past below, Eragon knew, were the remnants of the campsite where the Ra'zac had mortally wounded Brom. He allowed all of his anger and grief over the events of that day—as well as Garrow's murder and the destruction of their farm—to surge forth and give him the courage, nay, the *desire*, to face the Ra'zac in combat.

Eragon, said Saphira. *Today we need not guard our minds and keep our thoughts secret from one another, do we?*

Not unless another magician should appear.

A fan of golden light flared into existence as the top of the sun crested the horizon. In an instant, the full spectrum of colors enlivened the previously drab world: the mist glowed white, the water became a rich blue, the daubed-mud wall that encircled the center of Dras-Leona revealed its dingy yellow sides, the trees cloaked themselves in every shade of green, and the soil blushed red and orange. Helgrind, however, remained as it always was—black.

The mountain of stone rapidly grew larger as they approached. Even from the air, it was intimidating.

Diving toward the base of Helgrind, Saphira tilted so far to her left, Eragon and Roran would have fallen if they had not already strapped their legs to the saddle. Then she whipped around the apron of scree and over the altar where the priests of Helgrind observed their ceremonies. The lip of Eragon's helm caught the wind from her passage and produced a howl that almost deafened him.

"Well?" shouted Roran. He could not see in front of them.

"The slaves are gone!"

A great weight seemed to press Eragon into his seat as Saphira pulled out of her dive and spiraled up around Helgrind, searching for an entrance to the Ra'zac's hideout.

Not even a hole big enough for a woodrat, she declared. She slowed and hung in place before a ridge that connected the third lowest of the four peaks to the prominence above. The jagged buttress magnified the boom produced by each stroke of her wings until it was as loud as a thunderclap. Eragon's eyes watered as the air pulsed against his skin.

A web of white veins adorned the backside of the crags and pillars, where hoarfrost had collected in the cracks that furrowed the rock. Nothing else disturbed the gloom of Helgrind's inky, windswept ramparts. No trees grew among the slanting stones, nor shrubs, grass, or lichen, nor did eagles dare nest upon the tower's broken ledges. True to its name, Helgrind was a place of death, and stood cloaked in the razor-sharp, sawtooth folds of its scarps and clefts like a bony specter risen to haunt the earth.

Casting his mind outward, Eragon confirmed the presence of the two people whom he had discovered imprisoned within Helgrind the previous day, but he felt nothing of the slaves, and to his concern, he still could not locate the Ra'zac or the Lethrblaka. *If they aren't here, then where?* he wondered. Searching again, he noticed something that had eluded him before: a single flower, a gentian, blooming not fifty feet in front of them, where, by all rights, there ought to be solid rock. *How does it get enough light to live?*

Saphira answered his question by perching on a crumbling spur several feet to the right. As she did, she lost her balance for a moment and flared her wings to steady herself. Instead of brushing against the bulk of Helgrind, the tip of her right wing dipped into the rock and then back out again.

Saphira, did you see that!

I did.

Leaning forward, Saphira pushed the tip of her snout toward the sheer rock, paused an inch or two away—as if waiting for a trap to spring—then continued her advance. Scale by scale, Saphira's head slid into Helgrind, until all that was visible of her to Eragon was a neck, torso, and wings.

It's an illusion! exclaimed Saphira.

With a surge of her mighty thews, she abandoned the spur and flung the rest of her body after her head. It required every bit of Eragon's self-control not to cover his face in a desperate bid to protect himself as the crag rushed toward him.

An instant later, he found himself looking at a broad, vaulted

cave suffused with the warm glow of morning. Saphira's scales refracted the light, casting thousands of shifting blue flecks across the rock. Twisting around, Eragon saw no wall behind them, only the mouth of the cave and a sweeping view of the landscape beyond.

Eragon grimaced. It had never occurred to him that Galbatorix might have hidden the Ra'zac's lair with magic. *Idiot! I have to do better,* he thought. Underestimating the king was a sure way to get them all killed.

Roran swore and said, "Warn me before you do something like that again."

Hunching forward, Eragon began to unbuckle his legs from the saddle as he studied their surroundings, alert for danger.

The opening to the cave was an irregular oval, perhaps fifty feet high and sixty feet wide. From there the chamber expanded to twice that size before ending a good bowshot away in a pile of thick stone slabs that leaned against each other in a confusion of uncertain angles. A mat of scratches defaced the floor, evidence of the many times the Lethrblaka had taken off from, landed on, and walked about its surface. Like mysterious keyholes, five low tunnels pierced the sides of the cave, as did a lancet passageway large enough to accommodate Saphira. Eragon examined the tunnels carefully, but they were pitch-black and appeared vacant, a fact he confirmed with quick thrusts of his mind. Strange, disjointed murmurs echoed from within Helgrind's innards, suggesting unknown *things* scurrying about in the dark, and endlessly dripping water. Adding to the chorus of whispers was the steady rise and fall of Saphira's breathing, which was over-loud in the confines of the bare chamber.

The most distinctive feature of the cavern, however, was the mixture of odors that pervaded it. The smell of cold stone domi-nated, but underneath Eragon discerned whiffs of damp and mold and something far worse: the sickly sweet fetor of rotting meat.

Undoing the last few straps, Eragon swung his right leg over Saphira's spine, so he was sitting sidesaddle, and prepared to jump off her back. Roran did the same on the opposite side.

Before he released his hold, Eragon heard, amid the many rustlings that teased his ear, a score of simultaneous clicks, as if someone had struck the rock with a collection of hammers. The sound repeated itself a half second later.

He looked in the direction of the noise, as did Saphira.

A huge, twisted shape hurtled out of the lancet passageway. Eyes black, bulging, rimless. A beak seven feet long. Batlike wings. The torso naked, hairless, rippling with muscle. Claws like iron spikes.

Saphira lurched as she tried to evade the Lethrblaka, but to no avail. The creature crashed into her right side with what felt to Eragon like the strength and fury of an avalanche.

What exactly happened next, he knew not, for the impact sent him tumbling through space without so much as a half-formed thought in his jumbled brain. His blind flight ended as abruptly as it began when something hard and flat rammed against the back of him, and he dropped to the floor, banging his head a second time.

That last collision drove the remaining air clean out of Eragon's lungs. Stunned, he lay curled on his side, gasping and struggling to regain a semblance of control over his unresponsive limbs.

Eragon! cried Saphira.

The concern in her voice fueled Eragon's efforts as nothing else could. As life returned to his arms and legs, he reached out and grasped his staff from where it had fallen beside him. He planted the spike mounted on the staff's lower end into a nearby crack and pulled himself up the hawthorn rod and onto his feet. He swayed. A swarm of crimson sparks danced before him.

The situation was so confusing, he hardly knew where to look first.

Saphira and the Lethrblaka rolled across the cave, kicking and clawing and snapping at each other with enough force to gouge the rock beneath them. The clamor of their fight must have been unimaginably loud, but to Eragon they grappled in silence; his ears did not work. Still, he felt the vibrations through the soles of his feet as the colossal beasts thrashed from side to side, threatening to crush anyone who came near them.

A torrent of blue fire erupted from between Saphira's jaws and bathed the left side of the Lethrblaka's head in a ravening inferno hot enough to melt steel. The flames curved around the Lethrblaka without harming it. Undeterred, the monster pecked at Saphira's neck, forcing her to stop and defend herself.

Fast as an arrow loosed from a bow, the second Lethrblaka darted out of the lancet passageway, pounced upon Saphira's flank, and, opening its narrow beak, uttered a horrible, withering shriek that made Eragon's scalp prickle and a cold lump of dread form in his gut. He snarled in discomfort; *that* he could hear.

The smell now, with both Lethrblaka present, resembled the sort of overpowering stench one would get from tossing a half-dozen pounds of rancid meat into a barrel of sewage and allowing the mixture to ferment for a week in summer.

Eragon clamped his mouth shut as his gorge rose and turned his attention elsewhere to keep from retching.

A few paces away, Roran lay crumpled against the side of the cave, where he too had landed. Even as Eragon watched, his cousin lifted an arm and pushed himself onto all fours and then to his feet. His eyes were glazed, and he tottered as if drunk.

Behind Roran, the two Ra'zac emerged from a nearby tunnel. They wielded long, pale blades of an ancient design in their malformed hands. Unlike their parents, the Ra'zac were roughly the same size and shape as humans. An ebony exoskeleton encased them from top to bottom, although little of it showed, for even in Helgrind, the Ra'zac wore dark robes and cloaks.

They advanced with startling swiftness, their movements sharp and jerky like those of an insect.

And yet, Eragon still could not sense them or the Lethrblaka. *Are they an illusion too?* he wondered. But no, that was nonsense; the flesh Saphira tore at with her talons was real enough. Another explanation occurred to him: perhaps it was *impossible* to detect their presence. Perhaps the Ra'zac could conceal themselves from the minds of humans, their prey, just as spiders conceal themselves from flies. If so, then Eragon finally understood why the Ra'zac had been so successful hunting magicians and Riders for Galbatorix when they themselves could not use magic.

Blast! Eragon would have indulged in more colorful oaths, but it was time for action, not cursing their bad luck. Brom had claimed the Ra'zac were no match for him in broad daylight, and while that might have been true—given that Brom had had decades to invent spells to use against the Ra'zac—Eragon knew that, without the advantage of surprise, he, Saphira, and Roran would be hard-pressed to escape with their lives, much less rescue Katrina.

Raising his right hand above his head, Eragon cried, *"Brisingr!"* and threw a roaring fireball toward the Ra'zac. They dodged, and the fireball splashed against the rock floor, guttered for a moment, and then winked out of existence. The spell was silly and childish and could cause no conceivable damage if Galbatorix had protected the Ra'zac like the Lethrblaka. Still, Eragon found the attack immensely satisfying. It also distracted the Ra'zac long enough for Eragon to dash over to Roran and press his back against his cousin's.

"Hold them off for a minute," he shouted, hoping Roran would hear. Whether he did or not, Roran grasped Eragon's meaning, for he covered himself with his shield and lifted his hammer in preparation to fight.

The amount of force contained within each of the Lethrblaka's terrible blows had already depleted the wards against physical danger that Eragon had placed around Saphira. Without them, the Lethrblaka had inflicted several rows of scratches—long but shallow—along her thighs and had managed to stab her three times with their beaks; those wounds were short but deep and caused her a great deal of pain.

In return, Saphira had laid open the ribs of one Lethrblaka and had bitten off the last three feet of the other's tail. The Lethrblaka's blood, to Eragon's astonishment, was a metallic blue-green, not unlike the verdigris that forms on aged copper.

At the moment, the Lethrblaka had withdrawn from Saphira and were circling her, lunging now and then in order to keep her at bay while they waited for her to tire or until they could kill her with a stab from one of their beaks.

Saphira was better suited than the Lethrblaka to open combat by virtue of her scales—which were harder and tougher than the Lethrblaka's gray hide—and her teeth—which were far more lethal in close quarters than the Lethrblaka's beaks—but despite all that, she had difficulty fending off both creatures at once, especially since the ceiling prevented her from leaping and flying about and otherwise outmaneuvering her foes. Eragon feared that even if she prevailed, the Lethrblaka would maim her before she slew them.

Taking a quick breath, Eragon cast a single spell that contained every one of the twelve techniques of killing that Oromis had taught him. He was careful to phrase the incantation as a series of processes, so that if Galbatorix's wards foiled him, he could sever the flow of magic. Otherwise, the spell might consume his strength until he died.

It was well he took the precaution. Upon release of the spell, Eragon quickly became aware that the magic was having no effect upon the Lethrblaka, and he abandoned the assault. He had not expected to succeed with the traditional death-words, but he had to try, on the slight chance Galbatorix might have been careless or ignorant when he had placed wards upon the Lethrblaka and their spawn.

Behind him, Roran shouted, "Yah!" An instant later, a sword thudded against his shield, followed by the tinkle of rippling mail and the bell-like peal of a second sword bouncing off Roran's helm.

Eragon realized that his hearing must be improving.

The Ra'zac struck again and again, but each time their weapons glanced off Roran's armor or missed his face and limbs by a hairsbreadth, no matter how fast they swung their blades. Roran was too slow to retaliate, but neither could the Ra'zac harm him. They hissed with frustration and spewed a continuous stream of invectives, which seemed all the more foul because of how the creatures' hard, clacking jaws mangled the language.

Eragon smiled. The cocoon of charms he had spun around Roran had done its job. He hoped the invisible net of energy would hold until he could find a way to halt the Lethrblaka.

Everything shivered and went gray around Eragon as the two Lethrblaka shrieked in unison. For a moment, his resolve deserted him, leaving him unable to move, then he rallied and shook himself as a dog might, casting off their fell influence. The sound reminded him of nothing so much as a pair of children screaming in pain.

Then Eragon began to chant as fast as he could without mispronouncing the ancient language. Each sentence he uttered, and they were legion, contained the potential to deliver instant death, and each death was unique among its fellows. As he recited his

45

improvised soliloquy, Saphira received another cut upon her left flank. In return, she broke the wing of her assailant, slashing the thin flight membrane into ribbons with her claws. A number of heavy impacts transmitted themselves from Roran's back to Eragon's as the Ra'zac hacked and stabbed in a lightning-quick frenzy. The largest of the two Ra'zac began to edge around Roran, in order to attack Eragon directly.

And then, amid the din of steel against steel, and steel against wood, and claws against stone, there came the scrape of a sword sliding through mail, followed by a wet crunch. Roran yelled, and Eragon felt blood splash across the calf of his right leg.

Out of the corner of one eye, Eragon watched as a humpbacked figure leaped toward him, extending its leaf-bladed sword so as to impale him. The world seemed to contract around the thin, narrow point; the tip glittered like a shard of crystal, each scratch a thread of quicksilver in the bright light of dawn.

He only had time for one more spell before he would have to devote himself to stopping the Ra'zac from inserting the sword between his liver and kidneys. In desperation, he gave up trying to directly harm the Lethrblaka and instead cried, "Garjzla, letta!"

It was a crude spell, constructed in haste and poorly worded, yet it worked. The bulbous eyes of the Lethrblaka with the broken wing became a matched set of mirrors, each a perfect hemisphere, as Eragon's magic reflected the light that otherwise would have entered the Lethrblaka's pupils. Blind, the creature stumbled and flailed at the air in a vain attempt to hit Saphira.

Eragon spun the hawthorn staff in his hands and knocked aside the Ra'zac's sword when it was less than an inch from his ribs. The Ra'zac landed in front of him and jutted out its neck. Eragon recoiled as a short, thick beak appeared from within the depths of its hood. The chitinous appendage snapped shut just short of his right eye. In a rather detached way, Eragon noticed that the Ra'zac's tongue was barbed and purple and writhed like a headless snake.

Bringing his hands together at the center of the staff, Eragon drove his arms forward, striking the Ra'zac across its hollow chest and throwing the monster back several yards. It fell upon its hands and knees. Eragon pivoted around Roran, whose left side was slick with blood, and parried the sword of the other Ra'zac. He feinted, beat the Ra'zac's blade, and, when the Ra'zac stabbed at his throat, whirled the other half of the staff across his body and deflected the thrust. Without pausing, Eragon lunged forward and planted the wooden end of the staff in the Ra'zac's abdomen.

If Eragon had been wielding Zar'roc, he would have killed the Ra'zac then and there. As it was, something cracked inside the Ra'zac, and the creature went rolling across the cave for a dozen or more paces. It immediately popped up again, leaving a smear of blue gore on the uneven rock.

I need a sword, thought Eragon.

He widened his stance as the two Ra'zac converged upon him; he had no choice but to hold his ground and face their combined on-slaught, for he was all that stood between those hook-clawed carrion crows and Roran. He began to mouth the same spell that had proved itself against the Lethrblaka, but the Ra'zac executed high and low slashes before he could utter a syllable.

The swords rebounded off the hawthorn with a dull *bonk*. They did not dent or otherwise mar the enchanted wood.

Left, right, up, down. Eragon did not think; he acted and reacted as he exchanged a flurry of blows with the Ra'zac. The staff was ideal for fighting multiple opponents, as he could strike and block with both ends, and often simultaneously. That ability served him well now. He panted, each breath short and quick. Sweat dripped from his brow and gathered at the corners of his eyes, and a layer greased his back and the undersides of his arms. The red haze of battle dimmed his vision and throbbed in response to the convulsions of his heart.

He never felt so alive, or afraid, as he did when fighting.

Eragon's own wards were scant. Since he had lavished the bulk of his attention on Saphira and Roran, Eragon's magical defenses soon failed, and the smaller Ra'zac wounded him on the outside of his left knee. The injury was not life-threatening, but it was still serious, for his left leg would no longer support his full weight.

Gripping the spike at the bottom, Eragon swung the staff like a club and bashed one Ra'zac upside the head. The Ra'zac collapsed, but whether it was dead or only unconscious, Eragon could not tell. Advancing upon the remaining Ra'zac, he battered the creature's arms and shoulders and, with a sudden twist, knocked the sword out of its hand.

Before Eragon could finish off the Ra'zac, the blinded, broken-winged Lethrblaka flew the width of the cave and slammed against the far wall, knocking loose a shower of stone flakes from the ceiling. The sight and sound were so colossal, they caused Eragon, Roran, and the Ra'zac to flinch and turn, simply out of instinct.

Jumping after the crippled Lethrblaka, which she had just kicked, Saphira sank her teeth into the back of the creature's sinewy neck. The Lethrblaka thrashed in one final effort to free itself, and then Saphira whipped her head from side to side and broke its spine. Rising from her bloody kill, Saphira filled the cave with a savage roar of victory.

The remaining Lethrblaka did not hesitate. Tackling Saphira, it dug its claws underneath the edges of her scales and pulled her into an uncontrolled tumble. Together they rolled to the lip of the cave, teetered for a half second, and then dropped out of sight, battling the whole way. It was a clever tactic, for it carried the Lethrblaka out of the range of Eragon's senses, and that which he could not sense, he had difficulty casting a spell against.

Saphira! cried Eragon.

Tend to yourself. This one won't escape me.

With a start, Eragon whirled around just in time to see the two Ra'zac vanish into the depths of the nearest tunnel, the smaller supporting the larger. Closing his eyes, Eragon located the minds of the prisoners in Helgrind, muttered a burst of the ancient language, then said to Roran, "I sealed off Katrina's cell so the Ra'zac can't use her as a hostage. Only you and I can open the door now."

"Good," said Roran through clenched teeth. "Can you do something about this?" He jerked his chin toward the spot he had clamped his right hand over. Blood welled between his fingers. Eragon probed the wound. As soon as he touched it, Roran flinched and recoiled.

"You're lucky," said Eragon. "The sword hit a rib." Placing one hand on the injury and the other on the twelve diamonds concealed inside the belt of Beloth the Wise strapped around his waist, Eragon drew upon the power he had stored within the gems. "Waíse heill!" A ripple traversed Roran's side as the magic knit his skin and muscle back together again.

Then Eragon healed his own wound: the gash on his left knee.

Finished, he straightened and glanced in the direction that Saphira had gone. His connection with her was fading as she chased the Lethrblaka toward Leona Lake. He yearned to help her but knew that, for the time being, she would have to fend for herself.

"Hurry," said Roran. "They're getting away!"

"Right."

Hefting his staff, Eragon approached the unlit tunnel and flicked his gaze from one stone protrusion to another, expecting the Ra'zac to spring out from behind one of them. He moved slowly in order that his footsteps would not echo in the winding shaft. When he happened to touch a rock to steady himself, he found it coated in slime.

After a score of yards, several folds and twists in the passageway hid the main cavern and plunged them into a gloom so profound, even Eragon found it impossible to see.

"Maybe you're different, but I can't fight in the dark," whispered Roran.

"If I make a light, the Ra'zac won't come near us, not when I now know a spell that works on them. They'll just hide until we leave. We have to kill them while we have the chance."

"What am I supposed to do? I'm more likely to run into a wall and break my nose than I am to find those two beetles. . . . They could sneak around behind us and stab us in the back."

"Shh. . . . Hold on to my belt, follow me, and be ready to duck."

Eragon could not see, but he could still hear, smell, touch, and taste, and those faculties were sensitive enough that he had a fair idea of what lay nearby. The greatest danger was that the Ra'zac would attack from a distance, perhaps with a bow, but he trusted that his reflexes were sharp enough to save Roran and himself from an oncoming missile.

A current of air tickled Eragon's skin, then paused and reversed itself as pressure from the outside waxed and waned. The cycle repeated itself at inconsistent intervals, creating invisible eddies that brushed against him like fountains of roiling water.

His breathing, and Roran's, was loud and ragged compared with the odd assortment of sounds that propagated through the tunnel. Above the gusts of their respiration, Eragon caught the *tink, clink, clatter* of a stone falling somewhere in the tangle of branching tubes and the steady *doink . . . doink . . . doink* of condensed droplets striking the drumlike surface of a subterranean pool. He also heard the grind of pea-sized gravel crushed underneath the soles of his boots. A long, eerie moan wavered somewhere far ahead of them.

Of smells, none were new: sweat, blood, damp, and mold.

Step by step, Eragon led the way as they burrowed farther into the bowels of Helgrind. The tunnel slanted downward and often split or turned, so that Eragon would have soon been lost if he had not been able to use Katrina's mind as a reference point. The various knobby holes were low and cramped. Once, when Eragon bumped his head against the ceiling, a sudden flare of claustrophobia unnerved him.

I'm back, Saphira announced just as Eragon put his foot on a rugged step hewn out of the rock below him. He paused. She had escaped additional injury, which relieved him.

And the Lethrblaka?

Floating belly-up in Leona Lake. I'm afraid that some fishermen saw our battle. They were rowing toward Dras-Leona when I last saw them.

Well, it can't be helped. See what you can find in the tunnel the Lethrblaka came out of. And keep an eye out for the Ra'zac. They may try to slip past us and escape Helgrind through the entrance we used.

They probably have a bolt-hole at ground level.

Probably, but I don't think they'll run quite yet.

After what seemed like an hour trapped in the darkness—though Eragon knew it could not have been more than ten or fifteen minutes—and after descending more than a hundred feet through Helgrind, Eragon stopped on a level patch of stone. Transmitting his thoughts to Roran, he said, *Katrina's cell is about fifty feet in front of us, on the right.*

We can't risk letting her out until the Ra'zac are dead or gone.

What if they won't reveal themselves until we do let her out? For some reason, I can't sense them. They could hide from me until doomsday in here. So do we wait for who knows how long, or do we free Katrina while we still have the chance? I can place some wards around her that should protect her from most attacks.

Roran was quiet for a second. *Let's free her, then.*

They began to move forward again, feeling their way along the squat corridor with its rough, unfinished floor. Eragon had to devote most of his attention to his footing in order to maintain his balance.

As a result, he almost missed the swish of cloth sliding over cloth and then the faint *twang* that emanated from off to his right.

He recoiled against the wall, shoving Roran back. At the same time, something augered past his face, carving a groove of flesh from his right cheek. The thin trench burned as if cauterized.

"Kveykva!" shouted Eragon.

Red light, bright as the midday sun, flared into existence. It had no source, and thus it illuminated every surface evenly and without shadows, giving things a curious flat appearance. The sudden blaze dazzled Eragon, but it did more than that to the lone Ra'zac in front of him; the creature dropped its bow, covered its hooded face, and screamed high and shrill. A similar screech told Eragon that the second Ra'zac was behind them.

Roran!

Eragon pivoted just in time to see Roran charge the other Ra'zac, hammer held high. The disoriented monster stumbled backward but was too slow. The hammer fell. "For my father!" shouted Roran. He struck again. "For our home!" The Ra'zac was already dead, but Roran lifted the hammer once more. "For Carvahall!" His final blow shattered the Ra'zac's carapace like the rind of a dry gourd. In the merciless ruby glare, the spreading pool of blood appeared purple.

Spinning his staff in a circle to knock aside the arrow or sword that he was convinced was driving toward him, Eragon turned to confront the remaining Ra'zac. The tunnel before them was empty. He swore.

Eragon strode over to the twisted figure on the floor. He swung the staff over his head and brought it down across the chest of the dead Ra'zac with a resounding thud.

"I've waited a long time to do that," said Eragon.

"As have I."

He and Roran looked at each other.

"Ahh!" cried Eragon, and clutched his cheek as the pain intensified.

"It's bubbling!" exclaimed Roran. "Do something!"

The Ra'zac must have coated the arrowhead with Seithr oil, thought Eragon. Remembering his training, he cleansed the wound and surrounding tissue with an incantation and then repaired the damage to his face. He opened and closed his mouth several times to make sure the muscles were working properly. With a grim smile, he said, "Imagine the state we'd be in without magic."

"Without magic, we wouldn't have Galbatorix to worry about."

Talk later, said Saphira. *As soon as those fishermen reach Dras-Leona, the king may hear of our doings from one of his pet spellcasters in the city, and we do not want Galbatorix scrying Helgrind while we are still here.*

Yes, yes, said Eragon. Extinguishing the omnipresent red glow, he said, "Brisingr raudhr," and created a red werelight like that from the previous night, except that this one remained anchored six inches from the ceiling instead of accompanying Eragon wherever he went.

Now that he had an opportunity to examine the tunnel in some detail, Eragon saw that the stone hallway was dotted with twenty or so ironbound doors, some on either side. He pointed and said, "Ninth down, on the right. You go get her. I'll check the other cells. The Ra'zac might have left something interesting in them."

Roran nodded. Crouching, he searched the corpse at their feet but found no keys. He shrugged. "I'll do it the hard way, then." He sprinted to the proper door, abandoned his shield, and set to work on the hinges with his hammer. Each blow created a frightful crash.

Eragon did not offer to help. His cousin would not want or appreciate assistance now, and besides, there was something else Eragon had to do. He went to the first cell, whispered three words, then, after the lock snapped open, pushed aside the door. All that the small room contained was a black chain and a pile of rotting bones. Those sad remains were no more than he had expected; he already knew where the object of his search lay, but he maintained the charade of ignorance to avoid kindling Roran's suspicion.

Two more doors opened and closed beneath the touch of Eragon's fingers. Then, at the fourth cell, the door swung back to admit the shifting radiance of the werelight and reveal the very man Eragon had hoped he would not find: Sloan.

DIVERGENCE

The butcher sat slumped against the left-hand wall, both arms chained to an iron ring above his head.

His ragged clothes barely covered his pale, emaciated body; the corners of his bones stood out in sharp relief underneath his translucent skin. His blue veins were also prominent. Sores had formed on his wrists where the manacles chafed. The ulcers oozed a mixture of clear fluid and blood. What remained of his hair had turned gray or white and hung in lank, greasy ropes over his pock-marked face.

Roused by the clang of Roran's hammer, Sloan lifted his chin toward the light and, in a quavering voice, asked, "Who is it? Who's there?" His hair parted and slid back, exposing his eye sockets, which had sunk deep into his skull. Where his eyelids should have been, there were now only a few scraps of tattered skin draped over the raw cavities underneath. The area around them was bruised and scabbed.

With a shock, Eragon realized that the Ra'zac had pecked out Sloan's eyes.

What he then should do, Eragon could not decide. The butcher had told the Ra'zac that Eragon had found Saphira's egg. Furthermore, Sloan had murdered the watchman, Byrd, and had betrayed Carvahall to the Empire. If he were brought before his fellow villagers, they would undoubtedly find Sloan guilty and condemn him to death by hanging.

It seemed only right, to Eragon, that the butcher should die for his crimes. That was not the source of his uncertainty. Rather, it arose from the fact that Roran loved Katrina, and Katrina, whatever

Sloan had done, must still harbor a certain degree of affection for her father. Watching an arbitrator publicly denounce Sloan's offenses and then hang him would be no easy thing for her or, by extension, Roran. Such hardship might even create enough ill will between them to end their engagement. Either way, Eragon was convinced that taking Sloan back with them would sow discord between him, Roran, Katrina, and the other villagers, and might engender enough anger to distract them from their struggle against the Empire.

The easiest solution, thought Eragon, *would be to kill him and say that I found him dead in the cell.* . . . His lips trembled, one of the death-words heavy upon his tongue.

"What do you want?" asked Sloan. He turned his head from side to side in an attempt to hear better. "I already told you everything I know!"

Eragon cursed himself for hesitating. Sloan's guilt was not in dispute; he was a murderer and a traitor. Any lawgiver would sentence him to execution.

Notwithstanding the merit of those arguments, it was Sloan who was curled in front of him, a man Eragon had known his entire life. The butcher might be a despicable person, but the wealth of memories and experiences Eragon shared with him bred a sense of intimacy that troubled Eragon's conscience. To strike down Sloan would be like raising his hand against Horst or Loring or any of the elders of Carvahall.

Again Eragon prepared to utter the fatal word.

An image appeared in his mind's eye: *Torkenbrand, the slaver he and Murtagh had encountered during their flight to the Varden, kneeling on the dusty ground and Murtagh striding up to him and beheading him.* Eragon remembered how he had objected to Murtagh's deed and how it had troubled him for days afterward.

Have I changed so much, he asked himself, *that I can do the same thing now? As Roran said, I have killed, but only in the heat of battle . . . never like this.*

He glanced over his shoulder as Roran broke the last hinge to Katrina's cell door. Dropping his hammer, Roran prepared to charge the door and knock it inward but then appeared to think better of it and tried to lift it free of its frame. The door rose a fraction of an inch, then halted and wobbled in his grip. "Give me a hand here!" he shouted. "I don't want it to fall on her."

Eragon looked back at the wretched butcher. He had no more time for mindless wanderings. He had to choose. One way or another, he had to choose. . . .

"Eragon!"

I don't know what's right, realized Eragon. His own uncertainty told him that it would be wrong to kill Sloan or return him to the Varden. He had no idea what he should do instead, except to find a third path, one that was less obvious and less violent.

Lifting his hand, as if in benediction, Eragon whispered, "Slytha." Sloan's manacles rattled as he went limp, falling into a profound sleep. As soon as he was sure the spell had taken hold, Eragon closed and locked the cell door again and replaced his wards around it.

What are you up to, Eragon? asked Saphira.

Wait until we're together again. I'll explain then.

Explain what? You don't have a plan.

Give me a minute and I will.

"What was in there?" asked Roran as Eragon took his place opposite him.

"Sloan." Eragon adjusted his grip on the door between them. "He's dead."

Roran's eyes widened. "How?"

"Looks like they broke his neck."

For an instant, Eragon feared that Roran might not believe him. Then his cousin grunted and said, "It's better that way, I suppose. Ready? One, two, three—"

Together, they heaved the massive door out of its casing and threw it across the hallway. The stone passageway returned the resulting boom to them again and again. Without pause, Roran rushed into the cell, which was lit by a single wax taper. Eragon followed a step behind.

Katrina cowered at the far end of an iron cot. "Let me alone, you toothless bastards! I—" She stopped, struck dumb as Roran stepped forward. Her face was white from lack of sun and streaked with filth, yet at that moment, a look of such wonder and tender love blossomed upon her features, Eragon thought he had rarely seen anyone so beautiful.

Never taking her eyes off Roran, Katrina stood and, with a shaking hand, touched his cheek.

"You came."

"I came."

A laughing sob broke out of Roran, and he folded her in his arms, pulling her against his chest. They remained lost in their embrace for a long moment.

Drawing back, Roran kissed her three times on the lips. Katrina wrinkled her nose and exclaimed, "You grew a beard!" Of all the things she could have said, that was so unexpected—and she sounded so shocked and surprised—that Eragon chuckled in response.

For the first time, Katrina seemed to notice him. She glanced him over, then settled on his face, which she studied with evident puzzlement. "Eragon? Is that you?"

"Aye."

"He's a Dragon Rider now," said Roran.

"A Rider? You mean . . ." She faltered; the revelation seemed to overwhelm her. Glancing at Roran, as if for protection, she held him even closer and sidled around him, away from Eragon. To Roran, she said, "How . . . how did you find us? Who else is with you?"

"All that later. We have to get out of Helgrind before the rest of the Empire comes running after us."

"Wait! What about my father? Did you find him?"

Roran looked at Eragon, then returned his gaze to Katrina and gently said, "We were too late."

57

A shiver ran through Katrina. She closed her eyes, and a solitary tear leaked down the side of her face. "So be it."

While they spoke, Eragon frantically tried to figure out how to dispose of Sloan, although he concealed his deliberations from Saphira; he knew that she would disapprove of the direction his thoughts were taking. A scheme began to form in his mind. It was an outlandish concept, fraught with danger and uncertainty, but it was the only viable path, given the circumstances.

Abandoning further reflection, Eragon sprang into action. He had much to do in little time. "Jierda!" he cried, pointing. With a burst of blue sparks and flying fragments, the metal bands riveted around Katrina's ankles broke apart. Katrina jumped in surprise.

"Magic . . . ," she whispered.

"A simple spell." She shrank from his touch as he reached toward her. "Katrina, I have to make sure that Galbatorix or one of his magicians hasn't enchanted you with any traps or forced you to swear things in the ancient language."

"The ancient—"

Roran interrupted her: "Eragon! Do this when we make camp. We can't stay here."

"No." Eragon slashed his arm through the air. "We do it now." Scowling, Roran moved aside and allowed Eragon to put his hands on Katrina's shoulders. "Just look into my eyes," he told her. She nodded and obeyed.

That was the first time Eragon had a reason to use the spells Oromis had taught him for detecting the work of another spellcaster, and he had difficulty remembering every word from the scrolls in Ellesméra. The gaps in his memory were so serious that on three different instances he had to rely upon a synonym to complete an incantation.

For a long while, Eragon stared into Katrina's glistening eyes and mouthed phrases in the ancient language, occasionally—and with her permission—examining one of her memories for evidence that someone had tampered with it. He was as gentle as possible, unlike the Twins, who had ravaged his own mind in a similar procedure the day he arrived at Farthen Dûr.

Roran stood guard, pacing back and forth in front of the open doorway. Every second that went by increased his agitation; he twirled his hammer and tapped the head of it against his upper thigh, as if keeping time with a piece of music.

At last Eragon released Katrina. "I'm done."

"What did you find?" she whispered. She hugged herself, her forehead creased with worry lines as she waited for his verdict. Silence filled the cell as Roran came to a standstill.

"Nothing but your own thoughts. You are free of any spells."

"Of course she is," growled Roran, and again wrapped her in his arms.

Together, the three of them exited the cell. "Brisingr, iet tauthr," said Eragon, gesturing at the werelight that still floated near the ceiling of the hallway. At his command, the glowing orb darted to a spot directly over his head and remained there, bobbing like a piece of driftwood in the surf.

Eragon took the lead as they hurried back through the jumble of tunnels toward the cavern where they had landed. As he trotted across the slick rock, he watched for the remaining Ra'zac while, at the same time, erecting wards to safeguard Katrina. Behind him, he heard her and Roran exchange a series of brief phrases and lone words: "I love you . . . Horst and others safe . . . Always . . . For you . . . Yes . . . Yes . . . Yes . . . Yes." The trust and affection they shared were so obvious, it roused a dull ache of longing inside Eragon.

When they were about ten yards from the main cavern and could just begin to see by the faint glow ahead of them, Eragon extinguished the werelight. A few feet later, Katrina slowed, then pressed herself against the side of the tunnel and covered her face. "I can't. It's too bright; my eyes hurt."

Roran quickly moved in front of her, casting her in his shadow. "When was the last time you were outside?"

"I don't know. . . ." A hint of panic crept into her voice. "I don't know! Not since they brought me here. Roran, am I going blind?" She sniffed and began to cry.

Her tears surprised Eragon. He remembered her as someone of great strength and fortitude. But then, she had spent many weeks locked in the dark, fearing for her life. *I might not be myself either, if I were in her place.*

"No, you're fine. You just need to get used to the sun again." Roran stroked her hair. "Come on, don't let this upset you. Everything is going to be all right. . . . You're safe now. *Safe*, Katrina. You hear me?"

"I hear you."

Although he hated to ruin one of the tunics the elves had given him, Eragon tore off a strip of cloth from the bottom edge of his garment. He handed it to Katrina and said, "Tie this over your eyes. You should be able to see through it well enough to keep from falling or running into anything."

She thanked him and then blindfolded herself.

Once again advancing, the trio emerged into the sunny, blood-splattered main cavern—which stank worse than before, owing to the noxious fumes that drifted from the body of the Lethrblaka—even as Saphira appeared from within the depths of the lancet opening opposite them. Seeing her, Katrina gasped and clung to Roran, digging her fingers into his arms.

Eragon said, "Katrina, allow me to introduce you to Saphira. I am her Rider. She can understand if you speak to her."

"It is an honor, O dragon," Katrina managed to say. She dipped her knees in a weak imitation of a curtsy.

Saphira inclined her head in return. Then she faced Eragon. *I searched the Lethrblaka's nest, but all I found was bones, bones, and more bones, including several that smelled of fresh meat. The Ra'zac must have eaten the slaves last night.*

I wish we could have rescued them.

I know, but we cannot protect everyone in this war.

Gesturing at Saphira, Eragon said, "Go on; climb onto her. I'll join you in a moment."

Katrina hesitated, then glanced at Roran, who nodded and murmured, "It's all right. Saphira brought us here." Together, the couple skirted the corpse of the Lethrblaka as they went over to Saphira, who crouched flat upon her belly so that they could mount her. Cupping his hands to form a step, Roran lifted Katrina high enough to pull herself over the upper part of Saphira's left foreleg. From there Katrina clambered the looped leg straps of the saddle, as if a ladder, until she sat perched upon the crest of Saphira's shoulders. Like a mountain goat leaping from one ledge to another, Roran duplicated her ascent.

Crossing the cave after them, Eragon examined Saphira, assessing the severity of her various scrapes, gashes, tears, bruises, and stab wounds. To do so, he relied upon what she herself felt, in addition to what he could see.

For goodness' sake, said Saphira, *save your attentions until we are well out of danger. I'm not going to bleed to death.*

That's not quite true, and you know it. You're bleeding inside. Unless I stop it now, you may suffer complications I can't heal, and then we'll never get back to the Varden. Don't argue; you can't change my mind, and I won't take a minute.

As it turned out, Eragon required several minutes to restore Saphira to her former health. Her injuries were severe enough that in order to complete his spells, he had to empty the belt of Beloth the Wise of energy and, after that, draw upon Saphira's own vast reserves of strength. Whenever he shifted from a larger wound to a smaller one, she protested that he was being foolish and would he please leave off, but he ignored her complaints, much to her growing displeasure.

Afterward, Eragon slumped, tired from the magic and the fighting. Flicking a finger toward the places where the Lethrblaka had skewered her with their beaks, he said, *You should have Arya or another elf inspect my handiwork on those. I did my best, but I may have missed something.*

I appreciate your concern for my welfare, she replied, *but this is hardly the place for softhearted demonstrations. Once and for all, let us be gone!*

Aye. Time to leave. Stepping back, Eragon edged away from Saphira, in the direction of the tunnel behind him.

"Come on!" called Roran. "Hurry up!"

Eragon! exclaimed Saphira.

Eragon shook his head. "No. I'm staying here."

"You—" Roran started to say, but a ferocious growl from Saphira interrupted him. She lashed her tail against the side of the cave and raked the floor with her talons, so that bone and stone squealed in what sounded like mortal agony.

"Listen!" shouted Eragon. "One of the Ra'zac is still on the loose. And think what else might be in Helgrind: scrolls, potions, information about the Empire's activities—things that can help us! The Ra'zac may even have eggs of theirs stored here. If they do, I have to destroy them before Galbatorix can claim them for his own."

To Saphira, Eragon also said, *I can't kill Sloan, I can't let Roran or Katrina see him, and I can't allow him to starve to death in his cell or Galbatorix's men to recapture him. I'm sorry, but I have to deal with Sloan on my own.*

"How will you get out of the Empire?" demanded Roran.

"I'll run. I'm as fast as an elf now, you know."

The tip of Saphira's tail twitched. That was the only warning Eragon had before she leaped toward him, extending one of her glittering paws. He fled, dashing into the tunnel a fraction of a second before Saphira's foot passed through the space where he had been.

Saphira skidded to a stop in front of the tunnel and roared with frustration that she was unable to follow him into the narrow enclosure. Her bulk blocked most of the light. The stone shook around Eragon as she tore at the entrance with her claws and teeth, breaking off thick chunks. Her feral snarls and the sight of her lunging muzzle, filled with teeth as long as his forearm, sent a jolt of fear through Eragon. He understood then how a rabbit must feel when it cowers in its den while a wolf digs after it.

"Gánga!" he shouted.

No! Saphira placed her head on the ground and uttered a mournful keen, her eyes large and pitiful.

"Gánga! I love you, Saphira, but you have to go."

She retreated several yards from the tunnel and snuffled at him, mewling like a cat. *Little one . . .*

Eragon hated to make her unhappy, and he hated to send her away; it felt as if he were tearing himself apart. Saphira's misery flowed across their mental link and, coupled with his own anguish, almost paralyzed him. Somehow he mustered the nerve to say, "Gánga! And don't come back for me or send anyone else for me. I'll be fine. Gánga! Gánga!"

Saphira howled with frustration and then reluctantly walked to the mouth of the cave. From his place on her saddle, Roran said, "Eragon, come on! Don't be daft. You're too important to risk—"

A combination of noise and motion obscured the rest of his sentence as Saphira launched herself out of the cave. In the clear sky beyond, her scales sparkled like a multitude of brilliant blue diamonds. She was, Eragon thought, magnificent: proud, noble, and more beautiful than any other living creature. No stag or lion could compete with the majesty of a dragon in flight. She said, *A week: that is how long I shall wait. Then I shall return for you, Eragon, even if I must fight my way past Thorn, Shruikan, and a thousand magicians.*

Eragon stood there until she dwindled from sight and he could no longer touch her mind. Then, his heart heavy as lead, he squared his shoulders and turned away from the sun and all things bright and living and once more descended into the tunnels of shadow.

Rider and Ra'zac

Eragon sat bathed in the heatless radiance from his crimson werelight in the hall lined with cells near the center of Helgrind. His staff lay across his lap.

The rock reflected his voice as he repeated a phrase in the ancient language over and over again. It was not magic, but rather a message to the remaining Ra'zac. What he said meant this: "Come, O thou eater of men's flesh, let us end this fight of ours. You are hurt, and I am weary. Your companions are dead, and I am alone. We are a fit match. I promise that I shall not use gramarye against you, nor hurt or trap you with spells I have already cast. Come, O thou eater of men's flesh, let us end this fight of ours. . . ."

The time during which he spoke seemed endless: a neverwhen in a ghastly tinted chamber that remained unchanged through an eternity of cycling words whose order and significance ceased to matter to him. After a time, his clamoring thoughts fell silent, and a strange calm crept over him.

He paused with his mouth open, then closed it, watchful.

Thirty feet in front of him stood the Ra'zac. Blood dripped from the hem of the creature's ragged robes. "My massster does not want me to kill you," it hissed.

"But that does not matter to you now."

"No. If I fall to your staff, let Galbatorix deal with you as he will. He has more heartsss than you do."

Eragon laughed. "Hearts? I am the champion of the people, not him."

"Foolish boy." The Ra'zac cocked its head slightly, looking past him at the corpse of the other Ra'zac farther up the tunnel. "She was my hatchmate. You have become ssstrong since we firssst met, Shadeslayer."

"It was that or die."

"Will you make a pact with me, Shadeslayer?"

"What kind of a pact?"

"I am the lassst of my race, Shadeslayer. We are ancient, and I would not have us forgotten. Would you, in your songsss and in your hissstories, remind your fellow humans of the terror we inssspired in your kind? . . . Remember us as *fear*!"

"Why should I do that for you?"

Tucking its beak against its narrow chest, the Ra'zac clucked and chittered to itself for several moments. "Because," it said, "I will tell you sssomething secret, yesss I will."

"Then tell me."

"Give me your word firssst, lest you trick me."

"No. Tell me, and then I will decide whether or not to agree."

Over a minute passed, and neither of them moved, although Eragon kept his muscles taut and ready in expectation of a surprise attack. After another squall of sharp clicks, the Ra'zac said, "He has almossst found the *name*."

"Who has?"

"Galbatorix."

"The name of what?"

The Ra'zac hissed with frustration. "I cannot tell you! The *name*! The true *name*!"

"You have to give me more information than that."

"I cannot!"

"Then we have no pact."

"Curssse you, Rider! I curssse you! May you find no roossst nor den nor peace of mind in thisss land of yours. May you leave Alagaësia and never return!"

The nape of Eragon's neck prickled with the cold touch of dread.

In his mind, he again heard the words of Angela the herbalist when she had cast her dragon bones for him and told his fortune and predicted that selfsame fate.

A mare's tail of blood separated Eragon from his enemy as the Ra'zac swept back its sodden cloak, revealing a bow that it held with an arrow already fit to the string. Lifting and drawing the weapon, the Ra'zac loosed the bolt in the direction of Eragon's chest.

Eragon batted the shaft aside with his staff.

As if this attempt were nothing more than a preliminary gesture that custom dictated they observe before proceeding with their actual confrontation, the Ra'zac stooped, placed the bow on the floor, then straightened its cowl and slowly and deliberately pulled its leaf-bladed sword from underneath its robes. While it did, Eragon rose to his feet and took a shoulder-wide stance, his hands tight on the staff.

They lunged toward each other. The Ra'zac attempted to cleave Eragon from collarbone to hip, but Eragon twisted and stepped past the blow. Jamming the end of the staff upward, he drove its metal spike underneath the Ra'zac's beak and through the plates that protected the creature's throat.

The Ra'zac shuddered once and then collapsed.

Eragon stared at his most hated foe, stared at its lidless black eyes, and suddenly he went weak at the knees and retched against the wall of the corridor. Wiping his mouth, he yanked the staff free and whispered, "For our father. For our home. For Carvahall. For Brom. . . . I have had my fill of vengeance. May you rot here forever, Ra'zac."

Going to the appropriate cell, Eragon retrieved Sloan—who was still deep in his enchanted sleep—slung the butcher over his shoulder, and then began to retrace his steps back to the main cave of Helgrind. Along the way, he often lowered Sloan to the floor and left him to explore a chamber or byway that he had not visited before. In them he discovered many evil instruments, including four metal flasks of Seithr oil, which he promptly destroyed so that no one else could use the flesh-eating acid to further their malicious plans.

Hot sunlight stung Eragon's cheeks when he stumbled out of the network of tunnels. Holding his breath, he hurried past the dead Lethrblaka and went to the edge of the vast cave, where he gazed down the precipitous side of Helgrind at the hills far below. To the west, he saw a pillar of orange dust billowing above the lane that connected Helgrind to Dras-Leona, marking the approach of a group of horsemen.

His right side was burning from supporting Sloan's weight, so Eragon shifted the butcher onto his other shoulder. He blinked away the beads of sweat that clung to his eyelashes as he struggled to solve the problem of how he was supposed to transport Sloan and himself five thousand–some feet to the ground.

"It's almost a mile down," he murmured. "If there were a path, I could easily walk that distance, even with Sloan. So I must have the strength to lower us with magic. . . . Yes, but what you can do over a length of time may be too taxing to accomplish all at once without killing yourself. As Oromis said, the body cannot convert its stock-pile of fuel into energy fast enough to sustain most spells for more than a few seconds. I only have a certain amount of power available at any given moment, and once it's gone, I have to wait until I recover. . . . And talking to myself isn't getting me anywhere."

Securing his hold on Sloan, Eragon fixed his eyes on a narrow ledge about a hundred feet below. *This is going to hurt,* he thought, preparing himself for the attempt. Then he barked, "Audr!"

Eragon felt himself rise several inches above the floor of the cave. "Fram," he said, and the spell propelled him away from Helgrind and into open space, where he hung unsupported, like a cloud drifting in the sky. Accustomed as he was to flying with Saphira, the sight of nothing but thin air underneath his feet still caused him unease.

By manipulating the flow of magic, Eragon quickly descended

from the Ra'zac's lair—which the insubstantial wall of stone once again hid—to the ledge. His boot slipped on a loose piece of rock as he alighted. For a handful of breathless seconds, he flailed, searching for solid footing but unable to look down, as tilting his head could send him toppling forward. He yelped as his left leg went off the ledge and he began to fall. Before he could resort to magic to save himself, he came to an abrupt halt as his left foot wedged itself in a crevice. The edges of the rift dug into his calf behind his greave, but he did not mind, for it held him in place.

Eragon leaned his back against Helgrind, using it to help him prop up Sloan's limp body. "That wasn't too bad," he observed. The effort had cost him, but not so much that he was unable to continue. "I can do this," he said. He gulped fresh air into his lungs, waiting for his racing heart to slow; he felt as if he had sprinted a score of yards while carrying Sloan. "I can do this. . . ."

The approaching riders caught his eye again. They were noticeably closer than before and galloping across the dry land at a pace that worried him. *It's a race between them and me,* he realized. *I have to escape before they reach Helgrind. There are sure to be magicians among them, and I'm in no fit condition to duel Galbatorix's spellcasters.* Glancing over at Sloan's face, he said, "Perhaps you can help me a bit, eh? It's the least you can do, considering I'm risking death and worse for you." The sleeping butcher rolled his head, lost in the world of dreams.

With a grunt, Eragon pushed himself off Helgrind. Again he said, "Audr," and again he became airborne. This time he relied upon Sloan's strength—meager as it was—as well as his own. Together they sank like two strange birds along Helgrind's rugged flank toward another ledge whose width promised safe haven.

In such a manner Eragon orchestrated their downward climb. He did not proceed in a straight line, but rather angled off to his right, so that they curved around Helgrind and the mass of blocky stone hid him and Sloan from the horsemen.

The closer they got to the ground, the slower they went. A

crushing fatigue overcame Eragon, reducing the distance he was able to traverse in a single stretch and making it increasingly difficult for him to recuperate during the pauses between his bursts of exertion. Even lifting a finger became a task that he found irritating in the extreme, as well as one that was almost unbearably laborious. Drowsiness muffled him in its warm folds and dulled his thoughts and feelings until the hardest of rocks seemed as soft as pillows to his aching muscles.

When he finally dropped onto the sun-baked soil—too weak to keep Sloan and himself from ramming into the dirt—Eragon lay with his arms folded at odd angles underneath his chest and stared with half-lidded eyes into the yellow flecks of citrine embedded within the small rock an inch or two from his nose. Sloan weighed on his back like a pile of iron ingots. Air seeped from Eragon's lungs, but none seemed to return. His vision darkened as if a cloud had covered the sun. A deadly lull separated each beat of his heart, and the throb, when it came, was no more than a faint flutter.

Eragon was no longer capable of coherent thought, but somewhere in the back of his brain he was aware that he was about to die. It did not frighten him; to the contrary, the prospect comforted him, for he was tired beyond belief, and death would free him from the battered shell of his flesh and allow him to rest for all of eternity.

From above and behind his head, there came a bumblebee as big as his thumb. It circled his ear, then hovered by the rock, probing the nodes of citrine, which were the same bright yellow as the field-stars that bloomed among the hills. The bumblebee's mane glowed in the morning light—each hair sharp and distinct to Eragon—and its blurred wings generated a gentle bombilation, like a tattoo played on a drum. Pollen powdered the bristles on its legs.

The bumblebee was so vibrant, so alive, and so beautiful, its presence renewed Eragon's will to survive. A world that contained a creature as amazing as that bumblebee was a world he wanted to live in.

By sheer force of will, he pushed his left hand free of his chest and grasped the woody stem of a nearby shrub. Like a leech or a tick or some other parasite, he extracted the life from the plant, leaving it limp and brown. The subsequent rush of energy that coursed through Eragon sharpened his wits. Now he was scared; having regained his desire to continue existing, he found nothing but terror in the blackness beyond.

Dragging himself forward, he seized another shrub and transferred its vitality into his body, then a third shrub and a fourth shrub, and so on until he once again possessed the full measure of his strength. He stood and looked back at the trail of brown plants that stretched out behind him; a bitter taste filled his mouth as he saw what he had wrought.

Eragon knew that he had been careless with the magic and that his reckless behavior would have doomed the Varden to certain defeat if he had died. In hindsight, his stupidity made him wince. *Brom would box my ears for getting into this mess*, he thought.

Returning to Sloan, Eragon hoisted the gaunt butcher off the ground. Then he turned east and loped away from Helgrind and into the concealment of a draw. Ten minutes later, when he paused to check for pursuers, he saw a cloud of dirt swirling at the base of Helgrind, which he took to mean that the horsemen had arrived at the dark tower of stone.

He smiled. Galbatorix's minions were too far away for any lesser magicians among their ranks to detect his or Sloan's minds. *By the time they discover the Ra'zac's bodies,* he thought, *I shall have run a league or more. I doubt they will be able to find me then. Besides, they will be searching for a dragon and her Rider, not a man traveling on foot.*

Satisfied that he did not have to worry about an imminent attack, Eragon resumed his previous pace: a steady, effortless stride that he could maintain for the entire day.

Above him, the sun gleamed gold and white. Before him, trackless wilderness extended for many leagues before lapping against the outbuildings of some village. And in his heart, a new joy and hope flared.

At last the Ra'zac were dead!

At last his quest for vengeance was complete. At last he had fulfilled his duty to Garrow and to Brom. And at last he had cast off the pall of fear and anger that he had labored beneath ever since the Ra'zac first appeared in Carvahall. Killing them had taken far longer than he expected, but now the deed was done, and a mighty deed it was. He allowed himself to revel in satisfaction over having accomplished such a difficult feat, albeit with assistance from Roran and Saphira.

Yet, to his surprise, his triumph was bittersweet, tainted by an unexpected sense of loss. His hunt for the Ra'zac had been one of his last ties to his life in Palancar Valley, and he was loath to relinquish that bond, gruesome as it was. Moreover, the task had given him a purpose in life when he had none; it was the reason why he had originally left his home. Without it, a hole gaped inside of him where he had nurtured his hate for the Ra'zac.

That he could mourn the end of such a terrible mission appalled Eragon, and he vowed to avoid making the same mistake twice. *I refuse to become so attached to my struggle against the Empire and Murtagh and Galbatorix that I won't want to move on to something else when, and if, the time comes—or, worse, that I'll try to prolong the conflict rather than adapt to whatever happens next.* He chose then to push away his misbegotten regret and to concentrate instead on his relief: relief that he was free of the grim demands of his self-imposed quest and that his only remaining obligations were those born of his current position.

Elation lightened his steps. With the Ra'zac gone, Eragon felt as if he could finally make a life for himself based not on who he had been but on who he had become: a Dragon Rider.

He smiled at the uneven horizon and laughed as he ran, indifferent as to whether anyone might hear him. His voice rolled up and down the draw, and around him, everything seemed new and beautiful and full of promise.

TO WALK THE LAND ALONE

Eragon's stomach gurgled.

He was lying on his back, legs folded under at the knees—stretching his thighs after running farther and with more weight than he ever had before—when the loud, liquid rumble erupted from his innards.

The sound was so unexpected, Eragon bolted upright, groping for his staff.

Wind whistled across the empty land. The sun had set, and in its absence, everything was blue and purple. Nothing moved, save for the blades of grass that fluttered and Sloan, whose fingers slowly opened and closed in response to some vision in his enchanted slumber. A bone-biting cold heralded the arrival of true night.

Eragon relaxed and allowed himself a small smile.

His amusement soon vanished as he considered the source of his discomfort. Battling the Ra'zac, casting numerous spells, and bearing Sloan upon his shoulders for most of the day had left Eragon so ravenous, he imagined that if he could travel back in time, he could eat the entire feast the dwarves had cooked in his honor during his visit to Tarnag. The memory of how the roast Nagra, the giant boar, had smelled—hot, pungent, seasoned with honey and spices, and dripping with lard—was enough to make his mouth water.

The problem was, he had no supplies. Water was easy enough to come by; he could draw moisture from the soil whenever he wanted. Finding food in that desolate place, however, was not only far more difficult, it presented him with a moral dilemma that he had hoped to avoid.

Oromis had devoted many of his lessons to the various climates and geographic regions that existed throughout Alagaësia. Thus, when Eragon left their camp to investigate the surrounding area, he was able to identify most of the plants he encountered. Few were edible, and of those, none were large or bountiful enough for him to gather a meal for two grown men in a reasonable amount of time. The local animals were sure to have hidden away caches of seeds and fruit, but he had no idea where to begin searching for them. Nor did he think it was likely that a desert mouse would have amassed more than a few mouthfuls of food.

That left him with two options, neither of which appealed to him. He could—as he had before—drain the energy from the plants and insects around their camp. The price of doing so would be to leave a death-spot upon the earth, a blight where nothing, not even the tiny organisms in the soil, still lived. And while it might keep him and Sloan on their feet, transfusions of energy were far from satisfying, as they did nothing to fill one's stomach.

Or he could hunt.

Eragon scowled and twisted the butt of his staff into the ground. After sharing the thoughts and desires of numerous animals, it revolted him to consider eating one. Nevertheless, he was not about to weaken himself and perhaps allow the Empire to capture him just because he went without supper in order to spare the life of a rabbit. As both Saphira and Roran had pointed out, every living thing survived by eating something else. *Ours is a cruel world,* he thought, *and I cannot change how it is made. . . . The elves may be right to avoid flesh, but at the moment, my need is great. I refuse to feel guilty if circumstances drive me to this. It is not a crime to enjoy some bacon or a trout or what have you.*

He continued to reassure himself with various arguments, yet disgust at the concept still squirmed within his gut. For almost half an hour, he remained rooted to the spot, unable to do what logic told him was necessary. Then he became aware of how late it was and swore at himself for wasting time; he needed every minute of rest he could get.

Steeling himself, Eragon sent out tendrils from his mind and probed the land until he located two large lizards and, curled in a sandy den, a colony of rodents that reminded him of a cross between a rat, a rabbit, and a squirrel. "Deyja," said Eragon, and killed the lizards and one of the rodents. They died instantly and without pain, but he still gritted his teeth as he extinguished the bright flames of their minds.

The lizards he retrieved by hand, flipping over the rocks they had been hiding underneath. The rodent, however, he extracted from the den with magic. He was careful to not wake the other animals as he maneuvered the body up to the surface; it seemed cruel to terrify them with the knowledge that an invisible predator could kill them in their most secret havens.

He gutted, skinned, and otherwise cleaned the lizards and rodent, burying the offal deep enough to hide it from scavengers. Gathering thin, flat stones, he built a small oven, lit a fire within, and started the meat cooking. Without salt, he could not properly season any sort of food, but some of the native plants released a pleasant smell when he crushed them between his fingers, and those he rubbed over and packed into the carcasses.

The rodent was ready first, being smaller than the lizards. Lifting it off the top of the makeshift oven, Eragon held the meat in front of his mouth. He grimaced and would have remained locked in the grip of his revulsion, except that he had to continue tending the fire and the lizards. Those two activities distracted him enough that, without thinking, he obeyed the strident command of his hunger and ate.

The initial bite was the worst; it stuck in his throat, and the taste of hot grease threatened to make him sick. Then he shivered and dry-swallowed twice, and the urge passed. After that, it was easier. He was actually grateful the meat was rather bland, for the lack of flavor helped him to forget what he was chewing.

He consumed the entire rodent and then part of a lizard. Tearing the last bit of flesh off a thin leg bone, he heaved a sigh of contentment and then hesitated, chagrined to realize that, in spite of himself, he had enjoyed the meal. He was so hungry, the meager supper had seemed delicious once he overcame his inhibitions. *Perhaps*, he mused, *perhaps when I return . . . if I am at Nasuada's table, or King Orrin's, and meat is served . . . perhaps, if I feel like it and it would be rude to refuse, I might have a few bites. . . . I won't eat the way I used to, but neither shall I be as strict as the elves. Moderation is a wiser policy than zealotry, I think.*

By the light from the coals in the oven, Eragon studied Sloan's hands; the butcher lay a yard or two away, where Eragon had placed him. Dozens of thin white scars crisscrossed his long, bony fingers, with their oversized knuckles and long fingernails that, while they had been meticulous in Carvahall, were now ragged, torn, and blackened with accumulated filth. The scars testified to the relatively few mistakes Sloan had made during the decades he had spent wielding knives. His skin was wrinkled and weathered and bulged with wormlike veins, yet the muscles underneath were hard and lean.

Eragon sat on his haunches and crossed his arms over his knees. "I can't just let him go," he murmured. If he did, Sloan might track down Roran and Katrina, a prospect that Eragon considered unacceptable. Besides, even though he was not going to kill Sloan, he believed the butcher should be punished for his crimes.

Eragon had not been close friends with Byrd, but he had known him to be a good man, honest and steadfast, and he remembered Byrd's wife, Felda, and their children with some fondness, for Garrow, Roran, and Eragon had eaten and slept in their house on several occasions. Byrd's death, then, struck Eragon as being particularly cruel, and he felt the watchman's family deserved justice, even if they never learned about it.

What, however, would constitute proper punishment? *I refused to become an executioner*, thought Eragon, *only to make myself an arbiter. What do I know about the law?*

Rising to his feet, he walked over to Sloan and bent toward his ear and said, "Vakna."

With a jolt, Sloan woke, scrabbling at the ground with his sinewy hands. The remnants of his eyelids quivered as, by instinct, the butcher tried to lift them and look at his surroundings. Instead, he remained trapped in his own personal night.

Eragon said, "Here, eat this." He thrust the remaining half of his lizard toward Sloan, who, although he could not see it, surely must have smelled the food.

"Where am I?" asked Sloan. With trembling hands, he began to explore the rocks and plants in front of him. He touched his torn wrists and ankles and appeared confused to discover that his fetters were gone.

"The elves—and also the Riders in days gone by—called this place Mírnathor. The dwarves refer to it as Werghadn, and humans as the Gray Heath. If that does not answer your question, then perhaps it will if I say we are a number of leagues southeast of Helgrind, where you were imprisoned."

Sloan mouthed the word *Helgrind.* "You rescued me?"

"I did."

"What about—"

"Leave your questions. Eat this first."

His harsh tone acted like a whip on the butcher; Sloan cringed and reached with fumbling fingers for the lizard. Releasing it, Eragon retreated to his place next to the rock oven and scooped handfuls of dirt onto the coals, blotting out the glow so that it would not betray their presence in the unlikely event that anyone else was in the vicinity.

After an initial, tentative lick to determine what it was Eragon had given him, Sloan dug his teeth into the lizard and ripped a thick gobbet from the carcass. With each bite, he crammed as much flesh into his mouth as he could and only chewed once or twice before swallowing and repeating the process. He stripped each bone clean with the efficiency of a man who possessed an intimate understanding of how animals were constructed and what was the quickest way to disassemble them. The bones he dropped into a neat pile on his left. As the final morsel of meat from the lizard's tail vanished down Sloan's gullet, Eragon handed him the other reptile, which was yet whole. Sloan grunted in thanks and continued to gorge himself, making no attempt to wipe the fat from his mouth and chin.

The second lizard proved to be too large for Sloan to finish. He stopped two ribs above the bottom of the chest cavity and placed what was left of the carcass on the cairn of bones. Then he straightened his back, drew his hand across his lips, tucked his long hair behind his ears, and said, "Thank you, strange sir, for your hospitality. It has been so long since I had a proper meal, I think I prize your food even above my own freedom. . . . If I may ask, do you know of my daughter, Katrina, and what has happened to her? She was imprisoned with me in Helgrind." His voice contained a complex mixture of emotions: respect, fear, and submission in the presence of an unknown authority; hope and trepidation as to his daughter's fate; and determination as unyielding as the mountains of the Spine. The one element Eragon expected to hear but did not was the sneering disdain Sloan had used with him during their encounters in Carvahall.

"She is with Roran."

Sloan gaped. "Roran! How did he get here? Did the Ra'zac capture him as well? Or did—"

"The Ra'zac and their steeds are dead."

"You *killed* them? How? . . . Who—" For an instant, Sloan froze, as if he were stuttering with his entire body, and then his cheeks and mouth went slack and his shoulders caved in and he clutched at a bush to steady himself. He shook his head. "No, no, no. . . . *No.* . . . It can't be. The Ra'zac spoke of this; they demanded answers I didn't have, but I *thought* . . . That is, who would believe . . . ?" His sides heaved with such violence, Eragon wondered if he would hurt himself. In a gasping whisper, as if he were forced to speak after being punched in the middle, Sloan said, "You can't be *Eragon*."

A sense of doom and destiny descended upon Eragon. He felt as if he were the instrument of those two merciless overlords, and he replied in accordance, slowing his speech so each word struck like a hammer blow and carried all the weight of his dignity, station, and anger. "I am Eragon and far more. I am Argetlam and Shadeslayer and Firesword. My dragon is Saphira, she who is also known as Bjartskular and Flametongue. We were taught by Brom, who was a Rider before us, and by the dwarves and by the elves. We have fought the Urgals and a Shade and Murtagh, who is Morzan's son. We serve the Varden and the peoples of Alagaësia. And I have brought you here, Sloan Aldensson, to pass judgment upon you for murdering Byrd and for betraying Carvahall to the Empire."

"You lie! You cannot be—"

"Lie?" roared Eragon. "I do not lie!" Thrusting out with his mind, he engulfed Sloan's consciousness in his own and forced the butcher to accept memories that confirmed the truth of his statements. He also wanted Sloan to feel the power that was now his and to realize that he was no longer entirely human. And while Eragon was reluctant to admit it, he enjoyed having control over a man who had often made trouble for him and also tormented him with gibes, insulting both him and his family. He withdrew a half minute later.

Sloan continued to quiver, but he did not collapse and grovel as Eragon thought he might. Instead, the butcher's demeanor became cold and flinty. "Blast you," he said. "I don't have to explain myself to you, Eragon Son of None. Understand this, though: I did what I did for Katrina's sake and nothing else."

"I know. That's the only reason you're still alive."

"Do what you want with me, then. I don't care, so long as she's safe. . . . Well, go on! What's it to be? A beating? A branding? They already had my eyes, so one of my hands? Or will you leave me to starve or to be recaptured by the Empire?"

"I have not decided yet."

Sloan nodded with a sharp motion and pulled his tattered clothes tight around his limbs to ward off the night cold. He sat with military precision, gazing with blank, empty eye sockets into the shadows that ringed their camp. He did not beg. He did not ask for mercy. He did not deny his acts or attempt to placate Eragon. He but sat and waited, armored by his perfect stoic fortitude.

His bravery impressed Eragon.

The dark landscape around them seemed immense beyond reckoning to Eragon, and he felt as if the entire hidden expanse was converging upon him, a notion that heightened his anxiety over the choice that confronted him. *My verdict will shape the rest of his life*, he thought.

Abandoning for the moment the question of punishment, Eragon considered what he knew about Sloan: the butcher's overriding love for Katrina—obsessive, selfish, and generally unhealthy as it was, although it had once been something wholesome—his hate and fear of the Spine, which were the offspring of his grief for his late wife, Ismira, who had fallen to her death among those cloud-rending peaks; his estrangement from the remaining branches of his family; his pride in his work; the stories Eragon had heard about Sloan's childhood; and Eragon's own knowledge of what it was like to live in Carvahall.

Eragon took that collection of scattered, fragmented insights and turned them over in his mind, pondering their significance. Like the pieces of a puzzle, he tried to fit them together. He rarely succeeded, but he persisted, and gradually he traced a myriad of connections between the events and emotions of Sloan's life, and thereby he wove a tangled web, the patterns of which represented who Sloan was. Throwing the last line of his web, Eragon felt as if he finally comprehended the reasons for Sloan's behavior. Because of that, he empathized with Sloan.

More than empathy, he felt he understood Sloan, that he had isolated the core elements of Sloan's personality, those things one could not remove without irrevocably changing the man. There occurred to him, then, three words in the ancient language that seemed to embody Sloan, and without thinking about it, Eragon whispered the words under his breath.

The sound could not have reached Sloan, yet he stirred—his

hands gripping his thighs—and his expression became one of unease.

A cold tingle crawled down Eragon's left side, and goosebumps appeared on his arms and legs as he watched the butcher. He considered a number of different explanations for Sloan's reaction, each more elaborate than the last, but only one seemed plausible, and even it struck him as being unlikely. He whispered the trio of words again. As before, Sloan shifted in place, and Eragon heard him mutter, ". . . someone walking on my grave."

Eragon released a shaky breath. It was difficult for him to believe, but his experiment left no room for doubt: he had, quite by accident, chanced upon Sloan's true name. The discovery left him rather bewildered. Knowing someone's true name was a weighty responsibility, for it granted you absolute power over that person. Because of the inherent risks, the elves rarely revealed their true names, and when they did, it was only to those whom they trusted without reservation.

Eragon had never learned anyone's true name before. He had always expected that if he did, it would be as a gift from someone he cared about a great deal. Gaining Sloan's true name without his consent was a turn of events Eragon was unprepared for and uncertain how to deal with. It dawned upon Eragon that in order to guess Sloan's true name, he must understand the butcher better than he did himself, for he had not the slightest inkling what his own might be.

The realization was an uncomfortable one. He suspected that—given the nature of his enemies—not knowing everything he could about himself might well prove fatal. He vowed, then, to devote more time to introspection and to uncovering his true name. *Perhaps Oromis and Glaedr could tell me what it is*, he thought.

Whatever the doubts and confusion Sloan's true name roused within him, it gave Eragon the beginning of an idea for how to deal with the butcher. Even once he had the basic concept, it still took him another ten minutes to thrash out the rest of his plan and make sure that it would work in the manner he intended.

Sloan tilted his head in Eragon's direction as Eragon rose and walked out of their camp into the starlit land beyond. "Where are you going?" asked Sloan.

Eragon remained silent.

He wandered through the wilderness until he found a low, broad rock covered with scabs of lichen and with a bowl-like hollow in the middle. "Adurna rïsa," said he. Around the rock, countless minuscule droplets of water filtered up through the soil and coalesced into flawless silver tubes that arched over the edge of the rock and down into the hollow. When the water started to overflow and return to the earth, only to be again ensnared by his spell, Eragon released the flow of magic.

He waited until the surface of the water became perfectly still—so that it acted like a mirror and he stood before what looked like a basin of stars—and then he said, "Draumr kópa," and many other words besides, reciting a spell that would allow him to not only see but speak with others at a distance. Oromis had taught him the variation on scrying two days before he and Saphira had left Ellesméra for Surda.

The water went completely black, as if someone had extinguished the stars like candles. A moment or two later, an oval shape brightened in the middle of the water and Eragon beheld the interior of a large white tent, illuminated by the flameless light from a red Erisdar, one of the elves' magical lanterns.

Normally, Eragon would be unable to scry a person or place he had not seen before, but the elves' seeing glass was enchanted to transmit an image of its surroundings to anyone who contacted the glass. Likewise, Eragon's spell would project an image of himself and his surroundings onto the surface of the glass. The arrangement allowed strangers to contact each other from any location in the world, which was an invaluable ability in times of war.

A tall elf with silver hair and battle-worn armor entered Eragon's field of vision, and he recognized Lord Däthedr, who advised Queen Islanzadí and was a friend of Arya's. If Däthedr was surprised to see

Eragon, he did not show it; he inclined his head, touched the first two fingers of his right hand to his lips, and said in his lilting voice, "Atra esterní ono thelduin, Eragon Shur'tugal."

Mentally making the shift to conversing in the ancient language, Eragon duplicated the gesture with his fingers and replied, "Atra du evarínya ono varda, Däthedr-vodhr."

Continuing in his native tongue, Däthedr said, "I am glad to know you are well, Shadeslayer. Arya Dröttningu informed us of your mission some days ago, and we have been much concerned on your behalf and Saphira's. I trust nothing has gone amiss?"

"No, but I encountered an unforeseen problem, and if I may, I would consult with Queen Islanzadí and seek her wisdom in this matter."

Däthedr's catlike eyes drifted nearly shut, becoming two angled slashes that gave him a fierce and unreadable expression. "I know you would not ask this unless it is important, Eragon-vodhr, but beware: a drawn bow may just as easily snap and injure the archer as it may send the arrow flying. . . . If it so please you, wait, and I shall inquire after the queen."

"I shall wait. Your assistance is most welcome, Däthedr-vodhr." As the elf turned away from the seeing glass, Eragon grimaced. He disliked the elves' formality, but most of all, he hated trying to interpret their enigmatic statements. *Was he warning me that scheming and plotting around the queen is a dangerous pastime or that Islanzadí is a drawn bow about to snap? Or did he mean something else entirely?*

At least I'm able to contact the elves, thought Eragon. The elves' wards prevented anything from entering Du Weldenvarden by magical means, including the far-sight of scrying. So long as elves remained in their cities, one could communicate with them only by sending messengers into their forest. But now that the elves were on the move and had left the shade of their black-needled pine trees, their great spells no longer protected them and it was possible to use devices such as the seeing glass.

Eragon became increasingly anxious as first one minute and then another trickled past. "Come on," he murmured. He quickly glanced around to make sure that no person or beast was creeping up on him while he gazed into the pool of water.

With a sound akin to ripping cloth, the entrance flap to the tent flew open as Queen Islanzadí thrust it aside and stormed toward the seeing glass. She wore a bright corselet of golden scale armor, augmented with mail and greaves and a beautifully decorated helm—set with opals and other precious gemstones—that held back her flowing black tresses. A red cape trimmed with white billowed from her shoulders; it reminded Eragon of a looming storm front. In her left hand, Islanzadí wielded a naked sword. Her right hand was empty, but it appeared gloved in crimson, and after a moment, Eragon realized that dripping blood coated her fingers and wrist.

Islanzadí's slanting eyebrows narrowed as she looked upon Eragon. With that expression, she bore a striking resemblance to Arya, although her stature and bearing were even more impressive than her daughter's. She was beautiful and terrible, like a frightful goddess of war.

Eragon touched his lips with his fingers, then twisted his right hand over his chest in the elves' gesture of loyalty and respect and recited the opening line of their traditional greeting, speaking first, as was proper when addressing one of higher rank. Islanzadí made the expected response, and in an attempt to please her and demonstrate his knowledge of their customs, Eragon concluded with the optional third line of the salutation: "And may peace live in your heart."

The ferocity of Islanzadí's pose diminished somewhat, and a faint smile touched her lips, as if to acknowledge his maneuver. "And yours as well, Shadeslayer." Her low, rich voice contained hints of rustling pine needles and gurgling brooks and music played on reed pipes. Sheathing her sword, she moved across the tent to the folding table and stood at an angle to Eragon as she washed the blood off her skin with water from a pitcher. "Peace is difficult to come by these days, I fear."

83

"The fighting is heavy, Your Majesty?"

"It will be soon. My people are massing along the western edge of Du Weldenvarden, where we may prepare to kill and be killed while we are close to the trees we love so much. We are a scattered race and do not march in rank and file like others do—on account of the damage it inflicts upon the land—and so it takes time for us to assemble from the distant reaches of the forest."

"I understand. Only . . ." He searched for a way to ask his question without being rude. "If the fighting has not started yet, I cannot help but wonder why your hand is dyed with gore."

Shaking water droplets off her fingers, Islanzadí lifted her perfect gold-brown forearm for Eragon's inspection, and he realized that she had been the model for the sculpture of two intertwined arms that stood in the entryway to his tree house in Ellesméra. "Dyed no more. The only stain blood leaves on a person is on her soul, not her body. I said the fighting would escalate in the near future, *not* that we had yet to start." She pulled the sleeve of her corselet and the tunic underneath back down to her wrist. From the jeweled belt wrapped around her slim waist, she removed a gauntlet stitched with silver thread and worked her hand into it. "We have been observing the city of Ceunon, for we intend to attack there first. Two days ago, our rangers spotted teams of men and mules traveling from Ceunon into Du Weldenvarden. We thought they wished to collect timber from the edge of the forest, as is often done. 'Tis a practice we tolerate, for the humans must have wood, and the trees within the fringe are young and nearly beyond our influence, and we have not wanted to expose ourselves before. The teams did not stop at the fringe, however. They burrowed far into Du Weldenvarden, following game trails they were obviously familiar with. They were searching for the tallest, thickest trees—trees as old as Alagaësia itself, trees that were already ancient and fully grown when the dwarves discovered Farthen Dûr. When they found them, they began to saw them down." Her voice rippled with rage. "From their remarks, we learned why they were here. Galbatorix wanted the largest trees he could acquire to replace the siege engines and battering rams he lost during the battle on the Burning Plains. If their motive had been pure and honest, we might have forgiven the loss of one monarch of our forest. Maybe even two. But not eight-and-twenty."

A chill crept through Eragon. "What did you do?" he asked, although he already suspected the answer.

Islanzadí lifted her chin, and her face grew hard. "I was present with two of our rangers. Together, we *corrected* the humans' mistake. In the past, the people of Ceunon knew better than to intrude upon our lands. Today we reminded them why that was so." Without seeming to notice, she rubbed her right hand, as if it pained her, and she gazed past the seeing glass, looking at some vision of her own. "You have learned what it is like, Eragon-finiarel, to touch the life force of the plants and animals around you. Imagine how you would cherish them if you had possessed that ability for centuries. We give of ourselves to sustain Du Weldenvarden, and the forest is an extension of our bodies and minds. Any hurt it suffers is our hurt as well. . . . We are a slow people to rouse, but once roused we are like the dragons: we go mad with anger. It has been over a hundred years since I, or most any elf, shed blood in battle. The world has forgotten what we are capable of. Our strength may have declined since the Riders' fall, but we shall still give a full reckoning of ourselves; to our enemies, it will seem as if even the elements have turned against them. We are an Elder Race, and our skill and knowledge far exceed that of mortal men. Let Galbatorix and his allies beware, for we elves are about to forsake our forest, and we shall return in triumph, or never again."

Eragon shivered. Even during his confrontations with Durza, he had never encountered such implacable determination and ruthlessness. *It's not human*, he thought, then laughed mockingly to himself. *Of course not. And I would do well to remember that. However much we may look alike—and in my case, nigh on identical—we are not the same.* "If you take Ceunon," he said, "how will you control the people there? They may hate the Empire more than death itself, but I doubt they will trust you, if only because they are humans and you are elves."

Islanzadí waved a hand. "That is unimportant. Once we are within the city walls, we have ways to ensure that no one will oppose us. This is not the first time we have fought your kind." She removed her helm then, and her hair fell forward and framed her face between raven locks. "I was not pleased to hear of your raid on Helgrind, but I take it the assault is already over and was successful?"

"Yes, Your Majesty."

"Then my objections are for naught. I warn you, however, Eragon Shur'tugal, do not imperil yourself on such needlessly dangerous ventures. It is a cruel thing I must say, but true nevertheless, and it is this: your life is more important than your cousin's happiness."

"I swore an oath to Roran that I would help him."

"Then you swore recklessly, without considering the consequences."

"Would you have me abandon those I care about? If I did that, I would become a man to despise and distrust: an ill-formed vehicle for the hopes of the people who believe I will, *somehow*, bring low Galbatorix. And also, while Katrina was Galbatorix's hostage, Roran was vulnerable to his manipulation."

The queen lifted one dagger-sharp eyebrow. "A vulnerability that you could have prevented Galbatorix from exploiting by tutoring Roran in certain oaths in this, the language of magic. . . . I do not counsel you to cast away your friends or family. That would be folly indeed. But keep you firmly in mind what is at stake: the entirety of Alagaësia. If we fail now, then Galbatorix's tyranny will extend over all the races, and his reign shall have no conceivable end. You are the tip of the spear that is our effort, and if the tip should break and be lost, then our spear shall bounce off the armor of our foe, and we too shall be lost."

Folds of lichen cracked underneath Eragon's fingers as he gripped the edge of the rock basin and suppressed the urge to make an impertinent remark about how any well-equipped warrior ought to have a sword or another weapon to rely upon besides a spear. He was frustrated by the direction the conversation had taken and eager to change the topic as quickly as he could; he had not contacted the queen so she could berate him as if he were a mere child. Nevertheless, allowing his impatience to dictate his actions would do nothing to further his cause, so he remained calm and replied, "Please believe me, Your Majesty, I take your concerns very, very seriously. I can only say that if I hadn't helped Roran, I would have been as miserable as he, and more so if he attempted to rescue Katrina by himself and died as a result. In either case, I would have been too upset to be of any use to you or anyone. Cannot we at least agree to differ on the subject? Neither of us shall convince the other."

"Very well," said Islanzadí. "We shall lay the matter to rest . . . for the present. But do not think you have escaped a proper investigation of your decision, Eragon Dragon Rider. It seems to me you display a frivolous attitude toward your larger responsibilities, and that is a serious matter. I shall discuss it with Oromis; he will decide what is to be done about you. Now tell me, why did you seek this audience?"

Eragon clenched his teeth several times before he could bring himself to, in a civil tone, explain the day's events, the reasons for his actions in regard to Sloan, and the punishment he envisioned for the butcher.

When he finished, Islanzadí whirled around and paced the circumference of the tent—her movements as lithe as a cat's—then stopped and said, "You chose to stay behind, in the middle of the Empire, to save the life of a murderer and a traitor. You are alone with this man, on foot, without supplies or weapons, save for magic, and your enemies are close behind. I see my earlier admonishments were more than justified. You—"

"Your Majesty, if you must be angry with me, be angry with me later. I want to resolve this quickly so I can get some rest before dawn; I have many miles to cover tomorrow."

The queen nodded. "Your survival is all that matters. I shall be furious after we are done speaking. . . . As for your request, such a thing is unprecedented in our history. If I had been in your place, I would have killed Sloan and rid myself of the problem then and there."

"I know you would have. I once watched Arya slay a gyrfalcon who was injured, for she said its death was inevitable, and by killing it, she saved the bird hours of suffering. Perhaps I should have done the same with Sloan, but I couldn't. I think it would have been a choice I would have regretted for the rest of my life, or worse, one that would have made it easier for me to kill in the future."

Islanzadí sighed, and suddenly she appeared tired. Eragon reminded himself that she too had been fighting that day. "Oromis may have been your proper teacher, but you have proved yourself Brom's heir, not Oromis's. Brom is the only other person who managed to entangle himself in as many predicaments as you. Like him, you seem compelled to find the deepest patch of quicksand and then dive into it."

Eragon hid a smile, pleased by the comparison. "What of Sloan?" he asked. "His fate rests with you now."

Slowly, Islanzadí sat upon a stool next to the folding table, placed her hands in her lap, and gazed to one side of the seeing glass. Her countenance became one of enigmatic observation: a beautiful mask that concealed her thoughts and feelings, and one that Eragon could not penetrate, no matter how hard he strove. When she spoke, she said, "As you have seen fit to save this man's life, at no little trouble and effort on your own part, I cannot refuse your request and thereby render your sacrifice meaningless. If Sloan survives the ordeal you have set before him, then Gilderien the Wise shall allow him to pass, and Sloan shall have a room and a bed and food to eat. More I cannot promise, for what happens afterward will depend on Sloan himself, but if the conditions you named are met, then yes, we shall light his darkness."

"Thank you, Your Majesty. You are most generous."

"No, not generous. This war does not allow me to be generous, only practical. Go and do what you must, and be you careful, Eragon Shadeslayer."

"Your Majesty." He bowed. "If I may ask one last favor: would you please refrain from telling Arya, Nasuada, or any of the Varden of my current situation? I don't want them to worry about me any longer than they have to, and they'll learn of it soon enough from Saphira."

"I shall consider your request."

Eragon waited, but when she remained silent and it became clear she had no intention of announcing her decision, he bowed a second time and again said, "Thank you."

The glowing image on the surface of the water flickered and then vanished into darkness as Eragon ended the spell he had used to create it. He leaned back on his heels and gazed up at the multitude of stars, allowing his eyes to readjust to the faint, glimmering light they provided. Then he left the crumbling rock with the pool of water and retraced his path across the grass and scrub to the camp, where Sloan still sat upright, rigid as cast iron.

Eragon struck a pebble with his foot, and the resulting noise revealed his presence to Sloan, who snapped his head around, quick as a bird. "Have you made up your mind?" demanded Sloan.

"I have," said Eragon. He stopped and squatted in front of the butcher, steadying himself with one hand on the ground. "Hear me well, for I don't intend to repeat myself. You did what you did because of your love for Katrina, or so you say. Whether you admit it or not, I believe you also had other, baser motives in wanting to separate her from Roran: anger . . . hate . . . vindictiveness . . . and your own hurt."

Sloan's lips hardened into thin white lines. "You wrong me."

"No, I don't think so. Since my conscience prevents me from killing you, your punishment is to be the most terrible I could invent short of death. I'm convinced that what you said before is true, that Katrina is more important to you than anything else. Therefore, your punishment is this: you shall not see, touch, or talk with your daughter again, even unto your dying day, and you shall live with the knowledge that she is with Roran and they are happy together, without you."

Sloan inhaled through his clenched teeth. "*That* is your punishment? Ha! You cannot enforce it; you have no prison to put me in."

"I'm not finished. I will enforce it by having you swear oaths in the elves' tongue—in the language of truth and magic—to abide by the terms of your sentence."

"You can't force me to give my word," Sloan growled. "Not even if you torture me."

"I can, and I won't torture you. Furthermore, I will lay upon you a compulsion to travel northward until you reach the elf city of Ellesméra, which stands deep in the heart of Du Weldenvarden. You can try to resist the urge if you want, but no matter how long you fight it, the spell will irritate you like an unscratched itch until you obey its demands and travel to the elves' realm."

"Don't you have the guts to kill me yourself?" asked Sloan. "You're too much of a coward to put a blade to my neck, so you'll make me wander the wilderness, blind and lost, until the weather or the beasts do me in?" He spat to the left of Eragon. "You're nothing but the yellow-bellied offspring of a canker-ridden bunter. You're a bastard, you are, and an unlicked cub; a dung-splattered, tallow-faced rock-gnasher; a puking villain and a noxious toad; the runty, mewling spawn of a greasy sow. I wouldn't give you my last crust if you were starving, or a drop of water if you were burning, or a beggar's grave if you were dead. You have pus for marrow and fungus for brains, and you're a scug-backed cheek-biter!"

There was, Eragon thought, something rather obscenely impressive about Sloan's swearing, although his admiration did not prevent him from wanting to strangle the butcher, or to at least respond in kind. What stayed his desire for retaliation, however, was his suspicion that Sloan was deliberately trying to infuriate him enough to strike down the older man and thus give him a quick and undeserved end.

Eragon said, "Bastard I may be, but not a murderer." Sloan drew a sharp breath. Before he could resume his torrent of abuse, Eragon added: "Wherever you go, you shall not want for food, nor will wild animals attack you. I will place certain enchantments around you that will keep men and beasts from troubling you and will cause animals to bring you sustenance when you need it."

"You can't do this," whispered Sloan. Even in the starlight, Eragon could see the last remnants of color drain from his skin, leaving him bone white. "You don't have the means. You don't have the right."

"I am a Dragon Rider. I have as much right as any king or queen."

Then Eragon, who had no interest in continuing to chastise Sloan, uttered the butcher's true name loud enough for him to hear. An expression of horror and revelation crawled across Sloan's face, and he threw his arms up before him and howled as if he had been stabbed. His cry was raw and jagged and desolate: the scream of a man condemned by his own nature to a fate he could not escape. He fell forward onto the palms of his hands and remained in that position and began to sob, his face obscured by shocks of hair.

Eragon watched, transfixed by Sloan's reaction. *Does learning your true name affect everyone like this? Would this happen to me as well?*

Hardening his heart to Sloan's misery, Eragon set about doing what he said he would. He repeated Sloan's true name and, word by word, schooled the butcher in the ancient language oaths that would ensure Sloan never met or contacted Katrina again. Sloan resisted with much weeping and wailing and grinding of his teeth, but no matter how vigorously he struggled, he had no choice but to obey whenever Eragon invoked his true name. And when they finished with the oaths, Eragon cast the five spells that would drive Sloan toward Ellesméra, would protect him from unprovoked violence, and would entice the birds and the beasts and the fish that dwelled in the rivers and lakes to feed him. Eragon fashioned the spells so they would derive their energy from Sloan and not himself.

Midnight was a fading memory by the time Eragon completed the final incantation. Drunk with weariness, he leaned against the hawthorn staff. Sloan lay curled at his feet.

"Finished," said Eragon.

A garbled moan drifted up from the figure below. It sounded as if Sloan were attempting to say something. Frowning, Eragon knelt beside him. Sloan's cheeks were red and bloody where he had scraped them with his fingers. His nose ran, and tears dripped from the corner of his left eye socket, which was the less mutilated of the two. Pity and guilt welled up inside of Eragon; it gave him no pleasure to see Sloan reduced to such a low state. He was a broken man, stripped of everything he valued in life, including his self-delusions, and Eragon was the one who had broken him. The accomplishment left Eragon feeling soiled, as if he had done something shameful. *It was necessary,* he thought, *but no one should have to do what I did.*

Another moan emanated from Sloan, and then he said, ". . . only a piece of rope. I didn't mean to . . . Ismira . . . No, no, please no . . ." The butcher's ramblings subsided, and in the intervening silence, Eragon placed his hand on Sloan's upper arm. Sloan stiffened at the contact. "Eragon . . . ," he whispered. "Eragon . . . I am blind, and you send me to walk the land . . . to walk the land alone. I am forsaken and forsworn. I know who I am and I cannot bear it. Help me; kill me! Free me of this agony."

On an impulse, Eragon pressed the hawthorn rod into Sloan's right hand and said, "Take my staff. Let it guide you on your journey."

"Kill me!"

"No."

A cracked shout burst from Sloan's throat, and he thrashed from side to side and pounded the earth with his fists. "Cruel, cruel you are!" His meager strength depleted, he curled into an even tighter ball, panting and whimpering.

Bending over him, Eragon placed his mouth close to Sloan's ear and whispered, "I am not without mercy, so I give you this hope: If you reach Ellesméra, you will find a home waiting for you. The elves will care for you and allow you to do whatever you want for the rest of your life, with one exception: once you enter Du Weldenvarden, you cannot leave. . . . Sloan, listen to me. When I was among the elves, I learned that a person's true name often changes as they age. Do you understand what that means? Who you are is not fixed for all of eternity. A man could forge himself anew if he so wanted."

Sloan made no reply.

Eragon left the staff next to Sloan and crossed to the other side of the camp and stretched out his full length on the ground. His eyes already closed, he mumbled a spell that would rouse him before dawn and then allowed himself to drift into the soothing embrace of his waking rest.

The Gray Heath was cold, dark, and inhospitable when a low buzz sounded inside Eragon's head. "Letta," he said, and the buzzing ceased. Groaning as he stretched sore muscles, he got to his feet and lifted his arms over his head, shaking them to get the blood flowing. His back felt so bruised, he hoped it would be a long while before he had to swing a weapon again. He lowered his arms and then looked for Sloan.

The butcher was gone.

Eragon smiled as he saw a set of tracks, accompanied by the round imprint of the staff, leading away from the camp. The trail was confused and meandering, and yet its general direction was northward, toward the great forest of the elves.

I want him to succeed, Eragon thought with mild surprise. *I want him to succeed, because it will mean we may all have a chance to redeem ourselves from our mistakes. And if Sloan can mend the flaws in his character and come to terms with the evil he wrought, he will find his plight is not so bleak as he believes.* For Eragon had not told Sloan that if the butcher demonstrated that he truly regretted his crimes, reformed his ways, and lived as a better person, Queen Islanzadí would have her spellweavers restore his vision. However, it was a reward Sloan had to earn without knowing about its existence, else he might seek to trick the elves into bestowing it prematurely.

Eragon stared at the footprints for a long while, then lifted his gaze to the horizon and said, "Good luck."

Tired, but also content, he turned his back on Sloan's trail and began to run across the Gray Heath. To the southwest, he knew there stood the ancient sandstone formations where Brom lay encased in his diamond tomb. He longed to divert his path and to go pay his respects but dared not, for if Galbatorix had discovered the site, he would send his agents there to look for Eragon.

"I'll return," he said. "I promise you, Brom: someday I'll return."

He sped onward.

✦   ✦   ✦

THE TRIAL OF THE LONG KNIVES

"**B**ut we are your people!"

Fadawar, a tall, high-nosed, black-skinned man, spoke with the same heavy emphasis and altered vowels Nasuada remembered hearing during her childhood in Farthen Dûr, when emissaries from her father's tribe would arrive and she would sit on Ajihad's lap and doze while they talked and smoked cardus weed.

Nasuada gazed up at Fadawar and wished she were six inches taller so that she could look the warlord and his four retainers straight in the eyes. Still, she was accustomed to men looming over her. She found it rather more disconcerting to be among a group of people who were as dark as she was. It was a novel experience not to be the object of people's curious stares and whispered comments.

She was standing in front of the carved chair where she held her audiences—one of the only solid chairs the Varden had brought with them on their campaign—inside her red command pavilion. The sun was close to setting, and its rays filtered through the right side of the pavilion as through stained glass and gave the contents a ruddy glow. A long, low table covered with scattered reports and maps occupied one-half of the pavilion.

Just outside the entrance to the large tent, she knew the six members of her personal guard—two humans, two dwarves, and two Urgals—were waiting with drawn weapons, ready to attack if they received the slightest indication she was in peril. Jörmundur, her oldest and most trusted commander, had saddled her with guards since the day Ajihad died, but never so many for so long. However, the day after the battle on the Burning Plains, Jörmundur expressed his deep and abiding concern for her safety, a concern, he said, that often kept him up nights with a burning stomach. As an assassin had tried to kill her in Aberon, and Murtagh had actually accomplished the deed in regard to King Hrothgar less than a week past, it was Jörmundur's opinion that Nasuada ought to create a force dedicated to her own defense. She had objected that such a measure would be an overreaction but had been unable to convince Jörmundur; he had threatened to abdicate his post if she refused to adopt what he considered to be proper precautions. Eventually, she acceded, only to spend the next hour haggling over how many guards she was to have. He had wanted twelve or more at all times. She wanted four or fewer. They settled on six, which still struck Nasuada as too many; she worried about appearing afraid or, worse, as if she were attempting to intimidate those she met. Again her protestations had failed to sway Jörmundur. When she accused him of being a stubborn old worrywart, he laughed and said, "Better a stubborn old worrywart than a foolhardy youngling dead before his time."

As the members of her guard changed every six hours, the total number of warriors assigned to protect Nasuada was four-and-thirty, including the ten additional warriors who remained in readiness to replace their comrades in case of sickness, injury, or death.

It was Nasuada who had insisted upon recruiting the force from each of the three mortal races arrayed against Galbatorix. By doing so, she hoped to foster greater solidarity among them, as well as to convey that she represented the interests of all the races under her command, not just the humans. She would have included the elves as well, but at the moment, Arya was the only elf who fought alongside the Varden and their allies, and the twelve spellcasters Islanzadí had sent to protect Eragon had yet to arrive. To Nasuada's disappointment, her human and dwarf guards had been hostile to the Urgals they served with, a reaction she anticipated but had been unable to avert or mitigate. It would, she knew, take more than one shared battle to ease the tensions between races that had fought and hated each other for more generations than she cared to count. Still, she viewed it as encouraging that the warriors chose to name their corps the Nighthawks, for the title was a play upon both her coloring and the fact that the Urgals invariably referred to her as Lady Nightstalker.

Although she would never admit it to Jörmundur, Nasuada had quickly come to appreciate the increased sense of security her guards provided. In addition to being masters of their chosen weapons—whether they were the humans' swords, the dwarves' axes, or the Urgals' eccentric collection of instruments—many of the warriors were skilled spellweavers. And they had all sworn their undying loyalty to her in the ancient language. Since the day the Nighthawks first assumed their duties, they had not left Nasuada alone with another person, save for Farica, her handmaid.

That was, until now.

Nasuada had sent them out of the pavilion because she knew her meeting with Fadawar might lead to the type of bloodshed the Nighthawks' sense of duty would require them to prevent. Even so, she was not entirely defenseless. She had a dagger hidden in the folds of her dress, and an even smaller knife in the bodice of her undergarments, and the prescient witch-child, Elva, was standing just behind the curtain that backed Nasuada's chair, ready to intercede if need be.

Fadawar tapped his four-foot-long scepter against the ground. The chased rod was made of solid gold, as was his fantastic array of jewelry: gold bangles covered his forearms; a breastplate of hammered gold armored his chest; long, thick chains of gold hung around his neck; embossed disks of white gold stretched the lobes of his ears; and upon the top of his head rested a resplendent gold crown of such huge proportions, Nasuada wondered how Fadawar's neck could support the weight without buckling and how such a monumental piece of architecture remained fixed in place. It seemed one would have to bolt the edifice, which was at least two and a half feet tall, to its bony bedrock in order to keep it from toppling over.

Fadawar's men were garbed in the same fashion, although less opulently. The gold they wore served to proclaim not only their wealth but also the status and deeds of each individual and the skill of their tribe's far-famed craftsmen. As either nomads or city dwellers, the dark-skinned peoples of Alagaësia had long been renowned for the quality of their jewelry, which at its best rivaled that of the dwarves.

Nasuada owned several pieces of her own, but she had chosen not to wear them. Her poor raiment could not compete with Fadawar's splendor. Also, she believed it would not be wise to affiliate herself with any one group, no matter how rich or influential, when she had to deal with and speak for all the differing factions of the Varden. If she displayed partiality toward one or another, her ability to control the whole lot of them would diminish.

Which was the basis of her argument with Fadawar.

Fadawar again jabbed his scepter into the ground. "Blood is the most important thing! First come your responsibilities to your family, then to your tribe, then to your warlord, then to the gods above and below, and only then to your king and to your nation, if you have them. That is how Unulukuna intended men to live, and that is how we should live if we want to be happy. Are you brave enough to spit on the shoes of the Old One? If a man does not help his family, whom can he depend upon to help him? Friends are fickle, but family is forever."

"You ask me," said Nasuada, "to give positions of power to your fellow kinsmen because you are my mother's cousin and because my father was born among you. This I would be happy to do if your kinsmen could fulfill those positions better than anyone else in the Varden, but nothing you have said thus far has convinced me that is so. And before you squander more of your gilt-tongued eloquence, you should know that appeals based upon our shared blood are meaningless to me. I would give your request greater consideration if ever you had done more to support my father than send trinkets and empty promises to Farthen Dûr. Only now that victory and influence are mine have you made yourself known to me. Well, my parents are dead, and I say I have no family but myself. You are my people, yes, but nothing more."

Fadawar narrowed his eyes and lifted his chin and said, "A woman's pride is always without sense. You shall fail without our support."

He had switched to his native language, which forced Nasuada to respond in kind. She hated him for it. Her halting speech and uncertain tones exposed her unfamiliarity with her birth tongue, emphasizing that she had not grown up in their tribe but was an outsider. The ploy undermined her authority. "I always welcome new allies," she said. "However, I cannot indulge in favoritism, nor should you have need of it. Your tribes are strong and well gifted. They should be able to rise quickly through the ranks of the Varden without having to rely upon the charity of others. Are you starving dogs to sit whining at my table, or are you men who can feed themselves? If you can, then I look forward to working with you to better the Varden's lot and to defeat Galbatorix."

"Bah!" exclaimed Fadawar. "Your offer is as false as you are. We shall not do servants' work; we are the chosen ones. You insult us, you do. You stand there and you smile, but your heart is full of scorpion's poison."

Stifling her anger, Nasuada attempted to calm the warlord. "It was not my intent to cause offense. I was only trying to explain my position. I have no enmity for the wandering tribes, nor have I any special love for them. Is that such a bad thing?"

"It is worse than bad, it is bald-faced treachery! Your father made certain requests of us based upon our relation, and now you ignore our service and turn us away like empty-handed beggars!"

A sense of resignation overwhelmed Nasuada. *So Elva was right— it is inevitable,* she thought. A thrill of fear and excitement coursed through her. *If it must be, then I have no reason to maintain this charade.* Allowing her voice to ring forth, she said, "Requests that you did not honor half the time."

"We did!"

"You did not. And even if you were telling the truth, the Varden's position is too precarious for me to give you something for nothing. You ask for favors, yet tell me, what do you offer in return? Will you help fund the Varden with your gold and jewels?"

"Not directly, but—"

"Will you give me the use of your craftsmen, free of charge?"

"We could not—"

"How, then, do you intend to earn these boons? You cannot pay with warriors; your men already fight for me, whether in the Varden or in King Orrin's army. Be content with what you have, Warlord, and do not seek more than is rightfully yours."

"You twist the truth to suit your own selfish goals. I seek what is rightfully ours! That is why I am here. You talk and you talk, yet your words are meaningless, for by your actions, you have betrayed us." The bangles on his arms clattered together as he gestured, as if before an audience of thousands. "You admit we are your people. Then do you still follow our customs and worship our gods?"

Here is the turning point, thought Nasuada. She could lie and claim she had abandoned the old ways, but if she did, the Varden would lose Fadawar's tribes, and other nomads besides, once they heard of her statement. *We need them. We need everyone we can get if we're to have the slightest chance of toppling Galbatorix.*

"I do," she said.

"Then I say you are unfit to lead the Varden, and as is my right, I challenge you to the Trial of the Long Knives. If you are triumphant, we shall bow to you and never again question your authority. But if you lose, then you shall step aside, and I shall take your place as head of the Varden."

Nasuada noted the spark of glee that lit Fadawar's eyes. *This is what he wanted all along,* she realized. *He would have invoked the trial even if I had complied with his demands.* She said, "Perhaps I am mistaken, but I thought it was tradition that whoever won assumed command of his rival's tribes, as well as his own. Is that not so?" She almost laughed at the expression of dismay that flashed across Fadawar's face. *You didn't expect me to know that, did you?*

"It is."

"I accept your challenge, then, with the understanding that should I win, your crown and scepter will be mine. Are we agreed?"

Fadawar scowled and nodded. "We are." He stabbed his scepter deep enough into the ground that it stood upright by itself, then grasped the first bangle on his left arm and began to work it down over his hand.

"Wait," said Nasuada. Going to the table that filled the other side of the pavilion, she picked up a small brass bell and rang it twice, paused, and then rang it four times.

Only a moment or two passed before Farica entered the tent. She cast a frank gaze at Nasuada's guests, then curtsied to the lot of them and said, "Yes, Mistress?"

Nasuada gave Fadawar a nod. "We may proceed." Then she addressed her handmaid: "Help me out of my dress; I don't want to ruin it."

The older woman looked shocked by the request. "Here, Ma'am? In front of these . . . men?"

"Yes, here. And be quick about it too! I shouldn't have to argue with my own servant." Nasuada was harsher than she meant to be, but her heart was racing and her skin was incredibly, terribly sensitive; the soft linen of her undergarments seemed as abrasive as canvas. Patience and courtesy were beyond her now. All she could concentrate on was her upcoming ordeal.

Nasuada stood motionless as Farica picked and pulled at the laces to her dress, which extended from her shoulder blades to the base of her spine. When the cords were loose enough, Farica lifted Nasuada's arms out of the sleeves, and the shell of bunched fabric dropped in a pile around Nasuada's feet, leaving her standing almost naked in her white chemise. She fought back a shiver as the four warriors examined her, feeling vulnerable beneath their covetous looks. Ignoring them, she stepped forward, out of the dress, and Farica snatched the garment out of the dirt.

Across from Nasuada, Fadawar had been busy removing the bangles from his forearms, revealing the embroidered sleeves of his robes underneath. Finished, he lifted off his massive crown and handed it to one of his retainers.

The sound of voices outside the pavilion delayed further progress. Marching through the entrance, a message boy—Jarsha was his name, Nasuada remembered—planted himself a foot or two inside and proclaimed: "King Orrin of Surda, Jörmundur of the Varden, Trianna of Du Vrangr Gata, and Naako and Ramusewa of the Inapashunna tribe." Jarsha very pointedly kept his eyes fixed on the ceiling while he spoke.

Snapping about, Jarsha departed and the congregation he had announced entered, with Orrin at the vanguard. The king saw Fadawar first and greeted him, saying, "Ah, Warlord, this *is* unexpected. I trust you and—" Astonishment suffused his youthful face as he beheld Nasuada. "Why, Nasuada, what is the meaning of this?"

"I should like to know that as well," rumbled Jörmundur. He gripped the hilt of his sword and glowered at anyone who dared stare at her too openly.

"I have summoned you here," she said, "to witness the Trial of the Long Knives between Fadawar and myself and to afterward speak the truth of the outcome to everyone who asks."

The two gray-haired tribesmen, Naako and Ramusewa, appeared alarmed by her revelation; they leaned close together and began to whisper. Trianna crossed her arms—baring the snake bracelet coiled around one slim wrist—but otherwise betrayed no reaction. Jörmundur swore and said, "Have you taken leave of your senses, my Lady? This is madness. You cannot—"

"I can, and I will."

"My Lady, if you do, I—"

"Your concern is noted, but my decision is final. And I forbid anyone from interfering." She could tell he longed to disobey her order, but as much as he wanted to shield her from harm, loyalty had ever been Jörmundur's predominant trait.

"But, Nasuada," said King Orrin. "This trial, is not it where—"

"It is."

"Blast it, then; why don't you give up this mad venture? You would have to be addled to carry it out."

"I have already given my word to Fadawar."

The mood in the pavilion became even more somber. That she had given her word meant she could not rescind her promise without revealing herself to be an honorless oath-breaker that fairminded men would have no choice but to curse and shun. Orrin faltered for a moment, but he persisted with his questions: "To what end? That is, if you should lose—"

"If I should lose, the Varden shall no longer answer to me, but to Fadawar."

Nasuada had expected a storm of protest. Instead, there came a silence, wherein the hot anger that animated King Orrin's visage cooled and sharpened and acquired a brittle temper. "I do not appreciate your choice to endanger our entire cause." To Fadawar, he said, "Will you not be reasonable and release Nasuada from her obligation? I will reward you richly if you agree to abandon this ill-conceived ambition of yours."

"I am rich already," said Fadawar. "I have no need for your tin-tainted gold. No, nothing but the Trial of the Long Knives can compensate me for the slander Nasuada has aimed at my people and me."

"Bear witness now," said Nasuada.

Orrin clenched tight the folds of his robes, but he bowed and said, "Aye, I will bear witness."

From within their voluminous sleeves, Fadawar's four warriors produced small, hairy goat-hide drums. Squatting, they placed the drums between their knees and struck up a furious beat, pounding so fast, their hands were sooty smudges in the air. The rough music obliterated all other sound, as well as the host of frantic thoughts that had been bedeviling Nasuada. Her heart felt as if it were keeping pace with the manic tempo that assaulted her ears.

Without missing a single note, the oldest of Fadawar's men reached inside his vest and, from there, drew two long, curved knives that he tossed toward the peak of the tent. Nasuada watched the knives tumble haft over blade, fascinated by the beauty of their motion.

When it was close enough, she lifted her arm and caught her knife. The opal-studded hilt stung her palm.

Fadawar successfully intercepted his weapon as well.

He then grasped the left cuff of his garment and pushed the sleeve past his elbow. Nasuada kept her eyes fixed upon Fadawar's forearm as he did. His limb was thick and muscled, but she deemed that of no importance; athletic gifts would not help him win their contest. What she looked for instead were the telltale ridges that, if they existed, would lie across the belly of his forearm.

She observed five of them.

Five! she thought. *So many.* Her confidence wavered as she contemplated the evidence of Fadawar's fortitude. The only thing that kept her from losing her nerve altogether was Elva's prediction: the girl had said that, in this, Nasuada would prevail. Nasuada clung to the memory as if it were her only child. *She said I can do this, so I must be able to outlast Fadawar. . . . I must be able to!*

As he was the one who had issued the challenge, Fadawar went first. He held his left arm straight out from his shoulder, palm-upward; placed the blade of his knife against his forearm, just below the crease of his elbow; and drew the mirror-polished edge across his flesh. His skin split like an overripe berry, blood welling from within the crimson crevice.

He locked gazes with Nasuada.

She smiled and set her own knife against her arm. The metal was as cold as ice. Theirs was a test of wills to discover who could withstand the most cuts. The belief was that whoever aspired to become the chief of a tribe, or even a warlord, should be willing to endure more pain than anyone else for the sake of his or her people. Otherwise, how could the tribes trust their leaders to place the concerns of the community before their own selfish desires? It was Nasuada's opinion that the practice encouraged extremism, but she also understood the ability of the gesture to earn people's trust. Although the Trial of the Long Knives was specific to the dark-skinned tribes, besting Fadawar would solidify her standing among the Varden and, she hoped, King Orrin's followers.

She offered a quick plea for strength to Gokukara, the praying mantis goddess, and then pulled on the knife. The sharpened steel slid through her skin so easily, she struggled to avoid cutting too deeply. She shuddered at the sensation. She wanted to fling the knife away and clutch her wound and scream.

She did none of those things. She kept her muscles slack; if she tensed, the process would hurt all the more. And she kept smiling as, slowly, the blade mutilated her body. The cut ended after only three seconds, but in those seconds, her outraged flesh delivered a thousand shrieking complaints, and each one nearly made her stop. As she lowered the knife, she noticed that while the tribesmen still beat upon their drums, she heard naught but the pounding of her pulse.

Then Fadawar slashed himself a second time. The cords in his neck stood in high relief, and his jugular vein bulged as if it would burst while the knife carved its bloody path.

Nasuada saw it was her turn again. Knowing what to expect only increased her fear. Her instinct for self-preservation—an instinct that had served her well on all other occasions—warred against the commands she sent to her arm and hand. Desperate, she concentrated upon her desire to preserve the Varden and overthrow Galbatorix: the two causes to which she had devoted her entire being. In her mind, she saw her father and Jörmundur and Eragon and the people of the Varden, and she thought, *For them! I do this for them. I was born to serve, and this is my service.*

She made the incision.

A moment later, Fadawar opened up a third gash on his forearm, as did Nasuada on her own.

The fourth cut followed soon thereafter.

And the fifth . . .

A strange lethargy overtook Nasuada. She was so very tired, and cold as well. It occurred to her then that tolerance of pain might not decide the trial, but rather who would faint first from loss of blood. Shifting streams of it ran across her wrist and down her fingers, splashing into the thick pool by her feet. A similar, if larger, puddle gathered around Fadawar's boots.

The row of gaping red slits on the warlord's arm reminded Nasuada of the gills of a fish, a thought that for some reason seemed incredibly funny to her; she had to bite her tongue to keep from giggling.

With a howl, Fadawar succeeded in completing his sixth cut. "Best that, you feckless witch!" he shouted over the noise of the drums, and dropped to one knee.

She did.

Fadawar trembled as he transferred his knife from his right hand to his left; tradition dictated a maximum of six cuts per arm, else you risked severing the veins and tendons close to the wrist. As Nasuada imitated his movement, King Orrin sprang between them and said, "Stop! I won't allow this to continue. You're going to kill yourselves."

He reached toward Nasuada, then jumped back as she stabbed at him. "Don't meddle," she growled between her teeth.

Now Fadawar started on his right forearm, releasing a spray of blood from his rigid muscles. *He's clenching,* she realized. She hoped the mistake would be enough to break him.

Nasuada could not help herself; she uttered a wordless cry when the knife parted her skin. The razor edge burned like a white-hot wire. Halfway through the cut, her traumatized left arm twitched. The knife swerved as a result, leaving her with a long, jagged laceration twice as deep as the others. Her breath stopped while she weathered the agony. *I can't go on,* she thought. *I can't . . . I can't! It's too much to bear. I'd rather die. . . . Oh please, let it end!* It gave her some relief to indulge in those and other desperate complaints, but in the depths of her heart, she knew she would never give up.

For the eighth time, Fadawar positioned his blade above one of his forearms, and there he held it, the pale metal suspended a quarter of an inch away from his sable skin. He remained thus as sweat dripped over his eyes and his wounds shed ruby tears. It appeared as though his courage might have failed him, but then he snarled and, with a quick yank, sliced his arm.

His hesitation bolstered Nasuada's flagging strength. A fierce exhilaration overtook her, transmuting her pain into an almost pleasurable sensation. She matched Fadawar's effort and then, spurred onward by her sudden, heedless disregard for her own well-being, brought the knife down again.

"Best *that*," she whispered.

The prospect of having to make two cuts in a row—one to equal the number of Nasuada's and one to advance the contest—seemed to intimidate Fadawar. He blinked, licked his lips, and adjusted his grip on his knife three times before he raised the weapon over his arm.

His tongue darted out and moistened his lips again.

A spasm distorted his left hand, and the knife dropped from his contorted fingers, burying itself upright in the ground.

He picked it up. Underneath his robe, his chest rose and fell with frantic speed. Lifting the knife, he touched it to his arm; it promptly drew a small trickle of blood. Fadawar's jaw knotted and writhed, and then a shudder ran the length of his spine and he doubled over, pressing his injured arms against his belly. "I submit," he said.

The drums stopped.

The ensuing silence lasted for only an instant before King Orrin,

Jörmundur, and everyone else filled the pavilion with their overlapping exclamations.

Nasuada paid no attention to their remarks. Groping behind herself, she found her chair and sank into it, eager to take the weight off her legs before they gave way beneath her. She strove to remain conscious as her vision dimmed and flickered; the last thing she wanted to do was pass out in front of the tribesmen. A gentle pressure on her shoulder alerted her to the fact that Farica was standing next to her, holding a pile of bandages.

"My Lady, may I tend to you?" asked Farica, her expression both concerned and hesitant, as if she were uncertain how Nasuada would react.

Nasuada nodded her approval.

As Farica began to wind strips of linen around her arms, Naako and Ramusewa approached. They bowed, and Ramusewa said, "Never before has anyone endured so many cuts in the Trial of the Long Knives. Both you and Fadawar proved your mettle, but you are undoubtedly the victor. We shall tell our people of your achievement, and they shall give you their fealty."

"Thank you," said Nasuada. She closed her eyes as the throbbing in her arms increased.

"My Lady."

Around her, Nasuada heard a confused medley of sounds, which she made no effort to decipher, preferring instead to retreat deep inside herself, where her pain was no longer so immediate and menacing. She floated in the womb of a boundless black space, illuminated by formless blobs of ever-changing color.

Her respite was interrupted by the voice of Trianna as the sorceress said, "Leave off what you're doing, handmaid, and remove those bandages so I can heal your mistress."

Nasuada opened her eyes to see Jörmundur, King Orrin, and Trianna standing over her. Fadawar and his men had departed the pavilion. "No," said Nasuada.

The group looked at her with surprise, and then Jörmundur said,

"Nasuada, your thoughts are clouded. The trial is over. You don't have to live with these cuts any longer. In any event, we have to stanch your bleeding."

"Farica is doing that well enough as is. I shall have a healer stitch my wounds and make a poultice to reduce the swelling, and that is all."

"But why!"

"The Trial of the Long Knives requires participants to allow their wounds to heal at their natural pace. Otherwise, we won't have experienced the full measure of pain the trial entails. If I violate the rule, Fadawar will be declared the victor."

"Will you at least allow me to alleviate your suffering?" asked Trianna. "I know several spells that can eliminate any amount of pain. If you had consulted me beforehand, I could have arranged it so that you could lop off an entire limb without the slightest discomfort."

Nasuada laughed and allowed her head to loll to the side, feeling rather giddy. "My answer would have been the same then as it is now: trickery is dishonorable. I had to win the trial without deceit so no one can question my leadership in the future."

In a deadly soft tone, King Orrin said, "But what if you had lost?"

"I could not lose. Even if it meant my death, I never would have allowed Fadawar to gain control of the Varden."

Grave, Orrin studied her for a long while. "I believe you. Only, is the tribes' loyalty worth such a great sacrifice? You are not so common that we can easily replace you."

"The tribes' loyalty? No. But this will have an effect far beyond the tribes, as you must know. It should help unify our forces. And that is a prize valuable enough for me to willingly brave a host of unpleasant deaths."

"Pray tell, what would the Varden have gained if you *had* died today? No benefit would exist then. Your legacy would be discouragement, chaos, and likely ruin."

Whenever Nasuada drank wine, mead, and especially strong

109

spirits, she became most cautious with her speech and motions, for even if she did not notice it at once, she knew the alcohol degraded her judgment and coordination, and she had no desire to behave inappropriately or to give others an advantage in their dealings with her.

Pain-drunk as she was, she later realized she should have been as vigilant in her discussion with Orrin as if she had imbibed three tankards of the dwarves' blackberry-honey mead. If she had, her well-developed sense of courtesy would have prevented her from replying so: "You worry like an old man, Orrin. I had to do this, and it is done. 'Tis bootless to fret about it now. . . . I took a risk, yes. But we cannot defeat Galbatorix unless we dance along the very cliff edge of disaster. You are a king. You ought to understand that danger is the mantle a person assumes when he—or she—has the arrogance to decide the fates of other men."

"I understand well enough," growled Orrin. "My family and I have defended Surda against the Empire's encroachment every day of our lives for generations, while the Varden merely hid in Farthen Dûr and leeched off Hrothgar's generosity." His robes swirled about him as he turned and stalked out of the pavilion.

"That was badly handled, my Lady," observed Jörmundur.

Nasuada winced as Farica tugged on her bandages. "I know," she gasped. "I'll mend his broken pride tomorrow."

WINGED TIDINGS

A gap appeared then in Nasuada's memories: an absence of sensory information so complete, she only became aware of the missing time when it dawned upon her that Jörmundur was shaking her shoulder and saying something loudly. It took her several moments to decipher the sounds coming out of his mouth, and then she heard: ". . . keep looking at me, blast it! That's the thing! Don't go to sleep again. You won't wake up again if you do."

"You can let go of me, Jörmundur," she said, and mustered a weak smile. "I'm all right now."

"And my uncle Undset was an elf."

"Wasn't he?"

"Bah! You are the same as your father: always ignoring caution when it comes to your own safety. The tribes can rot in their bloody old customs, for all I care. Let a healer at you. You're in no condition to make decisions."

"That's why I waited until it was evening. See, the sun is almost down. I can rest tonight, and tomorrow I will be able to deal with the affairs that require my attention."

Farica appeared from the side and hovered over Nasuada. "Oh, Ma'am, you gave us quite a fright there."

"Still are, as a matter of fact," muttered Jörmundur.

"Well, I'm better now." Nasuada pushed herself upright in the chair, ignoring the heat from her forearms. "You can both go; I shall be fine. Jörmundur, send word to Fadawar that he may remain chief of his own tribe, so long as he swears loyalty to me as his warlord. He is too skilled a leader to waste. And, Farica, on your way back to your tent, please inform Angela the herbalist that I require her services. She agreed to mix some tonics and poultices for me."

"I won't leave you alone in this condition," declared Jörmundur.

Farica nodded. "Begging your pardon, my Lady, but I agree with him. It's not safe."

Nasuada glanced toward the entrance to the pavilion, to ensure none of the Nighthawks were close enough to overhear, and then dropped her voice into a low whisper. "I shall not *be* alone." Jörmundur's eyebrows shot up, and an alarmed expression crossed Farica's face. "I am *never* alone. Do you understand?"

"You have taken certain . . . precautions, my Lady?" asked Jörmundur.

"I have."

Both her caretakers appeared uneasy with her assurance, and Jörmundur said, "Nasuada, your safety is my responsibility; I need to know what additional protection you may have and who exactly has access to your person."

"No," she said gently. Seeing the hurt and indignation that appeared in Jörmundur's eyes, she continued. "It's not that I doubt your loyalty—far from it. Only, this I must have for myself. For the sake of my own peace of mind, I need to have a dagger no one else can see: a hidden weapon tucked up my sleeve, if you will. Consider it a flaw in my character, but do not torment yourself by imagining my choice is in any way a criticism of how you perform your duties."

"My Lady." Jörmundur bowed, a formality he almost never used with her.

Nasuada lifted her hand, indicating her permission for them to leave, and Jörmundur and Farica hurried from the red pavilion.

For a long minute, perhaps two, the only sound Nasuada heard was the harsh cry of gore-crows circling above the Varden's encampment. Then, from behind her, there came a slight rustling, like that of a mouse nosing about for food. Turning her head, she saw Elva slip out of her hiding place, emerging between two panels of fabric into the main chamber of the pavilion.

Nasuada studied her.

The girl's unnatural growth had continued. When Nasuada first met her but a short while ago, Elva had appeared between three and four years old. Now she looked closer to six. Her plain dress was black, with a few folds of purple around the neck and shoulders. Her long, straight hair was even darker: a liquid void that flowed down to the small of her back. Her sharp-angled face was bone white, for she rarely ventured outside. The dragon mark on her brow was silver. And her eyes, her violet eyes, contained a jaded, cynical air—the result of Eragon's blessing that was a curse, for it forced her to both endure other people's pain and also try to prevent it. The recent battle had almost killed her, what with the combined agony of thousands beating upon her mind, even though one of Du Vrangr Gata had placed her in an artificial slumber for the duration of the fighting, in an attempt to protect her. Only recently had the girl begun to speak and take interest in her surroundings again.

She wiped her rosebud mouth with the back of her hand, and Nasuada asked, "Were you ill?"

Elva shrugged. "The pain I'm used to, but it never gets any easier to resist Eragon's spell. . . . I am hard to impress, Nasuada, but you are a strong woman to withstand so many cuts."

Even though Nasuada had heard it many times, Elva's voice still inspired a thrill of alarm in her, for it was the bitter, mocking voice of a world-weary adult, not that of a child. She struggled to ignore it as she responded: "You are stronger. I did not have to suffer through Fadawar's pain as well. Thank you for staying with me. I know what it must have cost you, and I'm grateful."

"Grateful? Ha! There's an empty word for me, *Lady Nightstalker*." Elva's small lips twisted in a misshapen smile. "Have you anything to eat? I'm famished."

"Farica left some bread and wine behind those scrolls," said Nasuada, pointing across the pavilion. She watched the girl make her way to the food and begin wolfing down the bread, cramming large chunks into her mouth. "At least you won't have to live like this for much longer. As soon as Eragon returns, he'll remove the spell."

"Perhaps." After she had devoured half a loaf, Elva paused. "I lied about the Trial of the Long Knives."

"What do you mean?"

"I foresaw that you would lose, not win."

"What!"

"If I had allowed events to take their course, your nerve would have broken on the seventh cut and Fadawar would be sitting where you are now. So I told you what you needed to hear in order to prevail."

A chill crept over Nasuada. If what Elva said was true, then she was in the witch-child's debt more than ever. Still, she disliked being manipulated, even if it was for her own benefit. "I see. It seems I must thank you once again."

Elva laughed then, a brittle sound. "And you hate every moment of it, don't you? No matter. You need not worry about offending me, Nasuada. We are useful to each other, no more."

Nasuada was relieved when one of the dwarves guarding the pavilion, the captain of that particular watch, banged his hammer against his shield and proclaimed, "The herbalist Angela requests an audience with you, Lady Nightstalker."

"Granted," said Nasuada, raising her voice.

Angela bustled into the pavilion, carrying several bags and baskets looped over her arms. As always, her curly hair formed a stormy cloud around her face, which was pinched with concern. At her heels padded the werecat Solembum, in his animal form. He immediately angled toward Elva and began to rub against her legs, arching his back as he did.

Depositing her luggage on the ground, Angela rolled her shoulders and said, "Really! Between you and Eragon, I seem to spend most of my time among the Varden healing people too silly to realize they need to *avoid* getting chopped into tiny little pieces." While she spoke, the short herbalist marched over to Nasuada and began unwinding the bandages around her right forearm. She clucked with disapproval. "Normally, this is when the healer asks her patient how she is, and the patient lies through her teeth and says, 'Oh, not too bad,' and the healer says, 'Good, good. Be cheery and you'll make a fine recovery.' I think it's obvious, however, you're *not* about to start running around and leading charges against the Empire. Far from it."

"I will recover, won't I?" asked Nasuada.

"You would if I could use magic to seal up these wounds. Since I can't, it's a bit harder to tell. You'll have to muddle along like most people do and hope none of these cuts get infected." She paused in her work and gazed directly at Nasuada. "You do realize these will scar?"

"It will be what it will be."

"True enough."

Nasuada stifled a groan and gazed upward as Angela stitched each of her wounds and then covered them with a thick, wet mat of pulped plants. Out of the corner of her eye, she saw Solembum jump onto the table and sit next to Elva. Extending a large, shaggy paw, the werecat hooked a piece of bread off Elva's plate and nibbled on the morsel, his white fangs flashing. The black tassels on his oversized ears quivered as he swiveled his ears from side to side, listening to metal-clad warriors walking past the red pavilion.

"Barzûl," muttered Angela. "Only men would think of cutting themselves to determine who the pack leader is. Idiots!"

It hurt to laugh, but Nasuada could not help herself. "Indeed," she said after her fit subsided.

Just as Angela finished retying the last strip of cloth around Nasuada's arms, the dwarf captain outside the pavilion shouted, "Halt!" and there came a chorus of shimmering, bell-like notes as the human guards crossed their swords, barring the way to whoever sought entrance.

Without pausing to think, Nasuada drew the four-inch knife from the sheath sewn within the bodice of her chemise. It was difficult for her to grasp the hilt, as her fingers felt thick and clumsy and the muscles in her arm were slow to respond. It was as if the limb had fallen asleep, save for the sharp, burning lines scribed into her flesh.

Angela also pulled a dagger from somewhere in her clothes, and she placed herself before Nasuada and muttered a line of the ancient language. Leaping to the ground, Solembum crouched next to Angela. His fur stood on end, making him appear larger than most dogs. He growled low in his throat.

Elva continued eating, seemingly unperturbed by the commotion. She examined the morsel of bread she was holding between her thumb and index finger, as one might inspect a strange species of insect, and then dipped it into a goblet of wine and popped the bread into her mouth.

"My Lady!" shouted a man. "Eragon and Saphira fast approach from the northeast!"

Nasuada sheathed her knife. Pushing herself out of her chair, she said to Angela, "Help me dress."

Angela held the garment open in front of Nasuada, who stepped into it. Then Angela gently guided Nasuada's arms into the sleeves and, when they were in place, set about lacing up the back of the dress. Elva joined her. Together, they soon had Nasuada properly attired.

Nasuada surveyed her arms and saw no trace of her bandages. "Should I hide or reveal my injuries?" she asked.

"That depends," said Angela. "Do you think showing them will increase your standing or encourage your enemies, because they assume you are weak and vulnerable? The question is actually a rather philosophical one, predicated on whether when looking at a man who has lost a big toe, you say, 'Oh, he's a cripple' or 'Oh, he was smart or strong or lucky enough to escape worse injury.' "

"You make the strangest comparisons."

"Thank you."

"The Trial of the Long Knives is a contest of strength," said Elva.

"That is well known among the Varden and Surdans. Are you proud of your strength, Nasuada?"

"Cut off the sleeves," said Nasuada. When they hesitated, she said, "Go on! At the elbows. Don't mind the dress; I shall have it repaired later."

With a few deft movements, Angela removed the sections Nasuada had identified and dropped the excess fabric on the table.

Nasuada lifted her chin. "Elva, if you sense I'm about to faint, please tell Angela and have her catch me. Shall we, then?" The three of them gathered into a tight formation, with Nasuada at the lead. Solembum walked alone.

As they exited the red pavilion, the dwarf captain barked, "Stations!" and the six present members of the Nighthawks ranged themselves around Nasuada's group: the humans and dwarves fore and aft, and the hulking Kull—Urgals who stood eight feet and taller—on either side.

Dusk spread its gold and purple wings over the Varden's encampment, lending a sense of mystery to the rows of canvas tents that extended beyond the limits of Nasuada's sight. Deepening shadows presaged the advent of night, and countless torches and watchfires already glowed pure and bright in the warm twilight. The sky was clear to the east. South, a long, low cloud of black smoke hid the horizon and the Burning Plains, which were a league and a half away. West, a line of beeches and aspens marked the path of the Jiet River, upon which floated the *Dragon Wing*, the ship Jeod and Roran and the other villagers from Carvahall had pirated. But Nasuada had eyes only for the north, and the glittering shape of Saphira descending thence. Light from the fading sun still illuminated her, cloaking her in a blue halo. She appeared like a cluster of stars falling from the heavens.

The sight was so majestic, Nasuada stood transfixed for a moment, thankful she was fortunate enough to witness it. *They're safe!* she thought, and breathed a sigh of relief.

The warrior who had brought word of Saphira's arrival—a thin man with a large, untrimmed beard—bowed and then pointed. "My Lady, as you can see, I spoke the truth."

"Yes. You did well. You must have exceedingly sharp eyes to have spotted Saphira earlier. What is your name?"

"Fletcher, son of Harden, my Lady."

"You have my thanks, Fletcher. You may return to your post now."

With another bow, the man trotted off toward the edge of the camp.

Keeping her gaze fixed upon Saphira, Nasuada picked her way between the rows of tents toward the large clearing set aside as a place for Saphira to land and take off. Her guards and companions accompanied her, but she paid them little heed, eager as she was to rendezvous with Eragon and Saphira. She had spent much of the previous days worrying about them, both as the leader of the Varden and, somewhat to her surprise, as a friend.

Saphira flew as fast as any hawk or falcon Nasuada had seen, but she was still a number of miles away from the camp, and it took her almost ten minutes to traverse the remaining distance. In that time, a massive crowd of warriors gathered around the clearing: humans, dwarves, and even a contingent of gray-skinned Urgals, led by Nar Garzhvog, who spit at the men closest to them. Also in the congregation were King Orrin and his courtiers, who positioned themselves opposite Nasuada; Narheim, the dwarf ambassador who had assumed Orik's duties since Orik left for Farthen Dûr; Jörmundur; the other members of the Council of Elders; and Arya.

The tall elf woman wove her way through the crowd toward Nasuada. Even with Saphira nigh upon them, men and women alike tore their gaze from the sky to watch Arya's progress, she presented such a striking image. Dressed all in black, she wore leggings like a man, a sword on her hip, and a bow and quiver on her back. Her skin was the color of light honey. Her face was as angular as a cat's. And she moved with a slinking, muscular grace that bespoke her skill with a blade, and also her supernatural strength.

Her eccentric ensemble had always struck Nasuada as slightly indecent; it revealed so much of her form. But Nasuada had to admit that even if Arya donned a gown of rags, she would still appear more regal and dignified than any mortal-born noble.

Halting before Nasuada, Arya gestured with one elegant finger at Nasuada's wounds. "As the poet Earnë said, to place yourself in harm's way for the sake of the people and the country you love is the finest thing one can do. I have known every leader of the Varden, and they were all mighty men and women, and none so much as Ajihad. In this, though, I believe you have surpassed even him."

"You honor me, Arya, but I fear that if I burn so brightly, too few shall remember my father as he deserves."

"The deeds of the children are a testament of the upbringing they received from their parents. Burn like the sun, Nasuada, for the brighter you burn, the more people there shall be who will respect Ajihad for teaching you how to bear the responsibilities of command at such a tender age."

Nasuada dipped her head, taking to heart Arya's advice. Then she smiled and said, "A tender age? I'm a grown woman, by our reckoning."

Amusement gleamed in Arya's green eyes. "True. But if we judge by years, and not wisdom, no human would be considered an adult among my kind. Except for Galbatorix, that is."

"And me," Angela chimed in.

"Come now," said Nasuada, "you can't be much older than I am."

"Ha! You're confusing appearances with age. You ought to have more sense than that after being around Arya so long."

Before Nasuada could ask just how old Angela really was, she felt a hard tug on the back of her dress. Looking around, she saw that it was Elva who had taken such a liberty and that the girl was beckoning. Bending, Nasuada placed an ear close to Elva, who muttered, "Eragon's not on Saphira."

Nasuada's chest tightened, restricting her breathing. She peered upward: Saphira circled directly over the camp, some thousands of feet high. Her huge, batlike wings were black against the sky. Nasuada could see Saphira's underside, and her talons white against the lapped scales of her belly, but nothing of whoever might be riding her.

"How do you know?" she asked, keeping her voice low.

"I cannot feel his discomfort, nor his fears. Roran is there, and a woman I guess is Katrina. No one else."

Straightening, Nasuada clapped her hands and said, "Jörmundur!" allowing her voice to ring forth.

Jörmundur, who was almost a dozen yards away, came running, shoving aside those who got in his way; he was experienced enough to know when an emergency was at hand. "My Lady."

"Clear the field! Get everyone away from here before Saphira lands."

"Including Orrin and Narheim and Garzhvog?"

She grimaced. "No, but allow no one else to remain. Hurry!"

As Jörmundur began shouting orders, Arya and Angela converged upon Nasuada. They appeared as alarmed as she felt. Arya said, "Saphira would not be so calm if Eragon was hurt or dead."

"Where is he, then?" demanded Nasuada. "What trouble has he gotten himself into now?"

A raucous commotion filled the clearing as Jörmundur and his men directed the onlookers back to their tents, laying about them with swagger sticks whenever the reluctant warriors lingered or protested. Several scuffles broke out, but the captains under Jörmundur quickly overwhelmed the culprits, so as to prevent the violence from taking root and spreading. Fortunately, the Urgals, at the word of their war chief, Garzhvog, left without incident, although Garzhvog himself advanced toward Nasuada, as did King Orrin and the dwarf Narheim.

Nasuada felt the ground tremble under her feet as the eight-and-a-half-foot-tall Urgal approached her. He lifted his bony chin, baring his throat as was the custom of his race, and said, "What means this, Lady Nightstalker?" The shape of his jaws and teeth, coupled with his accent, made it difficult for Nasuada to understand him.

"Yes, I'd bloody well like an explanation myself," said Orrin. His face was red.

"And I," said Narheim.

It occurred to Nasuada, as she regarded them, that this was probably the first time in thousands of years that members of so many of the races of Alagaësia had gathered together in peace. The only ones missing were the Ra'zac and their mounts, and Nasuada knew no sane being would ever invite those foul creatures into their secret councils. She pointed at Saphira and said, "She shall provide the answers you desire."

Just as the last stragglers quit the clearing, a torrent of air rushed across Nasuada as Saphira swooped to the ground, raking her wings to slow herself before alighting upon her rear legs. She dropped to all fours, and a dull boom resounded across the camp. Unbuckling themselves from her saddle, Roran and Katrina quickly dismounted.

Striding forward, Nasuada examined Katrina. She was curious to see what kind of woman could inspire a man to undertake such extraordinary feats in order to rescue her. The young woman before her was strong-boned, with the pallid complexion of an invalid, a mane of copper hair, and a dress so torn and filthy, it was impossible to determine what it might have looked like originally. In spite of the toll her captivity had taken, it was apparent to Nasuada that Katrina was attractive enough, but not what the bards would call a great beauty. However, she possessed a certain force of gaze and bearing that made Nasuada think that if Roran had been the one captured, Katrina would have been just as capable of rousing the villagers of Carvahall, getting them south to Surda, fighting in the Battle of the Burning Plains, and then continuing on to Helgrind, all for the sake of her beloved. Even when she noticed Garzhvog, Katrina did not flinch or quail but remained standing where she was, next to Roran.

Roran bowed to Nasuada and, swiveling, also to King Orrin. "My Lady," he said, his face grave. "Your Majesty. If I may, this is my betrothed, Katrina." She curtsied to them both.

"Welcome to the Varden, Katrina," said Nasuada. "We have all heard your name here, on account of Roran's uncommon devotion. Songs of his love for you already spread across the land."

"You are most welcome," added Orrin. "Most welcome indeed."

Nasuada noticed that the king had eyes only for Katrina, as did every man present, including the dwarves, and Nasuada was certain they would be recounting tales of Katrina's charms to their comrades-in-arms before the night was out. What Roran had done on her behalf elevated her far above ordinary women; it made her an object of mystery, fascination, and allure to the warriors. That anyone should sacrifice so much for another person meant, by reason of the price paid, that person must be unusually precious.

Katrina blushed and smiled. "Thank you," she said. Along with her embarrassment at such attentions, a hint of pride colored her expression, as if she knew how remarkable Roran was and delighted in having captured his heart, of all the women in Alagaësia. He was hers, and that was all the status or treasure she desired.

A pang of loneliness shot through Nasuada. *I wish I had what they have,* she thought. Her responsibilities prevented her from entertaining girlish dreams of romance and marriage—and certainly children—unless she were to arrange a marriage of convenience for the good of the Varden. She had often considered doing that with Orrin, but her nerve always failed her. Still, she was content with her lot and did not begrudge Katrina and Roran their happiness. Her cause was what she cared about; defeating Galbatorix was far more important than something as trifling as marriage. Most everyone got married, but how many had the opportunity to oversee the birth of a new age?

I'm not myself this evening, realized Nasuada. *My wounds have set my thoughts ahumming like a nest of bees.* Shaking herself, she looked past Roran and Katrina to Saphira. Nasuada opened up the barriers she usually maintained around her mind so she might hear what Saphira had to say and then asked: "Where is he?"

With the dry rustle of scales sliding over scales, Saphira crept forward and lowered her neck so her head was directly in front of Nasuada, Arya, and Angela. The dragon's left eye sparkled with blue fire. She sniffed twice, and her crimson tongue darted out of her mouth. Hot, moist breath ruffled the lace collar on Nasuada's dress.

Nasuada swallowed as Saphira's consciousness brushed against her own. Saphira felt unlike any other being Nasuada had encountered: ancient, alien, and both ferocious and gentle. That, along with Saphira's imposing physical presence, always reminded Nasuada that if Saphira wanted to eat them, she could. It was impossible, Nasuada believed, to be complacent around a dragon.

I smell blood, said Saphira. *Who has hurt you, Nasuada? Name them, and I shall tear them from neck to groin and bring you their heads for trophies.*

"There's no need for you to tear anyone apart. Not yet, at least. I wielded the knife myself. However, this is the wrong time to delve into the matter. Right now, all I care about is Eragon's whereabouts."

Eragon, said Saphira, *decided to remain in the Empire.*

For a few seconds, Nasuada was unable to move or think. Then a mounting sense of doom replaced her stunned denial of Saphira's revelation. The others reacted in various ways as well, from which Nasuada deduced Saphira had spoken to them all at once.

"How . . . how could you allow him to stay?" she asked.

Small tongues of fire rippled in Saphira's nostrils as she snorted. *Eragon made his own choice. I could not stop him. He insists upon doing what he thinks is right, no matter the consequences for him or the rest of Alagaësia. . . . I could shake him like a hatchling, but I'm proud of him. Fear not; he can take care of himself. So far, no misfortune has befallen him. I would know if he was hurt.*

Arya spoke: "And why did he make this choice, Saphira?"

It would be faster for me to show you rather than explain with words. May I?

They all indicated their consent.

A river of Saphira's memories poured into Nasuada. She saw black Helgrind from above a layer of clouds; heard Eragon, Roran, and Saphira discussing how best to attack; watched them discover the Ra'zac's lair; and experienced Saphira's epic battle with the Lethrblaka. The procession of images fascinated Nasuada. She had been born in the Empire but could remember nothing of it; this was the first time as an adult that she had looked upon anything besides the wild fringes of Galbatorix's holdings.

Lastly came Eragon and his confrontation with Saphira. Saphira attempted to hide it, but the anguish she felt over leaving Eragon was still so raw and piercing, Nasuada had to dry her cheeks with the bandages on her forearms. However, the reasons Eragon gave for staying—killing the last Ra'zac and exploring the remainder of Helgrind—were reasons Nasuada deemed inadequate.

She frowned. *Eragon may be rash, but he's certainly not foolish enough to endanger everything we seek to accomplish merely so he could visit a few caves and drain the last bitter dregs of his revenge. There must be another explanation.* She wondered whether she should press Saphira for the truth, but she knew Saphira would not withhold such information on a whim. *Perhaps she wants to discuss it in private,* she thought.

"Blast it!" exclaimed King Orrin. "Eragon could not have picked a worse time to set off on his own. What matters a single Ra'zac when Galbatorix's entire army resides but a few miles from us? . . . We have to get him back."

Angela laughed. She was knitting a sock using five bone needles, which clicked and clacked and scraped against each other with a steady, if peculiar, rhythm. "How? He'll be traveling during the day, and Saphira daren't fly around searching for him when the sun's up and anyone might spot her and alert Galbatorix."

"Yes, but he's our Rider! We cannot sit by idly while he remains in the midst of our enemies."

"I agree," said Narheim. "However it is done, we must ensure his safe return. Grimstnzborith Hrothgar adopted Eragon into his family and clan—that is mine own clan, as you know—and we owe him the loyalty of our law and our blood."

Arya knelt and, to Nasuada's surprise, began to unlace and retie the upright sections of her boots. Holding one of the cords between her teeth, Arya said, "Saphira, where exactly was Eragon when you last touched his mind?"

In the entrance to Helgrind.

"And have you any idea what path he intended to follow?"

He did not yet know himself.

Springing to her feet, Arya said, "Then I shall have to look everywhere I can."

Like a deer, she bounded forward and ran across the clearing, vanishing among the tents beyond as she sped northward as fast and light as the wind itself.

"Arya, no!" shouted Nasuada, but the elf was already gone. Hopelessness threatened to engulf Nasuada as she stared after her. *The center is crumbling,* she thought.

Grasping the edges of the mismatched pieces of armor that covered his torso as if to tear them off, Garzhvog said to Nasuada, "Do you want me to follow, Lady Nightstalker? I cannot run as fast as little elves, but I can run as long."

"No . . . no, stay. Arya can pass for human at a distance, but soldiers would hunt you down the moment some farmer caught sight of you."

"I am used to being hunted."

"But not in the middle of the Empire, with hundreds of Galbatorix's men wandering the countryside. No, Arya will have to fend for herself. I pray that she can find Eragon and keep him safe, for without him, we are doomed."

◆ ◆ ◆

ESCAPE AND EVASION

Eragon's feet drummed against the ground.

The pounding beat of his stride originated in his heels and ran up his legs, through his hips, and along his spine until it terminated at the base of his skull, where the recurring impact jarred his teeth and exacerbated the headache that seemed to worsen with every passing mile. The monotonous music of his running had annoyed him at first, but before long, it lulled him into a trancelike state where he did not think, but moved.

As Eragon's boots descended, he heard brittle stalks of grass snap like twigs and glimpsed puffs of dirt rising from the cracked soil. He guessed it had been at least a month since it last rained in this part of Alagaësia. The dry air leached the moisture from his breath, leaving his throat raw. No matter how much he drank, he could not compensate for the amount of water the sun and the wind stole from him.

Thus his headache.

Helgrind was far behind him. However, he had made slower progress than he had hoped. Hundreds of Galbatorix's patrols—containing both soldiers and magicians—swarmed across the land, and he often had to hide in order to avoid them. That they were searching for him, he had no doubt. The previous evening, he had even spotted Thorn riding low on the western horizon. He had immediately shielded his mind, thrown himself into a ditch, and stayed there for half an hour, until Thorn dipped back down below the edge of the world.

Eragon had decided to travel on established roads and trails wherever possible. The events of the past week had pushed him to the limits of his physical and emotional endurance. He preferred to allow his body to rest and recover, rather than strain himself forging through brambles, over hills, and across muddy rivers. The time for desperate, violent exertion would come again, but now was not it.

So long as he held to the roads, he dared not run as fast as he was capable; indeed, it would be wiser to avoid running altogether. A fair number of villages and outbuildings were scattered throughout the area. If any of the inhabitants observed a lone man sprinting across the countryside as if a pack of wolves were chasing him, the spectacle would be sure to arouse curiosity and suspicion and might even inspire a frightened crofter to report the incident to the Empire. That could prove fatal for Eragon, whose greatest defense was the cloak of anonymity.

He only ran now because he had encountered no living creatures, except a long snake sunning itself, for over a league.

Returning to the Varden was Eragon's primary concern, and it rankled him to plod along like a common vagabond. Still, he appreciated the opportunity to be by himself. He had not been alone, truly alone, since he found Saphira's egg in the Spine. Always her thoughts had rubbed against his, or Brom or Murtagh or someone else had been at his side. In addition to the burden of constant companionship, Eragon had spent all the months since he had left Palancar Valley engaged in arduous training, breaking only for travel or to take part in the tumult of battle. Never before had he concentrated so intensely for so long or dealt with such huge amounts of worry and fear.

He welcomed his solitude, then, and the peace it brought. The absence of voices, including his own, was a sweet lullaby that, for a short while, washed away his fear of the future. He had no desire to scry Saphira—although they were too far apart to touch each other's minds, his bond with her would tell him if she was hurt—or to contact Arya or Nasuada and hear their angry words. Far better, he thought, to listen to the songs of the flitting birds and the sighing of the breeze through the grass and leafy branches.

The sound of jingling harnesses, clomping hooves, and men's voices jarred Eragon out of his reverie. Alarmed, he stopped and glanced around, trying to determine from what direction the men were approaching. A pair of cackling jackdaws spiraled upward from a nearby ravine.

The only cover close to Eragon was a small thicket of juniper trees. He sprinted toward it and dove under the drooping branches just as six soldiers emerged from the ravine and rode cantering out onto the thin dirt road not ten feet away. Normally, Eragon would have sensed their presence long before they got so close, but since Thorn's distant appearance, he had kept his mind walled off from his surroundings.

The soldiers reined in their horses and milled around in the middle of the road, arguing among themselves. "I'm telling you, I saw something!" one of them shouted. He was of medium height, with ruddy cheeks and a yellow beard.

His heart hammering, Eragon struggled to keep his breathing slow and quiet. He touched his brow to ensure the cloth strip he had tied around his head still covered his upswept eyebrows and pointed ears. *I wish I were still wearing my armor*, he thought. In order to avoid attracting unwanted attention, he had made himself a pack—using dead branches and a square of canvas he had bartered from a tinker—and placed his armor within it. Now he dared not remove and don his armor, for fear the soldiers would hear.

The soldier with the yellow beard climbed down from his bay charger and walked along the edge of the road, studying the ground and the juniper trees beyond. Like every member of Galbatorix's army, the soldier wore a red tunic embroidered with gold thread in the outline of a jagged tongue of fire. The thread sparkled as he moved. His armor was simple—a helmet, a tapered shield, and a leather brigandine—indicating he was little more than a mounted footman. As for arms, he bore a spear in his right hand and a longsword on his left hip.

As the soldier approached his location, spurs clinking, Eragon began to whisper a complex spell in the ancient language. The words poured off his tongue in an unbroken stream, until, to his alarm, he mispronounced a particularly difficult cluster of vowels and had to start the incantation anew.

The soldier took another step toward him.

And another.

Just as the soldier paused in front of him, Eragon completed the spell and felt his strength ebb as the magic took effect. He was an instant too late, however, to completely escape detection, for the soldier exclaimed, "Aha!" and brushed aside the branches, exposing Eragon.

Eragon did not move.

The soldier peered directly at him and frowned. "What the . . . ," he muttered. He jabbed his spear into the thicket, missing Eragon's face by less than an inch. Eragon dug his nails into his palms as a tremor racked his clenched muscles. "Ah, blast it," said the soldier, and released the branches, which sprang back to their original positions, hiding Eragon once more.

"What was it?" called another of the men.

"Nothing," said the soldier, returning to his companions. He removed his helmet and wiped his brow. "My eyes are playing tricks on me."

"What does that bastard Braethan expect of us? We've hardly gotten a wink of sleep these past two days."

"Aye. The king must be desperate to drive us so hard. . . . To be honest, I'd rather not find whoever it is we're searching for. It's not that I'm fainthearted, but anyone who gives Galbatorix pause is best avoided by the likes of us. Let Murtagh and his monster of a dragon catch our mysterious fugitive, eh?"

"Unless we be searching for Murtagh," suggested a third man. "You heard what Morzan's spawn said well as I did."

An uncomfortable silence settled over the soldiers. Then the one who was on the ground vaulted back onto his charger, wrapped the reins around his left hand, and said, "Keep your yap shut, Derwood. You talk too much."

With that, the group of six spurred their steeds forward and continued north on the road.

As the sound of the horses faded, Eragon ended the spell, then rubbed his eyes with his fists and rested his hands on his knees. A long, low laugh escaped him, and he shook his head, amused by how outlandish his predicament was compared with his upbringing in Palancar Valley. *I certainly never imagined this happening to me*, he thought.

The spell he had used contained two parts: the first bent rays of light around his body so he appeared invisible, and the second hopefully prevented other spellweavers from detecting his use of magic. The spell's main drawbacks were that it could not conceal footprints—therefore one had to remain stone-still while using it— and it often failed to completely eliminate a person's shadow.

Picking his way out of the thicket, Eragon stretched his arms high over his head and then faced the ravine from whence the soldiers had emerged. A single question occupied him as he resumed his journey:

What had Murtagh said?

"Ahh!"

The gauzelike illusion of Eragon's waking dreams vanished as he tore at the air with his hands. He twisted nearly in half as he rolled away from where he had been lying. Scrabbling backward, he pushed himself to his feet and raised his arms in front of himself to deflect oncoming blows.

The dark of night surrounded him. Above, the impartial stars continued to gyrate in their endless celestial dance. Below, not a creature stirred, nor could he hear anything but the gentle wind caressing the grass.

Eragon stabbed outward with his mind, convinced that someone was about to attack him. He extended himself over a thousand feet in every direction but found no one else in the vicinity.

At last he lowered his hands. His chest heaved, and his skin burned, and he stank of sweat. In his mind, a tempest roared: a whirlwind of flashing blades and severed limbs. For a moment, he thought he was in Farthen Dûr, fighting the Urgals, and then on the Burning Plains, crossing swords with men like himself. Each location was so real, he would have sworn some strange magic had transported him backward through space and time. He saw standing before him the men and the Urgals whom he had slain; they appeared so real, he wondered if they would speak. And while he no longer bore the scars of his wounds, his body remembered the many injuries he had suffered, and he shuddered as he again felt swords and arrows piercing his flesh.

With a shapeless howl, Eragon fell to his knees and wrapped his arms around his stomach, hugging himself as he rocked back and forth. *It's all right.* . . . *It's all right.* He pressed his forehead against the ground, curling into a hard, tight ball. His breath was hot against his belly.

"What's wrong with me?"

None of the epics Brom had recited in Carvahall mentioned that such visions had bedeviled the heroes of old. None of the warriors Eragon had met in the Varden seemed troubled by the blood they shed. And even though Roran admitted he disliked killing, he did not wake up screaming in the middle of the night.

I'm weak, thought Eragon. *A man should not feel like this. A Rider should not feel like this. Garrow or Brom would have been fine, I know. They did what needed to be done, and that was that. No crying about it, no endless worrying or gnashing of teeth.* . . . *I'm weak.*

Jumping up, he paced around his nest in the grass, trying to calm himself. After half an hour, when apprehension still clenched his chest in an iron grip and his skin itched as if a thousand ants crawled underneath it and he started at the slightest noise, Eragon grabbed his pack and set off at a dead run. He cared not what lay before him in the unknown darkness, nor who might notice his headlong flight.

He only sought to escape his nightmares. His mind had turned against him, and he could not rely upon rational thought to dispel his panic. His one recourse, then, was to trust in the ancient animal wisdom of his flesh, which told him to *move*. If he ran fast and hard enough, perhaps he could anchor himself in the moment. Perhaps the thrashing of his arms, the thudding of his feet on dirt, the slick chill of sweat under his arms, and a myriad of other sensations would, by their sheer weight and number, force him to forget.

Perhaps.

A flock of starlings darted across the afternoon sky, like fish through the ocean.

Eragon squinted at them. In Palancar Valley, when the starlings returned after winter, they often formed groups so large, they transformed day into night. This flock was not that large, yet it reminded him of evenings spent drinking mint tea with Garrow and Roran on the porch of their house, watching a rustling black cloud turn and twist overhead.

Lost in memory, he stopped and sat on a rock so he could retie the laces on his boots.

The weather had changed; it was cool now, and a gray smudge to the west hinted at the possibility of a storm. The vegetation was lusher, with moss and reeds and thick clumps of green grass. Several miles away, five hills dotted the otherwise smooth land. A stand of thick oak trees adorned the central hill. Above the hazy mounds of foliage, Eragon glimpsed the crumbling walls of a long-abandoned building, constructed by some race in ages past.

Curiosity aroused, he decided to break his fast among the ruins. They were sure to contain plentiful game, and foraging would provide him with an excuse to do a bit of exploring before continuing on his way.

Eragon arrived at the base of the first hill an hour later, where he found the remnants of an ancient road paved with squares of stone. He followed it toward the ruins, wondering at its strange construction, for it was unlike any human, elf, or dwarf work he was familiar with.

The shadows under the oak trees chilled Eragon as he climbed the central hill. Near the summit, the ground leveled off underneath his feet and the thicket opened up, and he entered a large glade. A broken tower stood there. The lower part of the tower was wide and ribbed, like the trunk of a tree. Then the structure narrowed and rose toward the sky for over thirty feet, ending in a sharp, jagged line. The upper half of the tower lay on the ground, shattered into innumerable fragments.

Excitement stirred within Eragon. He suspected that he had found an elven outpost, erected long before the destruction of the Riders. No other race had the skill or inclination to build such a structure.

Then he spotted the vegetable garden at the opposite side of the glade.

A single man sat hunched among the rows of plants, weeding a patch of snap peas. Shadows covered his downturned face. His gray beard was so long, it lay piled in his lap like a mound of uncombed wool.

Without looking up, the man said, "Well, are you going to help me finish these peas or not? There's a meal in it for you if you do."

Eragon hesitated, unsure what to do. Then he thought, *Why should I be afraid of an old hermit?* and walked over to the garden. "I'm Bergan. . . . Bergan, son of Garrow."

The man grunted. "Tenga, son of Ingvar."

The armor in Eragon's pack rattled as he dropped it to the ground. For the next hour, he labored in silence along with Tenga. He knew he should not stay for so long, but he enjoyed the task; it kept him from brooding. As he weeded, he allowed his mind to expand and touch the multitude of living things within the glade. He welcomed the sense of unity he shared with them.

When they had removed every last bit of grass, purslane, and dandelions from around the peas, Eragon followed Tenga to a narrow door set into the front of the tower, through which was a spacious kitchen and dining room. In the middle of the room, a circular staircase coiled up to the second story. Books, scrolls, and sheaves of loose-bound vellum covered every available surface, including a goodly portion of the floor.

Tenga pointed at the small pile of branches in the fireplace. With a pop and a crackle, the wood burst into flame. Eragon tensed, ready to grapple physically and mentally with Tenga.

The other man did not seem to notice his reaction but continued to bustle about the kitchen, procuring mugs, dishes, knives, and various leftovers for their lunch. He muttered to himself in an undertone while he did.

Every sense alert, Eragon sank onto the bare corner of a nearby chair. *He didn't utter the ancient language*, he thought. *Even if he said the spell in his head, he still risked death or worse to start a mere cookfire!* For as Oromis had taught Eragon, words were the means by which one controlled the release of magic. To cast a spell without the structure of language binding that motive power was to risk having a stray thought or emotion distort the result.

Eragon gazed around the chamber, searching for clues about his host. He spotted an open scroll that displayed columns of words from the ancient language and recognized it as a compendium of true names similar to those he had studied in Ellesméra. Magicians coveted such scrolls and books and would sacrifice almost anything to obtain them, for with them one could learn new words for a spell and also record therein words one had discovered. Few, however, were able to acquire a compendium, for they were exceedingly rare and those who already owned them almost never parted with them willingly.

It was unusual, then, for Tenga to possess one such compendium, but to Eragon's amazement, he saw six others throughout the room, in addition to writings on subjects ranging from history to mathematics to astronomy to botany.

A mug of ale and a plate with bread, cheese, and a slice of cold meat pie appeared in front of him as Tenga shoved the dishes under his nose.

"Thank you," said Eragon, accepting them.

Tenga ignored him and sat cross-legged next to the fireplace. He continued to grumble and mutter into his beard as he devoured his lunch.

After Eragon had scraped his plate clean and drained the last drops of the fine harvest ale, and Tenga had also nearly completed his repast, Eragon could not help but ask, "Did the elves build this tower?"

Tenga fixed him with a pointed gaze, as if the question made him doubt Eragon's intelligence. "Aye. The tricky elves built Edur Ithindra."

"What is it you do here? Are you all alone, or—"

"I search for the answer!" exclaimed Tenga. "A key to an unopened door, the secret of the trees and the plants. Fire, heat, lightning, light . . . Most do not know the question and wander in ignorance. Others know the question but fear what the answer will mean. Bah! For thousands of years we have lived like savages. Savages! I shall end that. I shall usher in the age of light, and all shall praise my deed."

"Pray tell, what exactly do you search for?"

A frown twisted Tenga's face. "You don't know the question? I thought you might. But no, I was mistaken. Still, I see you understand my search. You search for a different answer, but you search nevertheless. The same brand burns in your heart as burns in mine. Who else but a fellow pilgrim can appreciate what we must sacrifice to find the answer?"

"The answer to what?"

"To the question we choose."

He's mad, thought Eragon. Casting about for something with which he could distract Tenga, his gaze lit upon a row of small wood animal statues arranged on the sill below a teardrop-shaped window. "Those are beautiful," he said, indicating the statues. "Who made them?"

"*She* did . . . before she left. She was always making things." Tenga bounded upright and placed the tip of his left index finger on the first of the statues. "Here the squirrel with his waving tail, he so bright and swift and full of laughing gibes." His finger drifted to the next statue in line. "Here the savage boar, so deadly with his slashing tusks. . . . Here the raven with . . ."

Tenga paid no attention as Eragon backed away, nor when he lifted the latch to the door and slipped out of Edur Ithindra. Shouldering his pack, Eragon trotted down through the crown of oak trees and away from the cluster of five hills and the demented spellcaster who resided among them.

Throughout the rest of that day and the next, the number of people on the road increased until it seemed to Eragon as if a new group was always appearing over a hill. Most were refugees, although soldiers and other men of business were also present. Eragon avoided those he could and trudged along with his chin tucked against his collar the rest of the time.

That practice, however, forced him to spend the night in the village of Eastcroft, twenty miles north of Melian. He had intended to abandon the road long before he arrived at Eastcroft and find a sheltered hollow or cave where he might rest until morn, but because of his relative unfamiliarity with the land, he misjudged the distance and came upon the village while in the company of three men-at-arms. Leaving then, less than an hour from the safety of Eastcroft's walls and gates and the comfort of a warm bed, would have inspired even the slowest dullard to ask why he was trying to avoid the village. So Eragon set his teeth and silently rehearsed the stories he had concocted to explain his trip.

The bloated sun was two fingers above the horizon when Eragon first beheld Eastcroft, a medium-sized village enclosed by a tall palisade. It was almost dark by the time he finally arrived at the village and entered through the gate. Behind him, he heard a sentry ask the men-at-arms if anyone else had been close behind them on the road.

"Not that I could tell."

"That's good enough for me," replied the sentry. "If there are laggards, they'll have to wait until tomorrow to get in." To another man on the opposite side of the gate, he shouted, "Close it up!" Together they pushed the fifteen-foot-tall ironbound doors shut and barred them with four oak beams as thick as Eragon's chest.

They must expect a siege, thought Eragon, and then smiled at his own blindness. *Well, who doesn't expect trouble in these times?* A few months ago, he would have worried about being trapped in Eastcroft, but now he was confident he could scale the fortifications barehanded and, if he concealed himself with magic, escape unnoticed in the gloom of night. He chose to stay, however, for he was tired and casting a spell might attract the attention of nearby magicians, if there were any.

Before he took more than a few steps down the muddy lane that led to the town square, a watchman accosted him, thrusting a lantern toward his face. "Hold there! You've not been to Eastcroft before, have you?"

"This is my first visit," said Eragon.

The stubby watchman bobbed his head. "And have you family or friends here to welcome you?"

"No, I don't."

"What brings you to Eastcroft, then?"

"Nothing. I'm traveling south to fetch my sister's family and bring them back to Dras-Leona." Eragon's story seemed to have no effect on the watchman. *Perhaps he doesn't believe me,* Eragon speculated. *Or perhaps he's heard so many accounts like mine, they've ceased to matter to him.*

"Then you want the wayfarers' house, by the main well. Go there and you will find food and lodging. And while you stay here in Eastcroft, let me warn you, we don't tolerate murder, thievery, or lechery in these parts. We have sturdy stocks and gallows, and they have had their share of tenants. My meaning is clear?"

"Yes, sir."

"Then go, and be you of good fortune. But wait! What is your name, stranger?"

"Bergan."

With that, the watchman strode away, returning to his evening rounds. Eragon waited until the combined mass of several houses concealed the lantern the watchman carried before wandering over to the message board mounted to the left of the gates.

There, nailed over a half-dozen posters of various criminals, were two sheets of parchment almost three feet long. One depicted Eragon, one depicted Roran, and both labeled them traitors to the Crown. Eragon examined the posters with interest and marveled at the reward offered: an earldom apiece to whoever captured them. The drawing of Roran was a good likeness and even included the beard he had grown since fleeing Carvahall, but Eragon's portrait showed him as he had been before the Blood-oath Celebration, when he still appeared fully human.

How things have changed, thought Eragon.

Moving on, he slipped through the village until he located the wayfarers' house. The common room had a low ceiling with tar-stained timbers. Yellow tallow candles provided a soft, flickering light and thickened the air with intersecting layers of smoke. Sand and rushes covered the floor, and the mixture crunched underneath Eragon's boots. To his left were tables and chairs and a large fire-place, where an urchin turned a pig on a spit. Opposite this was a long bar, a fortress with raised drawbridges that protected casks of lager, ale, and stout from the horde of thirsty men who assailed it from all sides.

A good sixty people filled the room, crowding it to an uncomfortable level. The roar of conversation would have been startling enough to Eragon after his time on the road, but with his sensitive hearing, he felt as if he stood in the middle of a pounding waterfall. It was hard for him to concentrate upon any one voice. As soon as he caught hold of a word or a phrase, it was swept away by another utterance. Off in one corner, a trio of minstrels was singing and playing a comic version of "Sweet Aethrid o' Dauth," which did nothing to improve the clamor.

Wincing at the barrage of noise, Eragon wormed his way through the crowd until he reached the bar. He wanted to talk with the serving woman, but she was so busy, five minutes passed before she looked at him and asked, "Your pleasure?" Strands of hair hung over her sweaty face.

"Have you a room to let, or a corner where I could spend the night?"

"I wouldn't know. The mistress of the house is the one you should speak to about that. She'll be down directly," said the serving woman, and flicked a hand at a rank of gloomy stairs.

While he waited, Eragon rested against the bar and studied the people in the room. They were a motley assortment. About half he guessed were villagers from Eastcroft come to enjoy a night of drinking. Of the rest, the majority were men and women—families oftentimes—who were migrating to safer parts. It was easy for him to identify them by their frayed shirts and dirty pants and by how they huddled in their chairs and peered at anyone who came near. However, they studiously avoided looking at the last and smallest group of patrons in the wayfarers' house: Galbatorix's soldiers. The men in red tunics were louder than anyone else. They laughed and shouted and banged on tabletops with their armored fists while they quaffed beer and groped any maid foolish enough to walk by them.

Do they behave like that because they know no one dares oppose them and they enjoy demonstrating their power? wondered Eragon. *Or because they were forced to join Galbatorix's army and seek to dull their sense of shame and fear with their revels?*

Now the minstrels were singing:

> So with her hair aflying, sweet Aethrid o' Dauth
> Ran to Lord Edel and cried, "Free my lover,
> Else a witch shall turn you into a woolly goat!"
> Lord Edel, he laughed and said, "No witch shall turn me
>   into a woolly goat!"

The crowd shifted and granted Eragon a view of a table pushed against one wall. At it sat a lone woman, her face hidden by the drawn hood of her dark traveling cloak. Four men surrounded her, big, beefy farmers with leathery necks and cheeks flushed with the fever of alcohol. Two of them were leaning against the wall on either side of the woman, looming over her, while one sat grinning in a chair turned around backward and the fourth stood with his left foot on the edge of the table and was bent forward over his knee. The men spoke and gestured, their movements careless. Although Eragon could not hear or see what the woman said, it was obvious to him that her response angered the farmers, for they scowled and swelled their chests, puffing themselves up like roosters. One of them shook a finger at her.

To Eragon, they appeared decent, hardworking men who had lost their manners in the depths of their tankards, a mistake he had witnessed often enough on feast days in Carvahall. Garrow had had little respect for men who knew they could not hold their beer and yet insisted on embarrassing themselves in public. "It's unseemly," he had said. "What's more, if you drink to forget your lot in life and not for pleasure, you ought to do it where you won't disturb anyone."

The man to the left of the woman suddenly reached down and hooked a finger underneath the edge of her hood, as if to toss it back. So quickly that Eragon barely saw, the woman lifted her right hand and grasped the man's wrist, but then released it and returned to her previous position. Eragon doubted that anyone else in the common room, including the man she touched, had noticed her actions.

The hood collapsed around her neck, and Eragon stiffened, astounded. The woman was human, but she resembled Arya. The only differences between them were her eyes—which were round and level, not slanted like a cat's—and her ears, which lacked the pointed tips of an elf's. She was just as beautiful as the Arya Eragon knew, but in a less exotic, more familiar way.

Without hesitation, Eragon probed toward the woman with his mind. He had to know who she really was.

As soon as he touched her consciousness, a mental blow struck back at Eragon, destroying his concentration, and then in the confines of his skull, he heard a deafening voice exclaim, *Eragon!*

Arya?

Their eyes met for a moment before the crowd thickened again and hid her.

Eragon hurried across the room to her table, prying apart the bodies packed close together to clear himself a path. The farmers looked askance at him when he emerged from the press, and one said, "You're awful rude, barging in on us uninvited-like. Best make yourself scarce, eh?"

In as diplomatic a voice as he could muster, Eragon said, "It seems to me, gentlemen, that the lady would rather be left alone. Now, you wouldn't ignore the wishes of an honest woman, would you?"

"An honest woman?" laughed the nearest man. "No honest woman travels alone."

"Then let me set your concern to rest, for I am her brother, and we are going to live with our uncle in Dras-Leona."

The four men exchanged uneasy glances. Three of them began to edge away from Arya, but the largest planted himself a few inches in front of Eragon and, breathing upon his face, said, "I'm not sure I believe you, *friend*. You're just trying to drive us away so you can be with her yourself."

He's not far off, thought Eragon.

Speaking quietly enough that only that man could hear, Eragon said, "I assure you, she *is* my sister. Please, sir, I have no quarrel with you. Won't you go?"

"Not when I think you're a lying milksop."

"Sir, be reasonable. There's no need for this unpleasantness. The night is young, and there's drink and music aplenty. Let's not quarrel about such a petty misunderstanding. It's beneath us."

To Eragon's relief, the other man relaxed after a few seconds and uttered a scornful grunt. "I wouldn't want to fight a youngling like you anyway," he said. Turning around, he lumbered toward the bar with his friends.

Keeping his gaze fixed upon the crowd, Eragon slipped behind the table and sat next to Arya. "What are you doing here?" he asked, barely moving his lips.

"Searching for you."

Surprised, he glanced at her, and she raised a curved eyebrow. He looked back at the throng of people and, pretending to smile, asked, "Are you alone?"

"No longer. . . . Did you rent a bed for the night?"

He shook his head.

"Good. I already have a room. We can talk there."

They rose in unison, and he followed her to the stairs at the back of the common room. The worn treads creaked under their feet as they climbed to a hallway on the second story. A single candle illuminated the dingy, wood-paneled corridor. Arya led the way to the last door on the right, and from within the voluminous sleeve of her cloak, she produced an iron key. Unlocking the door, she entered the room, waited for Eragon to cross the threshold after her, and then closed and secured the door again.

A faint orange glow penetrated the lead-lined window across

from Eragon. The glow came from a lantern hanging on the other side of Eastcroft's town square. By it, he was able to make out the shape of an oil lamp on a low table to his right.

"Brisingr," whispered Eragon, and lit the wick with a spark from his finger.

Even with the lamp burning, the room was still dark. The chamber contained the same paneling as the hallway, and the chestnut-colored wood absorbed most of the light that struck it and made the room seem small and heavy, as if a great weight pressed inward. Aside from the table, the only other piece of furniture was a narrow bed with a single blanket thrown over the ticking. A small bag of supplies rested on the mattress.

Eragon and Arya stood facing each other. Then Eragon reached up and removed the cloth strip tied around his head, and Arya unfastened the brooch that held her cloak around her shoulders and placed the garment on the bed. She wore a forest-green dress, the first dress Eragon had seen her in.

It was a strange experience for Eragon to have their appearances reversed, so that he was the one who looked like an elf, and Arya a human. The change did nothing to diminish his regard for her, but it did make him more comfortable in her presence, for she was less alien to him now.

It was Arya who broke the silence. "Saphira said you stayed behind to kill the last Ra'zac and to explore the rest of Helgrind. Is that the truth?"

"It's part of the truth."

"And what is the whole truth?"

Eragon knew that nothing less would satisfy her. "Promise me that you won't share what I'm about to tell you with anyone unless I give you permission."

"I promise," she said in the ancient language.

Then he told her about finding Sloan, why he decided not to bring him back to the Varden, the curse he had laid upon the butcher, and the chance he had given Sloan to redeem himself—at least partially—and to regain his sight. Eragon finished by saying, "Whatever happens, Roran and Katrina can *never* learn that Sloan is still alive. If they do, there'll be no end of trouble."

Arya sat on the edge of the bed and, for a long while, stared at the lamp and its jumping flame. Then: "You should have killed him."

"Maybe, but I couldn't."

"Just because you find your task distasteful is no reason to shirk it. You were a coward."

Eragon bridled at her accusation. "Was I? Anyone with a knife could have killed Sloan. What I did was far harder."

"Physically, but not morally."

"I didn't kill him because I thought it was wrong." Eragon frowned with concentration as he searched for the words to explain himself. "I wasn't afraid . . . not that. Not after going into battle. . . . It was something else. I will kill in war. But I won't take it upon myself to decide who lives and who dies. I don't have the experience or the wisdom. . . . Every man has a line he won't cross, Arya, and I found mine when I looked upon Sloan. Even if I had Galbatorix as my captive, I would not kill him. I would take him to Nasuada and King Orrin, and if they condemned him to death, then I would happily lop off his head, but not before. Call it weakness if you will, but that is how I am made, and I won't apologize for it."

"You will be a tool, then, wielded by others?"

"I will serve the people as best I can. I've never aspired to lead. Alagaësia does not need another tyrant king."

Arya rubbed her temples. "Why does everything have to be so complicated with you, Eragon? No matter where you go, you seem to get yourself mired in difficult situations. It's as if you make an effort to walk through every bramble in the land."

"Your mother said much the same."

"I'm not surprised. . . . Very well, let it be. Neither of us is about to change our opinions, and we have more pressing concerns than arguing about justice and morality. In the future, though, you would do well to remember who you are and what you mean to the races of Alagaësia."

"I never forgot." Eragon paused, waiting for her response, but Arya let his statement pass unchallenged. Sitting on the edge of the table, he said, "You didn't have to come looking for me, you know. I was fine."

"Of course I did."

"How did you find me?"

"I guessed which route you would take from Helgrind. Luckily for me, my guess placed me forty miles west of here, and that was close enough for me to locate you by listening to the whispers of the land."

"I don't understand."

"A Rider does not walk unnoticed in this world, Eragon. Those who have the ears to hear and the eyes to see can interpret the signs easily enough. The birds sing of your coming, the beasts of the earth heed your scent, and the very trees and grass remember your touch. The bond between Rider and dragon is so powerful that those who are sensitive to the forces of nature can feel it."

"You'll have to teach that trick to me sometime."

"It is no trick, merely the art of paying attention to what is already around you."

"Why did you come to Eastcroft, though? It would have been safer to meet me outside the village."

"Circumstances forced me here, as I assume they did you. You did not come here willingly, no?"

"No. . . ." He rolled his shoulders, weary from the day's traveling. Pushing back sleep, he waved a hand at her dress and said, "Have you finally abandoned your shirt and trousers?"

A small smile appeared on Arya's face. "Only for the duration of this trip. I've lived among the Varden for more years than I care to recall, yet I still forget how humans insist upon separating their women from their men. I never could bring myself to adopt your customs, even if I did not conduct myself entirely as an elf. Who was to say yea or nay to me? My mother? She was on the other side of Alagaësia." Arya seemed to catch herself then, as if she had said more than she intended. She continued. "In any event, I had an unfortunate encounter with a pair of ox herders soon after I left the Varden, and I stole this dress directly afterward."

"It fits well."

"One of the advantages of being a spellcaster is that you never have to wait for a tailor."

Eragon laughed for a moment. Then he asked, "What now?"

"Now we rest. Tomorrow, before the sun rises, we shall slip out of Eastcroft, and no one shall be the wiser."

That night, Eragon lay in front of the door, while Arya took the bed. Their arrangement was not the result of deference or courtesy on Eragon's part—although he would have insisted on giving Arya the bed in any event—but rather caution. If anyone were to barge into the room, it would seem odd to find a woman on the floor.

As the empty hours crept by, Eragon stared at the beams above his head and traced the cracks in the wood, unable to calm his racing thoughts. He tried every method he knew to relax, but his mind kept returning to Arya, to his surprise at meeting her, to her comments about his treatment of Sloan, and, above all else, to the feelings he had for her. What those were exactly, he was unsure. He longed to be with her, but she had rejected his advances, and that tarnished his affection with hurt and anger, and also frustration, for while Eragon refused to accept that his suit was hopeless, he could not think of how to proceed.

An ache formed in his chest as he listened to the gentle rise and fall of Arya's breathing. It tormented him to be so close and yet be unable to approach her. He twisted the edge of his tunic between his fingers and wished there was something he could do instead of resigning himself to an unwelcome fate.

He wrestled with his unruly emotions deep into the night, until finally he succumbed to exhaustion and drifted into the waiting embrace of his waking dreams. There he wandered for a few fitful hours until the stars began to fade and it was time for him and Arya to leave Eastcroft.

Together, they opened the window and jumped from the sill to the ground twelve feet below, a small drop for one with an elf's abilities. As she fell, Arya grasped the skirt of her dress to keep it from billowing around her. They landed inches apart and then set off running between the houses toward the palisade.

"People will wonder where we went," said Eragon between strides. "Maybe we should have waited and left like normal travelers."

"It's riskier to stay. I paid for my room. That's all the innkeeper really cares about, not whether we snuck out early." The two of them parted for a few seconds as they circumvented a decrepit wagon, and then Arya added, "The most important thing is to keep moving. If we linger, the king will surely find us."

When they arrived at the outer wall, Arya ranged along it until she found a post that protruded somewhat. She wrapped her hands around it and pulled, testing the wood with her weight. The post swayed and rattled against its neighbors, but otherwise held.

"You first," said Arya.

"Please, after you."

With a sigh of impatience, she tapped her bodice. "A dress is somewhat breezier than a pair of leggings, Eragon."

Heat flooded his cheeks as he caught her meaning. Reaching above his head, he got a good grip and then began to climb the palisade, bracing himself with his knees and feet during the ascent. At the top, he stopped and balanced on the tips of the sharpened posts.

"Go on," whispered Arya.

"Not until you join me."

"Don't be so—"

"Watchman!" said Eragon, and pointed. A lantern floated in the darkness between a pair of nearby houses. As the light approached, the gilded outline of a man emerged from the gloom. He carried a naked sword in one hand.

Silent as a specter, Arya grasped the post and, using only the strength of her arms, pulled herself hand over hand toward Eragon. She seemed to glide upward, as if by magic. When she was close enough, Eragon seized her right forearm and lifted her above the remainder of the posts, setting her down next to him. Like two strange birds, they perched on the palisade, motionless and breathless as the watchman walked underneath them. He swung the lantern in either direction, searching for intruders.

Don't look at the ground, pleaded Eragon. *And don't look up.*

A moment later, the watchman sheathed his sword and continued on his rounds, humming to himself.

Without a word, Eragon and Arya dropped to the other side of the palisade. The armor in Eragon's pack rattled as he struck the grass-covered bank below and rolled to dissipate the force of the impact. Springing to his feet, he bent low and dashed away from Eastcroft over the gray landscape, Arya close behind. They kept to hollows and dry streambeds as they skirted the farms that surrounded the village. A half-dozen times, indignant dogs ran out to protest the invasion of their territories. Eragon tried to calm them with his mind, but the only way he found to stop the dogs from barking was to assure them that their terrible teeth and claws had scared him and Arya away. Pleased with their success, the dogs pranced with wagging tails back to the barns, sheds, and porches where they had been standing guard over their fiefdoms. Their smug confidence amused Eragon.

Five miles from Eastcroft, when it became apparent they were utterly alone and no one was trailing them, Eragon and Arya drew to a halt by a charred stump. Kneeling, Arya scooped several handfuls of dirt from the ground in front of her. "Adurna rïsa," she said. With a faint trickle, water welled out of the surrounding soil and poured into the hole she had dug. Arya waited until the water filled the cavity and then said, "Letta," and the flow ceased.

She intoned a spell of scrying, and Nasuada's face appeared upon the surface of the still water. Arya greeted her. "My Lady," Eragon said, and bowed.

"Eragon," she replied. She appeared tired, hollow-cheeked, as if she had suffered a long illness. A lock snapped free of her bun and coiled itself into a tight knot at her hairline. Eragon glimpsed a row of bulky bandages on her arm as she slid a hand over her head, pressing the rebellious hair flat. "You are safe, thank Gokukara. We were so worried."

"I'm sorry I upset you, but I had my reasons."

"You must explain them to me when you arrive."

"As you wish," he said. "How were you hurt? Did someone attack you? Why haven't any of Du Vrangr Gata healed you?"

"I ordered them to leave me alone. And that I will explain when you arrive." Thoroughly puzzled, Eragon nodded and swallowed his questions. To Arya, Nasuada said, "I'm impressed; you found him. I wasn't sure you could."

"Fortune smiled upon me."

"Perhaps, but I tend to believe your skill was as important as Fortune's generosity. How long until you rejoin us?"

"Two, three days, unless we encounter unforeseen difficulties."

"Good. I will expect you then. From now on, I want you to contact me at least once before noon and once before nightfall. If I fail to hear from you, I'll assume you've been captured, and I'll send Saphira with a rescue force."

"We may not always have the privacy we need to work magic."

"Find a way to get it. I need to know where you two are and whether you're safe."

Arya considered for a moment and then said, "If I can, I will do as you ask, but not if it puts Eragon in danger."

"Agreed."

Taking advantage of the ensuing pause in the conversation, Eragon said, "Nasuada, is Saphira near at hand? I would like to talk to her. . . . We haven't spoken since Helgrind."

"She left an hour ago to scout our perimeter. Can you maintain this spell while I find out if she has returned?"

"Go," said Arya.

A single step carried Nasuada out of their field of view, leaving behind a static image of the table and chairs inside her red pavilion. For a good while, Eragon appraised the contents of the tent, but then restlessness overtook him and he allowed his eyes to drift from the pool of water to the back of Arya's neck. Her thick black hair fell to one side, exposing a strip of smooth skin just above the collar of her dress. That transfixed him for the better part of a minute, and then he stirred and leaned against the charred stump.

There came the sound of breaking wood, and then a field of sparkling blue scales covered the pool as Saphira forced herself into the pavilion. It was hard for Eragon to tell what part of her he saw, it was such a small part. The scales slid past the pool and he glimpsed the underside of a thigh, a spike on her tail, the baggy membrane of a folded wing, and then the gleaming tip of a tooth as she turned and twisted, trying to find a position from which she could comfortably view the mirror Nasuada used for arcane communications. From the alarming noises that originated behind Saphira, Eragon guessed she was crushing most of the furniture. At last she settled in place, brought her head close to the mirror—so that one large sapphire eye occupied the entire pool—and peered out at Eragon.

They looked at each other for a full minute, neither of them moving. It surprised Eragon how relieved he was to see her. He had not truly felt safe since he and she had separated.

"I missed you," he whispered.

She blinked once.

"Nasuada, are you still there?"

The muffled answer floated toward him from somewhere to the right of Saphira: "Yes, barely."

"Would you be so kind as to relay Saphira's comments to me?"

"I'm more than happy to, but at the moment, I'm caught between a wing and a pole, and there's no path free, so far as I can tell. You may have difficulty hearing me. If you're willing to bear with me, though, I'll give it a try."

"Please do."

Nasuada was quiet for several heartbeats, and then in a tone so like Saphira's that Eragon almost laughed, she said, "You are well?"

"I'm healthy as an ox. And you?"

"To compare myself with a bovine would be both ridiculous and insulting, but I'm as fit as ever, if that is what you are asking. I'm pleased Arya is with you. It's good for you to have someone sensible around to watch your back."

"I agree. Help is always welcome when you're in danger." While Eragon was grateful that he and Saphira were able to talk, albeit in a roundabout fashion, he found the spoken word a poor substitute for the free exchange of thoughts and emotions they enjoyed when in close proximity. Furthermore, with Arya and Nasuada privy to their conversation, Eragon was reluctant to address topics of a more personal nature, such as whether Saphira had forgiven him for forcing her to leave him in Helgrind. Saphira must have shared in his reluctance, for she too refrained from broaching the subject. They chatted about other, inconsequential happenings and then bade each other farewell. Before he stepped away from the pool, Eragon touched his fingers to his lips and silently mouthed, *I'm sorry.*

A sliver of space appeared around each of the small scales that rimmed Saphira's eye as the underlying flesh softened. She blinked long and slow, and he knew she understood his message and that she bore him no ill will.

After Eragon and Arya took their leave of Nasuada, Arya

terminated her spell and stood. With the back of her hand, she knocked the dirt from her dress.

While she did, Eragon fidgeted, impatient as he had not been before; right then he wanted nothing else but to run straight to Saphira and curl up with her in front of a campfire.

"Let us be off," he said, already moving.

✦ ✦ ✦

A Delicate Matter

The muscles of Roran's back popped and rippled as he heaved the boulder off the ground.

He rested the large rock on his thighs for an instant and then, grunting, pressed it overhead and locked his arms straight. For a full minute, he held the crushing weight in the air. When his shoulders were trembling and about to fail, he threw the boulder onto the ground in front of him. It landed with a dull thud, leaving an indentation several inches deep in the dirt.

On either side of Roran, twenty of the Varden's warriors struggled to lift boulders of similar size. Only two succeeded; the rest returned to the lighter rocks they were accustomed to. It pleased Roran that the months he had spent in Horst's forge and the years of farmwork before had given him the strength to hold his own with men who had drilled with their weapons every day since they turned twelve.

Roran shook the fire from his arms and took several deep breaths, the air cool against his bare chest. Reaching up, he massaged his right shoulder, cupping the round ball of muscle and exploring it with his fingers, confirming once again that no trace remained of the injury he had suffered when the Ra'zac had bitten him. He grinned, glad to be whole and sound again, being as it had seemed no likelier to him than a cow dancing a jig.

A yelp of pain caused him to look over at Albriech and Baldor, who were sparring with Lang, a swarthy, battle-scarred veteran who taught the arts of war. Even two against one, Lang held his own, and with his wooden practice sword, he had disarmed Baldor, knocked him across the ribs, and jabbed Albriech so hard in the leg, he fell sprawling, all in the span of a few seconds. Roran empathized with them; he had just finished his own session with Lang, and it had left him with several new bruises to go with his faded ones from Helgrind. For the most part, he preferred his hammer over a sword, but he thought he should still be able to handle a blade if the occasion called for it. Swords required more finesse than he felt most fights deserved: bash a swordsman on the wrist and, armored or not, he would be too preoccupied with his broken bones to defend himself.

After the Battle of the Burning Plains, Nasuada had invited the villagers from Carvahall to join the Varden. They had all accepted her offer. Those who would have refused had already elected to stay in Surda when the villagers stopped in Dauth on their way to the Burning Plains. Every able-bodied man from Carvahall had taken up proper arms—discarding their makeshift spears and shields—and had worked to become warriors equal to any in Alagaësia. The people of Palancar Valley were accustomed to a hard life. Swinging a sword was no worse than chopping wood, and it was a far sight easier than breaking sod or hoeing acres of beets in the heat of summer. Those who knew a useful trade continued to ply their craft in service to the Varden, but in their spare time they still strove to master the weapons given to them, for every man was expected to fight when the call to battle sounded.

Roran had devoted himself to the training with unwavering dedication since returning from Helgrind. Helping the Varden defeat the Empire and, ultimately, Galbatorix was the one thing he could do to protect the villagers and Katrina. He was not arrogant enough to believe that he alone could tip the balance of the war, but he was confident in his ability to shape the world and knew that if he applied himself, he could increase the Varden's chances of victory. He had to stay alive, though, and that meant conditioning his body and mastering the tools and techniques of slaughter so as to avoid falling to a more experienced warrior.

As he crossed the practice field, on his way back to the tent he shared with Baldor, Roran passed a strip of grass sixty feet long whereon lay a twenty-foot log stripped of its bark and polished smooth by the thousands of hands that rubbed against it every day. Without breaking his stride, Roran turned, slipped his fingers under the thick end of the log, lifted it, and, grunting from the strain, walked it upright. He gave the log a push then, and it toppled over. Grabbing the thin end, he repeated the process twice more.

Unable to muster the energy to flip the log again, Roran left the field and trotted through the surrounding maze of gray canvas tents, waving to Loring and Fisk and others he recognized, as well as a half-dozen or so strangers who greeted him. "Hail, Stronghammer!" they cried in warm tones.

"Hail!" he replied. *It is a strange thing*, he thought, *to be known to people whom you have not met before*. A minute later, he arrived at the tent that had become his home and, ducking inside, stored away the bow, the quiver of arrows, and the short sword the Varden had given him.

He snared his waterskin from beside his bedding, then hurried back into the bright sunlight and, unstoppering the skin, poured the contents over his back and shoulders. Baths tended to be sporadic and infrequent events for Roran, but today was an important day, and he wanted to be fresh and clean for what was to come. With the sharp edge of a polished stick, he scraped the grime off his arms and legs and out from under his fingernails and then combed his hair and trimmed his beard.

Satisfied that he was presentable, he pulled on his freshly washed tunic, stuck his hammer through his belt, and was about to head off through the camp when he became aware of Birgit watching him from behind the corner of the tent. She clenched a sheathed dagger with both hands.

Roran froze, ready to draw his hammer at the slightest provocation. He knew that he was in mortal danger, and despite his prowess, he was not confident of defeating Birgit if she attacked, for like him, she pursued her enemies with single-minded determination.

"You once asked me to help you," said Birgit, "and I agreed

because I wanted to find the Ra'zac and kill them for eating my husband. Have I not upheld my bargain?"

"You have."

"And do you remember I promised that once the Ra'zac were dead, I would have my compensation from you for your role in Quimby's death?"

"I do."

Birgit twisted the dagger with increasing urgency, the back of her fists ridged with tendons. The dagger rose out of its sheath a full inch, baring the bright steel, and then slowly sank into darkness again. "Good," she said. "I would not want your memory to fail you. I *will* have my compensation, Garrowsson. Never you doubt that." With a swift, firm step, she departed, the dagger hidden among the folds of her dress.

Releasing his breath, Roran sat on a nearby stool and rubbed his throat, convinced that he had narrowly escaped being gutted by Birgit. Her visit had alarmed him but it did not surprise him; he had been aware of her intentions for months, since before they left Carvahall, and he knew that one day he would have to settle his debt with her.

A raven soared overhead, and as he tracked it, his mood lightened and he smiled. "Well," he said to himself. *A man rarely knows the day and hour when he will die. I could be killed at any moment, and there's not a blasted thing I can do about it. What will happen will happen, and I won't waste the time I have aboveground worrying. Misfortune always comes to those who wait. The trick is to find happiness in the brief gaps between disasters. Birgit will do what her conscience tells her to, and I will deal with it when I must.*

By his left foot, he noticed a yellowish stone, which he picked up and rolled between his fingers. Concentrating on it as hard as he could, he said, "Stenr rïsa." The stone ignored his command and remained immobile between his thumb and forefinger. With a snort, he tossed it away.

Standing, he strode north between the rows of tents. While he walked, he tried to untangle a knot in the lacing at his collar, but it resisted his efforts, and he gave up on it when he arrived at Horst's tent, which was twice as large as most. "Hello in there," he said, and knocked on the pole between the two entrance flaps.

Katrina burst out of the tent, copper hair flying, and wrapped her arms around him. Laughing, he lifted her by the waist and spun her in a circle, all the world a blur except her face, then gently set her down. She pecked him on the lips, once, twice, three times. Growing still, he gazed into her eyes, more happy than he could ever remember being.

"You smell nice," she said.

"How are you?" The only flaw in his joy was seeing how thin and pale imprisonment had left her. It made him want to resurrect the Ra'zac so they could endure the same suffering they had inflicted upon her and his father.

"Every day you ask me, and every day I tell you, 'Better.' Be patient; I will recover, but it will take time. . . . The best remedy for what ails me is being with you here under the sun. It does me more good than I can tell you."

"That was not all I was asking."

Crimson spots appeared on Katrina's cheeks, and she tilted her head back, her lips curving in a mischievous smile. "My, you are bold, dear sir. Most bold indeed. I'm not sure I should be alone with you, for fear you might take liberties with me."

The spirit of her reply set his concern to rest. "Liberties, eh? Well, since you already consider me a scoundrel, I might as well enjoy some of these *liberties*." And he kissed her until she broke the contact, although she remained in his embrace.

"Oh," she said, out of breath. "You're a hard man to argue with, Roran Stronghammer."

"That I am." Nodding toward the tent behind her, he lowered his voice and asked, "Does Elain know?"

"She would if she weren't so preoccupied with her pregnancy. I think the stress of the trip from Carvahall may cause her to lose the child. She's sick a good part of the day, and she has pains that . . . well, of an unfortunate nature. Gertrude has been tending her, but she can't do much to ease her discomfort. All the same, the sooner Eragon returns, the better. I'm not sure how long I can keep this secret."

"You'll do fine, I'm sure." He released her then and tugged on the hem of his tunic to smooth out the wrinkles. "How do I look?"

Katrina studied him with a critical eye and then wet the tips of her fingers and ran them through his hair, pushing it back off his forehead. Spotting the knot at his collar, she began to pick at it, saying, "You ought to pay closer attention to your clothes."

"Clothes haven't been trying to kill me."

"Well, things are different now. You're the cousin of a Dragon Rider, and you should look the part. People expect it of you."

He allowed her to continue fussing with him until she was pleased with his appearance. Kissing her goodbye, he walked the half mile to the center of the Varden's massive camp, where Nasuada's red command pavilion stood. The pennant mounted on the top bore a black shield and two parallel swords slanting underneath, and it whipped and snapped in a warm wind from the east.

The six guards outside the pavilion—two humans, two dwarves, and two Urgals—lowered their weapons as Roran approached, and one of the Urgals, a thickset brute with yellow teeth, challenged him, saying, "Who goes there?" His accent was nearly unintelligible.

"Roran Stronghammer, son of Garrow. Nasuada sent for me."

Pounding his breastplate with one fist, which produced a loud crash, the Urgal announced, "Roran Stronghammer requests an audience with you, Lady Nightstalker."

"You may admit him," came the answer from inside.

The warriors lifted their blades, and Roran carefully made his way past. They watched him, and he them, with the detached air of men who might have to fight each other at a moment's notice.

Inside the pavilion, Roran was alarmed to see that most of the furniture was broken and overturned. The only pieces that seemed unharmed were a mirror mounted on a pole and the grand chair in which Nasuada was sitting. Ignoring their surroundings, he knelt and bowed to her.

Nasuada's features and bearing were so different from those of the women Roran had grown up with, he was not sure how to act. She appeared strange and imperious, with her embroidered dress and the gold chains in her hair and her dusky skin, which at the moment had a reddish cast, due to the color of the fabric walls. In stark contrast to the rest of her apparel, linen bandages encased her forearms, a testament to her astounding courage during the Trial of the Long Knives. Her feat had been a topic of constant discussion among the Varden ever since Roran had returned with Katrina. It was the one aspect of her he felt as if he understood, for he too would make any sacrifice in order to protect those he cared about. It just so happened that she cared about a group of thousands, while he was committed to his family and his village.

159

"Please, rise," said Nasuada. He did as he was instructed and rested a hand on the head of his hammer, then waited while she inspected him. "My position rarely allows me the luxury of clear, direct speech, Roran, but I will be blunt with you today. You seem to be a man who appreciates candor, and we have much to discuss in a small amount of time."

"Thank you, my Lady. I have never enjoyed playing word games."

"Excellent. To be blunt, then, you have presented me with two difficulties, neither of which I can easily resolve."

He frowned. "What sort of difficulties?"

"One of character, and one of politics. Your deeds in Palancar Valley and during your flight thence with your fellow villagers are nigh on incredible. They tell me that you have a daring mind and that you are skilled at combat, strategy, and inspiring people to follow you with unquestioning loyalty."

"They may have followed me, but they certainly never stopped questioning me."

A smile touched her lips. "Perhaps. But you still got them here, didn't you? You possess valuable talents, Roran, and the Varden could use you. I assume you wish to be of service?"

"I do."

"As you know, Galbatorix has divided his army and sent troops south to reinforce the city of Aroughs, west toward Feinster, and north toward Belatona. He hopes to drag out this fight, to bleed us dry through slow attrition. Jörmundur and I cannot be in a dozen locations at once. We need captains whom we can trust to deal with the myriad conflicts springing up around us. In this, you could prove your worth to us. But . . ." Her voice faded.

"But you do not yet know if you can rely upon me."

"Indeed. Protecting one's friends and family stiffens a person's spine, but I wonder how you will fare without them. Will your nerve hold? And while you can lead, can you also obey orders? I cast no aspersions on your character, Roran, but the fate of Alagaësia is at stake, and I cannot risk putting someone incompetent in charge of my men. This war does not forgive such errors. Nor would it be fair to the men already with the Varden to place you over them without just cause. You must earn your responsibilities with us."

"I understand. What would you have me do, then?"

"Ah, but it's not that easy, for you and Eragon are practically brothers, and that complicates things immeasurably. As I'm sure you are aware, Eragon is the keystone of our hopes. It is important, then, to shelter him from distractions so he may concentrate upon the task before him. If I send you into battle and you die as a result, grief and anger might very well unbalance him. I've seen it happen before. Moreover, I must take great care with whom I allow you to serve, for there are those who will seek to influence you because of your relation to Eragon. So now you have a fair idea of the scope of my concerns. What have you to say about them?"

"If the land itself is at stake and this war is as hotly contested as you imply, then I say you cannot afford to let me sit idle. Employing me as a common swordsman would be just as much a waste. But I think you know that already. As for politics . . ." He shrugged. "I don't care one whit whom you put me with. No one shall get to Eragon through me. My only concern is breaking the Empire so that my kith and kin can return to our home and live in peace."

"You are determined."

"Very. Could you not allow me to remain in charge of the men from Carvahall? We are as close as family, and we work well together. Test me that way. The Varden would not suffer, then, if I failed."

She shook her head. "No. Perhaps in the future, but not yet. They require proper instruction, and I cannot judge your performance when you are surrounded by a group of people who are so loyal that at your urging they abandoned their homes and traversed the width of Alagaësia."

She considers me a threat, he realized. *My ability to influence the villagers makes her wary of me.* In an attempt to disarm her, he said, "They had their own sense to guide them. They knew it was folly to stay in the valley."

"You cannot explain away their behavior, Roran."

"What do you want of me, Lady? Will you let me serve or not? And if so, how?"

"Here is my offer. This morning, my magicians detected a patrol of twenty-three of Galbatorix's soldiers due east. I am sending out a contingent under the command of Martland Redbeard, the Earl of Thun, to destroy them and to do some scouting besides. If you are agreeable, you will serve under Martland. You will listen to and obey him and hopefully learn from him. He, in turn, will watch you and report to me whether he believes you are suitable for advancement. Martland is very experienced, and I have every confidence in his opinion. Does this strike you as fair, Roran Stronghammer?"

"It does. Only, when would I leave, and how long would I be gone?"

"You would leave today and return within a fortnight."

"Then I must ask, could you wait and send me on a different

expedition, in a few days? I would like to be here when Eragon returns."

"Your concern for your cousin is admirable, but events move apace, and we cannot delay. As soon as I know Eragon's fate, I will have one of Du Vrangr Gata contact you with the tidings, whether they be good or ill."

Roran rubbed his thumb along the sharp edges of his hammer as he tried to compose a reply that would convince Nasuada to change her mind and yet would not betray the secret he held. At last he abandoned the task as impossible and resigned himself to revealing the truth. "You're right. I am worried about Eragon, but of all people he can fend for himself. Seeing him safe and sound isn't why I want to stay."

"Why, then?"

"Because Katrina and I wish to be married, and we would like Eragon to perform the ceremony."

There was a cascade of sharp clicks as Nasuada tapped her fingernails against the arms of her chair. "If you believe I will allow you to loll about when you could be helping the Varden, just so you and Katrina can enjoy your wedding night a few days earlier, then you are sorely mistaken."

"It is a matter of some urgency, Lady Nightstalker."

Nasuada's fingers paused in midair, and her eyes narrowed. "How urgent?"

"The sooner we are wed, the better it will be for Katrina's honor. If you understand me at all, know that I would never ask favors for myself."

Light shifted on Nasuada's skin as she tilted her head. "I see. . . . Why Eragon? Why do you want him to perform the ceremony? Why not someone else: an elder from your village perhaps?"

"Because he is my cousin and I care for him, and because he is a Rider. Katrina lost nearly everything on my account—her home, her father, and her dowry. I cannot replace those things, but I at least want to give her a wedding worth remembering. Without gold or livestock, I cannot pay for a lavish ceremony, so I must find some other means besides wealth to make our wedding memorable, and it seems to me nothing could be more grand than having a Dragon Rider marry us."

Nasuada held her peace for so long, Roran began to wonder if she expected him to leave. Then: "It would indeed be an honor to have a Dragon Rider marry you, but it would be a sorry day if Katrina had to accept your hand without a proper dowry. The dwarves furnished me with many presents of gold and jewelry when I lived in Tronjheim. Some I have already sold to fund the Varden, but what I have left would still keep a woman clothed in mink and satin for many years to come. They shall be Katrina's, if you are amenable."

Startled, Roran bowed again. "Thank you. Your generosity is overwhelming. I don't know how I can ever repay you."

"Repay me by fighting for the Varden as you fought for Carvahall."

"I will, I swear it. Galbatorix will curse the day he ever sent the Ra'zac after me."

"I'm sure he already does. Now go. You may remain in camp until Eragon returns and marries you to Katrina, but then I expect you to be in the saddle the following morning."

✦ ✦ ✦

BLOODWOLF

What a proud man, thought Nasuada as she watched Roran leave the pavilion. *It's interesting; he and Eragon are alike in so many ways, and yet their personalities are fundamentally different. Eragon may be one of the most deadly warriors in Alagaësia, but he isn't a hard or cruel person. Roran, however, is made of sterner stuff. I hope that he never crosses me; I would have to destroy him in order to stop him.*

She checked her bandages and, satisfied that they were still fresh, rang for Farica and ordered her to bring a meal. After her handmaid delivered the food and then retired from the tent, Nasuada signaled Elva, who emerged from her hiding place behind the false panel at the rear of the pavilion. Together, the two of them shared a mid-morning repast.

Nasuada spent the next few hours reviewing the Varden's latest inventory reports, calculating the number of wagon trains she would need to move the Varden farther north, and adding and subtracting rows of figures that represented the finances of her army. She sent messages to the dwarves and Urgals, ordered the bladesmiths to increase their production of spearheads, threatened the Council of Elders with dissolution—as she did most every week—and otherwise attended to the Varden's business. Then, with Elva at her side, Nasuada rode out on her stallion, Battle-storm, and met with Trianna, who had captured and was busy interrogating a member of Galbatorix's spy network, the Black Hand.

As she and Elva left Trianna's tent, Nasuada became aware of a commotion to the north. She heard shouts and cheers, then a man appeared from among the tents, sprinting toward her. Without a word, her guards formed a tight circle around her, save for one of the Urgals, who planted himself in the path of the runner and hefted his club. The man slowed to a stop before the Urgal and, gasping, shouted, "Lady Nasuada! The elves are here! The elves have arrived!"

For a wild, improbable moment, Nasuada thought he meant Queen Islanzadí and her army, but then she remembered Islanzadí was near Ceunon; not even the elves could move a host across the width of Alagaësia in less than a week. *It must be the twelve spell-weavers Islanzadí sent to protect Eragon.*

"Quick, my horse," she said, and snapped her fingers. Her forearms burned as she swung herself onto Battle-storm. She waited only long enough for the nearest Urgal to hand her Elva, then drove her heels into the stallion. His muscles surged beneath her as he sprang into a gallop. Bending low over his neck, she steered him down a crude lane between two rows of tents, dodging men and animals and jumping a rain barrel that barred her way. The men did not seem to take offense; they laughed and scrambled after her so they could see the elves with their own eyes.

When she arrived at the northern entrance to the camp, she and Elva dismounted and scanned the horizon for motion.

"There," said Elva, and pointed.

Nearly two miles away, twelve long, lean figures emerged from behind a stand of juniper trees, their outlines wavering in the morning heat. The elves ran in unison, so light and fast, their feet raised no dust and they appeared to fly over the countryside. Nasuada's scalp prickled. Their speed was both beautiful and unnatural. They reminded her of a pack of predators chasing their prey. She felt the same sense of danger as when she had seen a Shrrg, a giant wolf, in the Beor Mountains.

"Awe-inspiring, aren't they?"

Nasuada started to find Angela next to her. She was annoyed and mystified by how the herbalist had been able to sneak up on her. She wished Elva had warned her of Angela's approach. "How is it you always manage to be present when something interesting is about to occur?"

"Oh well, I like to know what's going on, and being there is so much faster than waiting for someone to tell me about it afterward. Besides, people always leave out important pieces of information, like whether someone's ring finger is longer than their index finger, or whether they have magical shields protecting them, or whether the donkey they are riding happens to have a bald patch in the shape of a rooster's head. Don't you agree?"

Nasuada frowned. "You never reveal your secrets, do you?"

"Now, what good would that do? Everyone would get all excited over some piffle of a spell, and then I'd have to spend hours trying to explain, and in the end, King Orrin would want to chop off my head and I would have to fight off half your spellcasters during my escape. It's just not worth the effort, if you ask me."

"Your answer hardly inspires confidence. But—"

"That's because you are too serious, Lady Nightstalker."

"But tell me," Nasuada persisted, "why would you want to know if someone is riding a donkey with a bald patch shaped like a rooster's head?"

"Ah, that. Well, the man who owns that particular donkey cheated me at a game of knucklebones out of three buttons and a rather interesting shard of enchanted crystal."

"Cheated *you?*"

Angela pursed her lips, obviously irked. "The knucklebones were loaded. I switched them on him, but then he replaced them with a set of his own when I was distracted. . . . I'm still not quite sure how he tricked me."

"So you were both cheating."

"It was a valuable crystal! Besides, how can you cheat a cheater?"

Before Nasuada could respond, the six Nighthawks came pounding out of the camp and took up positions around her. She hid her distaste as the heat and smell of their bodies assailed her. The odor of the two Urgals was especially pungent. Then, somewhat to her surprise, the captain of the shift, a burly man with a crooked nose and the name of Garven, accosted her. "My Lady, may I have a word with you in private?" He spoke through close-set teeth, as if struggling to contain a great emotion.

Angela and Elva looked at Nasuada for confirmation that she wanted them to withdraw. She nodded, and they began walking west, toward the Jiet River. Once Nasuada was confident they were out of hearing, she began to speak, but Garven overrode her, exclaiming, "Blast it, Lady Nasuada, you shouldn't have left us as you did!"

"Peace, Captain," she replied. "It was a small enough risk, and I felt it was important to be here in time to greet the elves."

Garven's mail rustled as he struck his leg with a bunched fist. "A small risk? Not an hour ago, you received proof that Galbatorix still has agents hidden among us. He has been able to infiltrate us again and again, and yet you see fit to abandon your escort and go racing through a host of potential assassins! Have you forgotten the attack in Aberon, or how the Twins slew your father?"

"Captain Garven! You go too far."

"I'll go even further if it means ensuring your well-being."

The elves, Nasuada observed, had halved the distance between them and the camp. Angry, and eager to end the conversation, she said, "I am not without my own protection, Captain."

Flicking his eyes toward Elva, Garven said, "We have suspected as much, Lady." A pause followed, as if he were hoping she would volunteer more information. When she remained silent, he forged onward: "If you were actually safe, then I was wrong to accuse you of recklessness, and I apologize. Still, safety and the appearance of safety are two different things. For the Nighthawks to be effective, we have to be the smartest, toughest, meanest warriors in the land, and people have to *believe* that we're the smartest, the toughest, and the meanest. They have to believe that if they try to stab you or shoot you with a crossbow or use magic against you, that we *will* stop them. If they believe they have about as much chance of killing you as a mouse does a dragon, then they may very well give up the idea as hopeless, and we will have averted an attack without ever having to lift a finger.

"We cannot fight all your enemies, Lady Nasuada. That would take an army. Even Eragon couldn't save you if all who want you dead had the courage to act upon their hatred. You might survive a hundred attempts on your life or a thousand, but eventually one would succeed. The only way to keep that from happening is to convince the majority of your enemies that they will *never* get past the Nighthawks. Our reputation can protect you just as surely as our swords and our armor. It does us no good, then, for people to see you riding off without us. No doubt we looked a right bunch of fools back there, frantically trying to catch up. After all, if you do not respect us, Lady, why should anyone else?"

Garven moved closer, dropping his voice. "We will gladly die for you if we must. All we ask in return is that you allow us to perform our duties. It is a small favor, considering. And the day may come when you are grateful we are here. Your other protection is human, and therefore fallible, whatever her arcane powers may be. She has not sworn the same oaths in the ancient language that we of the Nighthawks have. Her sympathies could shift, and you would do well to ponder your fate if she turned against you. The Nighthawks, however, will never betray you. We are yours, Lady Nasuada, fully and completely. So please, let the Nighthawks do what they are supposed to do. . . . Let us protect you."

Initially, Nasuada was indifferent to his arguments, but his eloquence and the clarity of his reasoning impressed her. He was, she thought, a man she might have use for elsewhere. "I see Jörmundur has surrounded me with warriors as skilled with their tongues as they are with their swords," she said with a smile.

"My Lady."

"You are right. I should not have left you and your men behind, and I am sorry. It was careless and inconsiderate. I am still unaccustomed to having guards with me at all hours of the day, and sometimes I forget I cannot move about with the freedom I once did. You have my word of honor, Captain Garven, it shall not happen again. I do not wish to cripple the Nighthawks any more than you."

"Thank you, my Lady."

Nasuada turned back toward the elves, but they were hidden from sight below the bank of a dry stream a quarter of a mile away. "It strikes me, Garven, that you may have invented a motto for the Nighthawks a moment ago."

"Did I? If so, I cannot recall."

"You did. 'The smartest, the toughest, and the meanest,' you said. That would be a fine motto, although perhaps without the *and*. If the other Nighthawks approve of it, you should have Trianna translate the phrase into the ancient language, and I will have it inscribed on your shields and embroidered on your standards."

"You are most generous, my Lady. When we return to our tents, I shall discuss the matter with Jörmundur and my fellow captains. Only . . ."

He hesitated then, and guessing at what troubled him, Nasuada said, "But you are worried that such a motto may be too vulgar for men of your position, and you would prefer something more noble and high-minded, am I right?"

"Exactly, my Lady," he said with a relieved expression.

"It's a valid concern, I suppose. The Nighthawks represent the Varden, and you must interact with notables of every race and rank in the course of your duty. It would be regrettable if you were to convey the wrong impression. . . . Very well, I leave it to you and your compatriots to devise an appropriate motto. I am confident you will do an excellent job."

At that moment, the twelve elves emerged from the dry streambed, and Garven, after murmuring additional thanks, moved a discreet distance from Nasuada. Composing herself for a state visit, Nasuada signaled Angela and Elva to return.

When he was still several hundred feet away, the lead elf appeared soot-black from head to toe. At first Nasuada assumed he was dark-skinned, like herself, and wearing dark attire, but as he drew closer, she saw that the elf wore only a loincloth and a braided fabric belt with a small pouch attached. The rest of him was covered with midnight-blue fur that glistened with a healthy sheen under the glare of the sun. On average, the fur was a quarter-inch long—a smooth, flexible armor that mirrored the shape and movement of the underlying muscles—but on his ankles and the undersides of his forearms, it extended a full two inches, and between his shoulder blades, there was a ruffled mane that stuck out a handsbreadth from his body and tapered down along his back to the base of his spine. Jagged bangs shadowed his brow, and catlike tufts sprouted from the tips of his pointed ears, but otherwise the fur on his face was so short and flat, only its color betrayed its presence. His eyes were bright yellow. Instead of fingernails, a claw protruded from each of his middle fingers. And as he slowed to a stop before her, Nasuada noticed that a certain odor surrounded him: a salty musk reminiscent of dry juniper wood, oiled leather, and smoke. It was such a strong smell, and so obviously masculine, Nasuada felt her skin go hot and cold and crawl with anticipation, and she blushed and was glad it would not show.

The rest of the elves were more as she had expected, of the same general build and complexion as Arya, with short tunics of dusky orange and pine-needle green. Six were men, and six were women. They all had raven hair, save for two of the women whose hair was like starlight. It was impossible to determine their ages, for their faces were smooth and unlined. They were the first elves besides Arya that Nasuada had met in person, and she was eager to find out if Arya was representative of her race.

Touching his first two fingers to his lips, the lead elf bowed, as did his companions, and then twisted his right hand against his chest and said, "Greetings and felicitations, Nasuada, daughter of Ajihad. Atra esterní onto thelduin." His accent was more pronounced than Arya's: a lilting cadence that gave his words music.

"Atra du evarínya ono varda," replied Nasuada, as Arya had taught her.

The elf smiled, revealing teeth that were sharper than normal. "I am Blödhgarm, son of Ildrid the Beautiful." He introduced the other elves in turn before continuing. "We bring you glad tidings from Queen Islanzadí; last night our spellcasters succeeded in destroying the gates of Ceunon. Even as we speak, our forces advance through the streets toward the tower where Lord Tarrant has barricaded himself. Some few still resist us, but the city has fallen, and soon we shall have complete control over Ceunon."

Nasuada's guards and the Varden gathered behind her burst into cheers at the news. She too rejoiced at the victory, but then a sense of foreboding and disquiet tempered her celebratory mood as she pictured elves—especially ones as strong as Blödhgarm—invading human homes. *What unearthly forces have I unleashed?* she wondered. "These are glad tidings indeed," she said, "and I am well pleased to hear them. With Ceunon captured, we are that much closer to Urû'baen, and thus to Galbatorix and the fulfillment of our goals." In a more private voice, she said, "I trust that Queen Islanzadí will be gentle with the people of Ceunon, with those who have no love for Galbatorix but lack the means or the courage to oppose the Empire."

"Queen Islanzadí is both kind and merciful to her subjects, even if they are her unwilling subjects, but if anyone dares oppose us, we shall sweep them aside like dead leaves before an autumn storm."

"I would expect nothing less from a race as old and mighty as yours," Nasuada replied. After satisfying the demands of courtesy with several more polite exchanges of increasing triviality, Nasuada deemed it appropriate to address the reason for the elves' visit. She ordered the assembled crowd to disperse, then said, "Your purpose here, as I understand it, is to protect Eragon and Saphira. Am I right?"

"You are, Nasuada Svit-kona. And we are aware that Eragon is still inside the Empire but that he will return soon."

"Are you also aware that Arya left in search of him and that they are now traveling together?"

Blödhgarm flicked his ears. "We were informed of that as well. It is unfortunate that they should both be in such danger, but hopefully no harm will befall them."

"What do you intend to do, then? Will you seek them out and escort them back to the Varden? Or will you stay and wait and trust that Eragon and Arya can defend themselves against Galbatorix's minions?"

"We will remain as your guests, Nasuada, daughter of Ajihad. Eragon and Arya are safe enough as long as they avoid detection. Joining them in the Empire could very well attract unwanted attention. Under the circumstances, it seems best to bide our time where we can yet do some good. Galbatorix is most likely to strike here, at the Varden, and if he does, and if Thorn and Murtagh should reappear, Saphira will need all our help to drive them off."

Nasuada was surprised. "Eragon said you were among the strongest spellcasters of your race, but do you really have the wherewithal to thwart that accursed pair? Like Galbatorix, they have powers far beyond those of ordinary Riders."

"With Saphira helping us, yes, we believe that we can match or overcome Thorn and Murtagh. We know what the Forsworn were capable of, and while Galbatorix has probably made Thorn and Murtagh stronger than any individual member of the Forsworn, he certainly won't have made them his equals. In that regard, at least, his fear of treachery is to our benefit. Even three of the Forsworn could not conquer the twelve of us and a dragon. Therefore, we are confident that we can hold our own against all but Galbatorix."

"That is heartening. Since Eragon's defeat at the hands of Murtagh, I have been wondering if we should retreat and hide until Eragon's strength increases. Your assurances convince me that we are not entirely without hope. We may have no idea how to kill Galbatorix himself, but until we batter down the gates of his citadel in Urû'baen, or until he chooses to fly out on Shruikan and confront us on the field of battle, nothing shall stop us." She paused. "You have given me no reason to distrust you, Blödhgarm, but before you enter our camp, I must ask that you allow one of my men to touch each of your minds to confirm that you are actually elves, and not humans Galbatorix has sent here in disguise. It pains me to make such a request, but we have been plagued by spies and traitors, and we dare not take you, or anyone else, at their word. It is not my intention to cause offense, but war has taught us these precautions are necessary. Surely you, who have ringed the entire leafy expanse of Du Weldenvarden with protective spells, can understand my reasons. So I ask, will you agree to this?"

Blödhgarm's eyes were feral and his teeth were alarmingly sharp as he said, "For the most part, the trees of Du Weldenvarden have needles, not leaves. Test us if you must, but I warn you, whomever you assign the task should take great care he does not delve too deeply into our minds, else he may find himself stripped of his reason. It is perilous for mortals to wander among our thoughts; they can easily become lost and be unable to return to their bodies. Nor are our secrets available for general inspection."

Nasuada understood. The elves would destroy anyone who ventured into forbidden territory. "Captain Garven," she said.

Stepping forward with the expression of a man approaching his doom, Garven stood opposite Blödhgarm, closed his eyes, and frowned intensely as he searched out Blödhgarm's consciousness. Nasuada bit the inside of her lip as she watched. When she was a child, a one-legged man by the name of Hargrove had taught her how to conceal her thoughts from telepaths and how to block and divert the stabbing lances of a mental attack. At both those skills she excelled, and although she had never succeeded at initiating contact with the mind of another, she was thoroughly familiar with the principles involved. She empathized, then, with the difficulty and the delicacy of what Garven was trying to do, a trial only made harder by the strange nature of the elves.

Leaning toward her, Angela whispered, "You should have had me check the elves. It would have been safer."

"Perhaps," said Nasuada. Despite all the help the herbalist had given her and the Varden, she still felt uncomfortable relying upon her for official business.

For a few moments longer, Garven continued his efforts, and then his eyes snapped open and he released his breath in an explosive burst. His neck and face were mottled from the strain, and his pupils were dilated, as if it were night. In contrast, Blödhgarm appeared undisturbed; his fur was smooth, his breathing regular, and a faint smile of amusement flickered about the corners of his lips.

"Well?" asked Nasuada.

It seemed to take Garven a longish while to hear her question, and then the burly captain with the crooked nose said, "He is not human, my Lady. Of that I have no doubt. No doubt whatsoever."

Pleased and disturbed, for there was something uncomfortably remote about his reply, Nasuada said, "Very well. Proceed." Thereafter, Garven required less and less time to examine each elf, spending no more than a half-dozen seconds on the very last of the group.

174 Nasuada kept a close eye on him throughout the process, and she saw how his fingers became white and bloodless, and the skin at his temples sank into his skull like the eardrums of a frog, and he acquired the languid appearance of a person swimming deep underwater.

Having completed his assignment, Garven returned to his post beside Nasuada. He was, she thought, a changed man. His original determination and fierceness of spirit had faded into the dreamy air of a sleepwalker, and while he looked at her when she asked if he was well, and he answered in an even enough tone, she felt as if his spirit was far away, ambling among dusty, sunlit glades somewhere in the elves' mysterious forest. Nasuada hoped he would soon recover. If he did not, she would ask Eragon or Angela, or perhaps the two of them together, to attend to Garven. Until such time as his condition improved, she decided that he should no longer serve as an active member of the Nighthawks; Jörmundur would give him something simple to do, so she would not suffer guilt at causing him any further injury, and he might at least have the pleasure of enjoying whatever visions his contact with the elves had left him with.

Bitter at her loss, and furious with herself, with the elves, and with Galbatorix and the Empire for making such a sacrifice necessary, she had difficulty maintaining a soft tongue and good manners. "When you spoke of peril, Blödhgarm, you would have done well to mention that even those who return to their bodies do not escape entirely unscathed."

"My Lady, I am fine," said Garven. His protestation was so weak and ineffectual, hardly anyone noticed, and it only served to strengthen Nasuada's sense of outrage.

The fur on Blödhgarm's nape rippled and stiffened. "If I failed to explain myself clearly enough before, then I apologize. However, do not blame us for what has happened; we cannot help our nature. And do not blame yourself either, for we live in an age of suspicion. To allow us to pass unchallenged would have been negligent on your part. It is regrettable that such an unpleasant incident should mar this historic meeting between us, but at least now you may rest easy, confident that you have established our origins and that we are what we seem to be: elves of Du Weldenvarden."

A fresh cloud of his musk drifted over Nasuada, and even though she was hard with anger, her joints weakened and she was assailed by thoughts of bowers draped in silk, goblets of cherry wine, and the mournful dwarf songs she had often heard echoing through the empty halls of Tronjheim. Distracted, she said, "I would Eragon or Arya were here, for they could have looked at your minds without fear of losing their sanity."

Again she succumbed to the wanton attraction of Blödhgarm's odor, imagining what it would feel like to run her hands through his mane. She only returned to herself when Elva pulled on her left arm, forcing her to bend over and place her ear close to the witch-child's mouth. In a low, harsh voice, Elva said, "Horehound. Concentrate upon the taste of horehound."

Following her advice, Nasuada summoned a memory from the previous year, when she had eaten horehound candy during one of King Hrothgar's feasts. Just thinking about the acrid flavor of the candy dried out her mouth and counteracted the seductive qualities of Blödhgarm's musk. She attempted to conceal her lapse in concentration by saying, "My young companion here is wondering why you look so different from other elves. I must confess to some curiosity on the subject as well. Your appearance is not what we have come to expect from your race. Would you be so kind as to share with us the reason for your more *animalistic* features?"

A shiny ripple flowed through Blödhgarm's fur as he shrugged. "This shape pleased me," he said. "Some write poems about the sun and the moon, others grow flowers or build great structures or compose music. As much as I appreciate those various art forms, I believe that true beauty only exists in the fang of a wolf, in the pelt of the forest cat, in the eye of an eagle. So I adopted those attributes for myself. In another hundred years, I may lose interest in the beasts of the land and instead decide that the beasts of the sea embody all that is good, and then I will cover myself with scales, transform my hands into fins and my feet into a tail, and I will vanish beneath the surface of the waves and never again be seen in Alagaësia."

If he was jesting, as Nasuada believed, he showed no indication of it. Quite to the contrary, he was so serious, she wondered if he was mocking her. "Most interesting," she said. "I hope the urge to become a fish does not strike you in the near future, for we have need of you on dry ground. Of course, if Galbatorix should decide to also enslave the sharks and the rockfish, why, then, a spellcaster who can breathe underwater may be of some use."

Without warning, the twelve elves filled the air with their clear, bright laughter, and birds for over a mile in every direction burst into song. The sound of their mirth was like water falling on crystal. Nasuada smiled without meaning to, and around her she saw similar expressions on the faces of her guards. Even the two Urgals seemed giddy with joy. And when the elves fell silent and the world became mundane again, Nasuada felt the sadness of a fading dream. A film of tears obscured her vision for a clutch of heartbeats, and then that too was gone.

Smiling for the first time, and thereby presenting a visage both handsome and terrifying, Blödhgarm said, "It will be an honor to serve alongside a woman as intelligent, capable, and witty as yourself, Lady Nasuada. One of these days, when your duties permit, I would be delighted to teach you our game of Runes. You would make a formidable opponent, I'm sure."

The elves' sudden shift in behavior reminded her of a word she had occasionally heard the dwarves use to describe them: *capricious*. It had seemed a harmless enough description when she was a girl—it reinforced her concept of the elves as creatures who flitted from one delight to another, like fairies in a garden of flowers—but she now recognized that what the dwarves really meant was *Beware! Beware, for you never know what an elf will do.* She sighed to herself, depressed by the prospect of having to contend with another group of beings intent on controlling her for their own ends. *Is life always this complicated?* she wondered. *Or do I bring it upon myself?*

From within the camp, she saw King Orrin riding toward them at the head of a massive train of nobles, courtiers, functionaries major and minor, advisers, assistants, servants, men-at-arms, and a plethora of other species she did not bother identifying, while from the west, rapidly descending on outstretched wings, she saw Saphira. Girding herself for the loud tedium about to engulf them, she said, "It may be some months before I have the opportunity to accept your offer, Blödhgarm, but I appreciate it nevertheless. I would enjoy the distraction of a game after the work of a long day. For the present, however, it must remain a deferred pleasure. The entire weight of human society is about to crash down upon you. I suggest you prepare yourselves for an avalanche of names, questions, and requests. We humans are a curious lot, and none of us have seen so many elves before."

"We are prepared for this, Lady Nasuada," said Blödhgarm.

As King Orrin's thundering cavalcade drew near and Saphira prepared to land, flattening the grass with the wind from her wings, Nasuada's last thought was, *Oh dear. I'll have to put a battalion around Blödhgarm to keep him from being torn apart by the women in the camp. And even that might not solve the problem!*

◆　◆　◆

MERCY, DRAGON RIDER

It was midafternoon the day after they had left Eastcroft when Eragon sensed the patrol of fifteen soldiers ahead of them.

He mentioned it to Arya, and she nodded. "I noticed them as well." Neither he nor she voiced any concerns, but worry began to gnaw at Eragon's belly, and he saw how Arya's eyebrows lowered into a fierce frown.

The land around them was open and flat, devoid of any cover. They had encountered groups of soldiers before, but always in the company of other travelers. Now they were alone on the faint trail of a road.

"We could dig a hole with magic, cover the top with brush, and hide in it until they leave," said Eragon.

Arya shook her head without breaking stride. "What would we do with the excess dirt? They'd think they had discovered the biggest badger den in existence. Besides, I would rather save our energy for running."

Eragon grunted. *I'm not sure how many more miles I have left in me.* He was not winded, but the relentless pounding was wearing him down. His knees hurt, his ankles were sore, his left big toe was red and swollen, and blisters continued to break out on his heels, no matter how tightly he bound them. The previous night, he had healed several of the aches and pains troubling him, and while that had provided a measure of relief, the spells only exacerbated his exhaustion.

The patrol was visible as a plume of dust for half an hour before Eragon was able to make out the shapes of the men and the horses at the base of the yellow cloud. Since he and Arya had keener eyesight than most humans, it was unlikely the horsemen could see them at that distance, so they continued to run for another ten minutes. Then they stopped. Arya removed her skirt from her pack and tied it over the leggings she wore while running, and Eragon stored Brom's ring in his own pack and smeared dirt over his right palm to hide his silvery gedwëy ignasia. They resumed their journey with bowed heads, hunched shoulders, and dragging feet. If all went well, the soldiers would assume they were just another pair of refugees.

Although Eragon could feel the rumble of approaching hoofbeats and hear the cries of the men driving their steeds, it still took the better part of an hour for their two groups to meet on the vast plain. When they did, Eragon and Arya moved off the road and stood looking down between their feet. Eragon caught a glimpse of horse legs from under the edge of his brow as the first few riders pounded past, but then the choking dust billowed over him, obscuring the rest of the patrol. The dirt in the air was so thick, he had to close his eyes. Listening carefully, he counted until he was sure that more than half the patrol had gone by. *They're not going to bother questioning us!* he thought.

His elation was short-lived. A moment later, someone in the swirling blizzard of dust shouted, "Company, halt!" A chorus of *Whoas*, *Steady theres*, and *Hey there, Nells* rang out as the fifteen men coaxed their mounts to form a circle around Eragon and Arya. Before the soldiers completed their maneuver and the air cleared, Eragon pawed the ground for a large pebble, then stood back up.

"Be still!" hissed Arya.

While he waited for the soldiers to make their intentions known, Eragon strove to calm his racing heart by rehearsing the story he and Arya had concocted to explain their presence so close to the border with Surda. His efforts failed, for notwithstanding his strength, his training, the knowledge of the battles he had won, and the half-dozen wards protecting him, his flesh remained convinced that imminent injury or death awaited him. His gut twisted, his throat constricted, and his limbs were light and unsteady. *Oh, get on with it!* he thought. He longed to tear something apart with his hands, as if an act of destruction would relieve the pressure building inside of him, but the urge only heightened his frustration, for he dared not move. The one thing that steadied him was Arya's presence. He would sooner cut off a hand than have her consider him a coward. And although she was a mighty warrior in her own right, he still felt the desire to defend her.

The voice that had ordered the patrol to halt again issued forth. "Let me see your faces." Raising his head, Eragon saw a man sitting before them on a roan charger, his gloved hands folded over the pommel of his saddle. Upon his upper lip there sprouted an enormous curly mustache that, after descending to the corners of his mouth, extended a good nine inches in either direction and was in stark contrast to the straight hair that fell to his shoulders. How such a massive piece of sculpted foliage supported its own weight puzzled Eragon, especially since it was dull and lusterless and obviously had not been impregnated with warm beeswax.

The other soldiers held spears pointed at Eragon and Arya. So much dirt covered them, it was impossible to see the flames stitched on their tunics.

"Now then," said the man, and his mustache wobbled like an unbalanced set of scales. "Who are you? Where are you going? And what is your business in the king's lands?" Then he waved a hand. "No, don't bother answering. It doesn't matter. Nothing matters nowadays. The world is coming to an end, and we waste our days interrogating peasants. Bah! Superstitious vermin who scurry from place to place, devouring all the food in the land and reproducing at a ghastly rate. At my family's estate near Urû'baen, we would have the likes of you flogged if we caught you wandering around without permission, and if we learned that you had stolen from your master, why, then we'd hang you. Whatever you want to tell me is lies. It always is. . . .

"What have you got in that pack of yours, eh? Food and blankets, yes, but maybe a pair of gold candlesticks, eh? Silverware from the locked chest? Secret letters for the Varden? Eh? Cat got your tongue? Well, we'll soon sort the matter out. Langward, why don't you see what treasures you can excavate from yonder knapsack, there's a good boy."

Eragon staggered forward as one of the soldiers struck him across the back with the haft of a spear. He had wrapped his armor in rags to keep the pieces from rubbing against each other. The rags, however, were too thin to entirely absorb the force of the blow and muffle the clang of metal.

"Oho!" exclaimed the man with the mustache.

Grabbing Eragon from behind, the soldier unlaced the top of his pack and pulled out his hauberk, saying, "Look, sir!"

The man with the mustache broke out in a delighted grin. "Armor! And of fine make as well. Very fine, I should say. Well, you *are* full of surprises. Going to join the Varden, were you? Intent on treason and sedition, mmh?" His expression soured. "Or are you one of those who generally give honest soldiers a bad name? If so, you are a most incompetent mercenary; you don't even have a weapon. Was it too much trouble to cut yourself a staff or a club, eh? Well, how about it? Answer me!"

"No, sir."

"No, sir? Didn't occur to you, I suppose. It's a pity we have to accept such slow-minded wretches, but that's what this blasted war has reduced us to, scrounging for leftovers."

"Accept me where, sir?"

"Silence, you insolent rascal! No one gave you permission to speak!" His mustache quivering, the man gestured. Red lights exploded across Eragon's field of vision as the soldier behind him bashed him on the head. "Whether you are a thief, a traitor, a mercenary, or merely a fool, your fate will be the same. Once you swear the oath of service, you will have no choice but to obey Galbatorix and those who speak for him. We are the first army in history to be free of dissent. No mindless blathering about what we should do. Only orders, clear and direct. You too shall join our cause, and you shall have the privilege of helping to make real the glorious future our great king has foreseen. As for your lovely companion, there are other ways she can be of use to the Empire, eh? Now tie them up!"

Eragon knew then what he had to do. Glancing over, he found Arya already looking at him, her eyes hard and bright. He blinked once. She blinked in return. His hand tightened around the pebble.

Most of the soldiers Eragon had fought on the Burning Plains had possessed certain rudimentary wards intended to shield them from magical attacks, and he suspected these men were likewise equipped. He was confident he could break or circumvent any spells Galbatorix's magicians invented, but it would require more time than he now had. Instead, he cocked his arm and, with a flick of his wrist, threw the pebble at the man with the mustache.

The pebble punctured the side of his helm.

Before the soldiers could react, Eragon twisted around, yanked the spear from the hands of the man who had been tormenting him, and used it to knock him off his horse. As the man landed, Eragon stabbed him through the heart, breaking the blade of the spear on the metal plates of the soldier's gambeson. Releasing the spear, Eragon dove backward, his body parallel with the ground as he passed underneath seven spears that were flying toward where he had been. The lethal shafts seemed to float above him as he fell.

The instant Eragon had released the pebble, Arya bounded up the side of the horse nearest her, jumping from stirrup to saddle, and kicked the head of the oblivious soldier who was perched on the mare. He went hurtling more than thirty feet. Then Arya leaped from the back of horse to horse, killing the soldiers with her knees, her feet, and her hands in an incredible display of grace and balance.

Jagged rocks tore at Eragon's stomach as he tumbled to a stop. Grimacing, he sprang upright. Four soldiers who had dismounted confronted him with drawn swords. They charged. Dodging to the right, he caught the first soldier's wrist as the man swung his sword and punched him in the armpit. The man collapsed and was still. Eragon dispatched his next opponents by twisting their heads until their spines snapped. The fourth soldier was so close by then, running at him with sword held high, Eragon could not evade him.

Trapped, he did the one thing he could: he struck the man in the chest with all his might. A fount of blood and sweat erupted as his fist connected. The blow staved in the man's ribs and propelled him more than a dozen feet over the grass, where he fetched up against another corpse.

Eragon gasped and doubled over, cradling his throbbing hand. Four of his knuckles were disjointed, and white cartilage showed through his mangled skin. *Blast*, he thought as hot blood poured from the wounds. His fingers refused to move when he ordered them to; he realized that his hand would be useless until he could heal it. Fearing another attack, he looked around for Arya and the rest of the soldiers.

The horses had scattered. Only three soldiers remained alive. Arya was grappling with two of them some distance away while the third and final soldier fled south along the road. Gathering his strength, Eragon pursued him. As he narrowed the gap between them, the man began to plead for mercy, promising he would tell no one about the massacre and holding out his hands to show they were empty. When Eragon was within arm's reach, the man veered to the side and then a few steps later changed direction again, darting back and forth across the countryside like a frightened jackrabbit. All the while, the man continued to beg, tears streaming down his cheeks, saying that he was too young to die, that he had yet to marry and father a child, that his parents would miss him, and that he had been pressed into the army and this was only his fifth mission and why couldn't Eragon leave him alone? "What have you against me?" he sobbed. "I only did what I had to. I'm a good person!"

Eragon paused and forced himself to say: "You can't keep up with us. We can't leave you; you'll catch a horse and betray us."

"No, I won't!"

"People will ask what happened here. Your oath to Galbatorix and the Empire won't let you lie. I'm sorry, but I don't know how to release you from your bond, except . . ."

"Why are you doing this? You're a monster!" screamed the man. With an expression of pure terror, he made an attempt to dash around Eragon and return to the road. Eragon overtook him in less than ten feet, and as the man was still crying and asking for clemency, Eragon wrapped his left hand around his neck and squeezed. When he relaxed his grip, the soldier fell across his feet, dead.

Bile coated Eragon's tongue as he stared down at the man's slack face. *Whenever we kill, we kill a part of ourselves,* he thought. Shaking with a combination of shock, pain, and self-loathing, he walked back to where the fight had begun. Arya was kneeling beside a body, washing her hands and arms with water from a tin flask one of the soldiers had been carrying.

"How is it," asked Arya, "you could kill that man, but you could not bring yourself to lay a finger on Sloan?" She stood and faced him, her gaze frank.

Devoid of emotion, he shrugged. "He was a threat. Sloan wasn't. Isn't it obvious?"

Arya was quiet for a while. "It ought to be, but it isn't. . . . I am ashamed to be instructed in morality by one with so much less experience. Perhaps I have been too certain, too confident of my own choices."

Eragon heard her speak, but the words meant nothing to him as his gaze drifted over the corpses. *Is this all my life has become?* he wondered. *A never-ending series of battles?* "I feel like a murderer."

"I understand how difficult this is," said Arya. "Remember, Eragon, you have experienced only a small part of what it means to be a Dragon Rider. Eventually, this war will end, and you will see that your duties encompass more than violence. The Riders were not just warriors, they were teachers, healers, and scholars."

His jaw muscles knotted for a moment. "Why are we fighting these men, Arya?"

"Because they stand between us and Galbatorix."

"Then we should find a way to strike at Galbatorix directly."

"None exist. We cannot march to Urû'baen until we defeat his forces. And we cannot enter his castle until we disarm almost a century's worth of traps, magical and otherwise."

"There has to be a way," he muttered. He remained where he was as Arya strode forward and picked up a spear. But when she placed the tip of the spear under the chin of a slain soldier and thrust it into his skull, Eragon sprang toward her and pushed her away from the body. "What are you doing?" he shouted.

Anger flashed across Arya's face. "I will forgive that only because you are distraught and not of your right mind. Think, Eragon! It is too late in the day for anyone to be coddling you. Why is this necessary?"

The answer presented itself to him, and he grudgingly said, "If we don't, the Empire will notice that most of the men were killed by hand."

"Exactly! The only ones capable of such a feat are elves, Riders, and Kull. And since even an imbecile could figure out a Kull was not responsible for this, they'll soon know we are in the area, and in less than a day, Thorn and Murtagh will be flying overhead, searching for us." There was a wet squelch as she pulled the spear out of the body. She held it out to him until he accepted it. "I find this as repulsive as you do, so you might as well make yourself useful and help."

Eragon nodded. Then Arya scavenged a sword, and together they set out to make it appear as if a troop of ordinary warriors had killed the soldiers. It was grisly work, but it went quickly, for they both knew exactly what kinds of wounds the soldiers should have to ensure the success of the deception, and neither of them wished to linger. When they came to the man whose chest Eragon had destroyed, Arya said, "There's little we can do to disguise an injury like that. We will have to leave it as is and hope people assume a horse stepped on him." They moved on. The last soldier they dealt with was the commander of the patrol. His mustache was now limp and torn and had lost most of its former splendor.

After enlarging the pebble hole so it more closely resembled the triangular pit left by the spike of a war hammer, Eragon rested for a moment, contemplating the commander's sad mustache, then said, "He was right, you know."

"About what?"

"I need a weapon, a proper weapon. I need a sword." Wiping his palms on the edge of his tunic, he surveyed the plain around them, counting the bodies. "That's it, then, isn't it? We're done." He went and collected his scattered armor, rewrapped it in cloth, and returned it to the bottom of his pack. Then he joined Arya on the low hillock she had climbed.

"We had best avoid the roads from now on," she said. "We cannot risk another encounter with Galbatorix's men." Indicating his deformed right hand, which stained his tunic with blood, she said, "You should tend to that before we set forth." She gave him no time to respond but grasped his paralyzed fingers and said, "Waíse heill."

An involuntary groan escaped him as his fingers popped back into their sockets, and as his abraded tendons and crushed cartilage regained the fullness of their proper shapes, and as the flaps of skin hanging from his knuckles again covered the raw flesh below. When the spell ended, he opened and closed his hand to confirm that it was fully cured. "Thank you," he said. It surprised him that she had taken the initiative when he was perfectly capable of healing his own wounds.

Arya seemed embarrassed. Looking away, out over the plains, she said, "I am glad you were by my side today, Eragon."

"And you by mine."

She favored him with a quick, uncertain smile. They lingered on the hillock for another minute, neither of them eager to resume their journey. Then Arya sighed and said, "We should be off. The shadows lengthen, and someone else is bound to appear and raise a hue and cry when they discover this crows' feast."

Abandoning the hillock, they orientated themselves in a south-westerly direction, angling away from the road, and loped out across the uneven sea of grass. Behind them, the first of the carrion eaters dropped from the sky.

SHADOWS OF THE PAST

That night, Eragon sat staring at their meager fire, chewing on a dandelion leaf. Their dinner had consisted of an assortment of roots, seeds, and greens that Arya had gathered from the surrounding countryside. Eaten uncooked and unseasoned, they were hardly appetizing, but he had refrained from augmenting the meal with a bird or rabbit, of which there was an abundance in the immediate vicinity, for he did not wish Arya to regard him with disapproval. Moreover, after their fight with the soldiers, the thought of taking another life, even an animal's, sickened him.

It was late, and they would have to get an early start the next morning, but he made no move to retire, nor did Arya. She was situated at right angles to him, her legs pulled up, with her arms wrapped around them and her chin resting on her knees. The skirt of her dress spread outward, like the wind-battered petals of a flower.

His chin sunk low against his chest, Eragon massaged his right hand with his left, trying to dispel a deep-seated ache. *I need a sword,* he thought. *Short of that, I could use some sort of protection for my hands so I don't cripple myself whenever I hit something. The problem is, I'm so strong now, I would have to wear gloves with several inches of padding, which is ridiculous. They would be too bulky, too hot, and what's more, I can't go around with gloves on for the rest of my life.* He frowned. Pushing the bones of his hand out of their normal positions, he studied how they altered the play of light over his skin, fascinated by the malleability of his body. *And what happens if I get in a fight while I'm wearing Brom's ring? It's of elvish make, so I probably don't have to worry about breaking the sapphire. But if I hit anything with* the ring on my finger, I won't just dislocate a few joints, I'll splinter every bone in my hand. . . . I might not even be able to repair the damage. . . . He tightened his hands into fists and slowly turned them from side to side, watching the shadows deepen and fade between his knuckles. *I could invent a spell that would stop any object that was moving at a dangerous speed from touching my hands. No, wait, that's no good. What if it was a boulder? What if it was a mountain? I'd kill myself trying to stop it.*

Well, if gloves and magic won't work, I'd like to have a set of the dwarves' Ascûdgamln, their "fists of steel." With a smile, he remembered how the dwarf Shrrgnien had a steel spike threaded into a metal base that was embedded in each of his knuckles, excluding those on his thumbs. The spikes allowed Shrrgnien to hit whatever he wanted with little fear of pain, and they were convenient too, for he could remove them at will. The concept appealed to Eragon, but he was not about to start drilling holes in his knuckles. *Besides,* he thought, *my bones are thinner than dwarf bones, too thin, perhaps, to attach the base and still have the joints function as they should. . . . So Ascûdgamln are a bad idea, but maybe instead I can . . .*

Bending low over his hands, he whispered, "Thaefathan."

The backs of his hands began to crawl and prickle as if he had fallen into a patch of stinging nettles. The sensation was so intense and so unpleasant, he longed to jump up and scratch himself as hard as he could. With an effort of will, he stayed where he was and watched as the skin on his knuckles bulged, forming a flat, whitish callus half an inch thick over each joint. They reminded him of the hornlike deposits that appear on the inside of horses' legs. When he was pleased with the size and density of the knobs, he released the flow of magic and set about exploring, by touch and sight, the mountainous new terrain that loomed over his fingers.

His hands were heavier and stiffer than before, but he could still move his fingers through their full range of motion. *It may be ugly,* he thought, rubbing the rough protuberances on his right hand against the palm of his left, *and people may laugh and sneer if they notice, but I don't care, for it will serve its purpose and may keep me alive.*

Brimming with silent excitement, he struck the top of a domed rock that rose out of the ground between his legs. The impact jarred his arm and produced a muted thud but caused him no more discomfort than it would have to punch a board covered with several layers of cloth. Emboldened, he retrieved Brom's ring from his pack and slipped on the cool gold band, checking that the adjacent callus was higher than the face of the ring. He tested his observation by again ramming his fist against the rock. The only resulting sound was that of dry, compacted skin colliding with unyielding stone.

"What are you doing?" asked Arya, peering at him through a veil of her black hair.

"Nothing." Then he held out his hands. "I thought it would be a good idea, since I'll probably have to hit someone again."

Arya studied his knuckles. "You are going to have difficulty wearing gloves."

"I can always cut them open to make room."

She nodded and returned to gazing at the fire.

Eragon leaned back on his elbows and stretched out his legs, content that he was prepared for whatever fights might await him in the immediate future. Beyond that, he dared not speculate, for if he did, he would begin to ask himself how he and Saphira could possibly defeat Murtagh or Galbatorix, and then panic would sink its icy claws into him.

He fixed his gaze on the flickering depths of the fire. There, in that writhing inferno, he sought to forget his cares and responsibilities. But the constant motion of the flames soon lulled him into a passive state where unrelated fragments of thoughts, sounds, images, and emotions drifted through him like snowflakes falling from a calm winter's sky. And amid that flurry, there appeared the face of the soldier who had begged for his life. Again Eragon saw him crying, and again he heard his desperate pleas, and again he felt how his neck snapped like a wet branch of wood.

Tormented by the memories, Eragon clenched his teeth and breathed hard through flared nostrils. Cold sweat sprang up over his entire body. He shifted in place and strove to dispel the soldier's unfriendly ghost, but to no avail. *Go away!* he shouted. *It wasn't my fault. Galbatorix is the one you should blame, not me. I didn't want to kill you!*

Somewhere in the darkness surrounding them, a wolf howled. From various locations across the plains, a score of other wolves answered, raising their voices in a discordant melody. The eerie singing made Eragon's scalp tingle and goosebumps break out on his arms. Then, for a brief moment, the howls coalesced into a single tone that was similar to the battle-cry of a charging Kull.

Eragon shifted, uneasy.

"What's wrong?" asked Arya. "Is it the wolves? They shall not bother us, you know. They are teaching their pups how to hunt, and they won't allow their younglings near creatures who smell as strangely as we do."

"It's not the wolves out there," said Eragon, hugging himself. "It's the wolves in here." He tapped the middle of his forehead.

Arya nodded, a sharp, birdlike motion that betrayed the fact she was not human, even though she had assumed the shape of one. "It is always thus. The monsters of the mind are far worse than those that actually exist. Fear, doubt, and hate have hamstrung more people than beasts ever have."

"And love," he pointed out.

"And love," she admitted. "Also greed and jealousy and every other obsessive urge the sentient races are susceptible to."

Eragon thought of Tenga alone, in the ruined elf outpost of Edur Ithindra, hunched over his precious hoard of tomes, searching, always searching, for his elusive "answer." He refrained from mentioning the hermit to Arya, for it was not in him to discuss that curious encounter at the present. Instead, he asked, "Does it bother you when you kill?"

Arya's green eyes narrowed. "Neither I nor the rest of my people eat the flesh of animals because we cannot bear to hurt another creature to satisfy our hunger, and you have the effrontery to ask if killing disturbs us? Do you really understand so little of us that you believe we are coldhearted murderers?"

"No, of course not," he protested. "That's not what I meant."

"Then say what you mean, and do not give insult unless it is your intention."

Choosing his words with greater care now, Eragon said, "I asked this of Roran before we attacked Helgrind, or a question very like it. What I want to know is, how do you feel when you kill? How are you supposed to feel?" He scowled at the fire. "Do you see the warriors you have vanquished staring back at you, as real as you are before me?"

Arya tightened her arms around her legs, her gaze pensive. A flame jetted upward as the fire incinerated one of the moths circling the camp. "Gánga," she murmured, and motioned with a finger. With a flutter of downy wings, the moths departed. Never lifting her eyes from the clump of burning branches, she said, "Nine months after I became an ambassador, my mother's only ambassador, if truth be told, I traveled from the Varden in Farthen Dûr to the capital of Surda, which was still a new country in those days. Soon after my companions and I left the Beor Mountains, we encountered a band of roving Urgals. We were content to keep our swords in their sheaths and continue on our way, but as is their wont, the Urgals insisted on trying to win honor and glory to better their standing within their tribes. Our force was larger than theirs—for Weldon, the man who succeeded Brom as leader of the Varden, was with us—and it was easy for us to drive them off. . . . That day was the first time I took a life. It troubled me for weeks afterward, until I realized I would go mad if I continued to dwell upon it. Many do, and they become so angry, so grief-ridden, they can no longer be relied upon, or their hearts turn to stone and they lose the ability to distinguish right from wrong."

"How did you come to terms with what you had done?"

"I examined my reasons for killing to determine if they were just. Satisfied they were, I asked myself if our cause was important enough to continue supporting it, even though it would probably require me to kill again. Then I decided that whenever I began to think of the dead, I would picture myself in the gardens of Tialdarí Hall."

"Did it work?"

Brushing her hair out of her face, she tucked it behind one round ear. "It did. The only antidote for the corrosive poison of violence is finding peace within yourself. It's a difficult cure to obtain, but well worth the effort." She paused and then added, "Breathing helps too."

"Breathing?"

"Slow, regular breathing, as if you were meditating. It is one of the most effective methods for calming yourself."

Following her advice, Eragon began to consciously inhale and exhale, taking care to maintain a steady tempo and to expel all the air from his lungs with each breath. Within a minute, the knot inside his gut loosened, his frown eased, and the presence of his fallen enemies no longer seemed quite so tangible. . . . The wolves howled again, and after an initial burst of trepidation, he listened without fear, for their baying had lost the power to unsettle him. "Thank you," he said. Arya responded with a gracious tilt of her chin.

Silence reigned for a quarter of an hour until Eragon said, "Urgals." He let the statement stand for a while, a verbal monolith of ambivalence. "What do you think about Nasuada allowing them to join the Varden?"

Arya picked up a twig by the edge of her splayed dress and rolled it between her aquiline fingers, studying the crooked piece of wood as if it contained a secret. "It was a courageous decision, and I admire her for it. She always acts in the best interests of the Varden, no matter what the cost may be."

"She upset many of the Varden when she accepted Nar Garzhvog's offer of support."

"And she won back their loyalty with the Trial of the Long Knives. Nasuada is very clever when it comes to maintaining her position." Arya flicked the twig into the fire. "I have no love for Urgals, but neither do I hate them. Unlike the Ra'zac, they are not inherently evil, merely overfond of war. It is an important distinction, even if it can provide no consolation to the families of their victims. We elves have treated with Urgals before, and we shall again when the need arises. It is a futile prospect, however."

She did not have to explain why. Many of the scrolls Oromis had assigned Eragon to read were devoted to the subject of Urgals, and one in particular, *The Travels of Gnaevaldrskald*, had taught him that the Urgals' entire culture was based upon feats of combat. Male Urgals could only improve their standing by raiding another village—whether Urgal, human, elf, or dwarf mattered little—or by fighting their rivals one on one, sometimes to the death. And when it came to picking a mate, Urgal females refused to consider a ram eligible unless he had defeated at least three opponents. As a result, each new generation of Urgals had no choice but to challenge their peers, challenge their elders, and scour the land for opportunities to prove their valor. The tradition was so deeply ingrained, every attempt to suppress it had failed. *At least they are true to who they are,* mused Eragon. *That's more than most humans can claim.*

"How is it," he asked, "that Durza was able to ambush you, Glenwing, and Fäolin with Urgals? Didn't you have wards to protect yourself against physical attacks?"

"The arrows were enchanted."

"Were the Urgals spellcasters, then?"

Closing her eyes, Arya sighed and shook her head. "No. It was some dark magic of Durza's invention. He gloated about it when I was in Gil'ead."

"I don't know how you managed to resist him for so long. I saw what he did to you."

"It . . . it was not easy. I viewed the torments he inflicted on me as a test of my commitment, as a chance to demonstrate that I had not

195

made a mistake and I was indeed worthy of the yawë symbol. As such, I welcomed the ordeal."

"But still, even elves are not immune to pain. It's amazing you could keep the location of Ellesméra hidden from him all those months."

A touch of pride colored her voice. "Not just the location of Ellesméra but also where I had sent Saphira's egg, my vocabulary in the ancient language, and everything else that might be of use to Galbatorix."

The conversation lapsed, and then Eragon said, "Do you think about it much, what you went through in Gil'ead?" When she did not respond, he added, "You never talk about it. You recount the facts of your imprisonment readily enough, but you never mention what it was like for you, nor how you feel about it now."

"Pain is pain," she said. "It needs no description."

"True, but ignoring it can cause more harm than the original injury. . . . No one can live through something like that and escape unscathed. Not on the inside, at least."

"Why do you assume I have not already confided in someone?"

"Who?"

"Does it matter? Ajihad, my mother, a friend in Ellesméra."

"Perhaps I am wrong," he said, "but you do not seem that close to anyone. Where you walk, you walk alone, even among your own people."

Arya's countenance remained impassive. Her lack of expression was so complete, Eragon began to wonder if she would deign to respond, a doubt that had just transformed into conviction when she whispered, "It was not always so."

Alert, Eragon waited without moving, afraid that whatever he might do would stop her from saying more.

"Once, I had someone to talk to, someone who understood what I was and where I came from. Once . . . He was older than I, but we were kindred spirits, both curious about the world outside our forest, eager to explore and eager to strike against Galbatorix. Neither of us could bear to stay in Du Weldenvarden—studying, working magic, pursuing our own personal projects—when we knew the Dragon Killer, the bane of the Riders, was searching for a way to conquer our race. He came to that conclusion later than I—decades after I assumed my position as ambassador and a few years before Hefring stole Saphira's egg—but the moment he did, he volunteered to accompany me wherever Islanzadí's orders might take me." She blinked, and her throat convulsed. "I wasn't going to let him, but the queen liked the idea, and he was so very convincing. . . ." She pursed her lips and blinked again, her eyes brighter than normal.

As gently as he could, Eragon asked, "Was it Fäolin?"

"Yes," she said, releasing the confirmation almost as a gasp.

"Did you love him?"

Casting back her head, Arya gazed up at the twinkling sky, her long neck gold with firelight, her face pale with the radiance of the heavens. "Do you ask out of friendly concern or your own self-interest?" She gave an abrupt, choked laugh, the sound of water falling over cold rocks. "Never mind. The night air has addled me. It has undone my sense of courtesy and left me free to say the most spiteful things that occur to me."

"No matter."

"It does matter, because I regret it, and I shall not tolerate it. Did I love Fäolin? How would you define love? For over twenty years, we traveled together, the only immortals to walk among the short-lived races. We were companions . . . and friends."

A pang of jealousy afflicted Eragon. He wrestled with it, subdued it, and tried to eliminate it but was not altogether successful. A slight remnant of the feeling continued to aggravate him, like a splinter burrowing underneath his skin.

"Over twenty years," repeated Arya. Persisting in her survey of the constellations, she rocked back and forth, seemingly oblivious to Eragon. "And then in a single instant, Durza tore that away from me. Fäolin and Glenwing were the first elves to die in combat for nearly a century. When I saw Fäolin fall, I understood then that the true agony of war isn't being wounded yourself, it's having to watch those you care about being hurt. It was a lesson I thought I had already learned during my time with the Varden when, one after another, the men and women I had come to respect died from swords, arrows, poison, accidents, and old age. The loss had never been so personal, however, and when it happened, I thought, 'Now I must surely die as well.' For whatever danger we had encountered before, Fäolin and I had always survived it together, and if he could not escape, then why should I?"

Eragon realized she was crying, thick tears rolling from the outer corners of her eyes, down her temples, and into her hair. By the stars, her tears appeared like rivers of silvered glass. The intensity of her distress startled him. He had not thought it was possible to elicit such a reaction from her, nor had he intended to.

"Then Gil'ead," she said. "Those days were the longest of my life. Fäolin was gone, I did not know whether Saphira's egg was safe or if I had inadvertently returned her to Galbatorix, and Durza . . . Durza sated the bloodlust of the spirits that controlled him by doing the most horrible things he could imagine to me. Sometimes, if he went too far, he would heal me so he could begin anew the following morning. If he had given me a chance to collect my wits, I might have been able to fool my jailer, as you did, and avoid consuming the drug that kept me from using magic, but I never had more than a few hours' respite.

"Durza needed sleep no more than you or I, and he kept at me whenever I was conscious and his other duties permitted. While he worked on me, every second was an hour, every hour a week, and every day an eternity. He was careful not to drive me mad—Galbatorix would have been displeased with that—but he came close. He came very, very close. I began to hear birdsong where no birds could fly and to see things that could not exist. Once, when I was in my cell, gold light flooded the room and I grew warm all over. When I looked up, I found myself lying on a branch high in a tree near the center of Ellesméra. The sun was about to set, and the whole city glowed as if it were on fire. The Äthalvard were chanting on the path below, and everything was so calm, so peaceful . . . so beautiful, I would have stayed there forever. But then the light faded, and I was again on my cot. . . . I had forgotten, but once there was a soldier who left a white rose in my cell. It was the only kindness anyone ever showed me in Gil'ead. That night, the flower took root and matured into a huge rosebush that climbed the wall, forced its way between the blocks of stone in the ceiling, breaking them, and pushed its way out of the dungeon and into the open. It continued to ascend until it touched the moon and stood as a great, twisting tower that promised escape if I could but lift myself off the floor. I tried with every ounce of my remaining strength, but it was beyond me, and when I glanced away, the rosebush vanished. . . . That was my state of mind when you dreamed of me and I felt your presence hovering over me. Small wonder I disregarded the sensation as another delusion."

She gave him a wan smile. "And then you came, Eragon. You and Saphira. After hope had deserted me and I was about to be taken to Galbatorix in Urû'baen, a Rider appeared to rescue me. A Rider and dragon!"

"And Morzan's son," he said. "*Both* of Morzan's sons."

"Describe it how you will, it was such an improbable rescue, I occasionally think that I did go mad and that I've imagined everything since."

"Would you have imagined me causing so much trouble by staying behind at Helgrind?"

"No," she said. "I suppose not." With the cuff of her left sleeve, she dabbed her eyes, drying them. "When I awoke in Farthen Dûr, there was too much that needed doing for me to dwell on the past. But events of late have been dark and bloody, and increasingly I have found myself remembering that which I should not. It makes me grim and out of sorts, without patience for the ordinary delays of life." She shifted into a kneeling position and placed her hands on the ground on either side of her, as if to steady herself. "You say I walk alone. Elves do not incline toward the open displays of friendship humans and dwarves favor, and I have ever been of a solitary disposition. But if you had known me before Gil'ead, if you had known me as I was, you would not have considered me so aloof. Then I could sing and dance and not feel threatened by a sense of impending doom."

Reaching out, Eragon placed his right hand over her left. "The stories about the heroes of old never mention that this is the price you pay when you grapple with the monsters of the dark and the monsters of the mind. Keep thinking about the gardens of Tialdarí Hall, and I'm sure you will be fine."

Arya permitted the contact between them to endure for almost a minute, a time not of heat or passion for Eragon, but rather of quiet companionship. He made no attempt to press his suit with her, for he cherished her trust more than anything besides his bond with Saphira and he would sooner march into battle than endanger it. Then, with a slight lift of her arm, Arya let him know the moment had passed, and without complaint he withdrew his hand.

Eager to lighten her burden however he could, Eragon glanced about the ground nearest him and then murmured so softly as to be inaudible, "Loivissa." Guided by the power of the true name, he sifted through the earth by his feet until his fingers closed upon what he sought: a thin, papery disk half the size of his smallest fingernail. Holding his breath, he deposited it in his right palm, centering it over his gedwëy ignasia with as much delicacy as he could muster. He reviewed what Oromis had taught him concerning the sort of spell he was about to cast to ensure he would not make a mistake, and then he began to sing after the fashion of the elves, smooth and flowing:

Eldhrimner O Loivissa nuanen, dautr abr deloi,
Eldhrimner nen ono weohnataí medh solus un thringa,

Eldhrimner un fortha onr fëon vara,
Wiol allr sjon.

Eldhrimner O Loivissa nuanen . . .

Again and again, Eragon repeated the same four lines, directing them toward the brown flake in his hand. The flake trembled and then swelled and bulged, becoming spherical. White tendrils an inch or two long sprouted from the bottom of the peeling globe, tickling Eragon, while a thin green stem poked its way out of the tip and, at his urging, shot nearly a foot in the air. A single leaf, broad and flat, grew from the side of the stem. Then the tip of the stem thickened, drooped, and, after a moment of seeming inactivity, split into five segments that expanded outward to reveal the waxy petals of a deep-throated lily. The flower was pale blue and shaped like a bell.

When it reached its full size, Eragon released the magic and examined his handiwork. Singing plants into shape was a skill most every elf mastered at an early age, but it was one Eragon had practiced only a few times, and he had been uncertain whether his efforts would meet with success. The spell had exacted a heavy toll from him; the lily required a surprising amount of energy to feed what was the equivalent of a year and a half of growth.

Satisfied with what he had wrought, he handed the lily to Arya. "It's not a white rose, but . . ." He smiled and shrugged.

"You should not have," she said. "But I am glad you did." She caressed the underside of the blossom and lifted it to smell. The lines on her face eased. For several minutes, she admired the lily. Then she scooped a hole in the soil next to her and planted the bulb, pressing down the soil with the flat of her hand. She touched the petals again and kept glancing at the lily as she said, "Thank you. Giving flowers is a custom both our races share, but we elves attach greater importance to the practice than do humans. It signifies all that is good: life, beauty, rebirth, friendship, and more. I explain so you understand how much this means to me. You did not know, but—"

"I knew."

Arya regarded him with a solemn countenance, as if to decide what he was about. "Forgive me. That is twice now I have forgotten the extent of your education. I shall not make the mistake again."

She repeated her thanks in the ancient language, and—joining her in her native tongue—Eragon replied that it was his pleasure and he was happy she enjoyed his gift. He shivered, hungry despite the meal they had just eaten. Noticing, Arya said, "You used too much of your strength. If you have any energy left in Aren, use it to steady yourself."

It took Eragon a moment to remember that Aren was the name of Brom's ring; he had heard it uttered only once before, from Islanzadí, on the day he arrived in Ellesméra. *My ring now,* he told himself. *I have to stop thinking of it as Brom's.* He cast a critical gaze at the large sapphire that sparkled in its gold setting on his finger. "I don't know if there *is* any energy in Aren. I've never stored any there myself, and I never checked if Brom had." Even as he spoke, he extended his consciousness toward the sapphire. The instant his mind came into contact with the gem, he felt the presence of a vast, swirling pool of energy. To his inner eye, the sapphire thrummed with power. He wondered that it did not explode from the amount of force contained within the boundaries of its sharp-edged facets. After he used the energy to wash away his aches and pains and restore strength to his limbs, the treasure trove inside Aren was hardly diminished.

His skin tingling, Eragon severed his link with the gem. Delighted by his discovery and his sudden sense of well-being, he laughed out loud, then told Arya what he had found. "Brom must have squirreled away every bit of energy he could spare the whole time he was hiding in Carvahall." He laughed again, marveling. "All those years . . . With what's in Aren, I could tear apart an entire castle with a single spell."

"He knew he would need it to keep the new Rider safe when Saphira hatched," observed Arya. "Also, I am sure Aren was a way for him to protect himself if he had to fight a Shade or some other similarly powerful opponent. It was not by accident that he managed to frustrate his enemies for the better part of a century. . . . If I were you, I would save the energy he left you for your hour of greatest need, and I would add to it whenever I could. It is an incredibly valuable resource. You should not squander it."

No, thought Eragon, *that I will not.* He twirled the ring around his finger, admiring how it gleamed in the firelight. *Since Murtagh stole Zar'roc, this, Saphira's saddle, and Snowfire are the only things I have of Brom, and even though the dwarves brought Snowfire from Farthen Dûr, I rarely ride him nowadays. Aren is really all I have to remember him by. . . . My only legacy of him. My only inheritance. I wish he were still alive! I never had a chance to talk with him about Oromis, Murtagh, my father. . . . Oh, the list is endless. What would he have said about my feelings for Arya?* Eragon snorted to himself. *I know what he would have said: he would have berated me for being a love-struck fool and for wasting my energy on a hopeless cause. . . . And he would have been right too, I suppose, but, ah, how can I help it? She is the only woman I wish to be with.*

The fire cracked. A flurry of sparks flew upward. Eragon watched with half-closed eyes, contemplating Arya's revelations. Then his mind returned to a question that had been bothering him ever since the battle on the Burning Plains. "Arya, do male dragons grow any faster than female dragons?"

"No. Why do you ask?"

"Because of Thorn. He's only a few months old, and yet he's already nearly as big as Saphira. I don't understand it."

Picking a dry blade of grass, Arya began sketching in the loose soil, tracing the curved shapes of glyphs from the elves' script, the Liduen Kvaedhí. "Most likely Galbatorix accelerated his growth so Thorn would be large enough to hold his own with Saphira."

"Ah. . . . Isn't that dangerous, though? Oromis told me that if he used magic to give me the strength, speed, endurance, and other skills I needed, I would not understand my new abilities as well as if I had gained them the ordinary way: by hard work. He was right too. Even now, the changes the dragons made to my body during the Agaetí Blödhren still sometimes catch me by surprise."

Arya nodded and continued sketching glyphs in the dirt. "It is possible to reduce the undesirable side effects by certain spells, but it is a long and arduous process. If you wish to achieve true mastery of your body, it is still best to do so through normal means. The transformation Galbatorix has forced upon Thorn must be incredibly confusing for him. Thorn now has the body of a nearly grown dragon, and yet his mind is still that of a youngling."

Eragon fingered the newly formed calluses on his knuckles. "Do you also know why Murtagh is so powerful . . . more powerful than I am?"

"If I did, no doubt I would also understand how Galbatorix has managed to increase his own strength to such unnatural heights, but alas, I do not."

But Oromis does, Eragon thought. Or at least the elf had hinted as much. However, he had yet to share the information with Eragon and Saphira. As soon as they were able to return to Du Weldenvarden, Eragon intended to ask the elder Rider for the truth of the matter. *He has to tell us now! Because of our ignorance, Murtagh defeated us, and he could have easily taken us to Galbatorix.* Eragon almost mentioned Oromis's comments to Arya but held his tongue, for he realized that Oromis would not have concealed such an important fact for over a hundred years unless secrecy was of the utmost importance.

Arya signed a stop to the sentence she had been writing on the ground. Bending over, Eragon read, *Adrift upon the sea of time, the lonely god wanders from shore to distant shore, upholding the laws of the stars above.*

"What does it mean?"

"I don't know," she said, and smoothed out the line with a sweep of her arm.

"Why is it," he asked, speaking slowly as he organized his thoughts, "that no one ever refers to the dragons of the Forsworn by name? We say 'Morzan's dragon' or 'Kialandí's dragon,' but we never actually name the dragon. Surely they were as important as their Riders! I don't even remember seeing their names in the scrolls Oromis gave me . . . although they *must* have been there. . . . Yes, I'm certain they were, but for some reason, they don't stick in my head. Isn't that strange?" Arya started to answer, but before she could do more than open her mouth, he said, "For once I'm glad Saphira's not here. I'm ashamed I haven't noticed this before. Even you, Arya, and Oromis and every other elf I've met refuse to call them by name, as if they were dumb animals, undeserving of the honor. Do you do it on purpose? Is it because they were your enemies?"

"Did none of your lessons speak of this?" asked Arya. She seemed genuinely surprised.

"I think," he said, "Glaedr mentioned something about it to Saphira, but I'm not exactly sure. I was in the middle of a backbend during the Dance of Snake and Crane, so I wasn't really paying attention to what Saphira was doing." He laughed a little, embarrassed by his lapse and feeling as if he had to explain himself. "It got confusing at times. Oromis would be talking to me while I was listening to Saphira's thoughts while she and Glaedr communicated with their minds. What's worse, Glaedr rarely uses a recognizable language with Saphira; he tends to use images, smells, and feelings, rather than words. Instead of names, he sends impressions of the people and objects he means."

"Do you recall nothing of what he said, whether with words or not?"

Eragon hesitated. "Only that it concerned a name that was no name, or some such. I couldn't make heads or tails out of it."

"What he spoke of," said Arya, "was Du Namar Aurboda, The Banishing of the Names."

"The Banishing of the Names?"

Touching her dry blade of grass to the ground, she resumed writing in the dirt. "It is one of the most significant events that happened during the fighting between the Riders and the Forsworn. When the dragons realized that thirteen of their own had betrayed them—that those thirteen were helping Galbatorix to eradicate the rest of their race and that it was unlikely anyone could stop their rampage—the dragons grew so angry, every dragon not of the Forsworn combined their strength and wrought one of their inexplicable pieces of magic. Together, they stripped the thirteen of their names."

Awe crawled over Eragon. "How is that possible?"

"Did I not just say it was inexplicable? All we know is that after the dragons cast their spell, no one could utter the names of the thirteen; those who remembered the names soon forgot them; and while you can read the names in scrolls and letters where they are recorded and even copy them if you look at only one glyph at a time, they are as gibberish. The dragons spared Jarnunvösk, Galbatorix's first dragon, for it was not his fault he was killed by Urgals, and also Shruikan, for he did not choose to serve Galbatorix but was forced to by Galbatorix and Morzan."

What a horrible fate, to lose one's name, thought Eragon. He shivered. *If there's one thing I've learned since becoming a Rider, it's that you never, ever want to have a dragon for an enemy.* "What about their true names?" he asked. "Did they erase those as well?"

Arya nodded. "True names, birth names, nicknames, family names, titles. Everything. And as a result, the thirteen were reduced to little more than animals. No longer could they say, 'I like this' or 'I dislike that' or 'I have green scales,' for to say that would be to name themselves. They could not even call themselves dragons. Word by word, the spell obliterated everything that defined them as thinking creatures, and the Forsworn had no choice but to watch in silent misery as their dragons descended into complete ignorance. The experience was so disturbing, at least five of the thirteen, and several of the Forsworn, went mad as a result." Arya paused, considering the outline of a glyph, then rubbed it out and redrew it. "The Banishing of the Names is the main reason so many people now believe that dragons were nothing more than animals to ride from one place to another."

"They wouldn't believe that if they had met Saphira," said Eragon.

Arya smiled. "No." With a flourish, she completed the latest sentence she had been working on. He tilted his head and sidled closer in order to decipher the glyphs she had inscribed. They read: *The trickster, the riddler, the keeper of the balance, he of the many faces who finds life in death and who fears no evil; he who walks through doors.*

"What prompted you to write this?"

"The thought that many things are not what they appear." Dust billowed around her hand as she patted the ground, effacing the glyphs from the surface of the earth.

"Has anyone tried to guess Galbatorix's true name?" Eragon asked. "It seems as if that would be the fastest way to end this war. To be honest, I think it might be the only hope we have of vanquishing him in battle."

"Were you not being honest with me before?" asked Arya, a gleam in her eyes.

Her question forced him to chuckle. "Of course not. It's just a figure of speech."

"And a poor one at that," she said. "Unless you happen to be in the habit of lying."

Eragon floundered for a moment before he caught hold of his thread of speech again and could say, "I know it would be hard to find Galbatorix's true name, but if all the elves and all the members of the Varden who know the ancient language searched for it, we could not help but succeed."

Like a pale, sun-bleached pennant, the dry blade of grass hung from between Arya's left thumb and forefinger. It trembled in sympathy with each surge of blood through her veins. Pinching it at the top with her other hand, she tore the leaf in half lengthwise, then did the same with each of the resulting strips, quartering the leaf. Then she began to plait the strips, forming a stiff braided rod. She said, "Galbatorix's true name is no great secret. Three different elves—one a Rider, and two ordinary spellcasters—discovered it on their own and many years apart."

"They did!" exclaimed Eragon.

Unperturbed, Arya picked another blade of grass, tore it into strips, inserted the pieces into the gaps in her braided rod, and continued plaiting in a different direction. "We can only speculate whether Galbatorix himself knows his true name. I am of the opinion that he does not, for whatever it is, his true name must be so terrible, he could not go on living if he heard it."

"Unless he is so evil or so demented, the truth about his actions has no power to disturb him."

"Perhaps." Her nimble fingers flew so fast, twisting, braiding, weaving, that they were nearly invisible. She picked two more blades of grass. "Either way, Galbatorix is certainly aware that he has a true name, like all creatures and things, and that it is a potential weakness. At some point before he embarked upon his campaign against the Riders, he cast a spell that kills whoever uses his true name. And since we do not know exactly how this spell kills, we cannot shield ourselves from it. You see, then, why we have all but abandoned that line of inquiry. Oromis is one of the few who are brave enough to continue seeking out Galbatorix's name, albeit in a roundabout manner." With a pleased expression, she held out her hands, palms-upward. Resting on them was an exquisite ship made of green and white grass. It was no more than four inches long, but so detailed, Eragon descried benches for rowers, tiny railings along the edge of the deck, and portholes the size of raspberry seeds. The curved prow was shaped somewhat like the head and neck of a rearing dragon. There was a single mast.

"It's beautiful," he said.

Arya leaned forward and murmured, "Flauga." She gently blew upon the ship, and it rose from her hands and sailed around the fire and then, gathering speed, slanted upward and glided off into the sparkling depths of the night sky.

"How far will it go?"

"Forever," she said. "It takes the energy to stay aloft from the plants below. Wherever there are plants, it can fly."

The idea bemused Eragon, but he also found it rather sad to think of the pretty grass ship wandering among the clouds for the rest of eternity, with none but birds for company. "Imagine the stories people will tell about it in years to come."

Arya knit her long fingers together, as if to keep them from making something else. "Many such oddities exist in the world. The longer you live and the farther you travel, the more of them you will see."

Eragon gazed at the pulsing fire for a while, then said, "If it's so important to protect your true name, should I cast a spell to keep Galbatorix from using my true name against me?"

"You can if you wish to," said Arya, "but I doubt it's necessary. True names are not so easy to find as you think. Galbatorix does not know you well enough to guess your name, and if he were inside your mind and able to examine your every thought and memory, you would be already lost to him, true name or no. If it is any comfort, I doubt that even I could divine your true name."

"Couldn't you?" he asked. He was both pleased and displeased that she believed any part of him was a mystery to her.

She glanced at him and then lowered her eyes. "No, I do not think so. Could you guess mine?"

"No."

Silence enveloped their camp. Above, the stars gleamed cold and white. A wind sprang up from the east and raced across the plains, battering the grass and wailing with a long, thin voice, as if lamenting the loss of a loved one. As it struck, the coals burst into flame again and a twisting mane of sparks trailed off to the west. Eragon hunched his shoulders and pulled the collar of his tunic close around his neck. There was something unfriendly about the wind; it bit at him with unusual ferocity, and it seemed to isolate him and Arya from the rest of the world. They sat motionless, marooned on their tiny island of light and heat, while the massive river of air rushed past, howling its angry sorrows into the empty expanse of land.

When the gusts became more violent and began to carry the sparks farther away from the bare patch where Eragon had built the fire, Arya poured a handful of dirt over the wood. Moving forward onto his knees, Eragon joined her, scooping the dirt with both hands to speed the process. With the fire extinguished, he had difficulty seeing; the countryside had become a ghost of itself, full of writhing shadows, indistinct shapes, and silvery leaves.

Arya made as if to stand, then stopped in a half crouch, arms outstretched for balance, her expression alert. Eragon felt it as well: the air prickled and hummed, as if a bolt of lightning were about to strike. The hair on the back of his hands rose from his skin and waved freely in the wind.

"What is it?" he asked.

"We are being watched. Whatever happens, don't use magic or you may get us killed."

"Who—"

"Shh."

Casting about, he found a fist-sized rock, pried it out of the ground, and hefted it, testing its weight.

In the distance, a cluster of glowing multicolored lights appeared. They darted toward the camp, flying low over the grass. As they drew near, he saw that the lights were constantly changing in size—ranging from an orb no larger than a pearl to one several feet in diameter—and that their colors also varied, cycling through every hue in the rainbow. A crackling nimbus surrounded each orb, a halo of liquid tendrils that whipped and lashed, as if hungry to entangle something in their grasp. The lights moved so fast, he could not determine exactly how many there were, but he guessed it was about two dozen.

The lights hurtled into the camp and formed a whirling wall around him and Arya. The speed with which they spun, combined with the barrage of pulsing colors, made Eragon dizzy. He put a hand on the ground to steady himself. The humming was so loud now, his teeth vibrated against one another. He tasted metal, and his hair stood on end. Arya's did the same, despite its additional length, and when he glanced at her, he found the sight so ridiculous, he had to resist the urge to laugh.

"What do they want?" shouted Eragon, but she did not answer.

A single orb detached itself from the wall and hung before Arya at eye level. It shrank and expanded like a throbbing heart, alternating between royal blue and emerald green, with occasional flashes of red. One of its tendrils caught hold of a strand of Arya's hair. There was a sharp *pop*, and for an instant, the strand shone like a fragment of the sun, then it vanished. The smell of burnt hair drifted toward Eragon.

Arya did not flinch or otherwise betray alarm. Her face calm, she lifted an arm and, before Eragon could leap forward and stop her, laid her hand upon the lambent orb. The orb turned gold and white, and it swelled until it was over three feet across. Arya closed her eyes and tilted her head back, radiant joy suffusing her features. Her lips moved, but whatever she said, Eragon could not hear. When she finished, the orb flushed blood-red and then in quick succession shifted from red to green to purple to a ruddy orange to a blue so bright he had to avert his gaze and then to pure black fringed with a corona of twisting white tendrils, like the sun during an eclipse. Its appearance ceased to fluctuate then, as if only the absence of color could adequately convey its mood.

Drifting away from Arya, it approached Eragon, a hole in the fabric of the world, encircled by a crown of flames. It hovered in front of him, humming with such intensity, his eyes watered. His tongue seemed plated with copper, his skin crawled, and short filaments of electricity danced on the tips of his fingers. Somewhat frightened, he wondered whether he should touch the orb as Arya had. He looked at her for advice. She nodded and gestured for him to proceed.

He extended his right hand toward the void that was the orb. To his surprise, he encountered resistance. The orb was incorporeal, but it pushed against his hand the way a swift stream of water might. The closer he got, the harder it pushed. With an effort, he reached across the last few inches and came into contact with the center of the creature's being.

Bluish rays shot out from between Eragon's palm and the surface of the orb, a dazzling, fanlike display that overwhelmed the light from the other orbs and bleached everything a pale blue white. Eragon shouted with pain as the rays stabbed at his eyes, and he ducked his head, squinting. Then something moved inside the orb, like a sleeping dragon uncoiling, and a *presence* entered his mind, brushing aside his defenses as if they were dry leaves in an autumn storm. He gasped. Transcendent joy filled him; whatever the orb was, it seemed to be composed of distilled happiness. It enjoyed being alive, and everything around it pleased it to a greater or lesser degree. Eragon would have wept with sheer gladness, but he no longer had control of his body. The creature held him in place, the shimmering rays still blazing from underneath his hand while it flitted through his bones and muscles, lingering at the sites where he had been injured, and then returned to his mind. Euphoric as Eragon was, the creature's presence was so strange and so unearthly, he wanted to flee from it, but inside his consciousness, there was nowhere to hide. He had to remain in intimate contact with the fiery soul of the creature while it scoured his memories, dashing from one to the next with the speed of an elvish arrow. He wondered how it could comprehend so much information so quickly. While it searched, he tried to probe the orb's mind in return, to learn what he could about its nature and its origins, but it defied his attempts to understand it. The few impressions he gleaned were so different from those he had found in the minds of other beings, they were incomprehensible.

After a final, nearly instantaneous circuit through his body, the creature withdrew. The contact between them broke like a twisted cable under too much tension. The panoply of rays outlining Eragon's hand faded into oblivion, leaving behind lurid pink afterimages streaked across his field of vision.

Again changing colors, the orb in front of Eragon shrank to the size of an apple and rejoined its companions in the swirling vortex of light that encircled him and Arya. The humming increased to an almost unbearable pitch, and then the vortex exploded outward as the blazing orbs scattered in every direction. They regrouped a hundred feet or so from the dim camp, tumbling over each other like wrestling kittens, then raced off to the south and disappeared, as if they had never existed in the first place. The wind subsided to a gentle breeze.

Eragon fell to his knees, arm outstretched toward where the orbs had gone, feeling empty without the bliss they had given him. "What," he asked, and then had to cough and start over again, his throat was so dry. "What are they?"

"Spirits," said Arya. She sat.

"They didn't look like the ones that came out of Durza when I killed him."

"Spirits can assume many different guises, dictated by their whim."

He blinked several times and wiped the corners of his eyes with the back of a finger. "How can anyone bear to enslave them with magic? It's monstrous. I would be ashamed to call myself a sorcerer. Gah! And Trianna boasts of being one. I'll have her stop using spirits or I'll expel her from Du Vrangr Gata and ask Nasuada to banish her from the Varden."

"I would not be so hasty."

"Surely you don't think it's right for magicians to force spirits to

213

obey their will. . . . They are so beautiful that—" He broke off and shook his head, overcome with emotion. "Anyone who harms them ought to be thrashed within an inch of their life."

With a hint of a smile, Arya said, "I take it Oromis had yet to address the topic when you and Saphira left Ellesméra."

"If you mean spirits, he mentioned them several times."

"But not in any great detail, I dare say."

"Perhaps not."

In the darkness, the outline of her shape moved as she leaned to one side. "Spirits always induce a sense of rapture when they choose to communicate with we who are made of matter, but do not allow them to deceive you. They are not as benevolent, content, or cheerful as they would have you believe. Pleasing those they interact with is their way of defending themselves. They hate to be bound in one place, and they realized long ago that if the person they are dealing with is happy, then he or she will be less likely to detain the spirits and keep them as servants."

"I don't know," said Eragon. "They make you feel so good, I can understand why someone would want to keep them nearby, instead of releasing them."

Her shoulders rose and fell. "Spirits have as much difficulty predicting our behavior as we do theirs. They share so little in common with the other races of Alagaësia, conversing with them in even the simplest terms is a challenging prospect, and any meeting is fraught with peril, for one never knows how they will react."

"None of which explains why I shouldn't order Trianna to abandon sorcery."

"Have you ever seen her summon spirits to do her bidding?"

"No."

"I thought not. Trianna has been with the Varden for nigh on six years, and in that time she has demonstrated her mastery of sorcery exactly once, and that after much coaxing on Ajihad's part and much consternation and preparation on Trianna's. She has the necessary skills—she is no charlatan—but summoning spirits is exceedingly dangerous, and one does not embark upon it lightly."

Eragon rubbed his shining palm with his left thumb. The hue of light changed as blood rushed to the surface of his skin, but his efforts did nothing to reduce the amount of light radiating from his hand. He scratched at the gedwëy ignasia with his fingernails. *This had better not last more than a few hours. I can't go around shining like a lantern. It could get me killed. And it's silly too. Whoever heard of a Dragon Rider with a glowing body part?*

Eragon considered what Brom had told him. "They aren't human spirits, are they? Nor elf, nor dwarf, nor those of any other creature. That is, they aren't ghosts. We don't become them after we die."

"No. And please do not ask me, as I know you are about to, what, then, they really are. It is a question for Oromis to answer, not me. The study of sorcery, if properly conducted, is long and arduous and should be approached with care. I do not want to say anything that may interfere with the lessons Oromis has planned for you, and I certainly don't want you to hurt yourself trying something I mentioned when you lack the proper instruction."

"And when am I supposed to return to Ellesméra?" he demanded. "I can't leave the Varden again, not like this, not while Thorn and Murtagh are still alive. Until we defeat the Empire, or the Empire defeats us, Saphira and I have to support Nasuada. If Oromis and Glaedr really want to finish our training, they should join us, and Galbatorix be blasted!"

"Please, Eragon," she said. "This war shall not end as quickly as you think. The Empire is large, and we have but pricked its hide. As long as Galbatorix does not know about Oromis and Glaedr, we have an advantage."

"Is it an advantage if they never make full use of themselves?" he grumbled. She did not answer, and after a moment, he felt childish for complaining. Oromis and Glaedr wanted more than anyone else to destroy Galbatorix, and if they chose to bide their time in

Ellesméra, it was because they had excellent reasons for doing so. Eragon could even name several of them if he was so inclined, the most prominent being Oromis's inability to cast spells that required large amounts of energy.

Cold, Eragon pulled his sleeves down over his hands and crossed his arms. "What was it you said to the spirit?"

"It was curious why we had been using magic; that was what brought us to their attention. I explained, and I also explained that you were the one who freed the spirits trapped inside of Durza. That seemed to please them a great deal." Silence crept between them, and then she sidled toward the lily and touched it again. "Oh!" she said. "They were indeed grateful. Naina!"

At her command, a wash of soft light illuminated the camp. By it, he saw that the leaf and stem of the lily were solid gold, the petals were a whitish metal he failed to recognize, and the heart of the flower, as Arya revealed by tilting the blossom upward, appeared to have been carved out of rubies and diamonds. Amazed, Eragon ran a finger over the curved leaf, the tiny wire hairs on it tickling him. Bending forward, he discerned the same collection of bumps, grooves, pits, veins, and other minute details with which he had adorned the original version of the plant; the only difference was they were now made of gold.

"It's a perfect copy!" he said.

"And it is still alive."

"No!" Concentrating, he searched for the faint signs of warmth and movement that would indicate the lily was more than an inanimate object. He located them, strong as they ever were in a plant during the night. Fingering the leaf again, he said, "This is beyond everything I know of magic. By all rights, this lily ought to be dead. Instead, it is thriving. I cannot even imagine what would be involved in turning a plant into living metal. Perhaps Saphira could do it, but she would never be able to teach the spell to anyone else."

"The real question," said Arya, "is whether this flower will produce seeds that are fertile."

"It could spread?"

"I would not be surprised if it does. Numerous examples of self-perpetuating magic exist throughout Alagaësia, such as the floating crystal on the island of Eoam and the dream well in Mani's Caves. This would be no more improbable than either of those phenomena."

"Unfortunately, if anyone discovers this flower or the offspring it may have, they will dig them all up. Every fortune hunter in the land would come here to pick the golden lilies."

"They will not be so easy to destroy, I think, but only time will tell for sure."

A laugh bubbled up inside of Eragon. With barely contained glee, he said, "I've heard the expression 'to gild the lily' before, but the spirits actually did it! They gilded the lily!" And he fell to laughing, letting his voice boom across the empty plain.

Arya's lips twitched. "Well, their intentions were noble. We cannot fault them for being ignorant of human sayings."

"No, but . . . oh, ha, ha, ha!"

Arya snapped her fingers, and the wash of light faded into oblivion. "We have talked away most of the night. It is time we rested. Dawn is fast approaching, and we must depart soon thereafter."

Eragon stretched himself out on a rock-free expanse of the ground, still chuckling as he drifted into his waking dreams.

217

AMID THE RESTLESS CROWD

It was midafternoon when the Varden finally came into sight.

Eragon and Arya stopped on the crest of a low hill and studied the sprawling city of gray tents that lay before them, teeming as it was with thousands of men, horses, and smoking cookfires. To the west of the tents, there wound the tree-lined Jiet River. Half a mile to the east was a second, smaller camp—like an island floating close off the shore of its mother continent—where the Urgals led by Nar Garzhvog resided. Ranging for several miles around the perimeter of the Varden were numerous groups of horsemen. Some were riding patrol, others were banner-carrying messengers, and others were raiding parties either setting out on or returning from a mission. Two of the patrols spotted Eragon and Arya and, after sounding signal horns, galloped toward them with all possible speed.

A broad smile stretched Eragon's face, and he laughed, relieved. "We made it!" he exclaimed. "Murtagh, Thorn, hundreds of soldiers, Galbatorix's pet magicians, the Ra'zac—none of them could catch us. Ha! How's that for taunting the king? This'll tweak his beard for sure when he hears of it."

"He will be twice as dangerous then," warned Arya.

"I know," he said, grinning even wider. "Maybe he'll get so angry, he'll forget to pay his troops and they will all throw away their uniforms and join the Varden."

"You are in fine fettle today."

"And why shouldn't I be?" he demanded. Bouncing on the tips of his toes, he opened his mind as wide as he could and, gathering his strength, shouted, *Saphira!* sending the thought flying over the countryside like a spear.

A response was not long in coming:

Eragon!

They embraced with their minds, smothering each other with warm waves of love, joy, and concern. They exchanged memories of their time apart, and Saphira comforted Eragon over the soldiers he had killed, drawing off the pain and anger that had accumulated within him since the incident. He smiled. With Saphira so close, everything seemed right in the world.

I missed you, he said.

And I you, little one. Then she sent him an image of the soldiers he and Arya had fought and said, *Without fail, every time I leave you, you get yourself in trouble. Every time! I hate to so much as turn tail on you for fear you will be locked in mortal combat the moment I take my eyes off you.*

Be fair: I've gotten into plenty of trouble when I am with you. It's not something that just happens when I'm alone. We seem to be lodestones for unexpected events.

No, you are a lodestone for unexpected events, she sniffed. *Nothing out of the ordinary ever occurs to me when I'm by myself. But you attract duels, ambushes, immortal enemies, obscure creatures such as the Ra'zac, long-lost family members, and mysterious acts of magic as if they were starving weasels and you were a rabbit that wandered into their den.*

What about the time you spent as Galbatorix's possession? Was that an ordinary event?

I had not hatched yet, she said. *You cannot count that. The difference between you and me is that things happen to you, whereas I cause things to happen.*

Maybe, but that's because I'm still learning. Give me a few years, and I'll be as good as Brom at getting things done, eh? You can't say I didn't seize the initiative with Sloan.

Mmh. We still have to talk about that. If you ever surprise me like that again, I will pin you on the ground and lick you from head to toe.

Eragon shivered. Her tongue was covered with hooked barbs that could strip hair, hide, and meat off a deer with a single swipe. *I* know, but I wasn't sure myself whether I was going to kill Sloan or let him go free until I was standing in front of him. Besides, if I had told you I was going to stay behind, you would have insisted on stopping me.

He sensed a faint growl as it rumbled through her chest. She said, *You should have trusted me to do the right thing. If we cannot talk openly, how are we supposed to function as dragon and Rider?*

Would doing the right thing have involved taking me from Helgrind, regardless of my wishes?

It might not have, she said with a hint of defensiveness.

He smiled. *You're right, though. I should have discussed my plan with you. I'm sorry. From now on, I promise I will consult with you before I do anything you don't expect. Is that acceptable?*

Only if it involves weapons, magic, kings, or family members, she said.

Or flowers.

Or flowers, she agreed. *I don't need to know if you decide to eat some bread and cheese in the middle of the night.*

Unless a man with a very long knife is waiting for me outside of my tent.

If you could not defeat a single man with a very long knife, you would be a poor excuse for a Rider indeed.

Not to mention dead.

Well . . .

By your own argument, you should take comfort in the fact that while I may attract more trouble than most people, I am perfectly capable of escaping from situations that would kill most anyone else.

Even the greatest warriors can fall prey to bad luck, she said. *Remember the dwarf king Kaga, who was killed by a novice swordsman—swordsdwarf?—when he tripped on a rock. You should always remain cautious, for no matter your skills, you cannot anticipate and prevent every misfortune fate directs your way.*

Agreed. Now, can we please abandon such weighty conversation? I have become thoroughly exhausted with thoughts of fate, destiny, justice, and other, equally gloomy topics over the past few days. As far as I am concerned, philosophic questioning is just as likely to make you confused and depressed as it is to improve your condition. Swiveling his head, Eragon surveyed the plain and sky, searching for the distinctive blue glitter of Saphira's scales. *Where are you? I can feel you are nearby, but I can't see you.*

Right above you!

With a bugle of joy, Saphira dove out of the belly of a cloud several thousand feet overhead, spiraling toward the ground with her wings tucked close to her body. Opening her fearsome jaws, she released a billow of fire, which streamed back over her head and neck like a burning mane. Eragon laughed and held his arms outstretched to her. The horses of the patrol galloping toward him and Arya shied at the sight and sound of Saphira and bolted in the opposite direction while their riders frantically tried to rein them in.

"I had hoped we could enter the camp without attracting undue attention," Arya said, "but I suppose I should have realized we could not be unobtrusive with Saphira around. A dragon is hard to ignore."

I heard that, said Saphira, spreading her wings and landing with a thunderous crash. Her massive thighs and shoulders rippled as she absorbed the force of the impact. A blast of air struck Eragon's face, and the earth shuddered underneath him. He flexed his knees to maintain his balance. Folding her wings so they lay flat upon her back, she said, *I can be stealthy if I want.* Then she cocked her head and blinked, the tip of her tail whipping from side to side. *But I don't want to be stealthy today! Today I am a dragon, not a frightened pigeon trying to avoid being seen by a hunting falcon.*

When are you not a dragon? asked Eragon as he ran toward her. Light as a feather, he leaped from her left foreleg to her shoulder and thence to the hollow at the base of her neck that was his usual seat. Settling into place, he put his hands on either side of her warm neck, feeling the rise and fall of her banded muscles as she breathed.

He smiled again, with a profound sense of contentment. *This is where I belong, here with you.* His legs vibrated as Saphira hummed with satisfaction, her deep rumbling following a strange, subtle melody he did not recognize.

"Greetings, Saphira," said Arya, and twisted her hand over her chest in the elves' gesture of respect.

Crouching low and bending her long neck, Saphira touched Arya upon the brow with the tip of her snout, as she had when she blessed Elva in Farthen Dûr, and said, *Greetings, älfa-kona. Welcome, and may the wind rise under your wings.* She spoke to Arya with the same tone of affection that, until then, she had reserved for Eragon, as if she now considered Arya part of their small family and worthy of the same regard and intimacy as they shared. Her gesture surprised Eragon, but after an initial flare of jealousy, he approved. Saphira continued speaking: *I am grateful to you for helping Eragon to return without harm. If he had been captured, I do not know what I would have done!*

"Your gratitude means much to me," said Arya, and bowed. "As for what you would have done if Galbatorix had seized Eragon, why, you would have rescued him, and I would have accompanied you, even if it was to Urû'baen itself."

Yes, I like to think I would have rescued you, Eragon, said Saphira, turning her neck to look at him, *but I worry that I would have surrendered to the Empire in order to save you, no matter the consequences for Alagaësia.* Then she shook her head and kneaded the soil with her claws. *Ah, these are pointless meanderings. You are here and safe, and that is the true shape of the world. To while away the day contemplating evils that might have been is to poison the happiness we already have. . . .*

At that moment, a patrol galloped toward them and, halting thirty yards away because of their nervous horses, asked if they might escort the three to Nasuada. One of the men dismounted and gave his steed to Arya, and then as a group, they advanced toward the sea of tents to the southwest. Saphira set the pace: a leisurely crawl that allowed her and Eragon to enjoy the pleasure of each other's company before they immersed themselves in the noise and chaos that were sure to assault them once they neared the camp.

Eragon inquired after Roran and Katrina, then said, *Have you been eating enough fireweed? Your breath seems stronger than usual.*

Of course I have. You only notice it because you have been gone for many days. I smell exactly as a dragon should smell, and I'll thank you not to make disparaging comments about it unless you want me to drop you on your head. Besides, you humans have nothing to brag about, sweaty, greasy, pungent things that you are. The only creatures in the wild as smelly as humans are male goats and hibernating bears. Compared to you, the scent of a dragon is a perfume as delightful as a meadow of mountain flowers.

Come now, don't exaggerate. Although, he said, wrinkling his nose, *since the Agaetí Blödhren, I have noticed that humans tend to be rather smelly. But you cannot lump me in with the rest, for I am no longer entirely human.*

Perhaps not, but you still need a bath!

As they crossed the plain, more and more men congregated around Eragon and Saphira, providing them with a wholly unnecessary but very impressive honor guard. After so long spent in the wilds of Alagaësia, the dense press of bodies, the cacophony of high, excited voices, the storm of unguarded thoughts and emotions, and the confused motion of flailing arms and prancing horses were overwhelming for Eragon.

He retreated deep within himself, where the discordant mental chorus was no louder than the distant thunder of crashing waves. Even through the layers of barriers, he sensed the approach of twelve elves, running in formation from the other side of the camp, swift and lean as yellow-eyed mountain cats. Wanting to make a favorable impression, Eragon combed his hair with his fingers and squared his shoulders, but he also tightened the armor around his consciousness so that no one but Saphira could hear his thoughts.

The elves had come to protect him and Saphira, but ultimately their allegiance belonged to Queen Islanzadí. While he was grateful for their presence, and he doubted their inherent politeness would allow them to eavesdrop on him, he did not want to provide the queen of the elves with any opportunity to learn the secrets of the Varden, nor to gain a hold over him. If she could wrest him away from Nasuada, he knew she would. On the whole, the elves did not trust humans, not after Galbatorix's betrayal, and for that and other reasons, he was sure Islanzadí would prefer to have him and Saphira under her direct command. And of the potentates he had met, he trusted Islanzadí the least. She was too imperious and too erratic.

The twelve elves halted before Saphira. They bowed and twisted their hands as Arya had done and, one by one, introduced themselves to Eragon with the initial phrase of the elves' traditional greeting, to which he replied with the appropriate lines. Then the lead elf, a tall, handsome male with glossy blue-black fur covering his entire body, proclaimed the purpose of their mission to everyone within earshot and formally asked Eragon and Saphira if the twelve might assume their duties.

"You may," said Eragon.

You may, said Saphira.

Then Eragon asked, "Blödhgarm-vodhr, did I perchance see you at the Agaetí Blödhren?" For he remembered watching an elf with a similar pelt gamboling among the trees during the festivities.

Blödhgarm smiled, exposing the fangs of an animal. "I believe you met my cousin Liotha. We share a most striking family resemblance, although her fur is brown and flecked, whereas mine is dark blue."

"I would have sworn it was you."

"Unfortunately, I was otherwise engaged at the time and was unable to attend the celebration. Perhaps I shall have the opportunity when next the occasion occurs, a hundred years from now."

Would you not agree, Saphira said to Eragon, *that he has a pleasant aroma?*

Eragon sniffed the air. *I don't smell anything. And I would if there was anything to smell.*

That's odd. She provided him then with the range of odors she had detected, and at once he realized what she meant. Blödhgarm's musk surrounded him like a cloud, thick and heady, a warm, smoky scent that contained hints of crushed juniper berries and that set Saphira's nostrils to tingling. *All the women in the Varden seem to have fallen in love with him,* she said. *They stalk him wherever he goes, desperate to talk with him but too shy to utter so much as a squeak when he looks at them.*

Maybe only females can smell him. He cast a concerned glance at Arya. *She does not seem to be affected.*

She has protection against magical influences.

I hope so. . . . Do you think we should put a stop to Blödhgarm? What he is doing is a sneaky, underhanded way of gaining a woman's heart.

Is it any more underhanded than adorning yourself with fine clothing to catch the eye of your beloved? Blödhgarm has not taken advantage of the women who are fascinated by him, and it seems improbable that he would have composed the notes of his scent to appeal specifically to human women. Rather, I would guess it is an unintended consequence and that he created it to serve another purpose altogether. Unless he discards all semblance of decency, I think we should refrain from interfering.

What about Nasuada? Is she vulnerable to his charms?

Nasuada is wise and wary. She had Trianna place a ward around her that protects her against Blödhgarm's influence.

Good.

When they arrived at the tents, the crowd swelled in size until half the Varden appeared to be gathered around Saphira. Eragon raised his hand in response as people shouted, "Argetlam!" and "Shadeslayer!" and he heard others say, "Where have you been, Shadeslayer? Tell us of your adventures!" A fair number referred to him as the Bane of the Ra'zac, which he found so immensely satisfying, he repeated the phrase four times to himself under his breath.

225

People also shouted blessings upon his health and Saphira's too, and invitations to dine, and offers of gold and jewelry, and piteous requests for aid: would he please heal a son who had been born blind, or would he remove a growth that was killing a man's wife, or would he fix a horse's broken leg or repair a bent sword, for as the man bellowed, "It was my grandfather's!" Twice a woman's voice cried out, "Shadeslayer, will you marry me?" and while he looked, he was unable to identify the source.

Throughout the commotion, the twelve elves hovered close. The knowledge that they were watching for that which he could not see and listening for that which he could not hear was a comfort to Eragon and allowed him to interact with the massed Varden with an ease that had escaped him in the past.

Then from between the curving rows of woolen tents, the former villagers of Carvahall began to appear. Dismounting, Eragon walked among the friends and acquaintances of his childhood, shaking hands, slapping shoulders, and laughing at jokes that would be incomprehensible to anyone who had not grown up around Carvahall. Horst was there, and Eragon grasped the smith's brawny forearm. "Welcome back, Eragon. Well done. We're in your debt for avenging us on the monsters that drove us from our homes. I'm glad to see you are still in one piece, eh?"

"The Ra'zac would have had to move a sight faster to chop any parts off of me!" said Eragon. Then he found himself greeting Horst's sons, Albriech and Baldor; and then Loring the shoemaker and his three sons; Tara and Morn, who had owned Carvahall's tavern; Fisk; Felda; Calitha; Delwin and Lenna; and then fierce-eyed Birgit, who said, "I thank you, Eragon Son of None. I thank you for ensuring that the creatures who ate my husband were properly punished. My hearth is yours, now and forever."

Before Eragon could respond, the crowd swept them apart. *Son of None?* he thought. *Ha! I have a father, and everyone hates him.*

Then to his delight, Roran shouldered his way out of the throng,

Katrina beside him. He and Roran embraced, and Roran growled, "That was a fool thing to do, staying behind. I ought to knock your block off for abandoning us like that. Next time, give me advance warning before you traipse off on your own. It's getting to be a habit with you. And you should have seen how upset Saphira was on the flight back."

Eragon put a hand on Saphira's left foreleg and said, "I'm sorry I could not tell you beforehand that I planned to stay, but I did not realize it was necessary until the very last moment."

"And why was it exactly you remained in those foul caverns?"

"Because there was something I had to investigate."

When he failed to expand upon his answer, Roran's broad face hardened, and for a moment Eragon feared he would insist upon a more satisfactory explanation. But then Roran said, "Well, what hope has an ordinary man like myself of understanding the whys and wherefores of a Dragon Rider, even if he is my cousin? All that matters is that you helped free Katrina and you are here now, safe and sound." He craned his neck, as if he were trying to see what lay on top of Saphira, then he looked at Arya, who was several yards behind them, and said, "You lost my staff! I crossed the entire breadth of Alagaësia with that staff. Couldn't you manage to hold on to it for more than a few days?"

"It went to a man who needed it more than I," said Eragon.

"Oh, stop nipping at him," Katrina said to Roran, and after a moment's hesitation, she hugged Eragon. "He is really very glad to see you, you know. He just has difficulty finding the words to say it."

With a sheepish grin, Roran shrugged. "She's right about me, as always." The two of them exchanged a loving glance.

Eragon studied Katrina closely. Her copper hair had regained its original luster, and for the most part, the marks left by her ordeal had faded away, although she was still thinner and paler than normal.

Moving closer to him, so none of the Varden clustered around them could overhear, she said, "I never thought that I would owe you so much, Eragon. That *we* would owe you so much. Since Saphira brought us here, I have learned what you risked to rescue me, and I am most grateful. If I had spent another week in Helgrind, it would have killed me or stripped me of reason, which is a living death. For saving me from that fate, and for repairing Roran's shoulder, you have my utmost thanks, but more than that, you have my thanks for bringing the two of us back together again. If not for you, we never would have been reunited."

"Somehow I think Roran would have found a way to extricate you from Helgrind, even without me," commented Eragon. "He has a silver tongue when roused. He would have convinced another spellcaster to help him—Angela the herbalist, perhaps—and he would have succeeded all the same."

"Angela the herbalist?" scoffed Roran. "That prating girl would have been no match for the Ra'zac."

"You would be surprised. She's more than she appears . . . or sounds." Then Eragon dared to do something that he never would have attempted when he was living in Palancar Valley but that he felt was appropriate in his role as a Rider: he kissed Katrina upon her brow, and then he kissed Roran upon his, and he said, "Roran, you are as a brother to me. And, Katrina, you are as a sister to me. If ever you are in trouble, send for me, and whether you need Eragon the farmer or Eragon the Rider, everything I am shall be at your disposal."

"And likewise," said Roran, "if ever you are in trouble, you have but to send for us, and we shall rush to your aid."

Eragon nodded, acknowledging his offer, and refrained from mentioning that the troubles he was most likely to encounter would not be of a sort either of them could assist him with. He gripped them both by the shoulders and said, "May you live long, may you always be together and happy, and may you have many children." Katrina's smile faltered for a moment, and Eragon wondered at it.

At Saphira's urging, they resumed walking toward Nasuada's red pavilion in the center of the encampment. In due time, they and the host of cheering Varden arrived at its threshold, where Nasuada stood waiting, King Orrin to her left and scores of nobles and other notables gathered behind a double row of guards on either side.

Nasuada was garbed in a green silk dress that shimmered in the sun, like the feathers on the breast of a hummingbird, in bright contrast to the sable shade of her skin. The sleeves of the dress ended in lace ruffs at her elbows. White linen bandages covered the rest of her arms to her narrow wrists. Of all the men and women assembled before her, she was the most distinguished, like an emerald resting on a bed of brown autumn leaves. Only Saphira could compete with the brilliance of her appearance.

Eragon and Arya presented themselves to Nasuada and then to King Orrin. Nasuada gave them formal welcome on behalf of the Varden and praised them for their bravery. She finished by saying, "Aye, Galbatorix may have a Rider and dragon who fight for him even as Eragon and Saphira fight for us. He may have an army so large that it darkens the land. And he may be adept at strange and terrible magics, abominations of the spellcaster's art. But for all his wicked power, he could not stop Eragon and Saphira from invading his realm and killing four of his most favored servants, nor Eragon from crossing the Empire with impunity. The pretender's arm has grown weak indeed when he cannot defend his borders, nor protect his foul agents within their hidden fortress."

Amid the Varden's enthusiastic cheering, Eragon allowed himself a secret smile at how well Nasuada played upon their emotions, inspiring confidence, loyalty, and high spirits in spite of a reality that was far less optimistic than she portrayed it. She did not lie to them—to his knowledge, she did not lie, not even when dealing with the Council of Elders or other of her political rivals. What she did was report the truths that best supported her position and her arguments. In that regard, he thought, she was like the elves.

When the Varden's outpouring of excitement had subsided, King

Orrin greeted Eragon and Arya as Nasuada had. His delivery was staid compared with hers, and while the crowd listened politely and applauded afterward, it was obvious to Eragon that however much the people respected Orrin, they did not love him as they loved Nasuada, nor could he fire their imagination as Nasuada fired it. The smooth-faced king was gifted with a superior intellect. But his personality was too rarefied, too eccentric, and too subdued for him to be a receptacle for the desperate hopes of the humans that opposed Galbatorix.

If we overthrow Galbatorix, Eragon said to Saphira, *Orrin should not replace him in Urû'baen. He would not be able to unite the land as Nasuada has united the Varden.*

Agreed.

At length, King Orrin concluded. Nasuada whispered to Eragon, "Now it is your turn to address those who have assembled to catch a glimpse of the renowned Dragon Rider." Her eyes twinkled with suppressed merriment.

"Me!"

"It is expected."

Then Eragon turned and faced the multitude, his tongue dry as sand. His mind was blank, and for a handful of panic-stricken seconds, he thought the use of language would continue to elude him and he would embarrass himself in front of the entire Varden. Somewhere a horse nickered, but otherwise the camp seemed frightfully quiet. It was Saphira who broke his paralysis by nudging his elbow with her snout and saying, *Tell them how honored you are to have their support and how happy you are to be back among them.* With her encouragement, he managed to find a few fumbling words, and then, as soon as it was acceptable, he bowed and retreated a step.

Forcing a smile while the Varden clapped and cheered and beat their swords against their shields, he exclaimed, *That was horrible! I would rather fight a Shade than do that again.*

Really! It was not that hard, Eragon.

Yes, it was!

A puff of smoke drifted up from her nostrils as she snorted with amusement. *A fine Dragon Rider you are, afraid of talking to a large group! If only Galbatorix knew, he could have you at his mercy if he but asked you to make a speech to his troops. Ha!*

It's not funny, he grumbled, but she still continued to chuckle.

To Answer a King

After Eragon gave his address to the Varden, Nasuada gestured and Jörmundur leaped to her side. "Have everyone here return to their posts. If we were attacked now, we would be overwhelmed."

"Yes, my Lady."

Beckoning to Eragon and Arya, Nasuada placed her left hand on King Orrin's arm and, with him, entered the pavilion.

What about you? Eragon asked Saphira as he followed. Then he stepped inside the pavilion and saw that a panel at the back had been rolled up and tied to the wooden frame above so that Saphira might insert her head and participate in the goings-on. He had to wait but a moment before her glittering head and neck swung into view around the edge of the opening, darkening the interior as she settled into place. Purple flecks of light adorned the walls, projected by her blue scales onto the red fabric.

Eragon examined the rest of the tent. It was barren compared with when he had last visited, a result of the destruction Saphira had caused when she crawled into the pavilion to see Eragon in Nasuada's mirror. With only four pieces of furniture, the tent was austere even by military standards. There was the polished high-backed chair where Nasuada was sitting, King Orrin standing next to her; the selfsame mirror, which was mounted at eye level on a carved brass pole; a folding chair; and a low table strewn with maps and other documents of import. An intricately knotted dwarf rug covered the ground. Besides Arya and himself, a score of people were already gathered before Nasuada. They were all looking at him. Among them he recognized Narheim, the current commander of the dwarf troops; Trianna and other spellcasters from Du Vrangr Gata; Sabrae, Umérth, and the rest of the Council of Elders, save for Jörmundur; and a random assortment of nobles and functionaries from King Orrin's court. Those who were strangers to him he assumed also held positions of distinction in one of the many factions that made up the Varden's army. Six of Nasuada's guards were present—two stationed by the entrance and four behind Nasuada—and Eragon detected the convoluted pattern of Elva's dark and twisted thoughts from where the witch-child was hidden at the far end of the pavilion.

"Eragon," said Nasuada, "you have not met before, but let me introduce Sagabato-no Inapashunna Fadawar, chief of the Inapashunna tribe. He is a brave man."

For the next hour, Eragon endured what seemed like an endless procession of introductions, congratulations, and questions that he could not answer forthrightly without revealing secrets that were better left unsaid. When all of the guests had conversed with him, Nasuada bade them take their leave. As they filed out of the pavilion, she clapped her hands and the guards outside ushered in a second group and then, when the second group had enjoyed the dubious fruits of their visitation with him, a third. Eragon smiled the whole while. He shook hand after hand. He exchanged meaningless pleasantries and strove to memorize the plethora of names and titles that besieged him and otherwise acted with perfect civility the role he was expected to play. He knew that they honored him not because he was their friend but because of the chance of victory he embodied for the free peoples of Alagaësia, because of his power, and because of what they hoped to gain by him. In his heart, he howled with frustration and longed to break free of the stifling constraints of good manners and polite conduct and to climb on Saphira and fly away to somewhere peaceful.

The one part of the process Eragon enjoyed was watching how the supplicants reacted to the two Urgals who loomed behind Nasuada's chair. Some pretended to ignore the horned warriors—

although from the quickness of their motions and the shrill tones of their voices, Eragon could tell that the creatures unnerved them—while others glared at the Urgals and kept their hands on the pommels of their swords or daggers, and still others affected a false bravado and belittled the Urgals' notorious strength and boasted of their own. Only a few people truly seemed unaffected by the sight of the Urgals. Foremost among them was Nasuada, but their number also included King Orrin, Trianna, and an earl who said he had seen Morzan and his dragon lay waste to an entire town when he had been but a boy.

When Eragon could bear no more, Saphira swelled her chest and released a low, humming growl, so deep that it shook the mirror in its frame. The pavilion became as silent as a tomb. Her growl was not overtly threatening, but it captured everyone's attention and proclaimed her impatience with the proceedings. None of the guests were foolish enough to test her forbearance. With hurried excuses, they gathered their things and filed out of the pavilion, quickening their pace when Saphira tapped the tips of her claws against the ground.

Nasuada sighed as the entrance flap swung closed behind the last visitor. "Thank you, Saphira. I am sorry that I had to subject you to the misery of public presentation, Eragon, but as I am sure you are aware, you occupy an exalted position among the Varden, and I cannot keep you to myself anymore. You belong to the people now. They demand that you recognize them and that you give them what they consider their rightful share of your time. Neither you nor Orrin nor I can refuse the wishes of the crowd. Even Galbatorix in his dark seat of power at Urû'baen fears the fickle crowd, although he may deny it to everyone, including himself."

With the guests departed, King Orrin abandoned the guise of royal decorum. His stern expression relaxed into one of more human relief, irritation, and ferocious curiosity. Rolling his shoulders beneath his stiff robes, he looked at Nasuada and said, "I do not think we require your Nighthawks to wait on us any longer."

"Agreed." Nasuada clapped her hands, dismissing the six guards from the inside of the tent.

Dragging the spare chair over to Nasuada's, King Orrin seated himself in a tangle of sprawling limbs and billowing fabric. "Now," he said, switching his gaze between Eragon and Arya, "let us have a full account of your doings, Eragon Shadeslayer. I have heard only vague explanations for why you chose to delay at Helgrind, and I have had my fill of evasions and deceptive answers. I am determined to know the truth of the matter, so I warn you, do not attempt to conceal what actually transpired while you were in the Empire. Until I am satisfied you have told me everything there is to tell, none of us shall so much as step outside of this tent."

Her voice cold, Nasuada said, "You assume too much . . . Your Majesty. You do not have the authority to bind me in place; nor Eragon, who is my vassal; nor Saphira; nor Arya, who answers to no mortal lord but rather to one more powerful than the two of us combined. Nor do we have the authority to bind you. The five of us are as close to equals as any of us is likely to find in Alagaësia. You would do well to remember that."

King Orrin's response was equally flinty. "Do I exceed the bounds of my sovereignty? Well, perhaps I do. You are right: I have no hold over you. However, if we are equals, I have yet to see evidence of it in your treatment of me. Eragon answers to you and only you. By the Trial of the Long Knives, you have gained dominion over the wandering tribes, many of which I have long counted among my subjects. And you command as you will both the Varden and the men of Surda, who have long served my family with bravery and determination beyond that of ordinary men."

"It was you yourself who asked me to orchestrate this campaign," said Nasuada. "I have not deposed you."

"Aye, it was at my request you assumed command of our disparate forces. I am not ashamed to admit you have had more experience and success than I in waging war. Our prospects are too precarious for you, me, or any of us to indulge in false pride. However, since your investiture, you seem to have forgotten that I am still the king of Surda, and we of the Langfeld family can trace our line back to Thanebrand the Ring Giver himself, he who succeeded old, mad Palancar and who was the first of our race to sit on the throne in what is now Urû'baen.

"Considering our heritage and the assistance the House of Langfeld has rendered you in this cause, it is insulting of you to ignore the rights of my office. You act as if yours was the only verdict of moment and the opinions of others are of no account, to be trampled over in pursuit of whatever goal you have already determined is best for the portion of free humanity that is fortunate enough to have you as their leader. You negotiate treaties and alliances, such as that with the Urgals, of your own initiative and expect me, and others, to abide by your decisions, as if you speak for us all. You arrange preemptive visits of state, such as that with Blödhgarmvodhr, and do not trouble to alert me of his arrival, nor wait for me to join you so we might greet his embassy together as equals. And when I have the temerity to ask why Eragon—the man whose very existence is the reason I have staked my country in this venture—when I have the temerity to ask *why* this all-important person has elected to endanger the lives of Surdans and those of every creature who opposes Galbatorix by tarrying in the midst of our enemies, how is it you respond? By treating me as if I were no more than an overzealous, overinquisitive underling whose childish concerns distracted you from more pressing matters. Bah! I will not have it, I tell you. If you cannot bring yourself to respect my station and to accept a fair division of responsibility, as two allies ought to, then it is my opinion that you are unfit to command a coalition such as ours, and I shall set myself against you however I may."

What a long-winded fellow, Saphira observed.

Alarmed by the direction the conversation had taken, Eragon said, *What should I do? I had not intended to tell anyone else about Sloan, except for Nasuada. The fewer people who know he's alive, the better.*

A flickering sea-blue shimmer ran from the base of Saphira's head to the crest of her shoulders as the tips of the sharp, diamond-shaped scales along the sides of her neck rose a fraction of an inch from the underlying skin. The jagged layers of projecting scales gave her a fierce, ruffled appearance. *I cannot tell you what is best, Eragon. In this, you must rely upon your own judgment. Listen closely to what your heart says and perhaps it will become clear how to win free of these treacherous downdrafts.*

In response to King Orrin's sally, Nasuada clasped her hands in her lap, her bandages startling white against the green of her dress, and in a calm, even voice said, "If I have slighted you, Sire, then it was due to my own hasty carelessness and not to any desire on my part to diminish you or your house. Please forgive my lapses. They shall not happen again; that I promise you. As you have pointed out, I have but recently ascended to this post, and I have yet to master all of the accompanying niceties."

Orrin inclined his head in a cool but gracious acceptance of her words.

"As for Eragon and his activities in the Empire, I could not have provided you with specific details, for I have had no further intelligence myself. It was not, as I am sure you can appreciate, a situation that I wished to advertise."

"No, of course not."

"Therefore, it seems to me that the swiftest cure for the dispute that afflicts us is to allow Eragon to lay bare the facts of his trip that we may apprehend the full scope of this event and render judgment upon it."

"Of its own, that is not a cure," said King Orrin. "But it is the beginning of a cure, and I will gladly listen."

"Then let us tarry no longer," said Nasuada. "Let us begin this beginning and have done with our suspense. Eragon, it is time for your tale."

With Nasuada and the others gazing at him with wondering eyes, Eragon made his choice. Lifting his chin, he said, "What I tell you,

I tell you in confidence. I know I cannot expect either you, King Orrin, or you, Lady Nasuada, to swear that you will keep this secret bound within your hearts from now until the day you die, but I beg you to act as if you had. It could cause a great deal of grief if this knowledge were to be whispered in the wrong ears."

"A king does not remain king for long unless he appreciates the value of silence," said Orrin.

Without further ado, Eragon described everything that had happened to him in Helgrind and in the days that had followed. Afterward, Arya explained how she had gone about locating Eragon and then corroborated his account of their travels by providing several facts and observations of her own. When they had both said their fill, the pavilion was quiet as Orrin and Nasuada sat motionless upon their chairs. Eragon felt as if he were a child again, waiting for Garrow to tell him what his punishment would be for doing something foolish on their farm.

Orrin and Nasuada remained lost deep in reflection for several minutes, then Nasuada smoothed the front of her dress and said, "King Orrin may be of a different opinion, and if so, I look forward to hearing his reasons, but for my part, I believe that you did the right thing, Eragon."

"As do I," said Orrin, surprising them all.

"You do!" exclaimed Eragon. He hesitated. "I don't mean to sound impertinent, for I'm glad you approve, but I didn't expect you to look kindly upon my decision to spare Sloan's life. If I may ask, why—"

King Orrin interrupted. "Why do we approve? The rule of law must be upheld. If you had appointed yourself Sloan's executioner, Eragon, you would have taken for yourself the power that Nasuada and I wield. For he who has the audacity to determine who should live and who should die no longer serves the law but dictates the law. And however benevolent you might be, that would be no good thing for our species. Nasuada and I, at least, answer to the one lord even kings must kneel before. We answer to Angvard, in his realm of eternal twilight. We answer to the Gray Man on his gray horse. Death. We could be the worst tyrants in the whole of history, and given enough time, Angvard would bring us to heel. . . . But not you. Humans are a short-lived race, and we should not be governed by one of the Undying. We do not need another Galbatorix." A strange laugh escaped from Orrin then, and his mouth twisted in a humorless smile. "Do you understand, Eragon? You are so danger-ous, we are forced to acknowledge the danger to your face and hope that you are one of the few people able to resist the lure of power."

King Orrin laced his fingers together underneath his chin and gazed at a fold in his robes. "I have said more than I intended. . . . So, for all those reasons, and others besides, I agree with Nasuada. You were right to stay your hand when you discovered this Sloan in Helgrind. As inconvenient as this episode has been, it would have been far worse, and for you as well, if you had killed to please your-self and not in self-defense or in service to others."

Nasuada nodded. "That was well spoken."

Throughout, Arya listened with an inscrutable expression. Whatever her own thoughts on the matter were, she did not divulge them.

Orrin and Nasuada pressed Eragon with a number of questions about the oaths he had laid upon Sloan, as well as queries about the remainder of his trip. The interrogation continued for so long, Nasuada had a tray of cooled cider, fruit, and meat pies brought into the pavilion, along with the haunch of a steer for Saphira. Nasuada and Orrin had ample opportunity to eat between questions; how-ever, they kept Eragon so busy talking, he managed to consume only two bites of fruit and a few sips of cider to wet his throat.

At long last King Orrin bade them farewell and departed to re-view the status of his cavalry. Arya left a minute later, explaining that she needed to report to Queen Islanzadí and to, as she said, "heat a tub of water, wash the sand from my skin, and return my

239

features to their usual shape. I do not feel myself, with the tips of my ears missing, my eyes round and level, and the bones of my face in the wrong places."

When she was alone with Eragon and Saphira, Nasuada sighed and leaned her head against the back of the chair. Eragon was shocked by how tired she appeared. Gone were her previous vitality and strength of presence. Gone was the fire from her eyes. She had, he realized, been pretending to be stronger than she was in order to avoid tempting her enemies and demoralizing the Varden with the spectacle of her weakness.

"Are you ill?" he asked.

She nodded toward her arms. "Not exactly. It's taking me longer to recuperate than I had anticipated. . . . Some days are worse than others."

"If you want, I can—"

"No. Thank you, but no. Do not tempt me. One rule of the Trial of the Long Knives is that you must allow your wounds to heal at their own pace, without magic. Otherwise, the contestants will not have endured the full measure of pain from their cuts."

"That's barbaric!"

A slow smile touched her lips. "Maybe so, but it is what it is, and I would not fail so late in the trial merely because I could not withstand a bit of an ache."

"What if your wounds fester?"

"Then they fester, and I shall pay the price for my mistake. But I doubt they will while Angela ministers to me. She has an amazing storehouse of knowledge where medicinal plants are concerned. I half believe she could tell you the true name of every species of grass on the plains east of here merely by feeling their leaves."

Saphira, who had been so still she appeared asleep, now yawned—nearly touching the floor and the ceiling with the tips of her open jaws—and shook her head and neck, sending the flecks of light reflected by her scales spinning about the tent with dizzying speed.

Straightening in her seat, Nasuada said, "Ah, I am sorry. I know this has been tedious. You have both been very patient. Thank you."

Eragon knelt and placed his right hand over hers. "You do not need to worry about me, Nasuada. I know my duty. I have never aspired to rule; that is not my destiny. And if ever I am offered the chance to sit upon a throne, I shall refuse and see that it goes to someone who is better suited than I to lead our race."

"You are a good person, Eragon," murmured Nasuada, and pressed his hand between hers. Then she chuckled. "What with you, Roran, and Murtagh, I seem to spend most of my time worrying about members of your family."

Eragon bridled at the statement. "Murtagh is no family of mine."

"Of course. Forgive me. But still, you must admit it's startling how much bother the three of you have caused both the Empire *and* the Varden."

"It's a talent of ours," joked Eragon.

It runs in their blood, said Saphira. *Wherever they go, they get themselves entangled in the worst danger possible.* She nudged Eragon in the arm. *Especially this one. What else can you expect of people from Palancar Valley? Descendants all of a mad king.*

"But not mad themselves," said Nasuada. "At least I don't think so. It's hard to tell at times." She laughed. "If you, Roran, and Murtagh were locked in the same cell, I'm not sure who would survive."

Eragon laughed as well. "Roran. He's not about to let a little thing like death stand between him and Katrina."

Nasuada's smile became slightly strained. "No, I suppose he wouldn't at that." For a score of heartbeats, she was silent, then: "Goodness me, how selfish I am. The day is almost done, and here I am detaining you merely so I can enjoy a minute or two of idle conversation."

"The pleasure is mine."

"Yes, but there are better places than this for talk among friends. After what you have been through, I expect you would like a wash, a change, and a hearty meal, no? You must be famished!" Eragon glanced at the apple he still held and regretfully concluded it would be impolite to continue eating it when his audience with Nasuada was drawing to a close. Nasuada caught his look and said, "Your face answers for you, Shadeslayer. You have the guise of a winter-starved wolf. Well, I shall not torment you any longer. Go and bathe and garb yourself in your finest tunic. When you are presentable, I would be most pleased if you would consent to join me for my evening meal. Understand, you would not be my only guest, for the affairs of the Varden demand my constant attention, but you would brighten the proceedings considerably for me if you chose to attend."

Eragon fought back a grimace at the thought of having to spend hours more parrying verbal thrusts from those who sought to use him for their own advantage or to satisfy their curiosity about Riders and dragons. Still, Nasuada was not to be denied, so he bowed and agreed to her request.

242

A FEAST WITH FRIENDS

Eragon and Saphira left Nasuada's crimson pavilion with the contingent of elves ranged about them and walked to the small tent that had been assigned to him when they had joined the Varden at the Burning Plains. There he found a hogshead of boiling water waiting for him, the coils of steam opalescent in the oblique light from the large evening sun. Ignoring it for the moment, he ducked inside the tent.

After checking to ensure that none of his few possessions had been disturbed during his absence, Eragon unburdened himself of his pack and carefully removed his armor, storing it beneath his cot. It needed to be wiped and oiled, but that was a task that would have to wait. Then he reached even farther underneath the cot, his fingers scraping the fabric wall beyond, and groped in the darkness until his hand came into contact with a long, hard object. Grasping it, he lay the heavy cloth-wrapped bundle across his knees. He picked apart the knots in the wrapping, and then, starting at the thickest end of the bundle, began to unwind the coarse strips of canvas.

Inch by inch, the scuffed leather hilt of Murtagh's hand-and-a-half sword came into view. Eragon stopped when he had exposed the hilt, the crossguard, and a fair expanse of the gleaming blade, which was as jagged as a saw from where Murtagh had blocked Eragon's blows with Zar'roc.

Eragon sat and stared at the weapon, conflicted. He did not know what had prompted him, but the day after the battle, he had returned to the plateau and retrieved the sword from the morass of trampled dirt where Murtagh had dropped it. Even after only a single night exposed to the elements, the steel had acquired a mottled

243

veil of rust. With a word, he had dispelled the scrim of corrosion. Perhaps it was because Murtagh had stolen his own sword that Eragon felt compelled to take up Murtagh's, as if the exchange, unequal and involuntary though it was, minimized his loss. Perhaps it was because he wished to claim a memento of that bloody conflict. And perhaps it was because he still harbored a sense of latent affection for Murtagh, despite the grim circumstances that had turned them against each other. No matter how much Eragon abhorred what Murtagh had become, and pitied him for it too, he could not deny the connection that existed between them. Theirs was a shared fate. If not for an accident of birth, he would have been raised in Urû'baen, and Murtagh in Palancar Valley, and then their current positions might well have been reversed. Their lives were inexorably intertwined.

As he gazed at the silver steel, Eragon composed a spell that would smooth the wrinkles from the blade, close the wedge-shaped gaps along the edges, and restore the strength of the temper. He wondered, however, if he ought to. The scar that Durza had given him he had kept as a reminder of their encounter, at least until the dragons erased it during the Agaetí Blödhren. Should he keep this scar as well, then? Would it be healthy for him to carry such a painful memory on his hip? And what sort of message would it send to the rest of the Varden if he chose to wield the blade of another betrayer? Zar'roc had been a gift from Brom; Eragon could not have refused to accept it, nor was he sorry he had. But he was under no such compulsion to claim as his own the nameless blade that rested upon his thighs.

I need a sword, he thought. *But not this sword.*

He wrapped the blade again in its shroud of canvas and slid it back under the cot. Then, with a fresh shirt and tunic tucked under his elbow, he left the tent and went to bathe.

When he was clean and garbed in the fine lámarae shirt and tunic, he set out to meet with Nasuada near the tents of the healers, as she had requested. Saphira flew, for as she said, *It is too cramped for me on the ground; I keep knocking over tents. Besides, if I walk with you, such a herd of people will gather around us, we will hardly be able to move.*

Nasuada was waiting for him by a row of three flagpoles, upon which a half-dozen gaudy pennants hung limp in the cooling air. She had changed since they had parted and now wore a light summer frock, the color of pale straw. Her dense, mosslike hair she had piled high on her head in an intricate mass of knots and braids. A single white ribbon held the arrangement in place.

She smiled at Eragon. He smiled in return and quickened his pace. As he drew close, his guards mingled with her guards with a conspicuous display of suspicion on the part of the Nighthawks and studied indifference on the part of the elves.

Nasuada took his arm and, while they spoke in comfortable tones, guided his steps as they ambled through the sea of tents. Above, Saphira circled the camp, content to wait until they arrived at their destination before she went to the effort of landing. Eragon and Nasuada spoke of many things. Little of consequence passed between their lips, but her wit, her gaiety, and the thoughtfulness of her remarks charmed him. It was easy for him to talk to her and easier to listen, and that very ease caused him to realize how much he cared for her. Her hold on him far exceeded that of a liegelord over her vassal. It was a new feeling for him, their bond. Aside from his aunt Marian, of whom he had but faint memories, he had grown up in a world of men and boys, and he had never had the opportunity to be friends with a woman. His inexperience made him uncertain, and his uncertainty made him awkward, but Nasuada did not seem to notice.

She stopped him before a tent that glowed from within with the light of many candles and that hummed with a multitude of unintelligible voices. "Now we must dive into the swamp of politics again. Prepare yourself."

She swept back the entrance flap to the tent, and Eragon jumped as a host of people shouted, "Surprise!" A wide trestle table laden with food dominated the center of the tent, and at the table were sitting Roran and Katrina, twenty or so of the villagers from Carvahall—including Horst and his family—Angela the herbalist, Jeod and his wife, Helen, and several people Eragon did not recognize but who had the look of sailors. A half-dozen children had been playing on the ground next to the table; they paused in their games and stared at Nasuada and Eragon with open mouths, seemingly unable to decide which of these two strange figures deserved more of their attention.

Eragon grinned, overwhelmed. Before he could think of what to say, Angela raised her flagon and piped, "Well, don't just stand there gaping! Come in, sit down. I'm hungry!"

As everyone laughed, Nasuada pulled Eragon toward the two empty chairs next to Roran. Eragon helped Nasuada to her seat, and as she sank into the chair, he asked, "Did *you* arrange this?"

"Roran suggested whom you might want to attend, but yes, the original idea was mine. And I made a few additions of my own to the table, as you can see."

"Thank you," said Eragon, humbled. "Thank you so much."

He saw Elva sitting cross-legged in the far-left corner of the tent, a platter of food on her lap. The other children shunned her— Eragon could not imagine they had much in common—and none of the adults, save Angela, seemed comfortable in her presence. The small, narrow-shouldered girl gazed up at him from under her black bangs with her horrible violet eyes and mouthed what he guessed was "Greetings, Shadeslayer."

"Greetings, Farseer," he mouthed in return. Her small pink lips parted in what would have been a charming smile if not for the fell orbs that burned above them.

Eragon gripped the arms of his chair as the table shook, the dishes rattled, and the walls of the tent flapped. Then the back of the tent bulged and parted as Saphira pushed her head inside. *Meat!* she said. *I smell meat!*

For the next few hours, Eragon lost himself in a blur of food, drink, and the pleasure of good company. It was like returning home. The wine flowed like water, and after they had drained their cups once or twice, the villagers forgot their deference and treated him as one of their own, which was the greatest gift they could give. They were equally generous with Nasuada, although they refrained from making jokes at her expense, as they sometimes did with Eragon. Pale smoke filled the tent as the candles consumed themselves. Beside him, Eragon heard the boom of Roran's laughter ring forth again and again, and across the table the even deeper boom of Horst's laugh. Muttering an incantation, Angela set to dancing a small man she had fashioned from a crust of sourdough bread, much to everyone's amusement. The children gradually overcame their fear of Saphira and dared to walk up to her and pet her snout. Soon they were clambering over her neck, hanging from her spikes, and tugging at the crests above her eyes. Eragon laughed as he watched. Jeod entertained the crowd with a song he had learned from a book long ago. Tara danced a jig. Nasuada's teeth flashed as she tossed her head back. And Eragon, by popular request, recounted several of his adventures, including a detailed description of his flight from Carvahall with Brom, which was of special interest to his listeners.

"To think," said Gertrude, the round-faced healer tugging on her shawl, "we had a dragon in our valley and we never even knew it." With a pair of knitting needles produced from within her sleeves, she pointed at Eragon. "To think I nursed you when your legs had been scraped from flying on Saphira and I never suspected the cause." Shaking her head and clucking her tongue, she cast on with brown wool yarn and began to knit with speed born of decades of practice.

Elain was the first to leave the party, pleading exhaustion brought on by her advanced stage of pregnancy; one of her sons, Baldor, went with her. Half an hour later, Nasuada also made to leave, explaining that the demands of her position prevented her from staying as long as she would like but that she wished them health and happiness and hoped they would continue to support her in her fight against the Empire.

As she moved away from the table, Nasuada beckoned to Eragon. He joined her by the entrance. Turning her shoulder to the rest of the tent, she said, "Eragon, I know that you need time to recover from your journey and that you have affairs of your own that you must tend to. Therefore, tomorrow and the day after are yours to spend as you will. But on the morning of the third day, present yourself at my pavilion and we shall talk about your future. I have a most important mission for you."

"My Lady." Then he said, "You keep Elva close at hand wherever you go, do you not?"

"Aye, she is my safeguard against any danger that might slip past the Nighthawks. Also, her ability to divine what it is that pains people has proved enormously helpful. It is so much easier to obtain someone's cooperation when you are privy to all of their secret hurts."

"Are you willing to give that up?"

She studied him with a piercing gaze. "You intend to remove your curse from Elva?"

"I intend to try. Remember, I promised her I would."

"Yes, I was there." The crash of a falling chair distracted her for an instant, then she said, "Your promises will be the death of us. . . . Elva is irreplaceable; no one else has her skill. And the service she provides, as I just testified, is worth more than a mountain of gold. I have even thought that, of all of us, she alone might be able to defeat Galbatorix. She would be able to anticipate his every attack, and your spell would show her how to counter them, and as long as countering them did not require her to sacrifice her life, she would prevail. . . . For the good of the Varden, Eragon, for the good of everyone in Alagaësia, couldn't you feign your attempt to cure Elva?"

"No," he said, biting off the word as if it offended him. "I would not do it even if I could. It would be wrong. If we force Elva to remain as she is, she will turn against us, and I do not want her as an enemy." He paused, then at Nasuada's expression added, "Besides, there is a good chance I may not succeed. Removing such a vaguely worded spell is a difficult prospect at best. . . . If I may make a suggestion?"

"What?"

"Be honest with Elva. Explain to her what she means to the Varden, and ask her if she will continue to carry her burden for the sake of all free people. She may refuse; she has every right to, but if she does, her character is not one we would want to rely upon anyway. And if she accepts, then it shall be of her own free will."

With a slight frown, Nasuada nodded. "I shall speak with her tomorrow. You should be present as well, to help me persuade her and to lift your curse if we fail. Be at my pavilion three hours after dawn." And with that, she swept into the torch-lit night outside.

Much later, when the candles guttered in their sockets and the villagers began to disperse in twos and threes, Roran grasped Eragon's arm by the elbow and drew him through the back of the tent to stand by Saphira's side, where the others could not hear. "What you said earlier about Helgrind, was that all of it?" asked Roran. His grip was like a pair of iron pincers clamped around Eragon's flesh. His eyes were hard and questioning, and also unusually vulnerable.

Eragon held his gaze. "If you trust me, Roran, never ask me that question again. It's not something you want to know." Even as he spoke, Eragon felt a deep sense of unease over having to conceal Sloan's existence from Roran and Katrina. He knew the deception was necessary, but it still made him uncomfortable to lie to his family. For a moment, Eragon considered telling Roran the truth, but then he remembered all the reasons he had decided not to and held his tongue.

Roran hesitated, his face troubled, then he set his jaw and released Eragon. "I trust you. That's what family is for, after all, eh? Trust."

"That and killing each other."

Roran laughed and rubbed his nose with a thumb. "That too." He rolled his thick, round shoulders and reached up to massage his right one, a habit he had fallen into since the Ra'zac had bitten him. "I have another question."

"Oh?"

"It is a boon . . . a favor I seek of you." A wry smile touched his lips, and he shrugged. "I never thought I would speak to you of this. You're younger than I, you've barely reached your manhood, and you're my cousin to boot."

"Speak of what? Stop beating around the bush."

"Of marriage," said Roran, and lifted his chin. "Will you marry Katrina and me? It would please me if you would, and while I have refrained from mentioning it to her until I had your answer, I know Katrina would be honored and delighted if you would consent to join us as man and wife."

Astonished, Eragon was at a loss for words. At last he managed to stammer, "Me?" Then he hastened to say, "I would be happy to do it, of course, but . . . *me*? Is that really what you want? I'm sure Nasuada would agree to marry the two of you. . . . You could have King Orrin, a real king! He would leap at the chance to preside over the ceremony if it would help him earn my favor."

"I want you, Eragon," said Roran, and clapped him on the shoulder. "You are a Rider, and you are the only other living person who shares my blood; Murtagh does not count. I cannot think of anyone else I would rather have tie the knot around my wrist and hers."

"Then," said Eragon, "I shall." The air whooshed out of him as Roran embraced him and squeezed with all of his prodigious strength. He gasped slightly when Roran released him and then, once his breath had returned, said, "When? Nasuada has a mission planned for me. I don't know what it is yet, but I'm guessing it will keep me busy for some time. So . . . maybe early next month, if events allow?"

Roran's shoulders bunched and knotted. He shook his head like a bull sweeping its horns through a clump of brambles. "What about the day after tomorrow?"

"So soon? Isn't that rushing it a bit? There would hardly be any time to prepare. People will think it's unseemly."

Roran's shoulders rose, and the veins on his hands bulged as he opened and closed his fists. "It can't wait. If we're not married and quick, the old women will have something far more interesting to gossip about than my impatience. Do you understand?"

It took Eragon a moment to grasp Roran's meaning, but once he did, Eragon could not stop a broad smile from spreading across his face. *Roran's going to be a father!* he thought. Still smiling, he said, "I think so. The day after tomorrow it is." Eragon grunted as Roran hugged him again, pounding him on the back. With some difficulty, he freed himself.

Grinning, Roran said, "I'm in your debt. Thank you. Now I must go share the news with Katrina, and we must do what we can to ready a wedding feast. I will let you know the exact hour once we decide on it."

"That sounds fine."

Roran began walking toward the tent, then he spun around and threw his arms out in the air as if he would gather the entire world to his breast. "Eragon, I'm going to be married!"

With a laugh, Eragon waved his hand. "Go on, you fool. She's waiting for you."

Eragon climbed onto Saphira as the flaps of the tent closed over Roran. "Blödhgarm?" he called. Quiet as a shadow, the elf glided into the light, his yellow eyes glowing like coals. "Saphira and I are going to fly for a little while. We will meet you at my tent."

"Shadeslayer," said Blödhgarm, and tilted his head.

Then Saphira raised her massive wings, ran forward three steps, and launched herself over the rows of tents, battering them with wind as she flapped hard and fast. The movements of her body beneath him shook Eragon, and he gripped the spike in front of him for support. Saphira spiraled upward above the twinkling camp until it was an inconsequential patch of light dwarfed by the dark landscape that surrounded it. There she remained, floating between the heavens and the earth, and all was silent.

Eragon lay his head on her neck and stared up at the glittering band of dust that spanned the sky.

Rest if you want, little one, said Saphira. *I shall not let you fall.*

And he rested, and visions beset him of a circular stone city that stood in the center of an endless plain and of a small girl who wandered among the narrow, winding alleys within and who sang a haunting melody.

And the night wore on toward morning.

INTERSECTING SAGAS

It was just after dawn and Eragon was sitting on his cot, oiling his mail hauberk, when one of the Varden's archers came to him and begged him to heal his wife, who was suffering from a malignant tumor. Even though he was supposed to be at Nasuada's pavilion in less than an hour, Eragon agreed and accompanied the man to his tent. Eragon found his wife much weakened from the growth, and it took all of his skill to extract the insidious tendrils from her flesh. The effort left him tired, but he was pleased that he was able to save the woman from a long and painful death.

Afterward, Eragon rejoined Saphira outside of the archer's tent and stood with her for a few minutes, rubbing the muscles near the base of her neck. Humming, Saphira flicked her sinuous tail and twisted her head and shoulders so that he had better access to her smooth plated underside. She said, *While you were occupied in there, other petitioners came to seek an audience with you, but Blödhgarm and his ilk turned them away, for their requests were not urgent.*

Is that so? He dug his fingers under the edge of one of her large neck scales, scratching even harder. *Perhaps I should emulate Nasuada.*

How so?

On the sixth day of every week, from morning until noon, she grants an audience to everyone who wishes to bring requests or disputes before her. I could do the same.

I like the idea, said Saphira. *Only, you will have to be careful that you do not expend too much of your energy on people's demands. We must be ready to fight the Empire at a moment's notice.* She pushed her neck against his hand, humming even louder.

I need a sword, Eragon said.

Then get one.

Mmh. . . .

Eragon continued to scratch her until she pulled away and said, *You will be late for Nasuada unless you hurry.*

Together, they started toward the center of the camp and Nasuada's pavilion. It was less than a quarter of a mile away, so Saphira walked with him instead of soaring among the clouds, as she had before.

About a hundred feet from the pavilion, they chanced upon Angela the herbalist. She was kneeling between two tents, pointing at a square of leather draped across a low, flat rock. On the leather lay a jumbled pile of finger-length bones branded with a different symbol on each facet: the knucklebones of a dragon, with which she had read Eragon's future in Teirm.

Opposite Angela sat a tall woman with broad shoulders; tanned, weather-beaten skin; black hair braided in a long, thick rope down her back; and a face that was still handsome despite the hard lines that the years had carved around her mouth. She wore a russet dress that had been made for a shorter woman; her wrists stuck out several inches from the ends of her sleeves. She had tied a strip of dark cloth around each wrist, but the strip on the left had loosened and slipped toward her elbow. Eragon saw thick layers of scars where it had been. They were the sort of scars one could only get from the constant chafing of manacles. At some point, he realized, she had been captured by her enemies, and she had fought—fought until she had torn open her wrists to the bone, if her scars were anything to judge by. He wondered whether she had been a criminal or a slave, and he felt his countenance darken as he considered the thought of someone being so cruel as to allow such harm to befall a prisoner under his control, even if it was self-inflicted.

Next to the woman was a serious-looking teenage girl just entering into the full bloom of her adult beauty. The muscles of her forearms were unusually large, as if she had been an apprentice to a smith or a swordsman, which was highly improbable for a girl, no matter how strong she might be.

Angela had just finished saying something to the woman and her companion when Eragon and Saphira halted behind the curly-haired witch. With a single motion, Angela gathered up the knuckle-bones in the leather square and tucked them under the yellow sash at her waist. Standing, she flashed Eragon and Saphira a brilliant smile. "My, you both have the most impeccable sense of timing. You always seem to turn up whenever the drop spindle of fate begins to spin."

"The drop spindle of fate?" questioned Eragon.

She shrugged. "What? You can't expect brilliance all the time, not even from me." She gestured at the two strangers, who had also stood, and said, "Eragon, will you consent to give them your blessing? They have endured many dangers, and a hard road yet lies before them. I am sure they would appreciate whatever protection the benediction of a Dragon Rider may convey."

Eragon hesitated. He knew that Angela rarely cast the dragon bones for the people who sought her services—usually only for those whom Solembum deigned to speak with—as such a prognostication was no false act of magic but rather a true foretelling that could reveal the mysteries of the future. That Angela had chosen to do this for the handsome woman with the scars on her wrists and the teenage girl with the forearms of a swordfighter told him they were people of note, people who had had, and would have, important roles in shaping the Alagaësia to be. As if to confirm his suspicions, he spotted Solembum in his usual form of a cat with large, tufted ears lurking behind the corner of a nearby tent, watching the proceedings with enigmatic yellow eyes. And yet Eragon still hesitated, haunted by the memory of the first and last blessing he had bestowed—how, because of his relative unfamiliarity with the ancient language, he had distorted the life of an innocent child.

Saphira? he asked.

Her tail whipped through the air. *Do not be so reluctant. You have learned from your mistake, and you shall not make it again. Why, then, should you withhold your blessing from those who may benefit from it? Bless them, I say, and do it properly this time.*

"What are your names?" he asked.

"If it please you, Shadeslayer," said the tall, black-haired woman, with a hint of an accent he could not place, "names have power, and we would prefer ours remain unknown." She kept her gaze angled slightly downward, but her tone was firm and unyielding. The girl uttered a small gasp, as if shocked by the woman's effrontery.

Eragon nodded, neither upset nor surprised, although the woman's reticence had piqued his curiosity even more. He would have liked to know their names, but they were not essential for what he was about to do. Pulling the glove off his right hand, he placed his palm on the middle of the woman's warm forehead. She flinched at the contact but did not retreat. Her nostrils flared, the corners of her mouth thinned, a crease appeared between her eyebrows, and he felt her tremble, as if his touch pained her and she were fighting the urge to knock aside his arm. In the background, Eragon was vaguely aware of Blödhgarm stalking closer, ready to pounce on the woman should she prove to be hostile.

Disconcerted by her reaction, Eragon broached the barrier in his mind, immersed himself in the flow of magic, and, with the full power of the ancient language, said, "Atra guliä un ilian tauthr ono un atra ono waíse sköliro fra rauthr." By imbuing the phrase with energy, as he would the words of a spell, he ensured that it would shape the course of events and thereby improve the woman's lot in life. He was careful to limit the amount of energy he transferred into the blessing, for unless he put checks on it, a spell of that sort would feed off his body until it absorbed all of his vitality, leaving him an empty husk. Despite his caution, the drop in his strength was more than he expected; his vision dimmed and his legs wobbled and threatened to collapse underneath him.

A moment later, he recovered.

It was with a sense of relief that he lifted his hand from the woman's brow, a sentiment that she seemed to share, for she stepped back and rubbed her arms. She looked to him like a person trying to cleanse herself of some foul substance.

Moving on, Eragon repeated the procedure with the teenage girl. Her face widened as he released the spell, as if she could feel it becoming part of her body. She curtsied. "Thank you, Shadeslayer. We are in your debt. I hope that you succeed in defeating Galbatorix and the Empire."

She turned to leave but stopped when Saphira snorted and snaked her head past Eragon and Angela, so she loomed above the two women. Bending her neck, Saphira breathed first upon the face of the older woman and then upon the face of the younger, and projecting her thoughts with such force as to overwhelm all but the thickest defenses—for she and Eragon had noticed that the black-haired woman had a well-armored mind—she said, *Good hunting, O Wild Ones. May the wind rise under your wings, may the sun always be at your backs, and may you catch your prey napping. And, Wolf-Eyes, I hope that when you find the one who left your paws in his traps, you do not kill him too quickly.*

Both women stiffened when Saphira began to speak. Afterward, the elder clapped her fists against her chest and said, "That I shall not, O Beautiful Huntress." Then she bowed to Angela, saying, "Train hard, strike first, Seer."

"Bladesinger."

With a swirl of skirts, she and the teenager strode away and soon were lost from sight in the maze of identical gray tents.

What, no marks upon their foreheads? Eragon asked Saphira.

Elva was unique. I shall not brand anyone else in a like manner. What happened in Farthen Dûr just . . . happened. Instinct drove me. Beyond that, I cannot explain.

As the three of them walked toward Nasuada's pavilion, Eragon glanced at Angela. "Who were they?"

Her lips quirked. "Pilgrims on their own quest."

"That is hardly an answer," he complained.

"It is not my habit to hand out secrets like candied nuts on winter solstice. Especially not when they belong to others."

He was silent for a few paces. Then: "When someone refuses to tell me a certain piece of information, it only makes me that much more determined to find out the truth. I hate being ignorant. For me, a question unanswered is like a thorn in my side that pains me every time I move until I can pluck it out."

"You have my sympathy."

"Why is that?"

"Because if that is so, you must spend every waking hour in mortal agony, for life is full of unanswerable questions."

Sixty feet from Nasuada's pavilion, a contingent of pikemen marching through camp blocked their way. While they waited for the warriors to file past, Eragon shivered and blew on his hands. "I wish we had time for a meal."

Quick as ever, Angela said, "It's the magic, isn't it? It has worn you down." He nodded. Sticking a hand into one of the pouches that hung from her sash, Angela pulled out a hard brown lump flecked with shiny flaxseeds. "Here, this will hold you until lunch."

"What is it?"

She thrust it at him, insistent. "Eat it. You'll like it. Trust me." As he took the oily lump from between her fingers, she grasped his wrist with her other hand and held him in place while she inspected the half-inch-high calluses on his knuckles. "How very clever of you," she said. "They are as ugly as the warts on a toad, but who cares if they help keep your skin intact, eh? I like this. I like this quite a lot. Were you inspired by the dwarves' Ascûdgamln?"

"Nothing escapes you, does it?" he asked.

"Let it escape. I only concern myself with things that exist." Eragon blinked, thrown as he often was by her verbal trickery. She tapped a callus with the tip of one of her short fingernails. "I would do this myself, except that it would catch on the wool when I'm spinning or knitting."

"You knit with your own yarn?" he said, surprised that she would engage in anything so ordinary.

"Of course! It's a wonderful way to relax. Besides, if I didn't, where would I get a sweater with Dvalar's ward against mad rabbits knit in the Liduen Kvaedhí across the inside of the chest, or a snood that was dyed yellow, green, and bright pink?"

"Mad rabbits—"

She tossed her thick curls. "You would be amazed how many magicians have died after being bitten by mad rabbits. It's far more common than you might think."

Eragon stared at her. *Do you think she's jesting?* he asked Saphira.

Ask her and find out.

She would only answer with another riddle.

The pikemen having gone, Eragon, Saphira, and Angela continued toward the pavilion, accompanied by Solembum, who had joined them without Eragon noticing. Picking her way around piles of dung left by the horses of King Orrin's cavalry, Angela said, "So tell me: aside from your fight with the Ra'zac, did anything terribly interesting happen to you during your trip? You know how I love to hear about *interesting* things."

Eragon smiled, thinking of the spirits that had visited him and Arya. However, he did not want to discuss them, so instead he said, "Since you ask, quite a few interesting things happened. For example, I met a hermit named Tenga living in the ruins of an elf tower. He possessed the most amazing library. In it were seven—"

Angela stopped so abruptly, Eragon kept walking another three paces before he caught himself and turned back. The witch seemed stunned, as if she had taken a hard knock to her head. Padding toward her, Solembum leaned against her legs and gazed upward. Angela wet her lips, then said, "Are . . ." She coughed once. "Are you sure his name was Tenga?"

"Have you met him?"

Solembum hissed, and the hair on his back stood straight out.

Eragon edged away from the werecat, eager to escape the reach of his claws.

"Met him?" With a bitter laugh, Angela planted her hands on her hips. "Met him? Why, I did better than that! I was his apprentice for . . . for an unfortunate number of years."

Eragon had never expected Angela to willingly reveal anything about her past. Eager to learn more, he asked, "When did you meet him? And where?"

"Long ago and far away. However, we parted badly, and I have not seen him for many, many years." Angela frowned. "In fact, I thought he was already dead."

Saphira spoke then, saying, *Since you were Tenga's apprentice, do you know what question he's trying to answer?*

"I have not the slightest idea. Tenga always had a question he was trying to answer. If he succeeded, he immediately chose another one, and so on. He may have answered a hundred questions since I last saw him, or he may still be gnashing his teeth over the same conundrum as when I left him."

Which was?

"Whether the phases of the moon influence the number and quality of the opals that form in the roots of the Beor Mountains, as is commonly held among the dwarves."

"But how could you prove that?" objected Eragon.

Angela shrugged. "If anyone could, it would be Tenga. He may be deranged, but his brilliance is none the less for it."

He is a man who kicks at cats, said Solembum, as if that summed up Tenga's entire character.

Then Angela clapped her hands together and said, "No more! Eat your sweet, Eragon, and let us go to Nasuada."

MAKING AMENDS

"Y ou are late," said Nasuada as Eragon and Angela found seats in the row of chairs arranged in a semicircle before Nasuada's high-backed throne. Also seated in the semicircle were Elva and her caretaker, Greta, the old woman who had pleaded with Eragon in Farthen Dûr to bless her charge. As before, Saphira lay outside the pavilion and stuck her head through an opening at one end so that she could participate in the meeting. Solembum had curled up in a ball next to her head. He appeared to be sound asleep, except for occasional flicks of his tail.

Along with Angela, Eragon made his apologies for their tardiness, and then he listened as Nasuada explained to Elva the value of her abilities to the Varden—*As if she doesn't already know,* Eragon commented to Saphira—and entreated her to release Eragon from his promise to try to undo the effects of his blessing. She said she understood that what she was asking of Elva was difficult, but the fate of the entire land was at stake, and was it not worth sacrificing one's own comfort to help rescue Alagaësia from Galbatorix's evil clutches? It was a magnificent speech: eloquent, impassioned, and full of arguments intended to appeal to Elva's more noble sentiments.

Elva, who had been resting her small, pointed chin on her fists, raised her head and said, "No." Shocked silence pervaded the pavilion. Transferring her unblinking gaze from one person to the next, she elaborated: "Eragon, Angela, you both know what it is like to share someone's thoughts and emotions as they die. You know how horrible, how wrenching it is, how it feels as if part of yourself has vanished forever. And that is only from the death of one person.

Neither of you has to endure the experience unless you want to, whereas I . . . I have no choice but to share them all. I feel every death around me. Even now I can feel the life ebbing out of Sefton, one of your swordsmen, Nasuada, who was wounded on the Burning Plains, and I know what words I could say to him that would lessen his terror of obliteration. His fear is so great, oh, it makes me tremble!" With an incoherent cry, she cast up her arms before her face, as if to ward off a blow. Then: "Ah, he has gone. But there are others. There are always others. The line of dead never ends." The bitter mocking quality of her voice intensified, a travesty of a child's normal speech. "Do you truly understand, Nasuada, Lady Nightstalker . . . She Who Would Be Queen of the World? Do you truly understand? I am privy to all of the agony around me, whether physical or mental. I feel it as if it were my own, and Eragon's magic drives me to alleviate the discomfort of those who suffer, regardless of the cost to myself. And if I resist the urge, as I am this very moment, my body rebels against me: my stomach turns acid, my head throbs as if a dwarf is hammering on it, and I find it hard to move, much less think. Is this what you would wish on me, Nasuada?

"Night and day I have no respite from the pain of the world. Since Eragon *blessed* me, I have known nothing but hurt and fear, never happiness or pleasure. The lighter side of life, the things that make this existence bearable, these are denied me. Never do I see them. Never do I share in them. Only darkness. Only the combined misery of all the men, women, and children within a mile, battering at me like a midnight storm. This *blessing* has deprived me of the opportunity to be like other children. It has forced my body to mature faster than normal, and my mind even faster still. Eragon may be able to remove this ghastly ability of mine and the compulsion that accompanies it, but he cannot return me to what I was, nor what I should be, not without destroying who I have become. I am a freak, neither a child nor an adult, forever doomed to stand apart. I am not blind, you know. I see how you recoil when you hear me speak." She shook her head. "No, this is too much to ask of me. I will not continue like this for the sake of you, Nasuada, nor the Varden, nor the whole of Alagaësia, nor even for my dear mother, were she still alive today. It is not worth it, not for anything. I could go live by myself, so that I would be free of other people's afflictions, but I do not want to live like that. No, the only solution is for Eragon to attempt to correct his mistake." Her lips curved in a sly smile. "And if you disagree with me, if you think I am being stupid and selfish, why, then, you would do well to remember that I am hardly more than a swaddling babe and have yet to celebrate my second birthday. Only fools expect an infant to martyr herself for the greater good. But infant or not, I have made my decision, and nothing you can say will convince me otherwise. In this, I am as iron."

Nasuada reasoned with her further, but as Elva had promised, it proved to be a futile prospect. At last Nasuada asked Angela, Eragon, and Saphira to intervene. Angela refused on the grounds that she could not improve on Nasuada's words and that she believed Elva's choice was a personal one and therefore the girl ought to be able to do as she wished without being harried like an eagle by a flock of jays. Eragon was of a similar opinion, but he consented to say, "Elva, I cannot tell you what you should do—only you can determine that—but do not reject Nasuada's request out of hand. She is trying to save us all from Galbatorix, and she needs our support if we are to have any chance of success. The future is hidden to me, but I believe that your ability might be the perfect weapon against Galbatorix. You could predict his every attack. You could tell us exactly how to counteract his wards. And above all else, you would be able to sense where Galbatorix is vulnerable, where he is most weak, and what we could do to hurt him."

"You will have to do better than that, Rider, if you want to change my mind."

"I don't want to change your mind," said Eragon. "I only want to make sure you have given due consideration to the implications of your decision and that you are not being overly hasty."

The girl shifted but did not respond.

Then Saphira asked: *What is in your heart, O Shining Brow?*

Elva answered in a soft tone, with no trace of malice. "I have spoken my heart, Saphira. Any other words would be redundant."

If Nasuada was frustrated by Elva's obstinacy, she did not allow it to show, although her expression was stern, as befitted the discussion. She said, "I do not agree with your choice, Elva, but we will abide by it, for it is obvious that we cannot sway you. I suppose I cannot fault you, as I have no experience with the suffering you are exposed to on a daily basis, and if I were in your position, it is possible I would act no differently. Eragon, if you will . . ."

At her bidding, Eragon knelt in front of Elva. Her lustrous violet eyes bored into him as he placed her small hands between his larger ones. Her flesh burned against his as if she had a fever.

"Will it hurt, Shadeslayer?" Greta asked, the old woman's voice quavering.

"It shouldn't, but I do not know for sure. Removing spells is a much more inexact art than casting them. Magicians rarely if ever attempt it because of the challenges it poses."

The wrinkles on her face contorted with worry, Greta patted Elva on the head, saying, "Oh, be brave, my plum. Be brave." She did not seem to notice the look of irritation Elva directed at her.

Eragon ignored the interruption. "Elva, listen to me. There are two different methods for breaking an enchantment. One is for the magician who originally cast the spell to open himself to the energy that fuels our magic—"

"That's the part I always had difficulty with," said Angela. "It's why I rely more upon potions and plants and objects that are magical in and of themselves than upon incantations."

"*If* you don't mind . . ."

Her cheeks dimpling, Angela said, "I'm sorry. Proceed."

"Right," growled Eragon. "One is for the original magician to open himself—"

"Or herself," Angela interjected.

"Will you please let me finish?"

"Sorry."

Eragon saw Nasuada fight back a smile. "He opens himself to the flow of energy within his body and, speaking in the ancient language, recants not only the words of his spell but also the intention behind it. This can be quite difficult, as you might imagine. Unless the magician has the right intent, he will end up altering the original spell instead of lifting it. And then he would have to unsay *two* intertwined spells.

"The other method is to cast a spell that directly counteracts the effects of the original spell. It does not eliminate the original spell, but if done properly, it renders it harmless. With your permission, this is the method I intend to use."

"A most elegant solution," Angela proclaimed, "but who, pray tell, provides the continuous stream of energy needed to maintain this counterspell? And since someone must ask, what can go wrong with this particular method?"

Eragon kept his gaze fixed on Elva. "The energy will have to come from you," he told her, pressing her hands with his. "It won't be much, but it will still reduce your stamina by a certain amount. If I do this, you will never be able to run as far or lift as many pieces of firewood as someone who does not have a similar incantation leeching off them."

"Why can't you provide the energy?" asked Elva, arching an eyebrow. "You are the one who is responsible for my predicament, after all."

"I would, but the farther away I got from you, the harder it would be to send the energy to you. And if I went too far—a mile, say, or maybe a bit more—the effort would kill me. As for what can go wrong, the only risk is that I will word the counterspell improperly and it won't block all of my blessing. If that happens, I will simply cast another counterspell."

"And if that falls short as well?"

He paused. "Then I can always resort to the first method I explained. I would prefer to avoid that, however. It is the only way to completely do away with a spell, but if the attempt were to go amiss, and it very well might, you could end up worse off than you are now."

Elva nodded. "I understand."

"Have I your permission to proceed, then?"

When she dipped her chin again, Eragon took a deep breath, readying himself. His eyes half closed from the strength of his concentration, he began to speak in the ancient language. Each word fell from his tongue with the weight of a hammer blow. He was careful to enunciate every syllable, every sound that was foreign to his own language, so as to avoid a potentially tragic mishap. The counterspell was burned into his memory. He had spent many hours during his trip from Helgrind inventing it, agonizing over it, challenging himself to devise better alternatives, all in anticipation of the day he would attempt to atone for the harm he had caused Elva. As he spoke, Saphira channeled her strength into him, and he felt her supporting him and watching closely, ready to intervene if she saw in his mind that he was about to mangle the incantation. The counterspell was very long and very complicated, for he had sought to address every reasonable interpretation of his blessing. As a result, a full five minutes passed before Eragon uttered the last sentence, word, and then syllable.

In the silence that followed, Elva's face clouded with disappointment. "I can still sense them," she said.

Nasuada leaned forward in her seat. "Who?"

"You, him, her, everyone who's in pain. They haven't gone away! The urge to help them, that's gone, but this agony still courses through me."

Nasuada leaned forward in her throne. "Eragon?"

He frowned. "I must have missed something. Give me a little while to think, and I'll put together another spell that may do the trick. There are a few other possibilities I considered, but . . ." He trailed off, troubled by the fact that the counterspell had not performed as expected. Moreover, deploying a spell specifically to block the pain Elva was feeling would be far more difficult than trying to undo the blessing as a whole. One wrong word, one poorly constructed phrase, and he might destroy her sense of empathy, or preclude her from ever learning how to communicate with her mind, or inhibit her own sense of pain, so she would not immediately notice when she was injured.

Eragon was in the midst of consulting with Saphira when Elva said, "No!"

Puzzled, he looked at her.

An ecstatic glow seemed to emanate from Elva. Her round, pearl-like teeth gleamed as she smiled, her eyes flashing with triumphant joy. "No, don't try again."

"But, Elva, why would—"

"Because I don't want any more spells feeding off me. And because I just realized *I can ignore them!*" She gripped the arms of her chair, trembling with excitement. "Without the urge to aid everyone who is suffering, I can ignore their troubles, and it doesn't make me sick! I can ignore the man with the amputated leg, I can ignore the woman who just scalded her hand, I can ignore them all, and I feel no worse for it! It's true I can't block them perfectly, not yet at least, but oh, what a relief! Silence. Blessed silence! No more cuts, scrapes, bruises, or broken bones. No more petty worries of airheaded youths. No more anguish of abandoned wives or cuckolded husbands. No more the thousands of unbearable injuries of an entire war. No more the gut-wrenching panic that precedes the final darkness." With tears starting down her cheeks, she laughed, a husky warble that set Eragon's scalp atingle.

What madness is this? asked Saphira. *Even if you can put it out of your mind, why remain shackled to the pain of others when Eragon may yet be able to free you of it?*

Elva's eyes glowed with unsavory glee. "I will never be like ordinary people. If I must be different, then let me keep that which sets me apart. As long as I can control this power, as it seems I now can, I have no objection to carrying this burden, for it shall be by my

267

choice and not forced upon me by your magic, Eragon. Ha! From now on, I shall answer to no one and no thing. If I help anyone, it will be because I want to. If I serve the Varden, it will be because my conscience tells me I should and not because you ask me to, Nasuada, or because I'll throw up if I don't. I will do as I please, and woe unto those who oppose me, for I know all their fears and shall not hesitate to play upon them in order to fulfill my wishes."

"Elva!" exclaimed Greta. "Do not say such terrible things! You cannot mean them!"

The girl turned toward her so sharply, her hair fanned out behind her. "Ah yes, I had forgotten about you, my nursemaid. Ever faithful. Always fussing. I am grateful to you for adopting me after my mother died, and for the care you've given me since Farthen Dûr, but I do not require your assistance anymore. I will live alone, tend to myself, and be beholden to no one." Cowed, the old woman covered her mouth with the hem of a sleeve and shrank back.

What Elva said appalled Eragon. He decided that he could not allow her to retain her ability if she was going to abuse it. With Saphira's assistance, for she agreed with him, he picked the most promising of the new counterspells he had been contemplating earlier and opened his mouth to deliver the lines.

Quick as a snake, Elva clamped a hand over his lips, preventing him from speaking. The pavilion shook as Saphira snarled, nearly deafening Eragon, with his enhanced hearing. As everyone reeled, save for Elva, who kept her hand pressed against Eragon's face, Saphira said, *Let him go, hatchling!*

Drawn by Saphira's snarl, Nasuada's six guards charged inside, brandishing their weapons, while Blödhgarm and the other elves ran up to Saphira and stationed themselves on either side of her shoulders, pulling back the wall of the tent so they could all see what was happening. Nasuada gestured, and the Nighthawks lowered their weapons, but the elves remained poised for action. Their blades gleamed like ice.

Neither the commotion she had engendered nor the swords

268

leveled at her seemed to perturb Elva. She cocked her head and gazed at Eragon as if he were an unusual beetle she had found crawling along the edge of her chair, and then she smiled with such a sweet, innocent expression, he wondered why he did not have greater faith in her character. In a voice like warm honey, she said, "Eragon, cease. If you cast that spell, you will hurt me as you hurt me once before. You do not want that. Every night when you lay yourself down to sleep, you will think of me, and the memory of the wrong you have committed will torment you. What you were about to do was evil, Eragon. Are you the judge of the world? Will you condemn me in the absence of wrongdoing merely because you do not approve of me? That way lies the depraved pleasure of controlling others for your own satisfaction. Galbatorix would approve."

She released him then, but Eragon was too troubled to move. She had struck at his very core, and he had no counterarguments with which to defend himself, for her questions and observations were the very ones he directed at himself. Her understanding of him sent a chill crawling down his spine. "I am grateful to you also, Eragon, for coming here today to correct your mistake. Not everyone is as willing to acknowledge and confront their shortcomings. However, you have earned no favor with me today. You have righted the scales as best you could, but that is only what any decent person ought to have done. You have not compensated me for what I have endured, nor can you. So when next we cross paths, Eragon Shadeslayer, count me not as a friend or foe. I am ambivalent toward you, Rider; I am just as prepared to hate you as I am to love you. The outcome is yours alone to decide. . . . Saphira, you gave me the star upon my brow, and you have always been kind to me. I am and shall always remain your faithful servant."

Lifting her chin to maximize her three-and-a-half-foot height, Elva surveyed the interior of the pavilion. "Eragon, Saphira, Nasuada . . . Angela. Good day." And with that, she swept off toward the entrance. The Nighthawks parted ranks as she passed between them and went outside.

Eragon stood, feeling unsteady. "What sort of monster have I created?" The two Urgal Nighthawks touched the tip of each of their horns, which he knew was how they warded off evil. To Nasuada, he said, "I'm sorry. I seem to have only made things worse for you—for all of us."

Calm as a mountain lake, Nasuada arranged her robes before answering: "No matter. The game has gotten a little more complicated, that is all. It is to be expected the closer we get to Urû'baen and Galbatorix."

A moment later, Eragon heard the sound of an object rushing through the air toward him. He flinched, but fast as he was, he was too slow to avoid a stinging slap that knocked his head to one side and sent him staggering against a chair. He rolled across the seat of the chair and sprang upright, his left arm lifted to ward off an oncoming blow, his right arm pulled back, ready to stab with the hunting knife he had snatched from his belt during the maneuver. To his astonishment, he saw that it was Angela who had struck him. The elves were gathered inches behind the fortuneteller, ready to subdue her if she should attack him again or to escort her away should Eragon order it. Solembum was at her feet, teeth and claws bared, and his hair standing on end.

Right then, Eragon could care less about the elves. "What did you do that for?" he demanded. He winced as his split lower lip stretched, tearing the flesh farther apart. Warm, metallic-tasting blood trickled down his throat.

Angela tossed her head. "Now I'm going to have to spend the next ten years teaching Elva how to behave! That's *not* what I had in mind for the next decade!"

"Teach her?" exclaimed Eragon. "She won't let you. She'll stop you as easily as she stopped me."

"Humph. Not likely. She doesn't know what bothers me, nor what might be about to hurt me. I saw to that the day she and I first met."

"Would you share this spell with us?" Nasuada asked. "After how this has turned out, it seems prudent for us to have a means of protecting ourselves from Elva."

"No, I don't think I will," said Angela. Then she too marched out of the pavilion, and Solembum stalked after her, waving his tail ever so gracefully.

The elves sheathed their blades and retreated to a discreet distance from the tent.

Nasuada rubbed her temples with a circular motion. "Magic," she cursed.

"Magic," agreed Eragon.

The pair of them started as Greta cast herself upon the ground and began to weep and wail while pulling at her thin hair, beating herself on the face, and ripping at her bodice. "Oh, my poor dear! I've lost my lamb! Lost! What will become of her, all alone? Oh, woe is me, my own little blossom rejecting me. It's a shameful reward it is for the work I've done, bending my back like a slave I have. What a cruel, hard world, always stealing your happiness from you." She groaned. "My plum. My rose. My pretty sweet pea. Gone! And no one to look after her. . . . Shadeslayer! Will you watch over her?"

Eragon grasped her by the arm and helped her to her feet, consoling her with assurances that he and Saphira would keep a close eye on Elva. *If only*, as Saphira said to Eragon, *because she might attempt to slip a knife between our ribs.*

GIFTS OF GOLD

Eragon stood next to Saphira, fifty yards from Nasuada's crimson pavilion. Glad to be free of all the commotion that had surrounded Elva, he gazed up at the clear azure sky and rolled his shoulders, already tired from the events of the day. Saphira intended to fly out to the Jiet River and bathe herself in its deep, slow-moving water, but his own intentions were less definite. He still needed to finish oiling his armor, prepare for Roran and Katrina's wedding, visit with Jeod, locate a proper sword for himself, and also . . . He scratched his chin.

How long will you be gone? he asked.

Saphira unfurled her wings in preparation for flight. *A few hours. I'm hungry. Once I am clean, I am going to catch two or three of those plump deer I've seen nibbling the grass on the western bank of the river. The Varden have shot so many of them, though, I may have to fly a half-dozen leagues toward the Spine before I find any game worth hunting.*

Don't go too far, he cautioned, *else you might encounter the Empire.*

I won't, but if I happen upon a lone group of soldiers . . . She licked her chops. *I would enjoy a quick fight. Besides, humans taste just as good as deer.*

Saphira, you wouldn't!

Her eyes sparkled. *Maybe, maybe not. It depends on whether they are wearing armor. I hate biting through metal, and scooping my food out of a shell is just as annoying.*

I see. He glanced over at the nearest elf, a tall, silver-haired woman. *The elves won't want you to go alone. Will you allow a couple of them to ride on you? Otherwise, it will be impossible for them to keep pace.*

Not today. Today, I hunt alone! With a sweep of her wings, she took off, soaring high overhead. As she turned west, toward the Jiet River, her voice sounded in his mind, fainter than before because of the distance between them. *When I return, we will fly together, won't we, Eragon?*

Yes, when you return, we will fly together, just the two of us. Her pleasure at that caused him to smile as he watched her arrow away toward the west.

Eragon lowered his gaze as Blödhgarm ran up to him, lithe as a forest cat. The elf asked where Saphira was going and seemed displeased with Eragon's explanation, but if he had any objections, he kept them to himself.

"Right," Eragon said to himself as Blödhgarm rejoined his companions. "First things first."

He strode through the camp until he found a large square of open space where thirty-some Varden were practicing with a wide assortment of weapons. To his relief, they were too busy training to notice his presence. Crouching, he lay his right hand palm-upward on the trampled earth. He chose the words he would need from the ancient language, then murmured, "Kuldr, rïsa lam iet un malthinae unin böllr."

The soil beside his hand appeared unchanged, although he could feel the spell sifting through the dirt for hundreds of feet in every direction. Not more than five seconds later, the surface of the earth began to boil like a pot of water left to sit for too long over a high flame, and it acquired a bright yellow sheen. Eragon had learned from Oromis that wherever one went, the land was sure to contain minute particles of nearly every element, and while they would be too small and scattered to mine with traditional methods, a knowledgeable magician could, with great effort, extract them.

From the center of the yellow patch, a fountain of sparkling dust arched up and over, landing in the middle of Eragon's palm. There each glittering mote melded into the next, until three spheres of pure gold, each the size of a large hazelnut, rested on his hand.

"Letta," said Eragon, and released the magic. He sat back on his heels and braced himself against the ground as a wave of weariness washed over him. His head drooped forward, and his eyelids descended halfway as his vision flickered and dimmed. Taking a deep breath, he admired the mirror-smooth orbs in his hand while he waited for his strength to return. *So pretty,* he thought. *If only I could have done this when we were living in Palancar Valley. . . . It would almost be easier to mine the gold, though. A spell hasn't taken so much out of me since I carried Sloan down from the top of Helgrind.*

He pocketed the gold and set out again through the camp. He found a cook tent and ate a large lunch, which he needed after casting so many arduous spells, then headed toward the area where the villagers from Carvahall were staying. As he approached, he heard the ring of metal striking metal. Curious, he turned in that direction.

Eragon stepped around a line of three wagons parked across the mouth of the lane and saw Horst standing in a thirty-foot gap between the tents, holding one end of a five-foot-long bar of steel. The other end of the bar was bright cherry red and rested on the face of a massive two-hundred-pound anvil that was staked to the top of a low, wide stump. On either side of the anvil, Horst's burly sons, Albriech and Baldor, alternated striking the steel with sledgehammers, which they swung over their heads in huge circular blows. A makeshift forge glowed several feet behind the anvil.

The hammering was so loud, Eragon kept his distance until Albriech and Baldor had finished spreading the steel and Horst had returned the bar to the forge. Waving his free arm, Horst said, "Ho, Eragon!" Then he held up a finger, forestalling Eragon's reply, and pulled a plug of felted wool out of his left ear. "Ah, now I can hear again. What brings you about, Eragon?" While he spoke, his sons scooped more charcoal into the forge from a bucket and set about tidying up the tongs, hammers, dies, and other tools that lay on the ground. All three men gleamed with sweat.

"I wanted to know what was causing such a commotion," said

Eragon. "I should have guessed it was you. No one else can create as big an uproar as someone from Carvahall."

Horst laughed, his thick, spade-shaped beard pointed up toward the sky until his mirth was exhausted. "Ah, that tickles my pride, it does. And aren't you the living truth of it, eh?"

"We all are," Eragon replied. "You, me, Roran, everyone from Carvahall. Alagaësia will never be the same once the lot of us are done." He gestured at the forge and the other equipment. "Why are you here? I thought that all the smiths were—"

"So they are, Eragon. So they are. However, I convinced the captain who's in charge of this part of the camp to let me work closer to our tent." Horst tugged at the end of his beard. "It's on account of Elain, you know. This child, it goes hard with her, and no wonder, considering what we went through to get here. She's always been delicate, and now I worry that . . . well . . ." He shook himself like a bear ridding itself of flies. "Maybe you could look in on her when you get a chance and see if you can ease her discomfort."

"I'll do that," Eragon promised.

With a satisfied grunt, Horst lifted the bar partway out of the coals to better judge the color of the steel. Plunging the bar back into the center of the fire, he jerked his beard toward Albriech. "Here now, give it some air. It's almost ready." As Albriech began to pump the leather bellows, Horst grinned at Eragon. "When I told the Varden I was a smith, they were so happy, you would have thought I was another Dragon Rider. They don't have enough metalworkers, you see. And they gave me what tools I was missing, including that anvil. When we left Carvahall, I wept at the prospect that I would not have the opportunity to practice my craft again. I am no swordsmith, but here, ah, here there is enough work to keep Albriech, Baldor, and me busy for the next fifty years. It doesn't pay very well, but at least we're not stretched out on a rack in Galbatorix's dungeons."

"Or the Ra'zac could be nibbling on our bones," observed Baldor.

"Aye, that too." Horst motioned for his sons to take up the

sledgehammers again and then, holding the felt plug beside his left ear, said, "Is there anything else you wish of us, Eragon? The steel is ready, and I cannot leave it in the fire any longer without weakening it."

"Do you know where Gedric is?"

"Gedric?" The furrow between Horst's eyebrows deepened. "He should be practicing the sword and spear along with the rest of the men, thataway about a quarter of a mile." Horst pointed with a thumb.

Eragon thanked him and departed in the direction Horst had indicated. The repetitive ring of metal striking metal resumed, clear as the peals of a bell and as sharp and piercing as a glass needle stabbing the air. Eragon covered his ears and smiled. It comforted him that Horst had retained his strength of purpose and that, despite the loss of his wealth and home, he was still the same person he had been in Carvahall. Somehow the smith's consistency and resiliency renewed Eragon's faith that if only they could overthrow Galbatorix, everything would be all right in the end, and his life and those of the villagers from Carvahall would regain a semblance of normalcy.

Eragon soon arrived at the field where the men of Carvahall were drilling with their new weapons. Gedric was there, as Horst had suggested he would be, sparring with Fisk, Darmmen, and Morn. A quick word on the part of Eragon with the one-armed veteran who was leading the drills was sufficient to secure Gedric's temporary release.

The tanner ran over to Eragon and stood before him, his gaze lowered. He was short and swarthy, with a jaw like a mastiff's, heavy eyebrows, and arms thick and gnarled from stirring the foul-smelling vats where he had cured his hides. Although he was far from handsome, Eragon knew him to be a kind and honest man.

"What can I do for you, Shadeslayer?" Gedric mumbled.

"You have already done it. And I have come here to thank and repay you."

"I? How have I helped you, Shadeslayer?" He spoke slowly, cautiously, as if afraid Eragon were setting a trap for him.

"Soon after I ran away from Carvahall, you discovered that someone had stolen three ox hides from the drying hut by the vats. Am I right?"

Gedric's face darkened with embarrassment, and he shuffled his feet. "Ah, well now, I didn't lock that hut, you know. Anyone might have snuck in and carried those hides off. Besides, given what's happened since, I can't see as it's much important. I destroyed most of my stock before we trooped into the Spine, to keep the Empire and those filthy Ra'zac from getting their claws on anything of use. Whoever took those hides saved me from having to destroy three more. So let bygones be bygones, I say."

"Perhaps," said Eragon, "but I still feel honor-bound to tell you that it was I who stole your hides."

Gedric met his gaze then, looking at him as if he were an ordinary person, without fear, awe, or undue respect, as if the tanner were reevaluating his opinion of Eragon.

"I stole them, and I'm not proud of it, but I needed the hides. Without them, I doubt I would have survived long enough to reach the elves in Du Weldenvarden. I always preferred to think that I had borrowed the hides, but the truth is, I stole them, for I had no intention of returning them. Therefore, you have my apologies. And since I am keeping the hides, or what is left of them, it seems only right to pay you for them." From within his belt, Eragon removed one of the spheres of gold—hard, round, and warm from the heat of his flesh—and handed it to Gedric.

Gedric stared at the shiny metal pearl, his massive jaw clamped shut, the lines around his thin-lipped mouth harsh and unyielding. He did not insult Eragon by weighing the gold in his hand, nor by biting it, but when he spoke, he said, "I cannot accept this, Eragon. I was a good tanner, but the leather I made was not worth this much. Your generosity does you credit, but it would bother me to keep this gold. I would feel as if I hadn't earned it."

Unsurprised, Eragon said, "You would not deny another man the opportunity to haggle for a fair price, would you?"

"No."

"Good. Then you cannot deny me this. Most people haggle downward. In this case, I have chosen to haggle upward, but I will still haggle as fiercely as if I were trying to save myself a handful of coins. To me, the hides are worth every ounce of that gold, and I would not pay you a copper less, not even if you held a knife to my throat."

Gedric's thick fingers closed around the gold orb. "Since you insist, I will not be so churlish as to keep refusing you. No one can say that Gedric Ostvensson allowed good fortune to pass him by because he was too busy protesting his own unworthiness. My thanks, Shadeslayer." He placed the orb in a pouch on his belt, wrapping the gold in a patch of wool cloth to protect it from scratches. "Garrow did right by you, Eragon. He did right by both you and Roran. He may have been sharp as vinegar and as hard and dry as a winter rutabaga, but he raised the two of you well. He would be proud of you, I think."

Unexpected emotion clogged Eragon's chest.

As Gedric turned to rejoin the other villagers, he paused. "If I may ask, Eragon, why were those hides worth so much to you? What did you use them for?"

Eragon chuckled. "Use them for? Why, with Brom's help, I made a saddle for Saphira out of them. She doesn't wear it as often as she used to—not since the elves gave us a proper dragon's saddle—but it served us well through many a scrape and fight, and even the Battle of Farthen Dûr."

Astonishment raised Gedric's eyebrows, exposing pale skin that normally lay hidden in deep folds. Like a split in blue-gray granite, a wide grin spread across his jaw, transforming his features. "A saddle!" he breathed. "Imagine, me tanning the leather for a Rider's saddle! And without a hint of what I was doing at the time, no less! No, not *a* Rider, *the* Rider. He who will finally cast down the black tyrant himself! If only my father could see me now!" Kicking up his heels, Gedric danced an impromptu jig. With his grin undiminished, he bowed to Eragon and trotted back to his place among the villagers, where he began to relate his tale to everyone within earshot.

Eager to escape before the lot of them could descend upon him, Eragon slipped away between the rows of tents, pleased with what he had accomplished. *It might take me a while*, he thought, *but I always settle my debts.*

Before long, he arrived at another tent, close to the eastern edge of the camp. He knocked on the pole between the two front flaps.

With a sharp sound, the entrance was yanked aside to reveal Jeod's wife, Helen, standing in the opening. She regarded Eragon with a cold expression. "You've come to talk with *him*, I suppose."

"If he's here." Which Eragon knew perfectly well he was, for he could sense Jeod's mind as clearly as Helen's.

For a moment, Eragon thought Helen might deny the presence of her husband, but then she shrugged and moved aside. "You might as well come in, then."

Eragon found Jeod sitting on a stool, poring over an assortment of scrolls, books, and sheaves of loose papers that were piled high on a cot bare of blankets. A thin shock of hair hung across Jeod's forehead, mimicking the curve of the scar that stretched from his scalp to his left temple.

"Eragon!" he cried as he saw him, the lines of concentration on his face clearing. "Welcome, welcome!" He shook Eragon's hand and then offered him the stool. "Here, I shall sit on the corner of the bed. No, please, you are our guest. Would you care for some food or drink? Nasuada gives us an extra ration, so do not restrain yourself for fear that we will go hungry on your account. It is poor fare compared with what we served you in Teirm, but then no one should go to war and expect to eat well, not even a king."

"A cup of tea would be nice," said Eragon.

"Tea and biscuits it is." Jeod glanced at Helen.

Snatching the kettle off the ground, Helen braced it against her hip, fit the nipple of a waterskin in the end of the spout, and squeezed. The kettle reverberated with a dull roar as a stream of water struck the bottom. Helen's fingers tightened around the neck of the waterskin, restricting the flow to a languorous trickle. She remained thus, with the detached look of a person performing an unpleasant task, while the water droplets drummed out a maddening beat against the inside of the kettle.

An apologetic smile flickered across Jeod's face. He stared at a scrap of paper beside his knee as he waited for Helen to finish. Eragon studied a wrinkle in the side of the tent.

The bombastic trickle continued for over three minutes.

When the kettle was finally full, Helen removed the deflated waterskin from the spout, hung it on a hook on the center pole of the tent, and stormed out.

Eragon raised an eyebrow at Jeod.

Jeod spread his hands. "My position with the Varden is not as prominent as she had hoped, and she blames me for the fact. She agreed to flee Teirm with me, expecting, or so I believe, that Nasuada would vault me into the inner circle of her advisers, or grant me lands and riches fit for a lord, or some other extravagant reward for my help stealing Saphira's egg those many years ago. What Helen did not bargain on was the unglamorous life of a common swordsman: sleeping in a tent, fixing her own food, washing her own clothes, and so on. It's not that wealth and status are her only concerns, but you have to understand, she was born into one of the richest shipping families of Teirm, and for most of our marriage, I was not unsuccessful in my own ventures. She is unused to such privations as these, and she has yet to reconcile herself to them." His shoulders rose and fell a fraction of an inch. "My own hope was that this adventure—if it deserves such a romantic term—would narrow the rifts that have opened between us in recent years, but as always, nothing is ever as simple as it seems."

"Do *you* feel that the Varden ought to show you greater consideration?" asked Eragon.

"For myself, no. For Helen . . ." Jeod hesitated. "I want her to be happy. My reward was in escaping from Gil'ead with my life when Brom and I were attacked by Morzan, his dragon, and his men; in the satisfaction of knowing that I had helped strike a crippling blow against Galbatorix; in being able to return to my previous life and yet still help further the Varden's cause; and in being able to marry Helen. Those were my rewards, and I am more than content with them. Any doubts I had vanished the instant I saw Saphira fly out of the smoke of the Burning Plains. I do not know what to do about Helen, though. But I forget myself. These are not your troubles, and I should not lay them upon you."

Eragon touched a scroll with the tip of his index finger. "Then tell me, why so many papers? Have you become a copyist?"

The question amused Jeod. "Hardly, although the work is often as tedious. Since it was I who discovered the hidden passageway into Galbatorix's castle, in Urû'baen, and I was able to bring with me some of the rare books from my library in Teirm, Nasuada has set me to searching for similar weaknesses in the other cities of the Empire. If I could find mention of a tunnel that led underneath the walls of Dras-Leona, for example, it might save us a great deal of bloodshed."

"Where are you looking?"

"Everywhere I can." Jeod brushed back the lock of hair that was hanging over his forehead. "Histories; myths; legends; poems; songs; religious tracts; the writings of Riders, magicians, wanderers, madmen, obscure potentates, various generals, anyone who might have knowledge of a hidden door or a secret mechanism or something of that ilk that we might turn to our advantage. The amount of material I have to sift through is immense, for all of the cities have stood for hundreds of years, and some antedate the arrival of humans in Alagaësia."

"Is it likely you will actually find anything?"

"No, not likely. It is never likely that you will succeed in ferreting out the secrets of the past. But I may still prevail, given enough time. I have no doubt that what I am searching for exists in each of the cities; they are too old *not* to contain surreptitious ways in and out through their walls. However, it is another question entirely whether *records* of those ways exist and whether we possess those records. People who know about concealed trapdoors and the like usually want to keep the information to themselves." Jeod grasped a handful of the papers next to him on the cot and brought them closer to his face, then snorted and tossed the papers away. "I'm trying to solve riddles invented by people who didn't want them to be solved."

He and Eragon continued talking about other, less important matters until Helen reappeared, carrying three mugs of steaming-hot red-clover tea. As Eragon accepted his mug, he noted that her earlier anger seemed to have subsided, and he wondered if she had been listening outside to what Jeod had said about her. She handed Jeod his mug and, from somewhere behind Eragon, procured a tin plate laden with flat biscuits and a small clay pot of honey. Then she withdrew a few feet and stood leaning against the center pole, blowing on her own mug.

As was polite, Jeod waited until Eragon had taken a biscuit from the plate and consumed a bite of it before saying, "To what do I owe the pleasure of your company, Eragon? Unless I am mistaken, this is no idle visit."

Eragon sipped his tea. "After the Battle of the Burning Plains, I promised I would tell you how Brom died. That is why I have come."

A gray pallor replaced the color in Jeod's cheeks. "Oh."

"I don't have to, if that's not what you want," Eragon quickly pointed out.

With an effort, Jeod shook his head. "No, I do. You merely caught me by surprise."

When Jeod did not ask Helen to leave, Eragon was uncertain

whether he should continue, but then he decided that it did not matter if Helen or anyone else heard his story. In a slow, deliberate voice, Eragon began to recount the events that had transpired since he and Brom had left Jeod's house. He described their encounter with the band of Urgals, their search for the Ra'zac in Dras-Leona, how the Ra'zac had ambushed them outside the city, and how the Ra'zac had stabbed Brom as they fled from Murtagh's attack.

Eragon's throat constricted as he spoke of Brom's last hours, of the cool sandstone cave where he had lain, of the feelings of helplessness that had assailed Eragon as he watched Brom slipping away, of the smell of death that had pervaded the dry air, of Brom's final words, of the sandstone tomb Eragon had made with magic, and of how Saphira had transformed it into pure diamond.

"If only I had known what I know now," Eragon said, "then I could have saved him. Instead . . ." Unable to summon words past the tightness in his throat, he wiped his eyes and gulped at his tea. He wished it were something stronger.

A sigh escaped Jeod. "And so ended Brom. Alas, we are all far worse off without him. If he could have chosen the means of his death, though, I think he would have chosen to die like this, in the service of the Varden, defending the last free Dragon Rider."

"Were you aware that he had been a Rider himself?"

Jeod nodded. "The Varden told me before I met him."

"He seemed as if he was a man who revealed little about himself," observed Helen.

Jeod and Eragon laughed. "That he was," said Jeod. "I still have not recovered from the shock of seeing him and you, Eragon, standing on our doorstep. Brom always kept his own counsel, but we became close friends when we were traveling together, and I cannot understand why he let me believe he was dead for what, sixteen, seventeen years? Too long. What's more, since it was Brom who delivered Saphira's egg to the Varden after he slew Morzan in Gil'ead, the Varden couldn't very well tell me they had her egg without revealing that Brom was still alive. So I've spent the better part of two decades convinced that the one great adventure of my life had ended in failure and that, as a result, we had lost our only hope of having a Dragon Rider to help us overthrow Galbatorix. The knowledge was no easy burden, I can assure you. . . ."

With one hand, Jeod rubbed his brow. "When I opened our front door and realized whom I was looking at, I thought that the ghosts of my past had come to haunt me. Brom said he kept himself hidden to ensure that he would still be alive to train the new Rider when he or she should appear, but his explanation has never entirely satisfied me. Why was it necessary for him to cut himself off from nearly everyone he knew or cared about? What was he afraid of? What was he protecting?"

Jeod fingered the handle of his mug. "I cannot prove it, but it seems to me that Brom must have discovered something in Gil'ead when he was fighting Morzan and his dragon, something so momentous, it moved Brom to abandon everything that was his life up until then. It's a fanciful conjecture, I admit, but I cannot account for Brom's actions except by postulating that there was a piece of information he never shared with me nor another living soul."

Again Jeod sighed, and he drew a hand down his long face. "After so many years apart, I had hoped Brom and I might ride together once more, but fate had other ideas, it seems. And then to lose him a second time but a few weeks after discovering he was still alive was a cruel joke for the world to play." Helen swept past Eragon and went to stand by Jeod, touching him on the shoulder. He offered her a wan smile and wrapped an arm around her narrow waist. "I'm glad that you and Saphira gave Brom a tomb even a dwarf king might envy. He deserved that and more for all he did for Alagaësia. Although once people discover his grave, I have a horrible suspicion they will not hesitate to break it apart for the diamond."

"If they do, they will regret it," muttered Eragon. He resolved to return to the site at the earliest opportunity and place wards around Brom's tomb to protect it from grave robbers. "Besides, they will be too busy hunting gold lilies to bother Brom."

"What?"

"Nothing. It's not important." The three of them sipped their tea. Helen nibbled on a biscuit. Then Eragon asked, "You met Morzan, didn't you?"

"They were not the friendliest of occasions, but yes, I met him."

"What was he like?"

"As a person? I really couldn't say, although I'm well acquainted with tales of his atrocities. Every time Brom and I crossed paths with him, he was trying to kill us. Or rather, capture, torture, and *then* kill us, none of which are conducive to establishing a close relationship." Eragon was too intent to respond to Jeod's humor. Jeod shifted on the bed. "As a warrior, Morzan was terrifying. We spent a great deal of time running away from him, I seem to remember— him and his dragon, that is. Few things are as frightening as having an enraged dragon chasing you."

"How did he look?"

"You seem inordinately interested in him."

285

Eragon blinked once. "I'm curious. He was the last of the Forsworn to die, and Brom was the one who slew him. And now Morzan's son is my mortal enemy."

"Let me see, then," said Jeod. "He was tall, he had broad shoulders, his hair was dark like a raven's feathers, and his eyes were different colors. One was blue and one was black. His chin was bare, and he was missing the tip of one of his fingers; I forget which. Handsome he was, in a cruel, haughty manner, and when he spoke, he was most charismatic. His armor was always polished bright, whether mail or a breastplate, as if he had no fear of being spotted by his enemies, which I suppose he hadn't. When he laughed, it sounded as if he were in pain."

"What of his companion, the woman Selena? Did you meet her as well?"

Jeod laughed. "If I had, I would not be here today. Morzan may have been a fearsome swordsman, a formidable magician, and a murderous traitor, but it was that woman of his who inspired the most terror in people. Morzan only used her for missions that were so repugnant, difficult, or secretive that no one else would agree to undertake them. She was his Black Hand, and her presence always signaled imminent death, torture, betrayal, or some other horror." Eragon felt sick hearing his mother described thusly. "She was utterly ruthless, devoid of either pity or compassion. It was said that when she asked Morzan to enter his service, he tested her by teaching her the word for *heal* in the ancient language—for she was a spellcaster as well as a common fighter—and then pitting her against twelve of his finest swordsmen."

"How did she defeat them?"

"She healed them of their fear and their hate and all the things that drive a man to kill. And then while they stood grinning at each other like idiot sheep, she went up to the men and cut their throats. . . . Are you feeling well, Eragon? You are as pale as a corpse."

"I'm fine. What else do you remember?"

Jeod tapped the side of his mug. "Precious little concerning Selena. She was always somewhat of an enigma. No one besides Morzan even knew her real name until just a few months before Morzan's death. To the public at large, she has never been anything other than the Black Hand; the Black Hand we have now—the collection of spies, assassins, and magicians who carry out Galbatorix's low skulduggery—is Galbatorix's attempt to re-create Selena's usefulness to Morzan. Even among the Varden, only a handful of people were privy to her name, and most of them are moldering in graves now. As I recall, it was Brom who discovered her true identity. Before I went to the Varden with the information concerning the secret passageway into Castle Ilirea—which the elves built millennia ago and which Galbatorix expanded upon to form the black citadel that now dominates Urû'baen—before I went to them, Brom had spent a rather significant length of time spying on Morzan's estate in the hope he might unearth a hitherto unsuspected weakness of Morzan's. . . . I believe Brom gained admittance to Morzan's hall by disguising himself as a member of the serving staff. It was then that he found out what he did about Selena. Still, we never did learn why she was so attached to Morzan. Perhaps she loved him. In any event, she was utterly loyal to him, even to the point of death. Soon after Brom killed Morzan, word reached the Varden that sickness had taken her. It is as if the trained hawk was so fond of her master, she could not live without him."

She was not entirely loyal, thought Eragon. *She defied Morzan when it came to me, even though she lost her life as a result. If only she could have rescued Murtagh as well.* As for Jeod's accounts of her misdeeds, Eragon chose to believe that Morzan had perverted her essentially good nature. For the sake of his own sanity, Eragon could not accept that both his parents had been evil.

"She loved him," he said, staring at the murky dregs at the bottom of his mug. "In the beginning, she loved him; maybe not so much later. Murtagh is her son."

Jeod raised an eyebrow. "Indeed? You have it from Murtagh himself, I suppose?" Eragon nodded. "Well, that explains a number of questions I always had. Murtagh's mother . . . I'm surprised that Brom didn't uncover that particular secret."

"Morzan did everything he could to conceal Murtagh's existence, even from the other members of the Forsworn."

"Knowing the history of those power-hungry, backstabbing knaves, he probably saved Murtagh's life. More's the pity too."

Silence crept among them then, like a shy animal ready to flee at the slightest motion. Eragon continued to gaze into his mug. A host of questions bedeviled him, but he knew that Jeod could not answer them and it was unlikely anyone else could either: Why had Brom hidden himself in Carvahall? To keep watch over Eragon, the son of his most hated foe? Had it been some cruel joke giving Eragon Zar'roc, his father's blade? And why had Brom not told him the truth about his parentage? He tightened his grip on the mug and, without meaning to, shattered the clay.

The three of them started at the unexpected noise.

"Here, let me help you with that," said Helen, bustling forward and dabbing at his tunic with a rag. Embarrassed, Eragon apologized several times, to which both Jeod and Helen responded by assuring him it was a small mishap and not to worry himself about it.

While Helen picked up the shards of fire-hardened clay, Jeod began to dig through the layers of books, scrolls, and loose papers that covered the bed, saying, "Ah, it had nearly slipped my mind. I have something for you, Eragon, that might prove useful. If only I can find it here...." With a pleased exclamation, he straightened, flourishing a book, which he handed to Eragon.

It was *Domia abr Wyrda*, the *Dominance of Fate*, a complete history of Alagaësia written by Heslant the Monk. Eragon had first seen it in Jeod's library in Teirm. He had not expected that he would ever get a chance to examine it again. Savoring the feeling, he ran his hands over the carved leather on the front cover, which was shiny with age, then opened the book and admired the neat rows of runes within, lettered in glossy red ink. Awed by the size of the knowledge hoard he held, Eragon said, "You wish me to have this?"

"I do," asserted Jeod. He moved out of the way as Helen retrieved a fragment of the mug from under the bed. "I think you might profit by it. You are engaged in historic events, Eragon, and the roots of the difficulties you face lie in happenings from decades, centuries, and millennia ago. If I were you, I would study at every opportunity the lessons history has to teach us, for they may help you with the problems of today. In my own life, reading the record of the past has often provided me with the courage and the insight to choose the correct path."

Eragon longed to accept the gift, but still he hesitated. "Brom said that *Domia abr Wyrda* was the most valuable thing in your house. And rare as well.... Besides, what of your work? Don't you need this for your research?"

"*Domia abr Wyrda* is valuable and it is rare," said Jeod, "but only in the Empire, where Galbatorix burns every copy he finds and hangs their unfortunate owners. Here in the camp, I have already had six copies foisted upon me by members of King Orrin's court, and this is hardly what one would call a great center of learning. However, I do not part with it lightly, and only because you can put it to better use than I can. Books should go where they will be most appreciated, and not sit unread, gathering dust on a forgotten shelf, don't you agree?"

"I do." Eragon closed *Domia abr Wyrda* and again traced the intricate patterns on the front with his fingers, fascinated by the swirling designs that had been chiseled into the leather. "Thank you. I shall treasure it for as long as it is mine to watch over." Jeod dipped his head and leaned back against the wall of the tent, appearing satisfied. Turning the book on its edge, Eragon examined the lettering on the spine. "What was Heslant a monk of?"

"A small, secretive sect called the Arcaena that originated in the area by Kuasta. Their order, which has endured for at least five hundred years, believes that all knowledge is sacred." A hint of a smile lent Jeod's features a mysterious cast. "They have dedicated themselves to collecting every piece of information in the world and preserving it against a time when they believe an unspecified catastrophe will destroy all the civilizations in Alagaësia."

"It seems a strange religion," Eragon said.

"Are not all religions strange to those who stand outside of them?" countered Jeod.

Eragon said, "I have a gift for you as well, or rather, for you, Helen." She tilted her head, a quizzical frown on her face. "Your family was a merchant family, yes?" She jerked her chin in an affirmative. "Were you very familiar with the business yourself?"

Lightning sparked in Helen's eyes. "If I had not married him"— she motioned with a shoulder—"I would have taken over the family affairs when my father died. I was an only child, and my father taught me everything he knew."

That was what Eragon had hoped to hear. To Jeod, he said, "You claimed that you are content with your lot here with the Varden."

"And so I am. Mostly."

"I understand. However, you risked a great deal to help Brom and me, and you risked even more to help Roran and everyone else from Carvahall."

"The Palancar Pirates."

Eragon chuckled and continued. "Without your assistance, the Empire would surely have captured them. And because of your act of rebellion, you both lost all that was dear to you in Teirm."

"We would have lost it anyway. I was bankrupt and the Twins had betrayed me to the Empire. It was only a matter of time before Lord Risthart had me arrested."

"Maybe, but you still helped Roran. Who can blame you if you were protecting your own necks at the same time? The fact remains that you abandoned your lives in Teirm in order to steal the *Dragon Wing* along with Roran and the villagers. And for your sacrifice, I will always be grateful. So this is part of my thanks. . . ."

Sliding a finger underneath his belt, Eragon removed the second of the three gold orbs and presented it to Helen. She cradled it as gently as if it were a baby robin. While she gazed at it with wonder, and Jeod craned his neck to see over the edge of her hand, Eragon said, "It's not a fortune, but if you are clever, you should be able to make it grow. What Nasuada did with lace taught me that there is a great deal of opportunity for a person to prosper in war."

"Oh yes," breathed Helen. "War is a merchant's delight."

"For one, Nasuada mentioned to me last night at dinner that the dwarves are running low on mead, and as you might suspect, they have the means to buy as many casks as they want, even if the price were a thousandfold of what it was before the war. But then, that's just a suggestion. You may find others who are more desperate to trade if you look for yourself."

Eragon staggered back a step as Helen rushed at him and embraced him. Her hair tickled his chin. She released him, suddenly shy, then her excitement burst forth again and she lifted the honey-colored globe in front of her nose and said, "Thank you, Eragon! Oh, thank you!" She pointed at the gold. "This I can use. I know I can. With it, I'll build an empire even larger than my father's." The shiny orb disappeared within her clenched fist. "You believe my ambition exceeds my abilities? It shall be as I have said. I shall not fail!"

Eragon bowed to her. "I hope that you succeed and that your success benefits us all."

Eragon noticed that hard cords stood out in Helen's neck as she curtsied and said, "You are most generous, Shadeslayer. Again I thank you."

"Yes, thank you," said Jeod, rising from the bed. "I cannot think that we deserve this"—Helen shot him a furious look, which he ignored—"but it is most welcome nevertheless."

Improvising, Eragon added, "And for you, Jeod, your gift is not from me, but Saphira. She has agreed to let you fly on her when you both have a spare hour or two." It pained Eragon to share Saphira, and he knew that she would be upset he had not consulted her before volunteering her services, but after giving Helen the gold, he would have felt guilty about not giving Jeod something of equal value.

A film of tears glazed Jeod's eyes. He grasped Eragon's hand and shook it and, still holding it, said, "I cannot imagine a higher honor. Thank you. You don't know how much you have done for us."

Extricating himself from Jeod's grip, Eragon edged toward the entrance to the tent while excusing himself as gracefully as he could and making his farewells. Finally, after yet another round of thanks on their part and a self-deprecating "It was nothing," he managed to escape outdoors.

Eragon hefted *Domia abr Wyrda* and then glanced at the sun. It would not be long until Saphira returned, but he still had time to attend to one other thing. First, though, he would have to stop by his tent; he did not want to risk damaging *Domia abr Wyrda* by carrying it with him across the camp.

I own a book, he thought, delighted.

He set off at a trot, clasping the book against his chest, as Blödhgarm and the other elves followed close behind.

I Need a Sword!

Once *Domia abr Wyrda* was safely ensconced in his tent, Eragon went to the Varden's armory, a large open pavilion filled with racks of spears, swords, pikes, bows, and crossbows. Mounds of shields and leather armor filled slatted crates. The more expensive mail, tunics, coifs, and leggings hung on wooden stands. Hundreds of conical helmets gleamed like polished silver. Bales of arrows lined the pavilion, and among them sat a score or more fletchers, busy refurbishing arrows whose feathers had been damaged during the Battle of the Burning Plains. A constant stream of men rushed in and out of the pavilion: some bringing weapons and armor to be repaired, others new recruits coming to be outfitted, and still others ferrying equipment to different parts of the camp. Everyone seemed to be shouting at the top of their lungs. And in the center of the commotion stood the man Eragon had hoped to see: Fredric, the Varden's weapon master.

Blödhgarm accompanied Eragon as he strode into the pavilion toward Fredric. As soon as they stepped underneath the cloth roof, the men inside fell silent, their eyes fixed on the two of them. Then they resumed their activities, albeit with quicker steps and quieter voices.

Raising an arm in welcome, Fredric hurried to meet them. As always, he wore his suit of hairy oxhide armor—which smelled nearly as offensive as the animal must have in its original form—as well as a massive two-handed sword hung crosswise over his back, the hilt projecting above his right shoulder. "Shadeslayer!" he rumbled. "How can I help you this fine afternoon?"

"I need a sword."

Fredric's smile broke through his beard. "Ah, I wondered if you'd be visiting me about that. When you set out for Helgrind without a blade in hand, I thought, well, maybe you're beyond such things now. Maybe you can do all your fighting with magic."

"No, not yet."

"Well, I can't say as I'm sorry. Everyone needs a good sword, no matter how skilled they may be with conjuring. In the end, it always comes down to steel against steel. Just you watch, that's how this fight with the Empire will be resolved, with the point of a sword being driven through Galbatorix's accursed heart. Heh, I'd wager a year's wages that even Galbatorix has a sword of his own and that he *uses* it too, despite him being able to gut you like a fish with a flick of his finger. Nothing can quite compare to the feel of fine steel in your fist."

While he spoke, Fredric led them toward a rack of swords that stood apart from the others. "What kind of sword are you looking for?" he asked. "That Zar'roc you had was a one-handed sword, if I remember rightly. With a blade about two thumbs wide—two of my thumbs, in any case—and of a shape equally suited for both the cut and thrust, yes?" Eragon indicated that was so, and the weapon master grunted and began to pull swords off the rack and swing them through the air, only to replace them with seeming dissatisfaction. "Elf blades tend to be thinner and lighter than ours or the dwarves', on account of the enchantments they forge into the steel. If we made ours as delicate as theirs, the swords wouldn't last more than a minute in a battle before bending, breaking, or chipping so badly, you couldn't cut soft cheese with them." His eyes darted toward Blödhgarm. "Isn't that so, elf?"

"Even as you say, human," responded Blödhgarm in a perfectly modulated voice.

Fredric nodded and examined the edge of another sword, then snorted and dropped it back on the rack. "Which means whatever sword you choose will probably be heavier than you're used to. That shouldn't pose much difficulty for you, Shadeslayer, but the extra weight may still upset the timing of your blows."

"I appreciate the warning," said Eragon.

"Not at all," said Fredric. "That's what I'm here for: to keep as many of the Varden from getting killed as I can and to help them kill as many of Galbatorix's blasted soldiers as I can. It's a good job." Leaving the rack, he lumbered over to another one, hidden behind a pile of rectangular shields. "Finding the right sword for someone is an art unto itself. A sword should feel like an extension of your arm, as if it had grown out of your very flesh. You shouldn't have to think about how you want it to move; you should simply move it as instinctively as an egret his beak or a dragon her claws. The perfect sword is intent incarnate: what you want, so it does."

"You sound like a poet."

With a modest expression, Fredric half shrugged. "I've been picking weapons for men who are about to march into combat for twenty-six years. It seeps into your bones after a while, turns your mind to thoughts of fate and destiny and whether that young fellow I sent off with a billed pike would still be alive if I had given him a mace instead." Fredric paused with a hand hovering over the middle sword on the rack and looked at Eragon. "Do you prefer to fight with or without a shield?"

"With," Eragon said. "But I can't carry one around with me all the time. And there never seems to be one handy when I'm attacked."

Fredric tapped the hilt of the sword and gnawed on the edge of his beard. "Humph. So you need a sword you can use by itself but that's not too long to use with every kind of shield from a buckler to a wall shield. That means a sword of medium length, easy to wield with one arm. It has to be a blade you can wear at all occasions, elegant enough for a coronation and tough enough to fend off a band of Kull." He grimaced. "It's not natural, what Nasuada's done, allying us with those monsters. It can't last. The likes of us and them were never meant to mix. . . ." He shook himself. "It's a pity you only want a single sword. Or am I mistaken?"

"No. Saphira and I travel far too much to be lugging around a half-dozen blades."

"I suppose you're right. Besides, a warrior like you isn't expected to have more than one weapon. The curse of the named blade, I call it."

"What's that?"

"Every great warrior," said Fredric, "wields a sword—it's usually a sword—that has a name. Either he names it himself or, once he proves his prowess with some extraordinary feat, the bards name it for him. Thereafter, he *has* to use that sword. It's expected of him. If he shows up to a battle without it, his fellow warriors will ask where it is, and they will wonder if he is ashamed of his success and if he is insulting them by rejecting the acclaim they have bestowed upon him, and even his enemies may insist upon waiting to fight until he fetches his famed blade. Just you watch; as soon as you fight Murtagh or do anything else memorable with your new sword, the Varden will insist upon giving it a title. And they will look to see it on your hip from then on." He continued speaking while he proceeded to a third rack: "I never thought I would be fortunate enough to help a Rider choose his weapon. What an opportunity! It feels as if this is a culmination of my work with the Varden."

Plucking a sword from the rack, Fredric handed it to Eragon. Eragon tilted the tip of the sword up and down, then shook his head; the shape of the hilt was wrong for his hand. The weapon master did not seem disappointed. To the contrary, Eragon's rejection seemed to invigorate him, as if he relished the challenge Eragon posed. He presented another sword to Eragon, and again Eragon shook his head; the balance was too far forward for his liking.

"What worries me," Fredric said, returning to the rack, "is that any sword I give you will have to withstand impacts that would destroy an ordinary blade. What you need is dwarf-work. Their smiths are the finest besides the elves', and sometimes they even exceed them." Fredric peered at Eragon. "Hold now, I've been asking the wrong questions! How was it you were taught to block and parry? Was it edge on edge? I seem to recall you doing something of the kind when you dueled Arya in Farthen Dûr."

Eragon frowned. "What of it?"

"What of it?" Fredric guffawed. "Not to be disrespectful, Shadeslayer, but if you hit the edge of a sword against that of another, you will cause grave damage to both. That might not have been a problem with an enchanted blade like Zar'roc, but you can't do it with any of the swords I have here, not unless you want to replace your sword after every battle."

An image flashed in Eragon's mind of the chipped edges of Murtagh's sword, and he felt irritated with himself for having forgotten something so obvious. He had become accustomed to Zar'roc, which never dulled, never showed signs of wear, and, so far as he knew, was impervious to most spells. He was not even sure it was possible to destroy a Rider's sword. "You need not worry about that; I will protect the sword with magic. Must I wait all day for a weapon?"

"One more question, Shadeslayer. Will your magic last forever?"

Eragon's frown deepened. "Since you ask, no. Only one elf understands the making of a Rider's sword, and she has not shared her secrets with me. What I *can* do is transfer a certain amount of energy into a sword. The energy will keep it from getting damaged until the blows that *would* have damaged the sword exhaust the store of energy, at which point the sword will revert to its original state and, odds are, shatter in my grip the next time I close with my opponent."

Fredric scratched his beard. "I'll take your word for it, Shadeslayer. The point being, if you hammer on soldiers long enough, you'll wear out your spells, and the harder you hammer, the sooner the spells will vanish. Eh?"

"Exactly."

"Then you should still avoid going edge on edge, as it will wear out your spells faster than most any other move."

"I don't have time for this," Eragon snapped, his impatience overflowing. "I don't have the time to learn a completely different way of fighting. The Empire might attack at any moment. I have to concentrate on practicing what I *do* know, not trying to master a whole new set of forms."

Fredric clapped his hands. "I know just the thing for you, then!" Going to a crate filled with arms, he began digging through it, talking to himself as he did. "First *this*, then *that*, and then we'll see where we stand." From the bottom of the crate, he pulled out a large black mace with a flanged head.

Fredric rapped a knuckle against the mace. "You can break swords with this. You can split mail and batter in helms, and you won't do it the slightest bit of harm, no matter what you hit."

"It's a club," Eragon protested. "A metal club."

"What of it? With your strength, you can swing it as if it were light as a reed. You'll be a terror on the battlefield with this, you will."

Eragon shook his head. "No. Smashing things isn't how I prefer to fight. Besides, I would never have been able to kill Durza by stabbing him through the heart if I had been carrying a mace instead of a sword."

"Then I have only one more suggestion, unless you insist upon a traditional blade." From another part of the pavilion, Fredric brought Eragon a weapon he identified as a falchion. It was a sword, but not a type of sword Eragon was accustomed to, although he had seen them among the Varden before. The falchion had a polished, disk-shaped pommel, bright as a silver coin; a short grip made of wood covered with black leather; a curved crossguard carved with a line of dwarf runes; and a single-edged blade that was as long as his outstretched arm and had a thin fuller on either side, close to the spine. The falchion was straight until about six inches from the end, where the back of the blade flared upward in a small peak before gently curving down to the needle-sharp tip. This widening of the blade reduced the likelihood that the point would bend or snap when driven through armor and lent the end of the falchion a fanglike appearance. Unlike a double-edged sword, the falchion was made to be held with the blade and crossguard perpendicular to the ground. The most curious aspect of the falchion, though, was the bottom half inch of the blade, including the edge, which was pearly gray and substantially darker than the mirror-smooth steel above. The boundary between the two areas was wavy, like a silk scarf rippling in the wind.

Eragon pointed at the gray band. "I've not seen that before. What is it?"

"The thriknzdal," said Fredric. "The dwarves invented it. They temper the edge and the spine separately. The edge they make hard, harder than we dare with the whole of our blades. The middle of the blade and the spine they anneal so that the back of the falchion is softer than the edge, soft enough to bend and flex and survive the stress of battle without fracturing like a frost-ridden file."

298

"Do the dwarves treat all their blades thusly?"

Fredric shook his head. "Only their single-edged swords and the finest of their double-edged swords." He hesitated, and uncertainty crept into his gaze. "You understand why I chose this for you, Shadeslayer, yes?"

Eragon understood. With the blade of the falchion at right angles to the ground, unless he deliberately tilted his wrist, any blows he caught on the sword would strike the flat of the blade, saving the edge for attacks of his own. Wielding the falchion would require only a small adjustment to his fighting style.

Striding out of the pavilion, he assumed a ready position with the falchion. Swinging it over his head, he brought it down upon the head of an imaginary foe, then twisted and lunged, beat aside an invisible spear, sprang six yards to his left, and, in a brilliant but impractical move, spun the blade behind his back, passing it from one hand to the next as he did so. His breathing and heartbeat calm as ever, he returned to where Fredric and Blödhgarm were waiting. The speed and balance of the falchion had impressed Eragon. It was not the equal of Zar'roc, but it was still a superb sword.

"You chose well," he said.

Fredric detected the reticence in his bearing, however, for he said, "And yet you are not entirely pleased, Shadeslayer."

Eragon twirled the falchion in a circle, then grimaced. "I just wish it didn't look so much like a big skinning knife. I feel rather ridiculous with it."

"Ah, pay no heed if your enemies laugh. They'll not be able to once you lop off their heads."

Amused, Eragon nodded. "I'll take it."

"One moment, then," said Fredric, and disappeared into the pavilion, returning with a black leather scabbard decorated with silver scrollwork. He handed the scabbard to Eragon and asked, "Did you ever learn how to sharpen a sword, Shadeslayer? You wouldn't have had need with Zar'roc, would you?"

"No," Eragon admitted, "but I am a fair hand with a whetstone. I can hone a knife until it is so keen, it will cut a thread draped over it. Besides, I can always true up the edge with magic if I have to."

Fredric groaned and slapped his thighs, knocking loose a dozen or so hairs from his oxhide leggings. "No, no, a razor-thin edge is just what you *don't* want on a sword. The bevel has to be thick, thick and strong. A warrior has to be able to maintain his equipment properly, and that includes knowing how to sharpen his sword!"

Fredric insisted, then, on procuring a new whetstone for Eragon and showing him exactly how to put a battle-ready edge on the falchion while they sat in the dirt beside the pavilion. Once he was satisfied that Eragon could grind an entirely new edge on the sword, he said, "You can fight with rusty armor. You can fight with a dented helmet. But if you want to see the sun rise again, never fight with a dull sword. If you've just survived a battle and you're tired as a man who has climbed one of the Beor Mountains and your sword isn't sharp as it is now, it doesn't matter how you feel, you plunk yourself down the first chance you get and pull out your whetstone and strop. Just as you would see to your horse, or to Saphira, before you attended to your own needs, so too you should care for your sword before yourself. Because without it, you're no more than helpless prey for your enemies."

They had been sitting out in the late-afternoon sun for over an hour by the time the weapon master finally finished his instructions. As he did, a cool shadow slid over them and Saphira landed close by.

You waited, said Eragon. *You deliberately waited! You could have rescued me ages ago, but instead you left me here to listen to Fredric go on about water stones, oil stones, and whether linseed oil is better than rendered fat for protecting metal from water.*

And is it?

Not really. It's just not as smelly. But that's irrelevant! Why did you leave me to this doom?

One of her thick eyelids drooped in a lazy wink. *Don't exaggerate. Doom? You and I have far worse dooms to look forward to if we are not properly prepared. What the man with the smelly clothes was saying seemed important for you to know.*

Well, perhaps it was, he conceded. She arched her neck and licked the claws on her right foreleg.

After thanking Fredric and bidding him farewell, and agreeing upon a meeting place with Blödhgarm, Eragon fastened the falchion to the belt of Beloth the Wise and clambered onto Saphira's back. He whooped and she roared as she raised her wings and surged up into the sky.

Giddy, Eragon clung to the spike in front of him and watched the people and tents below dwindle away into flat, miniature versions of themselves. From above, the camp was a grid of gray, triangular peaks, the eastern faces of which were deep in shadow, giving the whole region a checkered appearance. The fortifications that encircled the camp bristled like a hedgehog, the white tips of the distant poles bright in the slanted sunlight. King Orrin's cavalry was a mass of milling dots in the northwestern quadrant of the camp. To the east was the Urgals' camp, low and dark on the rolling plain.

They soared higher.

The cold, pure air stung Eragon's cheeks and burned in his lungs. He took only shallow breaths. Beside them floated a thick column of clouds, looking as solid as whipped cream. Saphira spiraled around it, her ragged shadow racing across the plume. A lone scrap of moisture struck Eragon, blinding him for a few seconds and filling his nose and mouth with frigid droplets. He gasped and wiped his face.

They rose above the clouds.

A red eagle screeched at them as it flew past.

Saphira's flapping became labored, and Eragon began to feel light-headed. Stilling her wings, Saphira glided from one thermal to the next, maintaining her altitude but ascending no farther.

Eragon looked down. They were so high, height had ceased to matter and things on the ground no longer seemed real. The Varden's camp was an irregularly shaped playing board covered with tiny gray and black rectangles. The Jiet River was a silver rope fringed with green tassels. To the south, the sulfurous clouds rising from the Burning Plains formed a range of glowing orange mountains, home to shadowy monsters that flickered in and out of existence. Eragon quickly averted his gaze.

For perhaps half an hour, he and Saphira drifted with the wind, relaxing in the silent comfort of each other's company. An inaudible spell served to insulate Eragon from the chill. At last they were alone together, alone as they had been in Palancar Valley before the Empire had intruded upon their life.

Saphira was the first to speak. *We are the rulers of the sky.*

Here at the ceiling of the world. Eragon reached up, as if from where he sat he could brush the stars.

Banking to the left, Saphira caught a gust of warmer air from below, then leveled off again. *You will marry Roran and Katrina tomorrow.*

What a strange thought that is. Strange Roran should marry, and strange I should be the one to perform the ceremony. . . . Roran married. Thinking about it makes me feel older. Even we, who were boys but a short while ago, cannot escape the inexorable progress of time. So the generations pass, and soon it will be our turn to send our children out into the land to do the work that needs to be done.

But not unless we can survive the next few months.

Aye, there is that.

Saphira wobbled as turbulence buffeted them. Then she looked back at him and asked: *Ready?*

Go!

Tilting forward, she pulled her wings close against her sides and plummeted toward the ground, faster than a speeding arrow. Eragon laughed as the sensation of weightlessness overtook him. He tightened his legs around Saphira to keep himself from drifting away from her, then, overtaken by a surge of recklessness, released his grip and held his hands over his head. The disk of land below spun like a wheel as Saphira augered through the air. Slowing and then stopping her rotation, she rolled to the right until she was falling upside down.

"Saphira!" cried Eragon, and pounded her shoulder.

A ribbon of smoke streaming from her nostrils, she righted herself and again pointed herself at the fast-approaching ground. Eragon's ears popped, and he worked his jaw as the pressure increased. Less than a thousand feet above the Varden's camp, and only a few seconds from crashing into the tents and excavating a large and bloody crater, Saphira allowed the wind to catch her wings. The subsequent jolt threw Eragon forward, and the spike he had been holding nearly stabbed him in the eye.

With three powerful flaps, Saphira brought them to a complete halt. Locking her wings outstretched, she then began to gently circle downward.

Now that was fun! exclaimed Eragon.

There is no more exciting sport than flying, for if you lose, you die.

Ah, but I have complete confidence in your abilities; you would never run us into the ground. Her pleasure at his compliment radiated from her.

Angling toward his tent, she shook her head, jostling him, and said, *I ought to be accustomed to it by now, but every time I come out of a dive like that, it makes my chest and wing arms so sore, the next morning I can barely move.*

He patted her. *Well, you shouldn't have to fly tomorrow. The wedding is our only obligation, and you can walk to it.* She grunted and landed amid a billow of dust, knocking over an empty tent with her tail in the process.

Dismounting, Eragon left her grooming herself with six of the elves standing nearby, and with the other six, he trotted through the camp until he located the healer Gertrude. From her he learned the marriage rites he would need the following day, and he practiced them with her that he might avoid an embarrassing blunder when the moment arrived.

Then Eragon returned to his tent and washed his face and changed his clothes before going with Saphira to dine with King Orrin and his entourage, as promised.

Late that night, when the feast was finally over, Eragon and Saphira walked back to his tent, gazing at the stars and talking about what had been and what yet might be. And they were happy. When they arrived at their destination, Eragon paused and looked up at Saphira, and his heart was so full of love, he thought it might stop beating.

Good night, Saphira.

Good night, little one.

UNEXPECTED GUESTS

The next morning, Eragon went behind his tent, removed his heavy outer clothes, and began to glide through the poses of the second level of the Rimgar, the series of exercises the elves had invented. Soon his initial chill vanished. He began to pant from the effort, and sweat coated his limbs, which made it difficult for him to keep hold of his feet or his hands when contorted into a position that felt as if it were going to tear the muscles from his bones.

An hour later, he finished the Rimgar. Drying his palms on the corner of his tent, he drew the falchion and practiced his swordsmanship for another thirty minutes. He would have preferred to continue familiarizing himself with the sword for the rest of the day—for he knew his life might depend upon his skill with it—but Roran's wedding was fast approaching, and the villagers could use all the help they could get if they were to complete the preparations in time.

Refreshed, Eragon bathed in cold water and dressed, and then he and Saphira walked to where Elain was overseeing the cooking of Roran and Katrina's wedding feast. Blödhgarm and his companions followed a dozen or so yards behind, slipping between the tents with stealthy ease.

"Ah, good, Eragon," Elain said. "I had hoped you would come." She stood with both her hands pressed into the small of her back to relieve the weight of her pregnancy. Pointing with her chin past a row of spits and cauldrons suspended over a bed of coals, past a clump of men butchering a hog, past three makeshift ovens built of mud and stone, and past a pile of kegs toward a line of planks set on stumps that six women were using as a counter, she said, "There are still twenty loaves of bread dough that have to be kneaded. Will you see to it, please?" Then she frowned at the calluses on his knuckles. "And try not to get those in the dough, won't you?"

The six women standing at the planks, which included Felda and Birgit, fell silent when Eragon took his place among them. His few attempts to restart the conversation failed, but after a while, when he had given up on putting them at ease and was concentrating on his kneading, they resumed talking of their own accord. They spoke about Roran and Katrina and how lucky the two of them were and of the villagers' life in the camp and of their journey thence, and then without preamble, Felda looked over at Eragon and said, "Your dough looks a little sticky. Shouldn't you add some flour?"

Eragon checked the consistency. "You're right. Thank you." Felda smiled, and after that, the women included him in their conversation.

While Eragon worked the warm dough, Saphira lay basking on a nearby patch of grass. The children from Carvahall played on and around her; laughing shrieks punctuated the deeper thrum of the adults' voices. When a pair of mangy dogs started barking at Saphira, she lifted her head off the ground and growled at them. They ran away yipping.

Everyone in the clearing was someone Eragon had known while growing up. Horst and Fisk were on the other side of the spits, constructing tables for the feast. Kiselt was wiping the hog's blood off his forearms. Albriech, Baldor, Mandel, and several other of the younger men were carrying poles wound with ribbons toward the hill where Roran and Katrina wished to be married. The tavern-keeper Morn was off mixing the wedding drink, with his wife, Tara, holding three flagons and a cask for him. A few hundred feet away, Roran was shouting something at a mule-driver who was attempting to run his charges through the clearing. Loring, Delwin, and the boy Nolfavrell stood clustered nearby, watching. With a loud curse,

305

Roran grabbed the lead mule's harness and struggled to turn the animals around. The sight amused Eragon; he had never known Roran to get so flustered, nor to be so short-tempered.

"The mighty warrior is nervous ere his contest," observed Isold, one of the six women next to Eragon. The group laughed.

"Perhaps," Birgit said, stirring water into flour, "he is worried his sword may bend in the battle." Gales of merriment swept the women. Eragon's cheeks flushed. He kept his gaze fixed on the dough in front of him and increased the speed of his kneading. Bawdy jokes were common at weddings, and he had enjoyed his share before, but hearing them directed at his cousin disconcerted him.

The people who would not be able to attend the wedding were as much on Eragon's mind as those who could. He thought of Byrd, Quimby, Parr, Hida, young Elmund, Kelby, and the others who had died because of the Empire. But most of all, he thought of Garrow and wished his uncle were still alive to see his only son acclaimed a hero by the villagers and the Varden alike and to see him take Katrina's hand and finally become a man in full.

Closing his eyes, Eragon turned his face toward the noonday sun and smiled up at the sky, content. The weather was pleasant. The aroma of yeast, flour, roasting meat, freshly poured wine, boiling soups, sweet pastries, and melted candies suffused the clearing. His friends and family were gathered around him for celebration and not for mourning. And for the moment, he was safe and Saphira was safe. *This is how life ought to be.*

A single horn rang out across the land, unnaturally loud.

Then again.

And again.

Everyone froze, uncertain what the three notes signified.

For a brief interval, the entire camp was silent, except for the animals, then the Varden's war-drums began to beat. Chaos erupted. Mothers ran for their children and cooks dampened their fires while the rest of the men and women scrambled after their weapons.

Eragon sprinted toward Saphira even as she surged to her feet.

Reaching out with his mind, he found Blödhgarm and, once the elf lowered his defenses somewhat, said, *Meet us at the north entrance.*

We hear and obey, Shadeslayer.

Eragon flung himself onto Saphira. The instant he got a leg over her neck, she jumped four rows of tents, landed, and then jumped a second time, her wings half furled, not flying but rather bounding through the camp like a mountain cat crossing a fast-flowing river. The impact of each landing jarred Eragon's teeth and spine and threatened to knock him off his perch. As they rose and fell, frightened warriors dodging out of their path, Eragon contacted Trianna and the other members of Du Vrangr Gata, identifying the location of each spellcaster and organizing them for battle.

Someone who was not of Du Vrangr Gata touched his thoughts. He recoiled, slamming walls up around his consciousness, before he realized that it was Angela the herbalist and allowed the contact. She said, *I am with Nasuada and Elva. Nasuada wants you and Saphira to meet her at the north entrance—*

As soon as we can. Yes, yes, we're on our way. What of Elva? Does she sense anything?

Pain. Great pain. Yours. The Varden's. The others'. I'm sorry, she's not very coherent right now. It's too much for her to cope with. I'm going to put her to sleep until the violence is at an end. Angela severed the connection.

Like a carpenter laying out and examining his tools before beginning a new project, Eragon reviewed the wards he had placed around himself, Saphira, Nasuada, Arya, and Roran. They all seemed to be in order.

Saphira slid to a stop before his tent, furrowing the packed earth with her talons. He leaped off her back, rolling as he struck the ground. Bouncing upright, he dashed inside, undoing his sword belt as he went. He dropped the belt and the attached falchion into the dirt and, scrabbling under his cot, retrieved his armor. The cold, heavy rings of the mail hauberk slid over his head and settled on his shoulders with a sound like falling coins. He tied on his arming cap, placed the coif over it, and then jammed his head into his helm. Snatching up the belt, he refastened it around his waist. With his greaves and his bracers in his left hand, he hooked his little finger through the arm strap of his shield, grabbed Saphira's heavy saddle with his right hand, and burst out of the tent.

Releasing his armor in a noisy clatter, he threw the saddle onto the mound of Saphira's shoulders and climbed after it. In his haste and excitement, and his apprehension, he had trouble buckling the straps.

Saphira shifted her stance. *Hurry. You're taking too long.*

Yes! I'm moving as fast as I can! It doesn't help you're so blasted big!

She growled.

The camp swarmed with activity, men and dwarves streaming in jangling rivers toward the north, rushing to answer the summons of the war-drums.

Eragon collected his abandoned armor off the ground, mounted Saphira, and settled into the saddle. With a flash of down-swept wings, a jolt of acceleration, a blast of swirling air, and the bitter complaint of bracers scraping against shield, Saphira took to the air. While they sped toward the northern edge of the camp, Eragon strapped the greaves to his shins, holding himself on Saphira merely with the strength of his legs. The bracers he wedged between his belly and the front of the saddle. The shield he hung from a neck spike. When the greaves were secure, he slid his legs through the row of leather loops on either side of the saddle, then tightened the slipknot on each loop.

Eragon's hand brushed against the belt of Beloth the Wise. He groaned, remembering that he had emptied the belt while healing Saphira in Helgrind. *Argh! I should have stored some energy in it.*

We'll be fine, said Saphira.

He was just fitting on the bracers when Saphira arched her wings, cupping the air with the translucent membranes, and reared, stalling to a standstill as she alighted upon the crest of one of the embankments that ringed the camp. Nasuada was already there, sitting upon her massive charger, Battle-storm. Beside her was Jörmundur, also mounted; Arya, on foot; and the current watch of the Nighthawks, led by Khagra, one of the Urgals Eragon had met on the Burning Plains. Blödhgarm and the other elves emerged from the forest of tents behind them and stationed themselves close to Eragon and Saphira. From a different part of the camp galloped King Orrin and his retinue, reining in their prancing steeds as they drew near Nasuada. Close upon their heels came Narheim, chief of the dwarves, and three of his warriors, the group of them riding ponies clad with leather and mail armor. Nar Garzhvog ran out of the fields to the east, the Kull's thudding footsteps preceding his arrival by several seconds. Nasuada shouted an order, and the guards at the north entrance pulled aside the crude wooden gate to allow Garzhvog inside the camp, although if he had wanted, the Kull probably could have knocked open the gate by himself.

"Who challenges?" growled Garzhvog, scaling the embankment with four inhumanly long strides. The horses shied away from the gigantic Urgal.

"Look." Nasuada pointed.

Eragon was already studying their enemies. Roughly two miles away, five sleek boats, black as pitch, had landed upon the near bank of the Jiet River. From the boats there issued a swarm of men garbed in the livery of Galbatorix's army. The host glittered like wind-whipped water under a summer sun as swords, spears, shields, helmets, and mail ringlets caught and reflected the light.

Arya shaded her eyes with a hand and squinted at the soldiers. "I put their number between two hundred seventy and three hundred."

"Why so few?" wondered Jörmundur.

King Orrin scowled. "Galbatorix cannot be mad enough to believe he can destroy us with such a paltry force!" Orrin pulled off his helm, which was in the shape of a crown, and dabbed his brow with the corner of his tunic. "We could obliterate that entire group and not lose a man."

"Maybe," said Nasuada. "Maybe not."

Gnawing on the words, Garzhvog added, "The Dragon King is a false-tongued traitor, a rogue ram, but his mind is not feeble. He is cunning like a blood-hungry weasel."

The soldiers assembled themselves in orderly ranks and then began marching toward the Varden.

A messenger boy ran up to Nasuada. She bent in her saddle to listen, then dismissed him. "Nar Garzhvog, your people are safe within our camp. They are gathered near the east gate, ready for you to lead them."

Garzhvog grunted but remained where he was.

Looking back at the approaching soldiers, Nasuada said, "I can think of no reason to engage them in the open. We can pick them off with archers once they are within range. And when they reach our breastwork, they will break themselves against the trenches and the staves. Not a single one will escape alive," she concluded with evident satisfaction.

"When they have committed themselves," said Orrin, "my horsemen and I could ride out and attack them from the rear. They will be so surprised, they will not even have a chance to defend themselves."

"The tide of battle may—" Nasuada was replying when the brazen horn that had announced the arrival of the soldiers sounded once more, so loudly that Eragon, Arya, and the rest of the elves covered their ears. Eragon winced with pain from the blast.

Where is that coming from? he asked Saphira.

A more important question, I think, is why the soldiers would want to warn us of their attack, if they are indeed responsible for this baying.

Maybe it's a diversion or—

Eragon forgot what he was going to say as he saw a stir of motion on the far side of the Jiet River, behind a veil of sorrowful willow trees. Red as a ruby dipped in blood, red as iron hot to forge, red as a burning ember of hate and anger, Thorn appeared above the languishing trees. And upon the back of the glittering dragon, there sat Murtagh in his bright steel armor, thrusting Zar'roc high over his head.

They have come for us, said Saphira. Eragon's gut twisted, and he felt Saphira's own dread like a current of bilious water running through his mind.

FIRE IN THE SKY

As Eragon watched Thorn and Murtagh rise high in the northern sky, he heard Narheim whisper, "Barzûl," and then curse Murtagh for killing Hrothgar, the king of the dwarves.

Arya spun away from the sight. "Nasuada, Your Majesty," she said, her eyes flicking toward Orrin, "you have to stop the soldiers before they reach the camp. You cannot allow them to attack our defenses. If they do, they will sweep over these ramparts like a storm-driven wave and wreak untold havoc in our midst, among the tents, where we cannot maneuver effectively."

"Untold havoc?" Orrin scoffed. "Have you so little confidence in our prowess, Ambassador? Humans and dwarves may not be as gifted as elves, but we shall have no difficulty in disposing of these miserable wretches, I can assure you."

The lines of Arya's face tightened. "Your prowess is without compare, Your Majesty. I do not doubt it. But listen: this is a trap set for Eragon and Saphira. *They*"—she flung an arm toward the rising figures of Thorn and Murtagh—"have come to capture Eragon and Saphira and spirit them away to Urû'baen. Galbatorix would not have sent so few men unless he was confident they could keep the Varden occupied long enough for Murtagh to overwhelm Eragon. Galbatorix *must* have placed spells on those men, spells to aid them in their mission. What those enchantments might be, I do not know, but of this I am certain: the soldiers are more than they appear, and we must prevent them from entering this camp."

Emerging from his initial shock, Eragon said, "You don't want to let Thorn fly over the camp; he could set fire to half of it with a single pass."

Nasuada clasped her hands over the pommel of her saddle, seemingly oblivious to Murtagh and Thorn and to the soldiers, who were now less than a mile away. "But why not attack us while we were unawares?" she asked. "Why alert us to their presence?"

It was Narheim who answered. "Because they would not want Eragon and Saphira to get caught up in the fighting on the ground. No, unless I am mistaken, their plan is for Eragon and Saphira to meet Thorn and Murtagh in the air while the soldiers assail our position here."

"Is it wise, then, to accommodate their wishes, to willingly send Eragon and Saphira into this trap?" Nasuada raised an eyebrow.

"Yes," insisted Arya, "for we have an advantage they could not suspect." She pointed at Blödhgarm. "This time Eragon shall not face Murtagh alone. He will have the combined strength of thirteen elves supporting him. Murtagh will not be expecting that. Stop the soldiers before they reach us, and you will have frustrated part of Galbatorix's design. Send Saphira and Eragon up with the mightiest spellcasters of my race bolstering their efforts, and you will disrupt the remainder of Galbatorix's scheme."

"You have convinced me," said Nasuada. "However, the soldiers are too close for us to intercept them any distance from the camp with men on foot. Orrin—"

Before she finished, the king had turned his horse around and was racing toward the north gate of the camp. One of his retinue winded a trumpet, a signal for the rest of Orrin's cavalry to assemble for a charge.

To Garzhvog, Nasuada said, "King Orrin will require assistance. Send your rams to join him."

"Lady Nightstalker." Throwing back his massive horned head, Garzhvog loosed a wild wailing bellow. The skin on the back of Eragon's arms and neck prickled as he listened to the Urgal's savage howl. With a snap of his jaws, Garzhvog ceased his belling and then grunted, "They will come." The Kull broke into an earth-shattering trot and ran toward the gate where King Orrin and his horsemen were gathered.

Four of the Varden dragged open the gate. King Orrin raised his sword, shouted, and galloped out of the camp, leading his men toward the soldiers in their gold-stitched tunics. A plume of cream-colored dust billowed out from underneath the hooves of the horses, obscuring the arrowhead-shaped formation from view.

"Jörmundur," said Nasuada.

"Yes, my Lady?"

"Order two hundred swordsmen and a hundred spearmen after them. And have fifty archers station themselves seventy to eighty yards away from the fighting. I want these soldiers crushed, Jörmundur, obliterated, ground out of existence. The men are to understand that no quarter is to be given or accepted."

Jörmundur bowed.

"And tell them that although I cannot join them in this battle, on account of my arms, my spirit marches with them."

"My Lady."

As Jörmundur hurried off, Narheim urged his pony closer to Nasuada. "What of mine own people, Nasuada? What role shall we play?"

Nasuada frowned at the thick, choking dust that drifted across the rolling expanse of grass. "You can help guard our perimeter. If the soldiers should somehow win free of—" She was forced to pause as four hundred Urgals—more had arrived since the Battle of the Burning Plains—pounded out of the center of the camp, through the gate, and onto the field beyond, roaring incomprehensible war-cries the whole while. As they vanished into the dust, Nasuada resumed speaking: "If the soldiers should win free, your axes will be most welcome in the lines."

The wind gusted toward them, carrying with it the screams of dying men and horses, the shivery sound of metal sliding over metal, the clink of swords glancing off helmets, the dull impact of spears on shields, and, underlying it all, a horrible humorless laughter that issued from a multitude of throats and continued without pause throughout the mayhem. It was, Eragon thought, the laughter of the insane.

Narheim pounded his fist against his hip. "By Morgothal, we are not ones to stand by idly when there is a fight to be had! Release us, Nasuada, and let us hew a few necks for you!"

"No!" exclaimed Nasuada. "No, no, and no! I have given you my orders, and I expect you to abide by them. This is a battle of horses and men and Urgals and perhaps even dragons. It is not a fit place for dwarves. You would be trampled like children." At Narheim's outraged oath, she raised a hand. "I am well aware you are fearsome warriors. No one knows that better than I, who fought beside you in Farthen Dûr. However, not to put too fine a point on it, you are short by our standards, and I would rather not risk your warriors in a fray such as this, where your stature might be your undoing. Better to wait here, on the high ground, where you stand taller than anyone who tries to climb this berm, and let the soldiers come to you. If any soldiers do reach us, they shall be warriors of such tremendous skill, I want you and your people there to repel them, for one might as well try to uproot a mountain as defeat a dwarf."

315

Still displeased, Narheim grumbled some response, but whatever he said was lost as the Varden Nasuada had deployed filed through the cleft in the embankment where the gate had been. The noise of tramping feet and clattering equipment faded as the men drew away from the camp. Then the wind stiffened into a steady breeze, and from the direction of the fighting, the grim giggle again wafted toward them.

A moment later, a mental shout of incredible strength overwhelmed Eragon's defenses and tore through his consciousness, filling him with agony as he heard a man say, *Ah, no, help me! They won't die! Angvard take them, they won't die!* The link between their minds vanished then, and Eragon swallowed hard as he realized that the man had been killed.

Nasuada shifted in her saddle, her expression strained. "Who was that?"

"You heard him too?"

"It seems we all did," said Arya.

"I think it was Barden, one of the spellcasters who rides with King Orrin, but—"

"Eragon!"

Thorn had been circling higher and higher while King Orrin and his men engaged the soldiers, but now the dragon hung motionless in the sky, halfway between the soldiers and the camp, and Murtagh's voice, augmented with magic, echoed forth across the land: *"Eragon! I see you there, hiding behind Nasuada's skirts. Come fight me, Eragon! It is your destiny. Or are you a coward, Shadeslayer?"*

Saphira answered for Eragon by lifting her head and roaring even louder than Murtagh's thunderous speech, then discharging a twenty-foot-long jet of crackling blue fire. The horses close to Saphira, including Nasuada's, bolted away, leaving Saphira and Eragon alone on the embankment with the elves.

Walking over to Saphira, Arya placed a hand on Eragon's left leg and looked up at him with her slanted green eyes. "Accept this from me, Shur'tugal," she said. And he felt a surge of energy flow into him.

"Eka elrun ono," he murmured to her.

Also in the ancient language, she said, "Be careful, Eragon. I would not want to see you broken by Murtagh. I . . ." It seemed as if she were going to say more, but she hesitated, then removed her hand from his leg and retreated to stand by Blödhgarm.

"Fly well, Bjartskular!" the elves sang out as Saphira launched herself off the embankment.

As Saphira winged her way toward Thorn, Eragon joined his

mind first with her and then with Arya and, through Arya, with Blödhgarm and the eleven other elves. By having Arya serve as the focal point for the elves, Eragon was able to concentrate on the thoughts of Arya and Saphira; he knew them so well that their reactions would not distract him in the middle of a fight.

Eragon grasped the shield with his left hand and unsheathed his falchion, holding it upraised so he would not accidentally stab Saphira's wings as she flapped, nor slash her shoulders nor her neck, which were in constant motion. *I'm glad I took the time last night to reinforce the falchion with magic,* he said to Saphira and Arya.

Let us hope your spells hold, Saphira answered.

Remember, said Arya, *remain as close to us as you can. The more distance you place between us, the harder it is for us to maintain this bond with you.*

Thorn did not dive at Saphira or otherwise attack her as she neared him, but rather slid away on rigid wings, allowing her to rise to his level unmolested. The two dragons balanced upon the thermals, facing each other across a gap of fifty yards, the tips of their barbed tails twitching, both of their muzzles wrinkled with ferocious snarls.

He's bigger, observed Saphira. *It's not been two weeks since we last fought and he has grown another four feet, if not more.*

She was right. Thorn was longer from head to tail, and deeper in the chest, than he had been when they first clashed over the Burning Plains. He was barely older than a hatchling, but he was already nearly as large as Saphira.

Eragon reluctantly shifted his gaze from the dragon to the Rider.

Murtagh was bareheaded, and his long black hair billowed behind him like a sleek mane. His face was hard, harder than Eragon had ever seen before, and Eragon knew that this time Murtagh would not, could not, show him mercy. The volume of his voice substantially reduced, but still louder than normal, Murtagh said, "You and Saphira have caused us a great deal of pain, Eragon. Galbatorix was furious with us for letting you go. And after the two of you killed the Ra'zac, he was so angry, he slew five of his servants and then turned his wrath upon Thorn and me. We have both suffered horribly on account of you. We shall not do so again." He drew back his arm, as if Thorn were about to lunge forward and Murtagh were preparing to slash at Eragon and Saphira.

"Wait!" cried Eragon. "I know of a way you can both free yourselves of your oaths to Galbatorix."

An expression of desperate longing transformed Murtagh's features, and he lowered Zar'roc a few inches. Then he scowled and spat toward the ground and shouted, "I don't believe you! It's not possible!"

"It is! Just let me explain."

Murtagh seemed to be struggling with himself, and for a while Eragon thought he might refuse. Swinging his head around, Thorn looked back at Murtagh, and something passed between them. "Blast you, Eragon," said Murtagh, and lay Zar'roc across the front of his saddle. "Blast you for baiting us with this. We had already made peace with our lot, and you have to tantalize us with the specter of a hope we had abandoned. If this proves to be a false hope, *brother*, I swear I'll cut off your right hand before we present you to Galbatorix. . . . You won't need it for what you will be doing in Urû'baen."

A threat of his own occurred to Eragon, but he suppressed it. Lowering the falchion, he said, "Galbatorix would not have told you, but when I was among the elves—"

Eragon, do not reveal anything more about us! exclaimed Arya.

"—I learned that if your personality changes, so does your true name in the ancient language. Who you are isn't cast in iron, Murtagh! If you and Thorn can change something about yourselves, your oaths will no longer bind you, and Galbatorix will lose his hold on you."

Thorn drifted several yards closer to Saphira. "Why didn't you mention this before?" Murtagh demanded.

"I was too confused at the time."

A scant fifty feet separated Thorn and Saphira by then. The red dragon's snarl had subsided to a faint warning curl of his upper lip, and in his sparkling crimson eyes appeared a vast, puzzled sadness, as if he hoped Saphira or Eragon might know why he had been brought into the world merely so Galbatorix could enslave him, abuse him, and force him to destroy other beings' lives. The tip of Thorn's nose twitched as he sniffed at Saphira. She sniffed him in return, and her tongue darted out of her mouth as she tasted his scent. Pity for Thorn welled up inside Eragon and Saphira together, and they wished they could speak with him directly, but they dared not open their minds to him.

With so little distance between them, Eragon noticed the bundles of cords that ridged Murtagh's neck and the forked vein that pulsed in the middle of his forehead.

"I am not evil!" said Murtagh. "I've done the best I could under the circumstances. I doubt you would have survived as well as I did if our mother had seen fit to leave *you* in Urû'baen and hide *me* in Carvahall."

"Perhaps not."

Murtagh banged his breastplate with his fist. "Aha! Then how am I supposed to follow your advice? If I am already a good man, if I have already done as well as could be expected, how can I change? Must I become worse than I am? Must I embrace Galbatorix's darkness in order to free myself of it? That hardly seems like a reasonable solution. If I succeeded in so altering my identity, you would not like who I had become, and you would curse me as strongly as you curse Galbatorix now."

Frustrated, Eragon said, "Yes, but you do not have to become better or worse than you are now, only different. There are many kinds of people in the world and many ways to behave honorably. Look at someone whom you admire but who has chosen paths other than your own through life and model your actions upon his. It may take

319

a while, but if you can shift your personality enough, you can leave Galbatorix, and you can leave the Empire, and you and Thorn could join us in the Varden, where you would be free to do as you wish."

What of your own oaths to avenge Hrothgar's death? Saphira asked. Eragon ignored her.

Murtagh sneered at him. "So you are asking me to be that which I am not. If Thorn and I are to save ourselves, we must destroy our current identities. Your cure is worse than our affliction."

"I'm asking you to allow yourself to grow into something other than you are now. It's a difficult thing to do, I know, but people remake themselves all the time. Let go of your anger, for one, and you can turn your back on Galbatorix once and for all."

"Let go of my anger?" Murtagh laughed. "I'll let go of my anger when you forget yours over the Empire's role in the death of your uncle and the razing of your farm. Anger defines us, Eragon, and without it, you and I would be a feast for maggots. Still . . ." His eyes half lidded, Murtagh tapped Zar'roc's crossguard, the cords in his neck softening, although the vein that split his forehead remained swollen as ever. "The concept is intriguing, I admit. Perhaps we can work on it together when we are in Urû'baen. That is, if the king permits us to be alone with each other. Of course, he may decide to keep us permanently separated. I would if I were in his position."

Eragon tightened his fingers around the hilt of the falchion. "You seem to think we will accompany you to the capital."

"Oh, but you will, brother." A crooked smile stretched Murtagh's mouth. "Even if we wanted to, Thorn and I could not change who we are in an instant. Until such time as we may have that opportunity, we shall remain beholden to Galbatorix, and he has ordered us, in no uncertain terms, to bring him the two of you. Neither of us is willing to brave the king's displeasure again. We defeated you once before. It will be no great achievement to do so again."

A spurt of flame escaped from between Saphira's teeth, and Eragon had to stifle a similar response in words. If he lost control of his temper now, bloodshed would be unavoidable. "Please,

Murtagh, Thorn, will you not at least try what I've suggested? Have you no desire to resist Galbatorix? You will never cast off your chains unless you are willing to defy him."

"You underestimate Galbatorix, Eragon," growled Murtagh. "He has been creating name-slaves for over a hundred years, ever since he recruited our father. Do you think he is unaware that a person's true name may vary over the course of his life? He is sure to have taken precautions against that eventuality. If my true name were to change this very moment, or Thorn's, most likely it would trigger a spell that would alert Galbatorix to the change and force us to return to him in Urû'baen so he could bind us to him again."

"But only if he could guess your new names."

"He is most adept at the practice." Murtagh raised Zar'roc off the saddle. "We may make use of your suggestion in the future, but only after careful study and preparation, so that Thorn and I do not regain our freedom only to have Galbatorix steal it back from us directly afterward." He hefted Zar'roc, the sword's iridescent blade shimmering. "Therefore, we have no choice but to take you with us to Urû'baen. Will you go peacefully?"

Unable to contain himself any longer, Eragon said, "I would sooner tear out my own heart!"

"Better to tear out my hearts," Murtagh replied, then stabbed Zar'roc overhead and shouted a wild war cry.

Roaring in unison, Thorn flapped twice, fast, to climb above Saphira. He twisted in a half circle as he rose, so his head would be over Saphira's neck, where he could immobilize her with a single bite at the base of her skull.

Saphira did not wait for him. She tipped forward, rotating her wings in their shoulder sockets, so that, for the span of a heartbeat, she pointed straight down, her wings still parallel with the dust-smeared ground, supporting her entire unstable weight. Then she pulled in her right wing and swung her head to the left and her tail to the right, spinning in a clockwise direction. Her muscular tail struck Thorn across his left side just as he sailed over her, breaking his wing in five separate places. The jagged ends of Thorn's hollow flight bones pierced his hide and stuck out between his flashing scales. Globules of steaming dragon blood rained down upon Eragon and Saphira. A droplet splashed against the back of Eragon's coif and seeped through the mail to his bare skin. It burned like hot oil. He scrabbled at his neck, trying to wipe off the blood.

His roar converting into a whine of pain, Thorn tumbled past Saphira, unable to stay aloft.

"Well done!" Eragon shouted to Saphira as she righted herself.

Eragon watched from above as Murtagh removed a small round object from his belt and pressed it against Thorn's shoulder. Eragon sensed no surge of magic from Murtagh, but the object in his hand flared and Thorn's broken wing jerked as his bones snapped back in place and muscles and tendons rippled and the tears in them vanished. Lastly, the wounds in Thorn's hide sealed over.

How did he do that? Eragon exclaimed.

Arya answered, *He must have imbued the item with a spell of healing beforehand.*

We should have thought of that ourselves.

His injuries mended, Thorn halted his fall and began to ascend toward Saphira with prodigious speed, searing the air in front of him with a boiling spear of sullen red fire. Saphira dove at him, spiraling around the tower of flame. She snapped at Thorn's neck—causing him to shy away—and raked his shoulders and chest with her front claws and buffeted him with her huge wings. The edge of her right wing clipped Murtagh, knocking him sideways in his saddle. He recovered quickly and slashed at Saphira, opening up a three-foot rent in the membrane of her wing.

Hissing, Saphira kicked Thorn away with her hind legs and released a jet of fire, which split and passed harmlessly on either side of Thorn.

Eragon felt through Saphira the throbbing of her wound. He stared at the bloody gash, thoughts racing. If they had been fighting any magician besides Murtagh, he would not dare to cast a spell

322

while engaged in hostilities, for the magician would most likely be-lieve he or she was about to die and would counter with a desperate, all-out magical attack.

It was different with Murtagh. Eragon knew Galbatorix had or-dered Murtagh to capture, not kill, him and Saphira. *No matter what I do*, Eragon thought, *he will not attempt to slay me.* It was safe, then, Eragon decided, to heal Saphira. And, he belatedly realized, he could attack Murtagh with any spells he desired and Murtagh would not be able to respond with deadly force. But he wondered why Murtagh had used an enchanted object to cure Thorn's hurts in-stead of casting the spell himself.

Saphira said, *Perhaps he wants to preserve his strength. Or perhaps he wanted to avoid frightening you. It would not please Galbatorix if, by us-ing magic, Murtagh caused you to panic and you killed yourself or Thorn or Murtagh as a result. Remember, the king's great ambition is to have all four of us under his command, not dead, where we are beyond his reach.*

That must be it, Eragon agreed.

As he prepared to mend Saphira's wing, Arya said, *Wait. Do not.*

What? Why? Can't you feel Saphira's pain?

Let my brethren and I tend to her. It will confuse Murtagh, and this way, the effort shall not weaken you.

Aren't you too far away to work such a change?

Not when the lot of us pool our resources. And, Eragon? We recom-mend you refrain from striking at Murtagh with magic until he attacks with mind or magic himself. He may yet be stronger than you, even with the thirteen of us lending our strength. We do not know. It is better not to test yourself against him until there is no other alternative.

And if I cannot prevail?

All of Alagaësia will fall to Galbatorix.

Eragon sensed Arya concentrating, then the cut in Saphira's wing ceased weeping tears of blood and the raw edges of the delicate cerulean membrane flowed together without a scab or a scar. Saphira's relief was palpable. With a tinge of fatigue, Arya said, *Guard yourself better if you can. This was not easy.*

After Saphira had kicked him, Thorn flailed and lost altitude. He must have assumed that Saphira meant to harry him downward, where it would be harder for him to evade her attacks, because he fled west a quarter of a mile. When he finally noticed that Saphira was not pursuing him, he circled up and around until he was a good thousand feet higher than she was.

Drawing in his wings, Thorn hurtled toward Saphira, flames flickering in his open maw, his ivory talons outstretched, Murtagh brandishing Zar'roc on his back.

Eragon nearly lost his grip on the falchion as Saphira folded one wing and flipped upside down with a dizzying wrench, then extended the wing again to slow her descent. If he craned his head backward, Eragon could see the ground below them. Or was it above them? He gritted his teeth and concentrated on maintaining his hold on the saddle.

Thorn and Saphira collided, and to Eragon, it was as if Saphira had crashed into the side of a mountain. The force of the impact drove him forward, and he banged his helmet against the neck spike in front of him, denting the thick steel. Dazed, he hung loose from the saddle and watched as the disks of the heavens and the earth reversed themselves, spinning without a discernible pattern. He felt Saphira shudder as Thorn battered her exposed belly. Eragon wished there had been time to dress her in the armor the dwarves had given her.

A glittering ruby leg appeared around Saphira's shoulder, mauling her with bloody claws. Without thinking, Eragon hacked at it, shattering a line of scales and severing a bundle of tendons. Three of the toes on the foot went limp. Eragon hacked again.

Snarling, Thorn disengaged from Saphira. He arched his neck, and Eragon heard an inrush of air as the stocky dragon filled his lungs. Eragon ducked, burying his face in the corner of his elbow. A ravening inferno engulfed Saphira. The heat of the fire could not harm them—Eragon's wards prevented that—but the torrent of incandescent flames was still blinding.

324

Saphira veered to the left, out of the churning fire. By then, Murtagh had repaired the damage to Thorn's leg, and Thorn again flung himself at Saphira, grappling with her as they plummeted in sickening lurches toward the gray tents of the Varden. Saphira managed to clamp her teeth on the horned crest that projected from the rear of Thorn's head, despite the points of bone that punctured her tongue. Thorn bellowed and thrashed like a hooked fish, trying to pull away, but he was no match for the iron muscles of Saphira's jaws. The two dragons drifted downward side by side, like a pair of interlocked leaves.

Eragon leaned over and slashed crosswise at Murtagh's right shoulder, not intending to kill him but rather to injure him severely enough to end the fight. Unlike during their clash over the Burning Plains, Eragon was well rested; with his arm as fast as an elf's, he was confident Murtagh would be defenseless before him.

Murtagh lifted his shield and blocked the falchion.

His reaction was so unexpected, Eragon faltered, then barely had time to recoil and parry as Murtagh retaliated, swinging Zar'roc at him, the blade humming through the air with inordinate speed. The stroke jarred Eragon's shoulder. Pressing the attack, Murtagh struck at Eragon's wrist and then, when Eragon dashed aside Zar'roc, thrust underneath Eragon's shield and stabbed through the fringe of his mail hauberk and his tunic and the waist of his breeches and into his left hip. The tip of Zar'roc embedded itself in bone.

The pain shocked Eragon like a splash of frigid water, but it also lent his thoughts a preternatural clarity and sent a burst of uncommon strength coursing through his limbs.

As Murtagh withdrew Zar'roc, Eragon yelled and lunged at Murtagh, who, with a flip of his wrist, trapped the falchion beneath Zar'roc. Murtagh bared his teeth in a sinister smile. Without pause, Eragon yanked the falchion free, feinted toward Murtagh's right knee, then whipped the falchion in the opposite direction and sliced Murtagh across the cheek.

"You should have worn a helmet," said Eragon.

They were so close to the ground then—only a few hundred feet—that Saphira had to release Thorn, and the two dragons separated before Eragon and Murtagh could exchange any more blows.

As Saphira and Thorn spiraled upward, racing each other toward a pearl-white cloud gathering over the tents of the Varden, Eragon lifted his hauberk and tunic and examined his hip. A fist-sized patch of skin was discolored where Zar'roc had crushed the mail against his flesh. In the middle of the patch was a thin red line, two inches long, where Zar'roc had pierced him. Blood oozed from the wound, soaking the top of his breeches.

Being hurt by Zar'roc—a sword that had never failed him in moments of danger and that he still regarded as rightfully his—unsettled him. To have his own weapon turned against him was *wrong*. It was a warping of the world, and his every instinct rebelled against it.

Saphira wobbled as she flew through an eddy of air, and Eragon winced, renewed pain lancing up his side. It was fortunate, he concluded, that they were not fighting on foot, for he did not think his hip would bear his weight.

Arya, he said, *do you want to heal me, or shall I do it myself and let Murtagh stop me if he can?*

We shall attend to it for you, Arya said. *You may be able to catch Murtagh by surprise if he believes you are still wounded.*

Oh, wait.

Why?

I have to give you permission. Otherwise, my wards will block the spell. The phrase did not leap into Eragon's mind at first, but eventually he remembered the construction of the safeguard and, in the ancient language, whispered, "I agree to let Arya, daughter of Islanzadí, cast a spell on me."

We shall have to talk about your wards when you are not so distracted. What if you were unconscious? How could we minister to you then?

It seemed like a good idea after the Burning Plains. Murtagh immobi-

lized us both with magic. *I don't want him or anyone else to be able to cast spells on us without our consent.*

Nor should they, but there are more elegant solutions than yours.

Eragon squirmed in the saddle as the elves' magic took effect and his hip began to tingle and itch as if covered with flea bites. When the itching ceased, he slid a hand under his tunic and was delighted to feel nothing but smooth skin.

Right, he said, rolling his shoulders. *Let us teach them to fear our names!*

The pearl-white cloud looming large before them, Saphira twisted to the left and then, while Thorn was struggling to turn, plunged into the heart of the cloud. Everything went cold and damp and white, then Saphira shot out of the far side, exiting only a few feet above and behind Thorn.

Roaring with triumph, Saphira dropped upon Thorn and seized him by the flanks, sinking her claws deep into his thighs and along his spine. She snaked her head forward, caught Thorn's left wing in her mouth, and clamped down with the *snick* of razor teeth cutting through meat.

Thorn writhed and screamed, a horrible sound Eragon had not suspected dragons were capable of producing.

I have him, said Saphira. *I can tear off his wing, but I would rather not. Whatever you are going to do, do it before we fall too far.*

His face pale beneath smeared gore, Murtagh pointed at Eragon with Zar'roc—the sword trembling in the air—and a mental ray of immense power invaded Eragon's consciousness. The foreign presence groped after his thoughts, seeking to grab ahold and subdue them and subject them to Murtagh's approval. As on the Burning Plains, Eragon noticed that Murtagh's mind felt as if it contained multitudes, as if a confused chorus of voices was murmuring beneath the turmoil of Murtagh's own thoughts.

Eragon wondered if Murtagh had a group of magicians assisting him, even as the elves were him.

Difficult as it was, Eragon emptied his mind of everything but an image of Zar'roc. He concentrated on the sword with all his might, smoothing the plane of his consciousness into the calm of meditation so Murtagh would find no purchase with which to establish a foothold in Eragon's being. And when Thorn flailed underneath them and Murtagh's attention wavered for an instant, Eragon launched a furious counterattack, clutching at Murtagh's consciousness.

The two of them strove against each other in grim silence while they fell, wrestling back and forth in the confines of their minds. Sometimes Eragon seemed to gain the upper hand, sometimes Murtagh, but neither could defeat the other. Eragon glanced at the ground rushing up at them and realized that their contest would have to be decided by other means.

Lowering the falchion so it was level with Murtagh, Eragon shouted, "Letta!"—the same spell Murtagh had used on him during their previous confrontation. It was a simple piece of magic—it would do nothing more than hold Murtagh's arms and torso in place—but it would allow them to test themselves directly against one another and determine which of them had the most energy at their disposal.

Murtagh mouthed a counterspell, the words lost in Thorn's snarling and in the howling of the wind.

Eragon's pulse raced as the strength ebbed from his limbs. When he had nearly depleted his reserves and was faint from the effort, Saphira and the elves poured the energy from their bodies into his, maintaining the spell for him. Across from him, Murtagh had originally appeared smug and confident, but as Eragon continued to restrain him, Murtagh's scowl deepened, and he pulled back his lips, baring his teeth. And the whole while, they besieged each other's minds.

Eragon felt the energy Arya was funneling into him decrease once, then twice, and he assumed that two of the spellweavers under Blödhgarm's command had fainted. *Murtagh can't hold out much longer*, he thought, and then had to struggle to regain control of his mind, for his lapse of concentration had granted Murtagh entry.

The force from Arya and the other elves declined by half, and even Saphira began to shake with exhaustion. Just as Eragon became convinced Murtagh would prevail, Murtagh uttered an anguished shout, and a great weight seemed to lift off Eragon as Murtagh's resistance vanished. Murtagh appeared astonished by Eragon's success.

What now? Eragon asked Arya and Saphira. *Do we take them as hostages? Can we?*

Now, said Saphira, *I must fly.* She released Thorn and pushed herself away from him, raising her wings and laboriously flapping as she endeavored to keep them aloft. Eragon looked over her shoulder and had a brief impression of horses and sun-streaked grass hurtling toward them; then it was as if a giant struck him from underneath and his sight went black.

The next thing Eragon saw was a swath of Saphira's neck scales an inch or two in front of his nose. The scales shone like cobalt-blue ice. Eragon was dimly aware of someone reaching out to his mind from across a great distance, their consciousness projecting an intense sense of urgency. As his faculties returned, he recognized the other person as Arya. She said: *End the spell, Eragon! It will kill us all if you keep it up. End it; Murtagh is too far away! Wake up, Eragon, or you will pass into the void.*

With a jolt, Eragon sat upright in the saddle, barely noticing that Saphira was crouched amid a circle of King Orrin's horsemen. Arya was nowhere to be seen. Now that he was alert again, Eragon could feel the spell he had cast on Murtagh still draining his strength, and in ever-increasing amounts. If not for the aid of Saphira and Arya and the other elves, he would have already died.

Eragon released the magic, then looked for Thorn and Murtagh on the ground.

There, said Saphira, and motioned with her snout. Low in the northwestern sky, Eragon saw Thorn's glittering shape, the dragon winging his way up the Jiet River, fleeing toward Galbatorix's army some miles distant.

How?

Murtagh healed Thorn again, and Thorn was lucky enough to land on the slope of a hill. He ran down it, then took off before you regained consciousness.

From across the rolling landscape, Murtagh's magnified voice boomed: "Do not think you have won, Eragon, Saphira. We shall meet again, I promise, and Thorn and I shall defeat you then, for we shall be even stronger than we are now!"

Eragon clenched his shield and his falchion so tightly, he bled from underneath his fingernails. *Do you think you can overtake him?*

I could, but the elves would not be able to help you from so far away, and I doubt we could prevail without their support.

We might be able— Eragon stopped and pounded his leg in frustration. *Blast it, I'm an idiot! I forgot about Aren. We could have used the energy in Brom's ring to help defeat them.*

You had other things on your mind. Anyone might have made the same mistake.

Maybe, but I still wish I had thought of Aren sooner. We could still use it to capture Thorn and Murtagh.

And then what? asked Saphira. *How could we keep them as prisoners? Would you drug them like Durza drugged you in Gil'ead? Or do you just want to kill them?*

I don't know! We could help them to change their true names, to break their oaths to Galbatorix. Letting them wander around unchecked, though, is too dangerous.

Arya said, *In theory, you are right, Eragon, but you are tired, Saphira is tired, and I would rather Thorn and Murtagh escape than we lose the two of you because you were not at your best.*

But—

But we do not have the capabilities to safely detain a dragon and Rider for an extended period, and I do not think killing Thorn and Murtagh would be as easy as you assume, Eragon. Be grateful we have driven them off, and rest easy knowing we can do so again when next they dare to confront us. So saying, she withdrew from his mind.

Eragon watched until Thorn and Murtagh had vanished from sight, then he sighed and rubbed Saphira's neck. *I could sleep for a fortnight.*

As could I.

You should be proud; you outflew Thorn at nearly every turn.

Yes, I did, didn't I? She preened. *It was hardly a fair competition. Thorn does not have my experience.*

Nor your talent, I should think.

Twisting her neck, she licked the upper part of his right arm, the mail hauberk tinkling, and then gazed down at him with sparkling eyes.

He managed a ghost of a smile. *I suppose I should have expected it, but it still surprised me that Murtagh was as fast as me. More magic on the part of Galbatorix, no doubt.*

Why did your wards fail to deflect Zar'roc, though? They saved you from worse blows when we fought the Ra'zac.

I'm not sure. Murtagh or Galbatorix might have invented a spell I had not thought to guard against. Or it could just be that Zar'roc is a Rider's blade, and as Glaedr said—

—the swords Rhunön forged excel at—

—cutting through enchantments of every kind, and—

—it is only rarely they are—

—affected by magic. Exactly. Eragon stared at the streaks of dragon blood on the flat of the falchion, weary. *When will we be able to defeat our enemies on our own? I couldn't have killed Durza if Arya hadn't broken the star sapphire. And we were only able to prevail over Murtagh and Thorn with the help of Arya and twelve others.*

We must become more powerful.

Yes, but how? How has Galbatorix amassed his strength? Has he found a way to feed off the bodies of his slaves even when he is hundreds of miles away? Garr! I don't know.

A runnel of sweat coursed down Eragon's brow and into the corner of his right eye. He wiped off the perspiration with the palm of his hand, then blinked and again noticed the horsemen gathered around him and Saphira. *What are they doing here?* Looking beyond, he realized Saphira had landed close to where King Orrin had intercepted the soldiers from the boats. Not far off to her left, hundreds of men, Urgals, and horses milled about in panic and confusion. Occasionally, the clatter of swords or the scream of a wounded man broke through the uproar, accompanied by snatches of demented laughter.

I think they are here to protect us, said Saphira.

Us! From what? Why haven't they killed the soldiers yet? Where— Eragon abandoned his question as Arya, Blödhgarm, and four other haggard-looking elves sprinted up to Saphira from the direction of the camp. Raising a hand in greeting, Eragon called, "Arya! What's happened? No one seems to be in command."

To Eragon's alarm, Arya was breathing so hard, she was unable to speak for a few moments. Then: "The soldiers proved more dangerous than we anticipated. We do not know how. Du Vrangr Gata has heard nothing but gibberish from Orrin's spellcasters." Regaining her breath, Arya started examining Saphira's cuts and bruises.

Before Eragon could ask more, a collection of excited cries from within the maelstrom of warriors drowned out the rest of the tumult, and he heard King Orrin shout, "Back, back, all of you! Archers, hold the line! Blast you, no one move, we have him!"

Saphira had the same thought as Eragon. Gathering her legs under her, she leaped over the ring of horsemen—startling the horses so they bucked and ran—and made her way across the corpse-strewn battlefield toward the sound of King Orrin's voice, brushing aside men and Urgals alike as if they were so many stalks of grass. The rest of the elves hurried to keep up, swords and bows in hand.

Saphira found Orrin sitting on his charger at the leading edge of the tightly packed warriors, staring at a lone man forty feet away. The king was flushed and wild-eyed, his armor besmirched with filth from combat. He had been wounded under his left arm, and the shaft of a spear protruded several inches from his right thigh. When Saphira's approach caught his attention, his face registered sudden relief.

"Good, good, you're here," he muttered as Saphira crawled abreast of his charger. "We needed you, Saphira, and you, Shade-slayer." One of the archers edged forward a few inches. Orrin waved his sword at him and yelled, "Back! I'll have the head of anyone who doesn't remain where he is, I swear by Angvard's crown!" Then Orrin resumed glaring at the lone man.

Eragon followed his gaze. The man was a soldier of medium height, with a purple birthmark on his neck and brown hair plastered flat by the helmet he had been wearing. His shield was a splintered ruin. His sword was notched, bent, and broken, missing the last six inches. River mud caked his mail hose. Blood sheeted from a gash along his ribs. An arrow fletched with white swan feathers had impaled his right foot and pinned it to the ground, three-quarters of the shaft buried in the hard dirt. From the man's throat, a horrid gurgling laugh emanated. It rose and fell with a drunken cadence, pitching from note to note as if the man were about to begin shrieking with horror.

"What are you?" shouted King Orrin. When the soldier did not immediately respond, the king cursed and said, "Answer me, or I'll let my spellcasters at you. Be you man or beast or some ill-spawned demon? In what foul pit did Galbatorix find you and your brothers? Are you kin of the Ra'zac?"

The king's last question acted like a needle driven into Eragon; he straightened bolt upright, every sense tingling.

The laughter paused for a moment. "Man. I am a man."

"You are like no man I know."

"I wanted to assure the future of my family. Is that so foreign to you, Surdan?"

"Give me no riddles, you fork-tongued wretch! Tell me how you became as you are, and speak honestly, lest you convince me to pour boiling lead down your throat and see if *that* pains you."

The unbalanced chuckles intensified, then the soldier said, "You cannot hurt me, Surdan. No one can. The king himself made us impervious to pain. In return, our families will live in comfort for the rest of their lives. You can hide from us, but we will never stop pursuing you, even when ordinary men would drop dead from exhaustion. You can fight us, but we will continue killing you as long as we have an arm to swing. You cannot even surrender to us, for we take no prisoners. You can do nothing but die and return this land to peace."

With a gruesome grimace, the soldier wrapped his mangled shield hand around the arrow and, with the sound of tearing flesh, pulled the shaft out of his foot. Lumps of crimson meat clung to the arrowhead as it came free. The soldier shook the arrow at them, then threw the missile at one of the archers, wounding him in the hand. His laugh louder than ever, the soldier lurched forward, dragging his injured foot behind him. He raised his sword, as if he intended to attack.

"Shoot him!" shouted Orrin.

Bowstrings twanged like badly tuned lutes, then a score of spinning arrows leaped toward the soldier and, an instant later, struck him in the torso. Two of the arrows bounced off his gambeson; the remainder penetrated his rib cage. His laughter reduced to a wheezing chuckle as blood seeped into his lungs, the soldier continued moving forward, painting the grass underneath him bright scarlet. The archers shot again, and arrows sprouted from the man's shoulders and arms, but he did not stop. Another volley of arrows followed close upon the last. The soldier stumbled and fell as an arrow split his left kneecap and others skewered his upper legs and one passed entirely through his neck—punching a hole in his birthmark—and whistled out across the field, trailing a spray of blood. And still the soldier refused to die. He began to crawl, dragging himself forward with his arms, grinning and giggling as if the whole world were an obscene joke that only he could appreciate.

A cold tingle shivered down Eragon's spine as he watched.

King Orrin swore violently, and Eragon detected a hint of hysteria in his voice. Jumping off his charger, Orrin threw his sword and his shield into the dirt and then pointed at the nearest Urgal. "Give me your ax." Startled, the gray-skinned Urgal hesitated, then surrendered his weapon.

King Orrin limped over to the soldier, raised the heavy ax with both hands, and, with a single blow, chopped off the soldier's head.

The giggling ceased.

The soldier's eyes rolled and his mouth worked for another few seconds, and then he was still.

Orrin grasped the head by the hair and lifted it so all could see. "They *can* be killed," he declared. "Spread the word that the only sure way of stopping these abominations is to behead them. That or bash in their skulls with a mace or shoot them in the eye from a safe distance. . . . Graytooth, where are you?" A stout, middle-aged horseman urged his mount forward. Orrin threw him the head, which he caught. "Mount that on a pole by the north gate of the camp. Mount *all* of their heads. Let them serve as a message to Galbatorix that we do not fear his underhanded tricks and we shall prevail in spite of them." Striding back to his charger, Orrin returned the ax to the Urgal, then picked up his own weapons.

A few yards away, Eragon spotted Nar Garzhvog standing among a cluster of Kull. Eragon spoke a few words to Saphira, and she sidled over to the Urgals. After exchanging nods, Eragon asked Garzhvog, "Were all the soldiers like that?" He gestured toward the arrow-riddled corpse.

"All men with no pain. You hit them and you think them dead, turn your back and they hamstring you." Garzhvog scowled. "I lost many rams today. We have fought droves of humans, Firesword, but never before these laughing ghouls. It is not natural. It makes us think they are possessed by hornless spirits, that maybe the gods themselves have turned against us."

"Nonsense," scoffed Eragon. "It is merely a spell by Galbatorix, and we shall soon have a way to protect ourselves against it."

Notwithstanding his outer confidence, the concept of fighting enemies who felt no pain unsettled him as much as it did the Urgals. Moreover, from what Garzhvog had said, he guessed that maintaining morale among the Varden was going to be even more difficult for Nasuada once everyone learned about the soldiers.

While the Varden and the Urgals set about collecting their fallen comrades, stripping the dead of useful equipment, and beheading the soldiers and dragging their truncated bodies into piles to burn, Eragon, Saphira, and King Orrin returned to the camp, accompanied by Arya and the other elves.

Along the way, Eragon offered to heal Orrin's leg, but the king refused, saying, "I have my own physicians, Shadeslayer."

Nasuada and Jörmundur were waiting for them by the north gate. Accosting Orrin, Nasuada said, "What went wrong?"

Eragon closed his eyes as Orrin explained how at first the attack on the soldiers had seemed to go well. The horsemen had swept through their ranks, dealing what they had thought were death-blows left and right, and had suffered only one casualty during their charge. When they had engaged the remaining soldiers, however, many of those they had struck down before rose up and rejoined the fight. Orrin shuddered. "We lost our nerve then. Any man would have. We did not know if the soldiers were invincible, or if they were even men at all. When you see an enemy coming at you with bone sticking out of his calf, a javelin through his belly, and half his face sheared away, and he *laughs* at you, it's a rare man who can stand his ground. My warriors panicked. They broke formation. It was utter confusion. Slaughter. When the Urgals and your warriors, Nasuada, reached us, they became caught up in the madness." He shook his head. "I've never seen the like of it, not even on the Burning Plains."

Nasuada's face had grown pale, even with her dark skin. She looked at Eragon and then Arya. "How could Galbatorix have done this?"

It was Arya who answered, "Block most, but not all, of a person's ability to feel pain. Leave just enough sensation so they know where they are and what they are doing, but not so much that pain can incapacitate them. The spell would require only a small amount of energy."

Nasuada wet her lips. Again speaking to Orrin, she said, "Do you know how many we lost?"

A tremor racked Orrin. He doubled over, pressed a hand against his leg, gritted his teeth, and growled, "Three hundred soldiers against . . . What was the size of the force you sent?"

"Two hundred swordsmen. A hundred spearmen. Fifty archers."

"Those, plus the Urgals, plus my cavalry . . . Say around a thousand strong. Against three hundred foot soldiers on an open field. We slew every last one of the soldiers. What it cost us, though . . ." The king shook his head. "We won't know for sure until we count the dead, but it looked to me as if three-quarters of your swordsmen are gone. More of the spearmen. Some archers. Of my cavalry, few remain: fifty, seventy. Many of them were my friends. Perhaps a hundred, a hundred and fifty Urgals dead. Overall? Five or six hundred to bury, and the better part of the survivors wounded. I don't know . . . I don't know. I don't—" His jaw going slack, Orrin slumped to the side and would have fallen off his horse if Arya had not sprung forward and caught him.

Nasuada snapped her fingers, summoning two of the Varden from among the tents, and ordered them to take Orrin to his pavilion and then to fetch the king his healers.

"We have suffered a grievous defeat, no matter that we exterminated the soldiers," Nasuada murmured. She pressed her lips together, sorrow and despair mixed in equal portions in her expression. Her eyes glimmered with unshed tears. Stiffening her back, she fixed Eragon and Saphira with an iron gaze. "How fared it with the two of you?" She listened without moving while Eragon described their encounter with Murtagh and Thorn. Afterward, she nodded. "That you would be able to escape their clutches was all we dared hope. However, you accomplished more than that. You proved that Galbatorix has not made Murtagh so powerful that we have no hope of defeating him. With a few more spellcasters to help you, Murtagh would have been yours to do with as you pleased. For that reason, he will not dare confront Queen Islanzadí's army by himself, I think. If we can gather enough spellcasters around you, Eragon, I believe we can finally kill Murtagh and Thorn the next time they come to abduct the pair of you."

"Don't you want to capture them?" Eragon asked.

"I want a great number of things, but I doubt I shall receive very many of them. Murtagh and Thorn may not be trying to kill you, but if the opportunity presents itself, we must kill them without hesitation. Or do you see it otherwise?"

". . . No."

Shifting her attention to Arya, Nasuada asked, "Did any of your spellweavers die during the contest?"

"Some fainted, but they have all recovered, thank you."

Nasuada took a deep breath and looked northward, her eyes focused on infinity. "Eragon, please inform Trianna that I want Du Vrangr Gata to figure out how to replicate Galbatorix's spell. Despicable as it is, we must imitate Galbatorix in this. We cannot afford not to. It won't be practical for all of us to be unable to feel pain—we would hurt ourselves far too easily—but we should have a few hundred swordsmen, volunteers, who are immune to physical suffering."

"My Lady."

"So many dead," said Nasuada. She twisted her reins in her hands. "We have remained in one place for too long. It is time we force the Empire onto the defensive again." She spurred Battlestorm away from the carnage that lay before the camp, the stallion tossing his head and gnawing on his bit. "Your cousin, Eragon, begged me to allow him to take part in today's fighting. I refused, on account of his impending marriage, which pleased him not—although I suspect his betrothed feels otherwise. Would you do me the favor of notifying me if they still intend to proceed with the ceremony today? After so much bloodshed, it would hearten the Varden to attend a marriage."

"I will let you know as soon as I find out."

"Thank you. You may go now, Eragon."

The first thing Eragon and Saphira did upon leaving Nasuada was to visit the elves who had fainted during their battle with Murtagh and Thorn and thank them and their companions for their assistance. Then Eragon, Arya, and Blödhgarm attended to the hurts Thorn had dealt Saphira, mending her cuts and scratches and a few of her bruises. When they finished, Eragon located Trianna with his mind and conveyed Nasuada's instructions.

Only then did he and Saphira seek out Roran. Blödhgarm and his elves accompanied them; Arya left to attend to business of her own.

Roran and Katrina were arguing quietly and intensely when Eragon spotted them standing by the corner of Horst's tent. They fell silent as Eragon and Saphira drew near. Katrina crossed her arms and stared away from Roran, while Roran gripped the top of his hammer thrust through his belt and scuffed the heel of his boot against a rock.

Stopping in front of them, Eragon waited a few moments, hoping they would explain the reason for their quarrel, but instead Katrina said, "Are either of you injured?" Her eyes flicked from him to Saphira and back.

"We were, but no longer."

"That is so . . . strange. We heard tales of magic in Carvahall, but I never really believed them. They seemed so impossible. But here, there are magicians everywhere. . . . Did you wound Murtagh and Thorn badly? Is that why they fled?"

"We bested them, but we caused them no permanent harm." Eragon paused, and when neither Roran nor Katrina spoke, he asked if they still wanted to get married that day. "Nasuada suggested you proceed, but it might be better to wait. The dead have yet to be buried, and there is much that needs doing. Tomorrow would be more convenient . . . and more seemly."

"No," said Roran, and ground the tip of his boot against the rock. "The Empire could attack again at any moment. Tomorrow might be too late. If . . . if somehow I died before we were wed, what would become of Katrina or our . . ." He faltered and his cheeks reddened.

Her expression softening, Katrina turned to Roran and took his hand. She said, "Besides, the food has been cooked, the decorations have been hung, and our friends have gathered for our marriage. It would be a pity if all those preparations were for nothing." Reaching up, she stroked Roran's beard, and he smiled at her and placed an arm around her.

I don't understand half of what goes on between them, Eragon complained to Saphira. "When shall the ceremony take place, then?"

"In an hour," said Roran.

MAN AND WIFE

Four hours later, Eragon stood on the crest of a low hill dotted with yellow wildflowers.

Surrounding the hill was a lush meadow that bordered the Jiet River, which rushed past a hundred feet to Eragon's right. The sky was bright and clear; sunshine bathed the land with a soft radiance. The air was cool and calm and smelled fresh, as if it had just rained.

Gathered in front of the hill were the villagers from Carvahall, none of whom had been injured during the fighting, and what seemed to be half of the men of the Varden. Many of the warriors held long spears mounted with embroidered pennants of every color. Various horses, including Snowfire, were picketed at the far end of the meadow. Despite Nasuada's best efforts, organizing the assembly had taken longer than anyone had reckoned.

Wind tousled Eragon's hair, which was still wet from washing, as Saphira glided over the congregation and alighted next to him, fanning her wings. He smiled and touched her on the shoulder.

Little one.

Under normal circumstances, Eragon would have been nervous about speaking in front of so many people and performing such a solemn and important ceremony, but after the earlier fighting, everything had assumed an air of unreality, as if it were no more than a particularly vivid dream.

At the base of the hill stood Nasuada, Arya, Narheim, Jörmundur, Angela, Elva, and others of importance. King Orrin was absent, as his wounds had proved to be more serious than they had first appeared and his healers were still laboring over him in his pavilion. The king's prime minister, Irwin, was attending in his stead.

The only Urgals present were the two in Nasuada's private guard. Eragon had been there when Nasuada had invited Nar Garzhvog to the event, and he had been relieved when Garzhvog had had the good sense to decline. The villagers would never have tolerated a large group of Urgals at the wedding. As it was, Nasuada had difficulty convincing them to allow her guards to remain.

With a rustle of cloth, the villagers and the Varden parted, forming a long, open path from the hill to the edge of the crowd. Then, joining their voices, the villagers began to sing the ancient wedding songs of Palancar Valley. The well-worn verses spoke of the cycle of the seasons, of the warm earth that gave birth to a new crop each year, of the spring calving, of nesting robins and spawning fish, and of how it was the destiny of the young to replace the old. One of Blödhgarm's spellcasters, a female elf with silver hair, withdrew a small gold harp from a velvet case and accompanied the villagers with notes of her own, embellishing upon the simple themes of their melodies, lending the familiar music a wistful mood.

With slow, steady steps, Roran and Katrina emerged from either side of the crowd at the far end of the path, turned toward the hill, and, without touching, began to advance toward Eragon. Roran wore a new tunic he had borrowed from one of the Varden. His hair was brushed, his beard was trimmed, and his boots were clean. His face beamed with inexpressible joy. All in all, he seemed very handsome and distinguished to Eragon. However, it was Katrina who commanded Eragon's attention. Her dress was light blue, as befitted a bride at her first wedding, of a simple cut but with a lace train that was twenty feet long and carried by two girls. Against the pale fabric, her free-flowing locks glowed like polished copper. In her hands was a posy of wildflowers. She was proud, serene, and beautiful.

Eragon heard gasps from some of the women as they beheld Katrina's train. He resolved to thank Nasuada for having Du Vrangr

Gata make the dress for Katrina, for he assumed it was she who was responsible for the gift.

Three paces behind Roran walked Horst. And at a similar distance behind Katrina walked Birgit, careful to avoid stepping on the train.

When Roran and Katrina were halfway to the hill, a pair of white doves flew out from the willow trees lining the Jiet River. The doves carried a circlet of yellow daffodils clutched in their feet. Katrina slowed and stopped as they approached her. The birds circled her three times, north to east, and then dipped down and laid the circlet upon the crown of her head before returning to the river.

"Did you arrange that?" Eragon murmured to Arya.

She smiled.

At the top of the hill, Roran and Katrina stood motionless before Eragon while they waited for the villagers to finish singing. As the final refrain faded into oblivion, Eragon raised his hands and said, "Welcome, one and all. Today we have come together to celebrate the union between the families of Roran Garrowsson and Katrina Ismirasdaughter. They are both of good reputation, and to the best of my knowledge, no one else has a claim upon their hands. If that not be the case, however, or if any other reason exists that they should not become man and wife, then make your objections known before these witnesses, that we may judge the merit of your arguments." Eragon paused for an appropriate interval, then continued. "Who here speaks for Roran Garrowsson?"

Horst stepped forward. "Roran has neither father nor uncle, so I, Horst Ostrecsson, speak for him as my blood."

"And who here speaks for Katrina Ismirasdaughter?"

Birgit stepped forward. "Katrina has neither mother nor aunt, so I, Birgit Mardrasdaughter, speak for her as my blood." Despite her vendetta against Roran, by tradition it was Birgit's right and responsibility to represent Katrina, as she had been a close friend of Katrina's mother.

"It is right and proper. What, then, does Roran Garrowsson bring to this marriage, that both he and his wife may prosper?"

"He brings his name," said Horst. "He brings his hammer. He brings the strength of his hands. And he brings the promise of a farm in Carvahall, where they may both live in peace."

Astonishment rippled through the crowd as people realized what Roran was doing: he was declaring in the most public and binding way possible that the Empire would not stop him from returning home with Katrina and providing her with the life she would have had if not for Galbatorix's murderous interference. Roran was staking his honor, as a man and a husband, on the downfall of the Empire.

"Do you accept this offer, Birgit Mardrasdaughter?" Eragon asked. Birgit nodded. "I do."

"And what does Katrina Ismirasdaughter bring to this marriage, that both she and her husband may prosper?"

344

"She brings her love and devotion, with which she shall serve Roran Garrowsson. She brings her skills at running a household. And she brings a dowry." Surprised, Eragon watched as Birgit motioned and two men who were standing next to Nasuada came forward, carrying a metal casket between them. Birgit undid the clasp to the casket, then lifted open the lid and showed Eragon the contents. He gaped as he beheld the mound of jewelry inside. "She brings with her a gold necklace studded with diamonds. She brings a brooch set with red coral from the Southern Sea and a pearl net to hold her hair. She brings five rings of gold and electrum. The first ring—" As Birgit described each item, she lifted it from the casket so all might see she spoke the truth.

Bewildered, Eragon glanced at Nasuada and noted the pleased smile she wore.

After Birgit had finished her litany and closed the casket and fastened the lock again, Eragon asked, "Do you accept this offer, Horst Ostrecsson?"

"I do."

"Thus your families become one, in accordance with the law of the land." Then, for the first time, Eragon addressed Roran and Katrina directly: "Those who speak for you have agreed upon the terms of your marriage. Roran, are you pleased with how Horst Ostrecsson has negotiated on your behalf?"

"I am."

"And, Katrina, are you pleased with how Birgit Mardrasdaughter has negotiated on your behalf?"

"I am."

"Roran Stronghammer, son of Garrow, do you swear then, by your name and by your lineage, that you shall protect and provide for Katrina Ismirasdaughter while you both yet live?"

"I, Roran Stronghammer, son of Garrow, do swear, by my name and by my lineage, that I shall protect and provide for Katrina Ismirasdaughter while we both yet live."

"Do you swear to uphold her honor, to remain steadfast and faithful to her in the years to come, and to treat her with the proper respect, dignity, and gentleness?"

"I swear I shall uphold her honor, remain steadfast and faithful to her in the years to come, and treat her with the proper respect, dignity, and gentleness."

"And do you swear to give her the keys to your holdings, such as they may be, and to your strongbox where you keep your coin, by sunset tomorrow, so she may tend to your affairs as a wife should?"

Roran swore he would.

"Katrina, daughter of Ismira, do you swear, by your name and by your lineage, that you shall serve and provide for Roran Garrowsson while you both yet live?"

"I, Katrina, daughter of Ismira, do swear, by my name and by my lineage, that I shall serve and provide for Roran Garrowsson while we both yet live."

"Do you swear to uphold his honor, to remain steadfast and faithful to him in the years to come, to bear his children while you may, and to be a caring mother for them?"

"I swear I shall uphold his honor, remain steadfast and faithful to him in the years to come, bear his children while I may, and be a caring mother for them."

"And do you swear to assume charge of his wealth and his possessions, and to manage them responsibly, so he may concentrate upon those duties that are his alone?"

Katrina swore she would.

Smiling, Eragon drew a red ribbon from his sleeve and said, "Cross your wrists." Roran and Katrina extended their left and right arms, respectively, and did as he instructed. Laying the middle of the ribbon across their wrists, Eragon wound the strip of satin three times around and then tied the ends together with a bowknot. "As is my right as a Dragon Rider, I now declare you man and wife!"

The crowd erupted into cheers. Leaning toward each other, Roran and Katrina kissed, and the crowd redoubled their cheering.

Saphira dipped her head toward the beaming couple and, as Roran and Katrina separated, she touched each of them on the brow with the tip of her snout. *Live long, and may your love deepen with every passing year*, she said.

Roran and Katrina turned toward the crowd and raised their joined arms skyward. "Let the feast begin!" Roran declared.

Eragon followed the pair as they descended from the hill and walked through the press of shouting people toward two chairs that had been set at the forefront of a row of tables. There Roran and Katrina sat, as the king and queen of their wedding.

Then the guests lined up to offer their congratulations and present gifts. Eragon was first. His grin as large as theirs, he shook Roran's free hand and inclined his head toward Katrina.

"Thank you, Eragon," Katrina said.

"Yes, thank you," Roran added.

"The honor was mine." He looked at both of them, then burst out laughing.

"What?" demanded Roran.

"You! The two of you are as happy as fools."

346

Eyes sparkling, Katrina laughed and hugged Roran. "That we are!"

Growing sober, Eragon said, "You must know how fortunate you are to be here today, together. Roran, if you had not been able to rally everyone and travel to the Burning Plains, and if the Ra'zac had taken you, Katrina, to Urû'baen, neither of you would have—"

"Yes, but I did, and they didn't," interrupted Roran. "Let us not darken this day with unpleasant thoughts about what might have been."

"That is not why I mention it." Eragon glanced at the line of people waiting behind him, making sure they were not close enough to eavesdrop. "All three of us are enemies of the Empire. And as today has demonstrated, we are not safe, even here among the Varden. If Galbatorix can, he will strike at any one of us, including you, Katrina, in order to hurt the others. So I made these for you." From the pouch at his belt, Eragon withdrew two plain gold rings, polished until they shone. The previous night, he had molded them out of the last of the gold orbs he had extracted from the earth. He handed the larger one to Roran and the smaller one to Katrina.

Roran turned his ring, examining it, then held it up against the sky, squinting at the glyphs in the ancient language carved into the inside of the band. "It's very nice, but how can these help protect us?"

"I enchanted them to do three things," said Eragon. "If you ever need my help, or Saphira's, twist the ring once around your finger and say, 'Help me, Shadeslayer; help me, Brightscales,' and we will hear you, and we will come as fast as we can. Also, if either of you is close to death, your ring will alert us and you, Roran, or you, Katrina, depending on who is in peril. And so long as the rings are touching your skin, you will always know how to find each other, no matter how far apart you may be." He hesitated, then added, "I hope you will agree to wear them."

"Of course we will," said Katrina.

Roran's chest swelled, and his voice became husky. "Thank you," he said. "Thank you. I wish we had had these before she and I were separated in Carvahall."

Since they only had one free hand apiece, Katrina slid Roran's ring on for him, placing it on the third finger of his right hand, and he slid Katrina's on for her, placing it on the third finger of her left hand.

"I have another gift for you as well," said Eragon. Turning, he whistled and waved. Pushing his way through the crowd, a groom hurried toward them, leading Snowfire by the bridle. The groom handed Eragon the reins to the stallion, then bowed and withdrew. Eragon said, "Roran, you will need a good steed. This is Snowfire. He was Brom's to begin with, then mine, and now I am giving him to you."

Roran ran his eyes over Snowfire. "He's a magnificent beast."

"The finest. Will you accept him?"

"With pleasure."

Eragon summoned back the groom and returned Snowfire to his care, instructing him that Roran was the stallion's new owner. As the man and horse left, Eragon looked at the people in line who were carrying presents for Roran and Katrina. Laughing, he said, "The two of you may have been poor this morning, but you'll be rich by this evening. If Saphira and I ever have a chance to settle down, we'll have to come live with you in the giant hall you will build for all of your children."

"Whatever we build, it will hardly be large enough for Saphira, I think," said Roran.

"But you will always be welcome with us," said Katrina. "Both of you."

After congratulating them once more, Eragon ensconced himself at the end of a table and amused himself by throwing scraps of roast chicken toward Saphira and watching her snap them out of the air. He remained there until Nasuada had spoken with Roran and Katrina, handing them something small he could not see. Then he intercepted Nasuada as she was departing the festivities.

"What is it, Eragon?" she asked. "I cannot linger."

"Was it you who gave Katrina her dress and her dowry?"

"Aye. Do you disapprove?"

"I am grateful you were so kind to my family, but I wonder . . ."

"Yes?"

"Isn't the Varden desperate for gold?"

"We are," Nasuada said, "but not so desperate as before. Since my scheme with the lace, and since I triumphed in the Trial of the Long Knives and the wandering tribes swore absolute fealty to me and granted me access to their riches, we are less likely to starve to death and more likely to die because we don't have a shield or a spear." Her lips twitched in a smile. "What I gave Katrina is insignificant compared with the vast sums this army requires to function. And I do not believe I have squandered my gold. Rather, I believe I have made a valuable purchase. I have purchased prestige and self-respect for Katrina, and by extension, I have purchased Roran's goodwill. I may be overly optimistic, but I suspect his loyalty will prove far more valuable than a hundred shields or a hundred spears."

"You are always seeking to improve the Varden's prospects, aren't you?" Eragon said.

"Always. As you should be." Nasuada started to walk away from him, then returned and said, "Sometime before sunset, come to my pavilion, and we will visit the men who were wounded today. There are many we cannot heal, you know. It will do them good to see that we care about their welfare and that we appreciate their sacrifice."

Eragon nodded. "I will be there."

"Good."

Hours passed as Eragon laughed and ate and drank and traded stories with old friends. Mead flowed like water, and the wedding feast became ever more boisterous. Clearing a space between the tables, the men tested their prowess against one another with feats of wrestling and archery and bouts with quarterstaves. Two of the elves, a man and a woman, demonstrated their skill with swordplay—awing the onlookers with the speed and grace of their dancing blades—and even Arya consented to perform a song, which sent shivers down Eragon's spine.

Throughout, Roran and Katrina said little, preferring to sit and gaze at each other, oblivious to their surroundings.

When the bottom of the orange sun touched the distant horizon, however, Eragon reluctantly excused himself. With Saphira by his side, he left the sounds of revelry behind and walked to Nasuada's pavilion, breathing deeply of the cool evening air to clear his head. Nasuada was waiting for him in front of her red command tent, the Nighthawks gathered close around. Without saying a word, she, Eragon, and Saphira made their way across the camp to the tents of the healers, where the injured warriors lay.

For over an hour, Nasuada and Eragon visited with the men who had lost their limbs or their eyes or had contracted an incurable infection in the course of fighting the Empire. Some of the warriors had been injured that morning. Others, as Eragon discovered, had been wounded on the Burning Plains and had yet to recover, despite all the herbs and spells lavished upon them. Before they had set forth among the rows of blanket-covered men, Nasuada had warned Eragon not to tire himself further by attempting to heal everyone he met, but he could not help muttering a spell here and there to ease pain or to drain an abscess or to reshape a broken bone or to remove an unsightly scar.

One of the men Eragon met had lost his left leg below the knee, as well as two fingers on his right hand. His beard was short and gray, and his eyes were covered with a strip of black cloth. When Eragon greeted him and asked how he fared, the man reached out and grasped Eragon by the elbow with the three fingers of his right hand. In a hoarse voice, the man said, "Ah, Shadeslayer. I knew you would come. I have been waiting for you ever since the light."

"What do you mean?"

"The light that illuminated the flesh of the world. In a single instant, I saw every living thing around me, from the largest to the smallest. I saw my bones shining through my arms. I saw the worms in the earth and the gore-crows in the sky and the mites on the wings of the crows. The gods have touched me, Shadeslayer. They gave me this vision for a reason. I saw you on the field of battle, you and your dragon, and you were like a blazing sun among a forest of dim candles. And I saw your brother, your brother and his dragon, and they too were like a sun."

The nape of Eragon's neck prickled as he listened. "I have no brother," he said.

The maimed swordsman cackled. "You cannot fool me, Shade-slayer. I know better. The world burns around me, and from the fire, I hear the whisper of minds, and I learn things from the whispers. You hide yourself from me now, but I can still see you, a man of yellow flame with twelve stars floating around your waist and another star, brighter than the others, upon your right hand."

Eragon pressed his palm against the belt of Beloth the Wise, checking that the twelve diamonds sewn within were still concealed. They were.

"Listen to me, Shadeslayer," whispered the man, pulling Eragon toward his lined face. "I saw your brother, and he burned. But he did not burn like you. Oh no. The light from his soul shone *through* him, as if it came from somewhere else. He, *he* was a void, a shape of a man. And through that shape came the brilliance that burned. Do you understand? *Others* illuminated him."

"Where were these others? Did you see them as well?"

The warrior hesitated. "I could feel them close at hand, raging at the world as if they hated everything in it, but their bodies were hidden from my sight. They were there and not there. I cannot explain better than that. . . . I would not want to get any closer to those creatures, Shadeslayer. They aren't human, of that I'm sure, and their hate, it was like the largest thunderstorm you've ever seen crammed into a tiny glass bottle."

"And when the bottle breaks . . . ," Eragon murmured.

"Exactly, Shadeslayer. Sometimes I wonder if Galbatorix has managed to capture the gods themselves and make them his slaves, but then I laugh and call myself a fool."

"Whose gods, though? The dwarves'? Those of the wandering tribes?"

"Does it matter, Shadeslayer? A god is a god, regardless of where he comes from."

Eragon grunted. "Perhaps you're right."

As he left the man's pallet, one of the healers pulled Eragon aside. She said, "Forgive him, my Lord. The shock of his wounds has driven him quite mad. He's always ranting about suns and stars and glowing lights he claims to see. Sometimes it seems as if he knows things he shouldn't, but don't you be deceived, he gets them from the other patients. They gossip all the time, you know. It's all they have to do, poor things."

"I am not a lord," Eragon said, "and he is not mad. I'm not sure what he is, but he has an uncommon ability. If he gets better or worse, please inform one of Du Vrangr Gata."

The healer curtsied. "As you wish, Shadeslayer. I'm sorry for my mistake, Shadeslayer."

"How was he hurt?"

"A soldier cut off his fingers when he tried to block a sword with his hand. Later, one of the missiles from the Empire's catapults landed upon his leg, crushing it beyond repair. We had to amputate. The men who were beside him said that when the missile struck, he immediately began screaming about the light, and when they picked him up, they noticed that his eyes had turned pure white. Even his pupils have disappeared."

"Ah. You have been most helpful. Thank you."

It was dark when Eragon and Nasuada finally left the healers' tents. Nasuada sighed and said, "Now I could use a mug of mead." Eragon nodded, staring down between his feet. They started back to her pavilion, and after a while, she asked, "What are you thinking, Eragon?"

"That we live in a strange world, and I'll be lucky if I ever understand more than a small portion of it." Then he recounted his conversation with the man, which she found as interesting as he had.

"You should tell Arya about this," said Nasuada. "She might know what these 'others' could be."

They parted at her pavilion, Nasuada going inside to finish reading a report, while Eragon and Saphira continued on to Eragon's tent. There Saphira curled up on the ground and prepared to sleep as Eragon sat next to her and gazed at the stars, a parade of wounded men marching before his eyes.

What many of them had told him continued to reverberate through his mind: *We fought for you, Shadeslayer.*

✦ ✦ ✦

WHISPERS IN THE NIGHT

Roran opened his eyes and stared at the drooping canvas overhead.

A thin gray light pervaded the tent, leaching objects of their color, rendering everything a pale shadow of its daylight self. He shivered. The blankets had slid down to his waist, exposing his torso to the cold night air. As he pulled them back up, he noticed that Katrina was no longer by his side.

He saw her sitting by the entrance to the tent, staring up at the sky. She had a cloak wrapped over her shift. Her hair fell to the small of her back, a dark tangled bramble.

A lump formed in Roran's throat as he studied her.

Dragging the blankets with him, he sat beside her. He placed an arm around her shoulders, and she leaned against him, her head and neck warm against his chest. He kissed her on the brow. For a long while, he contemplated the glimmering stars with her and listened to the regular pattern of her breathing, the only sound besides his own in the sleeping world.

Then she whispered, "The constellations are shaped differently here. Have you noticed?"

"Aye." He shifted his arm, fitting it against the curve of her waist and feeling the slight bulge of her growing belly. "What woke you?"

She shivered. "I was thinking."

"Oh."

Starlight gleamed in her eyes as she twisted in his arms and gazed at him. "I was thinking about you and us . . . and our future together."

"Those are heavy thoughts for so late at night."

"Now that we are married, how do you plan to care for me and for our child?"

"Is that what worries you?" He smiled. "You won't starve; we have gold enough to assure that. Besides, the Varden will always see to it that Eragon's cousins have food and shelter. Even if something were to happen to me, they would continue to provide for you and the baby."

"Yes, but what do you intend to *do*?"

Puzzled, he searched her face for the source of her agitation. "I am going to help Eragon end this war so we can return to Palancar Valley and settle down without fear of soldiers dragging us off to Urû'baen. What else would I do?"

"You will fight with the Varden, then?"

"You know I will."

"As you would have fought today if Nasuada had let you?"

"Yes."

"What of our baby, though? An army on the march is no place to raise a child."

"We cannot run away and hide from the Empire, Katrina. Unless the Varden win, Galbatorix will find and kill us, or he will find and kill our children, or our children's children. And I do not think the Varden will achieve victory unless everyone does their utmost to help them."

She placed a finger over his lips. "You are my only love. No other man shall ever capture my heart. I will do everything I can to lighten your burden. I will cook your meals, mend your clothes, and clean your armor. . . . But once I give birth, I will leave this army."

"Leave!" He went rigid. "That's nonsense! Where would you go?"

"Dauth, perhaps. Remember, Lady Alarice offered us sanctuary, and some of our people are still there. I would not be alone."

"If you think I'm going to let you and our newborn child go tramping across Alagaësia by yourselves, then—"

"You don't need to shout."

"I'm not—"

"Yes, you are." Clasping his hand between hers and pressing it against her heart, she said, "It's not safe here. If it were only the two of us, I could accept the danger, but not when it is our baby who might die. I love you, Roran, I love you so much, but our child has to come before anything we want for ourselves. Otherwise, we do not deserve to be called parents." Tears shone in her eyes, and he felt his own eyes dampen. "It was you, after all, who convinced me to leave Carvahall and hide in the Spine when the soldiers attacked. This is no different."

The stars swam before Roran as his vision blurred. "I would rather lose an arm than be parted from you again."

Katrina began to cry then, her quiet sobs shaking his body. "I don't want to leave you either."

He tightened his embrace and rocked back and forth with her. When her weeping subsided, he whispered in her ear, "I would rather lose an arm than be parted from you, but I would rather die than allow anyone to hurt you . . . or our child. If you are going to leave, you should leave now, while it's still easy for you to travel."

She shook her head. "No. I want Gertrude as my midwife. She's the only one I trust. Besides, if I have any difficulty, I would rather be here, where there are magicians trained in healing."

"Nothing will go wrong," he said. "As soon as our child is born, you will go to Aberon, not Dauth; it is less likely to be attacked. And if Aberon becomes too dangerous, then you will go to the Beor Mountains and live with the dwarves. And if Galbatorix strikes at the dwarves, then you will go to the elves in Du Weldenvarden."

"And if Galbatorix attacks Du Weldenvarden, I will fly to the moon and raise our child among the spirits who inhabit the heavens."

"And they will bow down to you and make you their queen, as you deserve."

She snuggled closer to him.

Together, they sat and watched as, one by one, the stars vanished from the sky, obscured by the glow spreading in the east. When only the morning star remained, Roran said, "You know what this means, don't you?"

"What?"

"I'll just have to ensure we kill every last one of Galbatorix's soldiers, capture all the cities in the Empire, defeat Murtagh and Thorn, and behead Galbatorix and his turncoat dragon before your time comes. That way, there will be no need for you to go away."

She was silent for a moment, then said, "If you could, I would be very happy."

They were about to return to their cot when, out of the glimmering sky, there sailed a miniature ship, woven of dry strips of grass. The ship hovered in front of their tent, rocking upon invisible waves of air, and almost seemed to be looking at them with its dragon-head-shaped prow.

Roran froze, as did Katrina.

Like a living creature, the ship darted across the path before their tent, then it swooped up and around, chasing an errant moth. When the moth escaped, the ship glided back toward the tent, stopping only inches from Katrina's face.

Before Roran could decide if he should snatch the ship out of the air, it turned and flew off toward the morning star, vanishing once more into the endless ocean of the sky, leaving them to gaze after it in wonder.

✦ ✦ ✦

ORDERS

L ate that night, visions of death and violence gathered along the edges of Eragon's dreams, threatening to overwhelm him with panic. He stirred with unease, wanting to break free but unable to do so. Brief, disjointed images of stabbing swords and screaming men and Murtagh's angry face flashed before his eyes.

Then Eragon felt Saphira enter his mind. She swept through his dreams like a great wind, brushing aside his looming nightmare. In the silence that followed, she whispered, *All is well, little one. Rest easy; you are safe, and I am with you. . . . Rest easy.*

A sense of profound peace crept over Eragon. He rolled over and drifted off into happier memories, comforted by his awareness of Saphira's presence.

When Eragon opened his eyes, an hour before sunrise, he found himself lying underneath one of Saphira's vein-webbed wings. She had her tail wrapped around him, and her side was warm against his head. He smiled and crawled out from under her wing even as she lifted her head and yawned.

Good morning, he said.

She yawned again and stretched like a cat.

Eragon bathed, shaved with magic, cleaned the falchion's scabbard of dried blood from the previous day, and then dressed in one of his elf tunics.

Once he was satisfied he was presentable, and Saphira had finished her tongue bath, they walked to Nasuada's pavilion. All six of the current shift of Nighthawks were standing outside, their seamed faces set into their usual grim expressions. Eragon waited while a stocky dwarf announced them. Then he entered the tent, and Saphira crawled around to the open panel where she could insert her head and participate in the discussion.

Eragon bowed to Nasuada where she sat in her high-backed chair carved with blooming thistles. "My Lady, you asked me to come here to talk about my future; you said you had a most important mission for me."

"I did, and I do," said Nasuada. "Please, be seated." She indicated a folding chair next to Eragon. Tilting the sword at his waist so it would not catch, he settled into the chair. "As you know, Galbatorix has sent battalions to the cities of Aroughs, Feinster, and Belatona in an attempt to prevent us from taking them by siege or, failing that, to slow our progress and force us to divide our own troops so we would be more vulnerable to the depredations of the soldiers who were camped north of us. After yesterday's battle, our scouts reported that the last of Galbatorix's men withdrew to parts unknown. I was going to strike at those soldiers days ago, but I had to refrain since you were absent. Without you, Murtagh and Thorn could have slaughtered our warriors with impunity, and we had no way of discovering whether the two of them were among the soldiers. Now that you are with us again, our position is somewhat improved, although not as much as I had hoped, given that we must now also contend with Galbatorix's latest artifice, these men without pain. Our only encouragement is that the two of you, along with Islanzadí's spellcasters, have proved you can fend off Murtagh and Thorn. Upon that hope depends our plan for victory."

That red runt is no match for me, said Saphira. *If he did not have Murtagh protecting him, I would trap him against the ground and shake him by the neck until he submitted to me and acknowledged me as leader of the hunt.*

"I am sure you would," said Nasuada, smiling.

Eragon asked, "What course of action have you decided upon, then?"

"I have decided upon several courses, and we must undertake

them all simultaneously if any are to be successful. First, we cannot push farther into the Empire, leaving cities behind us that Galbatorix still controls. To do that would be to expose ourselves to attacks from both the front and the rear and to invite Galbatorix to invade and seize Surda while we were absent. So I have already ordered the Varden to march north, to the nearest place where we can safely cross the Jiet River. Once we are on the other side of the river, I will send warriors south to capture Aroughs while King Orrin and I continue with the remainder of our forces to Feinster, which, with your help and Saphira's, should fall before us without too much trouble.

"While we are engaged in the tedious business of tramping across the countryside, I have other responsibilities for you, Eragon." She leaned forward in her seat. "We need the full help of the dwarves. The elves are fighting for us in the north of Alagaësia, the Surdans have joined with us body and mind, and even the Urgals have allied themselves with us. But we need the dwarves. We cannot succeed without them. Especially now that we must contend with soldiers who cannot feel pain."

"Have the dwarves chosen a new king or queen yet?"

Nasuada grimaced. "Narheim assures me that the process is moving apace, but like the elves, dwarves take a longer view of time than we do. *Apace* for them might mean months of deliberations."

"Don't they realize the urgency of the situation?"

"Some do, but many oppose helping us in this war, and they seek to delay the proceedings as long as possible and to install one of their own upon the marble throne in Tronjheim. The dwarves have lived in hiding for so long, they have become dangerously suspicious of outsiders. If someone hostile to our aims wins the throne, we shall lose the dwarves. We cannot allow that to happen. Nor can we wait for the dwarves to resolve their differences at their usual pace. *But*"—she raised a finger—"from so far away, I cannot effectively intervene in their politics. Even if I were in Tronjheim, I could not ensure a favorable outcome; the dwarves do not take kindly to anyone who is not of their clans meddling in their government. So I want you, Eragon, to travel to Tronjheim in my stead and do what you can to ensure that the dwarves choose a new monarch in an expeditious manner—and that they choose a monarch who is sympathetic to our cause."

"Me! But—"

"King Hrothgar adopted you into Dûrgrimst Ingeitum. According to their laws and customs, you *are* a dwarf, Eragon. You have a legal right to participate in the hallmeets of the Ingeitum, and as Orik is set to become their chief, and as he is your foster brother and a friend of the Varden's, I am sure he will agree to let you accompany him into the secret councils of the thirteen clans where they elect their rulers."

Her proposal seemed preposterous to Eragon. "What about Murtagh and Thorn? When they return, as they surely will, Saphira and I are the only ones who can hold our own against them, albeit with some assistance. If we are not here, no one will be able to stop them from killing you or Arya or Orrin or the rest of the Varden."

The gap between Nasuada's eyebrows narrowed. "You dealt Murtagh a stinging defeat yesterday. Most likely, he and Thorn are winging their way back to Urû'baen even as we speak so Galbatorix may interrogate them about the battle and chastise them for their failure. He will not send them to attack us again until he is confident that they can overwhelm you. Murtagh is surely uncertain about the true limits of your strength now, so that unhappy event may yet be some while off. Between now and then, I believe you will have enough time to travel back and forth between Farthen Dûr."

"You could be wrong," argued Eragon. "Besides, how would you keep Galbatorix from learning about our absence and attacking while we are gone? I doubt you have found all of the spies he has seeded among us."

Nasuada tapped her fingers on the arms of her chair. "I said I wanted you to go to Farthen Dûr, Eragon. I did not say I wanted Saphira to go as well." Turning her head, Saphira released a small puff of smoke that drifted toward the peak of the tent.

"I'm not about to—"

"Let me finish, please, Eragon."

He clamped shut his jaw and glared at her, his left hand tight around the pommel of the falchion.

"You are not beholden to me, Saphira, but my hope is that you will agree to stay here while Eragon journeys to the dwarves so that we can deceive the Empire and the Varden as to Eragon's whereabouts. If we can hide your departure"—she gestured at Eragon—"from the masses, no one will have any reason to suspect you are not still here. We will only have to devise a suitable excuse, then, to account for your sudden desire to remain in your tent during the day—perhaps that you and Saphira are flying sorties into enemy territory at night and so must rest while the sun is up.

"In order for the ruse to work, however, Blödhgarm and his companions will have to stay here as well, both to avoid arousing suspicion and for reasons of defense. If Murtagh and Thorn reappear while you are gone, Arya can take your place on Saphira. Between her, Blödhgarm's spellcasters, and the magicians of Du Vrangr Gata, we should have a fair chance of thwarting Murtagh."

In a harsh voice, Eragon said, "If Saphira doesn't fly me to Farthen Dûr, then how am I supposed to travel there in a timely fashion?"

"By running. You told me yourself you ran much of the distance from Helgrind. I expect that without having to hide from soldiers or peasants you can traverse many more leagues each day on the way to Farthen Dûr than you were able to in the Empire." Again Nasuada drummed the polished wood of her chair. "Of course, it would be foolish to go alone. Even a powerful magician can die of a simple accident in the far reaches of the wilderness if he has no one to help him. Shepherding you through the Beor Mountains would be a waste of Arya's talents, and people would notice if one of Blödhgarm's elves disappeared without explanation. Therefore, I have decided that a Kull should accompany you, as they are the only other creatures capable of matching your pace."

"A Kull!" exclaimed Eragon, unable to contain himself any longer. "You would send me among the dwarves with a Kull by my side? I cannot think of any race the dwarves hate more than the Urgals. They make bows out of their horns! If I walked into Farthen Dûr with an Urgal, the dwarves would not pay heed to anything I had to say."

"I am well aware of that," said Nasuada. "Which is why you will not go directly to Farthen Dûr. Instead, you will first stop at Bregan Hold on Mount Thardûr, which is the ancestral home of the Ingeitum. There you will find Orik, and there you can leave the Kull while you continue on to Farthen Dûr in Orik's company."

Staring somewhat beyond Nasuada, Eragon said, "And what if I do not agree with the path you have chosen? What if I believe there are other, safer ways to accomplish what you desire?"

"What ways would those be, pray tell?" asked Nasuada, her fingers pausing in midair.

"I would have to think about it, but I am sure they exist."

"I *have* thought about it, Eragon, and at great length. Having you act as my emissary is our only hope of influencing the succession of the dwarves. I was raised among dwarves, remember, and I have a better understanding of them than most humans."

"I still believe it's a mistake," he growled. "Send Jörmundur instead, or one of your other commanders. I won't go, not while—"

"You *won't?*" said Nasuada, her voice rising. "A vassal who disobeys his lord is no better than a warrior who ignores his captain on the field of battle and may be punished similarly. As your liegelord, then, Eragon, I order you to run to Farthen Dûr, whether you want to or not, and to oversee the choosing of the next ruler of the dwarves."

Furious, Eragon breathed heavily through his nose, gripping and regripping the pommel of his falchion.

In a softer, although still guarded, tone, Nasuada said, "What will it be, Eragon? Will you do as I ask, or will you dispossess me and lead the Varden yourself? Those are your only options."

Shocked, he said, "No, I can reason with you. I can convince you otherwise."

"You cannot, because you cannot provide me with an alternative that is as likely to succeed."

He met her gaze. "I could refuse your order and let you punish me however you deem fit."

His suggestion startled her. Then she said, "To see you lashed to a whipping post would do irreparable harm to the Varden. And it would destroy my authority, for people would know you could defy me whenever you wanted, with the only consequence being a handful of stripes that you could heal an instant later, for we cannot execute you, as we would any other warrior who disobeyed a superior. I would rather abdicate my post and grant you command of the Varden than allow such a thing to occur. If you believe you are better suited for the task, then take my position, take my chair, and declare yourself master of this army! But so long as I speak for the Varden, I have the right to make these decisions. If they be mistakes, then that is my responsibility as well."

"Will you listen to no advice?" Eragon asked, troubled. "Will you dictate the course of the Varden regardless of what those around you counsel?"

Nasuada's middle fingernail clacked against the polished wood of her chair. "I do listen to advice. I listen to a continuous stream of advice every waking hour of my life, but sometimes my conclusions do not match those of my underlings. Now, you must decide whether you will uphold your oath of fealty and abide by my decision, even though you may not agree with it, or if you will set yourself up as a mirror image of Galbatorix."

"I only want what is best for the Varden," he said.

"As do I."

"You leave me no choice but one I dislike."

"Sometimes it is harder to follow than it is to lead."

"May I have a moment to think?"

"You may."

Saphira? he asked.

Flecks of purple light danced around the interior of the pavilion as she twisted her neck and fixed her eyes upon Eragon's. *Little one?*

Should I go?

I think you must.

He pressed his lips together in a rigid line. *And what of you?*

You know I hate to be separated from you, but Nasuada's arguments are well reasoned. If I can help keep Murtagh and Thorn away by remaining with the Varden, then perhaps I should.

His emotions and hers washed between their minds, tidal surges in a shared pool of anger, anticipation, reluctance, and tenderness. From him flowed the anger and reluctance; from her other, gentler sentiments—as rich in scope as his own—that moderated his choleric passion and lent him perspectives he would not otherwise have. Nevertheless, he clung with stubborn insistence to his opposition to Nasuada's scheme. *If you flew me to Farthen Dûr, I would not be gone for as long, meaning Galbatorix would have less of an opportunity to mount a new assault.*

But his spies would tell him the Varden were vulnerable the moment we left.

I do not want to part with you again so soon after Helgrind.

Our own desires cannot take precedence over the needs of the Varden, but no, I do not want to part with you either. Still, remember what Oromis said, that the prowess of a dragon and Rider is measured not only by how well they work together but also by how well they can function when apart. We are both mature enough to operate independently of each other, Eragon, however much we may dislike the prospect. You proved that yourself during your trip from Helgrind.

Would it bother you fighting with Arya on your back, as Nasuada mentioned?

Her I would mind least of all. We have fought together before, and it was she who ferried me across Alagaësia for nigh on twenty years when I was in my egg. You know that, little one. Why pose this question? Are you jealous?

What if I am?

An amused twinkle lit her sapphire eyes. She flicked her tongue at him. *Then it is very sweet of you. . . . Would you I should stay or go?*

It is your choice to make, not mine.

But it affects us both.

Eragon dug at the ground with the tip of his boot. Then he said, *If we must participate in this mad scheme, we should do everything we can to help it succeed. Stay, and see if you can keep Nasuada from losing her head over this thrice-blasted plan of hers.*

Be of good cheer, little one. Run fast, and we shall be reunited in short order.

Eragon looked up at Nasuada. "Very well," he said, "I will go."

Nasuada's posture relaxed somewhat. "Thank you. And you, Saphira? Will you stay or go?"

Projecting her thoughts to include Nasuada as well as Eragon, Saphira said, *I will stay, Nightstalker.*

Nasuada inclined her head. "Thank you, Saphira. I am most grateful for your support."

"Have you spoken to Blödhgarm of this?" asked Eragon. "Has he agreed to it?"

"No, I assumed you would inform him of the details."

Eragon doubted the elves would be pleased by the prospect of him traveling to Farthen Dûr with only an Urgal for company. He said, "If I might make a suggestion?"

"You know I welcome your suggestions."

That stopped him for a moment. "A suggestion and a request, then." Nasuada lifted a finger, motioning for him to continue. "When the dwarves have chosen their new king or queen, Saphira should join me in Farthen Dûr, both to honor the dwarves' new ruler and to fulfill the promise she made to King Hrothgar after the battle for Tronjheim."

Nasuada's expression sharpened into that of a hunting wildcat. "What promise was this?" she asked. "You have not told me of this before."

"That Saphira would mend the star sapphire, Isidar Mithrim, as recompense for Arya breaking it."

Her eyes wide with astonishment, Nasuada looked at Saphira and said, "You are capable of such a feat?"

I am, but I do not know if I will be able to summon the magic I will need when I am standing before Isidar Mithrim. My ability to cast spells is not subject to my own desires. At times, it is as if I have gained a new sense and I can feel the pulse of energy within my own flesh, and by directing it with my will, I can reshape the world as I wish. The rest of my life, however, I can no more cast a spell than a fish can fly. If I could mend Isidar Mithrim, though, it would go a long way toward earning us the goodwill of all the dwarves, not just a select few who have the breadth of knowledge to appreciate the importance of their cooperation with us.

"It would do more than you imagine," said Nasuada. "The star sapphire holds a special place in the hearts of dwarves. Every dwarf has a love of gemstones, but Isidar Mithrim they love and cherish above all others, because of its beauty, and most of all because of its immense size. Restore it to its previous glory and you will restore the pride of their race."

Eragon said, "Even if Saphira failed to repair Isidar Mithrim, she should be present for the coronation of the dwarves' new ruler. You could conceal her absence for a few days by letting it be known among the Varden that she and I have left on a brief trip to Aberon, or some such. By the time Galbatorix's spies realized you had deceived them, it would be too late for the Empire to organize an attack before we returned."

Nasuada nodded. "It is a good idea. Contact me as soon as the dwarves set a date for the coronation."

"I shall."

"You have made your suggestion, now out with your request. What is it you wish of me?"

"Since you insist I must make this trip, with your permission, I would like to fly with Saphira from Tronjheim to Ellesméra, after the coronation."

"For what purpose?"

"To consult with the ones who taught us during our last visit to Du Weldenvarden. We promised them that as soon as events allowed, we would return to Ellesméra to complete our training."

The line between Nasuada's eyebrows deepened. "There is not the time for you to spend weeks or months in Ellesméra continuing your education."

"No, but perhaps we have the time for a brief visit."

Nasuada leaned her head against the back of her carved chair and gazed down at Eragon from underneath heavy lids. "And who exactly are your teachers? I have noticed you always evade direct questions about them. Who was it that taught the two of you in Ellesméra, Eragon?"

Fingering his ring, Aren, Eragon said, "We swore an oath to Islanzadí that we would not reveal their identity without permission from her, Arya, or whoever may succeed Islanzadí to her throne."

"By all the demons above and below, how many oaths have you and Saphira sworn?" demanded Nasuada. "You seem to bind yourself to everyone you meet."

Feeling somewhat sheepish, Eragon shrugged and had opened his mouth to speak when Saphira said to Nasuada, *We do not seek them out, but how can we avoid pledging ourselves when we cannot topple Galbatorix and the Empire without the support of every race in Alagaësia? Oaths are the price we pay for winning the aid of those in power.*

"Mmh," said Nasuada. "So I must ask Arya for the truth of the matter?"

"Aye, but I doubt she will tell you; the elves consider the identity of our teachers to be one of their most precious secrets. They will not risk sharing it unless absolutely necessary, to keep word of it from reaching Galbatorix." Eragon stared at the royal-blue gemstone set in his ring, wondering how much more information his oath and his honor would allow him to divulge, then said, "Know this, though: we are not so alone as we once assumed."

Nasuada's expression sharpened. "I see. That is good to know, Eragon. . . . I only wish the elves were more forthcoming with me." After pursing her lips for a brief moment, Nasuada continued. "Why must you travel all the way to Ellesméra? Have you no means to communicate with your tutors directly?"

Eragon spread his hands in a gesture of helplessness. "If only we could. Alas, the spell has yet to be invented that can broach the wards that encircle Du Weldenvarden."

"The elves did not even leave an opening they themselves can exploit?"

"If they had, Arya would have contacted Queen Islanzadí as soon as she was revived in Farthen Dûr, rather than physically going to Du Weldenvarden."

"I suppose you are right. But then how was it you were able to consult Islanzadí about Sloan's fate? You implied that when you spoke with her, the elves' army was still situated within Du Weldenvarden."

"They were," he said, "but only in the fringe, beyond the protective measures of the wards."

The silence between them was palpable as Nasuada considered his request. Outside the tent, Eragon heard the Nighthawks arguing among themselves about whether a bill or a halberd was better suited for fighting large numbers of men on foot and, beyond them, the creak of a passing oxcart, the jangle of armor on men trotting in the opposite direction, and hundreds of other indistinct sounds that drifted through the camp.

When Nasuada spoke, she said, "What exactly do you hope to gain from such a visit?"

"I don't know!" growled Eragon. He struck the pommel of the

falchion with his fist. "And that's the heart of the problem: we don't know enough. It might accomplish nothing, but on the other hand, we might learn something that could help us vanquish Murtagh and Galbatorix once and for all. We barely won yesterday, Nasuada. Barely! And I fear that when we again face Thorn and Murtagh, Murtagh will be even stronger than before, and frost coats my bones when I consider the fact that Galbatorix's abilities far exceed Murtagh's, despite the vast amount of power he has already bestowed upon my *brother*. The elf who taught me, he . . ." Eragon hesitated, considering the wisdom of what he was about to say, then forged onward: "He hinted that he knows how it is Galbatorix's strength has been increasing every year, but he refused to reveal more at the time because we were not advanced enough in our training. Now, after our encounters with Thorn and Murtagh, I think he will share his knowledge with us. Moreover, there are entire branches of magic we have yet to explore, and any one of them might provide the means to defeat Galbatorix. If we are going to gamble upon this trip, Nasuada, then let us not gamble to maintain our current position; let us gamble to increase our standing and so win this game of chance."

Nasuada sat motionless for over a minute. "I cannot make this decision until after the dwarves hold their coronation. Whether you go to Du Weldenvarden will depend on the movements of the Empire then and on what our spies report about Murtagh and Thorn's activities."

Over the course of the next two hours, Nasuada instructed Eragon about the thirteen dwarf clans. She schooled him in their history and their politics; in the products upon which each clan based the majority of its trade; in the names, families, and personalities of the clan chiefs; in the list of important tunnels excavated and controlled by each clan; and in what she felt would be the best way to coax the dwarves to elect a king or queen friendly to the goals of the Varden.

"Ideally, Orik would be the one to take the throne," she said.

"King Hrothgar was highly regarded by most of his subjects, and Dûrgrimst Ingeitum remains one of the richest and most influential of clans, all of which is to Orik's benefit. Orik is devoted to our cause. He has served as one of the Varden, you and I both count him as a friend, and he is your foster brother. I believe he has the skills to become an excellent king for the dwarves." Amusement kindled in her expression. "Small matter, that. However, he is young by the standards of the dwarves, and his association with us may prove to be an insurmountable barrier for the other clan chiefs. Another obstacle is that the other great clans—Dûrgrimst Feldûnost and Dûrgrimst Knurlcarathn, to name but two—are eager, after over a hundred years of rule by the Ingeitum, to see the crown go to a different clan. By all means, support Orik if it can help him onto the throne, but if it becomes obvious that his attempt is doomed and your backing could guarantee the success of another clan chief who favors the Varden, then transfer your support, even if doing so will offend Orik. You cannot allow friendship to interfere with politics, not now."

371

When Nasuada finished her lecture on the dwarf clans, she, Eragon, and Saphira spent several minutes figuring out how Eragon could slip out of the camp without being noticed. After they had finally hammered out the details of the plan, Eragon and Saphira returned to their tent and told Blödhgarm what they had decided.

To Eragon's surprise, the fur-covered elf did not object. Curious, Eragon asked, "Do you approve?"

"It is not my place to say whether I approve or not," Blödhgarm replied, his voice a low purr. "But since Nasuada's stratagem does not seem to put either of you in unreasonable danger, and by means of this you may have the opportunity to further your learning in Ellesméra, neither I nor my brethren shall object." He inclined his head. "If you will excuse me, Bjartskular, Argetlam." Skirting Saphira, the elf exited the tent, allowing a bright flash of light to pierce the darkness inside as he pushed aside the entrance flap.

For a handful of minutes, Eragon and Saphira sat in silence, then

Eragon put his hand on the top of her head. *Say what you will, I will miss you.*

And I you, little one.

Be careful. If anything happened to you, I would . . .

And you as well.

He sighed. *We've been together only a few days, and already we must part again. I find it hard to forgive Nasuada for that.*

Do not condemn her for doing what she must.

No, but it leaves a bitter taste in my mouth.

Move swiftly then, so I may soon join you in Farthen Dûr.

I wouldn't mind being so far away from you if only I could still touch your mind. That's the worst part of it: the horrible sense of emptiness. We dare not even speak to each other through the mirror in Nasuada's tent, for people would wonder why you kept visiting her without me.

Saphira blinked and flicked out her tongue, and he sensed a strange shift in her emotions.

What? he asked.

I . . . She blinked again. *I agree. I wish we could remain in mental contact when we were at great distances from each other. It would reduce our worry and trouble and would allow us to confound the Empire more easily.* She hummed with satisfaction as he sat next to her and began to scratch the small scales behind the corner of her jaw.

FOOTPRINTS OF SHADOW

With a series of giddy leaps, Saphira carried Eragon through the camp to Roran and Katrina's tent. Outside the tent, Katrina was washing a shift in a bucket of soapy water, scrubbing the white fabric against a board of ridged wood. She lifted a hand to shield her eyes as a cloud of dust from Saphira's landing drifted over her.

Roran stepped out of the tent, buckling on his belt. He coughed and squinted in the dust. "What brings you here?" he asked as Eragon dismounted.

Speaking quickly, Eragon told them of his impending departure and impressed upon them the importance of keeping his absence a secret from the rest of the villagers. "No matter how slighted they feel because I supposedly refuse to see them, you cannot reveal the truth to them, not even to Horst or Elain. Let them think I have become a rude and ungrateful lout before you so much as utter a word about Nasuada's scheme. This I ask of you, for the sake of everyone who has pitted themselves against the Empire. Will you do it?"

"We would never betray you, Eragon," said Katrina. "Of that, you need have no doubts."

Then Roran said that he too was leaving.

"Where?" exclaimed Eragon.

"I just received my assignment a few minutes ago. We are going to raid the Empire's supply trains, somewhere well north of us, behind enemy lines."

Eragon gazed at the three of them in turn. First Roran, serious and determined, already tense with anticipation of battle; then Katrina, worried and trying to conceal it; and then Saphira, whose nostrils flickered with small tongues of flame, which sputtered as she breathed. "So we are all going our separate ways." What he did not say, but which hung over them like a shroud, was that they might never again see each other alive.

Grasping Eragon by the forearm, Roran pulled him close and hugged him for a moment. He released Eragon and stared deep into his eyes. "Guard your back, brother. Galbatorix isn't the only one who would like to slip a knife between your ribs when you aren't looking."

"Do the same yourself. And if you find yourself facing a spell-caster, run in the opposite direction. The wards I placed around you won't last forever."

Katrina hugged Eragon and whispered, "Don't take too long."

"I won't."

Together, Roran and Katrina went to Saphira and touched their foreheads to her long, bony snout. Her chest vibrated as she produced a pure bass note deep within her throat. *Remember, Roran,* she said, *do not make the mistake of leaving your enemies alive. And, Katrina? Do not dwell on that which you cannot change. It will only worsen your distress.* With a rustle of skin and scales, Saphira unfolded her wings and enveloped Roran, Katrina, and Eragon in a warm embrace, isolating them from the world.

As Saphira lifted her wings, Roran and Katrina stepped away while Eragon climbed onto her back. He waved at the newlywed couple, a lump in his throat, and continued waving even as Saphira took to the air. Blinking to clear his eyes, Eragon leaned against the spike behind him and gazed up at the tilting sky.

To the cook tents now? asked Saphira.

Aye.

Saphira climbed a few hundred feet before she aimed herself at the southwestern quadrant of the camp, where pillars of smoke drifted up from rows of ovens and large, wide pit fires. A thin stream of wind slipped past her and Eragon as she glided downward toward a clear patch of ground between two open-walled tents, each fifty feet long. Breakfast was over, so the tents were empty of men when Saphira landed with a loud thump.

Eragon hurried toward the fires beyond the plank tables, Saphira beside him. The many hundreds of men who were busy tending the fires, carving meat, cracking eggs, kneading dough, stirring cast-iron kettles full of mysterious liquids, scrubbing clean enormous piles of dirty pots and pans, and who were otherwise engaged in the enormous and never-ending task of preparing food for the Varden did not pause to gawk at Eragon and Saphira. For what importance was a dragon and Rider compared with the merciless demands of the ravenous many-mouthed creature whose hunger they were striving to sate?

A stout man with a close-cropped beard of white and black, who was almost short enough to pass for a dwarf trotted over to Eragon and Saphira and gave a curt bow. "I'm Quoth Merrinsson. How can I help you? If you want, Shadeslayer, we have some bread that just finished baking." He gestured toward a double row of sourdough loaves resting on a platter on a nearby table.

"I might have half a loaf, if you can spare it," said Eragon. "However, my hunger isn't the reason for our visit. Saphira would like something to eat, and we haven't time for her to hunt as she usually does."

Quoth looked past him and eyed Saphira's bulk, and his face grew pale. "How much does she normally . . . Ah, that is, how much do *you* normally eat, Saphira? I can have six sides of roast beef brought over immediately, and another six will be ready in about fifteen minutes. Will that be enough, or . . . ?" The knob in his throat jumped as he swallowed.

Saphira emitted a soft, rippling growl, which caused Quoth to squeak and hop backward. "She would prefer a live animal, if that's convenient," Eragon said.

In a high-pitched voice, Quoth said, "Convenient? Oh yes, it's convenient." He bobbed his head, twisting at his apron with his grease-stained hands. "Most convenient indeed, Shadeslayer,

Dragon Saphira. King Orrin's table will not be lacking this afternoon, then, oh no."

And a barrel of mead, Saphira said to Eragon.

White circles appeared around Quoth's irises as Eragon repeated her request. "I—I am afraid that the dwarves have purchased most of our stocks of m-m-mead. We have only a few barrels left, and those are reserved for King—" Quoth flinched as a four-foot-long flame leaped out of Saphira's nostrils and singed the grass in front of him. Snarled lines of smoke drifted up from the blackened stalks. "I—I—I will have a barrel brought to you at once. If you will f-follow me, I will take y-you to the livestock, where you may have whatever beast you like."

Skirting the fires and tables and groups of harried men, the cook led them to a collection of large wooden pens, which contained pigs, cattle, geese, goats, sheep, rabbits, and a number of wild deer the Varden's foragers had captured during their forays into the surrounding wilderness. Close to the pens were coops full of chickens, ducks, doves, quail, grouse, and other birds. Their squawking, chirping, cooing, and crowing formed a cacophony so harsh, it made Eragon grit his teeth with annoyance. In order to avoid being overwhelmed by the thoughts and feelings of so many creatures, he was careful to keep his mind closed to all but Saphira.

The three of them stopped over a hundred feet from the pens so Saphira's presence would not panic the imprisoned animals. "Is there any here catches your fancy?" Quoth asked, gazing up at her and rubbing his hands with nervous dexterity.

As she surveyed the pens, Saphira sniffed and said to Eragon, *What pitiful prey. . . . I'm not really that hungry, you know. I went hunting only the day before yesterday, and I'm still digesting the bones of the deer I ate.*

You're still growing quickly. The food will do you good.

Not if I can't stomach it.

Pick something small, then. A pig, maybe.

That would hardly be of any help to you. No . . . I'll take that one.

From Saphira, Eragon received the image of a cow of medium stature with a splattering of white splotches on her left flank.

After Eragon pointed out the cow, Quoth shouted at a line of men idling by the pens. Two of them separated the cow from the rest of the herd, slipped a rope over its head, and pulled the reluctant animal toward Saphira. Thirty feet from Saphira, the cow balked and lowed with terror and tried to shake free of the rope and flee. Before the animal could escape, Saphira pounced, leaping across the distance separating them. The two men who were pulling on the rope threw themselves flat as Saphira rushed toward them, her jaws gaping.

Saphira struck the cow broadside as it turned to run, knocking the animal over and holding it in place with her splayed feet. It uttered a single, terrified bleat before Saphira's jaws closed over its neck. With a ferocious shake of her head, she snapped its spine. She paused then, crouched low over her kill, and looked expectantly at Eragon.

Closing his eyes, Eragon reached out with his mind toward the cow. The animal's consciousness had already faded into darkness, but its body was still alive, its flesh thrumming with motive energy, which was all the more intense for the fear that had coursed through it moments before. Repugnance for what he was about to do filled Eragon, but he ignored it and, placing a hand over the belt of Beloth the Wise, transferred what energy he could from the body of the cow into the twelve diamonds hidden around his waist. The process took only a few seconds.

He nodded to Saphira. *I'm done.*

Eragon thanked the men for their assistance, and then the two of them left him and Saphira alone.

While Saphira gorged herself, Eragon sat against the barrel of mead and watched the cooks go about their business. Every time they or one of their assistants beheaded a chicken or cut the throat of a pig or a goat or any other animal, he transferred the energy from the dying animal into the belt of Beloth the Wise. It was grim work, for most of the animals were still aware when he touched their consciousness and the howling storm of their fear and confusion and pain battered at him until his heart pounded and sweat beaded his brow and he wished nothing more than to heal the suffering creatures. However, he knew it was their doom to die, lest the Varden should starve. He had depleted his reserve of energy during the past few battles, and Eragon wanted to replenish it before setting out on a long and potentially hazardous journey. If Nasuada had allowed him to remain with the Varden for another week, he could have stocked the diamonds with energy from his own body and still had time to recuperate before running to Farthen Dûr, but he could not in the few hours he had. And even if he had done nothing but lie in bed and pour the fire from his limbs into the gems, he would not have been able to garner as much force as he did then from the multitude of animals.

The diamonds in the belt of Beloth the Wise seemed to be able to absorb an almost unlimited amount of energy, so he stopped when he was unable to bear the prospect of immersing himself in the death throes of another animal. Shaking and dripping with sweat from head to toe, he leaned forward, his hands on his knees, and gazed at the ground between his feet, struggling not to be ill. Memories not his own intruded upon his thoughts, memories of Saphira soaring over Leona Lake with him on her back, of them plunging into the clear, cool water, a cloud of white bubbles swarming past them, of their shared delight in flying and swimming and playing together.

His breathing calmed, and he looked at Saphira where she sat among the remnants of her kill, chewing on the cow's skull. He smiled and sent her his gratitude for her help.

We can go now, he said.

Swallowing, she replied, *Take my strength as well. You may need it.*

No.

This is one argument you will not win. I insist.

And I insist otherwise. I won't leave you here weakened and unfit for battle. *What if Murtagh and Thorn attack later today? We both need to be ready to fight at any moment. You'll be in more danger than I will because Galbatorix and the whole of the Empire will still believe I'm with you.*

Yes, but you will be alone with a Kull in the middle of the wilderness.

I am as accustomed to the wilderness as you. Being away from civilization does not frighten me. As for a Kull, well, I don't know if I could beat one at a wrestling match, but my wards will protect me from any treachery. . . . I have enough energy, Saphira. You don't need to give me more.

She eyed him, considering his words, then lifted a paw and started licking it clean of blood. *Very well, I will keep myself . . . to myself?* The corners of her mouth seemed to lift with amusement. Lowering her paw, she said, *Would you be so kind as to roll that barrel over to me?* With a grunt, he got to his feet and did as she asked. She extended a single talon and punched two holes in the top of the barrel, which released the sweet smell of apple-honey mead. Arching her neck so her head was directly above the barrel, she grasped it between her massive jaws, then lifted it skyward and poured the gurgling contents down her gullet. The empty barrel shattered against the ground when she dropped it, and one of the iron hoops rolled several yards away. Her upper lip wrinkled, Saphira shook her head, then her breath hitched and she sneezed so hard that her nose struck the ground and a gout of fire erupted from both her mouth and her nostrils.

379

Eragon yelped with surprise and jumped sideways, batting at the smoking hem of his tunic. The right side of his face felt seared raw by the heat of the fire. *Saphira, be more careful!* he exclaimed.

Oops. She lowered her head and rubbed her dust-caked snout against the edge of one foreleg, scratching at her nostrils. *The mead tickles.*

Really, you ought to know better by now, he grumbled as he climbed onto her back.

After rubbing her snout against her foreleg once more, Saphira leaped high into the air and, gliding over the Varden's camp, returned Eragon to his tent. He slid off her, then stood looking up at Saphira. For a time, they said nothing, allowing their shared emotions to speak for them.

Saphira blinked, and he thought her eyes glistened more than normal. *This is a test*, she said. *If we pass it, we shall be the stronger for it, as dragon and Rider.*

We must be able to function by ourselves if necessary, else we will forever be at a disadvantage compared with others.

Yes. She gouged the earth with her clenching claws. *Knowing that does nothing to ease my pain, however.* A shiver ran the length of her sinuous body. She shuffled her wings. *May the wind rise under your wings and the sun always be at your back. Travel well and travel fast, little one.*

Goodbye, he said.

Eragon felt that if he remained with her any longer, he would never leave, so he whirled around and, without a backward glance, plunged into the dark interior of his tent. The connection between them—which had become as integral to him as the structure of his own flesh—he severed completely. They would soon be too far apart to sense each other's minds anyway, and he had no desire to prolong the agony of their parting. He stood where he was for a moment, gripping the hilt of the falchion and swaying as if he were dizzy. Already the dull ache of loneliness suffused him, and he felt small and isolated without the comforting presence of Saphira's consciousness. *I did this before, and I can do this again*, he thought, and forced himself to square his shoulders and lift his chin.

From underneath his cot, he removed the pack he had made during his trip from Helgrind. Into it he placed the carved wooden tube wrapped in cloth that contained the scroll of the poem he had written for the Agaetí Blödhren, which Oromis had copied for him in his finest calligraphy; the flask of enchanted faelnirv and the small soapstone box of nalgask that were also gifts from Oromis; the thick book, *Domia abr Wyrda*, which was Jeod's present; his whetstone and his strop; and, after some hesitation, the many pieces of his armor, for he reasoned, *If the occasion arises where I need it, I will be more happy to have it than I will be miserable carrying it all the way to Farthen Dûr.* Or so he hoped. The book and the scroll he took because—after having done so much traveling—he had concluded that the best way to avoid losing the objects he cared about was to keep them with him wherever he went.

The only extra clothes he decided to bring were a pair of gloves, which he stuffed inside his helmet, and his heavy woolen cloak, in case it got cold when they stopped nights. All the rest, he left rolled up in Saphira's saddlebags. *If I really am a member of Dûrgrimst Ingeitum,* he thought, *they will clothe me properly when I arrive at Bregan Hold.*

Cinching off the pack, he lay his unstrung bow and quiver across the top and lashed them to the frame. He was about to do the same with the falchion when he realized that if he leaned to the side, the sword could slide out of the sheath. Therefore, he tied the sword flat against the rear of the pack, angling it so the hilt would ride between his neck and his right shoulder, where he could still draw it if need be.

Eragon donned the pack and then stabbed through the barrier in his mind, feeling the energy surging in his body and in the twelve diamonds mounted on the belt of Beloth the Wise. Tapping into that flow of force, he murmured the spell he had cast but once before: that which bent rays of light around him and rendered him invisible. A slight pall of fatigue weakened his limbs as he released the spell.

He glanced downward and had the disconcerting experience of looking through where he knew his torso and legs to be and seeing the imprint of his boots on the dirt below. *Now for the difficult part,* he thought.

Going to the rear of the tent, he slit the taut fabric with his hunting knife and slipped through the opening. Sleek as a well-fed cat, Blödhgarm was waiting for him outside. He inclined his head in the general direction of Eragon and murmured, "Shadeslayer," then devoted his attention to mending the hole, which he did with a half-dozen short words in the ancient language.

Eragon drifted down the path between two rows of tents, using his knowledge of woodcraft to make as little noise as possible. Whenever anyone approached, Eragon darted off the path and stood motionless, hoping they would not notice the footprints of shadow in the dirt or on the grass. He cursed the fact that the land was so dry; his boots tended to raise small puffs of dust no matter how gently he lowered them. To his surprise, being invisible degraded his sense of balance; without the ability to see where his hands or his feet were, he kept misjudging distances and bumping into things, almost as if he had consumed too much ale.

Despite his uncertain progress, he reached the edge of the camp in fairly good time and without arousing any suspicion. He paused behind a rain barrel, hiding his footprints in its thick shadow, and

studied the packed-earth ramparts and ditches lined with sharpened stakes that protected the Varden's eastern flank. If he had been trying to enter the camp, it would have been extremely difficult to escape detection by one of the many sentinels who patrolled the ramparts, even while invisible. But since the trenches and the ramparts had been designed to repel attackers and not imprison the defenders, crossing them from the opposite direction was a far easier task.

Eragon waited until the two closest sentinels had their backs turned toward him, and then he sprinted forward, pumping his arms with all his might. Within seconds, he traversed the hundred or so feet that separated the rain barrel from the slope of the rampart and dashed up the embankment so fast, he felt as if he were a stone skipping across water. At the crest of the embankment, he drove his legs into the ground and, arms flailing, leaped out over the lines of the Varden's defenses. For three silent heartbeats, he flew, then landed with a bone-jarring impact.

As soon as he regained his balance, Eragon pressed himself flat against the ground and held his breath. One of the sentinels paused in his rounds, but he did not seem to notice anything out of the ordinary, and after a moment he resumed his pacing. Eragon released his breath and whispered, "Du deloi lunaea," and felt as the spell smoothed out the impressions his boots had left in the embankment.

Still invisible, he stood and trotted away from the camp, careful to step only on clumps of grass so he would not kick up more dust. The farther he got from the sentinels, the faster he ran, until he sped over the land more quickly than a galloping horse.

Almost an hour later, he danced down the steep side of a narrow draw that the wind and rain had etched into the surface of the grasslands. At the bottom was a trickle of water lined with rushes and cattails. He continued downstream, staying well away from the soft ground next to the water—in an attempt to avoid leaving traces of his passage—until the creek widened into a small pond, and there by the edge, he saw the bulk of a bare-chested Kull sitting on a boulder.

As Eragon pushed his way through a stand of cattails, the sound of rustling leaves and stalks alerted the Kull of his presence. The creature turned his massive horned head toward Eragon, sniffing at the air. It was Nar Garzhvog, leader of the Urgals who had allied themselves with the Varden.

"You!" exclaimed Eragon, becoming visible once more.

"Greetings, Firesword," Garzhvog rumbled. Heaving up his thick limbs and giant torso, the Urgal rose to his full eight and a half feet, his gray-skinned muscles rippling in the light of the noonday sun.

"Greetings, Nar Garzhvog," said Eragon. Confused, he asked, "What of your rams? Who will lead them if you go with me?"

"My blood brother, Skgahgrezh, will lead. He is not Kull, but he has long horns and a thick neck. He is a fine war chief."

"I see. . . . Why did *you* want to come, though?"

The Urgal lifted his square chin, baring his throat. "You are

Firesword. You must not die, or the Urgralgra—the Urgals, as you name us—will not have our revenge against Galbatorix, and our race will die in this land. Therefore, I will run with you. I am the best of our fighters. I have defeated forty-two rams in single combat."

Eragon nodded, not displeased by the turn of events. Of all the Urgals, he trusted Garzhvog the most, for he had probed the Kull's consciousness before the Battle of the Burning Plains and had discovered that, by the standards of his race, Garzhvog was honest and reliable. *As long as he doesn't decide that his honor requires him to challenge me to a duel, we should have no cause for conflict.*

"Very well, Nar Garzhvog," he said, tightening the strap of the pack around his waist, "let us run together, you and I, as has not happened in the whole of recorded history."

Garzhvog chuckled deep in his chest. "Let us run, Firesword."

Together they faced east, and together they set forth for the Beor Mountains, Eragon running light and swift, and Garzhvog loping beside him, taking one stride for every two of Eragon's, the earth shuddering beneath the burden of his weight. Above them, swollen thunderheads gathered along the horizon, portending a torrential storm, and circling hawks uttered lonesome cries as they hunted their prey.

OVER HILL AND MOUNTAIN

Eragon and Nar Garzhvog ran for the rest of the day, through the night, and through the following day, stopping only to drink and to relieve themselves.

At the end of the second day, Garzhvog said, "Firesword, I must eat, and I must sleep."

Eragon leaned against a nearby stump, panting, and nodded. He had not wanted to speak first, but he was just as hungry and exhausted as the Kull. Soon after leaving the Varden, he had discovered that while he was faster than Garzhvog at distances of up to five miles, beyond that, Garzhvog's endurance was equal to or greater than his own.

"I will help you hunt," he said.

"That is not needed. Make us a big fire, and I will bring us food."

"Fine."

As Garzhvog strode off toward a thicket of beech trees north of them, Eragon untied the strap around his waist and, with a sigh of relief, dropped his pack next to the stump. "Blasted armor," he muttered. Even in the Empire, he had not run so far while carrying such a load. He had not anticipated how arduous it would be. His feet hurt, his legs hurt, his back hurt, and when he tried to crouch, his knees refused to bend properly.

Trying to ignore his discomfort, he set about gathering grass and dead branches for a fire, which he piled on a patch of dry, rocky ground.

He and Garzhvog were somewhere just east of the southern tip of Lake Tüdosten. The land was wet and lush, with fields of grass that stood six feet high, through which there roamed herds of deer, gazelles, and wild oxen with black hides and wide, backswept horns. The riches of the area were due, Eragon knew, to the Beor Mountains, which caused the formation of huge banks of clouds that drifted for many leagues over the plains beyond, bringing rain to places that would otherwise have been as dry as the Hadarac Desert.

Although the two of them had already run an enormous number of leagues, Eragon was disappointed by their progress. Between the Jiet River and Lake Tüdosten, they had lost several hours while hiding and taking detours to avoid being seen. Now that Lake Tüdosten was behind them, he hoped that their pace would increase. *Nasuada didn't foresee this delay, now did she? Oh no. She thought I could run flat out from there to Farthen Dûr. Ha!* Kicking at a branch that was in his way, he continued to gather wood, grumbling to himself the entire time.

When Garzhvog returned an hour later, Eragon had built a fire a yard long and two feet wide and was sitting in front of it, staring at the flames and fighting the urge to slip into the waking dreams that were his rest. His neck cracked as he looked up.

Garzhvog strode toward him, holding the carcass of a plump doe under his left arm. As if it weighed no more than a sack of rags, he lifted the doe and wedged its head in the fork of a tree twenty yards from the fire. Then he drew a knife and began to clean the carcass.

Eragon stood, feeling as if his joints had turned to stone, and stumbled toward Garzhvog.

"How did you kill it?" he asked.

"With my sling," rumbled Garzhvog.

"Do you intend to cook it on a spit? Or do Urgals eat their meat raw?"

Garzhvog turned his head and gazed through the coil of his left horn at Eragon, a deep-set yellow eye gleaming with some enigmatic emotion. "We are not beasts, Firesword."

"I did not say you were."

With a grunt, the Urgal returned to his work.

"It will take too long to cook on a spit," said Eragon.

"I thought a stew, and we can fry what is left on a rock."

"Stew? How? We don't have a pot."

Reaching down, Garzhvog scrubbed his right hand clean on the ground, then removed a square of folded material from the pouch at his belt and tossed it at Eragon.

Eragon tried to catch it but was so tired he missed, and the object struck the ground. It looked like an exceptionally large piece of vellum. As he picked it up, the square fell open, and he saw it had the shape of a bag, perhaps a foot and a half wide and three feet deep. The rim was reinforced with a thick strip of leather, upon which were sewn metal rings. He turned the container over, amazed by its softness and the fact that it had no seams.

"What is it?" he asked.

"The stomach of the cave bear I killed the year I first got my horns. Hang it from a frame or put it in a hole, then fill it with water and drop hot stones in it. Stones heat water, and stew tastes good."

"Won't the stones burn through the stomach?"

"They have not yet."

"Is it enchanted?"

"No magic. Strong stomach." Garzhvog's breath huffed out as he grasped the deer's hips on either side and, with a single movement, broke its pelvis in two. The sternum he split using his knife.

"It must have been a big bear," Eragon said.

Garzhvog made a *ruk-ruk* sound deep in his throat. "It was bigger than I am now, Shadeslayer."

"Did you kill it with your sling as well?"

"I choked him to death with my hands. No weapons are allowed when you come of age and must prove your courage." Garzhvog paused for a moment, his knife buried to the hilt in the carcass. "Most do not try to kill a cave bear. Most hunt wolves or mountain goats. That is why I became war chief and others did not."

Eragon left him preparing the meat and went to the fire. Next to it, he dug a hole, which he lined with the bear stomach, pushing stakes through the metal rings to hold the stomach in place. He gathered a dozen apple-sized rocks from the surrounding field and tossed them into the center of the fire. While he waited for the rocks to heat, he used magic to fill the bear stomach two-thirds with water, and then he fashioned a pair of tongs out of a sapling willow and a piece of knotted rawhide.

When the rocks were cherry red, he shouted, "They're ready!"

"Put them in," Garzhvog replied.

Using the tongs, Eragon extracted the nearest stone from the fire and lowered it into the container. The surface of the water exploded into steam as the stone touched it. He deposited two more stones in the bear stomach, which brought the water to a rolling boil.

Garzhvog lumbered over and poured a double handful of meat into the water, then seasoned the stew with large pinches of salt from the pouch at his belt and several sprigs of rosemary, thyme, and other wild greens he had chanced upon while hunting. Then he placed a flat piece of shale across one side of the fire. When the stone was hot, he fried strips of meat on it.

While the food cooked, Eragon and Garzhvog carved themselves spoons from the stump where Eragon had dropped his pack.

Hunger made it seem longer to Eragon, but it was not many more minutes before the stew was done, and he and Garzhvog ate, ravenous as wolves. Eragon devoured twice as much as he thought he ever had before, and what he did not consume, Garzhvog did, eating enough for six large men.

Afterward, Eragon lay back, propping himself up on his elbows, and stared at the flashing fireflies that had appeared along the edge of the beech trees, swirling in abstract patterns as they chased one another. Somewhere an owl hooted, soft and throaty. The first few stars speckled the purple sky.

Eragon stared without seeing and thought of Saphira and then of Arya and then of Arya and Saphira, and then he closed his eyes, a dull throb forming behind his temples. He heard a cracking sound and, opening his eyes once more, saw that on the other side of the empty bear stomach, Garzhvog was cleaning his teeth with the pointed end of a broken thighbone. Eragon dropped his gaze to the bottom of the Urgal's bare feet—Garzhvog having removed his sandals before they began their meal—and to his surprise noticed that the Urgal had seven toes on each foot.

"The dwarves have the same number of toes as you do," he said.

Garzhvog spat a piece of meat into the coals of the fire. "I did not know that. I have never wanted to look at the feet of a dwarf."

"Don't you find it curious that Urgals and dwarves should both have fourteen toes, while elves and humans have ten?"

Garzhvog's thick lips lifted in a snarl. "We share no blood with those hornless mountain rats, Firesword. They have fourteen toes, and we have fourteen toes. It pleased the gods to shape us so when they created the world. There is no other explanation."

Eragon grunted in response and returned to watching the fireflies. Then: "Tell me a story your race is fond of, Nar Garzhvog."

389

The Kull pondered for a moment, then removed the bone from his mouth. He said, "Long ago, there lived a young Urgralgra, and her name was Maghara. She had horns that shone like polished stone, hair that hung past her waist, and a laugh that could charm the birds out of the trees. But she was not pretty. She was ugly. Now, in her village, there also lived a ram who was very strong. He had killed four rams in wrestling matches and had defeated twenty-three others besides. But although his feats had won him wide renown, he had yet to choose a brood-mate. Maghara wished to be his brood-mate, but he would not look at her, for she was ugly, and because of her ugliness, he did not see her bright horns, nor her long hair, and he did not hear her pleasant laugh. Sick at heart that he would not look at her, Maghara climbed the tallest mountain in the Spine, and she called out to Rahna to help her. Rahna is mother of us all, and it was she who invented weaving and farming and she who raised the Beor Mountains when she was fleeing the great dragon.

Rahna, She of the Gilded Horns, she answered Maghara, and she asked why Maghara had summoned her. 'Make me pretty, Honored Mother, so I can attract the ram I want,' said Maghara. And Rahna answered, 'You do not need to be pretty, Maghara. You have bright horns and long hair and a pleasant laugh. With those, you can catch a ram who is not so foolish as to look at only a female's face.' And Maghara, she threw herself down upon the ground and said, 'I will not be happy unless I can have this ram, Honored Mother. Please, make me pretty.' Rahna, she smiled then and said, 'If I do this, child, how will you repay me for this favor?' And Maghara said, 'I will give you anything you want.'

"Rahna was well pleased with her offer, and so she made Maghara pretty then, and Maghara returned to her village, and everyone wondered at her beauty. With her new face, Maghara became the brood-mate of the ram she wanted, and they had many children, and they lived in happiness for seven years. Then Rahna came to Maghara, and Rahna said, 'You have had seven years with the ram you wanted. Have you enjoyed them?' And Maghara said, 'I have.' And Rahna said, 'Then I have come for my payment.' And she looked around their house of stone, and she seized hold of Maghara's eldest son and said, 'I will have him.' Maghara begged She of the Gilded Horns not to take her eldest son, but Rahna would not relent. At last, Maghara took her brood-mate's club, and she struck at Rahna, but the club shattered in her hands. In punishment, Rahna stripped Maghara's beauty from her, and then Rahna left with Maghara's son for her hall where the four winds dwell, and she named the boy Hegraz and raised him to be one of the mightiest warriors who has ever walked this land. And so one should learn from Maghara to never fight one's fate, for you will lose that which you hold most dear."

Eragon watched the glowing rim of the crescent moon appear above the eastern horizon. "Tell me something about your villages."

"What?"

"Anything. I experienced hundreds of memories when I was in your mind and in Khagra's and in Otvek's, but I can recall only a handful of them, and those imperfectly. I am trying to make sense of what I saw."

"There is much I could tell you," rumbled Garzhvog. His heavy eyes pensive, he worked his makeshift toothpick around one of his fangs and then said, "We take logs, and we carve them with faces of the animals of the mountains, and these we bury upright by our houses so they will frighten away the spirits of the wild. Sometimes the poles almost seem to be alive. When you walk into one of our villages, you can feel the eyes of all the carved animals watching you. . . ." The bone paused in the Urgal's fingers, then resumed its back-and-forth motion. "By the doorway of each hut, we hang the namna. It is a strip of cloth as wide as my outstretched hand. The namna are brightly colored, and the patterns on them depict the history of the family that lives in that hut. Only the oldest and most skilled weavers are allowed to add to a namna or to reweave one if it becomes damaged. . . ." The bone disappeared inside of Garzhvog's fist. "During the months of winter, those who have mates work with them on their hearth rug. It takes at least five years to finish such a rug, so by the time it is done, you know whether you have made a good choice of mate."

"I've never seen one of your villages," said Eragon. "They must be very well hidden."

"Well hidden and well defended. Few who see our homes live to tell of it."

Focusing on the Kull and allowing an edge to creep into his voice, Eragon said, "How is it you learned this language, Garzhvog? Was there a human who lived among you? Did you keep any of us as slaves?"

Garzhvog returned Eragon's gaze without flinching. "We have no slaves, Firesword. I tore the knowledge from the minds of the men I fought, and I shared it with the rest of my tribe."

"You have killed many humans, haven't you?"

"You have killed many Urgralgra, Firesword. It is why we must be allies, or my race will not survive."

Eragon crossed his arms. "When Brom and I were tracking the Ra'zac, we passed through Yazuac, a village by the Ninor River. We found all of the people piled in the center of the village, dead, with a baby stuck on a spear at the top of the pile. It was the worst thing I've ever seen. And it was Urgals who killed them."

"Before I got my horns," said Garzhvog, "my father took me to visit one of our villages along the western fringes of the Spine. We found our people tortured, burnt, and slaughtered. The men of Narda had learned of our presence, and they had surprised the village with many soldiers. Not one of our tribe escaped. . . . It is true we love war more than other races, Firesword, and that has been our downfall many times before. Our women will not consider a ram for a mate unless he has proven himself in battle and killed at least three foes himself. And there is a joy in battle unlike any other joy. But though we love feats of arms, that does not mean we are not aware of our faults. If our race cannot change, Galbatorix will kill us all if he defeats the Varden, and you and Nasuada will kill us all if you overthrow that snake-tongued betrayer. Am I not right, Firesword?"

Eragon jerked his chin in a nod. "Aye."

"It does no good, then, to dwell upon past wrongs. If we cannot overlook what each of our races has done, there will never be peace between humans and the Urgralgra."

"How should we treat you, though, if we defeat Galbatorix and Nasuada gives your race the land you have asked for and, twenty years from now, your children begin to kill and plunder so they can win mates? If you know your own history, Garzhvog, then you know it has always been so when Urgals sign peace accords."

With a thick sigh, Garzhvog said, "Then we will hope that there are still Urgralgra across the sea and that they are wiser than us, for we will be no more in this land."

Neither of them spoke again that night. Garzhvog curled up on his side and slept with his massive head resting on the ground, while Eragon wrapped himself in his cloak and sat against the stump and gazed at the slowly turning stars, drifting in and out of his waking dreams.

By the end of the next day, they had come into sight of the Beor Mountains. At first the mountains were nothing more than ghostly shapes on the horizon, angled panes of white and purple, but as evening drew nigh, the distant range acquired substance, and Eragon was able to make out the dark band of trees along the base and, above that, the even wider band of gleaming snow and ice and, still higher yet, the peaks themselves, which were gray, bare stone, for they were so tall, no plants grew upon them and no snow fell upon them. As when he had first seen them, the sheer size of the Beor Mountains overwhelmed Eragon. His every instinct insisted that nothing that large could exist, and yet he knew his eyes did not deceive him. The mountains averaged ten miles high, and many were even taller.

Eragon and Garzhvog did not stop that night but continued running through the hours of darkness and through the day thereafter. When morning arrived, the sky grew bright, but because of the Beor Mountains, it was almost noon before the sun burst forth between two peaks and rays of light as wide as the mountains themselves streamed out over the land that was still caught in the strange twilight of shadow. Eragon paused then, on the bank of a brook, and contemplated the sight in silent wonderment for several minutes.

As they skirted the vast range of mountains, their journey began to seem to Eragon uncomfortably similar to his flight from Gil'ead to Farthen Dûr with Murtagh, Saphira, and Arya. He even thought he recognized the place where they had camped after crossing the Hadarac Desert.

The long days and longer nights slipped by with both excruciating slowness and surprising speed, for every hour was identical to the last, which made Eragon feel not only as if their ordeal would never end but also as if large portions of it had never taken place.

When he and Garzhvog arrived at the mouth of the great rift that split the range of mountains for many leagues from north to south, they turned to their right and passed between the cold and indifferent peaks. Arriving at the Beartooth River—which flowed out of the narrow valley that led to Farthen Dûr—they forded the frigid waters and continued southward.

That night, before they ventured east into the mountains proper, they camped by a small pond and rested their limbs. Garzhvog killed another deer with his sling, this time a buck, and they both ate their fill.

His hunger sated, Eragon was hunched over, mending a hole in the side of his boot, when he heard an eerie howl that set his pulse racing. He glanced around the darkened landscape, and to his alarm, he saw the silhouette of a huge beast loping around the pebble-lined shore of the pond.

"Garzhvog," said Eragon in a low voice, and reached over to his pack and drew his falchion.

Taking a fist-sized rock from the ground, the Kull placed it in the leather pocket of his sling, and then rising to his full height, he opened his maw and bellowed into the night until the land rang with echoes of his defiant challenge.

The beast paused, then proceeded at a slower pace, sniffing at the ground here and there. As it entered the circle of firelight, Eragon's breath caught in his throat. Standing before them was a gray-backed wolf as big as a horse, with fangs like sabers and burning yellow eyes that followed their every movement. The wolf's feet were the size of bucklers.

A *Shrrg!* thought Eragon.

As the giant wolf circled their camp, moving almost silently despite his great bulk, Eragon thought of the elves and how they would deal with a wild animal, and in the ancient language, he said, "Brother Wolf, we mean you no harm. Tonight our pack rests and does not hunt. You are welcome to share our food and the warmth of our den until morning." The Shrrg paused, and his ears swiveled forward while Eragon spoke in the ancient language.

"Firesword, what are you doing?" growled Garzhvog.

"Don't attack unless he does."

The heavy-shouldered beast slowly entered their camp, the tip of his huge wet nose twitching the whole while. The wolf poked his shaggy head toward the fire, seemingly curious about the writhing flames, then moved over to the scraps of meat and viscera scattered over the ground where Garzhvog had butchered the buck. Crouching, the wolf snapped up the gobbets of flesh, then rose and, without a backward glance, padded off into the depths of the night.

Eragon relaxed and sheathed the falchion. Garzhvog, however, remained standing where he was, his lips pulled back in a snarl, looking and listening for anything out of the ordinary in the surrounding darkness.

At dawn's first light, Eragon and Garzhvog left their camp, and running eastward, entered the valley that would lead them to Mount Thardûr.

As they passed underneath the boughs of the dense forest that guarded the interior of the mountain range, the air became noticeably cooler and the soft bed of needles on the ground muffled their footsteps. The tall, dark, grim trees that loomed over them seemed to be watching as they made their way between the thick trunks and around the twisted roots that knuckled up out of the moist earth, standing two, three, and often four feet high. Large black squirrels scampered among the branches, chattering loudly. A thick layer of moss blanketed the corpses of trees that had fallen. Ferns and thimbleberries and other green leafy plants flourished alongside mushrooms of every shape, size, and color.

The world narrowed once Eragon and Garzhvog were fully inside the long valley. The gigantic mountains pressed close on either side, oppressive with their bulk, and the sky was a distant, unreachable strip of sea blue, the highest sky Eragon had ever seen. A few thin clouds grazed the shoulders of the mountains.

An hour or so after noon, Eragon and Garzhvog slowed as a series of terrible roars echoed among the trees. Eragon pulled his sword from its sheath, and Garzhvog plucked a smooth river rock from the ground and fit it in the pocket of his sling.

"It is a cave bear," said Garzhvog. A furious, high-pitched squeal, similar to metal scraping over metal, punctuated his statement. "And Nagra. We must be careful, Firesword."

They proceeded at a slow pace and soon spotted the animals several hundred feet up the side of a mountain. A drove of reddish boars with thick, slashing tusks milled in squealing confusion before a huge mass of silver-brown fur, hooked claws, and snapping teeth that moved with deadly speed. At first the distance fooled Eragon, but then he compared the animals to the trees next to them and realized that each boar would have dwarfed a Shrrg and that the bear was nearly as large as his house in Palancar Valley. The boars had bloodied the cave bear's flanks, but that seemed to only enrage the beast. Rearing on his hind legs, the bear bellowed and swatted one of the boars with a massive paw, knocking it aside and tearing open its hide. Three more times the boar attempted to rise, and three more times the cave bear struck at it, until at last the boar gave up and lay still. As the bear bent to feed, the rest of the squealing pigs fled back under the trees, heading higher up the mountain and away from the bear.

Awed by the bear's strength, Eragon followed Garzhvog as the Urgal slowly walked across the bear's field of vision. Lifting his crimson snout from the belly of his kill, the bear watched them with small, beady eyes, then apparently decided they were no threat to him and resumed eating.

"I think even Saphira might not be able to overcome such a monster," Eragon murmured.

Garzhvog uttered a small grunt. "She can breathe fire. A bear cannot."

Neither of them looked away from the bear until trees hid it from view, and even then they kept their weapons at readiness, not knowing what other dangers they might encounter.

The day had passed into late afternoon when they became conscious of another sound: laughter. Eragon and Garzhvog halted, and then Garzhvog raised a finger and, with surprising stealth, crept through a wall of brush toward the laughter. Placing his feet with care, Eragon went with the Kull, holding his breath for fear his breathing would betray their presence.

Peering through a cluster of dogwood leaves, Eragon saw that there was now a well-worn path at the bottom of the valley, and next to the path, three dwarf children were playing, throwing sticks at each other and shrieking with laughter. No adults were visible. Eragon withdrew to a safe distance, exhaled, and studied the sky, where he spotted several plumes of white smoke perhaps a mile farther up the valley.

A branch snapped as Garzhvog squatted next to him, so that they were about level. Garzhvog said, "Firesword, here we part."

"You will not come to Bregan Hold with me?"

"No. My task was to keep you safe. If I go with you, the dwarves will not trust you as they should. Thardûr mountain is close at hand, and I am confident no one will dare hurt you between here and there."

Eragon rubbed the back of his neck and looked back and forth between Garzhvog and the smoke east of them. "Are you going to run straight back to the Varden?"

With a low chuckle, Garzhvog said, "Aye, but maybe not so fast as we did coming here."

Unsure of what to say, Eragon pushed at the rotten end of a log with the tip of his boot, exposing a clutch of white larvae squirming in the tunnels they had excavated. "Don't let a Shrrg or a bear eat you, eh? Then I would have to track down the beast and kill him, and I don't have the time for that."

Garzhvog pressed both his fists against his bony forehead. "May your enemies cower before you, Firesword." Standing and turning, Garzhvog loped away from Eragon. The forest soon hid the Kull's bulky form.

Eragon filled his lungs with the fresh mountain air, then pushed his way through the wall of brush. As he emerged from the thicket of brakes and dogwood, the tiny dwarf children froze, the expressions on their round-cheeked faces wary. Holding his hands out to his sides, Eragon said, "I am Eragon Shadeslayer, Son of None. I seek Orik, Thrifk's son, at Bregan Hold. Can you take me to him?" When the children did not respond, he realized they understood nothing of his own language. "I am a Dragon Rider," he said, speaking slowly and emphasizing the words. "Eka eddyr aí Shur'tugal . . . Shur'tugal . . . Argetlam."

At that, the children's eyes brightened, and their mouths formed round shapes of amazement. "Argetlam!" they exclaimed. "Argetlam!" And they ran over and threw themselves at him, wrapping their short arms around his legs and tugging at his clothes, shouting with merriment the entire time. Eragon stared down at them, feeling a foolish grin spread across his face. The children grasped his hands, and he allowed them to pull him down the path. Even though he could not understand, the children kept up a continuous stream of Dwarvish, telling him about what he knew not, but he enjoyed listening to their speech.

When one of the children—a girl, he thought—held her arms out toward him, he picked her up and placed her on his shoulders, wincing as she grasped fistfuls of his hair. She laughed, high and sweet, which made him smile again. Thus accoutered and accompanied, Eragon made his way toward Mount Thardûr and there to Bregan Hold and his foster brother, Orik.

✦ ✦ ✦

FOR MY LOVE

Roran stared at the round, flat stone he held cupped in his hands. His eyebrows met in a scowl of frustration.

"Stenr rïsa!" he growled under his breath.

The stone refused to budge.

"What are you up to, Stronghammer?" asked Carn, dropping onto the log where Roran sat.

Slipping the stone into his belt, Roran accepted the bread and cheese Carn had brought him and said, "Nothing. Just woolgathering."

Carn nodded. "Most do before a mission."

As he ate, Roran allowed his gaze to drift over the men he found himself with. Their group was thirty strong, himself included. They were all hardened warriors. Everyone carried a bow, and most also wore a sword, although a few chose to fight with a spear, or with a mace or a hammer. Of the thirty men, he guessed that seven or eight were close to his own age, while the rest were several years older. The eldest among them was their captain, Martland Redbeard, the deposed earl of Thun, who had seen enough winters that his famed beard had become frosted with silver hairs.

When Roran had first joined Martland's command, he had presented himself to Martland in his tent. The earl was a short man, with powerful limbs from a lifetime of riding horses and wielding swords. His titular beard was thick and well groomed and hung to the middle of his sternum. After looking Roran over, the earl had said, "Lady Nasuada has told me great things about you, my boy, and I have heard much else from the stories my men tell, rumors, gossip, hearsay, and the like. You know how it is. No doubt, you have accomplished notable feats; bearding the Ra'zac in their own den, for example, now there was a tricky piece of work. Of course, you had your cousin to help you, didn't you, hmm? . . . You may be accustomed to having your way with the people from your village, but you are part of the Varden now, my boy. More specifically, you are one of my warriors. We are not your family. We are not your neighbors. We are not even necessarily your friends. Our duty is to carry out Nasuada's orders, and carry them out we will, no matter how any one of us might feel about it. While you serve under me, you will do what I tell you, when I tell you, and how I tell you, or I swear upon the bones of my blessed mother—may she rest in peace—I will personally whip the skin off your back, no matter to whom you may be related. Do you understand?"

"Yes, sir!"

"Very good. If you behave yourself and show you have some common sense, and if you can manage to stay alive, it is possible for a man of determination to advance quickly among the Varden. Whether you do or not, however, depends entirely on if I deem you fit to command men of your own. But don't you believe, not for one moment, not *one* blasted moment, that you can flatter me into a good opinion of you. I don't care whether you like or hate me. My only concern is whether you can do what needs to be done."

"I understand perfectly, sir!"

"Yes, well, maybe you do at that, Stronghammer. We shall know soon enough. Leave and report to Ulhart, my right-hand man."

Roran swallowed the last of his bread and washed it down with a swig of wine from the skin he carried. He wished they could have had a hot dinner that night, but they were deep in the Empire's territory, and soldiers might have spotted a fire. With a sigh, he stretched out his legs. His knees were sore from riding Snowfire from dusk until dawn for the past three days.

In the back of his mind, Roran felt a faint but constant pressure, a mental itch that, night or day, pointed him in the same direction: the direction of Katrina. The source of the sensation was the ring

Eragon had given him, and it was a comfort to Roran knowing that, because of it, he and Katrina could find each other anywhere in Alagaësia, even if they were both blind and deaf.

Beside him, he heard Carn muttering phrases in the ancient language, and he smiled. Carn was their spellcaster, sent to ensure that an enemy magician could not kill them all with a wave of his hand. From some of the other men, Roran had gathered that Carn was not a particularly strong magician—he struggled to cast every spell—but that he compensated for his weakness by inventing extraordinarily clever spells and by excelling at worming his way into his opponents' minds. Carn was thin of face and thin of body, with drooping eyes and a nervous, excitable air. Roran had taken an immediate liking to him.

Across from Roran, two of the men, Halmar and Ferth, were sitting in front of their tent, and Halmar was telling Ferth, ". . . so when the soldiers came for him, he pulled all his men inside his estate and set fire to the pools of oil his servants had poured earlier, trapping the soldiers and making it appear to those who came later as if the whole lot of them had burned to death. Can you believe it? Five hundred soldiers he killed at one go, without even drawing a blade!"

"How did he escape?" Ferth asked.

"Redbeard's grandfather was a cunning bastard, he was. He had a tunnel dug all the way from the family hall to the nearest river. With it, Redbeard was able to get his family and all their servants out alive. He took them to Surda then, where King Larkin sheltered them. It was quite a number of years before Galbatorix learned they were still alive. We're lucky to be under Redbeard, to be sure. He's lost only two battles, and those because of magic."

Halmar fell silent as Ulhart stepped into the middle of the row of sixteen tents. The grim-faced veteran stood with his legs spread, immovable as a deep-rooted oak tree, and surveyed the tents, checking that everyone was present. He said, "Sun's down, get to sleep. We ride out two hours before first light. Convoy should be seven miles northwest of us. Make good time, we strike just as they start moving. Kill everyone, burn everything, an' we go back. You know how it goes. Stronghammer, you ride with me. Mess up, an' I'll gut you with a dull fishhook." The men chuckled. "Right, get to sleep."

Wind whipped Roran's face. The thunder of pulsing blood filled his ears, drowning out every other sound. Snowfire surged between his legs, galloping. Roran's vision had narrowed; he saw nothing but the two soldiers sitting on brown mares next to the second-to-last wagon of the supply train.

Raising his hammer overhead, Roran howled with all his might.

The two soldiers started and fumbled with their weapons and shields. One of them dropped his spear and bent to recover it.

Pulling on Snowfire's reins to slow him, Roran stood upright in his stirrups and, drawing abreast of the first soldier, struck him on the shoulder, splitting his mail hauberk. The man screamed, his arm going limp. Roran finished him off with a backhand blow.

The other soldier had retrieved his spear, and he jabbed at Roran, aiming at his neck. Roran ducked behind his round shield, the spear jarring him each time it buried itself in the wood. He pressed his legs against Snowfire's sides, and the stallion reared, neighing and pawing at the air with iron-shod hooves. One hoof caught the soldier in the chest, tearing his red tunic. As Snowfire dropped to all fours again, Roran swung his hammer sideways and crushed the man's throat.

Leaving the soldier thrashing on the ground, Roran spurred Snowfire toward the next wagon in the convoy, where Ulhart was battling three soldiers of his own. Four oxen pulled each wagon, and as Snowfire passed the wagon Roran had just captured, the lead ox tossed his head, and the tip of his left horn caught Roran in the lower part of his right leg. Roran gasped. He felt as if a red-hot iron had been laid against his shin. He glanced down and saw a flap of his boot hanging loose, along with a layer of his skin and muscle.

With another battle-cry, Roran rode up to the closest of the three soldiers Ulhart was fighting and felled him with a single swipe of his hammer. The next man evaded Roran's subsequent attack, then turned his horse and galloped away.

"Get him!" Ulhart shouted, but Roran was already in pursuit.

The fleeing soldier dug his spurs into the belly of his horse until the animal bled, but despite his desperate cruelty, his steed could not outrun Snowfire. Roran bent low over Snowfire's neck as the stallion extended himself, flying over the ground with incredible speed. Realizing flight was hopeless, the soldier reined in his mount, wheeled about, and slashed at Roran with a saber. Roran lifted his hammer and barely managed to deflect the razor-sharp blade. He immediately retaliated with a looping overhead attack, but the soldier parried and then slashed at Roran's arms and legs twice more. In his mind, Roran cursed. The soldier was obviously more experienced with swordplay than he was; if he could not win the engagement in the next few seconds, the soldier would kill him.

The soldier must have sensed his advantage, for he pressed the attack, forcing Snowfire to prance backward. On three occasions, Roran was sure the soldier was about to wound him, but the man's saber twisted at the last moment and missed Roran, diverted by an unseen force. Roran was thankful for Eragon's wards then.

Having no other recourse, Roran resorted to the unexpected: he stuck his head and neck out and shouted, "Bah!" just as he would if he were trying to scare someone in a dark hallway. The soldier flinched, and as he flinched, Roran leaned over and brought his hammer down on the man's left knee. The man's face went white with pain. Before he could recover, Roran struck him in the small of his back, and then as the soldier screamed and arched his spine, Roran ended his misery with a quick blow to the head.

Roran sat panting for a moment, then tugged on Snowfire's reins and spurred him into a canter as they returned to the convoy. His eyes darting from place to place, drawn by any flicker of motion, Roran took stock of the battle. Most of the soldiers were already dead, as were the men who had been driving the wagons. By the

403

lead wagon, Carn stood facing a tall man in robes, the two of them rigid except for occasional twitches, the only sign of their invisible duel. Even as Roran watched, Carn's opponent pitched forward and lay motionless on the ground.

By the middle of the convoy, however, five enterprising soldiers had cut the oxen loose from three wagons and had pulled the wagons into a triangle, from within which they were able to hold off Martland Redbeard and ten other Varden. Four of the soldiers poked spears between the wagons, while the fifth fired arrows at the Varden, forcing them to retreat behind the nearest wagon for cover. The archer had already wounded several of the Varden, some of whom had fallen off their horses, others of whom had kept their saddles long enough to find cover.

Roran frowned. They could not afford to linger out in the open on one of the Empire's main roads while they slowly picked off the entrenched soldiers. Time was against them.

All the soldiers were facing west, the direction from which the Varden had attacked. Aside from Roran, none of the Varden had crossed to the other side of the convoy. Thus, the soldiers were unaware that he was bearing down on them from the east.

A plan occurred to Roran. In any other circumstances, he would have dismissed it as ludicrous and impractical, but as it was, he accepted the plan as the only course of action that could resolve the standoff without further delay. He did not bother to consider the danger to himself; he had abandoned all fear of death and injury the moment their charge had begun.

Roran urged Snowfire into a full gallop. He placed his left hand on the front of his saddle, edged his boots almost out of the stirrups, and gathered his muscles in preparation. When Snowfire was fifty feet away from the triangle of wagons, he pressed downward with his hand and, lifting himself, placed his feet on the saddle and stood crouched on Snowfire. It took all his skill and concentration to maintain his balance. As Roran had expected, Snowfire lessened his speed and started to veer to the side as the cluster of wagons loomed large before them.

Roran released the reins just as Snowfire turned, and jumped off the horse's back, leaping high over the east-facing wagon of the triangle. His stomach lurched. He caught a glimpse of the archer's upturned face, the soldier's eyes round and edged with white, then slammed into the man, and they both crashed to the ground. Roran landed on top, the soldier's body cushioning his fall. Pushing himself onto his knees, Roran raised his shield and drove its rim through the gap between the soldier's helm and his tunic, breaking his neck. Then Roran shoved himself upright.

The other four soldiers were slow to react. The one to Roran's left made the mistake of trying to pull his spear inside the triangle of wagons, but in his haste, he wedged the spear between the rear of one wagon and the front wheel of another, and the shaft splintered in his hands. Roran lunged toward him. The soldier tried to retreat, but the wagons blocked his way. Swinging the hammer in an underhand blow, Roran caught the soldier beneath his chin.

The second soldier was smarter. He let go of his spear and reached for the sword at his belt but only succeeded in drawing the blade halfway out of the sheath before Roran staved in his chest.

The third and fourth soldiers were ready for Roran by then. They converged on him, naked blades outstretched, snarls on their faces. Roran tried to sidestep them, but his torn leg failed him, and he stumbled and fell to one knee. The closest soldier slashed downward. With his shield, Roran blocked the blow, then dove forward and crushed the soldier's foot with the flat end of his hammer. Cursing, the soldier toppled to the ground. Roran promptly smashed the soldier's face, then flipped onto his back, knowing that the last soldier was directly behind him.

Roran froze, his arms and legs splayed to either side.

The soldier stood over him, holding his sword extended, the tip of the gleaming blade less than an inch away from Roran's throat.

So this is how it ends, thought Roran.

Then a thick arm appeared around the soldier's neck, yanking him backward, and the soldier uttered a choked cry as a sword blade sprouted from the middle of his chest, along with a spray of blood. The soldier collapsed into a limp pile, and in his place, there stood Martland Redbeard. The earl was breathing heavily, and his beard and chest were splattered with gore.

Martland stuck his sword in the dirt, leaned on the pommel, and surveyed the carnage within the triangle of wagons. He nodded. "You'll do, I think."

Roran sat on the end of a wagon, biting his tongue as Carn cut off the rest of his boot. Trying to ignore the stabs of agony from his leg, Roran gazed up at the vultures circling overhead and concentrated on memories of his home in Palancar Valley.

He grunted as Carn probed especially deep into the gash.

"Sorry," said Carn. "I have to inspect the wound."

Roran kept staring at the vultures and did not answer. After a minute, Carn uttered a number of words in the ancient language, and a few seconds later, the pain in Roran's leg subsided to a dull ache. Looking down, Roran saw his leg was whole once more.

The effort of healing Roran and the two other men before him had left Carn gray-faced and shaking. The magician slumped against the wagon, wrapping his arms around his middle, his expression queasy.

"Are you all right?" Roran asked.

Carn lifted his shoulders in a minuscule shrug. "I just need a moment to recover. . . . The ox scratched the outer bone of your lower leg. I repaired the scratch, but I didn't have the strength to completely heal the rest of your injury. I stitched together your skin and muscle, so it won't bleed or pain you overmuch, but only lightly. The flesh there won't hold much more than your weight, not until it mends on its own, that is."

"How long will that take?"

"A week, perhaps two."

Roran pulled on the remains of his boot. "Eragon cast wards around me to protect me from injury. They saved my life several times today. Why didn't they protect me from the ox's horn, though?"

"I don't know, Roran," Carn said, sighing. "No one can prepare for every eventuality. That's one reason magic is so perilous. If you overlook a single facet of a spell, it may do nothing but weaken you, or worse, it may do some horrible thing you never intended. It happens to even the best magicians. There must be a flaw in your cousin's wards—a misplaced word or a poorly reasoned statement—that allowed the ox to gore you."

Easing himself off the wagon, Roran limped toward the head of the convoy, assessing the result of the battle. Five of the Varden had been wounded during the fighting, including himself, and two others had died: one a man Roran had barely met, the other Ferth, whom he had spoken with on several occasions. Of the soldiers and the men who steered the wagons, none remained alive.

Roran paused by the first two soldiers he had killed and studied their corpses. His saliva turned bitter, and his gut roiled with revulsion. *Now I have killed . . . I don't know how many.* He realized that during the madness of the Battle of the Burning Plains, he had lost count of the number of men he had slain. That he had sent so many to their deaths he could not remember the full number unsettled him. *Must I slaughter entire fields of men in order to regain what the Empire stole from me?* An even more disconcerting thought occurred to him: *And if I do, how could I return to Palancar Valley and live in peace when my soul was stained black with the blood of hundreds?*

Closing his eyes, Roran consciously relaxed all the muscles in his body, seeking to calm himself. *I kill for my love. I kill for my love of Katrina, and for my love of Eragon and everyone from Carvahall, and also for my love of the Varden, and my love of this land of ours. For my love, I will wade through an ocean of blood, even if it destroys me.*

"Never seen the likes o' that before, Stronghammer," said Ulhart. Roran opened his eyes to find the grizzled warrior standing in front of him, holding Snowfire by the reins. "No one else crazy enough to try a trick like that, jumping over the wagons, none that lived to tell the tale, nohow. Good job, that. Watch yourself, though. Can't go around leaping off horses an' taking on five men yourself an' expect to see another summer, eh? Bit of caution if you're wise."

"I'll keep that in mind," said Roran as he accepted Snowfire's reins from Ulhart.

In the minutes since Roran had disposed of the last of the soldiers, the uninjured warriors had been going to each of the wagons in the convoy, cutting open their bundles of cargo, and reporting the contents to Martland, who recorded what they found so Nasuada could study the information and perhaps gather from it some indication of Galbatorix's plans. Roran watched as the men examined the last few wagons, which contained bags of wheat and stacks of uniforms. That finished, the men slit the throats of the remaining oxen, soaking the road with blood. Killing the beasts bothered Roran, but he understood the importance of denying them to the Empire and would have wielded the knife himself if asked. They would have taken the oxen back to the Varden, but the animals were too slow and cumbersome. The soldiers' horses, however, could keep pace as they fled enemy territory, so they captured as many as they could and tied them behind their own steeds.

Then one of the men took a resin-soaked torch from his saddlebags and, after a few seconds of work with his flint and steel, lit it. Riding up and down the convoy, he pressed the torch against each wagon until it caught fire and then tossed the torch into the back of the last wagon.

"Mount up!" shouted Martland.

Roran's leg throbbed as he pulled himself onto Snowfire. He spurred the stallion over next to Carn as the surviving men assembled on their steeds in a double line behind Martland. The horses snorted and pawed at the ground, impatient to put distance between themselves and the fire.

Martland started forward at a swift trot, and the rest of the group followed, leaving behind them the line of burning wagons, like so many glowing beads strung out upon the lonely road.

✦ ✦ ✦

A Forest of Stone

A cheer went up from the crowd.

Eragon was sitting in the wooden stands that the dwarves had built along the base of the outer ramparts of Bregan Hold. The hold sat on a rounded shoulder of Thardûr mountain, over a mile above the floor of the mist-laden valley, and from it one could see for leagues in either direction, or until the ridged mountains obscured the view. Like Tronjheim and the other dwarf cities Eragon had visited, Bregan Hold was made entirely of quarried stone—in this case, a reddish granite that lent a sense of warmth to the rooms and corridors within. The hold itself was a thick, solid building that rose five stories to an open bell tower, which was topped by a teardrop of glass that was as large around as two dwarves and was held in place by four granite ribs that joined together to form a pointed capstone. The teardrop, as Orik had told Eragon, was a larger version of the dwarves' flameless lanterns, and during notable occasions or emergencies, it could be used to illuminate the entire valley with a golden light. The dwarves called it Az Sindriznarrvel, or The Gem of Sindri. Clustered around the flanks of the hold were numerous outbuildings, living quarters for the servants and warriors of Dûrgrimst Ingeitum, as well as other structures, such as stables, forges, and a church devoted to Morgothal, the dwarves' god of fire and their patron god of smiths. Below the high, smooth walls of Bregan Hold were dozens of farms scattered about clearings in the forest, coils of smoke drifting up from the stone houses.

All that and more, Orik had shown and explained to Eragon after the three dwarf children had escorted Eragon into the courtyard of Bregan Hold, shouting, "Argetlam!" to everyone within earshot.

Orik had greeted Eragon like a brother and then had taken him to the baths and, when he was clean, saw to it that he was garbed in a robe of deep purple, with a gold circlet for his brow.

Afterward, Orik surprised Eragon by introducing him to Hvedra, a bright-eyed, apple-faced dwarf woman with long hair, and proudly announcing that they had been married but two days past. While Eragon expressed his astonishment and congratulations, Orik shifted from foot to foot before replying, "It pained me that you were not able to attend the ceremony, Eragon. I had one of our spellcasters contact Nasuada, and I asked her if she would give you and Saphira my invitation, but she refused to mention it to you; she feared the offer might distract you from the task at hand. I cannot blame her, but I wish that this war would have allowed you to be at our wedding, and us at your cousin's, for we are all related now, by law if not by blood."

In her thick accent, Hvedra said, "Please, consider me as your kin now, Shadeslayer. So long as it is within mine power, you shall always be treated as family at Bregan Hold, and you may claim sanctuary of us whenever you need, even if it is Galbatorix who hunts you."

Eragon bowed, touched by her offer. "You are most kind." Then he asked, "If you don't mind my curiosity, why did you and Orik choose to marry now?"

"We had planned to join hands this spring, but . . ."

"But," Orik continued in his gruff manner, "the Urgals attacked Farthen Dûr, and then Hrothgar sent me traipsing off with you to Ellesméra. When I returned here and the families of the clan accepted me as their new grimstborith, we thought it the perfect time to consummate our betrothal and become husband and wife. None of us may survive the year, so why tarry?"

"So you *did* become clan chief," Eragon said.

"Aye. Choosing the next leader of Dûrgrimst Ingeitum was a contentious business—we were hard at it for over a week—but in the end, most of the families agreed that I should follow in

Hrothgar's footsteps and inherit his position since I was his only named heir."

Now Eragon sat next to Orik and Hvedra, devouring the bread and mutton the dwarves had brought him and watching the contest taking place in front of the stands. It was customary, Orik had said, for a dwarf family, if they had the gold, to stage games for the entertainment of their wedding guests. Hrothgar's family was so wealthy, the current games had already lasted for three days and were scheduled to continue for another four. The games consisted of many events: wrestling, archery, swordsmanship, feats of strength, and the current event, the Ghastgar.

From opposite ends of a grassy field, two dwarves rode toward each other on white Feldûnost. The horned mountain goats bounded across the sward, each leap over seventy feet long. The dwarf on the right had a small buckler strapped to his left arm but carried no weapons. The dwarf on the left had no shield, but in his right hand, he held a javelin poised to throw.

Eragon held his breath as the distance between the Feldûnost narrowed. When they were less than thirty feet apart, the dwarf with the spear whipped his arm through the air and launched the missile at his opponent. The other dwarf did not cover himself with his shield, but rather reached out and, with amazing dexterity, caught the spear by the shaft. He brandished it over his head. The crowd gathered around the lists let out a resounding cheer, which Eragon joined in, clapping vigorously.

"That was skillfully done!" exclaimed Orik. He laughed and drained his tankard of mead, his polished coat of mail sparkling in the early-evening light. He wore a helm embellished with gold, silver, and rubies and, on his fingers, five large rings. At his waist hung his ever-present ax. Hvedra was attired even more richly, with strips of embroidered cloth upon her sumptuous dress, strands of pearls and twisted gold around her neck, and in her hair, an ivory comb set with an emerald as large as Eragon's thumb.

A line of dwarves stood and winded a set of curved horns, the brassy notes echoing off the mountains. Then a barrel-chested dwarf stepped forward and, in Dwarvish, announced the winner of the last contest, as well as the names of the next pair to compete in the Ghastgar.

When the master of ceremonies finished speaking, Eragon bent over and asked, "Will you be accompanying us to Farthen Dûr, Hvedra?"

She shook her head and smiled widely. "I cannot. I must stay here and tend to the affairs of the Ingeitum while Orik is gone, so he does not return to find our warriors starving and all our gold spent."

Chuckling, Orik held out his tankard toward one of the servants standing several yards away. As the dwarf hurried over and refilled it with mead from a pitcher, Orik said to Eragon with obvious pride, "Hvedra does not boast. She is not only my wife, she is the . . . Ach, you have no word for it. She is the grimstcarvlorss of Dûrgrimst Ingeitum. *Grimstcarvlorss* means . . . 'the keeper of the house,' 'the arranger of the house.' It is her duty to ensure that the families of our clan pay their agreed-upon tithes to Bregan Hold, that our herds are driven to the proper fields at the proper times, that our stocks of feed and grain do not fall too low, that the women of the Ingeitum weave enough fabric, that our warriors are well equipped, that our smiths always have ore to smelt into iron, and in short, that our clan is well managed and will prosper and thrive. There is a saying among our people: a good grimstcarvlorss can make a clan—"

"And a bad grimstcarvlorss will destroy a clan," said Hvedra.

Orik smiled and clasped one of her hands in his. "And Hvedra is the best of grimstcarvlorssn. It is not an inherited title. You must prove that you are worthy of the post if you are to hold it. It is rare for the wife of a grimstborith to be grimstcarvlorss as well. I am most fortunate in that regard." Bending their heads together, he and Hvedra rubbed noses. Eragon glanced away, feeling lonely and excluded. Leaning back, Orik took a draught of mead, then said, "There have been many famous grimstcarvlorssn in our history. It is often said that the only thing we clan leaders are good for is declaring war on each other and that the grimstcarvlorssn prefer we

413

spend our time squabbling among ourselves so we do not have the time to interfere in the workings of the clan."

"Come now, Skilfz Delva," chided Hvedra. "You know that is not truth. Or it shall not be truth with us."

"Mmm," said Orik, and touched his forehead to Hvedra's. They rubbed noses again.

Eragon returned his attention to the crowd below as it erupted in a frenzy of hissing and jeering. He saw that one of the dwarves competing in the Ghastgar had lost his nerve and, at the last moment, had yanked his Feldûnost off to one side and even then was attempting to flee his opponent. The dwarf with the javelin pursued him twice around the lists. When they were close enough, he rose up in his stirrups and cast the spear, striking the cowardly dwarf in the back of his left shoulder. With a howl, the dwarf fell off his steed and lay on his side, clutching at the blade and shaft embedded in his flesh. A healer rushed toward him. After a moment, everyone turned their backs on the spectacle.

Orik's upper lip curved with disgust. "Bah! It will be many years before his family is able to erase the stain of their son's dishonor. I am sorry you have had to witness this contemptible act, Eragon."

"It's never enjoyable watching someone shame themselves."

The three of them sat in silence through the next two contests, then Orik startled Eragon by grasping him by the shoulder and asking, "How would you like to see a forest of stone, Eragon?"

"No such thing exists, unless it is carved."

Orik shook his head, his eyes twinkling. "It is not carved, and it does exist. So I ask again, would you like to see a forest of stone?"

"If you are not jesting . . . yes, I would."

"Ah, I am glad you accepted. I do not jest, and I promise you that tomorrow you and I shall walk among trees of granite. It is one of the wonders of the Beor Mountains. Everyone who is a guest of Dûrgrimst Ingeitum should have an opportunity to visit it."

* * *

The following morning, Eragon rose from his too-small bed in his stone room with its low ceiling and half-sized furniture, washed his face in a basin of cold water, and, out of habit, reached with his mind toward Saphira. He felt only the thoughts of the dwarves and the animals in and around the hold. Eragon faltered and leaned forward, gripping the rim of the basin, overcome by his sense of isolation. He remained in that position, unable to move or think, until his vision turned crimson and flashing spots floated in front of his eyes. With a gasp, he exhaled and refilled his lungs.

I missed her during the trip from Helgrind, he thought, *but at least I knew I was returning to her as fast as I could. Now I am traveling away from her, and I do not know when we will be reunited.*

Shaking himself, he dressed and made his way through the winding corridors of Bregan Hold, bowing to the dwarves he passed, who for their part greeted him with energetic reiterations of "Argetlam!"

He found Orik and twelve other dwarves in the courtyard of the hold, saddling a line of sturdy ponies, whose breath formed white plumes in the cold air. Eragon felt like a giant as the short, burly men moved about him.

Orik hailed him. "We have a donkey in our stables, if you would like to ride."

"No, I'll continue on foot, if it's all the same to you."

Orik shrugged. "As you wish."

When they were ready to depart, Hvedra descended the broad stone steps from the entrance to the main hall of Bregan Hold, her dress trailing behind her, and presented to Orik an ivory horn clad with gold filigree around the mouth and bell. She said, "This was mine father's when he rode with Grimstborith Aldhrim. I give it to you so you may remember me in the days to come." She said more in Dwarvish, so softly Eragon could not hear, and then she and Orik touched foreheads. Straightening in his saddle, Orik placed the horn to his lips and winded it. A deep, rousing note rang forth, increasing in volume until the air within the courtyard seemed to vibrate like a wind-sawed rope. A pair of black ravens rose from the tower above, cawing. The sound of the horn made Eragon's blood tingle. He shifted in place, eager to be gone.

Lifting the horn over his head and with a final look at Hvedra, Orik spurred his pony forward, trotted out of the main gates of Bregan Hold, and turned east, toward the head of the valley. Eragon and the twelve other dwarves followed close behind.

For three hours, they followed a well-worn trail across the side of Thardûr mountain, climbing ever higher above the valley floor. The dwarves drove the ponies as fast as they could without injuring the animals, but their pace was still only a fraction of Eragon's speed when he was free to run unchecked. Although he was frustrated, Eragon refrained from complaining, for he realized that it was inevitable he would have to travel slower with any but elves or Kull.

He shivered and pulled his cloak closer around himself. The sun had yet to appear over the Beor Mountains, and a damp chill pervaded the valley, even though noon was only a few hours away.

Then they came upon a flat expanse of granite over a thousand feet wide, bordered on the right by a slanting cliff of naturally formed octagonal pillars. Curtains of shifting mist obscured the far end of the stone field.

Orik raised a hand and said, "Behold, Az Knurldrâthn."

Eragon frowned. Stare as he might, he could discern nothing of interest in the barren location. "I see no forest of stone."

Clambering down from his pony, Orik handed the reins to the warrior behind him and said, "Walk with me, if you would, Eragon."

Together they strode toward the twisting bank of fog, Eragon shortening his steps to match Orik's. The mist kissed Eragon's face, cool and moist. The vapor became so thick that it obscured the rest of the valley, enveloping them in a featureless gray landscape where even up and down seemed arbitrary. Undaunted, Orik proceeded with a confident gait. Eragon, however, felt disoriented and slightly unsteady, and he walked with a hand held out in front of him, in case he should bump into anything hidden within the fog.

Orik stopped at the edge of a thin crack that defaced the granite they stood on and said, "What see you now?"

Squinting, Eragon swept his gaze back and forth, but the fog seemed as monotonous as ever. He opened his mouth to say as much but then noticed a slight irregularity in the texture of the mist to his right, a faint pattern of light and dark that held its shape even while the mist drifted past. He became aware of other areas that were static as well: strange, abstract patches of contrast that formed no recognizable objects.

"I don't . . . ," he started to say when a breath of wind ruffled his hair. Under the gentle encouragement of the newborn breeze, the fog thinned and the disjoined patterns of shade resolved into the boles of large, ash-colored trees with bare and broken limbs. Dozens of the trees surrounded him and Orik, the pale skeletons of an ancient forest. Eragon pressed his palm against a trunk. The bark was as cold and hard as a boulder. Blotches of pallid lichen clung to the surface of the tree. The back of Eragon's neck prickled. Although he did not consider himself overly superstitious, the ghostly mist and the eerie half-light and the appearance of the trees themselves— grim and foreboding and mysterious—ignited a spark of fear inside of him.

He wet his lips and asked, "How did these come to be?"

Orik shrugged. "Some claim that Gûntera must have placed them here when he created Alagaësia out of nothingness. Others claim Helzvog made them, for stone is his favorite element, and would not the god of stone have trees of stone for his garden? And still others say no, that once these were trees like any others, and a great catastrophe eons ago must have buried them in the ground, and that over time, wood became dirt, and dirt became stone."

"Is that possible?"

"Only the gods know for certain. Who besides them can hope to understand the whys and wherefores of the world?" Orik shifted his position. "Our ancestors discovered the first of the trees while

quarrying granite here, over a thousand years ago. The then grimstborith of Dûrgrimst Ingeitum, Hvalmar Lackhand, stopped the
mining and, instead, had his masons chisel out the trees from the
surrounding stone. When they had excavated nigh on fifty trees,
Hvalmar realized that there might be hundreds, or even thousands,
of stone trees entombed within the side of Mount Thardûr, and so
he ordered his men to abandon the project. This place, however,
captured the imagination of our race, and ever since, knurlan from
every clan have traveled here and labored to extricate more trees
from the grip of the granite. There are even knurlan who have dedicated their lives to the task. It has also become a tradition to send
troublesome offspring here to chisel out a tree or two while under
the supervision of a master mason."

"That sounds tedious."

"It gives them time to repent of their ways." With one hand, Orik
stroked his braided beard. "I spent some months here myself when I
was a rambunctious lad of four-and-thirty."

"And did you repent of your ways?"

"Eta. No. It was too . . . *tedious*. After all those weeks, I had freed
only a single branch from the granite, so I ran away and fell in with
a group of Vrenshrrgn—"

"Dwarves from the clan Vrenshrrgn?"

"Yes, knurlagn of the clan Vrenshrrgn, War Wolves, Wolves of
War, however you might say it in this tongue. I fell in with them,
became drunk on ale, and as they were hunting Nagran, decided
that I too should kill a boar and bring it to Hrothgar to appease his
anger at me. It wasn't the wisest thing I have done. Even our most
skilled warriors fear to hunt Nagran, and I was still more boy than
man. Once my mind cleared, I cursed myself for a fool, but I had
sworn I would, so I had no choice but to fulfill my oath."

When Orik paused, Eragon asked, "What happened?"

"Oh, I killed a Nagra, with help from the Vrenshrrgn, but the
boar gored me in the shoulder and tossed me into the branches of a
nearby tree. The Vrenshrrgn had to carry the both of us, the Nagra

and me, back to Bregan Hold. The boar pleased Hrothgar, and I . . . I, despite the ministrations of our best healers, I had to spend the next month resting in bed, which Hrothgar said was punishment enough for defying his orders."

Eragon watched the dwarf for a while. "You miss him."

Orik stood for a moment with his chin tucked against his stocky chest. Lifting his ax, he struck the granite with the end of the haft, producing a sharp clack that echoed among the trees. "It has been nigh on two centuries since the last dûrgrimstvren, the last clan war, racked our nation, Eragon. But by Morgothal's black beard, we stand on the brink of another one now."

"Now, of all times?" exclaimed Eragon, appalled. "Is it really that bad?"

Orik scowled. "It is worse. Tensions between the clans are higher than they have ever been in living memory. Hrothgar's death and Nasuada's invasion of the Empire have served to inflame passions, aggravate old rivalries, and lend strength to those who believe it is folly to cast our lot with the Varden."

"How can they believe that when Galbatorix has already attacked Tronjheim with the Urgals?"

"Because," said Orik, "they are convinced it is impossible to defeat Galbatorix, and their argument holds much sway with our people. Can you honestly tell me, Eragon, that if Galbatorix were to confront you and Saphira this very instant, that the two of you could best him?"

Eragon's throat tightened. "No."

"I thought not. Those who are opposed to the Varden have blinded themselves to Galbatorix's threat. They say that if we had refused shelter to the Varden, if we had not accepted you and Saphira into fair Tronjheim, then Galbatorix would have had no reason to make war on us. They say that if we just keep to ourselves and remain hidden in our caves and tunnels, we shall have nothing to fear from Galbatorix. They do not realize that Galbatorix's hunger for power is insatiable and that he will not rest until all of

Alagaësia lies at his feet." Orik shook his head, and the muscles in his forearms bunched and knotted as he pinched the ax blade between his wide fingers. "I will not allow our race to cower in tunnels like frightened rabbits until the wolf outside digs his way in and eats us all. We must continue fighting out of the hope that somehow we can find a way to kill Galbatorix. And I will not allow our nation to disintegrate into a clan war. With circumstances as they are, another dûrgrimstvren would destroy our civilization and possibly doom the Varden as well." His jaw set, Orik turned toward Eragon. "For the good of my people, I intend to seek the throne myself. Dûrgrimstn Gedthrall, Ledwonnû, and Nagra have already pledged their support to me. However, there are many who stand between me and the crown; it will not be easy to garner enough votes to become king. I need to know, Eragon, will you back me in this?"

Crossing his arms, Eragon walked from one tree to the next and then back again. "If I do, my support might turn the other clans against you. Not only will you be asking your people to ally themselves with the Varden, you will be asking them to accept a Dragon Rider as one of their own, which they have never done before and I doubt they will want to now."

"Aye, it may turn some against me," said Orik, "but it may also gain me the votes of others. Let me be the judge of that. All I wish to know is, Will you back me? . . . Eragon, why do you hesitate?"

Eragon stared at a gnarled root that rose out of the granite by his feet, avoiding Orik's eyes. "You are concerned about the good of your people, and rightly so. But my concerns are broader; they encompass the good of the Varden and the elves and everyone else who opposes Galbatorix. If . . . if it is not likely you can win the crown, and there is another clan chief who could, and who is not unsympathetic to the Varden—"

"No one would be a more sympathetic grimstnzborith than I!"

"I'm not questioning your friendship," Eragon protested. "But if what I said came to pass and my support might ensure that such a clan chief won the throne, for the good of your people and for the good of the rest of Alagaësia, shouldn't I back the dwarf who has the best chance of succeeding?"

In a deadly quiet voice, Orik said, "You swore a blood-oath on the Knurlnien, Eragon. By every law of our realm, you are a member of Dûrgrimst Ingeitum, no matter how greatly others may disapprove. What Hrothgar did by adopting you has no precedent in all of our history, and it cannot be undone unless, as grimstborith, I banish you from our clan. If you turn against me, Eragon, you will shame me in front of our entire race and none will ever trust my leadership again. Moreover, you will prove to your detractors that we cannot trust a Dragon Rider. Clan members do not betray each other to other clans, Eragon. It is not done, not unless you wish to wake up one night with a dagger buried in your heart."

"Are you threatening me?" asked Eragon, just as quietly.

Orik swore and banged his ax against the granite again. "No! I would never lift a hand against you, Eragon! You are my foster brother, you are the only Rider free of Galbatorix's influence, and blast it if I have not become fond of you during our travels together. But even though I would not harm you, that does not mean the rest of the Ingeitum would be so forbearing. I say that not as a threat but as a statement of fact. You must understand this, Eragon. If the clan hears you have given your support to another, I may not be able to restrain them. Even though you are our guest and the rules of hospitality protect you, if you speak out against the Ingeitum, the clan will see you as having betrayed them, and it is not our custom to allow traitors to remain within our midst. Do you understand me, Eragon?"

"What do you expect of me?" shouted Eragon. He flung his arms outward and paced back and forth in front of Orik. "I swore an oath to Nasuada as well, and those were the orders she gave me."

"And you also pledged yourself to Dûrgrimst Ingeitum!" roared Orik.

Eragon stopped and stared at the dwarf. "Would you have me doom all of Alagaësia just so you can maintain your standing among the clans?"

"Do not insult me!"

"Then don't ask the impossible of me! I will back you if it seems likely you can ascend to the throne, and if not, then I won't. You worry about Dûrgrimst Ingeitum and your race as a whole, while it is my duty to worry about them and all of Alagaësia as well." Eragon slumped against the cold trunk of a tree. "And I cannot afford to offend you or your—I mean, *our*—clan or the rest of dwarfdom."

In a kinder tone, Orik said, "There is another way, Eragon. It would be more difficult for you, but it would resolve your quandary."

"Oh? What wondrous solution would this be?"

Sliding his ax back under his belt, Orik walked over to Eragon, grasped him by the forearms, and gazed up at him through bushy eyebrows. "Trust me to do the right thing, Eragon Shadeslayer. Give me the same loyalty you would if you were indeed born of Dûrgrimst Ingeitum. Those under me would never presume to speak out against their own grimstborith in favor of another clan. If a grimstborith strikes the rock wrong, it is his responsibility alone, but that does not mean I am oblivious to your concerns." He glanced down for a moment, then said, "If I cannot be king, trust me not to be so blinded by the prospect of power that I cannot recognize when my bid has failed. If that should happen—not that I believe it shall—then I will, of my own volition, lend my support to one of the other candidates, for I have no more desire than you to see a grimstnzborith elected who is hostile to the Varden. And if I should help promote another to the throne, the status and prestige I will place at the service of that clan chief shall, of its very nature, include your own, since you are Ingeitum. Will you trust me, Eragon? Will you accept me as your grimstborith, as the rest of my hall-sworn subjects do?"

Eragon groaned and leaned his head against the rough tree and peered up at the crooked, bone-white branches wreathed in mist. *Trust.* Of all the things Orik could have asked of him, that was the most difficult to grant. Eragon liked Orik, but to subordinate himself to the dwarf's authority when so much was at stake would be to relinquish even more of his freedom, a prospect he loathed. And along with his freedom, he would also be relinquishing part of his responsibility for the fate of Alagaësia. Eragon felt as if he were hanging off the edge of a precipice and Orik was trying to convince him there was a ledge only a few feet below him, but Eragon could not bring himself to release his grip, for fear he would fall to his doom.

He said, "I would not be a mindless servant for you to order about. When it came to matters of Dûrgrimst Ingeitum, I would defer to you, but in all else, you would have no hold over me."

Orik nodded, his face serious. "I'm not worried about what mission Nasuada might send you on, nor whom you might kill while fighting the Empire. No, what gives me restless nights when I ought to be sleeping sound as Arghen in his cave is imagining you attempting to influence the clanmeet's voting. Your intentions are noble, I know, but noble or not, you are unfamiliar with our politics, no matter how well Nasuada may have schooled you. This is mine area of expertise, Eragon. Let me conduct it in the manner I deem appropriate. It is what Hrothgar groomed me for my entire life."

Eragon sighed, and with a sensation of falling, he said, "Very well. I will do as you think best about the succession, Grimstborith Orik."

A broad smile spread across Orik's face. He tightened his grip on Eragon's forearms, then released him, saying, "Ah, thank you, Eragon. You don't know what this means to me. It is good of you, very good of you, and I won't forget it, not if I live to be two hundred years old and my beard grows so long, it drags in the dirt."

Despite himself, Eragon chuckled. "Well, I hope it doesn't grow that long. You would trip over it all the time!"

"Perhaps I would at that," said Orik, laughing. "Besides, I rather think Hvedra would cut it short once it reached my knees. She has very definite opinions about the proper length of a beard."

* * *

Orik led the way as the two of them departed the forest of stone trees, striding through the colorless mist that swirled among the calcified trunks. They rejoined Orik's twelve warriors, then began to descend the side of Mount Thardûr. At the bottom of the valley, they continued in a straight line to the other side, and there the dwarves brought Eragon to a tunnel hidden so cleverly within the rock face, he never would have found the entrance on his own.

It was with regret that Eragon left behind the pale sunshine and fresh mountain air for the darkness of the tunnel. The passageway was eight feet wide and six feet high—which made it feel quite low to Eragon—and like all the dwarf tunnels he had visited, it was as straight as an arrow for as far as he could see. He looked back over his shoulder just in time to see the dwarf Farr swing closed the hinged slab of granite that served as a door to the tunnel, plunging their party into night. A moment later, fourteen glowing orbs of differing colors appeared as the dwarves removed flameless lanterns from their saddlebags. Orik handed one to Eragon.

Then they started forward under the roots of the mountain, and the ponies' hooves filled the tunnel with clashing echoes that seemed to shout at them like angry wraiths. Eragon grimaced, knowing they would have to listen to the din all the way to Farthen Dûr, for that was where the tunnel ended, many leagues thence. He hunched his shoulders and tightened his grip on the straps of his pack and wished he were with Saphira, flying high above the ground.

✦ ✦ ✦

THE LAUGHING DEAD

Roran squatted and gazed through the latticework of willow branches.

Two hundred yards away, fifty-three soldiers and wagon drivers sat around three separate cookfires, eating their dinner as dusk rapidly settled over the land. The men had stopped for the night on the broad, grass-covered bank next to a nameless river. The wagons full of supplies for Galbatorix's troops were parked in a rough half circle around the fires. Scores of hobbled oxen grazed behind the camp, lowing occasionally to each other. Twenty yards or so downstream, however, a soft earth shelf reared high out of the ground, which prevented any attack or escape from that quarter.

What were they thinking? Roran wondered. It was only prudent, when in hostile territory, to camp in a defensible location, which usually meant finding a natural formation to protect your back. Even so, you had to be careful to choose a resting place you could flee from if ambushed. As it was, it would be childishly easy for Roran and the other warriors under Martland's command to sweep out of the brush where they were hiding and pin the men of the Empire in the tip of the V formed by the earthen shelf and the river, where they could pick off the soldiers and drivers at their leisure. It puzzled Roran that trained soldiers would make such an obvious mistake. *Maybe they are from a city,* he thought. *Or maybe they are merely inexperienced.* He frowned. *Then why would they be entrusted with such a crucial mission?*

"Have you detected any traps?" he asked. He did not have to turn his head to know that Carn was close beside him, as well as Halmar and two other men. Save the four swordsmen who had joined Martland's company to replace those who had died or been irreparably wounded during their last engagement, Roran had fought alongside all of the men in their group. While he did not like every single one, he trusted them with his life, as he knew they trusted him. It was a bond that transcended age or upbringing. After his first battle, Roran had been surprised by how close he felt to his companions, as well as by how warm they were to him in turn.

"None that I can tell," murmured Carn. "But then—"

"They may have invented new spells you cannot detect, yes, yes. Is there a magician with them, though?"

"I can't tell for sure, but no, I don't think so."

Roran pushed away a shock of narrow willow leaves to better see the layout of the wagons. "I don't like it," he grumbled. "A magician accompanied the other convoy. Why not this one?"

"There are fewer of us than you might imagine."

"Mmh." Roran scratched his beard, still bothered by the soldiers' apparent disregard of common sense. *Could they be trying to invite an attack? They don't seem prepared for one, but appearances are hardly everything. What sort of trap could they have prepared for us? No one else is within thirty leagues, and Murtagh and Thorn were last spotted flying north from Feinster.* "Send the signal," he said. "But tell Martland it bothers me they camped here. Either they're idiots or they have some sort of defense invisible to us: magic or other trickery of the king."

Silence, then: "I sent it. Martland says he shares your concern, but unless you want to run back to Nasuada with your tail tucked between your legs, we try our luck."

Roran grunted and turned away from the soldiers. He gestured with his chin, and the other men scampered with him on hands and knees to where they had left their horses.

Standing, Roran mounted Snowfire.

"Whoa, steady, boy," he whispered, petting Snowfire as the stallion tossed his head. In the dim light, Snowfire's mane and hide gleamed like silver. Not for the first time, Roran wished his horse were a less visible shade, a nice bay or chestnut perhaps.

Taking his shield from where it hung by his saddle, Roran fit his left arm through the straps, then pulled his hammer from his belt.

He dry-swallowed, a familiar tightness between his shoulders, and readjusted his grip on the hammer.

When the five men were ready, Carn raised a finger and his eyelids drifted half closed and his lips twitched, as if he were talking with himself. A cricket sounded nearby.

Carn's eyelids snapped open. "Remember, keep your gaze directed downward until your vision adjusts, and even then, don't look at the sky." Then he began to chant in the ancient language, incomprehensible words that shivered with power.

Roran covered himself with his shield and squinted at his saddle as a pure white light, bright as the noonday sun, illuminated the landscape. The stark glow originated from a point somewhere above the camp; Roran resisted the temptation to see exactly where.

Shouting, he kicked Snowfire in the ribs and hunched over the horse's neck as his steed leaped forward. On either side, Carn and the other warriors did the same, brandishing their weapons. Branches tore at Roran's head and shoulders, and then Snowfire broke free of the trees and raced toward the camp at full gallop.

Two other groups of horsemen also thundered toward the camp, one led by Martland, the other Ulhart.

The soldiers and drivers cried out in alarm and covered their eyes. Staggering about like blind men, they scrabbled after their weapons while trying to position themselves to repel the attack.

Roran made no attempt to slow Snowfire. Spurring the stallion once more, he rose high in the stirrups and held on with all his strength as Snowfire jumped over the slight gap between two wagons. His teeth clattered as they landed. Snowfire kicked dirt into one of the fires, sending up a burst of sparks.

The rest of Roran's group jumped the wagons as well. Knowing they would attend to the soldiers behind him, Roran concentrated on those in front. Aiming Snowfire at one of the men, he jabbed at the soldier with the end of his hammer and broke the man's nose, splashing crimson blood across his face. Roran dispatched the man with a second blow to the head, then parried a sword from another soldier.

Farther down the curved line of wagons, Martland, Ulhart, and their men also jumped into the camp, alighting with a clack of hooves and a jangle of armor and weapons. A horse screamed and fell as a soldier wounded it with a spear.

Roran blocked the soldier's sword a second time, then rapped the man's sword hand, breaking bones and forcing the man to drop his weapon. Without pause, Roran struck the man in the center of his red tunic, cracking his sternum and felling the gasping, mortally wounded soldier.

Roran twisted in the saddle, searching the camp for his next opponent. His muscles vibrated with frantic excitement; every detail around him was as sharp and clear as if it were etched in glass. He felt invincible, invulnerable. Time itself seemed to stretch and slow, so that a confused moth that fluttered past him appeared to be flying through honey instead of air.

Then a pair of hands clamped down on the back of his mail hauberk and yanked him off Snowfire and slammed him into the hard ground, knocking the breath out of him. Roran's sight flickered and went black for a moment. When he recovered, he saw that the first soldier he had attacked was sitting on his chest, choking him. The soldier blotted out the source of light Carn had created in the sky. A white halo surrounded his head and shoulders, casting his features in such deep shadow, Roran could make out nothing of his face but the flash of bared teeth.

The soldier tightened his fingers around Roran's throat as Roran gasped for air. Roran groped after his hammer, which he had dropped, but it was not within reach. Tensing his neck to keep the soldier from crushing the life out of him, he drew his dagger from his belt and drove it through the soldier's hauberk, through his gambeson, and between the ribs on the soldier's left side.

The soldier did not even flinch, nor did his grip relax.

A continuous stream of gurgling laughter emanated from the soldier. The lurching, heart-stopping chuckle, hideous in the extreme, turned Roran's stomach cold with fear. He remembered the sound from before; he had heard it while watching the Varden fight the men who felt no pain on the grassy field beside the Jiet River. In a flash, he understood why the soldiers had chosen such a poor campsite: *They do not care if they are trapped or not, for we cannot hurt them.*

Roran's vision turned red, and yellow stars danced before his eyes. Teetering on the edge of unconsciousness, he yanked the dagger free and stabbed upward, into the soldier's armpit, twisting the blade in the wound. Gouts of hot blood spurted over his hand, but the soldier did not seem to notice. The world exploded in blotches of pulsing colors as the soldier smashed Roran's head against the ground. Once. Twice. Three times. Roran bucked his hips, trying without success to throw the man off. Blind and desperate, he slashed at where he guessed the man's face to be and felt the dagger catch in soft flesh. He pulled the dagger back slightly, then lunged in that direction, feeling the impact as the tip of the blade struck bone.

The pressure around Roran's neck vanished.

Roran lay where he was, his chest heaving, then rolled over and vomited, throat burning. Still gasping and coughing, he staggered upright and saw the soldier sprawled motionless next to him, the dagger protruding from the man's left nostril.

"Go for the head!" shouted Roran, despite his raw throat. "The head!"

He left the dagger buried in the soldier's nostril and retrieved his hammer from the trampled ground where it had fallen, pausing long enough to also grab an abandoned spear, which he held with his shield hand. Jumping over the fallen soldier, he ran toward Halmar, who was on foot as well and dueling three soldiers at once. Before the soldiers noticed him, Roran bashed the two closest ones in the head so hard, he split their helms. The third he left to Halmar, instead bounding over to the soldier whose sternum he had broken and whom he had left for dead. He found the man sitting against the wheel of a wagon, spitting up clotted blood and struggling to string a bow.

Roran gored him through an eye with the spear. Pieces of gray flesh clung to the blade of the spear as he pulled it free.

An idea occurred to Roran then. He threw the spear at a man in a red tunic on the other side of the nearest fire—impaling him through the torso—then slid the haft of his hammer under his belt and strung the soldier's bow. Placing his back against a wagon, Roran began to shoot the soldiers rushing about the encampment, attempting either to kill them with a lucky shot to the face, the throat, or the heart or to cripple them so his companions could more easily dispatch them. If nothing else, he reasoned that an injured soldier might bleed to death before the fight ended.

The initial confidence of the attack had faded into confusion. The Varden were scattered and dismayed, some on their steeds, some on foot, and most bloodied. At least five, so far as Roran could tell, had died when soldiers they had thought slain had returned to assail them. How many soldiers were left, it was impossible to tell in the throng of flailing bodies, but Roran could see that they still outnumbered the scant twenty-five or so of the remaining Varden. *They could tear us into pieces with their bare hands while we try to hack them apart,* he realized. He searched with his eyes among the frenzy for Snowfire and saw that the white horse had run farther down the river, where he now stood by a willow tree, nostrils flared and ears plastered flat against his skull.

With the bow, Roran killed four more soldiers and wounded over a score. When he had only two arrows left, he spotted Carn standing on the other side of the camp, dueling a soldier by the corner of a burning tent. Drawing the bow until the fletching on the arrow tickled his ear, Roran shot the soldier in the chest. The soldier stumbled, and Carn decapitated him.

Roran tossed the bow aside and, hammer in hand, ran over to Carn and shouted, "Can't you kill them with magic?"

For a moment, Carn could only pant, then he shook his head and said, "Every spell I cast was blocked." The light from the burning tent gilded the side of his face.

Roran cursed. "Together then!" he cried, and hefted his shield.

Shoulder to shoulder, the two of them advanced upon the nearest group of soldiers: a cluster of eight men surrounding three of the Varden. The next few minutes were a spasm of flashing weapons, tearing flesh, and sudden pains for Roran. The soldiers tired more slowly than ordinary men, and they never shirked from an attack, nor did they slacken in their efforts even when suffering from the most horrific injuries. The exertion of the fight was so great, Roran's nausea returned, and after the eighth soldier fell, he leaned over and vomited again. He spat to clear his mouth of bile.

One of the Varden they had sought to rescue had died in the struggle, slain by a knife in the kidneys, but the two who were still standing joined forces with Roran and Carn, and with them, they charged the next batch of soldiers.

"Drive them toward the river!" Roran shouted. The water and the mud would limit the soldiers' movement and perhaps allow the Varden to gain the upper hand.

Not far away, Martland had succeeded in rallying the twelve of the Varden who were still on their horses, and they were already doing what Roran had suggested: herding the soldiers back toward the shining water.

The soldiers and the few drivers who were still alive resisted. They shoved their shields against the men on foot. They jabbed spears at the horses. But in spite of their violent opposition, the Varden forced them to retreat a step at a time until the men in the crimson tunics stood knee-deep in the fast-flowing water, half blinded by the uncanny light shining down on them.

"Hold the line!" shouted Martland, dismounting and planting himself with spread legs on the edge of the riverbank. "Don't let them regain the shore!"

Roran dropped into a half crouch, ground his heels into the soft earth until he was comfortable with his stance, and waited for the large soldier standing in the cold water several feet in front of him to attack. With a roar, the soldier splashed out of the shallows, swinging his sword at Roran, which Roran caught on his shield. Roran retaliated with a stroke of his hammer, but the soldier blocked him with his own shield and then cut at Roran's legs. For several seconds, they exchanged blows, but neither wounded the other. Then Roran shattered the man's left forearm, knocking him back several paces. The soldier merely smiled and uttered a mirthless, soul-chilling laugh.

Roran wondered whether he or any of his companions would survive the night. *They're harder to kill than snakes. We can cut them to ribbons, and they'll still keep coming at us unless we hit something vital.* His next thought vanished as the soldier rushed at him again, his notched sword flickering in the pale light like a tongue of flame.

Thereafter, the battle assumed a nightmarish quality for Roran. The strange, baleful light gave the water and the soldiers an unearthly aspect, bleaching them of color and projecting long, thin, razor-sharp shadows across the shifting water, while beyond and all around, the fullness of night prevailed. Again and again, he repelled the soldiers who stumbled out of the water to kill him, hammering at them until they were barely recognizable as human, and yet they would not die. With every blow, medallions of black blood stained the surface of the river, like blots of spilled ink, and drifted away on the current. The deadly sameness of each clash numbed and horrified Roran. No matter how hard he strove, there was always another mutilated soldier there to slash and stab at him. And always the demented giggling of men who knew they were dead and yet continued to maintain a semblance of life even while the Varden destroyed their bodies.

And then silence.

Roran remained crouched behind his shield with his hammer half raised, gasping and drenched with sweat and blood. A minute passed before it dawned on him that no one stood in the water before him. He glanced left and right three times, unable to grasp that the soldiers were finally, blessedly, irrevocably dead. A corpse floated past him in the glittering water.

An inarticulate bellow escaped him as a hand gripped his right arm. He whipped around, snarling and pulling away, only to see Carn next to him. The wan, gore-smeared spellcaster was speaking. "We won, Roran! Eh? They're gone! We vanquished them!"

Roran let his arms drop and tilted his head back, too tired even to sit. He felt . . . he felt as if his senses were abnormally sharp, and yet his emotions were dull, muted things, tamped down somewhere deep inside of himself. He was glad it was so; otherwise, he thought he would go mad.

"Gather up and inspect the wagons!" shouted Martland. "The sooner you bestir yourselves, the sooner we can leave this accursed place! Carn, attend to Welmar. I don't like the look of that gash."

With an enormous effort of will, Roran turned and trudged across the bank to the nearest wagon. Blinking away the sweat that dripped from his brow, he saw that of their original force, only nine were still fit to stand. He pushed the observation out of his mind. *Mourn later, not now.*

433

As Martland Redbeard walked across the corpse-strewn encampment, a soldier who Roran had assumed was dead flipped over and, from the ground, lopped off the earl's right hand. With a movement so graceful it appeared practiced, Martland kicked the sword out of the soldier's grip, then knelt on the soldier's throat and, using his left hand, drew a dagger from his belt and stabbed the man through one of his ears, killing him. His face flushed and strained, Martland shoved the stump of his wrist under his left armpit and waved away everyone who rushed over to him. "Leave me alone! It's hardly a wound at all. Get to those wagons! Unless you wastrels hurry up, we'll be here so long, my beard will turn white as snow. Go on!" When Carn refused to budge, however, Martland scowled and shouted, "Begone with you, or I'll have you flogged for insubordination, I will!"

Carn held up Martland's wayward hand. "I might be able to re-attach it, but I'll need a few minutes."

"Ah, confound it, give me that!" exclaimed Martland, and snatched his hand away from Carn. He tucked it inside his tunic. "Stop fretting about me and save Welmar and Lindel if you can. You can try reattaching it once we've put a few leagues between us and these monsters."

"It might be too late then," said Carn.

"That was an order, spellcaster, not a request!" thundered Martland. As Carn retreated, the earl used his teeth to tie off the sleeve of his tunic over the stump of his arm, which he again stuck in his left armpit. Sweat beaded his face. "Right, then! What misbegotten items are hidden in those confounded wagons?"

"Rope!" someone shouted.

"Whiskey!" shouted someone else.

Martland grunted. "Ulhart, you record the figures for me."

Roran helped the others as they rifled through each of the wagons, calling out the contents to Ulhart. Afterward, they slaughtered the teams of oxen and lit the wagons on fire, as before. Then they rounded up their horses and mounted them, tying the injured into their saddles.

When they were ready to depart, Carn gestured toward the flare of light in the sky and murmured a long, tangled word. Night enveloped the world. Glancing up, Roran beheld a throbbing after-image of Carn's face superimposed over the faint stars, and then as he became accustomed to the darkness, he beheld the soft gray shapes of thousands of disoriented moths scattering across the sky like the shades of men's souls.

His heart heavy within him, Roran touched his heels to Snowfire's flanks and rode away from the remnants of the convoy.

◆ ◆ ◆

BLOOD ON THE ROCKS

Frustrated, Eragon stormed out of the circular chamber buried deep under the center of Tronjheim. The oak door slammed shut behind him with a hollow boom.

Eragon stood with his hands on his hips in the middle of the arched corridor outside the chamber and glared at the floor, which was tessellated with rectangles of agate and jade. Since he and Orik had arrived in Tronjheim, three days ago, the thirteen chiefs of the dwarf clans had done nothing but argue about issues that Eragon considered inconsequential, such as which clans had the right to graze their flocks in certain disputed pastures. As he listened to the clan chiefs debate obscure points of their legal code, Eragon often felt like shouting that they were being blind fools who were going to doom all of Alagaësia to Galbatorix's rule unless they put aside their petty concerns and chose a new ruler without further delay.

Still lost in thought, Eragon slowly walked down the corridor, barely noticing the four guards who followed him—as they did wherever he went—nor the dwarves he passed in the hall, who greeted him with variations of "Argetlam." *The worst one is Íorûnn,* Eragon decided. The dwarf woman was the grimstborith of Dûrgrimst Vrenshrrgn, a powerful, warlike clan, and she had made it clear, from the very beginning of the deliberations, that she intended to have the throne for herself. Only one other clan, the Urzhad, had openly pledged themselves to her cause, but as she had demonstrated on multiple occasions during the meetings between the clan chiefs, she was clever, cunning, and able to twist most any situation to her advantage. *She might make an excellent queen,* Eragon admitted to himself, *but she's so devious, it's impossible to know whether she would support the Varden once she was enthroned.* He allowed himself a wry smile. Talking with Íorûnn was always awkward for him. The dwarves considered her a great beauty, and even by the standards of humans, she cut a striking figure. Besides which, she seemed to have developed a fascination with Eragon that he was unable to fathom. In every conversation they had, she insisted upon making allusions to the dwarves' history and mythology that Eragon did not understand but that seemed to amuse Orik and the other dwarves to no end.

In addition to Íorûnn, two other clan chiefs had emerged as rivals for the throne: Gannel, chief of Dûrgrimst Quan, and Nado, chief of Dûrgrimst Knurlcarathn. As the custodians of the dwarves' religion, the Quan wielded enormous influence among their race, but so far, Gannel had obtained the support of but two other clans, Dûrgrimst Ragni Hefthyn and Dûrgrimst Ebardac—a clan primarily devoted to scholarly research. In contrast, Nado had forged a larger coalition, consisting of the clans Feldûnost, Fanghur, and Az Sweldn rak Anhûin.

Whereas Íorûnn seemed to want the throne merely for the power she would gain thereafter, and Gannel did not seem inherently hostile to the Varden—although neither was he friendly toward them—Nado was openly and vehemently opposed to any involvement with Eragon, Nasuada, the Empire, Galbatorix, Queen Islanzadí, or, so far as Eragon could tell, any living being outside of the Beor Mountains. The Knurlcarathn were the stoneworkers' clan and, in men and material goods, they had no equal, for every other clan depended upon their expertise for the tunneling and the building of their abodes, and even the Ingeitum needed them to mine the ore for their smiths. And if Nado's bid for the crown should falter, Eragon knew that many of the other, lesser clan chiefs who shared his views would leap up to take his place. Az Sweldn rak Anhûin, for example—whom Galbatorix and the Forsworn had nearly obliterated during their uprising—had declared themselves Eragon's blood enemies during his visit to the city of Tarnag and, in every action of theirs at the clanmeet, had demonstrated their implacable hatred of Eragon, Saphira, and all things to do with dragons and those who rode them. They had objected to Eragon's very presence at the meetings of the clan chiefs, even though it was perfectly legal by dwarf law, and forced a vote on the issue, thereby delaying the proceedings another six unnecessary hours.

One of these days, thought Eragon, *I will have to find a way to make peace with them. That or I'll have to finish what Galbatorix started. I refuse to live my entire life in fear of Az Sweldn rak Anhûin.* Again, as he had done so often in the past few days, he waited a moment for Saphira's response, and when it was not forthcoming, a familiar pang of unhappiness lanced his heart.

How secure the alliances between any of the clans were, however, was a question of some uncertainty. Neither Orik nor Íorûnn nor Gannel nor Nado had enough support to win a popular vote, so they were all actively engaged in trying to retain the loyalties of the clans who had already promised to help them while at the same time trying to poach their opponents' backers. Despite the importance of the process, Eragon found it exceedingly tedious and frustrating.

Based upon Orik's explanation, it was Eragon's understanding that before the clan chiefs could elect a ruler, they had to vote on whether they were *prepared* to choose a new king or queen and that the preliminary election had to garner at least nine votes in its favor if it was to pass. As of yet, none of the clan chiefs, Orik included, felt secure enough in their positions to bring the matter to a head and proceed to the final election. It was, as Orik had said, the most delicate part of the process and, in some instances, had been known to drag on for a frustratingly long time.

As he pondered the situation, Eragon wandered aimlessly through the warren of chambers below Tronjheim until he found himself in a dry, dusty room lined with five black arches on one side and a bas-relief carving of a snarling bear twenty feet high on the other. The bear had gold teeth and round, faceted rubies for eyes.

"Where are we, Kvîstor?" asked Eragon, glancing at his guards. His voice spawned hollow echoes in the room. Eragon could sense the minds of many of the dwarves in the levels above them, but he had no idea how to reach them.

The lead guard, a youngish dwarf no older than sixty, stepped forward. "These rooms were cleared millennia ago by Grimstnzborith Korgan, when Tronjheim was under construction. We have not used them much since, except when our entire race congregates in Farthen Dûr."

Eragon nodded. "Can you lead me back to the surface?"

"Of course, Argetlam."

Several minutes of brisk walking brought them to a broad staircase with shallow, dwarf-sized steps that climbed out of the ground to a passageway somewhere in the southwestern quadrant of Tronjheim's base. From there Kvîstor guided Eragon to the southern branch of the four mile-long hallways that divided Tronjheim along the cardinal compass points.

438

It was the same hallway through which Eragon and Saphira had first entered Tronjheim several months ago, and Eragon walked down it, toward the center of the city-mountain, with a strange sense of nostalgia. He felt as if he had aged several years in the interim.

The four-story-high avenue thronged with dwarves from every clan. All of them noticed Eragon, of that he was sure, but not all deigned to acknowledge him, for which he was grateful, as it saved him the effort of having to return even more greetings.

Eragon stiffened as he saw a line of Az Sweldn rak Anhûin cross the hallway. As one, the dwarves turned their heads and looked at him, their expressions obscured behind the purple veils those of their clan always wore in public. The last dwarf in line spat on the floor toward Eragon before filing through an archway and out of the hall along with his or her brethren.

If Saphira were here, they would not dare to be so rude, thought Eragon.

A half hour later, he reached the end of the majestic hallway, and although he had been there many times before, a sense of awe and wonder overwhelmed him as he stepped between the pillars of black onyx topped with yellow zircons thrice the size of a man and entered the circular chamber in the heart of Tronjheim.

The chamber was a thousand feet from side to side, with a floor of polished carnelian etched with a hammer surrounded by twelve pentacles, which was the crest of Dûrgrimst Ingeitum and of the dwarves' first king, Korgan, who had discovered Farthen Dûr while mining for gold. Opposite Eragon and to either side were the openings to the three other halls that radiated out through the city-mountain. The chamber had no ceiling but ascended all the way to the top of Tronjheim, a mile overhead. There it opened to the dragonhold where Eragon and Saphira had resided before Arya broke the star sapphire, and then to the sky beyond: a rich blue disk that seemed unimaginably distant, ringed as it was by the open mouth of Farthen Dûr, the hollow ten-mile-high mountain that sheltered Tronjheim from the rest of the world.

Only a scant amount of daylight filtered down to the base of Tronjheim. The City of Eternal Twilight, the elves called it. Since so little of the sun's radiance entered the city-mountain—except for a dazzling half hour before and after noon during the height of summer—the dwarves illuminated the interior with uncounted numbers of their flameless lanterns. Thousands of them were on glorious display in the chamber. A bright lantern hung from the outside of every other pillar of the curved arcades that lined each level of the city-mountain, and even more lanterns were mounted within the arcades, marking the entrances to strange and unknown rooms, as well as the path of Vol Turin, the Endless Staircase, which spiraled around the chamber from top to bottom. The effect was both moody and spectacular. The lanterns were of many different colors, making it appear as if the interior of the chamber were dotted with glowing jewels.

Their glory, however, paled beside the splendor of a real jewel, the greatest jewel of them all: Isidar Mithrim. On the floor of the chamber, the dwarves had built a wooden scaffold sixty feet in diameter, and within the enclosure of fitted oak beams, they were, piece by precious piece, reassembling the shattered star sapphire with the utmost care and delicacy. The shards they had yet to place they had stored in open-topped boxes padded with nests of raw wool, each box labeled with a line of spidery runes. The boxes were spread out across a large portion of the western side of the vast room. Perhaps three hundred dwarves sat hunched over them, intent on their work as they strove to fit the shards together into a cohesive whole. Another group bustled about the scaffolding, tending to the fragmented gem within, as well as building additional structures.

Eragon watched them at their labor for several minutes, then wandered over to the section of the floor Durza had broken when he and his Urgal warriors had entered Tronjheim from the tunnels below. With the tip of his boot, Eragon tapped the polished stone in front of him. No trace of the damage Durza had wrought remained. The dwarves had done a marvelous job of erasing the marks left by the Battle of Farthen Dûr, although Eragon hoped they would commemorate the battle with a memorial of some sort, for he felt it was important that future generations not forget the cost in blood the dwarves and the Varden had paid during the course of their struggle against Galbatorix.

As Eragon walked toward the scaffolding, he nodded at Skeg, who was standing on a platform overlooking the star sapphire. Eragon had met the thin, quick-fingered dwarf before. Skeg was of Dûrgrimst Gedthrall, and it was to him King Hrothgar had entrusted the restoration of the dwarves' most valuable treasure.

Skeg gestured for Eragon to climb up onto the platform. A sparkling vista of slanting, needle-sharp spires, glittering, paper-thin edges, and rippling surfaces confronted Eragon as he heaved himself onto the rough-hewn planks. The top of the star sapphire reminded him of the ice on the Anora River in Palancar Valley at the end of winter, when the ice had melted and refrozen multiple times and was treacherous to walk over, on account of the bumps and ridges the swings in temperature had cast up. Only instead of blue, white, or clear, the remnants of the star sapphire were a soft, rosy pink, shot through with traces of dusky orange.

"How goes it?" asked Eragon.

Skeg shrugged and fluttered his hands in the air like a pair of butterflies. "It goes as it does, Argetlam. You cannot hurry perfection."

"It looks to me as if you are making quick progress."

With a bony forefinger, Skeg tapped the side of his broad, flat nose. "The top of Isidar Mithrim, what is now the bottom, Arya broke it into large pieces, which are easy to fit together. The bottom of Isidar Mithrim, though, what is now the top . . ." Skeg shook his head, his lined face doleful. "The force of the break, all the pieces pushing against the face of the gem, pushing away from Arya and the dragon Saphira, pushing down toward you and that black-hearted Shade . . . it cracked the petals of the rose into ever-smaller fragments. And the rose, Argetlam, the rose is the key to the gem. It is the most complex, the most beautiful part of Isidar Mithrim. And it is in the most pieces. Unless we can reassemble it, every last speck where it ought to be, we might as well give the gem to our jewelers and have them grind it into rings for our mothers." The words spilled out of Skeg like water from an overflowing beaker. He shouted in Dwarvish at a dwarf carrying a box across the chamber, then tugged at his white beard and asked, "Have you ever heard recounted, Argetlam, the tale of how Isidar Mithrim was carved, in the Age of Herran?"

Eragon hesitated, thinking back to his history lessons in Ellesméra. "I know it was Dûrok who carved it."

"Aye," said Skeg, "it was Dûrok Ornthrond—Eagle-eye, as you say in this tongue. It was not he who discovered Isidar Mithrim, but it was he alone who extracted it from the surrounding stone, he who carved it, and he who polished it. Fifty-seven years he spent working on the Star Rose. The gem enthralled him as nothing else.

Every night he sat crouched over Isidar Mithrim until the wee hours of the morning, as he was determined that the Star Rose should be not just art but something that would touch the hearts of all who gazed upon it and would earn him a seat of honor at the table of the gods. His devotion was such that, in the thirty-second year of his labors, when his wife told him that either he had to share the burden of the project with his apprentices or she would leave his hall, Dûrok said not a word but turned his shoulder to her and continued grinding the contours of the petal he had begun earlier that year.

"Dûrok worked on Isidar Mithrim until he was pleased with its every line and curve. Then he dropped his polishing cloth, took one step back from the Star Rose, said, 'Gûntera, protect me; it is done,' and fell dead on the floor." Skeg tapped his chest, producing a hollow thump. "His heart gave out, for what else did he have to live for? . . . That is what we are trying to reconstruct, Argetlam: fifty-seven years of ceaseless concentration by one of the finest artists our race has known. Unless we can put Isidar Mithrim back together *exactly* the way it was, we shall diminish Dûrok's accomplishment for all who have yet to see the Star Rose." Knotting his right hand into a fist, Skeg bounced it off his thigh to emphasize his words.

Eragon leaned against the hip-high railing in front of him and watched as five dwarves on the opposite side of the gem lowered a sixth dwarf, who was bound in a rope harness, until he hung inches above the sharp edges of the fractured sapphire. Reaching inside his tunic, the suspended dwarf removed a sliver of Isidar Mithrim from a leather wallet and, grasping the sliver with a minuscule set of pincers, fit it into a small gap in the gem below.

"If the coronation were held three days from now," said Eragon, "could you have Isidar Mithrim ready by then?"

Skeg drummed the railing with all ten of his fingers, tapping out a melody Eragon failed to recognize. The dwarf said, "We would not rush so with Isidar Mithrim if not for the offer of your dragon. This haste is foreign to us, Argetlam. It is not our nature, as it is humans', to rush about like agitated ants. Still, we shall do our best to have Isidar Mithrim ready in time for the coronation. If that should be three days from now . . . well, I should not be too hopeful of our prospects. But if it were later in the week, I think we might be finished."

Eragon thanked Skeg for his prediction, then took his leave. With his guards trailing after him, Eragon walked to one of the many common eating halls in the city-mountain, a long, low room with stone tables arranged in rows on one side and dwarves busying themselves about soapstone ovens on the other.

There Eragon dined on sourdough bread, fish with white meat that the dwarves caught in underground lakes, mushrooms, and some sort of mashed tuber that he had eaten before in Tronjheim but whose provenance he had yet to learn. Before he began eating, though, he was careful to test the food for poison, using the spells Oromis had taught him.

As Eragon washed down the last crust of bread with a sip of thin, watered-down breakfast beer, Orik and his contingent of ten warriors entered the hall. The warriors sat at their own tables, positioning themselves where they could watch both entrances, while Orik joined Eragon, lowering himself onto the stone bench opposite him with a weary sigh. He placed his elbows on the table and rubbed his face with his hands.

Eragon cast several spells to prevent anyone from eavesdropping, then asked, "Did we suffer another setback?"

"No, no setback. Only, these deliberations are trying in the extreme."

"I noticed."

"And everyone noticed your frustration," said Orik. "You must control yourself better hereafter, Eragon. Revealing weakness of any sort to our opponents does nothing but further their cause. I—" Orik fell silent as a portly dwarf waddled up and deposited a plate of steaming food in front of him.

Eragon scowled at the edge of the table. "But are you any closer to the throne? Have we gained any ground with all of this long-winded prattle?"

Orik raised a finger while he chewed on a mouthful of bread. "We have gained a great deal. Do not be so gloomy! After you left, Havard agreed to lower the tax on the salt Dûrgrimst Fanghur sells to the Ingeitum, in exchange for summer access to our tunnel to Nalsvrid-mérna, so they may hunt the red deer that gather around the lake during the warm months of the year. You should have seen how Nado gritted his teeth when Havard accepted my offer!"

"Bah," spat Eragon. "Taxes, deer—what does any of it have to do with who succeeds Hrothgar as ruler? Be honest with me, Orik. What is your position compared with the other clan chiefs? And how much longer is this likely to drag on? With every day that passes, it becomes more likely that the Empire will discover our ruse and Galbatorix will strike at the Varden when I am not there to fend off Murtagh and Thorn."

Orik wiped his mouth on the corner of the tablecloth. "My position is sound enough. None of the grimstborithn have the support to call a vote, but Nado and I command the greatest followings. If either of us can win over, say, another two or three clans, the balance will quickly tip in that person's favor. Havard is already wavering. It won't take too much more encouragement, I think, to convince him to defect to our camp. Tonight we will break bread with him, and I will see what I can do toward providing that encouragement." Orik devoured a piece of roast mushroom, then said, "As for when the clanmeet will end, maybe after another week if we are lucky, and maybe two if we're not."

Eragon cursed in an undertone. He was so tense, his stomach churned and rumbled and threatened to reject the meal he had just eaten.

Reaching across the table, Orik caught Eragon by the wrist. "There is nothing you or I can do to further hasten the clanmeet's decision, so do not let it upset you overmuch. Worry about what you can change, and leave the rest to sort itself out, eh?" He released Eragon.

Eragon slowly exhaled and leaned on his forearms against the table. "I know. It's only that we have so little time, and if we fail . . ."

"What will be will be," said Orik. He smiled, but his eyes were sad and hollow. "No one can escape fate's design."

"Couldn't you seize the throne by force? I know you don't have that many troops in Tronjheim, but with my support, who could stand against you?"

Orik paused with his knife halfway between his plate and his mouth, then shook his head and resumed eating. Between mouthfuls, he said, "Such a ploy would prove disastrous."

"Why?"

"Must I explain? Our entire race would turn against us, and instead of seizing control of our nation, I would inherit an empty title. If that came to pass, I would not bet a broken sword we would live to see out the year."

"Ah."

Orik said nothing more until the food on his plate was gone. Then he downed a mouthful of beer, belched, and resumed the conversation: "We are balanced upon a windy mountain path with a mile-high drop on either side. So many of my race hate and fear Dragon Riders because of the crimes Galbatorix, the Forsworn, and now Murtagh have committed against us. And so many of them fear the world beyond the mountains and the tunnels and caverns wherein we hide." He turned his mug around on the table. "Nado and Az Sweldn rak Anhûin are only worsening the situation. They play upon people's fears and poison their minds against you, the Varden, and King Orrin. . . . Az Sweldn rak Anhûin is the epitome of what we must overcome if I am to be king. Somehow we must needs find a way to allay their concerns and the concerns of those like them, for even if I am king, I will have to give them a fair hearing if I am to retain the support of the clans. A dwarf king or queen is always at the mercy of the clans, no matter how strong a ruler they may be, just as the grimstborithn are at the mercy of the families of their clan." Tilting back his head, Orik drained the last of the beer from his mug, then set it down with a sharp clack.

"Is there anything I could do, any custom or ceremony of yours I could perform, that would appease Vermûnd and his followers?" asked Eragon, naming the current grimstborith of Az Sweldn rak Anhûin. "There must be *something* I can do to put their suspicions to rest and bring this feud to an end."

Orik laughed and stood from the table. "You could die."

Early the next morning, Eragon sat with his back against the curved wall of the round room set deep below the center of Tronjheim, along with a select group of warriors, advisers, servants, and family members of the clan chiefs who were privileged enough to attend the clanmeet. The clan chiefs themselves were seated in heavy, carved chairs arranged around the edge of a circular table, which like most objects of note in the lower levels of the city-mountain bore the crest of Korgan and the Ingeitum.

At the moment, Gáldhiem, grimstborith of Dûrgrimst Feldûnost, was speaking. He was short, even for a dwarf—hardly more than two feet in height—and wore patterned robes of gold, russet, and midnight blue. Unlike the dwarves of the Ingeitum, he did not trim or braid his beard, and it tumbled across his chest like a tangled bramble. Standing on the seat of his chair, he pounded the polished table with his gloved fist and roared, ". . . Eta! Narho ûdim etal os isû vond! Narho ûdim etal os formvn mendûnost brakn, az Varden, hrestvog dûr grimstnzhadn! Az Jurgenvren qathrid né dômar oen etal—"

". . . No," Eragon's translator, a dwarf named Hûndfast, whispered in his ear. "I will not let that happen. I will not let these beardless fools, the Varden, destroy our country. The Dragon War left us weak and not—"

Eragon stifled a yawn, bored. He allowed his gaze to drift around the granite table, from Gáldhiem to Nado, a round-faced dwarf with flaxen hair who was nodding with approval at Gáldhiem's thundering speech; to Havard, who was using a dagger to clean under the fingernails of the two remaining fingers on his right hand; to Vermûnd, heavy-browed but otherwise inscrutable behind his purple veil; to Gannel and Ûndin, who sat leaning toward each other, whispering, while Hadfala, an elderly dwarf woman who was the clan chief of Dûrgrimst Ebardac and the third member of Gannel's alliance, frowned at the sheaf of rune-covered parchment she brought with her to every meeting; and then to the chief of Dûrgrimst Ledwonnû, Manndrâth, who sat in profile to Eragon, displaying his long, drooping nose to good effect; to Thordris, grimstborith of Dûrgrimst Nagra, of whom he could see little but her wavy auburn hair, which fell past her shoulders and lay coiled on the floor in a braid twice as long as she was tall; to the back of Orik's head as he slouched to one side in his chair; to Freowin, grimstborith of Dûrgrimst Gedthrall, an immensely corpulent dwarf who kept his eyes fixed upon the block of wood he was busy carving into the likeness of a hunched raven; and then to Hreidamar, grimstborith of Dûrgrimst Urzhad, who, in contrast with Freowin, was fit and compact, with corded forearms, and who wore a mail hauberk and helm to every gathering; and finally to Íorûnn, she of the nut-brown skin marred only by a thin, crescent-shaped scar high upon her left cheekbone, she of the satin-bright hair bound underneath a silver helm wrought in the shape of a snarling wolf's head, she of the vermilion dress and the necklace of flashing emeralds set in squares of gold carved with lines of arcane runes.

447

Íorûnn noticed Eragon looking at her. A lazy smile appeared on her lips. With voluptuous ease, she winked at Eragon, obscuring one of her almond-shaped eyes for a pair of heartbeats.

Eragon's cheeks stung as blood suffused them, and the tips of his ears burned. He shifted his gaze and returned it to Gáldhiem, who was still busy pontificating, his chest puffed out like that of a strutting pigeon.

As Orik had asked, Eragon remained impassive throughout the meeting, concealing his reactions from those who were watching. When the clanmeet broke for their midday meal, he hastened over to Orik and, bending so that no one else could hear, said, "Do not look for me at your table. I have had my fill of sitting and talking. I am going to explore the tunnels for a bit."

Orik nodded, appearing distracted, and murmured in reply, "Do as you wish, only be sure you are here when we resume; it would not be meet for you to play truant, no matter how tedious these talks be."

"As you say."

Eragon edged out of the conference room, along with the press of dwarves eager to have their lunches, and rejoined his four guards in the hallway outside, where they had been playing dice with idle warriors from other clans. With his guards in tow, Eragon struck out in a random direction, allowing his feet to carry him where they would while he pondered methods of welding the dwarves' contentious factions into a whole united against Galbatorix. To his exasperation, the only methods he could envision were so far-fetched, it was absurd to imagine they might succeed.

Eragon paid little attention to the dwarves he met in the tunnels—aside from mumbled greetings that courtesy occasionally demanded—nor even to his exact surroundings, trusting that Kvîstor could guide him back to the conference room. Although Eragon did not study his surroundings in any great detail visually, he kept track of the minds of every living creature he was able to sense within a radius of several hundred feet, even down to the smallest spider crouched behind its web in the corner of a room, for Eragon had no desire to be surprised by anyone who might have cause to seek him out.

When at last he stopped, he was surprised to find himself in the same dusty room he had discovered during his wanderings the previous day. There to his left were the same five black arches that led to caverns unknown, while there to his right was the same bas-relief carving of the head and shoulders of a snarling bear. Bemused by the coincidence, Eragon sauntered over to the bronze sculpture and gazed up at the bear's gleaming fangs, wondering what had drawn him back.

After a moment, he went to the middle of the five archways and gazed through it. The narrow hallway beyond was devoid of lanterns and soon faded into the soft oblivion of shadow. Reaching out with his consciousness, Eragon probed the length of the tunnel and several of the abandoned chambers it opened to. A half-dozen spiders and a sparse collection of moths, millipedes, and blind crickets were the only inhabitants. "Hello!" called Eragon, and listened as the hall returned his voice to him with ever-decreasing volume. "Kvîstor," said Eragon, looking at him, "does no one at all live in these ancient parts?"

The fresh-faced dwarf answered, "Some do. A few strange knurlan, those to whom empty solitude is more pleasing than the touch of their wife's hand or the sound of their friends' voices. It was one such knurlag who warned us of the approach of the Urgal army, if you remember, Argetlam. Also, although we do not speak of it often, there are those who have broken the laws of our land and whom their clan chiefs have banished on pain of death for a term of years or, if the offense is severe, for the remainder of their lives. All such are as the walking dead to us; we shun them if we meet them outside of our lands and hang them if we catch them within our borders."

When Kvîstor had finished speaking, Eragon indicated that he was ready to leave. Kvîstor took the lead, and Eragon followed him out the doorway through which they had entered, the three other dwarves close behind. They had gone no more than twenty feet when Eragon heard a faint scuffing from the rear, so faint Kvîstor did not seem to notice.

Eragon glanced back. By the amber light cast by the flameless lanterns mounted on either side of the passageway, he saw seven dwarves garbed entirely in black, their faces masked with dark cloth and their feet muffled with rags, running toward his group with a speed that Eragon had assumed was the sole province of elves, Shades, and other creatures whose blood hummed with magic. In their right hands, the dwarves held long, sharp daggers with pale blades that flickered with prismatic colors, while in their left, each carried a metal buckler with a sharpened spike protruding from the boss. Their minds, like those of the Ra'zac, were hidden from Eragon.

Saphira! was Eragon's first thought. Then he remembered he was alone.

Twisting to face the black-garbed dwarves, Eragon reached for the hilt of his falchion while opening his mouth to shout a warning.

He was too late.

As the first word rang in his throat, three of the strange dwarves grabbed the hindmost of Eragon's guards and lifted their glimmering daggers to stab him. Faster than speech or conscious thought, Eragon plunged his whole being into the flow of magic and, without relying upon the ancient language to structure his spell, rewove the fabric of the world into a pattern more pleasing to him. The three guards who stood between him and the attackers flew toward him, as if yanked by invisible strings, and landed upon their feet beside him, unharmed but disoriented.

Eragon winced at the sudden decrease in his strength.

Two of the black-garbed dwarves rushed him, stabbing at his belly with their blood-hungry daggers. Sword in hand, Eragon parried both blows, stunned by the dwarves' speed and ferocity. One of his guards leaped forward, shouting and swinging his ax at the would-be assassins. Before Eragon could grab the dwarf's hauberk and yank him back to safety, a white blade, writhing as with spectral flame, pierced the dwarf's corded neck. As the dwarf fell, Eragon glimpsed his contorted face and was shocked to see Kvîstor—and that his throat was glowing molten red as it disintegrated around the dagger.

I can't let them so much as scratch me, Eragon thought.

Enraged by Kvîstor's death, Eragon stabbed at his killer so quickly, the black-garbed dwarf had no opportunity to evade the blow and dropped lifeless at Eragon's feet.

With all his strength, Eragon shouted, "Stay behind me!"

Thin cracks split the floors and walls, and flakes of stone fell from the ceiling as his voice reverberated through the corridor. The attacking dwarves faltered at the unbridled power of his voice, then resumed their offensive.

Eragon retreated several yards to give himself room to maneuver free of the corpses and settled into a low crouch, waving the falchion to and fro, like a snake preparing to strike. His heart was racing at twice its normal rate, and although the fight had just begun, he was already gasping for breath.

The hallway was eight feet wide, which was wide enough for three of his six remaining enemies to attack him at once. They spread out, two attempting to flank him on the right and the left, while the third charged straight at him, slashing with frenzied speed at Eragon's arms and legs.

Afraid to duel with the dwarves as he would have if they wielded normal blades, Eragon drove his legs against the floor and jumped up and forward. He spun halfway around and struck the ceiling feet-first. He pushed off, spun halfway around again, and landed on his hands and feet a yard behind the three dwarves. Even as they whirled toward him, he stepped forward and beheaded the lot of them with a single backhand blow.

Their daggers clattered against the floor an instant before their heads.

Leaping over their truncated bodies, Eragon twisted in midair and landed on the spot he had started from.

He was not a moment too soon.

A breath of wind tickled his neck as the tip of a dagger whipped past his throat. Another blade tugged at the cuff of his leggings, cutting them open. He flinched and swung the falchion, trying to gain space to fight. *My wards should have turned their blades away!* he thought, bewildered.

An involuntary cry escaped his throat as his foot struck a patch of slick blood and he lost his balance and toppled over backward.

With a sickening crunch, his head collided with the stone floor. Blue lights flashed before his eyes. He gasped.

His three remaining guards sprang over him and swung their axes in unison, clearing the air above Eragon and saving him from the bite of the flashing daggers.

That was all the time Eragon needed to recover. He flipped upright and, berating himself for not trying this sooner, shouted a spell laced with nine of the twelve death-words Oromis had taught him. However, the moment after he loosed his magic he abandoned the spell, for the black-garbed dwarves were protected by numerous wards. Given a few minutes, he might have been able to evade or defeat the wards, but minutes might as well have been days in a battle such as theirs, where every second was as long as an hour. Having failed with magic, Eragon hardened his thoughts into an iron-hard spear and launched it at where the consciousness of one of the black-garbed dwarves ought to be. The spear skated off mental armor of a sort Eragon had not encountered before: smooth and seamless, seemingly unbroken by the concerns natural to mortal creatures engaged in a struggle to the death.

Someone else is protecting them, Eragon realized. *There are more behind this attack than just these seven.*

Pivoting on one foot, Eragon lunged forward and with his falchion impaled his leftmost attacker in a knee, drawing blood. The dwarf stumbled, and Eragon's guards converged upon him, grasping the dwarf's arms so he could not swing his dire blade and hacking at him with their curved axes.

The nearest of the last two attackers raised his shield in anticipation of the blow Eragon was about to direct at him. Summoning the full measure of his might, Eragon cut at the shield, intending to shear it and the arm underneath in half, as he had often done with Zar'roc. In the fever of battle, though, he forgot to account for the dwarf's inexplicable speed. As the falchion neared its target, the dwarf tilted his shield, so as to deflect the blow to the side.

Two plumes of sparks erupted from the surface of the shield as the falchion glanced off the upper part and then the steel spike mounted in the center. Momentum carried the falchion farther than Eragon had intended, and it continued flying through the air until it struck edge-first against a wall, jarring Eragon's arm. With a crystalline sound, the blade of the falchion shattered into a dozen pieces, leaving him with a six-inch spike of jagged metal protruding from the hilt.

Dismayed, Eragon dropped the broken sword and gripped the rim of the dwarf's buckler, wresting with him back and forth and struggling to keep the shield between him and the dagger graced with a halo of translucent colors. The dwarf was incredibly tough; he matched Eragon's efforts and even succeeded in pushing him back a step. Releasing the buckler with his right hand but still holding on with his left, Eragon drew back his arm and struck the shield as hard as he could, punching through the tempered steel as easily as if it were made of rotten wood. Because of the calluses on his knuckles, he felt no pain from the impact.

The force of the blow threw the dwarf against the opposite wall. His head lolling upon a boneless neck, the dwarf dropped to the ground, like a puppet whose strings had been severed.

Eragon pulled his hand back through the jagged hole in the shield, scratching himself on the torn metal, and drew his hunting knife.

Then the last of the black-garbed dwarves was upon him. Eragon parried his dagger twice . . . thrice . . . and then cut through the dwarf's padded sleeve and scored his dagger arm from the elbow to the wrist. The dwarf hissed with pain, blue eyes furious above his cloth mask. He initiated a series of blows, the dagger whistling through the air faster than the eye could follow, which forced Eragon to hop away to avoid the deadly edge. The dwarf pressed the attack. For several yards, Eragon succeeded in evading him, until his heel struck a body and, in attempting to step around it, he stumbled and fell against a wall, bruising his shoulder.

With an evil laugh, the dwarf pounced, stabbing downward

453

toward Eragon's exposed chest. Throwing up an arm in a futile attempt to protect himself, Eragon rolled farther down the hallway, knowing that this time his luck had run out and he would not be able to escape.

As he completed a revolution and his face was momentarily turned toward the dwarf again, Eragon glimpsed the pale dagger descending toward his flesh, like a bolt of lightning from on high. Then, to his astonishment, the tip of the dagger caught on one of the flameless lanterns mounted on the wall. Eragon whirled away before he could see more, but an instant later, a burning hot hand seemed to strike him from behind, throwing him a good twenty feet through the hall, until he fetched up against the edge of an open archway, instantly accumulating a new collection of scrapes and bruises. A booming report deafened him. Feeling as if someone were driving splinters into his eardrums, Eragon clapped his hands over his ears and curled into a ball, howling.

When the noise and the pain had subsided, he lowered his hands and staggered to his feet, clenching his teeth as his injuries announced their presence with a myriad of unpleasant sensations. Groggy and confused, he gazed upon the site of the explosion.

The blast had blackened a ten-foot length of the hallway with soot. Soft flakes of ash tumbled through the air, which was as hot as the air from a heated forge. The dwarf who had been about to strike Eragon lay on the ground, thrashing, his body covered with burns. After a few more convulsions, he grew still. Eragon's three remaining guards lay at the edge of the soot, where the explosion had thrown them. Even as he watched, they staggered upright, blood dripping from their ears and gaping mouths, their beards singed and in disarray. The links along the fringe of their hauberks glowed red, but their leather under-armor seemed to have protected them from the worst of the heat.

Eragon took a single step forward, then stopped and groaned as a patch of agony bloomed between his shoulder blades. He tried to twist his arm around to feel the extent of the wound, but as his skin stretched, the pain became too great to continue. Nearly losing consciousness, he leaned against the wall for support. He glanced at the burnt dwarf again. *I must have suffered similar injuries on my back.*

Forcing himself to concentrate, he recited two of the spells designed to heal burns that Brom had taught him during their travels. As they took effect, it felt as if cool, soothing water were flowing across his back. He sighed with relief and straightened.

"Are you hurt?" he asked as his guards hobbled over.

The lead dwarf frowned, tapped his right ear, and shook his head.

Eragon muttered a curse and only then did he notice he could not hear his own voice. Again drawing upon the reserves of energy within his body, he cast a spell to repair the inner mechanisms of his ears and of theirs. As the incantation concluded, an irritating itch squirmed inside his ears, then faded along with the spell.

"Are you hurt?"

The dwarf on the right, a burly fellow with a forked beard, coughed and spat out a glob of congealed blood, then growled, "Nothing that time won't mend. What of you, Shadeslayer?"

"I'll live."

Testing the floor with every step, Eragon entered the soot-blackened area and knelt beside Kvîstor, hoping that he might still save the dwarf from the clutches of death. As soon as he beheld Kvîstor's wound again, he knew it was not to be.

Eragon bowed his head, the memory of recent and former bloodshed bitter to his soul. He stood. "Why did the lantern explode?"

"They are filled with heat and light, Argetlam," one of his guards replied. "If they are broken, all of it escapes at once and then it is better to be far away."

Gesturing at the crumpled corpses of their attackers, Eragon asked, "Do you know of which clan they are?"

The dwarf with the forked beard rifled through the clothes of several of the black-garbed dwarves, then said, "Barzûl! They carry no marks upon them such as you would recognize, Argetlam, but they carry this." He held up a bracelet made of braided horsehair set with polished cabochons of amethyst.

"What does it mean?"

"This amethyst," said the dwarf, and tapped one of the cabochons with a soot-streaked fingernail, "this particular variety of amethyst, it grows in only four parts of the Beor Mountains, and three of them belong to Az Sweldn rak Anhûin."

Eragon frowned. "Grimstborith Vermûnd ordered this attack?"

"I cannot say for sure, Argetlam. Another clan might have left the bracelet for us to find. They might want us to think it was Az Sweldn rak Anhûin so we do not realize who our foes really are. But . . . if I had to wager, Argetlam, I would wager a cartload of gold that it is Az Sweldn rak Anhûin who is responsible."

"Blast them," Eragon murmured. "Whoever it was, blast them." He clenched his fists to stop them from shaking. With the side of his boot, he nudged one of the prismatic daggers the assassins had

wielded. "The spells on these weapons and on the . . . on the men"—he motioned with his chin—"men, dwarves, be as it may, they must have required an incredible amount of energy, and I cannot even imagine how complex their wording was. Casting them would have been hard and dangerous. . . ." Eragon looked at each of his guards in turn and said, "As you are my witnesses, I swear I shall not let this attack, nor Kvîstor's death, go unpunished. Whichever clan or clans sent these dung-faced killers, when I learn their names, they will wish they had never thought to strike at me and, by striking at me, strike at Dûrgrimst Ingeitum. This I swear to you, as a Dragon Rider and as a fellow member of Dûrgrimst Ingeitum, and if any ask you of it, repeat my promise to them as I have given it to you."

The dwarves bowed before him, and he with the forked beard replied, "As you command, so we shall obey, Argetlam. You honor Hrothgar's memory by your words."

Then another of the dwarves said, "Whichever clan it was, they have violated the law of hospitality; they have attacked a guest.

They are not even so high as rats; they are *menknurlan*." He spat on the floor, and the other dwarves spat with him.

Eragon walked to where the remains of his falchion lay. He knelt in the soot and, with the tip of a finger, touched one of the pieces of metal, tracing its ragged edges. *I must have hit the shield and the wall so hard, I overwhelmed the spells I used to reinforce the steel*, he thought.

Then he thought, *I need a sword.*

I need a Rider's sword.

✦ ✦ ✦

A Matter of Perspective

The wind-of-morning-heat-above-flat-land, which was different from the wind-of-morning-heat-above-hills, shifted.

Saphira adjusted the angle of her wings to compensate for the changes in the speed and pressure of the air that supported her weight thousands of feet above the sun-bathed land below. She closed her double eyelids for a moment, luxuriating in the soft bed of the wind, as well as the warmth of the morning rays beating down upon her sinewy length. She imagined how the light must make her scales sparkle and how those who saw her circling in the sky must marvel at the sight, and she hummed with pleasure, content in the knowledge that she was the most beautiful creature in Alagaësia, for who could hope to match the glory of her scales; and her long, tapering tail; and her wings, so fair and well formed; and her curved claws; and her long white fangs, with which she could sever the neck of a wild ox with a single bite? Not Glaedr-of-the-gold-scales, who had lost a leg during the fall of the Riders. Nor could Thorn or Shruikan, for they were both slaves to Galbatorix, and their forced servitude had twisted their minds. A dragon who was not free to do as he or she wished was not a dragon at all. Besides, they were males, and while males might appear majestic, they could not embody the beauty she did. No, she was the most stunning creature in Alagaësia, and that was as it should be.

Saphira wriggled with satisfaction all the way from the base of her head to the tip of her tail. Today was a perfect day. The heat of the sun made her feel as if she were lying in a nest of coals. Her belly was full, the sky was clear, and there was nothing she needed to attend

458

to, besides watching for foes who might wish to fight, which she did anyway, as a matter of habit.

Her happiness had only one flaw, but it was a profound flaw, and the longer she considered it, the more discontented she grew, until she realized she was no longer satisfied; she wished Eragon were there to share the day with her. She growled and loosed a brief jet of blue flame from between her jaws, searing the air in front of her, then constricted her throat, cutting off the stream of liquid fire. Her tongue tingled from the flames that had run over it. When was Eragon, partner-of-her-mind-and-heart-Eragon, going to contact Nasuada from Tronjheim and ask for her, Saphira, to join him? She had urged him to obey Nasuada and travel to the mountains-higher-than-she-could-fly, but now too long had passed, and Saphira felt cold and empty in her gut.

There is a shadow in the world, she thought. *That is what has upset me. Something is wrong with Eragon. He is in danger, or he was in danger recently. And I cannot help him.* She was not a wild dragon. Since she had hatched, she had shared her entire life with Eragon, and without him, she was only half herself. If he died because she was not there to protect him, she would have no reason to continue living, save for revenge. She knew she would tear his killers apart and then she would fly on the black city of the egg-breaker-traitor who had kept her imprisoned for so many decades, and she would do her best to slay him, no matter that it would mean certain death for her.

Saphira growled again and snapped at a tiny sparrow that was foolish enough to fly within range of her teeth. She missed, and the sparrow darted past and continued on its way unmolested, which only exacerbated her foul mood. For a moment, she considered chasing the sparrow but then decided it was not worth bothering herself over such an inconsequential speck of bones and feathers. It would not even make a good snack.

Tilting on the wind and swinging her tail in the opposite direction to facilitate her turn, she wheeled around, studying the ground

459

far below and all the small scurrying things that strove to hide from her hunter's eyes. Even from her height of thousands of feet, she could count the number of feathers on the back of a chicken hawk that was skimming the fields of planted wheat west of the Jiet River. She could see the blur of brown fur as a rabbit dashed to the safety of its warren. She could pick out the small herd of deer cowering underneath the branches of the currant bushes clustered along a tributary of the Jiet River. And she could hear the high-pitched squeaks of frightened animals warning their brethren of her presence. Their wavering cries gratified her; it was only right that her food should fear her. If ever she should fear it, she would know it was her time to die.

A league farther upstream, the Varden were packed against the Jiet River like a herd of red deer against the edge of a cliff. The Varden had arrived at the crossing yesterday, and since then, perhaps a third of the men-who-were-friends and the Urgals-who-were-friends and the horses-she-must-not-eat had forded the river. The army moved so slowly, she sometimes wondered how humans ever had time to do anything other than travel, considering how short their lives were. *It would be much more convenient if they could fly,* she thought, and wondered why they did not choose to. Flying was so easy, it never ceased to puzzle her why any creature would remain earthbound. Even Eragon retained his attachment to the soft-hard-ground, when she knew he could join her in the sky at any time merely by uttering a few words in the ancient language. But then, she did not always understand the actions of those who tottered about on two legs, whether they had round ears, pointed ears, or horns or were so short she could squash them under her feet.

A flicker of movement to the northeast caught her attention, and she angled toward it, curious. She saw a line of five-and-forty weary horses trudging toward the Varden. Most of the horses were riderless; therefore, it did not occur to her until another half hour had elapsed and she could make out the faces of the men in the saddles that the group might be Roran's returning from their raid. She wondered what had happened to so reduce their numbers and felt a momentary twinge of unease. She was not bonded to Roran, but Eragon cared for him, and that was reason enough for her to worry about his well-being.

Pushing her consciousness down toward the disorganized Varden, she searched until she found the music of Arya's mind, and once the elf acknowledged her and allowed access to her thoughts, Saphira said, *Roran shall be here by late afternoon. However, his company is sore diminished. Some great evil befell them this trip.*

Thank you, Saphira, said Arya. *I shall inform Nasuada.*

As Saphira withdrew from Arya's mind, she felt the questing touch of black-blue-wolf-hair-Blödhgarm. *I am not a hatchling*, she snapped. *You need not check on my health every few minutes.*

You have my most humble apologies, Bjartskular, only you have been gone for quite some time now, and if any are watching, they will begin to wonder why you and—

Yes, I know, she growled. Shortening her wingspan, she tilted downward, the sensation of weight leaving her, and gyrated in slow spirals as she dove toward the turgid river. *I shall be there shortly.*

A thousand feet above the water, she flared her wings and felt the strain in her flight membranes as the wind pressed against them with immense force. She slowed to a near standstill, then spilled air from her wings and accelerated once more, gliding to within a hundred feet of the brown not-good-to-drink-water. With an occasional flap to maintain her altitude, she flew up the Jiet River, alert for the sudden changes of pressure that plagued cool-air-above-flowing-water and that could push her in an unexpected direction or, worse, into sharp-pointy-trees or the break-bone-ground.

She swept high above the Varden gathered next to the river, high enough that her arrival would not unduly frighten the silly horses. Then, drifting downward upon still wings, she landed in a clearing among the tents—a clearing Nasuada had ordered set aside just for her—and crawled through the camp to Eragon's empty tent, where Blödhgarm and the eleven other elves he commanded were waiting for her. She greeted them with a blink of her eyes and a flick of her tongue and then curled up in front of Eragon's tent, resigned to dozing and waiting for dark as she would if Eragon were actually in the tent and he and she were flying missions at night. It was dull, tedious work, lying there day after day, but it was necessary in order to maintain the deception that Eragon was still with the Varden, so Saphira did not complain, even if after twelve or more hours spent on the rough-hard-ground dirtying her scales, she felt like fighting a thousand soldiers, or razing a forest with tooth and claw and fire, or leaping up and flying until she could fly no more or until she reached the end of earth, water, and air.

Growling to herself, she kneaded the ground with her claws, softening it, then lay her head across her forelegs and closed her inner eyelids so she could rest and still watch those who walked by. A dragonfly buzzed over her head, and not for the first time she wondered what could have possibly inspired some feebleminded runtling to name the insect after her race. *It looks nothing like a dragon*, she grumbled, then drifted off into a light sleep.

The big-round-fire-in-the-sky was close to the horizon when Saphira heard the shouts and cries of welcome that meant Roran and his fellow warriors had reached the camp. She roused herself. As he had before, Blödhgarm half sang, half whispered a spell that created an insubstantial likeness of Eragon, which the elf caused to walk out of the tent and climb onto Saphira's back, where it sat looking around in a perfect imitation of independent life. Visually, the apparition was flawless, but it had no mind of its own, and if any of Galbatorix's agents tried to eavesdrop upon Eragon's thoughts, they would discover the deceit forthwith. Therefore, the success of the ploy depended upon Saphira ferrying the apparition through the camp and out of sight as quickly as possible, and upon the hope that Eragon's reputation was so formidable, it would discourage clandestine observers from attempting to glean information about the Varden from his consciousness, for fear of his vengeance.

Saphira started up and bounded through the camp, the twelve elves running in formation around her. Men leaped out of their path, shouting, "Hail, Shadeslayer!" and "Hail, Saphira!" which kindled a warm glow in her belly.

When she arrived at Nasuada's folded-wing-red-butterfly-chrysalis-tent, she crouched and stuck her head inside the dark gap along one wall, where Nasuada's guards had pulled aside a panel of fabric to allow her access. Blödhgarm resumed his soft singing then, and the Eragon-wraith climbed down off Saphira, entered the crimson tent, and, once it was out of sight of the gawking onlookers outside, dissolved into nothingness.

"Do you think our ruse was discovered?" Nasuada asked from her high-backed chair.

Blödhgarm bowed with an elegant gesture. "Again, Lady Nasuada, I cannot say for sure. We will have to wait and see if the Empire moves to take advantage of Eragon's absence before we will know the answer to that question."

"Thank you, Blödhgarm. That will be all."

With another bow, the elf withdrew from the tent and took up a position several yards behind Saphira, guarding her flank.

Saphira settled down onto her underside and began to lick clean the scales around the third claw on her left forefoot, between which there had accumulated unsightly lines of the dry white clay she remembered standing in when she ate her last kill.

Not a minute later, Martland Redbeard, Roran, and a man-with-round-ears, whom she did not recognize, entered the red tent and bowed to Nasuada. Saphira paused in her cleaning to taste the air with her tongue and discerned the tang of dried blood, the bitter-sour musk of sweat, the scent of horse and leather intermingled, and, faint but unmistakable, the sharp spike of man-fear. She examined the trio again and saw that the red-long-beard-man had lost his right hand, then returned to excavating the clay from around her scales.

She continued licking her foot, restoring every scale to pristine brilliance, while first Martland, then the man-with-round-ears-who-was-Ulhart, then Roran, told a tale of blood and fire and of laughing men who refused to die at their allotted times but insisted upon continuing to fight long past when Angvard had called their names. As was her wont, Saphira held her peace while others—specifically Nasuada and her adviser, long-man-gaunt-face-Jörmundur—questioned the warriors about the details of their ill-fated mission. Saphira knew it sometimes puzzled Eragon why she did not participate more in conversations. Her reasons for silence were simple: save for Arya or Glaedr, she felt most comfortable communicating only with Eragon, and in her opinion, most conversations were nothing more than pointless dithering. Whether round-ear, pointed-ear, horned, or short, two-legs seemed addicted to dithering. Brom had not dithered, which was something Saphira had liked about him. For her, choices were simple; either there was an action she could take to improve the situation, in which case she took it, or there was not, and everything else said on the subject was so much meaningless noise. In any event, she did not worry herself about the future, except where Eragon was concerned. Him, she always worried about.

When the questions were finished, Nasuada expressed her condolences to Martland for his lost hand, then dismissed Martland and Ulhart, but not Roran, to whom she said, "You have demonstrated your prowess once again, Stronghammer. I am well pleased with your abilities."

"Thank you, my Lady."

"Our best healers will attend to him, but Martland will still need time to recover from his injury. Even once he does, he cannot lead raids such as these with only one hand. From now on, he will have to serve the Varden from the back of the army, not the front. I think, perhaps, that I shall promote him and make him one of my battle advisers. Jörmundur, what think you of that idea?"

"I think it an excellent idea, my Lady."

Nasuada nodded, appearing satisfied. "This means, however, that I must find another captain for you to serve under, Roran."

Then Roran said, "My Lady, what of my own command? Have I not proven myself to your satisfaction with these two raids, as well as with my past accomplishments?"

"If you continue to distinguish yourself as you have, Stronghammer, you will win your command soon enough. However, you must be patient and abide awhile longer. Two missions alone, however impressive, may not reveal the full scope of a man's character. I am a cautious person when it comes to entrusting my people to others, Stronghammer. In this, you must humor me."

Roran gripped the head of the hammer stuck through his belt, veins and tendons standing out on his hand, but his tone remained polite. "Of course, Lady Nasuada."

"Very good. A page will bring you your new assignment later today. Oh, and see to it that you have a large meal once you and Katrina finish celebrating your reunion. That's an order, Stronghammer. You look as if you're about to fall over."

"My Lady."

As Roran started to leave, Nasuada raised a hand and said, "Roran." He paused. "Now that you have fought these men who feel no pain, do you believe that having similar protection from the agonies of the flesh would make it easier to defeat them?"

Roran hesitated, then shook his head. "Their strength is their weakness. They do not shield themselves as they would if they feared the bite of a sword or the stab of an arrow, and thus they are careless with their lives. It is true they can continue fighting long past when an ordinary man would have dropped dead, and that is no small advantage in battle, but they also die in greater numbers, because they do not protect their bodies as they ought. In their numb confidence, they will walk into traps and peril we would go to great lengths to avoid. As long as the Varden's spirits remain high, I believe that with the right tactics we can prevail against these laughing monsters. If we were like them, though, we would hack each other into oblivion, and neither of us would care, since we would have no thought for self-preservation. Those are my thoughts."

"Thank you, Roran."

When Roran had gone, Saphira said, *Nothing yet from Eragon?*

Nasuada shook her head. "No, nothing yet from him, and his silence is beginning to concern me. If he has not contacted us by the day after tomorrow, I will have Arya send a message to one of Orik's spellcasters demanding a report from him. If Eragon is unable to hasten the end of the dwarves' clanmeet, then I fear we will no longer be able to count on the dwarves as allies during the battles to come. The only good of such a disastrous outcome would be that Eragon could return to us without further delay."

When Saphira was ready to leave the red-chrysalis-tent, Blödhgarm again summoned up the apparition of Eragon and placed it on Saphira's back. Then Saphira withdrew her head from the confines of the tent and, as she had before, bounded through the camp, the lithe elves keeping step with her the entire way.

Once she reached Eragon's tent and the colored-shadow-Eragon disappeared inside it, Saphira lowered herself to the ground and resigned herself to waiting out the remainder of the day in unrelieved monotony. Before she resumed her reluctant nap, however, she extended her mind toward Roran and Katrina's tent and pressed against Roran's mind until he lowered the barriers around his consciousness.

Saphira? he asked.

Do you know another such as me?

Of course not. You just surprised me. I am . . . ah, somewhat occupied at the moment.

She studied the color of his emotions, as well as those of Katrina, and was amused by her findings. *I only wished to welcome you back. I am glad you were not injured.*

Roran's thoughts flashed quick-hot-muddled-cold, and he seemed to have difficulty forming a coherent answer. Eventually, he said, *That's very kind of you, Saphira.*

If you can, come visit me tomorrow, when we may speak at greater length. I grow restless sitting here day after day. Perhaps you could tell me more about how Eragon was before I hatched for him.

It . . . it would be my honor.

Satisfied she had fulfilled the demands of round-ears-two-legs courtesy by welcoming Roran, and heartened by the knowledge that the following day would not be as boring—for it was unthinkable anyone would dare ignore her request for an audience—Saphira made herself as comfortable as she could on the bare earth, wishing as she often did for the soft nest that was hers in Eragon's wind-rocked-tree-house in Ellesméra. A puff of smoke escaped her as she sighed and fell asleep and dreamed that she flew higher than she ever had before.

She flapped and she flapped until she rose above the unreachable peaks of the Beor Mountains. There she circled for a time, gazing down at the whole of Alagaësia laid out before her. Then an uncontrollable desire entered her to climb even higher and see what she might, and so she began flapping again, and in what seemed like the blink of an eye, she soared past the glaring moon, until only she and the silver stars hung in the black sky. She drifted among the heavens for an indeterminate period, queen of the bright, jewel-like world below, but then disquiet entered her soul, and she cried out with her thoughts:

Eragon, where are you!

✦ ✦ ✦

KISS ME SWEET

Waking, Roran extricated himself from Katrina's smooth arms and sat bare-chested on the edge of the cot they shared. He yawned and rubbed his eyes, then gazed at the pale strip of firelight that glowed between the two entrance flaps, feeling dull and stupid with accumulated exhaustion. A chill crept over him, but he remained where he was, motionless.

"Roran?" Katrina asked in a sleep-smeared voice. She propped herself up on one arm and reached for him with the other. He did not react as she touched him, sliding her hand across his upper back and rubbing his neck. "Sleep. You need your rest. You'll be gone again before long."

He shook his head, not looking at her.

"What is it?" she asked. Sitting upright, she pulled a blanket over his shoulders, then leaned against him, her cheek warm against his arm. "Are you worried about your new captain or where Nasuada may send you next?"

"No."

She was silent for a while. "Every time you leave, I feel as if less of you returns to me. You have become so grim and quiet. . . . If you want to tell me about what is troubling you, you can, you know, no matter how terrible it is. I am the daughter of a butcher, and I have seen my share of men fall in battle."

"Want!" Roran exclaimed, choking on the word. "I don't ever want to think about it again." He clenched his fists, his breathing uncertain. "A true warrior would not feel as I do."

"A true warrior," she said, "does not fight because he wishes to but because he has to. A man who yearns for war, a man who *enjoys* his killing, he is a brute and a monster. No matter how much glory he wins on the battlefield, that cannot erase the fact that he is no better than a rabid wolf who will turn on his friends and family as soon as his foes." She brushed his hair away from his brow and stroked the top of his head, light and slow. "You once told me that 'The Song of Gerand' was your favorite of Brom's stories, that it was why you fight with a hammer instead of a blade. Remember how Gerand disliked killing and how reluctant he was to take up arms again?"

"Aye."

"And yet he was considered the greatest warrior of his age." She cupped his cheek in her hand and turned his face toward her so that he was forced to gaze into her solemn eyes. "And you are the greatest warrior I know of, Roran, here or anywhere."

With a dry mouth, he said, "What of Eragon or—"

"They are not half so valorous as you. Eragon, Murtagh, Galbatorix, the elves . . . all of them march into battle with spells upon their lips and might that far exceeds ours. But you"—she kissed him on the nose—"you are no more than a man. You face your foes on your own two feet. You are not a magician, and yet you slew the Twins. You are only as fast and as strong as a human may be, and yet you did not shirk from attacking the Ra'zac in their lair and freeing me from their dungeon."

He swallowed. "I had wards from Eragon to protect me."

"But no longer. Besides, you did not have any wards in Carvahall either, and did you flee from the Ra'zac then?" When he was unresponsive, she said, "You are no more than a man, but you have done things not even Eragon or Murtagh could have. To me, that makes you the greatest warrior in Alagaësia. . . . I cannot think of anyone else in Carvahall who would have gone to the lengths you did to rescue me."

"Your father would have," he said.

He felt her shiver against him. "Yes, he would have," she whispered. "But he never would have been able to convince others to follow him, as you did." She tightened her arm around him. "Whatever you have seen or done, you will always have me."

"That is all I will ever need," he said, and clasped her in his arms and held her for a span. Then he sighed. "Still, I wish this war were at an end. I wish I could till a field again and sow my crops and harvest them when they ripened. Farming is backbreaking work, but at least it is honest labor. This killing isn't honest. It is thievery . . . the thievery of men's lives, and no right-minded person should aspire to it."

"As I said."

"As you said." Difficult as it was, he made himself smile. "I have forgotten myself. Here I am burdening you with my troubles when you have worries enough of your own." And he placed a hand over her rounding womb.

"Your troubles shall always be my troubles, so long as we are married," she murmured, and nuzzled his arm.

"Some troubles," he said, "no one else should have to endure, especially not those you love."

She withdrew an inch or two from him, and he saw her eyes become bleak and listless, as they did whenever she fell to brooding over the time she had spent imprisoned in Helgrind. "No," she whispered, "some troubles no one else should have to endure."

"Ah, do not be sad." He pulled her closer and rocked back and forth with her and wished with all his might that Eragon had not found Saphira's egg in the Spine. After a while, when Katrina had grown soft in his arms again, and even he no longer felt quite so tense, he caressed the curve of her neck. "Come, kiss me sweet, and then let us return to bed, for I am tired, and I would sleep."

She laughed at him then, and kissed him most sweetly, and then they lay upon the cot as they had before, and outside the tent all was still and quiet except for the Jiet River, which flowed past the camp, never pausing, never stopping, and poured itself into Roran's dreams, where he imagined himself standing at the prow of a ship, Katrina by his side, and gazing into the maw of the giant whirlpool, the Boar's Eye.

And he thought, *How can we hope to escape?*

GLÛMRA

H undreds of feet below Tronjheim, the stone opened up into a cavern thousands of feet long with a still black lake of unknown depth along one side and a marble shore on the other. Brown and ivory stalactites dripped from the ceiling, while stalagmites stabbed upward from the ground, and in places the two joined to form bulging pillars thicker around than even the largest trees in Du Weldenvarden. Scattered among the pillars were mounds of compost studded with mushrooms, as well as three-and-twenty low stone huts. A flameless lantern glowed iron red next to each of their doors. Beyond the reach of the lanterns, shadows abounded.

Inside one of the huts, Eragon sat in a chair that was too small for him, at a granite table no higher than his knees. The smell of soft goat cheese, sliced mushrooms, yeast, stew, pigeon eggs, and coal dust pervaded the air. Across from him, Glûmra, a dwarf woman of the Family of Mord, she who was the mother of Kvîstor, Eragon's slain guard, wailed and tore at her hair and beat at her breast with her fists. Glistening tracks marked where her tears had rolled down her plump face.

The two of them were alone in the hut. Eragon's four guards— their numbers replenished by Thrand, a warrior from Orik's retinue—were waiting outside, along with Hûndfast, Eragon's translator, whom Eragon had dismissed from the hut once he learned that Glûmra could speak his language.

After the attempt on his life, Eragon had contacted Orik with his mind, whereupon Orik insisted Eragon run as fast as he could to the chambers of the Ingeitum, where he would be safe from any more assassins. Eragon had obeyed, and there he had remained while

Orik forced the clanmeet to adjourn until the following morning, on the grounds that an emergency had arisen within his clan that required his immediate attention. Then Orik marched with his stoutest warriors and most adept spellcaster to the site of the ambush, which they studied and recorded with means both magical and mundane. Once Orik was satisfied they had learned all they could, he had hurried back to his chambers, where he said to Eragon, "We have much to do and little time in which to do it. Before the clanmeet resumes upon the third morning hour of tomorrow, we must attempt to establish beyond all doubt who ordered the attack. If we can, then we will have leverage to use against them. If not, then we will be flailing in the dark, uncertain of our enemies. We can keep the attack a secret until the clanmeet, but no longer. Knurlan will have heard echoes of your fight throughout the tunnels under Tronjheim, and even now, I know they will be searching for the source of the disturbance, for fear there may have been a cave-in or similar catastrophe that might undermine the city above." Orik stamped his feet and cursed the ancestors of whoever had sent the assassins, then planted his fists on his hips and said, "A clan war was already threatening us, but now it stands upon our very threshold. We must move quickly if we are to avert that dread fate. There are knurlan to find, questions to ask, threats to make, bribes to offer, and scrolls to steal—and all before morn."

"What of me?" Eragon asked.

"You should remain here until we know if Az Sweldn rak Anhûin or some other clan has a larger force massed elsewhere to kill you. Also, as long as we can hide from your attackers whether you are alive, dead, or wounded, the longer we may keep them uncertain as to the safety of the rock beneath their feet."

At first Eragon agreed with Orik's proposal, but as he watched the dwarf bustle about issuing orders, he felt increasingly uneasy and helpless. Finally, he caught Orik by the arm and said, "If I have to sit here and stare at the wall while you search for the villains who did this, I'll grind my teeth down to nubs. There must be something I can do to help. . . . What of Kvîstor? Do any of his family live in Tronjheim? Has anyone told them of his death yet? Because if not, I would be the one to bring them the tidings, for it was me he died defending."

Orik inquired of his guards, and from them they learned that Kvîstor did indeed have family in Tronjheim, or more accurately, underneath Tronjheim. When he heard, Orik frowned and muttered a strange word in Dwarvish. "They are deep dwellers," he said, "knurlan who have forsaken the surface of the land for the world below, except for occasional forays above. More of them live here, below Tronjheim and Farthen Dûr, than anywhere else, because they can come out in Farthen Dûr and not feel as if they are actually outside, which most of them cannot bear, they are so accustomed to closed-in spaces. I had not known Kvîstor was of their number."

"Would you mind if I go to visit his family?" Eragon asked. "Among these rooms, there are stairs that lead below, am I right? We could leave without anyone being the wiser."

Orik thought for a moment, then nodded. "You're right. The path is safe enough, and no one would think to look for you among the deep dwellers. They would come here first, and here they would otherwise find you. . . . Go, and do not return until I send a messenger for you, even if the Family of Mord turns you away and you must sit on a stalagmite until morn. But, Eragon, be you careful; the deep dwellers keep to themselves for the most part, and they are prickly to an extreme about their honor, and they have strange customs of their own. Tread carefully, as if you were on rotten shale, eh?"

And so, with Thrand added to his guards, and Hûndfast accompanying them—and with a short dwarf sword belted around his waist—Eragon went to the nearest staircase leading downward, and following it, he descended farther into the bowels of the earth than ever he had before. And in due time, he found Glûmra and informed her of Kvîstor's demise, and now he sat listening as she grieved for her slain child, alternating between wordless howls and scraps of Dwarvish sung in a haunting, dissonant key.

Discomfited by the strength of her sorrow, Eragon glanced away from her face. He looked at the green soapstone stove that stood against one wall and the worn carvings of geometric design that adorned its edges. He studied the green and brown rug that lay before the hearth, and the churn in the corner, and the provisions hanging from the beams of the ceiling. He gazed at the heavy-timbered loom that stood underneath a round window with panes of lavender glass.

Then, at the height of her wailing, Glûmra caught Eragon's eye as she rose from the table, went to the counter, and placed her left hand on the cutting board. Before Eragon could stop her, she took a carving knife and cut off the first joint of her little finger. She groaned and doubled over.

Eragon sprang halfway up with an involuntary exclamation. He wondered what madness had overcome the dwarf woman and whether he should attempt to restrain her, lest she should do herself additional harm. He opened his mouth to ask if she wanted him to heal the wound, but then he thought better of it, remembering Orik's admonishments about the deep dwellers' strange customs and strong sense of honor. *She might consider the offer an insult,* he realized. Closing his mouth, he sank back into his too-small chair.

After a minute, Glûmra straightened out of her hunched position, took a deep breath, and then quietly and calmly washed the raw end of her finger with brandy, smeared it with a yellow salve, and bandaged the wound. Her moon-face still pale from the shock, she lowered herself into the chair opposite Eragon. "I thank you, Shadeslayer, for bringing me news of mine son's fate yourself. I am glad to know that he died proudly, as a warrior ought to."

"He was most brave," Eragon said. "He could see that our enemies were as fast as elves, and yet he still leaped forward to protect me. His sacrifice bought me time to escape their blades and also revealed the danger of the enchantments they had placed on their weapons. If not for his actions, I doubt I would be here now."

Glûmra nodded slowly, eyes downcast, and smoothed the front of her dress. "Do you know who was responsible for this attack on our clan, Shadeslayer?"

"We have only suspicions. Grimstborith Orik is trying to determine the truth of the matter even as we speak."

"Was it Az Sweldn rak Anhûin?" Glûmra asked, surprising Eragon with the astuteness of her guess. He did his best to conceal his reaction. When he remained silent, she said, "We all know of their blood feud with you, Argetlam; every knurla within these mountains knows. Some of us have looked with favor upon their opposition of you, but if they thought to actually kill you, then they have misjudged the lay of the rock and doomed themselves because of it."

Eragon raised an eyebrow, interested. "Doomed? How?"

"It was you, Shadeslayer, who slew Durza and so allowed us to save Tronjheim and the dwellings below from the clutches of Galbatorix. Our race shall never forget that so long as Tronjheim remains standing. And then there is word come by the tunnels that your dragon shall make whole again Isidar Mithrim?"

Eragon nodded.

"That is good of you, Shadeslayer. You have done much for our race, and whichever clan it was attacked you, we shall turn against them and have our vengeance."

"I swore before witnesses," Eragon said, "and I swear to you as well, that I will punish whoever sent those backstabbing murderers and that I'll make them wish they had never thought of such a foul deed. However—"

"Thank you, Shadeslayer."

Eragon hesitated, then inclined his head. "However, we must not do anything that would ignite a clan war. Not now. If force is to be used, it should be Grimstborith Orik who decides when and where we draw our swords, don't you agree?"

"I will think upon what you have said, Shadeslayer," Glûmra replied. "Orik is . . ." Whatever she was going to say next caught in her mouth. Her thick eyelids drooped and she sagged forward for a moment, pressing her maimed hand against her abdomen. When the bout passed, she pushed herself upright and held the back of the hand against her opposite cheek and swayed from side to side, moaning, "Oh, mine son . . . mine beautiful son."

Standing, she staggered around the table, heading toward a small collection of swords and axes mounted on the wall behind Eragon, next to an alcove covered by a curtain of red silk. Afraid that she intended to cause herself further injury, Eragon leaped to his feet, knocking over the oak chair in his haste. He reached for her and then saw that she was walking toward the curtained alcove, not the weapons, and he snatched his arm back before he caused offense.

The brass rings sewn on top of the silk drapery clattered against one another as Glûmra swept aside the cloth to expose a deep, shadowed shelf carved with runes and shapes of such fantastic detail, Eragon thought he could stare at them for hours and still not grasp them in their entirety. On the low shelf rested statues of the six major dwarf gods, as well as nine other entities Eragon was unfamiliar with, all carved with exaggerated features and postures to better convey the character of the being portrayed.

Glûmra removed an amulet of gold and silver from within her bodice, which she kissed and then held against the hollow of her throat as she knelt before the alcove. Her voice rising and falling in the strange patterns of dwarf music, she began to croon a dirge in her native language. The melody brought tears to Eragon's eyes. For several minutes, Glûmra sang, and then she fell silent and continued to gaze at the figurines, and as she gazed, the lines of her grief-ravaged face softened, and where before Eragon had perceived only anger, distress, and hopelessness, her countenance assumed an air of calm acceptance, of peacefulness, and of sublime transcendence. A soft glow seemed to emanate from her features. So complete was Glûmra's transformation, Eragon almost did not recognize her.

She said, "Tonight Kvîstor will dine in Morgothal's hall. That I know." She kissed her amulet again. "I wish I might break bread with him, along with mine husband, Bauden, but it is not mine time to sleep in the catacombs of Tronjheim, and Morgothal refuses entry to his hall to those who quicken their arrival. But in time, our family shall be reunited, including all of our ancestors since Gûntera created the world from darkness. That I know."

Eragon knelt next to her, and in a hoarse voice, he asked, "How do you know this?"

"I know because it is so." Her movements slow and respectful, Glûmra touched the chiseled feet of each of the gods with the tips of her fingers. "How could it be otherwise? Since the world could not have created itself any more than a sword or a helm might, and since the only beings with the wherewithal to forge the earth and the heavens into shape are those with divine power, it is to the gods we must look for our answers. Them I trust to ensure the rightness of the world, and by mine trust, I free myself of the burdens of mine flesh."

She spoke with such conviction, Eragon felt a sudden desire to share in her belief. He longed to toss aside his doubts and fears and to know that, however horrible the world might seem at times, life was not mere confusion. He wished to know for certain that who he was would not end if a sword should shear off his head and that one day he would meet again with Brom, Garrow, and everyone else he had cared for and lost. A desperate yearning for hope and comfort filled him, confused him, left him unsteady upon the face of the earth.

And yet.

Part of himself held back and would not allow him to commit to the dwarf gods and bind his identity and his sense of well-being to something he did not understand. He also had difficulty accepting that if gods did exist, the dwarf gods were the only ones. Eragon was certain that if he asked Nar Garzhvog or a member of the nomad tribes, or even the black priests of Helgrind, if their gods were real, they would uphold the supremacy of their deities just as vigorously as Glûmra would uphold hers. *How am I supposed to know which religion is the true religion?* he wondered. *Just because someone follows a certain faith does not necessarily mean it is the right path. . . . Perhaps*

no one religion contains all of the truth of the world. Perhaps every reli-
gion contains fragments of the truth and it is our responsibility to identify
those fragments and piece them together. Or perhaps the elves are right
and there are no gods. But how can I know for sure?

With a long sigh, Glûmra murmured a phrase in Dwarvish, then rose from her knees and drew closed the silk curtain over the al-cove. Eragon likewise stood, wincing as his battle-sore muscles stretched, and followed her to the table, where he returned to his chair. From a stone cupboard set into the wall, the dwarf woman took two pewter mugs, then retrieved a bladder full of wine from where it hung from the ceiling and poured a drink for both her and Eragon. She raised her mug and uttered a toast in Dwarvish, which Eragon struggled to imitate, and then they drank.

"It is good," said Glûmra, "to know that Kvîstor still lives on, to know that even now he is garbed in robes fit for a king while he en-joys the evening feast in Morgothal's hall. May he win much honor in the service of the gods!" And she drank again.

Once he had emptied his mug, Eragon began to bid farewell to Glûmra, but she forestalled him with a motion of her hand. "Have you a place to stay, Shadeslayer, safe from those who wish you dead?" Whereupon Eragon told her how he was supposed to remain hidden underneath Tronjheim until Orik sent a messenger for him. Glûmra nodded with a short, definitive jerk of her chin and said, "Then you and your companions must wait here until the messen-ger arrives, Shadeslayer. I insist upon it." Eragon started to protest, but she shook her head. "I could not allow the men who fought with mine son to languish in the damp and the dark of the caves while I yet have life in mine bones. Summon your companions, and we shall eat and be merry this gloomy night."

Eragon realized that he could not leave without upsetting Glûmra, so he called to his guards and his translator. Together, they helped Glûmra to prepare a dinner of bread, meat, and pie, and when it was ready, the lot of them ate and drank and talked late into the night. Glûmra was particularly lively; she drank the most, laughed the loudest, and was always the first to make a witty remark. At first Eragon was shocked by her behavior, but then he noticed how her smiles never reached her eyes and how, if she thought no one was looking, the mirth would drain from her face and her expression would become one of somber quietude. Entertaining them, he concluded, was her way of celebrating her son's memory, as well as fending off her grief at Kvîstor's death.

I have never met anyone like you before, he thought as he watched her.

Long after midnight, someone knocked on the door of the hut. Hûndfast ushered in a dwarf who was garbed in full armor and who seemed edgy and ill at ease; he kept glancing at the doors and windows and shadowed corners. With a series of phrases in the ancient language, he convinced Eragon that he was Orik's messenger, and then he said, "I am Farn, son of Flosi. . . . Argetlam, Orik bids you return with all possible haste. He has most important tidings concerning the events of today."

At the doorway, Glûmra grasped Eragon's left forearm with fingers like steel, and as he gazed down into her flinty eyes, she said, "Remember your oath, Shadeslayer, and do not let the killers of mine son escape without retribution!"

"That I shall not," he promised.

CLANMEET

The dwarves standing watch outside of Orik's chambers threw open the double doors that led inside as Eragon strode toward them.

The entryway beyond was long and ornate, furnished with three circular seats upholstered with red fabric set in a line down the middle of the room. Embroidered hangings decorated the walls, along with the dwarves' ubiquitous flameless lanterns, while the ceiling had been carved to depict a famous battle from dwarven history.

Orik stood consulting with a group of his warriors and several gray-bearded dwarves of Dûrgrimst Ingeitum. As Eragon approached, Orik turned toward him, his face grim. "Good, you did not delay! Hûndfast, you may retire to your quarters now. We must needs speak in private."

Eragon's translator bowed and disappeared through an archway to the left, his footsteps echoing on the polished agate floor. Once he was out of hearing, Eragon said, "You don't trust him?"

Orik shrugged. "I do not know whom to trust at the moment; the fewer people who know what we have discovered, the better. We cannot risk the news escaping to another clan before tomorrow. If it does, it will certainly mean a clan war." The dwarves behind him muttered among themselves, appearing disconcerted.

"What is your news, though?" asked Eragon, worried.

The warriors gathered behind Orik moved aside as he gestured at them, revealing as they did so three bound and bloodied dwarves stacked on top of one another in the corner. The dwarf on the bottom groaned and kicked his feet in the air but was unable to extricate himself from under his fellow prisoners.

"Who are they?" asked Eragon.

Orik replied, "I had several of our smiths examine the daggers your attackers carried. They identified the craftsmanship as that of one Kiefna Long-nose, a bladesmith of our clan who has achieved great renown among our people."

"So he can tell us who bought the daggers and thus who our enemies are?"

A brusque laugh shook Orik's chest. "Hardly, but we were able to track the daggers from Kiefna to an armorer in Dalgon, many leagues from here, who sold them to a knurlaf with—"

"A knurlaf?" Eragon asked.

Orik scowled. "A woman. A woman with seven fingers on each hand bought the daggers two months ago."

"And did you find her? There can't be very many women with that number of fingers."

"Actually, the condition is fairly common among our people," said Orik. "Be that as it may, after quite a bit of difficulty, we managed to locate the woman in Dalgon. My warriors there questioned her most closely. She is of Dûrgrimst Nagra, but so far as we can determine, she was acting of her own accord, and not under orders from the leaders of her clan. From her, we learned that a dwarf had engaged her to buy the daggers and then to deliver them to a wine merchant who would take them with him from Dalgon. The woman's employer did not tell her where the daggers were destined, but by asking among the merchants of the city, we discovered that he traveled directly from Dalgon to one of the cities held by Dûrgrimst Az Sweldn rak Anhûin."

"So it *was* them!" Eragon exclaimed.

"That or it could have been someone who wished us to think it was them. We needed more evidence before we could establish Az Sweldn rak Anhûin's guilt for certain." A twinkle appeared in Orik's eyes, and he raised a finger. "So, by means of a very, very clever spell, we retraced the path of the assassins back through the tunnels and caves and up to a deserted area on the twelfth level of

Tronjheim, off the subadjunct auxiliary hall of the southern spoke in the western quadrant, along the . . . ah, well, it does not matter. But someday I will have to teach you how the rooms are arranged in Tronjheim, so that if ever you need to find a place within the city by yourself, you can. In any event, the trail led us to an abandoned storeroom where those three"—he gestured toward the bound dwarves—"had been staying. They were not expecting us, and so we were able to capture them alive, although they tried to kill themselves. It was not easy, but we broke the minds of two of them—leaving the third for the other grimstborithn to interrogate at their pleasure—and we took from them everything they knew about this matter." Orik pointed at the prisoners again. "It was they who equipped the assassins for the attack, gave them the daggers and their black clothes, and fed and sheltered them last night."

"Who are they?" asked Eragon.

"Bah!" exclaimed Orik, and spat on the floor. "They are Vargrimstn, warriors who have disgraced themselves and are now clanless. No one deals with such filth unless they are engaged in villainy themselves and do not wish others to know of it. And so it was with those three. They took their orders directly from Grimstborith Vermûnd of Az Sweldn rak Anhûin."

"There is no doubt?"

Orik shook his head. "There is no doubt; it is Az Sweldn rak Anhûin who tried to kill you, Eragon. We will probably never know if any other clans joined them in the attempt, but if we expose Az Sweldn rak Anhûin's treachery, it will force everyone else who might have been involved in the plot to disparage their former confederates; to abandon, or at least delay, further attacks on Dûrgrimst Ingeitum; and, if this is handled properly, to give me their vote for king."

An image flashed in Eragon's mind of the prismatic blade emerging from the back of Kvîstor's neck and of the dwarf's agonized expression as he had fallen to the floor, dying. "How will we punish Az Sweldn rak Anhûin for this crime? Should we kill Vermûnd?"

"Ah, leave that to me," said Orik, and tapped the side of his nose. "I have a plan. But we must tread carefully, for this is a situation of the utmost delicacy. Such a betrayal has not occurred in many long years. As an outsider, you cannot know how abhorrent we find it that one of our own should attack a guest. You being the only free Rider left to oppose Galbatorix only worsens the offense. Further bloodshed may yet be necessary, but at the moment, it would only bring about another clan war."

"A clan war might be the only way to deal with Az Sweldn rak Anhûin," Eragon pointed out.

"I think not, but if I am mistaken and war is unavoidable, we must ensure it is a war between the rest of the clans and Az Sweldn rak Anhûin. That would not be so bad. Together, we could crush them inside of a week. A war with the clans split into two or three factions, however, would destroy our country. It is crucial, then, that before we draw our swords, we convince the other clans of what Az Sweldn rak Anhûin has done. Toward that end, will you allow magicians from different clans to examine your memories of the attack so they may see it happened as we shall say it did and that we did not stage it for our own benefit?"

Eragon hesitated, reluctant to open his mind to strangers, then nodded toward the three dwarves stacked on top of one another. "What about them? Won't their memories be enough to convince the clans of Az Sweldn rak Anhûin's guilt?"

Orik grimaced. "They ought to be, but in order to be thorough, the clan chiefs will insist upon verifying their memories against yours, and if you refuse, Az Sweldn rak Anhûin will claim we are hiding something from the clanmeet and that our accusations are nothing more than slanderous fiction."

"Very well," said Eragon. "If I must, I must. But if any of the magicians stray where they are not supposed to, even if by accident, I will have no choice but to burn what they have seen out of their minds. There are some things I cannot allow to become common knowledge."

Nodding, Orik said, "Aye, I can think of at least one three-legged piece of information that would cause us some consternation if it were to be trumpeted throughout the land, eh? I am sure the clan chiefs will accept your conditions—for they all have secrets of their own they would not want bandied about—just as I am sure they will order their magicians to proceed, regardless of the danger. This attack has the potential to incite such turmoil among our race, the grimstborithn will feel compelled to determine the truth about it, though it may cost them their most skilled spellcasters."

Drawing himself upright then, to the full extent of his limited height, Orik ordered the prisoners removed from the ornate entryway and dismissed all of his vassals, save for Eragon and a contingent of twenty-six of his finest warriors. With a graceful flourish, Orik grasped Eragon's left elbow and conducted him toward the inner rooms of his chambers. "Tonight you must remain here, with me, where Az Sweldn rak Anhûin will not dare to strike."

"If you intend to sleep," said Eragon, "I must warn you, I cannot rest, not tonight. My blood still churns from the tumult of the fight, and my thoughts are likewise uneasy."

Orik replied, "Rest or not as you will; you shall not disturb my slumber, for I shall pull a thick woolen cap low over my eyes. I urge you to try and calm yourself, however—perhaps with some of the techniques the elves taught you—and recover what strength you may. The new day is already upon us, and but a few hours remain until the clanmeet shall be assembled. We should both be as fresh as possible for what is to come. What we do and say today shall determine the ultimate fate of mine people, mine country, and the rest of Alagaësia. . . . Ah, do not look so grim about the mouth! Think of this instead: whether success or failure awaits us, and I surely hope we prevail, our names shall be remembered until the end of time for how we comport ourselves at this clanmeet. That at least is an accomplishment to fill your belly with pride! The gods are fickle, and the only immortality we can count on is that which we win through our deeds. Fame or infamy, either one is preferable to being forgotten when you have passed from this realm."

Later that night, in the dead hours before morning, Eragon's thoughts wandered as he sat slumped within the embrace of the padded arms of a dwarf couch, and the frame of his consciousness dissolved into the disordered fantasy of his waking dreams. Yet conscious of the mosaic of colored stones mounted upon the wall opposite him, he also beheld, as if a glowing scrim draped over the mosaic, scenes of his life in Palancar Valley before momentous and bloody fate had intervened in his existence. The scenes diverged from established fact, however, and immersed him in imaginary situations constructed piecemeal from fragments of what had actually been. In the last few moments before he roused himself from his stupor, his vision flickered and the images acquired a sense of heightened reality.

He was standing in Horst's workshop, the doors of which hung open, loose upon their hinges, like an idiot's slackjaw grin. Outside was a starless night, and the all-consuming darkness seemed to press against the edges of the dull red light cast by the coals, as if eager to devour everything within the scope of that ruddy sphere. Next to the forge, Horst loomed like a giant, the shifting shadows upon his face and beard fearsome to behold. His burly arm rose and fell, and a bell-like clang shivered the air as the hammer he wielded struck the end of a yellow-glowing bar of steel. A burst of sparks extinguished itself on the ground. Four more times the smith smote the metal; then he lifted the bar from his anvil and plunged it into a barrel of oil. Wraithlike flames, blue and gossamer, flickered across the surface of the oil and then vanished with small shrieks of fury. Removing the bar from the barrel, Horst turned toward Eragon and frowned at him. He said, "Why have you come here, Eragon?"

"I need a Dragon Rider's sword."

"Begone with you. I have no time to forge you a Rider's sword. Cannot you see I am working on a pothook for Elain? She must have it for the battle. Are you alone?"

"I do not know."

"Where is your father? Where is your mother?"

"I do not know."

Then a new voice sounded, a well-polished voice of strength and power, and it said, "Good smith, he is not alone. He came with me."

"And who might you be?" demanded Horst.

"I am his father."

Between the gaping doors, a huge figure rimmed with pale light emerged from the clotted darkness and stood upon the threshold of the workshop. A red cape billowed from shoulders wider than a Kull's. In the man's left hand gleamed Zar'roc, sharp as pain. Through the slits of his brightly polished helm, his blue eyes bored into Eragon, pinning him into place, like an arrow through a rabbit. He lifted his free hand and held it out toward Eragon. "My son, come with me. Together, we can destroy the Varden, kill Galbatorix, and conquer all of Alagaësia. But give me your heart, and we shall be invincible.

"Give me your heart, my son."

With a strangled exclamation, Eragon leaped out of the couch and stood staring at the floor, his fists clenched, his chest heaving. Orik's guards gave him inquisitive glances, but he ignored them, too upset to explain his outburst.

The hour was still early, so after a time, Eragon settled back onto the couch, but thereafter, he remained alert and did not allow himself to sink into the land of dreams, for fear of what manifestations might torment him.

Eragon stood with his back to the wall, his hand on the pommel of his dwarf sword, as he watched the various clan chiefs file into the round conference room buried beneath Tronjheim. He kept an especially close eye on Vermûnd, the grimstborith of Az Sweldn rak Anhûin, but if the purple-veiled dwarf was surprised to see Eragon alive and well, he did not show it.

Eragon felt Orik's boot nudge his own. Without looking away from Vermûnd, Eragon leaned over toward Orik and heard him

whisper, "Remember, to the left and three doorways down," referring to the place where Orik had stationed a hundred of his warriors
without the other clan chiefs knowing.

Whispering as well, Eragon said, "If blood is shed, should I seize
the opportunity to kill that snake, Vermûnd?"

"Unless he is attempting the same with you or me, please do not."
A low chuckle emanated from Orik. "It would hardly *endear* you to
the other grimstborithn. . . . Ah, I must go now. Pray to Sindri for
luck, would you? We are about to venture into a lava field none
have dared cross before."

And Eragon prayed.

When all of the clan chiefs were seated around the table in the
center of the room, those watching from the perimeter, including
Eragon, took their own seats from among the ring of chairs set
against the curving wall. Eragon did not relax into his, however, as
many of the dwarves did, but sat upon the edge, ready to fight at the
slightest hint of danger.

As Gannel, the black-eyed warrior-priest of Dûrgrimst Quan,
rose from the table and began to speak in Dwarvish, Hûndfast sidled
closer to Eragon's right side and murmured a continuous translation. The dwarf said, "Greetings again, mine fellow clan chiefs. But
whether 'tis well met or not, I am undecided, for certain disturbing
rumors—rumors of rumors, if truth be told—have reached mine
ears. I have no information beyond these vague and worrisome mut-
terings, nor proof upon which to found an accusation of misdeeds.
However, as today is mine day to preside over this, our congregation, I propose that we delay our most serious debates for the moment, and if you are agreeable, allow me to pose a few questions to
the meet."

The clan chiefs muttered among themselves, and then Íorûnn,
bright, dimpling Íorûnn, said, "I have no objection, Grimstborith
Gannel. You have aroused mine curiosity with these cryptic insinu-
ations. Let us hear what questions you have."

"Aye, let us hear them," said Nado.

"Let us hear them," agreed Manndrâth and all the rest of the clan chiefs, including Vermûnd.

Having received the permission he sought, Gannel rested his knuckles upon the table and was silent for a span, garnering the attention of everyone in the room. Then he spoke. "Yesterday, while we were lunching in our chosen places of repast, knurlan throughout the tunnels underneath the southern quadrant of Tronjheim heard a noise. Reports of its loudness differ, but that so many noticed it over so large an area proves that it was no small disturbance. Like you, I received the usual warnings of a possible cave-in. What you may not be aware of, however, is that just two hours past—"

Hûndfast hesitated, and quickly whispered, "The word is difficult to render in this tongue. *Runners-of-the-tunnels*, I think." And then he resumed translating as before:

"—runners-of-the-tunnels discovered evidence of a mighty fight within one of the ancient tunnels that our famed forefather, Korgan Longbeard, excavated. The floor was painted with blood, the walls were dark with soot from a lantern a warrior of careless blade did breach, cracks split the surrounding stone, and sprawled throughout were seven charred and mangled bodies, with signs that others may have been removed. Nor were these the remnants of some obscure skirmish from the Battle of Farthen Dûr. No! For the blood had yet to dry, the soot was soft, the cracks were most obviously freshly broken, and, I am told, the residue of powerful magics could still be detected within the area. Even now, several of our most accomplished spellcasters are attempting to reconstruct a pictorial facsimile of what occurred, but they have little hope of success, as those involved were wrapped about with such devious enchantments. So my first question for the meet is this: do any of you possess further knowledge of this mysterious action?"

As Gannel concluded his speech, Eragon tensed his legs, ready to spring up if the purple-veiled dwarves of Az Sweldn rak Anhûin should reach for their blades.

Orik cleared his throat and said, "I believe that I can satisfy some

489

of your curiosity upon that point, Gannel. However, since my answer must of necessity be a lengthy one, I suggest you ask your other questions before I begin."

A frown darkened Gannel's brow. Rapping his knuckles against the table, he said, "Very well. . . . In what is undoubtedly related to the clash of arms in Korgan's tunnels, I have had reports of numerous knurlan moving through Tronjheim and, with furtive intent, gathering here and there into large bands of armed men. My agents were unable to ascertain the clan of the warriors, but that any of this council should attempt to surreptitiously marshal their forces whilst we are engaged in a meet to decide who should succeed King Hrothgar suggests motives of the darkest kind. So my second question for the meet is this: who is responsible for this ill-thought-of maneuvering? And if none are willing to admit their misconduct, I move most strongly that we order all warriors, regardless of their clan, expelled from Tronjheim for the duration of the meet and that we immediately appoint a reader-of-law to investigate these doings and determine whom we should censure."

Gannel's revelation, question, and subsequent proposal aroused a flurry of heated conversation among the clan chiefs, with the dwarves hurling accusations, denials, and counteraccusations at each other with increasing vitriol, until, at last, when an infuriated Thordris was shouting at a red-faced Gáldhiem, Orik cleared his throat again, causing everyone to stop and stare at him.

In a mild tone, Orik said, "This too I believe I can explain to you, Gannel, at least in part. I cannot speak to the activities of the other clans, but several hundred of the warriors who have been hurrying through the servants' halls in Tronjheim have been of Dûrgrimst Ingeitum. This I freely admit."

All was silent until Íorûnn said, "And what explanation have you for this belligerent behavior, Orik, Thrifk's son?"

"As I said before, fair Íorûnn, my answer must of necessity be a lengthy one, so if you, Gannel, have any other questions to ask, I suggest you proceed forthwith."

Gannel's frown deepened until his projecting eyebrows nearly touched. He said, "I will withhold mine other questions for the time being, for they all pertain to those I have already put to the meet, and it seems we must wait upon your pleasure to learn any more of those subjects. However, since you are involved fist and foot with these doubtful activities, a new question has occurred to me that I would ask of you specifically, Grimstborith Orik. For what reason did you desert yesterday's meet? And let me warn you, I will brook no evasions. You have already intimated you have knowledge of these affairs. Well, time is for you to provide a full accounting of yourself, Grimstborith Orik."

Orik stood even as Gannel sat, and he said, "It shall be mine pleasure."

Lowering his bearded chin until it rested upon his chest, Orik paused for a brief span and then began to speak in a sonorous voice, but he did not begin as Eragon had expected, nor, Eragon surmised, as the rest of the congregation had expected. Instead of describing the attempt on Eragon's life, and thus explaining why he had terminated the previous clanmeet prematurely, Orik commenced by recounting how, at the dawn of history, the race of dwarves had migrated from the once-verdant fields of the Hadarac Desert to the Beor Mountains, where they had excavated their uncounted miles of tunnels, built their magnificent cities both above and below the ground, and waged lusty war between their various factions, as well as with the dragons, whom, for thousands of years, the dwarves had regarded with a combination of hate, fear, and reluctant awe.

Then Orik spoke of the elves' arrival in Alagaësia and of how the elves had fought with the dragons until they nearly destroyed each other and of how, as a result, the two races had agreed to create the Dragon Riders to maintain the peace thereafter.

"And what was our response when we learned of their intentions?" demanded Orik, his voice ringing loud in the chamber. "Did we ask to be included in their pact? Did we aspire to share in the power that would be the Dragon Riders'? No! We clung to our old ways, our old hatreds, and we rejected the very thought of bonding with the dragons or allowing anyone outside our realm to police us. To preserve our authority, we sacrificed our future, for I am convinced that if some of the Dragon Riders had been knurlan, Galbatorix might have never risen to power. Even if I am wrong—and I mean not to belittle Eragon, who has proven himself a fine Rider—the dragon Saphira might have hatched for one of our race and not a human. And then what glory might have been ours?

"Instead, our importance in Alagaësia has diminished ever since Queen Tarmunora and Eragon's namesake made peace with the dragons. At first our lessened status was not so bitter a draught to swallow, and often it was easier to deny than to accept. But then came the Urgals, and then the humans, and the elves amended their spells so humans might be Riders as well. And then did we seek to be included in their accord, as well we might have . . . as was our right?" Orik shook his head. "Our pride would not allow it. Why should we, the oldest race in the land, beg the elves for the favor of their magic? We did not need to chain our fate to the dragons' in order to save our race from destruction, as had the elves and humans. We ignored, of course, the battles we waged among ourselves. Those, we reasoned, were private affairs and of no concern to anyone else."

The listening clan chiefs stirred. Many of them bore expressions of dissatisfaction at Orik's criticism, whereas the rest seemed more receptive to his comments and were thoughtful of countenance.

Orik continued: "While the Riders watched over Alagaësia, we enjoyed the greatest period of prosperity ever recorded in the annals of our realm. We flourished as never before, and yet we had no share in the cause of it: the Dragon Riders. When the Riders fell, our fortunes faltered, but again we had no share in the cause of it: the Riders. Neither state of affairs is, I deem, fitting for a race of our stature. We are not a country of vassals subject to the whims of foreign masters. Nor should those who are not the descendants of Odgar and Hlordis dictate our fate."

This line of reasoning was more to the liking of the clan chiefs; they nodded and smiled, and Havard even clapped a few times at the final line.

"Consider now our present era," said Orik. "Galbatorix is ascendant, and every race fights to remain free of his rule. He has grown so powerful, the only reason we are not already his slaves is that, so far, he has not chosen to fly out upon his black dragon and attack us directly. If he did, we would fall before him like saplings before an avalanche. Fortunately, he seems content to wait for us to slaughter our way to the gates of his citadel in Urû'baen. Now, I remind you that before Eragon and Saphira turned up wet and bedraggled on our front doorstep, with a hundred yammering Kull hard upon their heels, our only hope of defeating Galbatorix was that someday, somewhere, Saphira would hatch for her chosen Rider and that this unknown person would, perhaps, perchance, if we were luckier than every gambler who has ever won a toss of dice, be able to overthrow Galbatorix. Hope? Ha! We did not even have hope; we had a hope of a hope. When Eragon first presented himself, many of us were dismayed by his appearance, myself included. 'He is but a boy,' we said. 'It would have been better if he had been an elf,' we said. But lo, he has shown himself to be the embodiment of our every hope! He slew Durza, and so allowed us to save our most beloved city, Tronjheim. His dragon, Saphira, has promised to restore the Star Rose to its former glory. During the Battle of the Burning Plains, he drove off Murtagh and Thorn, and so allowed us to win the day. And look! He even now wears the semblance of an elf, and through their strange magics, he has acquired their speed and their strength."

Orik raised a finger for emphasis. "Moreover, King Hrothgar, in his wisdom, did what no other king or grimstborith has ever done; he offered to adopt Eragon into Dûrgrimst Ingeitum and to make him a member of his own family. Eragon was under no obligation to accept this offer. Indeed, he was aware that many of the families of the Ingeitum objected to it and that, in general, many knurlan would not regard it with favor. Yet in spite of that discouragement,

493

and in spite of the fact that he was already bound in fealty to Nasuada, Eragon accepted Hrothgar's gift, knowing full well that it would only make his life harder. As he has told me himself, Eragon swore the hall-oath upon the Heart of Stone because of the sense of obligation he feels toward all the races of Alagaësia, and especially toward us, since we, by the actions of Hrothgar, showed him and Saphira such kindness. Because of Hrothgar's genius, the last free Rider of Alagaësia, and our one and only hope against Galbatorix, freely chose to become a knurla in all but blood. Since then, Eragon has abided by our laws and traditions to the best of his knowledge, and he has sought to learn ever more about our culture so that he may honor the true meaning of his oath. When Hrothgar fell, struck down by the traitor Murtagh, Eragon swore to me upon every stone in Alagaësia, and also as a member of Dûrgrimst Ingeitum, that he would strive to avenge Hrothgar's death. He has given me the respect and obedience I am due as grimstborith, and I am proud to regard him as mine foster brother."

Eragon glanced downward, his cheeks and the tips of his ears burning. He wished Orik were not so free with his praise; it would only make his position harder to maintain in the future.

Sweeping his arms out to include the other clan chiefs, Orik exclaimed, "Everything we could have ever wished for in a Dragon Rider we have received in Eragon! He exists! He is powerful! And he has embraced our people as no other Dragon Rider ever has!" Then Orik lowered his arms and, with them, the volume of his voice, until Eragon had to strain to hear his words. "How have we responded to his friendship, though? In the main, with sneers and slights and surly resentment. We are an ungrateful race, I say, and our memories are too long for our own good. . . . There are even those who have become so filled with festering hatred, they have turned to violence to slake the thirst of their anger. Perhaps they still believe they are doing what is best for our people, but if so, then their minds are as moldy as a lump of year-old cheese. Otherwise, why would they try to kill Eragon?"

The listening clan chiefs became perfectly still, their eyes riveted to Orik's face. So intense was their concentration, the corpulent grimstborith, Freowin, had set aside his carving of a raven and folded his hands on top of his ample belly, appearing for all the world like one of the dwarves' statues.

As they gazed at him with unblinking eyes, Orik related to the clanmeet how the seven black-clad dwarves had attacked Eragon and his guards while they were meandering among the tunnels underneath Tronjheim. Then Orik told them of the braided horsehair bracelet set with amethyst cabochons that Eragon's guards had found upon one of the corpses.

"Do not think to blame this attack upon mine clan based upon such paltry evidence!" exclaimed Vermûnd, bolting upright. "One can buy similar trinkets in most every market of our realm!"

"Quite so," said Orik, and inclined his head toward Vermûnd. In a dispassionate voice, and with a quick pace, Orik proceeded to tell his audience, as he had told Eragon the previous night, how his subjects in Dalgon had confirmed for him that the strange flickering daggers the assassins had wielded had been forged by the smith Kiefna, and also how his subjects had discovered that the dwarf who had bought the weapons had arranged for them to be transported from Dalgon to one of the cities held by Az Sweldn rak Anhûin.

Uttering a low, growling oath, Vermûnd leaped to his feet again. "Those daggers might never have reached our city, and even if they did, you can draw no conclusions from that fact! Knurlan of many clans stay within our walls, as they do within the walls of Bregan Hold, for example. It signifies *nothing*. Be careful what you say next, Grimstborith Orik, for you have no grounds upon which to level accusations against mine clan."

"I was of the same opinion as you, Grimstborith Vermûnd," Orik replied. "Therefore, last night, my spellcasters and I retraced the assassins' path back to their place of origin, and on the twelfth level of Tronjheim, we captured three knurlan who were hiding in a dusty storeroom. We broke the minds of two of them and, from them, we learned they provisioned the assassins for their attack. And," said Orik, his voice growing harsh and terrible, "from them we learned the identity of their master. I name you, Grimstborith Vermûnd! I name you Murderer and Oath-breaker. I name you an enemy of Dûrgrimst Ingeitum, and I name you a traitor to your kind, for it was you and your clan who attempted to kill Eragon!"

The clanmeet erupted into chaos as every clan chief except Orik and Vermûnd began to shout and wave their hands and otherwise attempt to dominate the conversation. Eragon stood and loosened his borrowed sword in its sheath, drawing it out a half inch, so he could respond with all possible speed if Vermûnd or one of his dwarves chose that moment to attack. Vermûnd did not move, however, nor did Orik; they stared at each other like rival wolves and paid no attention to the commotion around them.

When at last Gannel succeeded in restoring order, he said, "Grimstborith Vermûnd, can you refute these charges?"

In a flat, emotionless voice, Vermûnd replied, "I deny them with every bone in my body, and I challenge anyone to prove them to the satisfaction of a reader-of-law."

Gannel turned toward Orik. "Present your evidence, then, Grimstborith Orik, that we may judge whether it is valid or not. There are five readers-of-law here today, if I am not mistaken." He motioned toward the wall, where five white-bearded dwarves stood and bowed. "They will ensure that we do not stray beyond the boundaries of the law in our investigation. Are we agreed?"

"I am agreed," said Ûndin.

"I am agreed," said Hadfala and all the rest of the clan chiefs after her save Vermûnd.

First, Orik placed the amethyst bracelet upon the table. Every clan chief had one of their magicians examine it, and all agreed that as evidence it was inconclusive.

Then Orik had an aide bring in a mirror mounted on a bronze tripod. One of the magicians within his retinue cast a spell, and upon the glossy surface of the mirror there appeared the image of a small, book-filled room. A moment passed, and then a dwarf rushed into the room and bowed toward the clanmeet from within the mirror. In a breathless voice, he introduced himself as Rimmar, and after swearing oaths in the ancient language to ensure his honesty, he told the clanmeet how he and his assistants had made their discoveries concerning the daggers Eragon's attackers had wielded.

When the clan chiefs finished questioning Rimmar, Orik had his warriors bring in the three dwarves the Ingeitum had captured. Gannel ordered them to swear the oaths of truthfulness in the ancient language, but they cursed at him and spat on the floor and refused. Then magicians from all of the different clans joined their thoughts, invaded the prisoners' minds, and wrested from them the information the clanmeet desired. Without exception, the magicians confirmed what Orik had already said.

Lastly, Orik called upon Eragon to testify. Eragon felt nervous as he walked over to the table and the thirteen grim clan chiefs stared at him. He gazed across the room at a small whorl of color on a marble pillar and tried to ignore his discomfort. He repeated the oaths of truthfulness as one of the dwarf magicians gave them to him, and then, speaking no more than was necessary, Eragon told the clan chiefs how he and his guards had been attacked. Afterward, he answered the dwarves' inevitable questions and then allowed two of the magicians—whom Gannel chose at random from among those assembled—to examine his memories of the event. As Eragon lowered the barriers around his mind, he noted that the two magicians appeared apprehensive, and he drew some comfort from the observation. *Good*, he thought. *They will be less likely to wander where they should not if they fear me.*

To Eragon's relief, the inspection went without incident, and the magicians corroborated his account to the clan chiefs.

Gannel rose from his chair and addressed the readers-of-law, asking them: "Are you satisfied with the quality of the evidence Grimstborith Orik and Eragon Shadeslayer have shown us?"

The five white-bearded dwarves bowed, and the middle dwarf said, "We are, Grimstborith Gannel."

Gannel grunted, seeming unsurprised. "Grimstborith Vermûnd, you are responsible for the death of Kvîstor, son of Bauden, and you attempted to kill a guest. By doing so, you have brought shame upon our entire race. What say you to this?"

The clan chief of Az Sweldn rak Anhûin pressed his hands flat against the table, veins bulging underneath his tanned skin. "If this *Dragon Rider* is a knurla in all but blood, then he is no guest and we may treat him as we would any of our enemies from a different clan."

"Why, that's preposterous!" exclaimed Orik, almost sputtering with outrage. "You can't say he—"

"Still your tongue, if you please, Orik," said Gannel. "Shouting will not settle this point. Orik, Nado, Íorûnn, if you will come with me."

Worry began to gnaw at Eragon as the four dwarves went and conferred with the readers-of-law for several minutes. *Surely they won't let Vermûnd escape punishment just because of some verbal trickery!* he thought.

Returning to the table, Íorûnn said, "The readers-of-law are unanimous. Even though Eragon is a sworn member of Dûrgrimst Ingeitum, he also holds positions of importance beyond our realm: namely, that of Dragon Rider, but also that of an official envoy of the Varden, sent by Nasuada to witness the coronation of our next ruler, and also that of a friend of high influence with Queen Islanzadí and her race as a whole. For those reasons, Eragon is due the same hospitality we would extend to any visiting ambassador, prince, monarch, or other person of significance." The dwarf woman glanced sidelong at Eragon, her dark, flashing eyes bold upon his limbs. "In short, he is our honored guest, and we should treat him as such . . . which every knurla who is not cave-mad ought to know."

"Aye, he is our guest," concurred Nado. His lips were pinched and white and his cheeks drawn, as if he had just bitten into an apple only to discover it was not yet ripe.

"What say you now, Vermûnd?" demanded Gannel.

Rising from his seat, the purple-veiled dwarf looked around the table, gazing at each of the clan chiefs in turn. "I say this, and hear me well, grimstborithn: if any clan turns their ax against Az Sweldn rak Anhûin because of these false accusations, we shall consider it an act of war, and we shall respond appropriately. If you imprison me, that too we shall consider an act of war, and we shall respond appropriately." Eragon saw Vermûnd's veil twitch, and he thought the dwarf might have smiled underneath. "If you strike at us in any possible way, whether with steel or with words, no matter how mild your rebuke, we shall consider it an act of war, and we shall respond appropriately. Unless you are eager to rend our country into a thousand bloody scraps, I suggest you let the wind waft away this morning's discussion and, in its place, fill your minds with thoughts of who should next rule from upon the granite throne."

The clan chiefs sat in silence for a long while.

Eragon had to bite his tongue to keep from jumping onto the table and railing against Vermûnd until the dwarves agreed to hang him for his crimes. He reminded himself that he had promised Orik that he would follow Orik's lead when dealing with the clanmeet. *Orik is my clan chief, and I must let him respond to this as he sees fit.*

Freowin unfolded his hands and slapped the table with a meaty palm. With his hoarse baritone voice, which carried throughout the room, although it seemed no louder than a whisper, the corpulent dwarf said, "You have shamed our race, Vermûnd. We cannot retain our honor as knurlan and ignore your trespass."

The elderly dwarf woman, Hadfala, shuffled her sheaf of rune-covered pages and said, "What did you think to accomplish, besides our doom, by killing Eragon? Even if the Varden could unseat Galbatorix without him, what of the sorrow the dragon Saphira would rain down upon us if we slew her Rider? She would fill Farthen Dûr with a sea of our own blood."

Not a word came from Vermûnd.

Laughter broke the quiet. The sound was so unexpected, at first Eragon did not realize it was coming from Orik. His mirth subsiding, Orik said, "If we move against you or Az Sweldn rak Anhûin, you will consider it an act of war, Vermûnd? Very well, then we shall not move against you, not at all."

Vermûnd's brow beetled. "How can this provide you with a source of amusement?"

Orik chuckled again. "Because I have thought of something you have not, Vermûnd. You wish us to leave you and your clan alone? Then I propose to the clanmeet that we do as Vermûnd wishes. If Vermûnd had acted upon his own and not as a grimstborith, he would be banished for his offenses upon pain of death. Therefore, let us treat the clan as we would treat the person; let us banish Az Sweldn rak Anhûin from our hearts and minds until they choose to replace Vermûnd with a grimstborith of a more moderate temperament and until they acknowledge their villainy and repent of it to the clanmeet, even if we must wait a thousand years."

The wrinkled skin around Vermûnd's eyes went pale. "You would not dare."

Orik smiled. "Ah, but we would not lay a finger upon you or your kind. We will simply ignore you and refuse to trade with Az Sweldn rak Anhûin. Will you declare war upon us for doing nothing, Vermûnd? For if the meet agrees with me, that is exactly what we shall do: *nothing*. Will you force us at swordpoint to buy your honey and your cloth and your amethyst jewelry? You have not the warriors to compel us so." Turning to the rest of the table, Orik asked, "What say the rest of you?"

The clanmeet did not take long to decide. One by one, the clan chiefs stood and voted to banish Az Sweldn rak Anhûin.

Even Nado, Gáldhiem, and Havard—Vermûnd's erstwhile allies—supported Orik's proposal. With every vote of affirmation, what skin was visible of Vermûnd's face grew ever whiter, until he appeared like a ghost dressed in the clothes of his former life.

When the vote was finished, Gannel pointed toward the door and said, "Begone, Vargrimstn Vermûnd. Leave Tronjheim this very day and may none of Az Sweldn rak Anhûin trouble the clanmeet until they have fulfilled the conditions we have set forth. Until such time as that happens, we shall shun every member of Az Sweldn rak Anhûin. Know this, however: while your clan may absolve themselves of their dishonor, you, Vermûnd, shall always remain Vargrimstn, even unto your dying day. Such is the will of the clanmeet." His declaration concluded, Gannel sat.

Vermûnd remained where he was, his shoulders quivering with an emotion Eragon could not identify. "It is you who have shamed and betrayed our race," he growled. "The Dragon Riders killed all of our clan, save Anhûin and her guards. You expect us to forget this? You expect us to forgive this? Bah! I spit on the graves of your ancestors. We at least have not lost our beards. We shall not cavort with this puppet of the elves while our dead family members still cry out for vengeance."

Outrage gripped Eragon when none of the other clan chiefs replied, and he was about to answer Vermûnd's tirade with harsh words of his own when Orik glanced over at him and shook his head ever so slightly. Difficult as it was, Eragon kept his anger in check, although he wondered why Orik would allow such dire insults to pass uncontested.

It is almost as if . . . Oh.

Pushing himself away from the table, Vermûnd stood, his hands balled into fists and his shoulders hunched high. He resumed speaking, berating and disparaging the clan chiefs with increasing passion until he was shouting at the top of his lungs.

No matter how vile Vermûnd's imprecations were, however, the clan chiefs did not respond. They gazed into the distance, as if pondering complex dilemmas, and their eyes slid over Vermûnd without pause. When, in his fury, Vermûnd grasped Hreidamar by the front of his mail hauberk, three of Hreidamar's guards jumped forward and pulled Vermûnd away, but as they did, Eragon noticed their expressions remained bland and unchanging, as if they were merely helping Hreidamar to straighten his hauberk. Once they released Vermûnd, the guards did not look at him again.

A chill crept up Eragon's spine. The dwarves acted as if Vermûnd had ceased to exist. *So this is what it means to be banished among the dwarves.* Eragon thought he would rather be killed than suffer such a fate, and for a moment, he felt a stir of pity for Vermûnd, but his pity vanished an instant later as he remembered Kvîstor's dying expression.

With a final oath, Vermûnd strode out of the room, followed by those of his clan who had accompanied him to the meet.

The mood among the remaining clan chiefs eased as the doors swung shut behind Vermûnd. Once again the dwarves gazed around without restriction, and they resumed talking in loud voices, discussing what else they would need to do with regard to Az Sweldn rak Anhûin.

Then Orik rapped the pommel of his dagger against the table, and everyone turned to hear what he had to say. "Now that we have dealt with Vermûnd, there is another issue I wish the meet to consider. Our purpose in assembling here is to elect Hrothgar's successor. We have all had much to say upon the topic, but now I believe the time is ripe to put words behind us and allow our actions to speak for us. So I call upon the meet to decide whether we are ready—and we are more than ready, in mine opinion—to proceed to the final vote three days hence, as is our law. My vote, as I cast it, is aye."

Freowin looked at Hadfala, who looked at Gannel, who looked at Manndrâth, who tugged on his drooping nose and looked at Nado, sunk low in his chair and biting the inside of his cheek.

"Aye," said Íorûnn.

"Aye," said Ûndin.

". . . Aye," said Nado, and so did the eight other clan chiefs.

Hours later, when the clanmeet broke for lunch, Orik and Eragon returned to Orik's chambers to eat. Neither of them spoke until they entered his rooms, which were proofed against eavesdroppers. There Eragon allowed himself to smile. "You planned all along to banish Az Sweldn rak Anhûin, didn't you?"

A satisfied expression on his face, Orik smiled as well and slapped his stomach. "That I did. It was the only action I could take that would not inevitably lead to a clan war. We may still have a clan war, but it shall not be of our making. I doubt such a calamity will come to pass, though. As much as they hate you, most of Az Sweldn rak Anhûin will be appalled by what Vermûnd has done in their name. He will not remain grimstborith for long, I think."

"And now you have ensured that the vote for the new king—"

"Or queen."

"—or queen shall take place." Eragon hesitated, reluctant to tarnish Orik's enjoyment of his triumph, but then he asked, "Do you really have the support you need to win the throne?"

Orik shrugged. "Before this morning, no one had the support they needed. Now the balance has shifted, and for the time being, sympathies lie with us. We might as well strike while the iron is hot; we shall never have a better opportunity than this. In any case, we cannot allow the clanmeet to drag on any longer. If you do not return to the Varden soon, all may be lost."

"What shall we do while we wait for the vote?"

"First, we shall celebrate our success with a feast," Orik declared. "Then, when we are sated, we shall continue as before: attempting to gather additional votes while defending those we have already won." Orik's teeth flashed white underneath the fringe of his beard as he smiled again. "But before we consume so much as a single sip of mead, there is something you must attend to, which you have forgotten."

"What?" asked Eragon, puzzled by Orik's obvious delight.

"Why, you must summon Saphira to Tronjheim, of course! Whether I become king or not, we shall crown a new monarch in three days' time. If Saphira is to attend the ceremony, she will need to fly quickly in order to arrive here before then."

With a wordless exclamation, Eragon ran to find a mirror.

INSUBORDINATION

The rich black soil was cool against Roran's hand.

He picked up a loose clod and crumbled it between his fingers, noting with approval that it was moist and full of decomposing leaves, stems, moss, and other organic matter that would provide excellent food for crops. He pressed it to his lips and tongue. The soil tasted alive, full of hundreds of flavors, from pulverized mountains to beetles and punky wood and the tender tips of grass roots.

This is good farmland, thought Roran. He cast his mind back to Palancar Valley, and again he saw the autumn sun streaming through the field of barley outside his family's house—neat rows of golden stalks shifting in the breeze—with the Anora River to the west and the snowcapped mountains rising high on either side of the valley. *That is where I should be, plowing the earth and raising a family with Katrina, not watering the ground with the sap of men's limbs.*

"Ho there!" cried Captain Edric, pointing toward Roran from on his horse. "Have an end to your dawdling, Stronghammer, lest I change my mind about you and leave you to stand guard with the archers!"

Dusting his hands on his leggings, Roran rose from a kneeling position. "Yes, sir! As you wish, sir!" he said, suppressing his dislike for Edric. Since he had joined Edric's company, Roran had attempted to learn what he could of the man's history. From what he heard, Roran had concluded Edric was a competent commander—Nasuada never would have put him in charge of such an important mission otherwise—but he had an abrasive personality, and he disciplined his warriors for even the slightest deviation from established practice, as Roran had learned to his chagrin upon three separate occasions during his first day with Edric's company. It was, Roran believed, a style of command that undermined a man's morale, as well as discouraged creativity and invention from those underneath you. *Perhaps Nasuada gave me to him for those very reasons,* thought Roran. *Or perhaps this is another test of hers. Perhaps she wants to know whether I can swallow my pride long enough to work with a man like Edric.*

Getting back onto Snowfire, Roran rode to the front of the column of two hundred and fifty men. Their mission was simple; since Nasuada and King Orrin had withdrawn the bulk of their forces from Surda, Galbatorix had apparently decided to take advantage of their absence and wreak havoc throughout the defenseless country, sacking towns and villages and burning the crops needed to sustain the invasion of the Empire. The easiest way to eliminate the soldiers would have been for Saphira to fly out and tear them to pieces,

but unless she was winging her way toward Eragon, everyone agreed it would be too dangerous for the Varden to be without her for so long. So Nasuada had sent Edric's company to repel the soldiers, whose number her spies had initially estimated to be around three hundred. However, two days ago, Roran and the rest of the warriors had been dismayed when they came across tracks that indicated the size of Galbatorix's force was closer to seven hundred.

Roran reined in Snowfire next to Carn on his dappled mare and scratched his chin while he studied the lay of the land. Before them was a vast expanse of undulating grass, dotted with occasional stands of willow and cottonwood trees. Hawks hunted above, while below, the grass was full of squeaking mice, rabbits, burrowing rodents, and other wildlife. The only evidence that men had ever visited the place before was the swath of trampled vegetation that led toward the eastern horizon, marking the soldiers' trail.

Carn glanced up at the noonday sun, the skin pulling tight around his drooping eyes as he squinted. "We should overtake them before our shadows are longer than we are tall."

"And then we'll discover whether there are enough of us to drive them away," muttered Roran, "or whether they will just massacre us. For once I'd like to outnumber our enemies."

A grim smile appeared on Carn's face. "It is always thus with the Varden."

"Form up!" shouted Edric, and spurred his horse down the trail trampled through the grass. Roran clamped his jaw shut and touched his heels to Snowfire's flanks as the company followed their captain.

Six hours later, Roran sat on Snowfire, hidden within a cluster of beech trees that grew along the edge of a small, flat stream clotted with rushes and strands of floating algae. Through the net of branches that hung before him, Roran gazed upon a crumbling, gray-sided village of no more than twenty houses. Roran had watched with ever-increasing fury as the villagers had spotted the soldiers advancing from the west and then had gathered up a few bundles of possessions and fled south, toward the heart of Surda. If it had been up to him, Roran would have revealed their presence to the villagers and assured them they were not about to lose their houses, not if he and the rest of his companions could prevent it, for he well remembered the pain and desperation and sense of hope-lessness that abandoning Carvahall had caused him, and he would have spared them that if he could. Also, he would have asked the men of the village to fight with them. Another ten or twenty sets of arms might mean the difference between victory or defeat, and Roran knew better than most the fervor with which people would fight to defend their homes. However, Edric had rejected the idea and insisted that the Varden remain concealed in the hills southeast of the village.

"We're lucky they're on foot," murmured Carn, indicating the red column of soldiers marching toward the village. "We would not have been able to get here first otherwise."

Roran glanced back at the men gathered behind them. Edric

had given him temporary command over eighty-one warriors. They consisted of swordsmen, spearmen, and a half-dozen archers. One of Edric's familiars, Sand, led another eighty-one of the company, while Edric headed the rest himself. All three groups were pressed against one another among the beech trees, which Roran thought was a mistake; the time it took to organize themselves once they broke from cover would be extra time the soldiers would have to marshal their defenses.

Leaning over toward Carn, Roran said, "I don't see any of them with missing hands or legs or other injuries of note, but that proves nothing one way or another. Can you tell if any of them are men who cannot feel pain?"

Carn sighed. "I wish I could. Your cousin might be able to, for Murtagh and Galbatorix are the only spellcasters Eragon need fear, but I am a poor magician, and I dare not test the soldiers. If there are any magicians disguised among the soldiers, they would know of my spying, and there is every chance I would not be able to break their minds before they alerted their companions we are here."

"We seem to have this discussion every time we are about to fight," Roran observed, studying the soldiers' armaments and trying to decide how best to deploy his men.

With a laugh, Carn said, "That's all right. I only hope we keep having it, because if not—"

"One or both of us will be dead—"

"Or Nasuada will have reassigned us to different captains—"

"And then we might as well be dead, because no one else will guard our backs as well," Roran concluded. A smile touched his lips. It had become an old joke between them. He drew his hammer from his belt and then winced as his right leg twinged where the ox had ripped his flesh with its horn. Scowling, he reached down and massaged the location of the wound.

Carn saw and asked, "Are you well?"

"It won't kill me," said Roran, then reconsidered his words.

"Well, maybe it will, but I'll be blasted if I'm going to wait here while you go off and cut those bumbling oafs to pieces."

When the soldiers reached the village, they marched straight through it, pausing only to break down the door to each house and tramp through the rooms to see if anyone was hiding inside. A dog ran out from behind a rain barrel, his ruff standing on end, and began barking at the soldiers. One of the men stepped forward and threw his spear at the dog, killing it.

As the first of the soldiers reached the far side of the village, Roran tightened his hand around the haft of his hammer in preparation for the charge, but then he heard a series of high-pitched screams, and a sense of dread gripped him. A squad of soldiers emerged from the second-to-last house, dragging three struggling people: a lanky, white-haired man, a young woman with a torn blouse, and a boy no older than eleven.

Sweat sprang up on Roran's brow. In a low, slow monotone, he began to swear, cursing the three captives for not having fled with their neighbors, cursing the soldiers for what they had done and might yet do, cursing Galbatorix, and cursing whatever whim of fate had resulted in the situation as it was. Behind him, he was aware of his men shifting and muttering with anger, eager to punish the soldiers for their brutality.

Having searched all of the houses, the mass of soldiers retraced their steps to the center of the village and formed a rough semicircle around their prisoners.

Yes! crowed Roran to himself as the soldiers turned their backs to the Varden. Edric's plan had been to wait for them to do just that. In anticipation of the order to charge, Roran rose up several inches above his saddle, his entire body tense. He tried to swallow, but his throat was too dry.

The officer in charge of the soldiers, who was the only man among them on a horse, dismounted his steed and exchanged a few inaudible words with the white-haired villager. Without warning, the officer drew his saber and decapitated the man, then hopped backward to avoid the resulting spray of blood. The young woman screamed even louder than before.

"Charge," said Edric.

It took Roran a half second to comprehend that the word Edric had uttered so calmly was the command he had been waiting for.

"Charge!" shouted Sand on the other side of Edric, and galloped out of the copse of beech trees along with his men.

"Charge!" shouted Roran, and dug his heels into Snowfire's sides. He ducked behind his shield as Snowfire carried him through the net of branches, then lowered it again when they were in the open, fly-ing down the side of the hill, with the thunder of hoofbeats sur-rounding them. Desperate to save the woman and the boy, Roran urged Snowfire to the limit of his speed. Looking back, he was heart-ened to see that his contingent of men had separated from the rest of the Varden without too much trouble; aside from a few stragglers, the majority were in a single bunch not thirty feet behind him.

Roran glimpsed Carn riding at the vanguard of Edric's men, his gray cloak flapping in the wind. Once again, Roran wished Edric had allowed them to remain in the same group.

As were his orders, Roran did not enter the village head-on, but rather veered to the left and rode around the buildings, so as to flank the soldiers and attack them from another direction. Sand did the same on the right, while Edric and his warriors drove straight into the village.

A line of houses concealed the initial clash from Roran, but he heard a chorus of frantic shouts, then a series of strange, metallic twangs, and then the screams of men and horses.

Worry knotted Roran's gut. *What was that noise? Could it be metal bows? Do they exist?* Regardless of the cause, he knew there should not have been so many horses crying out in agony. Roran's limbs went cold as he realized with utter certainty that the attack had somehow gone wrong and that the battle might already be lost.

He pulled hard on Snowfire's reins as they passed the last house, steering him toward the center of the village. Behind him, his men did the same. Two hundred yards ahead, Roran saw a triple line of soldiers positioned between two houses, so as to block their way. The soldiers seemed unafraid of the horses racing toward them.

Roran hesitated. His orders were clear: he and his men were to charge the western flank and cut their way through Galbatorix's troops until they rejoined Sand and Edric. However, Edric had not told Roran what he should do if riding straight up to the soldiers no longer seemed a good idea once he and his men were in position. And Roran knew that if he deviated from his orders, even if it was to prevent his men from being massacred, he would be guilty of insubordination and Edric could punish him accordingly.

Then the soldiers swept aside their voluminous cloaks and raised drawn crossbows to their shoulders.

In that instant, Roran decided that he would do whatever was necessary in order to ensure the Varden won the battle. He was not about to let the soldiers destroy his force with a single volley of arrows just because he wished to avoid the unpleasant consequences of defying his captain.

"Take cover!" shouted Roran, and wrenched Snowfire's head to the right, forcing the animal to swerve behind a house. A dozen quarrels buried themselves in the side of the building a second later. Turning around, Roran saw that all but one of his warriors had managed to duck behind nearby houses before the soldiers fired. The man who had been too slow lay bleeding in the dirt, a pair of quarrels projecting from his chest. The bolts had torn through his mail hauberk as if it were no thicker than a sheet of tissue. Frightened by the smell of blood, his horse kicked up its heels and fled the village, leaving a plume of dust rising in its wake.

Roran reached over and grasped the edge of a beam in the side of the house, holding Snowfire in place while he desperately tried to figure out how to proceed. The soldiers had him and his men pinned down; they could not step back out into the open without being shot so full of quarrels, they would resemble hedgehogs.

A group of Roran's warriors rode up to him from a house that his own building partially shielded from the soldiers' line of sight. "What should we do, Stronghammer?" they asked him. They did not seem bothered by the fact that he had disobeyed his orders; to the contrary, they looked at him with expressions of newfound trust.

Thinking as fast as he could, Roran cast his gaze around. By chance, his eyes alighted upon the bow and quiver strapped behind one of the men's saddles. Roran smiled. Only a few of the warriors fought as archers, but they all carried a bow and arrows so they could hunt for food and help feed the company when they were alone in the wilderness, without support from the rest of the Varden.

Roran pointed toward the house he was leaning against and said, "Take your bows and climb onto the roof, as many of you as will fit, but if you value your lives, stay out of sight until I say otherwise. When I tell you to, start shooting and keep shooting until you run out of arrows or until every last soldier is dead. Understood?"

"Yes, sir!"

"Get going, then. The rest of you, find buildings of your own where you can pick off the soldiers. Harald, spread the word to everyone else, and find ten of our best spearmen and ten of our best swordsmen and bring them here as fast as you can."

"Yes, sir!"

With a flurry of motion, the warriors hurried to obey. Those who were closest to Roran retrieved their bows and quivers from behind their saddles and then, standing upon the backs of their horses, pulled themselves onto the thatched roof of the house. Four minutes later, the majority of Roran's men were in place on the roofs of seven different houses—with about eight men per roof—and Harald had returned with the requested swordsmen and spearmen in tow.

To the warriors gathered around him, Roran said, "Right, now listen. When I give the order, the men up there will start shooting. As soon as the first flight of arrows strikes the soldiers, we're going to ride out and attempt to rescue Captain Edric. If we can't, we'll have to settle for giving the red-tunics a taste of good cold steel. The archers should provide enough confusion for us to close with the soldiers before they can use their crossbows. Am I understood?"

"Yes, sir!"

"Then fire!" Roran shouted.

With full-throated yells, the men stationed on the houses rose up above the ridges of the roofs and, as one, fired their bows at the soldiers below. The swarm of arrows whistled through the air like bloodthirsty shrikes diving toward their prey.

An instant later, when soldiers began to howl with agony at their wounds, Roran said, "Now *ride!*" and jabbed his heels into Snowfire.

Together, he and his men galloped around the side of the house, pulling their steeds into such a tight turn that they nearly fell over. Relying on his speed and the skill of the archers for protection, Roran skirted the soldiers, who were flailing in disarray, until he came upon the site of Edric's disastrous charge. There the ground was slick with blood, and the corpses of many good men and fine horses littered the space between the houses. Edric's remaining forces were engaged in hand-to-hand combat with the soldiers. To Roran's surprise, Edric was still alive, fighting back to back with five of his men.

"Stay with me!" Roran shouted to his companions as they raced into the battle.

Lashing out with his hooves, Snowfire knocked two soldiers to the ground, breaking their sword arms and staving in their rib cages. Pleased with the stallion, Roran laid about himself with his hammer, snarling with the fierce joy of battle as he felled soldier after soldier, none of whom could withstand the ferocity of his assault. "To me!" he shouted as he drew abreast of Edric and the other survivors. "To me!" In front of him, arrows continued to rain down upon the mass of soldiers, forcing them to cover themselves with their shields while at the same time trying to fend off the Varden's swords and spears.

Once he and his warriors had surrounded the Varden who were on foot, Roran shouted, "Back! Back! To the houses!" Step by step, the lot of them withdrew until they were out of reach of the soldiers' blades, and then they turned and ran toward the nearest house. The soldiers shot and killed three of the Varden along the way, but the rest arrived at the building unharmed.

Edric slumped against the side of the house, gasping for breath. When again he was able to speak, he gestured at Roran's men and said, "Your intervention is most timely and welcome, Stronghammer, but why do I see you here, and not riding out from among the soldiers, as I expected?"

Then Roran explained what he had done and pointed out the archers on the roofs.

A dark scowl appeared on Edric's brow as he listened to Roran's account. However, he did not chastise Roran for his disobedience but merely said, "Have those men come down at once. They have succeeded in breaking the soldiers' discipline. Now we must rely upon honest blade-work to dispose of them."

"There are too few of us left to attack the soldiers directly!" protested Roran. "They outnumber us better than three to one."

"Then we shall make up in valor what we lack in numbers!" Edric bellowed. "I was told you had courage, Stronghammer, but obviously rumor is mistaken and you are as timid as a frightened rabbit. Now do as you're told, and do not question me again!" The captain indicated one of Roran's warriors. "You there, lend me your steed." After the man dismounted, Edric pulled himself into the saddle and said, "Half of you on horse, follow me; I go to reinforce Sand. Everyone else, remain with Roran." Kicking his mount in the sides, Edric galloped away with the men who chose to follow him, racing from building to building as they worked their way around the soldiers clumped in the center of the village.

Roran shook with fury as he watched them depart. Never before had he allowed anyone to question his courage without answering his critic with words or blows. So long as the battle persisted, however, it would be inappropriate for him to confront Edric. *Very well*, Roran thought, *I shall demonstrate to Edric the courage he thinks I lack. But that is all he shall have from me. I will not send the archers to fight the soldiers face to face when they are safer and more effective where they are.*

Roran turned and inspected the men Edric had left to him. Among those they had rescued, Roran was delighted to see Carn, who was scratched and bloody but, on the whole, unharmed. They nodded to each other, and then Roran addressed the group: "You have heard what Edric said. I disagree. If we do as he wishes, all of us will end up piled in a cairn before sunset. We can still win this battle, but not by marching to our own deaths! What we lack in numbers, we can make up with cunning. You know how I came to join the Varden. You know I have fought and defeated the Empire before, and in just such a village! This I can do, I swear to you. But I cannot do it alone. Will you follow me? Think carefully. I will claim responsibility for ignoring Edric's orders, but he and Nasuada may still punish everyone who was involved."

"Then they would be fools," growled Carn. "Would they prefer that we died here? No, I think not. You may count on me, Roran."

As Carn made his declaration, Roran saw how the other men squared their shoulders and set their jaws and how their eyes burned with renewed determination, and he knew they had decided to cast their lot with him, if only because they would not want to be parted from the only magician in their company. Many was the warrior of the Varden who owed his life to a member of Du Vrangr Gata, and the men-at-arms Roran had met would sooner stab themselves in a foot than go into battle without a spellcaster close at hand.

"Aye," said Harald. "You may count on us as well, Stronghammer."

"Then follow me!" said Roran. Reaching down, he pulled Carn up onto Snowfire behind himself, then hurried with his group back around the village to where the bowmen on the roofs continued to fire arrows at the soldiers. As Roran and the men with him dashed from house to house, quarrels buzzed past them—sounding like giant, angry insects—and one even buried itself halfway through Harald's shield.

Once they were safely behind cover, Roran had the men who were still mounted give their bows and arrows to the men on foot, whom he then sent to climb the houses and join the other archers. As they scrambled to obey him, Roran beckoned to Carn, who had jumped off Snowfire the moment they ceased moving, and said, "I need a spell of you. Can you shield me and ten others from these bolts?"

Carn hesitated. "For how long?"

"A minute? An hour? Who knows?"

"Shielding that many people from more than a handful of bolts would soon exceed the bounds of my strength. . . . Although, if you don't care if I stop the bolts in their tracks, I could deflect them from you, which—"

"That would be fine."

"Who exactly do you want me to protect?"

Roran pointed at the men he had picked to join him, and Carn asked each of them their names. Standing with his shoulders hunched inward, Carn began to mutter in the ancient language, his face pale and strained. Three times he tried to cast the spell, and three times he failed. "I'm sorry," he said, and released an unsteady breath. "I can't seem to concentrate."

"Blast it, don't apologize," growled Roran. "Just do it!" Leaping down from Snowfire, he grasped Carn on either side of his head, holding him in place. "Look at me! Look into the center of my eyes. That's it. Keep staring at me. . . . Good. Now place the ward around us."

Carn's features cleared and his shoulders loosened, and then, in a confident voice, he recited the incantation. As he uttered the last word, he sagged slightly in Roran's grip before recovering. "It is done," he said.

Roran patted him on the shoulder, then clambered into

516

Snowfire's saddle again. Sweeping his gaze over the ten horsemen, he said, "Guard my sides and my back, but otherwise keep behind me so long as I am able to swing my hammer."

"Yes, sir!"

"Remember, the bolts cannot harm you now. Carn, you stay here. Don't move too much; conserve your strength. If you feel like you can't maintain the spell any longer, signal us before you end it. Agreed?"

Carn sat on the front step of the house and nodded. "Agreed."

Renewing his grip on his shield and hammer, Roran took a deep breath, attempting to calm himself. "Brace yourselves," he said, and clucked his tongue to Snowfire.

With the ten horsemen following, Roran rode out into the middle of the dirt street that ran between the houses and faced the soldiers once more. Five hundred or so of Galbatorix's troops remained in the center of the village, most of them crouching or kneeling behind their shields while they struggled to reload their crossbows. Occasionally, a soldier would stand and loose a bolt at one of the archers on the roofs before dropping back behind his shield as a flight of arrows sliced through the air where he had just been. Throughout the corpse-strewn clearing, patches of arrows studded the ground, like reeds sprouting from the bloody soil. Several hundred feet away, on the far side of the soldiers, Roran could see a knot of thrashing bodies, and he assumed that was where Sand, Edric, and whatever remained of their forces were fighting the soldiers. If the young woman and the boy were still in the clearing, he did not notice them.

A quarrel buzzed toward Roran. When the bolt was less than a yard from his chest, it abruptly changed direction and hurtled off at an angle, missing him and his men. Roran flinched, but the missile was already past. His throat constricted, and his heartbeat doubled.

Glancing around, Roran spotted a broken wagon leaning against a house off to his left. He pointed at it and said, "Pull that over here and lay it upside down. Block as much of the street as you can." To

517

the archers, he shouted, "Don't let the soldiers sneak around and attack us from the sides! When they come at us, thin out their ranks as much as you can. And as soon as you run out of arrows, come join us."

"Yes, sir!"

"Just be careful you don't shoot us by accident, or I swear I'll haunt your halls for the rest of time!"

"Yes, sir!"

More quarrels flew at Roran and the other horsemen in the street, but in every case, the bolts glanced off Carn's ward and veered into a wall or the ground or vanished into the sky.

Roran watched his men drag the wagon into the street. When they were nearly finished, he lifted his chin, filled his lungs, and then, projecting his voice toward the soldiers, he roared, "Ho there, you cowering carrion dogs! See how only eleven of us bar your way. Win past us, and you win your freedom. Try your hand if you have the guts. What? You hesitate? Where is your manhood, you deformed maggots, you bilious, swine-faced murderers? Your fathers were dribbling half-wits who should have been drowned at birth! Aye, and your mothers were poxy trollops and the consorts of Urgals!" Roran smiled with satisfaction as several of the soldiers howled with outrage and began to insult him in return. One of the soldiers, however, seemed to lose his will to continue fighting, for he sprang to his feet and ran northward, covering himself with his shield and darting from side to side in a desperate attempt to avoid the archers. Despite his efforts, the Varden shot him dead before he had gone more than a hundred feet. "Ha!" exclaimed Roran. "Cowards you are, every last one of you, you verminous river rats! If it will give you spine, then know this: Roran Stronghammer is my name, and Eragon Shadeslayer is my cousin! Kill me, and that foul king of yours will reward you with an earldom, or more. But you will have to kill me with a blade; your crossbows are of no use against me. Come now, you slugs; you leeches; you starving, white-bellied ticks! Come and best me if you can!"

With a flurry of battle-cries, a group of thirty soldiers dropped their crossbows, drew their flashing swords, and, with shields held high, ran toward Roran and his men.

From over his right shoulder, Roran heard Harald say, "Sir, there are many more of them than us."

"Aye," Roran said, keeping his eyes fixed on the approaching soldiers. Four of them stumbled and then lay motionless on the ground, pierced through by numerous shafts.

"If they all charge us at once, we won't stand a chance."

"Yes, but they won't. Look, they're confused and disorganized. Their commander must have fallen. As long as we maintain order, they cannot overwhelm us."

"But, Stronghammer, we cannot kill that many men ourselves!"

Roran glanced back at Harald. "Of course we can! We fight to protect our families and to reclaim our homes and our lands. They fight because Galbatorix forces them to. They have not the heart for this battle. So think of your families, think of your homes, and remember it is they you are defending. A man who fights for something greater than himself may kill a hundred enemies with ease!" As he spoke, Roran saw in his mind an image of Katrina clad in her blue wedding dress, and he smelled the scent of her skin, and he heard the muted tones of her voice from their discussions late at night.

Katrina.

Then the soldiers were upon them, and for a span Roran heard nothing but the thud of swords bouncing off his shield and the clang of his hammer as he struck the soldiers' helms and the cries of the soldiers as they crumpled underneath his blows. The soldiers threw themselves against him with desperate strength, but they were no match for him or his men. When he vanquished the last of the attacking soldiers, Roran burst out laughing, exhilarated. What a joy it was to crush those who would harm his wife and his unborn child!

He was pleased to see that none of his warriors had been seriously injured. He also noticed that during the fray, several of the archers had descended from the roofs to fight on horseback with them. Roran grinned at the newcomers and said, "Welcome to the battle!"

"A warm welcome indeed!" one of them replied.

Pointing with his gore-covered hammer toward the right side of the street, Roran said, "You, you, and you, pile the bodies over there. Make a funnel out of them and the wagon, so that only two or three soldiers can get to us at once."

"Yes, sir!" the warriors answered, swinging down from their horses.

A quarrel whizzed toward Roran. He ignored it and focused on the main body of soldiers, where a group, perhaps a hundred strong, was massing in preparation for a second onslaught. "Hurry!" he shouted to the men shifting the corpses. "They're almost upon us. Harald, go help."

Roran wet his lips, nervous, as he watched his men labor while the soldiers advanced. To his relief, the four Varden dragged the last body into place and clambered back onto their steeds moments before the wave of soldiers struck.

The houses on either side of the street, as well as the overturned wagon and the gruesome barricade of human remains, slowed and compressed the flow of soldiers, until they were nearly at a standstill when they reached Roran. The soldiers were packed so tightly, they were helpless to escape the arrows that streaked toward them from above.

The first two ranks of soldiers carried spears, with which they menaced Roran and the other Varden. Roran parried three separate thrusts, cursing the whole while as he realized that he could not reach past the spears with his hammer. Then a soldier stabbed Snowfire in the shoulder, and Roran leaned forward to keep from being thrown as the stallion squealed and reared.

As Snowfire landed on all fours, Roran slid out of the saddle, keeping the stallion between him and the hedge of spear-wielding soldiers. Snowfire bucked as another spear pierced his hide. Before the soldiers could wound him again, Roran pulled on Snowfire's reins and forced him to prance backward until there was enough room among the other horses for the stallion to turn around. "Yah!" he shouted, and slapped Snowfire on the rump, sending him galloping out of the village.

"Make way!" Roran bellowed, waving at the Varden. They cleared a path for him between their steeds, and he bounded to the forefront of the fight again, sticking his hammer through his belt as he did.

A soldier jabbed a spear at Roran's chest. He blocked it with his wrist, bruising himself on the hard wooden shaft, and then yanked the spear out of the soldier's hands. The man fell flat on his face. Twirling the weapon, Roran stabbed the man, then lunged forward and lanced two more soldiers. Roran took a wide stance, planting his feet firmly in the rich soil where once he would have sought to raise crops, and shook the spear at his foes, shouting, "Come, you misbegotten bastards! Kill me if you can! I am Roran Strong-hammer, and I fear no man alive!"

The soldiers shuffled forward, three men stepping over the bodies of their former comrades to exchange blows with Roran. Dancing to the side, Roran drove his spear into the jaw of the rightmost soldier, shattering his teeth. A pennant of blood trailed the blade as Roran withdrew the weapon and, dropping to one knee, impaled the central soldier through an armpit.

An impact jarred Roran's left shoulder. His shield seemed to double in weight. Rising, he saw a spear buried in the oak planks of his shield and the remaining soldier of the trio rushing at him with a drawn sword. Roran lifted his spear above his head as if he were about to throw it and, when the soldier faltered, kicked him between the fork of his legs. He dispatched the man with a single blow. During the momentary lull in combat that followed, Roran disengaged his arm from the useless shield and cast it and the attached spear under the feet of his enemies, hoping to tangle their legs.

More soldiers shuffled forward, quailing before Roran's feral grin

521

and stabbing spear. A mound of bodies grew before him. When it reached the height of his waist, Roran bounded to the top of the blood-soaked berm, and there he remained, despite the treacherous footing, for the height gave him an advantage. Since the soldiers were forced to climb up a ramp of corpses to reach him, he was able to kill many of them when they stumbled over an arm or a leg or stepped upon the soft neck of one of their predecessors or slipped on a slanting shield.

From his elevated position, Roran could see that the rest of the soldiers had chosen to join the assault, save for a score across the village who were still battling Sand's and Edric's warriors. He realized he would have no more rest until the battle had concluded.

Roran acquired dozens of wounds as the day wore on. Many of his injuries were minor—a cut on the inside of a forearm, a broken finger, a scratch across his ribs where a dagger had shorn through his mail—but others were not. From where he lay on the pile of bodies, a soldier stabbed Roran through his right calf muscle, hobbling him. Soon afterward, a heavyset man smelling of onions and cheese fell against Roran and, with his dying breath, shoved the bolt of a crossbow into Roran's left shoulder, which thereafter prevented Roran from lifting his arm overhead. Roran left the bolt embedded in his flesh, for he knew he might bleed to death if he pulled it out. Pain became Roran's ruling sensation; every movement caused him fresh agony, but to stand still was to die, and so he kept dealing death-blows, regardless of his wounds and regardless of his weariness.

Roran was sometimes aware of the Varden behind or beside him, such as when they threw a spear past him, or when the blade of a sword would dart around his shoulder to fell a soldier who was about to brain him, but for the most part Roran faced the soldiers alone, because of the pile of bodies he stood on and the restricted amount of space between the overturned wagon and the sides of the houses. Above, the archers who still had arrows maintained their lethal barrage, their gray-goose shafts penetrating bone and sinew alike.

Late in the battle, Roran thrust his spear at a soldier, and as the tip struck the man's armor, the haft cracked and split along its length. That he was still alive seemed to catch the soldier by surprise, for he hesitated before swinging his sword in retaliation. His imprudent delay allowed Roran to duck underneath the length of singing steel and seize another spear from the ground, with which he slew the soldier. To Roran's dismay and disgust, the second spear lasted less than a minute before it too shattered in his grip. Throwing the splintered remains at the soldiers, Roran took a shield from a corpse and drew his hammer from his belt. His hammer, at least, had never failed him.

Exhaustion proved to be Roran's greatest adversary as the last of the soldiers gradually approached, each man waiting his turn to duel him. Roran's limbs felt heavy and lifeless, his vision flickered, and he could not seem to get enough air, and yet he somehow always managed to summon the energy to defeat his next opponent. As his reflexes slowed, the soldiers dealt him numerous cuts and bruises that he could have easily avoided earlier.

When gaps appeared between the soldiers, and through them Roran could see open space, he knew his ordeal was nearly at an end. He did not offer the final twelve men mercy, nor did they ask it of him, even though they could not have hoped to battle their way past him as well as the Varden beyond. Nor did they attempt to flee. Instead, they rushed at him, snarling, cursing, desiring only to kill the man who had slain so many of their comrades before they too passed into the void.

In a way, Roran admired their courage.

Arrows sprouted from the chests of four of the men, downing them. A spear thrown from somewhere behind Roran took a fifth man under the collarbone, and he too toppled onto a bed of corpses. Two more spears claimed their victims, and then the men reached Roran. The lead soldier hewed at Roran with a spiked ax. Although Roran could feel the head of the crossbow bolt grating against his bone, he threw up his left arm and blocked the ax with his shield. Howling with pain and anger, as well as an overwhelming desire for the battle to end, Roran whipped his hammer around and slew the soldier with a blow to the head. Without pause, Roran hopped forward on his good leg and struck the next soldier twice in the chest before he could defend himself, cracking his ribs. The third man parried two of Roran's attacks, but then Roran deceived him with a feint and slew him as well. The final two soldiers converged on Roran from either side, swinging at his ankles as they climbed to the summit of the piled corpses. His strength flagging, Roran sparred with them for a long and wearisome while, both giving and receiving wounds, until at last he killed one man by caving in his helm and the other by breaking his neck with a well-placed blow.

Roran swayed and then collapsed.

He felt himself being lifted up and opened his eyes to see Harald holding a wineskin to his lips. "Drink this," Harald said. "You'll feel better."

His chest heaving, Roran consumed several draughts between gasps. The sun-warmed wine stung the inside of his battered mouth. He felt his legs steady and said, "It's all right; you can let go of me now."

Roran leaned against his hammer and surveyed the battleground. For the first time he appreciated how high the mound of bodies had grown; he and his companions stood at least twenty feet in the air, which was nearly level with the tops of the houses on either side. Roran saw that most of the soldiers had died of arrows, but even so, he knew that he had slain a vast number by himself.

"How . . . how many?" he asked Harald.

The blood-spattered warrior shook his head. "I lost count after thirty-two. Perhaps another can say. What you did, Stronghammer . . . Never have I seen such a feat before, not by a man of human abilities. The dragon Saphira chose well; the men of your family are fighters like no others. Your prowess is unmatched by any mortal, Stronghammer. However many you slew here today, I—"

"It was one hundred and ninety-three!" cried Carn, clambering toward them from below.

"Are you sure?" asked Roran, unbelieving.

Carn nodded as he reached them. "Aye! I watched, and *I* kept careful count. One hundred and ninety-three, it was—ninety-four if you count the man you stabbed through the gut before the archers finished him off."

The tally astounded Roran. He had not suspected the total was quite so large. A hoarse chuckle escaped him. "A pity there are no more of them. Another seven and I would have an even two hundred."

The other men laughed as well.

His thin face furrowed with concern, Carn reached for the bolt sticking out of Roran's left shoulder, saying, "Here, let me see to your wounds."

"No!" said Roran, and brushed him away. "There may be others who are more seriously injured than I am. Tend to them first."

"Roran, several of those cuts could prove fatal unless I stanch the bleeding. It won't take but a—"

"I'm fine," he growled. "Leave me alone."

"Roran, just look at yourself!"

He did and averted his gaze. "Be quick about it, then." Roran stared into the featureless sky, his mind empty of thought while Carn pulled the bolt out of his shoulder and muttered various spells. In every spot where the magic took effect, Roran felt his skin itch and crawl, followed by a blessed cessation of pain. When Carn had finished, Roran still hurt, but he did not hurt quite so badly, and his mind was clearer than before.

The healing left Carn gray-faced and shaking. He leaned against his knees until his tremors stopped. "I will go . . ." He paused for breath. ". . . go help the rest of the wounded now." He straightened and picked his way down the mound, lurching from side to side as if he were drunk.

Roran watched him go, concerned. Then it occurred to him to wonder about the fate of the rest of their expedition. He looked toward the far side of the village and saw nothing but scattered bodies, some clad in the red of the Empire, others in the brown wool favored by the Varden. "What of Edric and Sand?" he asked Harald.

"I'm sorry, Stronghammer, but I saw nothing beyond the reach of my sword."

Calling to the few men who still stood on the roofs of the houses, Roran asked, "What of Edric and Sand?"

"We do not know, Stronghammer!" they replied.

Steadying himself with his hammer, Roran slowly picked his way down the tumbled ramp of bodies and, with Harald and three other men by his side, crossed the clearing in the center of the village, executing every soldier they found still alive. When they arrived at the edge of the clearing, where the number of slain Varden surpassed the number of slain soldiers, Harald banged his sword on his shield and shouted, "Is anyone still alive?"

After a moment, a voice came back at them from among the houses: "Name yourself!"

"Harald and Roran Stronghammer and others of the Varden. If you serve the Empire, then surrender, for your comrades are dead and you cannot defeat us!"

From somewhere between the houses came a crash of falling metal, and then in ones and twos, warriors of the Varden emerged from hiding and limped toward the clearing, many of them supporting their wounded comrades. They appeared dazed, and some were stained with so much blood, Roran at first mistook them for captured soldiers. He counted four-and-twenty men. Among the final group of stragglers was Edric, helping along a man who had lost his right arm during the fighting.

Roran motioned, and two of his men hurried to relieve Edric of his burden. The captain straightened from under the weight. With slow steps, he walked over to Roran and looked him straight in the eye, his expression unreadable. Neither he nor Roran moved, and Roran was aware that the clearing had grown exceptionally quiet.

Edric was the first to speak. "How many of your men survived?"

"Most. Not all, but most."

Edric nodded. "And Carn?"

"He lives. . . . What of Sand?"

"A soldier shot him during his charge. He died but a few minutes ago." Edric looked past Roran, then toward the mound of bodies. "You defied my orders, Stronghammer."

"I did."

Edric held out an open hand toward him.

"Captain, no!" exclaimed Harald, stepping forward. "If it weren't for Roran, none of us would be standing here. And you should have seen what he did; he slew nearly two hundred by himself!"

Harald's pleas made no impression on Edric, who continued to hold out his hand. Roran remained impassive as well.

Turning to him then, Harald said, "Roran, you know the men are yours. Just say the word, and we will—"

Roran silenced him with a glare. "Don't be a fool."

Between thin lips, Edric said, "At least you are not completely devoid of sense. Harald, keep your teeth shut unless you want to lead the packhorses the whole way back."

Lifting his hammer, Roran handed it to Edric. Then he unbuckled his belt, upon which hung his sword and his dagger, and those too he surrendered to Edric. "I have no other weapons," he said.

Edric nodded, grim, and slung the sword belt over one shoulder. "Roran Stronghammer, I hereby relieve you of command. Have I your word of honor you will not attempt to flee?"

"You do."

"Then you will make yourself useful where you may, but in all else, you will comport yourself as a prisoner." Edric looked around and pointed at another warrior. "Fuller, you will assume Roran's position until we return to the main body of the Varden and Nasuada can decide what is to be done about this."

"Yes, sir," said Fuller.

✳ ✳ ✳

For several hours, Roran bent his back alongside the other warriors as they collected their dead and buried them on the outskirts of the village. During the process, Roran learned that only nine of his eighty-one warriors had died in the battle, while between them, Edric and Sand had lost almost a hundred and fifty men, and Edric would have lost more, except that a handful of his warriors had remained with Roran after he rode to their rescue.

When they finished interring their casualties, the Varden retrieved their arrows, then built a pyre in the center of the village, stripped the soldiers of their gear, dragged them onto the pile of wood, and set it ablaze. The burning bodies filled the sky with a pillar of greasy black smoke that drifted upward for what seemed like miles. Through it, the sun appeared as a flat red disk.

The young woman and the boy the soldiers had captured were nowhere to be found. Since their bodies were not among the dead, Roran guessed the two had fled the village when the fighting broke out, which, he thought, was probably the best thing they could have done. He wished them luck, wherever they had gone.

To Roran's pleased surprise, Snowfire trotted back into the village minutes before the Varden were to depart. At first the stallion was skittish and standoffish, allowing no one to approach, but by talking to him in a low voice, Roran managed to calm the stallion enough to clean and bandage the wounds in the horse's shoulder. Since it would be unwise to ride Snowfire until he was fully healed, Roran tied him to the front of the packhorses, which the stallion took an immediate dislike to, flattening his ears, flicking his tail from side to side, and curling his lips to bare his teeth.

"Behave yourself," said Roran, stroking his neck. Snowfire rolled an eyeball at him and nickered, his ears relaxing slightly.

Then Roran pulled himself onto a gelding that had belonged to one of the dead Varden and took his place at the rear of the line of men assembled between the houses. Roran ignored the many glances they directed at him, although it heartened him when several of the warriors murmured, "Well done."

As he sat waiting for Edric to give the command to start forward, Roran thought of Nasuada and Katrina and Eragon, and a cloud of dread shadowed his thoughts as he wondered how they would react when they learned of his mutiny. Roran pushed away his worries a second later. *I did what was right and necessary,* he told himself. *I won't regret it, no matter what may come of it.*

"Move on out!" shouted Edric from the head of the procession.

Roran spurred his steed into a brisk walk, and as one, he and the other men rode west, away from the village, leaving the pile of soldiers to burn itself to extinction.

MESSAGE IN A MIRROR

The morning sun beat down on Saphira, suffusing her with a pleasant warmth.

She lay basking on a smooth shelf of stone several feet above Eragon's empty cloth-shell-tent. The night's activities, flying around scouting the Empire's locations—as she had every night since Nasuada sent Eragon to the big-hollow-mountain-Farthen Dûr—had left her drowsy. The flights were necessary to conceal Eragon's absence, but the routine wore on her, for while the dark held no terrors for her, she was not nocturnal by habit, and she disliked having to do anything with such regularity. Also, since it took the Varden so long to move from place to place, she spent most of her time soaring over much the same landscape every night. The only recent excitement was when she spotted stunted-thoughts-red-scales-Thorn low on the northeastern horizon the previous morning. He had not turned to confront her, however, but had continued on his way, heading deeper into the Empire. When Saphira had reported what she had seen, Nasuada, Arya, and the elves guarding Saphira had reacted like a flock of frightened jays, screaming and yammering at each other while darting every which way. They had even insisted that black-blue-wolf-hair-Blödhgarm fly with her in the guise of Eragon, which of course she had refused to allow. It was one thing to permit the elf to place a water-shadow-ghost of Eragon on her back every time she took off from or landed among the Varden, but she was not about to let anyone other than Eragon ride her unless a battle was imminent, and perhaps not even then.

Saphira yawned and stretched out her right foreleg, spreading the clawed fingers of her paw. Relaxing again, she wrapped her tail around her body and adjusted the position of her head on her paws, visions of deer and other prey drifting through her mind.

Not long afterward, she heard the patter of feet as someone ran through the camp, heading toward Nasuada's folded-wing-red-butterfly-chrysalis-tent. Saphira paid little attention to the sound; messengers were always hurrying to and fro.

Just as she was about to fall asleep, Saphira heard another runner dash past, then, after a brief interval, two more. Without opening her eyes, she extended the tip of her tongue and tasted the air. She detected no unusual odors. Deciding that the disturbance was not worth investigating, she drifted off into dreams of diving for fish in a cool green lake.

Angry shouting woke Saphira.

She did not stir as she listened to a large number of round-ear-two-legs arguing with each other. They were too far away for her to make out the words, but from the tone of their voices, she could tell they were angry enough to kill. Disputes sometimes broke out among the Varden, just as they did in any large herd, but never before had she heard so many two-legs argue for so long and with so much passion.

531

A dull throbbing formed at the base of Saphira's skull as the two-legs' shouting intensified. She tightened her claws against the stone beneath her, and with sharp cracks, thin wafers of the quartz-laden rock flaked off around the tips of her talons.

I shall count to thirty-three, she thought, *and if they have not stopped by then, they had better hope that whatever upset them was worth disrupting the rest of a daughter-of-the-wind!*

When Saphira reached the count of seven-and-twenty, the two-legs fell silent. *At last!* Shifting to a more comfortable position, she prepared to resume her much-needed slumber.

Metal clinked, plant-cloth-hides swished, skin-paw-coverings thudded against the ground, and the unmistakable scent of dark-skin-warrior-Nasuada wafted over Saphira. *What now?* she wondered, and briefly considered roaring at everyone until they fled in terror and left her alone.

Saphira opened a single eye and saw Nasuada and her six guards striding toward where she lay. At the lower end of the slab of stone, Nasuada ordered her guards to remain behind with Blödhgarm and the other elves—who were sparring with each other on a small expanse of grass—and then she climbed the slab by herself.

"Greetings, Saphira," Nasuada said. She wore a red dress, and the color seemed unnaturally strong against the green leaves of the apple trees behind her. Glints of light from Saphira's scales mottled her face.

Saphira blinked once, feeling no inclination to answer with words.

After glancing around, Nasuada stepped closer to Saphira's head and whispered, "Saphira, I must speak to you in private. You can reach into my mind, but I cannot reach into yours. Can you remain inside me, so I can think what I need to say and you will hear?"

Extending herself toward the woman's tense-hard-tired-consciousness, Saphira allowed her irritation at being kept from her sleep to wash over Nasuada, and then she said, *I can if I so choose, but I would never do so without your permission.*

Of course, Nasuada replied. *I understand.* At first Saphira received nothing but disjointed images and emotions from the woman: a gallows with an empty noose, blood on the ground, snarling faces, dread, weariness, and an undercurrent of grim determination. *Forgive me*, said Nasuada. *I have had a trying morning. If my thoughts wander overmuch, please bear with me.*

Saphira blinked again. *What is it that has stirred up the Varden so? A group of men roused me from my sleep with their ill-tempered wrangling, and before that, I heard an unusual number of messengers racing through the camp.*

Pressing her lips together, Nasuada turned away from Saphira and crossed her arms, cradling her healing forearms with cupped hands. The coloring of her mind became black as a midnight cloud, full of intimations of death and violence. After an uncharacteristically long pause, she said, *One of the Varden, a man by the name of Othmund, crept into the Urgals' camp last night and killed three of them while they were asleep around their fire. The Urgals failed to catch Othmund at the time, but this morning, he claimed credit for the deed and was boasting of it throughout the army.*

Why did he do this? Saphira asked. *Did the Urgals kill his family?*

Nasuada shook her head. *I almost wish they had, because then the Urgals would not be so upset; revenge, at least, they understand. No, that's the strange part of this affair; Othmund hates the Urgals for no other reason than they are Urgals. They have never wronged him, nor his kin, and yet he loathes Urgals with every fiber of his body. Or so I gather after having spoken with him.*

How will you deal with him?

Nasuada looked at Saphira again, a profound sadness in her eyes. *He will hang for his crimes. When I accepted the Urgals into the Varden, I decreed that anyone who attacked an Urgal would be punished as if he had attacked a fellow human. I cannot go back on my word now.*

Do you regret your promise?

No. The men needed to know I would not condone such acts. Otherwise, they might have turned against the Urgals the very day Nar Garzhvog and I made our pact. Now, however, I must show them I meant what I said. If I don't, there will be even more murders, and then the Urgals will take matters into their own hands, and once again, our two races shall be snapping at each other's throats. It is only right Othmund should die for killing the Urgals and for defying my order, but oh, Saphira, the Varden will not like this. I have sacrificed my own flesh to win their loyalty, but now they will hate me for hanging Othmund. . . . They will hate me for equating the lives of Urgals with the lives of humans. Lowering her arms, Nasuada tugged at the cuffs of her sleeves. *And I cannot say I like it any more than they will. For all my attempts to treat the Urgals openly and fairly and as equals, as my father would have, I cannot help but remember how they killed him. I cannot help but remember the sight of all those Urgals slaughtering the*

Varden during the Battle of Farthen Dûr. I cannot help but remember the many stories I heard when I was a child, stories of Urgals sweeping out of the mountains and murdering innocent people in their beds. Always Urgals were the monsters to be feared, and here I have joined our fate with theirs. I cannot help but remember all that, Saphira, and I find myself wondering if I have made the right decision.

You cannot help but be human, said Saphira, attempting to comfort Nasuada. *Yet you do not have to be bound by what those around you believe. You can grow beyond the limits of your race if you have the will. If the events of the past can teach us anything, it is that the kings and queens and other leaders who have brought the races closer together are the ones who have accomplished the greatest good in Alagaësia. It is strife and anger we must guard against, not closer relations with those who were once our foes. Remember your distrust of the Urgals, for they have well earned it, but also remember that once dwarves and dragons loved one another no more than humans and Urgals. And once dragons fought against the elves and would have driven their race extinct if we could have. Once those things were true, but no more, because people like you had the courage to set aside past hatreds and forge bonds of friendship where, previously, none existed.*

Nasuada pressed her forehead against the side of Saphira's jaw, then said, *You are very wise, Saphira.*

Amused, Saphira lifted her head off her paws and touched Nasuada on the brow with the tip of her snout. *I speak the truth as I see it, no more. If that is wisdom, then you are welcome to it; however, I believe you already possess all the wisdom you need. Executing Othmund may not please the Varden, but it will take more than this to break their devotion to you. Besides, I am sure you can find a way to mollify them.*

Aye, said Nasuada, wiping the corners of her eyes with her fingers. *I will have to, I think.* Then she smiled and her face was transformed. *But Othmund was not why I came to see you. Eragon just contacted me and asked for you to join him in Farthen Dûr. The dwarves—*

Arching her neck, Saphira roared toward the sky, sending the fire from her belly rippling out through her mouth in a flickering sheet of flame. Nasuada staggered back from her while everyone else within earshot froze and stared at Saphira. Rising to her feet, Saphira shook herself from head to tail, her weariness forgotten, and spread her wings in preparation for flight.

Nasuada's guards started toward her, but she waved them back. A patch of smoke swept over her, and she pressed the underside of a sleeve over her nose, coughing. *Your enthusiasm is commendable, Saphira, but—*

Is Eragon injured or hurt? Saphira asked. Alarm shot through her when Nasuada hesitated.

He's as healthy as ever, Nasuada replied. *However, there was an . . . incident . . . yesterday.*

What kind of incident?

He and his guards were attacked.

Saphira held herself motionless while Nasuada recalled for her everything Eragon had said during their conversation. Afterward, Saphira bared her teeth. *Dûrgrimst Az Sweldn rak Anhûin should be grateful I was not with Eragon; I would not have let them escape so easily for attempting to kill him.*

With a small smile, Nasuada said, *For that reason, it is probably better you were here.*

Perhaps, Saphira admitted, and then released a puff of hot smoke and lashed her tail from side to side. *It does not surprise me, though. Always this happens; whenever Eragon and I part, someone attacks him. It's gotten so it makes my scales itch to let him out of my sight for more than a few hours.*

He's more than capable of defending himself.

True, but our enemies are not without skill either. Impatient, Saphira shifted her stance, raising her wings even higher. *Nasuada, I am eager to be gone. Is there anything else I should know?*

No, said Nasuada. *Fly swift and fly true, Saphira, but do not tarry when you arrive in Farthen Dûr. As soon as you leave our camp, we shall have only a few days' grace before the Empire realizes I have not sent you and Eragon on a brief scouting trip. Galbatorix may or may not decide to* strike while you are away, but every hour you are absent will increase the possibility. Also, I would much prefer to have the two of you with us when we attack Feinster. We could take the city without you, but it will cost us many more lives. In short, the fate of the entire Varden depends upon your speed.

We shall be as swift as the storm-driven wind, Saphira assured her.

Then Nasuada bade her farewell and retreated from the stone slab, whereupon Blödhgarm and the other elves rushed to Saphira's side and strapped her uncomfortable-leather-patch-Eragon-seat-saddle onto her and filled the saddlebags with the food and equipment she would normally carry if embarking upon a trip with Eragon. She would not need the supplies—she could not even access them herself—but for the sake of appearances, she had to carry them. Once she was ready, Blödhgarm twisted his hand in front of his chest in the elves' gesture of respect and said in the ancient language, "Fare thee well, Saphira Brightscales. May you and Eragon return to us unharmed."

Fare thee well, Blödhgarm.

Saphira waited while the black-blue-wolf-hair-elf created a water-shadow-ghost of Eragon and the apparition walked out of Eragon's tent and climbed onto her back. She felt nothing as the insubstantial wraith stepped from her left foreleg to the upper part of her leg and then to her shoulder. When Blödhgarm nodded to her, indicating the not-Eragon was in place, she lifted her wings until they touched overhead, then leaped forward, off the end of the stone slab.

As Saphira fell toward the gray tents below, she drove her wings downward, propelling herself away from the break-bone-ground. She turned in the direction of Farthen Dûr and began climbing up to the layer of thin-cold-air high above, where she hoped to find a steady wind to aid her on her journey.

She circled over the wooded riverbank where the Varden had chosen to stop for the night and wriggled with a fierce joy. No longer did she have to wait while Eragon went off adventuring without her! No longer would she have to spend the entire night flying over the same patches of land again and again! And no longer would those who wished to hurt her partner-of-her-mind-and-heart be able to escape her wrath! Opening her jaws, Saphira roared her joy and confidence to the world, daring whatever gods there might be to challenge *her*, she who was the daughter of Iormûngr and Vervada, two of the greatest dragons of their age.

When she was more than a mile above the Varden and a strong southwestern wind was pressing against her, Saphira aligned herself with the torrent of air and allowed it to propel her forward, soaring over the sun-drenched land below.

Casting her thoughts out before her, she said, *I'm on my way, little one!*

✦ ✦ ✦

Four Strokes upon the Drum

Eragon leaned forward, every muscle in his body tense, as the white-haired dwarf woman Hadfala, chief of Dûrgrimst Ebardac, rose from the table where the clanmeet was gathered and uttered a short line in her native language.

Murmuring into Eragon's left ear, Hûndfast translated: "On behalf of mine clan, I vote for Grimstborith Orik as our new king."

Eragon released his pent-up breath. *One.* In order to become ruler of the dwarves, a clan chief had to win a majority of the votes from the other chiefs. If none achieved that feat, then according to Dwarvish law, the clan chief with the least votes would be eliminated from the competition and the meet could adjourn for up to three days before voting again. The process would continue as needed until a clan chief had achieved the necessary majority, at which point, the meet would swear fealty to him or her as their new monarch. Considering how pressed for time the Varden were, Eragon fervently hoped that the voting would not require more than one round, and if it did, that the dwarves would not insist upon taking a recess of more than a few hours. If that happened, he thought he might break the stone table in the center of the room out of frustration.

That Hadfala, the first clan chief to vote, had cast her lot with Orik boded well. Hadfala, as Eragon knew, had been backing Gannel of Dûrgrimst Quan before the attempt on Eragon's life. If Hadfala's allegiances had shifted, then it was also possible that the other member of Gannel's cohort—namely, Grimstborith Ûndin—might also give his vote to Orik.

Next, Gáldhiem of Dûrgrimst Feldûnost rose from the table, although he was so short, he was taller sitting than he was standing.

"On behalf of mine clan," he declared, "I vote for Grimstborith Nado as our new king."

Turning his head to one side, Orik looked back at Eragon and said to him in an undertone, "Well, that was as we expected."

Eragon nodded and glanced over at Nado. The round-faced dwarf was stroking the end of his yellow beard, appearing pleased with himself.

Then Manndrâth of Dûrgrimst Ledwonnû said, "On behalf of mine clan, I vote for Grimstborith Orik as our new king." Orik nodded toward him in thanks, and Manndrâth nodded in return, the tip of his long nose bobbing.

As Manndrâth sat, Eragon and everyone else looked at Gannel, and the room became so quiet, Eragon could not even hear the dwarves breathing. As chief of the religious clan, the Quan, and the high priest of Gûntera, king of the dwarf gods, Gannel carried enormous influence among his race; however he chose, so the crown was likely to go.

"On behalf of mine clan," Gannel said, "I vote for Grimstborith Nado as our new king."

A wave of soft exclamations broke out among the dwarves watching from the perimeter of the circular room, and Nado's pleased expression broadened. Clenching his interlaced hands, Eragon silently cursed.

"Don't give up hope yet, lad," Orik muttered. "We may yet pull through. It's happened before that the grimstborith of the Quan has lost the vote."

"How often does it happen, though?" whispered Eragon.

"Often enough."

"When did it *last* happen?"

Orik shifted and glanced away. "Eight hundred and twenty-four years ago, when Queen—"

He fell silent as Ûndin of Dûrgrimst Ragni Hefthyn proclaimed, "On behalf of mine clan, I vote for Grimstborith Nado as our new king."

Orik crossed his arms. Eragon could only see his face from the side, but it was obvious that Orik was scowling.

Biting the inside of his cheek, Eragon stared at the patterned floor, counting the votes that had been cast, as well as those that remained, trying to determine if Orik could still win the election. Even in the best of circumstances, it would be a close thing. Eragon tightened his grip, his fingernails digging into the back of his hands.

Thordris of Dûrgrimst Nagra stood and draped her long, thick braid over one arm. "On behalf of mine clan, I vote for Grimstborith Orik as our new king."

"That makes three to three," Eragon said in a low voice. Orik nodded.

It was Nado's turn to speak then. Smoothing his beard with the flat of a hand, the chief of Dûrgrimst Knurlcarathn smiled at the assembly, a predatory gleam in his eyes. "One behalf of mine clan, I vote for myself as our new king. If you will have me, I promise to rid our country of the outlanders who have polluted it, and I promise to devote our gold and warriors to protecting our own people, and not the necks of elves, humans, and *Urgals*. This I swear upon mine family's honor."

"Four to three," Eragon noted.

"Aye," said Orik. "I suppose it would have been too much to ask for Nado to vote for anyone but himself."

Setting aside his knife and wood, Freowin of Dûrgrimst Gedthrall heaved his bulk halfway out of his chair and, keeping his gaze angled downward, said in his whispering baritone, "On behalf of mine clan, I vote for Grimstborith Nado as our new king." Then he lowered himself back into his seat and resumed carving his raven, ignoring the stir of astonishment that swept through the room.

Nado's expression changed from pleased to smug.

"Barzûl," growled Orik, his scowl deepening. His chair creaked as he pressed his forearms down against the armrests, the tendons in his hands rigid with strain. "That false-faced traitor. He promised his vote to me!"

Eragon's stomach sank. "Why would he betray you?"

"He visits Sindri's temple twice a day. I should have known he would not go against Gannel's wishes. Bah! Gannel's been playing me this whole time. I—" At that moment, the attention of the clanmeet turned to Orik. Concealing his anger, Orik got to his feet and looked around the table at each of the other clan chiefs, and in his own language, he said, "On behalf of mine clan, I vote for myself as our new king. If you will have me, I promise to bring our people gold and glory and the freedom to live above the ground without fear of Galbatorix destroying our homes. This I swear upon mine family's honor."

"Five to four," Eragon said to Orik as he returned to his seat. "And not in our favor."

Orik grunted. "I can count, Eragon."

Eragon rested his elbows on his knees, his eyes darting from one dwarf to another. The desire to act gnawed at him. How, he knew not, but with so much at stake, he felt that he ought to find a way to ensure Orik would become king and, thus, that the dwarves would continue to aid the Varden in their struggle against the Empire. For all he tried, however, Eragon could think of nothing to do but sit and wait.

The next dwarf to rise was Havard of Dûrgrimst Fanghur. With his chin tucked against his breastbone, Havard pushed out his lips and tapped the table with the two fingers he still had on his right hand, appearing thoughtful. Eragon inched forward on his seat, his heart pounding. *Will he uphold his bargain with Orik?* Eragon wondered.

Havard tapped the table once more, then slapped the stone with the flat of his hand. Lifting his chin, he said, "On behalf of mine clan, I vote for Grimstborith Orik as our new king."

It gave Eragon immense satisfaction to watch as Nado's eyes widened, and then the dwarf gnashed his teeth together, a muscle in his cheek twitching. "Ha!" muttered Orik. "That put a burr in his beard."

The only two clan chiefs who had yet to vote were Hreidamar and Íorûnn. Hreidamar, the compact, muscular grimstborith of the Urzhad, appeared uneasy with the situation, while Íorûnn—she of Dûrgrimst Vrenshrrgn, the War Wolves—traced the crescent-shaped scar on her left cheekbone with the tip of a pointed finger-nail and smiled like a self-satisfied cat.

Eragon held his breath as he waited to hear what the two of them would say. *If Íorûnn votes for herself,* he thought, *and if Hreidamar is still loyal to her, then the election will have to proceed to a second round. There's no reason for her to do that, however, other than to delay events, and so far as I know, she would not profit from a delay. She cannot hope to become queen at this point; her name would be eliminated from con-sideration before the beginning of the second round, and I doubt she would be so foolish as to squander the power she has now merely so she can boast to her grandchildren that she was once a candidate for the throne. But if Hreidamar does part ways with her, then the vote will re-main tied and we will continue on to a second round regardless. . . . Argh! If only I could scry into the future! What if Orik loses? Should I seize control of the clanmeet then? I could seal the chamber so no one could enter or leave, and then . . . But no, that would be—*

Íorûnn interrupted Eragon's thoughts by nodding at Hreidamar and then directing her heavy-lidded gaze toward Eragon, which made him feel as if he were a prize ox she was examining. The rings of his mail hauberk clinking, Hreidamar stood upright and said, "On behalf of mine clan, I vote for Grimstborith Orik as our new king."

Eragon's throat constricted.

Her red lips curving with amusement, Íorûnn rose from her chair with a sinuous motion and in a low, husky voice said, "It seems it falls to me to decide the outcome of today's meet. I have listened most carefully to your arguments, Nado, and your arguments, Orik. While you have both made points I agree with upon a wide range of subjects, the most important issue we must decide is whether to commit ourselves to the Varden's campaign against the Empire. If theirs were merely a war between rival clans, it would not matter to me which side won, and I certainly would not consider sacrificing our warriors for the benefit of outlanders. However, this is not the case. Far from it. If Galbatorix emerges triumphant from this war, not even the Beor Mountains will protect us from his wrath. If our realm is to survive, we must see Galbatorix overthrown. Moreover, it strikes me that hiding in caves and tunnels while others decide the fate of Alagaësia is unbecoming for a race as old and as powerful as ours. When the chronicles of this age are written, shall they say we fought alongside the humans and the elves, as the heroes of old, or that we sat cowering in our halls like frightened peasants while a battle raged outside our doors? I, for one, know mine answer." Íorûnn tossed back her hair, then said, "On behalf of mine clan, I vote for Grimstborith Orik as our new king!"

The eldest of the five readers-of-law who stood against the circular wall stepped forward and struck the end of his polished staff against the stone floor and proclaimed, "All hail King Orik, the forty-third king of Tronjheim, Farthen Dûr, and every knurla above and below the Beor Mountains!"

"All hail King Orik!" the clanmeet roared, rising to their feet with a loud rustle of clothes and armor. His head swimming, Eragon did likewise, aware that he was now in the presence of royalty. He glanced at Nado, but the dwarf's face was a dead-eyed mask.

The white-bearded reader-of-law struck his staff against the floor again. "Let the scribes record at once the clanmeet's decision, and let the news be spread to every person throughout the realm. Heralds! Inform the mages with their scrying mirrors of what has transpired here today, and then seek out the wardens of the mountain and tell them, 'Four beats upon the drum. Four beats, and swing your mallets as you have never swung them before in all your lives, for we have a new king. Four beats of such strength, Farthen Dûr itself shall ring with the news.' Tell them this, I charge you. Go!"

After the heralds departed, Orik pushed himself out of his chair and stood looking at the dwarves around him. His expression, to

Eragon, seemed somewhat dazed, as if he had not actually expected to win the crown. "For this great responsibility," he said, "I thank you." He paused, then continued, "Mine only thought now is for the betterment of our nation, and I shall pursue that goal without faltering until the day I return to the stone."

Then the clan chiefs came forward, one by one, and they knelt before Orik and swore their fealty to him as his loyal subjects. When the time came for Nado to pledge himself, the dwarf displayed nothing of his sentiments but merely recited the phrases of the oath without inflection, the words dropping from his mouth like bars of lead. A palpable sense of relief rippled through the clanmeet once he had finished.

Upon the conclusion of the oath giving, Orik decreed that his coronation would take place the following morning, and then he and his attendants retired to an adjacent chamber. There Eragon looked at Orik, and Orik looked at Eragon, and neither made a sound until a broad smile appeared on Orik's face and he broke out laughing, his cheeks turning red. Laughing with him, Eragon grasped him by a forearm and embraced him. Orik's guards and advisers gathered around them, clapping Orik on the shoulder and congratulating him with hearty exclamations.

Eragon released Orik, saying, "I didn't think Íorûnn would side with us."

"Aye. I'm glad she did, but it complicates matters, it does." Orik grimaced. "I suppose I'll have to reward her for her assistance with a place within my council, at the very least."

"It may be for the best!" said Eragon, straining to make himself heard over the commotion. "If the Vrenshrrgn are equal to their name, we shall have great need of them before we reach the gates of Urû'baen."

Orik started to answer, but then a long, low note of portentous volume reverberated throughout the floor and the ceiling and the air of the room, causing Eragon's bones to vibrate with its force. "Listen!" cried Orik, and raised a hand. The group fell silent.

Four times in total the bass note sounded, shaking the room with each repetition, as if a giant were pounding against the side of Tronjheim. Afterward, Orik said, "I never thought to hear the Drums of Derva announce mine kingship."

"How large are the drums?" asked Eragon, awed.

"Close to fifty feet across, if memory serves."

It occurred to Eragon that although the dwarves were the shortest of the races, they built the biggest structures in Alagaësia, which seemed odd to him. *Perhaps*, he thought, *by making such enormous objects, they do not feel so small themselves.* He almost mentioned his theory to Orik but at the last moment decided that it might offend him, so he held his tongue.

Closing ranks around him, Orik's attendants began to consult with him in Dwarvish, often speaking over one another in a loud tangle of voices, and Eragon, who had been about to ask Orik another question, found himself relegated to a corner. He tried to wait patiently for a lull in the conversation, but after a few minutes, it became plain the dwarves were not about to stop plying Orik with questions and advice, for such, he assumed, was the nature of their discourse.

Therefore, Eragon said, "Orik Könungr," and he imbued the ancient language word for *king* with energy, that it would capture the attention of everyone present. The room fell silent, and Orik looked at Eragon and lifted an eyebrow. "Your Majesty, may I have your permission to withdraw? There is a certain . . . *matter* I would like to attend to, if it is not already too late."

Comprehension brightened Orik's brown eyes. "By all means, make haste! But you need not call me *majesty*, Eragon, nor *sire*, nor by any other title. We are friends and foster brothers, after all."

"We are, Your Majesty," Eragon replied, "but for the time being, I believe it is only proper I should observe the same courtesies as everyone else. You are the king of your race now, and my own king as well, seeing as how I am a member of Dûrgrimst Ingeitum, and that is not something I can ignore."

Orik studied him for a moment, as if from a great distance, and then nodded and said, "As you wish, Shadeslayer."

Eragon bowed and left the room. Accompanied by his four guards, he bounded through the tunnels and up the stairs that led to the ground floor of Tronjheim. Once they arrived at the southern branch of the four main hallways that divided the city-mountain, Eragon turned to Thrand, the captain of his guards, and said, "I mean to run the rest of the way. Since you won't be able to keep pace with me, I suggest you stop when you reach the south gate of Tronjheim and wait there for my return."

Thrand said, "Argetlam, please, you should not go alone. Cannot I convince you to slow yourself so we can accompany you? We may not be as fleet as the elves, but we can run from sunup to sundown, and in full armor too."

"I appreciate your concern," said Eragon, "but I would not tarry a minute longer, even if I knew there were assassins hiding behind every pillar. Farewell!"

And with that, he dashed down the broad hallway, dodging around the dwarves who blocked his way.

REUNION

It was nearly a mile from where Eragon started to the south gate of Tronjheim. He covered the distance in only a few minutes, his footsteps loud upon the stone floor. As he ran, he caught glimpses of the rich tapestries that hung above the arched entrances to the corridors on either side and of the grotesque statues of beasts and monsters that lurked between the pillars of blood-red jasper that lined the vaulted avenue. The four-story-high thoroughfare was so large, Eragon had little difficulty evading the dwarves who populated it, although at one point, a line of Knurlcarathn stepped in front of him, and he had no choice but to leap over the dwarves, who ducked, uttering startled exclamations. Eragon savored their looks of astonishment as he sailed over them.

With an easy, loping stride, Eragon ran underneath the massive timber gate that protected the southern entrance to the city-mountain, hearing the guards cry, "Hail, Argetlam!" as he flew past. Twenty yards beyond, for the gate was recessed into the base of Tronjheim, he sped between the pair of giant gold griffins that stared with sightless eyes toward the horizon and then emerged into the open.

The air was cool and moist and smelled like fresh-fallen rain. Though it was morning, gray twilight enveloped the flat disk of land that surrounded Tronjheim, land upon which no grass grew, only moss and lichen and the occasional patch of pungent toadstools. Above, Farthen Dûr rose over ten miles to a narrow opening, through which pale, indirect light entered the immense crater. Eragon had difficulty grasping the scale of the mountain when he gazed upward.

As he ran, he listened to the monotonous pattern of his breathing and to his light, quick footsteps. He was alone, save for a curious bat that swooped overhead, emitting shrill squeaks. The tranquil mood that permeated the hollow mountain comforted him, freed him of his usual worries.

He followed the cobblestone path that extended from Tronjheim's south gate all the way to the two black thirty-foot-high doors set into the southern base of Farthen Dûr. As he drew to a halt, a pair of dwarves emerged from hidden guardrooms and hurried to open the doors, revealing the seemingly endless tunnel beyond.

Eragon continued forward. Marble pillars studded with rubies and amethysts lined the first fifty feet of the tunnel. Past them the tunnel was bare and desolate, the smooth walls broken only by a single flameless lantern every twenty yards and at infrequent intervals by a closed gate or door. *I wonder where they lead*, Eragon thought. Then he imagined the miles of stone pressing down on him from overhead, and for a moment, the tunnel seemed unbearably oppressive. He quickly pushed the image away.

Halfway through the tunnel, Eragon felt her.

"Saphira!" he shouted, with both his mind and his voice, her name echoing off the stone walls with the force of a dozen yells.

Eragon! An instant later, the faint thunder of a distant roar rolled toward him from the other end of the tunnel.

Redoubling his speed, Eragon opened his mind to Saphira, removing every barrier around who he was, so that they might join together without reservation. Like a flood of warm water, her consciousness rushed into him, even as his rushed into her. Eragon gasped and tripped and nearly fell. They enveloped each other within the folds of their thoughts, holding each other with an intimacy no physical embrace could replicate, allowing their identities to merge once again. Their greatest comfort was a simple one: they were no longer alone. To know that you were with one who cared for you, and who understood every fiber of your being, and who would not abandon you in even the most desperate of circumstances, *that* was the most precious relationship a person could have, and both Eragon and Saphira cherished it.

It was not long before Eragon sighted Saphira hurrying toward him as swiftly as she could without banging her head on the ceiling or scraping her wings against the walls. Her claws screeched on the stone floor as she slid to a stop in front of Eragon, fierce, sparkling, glorious.

Crying out with joy, Eragon leaped upward and, ignoring her sharp scales, wrapped his arms around her neck and hugged her as tightly as he could, his feet dangling several inches in the air. *Little one*, said Saphira, her tone warm. She lowered him to the floor, then snorted and said, *Little one, unless you wish to choke me, you should loosen your arms.*

Sorry. Grinning, he stepped back, then laughed and pressed his forehead against her snout and began to scratch behind both corners of her jaw.

Saphira's low humming filled the tunnel.

You're tired, he said.

I have never flown so far so fast. I stopped only once after I left the Varden, and I would not have stopped at all except I became too thirsty to continue.

Do you mean you haven't slept or eaten for three days?

She blinked at him, concealing her brilliant sapphire eyes for an instant.

You must be starving! Eragon exclaimed, worried. He looked her over for signs of injury. To his relief, he found none.

I am tired, she admitted, *but not hungry. Not yet. Once I have rested, then I will need to eat. Right now, I do not think I could stomach so much as a rabbit. . . . The earth is unsteady beneath me; I feel as if I am still flying.*

If they had not been apart for so long, Eragon might have reproached her for being reckless, but as it was, he was touched and grateful that she had pushed herself. *Thank you*, he said. *I would have hated to wait another day for us to be together again.*

As would have I. She closed her eyes and pressed her head against his hands as he continued to scratch behind her jaw. *Besides, I could hardly be late for the coronation, now could I? Who did the clanmeet—*

Before she could finish the question, Eragon sent her an image of Orik.

Ah, she sighed, her satisfaction flowing through him. *He will make a fine king.*

I hope so.

Is the star sapphire ready for me to mend?

If the dwarves have not already finished piecing it together, I'm sure they will have by tomorrow.

That is good. Cracking open an eyelid, she fixed him with her piercing gaze. *Nasuada told me of what Az Sweldn rak Anhûin attempted. Always you get into trouble when I am not with you.*

His smile widened. *And when you are?*

I eat the trouble before it eats you.

So you say. What about when the Urgals ambushed us by Gil'ead and took me captive?

A plume of smoke escaped from between Saphira's fangs. *That does not count. I was smaller then, and not as experienced. It would not happen now. And you are not as helpless as you once were.*

I've never been helpless, he protested. *I just have powerful enemies.*

For some reason, Saphira found his last statement enormously amusing; she started laughing deep within her chest, and soon Eragon was laughing as well. Neither of them was able to stop until Eragon was lying on his back, gasping for air, and Saphira was struggling to contain the darts of flame that kept shooting out of her nostrils. Then Saphira made a sound Eragon had never heard before, a strange jumping growl, and he noticed the oddest feeling through their connection.

Saphira made the sound again, then shook her head, as if trying to rid herself of a swarm of flies. *Oh dear,* she said. *I seem to have the hiccups.*

Eragon's mouth dropped open. He held that pose for a moment, then he doubled over, laughing so hard, tears streamed down his face. Every time he was about to recover, Saphira would hiccup, bobbing her head forward like a stork, and he would go off into convulsions again. At last he plugged his ears with his fingers and stared at the ceiling and recited the true names of every metal and stone he could remember.

When he finished, he took a deep breath and stood.

Better? Saphira asked. Her shoulders shook as another hiccup racked her.

Eragon bit his tongue. *Better. . . . Come on, let's go to Tronjheim. You should have some water. That might help. And then you should sleep.*

Cannot you cure hiccups with a spell?

Maybe. Probably. But neither Brom nor Oromis taught me how. Saphira grunted her understanding, and a hiccup followed an instant later. Biting his tongue even harder, Eragon stared at the tips of his boots. *Shall we?*

Saphira extended her right foreleg in invitation. Eragon eagerly climbed up onto her back and settled into the saddle at the base of her neck.

Together, they continued through the tunnel toward Tronjheim, both of them happy, and both of them sharing in each other's happiness.

551

ASCENSION

The Drums of Derva sounded, summoning the dwarves of Tronjheim to witness the coronation of their new king.

"Normally," Orik had told Eragon the previous night, "when the clanmeet elects a king or queen, the knurla begins their rule at once, but we do not hold the coronation for at least three months, so that all who wish to attend the ceremony may have time to place their affairs in order and to travel to Farthen Dûr from even the most distant parts of our realm. It is not often we crown a monarch, so when we do, it is our custom to make much of the event, with weeks of feasting and song, and with games of wit and strength and contests of skill at forging, carving, and other forms of art. . . . However, these are hardly normal times."

Eragon stood next to Saphira just outside the central chamber of Tronjheim, listening to the pounding of the giant drums. On either side of the mile-long hall, hundreds of dwarves crowded the archways of each level, peering at Eragon and Saphira with dark gleaming eyes.

Saphira's barbed tongue rasped against her scales as she licked her chops, which she had been doing ever since she finished devouring five full-grown sheep earlier that morning. Then she lifted her left foreleg and rubbed her muzzle against it. The smell of burnt wool clung to her.

Stop fidgeting, said Eragon. *They're looking at us.*

A soft growl emanated from Saphira. *I can't help it. I have wool stuck between my teeth. Now I remember why I hate eating sheep. Horrible, fluffy things that give me hair balls and indigestion.*

I'll help you clean your teeth when we are finished here. Just hold still until then.

Hmph.

Did Blödhgarm pack any fireweed in the saddlebags? That would settle your stomach.

I don't know.

Mmm. Eragon thought for a moment. *If not, I'll ask Orik if the dwarves have any stored in Tronjheim. We ought to—*

He cut himself off as the final note from the drums faded into silence. The crowd shifted, and he heard the soft rustle of clothes and the occasional phrase of murmured Dwarvish.

A fanfare of dozens of trumpets rang forth, filling the city-mountain with its rousing call, and somewhere a choir of dwarves began to chant. The music made Eragon's scalp tingle and prickle and his blood flow faster, as if he were about to embark upon a hunt. Saphira whipped her tail from side to side, and he knew she felt the same.

Here we go, he thought.

As one, he and Saphira advanced into the central chamber of the city-mountain and took their place among the ring of clan chiefs, guild leaders, and other notables who girded the vast, towering room. In the center of the chamber rested the reconstructed star sapphire, encased within a framework of wooden scaffolding. An hour before the coronation, Skeg had sent a message to Eragon and Saphira, telling them that he and his team of artisans had just finished fitting together the last fragments of the gem and that Isidar Mithrim was ready for Saphira to make whole once more.

The black granite throne of the dwarves had been carried from its customary resting place underneath Tronjheim and placed upon a raised dais next to the star sapphire, facing the eastern branch of the four main hallways that divided Tronjheim, east because it was the direction of the rising sun and that symbolized the dawning of a new age. Thousands of dwarf warriors clad in burnished mail armor stood at attention in two large blocks before the throne, as well as in double rows along either side of the eastern hallway all the way to Tronjheim's eastern gate, a mile away. Many of the warriors carried spears mounted with pennants that bore curious designs. Hvedra, Orik's wife, stood at the forefront of the congregation; after the clanmeet had banished Grimstborith Vermûnd, Orik had sent for her in anticipation of becoming king. She had arrived in Tronjheim only that morning.

For half an hour, the trumpets played and the unseen choir sang as, step by deliberate step, Orik walked from the eastern gate to the center of Tronjheim. His beard was brushed and curled, and he wore buskins of the finest polished leather with silver spurs mounted upon the heels, gray wool leggings, a shirt of purple silk that shimmered in the lantern light, and, over his shirt, a mail hauberk, each link of which was wrought of pure white gold. A long ermine-trimmed cloak embroidered with the insignia of Dûrgrimst Ingeitum flowed over Orik's shoulders and onto the floor behind him. Volund, the war hammer that Korgan, first king of the dwarves, had forged, hung at Orik's waist from a wide, ruby-studded belt. Because of his lavish raiment and his magnificent armor, Orik seemed to glow from within; to look at him dazzled Eragon's eyes.

Twelve dwarf children followed Orik, six male and six female, or so Eragon assumed based upon the cut of their hair. The children were garbed in tunics of red and brown and gold, and they each carried in their cupped hands a polished orb six inches across, every orb a different species of stone.

As Orik entered the center of the city-mountain, the chamber dimmed and a pattern of dappled shadows appeared on everything within. Confused, Eragon glanced upward and was astonished to behold pink rose petals drifting downward from the top of Tronjheim. Like soft, thick snowflakes, the velvety petals settled upon the heads and shoulders of those in attendance, and also upon the floor, suffusing the air with their sweet fragrance.

The trumpets and the choir fell silent as Orik knelt on one knee before the black throne and bowed his head. Behind him, the twelve children stopped and stood motionless.

Eragon placed his hand on Saphira's warm side, sharing his concern and excitement with her. He had no idea what would happen next, for Orik had refused to describe the ceremony past that point.

Then Gannel, clan chief of Dûrgrimst Quan, stepped forward, breaking the ring of people around the chamber, and walked to stand on the right-hand side of the throne. The heavy-shouldered dwarf was appareled in sumptuous red robes, the borders of which gleamed with runes outlined with metal thread. In one hand, Gannel bore a tall staff with a clear, pointed crystal mounted on the top.

Lifting the staff over his head with both hands, Gannel brought it down upon the stone floor with a resounding crack. "Hwatum il skilfz gerdûmn!" he exclaimed. He continued to speak in the tongue of the dwarves for some minutes, and Eragon listened without comprehending, for his translator was not with him. But then the tenor of Gannel's voice shifted, and Eragon recognized his words as belonging to the ancient language, and he realized Gannel was weaving a spell, although it was a spell unlike any Eragon was familiar with. Instead of directing the incantation at an object or an element of the world around them, the priest said, in the language of mystery and power: "Gûntera, creator of the heavens and the earth and the boundless sea, hear now the cry of your faithful servant! We thank you for your magnanimity. Our race flourishes. This and every year, we have offered to you the finest rams of our flocks and also flagons of spiced mead and a portion of our harvests of fruits and vegetables and grain. Your temples are the richest in the land, and none may hope to compete with the glory that is yours. O mighty Gûntera, king of the gods, hear now mine plea and grant me this request: time is for us to name a mortal ruler of our earthly affairs. Will you deign to bestow your blessing upon Orik, Thrifk's son, and to crown him in the tradition of his predecessors?"

At first Eragon thought Gannel's request would go unanswered, for he felt no surge of magic from the dwarf when he finished speaking. However, Saphira nudged him then and said, *Look.*

Eragon followed her gaze and, thirty feet above, saw a disturbance among the tumbling petals: a gap, a void where the petals would not fall, as if an invisible object occupied the space. The disturbance spread, extending all the way to the floor, and the void outlined by the petals assumed the shape of a creature with arms and legs like a dwarf or a man or an elf or an Urgal, but of different proportions than any race Eragon had knowledge of; the head was nearly the width of the shoulders, the massive arms hung below the knees, and while the torso was bulky, the legs were short and crooked.

Thin, needle-sharp rays of watery light radiated outward from the shape, and there appeared the nebulous image of a gigantic, shaggy-haired male figure of the form the petals had traced. The god, if god he was, wore nothing but a knotted loincloth. His face was dark and heavy and seemed to contain equal amounts of cruelty and kindness, as if he might veer between the extremes of both without warning.

As he noticed those details, Eragon also became aware of the presence of a strange, far-reaching consciousness within the chamber, a consciousness of unreadable thoughts and unfathomable depths, a consciousness that flashed and growled and billowed in unexpected directions, like a summer thunderstorm. Eragon quickly sequestered his mind from the touch of the other. His skin prickled, and a cold shiver ran down him. He did not know what he had felt, but fear gripped him, and he looked at Saphira for comfort. She was staring at the figure, her blue cat eyes sparkling with unusual intensity.

With a single motion, the dwarves sank to their knees.

The god spoke then, and his voice sounded like the grinding of boulders and the sweep of the wind over barren mountain peaks and the slap of waves against a stony shore. He spoke in Dwarvish, and though Eragon knew not what was said, he shrank from the power of the god's speech. Three times the god questioned Orik, and three times Orik replied, his own voice faint in comparison. Apparently pleased with Orik's answers, the apparition extended his glowing arms and placed his forefingers on either side of Orik's bare head.

The air between the god's fingers rippled, and upon Orik's brow materialized the gem-encrusted helm of gold that Hrothgar had worn. The god slapped his belly and uttered a booming chuckle and then faded into oblivion. The rose petals resumed their fall un-interrupted.

"Ûn qroth Gûntera!" Gannel proclaimed. Loud and brassy, the trumpets blared.

Rising from his knee, Orik ascended the dais, turned to face the assembly, and then he sank into the hard black throne.

"Nal, Grimstnzborith Orik!" the dwarves shouted, and struck their shields with their axes and their spears and stamped the floor with their feet. "Nal, Grimstnzborith Orik! Nal, Grimstnzborith Orik!"

"All hail King Orik!" cried Eragon. Arching her neck, Saphira roared her tribute and released a jet of flame over the heads of the dwarves, incinerating a swath of rose petals. Eragon's eyes watered as a blast of heat washed over him.

Then Gannel knelt before Orik and spoke some more in Dwarvish. When he finished, Orik touched him upon the crown of his head, and then Gannel returned to his place at the edge of the chamber. Nado approached the throne and said many of the same things, and after him, so did Manndrâth and Hadfala and all the other clan chiefs, with the sole exception of Grimstborith Vermûnd, who had been banned from the coronation.

They must be pledging themselves to Orik's service, Eragon said to Saphira.

Did not they already give him their word?

Aye, but not in public. Eragon watched Thordris walk toward the throne before saying, *Saphira, what do you think we just saw? Could that really have been Gûntera, or was it an illusion? His mind seemed real enough, and I do not know how one might fake that, but . . .*

It may have been an illusion, she said. The dwarves' gods have never helped them upon the field of battle, nor in any other endeavor I am aware of. Nor do I believe that a true god would come running at Gannel's summons like a trained hound. I would not, and should not a god be greater than a dragon? . . . But then, there are many inexplicable things in Alagaësia. It is possible we have seen a shade from a long-forgotten age, a pale remnant of what once was that continues to haunt the land, longing for the return of its power. Who can know for sure?

Once the final clan chief had presented himself to Orik, the guild leaders did the same, and then Orik gestured toward Eragon. With a slow, measured pace, Eragon walked forward between the rows of dwarf warriors until he reached the base of the throne, where he knelt and, as a member of Dûrgrimst Ingeitum, acknowledged Orik as his king and swore to serve and protect him. Then, acting as Nasuada's emissary, Eragon congratulated Orik on behalf of Nasuada and the Varden and promised him the Varden's friendship.

Others went to speak with Orik as Eragon withdrew, a seemingly endless train of dwarves eager to demonstrate their loyalty to their new king.

The procession continued for hours, and then the gift giving began. Each of the dwarves brought Orik an offering from their clan or their guild: a goblet of gold filled to the brim with rubies and diamonds, a corselet of enchanted mail that no blade could pierce, a tapestry twenty feet long woven of the soft wool the dwarves combed from the beards of the Feldûnost goats, a tablet of agate inscribed with the names of every one of Orik's ancestors, a curved dagger ground from the tooth of a dragon, and many other treasures. In exchange, Orik presented the dwarves with rings as tokens of his gratitude.

Eragon and Saphira were the last to go before Orik. Once again kneeling at the base of the dais, Eragon drew from his tunic the gold armband he had begged from the dwarves the previous night. He held it up toward Orik, saying, "Here is my gift, King Orik. I did not make the armlet, but I have set on it spells to protect you. So long as you wear it, you need fear no poison. If an assassin tries to hit or stab you or throw any kind of object at you, the weapon will miss. The band will even shield you from most hostile magic. And it has other properties as well, which you may find of use if your life is in danger."

Inclining his head, Orik accepted the band from Eragon and said, "Your gift is most appreciated, Eragon Shadeslayer." In full view of everyone, Orik slid the band onto his left arm.

Saphira spoke next, projecting her thoughts to everyone who was watching: *My gift is this, Orik.* She walked past the throne, her claws clacking against the floor, and reared up and placed her forefeet upon the edge of the scaffolding around the star sapphire. The stout wood beams creaked under her weight, but held. Minutes passed and nothing happened, but Saphira remained where she was, gazing at the huge gemstone.

The dwarves watched her, never blinking, hardly breathing.

Are you sure you can do this? Eragon asked, reluctant to break her concentration.

I don't know. The few times I used magic before, I didn't pause to consider whether I was casting a spell or not. I just willed the world to change, and it did. It was not a deliberate process. . . . I suppose I will have to wait until the moment feels right for me to mend Isidar Mithrim.

Let me help. Let me work a spell through you.

No, little one. This is my task, not yours.

A single voice, low and clear, wafted across the chamber, singing a slow, wistful melody. One by one, the other members of the hidden dwarf choir joined in the song, filling Tronjheim with the plaintive beauty of their music. Eragon was going to ask for them to be silent, but Saphira said, *It's all right. Leave them alone.*

Although he did not understand what the choir sang, Eragon could tell from the tone of the music that it was a lamentation for things that had been and were no more, such as the star sapphire.

As the song built toward its conclusion, he found himself thinking of his lost life in Palancar Valley, and tears welled in his eyes.

To his surprise, he sensed a similar strain of pensive melancholy from Saphira. Neither sorrow nor regret was a normal part of her personality, so he wondered at it and would have questioned her, except that he also sensed a stirring of something deep within her, like the awakening of some ancient part of her being.

The song ended on a long, wavering note, and as it faded into oblivion, a surge of energy rushed through Saphira—so much energy, Eragon gasped at its magnitude—and she bent and touched the star sapphire with the tip of her snout. The branching cracks within the giant gemstone flared bright as bolts of lightning, and then the scaffolding shattered and fell to the floor, revealing Isidar Mithrim whole and sound again.

But not quite the same. The color of the jewel was a deeper, richer shade of red than before, and the innermost petals of the rose were shot through with streaks of dusky gold.

The dwarves stared in wonder at Isidar Mithrim. Then they leaped to their feet, cheering and applauding Saphira with such enthusiasm, it sounded like the pounding roar of a waterfall. She dipped her head toward the crowd and then walked back to Eragon, crushing rose petals under her feet. *Thank you,* she said to him.

For what?

For helping me. It was your emotions that showed me the way. Without them, I might have stayed there for weeks before I felt inspired to fix Isidar Mithrim.

Lifting his arms, Orik quieted the crowd, and then he said, "On behalf of our entire race, I thank you for your gift, Saphira. Today you have restored the pride of our realm, and we shall not forget your deed. Let it not be said that knurlan are an ungrateful lot; from now until the end of time, your name shall be recited at the winter festivals, along with the lists of Master Makers, and when Isidar Mithrim is returned to its setting at the peak of Tronjheim, your name will be engraved in the collar surrounding the Star Rose, along with that of Dûrok Ornthrond, who first gave shape to the jewel."

To both Eragon and Saphira, Orik said, "Once again you have demonstrated your friendship to mine people. It pleases me that, by your actions, you have vindicated my foster father's decision to adopt you into Dûrgrimst Ingeitum."

After the conclusion of the multitude of rituals that followed the coronation, and after Eragon had helped remove the wool caught between Saphira's teeth—a slippery, slimy, smelly task that left him needing a bath—the two of them attended the banquet held in Orik's honor. The feasting was loud and boisterous and lasted long into the night. Jugglers and acrobats entertained the guests, as well as a troupe of actors who performed a play called *Az Sartosvrenht rak Balmung, Grimstnzborith rak Kvisagûr*, which Hûndfast told Eragon meant *The Saga of King Balmung of Kvisagûr*.

When the celebrations had died down some and most of the dwarves were deep in their cups, Eragon leaned toward Orik, who sat at the head of the stone table, and said, "Your Majesty."

Orik waved a hand. "I won't have you calling me *Your Majesty* all the time, Eragon. It won't do. Unless the occasion demands it, use mine name as you always have. That's an order." He reached for his goblet but missed and nearly knocked the container over. He laughed.

Smiling, Eragon said, "Orik, I have to ask, Was that really Gûntera who crowned you?"

Orik's chin sank to his chest, and he fingered the stem of the goblet, his expression growing serious. "It was as close to Gûntera as we are ever likely to see on this earth. Does that answer your question, Eragon?"

"I . . . I think so. Does he always answer when called upon? Has he ever refused to crown one of your rulers?"

The gap between Orik's eyebrows narrowed. "Have you ever heard of the Heretic Kings and the Heretic Queens before?"

Eragon shook his head.

"They are knurlan who failed to secure Gûntera's blessing as our next ruler and yet who nevertheless insisted upon taking the throne." Orik's mouth twisted. "Without exception, their reigns were short and unhappy ones."

A band seemed to tighten around Eragon's chest. "So, even though the clanmeet elected you their leader, if Gûntera had failed to crown you, you would not be king now."

"That or I would be king of a nation at war with itself." Orik shrugged. "I was not overly worried about the possibility. With the Varden in the midst of invading the Empire, only a madman would risk tearing our country apart merely to deny me the throne, and while *Gûntera* is many things, he is not mad."

"But you did not know for certain," said Eragon.

Orik shook his head. "Not until he placed the helm upon mine head."

WORDS OF WISDOM

"**S**orry," said Eragon as he bumped the basin.

Nasuada frowned, her face shrinking and elongating as a row of ripples ran through the water in the basin. "What for?" she asked. "I should think congratulations are in order. You have accomplished everything I sent you to do and more."

"No, I—" Eragon stopped as he realized she could not see the disturbance in the water. The spell was designed so that Nasuada's mirror would provide her with an unobstructed view of him and Saphira, not the objects they were gazing at. "I struck the basin with my hand, that is all."

"Oh. In that case, let me formally congratulate you, Eragon. By ensuring Orik became king—"

"Even if it was by getting myself attacked?"

Nasuada smiled. "Yes, even if it was by getting yourself attacked, you have preserved our alliance with the dwarves, and that might mean the difference between victory and defeat. The question now becomes, How long until the rest of the dwarves' army will be able to join us?"

"Orik has already ordered the warriors to ready themselves for departure," said Eragon. "It will probably take the clans a few days to muster their forces, but once they do, they'll march immediately."

"It's a good thing too. We can use their assistance as soon as possible. Which reminds me, when can we expect you to return? Three days? Four days?"

Saphira shuffled her wings, her breath hot on the back of Eragon's neck. Eragon glanced at her, and then, choosing his words with care, he said, "That depends. Do you remember what we discussed before I left?"

Nasuada pursed her lips. "Of course I do, Eragon. I—" She looked off to the side of the image and listened as a man addressed her, his voice an unintelligible murmur to Eragon and Saphira. Returning her attention to them, Nasuada said, "Captain Edric's company has just returned. They appear to have suffered heavy casualties, but our watchmen say that Roran survived."

"Was he injured?" asked Eragon.

"I'll let you know once I find out. I would not worry too much, though. Roran has the luck of—" Once again, the voice of an unseen person distracted Nasuada, and she stepped out of view.

Eragon fidgeted while he waited.

"My apologies," said Nasuada, her visage reappearing in the basin. "We are closing in on Feinster, and we are having to fight off marauding groups of soldiers Lady Lorana sends from the city to harass us. . . . Eragon, Saphira, we need you for this battle. If the people of Feinster see only men, dwarves, and Urgals gathered outside their walls, they may believe they have a chance of holding the city, and they will fight all the harder because of it. They can't hold Feinster, of course, but they have yet to realize that. If they see a dragon and Rider leading the charges against them, however, they will lose the will to fight."

"But—"

Nasuada raised her hand, cutting him off. "There are other reasons for you to return as well. Because of my wounds from the Trial of the Long Knives, I cannot ride into battle with the Varden, as I have before. I need *you* to take my place, Eragon, in order to see that my commands are carried out as I intend and also to prop up the spirits of our warriors. What's more, rumors of your absence are already coursing through the camp, despite our best efforts to the contrary. If Murtagh and Thorn attack us directly as a result, or if Galbatorix sends them to reinforce Feinster . . . well, even with the elves by our sides, I doubt we could withstand them. I'm sorry,

Eragon, but I cannot allow you to return to Ellesméra right now. It's too dangerous."

Pressing his hands against the edge of the cold stone table upon which the basin rested, Eragon said, "Nasuada, please. If not now, then when?"

"Soon. You must be patient."

"Soon." Eragon drew a deep breath, tightening his grip on the table. "How soon exactly?"

Nasuada frowned at him. "You cannot expect me to know that. First we must take Feinster, and then we must secure the country-side, and then—"

"And then you intend to march on Belatona or Dras-Leona, and then to Urû'baen," said Eragon. Nasuada attempted to reply, but he did not allow her the opportunity. "And the closer you get to Galbatorix, the likelier it will be that Murtagh and Thorn will at-tack you, or even the king himself, and you will be ever more reluc-tant to let us go. . . . Nasuada, Saphira and I do not have the skill, the knowledge, nor the strength to kill Galbatorix. You know that! Galbatorix could end this war at any time if he was willing to leave his castle and confront the Varden directly. We *have* to talk with our teachers again. They can tell us where Galbatorix's power is coming from, and they might be able to show us a trick or two that will al-low us to defeat him."

Nasuada gazed downward, studying her hands. "Thorn and Murtagh could destroy us while you were gone."

"And if we do not go, Galbatorix will destroy us when we reach Urû'baen. . . . Could you wait a few days before you attack Feinster?"

"We could, but every day we camp outside the city will cost us lives." Nasuada rubbed her temples with the heels of her palms. "You are asking a lot in exchange for an uncertain reward, Eragon."

"The reward may be uncertain," he said, "but our doom is in-evitable unless we try."

"Is it? I am not so sure. Still . . ." For an uncomfortably long time, Nasuada was silent, gazing past the edge of the image. Then she nodded once, as if confirming something to herself, and said, "I can delay our arrival at Feinster for two or three days. There are several towns in the area we can seize first. Once we do reach the city, I can pass another two or three days having the Varden build siege engines and prepare fortifications. No one will think strangely of it. After that, though, I will have to set upon Feinster, if for no other reason but that we need their supplies. An army that sits still in enemy territory is an army that starves. At the most, I can give you six days, and perhaps only four."

As she spoke, Eragon made several quick calculations. "Four days won't be long enough," he said, "and six might not be either. It took Saphira three days to fly to Farthen Dûr, and that was without stopping to sleep and without having to carry my weight. If the maps I have seen are accurate, it's at least as far from here to Ellesméra, maybe farther, and about the same from Ellesméra to Feinster. And with me on her back, Saphira won't be able to cover the distance as quickly."

No, I won't, Saphira said to him.

Eragon continued: "Even under the best of circumstances, it would still take us a week to reach you at Feinster, and that would be without staying for more than a minute in Ellesméra."

An expression of profound exhaustion crossed Nasuada's face. "Must you fly all the way to Ellesméra? Wouldn't it be sufficient to scry with your mentors once you are past the wards along the edge of Du Weldenvarden? The time you would save could be crucial."

"I don't know. We can try."

Nasuada closed her eyes for a moment. In a hoarse voice, she said, "I may be able to delay our arrival at Feinster for four days. . . . Go to Ellesméra or don't; I leave the decision up to you. If you do, then stay however long is needed. You're right; unless you find a way to defeat Galbatorix, we have no hope of victory. Even so, keep you in mind the tremendous risk we are taking, the lives of the Varden I will be sacrificing in order to buy you this time, and how many more of the Varden will die if we lay siege to Feinster without you."

Somber, Eragon nodded. "I won't forget."

"I should hope not. Now go! Do not tarry any longer! Fly. Fly! Fly faster than a diving hawk, Saphira, and do not let anything slow you." Nasuada touched the tips of her fingers to her lips and then pressed them against the invisible surface of the mirror, where he knew she beheld the moving likeness of him and Saphira. "Luck on your journey, Eragon, Saphira. If we meet again, I fear it will be on the field of battle."

And then she hurried from their sight, and Eragon released his spell, and the water in the basin cleared.

✦ ✦ ✦

THE WHIPPING POST

Roran sat bolt upright and stared past Nasuada, his eyes fixed upon a wrinkle in the side of the crimson pavilion.

He could feel Nasuada studying him, but he refused to meet her gaze. During the long, dull silence that enveloped them, he contemplated a host of dire possibilities, and his temples throbbed with a feverish intensity. He wished he could leave the stifling pavilion and breathe the cool air outside.

At last Nasuada said, "What am I going to do with you, Roran?"

He straightened his spine even more. "Whatever you wish, my Lady."

"An admirable answer, Stronghammer, but in no way does it resolve my quandary." Nasuada sipped wine from a goblet. "Twice you defied a direct order from Captain Edric, and yet if you hadn't, neither he nor you nor the rest of your band might have survived to tell the tale. However, your success does not negate the reality of your disobedience. By your own account, you knowingly committed insubordination, and I *must* punish you if I am to maintain discipline among the Varden."

"Yes, my Lady."

Her brow darkened. "Blast it, Stronghammer. If you were anyone else but Eragon's cousin, and if your gambit had been even one whit less effective, I would have you strung up and hanged for your misconduct."

Roran swallowed as he imagined a noose tightening around his neck.

With the middle finger of her right hand, Nasuada tapped the arm of her high-backed chair with increasing speed until, stopping, she said, "Do you wish to continue fighting with the Varden, Roran?"

"Yes, my Lady," he replied without hesitation.

"What are you willing to endure in order to remain within my army?"

Roran did not allow himself to dwell upon the implications of her question. "Whatever I must, my Lady."

The tension in her face eased, and Nasuada nodded, appearing satisfied. "I hoped you would say that. Tradition and established precedent leave me only three choices. One, I can hang you, but I won't . . . for a multitude of reasons. Two, I can give you thirty lashes and then discharge you from the ranks of the Varden. Or three, I can give you fifty lashes and keep you under my command."

Fifty lashes isn't that many more than thirty, Roran thought, trying to bolster his courage. He wet his lips. "Would I be flogged where all could see?"

Nasuada's eyebrows rose a fraction of an inch. "Your pride has no part in this, Stronghammer. The punishment must be severe so that others are not tempted to follow in your footsteps, and it must be held in public so that the whole of the Varden can profit by it. If you are even half as intelligent as you seem, you knew when you defied Edric that your decision would have consequences and that those consequences would most likely be unpleasant. The choice you must now make is simple: will you stay with the Varden, or will you abandon your friends and family and go your own way?"

Roran lifted his chin, angry that she would question his word. "I shall not leave, Lady Nasuada. No matter how many lashes you assign me, they cannot be as painful as losing my home and my father was."

"No," said Nasuada softly. "They could not. . . . One of the magicians of Du Vrangr Gata will oversee the flogging and attend to you afterward, to ensure that the whip causes you no permanent damage. However, they shall not entirely heal your wounds, nor may you seek out a magician on your own to mend your back."

"I understand."

"Your flogging will be held as soon as Jörmundur can marshal the troops. Until then, you will remain under guard in a tent by the whipping post."

It relieved Roran that he would not have to wait any longer; he did not want to have to labor for days under the shadow of what lay before him. "My Lady," he said, and she dismissed him with a motion of her finger.

Turning on his heel, Roran marched out of the pavilion. Two guards took up positions on either side of him as he emerged. Without looking at or speaking to him, they led Roran through the camp until they arrived at a small, empty tent not far from the blackened whipping post, which stood upon a slight rise just beyond the edge of the camp.

The post was six and a half feet high and had a thick crossbeam near the top, to which prisoners' wrists were tied. Rows of scratches from the fingernails of scourged men covered the crossbeam.

Roran forced himself to look away and then ducked inside the tent. The only piece of furniture inside was a battered wooden stool. He sat and concentrated upon his breathing, determined to remain calm.

As the minutes passed, Roran began to hear the tromp of boots and the clink of mail as the Varden assembled around the whipping post. Roran imagined the thousands of men and women staring at him, including the villagers from Carvahall. His pulse quickened, and sweat sprang up upon his brow.

After about half an hour, the sorceress Trianna entered the tent and had him strip down to his trousers, which embarrassed Roran, although the woman seemed to take no notice. Trianna examined him all over, and even cast an additional spell of healing on his left shoulder, where the soldier had stabbed him with the bolt of a crossbow. Then she declared him fit to continue and gave him a shirt made of sackcloth to wear in place of his own.

Roran had just pulled the shirt over his head when Katrina

pushed her way into the tent. As he beheld her, an equal measure of joy and dread filled Roran.

Katrina glanced between him and Trianna, then curtsied to the sorceress. "May I please speak with my husband alone?"

"Of course. I shall wait outside."

Once Trianna had departed, Katrina rushed to Roran and threw her arms around him. He hugged her just as fiercely as she hugged him, for he had not seen her since he had returned to the Varden.

"Oh, how I've missed you," Katrina whispered in his right ear.

"And I you," he murmured.

They drew apart just far enough so that they could gaze into each other's eyes, and then Katrina scowled. "This is wrong! I went to Nasuada, and I begged her to pardon you, or at least to reduce the number of lashes, but she refused to grant my request."

Running his hands up and down Katrina's back, Roran said, "I wish that you hadn't."

"Why not?"

"Because I said that I would remain with the Varden, and I will not go back on my word."

"But this is wrong!" said Katrina, gripping him by his shoulders. "Carn told me what you did, Roran: you slew almost two hundred soldiers by yourself, and if not for your heroism, none of the men with you would have survived. Nasuada ought to be plying you with gifts and praise, not having you whipped like a common criminal!"

"It does not matter whether this is right or wrong," he told her. "It is necessary. If I were in Nasuada's position, I would have given the same order myself."

Katrina shuddered. "Fifty lashes, though. . . . Why does it have to be so many? Men have died from being whipped that many times."

"Only if they had weak hearts. Don't be so worried; it will take more than that to kill me."

A false smile flickered across Katrina's lips, and then a sob escaped her and she pressed her face against his chest. He cradled her in his arms, stroking her hair and reassuring her as best he could, even though he felt no better than she. After several minutes, Roran heard a horn being winded outside the tent, and he knew that their time together was drawing to a close. Extricating himself from Katrina's embrace, he said, "There is something I want you to do for me."

"What?" she asked, dabbing at her eyes.

"Go back to our tent and do not leave it until after my flogging."

Katrina appeared shocked by his request. "No! I shall not leave you . . . not now."

"Please," he said, "you should not have to see this."

"And you should not have to endure it," she retorted.

"Leave that. I know you wish to stay by my side, but I can bear this better if I know that you aren't here watching me. . . . I brought this upon myself, Katrina, and I do not want you to suffer because of it as well."

Her expression became strained. "The knowledge of your fate shall pain me regardless of where I am standing. However . . . I shall do as you ask, but only because it will help you through this ordeal. . . . You know that I would have the whip fall upon my own body instead of yours, if I could."

"And you know," he said, kissing her on both cheeks, "that I would refuse to let you take my place."

Tears welled up in her eyes again, and she pulled him closer, hugging him so tightly, he had difficulty breathing.

They were still wrapped in each other's arms when the entrance flap to the tent was swept back and Jörmundur entered, along with two of the Nighthawks. Katrina disengaged herself from Roran, curtsied to Jörmundur, and then, without a word, slipped out of the tent.

Jörmundur extended a hand toward Roran. "It's time."

Nodding, Roran rose and allowed Jörmundur and the guards to escort him to the whipping post outside. Row after row of the Varden boxed in the area around the post, every man, woman, dwarf, and Urgal standing with stiff spines and squared shoulders. After his initial glimpse of the assembled army, Roran gazed off toward the horizon and did his best to ignore the onlookers.

The two guards lifted Roran's arms above his head and secured his wrists to the crossbeam of the whipping post. While they did, Jörmundur walked around in front of the post and held up a leather-wrapped dowel. "Here, bite down on this," he said in a low voice. "It will keep you from hurting yourself." Grateful, Roran opened his mouth and allowed Jörmundur to fit the dowel between his teeth. The tanned leather tasted bitter, like green acorns.

Then a horn and a drumroll sounded, and Jörmundur read out the charges against Roran, and the guards cut off Roran's sackcloth shirt.

He shivered as the cold air washed across his bare torso.

An instant before it struck, Roran heard the whip whistling through the air.

It felt as if a rod of hot metal had been laid across his flesh. Roran arched his back and bit down on the dowel. An involuntary groan escaped him, although the dowel muffled the sound so he thought no one else heard.

"One," said the man wielding the whip.

The shock of the second blow caused Roran to groan again, but thereafter he remained silent, determined not to appear weak before the whole of the Varden.

The whipping was as painful as any of the numerous wounds Roran had suffered over the past few months, but after a dozen or so blows, he gave up trying to fight the pain and, surrendering to it, entered a bleary trance. His field of vision narrowed until the only thing he saw was the worn wood in front of him; at times, his sight flickered and went blank as he drifted into brief spates of unconsciousness.

After an interminable time, he heard the dim and faraway voice intone, "Thirty," and despair gripped him as he wondered, *How can I possibly withstand another twenty lashes?* Then he thought of Katrina and their unborn child, and the thought gave him strength.

✳ ✳ ✳

Roran woke to find himself lying on his stomach on the cot inside the tent he and Katrina shared. Katrina was kneeling next to him, stroking his hair and murmuring in his ear, while someone daubed a cold, sticky substance over the stripes on his back. He winced and stiffened as the anonymous person poked a particularly sensitive spot.

"That is *not* how I would treat a patient of mine," he heard Trianna say in a haughty tone.

"If you treat all of your patients as you were treating Roran," another woman replied, "I'm amazed that any survived your attentions." After a moment, Roran recognized the second voice as belonging to the strange, bright-eyed herbalist Angela.

"I beg your pardon!" said Trianna. "I will not stand here and be insulted by a lowly *fortuneteller* who struggles to cast even the most basic spell."

"Sit, then, if it pleases you, but whether you sit or stand, I will continue to insult you until you admit that his back muscle attaches *here* and not *there*." Roran felt a finger touch him in two different places, each a half inch apart.

"Oh!" said Trianna, and left the tent.

Katrina smiled at Roran, and for the first time, he noticed the tears streaking her face. "Roran, do you understand me?" she asked. "Are you awake?"

"I . . . I think so," he said, his voice raspy. His jaw ached from biting the dowel so hard for so long. He coughed, then grimaced as every one of the fifty stripes on his back throbbed in unison.

"There we go," said Angela. "All finished."

"It's amazing. I didn't expect you and Trianna to do so much," said Katrina.

"On Nasuada's orders."

"Nasuada? . . . Why would—"

"You'll have to ask her yourself. Tell him to stay off his back if he can help it. And he ought to be careful twisting from side to side, or he might tear open the scabs."

"Thank you," Roran mumbled.

Behind him, Angela laughed. "Think nothing of it, Roran. Or rather, think something of it, but do not consider it overly important. Besides, it amuses me to have tended injuries on both your back and Eragon's. Right, then, I'll be off. Watch out for ferrets!"

When the herbalist had gone, Roran closed his eyes again. Katrina's smooth fingers stroked his forehead. "You were very brave," she said.

"Was I?"

"Aye. Jörmundur and everyone else I spoke to said that you never cried out or begged for the flogging to stop."

"Good." He wanted to know how serious his wounds were, but he was reluctant to force her to describe the damage to his back.

Katrina seemed to sense his desire, however, for she said, "Angela believes that with a bit of luck, you won't scar too badly. In either case, once you're completely healed, Eragon or another magician can remove the scars from your back and it will be as if you were never whipped in the first place."

"Mmh."

"Would you like something to drink?" she asked. "I have a pot of yarrow tea steeping."

"Yes, please."

As Katrina rose, Roran heard another person enter the tent. He opened one eye and was surprised to see Nasuada standing next to the pole at the front of the tent.

"My Lady," Katrina said, her voice razor-sharp.

In spite of the lances of pain from his back, Roran pushed himself partially up and, with Katrina's help, swung himself into a sitting position. Leaning on Katrina, he started to stand, but Nasuada lifted a hand. "Please don't. I do not wish to cause you any more distress than I already have."

"Why have you come, Lady Nasuada?" asked Katrina. "Roran needs to rest and recover, not to spend his time talking when he does not have to."

Roran placed a hand on Katrina's left shoulder. "I can talk if I must," he said.

Moving farther into the tent, Nasuada lifted the hem of her green dress and sat on the small chest of belongings Katrina had brought with her from Carvahall. After arranging the folds of her skirt, she said, "I have another mission for you, Roran: a small raid similar to those you have already participated in."

"When will I leave?" he asked, puzzled that she would bother to inform him in person of such a simple assignment.

"Tomorrow."

Katrina's eyes widened. "Are you mad?" she exclaimed.

"Katrina . . . ," Roran murmured, attempting to placate her, but she shrugged off his hand and said, "The last trip you sent him on nearly killed him, and you've just had him whipped within an inch of his life! You can't order him back into combat so soon; he wouldn't last more than a minute against Galbatorix's soldiers!"

"I can, and I must!" said Nasuada with such authority, Katrina held her tongue and waited to hear Nasuada's explanation, although Roran could tell that her anger had not subsided. Gazing at him intensely, Nasuada said, "Roran, as you may or may not be aware, our alliance with the Urgals is upon the verge of collapse. One of our own murdered three of the Urgals while you were serving under Captain Edric, who, you may be pleased to know, is a captain no more. Anyway, I had the miserable wretch who killed the Urgals hanged, but ever since, our relations with Garzhvog's rams have become increasingly precarious."

"What does this have to do with Roran?" Katrina demanded.

Nasuada pressed her lips together, then said, "I need to convince the Varden to accept the presence of the Urgals without further bloodshed, and the best way I can do that is to *show* the Varden that our two races can work together in peaceful pursuit of a common goal. Toward that end, the group you shall be traveling with will contain equal numbers of both humans and Urgals."

"But that still doesn't—" Katrina started to say.

"And I am placing the whole lot of them under your command, Stronghammer."

"Me?" Roran rasped, astonished. "Why?"

With a wry smile, Nasuada said, "Because you will do whatever you have to in order to protect your friends and family. In this, you are like me, although my family is larger than yours, for I consider the whole of the Varden my kin. Also, because you are Eragon's cousin, I cannot afford to have you commit insubordination again, for then I will have no choice but to execute you or expel you from the Varden. Neither of which I wish to do.

"Therefore, I am giving you your own command so that there is no one above you to disobey, except me. If you ignore *my* orders, it had better be to kill Galbatorix; no other reason will save you from far worse than the lashes you earned today. And I am giving you *this* command, because you have proven that you are able to convince others to follow you, even in the face of the most daunting circumstances. You have as good a chance as any of maintaining control over a group of Urgals and humans. I would send Eragon if I could, but since he is not here, the responsibility falls to you. When the Varden hear that Eragon's own cousin, Roran Stronghammer—he who slew nigh on two hundred soldiers by himself—went on a mission with Urgals and that the mission was a success, then we may yet keep the Urgals as our allies for the duration of this war. *That* is why I had Angela and Trianna heal you more than is customary: not to spare you your punishment, but because I need you fit to command. Now, what say you, Stronghammer? Can I count on you?"

Roran looked at Katrina. He knew she desperately wished he would tell Nasuada that he was incapable of leading the raid. Dropping his gaze so he did not have to see her distress, Roran thought of the immense size of the army that opposed the Varden, and then, in a hoarse whisper, he said:

"You may count on me, Lady Nasuada."

◆ ◆ ◆

AMONG THE CLOUDS

From Tronjheim, Saphira flew the five miles to Farthen Dûr's inner wall, then she and Eragon entered the tunnel that burrowed east, miles through Farthen Dûr's base. Eragon could have run the length of the tunnel in about ten minutes, but since the height of the ceiling prevented Saphira from flying or jumping, she would not have been able to keep up, so he limited himself to a brisk walk.

An hour later, they emerged in Odred Valley, which ran north to south. Nestled among the foothills at the head of the narrow, fern-filled valley was Fernoth-mérna, a fair-sized lake that was like a drop of dark ink between the towering mountains of the Beor range. From the northern end of Fernoth-mérna flowed the Ragni Darmn, which wound its way up the valley until it joined with the Az Ragni by the flanks of Moldûn the Proud, the northernmost mountain of the Beors.

They had departed Tronjheim well before dawn, and although the tunnel had slowed them, it was still early morning. The ragged strip of sky overhead was barred with rays of pale yellow where sunlight streamed between the peaks of the towering mountains. Within the valley below, ridges of heavy clouds clung to the sides of the mountains like vast gray snakes. Coils of white mist drifted up from the glassy surface of the lake.

Eragon and Saphira stopped at the edge of Fernoth-mérna to drink and to replenish their waterskins for the next leg of their journey. The water came from melted snow and ice high in the mountains. It was so cold, it made Eragon's teeth hurt. He screwed up his eyes and stamped the ground, groaning as a spike of cold-induced pain shot through his skull.

As the throbbing subsided, he gazed across the lake. Between the curtains of shifting mist, he spotted the ruins of a sprawling castle built upon a bare stone spur on one mountain. Thick ropes of ivy strangled the crumbling walls, but aside from that, the structure appeared lifeless. Eragon shivered. The abandoned building seemed gloomy, ominous, as if it were the decaying carcass of some foul beast.

Ready? Saphira asked.

Ready, he said, and climbed into the saddle.

From Fernoth-mérna, Saphira flew northward, following Odred Valley out of the Beor Mountains. The valley did not lead directly toward Ellesméra, which was farther west, yet they had no choice but to remain in the valley, as the passes between the mountains were over five miles high.

Saphira flew at as lofty an altitude as Eragon could endure because it was easier for her to traverse long distances in the rarefied upper atmosphere than in the thick, moist air near the ground. Eragon protected himself against the freezing temperatures by wearing several layers of clothes and by shielding himself from the wind with a spell that split the stream of freezing air so it flowed harmlessly to either side.

Riding Saphira was far from restful, but since she flapped in a slow and steady rhythm, Eragon did not have to concentrate upon maintaining his balance as he did when she turned or dove or engaged in other, more elaborate maneuvers. For the most part, he divided his time between talking with Saphira, thinking back upon the events of the past few weeks, and studying the ever-changing vista below them.

You used magic without the ancient language when the dwarves attacked you, said Saphira. *That was a dangerous thing to do.*

I know, but I didn't have time to think of the words. Besides, you never use the ancient language when you cast a spell.

That's different. I'm a dragon. We do not need the ancient language to state our intentions; we know what we want, and we do not change our minds as easily as elves or humans.

The orange sun was a handsbreadth above the horizon when Saphira sailed through the mouth of the valley and out over the flat, empty grasslands that abutted the Beor Mountains. Straightening in the saddle, Eragon gazed around them and shook his head, amazed by how much distance they had covered. *If only we could have flown to Ellesméra the first time,* he said. *We would have had so much more time to spend with Oromis and Glaedr.* Saphira indicated her agreement with a silent mental nod.

Saphira flew until the sun had set and the stars covered the sky and the mountains were a dark purple smudge behind them. She would have continued on until morning, but Eragon insisted they stop to rest. *You are still tired from your trip to Farthen Dûr. We can fly through the night tomorrow, and the day after as well, if necessary, but tonight you must sleep.*

580

Although Saphira did not like his proposal, she agreed to it and landed by a patch of willow trees growing alongside a stream. As he dismounted, Eragon discovered his legs were so stiff, he had difficulty remaining on his feet. He unsaddled Saphira, then spread his bedroll on the ground next to her and curled up with his back against her warm body. He had no need of a tent, for she sheltered him with a wing, like a mother hawk protecting her brood. The two of them soon sank into their respective dreams, which mingled in strange and wonderful ways, for their minds remained linked even then.

As soon as the first hint of light appeared in the east, Eragon and Saphira continued on their way, soaring high above the verdant plains.

A fierce headwind sprang up in midmorning, which slowed Saphira to half her normal speed. Try as she might, she could not rise above the wind. All day she fought against the rushing air. It was arduous work, and although Eragon gave her as much of his strength as he dared, by afternoon her exhaustion was profound. She swooped down and alighted on a knoll in the grasslands and sat there with her wings draped across the ground, panting and trembling.

We should stay here for the night, Eragon said.

No.

Saphira, you're in no condition to go on. Let's make camp until you recover. Who knows, the wind might die down by evening.

He heard the wet rasp of her tongue as she licked her chops and then the heave of her lungs as she resumed panting.

No, she said. *On these plains, it might blow for weeks or even months on end. We cannot wait for calm.*

But—

I will not give up merely because I hurt, Eragon. Too much is at stake. . . .

Then let me give you energy from Aren. There is more than enough in the ring to sustain you from here to Du Weldenvarden.

No, she repeated again. *Save Aren for when we have no other recourse. I can rest and recover in the forest. Aren, however, we may have need of at any moment; you should not deplete it merely to ease my discomfort.*

I hate to see you in such pain, though.

A faint growl escaped her. *My ancestors, the wild dragons, would not have shrunk from a puny breeze like this, and neither will I.*

And with that, she jumped back into the air, carrying him with her as she drove herself into the gale.

As the day was drawing to an end and the wind still howled around them, pushing against Saphira as if fate were determined to keep them from reaching Du Weldenvarden, Eragon thought of the dwarf woman Glûmra and of her faith in the dwarven gods, and for the first time in his life, he felt the desire to pray. Withdrawing from his mental contact with Saphira—who was so tired and preoccupied, she did not notice—Eragon whispered, "Gûntera, king of the gods, if you exist, and if you can hear me, and if you have the power, then, please, still this wind. I know I'm not a dwarf, but King Hrothgar adopted me into his clan, and I think that gives me the right to pray to you. Gûntera, please, we have to get to Du Weldenvarden as fast as possible, not only for the good of the Varden but also for the good of your people, the knurlan. Please, I beg of you, still this wind. Saphira cannot keep this up much longer." Then, feeling slightly foolish, Eragon extended himself toward Saphira's consciousness, wincing in sympathy as he felt the burning within her muscles.

Late that night, when all was cold and black, the wind abated and, thereafter, only occasionally buffeted them with a gust.

When morning came, Eragon looked down and saw the hard, dry land of the Hadarac Desert. *Blast it*, he said, for they had not come as far as he had hoped. *We won't make it to Ellesméra today, will we?*

Not unless the wind decides to blow in the opposite direction and carry us there upon its back. Saphira labored in silence for another few minutes, then added, *However, barring any other unpleasant surprises, we should arrive at Du Weldenvarden by evening.*

Eragon grunted.

They landed only twice that day. Once, while they were on the ground, Saphira devoured a brace of ducks that she caught and killed with a burst of fire, but other than that, she went without food. To save time, Eragon ate his own meals in the saddle.

As Saphira had predicted, Du Weldenvarden came into sight even as the sun neared setting. The forest appeared before them as an endless expanse of green. Deciduous trees—oaks and beeches and maples—dominated the outer parts of the forest, but farther in, Eragon knew, they gave way to the forbidding pine trees that formed the bulk of the woods.

Dusk had settled over the countryside by the time they arrived at the edge of Du Weldenvarden, and Saphira glided to a soft landing under the outstretched branches of a massive oak. She folded her wings and sat still for a while, too tired to continue. Her crimson tongue hung loose from her mouth. While she rested, Eragon listened to the rustle of leaves overhead and to the hoot of owls and the chirp of evening insects.

When she was sufficiently recovered, Saphira walked forward and passed between two giant, moss-covered oak trees and so crossed into Du Weldenvarden on foot. The elves had made it impossible for anyone or anything to enter the forest by means of magic, and since dragons did not rely upon their bodies alone to fly, Saphira could not enter while in the air, else her wings would fail her and she would fall from the sky.

That should be far enough, Saphira said, stopping in a small meadow several hundred feet from the perimeter of the forest.

Eragon unbuckled the straps from around his legs and slid down Saphira's side. He searched the meadow until he found a bare patch of earth. With his hands, he scooped out a shallow hole a foot and a half wide. He summoned forth water to fill the hole, then uttered a spell of scrying.

The water shimmered and acquired a soft yellow glow as Eragon beheld the interior of Oromis's hut. The silver-haired elf was sitting at his kitchen table, reading a tattered scroll. Oromis looked up at Eragon and nodded with unsurprised recognition.

"Master," Eragon said, and twisted his hand over his chest.

"Greetings, Eragon. I have been expecting you. Where are you?"

"Saphira and I just reached Du Weldenvarden. . . . Master, I know we promised to return to Ellesméra, but the Varden are only a few days away from the city of Feinster, and they are vulnerable without us. We don't have the time to fly all the way to Ellesméra. Could you answer our questions here, through the scrying pool?"

Oromis leaned back in his chair, his angled face grave and pensive. Then he said, "I will not instruct you at a distance, Eragon. I can guess at some of the things you wish to ask me, and they are subjects we must discuss in person."

"Master, please. If Murtagh and Thorn—"

"No, Eragon. I understand the reason for your urgency, but your studies are just as important as protecting the Varden, maybe even more so. We must do this properly, or not at all."

Eragon sighed and slumped forward. "Yes, Master."

Oromis nodded. "Glaedr and I will be waiting for you. Fly safe and fly fast. We have much to talk about."

"Yes, Master."

Feeling numb and worn-out, Eragon ended the spell. The water soaked back into the ground. He held his head in his hands, staring at the patch of moist dirt between his feet. Saphira's heavy breathing was loud beside him. *I guess we have to keep going,* he said. *I'm sorry.*

Her breathing paused for a moment as she licked her chops. *It's all right. I'm not about to collapse.*

He looked up at her. *Are you sure?*

Yes.

Eragon reluctantly hoisted himself upright and climbed onto her back. *As long as we're going to Ellesméra,* he said, tightening the straps around his legs, *we should visit the Menoa tree again. Maybe we can finally figure out what Solembum meant. I could certainly use a new sword.*

When Eragon had first met Solembum in Teirm, the werecat had told him, *When the time comes and you need a weapon, look under the roots of the Menoa tree. Then, when all seems lost and your power is insufficient, go to the Rock of Kuthian and speak your name to open the Vault of Souls.* Eragon still did not know where the Rock of Kuthian was, but during their first stay in Ellesméra, he and Saphira had had several chances to examine the Menoa tree. They had discovered no clue as to the exact whereabouts of the supposed weapon. Moss, dirt, bark, and the occasional ant were the only things they had seen among the roots of the Menoa tree, and none of them indicated where to excavate.

Solembum might not have meant a sword, Saphira pointed out. *Werecats love riddles nearly as much as dragons do. If it even exists, this weapon might be a scrap of parchment with a spell inscribed on it, or a book, or a painting, or a sharp piece of rock, or any other dangerous thing.*

Whatever it is, I hope we can find it. Who knows when we will have the chance to return to Ellesméra again?

Saphira raked aside a fallen tree that lay before her, then crouched and unfurled her velvety wings, her massive shoulder muscles bunching. Eragon yelped and grabbed the front of his saddle as she surged up and forward with unexpected force, rising above the tops of the trees in a single vertiginous bound.

Wheeling over the sea of shifting branches, Saphira oriented herself in a northwesterly direction and then set out toward the elves' capital, the beats of her wings slow and heavy.

✦ ✦ ✦

BUTTING HEADS

The raid on the supply train went almost exactly as Roran had planned: three days after leaving the main body of the Varden, he and his fellow horsemen rode down from the lip of a ravine and struck the meandering line of wagons broadside. Meanwhile, the Urgals sprang out from behind boulders scattered across the floor of the ravine and attacked the supply train from the front, stopping the procession in its tracks. The soldiers and wagoners put up a brave fight, but the ambush had caught them while sleepy and disorganized, and Roran's force soon overwhelmed them. None of the humans or Urgals died in the attack, and only three suffered wounds: two humans and one Urgal.

Roran killed several of the soldiers himself, but for the most part, he hung back and concentrated upon directing the assault, as was his responsibility now. He was still stiff and sore from the flogging he had endured, and he did not want to exert himself any more than necessary, for fear of cracking the mat of scabs that covered his back.

Until that point, Roran had had no difficulty maintaining discipline among the twenty humans and twenty Urgals. Although it was obvious that neither group liked nor trusted the other—an attitude he shared, for he regarded the Urgals with the same degree of suspicion and distaste as would any man who had been raised in proximity to the Spine—they had succeeded in working together during the past three days with nary a raised voice. That both groups had managed to cooperate so well had, he knew, little to do with his prowess as a commander. Nasuada and Nar Garzhvog had taken great care in picking the warriors who were to travel with him, selecting only those with a reputation for a quick blade, sound judgment, and, above all, a calm and even disposition.

However, in the aftermath of the attack on the supply train, as his men were busy dragging the bodies of the soldiers and the wagoners into a pile, and Roran was riding up and down the line of wagons overseeing the work, he heard an agonized howl from somewhere by the far end of the train. Thinking that perhaps another contingent of soldiers had chanced upon them, Roran shouted to Carn and several other men to join him and then touched his spurs to Snowfire's flanks and galloped toward the rear of the wagons.

Four Urgals had tied an enemy soldier to the trunk of a gnarled willow tree and were amusing themselves by poking and prodding him with their swords. Swearing, Roran jumped down from Snowfire and, with a single blow of his hammer, put the man out of his misery.

A swirling cloud of dust swept over the group as Carn and four other warriors galloped up to the willow tree. They reined in their steeds and spread out on either side of Roran, holding their weapons at the ready.

The largest Urgal, a ram named Yarbog, stepped forward. "Stronghammer, why did you stop our sport? He would have danced for us for many more minutes."

From between clenched teeth, Roran said, "So long as you are under my command, you will not torture captives without cause. Am I understood? Many of these soldiers have been forced to serve Galbatorix against their will. Many of them are our friends or family or neighbors, and while we must fight them, I will not have you treat them with unnecessary cruelty. If not for the whims of fate, any one of us humans might be standing in their place. They are not our enemy; Galbatorix is, as he is yours."

The Urgal's heavy brow beetled, nearly obscuring his deep-set yellow eyes. "But you will still kill them, yes? Why cannot we enjoy seeing them wriggle and dance first?"

Roran wondered if the Urgal's skull was too thick to crack with his hammer. Struggling to restrain his anger, he said, "Because it is wrong, if nothing else!" Pointing at the dead soldier, he said, "What if *he* had been one of your own race who had been enthralled by the Shade, Durza? Would you have tormented him as well?"

"Of course," said Yarbog. "They would want us to tickle them with our swords so that they would have an opportunity to prove their bravery before they died. Is it not the same with you hornless humans, or have you no stomach for pain?"

Roran was not sure how serious an insult it was among the Urgals to call another *hornless*, but even so, he had no doubt that questioning someone's courage was as offensive to Urgals as it was to humans, if not more so. "Any one of us could withstand more pain without crying out than you, Yarbog," he said, tightening his grip on his hammer and shield. "Now, unless you wish to experience agony the likes of which you cannot imagine, surrender your sword to me, then untie that poor wretch and carry him over to the rest of the bodies. After that, go see to the packhorses. They are yours to care for until we return to the Varden."

Without waiting for an acknowledgment from the Urgal, Roran turned and grasped Snowfire's reins and prepared to climb back onto the stallion.

"No," growled Yarbog.

Roran froze with one foot in a stirrup and silently swore to himself. He had hoped that just such a situation would not arise during the trip. Swinging around, he said, "No? Are you refusing to obey my orders?"

Drawing back his lips to expose his short fangs, Yarbog said, "No. I challenge you for leadership of this tribe, Stronghammer." And the Urgal threw back his massive head and bellowed so loudly that the rest of the humans and Urgals stopped what they were doing and ran toward the willow tree until all forty of them were clustered around Yarbog and Roran.

"Shall we attend to this creature for you?" Carn asked, his voice ringing out.

Wishing that there were not so many onlookers, Roran shook his head. "No, I shall deal with him myself." Despite his words, he was glad to have his men beside him, opposite the line of hulking, gray-skinned Urgals. The humans were smaller than the Urgals, but all except Roran were mounted on horses, which would give them a slight advantage if there were a fight between the two groups. If that came to pass, Carn's magic would be of little help, for the Urgals had a spellcaster of their own, a shaman named Dazhgra, and from what Roran had seen, Dazhgra was the more powerful magician, if not as skilled in the nuances of their arcane art.

To Yarbog, Roran said, "It is not the custom of the Varden to award leadership based upon trial by combat. If you wish to fight, I will fight, but you will gain nothing by it. If I lose, Carn will assume my command, and you will answer to him instead of me."

"Bah!" said Yarbog. "I do not challenge you for the right to lead your own race. I challenge you for the right to lead us, the fighting rams of the Bolvek tribe! You have not proven yourself, Strong-hammer, so you cannot claim the position of chieftain. If you lose, I will become chieftain here, and we shall not lift our chins to you, Carn, or any other creature too weak to earn our respect!"

Roran pondered his situation before accepting the inevitable. Even if it cost him his life, he had to try to maintain his authority over the Urgals, else the Varden would lose them as allies. Taking a breath, he said, "Among my race, it is customary for the person who has been challenged to choose the time and place for the fight, as well as the weapons both parties will use."

Chortling deep in his throat, Yarbog said, "The time is now, Stronghammer. The place is here. And among my race, we fight in a loincloth and without weapons."

"That is hardly fair, since I have no horns," Roran pointed out. "Will you agree to let me use my hammer to compensate for my lack?"

Yarbog thought about it, then said, "You may keep your helmet and shield, but no hammer. Weapons are not allowed when we fight to be chief."

"I see. . . . Well, if I can't have my hammer, I will forgo my helmet and shield as well. What are the rules of combat, and how shall we decide the winner?"

"There is only one rule, Stronghammer: if you flee, you forfeit the match and are banished from your tribe. You win by forcing your rival to submit, but since I will never submit, we will fight to the death."

Roran nodded. *That might be what he intends to do, but I won't kill him if I can help it.* "Let us begin," he cried, and banged his hammer against his shield.

At his direction, the men and Urgals cleared a space in the middle of the ravine and pegged out a square, twelve paces by twelve paces. Then Roran and Yarbog stripped, and two Urgals slathered bear grease over Yarbog's body while Carn and Loften, another human, did the same for Roran.

"Rub as much as you can into my back," Roran murmured. He wanted his scabs to be as soft as possible so as to minimize the number of places they would crack.

Leaning close to him, Carn said, "Why did you refuse the shield and helmet?"

"They would only slow me. I'll have to be as fast as a frightened hare if I'm to avoid being crushed by him." As Carn and Loften worked their way down his limbs, Roran studied his opponent, searching for any vulnerability that would help him defeat the Urgal.

Yarbog stood well over six feet tall. His back was broad, his chest deep, and his arms and legs covered with knotted muscles. His neck was as thick as a bull's, as it had to be in order to sustain the weight of his head and his curled horns. Three slanting scars marked the left side of his waist, where he had been clawed by an animal. Sparse black bristles grew over the whole of his hide.

At least he's not a Kull, thought Roran. He was confident of his own strength, but even so, he did not believe that he could overpower Yarbog with sheer force. Rare was the man who could hope to match the physical prowess of a healthy Urgal ram. Also, Roran knew that Yarbog's large black fingernails, his fangs, his horns, and his leathery hide would all provide Yarbog with considerable advantages in the unarmed combat they were about to engage in. *If I can, I will*, Roran decided, thinking of all the low tricks he could use against the Urgal, for fighting Yarbog would not be like wrestling with Eragon or Baldor or any other man from Carvahall; rather, Roran was sure that it would be like the ferocious and unrestrained brawling between two wild beasts.

Again and again, Roran's eyes returned to Yarbog's immense horns, for those, he knew, were the most dangerous of the Urgal's features. With them, Yarbog could butt and gore Roran with impunity, and they would also protect the sides of Yarbog's head from any blows Roran could deliver with his bare hands, although they limited the Urgal's peripheral vision. Then it occurred to Roran that just as the horns were Yarbog's greatest natural gift, so too they might be his undoing.

Roran rolled his shoulders and bounced on the balls of his feet, eager for the contest to be over.

591

When both Roran and Yarbog were completely covered with bear grease, their seconds retreated and they stepped into the confines of the square pegged out on the ground. Roran kept his knees partially flexed, ready to leap in any direction at the slightest hint of movement from Yarbog. The rocky soil was cold, hard, and rough beneath the soles of his bare feet.

A slight gust stirred the branches of the nearby willow tree. One of the oxen harnessed to the wagons pawed at a clump of grass, his tack creaking.

With a rippling bellow, Yarbog charged Roran, covering the distance between them with three thundering steps. Roran waited until Yarbog was nearly upon him, then jumped to the right. He underestimated Yarbog's speed, however. Lowering his head, the Urgal rammed his horns into Roran's left shoulder and tossed him sprawling across the square.

Sharp rocks poked into Roran's side as he landed. Lines of pain flashed across his back, tracing the paths of his half-healed wounds. He grunted and rolled upright, feeling several scabs break open, exposing his raw flesh to the stinging air. Dirt and small pebbles clung to the film of grease on his body. Keeping both feet on the ground, he shuffled toward Yarbog, never taking his eyes off the snarling Urgal.

Again Yarbog charged him, and again Roran attempted to jump out of the way. This time his maneuver succeeded, and he slipped past the Urgal with inches to spare. Whirling around, Yarbog ran at him for a third time, and once more, Roran managed to evade him.

Then Yarbog changed tactics. Advancing sideways, like a crab, he thrust out his large, hooked hands to catch Roran and pull him into his deadly embrace. Roran flinched and retreated. Whatever happened, he had to avoid falling into Yarbog's clutches; with his immense strength, the Urgal could soon dispatch him.

The men and Urgals gathered around the square were silent, their faces impassive as they watched Roran and Yarbog scuffle back and forth in the dirt.

For several minutes, Roran and Yarbog exchanged quick glancing blows. Roran avoided closing with the Urgal wherever possible, trying to wear him out from a distance, but as the fight dragged on and Yarbog seemed no more tired than when they had begun, Roran realized that time was not his friend. If he was going to win, he had to end the fight without further delay.

Hoping to provoke Yarbog into charging again—for his strategy depended upon just that—Roran withdrew to the far corner of the square and began to taunt him, saying, "Ha! You are as fat and slow as a milk cow! Can't you catch me, Yarbog, or are your legs made of lard? You should cut off your horns in shame for letting a human make a fool of you. What will your prospective mates think when they hear of this? Will you tell them—"

Yarbog drowned out Roran's words with a roar. The Urgal sprinted toward him, turning slightly, so as to crash into Roran with his full weight. Skipping out of the way, Roran reached out for the tip of Yarbog's right horn but missed his mark and fell stumbling into the middle of the square, skinning both knees. He cursed to himself as he regained his footing.

Checking his headlong rush just before momentum carried him beyond the boundaries of the square, Yarbog turned back, his small yellow eyes searching for Roran. "Yah!" shouted Roran. He stuck out his tongue and made every rude gesture he could think of. "You couldn't hit a tree even if it was in front of you!"

"Die, puny human!" Yarbog growled, and sprang at Roran, arms outstretched.

Two of Yarbog's nails carved bloody furrows across Roran's ribs as Roran darted to his left, but he still managed to grasp and hang on to one of the Urgal's horns. Roran grabbed the other horn as well before Yarbog could throw him off. Using the horns as handles, Roran wrenched Yarbog's head to one side and, straining every muscle, cast the Urgal to the ground. Roran's back flared in angry protest at the motion.

As soon as Yarbog's chest touched the dirt, Roran placed a knee on top of his right shoulder, pinning him in place. Yarbog snorted and bucked, trying to break Roran's grip, but Roran refused to let go. He braced his feet against a rock and twisted the Urgal's head as far around as it would go, pulling so hard he would have broken the neck of any human. The grease on his palms made it difficult to hold on to Yarbog's horns.

Yarbog relaxed for a moment, then pushed himself off the ground with his left arm, lifting Roran as well, and scrabbled with his legs in an effort to get them underneath his body. Roran grimaced and leaned against Yarbog's neck and shoulder. After a handful of seconds, Yarbog's left arm buckled and he fell flat on his stomach again.

Both Roran and Yarbog were panting as heavily as if they had run a race. Where they touched, the bristles on the Urgal's hide poked Roran like pieces of stiff wire. Dust coated their bodies. Thin streams of blood ran down from the scratches on Roran's side and from his aching back.

Yarbog resumed kicking and flailing once he had regained his breath, flopping around in the dirt like a hooked fish. It took all of Roran's strength, but he hung on, trying to ignore the stones that cut his feet and legs. Unable to free himself by those methods, Yarbog let his limbs go limp and then began to flex his neck again and again, in an attempt to exhaust Roran's arms.

They lay there, neither of them moving more than a few inches as they struggled against each other.

A fly buzzed over them and landed on Roran's ankle.

Oxen lowed.

After nearly ten minutes, sweat drenched Roran's face. He could not seem to get enough air into his lungs. His arms seared with agony. The stripes on his back felt as if they were about to tear asunder. His ribs throbbed where Yarbog had clawed him.

Roran knew he could not continue for much longer. *Blast it!* he thought. *Won't he ever give up?*

Just then, Yarbog's head quivered as a muscle in the Urgal's neck cramped. Yarbog grunted, the first sound he had made in over a minute, and in an undertone, he muttered, "Kill me, Strong-hammer. I cannot best you."

Adjusting his grip on Yarbog's horns, Roran growled in an equally low tone, "No. If you want to die, find someone else to kill you. I have fought by your rules, now you will accept defeat according to mine. Tell everyone that you submit to me. Say you were wrong to challenge me. Do that, and I'll let you go. If not, I'll keep you here until you change your mind, no matter how long it takes."

Yarbog's head twitched under Roran's hands as the Urgal tried once more to free himself. He huffed, blowing a small cloud of dust into the air, then rumbled, "The shame would be too great, Stronghammer. Kill me."

"I don't belong to your race, and I won't abide by your customs," said Roran. "If you are so worried about your honor, tell those who are curious that you were defeated by the cousin of Eragon Shadeslayer. Surely there is no shame in that." When several minutes had passed and Yarbog still had not replied, Roran yanked on Yarbog's horns and growled, "Well?"

Raising his voice so that all of the men and Urgals could hear, Yarbog said, "Gar! Svarvok curse me; I submit! I should not have challenged you, Stronghammer. You are worthy to be chief, and I am not."

As one, the men cheered and shouted, banging the pommels of their swords on their shields. The Urgals shifted in place and said nothing.

Satisfied, Roran released Yarbog's horns and rolled away from the gray Urgal. Feeling almost as if he had endured another flogging, Roran slowly got to his feet and hobbled out of the square to where Carn was waiting.

Roran winced as Carn draped a blanket over his shoulders and the fabric rubbed against his abused skin. Grinning, Carn handed him a wineskin. "After he knocked you down, I thought for sure he would kill you. I should have learned by now to never count you out, eh, Roran? Ha! That was just about the finest fight I've ever seen. You must be the only man in history to have wrestled an Urgal."

"Maybe not," Roran said between sips of wine. "But I might be the only man who has survived the experience." He smiled as Carn laughed. Roran looked over at the Urgals, who were clustered around Yarbog, talking with him in low grunts while two of their brethren wiped the grease and grime from Yarbog's limbs. Although the Urgals appeared subdued, they did not seem angry or resentful, so far as he was able to judge, and he was confident that he would have no more trouble from them.

Despite the pain of his wounds, Roran felt pleased with the outcome of the match. *This won't be the last fight between our two races,* he thought, *but as long as we can return safely to the Varden, the Urgals won't break off our alliance, at least not on account of me.*

After taking one last sip, Roran stoppered the wineskin and handed it back to Carn, then shouted, "Right, now stop standing around yammering like sheep and finish drawing up a list of what's in those wagons! Loften, round up the soldiers' horses, if they haven't already wandered too far away! Dazhgra, see to the oxen. Make haste! Thorn and Murtagh could be flying here even now. Go on, snap to!

"And, Carn, where the blazes are my clothes?"

✦   ✦   ✦

GENEALOGY

On the fourth day after leaving Farthen Dûr, Eragon and Saphira arrived in Ellesméra.

The sun was clear and bright overhead when the first of the city's buildings—a narrow, twisting turret with glittering windows that stood between three tall pine trees and was grown out of their intermingled branches—came into view. Beyond the bark-sheathed turret, Eragon spotted the seemingly random collection of clearings that marked the location of the sprawling city.

As Saphira planed over the uneven surface of the forest, Eragon quested with his mind for the consciousness of Gilderien the Wise, who, as the wielder of the White Flame of Vándil, had protected Ellesméra from the elves' enemies for over two and a half millennia. Projecting his thoughts toward the city, Eragon said in the ancient language, *Gilderien-elda, may we pass?*

A deep, calm voice sounded in Eragon's mind. *You may pass, Eragon Shadeslayer and Saphira Brightscales. So long as you keep the peace, you are welcome to stay in Ellesméra.*

Thank you, Gilderien-elda, said Saphira.

Her claws brushed the crowns of the dark-needled trees, which rose over three hundred feet above the ground, as she glided across the pinewood city and headed toward the slope of inclined land on the other side of Ellesméra. Between the latticework of branches below, Eragon caught brief glimpses of the flowing shapes of buildings made of living wood, colorful beds of blooming flowers, rippling streams, the auburn glow of a flameless lantern, and, once or twice, the pale flash of an elf's upturned face.

Tilting her wings, Saphira soared up the slope of land until she reached the Crags of Tel'naeír, which dropped over a thousand feet to the rolling forest at the base of the bare white cliff and extended for a league in either direction. Then she turned right and flew north along the ridge of stone, flapping twice to maintain her speed and altitude.

A grass-covered clearing appeared at the edge of the cliff. Set against the backdrop of the surrounding trees was a modest, single-story house grown out of four different pines. A chuckling, gurgling stream wandered out of the mossy forest and passed underneath the roots of one of the pines before disappearing into Du Weldenvarden once again. And curled up next to the house, there lay the golden dragon Glaedr, massive, glittering, his ivory teeth as thick around as Eragon's chest, his claws like scythes, his folded wings soft as suede, his muscled tail nearly as long as all of Saphira, and the striations of his one visible eye sparkling like the rays within a star sapphire. The stump of his missing foreleg was concealed on the other side of his body. A small round table and two chairs had been placed in front of Glaedr. Oromis sat in the chair closest to him, the elf's silver hair gleaming like metal in the sunlight.

Eragon leaned forward in his saddle as Saphira reared upright, slowing herself. She descended with a jolt upon the sward of green grass and ran forward several steps, raking her wings backward before she came to a halt.

His fingers clumsy from exhaustion, Eragon loosened the slip-knots that bound the straps around his legs and then attempted to climb down Saphira's right front leg. As he lowered himself, his knees buckled and he fell. He raised his hands to protect his face and landed upon all fours, scraping his shin on a rock hidden within the grass. He grunted with pain and, feeling as stiff as an old man, started to push himself onto his feet.

A hand entered his field of vision.

Eragon looked up and saw Oromis standing over him, a faint smile upon his timeless face. In the ancient language, Oromis said,

"Welcome back to Ellesméra, Eragon-finiarel. And you as well, Saphira Brightscales, welcome. Welcome, both of you."

Eragon took his hand, and Oromis pulled him upright without apparent effort. At first Eragon was unable to find his tongue, for he had barely spoken aloud since they had left Farthen Dûr and because fatigue blurred his mind. He touched the first two fingers of his right hand to his lips and, also in the ancient language, said, "May good fortune rule over you, Oromis-elda," and then he twisted his hand over his sternum in the gesture of courtesy and respect the elves used.

"May the stars watch over you, Eragon," replied Oromis.

Then Eragon repeated the ceremony with Glaedr. As always, the touch of the dragon's sanguine consciousness awed and humbled Eragon.

Saphira did not greet either Oromis or Glaedr; she remained where she was, her neck drooping until her nose brushed the ground and her shoulders and haunches trembling as if with cold. Dry yellow foam encrusted the corners of her open mouth. Her barbed tongue hung limp from between her fangs.

By way of explanation, Eragon said, "We ran into a headwind the day after we left Farthen Dûr, and . . ." He fell silent as Glaedr lifted his giant head and swung it across the clearing until he was looking down upon Saphira, who made no attempt to acknowledge his presence. Then Glaedr breathed out upon her, fingers of flame burning within the pits of his nostrils. A sense of relief washed over Eragon as he felt energy pour into Saphira, stilling her tremors and strengthening her limbs.

The flames in Glaedr's nostrils vanished with a wisp of smoke. *I went hunting this morning,* he said, his mental voice resonating throughout Eragon's being. *You will find what is left of my kills by the tree with the white branch at the far end of the field. Eat what you want.*

Silent gratitude emanated from Saphira. Dragging her limp tail across the grass, she crawled over to the tree Glaedr had indicated and then settled down and began to tear at the carcass of a deer.

"Come," said Oromis, and gestured toward the table and chairs. On the table was a tray with bowls of fruit and nuts, half a round of cheese, a loaf of bread, a decanter of wine, and two crystal goblets. As Eragon sat, Oromis indicated the decanter and asked, "Would you care for a drink to wash the dust from your throat?"

"Yes, please," said Eragon.

With an elegant motion, Oromis unstoppered the decanter and filled both goblets. He handed one to Eragon and then settled back into his chair, arranging his white tunic with long, smooth fingers.

Eragon sipped the wine. It was mellow and tasted of cherries and plums. "Master, I—"

An upraised finger from Oromis stopped him. "Unless it is unbearably urgent, I would wait until Saphira joins us before we discuss what has brought you here. Are you agreed?"

After a moment's hesitation, Eragon nodded and concentrated upon eating, savoring the flavor of the fresh fruit. Oromis seemed content to sit beside him in silence, drinking his wine and gazing out over the edge of the Crags of Tel'naeír. Behind him, Glaedr watched over the proceedings like a living statue of gold.

The better part of an hour passed before Saphira rose from her meal, crawled over to the stream, and lapped the water for another ten minutes. Drops of water still clung to her jaws when she turned away from the stream and, with a sigh, sprawled next to Eragon, her eyes heavy-lidded. She yawned, her teeth flashing, then exchanged salutations with Oromis and Glaedr. *Talk as you want,* she said. *However, do not expect me to say much. I may fall asleep at any moment.*

If you do, we shall wait for you to wake before we continue, said Glaedr.

That is most . . . kind, replied Saphira, and her eyelids drifted even lower.

"More wine?" Oromis asked, and lifted the decanter an inch off the table. When Eragon shook his head, Oromis replaced the decanter, then pressed the tips of his fingers together, his round fingernails like polished opals. He said, "You do not need to tell me what has befallen you these past weeks, Eragon. Since Islanzadí left the forest, Arya has kept her informed of the news of the land, and every three days, Islanzadí sends a runner from our army back to Du Weldenvarden. Thus, I know of your duel with Murtagh and Thorn on the Burning Plains. I know of your trip to Helgrind and how you punished the butcher from your village. And I know you attended the dwarves' clanmeet in Farthen Dûr and the outcome thereof. Whatever you wish to say, then, you may say without fear of having to educate me about your recent doings."

Eragon rolled a plump blueberry in the palm of his hand. "Do you know of Elva and what happened when I tried to free her of my curse?"

"Yes, even that. You may not have succeeded in removing the whole of the spell from her, but you paid your debt to the child, and that is what a Dragon Rider is supposed to do: fulfill his obligations, no matter how small or difficult they be."

"She still feels the pain of those around her."

"But now it is by her own choice," said Oromis. "No longer does your magic force it upon her. . . . You did not come here to seek my opinion concerning Elva. What is it that weighs upon your heart, Eragon? Ask what you will, and I promise I shall answer all of your questions to the best of my knowledge."

"What," said Eragon, "if I don't know the right questions to ask?"

A twinkle appeared in Oromis's gray eyes. "Ah, you begin to think like an elf. You must trust us as your mentors to teach you and Saphira those things of which you are ignorant. And you must also trust us to decide when it is appropriate to broach those subjects, for there are many elements of your training that should not be spoken of out of turn."

Eragon placed the blueberry in the precise center of the tray, then in a quiet but firm voice said, "It seems as if there is much you have not spoken of."

For a moment, the only sounds were the rustle of branches and the burble of the stream and the chatter of distant squirrels.

601

If you have a quarrel with us, Eragon, said Glaedr, *then give voice to it and do not gnaw on your anger like a dry old bone.*

Saphira shifted her position, and Eragon imagined he heard a growl from her. He glanced at her, and then, fighting to control the emotions coursing through him, he asked, "When I was last here, did you know who my father was?"

Oromis nodded once. "We did."

"And did you know that Murtagh was my brother?"

Oromis nodded once more. "We did, but—"

"Then why didn't you tell me!" exclaimed Eragon, and jumped to his feet, knocking over his chair. He pounded a fist against his hip, strode several feet away, and stared at the shadows within the tangled forest. Whirling around, Eragon's anger swelled as he saw that Oromis appeared as calm as before. "Were you ever going to tell me? Did you keep the truth about my family a secret because you were afraid it would distract me from my training? Or was it that you were afraid I would become like my father?" A worse thought occurred to Eragon. "Or did you not even consider it important enough to mention? And what of Brom? Did he know? Did he choose Carvahall to hide in because of me, because I was the son of his enemy? You can't expect me to believe it was coincidence he and I happened to be living only a few miles apart and that Arya just *happened* to send Saphira's egg to me in the Spine."

"What Arya did was an accident," asserted Oromis. "She had no knowledge of you then."

Eragon gripped the pommel of his dwarf sword, every muscle in his body as hard as iron. "When Brom first saw Saphira, I remember he said something to himself about being unsure whether 'this' was a farce or a tragedy. At the time, I thought he was referring to the fact that a common farmer like myself had become the first new Rider in over a hundred years. But that's not what he meant, was it? He was wondering whether it was a farce or a tragedy that Morzan's youngest son should be the one to take up the Riders' mantle!

"Is that why you and Brom trained me, to be nothing more than a weapon against Galbatorix so that I may atone for the villainy of my father? Is that all I am to you, a balancing of the scales?" Before Oromis could respond, Eragon swore and said, "My whole life has been a lie! Since the moment I was born, no one but Saphira has wanted me: not my mother, not Garrow, not Aunt Marian, not even Brom. Brom showed interest in me only because of Morzan and Saphira. I have always been an inconvenience. Whatever you think of me, though, I am *not* my father, nor my brother, and I refuse to follow in their footsteps." Placing his hands on the edge of the table, Eragon leaned forward. "I'm not about to betray the elves or the dwarves or the Varden to Galbatorix, if that's what you are worried about. I will do what I must, but from now on, you have neither my loyalty nor my trust. I will not—"

The ground and the air shook as Glaedr growled, his upper lip pulling back to reveal the full length of his fangs. *You have more reason to trust us than anyone else, hatchling,* he said, his voice thundering in Eragon's mind. *If not for our efforts, you would be long dead.*

Then, to Eragon's surprise, Saphira said to Oromis and Glaedr, *Tell him,* and it alarmed him to feel the distress in her thoughts.

Saphira? he asked, puzzled. *Tell me what?*

She ignored him. *This arguing is without cause. Do not prolong Eragon's discomfort anymore.*

One of Oromis's slanted eyebrows rose. "You know?"

I know.

"You know what?" Eragon bellowed, on the verge of tearing his sword from its sheath and threatening all of them until they explained themselves.

With one slim finger, Oromis pointed toward the fallen chair. "Sit." When Eragon remained standing, too angry and full of resentment to obey, Oromis sighed. "I understand this is difficult for you, Eragon, but if you insist upon asking questions and then refuse to listen to the answers, frustration will be your only reward. Now, please sit, so we can talk about this in a civilized manner."

Glaring, Eragon righted the chair and dropped into it. "Why?" he asked. "Why didn't you tell me that my father was Morzan, the first of the Forsworn?"

"In the first place," said Oromis, "we shall be fortunate if you are anything like your father, which, indeed, I believe you are. And, as I was about to say before you interrupted me, Murtagh is not your brother, but rather your half brother."

The world seemed to tilt around Eragon; the sensation of vertigo was so intense, he had to grab the edge of the table to steady himself. "My half brother . . . But then, who . . . ?"

Oromis plucked a blackberry from a bowl, contemplated it for a moment, and then ate it. "Glaedr and I did not wish to keep this a secret from you, but we had no choice. We both promised, with the most binding of oaths, that we would never reveal to you the identity of your father or of your half brother, nor discuss your lineage, unless you had discovered the truth on your own or unless the identity of your relatives had placed you in danger. What transpired between you and Murtagh during the Battle of the Burning Plains satisfies enough of those requirements that we can now speak freely on this topic."

Trembling with barely restrained emotion, Eragon said, "Oromis-elda, if Murtagh is my half brother, then who is my father?"

Look into your heart, Eragon, said Glaedr. *You already know who he is, and you have known for a long time.*

Eragon shook his head. "I don't know! I don't know! Please . . ."

A gout of smoke and flame jetted from Glaedr's nostrils as he snorted. *Is it not obvious? Your father is Brom.*

TWO LOVERS DOOMED

Eragon gaped at the gold dragon.

"But how?" he exclaimed. Before either Glaedr or Oromis could respond, Eragon whirled toward Saphira and, with both his mind and his voice, he said, "You knew? You knew, and yet you let me believe Morzan was my father this whole time, even though it . . . even though I—I . . ." His chest heaving, Eragon stuttered and trailed off, unable to speak coherently. Unbidden, memories of Brom flooded through him, washing away his other thoughts. He reconsidered the meaning of Brom's every word and expression, and in that instant, a sense of rightness settled over Eragon. He still wanted explanations, but he did not need them in order to determine the veracity of Glaedr's claim, for in his bones, Eragon felt the truth of what Glaedr had said.

Eragon started as Oromis touched him on the shoulder. "Eragon, you need to calm yourself," said the elf in a soothing tone. "Remember the techniques I taught you for meditating. Control your breathing, and concentrate upon letting the tension drain out of your limbs into the ground beneath you. . . . Yes, like that. Now again, and breathe deeply."

Eragon's hands grew still and his heartbeat slowed as he followed Oromis's instructions. Once his thoughts had cleared, he looked at Saphira again and in a soft voice said, "You knew?"

Saphira lifted her head from the ground. *Oh, Eragon, I wanted to tell you. It pained me to see how Murtagh's words tormented you and yet to be unable to help you. I tried to help—I tried so many times—but like Oromis and Glaedr, I too swore in the ancient language to keep Brom's identity a secret from you, and I could not break my oath.*

"Wh-when did he tell you?" Eragon asked, so agitated that he continued speaking out loud.

The day after the Urgals attacked us outside of Teirm, while you were still unconscious.

"Was that also when he told you how to contact the Varden in Gil'ead?"

Yes. Before I knew what Brom wished to say, he had me swear to never speak of this with you unless you found out on your own. To my regret, I agreed.

"Is there anything else he told you?" demanded Eragon, his anger rising again. "Any other secrets I ought to know, like that Murtagh isn't my only sibling, or perhaps how to defeat Galbatorix?"

During the two days Brom and I spent hunting the Urgals, Brom re-counted the details of his life to me so that if he died, and if ever you learned of your relation to him, his son could know what kind of a man he was and why he had acted as he did. Also, Brom gave me a gift for you.

A gift?

A memory of him speaking to you as your father and not as Brom the storyteller.

"Before Saphira shares this memory with you, however," said Oromis, and Eragon realized she had allowed the elf to hear her words, "it would be best, I think, if you knew how this came to pass. Will you listen to me for a while, Eragon?"

Eragon hesitated, unsure of what he wanted, then nodded.

Lifting his crystal goblet, Oromis drank of his wine, then returned the goblet to the table and said: "As you know, both Brom and Morzan were my apprentices. Brom, who was the younger by three years, held Morzan in such high esteem, he allowed Morzan to be-little him, order him about, and otherwise treat him most shame-fully."

In a raspy voice, Eragon said, "It's hard to imagine Brom letting anyone order him about."

Oromis inclined his head in a quick, birdlike dip. "And yet, so it was. Brom loved Morzan as a brother, despite his behavior. It was only once Morzan betrayed the Riders to Galbatorix and the Forsworn killed Saphira, Brom's dragon, that Brom realized the true nature of Morzan's character. As strong as Brom's affection for Morzan had been, it was like a candle before an inferno compared with the hatred that replaced it. Brom swore to thwart Morzan however and wherever he could, to undo his accomplishments and reduce his ambitions to bitter regrets. I cautioned Brom against a path so full of hate and violence, but he was mad with grief from the death of Saphira, and he would not listen to me.

"In the decades that followed, Brom's hatred never weakened, nor did he falter in his efforts to depose Galbatorix, kill the Forsworn, and, above all else, to repay Morzan the hurts he had suffered. Brom was persistence embodied, his name a nightmare for the Forsworn and a beacon of hope for those who still had the spirit to resist the Empire." Oromis looked toward the white line of the horizon and took another draught of his wine. "I am rather proud of what he achieved on his own and without the aid of his dragon. It is always heartening for a teacher to see one of his students excel, however it might be. . . . But I digress. It so happened, then, that some twenty years ago, the Varden began to receive reports from their spies within the Empire about the activities of a mysterious woman known only as the Black Hand."

"My mother," said Eragon.

"Your mother and Murtagh's," said Oromis. "At first the Varden knew nothing about her, save that she was extremely dangerous and that she was loyal to the Empire. In time, and after a great deal of bloodshed, it became apparent that she served Morzan, and Morzan alone, and that he had come to depend upon her to carry out his will throughout the Empire. Upon learning of this, Brom set out to kill the Black Hand and so to strike at Morzan. Since the Varden could not predict where your mother might appear next, Brom traveled to Morzan's castle and spied upon it until he was able to devise a means of infiltrating the hold."

"Where was Morzan's castle?"

"*Is*, not *was*; the castle still stands. Galbatorix uses it for himself now. It is situated among the foothills of the Spine, near the northwestern shore of Leona Lake, hidden well away from the rest of the land."

Eragon said, "Jeod told me that Brom snuck into the castle by pretending to be one of the servants."

"He did, and it was no easy task. Morzan had impregnated his fortress with hundreds of spells designed to protect him from his enemies. He also forced everyone who served him to swear oaths of fealty, and often with their true names. However, after much experimentation, Brom managed to find a flaw in Morzan's wards that allowed him to procure a position as a gardener on his estate, and it was in that guise he first met your mother."

Glancing down at his hands, Eragon said, "And then he seduced her to hurt Morzan, I suppose."

"Not at all," replied Oromis. "That may have been his intention to begin with, but then something happened neither he nor your mother anticipated: they fell in love. Whatever affection your mother once had for Morzan had vanished by then, expunged by his cruel treatment of her and their newborn child, Murtagh. I do not know the exact sequence of events, but at some point Brom revealed his true identity to your mother. Instead of betraying him, she began to supply the Varden with information about Galbatorix, Morzan, and the rest of the Empire."

"But," said Eragon, "didn't Morzan have her swear oaths of fealty to him in the ancient language? How could she turn against him?"

A smile appeared on Oromis's thin lips. "She could because Morzan allowed her somewhat more freedom than his other servants so that she could use her own ingenuity and initiative while carrying out his orders. In his arrogance, Morzan believed that her love for him would ensure her loyalty better than any oath. Also, she was not the same woman who had bound herself to Morzan; becoming a mother and meeting Brom altered her character to such a degree that her true name changed, which released her from her previous commitments. If Morzan had been more careful—if, for example, he had cast a spell that would alert him if ever she failed to abide by her promises—he would have known the moment he lost control over her. But that was always a shortcoming of Morzan's; he would devise a cunning spell, but then it would fail because, in his impatience, he overlooked some crucial detail."

Eragon frowned. "Why didn't my mother leave Morzan once she had the chance?"

"After all she had done in Morzan's name, she felt it was her duty to help the Varden. But more importantly, she could not bring herself to abandon Murtagh to his father."

"Couldn't she have taken him with her?"

"If it had been within her power, I am sure she would have. Morzan realized that the child gave him a vast amount of control over your mother. He forced her to surrender Murtagh to a wet nurse and only allowed her to visit him at infrequent intervals. What Morzan did not know is that, during those intervals, she also visited Brom."

Oromis turned to watch a pair of swallows cavorting in the blue sky. In profile, his delicate, slanted features reminded Eragon of a hawk or a sleek cat. Still gazing at the swallows, Oromis said, "Not even your mother could anticipate where Morzan would send her next, nor when she could return to his castle. Therefore, Brom had to remain on Morzan's estate for extended lengths of time if he wished to see her. For nigh on three years, Brom served as one of Morzan's gardeners. Now and then, he would slip away to send a message to the Varden or to communicate with his spies throughout the Empire, but other than that, he did not leave the castle grounds."

"Three years! Wasn't he afraid that Morzan might see him and recognize him?"

Oromis lowered his gaze from the heavens, returning it to Eragon. "Brom was most adept at disguising himself, and it had been many years since he and Morzan had last stood face to face."

"Ah." Eragon twisted his goblet between his fingers, studying how the light refracted through the crystal. "Then what happened?"

"Then," said Oromis, "one of Brom's agents in Teirm made contact with a young scholar by the name of Jeod who wished to join the Varden and who claimed to have discovered evidence of a hitherto-secret tunnel that led into the elf-built portion of the castle in Urû'baen. Brom rightly felt that Jeod's discovery was too important to ignore, so he packed his bags, made his excuses to his fellow servants, and then departed for Teirm with all possible haste."

"What of my mother?"

"She had left a month before on another of Morzan's missions."

Struggling to weld a cohesive whole out of the fragmented accounts he had heard from various people, Eragon said, "So then . . . Brom met with Jeod, and once he was convinced the tunnel was real, he arranged for one of the Varden to attempt to steal the three dragon eggs Galbatorix was holding in Urû'baen."

Oromis's face darkened. "Unfortunately, for reasons that have never become entirely clear, the man they selected for the task, a certain Hefring of Furnost, succeeded in filching only one egg—Saphira's—from Galbatorix's treasury, and once he had possession of it, he fled from both the Varden and Galbatorix's servants. Because of his betrayal, Brom had to spend the next seven months chasing Hefring back and forth across the land in a desperate attempt to recapture Saphira."

"And during that time, my mother traveled in secret to Carvahall, where she gave birth to me five months later?"

Oromis nodded. "You were conceived just before your mother set forth upon her last mission. As a result, Brom knew nothing of her condition while he was pursuing Hefring and Saphira's egg. . . . When Brom and Morzan finally confronted each other in Gil'ead, Morzan asked Brom whether he had been responsible for the disappearance of his Black Hand. It is understandable that Morzan would suspect Brom's involvement, since Brom had arranged the deaths of several of the Forsworn. Brom, of course, immediately concluded that something terrible had befallen your mother. He later told me it was that belief which gave him the strength and fortitude he needed to kill Morzan and his dragon. Once they were dead, Brom took Saphira's egg from Morzan's corpse—for Morzan had already located Hefring and seized the egg from him—and then Brom left the city, pausing only long enough to hide Saphira where he knew the Varden would eventually find her."

"So that's why Jeod thought Brom died in Gil'ead," said Eragon.

Again Oromis nodded. "Stricken by fear, Brom dared not wait for his companions. Even if your mother was alive and well, Brom worried that Galbatorix would decide to make Selena his own Black Hand and that she would never again have the chance to escape her service to the Empire."

Eragon felt tears wet his eyes. *How Brom must have loved her, to leave everyone behind as soon as he knew she was in danger.*

"From Gil'ead, Brom rode straight to Morzan's estate, stopping only to sleep. For all his speed, however, he was still too slow. When he reached the castle, he discovered that your mother had returned a fortnight prior, sick and weary from her mysterious journey. Morzan's healers tried to save her, but in spite of their efforts, she had passed into the void just hours before Brom arrived at the castle."

"He never saw her again?" Eragon asked, his throat tightening.

"Never again." Oromis paused, and his expression softened. "Losing her was, I think, almost as difficult for Brom as losing his dragon, and it quenched much of the fire within his soul. He did not give up, though, nor did he go mad as he had for a time when the Forsworn slew Saphira's namesake. Instead, he decided to discover the reason for your mother's death and to punish those who were responsible if he could. He questioned Morzan's healers and forced them to describe your mother's ailments. From what they said, and also from gossip he heard among the servants on the estate, Brom guessed the truth about your mother's pregnancy. Possessed of that hope, he rode to the one place he knew to look: your mother's home in Carvahall. And there he found you in the care of your aunt and uncle.

"Brom did not stay in Carvahall, however. As soon as he assured himself that no one in Carvahall knew your mother had been the Black Hand and that you were in no imminent danger, Brom returned in secret to Farthen Dûr, where he revealed himself to Deynor, who was the leader of the Varden at that time. Deynor was astounded to see him, for until that moment, everyone had believed that Brom had perished in Gil'ead. Brom convinced Deynor to keep his presence a secret from all but a select few, and then—"

Eragon raised a finger. "But why? Why pretend to be dead?"

"Brom wanted to live long enough to help instruct the new Rider, and he knew the only way he could avoid being assassinated in re-taliation for killing Morzan would be if Galbatorix believed he was already dead and buried. Also, Brom hoped to avoid attracting un-warranted attention to Carvahall. He intended to settle there in or-der to be close to you, as indeed he did, but he was determined that the Empire should not learn of your existence as a result.

"While in Farthen Dûr, Brom helped the Varden negotiate the agreement with Queen Islanzadí over how the elves and the hu-mans would share custody of the egg and how the new Rider would be trained, if and when the egg should hatch. Then Brom accompa-nied Arya as she carried the egg from Farthen Dûr to Ellesméra. When he arrived, he told Glaedr and me what I have now told you, so that the truth about your parentage would not be forgotten if he should die. That was the last time I ever saw him. From here, Brom returned to Carvahall, where he introduced himself as a bard and storyteller. What happened thereafter, you know better than I."

Oromis fell silent, and for a time, no one spoke.

Staring at the ground, Eragon reviewed everything Oromis had told him and tried to sort out his feelings. At last he said, "And Brom really is my father, not Morzan? I mean, if my mother was Morzan's consort, then . . ." He trailed off, too embarrassed to continue.

"You are your father's son," Oromis said, "and your father is Brom. Of that there is no doubt."

"No doubt whatsoever?"

Oromis shook his head. "None."

A sense of giddiness gripped Eragon, and he realized he had been holding his breath. Exhaling, he said, "I think I understand why"—he paused to fill his lungs—"why Brom didn't say anything about this before I found Saphira's egg, but why didn't he tell me afterward? And why did he swear you and Saphira to such secrecy? . . . Didn't he want to claim me as his son? Was he ashamed of me?"

"I cannot pretend to know the reasons for everything Brom did, Eragon. However, of this much I am confident: Brom wanted nothing more than to name you his son and to raise you, but he dared not reveal that you were related, lest the Empire should find out and try to hurt him through you. His prudence was warranted too. Look how Galbatorix strove to capture your cousin so that he could use Roran to force you to surrender."

"Brom could have told my uncle," Eragon protested. "Garrow wouldn't have betrayed Brom to the Empire."

"Think, Eragon. If you had been living with Brom, and if word of Brom's survival had reached the ears of Galbatorix's spies, you both would have had to flee Carvahall for fear of your lives. By keeping the truth hidden from you, Brom hoped to protect you from those dangers."

"He didn't succeed. We had to flee Carvahall anyway."

"Yes," said Oromis. "Brom's mistake, as it were, although I judge it has yielded more good than ill, was that he could not bear to separate himself entirely from you. If he had had the strength to refrain from returning to Carvahall, you never would have found Saphira's egg, the Ra'zac would not have killed your uncle, and many things that were not, would have been; and many things that are, would not be. He could not cut you out of his heart, though."

Eragon clenched his jaw as a tremor coursed through him. "And after he learned Saphira had hatched for me?"

Oromis hesitated, and his calm expression became somewhat troubled. "I am not sure, Eragon. It may have been that Brom was still trying to protect you from his enemies, and he did not tell you for the same reason he did not bring you to the Varden straightaway: because it would have been more than you were ready for. Perhaps he was planning to tell you just before you went to the Varden. If I had to guess, though, I would guess that Brom held his tongue not because he was ashamed of you but because he had become accustomed to living with his secrets and was loath to part with them. And because—and this is no more than speculation—because he was uncertain how you might react to his revelation. By your own account, you were not that well acquainted with Brom before you left Carvahall with him. It is quite possible he was afraid that you might hate him if he told you he was your father."

"Hate him?" exclaimed Eragon. "I wouldn't have hated him. Although . . . I might not have believed him."

"And would you have trusted him after such a revelation?"

Eragon bit the inside of his cheek. *No, I wouldn't have.*

Continuing, Oromis said, "Brom did the best he could in what were incredibly trying circumstances. Before all else, it was his responsibility to keep the two of you alive and to teach and advise you, Eragon, so that you would not use your power for selfish means, as Galbatorix has done. In that, Brom acquitted himself with distinction. He may not have been the father you wished him to be, but he gave you as great an inheritance as any son has ever had."

"It was no more than he would have done for whoever became the new Rider."

"That does not diminish its value," Oromis pointed out. "But you are mistaken; Brom did more for you than he would have for anyone else. You need only think of how he sacrificed himself to save your life to know the truth of that."

With the nail of his right index finger, Eragon picked at the edge of the table, following a faint ridge formed by one of the rings in the wood. "And it really was an accident that Arya sent Saphira to me?"

"It was," Oromis confirmed. "But it was not entirely a coincidence. Instead of transporting the egg to the father, Arya made it appear before the son."

"How could that be if she had no knowledge of me?"

Oromis's thin shoulders rose and fell. "Despite thousands of years of study, we still cannot predict or explain all of the effects of magic."

Eragon continued to finger the small ridge in the edge of the table. *I have a father,* he thought. *I watched him die, and I had no idea who he was to me. . . .* "My parents," he said, "were they ever married?"

"I know why you ask, Eragon, and I do not know if my answer will satisfy you. Marriage is not an elvish custom, and the subtleties of it often escape me. No one joined Brom's and Selena's hands in marriage, but I know that they considered themselves to be husband and wife. If you are wise, you will not worry that others of your race may call you a bastard but rather be content to know that you are your parents' child and that they both gave their lives that you might live."

It surprised Eragon how calm he felt. His entire life he had speculated about the identity of his father. When Murtagh had claimed it was Morzan, the revelation had shocked Eragon as deeply as had the death of Garrow. Glaedr's counterclaim that Eragon's father was Brom had also shocked him, but the shock did not seem to have lasted, perhaps because, this time, the news was not as upsetting. Calm as he was, Eragon thought that it might be many years before he was certain of his feelings toward either of his parents. *My father was a Rider and my mother was Morzan's consort and Black Hand.*

"Could I tell Nasuada?" he asked.

Oromis spread his hands. "Tell whomever you wish; the secret is now yours to do with as you please. I doubt you would be in any more danger if the whole world knew you were Brom's heir."

"Murtagh," Eragon said. "He believes we are full brothers. He told me so in the ancient language."

"And I am sure Galbatorix does as well. It was the Twins who figured out that Murtagh's mother and your mother were one and the same person, and this they conveyed to the king. But they could not have informed him of Brom's involvement, for there was no one among the Varden who was privy to that information."

Eragon glanced up as a pair of swallows swooped by overhead, and he allowed himself a wry half smile.

"Why do you smile?" Oromis asked.

"I'm not sure you would understand."

The elf folded his hands in his lap. "I might not; that is true. But then, you cannot know for certain unless you try to explain."

It took Eragon a while to find the words he needed. "When I was younger, before . . . all of *this*"—he gestured at Saphira and Oromis and Glaedr and the world in general—"I used to amuse myself by imagining that, because of her great wit and beauty, my mother had been taken in among the courts of Galbatorix's nobles. I imagined that she had traveled from city to city and supped with the earls and ladies in their halls and that . . . well, she had fallen desperately in love with a rich and powerful man, but for some reason, she was forced to hide me from him, so she gave me to Garrow and Marian for safekeeping, and one day she would return and tell me who I was and that she had never wanted to leave me behind."

"That is not so different from what happened," said Oromis.

"No, it isn't, but . . . I imagined that my mother and my father were people of importance and I was someone of importance as well. Fate gave me what I wanted, but the truth of it is not as grand or as happy as I thought it would be. . . . I was smiling at my own ignorance, I suppose, and also at the unlikeliness of everything that has befallen me."

A light breeze swept across the clearing, feathering the grass at their feet and stirring the branches of the forest around them.

Eragon watched the fluttering of the grass for a few moments, then slowly asked, "Was my mother a good person?"

"I could not say, Eragon. The events of her life were complicated. It would be foolish and arrogant of me to presume to pass judgment on one I know so little of."

"But I need to know!" Eragon clasped his hands, pressing his fingers between the calluses on his knuckles. "When I asked Brom if he had known her, he said that she was proud and dignified and that she always helped the poor and those less fortunate than her. How could she, though? How could she be that person and also the Black Hand? Jeod told me stories about some of the things— horrible, terrible things—she did while she was in Morzan's service. . . . Was she evil, then? Did she not care if Galbatorix ruled or not? Why did she go with Morzan in the first place?"

Oromis paused. "Love can be a terrible curse, Eragon. It can make you overlook even the largest flaws in a person's behavior. I doubt that your mother was fully aware of Morzan's true nature when she left Carvahall with him, and once she had, he would not have allowed her to disobey his wishes. She became his slave in all but name, and it was only by changing her very identity that she was able to escape his control."

"But Jeod said that she enjoyed what she did as the Black Hand."

An expression of faint disdain altered Oromis's features. "Accounts of past atrocities are often exaggerated and distorted. That much you should keep in mind. No one but your mother knows exactly what she did, nor why, nor how she felt about it, and she is not still among the living to explain herself."

"Whom should I believe, though?" pleaded Eragon. "Brom or Jeod?"

"When you asked Brom about your mother, he told you what he thought were her most important qualities. My advice would be to trust in his knowledge of her. If that does not quell your doubts, remember that whatever crimes she may have committed while acting as the Hand of Morzan, ultimately your mother sided with the Varden and went to extraordinary lengths to protect you. Knowing that, you should not torment yourself further about the nature of her character."

Propelled by the breeze, a spider hanging from a gossamer strand of silk drifted past Eragon, rising and falling on the invisible eddies of air. When the spider had floated out of view, Eragon said, "The first time we visited Tronjheim, the fortuneteller Angela told me that it was Brom's wyrd to fail at everything he attempted, except for killing Morzan."

Oromis inclined his head. "One might think that. Another might conclude that Brom achieved many great and difficult things. It depends upon how you choose to view the world. The words of fortunetellers are rarely easy to decipher. It has been my experience that their predictions are never conducive to peace of mind. If you wish to be happy, Eragon, think not of what is to come nor of that which you have no control over but rather of the now and of that which you are able to change."

A thought occurred to Eragon then. "Blagden," he said, referring to the white raven who was Queen Islanzadí's companion. "He knows about Brom as well, doesn't he?"

One of Oromis's sharp eyebrows lifted. "Does he? I never spoke of it to him. He is a fickle creature and not to be relied upon."

"The day Saphira and I left for the Burning Plains, he recited a riddle to me. . . . I can't remember every line, but it was something about one of two being one, while one might be two. I think he might have been hinting that Murtagh and I only share a single parent."

"It is not impossible," said Oromis. "Blagden was here in Ellesméra when Brom told me about you. I would not be surprised if that sharp-beaked thief happened to be perched in a nearby tree during our conversation. Eavesdropping is an unfortunate habit of his. It might also be that his riddle was the result of one of his sporadic fits of foresight."

A moment later, Glaedr stirred, and Oromis turned and glanced back at the golden dragon. The elf rose from his chair with a graceful motion, saying, "Fruit, nuts, and bread are fine fare, but after your trip, you should have something more substantial to fill your belly. I have a soup that needs tending simmering in my hut, but please, do not bestir yourself. I will bring it to you when it is ready." His footsteps soft upon the grass, Oromis walked to his bark-covered house and disappeared inside. As the carved door closed, Glaedr huffed out his breath and closed his eyes, seeming to fall asleep.

And all was silent, save the rustle of the wind-tossed branches.

INHERITANCE

E ragon remained sitting at the round table for several minutes, then he stood and walked to the edge of the Crags of Tel'naeír, where he gazed out over the rolling forest a thousand feet below. With the tip of his left boot, he pushed a pebble over the cliff and watched it bounce off the slanted face of the stone until it vanished into the depths of the canopy.

A branch cracked as Saphira approached from behind. She crouched by his side, her scales painting him with hundreds of shifting flecks of blue light, and stared in the same direction as he. *Are you angry with me?* she asked.

No, of course not. I understand that you could not break your oath in the ancient language. . . . I just wish that Brom could have told me this himself and that he hadn't felt it necessary to hide the truth from me.

She swung her head toward him. *And how do you feel, Eragon?*

You know as well as I.

A few minutes ago, I did, but not now. You have grown still, and looking into your mind is like peering into a lake so deep, I cannot see the bottom. What is in you, little one? Is it rage? Is it happiness? Or have you no emotions to give?

What is in me is acceptance, he said, and turned to face her. *I cannot change who my parents are; I reconciled myself with that after the Burning Plains. What is is, and no amount of gnashing teeth on my part will change that. I am . . . glad, I think, to consider Brom my father. But I'm not sure. . . . It's too much to grasp all at once.*

Perhaps what I have to give you will help. Would you like to see the memory Brom left for you, or would you prefer to wait?

No, no waiting, he said. *If we delay, you may never have the opportunity.*

Then close your eyes and let me show you what once was.

Eragon did as she directed, and from Saphira, there flowed a stream of sensations: sights, sounds, smells, and more, everything that she had been experiencing at the time of the memory.

Before him, Eragon beheld a glade in the forest somewhere among the foothills piled against the western side of the Spine. The grass was thick and lush, and veils of chartreuse lichen hung from the tall, drooping, moss-covered trees. Due to the rains that swept inland from the ocean, the woods were far greener and wetter than those of Palancar Valley. As seen through Saphira's eyes, the greens and reds were more subdued than they would have been to Eragon, while every hue of blue shone with additional intensity. The smell of moist soil and punky wood suffused the air.

And in the center of the glade lay a fallen tree, and upon the fallen tree sat Brom.

The hood of the old man's robe was pulled back to expose his bare head. Across his lap lay his sword. His twisted, rune-carved staff stood propped against the log. The ring Aren glittered on his right hand.

For a long while, Brom did not move, and then he squinted up at the sky, his hooked nose casting a long shadow across his face. His voice rasped, and Eragon swayed, feeling disjointed in time.

Brom said, "Ever the sun traces its path from horizon to horizon, and ever the moon follows, and ever the days roll past without care for the lives they grind away, one by one." Lowering his eyes, Brom gazed straight at Saphira and, through her, Eragon. "Try though they might, no being escapes death forever, not even the elves or the spirits. To all, there is an end. If you are watching me, Eragon, then my end has come and I am dead and you know that I am your father."

From the leather pouch by his side, Brom drew forth his pipe, filled it with cardus weed, then lit it with a soft muttering of "Brisingr." He puffed on the pipe several times to set the fire before he resumed talking. "If you do see this, Eragon, I hope that you are safe and happy and that Galbatorix is dead. However, I realize that's unlikely, if for no other reason than you are a Dragon Rider, and a Dragon Rider may never rest while there is injustice in the land."

A chuckle escaped Brom and he shook his head, his beard rippling like water. "Ah, I have not the time to say even half of what I would like; I would be twice my current age before I finished. In the pursuit of brevity, I shall assume that Saphira has already told you how your mother and I met, how Selena died, and how I came to be in Carvahall. I wish that you and I could have this talk face to face, Eragon, and perhaps we still shall and Saphira will have no need to share this memory with you, but I doubt it. The sorrows of my years press on me, Eragon, and I feel a cold creeping into my limbs the likes of which has never troubled me before. I think it is because I know it is now your turn to take up the standard. There is much I still hope to accomplish, but none of it is for myself, only for you, and you shall eclipse everything I have done. Of that, I am sure. Before my grave closes over me, though, I wanted to be able, at least this once, to call you my son. . . . My son. . . . Your whole life, Eragon, I have longed to reveal to you who I was. It has been a pleasure like no other for me to watch you growing up, but also a torture like no other because of the secret I held in my heart."

Brom laughed then, a harsh, barking sound. "Well, I didn't exactly manage to keep you safe from the Empire, now did I? If you are still wondering who was responsible for Garrow's death, you need look no further, for here he sits. It was my own foolishness. I should never have returned to Carvahall. And now look: Garrow dead, and you a Dragon Rider. I warn you, Eragon, beware of whom you fall in love with, for fate seems to have a morbid interest in our family."

Wrapping his lips around the stem of his pipe, Brom drew on the smoldering cardus weed several times, blowing the chalk-white

622

smoke off to one side. The pungent smell was heavy in Saphira's nostrils. Brom said, "I have my share of regrets, but you are not one of them, Eragon. You may occasionally behave like a moon-addled fool, such as letting these blasted Urgals escape, but you are no more of an idiot than I was at your age." He nodded. "Less of an idiot, in fact. I am proud to have you as my son, Eragon, prouder than you will ever know. I never thought that you would become a Rider as I was, nor wished that future upon you, but seeing you with Saphira, ah, it makes me feel like crowing at the sun like a rooster."

Brom drew on the pipe again. "I realize you may be angry at me for keeping this from you. I can't say I would have been happy to discover the name of my own father this way. Whether you like it or not, though, we are family, you and I. Since I could not give you the care I owed you as your father, I will give you the one thing I can instead, and that is advice. Hate me if you wish, Eragon, but heed what I have to say, for I know whereof I speak."

With his free hand, Brom grasped the sheath of his sword, the veins prominent on the back of his hand. He fixed the pipe in one corner of his mouth. "Right. Now, my advice is twofold. Whatever you do, protect those you care for. Without them, life is more miserable than you can imagine. An obvious statement, I know, but no less true because of it. There, that is the first part of my advice. As for the rest . . . If you are so fortunate as to have already killed Galbatorix—or if *anyone* has succeeded in slitting that traitor's throat—then congratulations. If *not*, then you must realize that Galbatorix is your greatest and most dangerous enemy. Until he is dead, neither you nor Saphira will ever find peace. You may run to the farthest corners of the earth, but unless you join the Empire, one day you will have to confront Galbatorix. I am sorry, Eragon, but that is the truth of it. I have fought many magicians, and several of the Forsworn, and so far, I have always defeated my opponents." The lines on Brom's forehead deepened. "Well, all but once, but that was because I was not yet fully grown. Anyway, the reason I have always emerged triumphant is that I use my brain, unlike most.

I am not a strong spellcaster, nor are you, compared with Galbatorix, but when it comes to a wizards' duel, *intelligence* is even more important than strength. The way to defeat another magician is not by battering blindly against his mind. No! In order to ensure victory, you have to figure out how your enemy interprets information and reacts to the world. Then you will know his weaknesses, and there you strike. The trick isn't inventing a spell no one else has ever thought of before; the trick is finding a spell your enemy has overlooked and using it against him. The trick isn't plowing your way through the barriers in someone's mind; the trick is slipping underneath or around the barriers. No one is omniscient, Eragon. Remember that. Galbatorix may have immense power, but he cannot anticipate every possibility. Whatever you do, you must remain nimble in your thinking. Do not become so attached to any one belief that you cannot see past it to another possibility. Galbatorix is mad and therefore unpredictable, but he also has gaps in his reasoning that an ordinary person would not. If you can find those, Eragon, then perhaps you and Saphira can defeat him."

624

Brom lowered his pipe, his face grave. "I hope you do. My greatest desire, Eragon, is that you and Saphira will live long and fruitful lives, free from fear of Galbatorix and the Empire. I wish that I could protect you from all of the dangers that threaten you, but alas, that is not within my ability. All I can do is give you my advice and teach you what I can *now* while I am still here. . . . My son. Whatever happens to you, know that I love you, and so did your mother. May the stars watch over you, Eragon Bromsson."

As Brom's final words echoed in Eragon's mind, the memory faded away, leaving behind empty darkness. Eragon opened his eyes and was embarrassed to find tears running down his cheeks. He uttered a choked laugh and wiped his eyes on the edge of his tunic. *Brom really was afraid that I would hate him,* he said, and sniffed.

Are you going to be all right? Saphira asked.

Yes, said Eragon, and lifted his head. *I think I will, actually. I don't like some of the things Brom did, but I am proud to call him my father and* to carry his name. He was a great man. . . . It bothers me, though, that I never had the opportunity to talk to either of my parents as my parents.

At least you were able to spend time with Brom. I am not so fortunate; both my sire and my mother died long before I hatched. The closest I can come to meeting them are a few hazy memories from Glaedr.

Eragon put a hand on her neck, and they comforted each other as best they could while they stood upon the edge of the Crags of Tel'naeír and gazed out over the forest of the elves.

Not long afterward, Oromis emerged from his hut, carrying two bowls of soup, and Eragon and Saphira turned away from the crags and slowly walked back to the small table in front of Glaedr's immense bulk.

SOULS OF STONE

As Eragon pushed away his empty bowl, Oromis said, "Would you like to see a fairth of your mother, Eragon?"

Eragon froze for a moment, astonished. "Yes, please."

From within the folds of his white tunic, Oromis withdrew a shingle of thin gray slate, which he passed to Eragon.

The stone was cool and smooth between Eragon's fingers. On the other side of it, he knew he would find a perfect likeness of his mother, painted by means of a spell with pigments an elf had set within the slate many years ago. A flutter of uneasiness ran through Eragon. He had always wanted to see his mother, but now that the opportunity was before him, he was afraid that the reality might disappoint him.

With an effort, he turned the slate over and beheld an image— clear as a vision seen through a window—of a garden of red and white roses lit by the pale rays of dawn. A gravel path ran through the beds of roses. And in the middle of the path was a woman, kneeling, cupping a white rose between her hands and smelling the flower, her eyes closed and a faint smile upon her lips. She was very beautiful, Eragon thought. Her expression was soft and tender, yet she wore clothes of padded leather, with blackened bracers upon her forearms and greaves upon her shins and a sword and dagger hanging from her waist. In the shape of her face, Eragon could detect a hint of his own features, as well as a certain resemblance to Garrow, her brother.

The image fascinated Eragon. He pressed his hand against the surface of the fairth, wishing that he could reach into it and touch her on the arm.

Mother.

Oromis said, "Brom gave me the fairth for safekeeping before he left for Carvahall, and now I give it to you."

Without looking up, Eragon asked, "Would you keep it safe for me as well? It might get broken during our traveling and fighting."

The pause that followed caught Eragon's attention. He wrenched his gaze away from his mother to see that Oromis appeared melancholy and preoccupied. "No, Eragon, I cannot. You will have to make other arrangements for the preservation of the fairth."

Why? Eragon wanted to ask, but the sorrow in Oromis's eyes dissuaded him.

Then Oromis said, "Your time here is limited, and we still have many matters to discuss. Shall I guess which subject you would like to address next, or will you tell me?"

With great reluctance, Eragon placed the fairth on the table and rotated it so that the image was upside down. "The two times we have fought Murtagh and Thorn, Murtagh has been more powerful than any human ought to be. On the Burning Plains, he defeated Saphira and me because we did not realize how strong he was. If not for his change of heart, we would be prisoners in Urû'baen right now. You once mentioned that you know how Galbatorix has become so powerful. Will you tell us now, Master? For our own safety, we need to know."

"It is not my place to tell you this," said Oromis.

"Then whose is it?" demanded Eragon. "You can't—"

Behind Oromis, Glaedr opened one of his molten eyes, which was as large as a round shield, and said, *It is mine. . . . The source of Galbatorix's power lies in the hearts of dragons. From us, he steals his strength. Without our aid, Galbatorix would have fallen to the elves and the Varden long ago.*

Eragon frowned. "I don't understand. Why would you help Galbatorix? And how could you? There are only four dragons and an egg left in Alagaësia . . . aren't there?"

Many of the dragons whose bodies Galbatorix and the Forsworn slew are still alive today.

"Still alive . . . ?" Bewildered, Eragon glanced at Oromis, but the elf remained quiet, his face inscrutable. Even more disconcerting was that Saphira did not seem to share Eragon's confusion.

The gold dragon turned his head on his paws to better look at Eragon, his scales scraping against one another. *Unlike with most creatures,* he said, *a dragon's consciousness does not reside solely within our skulls. There is in our chests a hard, gemlike object, similar in composition to our scales, called the Eldunarí, which means "the heart of hearts." When a dragon hatches, their Eldunarí is clear and lusterless. Usually it remains so all through a dragon's life and dissolves along with the dragon's corpse when they die. However, if we wish, we can transfer our consciousness into the Eldunarí. Then it will acquire the same color as our scales and begin to glow like a coal. If a dragon has done this, the Eldunarí will outlast the decay of their flesh, and a dragon's essence may live on indefinitely. Also, a dragon can disgorge their Eldunarí while they are still alive. By this means, a dragon's body and a dragon's consciousness can exist separately and yet still be linked, which can be most useful in certain circumstances. But to do this exposes us to great danger, for whosoever holds our Eldunarí holds our very soul in their hands. With it, they could force us to do their bidding, no matter how vile.*

628

The implications of what Glaedr had said astounded Eragon. Shifting his gaze to Saphira, he asked, *Did you already know about this?*

The scales on her neck rippled as she made an odd, serpentine motion with her head. *I have always been aware of my heart of hearts. Always I have been able to feel it inside of me, but I never thought to mention it to you.*

How could you not when it's of such significance?

Would you think it worthy of mention that you have a stomach, Eragon? Or a heart or a liver or any other organ? My Eldunarí is an integral part of who I am. I never considered its existence worthy of note. . . . At least not until we last came to Ellesméra.

So you did know!

Only a little. Glaedr hinted that my heart of hearts was more impor-

tant than I had originally believed, and he warned me to protect it, lest I inadvertently deliver myself into the hands of our enemies. More than that he did not explain, but since then, I inferred much of what he just said.

Yet you still did not think this was worth mentioning? demanded Eragon.

I wanted to, she growled, *but as with Brom, I gave my word to Glaedr that I would speak of this to no one, not even to you.*

And you agreed?

I trust Glaedr, and I trust Oromis. Do you not?

Eragon scowled and turned back to the elf and the golden dragon. "Why didn't you tell us of this sooner?"

Unstoppering the decanter, Oromis refilled his goblet with wine and said, "In order to protect Saphira."

"Protect her? From what?"

From you, Glaedr said. Eragon was so surprised and outraged, he failed to regain his composure well enough to protest before Glaedr resumed speaking. *In the wild, a dragon would learn about his Eldunarí from one of his elders when he was old enough to understand the use of it. That way, a dragon would not transfer themself into their heart of hearts without knowing the full import of their actions. Among the Riders, a different custom arose. The first few years of partnership between a dragon and a Rider are crucial to establishing a healthy relationship between the two, and the Riders discovered that it was better to wait until newly joined Riders and dragons were well familiar with each other before informing them of the Eldunarí. Otherwise, in the reckless folly of youth, a dragon might decide to disgorge his heart of hearts merely to appease or impress his Rider. When we give up our Eldunarí, we are giving up a physical embodiment of our entire being. And we cannot return it to its original place within our bodies once it is gone. A dragon should not undertake the separation of their consciousness lightly, for it will change how they live the rest of their lives, even if they should endure for another thousand years.*

"Do you still have your heart of hearts within you?" Eragon asked.

The grass around the table bent under the blast of hot air that erupted from Glaedr's nostrils. *That is not a meet question to ask any dragon but Saphira. Do not presume to put it to me again, hatchling.*

Although Glaedr's rebuke made Eragon's cheeks sting, he still had the wherewithal to respond as he should, with a seated bow and the words "No, Master." Then he asked, "What . . . what happens if your Eldunarí breaks?"

If a dragon has already transferred their consciousness to their heart of hearts, then they will die a true death. With an audible click, Glaedr blinked, his inner and outer eyelids flashing across the rayed orb of his iris. *Before we formed our pact with the elves, we kept our hearts in Du Fells Nángoröth, the mountains in the center of the Hadarac Desert. Later, after the Riders established themselves on the island of Vroengard and therein built a repository for the Eldunarí, wild dragons and paired dragons both entrusted their hearts to the Riders for safekeeping.*

"So then," said Eragon, "Galbatorix captured the Eldunarí?"

Contrary to Eragon's expectations, it was Oromis who replied. "He did, but not all at once. It had been so long since anyone had truly threatened the Riders, many of our order had become careless about protecting the Eldunarí. At the time Galbatorix turned against us, it was not uncommon for a Rider's dragon to disgorge their Eldunarí merely for the sake of convenience."

"Convenience?"

Anyone who holds one of our hearts, said Glaedr, *may communicate with the dragon from which it came without regard for distance. The whole of Alagaësia might separate a Rider and dragon, and yet if the Rider had with him his dragon's Eldunarí, they could share thoughts as easily as you and Saphira do now.*

"In addition," said Oromis, "a magician who possesses an Eldunarí can draw upon the dragon's strength to bolster his spells, again without regard for where the dragon might be. When—"

A brilliantly colored hummingbird interrupted their conversation by darting across the table. Its wings a throbbing blur, the bird hovered over the bowls of fruit and lapped at the liquid oozing from a crushed blackberry, then flitted up and away, vanishing among the trunks of the forest.

Oromis resumed speaking: "When Galbatorix killed his first Rider, he also stole the heart of the Rider's dragon. During the years Galbatorix spent hiding in the wilderness thereafter, he broke the dragon's mind and bent it to his will, likely with the help of Durza. And when Galbatorix began his insurrection in earnest, with Morzan by his side, he was already stronger than most every other Rider. His strength was not merely magical but mental, for the force of the Eldunarí's consciousness augmented his own.

"Galbatorix did not just try to kill the Riders and dragons. He made it his goal to acquire as many of the Eldunarí as he could, either by seizing them from Riders or by torturing a Rider until his dragon disgorged its heart of hearts. By the time we realized what Galbatorix was doing, he was already too powerful to stop. It helped Galbatorix that many Riders traveled not only with the Eldunarí of their own dragon but also with Eldunarí of dragons whose bodies were no more, for such dragons often became bored with sitting in an alcove and yearned for adventure. And of course, once Galbatorix and the Forsworn sacked the city of Doru Araeba on the island of Vroengard, he gained possession of the entire hoard of Eldunarí stored therein.

"Galbatorix engineered his success by using the might and wisdom of the dragons against all of Alagaësia. At first he was unable to control more than a handful of the Eldunarí he had captured. It is no easy thing to force a dragon to submit to you, no matter how powerful you might be. As soon as Galbatorix crushed the Riders and had installed himself as king in Urû'baen, he dedicated himself to subduing the rest of the hearts, one by one.

"We believe the task preoccupied him for the main part of the next forty years, during which time he paid little attention to the affairs of Alagaësia—which is why the people of Surda were able to secede from the Empire. When he finished, Galbatorix emerged from seclusion and began to reassert his control over the Empire and the lands beyond. For some reason, after two and a half years of additional slaughter and sorrow, he withdrew to Urû'baen again, and there he has dwelt ever since, not so solitary as before, but obviously focused upon some project known only to him. His vices are many, but he has not abandoned himself to debauchery; that much the Varden's spies have determined. More than that, though, we have not been able to discover."

Lost deep in thought, Eragon stared off into the distance. For the first time, all of the stories he had heard about Galbatorix's unnatural power made sense. A faint feeling of optimism welled up within Eragon as he said to himself, *I'm not sure how, but if we could release the Eldunarí from Galbatorix's control, he would be no more powerful than any normal Dragon Rider.* Unlikely as the prospect seemed, it heartened Eragon to know that the king did have a vulnerability, no matter how slight.

As Eragon continued to muse upon the subject, another question occurred to him. "Why is it that I've never heard mention of the hearts of dragons in the stories of old? Surely if they are so important, the bards and scholars would speak of them."

Oromis laid a hand flat on the table then and said, "Of all the secrets in Alagaësia, that of the Eldunarí is one of the most closely guarded, even among my own people. Throughout history, dragons have striven to hide their hearts from the rest of the world. They revealed their existence to us only after the magical pact between our races was established, and then only to a select few."

"But why?"

Ah, said Glaedr, *often we despised the need for secrecy, but if ever the Eldunarí had become common knowledge, every low-minded scoundrel in the land would have attempted to steal one, and eventually some would have achieved their goal. It was an outcome we went to great lengths to prevent.*

"Is there no way for a dragon to defend themselves through their Eldunarí?" Eragon asked.

Glaedr's eye seemed to twinkle brighter than ever. *An apt question. A dragon who has disgorged their Eldunarí but who still enjoys the use of their flesh can, of course, defend their heart with their claws and their fangs and their tail and with the battering of their wings. A dragon whose body is dead, however, possesses none of those advantages. Their only weapon is the weapon of their mind and, perhaps, if the moment is right, the weapon of magic, which we cannot command at will. That is one reason why many dragons did not choose to prolong their existence beyond the demise of their flesh. To be unable to move of your own volition, to be unable to sense the world around you except through the minds of others, and to only be able to influence the course of events with your thoughts and with rare and unpredictable flashes of magic; it would be a difficult existence to embrace for most any creature, but especially dragons, who are the freest of all beings.*

"Why would they, then?" asked Eragon.

Sometimes it happened by accident. As their body was failing, a dragon might panic and flee into their Eldunarí. Or if a dragon had disgorged their heart before their body died, they would have no choice but to continue to endure. But mostly, the dragons who chose to live on in their Eldunarí were those who were old beyond measure, older than Oromis and I are now, old enough that the concerns of the flesh had ceased to matter to them and they had turned in on themselves and wished to spend the rest of eternity pondering questions younger beings could not comprehend. We revered and treasured the hearts of such dragons on account of their vast wisdom and intelligence. It was common for wild dragons and paired dragons alike, as well as Riders, to seek advice from them on matters of importance. That Galbatorix enslaved them is a crime of almost unimaginable cruelty and evil.

Now I have a question, said Saphira, the rich thrum of her thoughts running through Eragon's mind. *Once one of our kind becomes confined to their Eldunarí, must they continue to exist, or is it possible for them, if they could no longer endure their condition, to release their hold on the world and pass into the darkness beyond?*

633

"Not on their own," said Oromis. "Not unless the inspiration to use magic should sweep over the dragon and allow them to break their Eldunarí from within, which to my knowledge has happened but rarely. The only other option would be for the dragon to convince someone else to smash the Eldunarí for them. That lack of control is another reason why dragons were extremely wary of transferring themselves into their heart of hearts, lest they trap themselves in a prison from which there was no escape."

Eragon could feel Saphira's loathing at the thought of that prospect. She did not speak of it, however, but asked, *How many Eldunarí does Galbatorix hold in his thrall?*

"We do not know the exact number," said Oromis, "but we estimate that his hoard contains many hundreds."

A wriggle shimmered down Saphira's glittering length. *So then, our race is not on the verge of extinction after all?*

Oromis hesitated, and it was Glaedr who answered. *Little one,* he said, startling Eragon with the use of the epithet, *even if the ground were covered with Eldunarí, our race would still be doomed. A dragon preserved within an Eldunarí is still a dragon, but they possess neither the urges of the flesh nor the organs with which to fulfill them. They cannot reproduce.*

The base of Eragon's skull began to throb, and he became increasingly aware of his weariness from the past four days of traveling. His exhaustion made it difficult to keep hold of thoughts for more than a few moments; at the slightest distraction, they slipped out of his grasp.

The tip of Saphira's tail twitched. *I am not so ignorant as to believe that Eldunarí could beget offspring. However, it comforts me to know I am not as alone as I once thought. . . . Our race may be doomed, but at least there are more than four dragons alive in the world, whether they be cloaked in their flesh or not.*

"That is true," said Oromis, "but they are as much Galbatorix's captives as Murtagh and Thorn."

*Freeing them gives me something to strive for, though, along with res-
cuing the last egg,* said Saphira.

"It is something for us both to strive for," said Eragon. "We are
their only hope." He rubbed his brow with his right thumb, then
said, "There is still something I don't understand."

"Oh?" asked Oromis. "Wherein lies your confusion?"

"If Galbatorix draws his power from these hearts, how do they
produce the energy he uses?" Eragon paused, searching for a better
way to phrase his question. He gestured at the swallows flitting
about in the sky. "Every living thing eats and drinks to sustain itself,
even plants. Food provides the energy our bodies need to function
properly. It also provides the energy we need to work magic,
whether we rely upon our own strength to cast a spell or make use of
the strength of others. How can that be, though, with these
Eldunarí? They don't have bones and muscles and skin, do they?
They don't eat, do they? So then, how do they survive? Where does
their energy come from?"

Oromis smiled, his longish teeth glossy as enameled porcelain.
"From magic."

"Magic?"

"If one defines magic as the manipulation of energy, which properly it is, then yes, magic. Where exactly the Eldunarí acquire their
energy is a mystery to both us and the dragons; no one has ever
identified the source. It may be they absorb sunlight, as do plants, or
that they feed off the life forces of the creatures closest to them.
Whatever the answer, it has been proven that when a dragon un-
dergoes body death and their consciousness takes up sole residence
in their heart of hearts, they bring with them however much spare
strength was available within their body when it ceased to function.
Thereafter, their store of energy increases at a steady pace for the
next five to seven years, until they attain the full height of their
power, which is immense indeed. The total amount of energy an
Eldunarí can hold depends upon the size of the heart; the older a

635

dragon, the larger their Eldunarí and the more energy it can absorb before becoming saturated."

Thinking back to when he and Saphira had battled Murtagh and Thorn, Eragon said, "Galbatorix must have given Murtagh several Eldunarí. That's the only explanation for his increase in strength."

Oromis nodded. "You are fortunate Galbatorix did not lend him any more hearts, else it would have been easy for Murtagh to overwhelm you, Arya, and all the other spellcasters with the Varden."

Eragon remembered how, both times he and Saphira had encountered Murtagh and Thorn, Murtagh's mind had felt as if it contained multiple beings. Eragon shared his recollection with Saphira and said, *Those must have been the Eldunarí I sensed. . . . I wonder where Murtagh put them? Thorn carried no saddlebags, and I didn't see any odd bulges in Murtagh's clothing.*

I don't know, said Saphira. *You do realize that Murtagh must have been referring to his Eldunarí when he said that instead of tearing out your own heart, it would be better to tear out his hearts. Hearts, not heart.*

You're right! Maybe he was trying to warn me. Inhaling, Eragon loosened the knot between his shoulder blades and leaned back in his chair. "Aside from Saphira's heart of hearts, and Glaedr's, are there any Eldunarí that Galbatorix hasn't captured?"

Faint lines appeared around the corners of Oromis's down-turned mouth. "None that we know of. After the fall of the Riders, Brom went searching for Eldunarí that Galbatorix might have overlooked, but without success. Nor, in all my years of scouring Alagaësia with my mind, have I detected so much as a whisper of a thought from an Eldunarí. Every Eldunarí was well accounted for when Galbatorix and Morzan initiated their attack on us, and none of them vanished without explanation. It is inconceivable that any great store of Eldunarí might be lying hidden somewhere, ready to help us if we could but locate them."

Although Eragon had expected no other answer, he still found it disappointing. "One last question. When either a Rider or a Rider's dragon dies, the surviving member of the pair would often waste away or commit suicide soon afterward. And those that didn't usually went mad from the loss. Am I right?"

You are, said Glaedr.

"What would happen, though, if the dragon transferred their consciousness to their heart and then their body died?"

Through the soles of his boots, Eragon felt a faint tremor shake the ground as Glaedr shifted his position. The gold dragon said, *If a dragon experienced body death and yet their Rider still lived, together they became known as Indlvarn. The transition would hardly be a pleasant one for the dragon, but many Riders and dragons successfully adapted to the change and continued to serve the Riders with distinction. If, however, it was a dragon's Rider who died, then the dragon would often smash their Eldunarí, or arrange for another to smash it for them if their body was no more, thus killing themselves and following their Rider into the void. But not all. Some dragons were able to overcome their loss—as were some Riders, such as Brom—and continue to serve our order for many years afterward, either through their flesh or through their heart of hearts.*

You have given us much to think about, Oromis-elda, said Saphira. Eragon nodded but stayed silent, for he was busy pondering all that had been said.

HANDS OF A WARRIOR

Eragon nibbled on a warm, sweet strawberry while he stared into the fathomless depths of the sky. When he finished eating the berry, he set the stem on the tray before him, pushing it into just the right spot with the tip of his forefinger, and then opened his mouth to speak.

Before he could, Oromis said, "What now, Eragon?"

"What now?"

"We have spoken at length on those subjects about which you were curious. What now do you and Saphira wish to accomplish? You cannot linger in Ellesméra, so I wonder what else you hope to achieve by your visit, or is it your intention to depart again tomorrow morning?"

"We had hoped," Eragon said, "that, when we returned, we would be able to continue our training as before. Obviously, we haven't time for that now, but there is something else I would like to do."

"And that would be?"

". . . Master, I have not told you everything that happened to me when Brom and I were in Teirm." And then Eragon recounted how curiosity had lured him into Angela's shop and how she had told him his fortune, and the advice Solembum had given him afterward.

Oromis drew a finger across his upper lip, his demeanor contemplative. "I have heard this fortuneteller mentioned with increasing frequency throughout this past year, both by you and in Arya's reports from the Varden. This Angela seems to be most adept at turning up whenever and wherever events of significance are about to take place."

That she is, confirmed Saphira.

Continuing, Oromis said, "Her behavior reminds me very much of a human spellcaster who once visited the halls of Ellesméra, although she did not go by the name of Angela. Is Angela a woman of short stature, with thick, curly brown hair, flashing eyes, and a wit that is as sharp as it is odd?"

"You have described her perfectly," said Eragon. "Is she the same person?"

Oromis made a small flicking motion with his left hand. "If she is, she is an extraordinary person. . . . As for her prophecies, I would not devote much thought to them. Either they will come true or they will not, and without knowing more, none of us can influence the outcome.

"What the werecat said, though, is worthy of far more consideration. Unfortunately, I cannot elucidate either of his statements. I have never heard of any such place as the Vault of Souls, and while the Rock of Kuthian strikes a familiar chord in my memory, I cannot recall where I have encountered the name. I will search my scrolls for it, but instinct tells me I will find no mention of it in elvish writings."

"What of the weapon underneath the Menoa tree?"

"I know of no such weapon, Eragon, and I am well acquainted with the lore of this forest. In all of Du Weldenvarden, there are perhaps only two elves whose learning exceeds my own where the forest is concerned. I will inquire of them, but I suspect it will be a futile endeavor." When Eragon expressed his disappointment, Oromis said, "I understand that you require a suitable replacement for Zar'roc, Eragon, and this I can help you with. Besides my own blade, Naegling, we elves have preserved two other swords of the Dragon Riders. They are Arvindr and Támerlein. Arvindr is currently held in the city of Nädindel, which you have not the time to visit. But Támerlein is here, in Ellesméra. It is a treasure of House Valtharos, and while the lord of their house, Lord Fiolr, would not part with it eagerly, I think he would give it to you if you asked him respectfully. I will arrange for you to meet with him tomorrow morning."

"And what if the sword does not fit me?" asked Eragon.

"Let us hope it does. However, I shall also send word to the smith Rhunön that she may expect you later in the day."

"But she swore she would never forge another sword."

Oromis sighed. "She did, but her advice would still be worth seeking out. If anyone can recommend the proper weapon for you, it would be she. Besides, even if you like the feel of Támerlein, I am sure Rhunön would want to examine the sword before you left with it. Over a hundred years have elapsed since Támerlein was last used in battle, and it might need some slight refurbishing."

"Could another elf forge me a blade?" asked Eragon.

"Nay," said Oromis. "Not if it were to match the craftsmanship of Zar'roc or whichever stolen sword Galbatorix has chosen to wield. Rhunön is one of the very oldest of our race, and it is she alone who has made the swords for our order."

"She is as old as the Riders?" said Eragon, amazed.

"Older even."

Eragon paused. "What shall we do between now and tomorrow, Master?"

Oromis looked over Eragon and Saphira, then said, "Go and visit the Menoa tree; I know you will not rest easy until you have. See there if you can find the weapon the werecat enticed you with. When you have satisfied your curiosity, retire to the quarters of your tree house, which Islanzadí's servants keep in readiness for you and Saphira. Tomorrow we shall do what we can."

"But, Master, we have so little time—"

"And the pair of you are far too tired for any more excitement today. Trust me, Eragon; you will do better for the rest. I think the hours between will help you to digest all we have spoken of. Even by the measure of kings, queens, and dragons, this conversation of ours has been no light exchange."

Despite Oromis's assurances, Eragon felt uneasy about spending the remainder of the day in leisure. His sense of urgency was so great, he wanted to continue working even when he knew he ought to be recuperating.

Eragon shifted in his chair, and by the motion he must have revealed something of his ambivalence, for Oromis smiled and said, "If it will help you relax, Eragon, I promise you this: before you and Saphira leave for the Varden, you may pick any use of magic, and in the brief while we have, I will teach you everything I can concerning it."

With his thumb, Eragon pushed his ring around his right index finger and considered Oromis's offer, trying to decide what, of all areas of magic, he would most like to learn. At last he said, "I would like to know how to summon spirits."

A shadow passed over Oromis's face. "I shall keep my word, Eragon, but sorcery is a dark and unseemly art. You should not seek to control other beings for your own gain. Even if you ignore the immorality of sorcery, it is an exceptionally dangerous and fiendishly complicated discipline. A magician requires at least three years of intensive study before he can hope to summon spirits and not have them possess him.

"Sorcery is not like other magics, Eragon; by it, you attempt to force incredibly powerful and hostile beings to obey your commands, beings who devote every moment of their captivity to finding a flaw in their bonds so that they can turn on you and subjugate you in revenge. Throughout history, never has there been a Shade who was also a Rider, and of all the horrors that have stalked this fair land, such an abomination could easily be the worst, worse even than Galbatorix. Please choose another subject, Eragon: one less perilous for you and for our cause."

"Then," said Eragon, "could you teach me my true name?"

"Your requests," said Oromis, "grow ever more difficult, Eragon-finiarel. I might be able to guess your true name if I so wished." The silver-haired elf studied Eragon with increased intensity, his eyes heavy upon him. "Yes, I believe I could. But I will not. A true name can be of great importance magically, but it is not a spell in and of itself, and so it is exempt from my promise. If your desire is to better understand yourself, Eragon, then seek to discover your true name on your own. If I gave you it, you might profit thereof, but you would do so without the wisdom you would otherwise acquire during the journey to find your true name. A person must earn enlightenment, Eragon. It is not handed down to you by others, regardless of how revered they be."

Eragon fiddled with his ring for another moment, then made a noise in his throat and shook his head. "I don't know. . . . My questions have run dry."

"That I very much doubt," said Oromis.

Eragon found it difficult to concentrate upon the matter at hand; his thoughts kept returning to the Eldunarí and to Brom. Again Eragon marveled at the strange series of events that had led Brom to settle in Carvahall and, eventually, to Eragon himself becoming a Dragon Rider. *If Arya hadn't . . .* Eragon stopped and smiled as a thought occurred to him. "Will you teach me how to move an object from place to place without delay, just as Arya did with Saphira's egg?"

Oromis nodded. "An excellent choice. The spell is costly, but it has many uses. I am sure it will prove most helpful to you in your dealings with Galbatorix and the Empire. Arya, for one, can attest to its effectiveness."

Lifting his goblet from the table, Oromis held it up to the sun, and the radiance from above rendered the wine transparent. He studied the liquid for a long while, then lowered the goblet and said, "Before you venture into the city, you should know that he whom you sent to live among us arrived here some time ago."

A moment passed before Eragon realized to whom Oromis was referring. "Sloan is in Ellesméra?" said Eragon, astonished.

"He lives alone in a small dwelling by a stream on the western edge of Ellesméra. Death was close upon him when he staggered out of the forest, but we tended the wounds of his flesh, and he is healthy now. The elves in the city bring him food and clothes and otherwise see to it he is well cared for. They escort him wherever he wishes to go, and sometimes they read to him, but for the most part, he prefers to sit alone, saying nothing to those who approach. Twice he has attempted to leave, but your spells prevented it."

I'm surprised he arrived here so quickly, Eragon said to Saphira.

The compulsion you placed upon him must have been stronger than you realized.

Aye. In a quiet voice, Eragon asked, "Have you seen fit to restore his vision?"

"We have not."

The weeping man is broken inside, Glaedr said. *He cannot see clearly enough for his eyes to be of any use.*

"Should I go and visit him?" asked Eragon, unsure of what Oromis and Glaedr expected.

"That is for you to decide," said Oromis. "Meeting you again might only upset him. However, you are responsible for his punishment, Eragon. It would be wrong for you to forget him."

"No, Master, I won't."

With a brisk motion of his head, Oromis set his goblet on the table and moved his chair closer to Eragon. "The day grows old, and I would keep you here no longer, lest I interfere with your rest, but there is one more thing I wish to attend to before you depart: your hands, may I examine them? I would like to see what they say about you now." And Oromis held out his own hands toward Eragon.

Extending his arms, Eragon placed his hands palm-downward on top of Oromis's, shivering at the touch of the elf's thin fingers against the inside of his wrists. The calluses on Eragon's knuckles cast long shadows across the backs of his hands as Oromis tilted them from side to side. Then, exerting a slight but firm pressure, Oromis turned Eragon's hands over and inspected his palms and the undersides of his fingers.

"What do you see?" asked Eragon.

Oromis twisted Eragon's hands around again and gestured at his calluses. "You now have the hands of a warrior, Eragon. Take care they do not become the hands of a man who revels in the carnage of war."

THE TREE OF LIFE

From the Crags of Tel'naeír, Saphira flew low over the swaying forest until she arrived at the clearing wherein stood the Menoa tree. Thicker than a hundred of the giant pines that encircled it, the Menoa tree rose toward the sky like a mighty pillar, its arching canopy thousands of feet across. The gnarled net of its roots radiated outward from the massive, moss-bound trunk, covering more than ten acres of forest floor before the roots delved deeper into the soft soil and vanished beneath those of lesser trees. Close to the Menoa tree, the air was moist and cool, and a faint but constant mist drifted down from the mesh of needles above, watering the broad ferns clustered about the base of its trunk. Red squirrels raced along the branches of the ancient tree, and the bright calls and chirrups of hundreds of birds burst forth from the bramble-like depths of its foliage. And throughout the clearing, the sense of a watchful presence pervaded, for the tree contained within it the remnants of the elf once known as Linnëa, whose consciousness now guided the growth of the tree and that of the forest beyond.

Eragon searched the uneven field of roots for any sign of a weapon, but as before, he found no object he would consider carrying into battle. He pried a loose slab of bark from the moss at his feet and held it up to Saphira. *What do you think?* he asked. *If I imbued it with enough spells, could I kill a soldier with this?*

You could kill a soldier with a blade of grass if you wanted to, she answered. *However, against Murtagh and Thorn, or the king and his black dragon, you might as well attack them with a strand of wet wool as that bark.*

You're right, he said, and tossed it away.

It seems to me, she said, *that you should not need to make a fool of yourself in order for Solembum's advice to prove true.*

No, but perhaps I should approach the problem differently if I am going to find this weapon. As you pointed out before, it could just as easily be a stone or a book as a blade of some sort. A staff carved from the branch of the Menoa tree would be a worthy weapon, I would think.

But hardly equal to a sword.

No. . . . And I would not dare lop off a branch without permission from the tree herself, and I have no idea how I could go about convincing her to grant my request.

Saphira arched her sinuous neck and gazed upward at the tree, then shook her head and shoulders to rid herself of the droplets that had accumulated on the sharp edges of her faceted scales. As the spray of cold water struck him, Eragon yelped and jumped backward, shielding his face with his arm. *If any creature tried to harm the Menoa tree,* she said, *I doubt they would live long enough to regret their mistake.*

For several more hours, the two of them prowled the clearing. Eragon continued to hope they would stumble across some nook or cranny among the knotted roots where they would find the exposed corner of a buried chest, which would contain a sword. *Since Murtagh has Zar'roc, which is his father's sword,* Eragon thought, *by all rights, I ought to have the sword Rhunön made for Brom.*

It would be the right color too, Saphira added. *His dragon, my namesake, was blue as well.*

At last, in desperation, Eragon reached out with his mind toward the Menoa tree and attempted to attract the attention of her slow-moving consciousness, to explain his search and ask for her help. But he might as well have been trying to communicate with the wind or the rain, for the tree took no more notice of him than he would of an ant flailing its feelers by his boots.

Disappointed, he and Saphira left the Menoa tree even as the rim of the sun kissed the horizon. From the clearing, Saphira flew to the center of Ellesméra, where she glided to a landing within the bedroom of the tree house the elves had given them to stay in. The house was a cluster of several globular rooms that rested in the crown of a sturdy tree, several hundred feet above the ground.

A meal of fruit, vegetables, cooked beans, and bread was waiting for Eragon in the dining room. After eating a little, Eragon curled up next to Saphira on the blanket-lined basin set into the floor, ignoring the bed in preference for Saphira's company. He lay there, alert and aware of his surroundings, while Saphira sank into a deep sleep. From his place by her side, Eragon watched the stars rise and set above the moonlit forest and thought of Brom and the mystery of his mother. Late in the night, he slipped into the trancelike state of his waking dreams, and there he spoke with his parents. Eragon could not hear what they said, for his voice and theirs were muted and indistinct, but somehow he was aware of the love and pride his parents felt for him, and although he knew they were no more than phantoms of his restless mind, ever after he treasured the memory of their affection.

At dawn, a slim elf maid led Eragon and Saphira through the paths of Ellesméra to the compound of the family Valtharos. As they passed between the dark boles of the gloomy pines, it struck Eragon how very empty and quiet the city was compared with their last visit; he descried only three elves among the trees: tall, graceful figures who glided away on silent footsteps.

When the elves march to war, Saphira observed, *few remain behind.*

Aye.

Lord Fiolr was waiting for them inside an arched hall illuminated by several floating werelights. His face was long and stern and angled more sharply than those of most elves, so that his features reminded Eragon of a thin-bladed spear. He wore a robe of green and gold, the collar of which flared high behind his head, like the neck feathers of an exotic bird. In his left hand, he carried a wand of white wood carved with glyphs from the Liduen Kvaedhí. Mounted upon the end was a lustrous pearl.

Bending at the waist, Lord Fiolr bowed, as did Eragon. Then they exchanged the elves' traditional greetings, and Eragon thanked the lord for being so generous as to allow him to inspect the sword Támerlein.

And Lord Fiolr said, "Long has Támerlein been a prized possession of my family, and it is especially dear to my own heart. Know you the history of Támerlein, Shadeslayer?"

"No," said Eragon.

"My mate was the most wise and fair Naudra, and her brother, Arva, was a Dragon Rider at the time of the Fall. Naudra was visiting with him in Ilirea when Galbatorix and the Forsworn did sweep down upon the city like a storm from the north. Arva fought alongside the other Riders to defend Ilirea, but Kialandí of the Forsworn dealt him a mortal blow. As he lay dying on the battlements of Ilirea, Arva gave his sword, Támerlein, to Naudra that she might protect herself. With Támerlein, Naudra fought free of the Forsworn and returned here with another dragon and Rider, although she died soon afterward of her wounds."

With a single finger, Lord Fiolr stroked the wand, eliciting a soft glow from the pearl in response. "Támerlein is as precious to me as the air in my lungs; I would sooner part with life than part with it. Unfortunately, neither I nor my kin are worthy of wielding it. Támerlein was forged for a Rider, and Riders we are not. I am willing to lend you it, Shadeslayer, in order to aid you in your fight against Galbatorix. However, Támerlein will remain the property of House Valtharos, and you must promise to return the sword if ever I or my heirs ask for it."

Eragon gave his word, and then Lord Fiolr led him and Saphira to a long, polished table grown out of the living wood of the floor. At one end of the table was an ornate stand, and resting upon the stand was the sword Támerlein and its sheath.

The blade of Támerlein was colored a dark, rich green, as was its sheath. A large emerald adorned the pommel. The furniture of the sword had been wrought of blued steel. A line of glyphs adorned the crossguard. In Elvish, they said, *I am Támerlein, bringer of the final sleep.* In length, the sword was equal to Zar'roc, but the blade was wider and the tip rounder and the build of the hilt was heavier. It was a beautiful, deadly weapon, but just by looking at it, Eragon could see that Rhunön had forged Támerlein for a person with a fighting style different from his own, a style that relied more on cutting and slashing than the faster, more elegant techniques Brom had taught him.

As soon as Eragon's fingers closed around Támerlein's hilt, he realized that the hilt was too large for his hand, and at that moment he knew that Támerlein was not the sword for him. It did not feel like an extension of his arm, as had Zar'roc. And yet, despite his realization, Eragon hesitated, for where else could he hope to find so fine a sword? Arvindr, the other blade Oromis had mentioned, lay in a city hundreds of miles distant.

Then Saphira said, *Do not take it. If you are to carry a sword into battle, if your life and mine are to depend upon it, then the sword must be perfect. Nothing else will suffice. Besides, I do not like the conditions Lord Fiolr has attached to his gift.*

And so Eragon replaced Támerlein on its stand and apologized to Lord Fiolr, explaining why he could not accept the sword. The narrow-faced elf did not appear overly disappointed; to the contrary, Eragon thought he saw a flash of satisfaction appear in Fiolr's fierce eyes.

From the halls of the family Valtharos, Eragon and Saphira made their own way through the dim caverns of the forest to the tunnel of dogwood trees that led to the open atrium in the center of Rhunön's house. As they emerged from the tunnel, Eragon heard the clink of a hammer on a chisel, and he saw Rhunön sitting at a bench by the open-walled forge in the middle of the atrium. The elf woman was busy carving a block of polished steel that lay before her. Whatever she was sculpting, Eragon could not guess, for the piece was still rough and indistinct.

"So, Shadeslayer, you are still alive," said Rhunön, without taking her eyes off her work. Her voice grated like pitted millstones. "Oromis told me that you lost Zar'roc to the son of Morzan."

Eragon winced and nodded, even though she was not looking at him. "Yes, Rhunön-elda. He took it from me on the Burning Plains."

"Hmph." Rhunön concentrated on her hammering, tapping the back of her chisel with inhuman speed, then she paused and said, "The sword has found its rightful owner, then. I do not like the use to which—what is his name? ah yes—*Murtagh* is putting Zar'roc, but every Rider deserves a proper sword, and I can think of no better sword for the son of Morzan than Morzan's own blade." The elf woman glanced up at Eragon from underneath her lined brow. "Understand me, Shadeslayer, I would prefer it if you had kept hold of Zar'roc, but it would please me even more if you had a sword that was made for you. Zar'roc may have served you well, but it was the wrong shape for your body. And do not even speak to me of Támerlein. You would have to be a fool to think you could wield it."

"As you can see," said Eragon, "I did not bring it with me from Lord Fiolr."

Rhunön nodded and resumed chiseling. "Well then, good."

"If Zar'roc is the right sword for Murtagh," said Eragon, "wouldn't Brom's sword be the right weapon for me?"

A frown pinched Rhunön's eyebrows together. "Undbitr? Why would you think of Brom's blade?"

"Because Brom was my father," said Eragon, and felt a thrill at being able to say that.

"Is that so now?" Laying down her hammer and chisel, Rhunön walked out from under the roof of her forge until she stood opposite Eragon. Her posture was slightly stooped from the centuries she had spent hunched over her work, and because of it, she appeared an inch or two shorter than he. "Mmh, yes, I can see the similarity. He was a rude one, he was, Brom; he said what he meant and wasted no words. I rather liked it. I cannot abide how my race has become. They are too polite, too refined, too precious. Ha! I remember when elves used to laugh and fight like normal creatures. Now they have become so withdrawn, some seem to have no more emotion than a marble statue!"

Saphira said, *Are you referring to how elves were before our races joined themselves to one another?*

Rhunön turned her scowl onto Saphira. "Brightscales. Welcome. Yes, I was speaking of a time before the bond between elves and dragons was sealed. The changes I have seen in our races since, you would hardly credit as possible, but so they are, and here I am, one of the few still alive who can remember what we were like before."

Then Rhunön whipped her gaze back to Eragon. "Undbitr is not the answer to your need. Brom lost his sword during the fall of the Riders. If it does not reside in Galbatorix's collection, then it may have been destroyed or it may be buried in the earth somewhere, underneath the crumbling bones of a long-forgotten battlefield. Even if it could be found, you could not retrieve it before you would have to face your enemies again."

"What, then, should I do, Rhunön-elda?" asked Eragon. And he told her of the falchion he had chosen when he was among the Varden and of the spells he had reinforced the falchion with and of how it had failed him in the tunnels underneath Farthen Dûr.

Rhunön snorted. "No, that would never work. Once a blade has been forged and quenched, you can protect it with an endless array of spells, but the metal itself remains as weak as ever. A Rider needs something more: a blade that can survive the most violent of impacts and one that is unaffected by most any magic. No, what you must do is sing spells over the hot metal while you are extracting it from the ore and also while you are forging it, so as to alter and improve the structure of the metal."

"How can I get such a sword, though?" Eragon asked. "Would you make me one, Rhunön-elda?"

The wire-thin lines on Rhunön's face deepened. She reached over and rubbed her left elbow, the thick muscles in her bare forearm writhing. "You know that I swore that I would never create another weapon so long as I live."

"I do."

"My oath binds me; I cannot break it, no matter how much I might wish to." Continuing to hold her elbow, Rhunön walked back to her bench and sat before her sculpture. "And why should I, Dragon Rider? Tell me that. Why should I loose another soul-reaver upon the world?"

Choosing his words with care, Eragon said, "Because if you did, you could help put an end to Galbatorix's reign. Would not it be fitting if I killed him with a blade you forged when it was with your swords he and the Forsworn slew so many dragons and Riders? You hate how they have used your weapons. How better to balance the scales, then, than by forging the instrument of Galbatorix's doom?"

Rhunön crossed her arms and looked up at the sky. "A sword . . . a new sword. After so long, to again ply my craft. . . ." Lowering her gaze, she jutted her chin out at Eragon and said, "It is possible, just possible, that there might be a way I could help you, but it is futile to speculate, for I cannot try."

Why not? asked Saphira.

"Because I have not the metal I need!" Rhunön growled. "You do not think that I forged the Riders' swords out of ordinary steel, do you? No! Long ago, while I was wandering through Du Welden-varden, I happened upon fragments of a shooting star that had fallen to the earth. The pieces contained an ore unlike any I had handled before, and so I returned with it to my forge, and I refined it, and I discovered that the mix of steel that resulted was stronger, harder, and more flexible than any of earthly origin. I named the metal *brightsteel*, on account of its uncommon brilliance, and when Queen Tarmunora asked me to forge the first of the Riders' swords, it was brightsteel I used. Thereafter, whenever I had the opportunity, I would search the forest for more fragments of the star metal. I did not often find any, but when I did, I would save them for the Riders.

"Over the centuries, the fragments became ever more rare, until at last I began to think none were left. It took me four-and-twenty years to find the last deposit. From it, I forged seven swords, among them Undbitr and Zar'roc. Since the Riders fell, I have searched for brightsteel only once more, and that was last night, after Oromis spoke to me about you." Rhunön tilted her head, and her watery eyes bored into Eragon. "I wandered far and wide, and I cast many spells of finding and binding, but I came across not a single speck of brightsteel. If some could be procured, then we might begin to consider a sword for you, Shadeslayer. Otherwise, this discussion is no more than pointless blathering."

Eragon bowed to the elf woman and thanked her for her time, then he and Saphira left the atrium through the green leafy tunnel of dogwood.

As they walked side by side toward a glade from which Saphira could take off, Eragon said, *Brightsteel; that has to be what Solembum meant. There must be brightsteel underneath the Menoa tree.*

How would he know?

Perhaps the tree told him herself. Does it matter?

Brightsteel or not, she said, *how are we supposed to get at anything that the roots of the Menoa tree cover? We cannot chop through them. We do not even know where to chop.*

I have to think about it.

From the glade by Rhunön's house, Saphira and Eragon flew over Ellesméra back to the Crags of Tel'naeír, where Oromis and Glaedr were waiting. Once Saphira had landed and Eragon climbed down, she and Glaedr leaped off the cliff and spiraled high overhead, not really going anywhere, but rather enjoying the pleasure of each other's presence.

While the two dragons danced among the clouds, Oromis taught Eragon how a magician could transport an object from one place to another without having the object traverse the intervening distance. "Most forms of magic," said Oromis, "require ever more energy to sustain as the distance between you and your target increases. However, that is not the case in this particular instance. It would require the same amount of energy to send the rock in my hand to the other side of that stream as it would to send it all the way to the Southern Isles. For that reason, the spell is most useful when you need to transport an item with magic across a distance so vast, it would kill you to move it normally through space. Even so, it is a demanding spell, and you should only resort to it if all else has failed. To shift something as large as Saphira's egg, for example, would leave you too exhausted to move."

Then Oromis taught Eragon the wording of the spell and several variations on it. Once he had memorized the incantations to Oromis's satisfaction, the elf had him attempt to shift the small rock he was holding.

As soon as Eragon uttered the spell in its entirety, the rock vanished from the palm of Oromis's hand and, an instant later, reappeared in the middle of the clearing with a flash of blue light, a loud detonation, and a surge of burning hot air. Eragon flinched from the noise and then gripped the branch of a nearby tree to steady himself as his knees buckled and cold crept over his limbs. His scalp tingled as he gazed at the rock, which lay in a circle of charred and flattened grass, and he remembered the moment when he had first beheld Saphira's egg.

"Well done," said Oromis. "Now, can you tell me why the stone made that sound when it materialized in the grass?"

Eragon paid close attention to everything Oromis said, but throughout the lesson, he continued to ponder the question of the Menoa tree, even as he knew Saphira did as she soared high above. The longer he considered it, the more he despaired of ever finding a solution.

When Oromis had finished teaching him how to shift objects, the elf asked, "Since you have declined Lord Fiolr's offer of Támerlein, will you and Saphira stay in Ellesméra much longer?"

"I don't know, Master," replied Eragon. "There is something more

I wish to try with the Menoa tree, but if it does not succeed, then I suppose we will have no choice but to depart for the Varden empty-handed."

Oromis nodded. "Before you leave, return here with Saphira one last time."

"Yes, Master."

As Saphira winged her way toward the Menoa tree with Eragon on her back, she said, *It didn't work before. Why should it now?*

It will work because it must. Besides, do you have a better idea?

No, but I like it not. We do not know how she might react. Remember, before Linnëa sang herself into the tree, she killed the young man who betrayed her affections. She might resort to violence again.

She won't dare, not while you are there to protect me.

Mmh.

With a faint whisper of wind, Saphira alighted upon a knuckle-like root several hundred feet from the base of the Menoa tree. The squirrels in the enormous pine screamed warnings to their brethren as they noticed her arrival.

Sliding down onto the root, Eragon rubbed his palms on his thighs, then muttered, "Right, let's not waste time." With light footsteps, he ran up the root to the trunk of the tree, holding his arms out on either side to maintain his balance. Saphira followed at a slower pace, her claws splitting and cracking the bark she trod over.

Eragon squatted on a slippery patch of wood and hooked his fingers through a crevice in the trunk of the tree in order to keep himself from toppling over. He waited until Saphira was standing above him, and then he closed his eyes, breathed deeply of the cool, moist air, and pushed his thoughts out toward the tree.

The Menoa tree made no attempt to stop him from touching her mind, for her consciousness was so large and alien, and so intertwined with that of the other plant life of the forest, it did not need to defend itself. Anyone who attempted to seize control of the tree would also have to establish their mental dominance over a large swath of Du Weldenvarden, a feat which no single person could hope to achieve.

From the tree, Eragon felt a sense of warmth and light and of the earth pressing against her roots for hundreds of yards in every direction. He felt the stir of a breeze through the tree's tangled branches and the flow of sticky sap seeping over a small cut in its bark, and he received a host of similar impressions from the other plants the Menoa tree watched over. Compared with the awareness it had displayed during the Blood-oath Celebration, the tree almost seemed to be asleep; the only sentient thought Eragon could detect was so long and slow-moving, it was impossible to decipher.

Summoning all of his resources, Eragon flung a mental shout at the Menoa tree. *Please, listen to me, O great tree! I need your help! The entire land is at war, the elves have left the safety of Du Weldenvarden, and I do not have a sword to fight with! The werecat Solembum told me to look under the Menoa tree when I needed a weapon. Well, that time has come! Please, listen to me, O mother of the forest! Help me in my quest!* While he spoke, Eragon pressed against the tree's consciousness images of Thorn and Murtagh and the armies of the Empire. Adding several more memories to the mix, Saphira bolstered his efforts with the force of her own mind.

Eragon did not rely on words and images alone. From within himself and Saphira, he funneled a steady stream of energy into the tree: a gift of good faith that he hoped might also rouse the Menoa tree's curiosity.

Several minutes elapsed, and still the tree did not acknowledge them, but Eragon refused to abandon their attempt. The tree, he reasoned, moved at a slower pace than humans or elves; it was only to be expected that it would not immediately respond to their request.

We cannot spare much more of our strength, said Saphira, *not if we are to return to the Varden in a timely fashion.*

Eragon agreed and reluctantly stemmed the flow of energy.

While they continued to plead with the Menoa tree, the sun

reached its zenith and then began to descend. Clouds billowed and shrank and scuttled across the dome of the sky. Birds darted over the trees, angry squirrels chattered, butterflies meandered from spot to spot, and a line of red ants marched past Eragon's boot, carrying small white larvae in their pincers.

Then Saphira snarled, and every bird within hearing fled in fright. *Enough of this groveling!* she declared. *I am a dragon, and I will not be ignored, not even by a tree!*

"No, wait!" Eragon cried, sensing her intentions, but she ignored him.

Stepping back from the trunk of the Menoa tree, Saphira crouched, sank her claws deep into the root underneath her, and, with a mighty wrench, tore three huge strips of wood out of the root. *Come out and speak with us, elf-tree!* she roared. She drew back her head like a snake about to strike, and a pillar of flame erupted from between her jaws, bathing the trunk in a storm of blue and white fire.

Covering his face, Eragon leaped away to escape the heat.

"Saphira, stop!" he shouted, horrified.

I will stop when she answers us.

A thick cloud of water droplets fell to the ground. Looking up, Eragon saw the branches of the pine trembling and swaying with increasing agitation. The groan of wood rubbing against wood filled the air. At the same time, an ice-cold breeze struck Eragon's cheek, and he thought he felt a low rumble beneath his feet. Glancing around, he saw that the trees that ringed the clearing seemed taller and more angular than before, and they seemed to be leaning inward, their crooked branches reaching toward him like talons.

And Eragon was afraid.

Saphira . . . , he said, and sank into a half crouch, ready to either run or fight.

Closing her jaws and thus ending the stream of fire, Saphira looked away from the Menoa tree. As she beheld the ring of menacing trees, her scales rippled and the tips rose from her hide like the ruff on a riled cat. She growled at the forest, swinging her head from side to side, then unfolded her wings and began to retreat from the Menoa tree. *Quick, get on my back.*

Before Eragon could take a single step, a root as thick as his arm sprouted out of the ground and coiled itself around his left ankle, immobilizing him. Even thicker roots appeared on either side of Saphira and grasped her by the legs and tail, holding her in place. Saphira roared in fury and arched her neck to loose another deluge of fire.

The flames in her mouth flickered and went out as a voice sounded in her mind and Eragon's, a slow, whispering voice that reminded Eragon of rustling leaves, and the voice said: *Who dares to disturb my peace? Who dares to bite me and burn me? Name yourselves, so I will know who it is I have killed.*

Eragon grimaced in pain as the root tightened around his ankle. A little more pressure and it would break the bone. *I am Eragon Shadeslayer, and this is the dragon with whom I am bonded, Saphira Brightscales.*

Die well, Eragon Shadeslayer and Saphira Brightscales.

Wait! Eragon said. *I have not finished naming us.*

A long silence followed, then the voice said, *Continue.*

I am the last free Dragon Rider in Alagaësia, and Saphira is the last female dragon in all of existence. We are perhaps the only ones who can defeat Galbatorix, the traitor who has destroyed the Riders and conquered half of Alagaësia.

Why did you hurt me, dragon? the voice sighed.

Saphira bared her teeth as she answered: *Because you would not talk with us, elf-tree, and because Eragon has lost his sword and a werecat told him to look under the Menoa tree when he needed a weapon. We have looked and looked, but we cannot find it on our own.*

Then you die in vain, dragon, for there is no weapon under my roots.

Desperate to keep the tree talking, Eragon said, *We believe the werecat might have meant brightsteel, the star metal Rhunön uses to forge the blades of the Riders. Without it, she cannot replace my sword.*

The surface of the earth rippled as the network of roots that covered the clearing shifted slightly. The disturbance flushed hundreds of panicked rabbits, mice, voles, shrews, and other small creatures from their burrows and dens, and sent them scampering across the open ground toward the main body of the forest.

Out of the corner of his eye, Eragon saw dozens of elves running toward the clearing, their hair streaming behind them like silk pennants. Silent as apparitions, the elves stopped underneath the boughs of the encircling trees and stared at him and Saphira but made no move to approach or to assist them.

Eragon was about to call with his mind for Oromis and Glaedr when the voice returned. *The werecat knew whereof he spoke; there is a nodule of brightsteel ore buried at the very edge of my roots, but you shall not have it. You bit me and you burned me, and I do not forgive you.*

Alarm tempered Eragon's excitement at hearing of the ore's existence. *But Saphira is the last female dragon!* he exclaimed. *Surely you would not kill her!*

Dragons breathe fire, whispered the voice, and a shudder ran through the trees at the edge of the clearing. *Fires must be extinguished.*

Saphira growled again and said, *If we cannot stop the man who destroyed the Dragon Riders, he will come here and he will burn the forest around you, and then he will destroy you as well, elf-tree. If you help us, though, we may be able to stop him.*

A screech echoed among the trees as two branches scraped against each other. *If he tries to kill my seedlings, then he will die*, said the voice. *No one is as strong as the whole of the forest. No one can hope to defeat the forest, and I speak for the forest.*

Is not the energy we gave you enough to repair your wounds? asked Eragon. *Is not it compensation enough?*

The Menoa tree did not answer but rather probed at Eragon's mind, sweeping through his thoughts like a gust of wind. *What are you, Rider?* said the tree. *I know every creature that lives among this forest, but never have I encountered one like you.*

I am neither elf nor human, said Eragon. *I am something in between. The dragons changed me during the Blood-oath Celebration.*

Why did they change you, Rider?

So that I could better fight Galbatorix and his empire.

I remember I felt a warping in the world during the celebration, but I did not think it was important. . . . So little seems important now, save the sun and the rain.

Eragon said, *We will heal your root and trunk if that will satisfy you, but please, may we have the brightsteel?*

The other trees creaked and moaned like abandoned souls, and then, soft and fluttering, the voice came again. *Will you give me what I want in return, Dragon Rider?*

I will, Eragon said without hesitation. Whatever the price, he would gladly pay it for a Rider's sword.

The canopy of the Menoa tree grew still, and for several minutes, all was quiet in the clearing. Then the ground began to shake and the roots in front of Eragon began to twist and grind, shedding flakes of bark as they pulled aside to reveal a bare patch of dirt, out of which emerged what appeared to be a lump of corroded iron roughly two feet long and a foot and a half wide. As the ore came to rest on the surface of the rich black soil, Eragon felt a slight twinge in his lower belly. He winced and rubbed at the spot, but the momentary flare of discomfort had already vanished. Then the root around his ankle loosened and retreated into the ground, as did those that had been holding Saphira in place.

Here is your metal, whispered the Menoa tree. *Take it and go. . . .*

But— Eragon started to ask.

Go . . . , said the Menoa tree, its voice fading away. *Go. . . .* And the tree's consciousness withdrew from him and Saphira, receding deeper and deeper into itself until Eragon could barely sense its presence. Around them, looming pines relaxed and resumed their usual positions.

"But . . . ," Eragon said out loud, puzzled that the Menoa tree had not told him what she wanted.

Still perplexed, he went over to the ore, slid his fingers under the edge of the metal-laced stone, and hoisted the irregular mass into his arms, grunting at its weight. Hugging it against his chest, he turned away from the Menoa tree and started the long walk toward Rhunön's house.

Saphira sniffed the brightsteel as she joined him. *You were right,* she said. *I should not have attacked her.*

At least we got the brightsteel, said Eragon, *and the Menoa tree . . . well, I don't know what she got, but we have what we came for, and that's what matters.*

The elves gathered alongside the path Eragon had chosen to follow and gazed at Eragon and Saphira with an intensity that made Eragon quicken his pace and the skin on the nape of his neck prickle. Not once did the elves speak, only stared with their slanting eyes, stared as if they were watching a dangerous animal stalk through their homes.

A puff of smoke billowed from Saphira's nostrils. *If Galbatorix does not kill us first,* she said, *I think we shall live to regret this.*

MIND OVER METAL

"**W**here did you find that?" demanded Rhunön as Eragon staggered into the atrium of her house and dropped the lump of brightsteel ore onto the ground by her feet.

In as few words as possible, Eragon explained about Solembum and the Menoa tree.

Squatting next to the ore, Rhunön caressed the pitted surface, her fingers lingering over the metallic patches interspersed among the stone. "You were either very foolish or very brave to test the Menoa tree as you did. She is not one to trifle with."

Is there enough ore for a sword? Saphira asked.

"Several swords, if past experience is anything to judge by," said Rhunön, rising to her full height. The elf woman glanced at her forge in the center of the atrium, then clapped her hands together, her eyes lighting up with a combination of eagerness and determination. "Let us to it, then! You need a sword, Shadeslayer? Very well, I shall give you a sword the likes of which has never been seen before in Alagaësia."

"But what of your oath?" Eragon asked.

"Think not of it for the time being. When must the two of you return to the Varden?"

"We should have left the day we arrived," said Eragon.

Rhunön paused, her expression introspective. "Then I shall have to hurry that which I do not normally hurry and use magic to craft that which would otherwise require weeks of work by hand. You and Brightscales will help me." It was not a question, but Eragon nodded in agreement. "We shall not rest tonight, but I promise you, Shadeslayer, you shall have your sword by tomorrow morning." Bending at

661

the knees, Rhunön lifted the ore from the ground without discernible effort and carried it to the bench with her carving in progress.

Eragon removed his tunic and shirt, so he would not ruin them during the work to come, and in their place Rhunön gave him a tight-fitting jerkin and a fabric apron treated so that it was impervious to fire. Rhunön wore the same. When Eragon asked her about gloves, she laughed and shook her head. "Only a clumsy smith uses gloves."

Then Rhunön led him to a low, grotto-like chamber set within the trunk of one of the trees out of which her house was grown. Inside the chamber were bags of charcoal and loose piles of whitish clay bricks. By means of a spell, Eragon and Rhunön lifted several hundred bricks and carried them outside, next to the open-walled forge, then did the same with the bags of charcoal, each of which was as large as a man.

Once the supplies were arranged to Rhunön's satisfaction, she and Eragon built a smelter for the ore. The smelter was a complex structure, and Rhunön refused to use much magic to construct it, so the project took them most of the afternoon. First they dug a rectangular pit five feet deep, which they filled with layers of sand, gravel, clay, charcoal, and ash, and in which they embedded a number of chambers and channels to wick away moisture that would otherwise dampen the heat of the smelting fire. When the contents of the pit were level with the ground, they assembled a trough of bricks on top of the layers below, using water and unfired clay as their mortar. Ducking inside her house, Rhunön returned with a pair of bellows, which they attached to holes at the base of the trough.

They broke then to drink and to eat a few bites of bread and cheese.

After the brief repast, Rhunön placed a handful of small branches in the trough, lit them on fire with a murmured word, and, when the flames were well set, laid medium-sized pieces of seasoned oak along the bottom. For nearly an hour, she tended the fire, cultivating it with the care of a gardener growing roses, until the wood had burned down to an even bed of coals. Then Rhunön nodded to Eragon and said, "Now."

Eragon lifted the lump of ore and gently lowered it into the trough. When the heat on his fingers became unbearable, he released the ore and jumped back as a fountain of sparks swirled upward like a swarm of fireflies. On top of the ore and the coals, he shoveled a thick blanket of charcoal as fuel for the fire.

Eragon brushed the charcoal dust from his palms, then grasped the handles of one set of bellows and began to pump it, as did Rhunön the bellows on the other side of the smelter. Between them, they supplied the fire with a steady stream of fresh air so that it burned ever hotter.

The scales on Saphira's chest, as well as on the underside of her head and neck, sparkled with dazzling flashes of light as the flames in the smelter danced. She crouched several yards away, her eyes fixed upon the molten heart of the fire. *I could help with this, you know*, she said. *It would take me but a minute to melt the ore.*

"Yes," said Rhunön, "but if we melt it too quickly, the metal will not combine with the charcoal and become hard and flexible enough for a sword. Save your fire, dragon. We shall need it later."

The heat from the smelter and the effort of pumping the bellows soon had Eragon covered in a sheen of sweat; his bare arms shone in the light from the fire.

Every now and then, he or Rhunön would abandon their bellows to shovel a new layer of charcoal over the fire.

The work was monotonous, and as a result, Eragon soon lost track of the time. The constant roar of the fire, the feel of the bellows' handle in his hands, the whoosh of rushing air, and Saphira's vigilant presence were the only things he was aware of.

It came as a surprise to him, then, when Rhunön said, "That should be sufficient. Leave the bellows."

Wiping his brow, Eragon helped as she shoveled the incandescent coals out of the smelter and into a barrel filled with water. The coals sizzled and emitted an acrid smell as they struck the liquid.

When they finally exposed the glowing pool of white-hot metal at the bottom of the trough—the slag and other impurities having run off during the process—Rhunön covered the metal with an inch of fine white ash, then leaned her shovel against the side of the smelter and went to sit on the bench by her forge. "What now?" Eragon asked as he joined her.

"Now we wait."

"For what?"

Rhunön gestured toward the sky, where the light from the setting sun painted a tattered array of clouds red and purple and gold. "It must be dark when we work the metal if we are to correctly judge its color. Also, the brightsteel needs time to cool so that it will be soft and easy to shape."

Reaching around behind her head, Rhunön undid the cord that held back her hair, then gathered up her hair again and retied the cord. "In the meantime, let us talk about your sword. How do you fight, with one hand or two?"

Eragon thought for a minute, then said, "It varies. If I have a choice, I prefer to wield a sword with one hand and carry a shield with my other. However, circumstances have not always been favorable to me, and I have often had to fight without a shield. Then I like being able to grip the hilt with both hands, so I can deliver a more powerful stroke. The pommel on Zar'roc was large enough to grasp with my left hand if I had to, but the ridges around the ruby were uncomfortable and they did not afford me a secure hold. It would be nice to have a slightly longer hilt."

"I take it you do not want a true two-handed sword?" said Rhunön.

Eragon shook his head. "No, it would be too big for fighting indoors."

"That depends upon the size of the hilt and the blade combined, but in general, you are correct. Would you be amenable to a hand-and-a-half sword instead?"

An image flashed in Eragon's mind of Murtagh's original sword, and he smiled. *Why not?* thought Eragon. "Yes, a hand-and-a-half sword would be perfect, I think."

"And how long would you like the blade?"

"No longer than Zar'roc's."

"Mmh. Do you want a straight blade or a curved blade?"

"Straight."

"Have you any preferences as to the guard?"

"Not especially."

Crossing her arms, Rhunön sat with her chin touching her breastbone, her eyes heavy-lidded. Her lips twitched. "What of the width of the blade? Remember, no matter how narrow it is, the sword shall not break."

"Perhaps it could be a little wider at the guard than Zar'roc was."

"Why?"

"I think it might look better."

A harsh, cracked laugh broke from Rhunön's throat. "But how would that improve the use of the sword?"

Embarrassed, Eragon shifted on the bench, at a loss for words.

"Never ask me to alter a weapon merely in order to improve its appearance," admonished Rhunön. "A weapon is a tool, and if it is beautiful, then it is beautiful because it is useful. A sword that could not fulfill its function would be ugly to my eyes no matter how fair its shape, not even if it were adorned with the finest jewels and the most intricate engraving." The elf woman pursed her lips, pushing them out as she thought. "So, a sword equally suited for the unrestrained bloodshed of a battlefield as it is for defending yourself in the narrow tunnels under Farthen Dûr. A sword for all occasions, of middling length, but for the hilt, which shall be longer than average."

"A sword for killing Galbatorix," said Eragon.

Rhunön nodded. "And as such, it must be well protected against magic. . . ." Her chin sank to her chest again. "Armor has improved a great deal in the past century, so the tip will need to be narrower than I used to make them, the better to pierce plate and mail and to slip into the gaps between the various pieces. Mmh." From a pouch by her side, Rhunön withdrew a knotted piece of twine, with which she took numerous measurements of Eragon's hands and arms. Afterward, she retrieved a wrought-iron poker from the forge and tossed it toward Eragon. He caught it with one hand and raised an eyebrow at the elf woman. She motioned toward him with a finger and said, "Go on now. Up on your feet and let me see how you move with a sword."

Walking out from under the roof of the open-walled forge, Eragon obliged her by demonstrating several of the forms Brom had taught him. After a minute, he heard the clink of metal on stone, then Rhunön coughed and said, "Oh, this is hopeless." She stepped in front of Eragon, holding another poker. Her brow furrowed with a fierce scowl as she raised the poker before her in a salute and shouted, "Have at you, Shadeslayer!"

Rhunön's heavy poker whistled through the air as she swung at him with a strong slashing blow. Dancing to the side, Eragon parried the attack. The poker jumped in his hand as the two rods of metal collided. For a brief while, he and Rhunön sparred. Although it was obvious she had not practiced her swordsmanship for some time, Eragon still found her a formidable opponent. At last they were forced to stop because the soft iron of the pokers had bent until the rods were as crooked as the branches of a yew tree.

Rhunön collected Eragon's poker, then carried the two mangled pieces of metal over to a pile of broken tools. When she returned, the elf woman lifted her chin and said, "Now I know exactly what shape your sword should have."

"But how will you make it?"

A twinkle of amusement appeared in Rhunön's eyes. "I won't. You shall make the sword instead of me, Shadeslayer."

Eragon gaped at her for a moment, then sputtered and said, "Me? But I was never apprenticed to a blacksmith or a bladesmith. I have not the skill to forge even a common brush knife."

The twinkle in Rhunön's eyes brightened. "Nevertheless, you shall be the one to make this sword."

"But how? Will you stand beside me and give me orders as I hammer the metal?"

"Hardly," said Rhunön. "No, I shall guide your actions from within your mind so that your hands may do what mine cannot. It is not a perfect solution, but I can think of no other means of evading my oath that will also allow me to ply my craft."

Eragon frowned. "If you move my hands for me, how is that any different from making the sword yourself?"

Rhunön's expression darkened and, in a brusque voice, she said, "Do you want this sword or not, Shadeslayer?"

"I do."

"Then refrain from pestering me with such questions. Making the sword through you is different because I think it is different. If I believed otherwise, then my oath would prevent me from participating in the process. So, unless you wish to return to the Varden empty-handed, you would be wise to remain silent on the subject."

"Yes, Rhunön-elda."

They went to the smelter then, and Rhunön had Saphira pry the still-warm mass of congealed brightsteel from the bottom of the brick trough. "Break it into fist-sized pieces," Rhunön directed, and withdrew to a safe distance.

Lifting her front leg, Saphira stamped upon the rippled beam of brightsteel with all her strength. The earth shook, and the brightsteel cracked in several places. Three more times Saphira stamped upon the metal before Rhunön was satisfied with the results.

The elf woman gathered up the sharp lumps of metal in her apron and carried them to a low table next to her forge. There she sorted the metal according to its hardness, which, or so she told Eragon, she was able to determine by the color and texture of the fractured metal. "Some is too hard and some is too soft," she said, "and while

I could remedy that if I wanted to, it would require another heating. So we will only use the pieces that are already suitable for a sword. On the edges of the sword will go a slightly harder steel"—she touched a cluster of pieces that had a brilliant, sparkling grain—"the better to take a keen edge. The middle of the sword shall be made of a slightly softer steel"—she touched a cluster of pieces that were grayer and not so bright—"the better to bend and to absorb the shock of a blow. Before the metal can be forged into shape, though, it must be worked to rid it of the remaining impurities."

How is that done? asked Saphira.

"That you shall see momentarily." Rhunön went to one of the poles that supported the roof of the forge, sat with her back against it, crossed her legs, and closed her eyes, her face still and composed. "Are you ready, Shadeslayer?" she asked.

"I am," said Eragon, despite the tension gathered in his belly.

The first thing Eragon noticed about Rhunön as their minds met was the low chords that echoed through the dark and tangled landscape of her thoughts. The music was slow and deliberate and cast in a strange and unsettling key that scraped on his nerves. What it implied about Rhunön's character, Eragon was not sure, but the eerie melody caused him to reconsider the wisdom of allowing her to control his flesh. But then he thought of Saphira sitting next to the forge, watching over him, and his trepidation receded, and he lowered the last of the defenses around his consciousness.

It felt to Eragon like a piece of raw wool sliding over his skin as Rhunön enveloped his mind with hers, insinuating herself into the most private areas of his being. He shivered at the contact and almost withdrew from it, but then Rhunön's rough voice sounded within his skull: *Relax, Shadeslayer, and all shall be well.*

Yes, Rhunön-elda.

Then Rhunön began to lift his arms, shift his legs, roll his head, and otherwise experiment with the abilities of his body. Strange as it was for Eragon to feel his head and limbs move without his direction, it was stranger still when his eyes began to flick from place to place, seemingly of their own accord. The sensation of helplessness kindled a burst of sudden panic within Eragon. When Rhunön walked him forward and his foot struck the corner of the forge and it seemed as if he were going to fall, Eragon immediately reasserted command over his faculties and grabbed the horn of Rhunön's anvil to steady himself.

Do not interfere, snapped Rhunön. *If your nerve fails you at the wrong moment during the forging, you could cause yourself irreparable harm.*

So could you if you're not careful, Eragon retorted.

Be patient, Shadeslayer. I shall have mastered this by the time it is dark.

While they waited for the last of the light to fade from the velvet sky, Rhunön prepared the forge and practiced wielding various tools. Her initial clumsiness with Eragon's body soon disappeared, although once she reached for a hammer and rammed the tips of his fingers into the top of a table. The pain made Eragon's eyes water. Rhunön apologized and said, *Your arms are longer than mine.* A few minutes later, when they were about to begin, she commented, *It is fortunate you have the speed and strength of an elf, Shadeslayer, else we would have no hope of finishing this tonight.*

669

Taking the pieces of hard and soft brightsteel she had decided to use, Rhunön placed them into the forge. At the elf's request, Saphira heated the steel, opening her jaws only a fraction of an inch so that the blue and white flames that poured from her mouth remained focused in a narrow stream and did not spill over into the rest of the workshop. The roaring pillar of fire illuminated the entire atrium with a fierce blue light and made Saphira's scales sparkle and flash with blinding brilliance.

Rhunön had Eragon remove the brightsteel from the torrent of flames with a pair of tongs once the metal began to glow cherry red. She laid it on her anvil and, with a series of quick blows from a sledgehammer, flattened the lumps of metal into plates that were no more than a quarter of an inch thick. The surface of the red-hot steel glittered with incandescent motes. As she finished with each plate, Rhunön dropped it into a nearby trough of brine.

Having flattened all of the brightsteel, Rhunön pulled the plates out of the trough, the brine warm against Eragon's arm, and scoured each plate with a piece of sandstone to remove the black scales that had formed on the surface of the metal. The scouring exposed the crystalline structure of the metal, which Rhunön examined with great attentiveness. She further sorted the metal by relative hardness and purity according to the qualities the crystals displayed.

Eragon was privy to Rhunön's every thought and feeling, by reason of their closeness. The depth of her knowledge amazed him; she saw things within the metal he had not suspected existed, and the calculations she made concerning its treatment were beyond his understanding. He also sensed she was dissatisfied with how she had handled the sledgehammer while flattening the steel.

Rhunön's dissatisfaction continued to grow until she said, *Bah! Look at these dents in the metal! I cannot forge a blade like this. My control over your arms and hands is not fine enough to craft a sword worthy of note.*

Before Eragon could attempt to reason with her, Saphira said, *The tools do not the artist make, Rhunön-elda. Surely you can find a way to compensate for this inconvenience.*

Inconvenience? snorted Rhunön. *I have no more coordination than a fledgling. I am a stranger in a stranger's house.* Still grumbling, she subsided into mental deliberations that were incomprehensible to Eragon, then said, *Well, I may have a solution, but I warn you, I shall not continue if I am unable to maintain my usual level of craftsmanship.*

She did not explain the solution to either Eragon or Saphira but, one by one, placed the plates of steel on the anvil and cracked them into flakes no wider than rose petals. Gathering up half the flakes of the harder brightsteel, Rhunön stacked them into a brick, which she then coated with clay and birch bark to hold them together.

The brick went on a thick steel paddle with a seven-foot-long handle, similar to those used by bakers to insert and remove loaves of bread from a hot oven.

Rhunön laid the end of the paddle in the center of the forge and then backed Eragon as far away as she could and still have him hold on to the handle. Then she asked Saphira to resume breathing fire, and again the atrium glowed with a flickering blue radiance. The heat was so intense, Eragon felt as if his exposed skin were crisping, and he saw that the granite stones of which the forge was made had acquired a bright yellow glow.

The brightsteel could easily have taken over half an hour to reach the appropriate temperature in a charcoal fire, but it required only a few minutes in the withering inferno of Saphira's flames before it turned white. The moment it did, Rhunön ordered Saphira to cease breathing fire. Darkness engulfed the forge as Saphira closed her jaws.

Rushing Eragon forward, Rhunön had him transport the glowing brick of clay-covered steel to the anvil, where she seized a hammer and welded the disparate flakes of brightsteel into a cohesive whole. She continued to pound on the metal, elongating it out into a bar, then made a cut in the middle, folded the metal back on itself, and welded the two pieces together. The bell-like peals of ringing metal echoed off the ancient trees that surrounded the atrium.

Rhunön had Eragon return the brightsteel to the forge once its color had faded from white to yellow, and again Saphira bathed the metal with the fire from her belly. Six times Rhunön heated and folded the brightsteel, and each time the metal became smoother and more flexible, until it could bend without tearing.

As Eragon hammered the steel, his every action dictated by Rhunön, the elf woman began to sing, both with his tongue and her own. Together, their voices formed a not-unpleasant harmony that rose and fell with the beats of the hammer. A tingle crawled down Eragon's spine as he felt Rhunön channel a steady flow of energy into the words they were mouthing, and he realized that the song contained spells of making, shaping, and binding. With their voices two, Rhunön sang of the metal that lay on the anvil, describing its properties—altering them in ways that exceeded Eragon's understanding—and imbuing the brightsteel with a complex web of enchantments designed to give it strength and resilience beyond that of any ordinary metal. Of Eragon's hammer arm Rhunön also sang, and under the gentle influence of her crooning, every blow she struck with his arm landed upon its intended target.

Rhunön quenched the bar of brightsteel after the sixth and final fold was complete. She repeated the entire process with the other half of the hard brightsteel, forging an identical bar to the first. Then she gathered up the fragments of the softer steel, which she folded and welded ten times before forming it into a short, heavy wedge.

Next, Rhunön had Saphira reheat the two bars of harder steel. Rhunön lay the shining rods side by side on her anvil, grasped both of them at either end with a pair of tongs, and then twisted the rods around each other seven times. Sparks shot into the air as she hammered upon the twists to weld them into a single piece of metal. The resulting mass of brightsteel Rhunön folded, welded, and pounded back out to length another six times. When she was pleased with the quality of the metal, Rhunön flattened the brightsteel into a thick rectangular sheet, cut the sheet in half lengthwise with a sharp chisel, and bent each of the two halves down their middle, so they were in the shape of long, shallow V's.

And all that, Eragon estimated, Rhunön was able to accomplish within the course of an hour and a half. He marveled at her speed, even though it was his own body that carried out the tasks. Never before had he seen a smith shape metal with such ease; what would have taken Horst hours took her only minutes. And yet no matter how demanding the forging was, Rhunön continued to sing, weaving a fabric of spells within the brightsteel and guiding Eragon's arm with infallible accuracy.

Amid the frenzy of noise, fire, sparks, and exertion, Eragon thought he glimpsed, as Rhunön raked his eyes across the forge, a trio of slender figures standing by the edge of the atrium. Saphira confirmed his suspicion a moment later when she said, *Eragon, we are not alone.*

Who are they? he asked. Saphira sent him an image of the short, wizened werecat Maud, in human form, standing between two pale elves who were no taller than she. One of the elves was male, the other female, and they were both extraordinarily beautiful, even by the standards of the elves. Their solemn teardrop faces seemed wise and innocent in equal measure, which made it impossible for Eragon to judge their age. Their skin displayed a faint, silvery sheen, as if the two elves were so filled with energy, it was seeping out of their very flesh.

Eragon queried Rhunön as to the identity of the elves when she paused to allow his body a brief rest. Rhunön glanced at them, affording him a slightly better view, then, without interrupting her song, she said with her thoughts, *They are Alanna and Dusan, the only elf children in Ellesméra. There was much rejoicing when they were conceived twelve years ago.*

They are like no other elves I have met, he said.

Our children are special, Shadeslayer. They are blessed with certain gifts—gifts of grace and gifts of power—which no grown elf can hope to match. As we age, our blossom withers somewhat, although the magic of our early years never completely abandons us.

Rhunön wasted no more time talking. She had Eragon place the wedge of brightsteel between the two V-shaped strips and hammer on them until the strips nearly enveloped the wedge and friction held the three pieces together. Then Rhunön welded the pieces into a whole, and while the metal was still hot, she began to draw it out and form a rough blank of the sword. The soft wedge became the spine of the blade, while the two harder strips became the sides, edges, and point. Once the blank was nearly as long as the finished sword, the work slowed as Rhunön returned to the tang and carefully hammered her way up the blade, establishing the final angles and proportions.

Rhunön had Saphira heat the blade in segments of no more than six or seven inches at a time, which Rhunön arranged by holding the blade over one of Saphira's nostrils, through which Saphira would release a single jet of fire. A host of writhing shadows fled toward the perimeter of the atrium every time the fire sprang into existence.

Eragon watched with amazement as his hands transformed the crude lump of metal into an elegant instrument of war. With every blow, the outline of the blade became clearer, as if the brightsteel *wanted* to be a sword and was eager to assume the shape Rhunön desired.

At last the forging came to a close, and there on the anvil lay a long black blade, which, although it was still rough and incomplete, already radiated a sense of deadly purpose.

Rhunön allowed Eragon's tired arms to rest while the blade cooled by air, then she had Eragon take the blade to another corner of her workshop, where she had arranged six different grinding wheels and, on a small bench, a wide assortment of files, scrapers, and abrasive stones. She fixed the blade between two blocks of wood and spent the next hour planing the sides of the sword with a drawknife, as well as refining the contours of the blade with files. As with the hammering, every stroke of the drawknife and every scrape of a file seemed to have twice the effect it normally would; it was as if the tools knew exactly how much steel to remove and would remove no more.

When she was done filing, Rhunön built a charcoal fire in her forge, and while she waited for the fire to mature, she mixed a slurry of dark, fine-grained clay, ash, powdered pumice, and crystallized juniper sap. She painted the blade with the concoction, slathering twice as much on the spine as she did along the edges and by the point. The thicker the solution of clay, the slower the underlying metal would cool when it was quenched and, as a result, the softer that area of the sword would become.

The clay lightened as Rhunön dried it with a quick incantation. At the direction of the elf woman, Eragon went to the forge. He lay the sword flat upon the bed of scintillating coals and, pumping the bellows with his free hand, slowly pulled it toward his hip. Once the tip of the blade came free of the fire, Rhunön turned it over and repeated the sequence. She continued to draw the blade through the coals until both edges had acquired an even orange tone and the spine of the sword was bright red in color. Then, with a single smooth motion, Rhunön lifted the sword from the coals, swept the glowing bar of steel through the air, and plunged it into the trough of water next to the forge.

An explosive cloud of steam erupted from the surface of the water, which hissed and sizzled and bubbled around the blade. After a minute, the roiling water subsided, and Rhunön withdrew the now pearl-gray sword. Returning it to the fire, she brought the whole sword to the same low heat, so as to reduce the brittleness of the edges, and then quenched it once more.

Eragon had expected Rhunön to relinquish her hold on his body after they had forged, hardened, and tempered the blade, but to his surprise, she remained in his mind and continued to control his limbs.

Rhunön had him douse the forge, then she walked Eragon back to the bench with the files and scrapers and abrasive stones. There she sat him, and making use of ever finer stones, she polished the blade. From her memories, Eragon learned that she would normally spend a week or more polishing a blade, but because of the song they sang, she, through him, was able to complete the task in a mere four hours, in addition to carving a narrow groove down the middle of each side of the blade. As the brightsteel grew smoother, the true beauty of the metal was revealed; within it, Eragon could see a shimmering, cable-like pattern, every line of which marked the transition between two layers of the velvety steel. And along each edge of the sword was a rippling, silvery white band as wide as his thumb, which made it appear as if the edges burned with tongues of frozen fire.

The muscles in Eragon's right arm gave way as Rhunön was covering the tang with decorative cross-hatching, and the file he was holding slipped off the tang and fell from his fingers. The extent of his exhaustion surprised him, for he had been concentrating upon the sword to the exclusion of all else.

Enough, said Rhunön, and she removed herself from Eragon's mind without further ado.

Shocked by her sudden absence, Eragon swayed on his seat and nearly lost his balance before he regained control over his rebellious limbs. "But we're not finished!" he protested, turning toward Rhunön. The night sounded unnaturally quiet to him without the strains of their extended duet.

Rhunön rose from where she had been sitting cross-legged against the pole and shook her head. "I have no more need of you, Shadeslayer. Go and dream until dawn."

"But—"

"You are tired, and even with my magic, you are liable to ruin the sword if you continue to work on it. Now that the blade is done, I can attend to the rest without interference from my oath, so go. You will find a bed on the second floor of my house. If you are hungry, there is food in the pantry."

Eragon hesitated, reluctant to leave, then nodded and shambled away from the bench, his feet dragging in the dirt. As he passed her, he ran a hand over Saphira's wing and bade her good night, too weary to say more. In return, she tousled his hair with a warm puff of air and said, *I shall watch and remember for you, little one.*

Eragon paused on the threshold of Rhunön's house and looked across the shadowy atrium to where Maud and the two elf children were still standing. He raised a hand in greeting, and Maud smiled at him, baring her sharp, pointed teeth. A tingle crawled down Eragon's neck as the elf children gazed at him; their large, slanted eyes were slightly luminous in the gloom. When they made no other motion, he ducked his head and hurried inside, eager to lie down upon a soft mattress.

A Rider in Full

Wake, little one, *said Saphira.* The sun has risen and Rhunön is impatient.

Eragon bolted upright, throwing off his blankets as easily as he cast off his waking dreams. His arms and shoulders were sore from his exertions of the previous day. He pulled on his boots, fumbling with the laces in his excitement, grabbed his grimy apron from the floor, and bounded down the elaborately carved stairs to the entryway of Rhunön's curved house.

Outside, the sky was bright with the first light of dawn, although shadow still enveloped the atrium. Eragon spotted Rhunön and Saphira by the open-walled forge and trotted over to them, combing his hair into place with his fingers.

Rhunön stood leaning against the edge of the bench. There were dark bags under her eyes, and the lines on her face were heavier than before.

The sword lay before her, concealed beneath a length of white cloth.

"I have done the impossible," she said, the words hoarse and broken. "I made a sword when I swore I would not. What is more, I made it in less than a day and with hands that were not my own. Yet the sword is not crude or shoddy. No! It is the finest sword I have ever forged. I would have preferred to use less magic during the process, but that is my only qualm, and it is a small one compared with the perfection of the results. Behold!"

Grasping the corner of the cloth, Rhunön pulled it aside, revealing the sword.

Eragon gasped.

He had thought that in the handful of hours since he had left her, Rhunön would only have had enough time to fabricate a plain hilt and crossguard for the sword, and maybe a simple wooden scabbard. Instead, the sword Eragon saw on the bench was as magnificent as Zar'roc, Naegling, and Támerlein and, in his opinion, more beautiful than any of them.

Covering the blade was a glossy scabbard of the same dark blue as the scales on Saphira's back. The color displayed a slight variegation, like the mottled light at the bottom of a clear forest pond. A piece of blued brightsteel carved in the shape of a leaf capped the end of the scabbard while a collar decorated with stylized vines encircled the mouth. The curved crossguard was also made of blued brightsteel, as were the four ribs that held in place the large sapphire that formed the pommel. The hand-and-a-half hilt was made of hard black wood.

Overcome by a sense of reverence, Eragon reached out toward the sword, then paused and glanced at Rhunön. "May I?" he asked.

She inclined her head. "You may. I give it to thee, Shadeslayer."

Eragon lifted the sword from the bench. The scabbard and the wood of the hilt were cool to the touch. For several minutes, he marveled at the details on the scabbard and the guard and the pommel. Then he tightened his grip around the hilt and unsheathed the blade.

Like the rest of the sword, the blade was blue, but of a slightly lighter shade; it was the blue of the scales in the hollow of Saphira's throat rather than the blue of those on her back. And as it was on Zar'roc, the color was iridescent; as Eragon moved the sword about, the color would shimmer and shift, displaying any of the many tones of blue present on Saphira herself. Through the wash of color, the cable-like patterns within the brightsteel and the pale bands along the edges were still visible.

With a single hand, Eragon swung the sword through the air, and he laughed at how light and fast it felt. The sword almost seemed alive. He grasped the sword with both his hands then and was delighted to find that they fit perfectly on the longer hilt. Lunging forward, he stabbed at an imaginary enemy and was confident they would have died from the attack.

"Here," said Rhunön, and pointed at a bundle of three iron rods planted upright in the ground outside the forge. "Try it on those."

Eragon allowed himself a moment to focus his thoughts, then took a single step toward the rods. With a yell, he slashed downward and cut through all three rods. The blade emitted a single pure note that slowly faded into silence. When Eragon examined the edge where it had struck the iron, he saw that the impact had not damaged it in the slightest.

"Are you well pleased, Dragon Rider?" Rhunön asked.

"More than pleased, Rhunön-elda," said Eragon, and bowed to her. "I do not know how I can thank you for such a gift."

"You may thank me by killing Galbatorix. If there is any sword destined to slay that mad king, it is this one."

"I shall try my hardest, Rhunön-elda."

The elf woman nodded, appearing satisfied. "Well, you finally have a sword of your own, which is as it ought to be. *Now* you are truly a Dragon Rider!"

"Yes," said Eragon, and held the sword up toward the sky, admiring it. "Now I am truly a Rider."

"Before you leave, one last thing remains for you to do," said Rhunön.

"Oh?"

She flicked a finger toward the sword. "You must name it so I can mark the blade and scabbard with the appropriate glyph."

Eragon walked over to Saphira and said, *What do you think?*

I am not the one who must carry the blade. Name it as you see fit.

Yes, but you must have some ideas!

She lowered her head toward him and sniffed at the sword, then said, *Blue-gem-tooth is what I would name it. Or Blue-claw-red.*

That would sound ridiculous to humans.

Then what of Reaver or Gutripper? Or maybe Battleclaw or Glitter-

thorn or Limbhacker? *You could name it Terror or Pain or Armbiter or Eversharp or Ripplescale: that on account of the lines in the steel. There is also Tongue of Death and Elfsteel and Starmetal and many others besides.*

Her sudden outpouring surprised Eragon. *You have a talent for this,* he said.

Inventing random names is easy. Inventing the right name, however, can try the patience of even an elf.

What of Kingkiller? he asked.

And what if we actually kill Galbatorix? What, then? Will you do nothing else of worth with your sword?

Mmh. Placing the sword alongside Saphira's left foreleg, Eragon said, *It's exactly the same color as you. . . . I could name it after you.*

A low growl sounded in Saphira's chest. *No.*

He fought back a smile. *Are you sure? Just imagine if we were in battle and—*

Her claws sank into the earth. *No. I am not a thing for you to wave about and make fun of.*

681

No, you're right. I'm sorry. . . . Well, what if I named it Hope in the ancient language? Zar'roc means "misery," so wouldn't it be fitting if I were to wield a sword that by its very name would counteract misery?

A noble sentiment, said Saphira. *But do you really want to give your enemies hope? Do you want to stab Galbatorix with hope?*

It's an amusing pun, he said, chuckling.

Once, maybe, but no more.

Stymied, Eragon grimaced and rubbed his chin, studying the play of light across the glittering blade. As he gazed into the depths of the steel, his eye chanced upon the flamelike pattern that marked the transition between the softer steel of the spine and that of the edges, and he recalled the word Brom had used to light his pipe during the memory Saphira had shared with him. Then Eragon thought of Yazuac, where he had first used magic, and also of his duel with Durza in Farthen Dûr, and in that instant he knew without doubt that he had found the right name for his sword.

Eragon consulted with Saphira, and when she agreed with his

choice, he lifted the weapon to shoulder level and said, "I am decided. Sword, I name thee Brisingr!"

And with a sound like rushing wind, the blade burst into fire, an envelope of sapphire-blue flames writhing about the razor-sharp steel.

Uttering a startled cry, Eragon dropped the sword and jumped back, afraid of being burned. The blade continued to blaze on the ground, the translucent flames charring a nearby clump of grass. It was then that Eragon realized it was he who was providing the energy to sustain the unnatural fire. He quickly ended the magic, and the fire vanished from the sword. Puzzled by how he could have cast a spell without intending to, he picked up the sword again and tapped the blade with the tip of a finger. It was no hotter than before.

A heavy scowl on her brow, Rhunön stalked forward, seized the sword from Eragon, and examined it from tip to pommel. "You are fortunate I have already protected it with wards against heat and damage, else you would have just scratched the guard and destroyed the temper of the blade. Do not drop the sword again, Shadeslayer—even if it should turn into a snake—or else I shall take it back and give you a worn-out hammer instead." Eragon apologized, and appearing somewhat mollified, Rhunön handed the sword back to him. "Did you set fire to it on purpose?" she asked.

"No," said Eragon, unable to explain what had happened.

"Say it again," ordered Rhunön.

"What?"

"The name, the name, say it again."

Holding the sword as far away from his body as he could, Eragon exclaimed, "Brisingr!"

A column of flickering flames engulfed the blade of the sword, the heat warming Eragon's face. This time Eragon noticed the slight drain on his strength from the spell. After a few moments, he extinguished the smokeless fire.

Once more Eragon exclaimed, "Brisingr!" And once more the blade shimmered with blue, wraithlike tongues of flame.

Now there is a fitting sword for a Rider and dragon! said Saphira in a delighted tone. *It breathes fire as easily as I do.*

"But I wasn't trying to cast a spell!" protested Eragon. "All I did was say *Brisingr* and—" He yelped and swore as the sword again caught fire, which he put out for the fourth time.

"May I?" asked Rhunön, extending a hand toward Eragon. He gave her the sword, and she too said, "Brisingr!" A shiver seemed to run down the blade, but other than that, it remained inanimate. Her expression contemplative, Rhunön returned the sword to Eragon and said, "I can think of two explanations for this marvel. One is that because you were involved with the forging, you imbued the blade with a portion of your personality and therefore it has become attuned to your wishes. My other explanation is that you have discovered the true name of your sword. Perhaps both those things are what has happened. In any event, you have chosen well, Shadeslayer. Brisingr! Yes, I like it. It is a good name for a sword."

A very good name, Saphira agreed.

Then Rhunön placed her hand over the middle of Brisingr's blade and murmured an inaudible spell. The Elvish glyph for *fire* appeared upon both sides of the blade. She did the same to the front of the scabbard.

Again Eragon bowed to the elf woman, and both he and Saphira expressed their gratitude to her. A smile appeared on Rhunön's aged face, and she touched each of them upon their brows with her callused thumb. "I am glad I was able to help the Riders this once more. Go, Shadeslayer. Go, Brightscales. Return to the Varden, and may your enemies flee with fear when they see the sword you now wield."

So Eragon and Saphira bade her farewell, and together they departed Rhunön's house, Eragon cradling Brisingr in his arms as he would a newborn child.

683

✦ ✦ ✦

GREAVES AND BRACERS

A single candle lit the inside of the gray wool tent, a poor substitute for the radiance of the sun.

Roran stood with his arms outstretched while Katrina laced up the sides of the padded jerkin she had fitted for him. When she finished, she tugged on the hem of the jerkin, smoothing out the wrinkles, and said, "There now. Is it too tight?"

He shook his head. "No."

She retrieved his greaves from the cot they shared and knelt before him in the flickering candlelight. Roran watched as she buckled the greaves onto his lower legs. She cupped the curve of his calf with her hand as she secured the second piece of armor, her flesh warm against his through the fabric of his trousers.

Standing, she turned to the cot again and picked up his bracers. Roran held out his arms toward her and stared into her eyes, even as she stared into his. With slow, deliberate motions, she fastened the bracers onto his forearms, then drew her hands from the inside of his elbow down to his wrists, where he clasped her hands with his own.

She smiled and pulled free of his gentle grip.

Next from the cot, she took his shirt of mail. She rose up onto the tips of her toes and lifted the hauberk over his head and held it there while he fit his arms into the sleeves. The mail tinkled like ice as she released it and it fell onto his shoulders, unfurling so that the lower edge hung level with his knees.

On his head, she set his leather arming cap, tying it firmly in place with a knot under his chin. She held his face between her hands for a moment, then kissed him once upon the lips and fetched his peaked helm, which she carefully slid over the arming cap.

Roran slipped his arm around her thickening waist as she started back toward the cot, stopping her. "Listen to me," he said. "I'll be fine." He tried to convey all his love for her through the tone of his voice and the strength of his gaze. "Don't just sit here all alone. Promise me that. Go to Elain; she could use your help. She's sick, and her child is overdue."

Katrina lifted her chin, her eyes gleaming with tears he knew she would not shed until after he had left. "Must you march in the front line?" she whispered.

"Someone must, and it might as well be me. Whom would you send in my stead?"

"Anyone . . . anyone at all." Katrina looked down and was silent for a span, then she removed a red kerchief from the bodice of her dress and said, "Here, carry this favor of mine, so that the whole world may know how proud I am of you." And she tied the kerchief to his sword belt.

Roran kissed her twice and released her, and she fetched his shield and spear from the cot. He kissed her a third time as he took them from her, then fit his arm through the strap on his shield.

"If something does happen to me—" he began to say.

Katrina placed a finger upon his lips. "Shh. Speak not of it, lest it should come true."

"Very well." He hugged her one last time. "Be safe."

"And you."

Although he hated to leave her, Roran raised his shield and strode out of the tent into the pale light of dawn. Men, dwarves, and Urgals streamed westward through the camp, heading toward the trampled field where the Varden were assembling.

Roran filled his lungs with the cool morning air and then followed, knowing that his band of warriors would be waiting for him. Once he arrived at the field, he sought out Jörmundur's division and, after reporting to Jörmundur, made his way to the front of the group, where he chose to stand next to Yarbog.

The Urgal glanced at him, then grunted, "A good day for a battle."

"A good day."

A horn sounded at the forefront of the Varden as soon as the sun broke over the horizon. Roran hefted his spear and began to run forward, like everyone else around him, howling at the top of his lungs as arrows rained down upon them and boulders whistled past overhead, flying in either direction. Ahead of him, a stone wall eighty feet tall loomed.

The siege of Feinster had begun.

✦ ✦ ✦

LEAVE-TAKING

From Rhunön's house, Saphira and Eragon flew back to their tree house. Eragon gathered up his belongings from the bedroom, saddled Saphira, and then returned to his usual place upon the crest of her shoulders.

Before we go to the Crags of Tel'naeír, he said, *there is one more thing I must do in Ellesméra.*

Must you? she asked.

I won't be content unless I do.

Saphira leaped out from the tree house. She glided westward until the number of buildings began to diminish, and then she angled downward for a soft landing upon a narrow, moss-covered path. After asking for, and getting, directions from an elf who was sitting in the branches of a nearby tree, Eragon and Saphira continued through the woods until they arrived at a small one-room house grown out of the bole of a fir tree that stood at an acute angle, as if a constant wind pressed against it.

To the left of the house was a soft bank of earth taller by several feet than Eragon. A rivulet of water tumbled over the edge of the bank and poured itself into a limpid pool before meandering off into the dim recesses of the forest. White orchids lined the pool. A bulbous root protruded out of the ground from among the slender flowers that grew along the near shore, and sitting cross-legged upon the root was Sloan.

Eragon held his breath, not wanting to alert the other man to his presence.

The butcher wore robes of brown and orange, after the fashion of the elves. A thin black strip of cloth was tied around his head, concealing the gaping holes where his eyes had been. In his lap, he held a length of seasoned wood, which he was whittling with a small, curved knife. His face was covered with far more lines than Eragon remembered, and upon his hands and arms were several new scars, livid against the surrounding skin.

Wait here, Eragon said to Saphira, and slipped off her back.

As Eragon approached him, Sloan paused in his carving and cocked his head. "Go away," he rasped.

Not knowing how to respond, Eragon stopped where he was and remained silent.

The muscles in his jaw rippling, Sloan removed another few curls from the wood he held, then tapped the tip of his knife against the root and said, "Blast you. Can you not leave me alone with my misery for a few hours? I don't want to listen to any bard or minstrel of yours, and no matter how many times you ask me, I won't change my mind. Now go on. Away with you."

Pity and anger welled up inside Eragon, and also a sense of displacement at seeing a man he had grown up around, and had so often feared and disliked, brought to such a state. "Are you comfortable?" Eragon asked in the ancient language, adopting a light, lilting tone.

Sloan uttered a growl of disgust. "You know I cannot understand your tongue and I do not wish to learn it. The words ring in my ears longer than they ought to. If you will not speak in the language of my race, then do not speak to me at all."

Despite Sloan's entreaty, Eragon did not repeat the question in their common language, nor did he depart.

With a curse, Sloan resumed his whittling. After every other stroke, he ran his right thumb over the surface of the wood, checking the progress of whatever he was carving. Several minutes passed, and then in a softer voice, Sloan said, "You were right; having something to do with my hands calms my thoughts. Sometimes . . . sometimes I can almost forget what I have lost, but the memories always return, and I feel as if I am choking on them. . . .

I am glad you sharpened the knife. A man's knives should always be sharp."

Eragon watched him for a minute more, then he turned away and walked back to where Saphira was waiting. As he pulled himself into the saddle, he said, *Sloan does not seem to have changed very much.*

And Saphira replied, *You cannot expect him to become someone else entirely in such a short time.*

No, but I had hoped he would learn something of wisdom here in Ellesméra and that maybe he would repent of his crimes.

If he does not wish to acknowledge his mistakes, Eragon, nothing can force him to. In any event, you have done all you can for him. Now he must find a way to reconcile himself with his lot. If he cannot, then let him seek the solace of the everlasting grave.

From a clearing close to Sloan's house, Saphira launched herself up and over the surrounding trees and headed north toward the Crags of Tel'naeír, flapping as hard and fast as she could. The morning sun sat full upon the horizon, and the rays of light that streamed out over the treetops created long, dark shadows that, as one, pointed to the west like purple pennants.

Saphira descended toward the clearing by Oromis's pinewood house, where Glaedr and Oromis stood waiting for them. Eragon was startled to see that Glaedr was wearing a saddle nestled between two of the towering spikes on his back and that Oromis was garbed in heavy traveling robes of blue and green, over which he wore a corselet of golden scale armor, as well as bracers upon his arms. A tall, diamond-shaped shield was slung across his back, an archaic helm rested in the crook of his left arm, and around his waist was belted his bronze-colored sword, Naegling.

With a gust of wind from her wings, Saphira alighted upon the sward of grass and clover. She flicked out her tongue, tasting the air as Eragon slid to the ground. *Are you going to fly with us to the Varden?* she asked. The tip of her tail twitched with excitement.

"We shall fly with you as far as the edge of Du Weldenvarden, but there our paths must part," said Oromis.

Disappointed, Eragon asked, "Will you return to Ellesméra then?"

Oromis shook his head. "No, Eragon. Then we shall continue onward to the city of Gil'ead."

Saphira hissed with surprise, a sentiment Eragon shared. "Why to Gil'ead?" he asked, bewildered.

Because Islanzadí and her army have marched there from Ceunon, and they are about to lay siege to the city, said Glaedr. The strange, gleaming structures of his mind brushed against Eragon's consciousness.

But do not you and Oromis wish to keep your existence hidden from the Empire? Saphira asked.

Oromis closed his eyes for a moment, his expression withdrawn and enigmatic. "The time for hiding has passed, Saphira. Glaedr and I have taught the two of you everything we could in the brief while you were able to study under us. It was a paltry education compared with that you would have received of old, but given how events press on us, we are fortunate to have been able to teach you as much as we did. Glaedr and I are satisfied that you now know everything that might help you to defeat Galbatorix.

"Therefore, since it seems unlikely that either of you will have a chance to return here for further instruction before the conclusion of this war, and since it seems even more unlikely that there shall ever be another dragon and Rider for us to instruct while Galbatorix still bestrides the warm earth, we have decided that we no longer have any reason to remain sequestered in Du Weldenvarden. It is more important that we help Islanzadí and the Varden overthrow Galbatorix than we tarry here in idle comfort while we wait for another Rider and dragon to seek us out.

"When Galbatorix learns that we are still alive, it shall undermine his confidence, for he shall not know if other dragons and Riders have survived his attempt to exterminate them. Also, knowledge of our existence shall bolster the spirits of the dwarves and the Varden and counteract any adverse effects Murtagh and

Thorn's appearance on the Burning Plains may have had upon the resolution of their warriors. And it may well increase the number of recruits Nasuada receives from the Empire."

Eragon glanced at Naegling and said, "Surely, though, Master, you do not intend to venture into battle yourselves."

"And why should we not?" inquired Oromis, tilting his head to one side.

Since he did not want to offend Oromis or Glaedr, Eragon was uncertain how to respond. At last he said, "Forgive me, Master, but how can you fight when you cannot cast spells that require more than a small amount of energy? And what of the spasms you sometimes suffer? If one were to strike in the middle of a battle, it could prove fatal."

Oromis replied, "As you ought to know well by now, mere strength rarely decides the victor when two magicians duel. Even so, I have all the strength I need here, in the jewel of my sword." And he reached across his body and placed the palm of his right hand on the yellow diamond that formed the pommel of Naegling. "For over a hundred years, Glaedr and I have stored every iota of our excess strength in this diamond, and others have added their strength to the pool as well; twice a week, several elves from Ellesméra visit me here and transfer as much of their life force into the gem as they can without killing themselves. The amount of energy contained within this stone is formidable, Eragon; with it, I could shift an entire mountain. It is a small matter, then, to defend Glaedr and myself from swords and spears and arrows, or even from a boulder cast by a siege engine. As for my seizures, I have attached certain wards to the stone in Naegling that will protect me from harm if I become incapacitated upon the battlefield. So you see, Eragon, Glaedr and I are far from helpless."

Chastened, Eragon dipped his head and murmured, "Yes, Master."

Oromis's expression softened somewhat. "I appreciate your concern, Eragon, and you are right to be concerned, for war is a perilous endeavor and even the most accomplished warrior may find death waiting for him amid the heated frenzy of battle. However, our cause is a worthy one. If Glaedr and I go to our deaths, then we go willingly, for by our sacrifice, we may help to free Alagaësia from the shadow of Galbatorix's tyranny."

"But if you die," said Eragon, feeling very small, "and yet we still succeed in killing Galbatorix and freeing the last dragon egg, who will train that dragon and his Rider?"

Oromis surprised Eragon by reaching out and clasping him by the shoulder. "If that should come to pass," said the elf, his face grave, "then it shall be your responsibility, Eragon, and yours, Saphira, to instruct the new dragon and Rider in the ways of our order. Ah, do not look so apprehensive, Eragon. You would not be alone in the task. No doubt Islanzadí and Nasuada would ensure that the wisest scholars of both our races would be there to help you."

A strange sense of unease troubled Eragon. He had often longed to be treated as more of an adult, but nevertheless, he did not feel

ready to take Oromis's place. It seemed wrong to even contemplate the notion. For the first time, Eragon understood that he would eventually become part of the older generation, and that when he did, he would have no mentor to rely upon for guidance. His throat tightened.

Releasing Eragon's shoulder, Oromis gestured at Brisingr, which lay in Eragon's arms, and said, "The entire forest shuddered when you woke the Menoa tree, Saphira, and half the elves in Ellesméra contacted Glaedr and me with frantic pleas for us to rush to her aid. Moreover, we had to intervene on your behalf with Gilderien the Wise, so as to prevent him from punishing you for employing such violent methods."

I shall not apologize, said Saphira. *We had not the time to wait for gentle persuasion to work.*

Oromis nodded. "I understand, and I am not criticizing you, Saphira. I only wanted you to be aware of the consequences of your actions." At his request, Eragon handed his newly forged sword to

Oromis and held his helm for him while the elf examined the sword. "Rhunön has outdone herself," Oromis declared. "Few weapons, swords or otherwise, are the equal of this. You are fortunate to wield such an impressive blade, Eragon." One of Oromis's sharp eyebrows rose a fraction of an inch as he read the glyph on the blade. "Brisingr . . . a most apt name for the sword of a Dragon Rider."

"Aye," said Eragon. "But for some reason, every time I utter its name, the blade bursts into . . . ," he hesitated, and instead of saying *fire*—which, of course, was *brisingr* in the ancient language—he said, "flames."

Oromis's eyebrow climbed even higher. "Indeed? Did Rhunön have an explanation for this unique phenomenon?" As he spoke, Oromis returned Brisingr to Eragon in exchange for his helm.

"Yes, Master," said Eragon. And he recounted Rhunön's two theories.

When he had finished, Oromis murmured, "I wonder . . . ," and his gaze drifted past Eragon toward the horizon. Then Oromis gave a brief shake of his head and again focused his gray eyes upon Eragon and Saphira. His face became even more solemn than before. "I am afraid I have let my pride speak for me. Glaedr and I may not be helpless, but neither, as you pointed out, Eragon, are we entirely whole. Glaedr has his wound, and I have my own . . . impairments. It is not for nothing I am called the Cripple Who Is Whole.

"Our disabilities would not be a problem if our only enemies were mortal men. Even in our current state, we could easily slay a hundred ordinary humans—a hundred or a thousand, it would matter little which. However, our enemy is the most dangerous foe we or this land has ever faced. As much as I dislike acknowledging it, Glaedr and I are at a disadvantage, and it is quite possible that we shall not survive the battles yet to come. We have lived long and full lives, and the sorrows of centuries press upon us, but the two of you are young and fresh and full of hope, and I believe your

693

prospects of defeating Galbatorix are greater than those of anyone else."

Oromis glanced at Glaedr, and the elf's face became troubled. "Therefore, in order to help ensure your survival, and as a precaution against our possible demise, Glaedr has, with my blessing, decided to . . ."

I have decided, said Glaedr, *to give you my heart of hearts, Saphira Brightscales, Eragon Shadeslayer.*

Saphira's astonishment was no less than Eragon's. Together, they stared at the majestic gold dragon who towered high above them. Saphira said, *Master, you honor us beyond words, but . . . are you sure that you wish to entrust your heart to us?*

I am sure, said Glaedr, and lowered his massive head until it was only slightly above Eragon. *For many reasons, I am sure. If you hold my heart, you shall be able to communicate with Oromis and me—no matter how far apart we may be—and I shall be able to aid you with my strength whenever you are in difficulty. And if Oromis and I should fall in battle, our knowledge and experience, and also my strength, shall still be at your disposal. Long have I pondered this choice, and I am confident it is the right one.*

"But if Oromis were to die," said Eragon in a soft voice, "would you really want to live on without him, and as an Eldunarí?"

Glaedr turned his head and focused one of his immense eyes upon Eragon. *I do not wish to be parted from Oromis, but whatever happens, I shall continue to do what I can to topple Galbatorix from his throne. That is our only goal, and not even death shall deter us from pursuing it. The idea of losing Saphira horrifies you, Eragon, and rightly so. However, Oromis and I have had centuries to reconcile ourselves with the fact that such a parting is inevitable. No matter how careful we are, if we live long enough, eventually one of us will die. It is not a happy thought, but it is the truth. Such is the way of the world.*

Shifting his stance, Oromis said, "I cannot pretend that I regard this with favor, but the purpose of life is not to do what we want but what needs to be done. This is what fate demands of us."

So now I ask you, said Glaedr, *Saphira Brightscales and Eragon Shadeslayer, will you accept my gift and all that it entails?*

I will, said Saphira.

I will, replied Eragon after a brief hesitation.

Then Glaedr drew back his head. The muscles of his abdomen rippled and clenched several times, and his throat began to convulse, as if something were stuck in it. Widening his stance, the gold dragon extended his neck straight out in front of him, every cord and sinew of his body standing in high relief underneath the armor of his sparkling scales. Glaedr's throat continued to flex and relax with increasing speed until at last he lowered his head so that it was level with Eragon and opened his jaws, hot, pungent air pouring from his massive maw. Eragon squinted and tried not to gag. As he gazed into the depths of Glaedr's mouth, Eragon saw the dragon's throat contract one last time, and then a hint of gold light appeared between the folds of dripping, blood-red tissue. A second later, a round object about a foot in diameter slid down Glaedr's crimson tongue and out of his mouth so fast, Eragon nearly missed catching it.

As his hands closed around the slippery, saliva-covered Eldunarí, Eragon gasped and staggered backward, for he suddenly felt Glaedr's every thought and emotion, and all of the sensations of his body. The amount of information was overwhelming, as was the closeness of their contact. Eragon had expected as much, but it still shocked him to realize he was holding Glaedr's entire being between his hands.

Glaedr flinched, shaking his head as if he had been stung, and quickly shielded his mind from Eragon, although Eragon could still sense the flicker of his shifting thoughts, as well as the general color of his emotions.

The Eldunarí itself was like a giant gold jewel. Its surface was warm and covered with hundreds of sharp facets, which varied somewhat in size and sometimes projected at odd, slanting angles. The center of the Eldunarí glowed with a dull radiance, similar to

695

that of a shuttered lantern, and the diffuse light throbbed with a slow, steady beat. Upon first inspection, the light appeared uniform, but the longer Eragon gazed at it, the more details he saw within it: small eddies and currents that coiled and twisted in seemingly random directions, darker motes that barely moved at all, and flurries of bright flashes no larger than the head of a pin that would flare for a moment, then fade back into the underlying field of light. It was alive.

"Here," said Oromis, and handed Eragon a sturdy cloth sack.

To Eragon's relief, his connection with Glaedr vanished as soon as he placed the Eldunarí in the bag and his hands were no longer touching the gemlike stone. Still somewhat shaken, Eragon clasped the cloth-covered Eldunarí against his chest, awed by the knowledge that his arms were wrapped around Glaedr's essence and afraid of what might happen to it if he allowed the heart of hearts out of his grasp.

"Thank you, Master," Eragon managed to say, bowing his head toward Glaedr.

We shall guard your heart with our lives, Saphira added.

"No!" exclaimed Oromis, his voice fierce. "Not with your lives! That is the very thing we wish to avoid. Do not allow any misfortune to befall Glaedr's heart because of carelessness on your part, but neither should you sacrifice yourself to protect him or me or anyone else. You have to stay alive at all costs, else our hopes shall be dashed and all will be darkness."

"Yes, Master," Eragon and Saphira said at the same time, he with his tongue and she with her thoughts.

Said Glaedr, *Because you swore fealty to Nasuada, and you owe her your loyalty and obedience, you may tell her of my heart if you must, but only if you must. For the sake of dragons everywhere, what few of us remain, the truth about the Eldunarí cannot become common knowledge.*

May we tell Arya? asked Saphira.

"And what about Blödhgarm and the other elves Islanzadí sent to protect me?" asked Eragon. "I allowed them into my mind when

Saphira and I last fought Murtagh. They will notice your presence, Glaedr, if you help us in the midst of a battle."

You may inform Blödhgarm and his spellcasters of the Eldunarí, said Glaedr, *but only after they have sworn oaths of secrecy to you.*

Oromis placed his helm on his head. "Arya is Islanzadí's daughter, and so I suppose it is proper she should know. However, as with Nasuada, do not tell her unless it becomes absolutely necessary. A secret shared is no secret at all. If you can be so disciplined, do not even think of it, nor of the very fact of the Eldunarí, so that no one may steal the information from your minds."

"Yes, Master."

"Now let us be gone from here," said Oromis, and drew a pair of thick gauntlets over his hands. "I have heard from Islanzadí that Nasuada has laid siege to the city of Feinster, and the Varden have great need of you."

We have spent too long in Ellesméra, said Saphira.

Perhaps, said Glaedr, *but it was time well spent.*

Taking a short running start, Oromis bounded up Glaedr's single foreleg and onto his high, jagged back, where Oromis settled into his saddle and began to tighten the straps around his legs. "As we fly," said the elf, calling down to Eragon, "we can review the lists of true names you learned during your last visit."

Eragon went to Saphira and carefully climbed onto her back, wrapped one of his blankets around Glaedr's heart, and packed the bundle in his saddlebags. Then he secured his legs in the same manner as had Oromis. Behind him, he could feel a constant thrum of energy radiating from the Eldunarí.

Glaedr walked to the edge of the Crags of Tel'naeír and unfurled his voluminous wings. The earth shook as the gold dragon leaped toward the cloud-streaked sky, and the air boomed and shuddered as Glaedr drove his wings downward, pulling away from the ocean of trees below. Eragon gripped the spike in front of him as Saphira followed, flinging herself out into open space and falling several hundred feet in a steep dive before she ascended to Glaedr's side.

Glaedr assumed the lead as the two dragons oriented themselves toward the southwest. Each of them flapping at a different tempo, Saphira and Glaedr sped over the rolling forest.

Saphira arched her neck and uttered a ringing roar. Ahead, Glaedr responded likewise. Their fierce cries echoed across the vast dome of the sky, frightening the birds and beasts below.

FLIGHT

From Ellesméra, Saphira and Glaedr flew without stopping over the ancient forest of the elves, soaring high above the tall, dark pine trees. Sometimes the forest would break, and Eragon would see a lake or a contorted river winding across the land. Often there was a herd of small roe deer gathered along the edge of the water, and the animals would stop and lift their heads to watch the dragons soar past. For the most part, however, Eragon paid little attention to the scenery because he was busy reciting within his mind every word of the ancient language Oromis had taught him, and if he forgot any or made a mistake in pronunciation, Oromis would have him repeat the word until he had memorized it.

They arrived at the edge of Du Weldenvarden by late afternoon of the first day. There, above the shadowed boundary between the trees and the fields of grass beyond, Glaedr and Saphira circled one another, and Glaedr said, *Keep safe your heart, Saphira, and mine as well.*

I will, Master, Saphira replied.

And Oromis shouted from Glaedr's back, "Fair winds to you both, Eragon, Saphira! When next we meet, let it be before the gates of Urû'baen."

"Fair winds to you as well!" Eragon called in return.

Then Glaedr turned and followed the line of the forest westward—which would lead him to the northernmost tip of Isenstar Lake, and the lake thence to Gil'ead—while Saphira continued in the same southwesterly direction as before.

Saphira flew all through that night, landing only to drink and so Eragon could stretch his legs and relieve himself. Unlike during their flight to Ellesméra, they encountered no headwinds; the air remained clear and smooth, as if even nature were eager for them to return to the Varden. When the sun rose on their second day, it found them already deep within the Hadarac Desert and heading straight south, so as to skirt the eastern border of the Empire. And by the time darkness had again engulfed the land and sky and held them in its cold embrace, Saphira and Eragon were beyond the confines of the sandy wastes and were again soaring over the verdant fields of the Empire, their course such that they would pass between Urû'baen and Lake Tüdosten on their way to the city of Feinster.

After flying for two days and two nights without sleep, Saphira was unable to continue. Swooping down to a small thicket of white birch trees by a pond, she curled up in their shade and napped for a few hours while Eragon kept watch and practiced his swordsmanship with Brisingr.

Ever since they had parted with Oromis and Glaedr, a sense of constant anxiety had troubled Eragon as he pondered what awaited him and Saphira at Feinster. He knew that they were better protected than most from death and injury, but when he thought back to the Burning Plains, and to the Battle of Farthen Dûr, and when he remembered the sight of blood spurting from severed limbs and the screams of wounded men and the white-hot lash of a sword slicing through his own flesh, then Eragon's gut would roil and his muscles would shake with suppressed energy, and he did not know whether he wished to fight every soldier in the land or flee in the opposite direction and hide in a deep, dark hole.

His dread only worsened when he and Saphira resumed their journey and spotted lines of armed men marching over the fields below. Here and there, pillars of pale smoke rose from sacked villages. The sight of so much wanton destruction sickened him. Averting his gaze, he squeezed the neck spike in front of him and squinted until the only thing visible through the bars of his blurry eyelashes was the white calluses on his knuckles.

Little one, said Saphira, her thoughts slow and tired. *We have done this before. Do not allow it to disturb you so.*

Regretting that he had distracted her from flying, he said, *I'm sorry. . . . I'll be fine when we get there. I just want it to be over.*

I know.

Eragon sniffed and wiped his cold nose on the cuff of his tunic. *Sometimes I wish I enjoyed fighting as much as you do. Then this would be so much easier.*

If you did, she said, *the entire world would cower before our feet, including Galbatorix. No, it is good you do not share my love of blood. We balance each other out, Eragon. . . . Apart we are incomplete, but together we are whole. Now clear your mind of these poisonous thoughts and tell me a riddle that will keep me awake.*

Very well, he said after a moment. *I am colored red and blue and yellow and every other hue of the rainbow. I am long and short, thick and thin, and I often rest coiled up. I can eat a hundred sheep in a row and still be hungry. What am I?*

A dragon, of course, she said without hesitation.

No, a woolen rug.

Bah!

Their third day of traveling crept past with agonizing slowness. The only sounds were those of Saphira's wings flapping, the steady rasp of her panting, and the dull roar of air rushing past Eragon's ears. His legs and lower back ached from sitting in the saddle for so long, but his discomfort was slight compared with Saphira's; her flight muscles burned with an almost unbearable amount of pain. Still, she persevered and did not complain, and she refused his offer to alleviate her suffering with a spell, saying, *You will need the strength when we arrive.*

Hours after dusk, Saphira wobbled and dropped several feet in a single, sickening lurch. Eragon straightened, alarmed, and looked around for any clues as to what had caused the disturbance but saw only blackness below and the glittering stars above.

I think we just reached the Jiet River, said Saphira. *The air here is cool and moist, as it would be over water.*

Then Feinster shouldn't be much farther ahead. Are you sure you can find the city in the dark? We could be a hundred miles north or south of it!

No, we could not. My sense of direction may not be infallible, but it is certainly better than yours or that of any other earthbound creature. If the elf maps we have seen were accurate, then we cannot be off by more than fifty miles north or south of Feinster, and at this height, we can easily see the city over that distance. We may even be able to smell the smoke from their chimneys.

And so it was. Later that night, when dawn was only a few hours away, a dull red glow appeared upon the western horizon. Seeing it, Eragon twisted around and removed his armor from the saddlebags, then donned his mail hauberk, his arming cap, his helm, his bracers, and his greaves. He wished he had his shield, but he had left it with the Varden before running to Mount Thardûr with Nar Garzhvog.

Then Eragon rummaged with one hand through the contents of his bags until he found the silver flask of faelnirv Oromis had given him. The metal container was cool to the touch. Eragon drank a small sip of the enchanted liqueur, which seared the inside of his mouth and which tasted of elderberries and mead and mulled cider. Heat suffused his face. Within seconds, his weariness began to recede as the restorative properties of the faelnirv took effect.

Eragon shook the flask. To his concern, it felt as if a third of the precious liqueur was already gone, even though he had only consumed a single mouthful once before. *I have to be more careful with it in the future,* he thought.

As he and Saphira drew closer, the glow on the horizon resolved into thousands of individual points of light, from small handheld lanterns to cookfires to bonfires to huge patches of burning pitch that poured a foul black smoke into the night sky. By the ruddy light of the fires, Eragon saw a sea of flashing spearpoints and gleaming helmets surging against the base of the large, well-fortified city, the walls of which teemed with tiny figures busy firing arrows at the army below, pouring cauldrons of boiling oil between the merlons of the parapet, cutting ropes thrown over the walls, and pushing away the rickety wooden ladders the besiegers kept leaning against the ramparts. Faint calls and cries floated upward from the ground, as well as the boom of a battering ram crashing against the city's iron gates.

The last of Eragon's weariness vanished as he studied the battlefield and noted the placement of the men and the buildings and the various pieces of war machinery. Extending outward from the walls of Feinster were hundreds of ramshackle hovels crammed one against another, with hardly enough room for a horse to pass between: the dwellings of those too poor to afford a house within the main part of the city. Most of the hovels appeared deserted, and a wide swath had been demolished so that the Varden could approach the city walls in force. A score or more of the mean huts were burning, and even as he watched, the fires spread, leaping from one thatched roof to another. East of the hovels, curved black lines scored the earth where trenches had been excavated to protect the Varden's camp. On the other side of the city were docks and wharves similar to those Eragon remembered from Teirm, and then the dark and restless ocean that seemed to extend to infinity.

A thrill of feral excitement ran through Eragon, and he felt Saphira shiver underneath him at the same time. He gripped the hilt of Brisingr. *They don't seem to have noticed us yet. Shall we announce our arrival?*

Saphira answered him by loosing a roar that made his teeth rattle and by painting the sky in front of them with a thick sheet of blue fire.

Below, the Varden at the foot of the city and the defenders upon the ramparts paused, and for a moment, silence enveloped the battlefield. Then the Varden began to cheer and bang their spears and swords against their shields while great groans of despair wafted from the people of the city.

Ah! exclaimed Eragon, blinking. *I wish you hadn't done that. Now I can't see anything.*

Sorry.

Still blinking, he said, *The first thing we should do is find a horse that just died, or some other animal, so that I can replenish your strength with theirs.*

You don't have—

Saphira stopped talking as another mind touched theirs. After a half second of panic, Eragon recognized the consciousness as that of Trianna. *Eragon, Saphira!* cried the sorceress. *You're just in time! Arya and another elf scaled the walls, but they were trapped by a large group of soldiers. They won't survive another minute unless someone helps them! Hurry!*

BRISINGR!

Saphira tucked her wings close to her body and tipped into a steep dive, hurtling toward the dark buildings of the city. Eragon ducked his head against the blast of wind that tore at his face. The world spun around them as Saphira rolled to her right so that the archers on the ground would have difficulty shooting her.

Eragon's limbs grew heavy as Saphira pulled out of the dive. Then she leveled out and the weight pressing down on him vanished. Like strange, shrieking hawks, arrows whistled past them, some missing their mark, while Eragon's wards deflected the rest.

Swooping low over the outer city walls, Saphira roared again and lashed out with her claws and tail, knocking groups of screaming men off the parapet and toward the hard ground eighty feet below.

A tall, square tower armed with four ballistae stood at the far end of the southern wall. The huge crossbows fired twelve-foot-long javelins toward the Varden massed before the city gates. Inside the curtain wall, Eragon and Saphira spotted a hundred or so soldiers gathered around a pair of warriors, who stood with their backs pressed against the base of the tower, desperately trying to fend off a thicket of thrusting blades.

Even in the gloom and from high above, Eragon recognized one of the warriors as Arya.

Saphira leaped down from the parapet and landed in the midst of the soldiers, crushing several men beneath her feet. The rest scattered, screaming with fear and surprise. Saphira roared, frustrated that her prey was escaping, and whipped her tail across the dirt, flattening a dozen more soldiers. A man tried to run past her. Fast as a striking snake, she caught him between her jaws and shook her head, snapping his spine. She disposed of another four in a similar manner.

By then the remaining men had vanished among the buildings.

Eragon quickly pulled loose his leg straps, then jumped to the ground. The additional weight of his armor drove him to one knee as he landed. He grunted and pushed himself up onto his feet.

"Eragon!" cried Arya, running up to him. She was panting and drenched with sweat. Her only armor was a padded jerkin and a light helm painted black so it would not cast unwanted reflections.

"Welcome, Bjartskular. Welcome, Shadeslayer," purred Blödhgarm from by her side, his short fangs orange and glistening in the torchlight, his yellow eyes glowing. The ruff of fur on the elf's back and neck stood on end, which made him appear even fiercer than usual. Both he and Arya were stained with blood, although Eragon could not tell if the blood was theirs.

"Are you hurt?" he asked.

Arya shook her head, and Blödhgarm said, "A few scratches, but nothing serious."

What are you doing here without reinforcements? asked Saphira.

"The gates," said Arya, gasping. "For three days, we've tried to break them, but they're impervious to magic, and the battering ram has barely dented the wood. So I convinced Nasuada to . . ."

When Arya paused to regain her breath, Blödhgarm picked up the thread of her narrative. "Arya convinced Nasuada to stage tonight's attack so that we could sneak into Feinster without being noticed and open the gates from within. Unfortunately, we encountered a trio of spellcasters. They engaged us with their minds and prevented us from using magic while they summoned soldiers to overwhelm us with sheer numbers."

While Blödhgarm spoke, Eragon placed a hand on the chest of one of the dead soldiers and transferred what energy remained in the man's flesh into his own body, and thence to Saphira. "Where are the spellcasters now?" he asked, proceeding to another corpse.

Blödhgarm's fur-covered shoulders rose and fell. "They seem to have taken fright at your appearance, Shur'tugal."

As well they should, growled Saphira.

Eragon drained the energy from three more soldiers, and from the last, he also took the man's round wooden shield. "Well then," he said, standing, "let us go open the gates for the Varden, shall we?"

"Yes, and without delay," said Arya. She started forward, then cast a sideways glance at Eragon. "You have a new sword." It was not a question.

He nodded. "Rhunön helped me to forge it."

"And what is the name of your weapon, Shadeslayer?" asked Blödhgarm.

Eragon was about to answer when four soldiers ran out from the mouth of a dark alleyway, spears lowered. In a single, smooth motion, he drew Brisingr from its sheath and slashed through the haft of the lead man's spear and, continuing with the blow, decapitated the soldier. Brisingr seemed to shimmer with savage delight. Arya lunged forward and stabbed two of the other men before they could react while Blödhgarm leaped sideways and tackled the last soldier, killing him with his own dagger.

"Hurry!" cried Arya, and started to run toward the city gates.

Eragon and Blödhgarm raced after her while Saphira followed close behind, her claws loud against the paving stones of the street. Archers fired arrows at them from the parapet above, and three different times, soldiers rushed out from the main bulk of the city and flung themselves against them. Without slowing, Eragon, Arya, and Blödhgarm cut down the attackers, or else Saphira blasted them with a withering torrent of fire.

The steady boom of the battering ram became ever louder as they approached the forty-foot-tall gates of the city. Eragon saw two men and a woman, who were garbed in dark robes, standing before the ironbound doors, chanting in the ancient language and swaying from side to side with upheld arms. The three spellcasters fell silent when they noticed Eragon and his companions and, with their robes flapping, ran up the main street of Feinster, which led to the keep at the far side of the city.

Eragon longed to pursue them. However, it was more important to let the Varden into the city, where they would no longer be at the mercy of the men on the walls. *I wonder what mischief they have planned,* he thought, worried as he watched the spellcasters depart.

Before Eragon, Arya, Blödhgarm, and Saphira arrived at the gates, fifty soldiers in gleaming armor streamed out of the guard towers and positioned themselves in front of the huge wooden doors.

One of the soldiers pounded the hilt of his sword against his shield and shouted, "Never shall you pass, foul demons! This is our home, and we shall not allow Urgals and elves and other inhuman monsters to enter! Begone, for you shall find nothing but blood and sorrow in Feinster!"

Arya pointed at the guard towers and murmured to Eragon, "The gears for opening the gates are hidden within there."

"Go," he said. "You and Blödhgarm sneak around the men and slip into the towers. Saphira and I will keep them occupied in the meantime."

Arya nodded, then she and Blödhgarm disappeared into the pools of inky shadows that surrounded the houses behind Eragon and Saphira.

Through his bond with her, Eragon sensed that Saphira was gathering herself to pounce upon the group of soldiers. He put a hand on one of her forelegs. *Wait,* he said. *Let me try something first.*

If it doesn't work, then may I tear them to shreds? she asked, licking her fangs.

Yes, then you may do what you wish with them.

Eragon slowly walked toward the soldiers, holding his sword and shield out to either side. An arrow shot toward him from above, only to stop dead in the air three feet from his chest and drop straight to the ground. Eragon looked over the soldiers' frightened faces, then raised his voice and said, "My name is Eragon Shade-slayer! Perhaps you have heard of me, and perhaps not. In either case, know this: I am a Dragon Rider, and I have sworn to help the Varden remove Galbatorix from his throne. Tell me, have any of you sworn fealty in the ancient language to Galbatorix or the Empire? . . . Well, have you?"

The same man who had spoken before, who appeared to be the captain of the soldiers, said, "We would not swear fealty to the king even if he held a sword to our necks! Our loyalty belongs to Lady Lorana. She and her family have ruled us for four generations, and they've done a fine job of it too!" The other soldiers muttered in agreement.

"Then join us!" cried Eragon. "Lay down your weapons, and I promise no harm shall come to you or your families. You cannot hope to hold Feinster against the combined might of the Varden, Surda, the dwarves, and the elves."

"So you say," shouted one of the soldiers. "But what if Murtagh and that red dragon of his should come here again?"

Eragon hesitated, then said in a confident tone, "He is no match for me and the elves who fight with the Varden. We have already driven him off once before." To the left of the soldiers, Eragon saw Arya and Blödhgarm sidle out from behind one of the stone staircases that led to the top of the walls and, with silent footsteps, creep toward the leftmost guard tower.

The captain of the soldiers said, "We may not have pledged ourselves to the king, but Lady Lorana has. What will you do to her, then? Kill her? Imprison her? No, we will not betray our trust and allow you to pass, nor the monsters clawing at our walls. You and the Varden hold nothing but the promise of death for those who have been forced to serve the Empire!

"Why couldn't you have left well enough alone, eh, Dragon Rider? Why couldn't you have kept your head down so the rest of us could live in peace? But no, the lure of fame and glory and riches was too great. You had to bring wrack and ruin to our homes so that you could satisfy your ambitions. Well, I curse you, Dragon Rider! I curse you with all my heart! May you leave Alagaësia and never return!"

A chill crept over Eragon, for the man's curse echoed that which the last Ra'zac had cast upon him in Helgrind, and he remembered how Angela had foretold that very future for him. With an effort, he put aside such thoughts and said, "I do not wish to kill you, but I will if I must. Lay down your weapons!"

Arya silently opened the door at the bottom of the leftmost guard tower and slipped inside. Stealthy as a hunting wildcat, Blödhgarm crept behind the soldiers toward the other tower. If any of the men had turned around, they would have seen him.

The captain of the soldiers spat on the ground by Eragon's feet. "You don't even look human yourself! You're a traitor to your race, you are!" And with that, the man raised his shield and hefted his sword and slowly walked toward Eragon. "Shadeslayer," growled the soldier. "Ha! I'd as soon believe my brother's twelve-year-old son had killed a Shade as a youth like you."

Eragon waited until the captain was only a few feet away. Then he took a single step forward and stabbed Brisingr through the center of the man's embossed shield, through his arm underneath, and then through the man's chest and out his back. The man convulsed once and was still. As Eragon pulled his blade free of the corpse, there was a discordant clamor from within the guard towers as gears and chains began to turn and the massive beams that held closed the city gates began to withdraw.

"Lay down your weapons or die!" Eragon shouted.

Bellowing in unison, twenty soldiers ran at him, brandishing their swords. The others either dispersed and fled toward the heart of the city or else took Eragon's advice and placed their swords and spears and their shields on the gray paving stones and knelt by the side of the street with their hands on their knees.

A fine mist of blood formed around Eragon as he cut his way through the soldiers, dancing from one to the next faster than they could react. Saphira knocked two of the soldiers over, then set another two on fire with a short burst of flame from her nostrils, cooking them in their armor. Eragon slid to a stop several feet beyond the rearmost soldier and held his position, his sword arm out-stretched from the blow he had just dealt, and waited until he heard the man topple to the ground, first one half, and then the other.

Arya and Blödhgarm emerged from the guard towers just as the gates groaned and swung outward, revealing the blunt and splintered end of the Varden's massive battering ram. Above, the archers on the parapet cried out in dismay and retreated toward more defensible positions. Dozens of hands appeared around the edges of the gates and pulled them farther apart, and Eragon saw a mass of grim-faced Varden, men and dwarves alike, crowded in the archway beyond.

"Shadeslayer!" they shouted, and also "Argetlam!" and "Wel-come back! The hunting is good today!"

"These are my prisoners!" Eragon said, and pointed with Brisingr at the soldiers kneeling by the side of the street. "Bind them and see that they are treated well. I gave my word that no harm would come to them."

Six warriors hurried to follow his order.

The Varden rushed forward, streaming into the city, their jan-gling armor and pounding boots creating a continuous, rolling thunder. Eragon was pleased to see Roran and Horst and several other men from Carvahall in the fourth rank of the warriors. He hailed them, and Roran raised his hammer in greeting and ran toward him.

Eragon grasped Roran's right forearm and pulled him into a rough hug. Drawing back, he noticed that Roran seemed older and hollow-eyed compared with before.

"About time you got here," Roran grunted. "We've been dying by the hundreds trying to take the walls."

"Saphira and I came as fast as we could. How's Katrina?"

"She's fine."

"Once this is over, you'll have to tell me everything that's hap-pened to you since I left."

Roran pressed his lips together and nodded. Then he pointed at Brisingr and said, "Where did you get the sword?"

"From the elves."

"What's it called?"

"Bris—" Eragon started to say, but then the eleven other elves whom Islanzadí had assigned to protect him and Saphira sprinted out of the column of men and surrounded the two of them. Arya and Blödhgarm rejoined them as well, Arya wiping clean the slim blade of her sword.

Before Eragon could resume speaking, Jörmundur rode through the gates and hailed him, shouting, "Shadeslayer! Well met indeed!"

Eragon greeted him in return and asked, "What should we do now?"

"Whatever you see fit," Jörmundur replied, reining in his brown charger. "We have to fight our way up to the keep. It doesn't look as if Saphira would fit between most of the houses, so fly around and harry their forces where you can. If you could break open the keep or capture Lady Lorana, it would be a great help."

"Where's Nasuada?"

Jörmundur gestured over his shoulder. "At the rear of the army, coordinating our forces with King Orrin." Jörmundur glanced out over the influx of warriors, then looked back at Eragon and Roran. "Stronghammer, your place is with your men, not gossiping with your cousin." Then the lean, wiry commander spurred his horse forward and rode up the gloomy street, shouting orders to the Varden.

As Roran and Arya started to follow, Eragon grabbed Roran by the shoulder and tapped Arya's blade with his own. "Wait," he said.

"What!" both Arya and Roran demanded in exasperated tones.

Yes, what? Saphira asked. *We should not be sitting and talking when there is sport to be had.*

"My father," Eragon exclaimed. "It's not Morzan, it's Brom!"

Roran blinked. "Brom?"

"Yes, Brom!"

Even Arya appeared surprised. "Are you sure, Eragon? How do you know?"

"Of course I'm sure! I'll explain later, but I couldn't wait to tell you the truth."

Roran shook his head. "Brom. . . . I never would have guessed, but I suppose it makes sense. You must be glad to be rid of Morzan's name."

"More than glad," Eragon said, grinning.

Roran clapped him on the back, then said, "Watch yourself, eh?" and trotted after Horst and the other villagers.

Arya moved away in the same direction, but before she went more than a few steps, Eragon called her name and said, "The Cripple Who Is Whole has left Du Weldenvarden and joined Islanzadí at Gil'ead." Arya's green eyes widened and her lips parted, as if she were about to ask a question. Before she could, the column of inrushing warriors swept her deeper into the city.

Blödhgarm sidled closer to Eragon. "Shadeslayer, why did the Mourning Sage leave the forest?"

"He and his companion felt that the time had come to strike against the Empire and to reveal their presence to Galbatorix."

The elf's fur rippled. "That is indeed momentous news."

Eragon climbed back onto Saphira. To Blödhgarm and his other guards, he said, "Work your way up to the keep. We'll meet you there."

Without waiting for the elf to answer, Saphira jumped onto the stairs leading to the top of the city walls. The stone steps cracked under her weight as she climbed up to the wide parapet, from which she took flight over the burning hovels outside Feinster, flapping quickly to gain altitude.

Arya will have to give us permission before we can tell anyone else about Oromis and Glaedr, said Eragon, remembering the oath of secrecy he, Orik, and Saphira had sworn to Queen Islanzadí during their first visit to Ellesméra.

I am sure she will once she hears our account, said Saphira.

Aye.

Eragon and Saphira flew from place to place within Feinster, landing wherever they spotted a large clump of men or wherever members of the Varden appeared beleaguered. Unless someone immediately attacked, Eragon attempted to convince each group of enemies to surrender. He failed as often as he succeeded, but he felt better for having tried, for many of the men who thronged the streets were ordinary citizens of Feinster, and not trained soldiers. To each, Eragon said, "The Empire is our foe, not you. Do not take up arms against us and you shall have no cause to fear us." The few times Eragon saw a woman or child running through the dark city, he ordered them to hide in the nearest house, and without exception, they obeyed.

Eragon examined the minds of every person around him and Saphira, searching for magicians who might mean them harm, but he found no other spellcaster besides the three they had already seen, and the three were careful to keep their thoughts hidden from him. It concerned him that they did not seem to have rejoined the fight in any noticeable way.

Maybe they intend to abandon the city, he said to Saphira.

Would Galbatorix let them leave in the middle of a battle?

I doubt he wants to lose any of his spellcasters.

Maybe, but we should still tread with care. Who knows what they are planning?

Eragon shrugged. *For now, the best thing we can do is help the Varden secure Feinster as quickly as possible.*

She agreed and angled toward a skirmish in a nearby square.

Fighting in a city was different from fighting in the open, as Eragon and Saphira were accustomed to. The narrow streets and close-set buildings hampered Saphira's movements and made it difficult to react when soldiers attacked, even though Eragon could sense the men approaching long before they arrived. Their encounters with the soldiers devolved into dark and desperate struggles, broken only by the occasional burst of fire or magic. More than once, Saphira wrecked the front of a house with a careless sweep of her tail. She and Eragon always managed to escape permanent injury—through a combination of luck, skill, and Eragon's wards—but the attacks made them even more cautious and tense than they normally were in battle.

The fifth such confrontation left Eragon so enraged that when the soldiers began to withdraw, as they always did in the end, he gave chase, determined to kill every last one. They surprised him by swerving off the street and crashing through the barred door of a millinery shop.

Eragon followed, leaping over the cracked wreckage of the door. The inside of the shop was pitch-black and smelled like chicken feathers and stale perfume. He could have lit the shop with magic, but since he knew the soldiers were at a greater disadvantage than he was, he refrained. Eragon felt their minds nearby, and he could hear their ragged breathing, but he was uncertain of what lay between him and them. He inched deeper into the inky shop, feeling his way with his feet. He held his shield in front of him and Brisingr over his head, ready to strike.

Faint as a line of thread falling to the floor, Eragon heard an object flying through the air.

He jerked backward and staggered as a mace or a hammer struck his shield, breaking it into pieces. Shouts erupted. A man knocked over a chair or a table and something shattered against a wall. Eragon lashed out and felt Brisingr sink into flesh and bury itself in bone. A weight dragged on the end of his sword. Eragon yanked it free, and the man he had struck collapsed across his feet.

Eragon dared a glance back at Saphira, who was waiting for him in the narrow street outside. Only then did Eragon see that there was a lantern mounted on an iron post beside the street and that the light it cast rendered him visible to the soldiers. He quickly moved from the open doorway and threw away the remnants of his shield.

Another crash echoed through the shop, and there was a confusion of footsteps as the soldiers rushed out the back and up a flight of stairs. Eragon scrambled after them. The second story was the living quarters of the family who owned the store below. Several people screamed and a baby began to wail as Eragon bounded through a maze of small rooms, but he ignored them, intent as he was on his prey. At last he cornered the soldiers in a cramped sitting room illuminated by a single flickering candle.

Eragon slew the four soldiers with four strokes of his sword, wincing as their blood splattered him. He scavenged a new shield from one, then paused and studied the corpses. It seemed rude to leave them lying in the middle of the sitting room, so he threw them out a nearby window.

On his way back to the stairs, a figure stepped around a corner and stabbed a dagger toward Eragon's ribs. The tip of the dagger stopped a fraction of an inch from Eragon's side, halted by his wards. Startled, Eragon swept Brisingr upward and was about to strike his attacker's head from his shoulders when he realized that the holder of the dagger was a thin boy of no more than thirteen.

Eragon froze. *That could be me,* he thought. *I would have done the same if I were in his shoes.* Looking past the boy, he saw a man and a woman standing in their nightgowns and knit caps, clutching each other and staring at him with horror.

A tremor ran through Eragon. He lowered Brisingr and, with his free hand, removed the dagger from the boy's now-soft grip. "If I were you," Eragon said, and the loudness of his voice shocked him, "I would not go outside until the battle is over." He hesitated, then added, "I'm sorry."

Feeling ashamed, he hurried from the shop and rejoined Saphira.

They continued along the street.

Not far from the millinery shop, Eragon and Saphira came across several of King Orrin's men carrying gold candlesticks, silver plates and utensils, jewelry, and an assortment of furnishings out of a well-appointed mansion the men had broken into.

Eragon dashed a pile of rugs from the arms of one man. "Put these things back!" he shouted to the entire group. "We're here to *help* these people, not steal from them! They are our brothers and sisters, our mothers and fathers. I'll let you off this once, but spread the word that if you or anyone else goes looting, I'll have you strung up and whipped as the thieves you are!" Saphira growled, emphasizing his point. Under their watchful gaze, the chastened warriors returned the spoils to the marble-clad mansion.

Now, Eragon said to Saphira, *maybe we can—*

"Shadeslayer! Shadeslayer!" shouted a man, running toward them from deeper within the city. His arms and armor identified him as one of the Varden.

Eragon tightened his grip on Brisingr. "What?"

"We need your help, Shadeslayer. And yours too, Saphira!"

They followed the warrior through Feinster until they arrived at a large stone building. Several dozen Varden sat hunched behind a low wall in front of the building. They appeared relieved to see Eragon and Saphira.

"Stay back!" said one of the Varden, gesturing. "There's a whole group of soldiers inside, and they have bows aimed at us."

Eragon and Saphira halted just out of sight of the building. The warrior who had brought them said, "We can't get at them. The doors and windows are blocked, and they shoot at us if we try to chop our way in."

Eragon looked at Saphira. *Shall I, or shall you?*

I'll attend to it, she said, and jumped into the air with a rush of spreading wings.

The building shook, windows shattering, as Saphira landed on the roof. Eragon and the other warriors watched with awe as she fit the tips of her claws into the mortared grooves between the stones and, snarling from the effort, tore the building apart until she exposed the terrified soldiers, whom she killed like a terrier kills rats.

When Saphira returned to Eragon's side, the Varden edged away from her, clearly frightened by her display of ferocity. She ignored them and began licking her paws, cleaning the gore from her scales.

Have I ever told you how glad I am we're not enemies? Eragon asked.

No, but it's very sweet of you.

Throughout the city, the soldiers fought with a tenacity that impressed Eragon; they gave ground only when forced and made every attempt to slow the Varden's advance. Because of their determined resistance, the Varden did not arrive at the western side of the city, where the keep stood, until the first faint light of dawn began to spread across the sky.

The keep was an imposing structure. It was tall and square and adorned with numerous towers of differing height. The roof was made of slate, so attackers could not set it on fire. In front of the keep was a large courtyard—in which were several low outbuildings and a row of four catapults—and encircling the lot was a thick curtain wall interspersed with smaller towers of its own. Hundreds of soldiers manned the battlements and hundreds more teemed within the courtyard. The only way to enter the courtyard on the ground was through a wide, arched passageway in the curtain wall, which was closed off by both an iron portcullis and a set of thick oaken doors.

Several thousand of the Varden stood pressed against the curtain wall, striving to break through the portcullis with the battering ram they had brought from the main gate of the city or else to surmount the walls with grappling hooks and ladders, which the defenders kept pushing away. Flocks of whining arrows arched back and forth over the wall. Neither side seemed to have the advantage.

The gate! said Eragon, pointing.

Saphira swept down from on high and cleared the parapet above the portcullis with a jet of billowing fire, smoke venting from her nostrils. She dropped onto the top of the wall, jarring Eragon, and said, Go. *I'll see to the catapults before they start lobbing rocks at the Varden.*

Be careful. He lowered himself to the parapet from her back.

It is they *who must be careful!* she replied. She snarled at the pikemen gathering around the catapults. Half of them turned and fled inside.

The wall was too high for Eragon to comfortably jump to the street below, so Saphira draped her tail over the side and wedged it between two merlons. Eragon sheathed Brisingr, then climbed down, using the spikes on her tail like rungs on a ladder. When he reached the tip, he released his hold and fell the remaining twenty feet. He rolled to lessen the impact as he landed amid the press of Varden.

"Greetings, Shadeslayer," said Blödhgarm, emerging from the crowd, along with the eleven other elves.

"Greetings." Eragon drew Brisingr again. "Why haven't you already opened the gate for the Varden?"

"The gate is protected by many spells, Shadeslayer. It would require much strength to break and shatter. My companions and I are here to protect you and Saphira, and we cannot fulfill our duty if we exhaust ourselves on other tasks."

Biting back a curse, Eragon said, "Would you rather Saphira and I exhaust ourselves, Blödhgarm? Will that make us safer?"

The elf stared at Eragon for a moment, his yellow eyes inscrutable, then he bowed his head slightly. "We shall open the gate at once, Shadeslayer."

"No, don't," growled Eragon. "Wait here."

Eragon pushed his way to the front of the Varden and strode toward the lowered portcullis. "Give me room!" he shouted, gesturing at the warriors. The Varden backed away from him, forming an open area twenty feet across. A javelin shot from a ballista glanced off his wards and flew spinning down a side street. Saphira roared from inside the courtyard, and there came the sounds of timbers breaking and of taut rope snapping in twain.

Grasping his sword with both hands, Eragon lifted it overhead and shouted, "Brisingr!" The blade burst into blue fire, and the warriors behind him uttered exclamations of amazement. Eragon stepped forward then and smote one of the crossbars of the portcullis. A blinding flash lit the wall and surrounding buildings as the sword sliced through the thick piece of metal. At the same time,

Eragon noticed a sudden increase in his fatigue as Brisingr severed the wards protecting the portcullis. He smiled. As he had hoped, the spells of countermagic with which Rhunön had imbued Brisingr were more than sufficient to defeat the enchantments.

Moving at a quick but steady pace, Eragon cut as large a hole as he could in the portcullis, then stood aside as the loose piece of grating fell flat onto the stones of the street with a discordant clang. He stepped past the grating and walked forward to the oaken doors recessed farther within the curtain wall. He aligned Brisingr with the hairline crack between the two doors, put his weight behind the sword, and pushed the blade through the narrow gap and out the other side. Then he increased the flow of energy to the fire blazing around the blade until it was hot enough to burn its way through the dense wood as easily as a knife cuts through fresh bread. Copious amounts of smoke billowed from around the blade, making his throat sting and his eyes smart.

Eragon worked the sword upward, burning through the immense wooden beam that barred the doors shut from the inside. As soon as he felt the resistance against Brisingr's blade lessen, he withdrew the sword and extinguished the flame. He wore thick gloves, so he did not shrink from grasping the glowing edges of one door and pulling it open with a mighty heave. The other door also swung outward, seemingly of its own accord, although a moment later, Eragon saw that it was Saphira who had pushed it open; she sat to the right of the entryway, peering at him with sparkling sapphire eyes. Behind her, the four catapults lay in ruins.

Eragon went to stand with Saphira as the Varden poured into the courtyard, filling the air with their clamorous battle-cries. Exhausted by his efforts, Eragon placed a hand over the belt of Beloth the Wise and bolstered his flagging strength with some of the energy he had stored within the twelve diamonds hidden inside the belt. He offered the rest of it to Saphira, who was equally tired, but she declined, saying, *Keep it for yourself. You haven't that much left. Besides, what I really need is a meal and a full night's sleep.*

Eragon leaned against her and allowed his eyelids to drift halfway closed. *Soon,* he said. *Soon this will all be over.*

I hope so, she replied.

Among the warriors who streamed past was Angela, garbed in her strange, flanged armor of green and black and carrying her hûthvír, the double-bladed staff weapon of the dwarf priests. The herbalist paused next to Eragon and, with an impish expression, said, "An impressive display, but don't you think you're overdoing it a bit?"

"What do you mean?" asked Eragon, frowning.

She lifted an eyebrow. "Come now, was it really necessary to set your sword on fire?"

Eragon's expression cleared as he understood her objection. He laughed. "Not for the portcullis, no, but I enjoyed it. Besides, I can't help it. I named the sword *Fire* in the ancient language, and every time I say the word, the blade flares up like a branch of dry wood in a bonfire."

"You named your sword Fire?" Angela exclaimed with a note of incredulity. "Fire? What kind of a boring name is that? You might as well name your sword Blazing Blade and be done with it. Fire indeed. Humph. Wouldn't you rather have a sword called Sheepbiter or Chrysanthemum Cleaver or something else with imagination?"

"I already have one Sheepbiter here," said Eragon, and laid a hand on Saphira. "Why would I need another?"

Angela broke out into a wide smile. "So you're not entirely devoid of wit after all! There just might be hope for you." And she danced off toward the keep, twirling her double-bladed staff by her side and muttering, "Fire? Bah!"

A soft growl emanated from Saphira, and she said, *Be careful whom you call Sheepbiter, Eragon, or you might get bitten yourself.*

Yes, Saphira.

SHADOW OF DOOM

By then, Blödhgarm and his fellow elves had joined Eragon and Saphira in the courtyard, but Eragon ignored them and looked for Arya. When he spotted her, running alongside Jörmundur on his charger, Eragon hailed her and brandished his shield to attract her attention.

Arya heeded his call and loped over, her stride as graceful as a gazelle's. She had acquired a shield, a full-sized helm, and a mail hauberk since they had parted, and the metal of her armor gleamed in the gray half-light that pervaded the city. As she drew to a stop, Eragon said, "Saphira and I are going to enter the keep from above and try to capture Lady Lorana. Do you want to come with us?"

Arya agreed with a terse nod.

Springing from the ground onto one of Saphira's front legs, Eragon climbed into her saddle. Arya followed his example an instant later and sat close behind him, the links of her hauberk pressing against his back.

Saphira unfurled her velvety wings and took flight, leaving Blödhgarm and the other elves gazing up at her with looks of frustration.

"You should not abandon your guards so lightly," Arya murmured in Eragon's left ear. She wrapped her sword arm around his waist and held him tightly as Saphira wheeled above the courtyard.

Before Eragon could respond, he felt the touch of Glaedr's vast mind. For a moment, the city below vanished, and he saw and felt only what Glaedr saw and felt.

Little-stinging-hornet-arrows bounced off his belly as he rose above the scattered wood-caves of the two-legs-round-ears. The air was smooth and firm beneath his wings, perfect for the flying he would need to do. On his back, the saddle rubbed against his scales as Oromis altered his position.

Glaedr flicked his tongue out and tasted the enticing aroma of burnt-wood-cooked-meat-spilled-blood. He had been to this place many times before. In his youth, it had been known by a different name than Gil'ead, and then the only inhabitants had been the somber-laughing-quick-tongued-elves and the friends of elves. His previous visits had always been pleasant, but it pained him to remember the two nest-mates who had died here, slain by the twisted-mind-Forsworn.

The lazy-one-eye-sun hovered just above the horizon. To the north, the big-water-Isenstar was a rippling sheet of polished silver. Below, the herd of pointed-ears commanded by Islanzadí was arrayed around the broken-anthill-city. Their armor glittered like crushed ice. A pall of blue smoke lay over the whole area, thick as cold morning mist.

And from the south, the small-angry-rip-claw-Thorn winged his way toward Gil'ead, bellowing his challenge for all to hear. Morzan-son-Murtagh sat upon his back, and in Murtagh's right hand, Zar'roc shone as bright as a nail.

Sorrow filled Glaedr as he beheld the two miserable hatchlings. He wished he and Oromis did not have to kill them. Once more, he thought, dragon must fight dragon and Rider must fight Rider, and all because of that egg-breaker-Galbatorix. His mood grim, Glaedr quickened his flapping and spread his claws in preparation for tearing at his oncoming foes.

Eragon's head whipped on his neck as Saphira lurched to one side and dropped a score of feet before she regained her equilibrium. *Did you see that as well?* she asked.

I did. Worried, Eragon glanced back at the saddlebags, where Glaedr's heart of hearts was hidden, and wondered if he and Saphira should try to help Oromis and Glaedr but then reassured himself with the knowledge that there were numerous spellcasters among the elves. His teachers would not want for assistance.

"What is wrong?" asked Arya, her voice loud in Eragon's ear.

Oromis and Glaedr are about to fight Thorn and Murtagh, said Saphira.

Eragon felt Arya stiffen against him. "How do you know?" she asked.

"I'll explain later. I just hope they don't get hurt."

"As do I," said Arya.

Saphira flew high above the keep, then floated downward on silent wings and alighted upon the spire of the tallest tower. As Eragon and Arya clambered onto the steep roof, Saphira said, *I will meet you in the chamber below. The window here is too small for me.* And she took off, the gusts from her wings buffeting them.

Eragon and Arya lowered themselves over the edge of the roof and dropped to a narrow stone ledge eight feet below. Ignoring the vertigo-inducing fall that awaited him if he slipped, Eragon inched along the ledge to a cross-shaped window, where he pulled himself into a large square room lined with sheaves of quarrels and racks of heavy crossbows. If anyone had been in the room when Saphira landed, they had already fled.

Arya climbed through the window after him. She inspected the room, then gestured at the stairs in the far corner and padded toward them, her leather boots silent on the stone floor.

As Eragon followed her, he sensed a strange confluence of energies below them and also the minds of five people whose thoughts were closed to him. Wary of a mental attack, Eragon withdrew into himself and concentrated upon reciting a scrap of elvish poetry. He touched Arya on the shoulder and whispered, "Do you feel that?"

She nodded. "We should have brought Blödhgarm with us."

Together, they descended the stairs, making every effort to be quiet. The next room in the tower was much larger than the last; the ceiling was over thirty feet high, and from it hung a lantern with faceted panes of glass. A yellow flame burned inside. Hundreds of oil paintings covered the walls: portraits of bearded men in ornate robes and expressionless women sitting amid children with sharp, flat teeth; gloomy, windswept seascapes depicting the drowning of sailors; and scenes of battle, where humans slaughtered bands of grotesque Urgals. A row of tall wooden shutters set within the northern wall opened onto a balcony with a stone balustrade. Opposite the window, near the far wall, was a collection of small round tables littered with scrolls, three padded chairs, and two oversized brass urns filled with bouquets of dried flowers. A stout, gray-haired woman garbed in a lavender dress sat in one of the chairs. She bore a strong resemblance to several of the men in the paintings. A silver diadem adorned with jade and topaz rested upon her head.

In the center of the room stood the three magicians Eragon had glimpsed before in the city. The two men and a woman were facing each other, the hoods of their robes thrown back and their arms extended out to each side, so that the tips of their fingers touched. They swayed in unison, murmuring an unfamiliar spell in the ancient language. A fourth person sat in the middle of the triangle they formed: a man garbed in an identical fashion, but who said nothing, and who grimaced as if in pain.

Eragon threw himself at the mind of one of the male spellcasters, but the man was so focused on his task, Eragon failed to gain entry to his consciousness and thus was unable to subordinate him to his will. The man did not even seem to notice the attack. Arya must have attempted the same thing, for she frowned and whispered, "They were trained well."

"Do you know what they are doing?" he murmured.

She shook her head.

Then the woman in the lavender dress looked up and saw Eragon and Arya crouched upon the stone stairs. To Eragon's surprise, the woman did not call for help but rather placed a finger upon her lips, then beckoned.

Eragon exchanged a perplexed glance with Arya. "It could be a trap," he whispered.

"It most likely is," she said.

"What should we do?"

"Is Saphira almost here?"

"Yes."

"Then let us go and greet our host."

Matching their steps, they padded down the remaining stairs and snuck across the room, never taking their eyes off the engrossed magicians. "Are you Lady Lorana?" asked Arya in a soft voice as they halted before the seated woman.

The woman inclined her head. "That I am, fair elf." She turned her gaze upon Eragon then and said, "And are you the Dragon Rider of whom we have heard so much about recently? Are you Eragon Shadeslayer?"

"I am," said Eragon.

A relieved expression appeared upon the woman's distinguished face. "Ah, I had hoped you would come. You must stop them, Shadeslayer." And she gestured at the magicians.

"Why don't you order them to surrender?" whispered Eragon.

"I cannot," said Lorana. "They answer only to the king and his new Rider. I have sworn myself to Galbatorix—I had no choice in the matter—so I cannot raise a hand against him or his servants; otherwise, I would have arranged their destruction myself."

"Why?" asked Arya. "What is it you fear so much?"

The skin around Lorana's eyes tightened. "They know they cannot hope to drive off the Varden as they are, and Galbatorix has not sent reinforcements to our aid. So they are attempting, I do not know how, to create a Shade in the hope that the monster will turn against the Varden and spread sorrow and confusion throughout your ranks."

Horror enveloped Eragon. He could not imagine having to fight another Durza. "But a Shade might just as easily turn against them and everyone else in Feinster as it would against the Varden."

Lorana nodded. "They do not care. They only wish to cause as much pain and destruction as they can before they die. They are insane, Shadeslayer. Please, you must stop them, for the sake of my people!"

As she finished speaking, Saphira landed upon the balcony outside the room, cracking the balustrade with her tail. She knocked aside the shutters with a single blow of her paw, breaking their frames like so much tinder, and then pushed her head and shoulders into the chamber and growled.

The magicians continued to chant, seemingly oblivious to her presence.

"Oh my," said Lady Lorana, gripping the arms of her chair.

"Right," said Eragon. He hefted Brisingr and started toward the magicians, as did Saphira from the opposite direction.

The world reeled around Eragon, and again he found himself peering through Glaedr's eyes.

Red. Black. Flashes of throbbing yellow. Pain . . . Bone-bending pain in his belly and in the shoulder of his left wing. Pain as he had not felt for over a hundred years. Then relief as partner-of-his-life-Oromis healed his injuries.

727

Glaedr regained his balance and looked for Thorn. The little-red-shrike-dragon was stronger and faster than Glaedr had anticipated, due to Galbatorix's meddling.

Thorn slammed into Glaedr's left side, his weak side, where he had lost his foreleg. They spun around each other, plummeting toward the hard-flat-wing-crushing-ground. Glaedr snapped and tore and raked with his hind feet, trying to batter the smaller dragon into submission.

You will not best me, *youngling, he vowed to himself. I was old before you were born.*

White-dagger-claws scratched Glaedr along his ribs and underside. He flexed his tail and struck snarling-long-fang-Thorn across one leg, stabbing him in the thigh with a spike on his tail. The fighting had long since exhausted both of their invisible-spell-shields, leaving them vulnerable to every sort of wound.

When the twirling ground was only a few thousand feet away, Glaedr inhaled and drew back his head. He tightened his neck, clenched his belly, and drew forth the dense-liquid-of-fire from deep within his gut. The liquid ignited as it combined with the air in his throat. He opened his jaws to their full extent and sprayed the red dragon with fire, engulfing him in a blistering cocoon. The torrent of hungry-grasping-writhing-flames tickled the inside of Glaedr's cheeks.

He closed off his throat, terminating the flow of fire as he and the squirming-squealing-slash-claw-dragon pulled away from each other. From on his back, Glaedr heard Oromis say, "Their strength is fading; I can see it in their bearing. Another few minutes and Murtagh's concentration shall fail and I will be able to assume control over his thoughts. That or we shall slay them with sword and fang."

Glaedr growled in agreement, frustrated that he and Oromis dared not communicate with their minds, as they usually did. Rising on warm-wind-from-tilled-earth, he turned toward Thorn, whose limbs dripped with crimson blood, and roared and prepared to grapple with him once more.

Eragon stared at the ceiling, disoriented. He was lying on his back within the keep tower. Kneeling next to him was Arya, concern etched upon her face. She grasped him by an arm and helped him upright, steadying him as he wobbled. Across the room, Eragon saw Saphira shake her head, and he felt her own confusion.

The three magicians still stood with their arms outstretched, swaying and chanting in the ancient language. The words of their spell rang with unusual force and lingered in the air long after they should have faded to silence. The man who sat at their feet gripped his knees, his entire body shuddering as he thrashed his head from side to side.

"What happened?" asked Arya in a strained undertone. She pulled Eragon closer and lowered her voice even further. "How can you know what Glaedr is thinking from so far away, and when his mind is closed even to Oromis? Forgive me for touching your thoughts without your permission, Eragon, but I was worried about your welfare. What sort of a bond do you and Saphira share with Glaedr?"

"Later," he said, and squared his shoulders.

"Did Oromis give you an amulet or some other trinket that allows you to contact Glaedr?"

"It would take too long to explain. Later, I promise."

Arya hesitated, then nodded and said, "I shall hold you to that."

Together, Eragon, Saphira, and Arya advanced toward the magicians and struck at a separate one each. A metallic peal filled the room as Brisingr glanced aside before it reached its intended target, wrenching Eragon's shoulder. Likewise, Arya's sword rebounded off a ward, as did Saphira's right front paw. Her claws screeched against the stone floor.

"Concentrate on this one!" Eragon shouted, and pointed at the tallest spellcaster, a pale man with a snarled beard. "Hurry, before they manage to summon any spirits!" Eragon or Arya could have attempted to circumvent or deplete the spellcasters' wards with spells of their own, but using magic against another magician was always a perilous proposition unless the magician's mind was under your control. Neither Eragon nor Arya wanted to risk being killed by a ward they were as yet ignorant of.

Attacking in turns, Eragon, Saphira, and Arya cut, stabbed, and battered at the bearded spellcaster for nearly a minute. None of their blows touched the man. Then, at last, after only the slightest hint of resistance, Eragon felt something give way beneath Brisingr, and the sword continued on its way and lopped off the spellcaster's head. The air in front of Eragon shimmered. At the same instant, he felt a sudden drain on his strength as his wards defended him from an unknown spell. The assault ceased after a few seconds, leaving him dizzy and light-headed. His stomach rumbled. He grimaced and fortified himself with energy from the belt of Beloth the Wise.

The only response the other two magicians evinced at the death of their companion was to increase the speed of their invocation.

Yellow foam encrusted the corners of their mouths, and spittle flew from their lips, and the whites of their eyes showed, but still they made no attempt to flee or to attack.

Continuing on to the next spellcaster—a corpulent man with rings on his thumbs—Eragon, Saphira, and Arya repeated the process they had used on the first magician: alternating blows until they succeeded in wearing down his wards. It was Saphira who slew the man, knocking him through the air with a swipe of her claws. He hit the side of the staircase and cracked open his skull on the corner of a step. This time there was no magical retaliation.

As Eragon moved toward the female spellcaster, a cluster of multicolored lights hurtled into the room through the broken shutters and converged upon the man seated on the floor. The glowing spirits flashed with angry virulence as they whirled around the man, forming an impenetrable wall. He threw up his arms as if to shield himself and screamed. The air hummed and crackled with the energy that radiated from the flickering orbs. A sour, ironlike taste coated Eragon's tongue, and his skin prickled. The hair on the female spellcaster's head was standing on end. Across from her, Saphira hissed and arched her back, every muscle in her body rigid.

A bolt of fear shot through Eragon. *No!* he thought, feeling sick. *Not now. Not after all we've gone through.* He was stronger than he had been when he faced Durza in Tronjheim, but if anything, he was even more aware of just how dangerous a Shade could be. Only three warriors had ever survived the killing of a Shade: Laetrí the Elf, Irnstad the Rider, and himself—and he had no confidence he could duplicate the feat. *Blödhgarm, where are you?* Eragon shouted with his mind. *We need your help!*

And then everything around Eragon winked out of existence, and in its place he beheld:

Whiteness. Blank whiteness. The cold-soft-sky-water was soothing against Glaedr's limbs after the stifling heat of combat. He lapped at the air, welcoming the thin coat of moisture that accumulated on his dry-sticky-tongue.

He flapped once more and the sky-water parted before him, revealing the glaring-scorchback-sun and the hazy-green-brown-earth. Where is he? *Glaedr wondered. He swung his head, looking for Thorn. The little-red-shrike-dragon had fled high above Gil'ead, higher than any bird normally flew, where the air was thin and one's breath water-smoked.*

"Glaedr, behind us!" Oromis shouted.

Glaedr twisted, but he was too slow. The red dragon crashed into his right shoulder, knocking him tumbling. Snarling, Glaedr wrapped his single remaining foreleg around the nipping-scratching-ferocious-hatchling and strove to crush the life out of Thorn's squirming body. The red dragon bellowed and climbed halfway out of Glaedr's embrace, digging his claws into Glaedr's chest. Glaedr arched his neck and sank his teeth into Thorn's left hind leg and, with it, held him in place, although the red dragon writhed and kicked like a pinned wildcat. Hot-salty-blood filled Glaedr's mouth.

As they plummeted downward, Glaedr heard the sound of swords striking shields as Oromis and Murtagh exchanged a flurry of blows. Thorn convulsed, and Glaedr glimpsed Morzan-son-Murtagh. Glaedr thought the human appeared frightened, but he was not entirely sure. Even after so long bonded with Oromis, he still had difficulty deciphering the expressions of two-legs-no-horns, what with their soft, flat faces and their lack of tails.

The clanging of metal ceased, and Murtagh shouted, "Curse you for not showing yourself sooner! Curse you! You could have helped us! You could have—" Murtagh seemed to choke on his tongue for a moment.

Glaedr grunted as an unseen force brought their fall to an abrupt halt, nearly shaking him loose from Thorn's leg, and then lifted the four of them up through the sky, higher and higher, until the broken-anthill-city was only a faint blotch below and even Glaedr had difficulty breathing in the rarefied air.

What is the youngling doing? *Glaedr wondered, concerned.* Is he trying to kill himself?

Then Murtagh resumed speaking, and when he did, his voice was richer and deeper than before, and it echoed as if he were standing in an empty hall. Glaedr felt the scales on his shoulders crawl as he recognized the voice of their ancient foe.

"So you survived, Oromis, Glaedr," said Galbatorix. His words were round and smooth, like those of a practiced orator, and their tone was deceptively friendly. "Long have I thought that the elves might be hiding a dragon or a Rider from my sight. It is gratifying to have my suspicions confirmed."

"Begone, foul oath-breaker!" cried Oromis. "You shall not have any satisfaction from us!"

Galbatorix chuckled. "Such a harsh greeting. For shame, Oromis-elda. Have the elves forgotten their fabled courtesy over the past century?"

"You deserve no more courtesy than a rabid wolf."

"Tut-tut, Oromis. Remember what you said to me when I stood before you and the other Elders: 'Anger is a poison. You must purge it from your mind or else it will corrupt your better nature.' You should heed your own advice."

"You cannot confuse me with your snake's tongue, Galbatorix. You are an abomination, and we shall see to it that you are eliminated, even if it costs us our lives."

"But why should it, Oromis? Why should you pit yourself against me? It saddens me that you have allowed your hate to distort your wisdom, for you were wise once, Oromis, perhaps the wisest member of our entire order. You were the first to recognize the madness eating away at my soul, and it was you who convinced the other Elders to deny my request for another dragon egg. That was very wise of you, Oromis. Futile, but wise. And somehow you managed to escape from Kialandí and Formora, even after they had broken you, and then you hid until all but one of your enemies had died. That too was wise of you, elf."

A brief pause marked Galbatorix's speech. "There is no need to continue fighting me. I freely admit that I committed terrible crimes in my youth, but those days are long past, and when I reflect upon the blood I have shed, it torments my conscience. Still, what would you have of me? I cannot undo my deeds. Now, my greatest concern is ensuring the peace and prosperity of the empire over which I find myself lord and master. Cannot you see that I have lost my thirst for vengeance? The rage that drove me for so many years has burned itself to ashes. Ask yourself this, Oromis: who is responsible for the war that has swept across Alagaësia? Not I. The Varden were the ones who provoked this conflict. I would have been content to rule my people and leave the elves and the dwarves and the Surdans to their own devices. But the Varden could not leave well enough alone. It was they who chose to steal Saphira's egg, and they who cover the earth with mountains of corpses. Not I. You were wise once before, Oromis, and you can become wise once again. Give up your hatred and join me in Ilirea. With you by my side, we can bring an end to this conflict and usher in an era of peace that will endure for a thousand years or more."

Glaedr was not persuaded. He tightened his crushing-piercing-jaws, causing Thorn to yowl. The pain-noise seemed incredibly loud after Galbatorix's speech.

In clear, ringing tones, Oromis said, "No. You cannot make us forget your atrocities with a balm of honeyed lies. Release us! You have not the means to hold us here much longer, and I refuse to exchange pointless banter with a traitor like yourself."

"Bah! You are a senile old fool," said Galbatorix, and his voice acquired a harsh, angry cast. "You should have accepted my offer; you would have been first and foremost among my slaves. I will make you regret your mindless devotion to your so-called justice. And you are wrong. I can keep you thus as long as I want, for I have become as powerful as a god, and there are none who can stop me!"

"You shall not prevail," said Oromis. "Even gods do not endure forever."

At that Galbatorix uttered a foul oath. "Your philosophy does not constrain me, elf! I am the greatest of magicians, and soon I will be even greater still. Death will not take me. You, however, shall die. But first you will suffer. You will both suffer beyond imagining, and then I will kill you, Oromis, and I shall take your heart of hearts, Glaedr, and you will serve me until the end of time."

"Never!" exclaimed Oromis.

And Glaedr again heard the clash of swords on armor.

Glaedr had excluded Oromis from his mind for the duration of the fight, but their bond ran deeper than conscious thought, so he felt it when Oromis stiffened, incapacitated by the searing pain of his bone-blight-nerve-rot. Alarmed, Glaedr released Thorn's leg and tried to kick the red dragon away. Thorn howled at the impact but remained where he was. Galbatorix's spell held the two of them in place—neither able to move more than a few feet in any direction.

There was another metallic clang from above, and then Glaedr saw Naegling fall past him. The golden sword flashed and gleamed as it tumbled toward the ground. For the first time, the cold claw of fear gripped Glaedr. Most of Oromis's word-will-energy was stored within the sword, and his wards were bound to the blade. Without it, he would be defenseless.

Glaedr threw himself against the limits of Galbatorix's spell, struggling with all his might to break free. In spite of his efforts, however, he could not escape. And just as Oromis began to recover, Glaedr felt Zar'roc slash Oromis from shoulder to hip.

Glaedr howled.

He howled as Oromis had howled when Glaedr lost his leg.

An inexorable force gathered inside of Glaedr's belly. Without pausing to consider whether it was possible, he pushed Thorn and Murtagh away with a blast of magic, sending them flying like windblown leaves, and then tucked his wings against his sides and dove toward Gil'ead. If he could get there fast enough, then Islanzadí and her spellcasters would be able to save Oromis.

The city was too far away, though. Oromis's consciousness was faltering . . . fading . . . slipping away. . . .

Glaedr poured his own strength into Oromis's ruined frame, trying to sustain him until they reached the ground. But for all the energy he gave to Oromis, he could not stop the bleeding, the terrible bleeding.

Glaedr . . . release me, Oromis murmured with his mind.

A moment later, in an even fainter voice, he whispered, *Do not mourn me.*

And then the partner of Glaedr's life passed into the void.

Gone.

Gone!

GONE!

Blackness. Emptiness.

He was alone.

A crimson haze descended over the world, throbbing in unison with his pulse. He flared his wings and looped back the way he had come, searching for Thorn and his Rider. He would not let them escape; he would catch them and tear at them and burn them until he had eradicated them from the world.

Glaedr saw the red-shrike-dragon diving toward him, and he roared his grief and redoubled his speed. The red dragon swerved at the last moment, in an attempt to flank him, but he was not fast enough to evade Glaedr, who lunged and snapped and bit off the last three feet of the red dragon's tail. A fountain of blood sprayed from the stump. Yelping in agony, the red dragon wriggled away and darted behind Glaedr. Glaedr started to twist around to face him, but the smaller dragon was too quick, too nimble. Glaedr felt a sharp pain at the base of his skull, and then his vision flickered and failed.

Where was he?

He was alone.

He was alone and in the dark.

He was alone and in the dark, and he could not move or see.

He could feel the minds of other creatures close by, but they were not the minds of Thorn and Murtagh but of Arya, Eragon, and Saphira.

And then Glaedr realized where he was, and the true horror of the situation broke upon him, and he howled into the darkness. He howled and he howled, and he abandoned himself to his agony, not caring what the future might bring, for Oromis was dead, and he was alone.

Alone!

With a start, Eragon returned to himself.

He was curled into a ball. Tears streaked his face. Gasping, he pushed himself up off the floor and looked for Saphira and Arya.

It took him a moment to comprehend what he saw.

The female spellcaster Eragon had been about to attack lay before him, slain by a single sword thrust. The spirits she and her companions had summoned were nowhere to be seen. Lady Lorana was still ensconced in her chair. Saphira was in the process of struggling to her feet on the opposite side of the room. And the man who had been sitting on the floor amid the three other spellcasters was standing next to him, holding Arya in the air by her throat.

The color had vanished from the man's skin, leaving him bone white. His hair, which had been brown, was now bright crimson, and when he looked at Eragon and smiled, Eragon saw that his eyes had become maroon. In every aspect of appearance and bearing, the man resembled Durza.

"Our name is Varaug," said the Shade. "Fear us." Arya kicked at him, but her blows seemed to have no effect.

The burning pressure of the Shade's consciousness pressed against Eragon's mind, trying to break down his defenses. The force of the attack immobilized Eragon; he could barely repel the burrowing tendrils of the Shade's mind, much less walk or swing a sword. For whatever reason, Varaug was even stronger than Durza, and Eragon was not sure how long he could withstand the Shade's might. He saw that Saphira was also under attack; she sat stiff and motionless by the balcony, a snarl carved on her face.

The veins in Arya's forehead bulged, and her face turned red and purple. Her mouth was open, but she was not breathing. With the palm of her right hand, she struck the Shade's locked elbow and broke the joint with a loud crack. Varaug's arm sagged, and for a moment, Arya's toes brushed the floor, but then the bones in the Shade's arm popped back into place, and he lifted her even higher.

"You shall die," growled Varaug. "You shall all die for imprisoning us in this cold, hard clay."

Knowing that Arya's and Saphira's lives were in peril stripped Eragon of every emotion, save that of implacable determination. His thoughts as sharp and clear as a shard of glass, he drove himself at the Shade's seething consciousness. Varaug was too powerful, and the spirits that resided within him too disparate, for Eragon to overwhelm and control, so Eragon sought to isolate the Shade. He surrounded Varaug's mind with his own: every time Varaug attempted to reach out toward Saphira or Arya, Eragon blocked the mental ray, and every time the Shade attempted to shift his body, Eragon counteracted the urge with a command of his own.

They battled at the speed of thought, fighting back and forth along the perimeter of the Shade's mind, which was a landscape so jumbled and incoherent, Eragon feared it would drive him mad if he gazed at it for long. Eragon pushed himself to the utmost as he dueled with Varaug, striving to anticipate the Shade's every move, but he knew that their contest could only end with his own defeat. As fast as he was, Eragon could not outthink the numerous intelligences contained within the Shade.

Eragon's concentration eventually wavered, and Varaug seized upon the opportunity to force himself further into Eragon's mind, trapping him . . . transfixing him . . . suppressing his thoughts until Eragon could do no more than stare at the Shade with dumb rage. An excruciating tingling filled Eragon's limbs as the spirits raced through his body, coursing down every one of his nerves.

"Your ring is full of light!" exclaimed Varaug, his eyes widening with pleasure. "Beautiful light! It will feed us for a long time!"

Then he growled with anger as Arya grabbed his wrist and broke it in three places. She twisted free of Varaug's grip before he could heal himself and dropped to the ground, gasping for air. Varaug kicked at her, but she rolled out of the way. She reached for her fallen sword.

Eragon trembled as he struggled to cast off the Shade's oppressive presence.

Arya's hand closed around the hilt of her sword. A wordless bellow escaped the Shade. He pounced on her, and they rolled across the floor, wrestling for control of the weapon. Arya shouted and struck Varaug in the side of his head with the pommel of the sword.

The Shade went limp for an instant, and Arya scrambled backward, pushing herself upright.

In a flash, Eragon freed himself from Varaug. Without consideration for his own safety, he resumed his attack on the Shade's consciousness, his only thought to restrain the Shade for a few moments.

Varaug rose onto one knee, then faltered as Eragon redoubled his efforts.

"Get him!" Eragon shouted.

Arya lunged forward, her dark hair flying. . . .

And she stabbed the Shade through his heart.

Eragon winced and extricated himself from Varaug's mind even as the Shade recoiled from Arya, pulling himself off her blade. The Shade opened his mouth and uttered a piercing, dithering wail that shattered the panes of glass in the lantern above. He reached out toward Arya and tottered in her direction, then stopped as his skin faded and became transparent, revealing the dozens of glittering spirits trapped within the confines of his flesh. The spirits throbbed, growing in size, and Varaug's skin split along the bellies of his muscles. With a final burst of light, the spirits tore Varaug apart and fled the tower room, passing through the walls as if the stone were insubstantial.

Eragon's pulse gradually slowed. Then, feeling very old and very tired, he walked over to Arya, who stood leaning against a chair, cupping the front of her neck with a hand. She coughed, spitting up blood. Since she seemed incapable of talking, Eragon placed his hand over hers and said, "Waíse heill." As the energy to mend her injuries flowed out of him, Eragon's legs weakened, and he had to brace himself against the chair.

"Better?" he asked as the spell finished its work.

"Better," Arya whispered, and favored him with a weak smile. She motioned toward where Varaug had been. "We killed him. . . . We killed him, and yet we did not die." She sounded surprised. "So few have ever killed a Shade and lived."

"That is because they fought alone, not together, like us."

"No, not like us."

"I had you to help me in Farthen Dûr, and you had me to help you here."

"Yes."

"Now I shall have to call *you* Shadeslayer."

"We are both—"

Saphira startled them by loosing a long, mournful keen. Still keening, she raked her claws across the floor, chipping and scratching the stones. Her tail whipped from side to side, smashing the furniture and the grim paintings on the walls. *Gone!* she said. *Gone! Gone forever!*

"Saphira, what's wrong?" exclaimed Arya. When Saphira did not answer, Arya repeated the question to Eragon.

Hating the words he spoke, Eragon said, "Oromis and Glaedr are dead. Galbatorix killed them."

Arya staggered as if she had been hit. "Ah," she said. She gripped the back of the chair so hard, her knuckles turned white. Tears filled her slanted eyes, then spilled over onto her cheeks and coursed down her face. "Eragon." She reached out and grasped his shoulder, and almost by accident, he found himself holding her in his arms. Eragon felt his own eyes grow wet. He clenched his jaw in an effort to maintain his composure; if he started crying, he knew he would not be able to stop.

He and Arya remained locked together for a long while, consoling each other, then Arya withdrew and said, "How did it happen?"

"Oromis had one of his seizures, and while he was paralyzed, Galbatorix used Murtagh to—" Eragon's voice broke, and he shook his head. "I'll tell you about it along with Nasuada. She should know about this, and I don't want to have to describe it more than once."

Arya nodded. "Then let us go and see her."

SUNRISE

As Eragon and Arya escorted Lady Lorana down from the room in the tower, they encountered Blödhgarm and the eleven other elves running up the staircase four steps at a time.

"Shadeslayer! Arya!" exclaimed a female elf with long black hair. "Are you hurt? We heard Saphira's lament, and we thought one of you might have died."

Eragon glanced at Arya. His oath of secrecy to Queen Islanzadí would not allow him to discuss Oromis or Glaedr while in the presence of anyone not from Du Weldenvarden—such as Lady Lorana—without permission from the queen, Arya, or whoever might succeed Islanzadí to the knotted throne in Ellesméra.

She nodded and said, "I release you from your vow, Eragon, both of you. Speak of them to whomever you choose."

"No, we are not hurt," Eragon said. "However, Oromis and Glaedr have just died, slain in battle over Gil'ead."

As one, the elves cried out in shock and then began to ply Eragon with dozens of questions. Arya raised a hand and said, "Restrain yourselves. Now is not the time or place to satisfy your curiosity. There are still soldiers about, and we do not know who might be listening. Keep your sorrow hidden within your hearts until we are safe and secure." She paused and looked at Eragon, then said, "I will explain the full circumstances of their deaths to you once I know them myself."

"Nen ono weohnata, Arya Dröttningu," they murmured.

"Did you hear my call?" Eragon asked Blödhgarm.

"I did," the fur-covered elf said. "We came as fast as we could, but there were many soldiers between there and here."

Eragon twisted his hand over his chest in the elves' traditional gesture of respect. "I apologize for leaving you behind, Blödhgarm-elda. The heat of battle made me foolish and overconfident, and we nearly died because of my mistake."

"You need not apologize, Shadeslayer. We too made a mistake today, one which I promise we shall not repeat. From now on, we will fight alongside you and the Varden without reserve."

Together, they all trooped down the stairs to the courtyard outside. The Varden had killed or captured most of the soldiers within the keep, and the few men who were still fighting surrendered once they saw that Lady Lorana was in the custody of the Varden. Since the stairwell was too small for her, Saphira had descended by wing to the courtyard and was waiting for them when they arrived.

Eragon stood with Saphira, Arya, and Lady Lorana while one of the Varden fetched Jörmundur. When Jörmundur joined them, they informed him of what had happened within the tower—which amazed him greatly—and then gave over Lady Lorana to his custody.

Jörmundur bowed to her. "You may rest assured, Lady, we shall treat you with the respect and dignity due your station. We may be your enemies, but we are still civilized men."

"Thank you," she replied. "I am relieved to hear it. However, my main concern now is for the safety of my subjects. If I might, I would like to speak with your leader, Nasuada, about her plans for them."

"I believe she wishes to speak with you as well."

As they parted, Lady Lorana said, "I am most grateful to you, elf, and to you as well, Dragon Rider, for killing that monster before he could wreak sorrow and destruction upon Feinster. Fate has placed us on opposite sides of this conflict, but that does not mean I cannot admire your bravery and prowess. We may never meet again, so fare thee well, both of you."

Eragon bowed and said, "Fare thee well, Lady Lorana."

"May the stars watch over you," said Arya.

Blödhgarm and the elves under his command accompanied

Eragon, Saphira, and Arya as they searched Feinster for Nasuada. They found her riding her stallion through the gray streets, inspecting the damage to the city.

Nasuada greeted Eragon and Saphira with evident relief. "I'm glad you have finally returned. We've needed you here these past few days. I see you have a new sword, Eragon, a Dragon Rider's sword. Did the elves give it to you?"

"In an indirect way, yes." Eragon eyed the various people standing nearby and lowered his voice. "Nasuada, we must talk with you alone. It's important."

"Very well." Nasuada studied the buildings that lined the street, then pointed at a house that appeared abandoned. "Let us talk in there."

Two of Nasuada's guards, the Nighthawks, ran forward and entered the house. They reappeared a few minutes later and bowed to Nasuada, saying, "It's empty, my Lady."

"Good. Thank you." She dismounted her steed, handed the reins to one of the men in her retinue, and strode inside. Eragon and Arya followed.

The three of them wandered through the shabby building until they found a room, the kitchen, with a window large enough to accommodate Saphira's head. Eragon pushed opened the shutters, and Saphira laid her head on the wooden counter. Her breath filled the kitchen with the smell of charred meat.

"We may speak without fear," Arya announced after casting spells that would prevent anyone from eavesdropping on their conversation.

Nasuada rubbed her arms and shivered. "What is this all about, Eragon?" she asked.

Eragon swallowed, wishing that he did not have to dwell upon Oromis and Glaedr's fate. Then he said, "Nasuada . . . Saphira and I were not alone. . . . There was another dragon and another Rider fighting against Galbatorix."

"I knew it," breathed Nasuada, her eyes shining. "It was the only explanation that made sense. They were your teachers in Ellesméra, weren't they?"

They were, said Saphira, *but no more.*

"No more?"

Eragon pressed his lips together and shook his head, tears blurring his vision. "Just this morning they died at Gil'ead. Galbatorix used Thorn and Murtagh to kill them; I heard him speak to them with Murtagh's tongue."

The excitement drained from Nasuada's face, replaced by a dull, empty expression. She sank into the nearest chair and stared at the cinders in the cold fireplace. The kitchen was silent. At last she stirred and said, "Are you sure they are dead?"

"Yes."

Nasuada wiped her eyes on the hem of her sleeve. "Tell me about them, Eragon. Would you, please?"

So for the next half hour, Eragon spoke of Oromis and Glaedr. He explained how they had survived the fall of the Riders and why they had chosen to keep themselves hidden thereafter. He explained about their respective disabilities, and he spent some time describing their personalities and what it had been like to study under them. Eragon's sense of loss deepened as he remembered the long days he had spent with Oromis on the Crags of Tel'naeír and the many things the elf had done for him and Saphira. As he came to their encounter with Thorn and Murtagh at Gil'ead, Saphira lifted her head off the counter and began to keen again, her mournful wail soft and persistent.

743

Afterward, Nasuada sighed and said, "I wish I could have met Oromis and Glaedr, but alas, it was not to be. . . . There is one thing I still do not understand, Eragon. You said you *heard* Galbatorix speaking to them. How could you?"

"Yes, I would like to know that as well," said Arya.

Eragon looked for something to drink, but there was no water or wine in the kitchen. He coughed, then launched into an account of their recent trip to Ellesméra. Saphira occasionally made a comment, but for the most part, she left it to him to tell the story. Starting with the truth about his parentage, Eragon proceeded in quick succession through the events of their stay, from their discovery of the brightsteel under the Menoa tree to the forging of Brisingr to his visit with Sloan. Last of all, he told Arya and Nasuada about the dragons' heart of hearts.

"Well," said Nasuada. She stood and walked the length of the kitchen and then back again. "You the son of Brom, and Galbatorix leeching off the souls of dragons whose bodies have died. It's almost too much to comprehend. . . ." She rubbed her arms again. "At least we now know the true source of Galbatorix's power."

Arya stood motionless, breathless, her expression stunned. "The dragons are still alive," she whispered. She clasped her hands together in a prayer-like fashion and held them against her chest. "They are still alive after all these years. Oh, if only we could tell the rest of my race. How they would rejoice! And how terrible their wrath would be when they heard of the enslavement of the Eldunarí! We would run straight to Urû'baen, and we would not rest until we had freed the hearts of Galbatorix's control, no matter how many of us died in the process."

But we cannot tell them, said Saphira.

"No," said Arya, and lowered her gaze. "We cannot. But I wish we could."

Nasuada looked at her. "Please do not take offense, but I wish that your mother, Queen Islanzadí, had seen fit to share this information with us. We could have made use of it long ago."

"I agree," said Arya, frowning. "On the Burning Plains, Murtagh was able to defeat the two of you"—she indicated Eragon and Saphira—"because you did not know that Galbatorix might have given him some of the Eldunarí and thus you failed to act with appropriate caution. If not for Murtagh's conscience, you would both be trapped in Galbatorix's service even now. Oromis and Glaedr, and my mother too, had sound reasons for keeping the Eldunarí a secret, but their reticence was nearly our undoing. I will discuss this with my mother when next we speak."

Nasuada paced between the counter and the fireplace. "You have given me much to think about, Eragon. . . ." She tapped the floor with the tip of her boot. "For the first time in the history of the Varden, we know of a way to kill Galbatorix that might actually succeed. If we can separate him from these heart of hearts, he will lose the better part of his strength, and then you and our other spell-casters will be able to overpower him."

"Yes, but how can we separate him from his hearts?" Eragon asked.

Nasuada shrugged. "I could not say, but I am sure it must be possible. From now on, you will work on devising a method. Nothing else is as important."

Eragon felt Arya studying him with unusual concentration. Unsettled, he made a questioning face at her.

"I always wondered," said Arya, "why Saphira's egg appeared to you, and not somewhere in an empty field. It seemed too great a co-incidence to have occurred purely by chance, but I could not think of any plausible explanation. Now I understand. I should have guessed that you were Brom's son. I did not know Brom well, but I did know him, and you share a certain resemblance."

"I do?"

"You should be proud to call Brom your father," said Nasuada. "By all accounts, he was a remarkable man. If not for him, the Varden wouldn't exist. It seems fitting that you are the one to carry on his work."

Then Arya said, "Eragon, may we see Glaedr's Eldunarí?"

Eragon hesitated, then went outside and retrieved the pouch from Saphira's saddlebags. Careful not to touch the Eldunarí, he loosened the drawstring at the top and allowed the pouch to slide down around the golden, gemlike stone. In contrast to when he had last seen it, the glow within the heart of hearts was dim and feeble, as if Glaedr were barely conscious.

Nasuada leaned forward and stared into the swirling center of the Eldunarí, her eyes gleaming with reflected light. "And Glaedr is really inside of here?"

He is, said Saphira.

"Can I speak with him?"

"You could try, but I doubt he would respond. He just lost his Rider. It will take him a long time to recover from the shock, if ever. Please leave him be, Nasuada. If he wished to speak with you, he would have done so already."

"Of course. It was not my intention to disturb him in his time of grief. I shall wait to meet him until such time as he has regained his composure."

Arya moved closer to Eragon and placed her hands on either side of the Eldunarí, her fingers less than an inch away from its surface. She gazed at the stone with an expression of reverence, seemingly lost within its depths, then whispered something in the ancient language. Glaedr's consciousness flared slightly, as if in response.

Arya lowered her hands. "Eragon, Saphira, you have been given the most solemn responsibility: the safekeeping of another life. Whatever happens, you must protect Glaedr. With Oromis gone, we shall need his strength and wisdom more than ever before."

Do not worry, Arya, we won't allow any misfortune to befall him, Saphira promised.

Eragon covered the Eldunarí with the pouch again and fumbled with the drawstring, exhaustion rendering him clumsy. The Varden had won an important victory and the elves had taken Gil'ead, but the knowledge brought him little joy. He looked at Nasuada and asked, "What now?"

Nasuada lifted her chin. "Now," she said, "we will march north to Belatona, and when we have captured it, we will proceed onward to Dras-Leona and seize it as well, and then to Urû'baen, where we will cast down Galbatorix or die trying. That is what we shall do now, Eragon."

After they left Nasuada, Eragon and Saphira agreed to leave Feinster for the Varden's camp so that they could both rest undisturbed by the cacophony of noises within the city. With Blödhgarm and the rest of Eragon's guards ranged around them, they walked toward the main gates of Feinster, Eragon still carrying Glaedr's heart of hearts in his arms. Neither of them spoke.

Eragon stared at the ground between his feet. He paid little attention to the men who ran or marched past; his part in the battle was finished, and all he wanted to do was lie down and forget the sorrows of the day. The last sensations he had felt from Glaedr still reverberated through his mind: *He was alone. He was alone and in the dark. . . . Alone!* Eragon's breath caught as a wave of nausea swept over him. *So that is what it's like to lose your Rider or your dragon. No wonder Galbatorix went insane.*

We are the last, Saphira said.

Eragon frowned, not understanding.

The last free dragon and Rider, she explained. *We are the only ones left. We are . . .*

Alone.

Yes.

Eragon stumbled as his foot struck a loose stone he had overlooked. Miserable, he closed his eyes for a moment. *We can't do this by ourselves,* he thought. *We can't! We're not ready.* Saphira agreed, and her grief and anxiety, combined with his, nearly incapacitated him.

When they arrived at the city gates, Eragon paused, reluctant to push his way through the large crowd gathered in front of the opening, trying to flee Feinster. He glanced around for another route. As his eyes passed over the outer walls, a sudden desire gripped him to see the city in the light of day.

Veering away from Saphira, he ran up a staircase that led to the top of the walls. Saphira uttered a short growl of annoyance and followed, half opening her wings as she jumped from the street to the parapet in a single bound.

They stood together on the battlements for the better part of an hour and watched as the sun rose. One by one, rays of pale gold light streaked across the verdant fields from the east, illuminating the countless motes of dust that drifted through the air. Where the rays struck a column of smoke, the smoke glowed orange and red and billowed with renewed urgency. The fires among the hovels outside the city walls had mostly died out, although since Eragon and Saphira had arrived, the fighting had set a score of houses within Feinster ablaze, and the pillars of flame that leaped up from the disintegrating houses lent the cityscape an eerie beauty. Behind Feinster, the shimmering sea stretched out to the far, flat horizon, where the sails of a ship plowing its way northward were just visible.

As the sun warmed Eragon through his armor, his melancholy gradually dissipated like the wreaths of mist that adorned the rivers below. He took a deep breath and exhaled, relaxing his muscles.

No, he said, *we are not alone. I have you, and you have me. And there is Arya and Nasuada and Orik, and many others besides who will help us along our way.*

And Glaedr too, said Saphira.

Aye.

748

Eragon gazed down at the Eldunarí that lay covered within his arms and felt a rush of sympathy and protectiveness toward the dragon who was trapped inside the heart of hearts. He hugged the stone closer to his chest and laid a hand upon Saphira, grateful for their companionship.

We can do this, he thought. *Galbatorix isn't invulnerable. He has a weakness, and we can use that weakness against him. . . . We can do this.*

We can, and we must, said Saphira.

For the sake of our friends and our family—

—and for the rest of Alagaësia—

—we must do this.

Eragon lifted Glaedr's Eldunarí over his head, presenting it to the sun and the new day, and he smiled, eager for the battles yet to come, so that he and Saphira might finally confront Galbatorix and kill the dark king.

HERE ENDS THE THIRD BOOK

OF THE INHERITANCE CYCLE.

THE STORY WILL CONTINUE AND CONCLUDE

IN BOOK FOUR.

ON THE ORIGIN OF NAMES:

To the casual observer, the various names an intrepid traveler will encounter throughout Alagaësia might seem but a random collection of labels with no inherent integrity, culture, or history. However, as with any land that different cultures—and in this case, different species—have repeatedly colonized, Alagaësia acquired names from a wide array of unique sources, among them the languages of the dwarves, elves, humans, and even Urgals. Thus, we can have Palancar Valley (a human name), the Anora River and Ristvak'baen (elven names), and Utgard Mountain (a dwarf name) all within a few square miles of each other.

While this is of great historical interest, practically it often leads to confusion as to the correct pronunciation. Unfortunately, there are no set rules for the neophyte. You must learn each name upon its own terms, unless you can immediately place its language of origin. The matter grows even more confusing when you realize that in many places the resident population altered the spelling and pronunciation of foreign words to conform to their own language. The Anora River is a prime example. Originally *anora* was spelled *äenora*, which means *broad* in the ancient language. In their writings, the humans simplified the word to *anora*, and this, combined with a vowel shift wherein *äe* (ay-eh) was said as the easier *a* (uh), created the name as it appears in Eragon's time.

To spare readers as much difficulty as possible, I have compiled the following list, with the understanding that these are only rough guidelines to the actual pronunciation. The enthusiast is encouraged to study the source languages in order to master their true intricacies.

PRONUNCIATION:

Ajihad—AH-zhi-hod
Alagaësia—al-uh-GAY-zee-uh
Arya—AR-ee-uh
Blödhgarm—BLAWD-garm
Brisingr—BRISS-ing-gur
Carvahall—CAR-vuh-hall
Dras-Leona—DRAHS-lee-OH-nuh
Du Weldenvarden—doo WELL-den-VAR-den
Ellesméra—el-uhs-MEER-uh
Eragon—EHR-uh-gahn
Farthen Dûr—FAR-then DURE (*dure* rhymes with *lure*)
Galbatorix—gal-buh-TOR-icks
Gil'ead—GILL-ee-id
Glaedr—GLAY-dur
Hrothgar—HROTH-gar
Islanzadí—iss-lan-ZAH-dee
Jeod—JODE (rhymes with *load*)

Murtagh—MUR-tag (*mur* rhymes with *purr*)
Nasuada—nah-soo-AH-dah
Nolfavrell—NOLL-fah-vrel (*noll* rhymes with *toll*)
Oromis—OR-uh-miss
Ra'zac—RAA-zack
Saphira—suh-FEAR-uh
Shruikan—SHREW-kin
Sílthrim—SEAL-thrim (*síl* is a hard sound to transcribe; it's made
    by flicking the tip of the tongue off the roof of the mouth)
Skgahgrezh—skuh-GAH-grezh
Teirm—TEERM
Trianna—TREE-ah-nuh
Tronjheim—TRONJ-heem
Urû'baen—OO-roo-bane
Vrael—VRAIL
Yazuac—YAA-zoo-ack
Zar'roc—ZAR-rock

THE ANCIENT LANGUAGE:

Adurna rïsa.—Water, rise.
Agaetí Blödhren—Blood-oath Celebration (held once a century to
    honor the original pact between elves and dragons)
älfa-kona—elf woman
Äthalvard—an organization of elves dedicated to the preservation
    of their songs and poems
Atra du evarínya ono varda, Däthedr-vodhr.—May the stars watch
    over you, honored Däthedr.
Atra esterní ono thelduin, Eragon Shur'tugal.—May good fortune
    rule over you, Eragon Dragon Rider.
Atra guliä un ilian tauthr ono un atra ono waíse sköliro fra rauthr.—
    May luck and happiness follow you and may you be shielded
    from misfortune.

audr—up

Bjartskular—Brightscales

Blödhgarm—Bloodwolf

brisingr—fire

Brisingr, iet tauthr.—Fire, follow me.

Brisingr raudhr!—Red fire!

deyja—die

draumr kópa—dream stare

dröttningu—princess

Du deloi lunaea.—Smooth the earth/dirt.

Du Namar Aurboda—The Banishing of the Names

Du Vrangr Gata—The Wandering Path

edur—a tor or prominence

Eka eddyr aí Shur'tugal . . . Shur'tugal . . . Argetlam.—I am a
    Dragon Rider . . . Dragon Rider . . . Silver Hand.

Eka elrun ono.—I thank you.

elda—a gender-neutral honorific suffix of great praise, attached
    with a hyphen

Eldhrimner O Loivissa nuanen, dautr abr deloi/Eldhrimner nen
    ono weohnataí medh solus un thringa/Eldhrimner un fortha onr
    fëon vara/Wiol allr sjon.—Grow, O beautiful Loivissa, daughter
    of the earth/Grow as you would with sun and rain/Grow and put
    forth your flower of spring/For all to see.

Eldunarí—the heart of hearts

Erisdar—the flameless lanterns both the elves and the dwarves use
    (named after the elf who invented them)

faelnirv—elven liqueur

fairth—a picture taken by magical means on a shingle of slate

fell—mountain

finiarel—an honorific suffix for a young man of great promise,
    attached with a hyphen

flauga—fly

fram—forward

Fricai onr eka eddyr.—I am your friend.

gánga—go

Garjzla, letta!—Light, stop!

gedwëy ignasia—shining palm

Helgrind—The Gates of Death

Indlvarn—a certain type of pairing between a Rider and dragon

jierda—break; hit

könungr—king

Kuldr, rïsa lam iet un malthinae unin böllr.—Gold, rise to my hand
and bind into an orb.

kveykva—lightning

lámarae—a fabric made by cross-weaving wool and nettle threads
(similar in construction to linsey-woolsey, but of higher
quality)

letta—stop

Liduen Kvaedhí—Poetic Script

loivissa—a blue, deep-throated lily that grows in the Empire

maela—quiet

naina—make bright

nalgask—a mixture of beeswax and hazelnut oil used to moisten
the skin

Nen ono weohnata, Arya Dröttningu.—As you will, Princess Arya.

seithr—witch

Shur'tugal—Dragon Rider

slytha—sleep

Stenr rïsa!—Stone, rise!

svit-kona—a formal honorific for an elf woman of great wisdom

talos—a cactus found near Helgrind

thaefathan—thicken

Thorta du ilumëo!—Speak the truth!

vakna—awaken

vodhr—a male honorific suffix of middling praise, attached with a
hyphen

Waíse heill!—Be healed!

yawë—a bond of trust

THE DWARF LANGUAGE:

Ascûdgamln—fists of steel

Az Knurldrâthn—The Trees of Stone

Az Ragni—The River

Az *Sartosvrenht rak Balmung, Grimstnzborith rak Kvisagûr*—The Saga
   of King Balmung of Kvisagûr

Az Sindriznarrvel—The Gem of Sindri

barzûl—curse someone with ill fate

delva—a term of endearment among the dwarves; also a form of
   gold nodule indigenous to the Beor Mountains that the dwarves
   greatly prize

dûr—our

dûrgrimst—clan (literally, "our hall," or "our home")

dûrgrimstvren—clan war

eta—no

Eta! Narho ûdim etal os isû vond! Narho ûdim etal os formvn
   mendûnost brakn, az Varden, hrestvog dûr grimstnzhadn! Az
   Jurgenvren qathrid né dômar oen etal— No! I will not let that
   happen! I will not let these beardless fools, the Varden, destroy
   our country. The Dragon War left us weak and not—

Fanghur—dragon-like creatures that are smaller and less
   intelligent than their cousins (native to the Beor Mountains)

Farthen Dûr—Our Father

Feldûnost—frostbeard (a species of goat native to the Beor Mountains)

Gáldhiem—Bright/shining head

Ghastgar—spear-throwing contest akin to jousting and fought on
   the backs of Feldûnost

grimstborith—clan chief (literally, "hall chief"; plural is *grimstborithn*)

grimstcarvlorss—arranger of the house

grimstnzborith—ruler of the dwarves, whether king or queen
   (literally, "halls' chief")

hûthvír—double-bladed staff weapon used by Dûrgrimst Quan

Hwatum il skilfz gerdûmn!—Listen to mine words!

Ingeitum—fire workers; smiths

Isidar Mithrim—Star Rose (the star sapphire)

knurla—dwarf (literally, "one of stone"; plural is *knurlan*)

knurlaf—woman/she/her

knurlag—man/he/him

knurlagn—men

Knurlcarathn—stoneworkers; masons

Knurlnien—Stone Heart

Ledwonnû—Kílf's necklace; also used as a general term for *necklace*

menknurlan—unstone ones/those who are not, or are without, stone (the worst insult in Dwarvish; cannot be directly translated into English)

mérna—lake/pool

Nagra—giant boar, native to the Beor Mountains

Nal, Grimstnzborith Orik!—Hail, King Orik!

ornthrond—eagle eye

Ragni Darmn—River of Small Red Fish

Ragni Hefthyn—River Guard

Shrrg—giant wolf, native to the Beor Mountains

Skilfz Delva—Mine Delva (see *delva* for translation)

thriknzdal—the temper line on the blade of a differentially tempered weapon

Tronjheim—Helm of Giants

Ûn qroth Gûntera!—Thus spoke Gûntera!

Urzhad—giant cave bear, native to the Beor Mountains

Vargrimst—clanless/banished

Vrenshrrgn—War Wolves

werg—the dwarves' equivalent of *ugh* (used humorously in the place name Werghadn; *Werghadn* translates as either "the land of ugh" or, more liberally, "the ugly land")

The Nomad Language:

no—an honorific suffix attached with a hyphen to the main name
of someone you respect

The Urgal Language:

Herndall—Urgal dams who rule their tribes
namna—woven strips containing Urgal family narratives that are
placed by the entrances to their huts
nar—a title of great respect
Urgralgra—Urgals' name for themselves (literally, "those with
horns")

ACKNOWLEDGMENTS

Kvetha Fricaya. Greetings, Friends.

Brisingr was a fun, intense, and sometimes difficult book to write. When I started, I felt as if the story were a vast, three-dimensional puzzle that I had to solve without hints or instructions. I found the experience to be immensely satisfying, despite the challenges it occasionally posed.

Because of its complexity, *Brisingr* ended up much larger than I anticipated—so much larger, in fact, that I had to expand the series from three books to four. Thus, the Inheritance trilogy became the Inheritance cycle. I'm pleased with the change too. Having another volume in the series has allowed me to explore and develop the characters' personalities and relationships at a more natural pace.

As with *Eragon* and *Eldest*, I never would have been able to complete this book without the support of a whole host of talented people, to whom I am ever grateful. They are:

At home: Mom, for her food, tea, advice, sympathy, endless patience, and optimism; Dad, for his unique perspective, razor-sharp observations on story and prose, helping me to name the book, and for coming up with the idea of having Eragon's sword burst into flame every time he says its name (very cool); and my one and only sister, Angela, for once again consenting to reprise her character and for numerous pieces of information on names, plants, and all things wool.

At Writers House: Simon Lipskar, my agent, for his friendship, his hard work, and for giving me a much-needed kick in the pants early on in *Brisingr* (without which I might have taken another two years to finish the book); and his assistant Josh Getzler for all he does on behalf of Simon and the Inheritance cycle.

At Knopf: my editor, Michelle Frey, who did an awesome job of helping me to clean up and tighten the manuscript (the first draft was *much* longer); associate editor Michele Burke, who also labored over the editing and who helped pull together the synopsis of *Eragon* and *Eldest*; head of communications and marketing Judith Haut, who from the beginning spread word of the series throughout the land; publicity director Christine Labov; art director Isabel Warren-Lynch and her team for again putting together such a classy-looking book; John Jude Palencar for a majestic cover painting (I don't know how he can top it with the fourth book!); executive copy editor Artie Bennett for checking every word, real or invented, in *Brisingr* with such consummate care; Chip Gibson, head of the children's division at Random House; Knopf publishing director Nancy Hinkel for her unwavering support; Joan DeMayo, director of sales and her team (huzzah and many thanks!); head of marketing John Adamo, whose team designed such impressive materials; Linda Leonard, new media, for all her efforts with online marketing; Linda Palladino, Milton Wackerow, and Carol Naughton, production; Pam White, Jocelyn Lange, and the rest of the subsidiary rights team, who have done a truly extraordinary job of selling the Inheritance cycle in countries and languages throughout the world; Janet Renard, copyediting; and everyone else at Knopf who has supported me.

At Listening Library: Gerard Doyle, who brings the world of Alagaësia to life with his voice; Taro Meyer for getting the pronunciation of my languages just right; Orli Moscowitz for pulling all the threads together; and Amanda D'Acierno, publisher of Listening Library.

Thank you all.

The Craft of the Japanese Sword by Leon and Hiroko Kapp and Yoshindo Yoshihara provided me with much of the information I needed to accurately describe the smelting and forging process in the chapter "Mind over Metal." I highly recommend the book to anyone who is interested in learning more about (specifically Japanese) swordmaking. Did you know that Japanese smiths used to start their fires by hammering on the end of a bar of iron until it was red-hot, then touching it to a cedar shingle that was coated with sulfur?

Also, for those who understood the reference to a "lonely god" when Eragon and Arya are sitting around the campfire, my only excuse is that the Doctor can travel everywhere, even alternate realities.

Hey, I'm a fan too!

Finally, and most importantly, thank you. Thank you for reading *Brisingr*. And thank you for sticking with the Inheritance cycle through all these years. Without your support, I never would have been able to write this series, and I can't imagine anything else I would rather be doing.

Once again Eragon and Saphira's adventures are over, and once again we have arrived at the end of this wandering path . . . but only for the time being. Many more miles still lie before us. Book Four will be published just as soon as I can finish it, and I can promise you, it's going to be the most exciting installment in the series. I can't wait for you to read it!

Sé onr sverdar sitja hvass!

Christopher Paolini
September 20, 2008

BRISINGR

is also available in an unabridged
audio edition from Listening Library

CD ISBN 978-0-739-36804-6
$60.00 U.S. / $69.00 CAN.

Audiobook download ISBN 978-0-739-36805-3
$30.00 U.S. / $34.00 CAN.